SSC

STAFF SELECTION COMMISSION

CONSTABLE (G.D.)

(Male/Female)

SSC

STAFF SELECTION COMMISSION

CONSTABLE (G.D.)

(Male/Female)

TEAM PRABHAT

PRABHAT EXAMS

Publisher

PRABHAT EXAMS

4/19 Asaf Ali Road, New Delhi–110 002

Ph. 23289555 • 23289666 • 23289777 • Helpline/ 7827007777

e-mail: prabhatbooks@gmail.com • Website: www.prabhatexam.com

Price

Four Hundred Fifty Rupees

ISBN 978-93-5488-954-7

Printed at

Siddhi Press, Delhi

SSC
STAFF SELECTION COMMISSION
CONSTABLE (GD)
(MALE/FEMALE)
by Team Prabhat

ISBN 978-93-5488-954-7

₹ 450.00

CONTENTS

SSC Constable (GD)
Solved Paper-2022
Exam Date 12-01-2023

Part-A: General Intelligence and Reasoning

1. Select the correct mirror image of the given figure when the mirror is placed at MN as shown below.

(a) 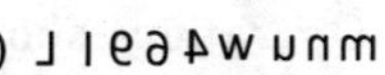
(b) 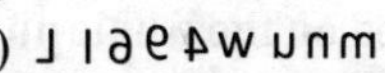
(c) 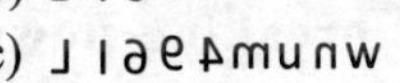
(d) 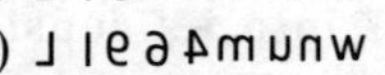

2. 6 people – A, B, C, D, E and F are sitting in front of a mirror shaped table facing the center. B sits right or next to A. F sits to the right or right next to A. E sits immediately next to F and D. C sits to the right or right next to D. Who among them sits immediately next to A and C?

(a) B (b) F
(c) E (d) D

3. Eight friends P, Q, R, S, T, U, V and W are sitting in two rows facing each other. Each row has four persons. Q and R are sitting in front of each other. R is the immediate neighbour of S and T. W is sitting to the immediate left of T. W and U are diagonally opposite. V and Q are not next to each other. Who is in front of T?

(a) Q (b) R
(c) P (d) S

4. The sequence of folding a piece of paper and the manner in which the folded paper has been cut is shown below. Select the figure which would most closely resemble the unfolded form of the paper.

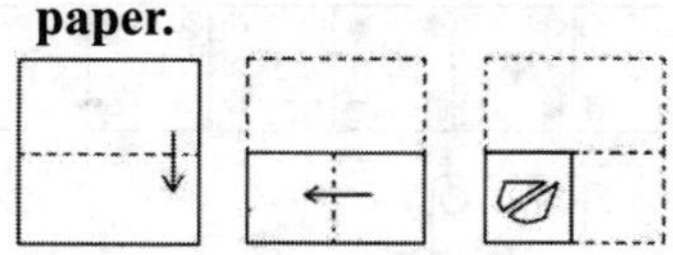

(a) 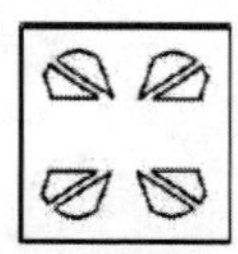

(b) 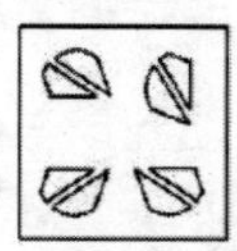

(c) 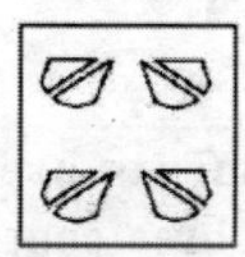

(d) 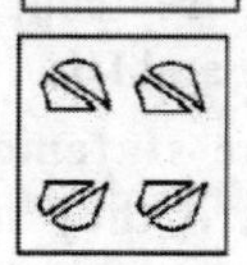

5. Select the option that is related to the fifth letter-cluster in the same way as the second letter-cluster is related to the first letter-cluster and the fourth letter-cluster is related to the third letter-cluster.

KSW : NUX :: AGP : DIQ :: EOV : ?

(a) BQU
(b) HQW
(c) BQW
(d) HOW

6. In a certain code language, 'FAVOUR' is written as 'RUOVAF' and 'REVEAL' is written as 'LAEVER'. How will 'MIRACLE' be written in that language?

(a) ECLRAIM
(b) ELCARIM
(c) ECLARMI
(d) EMLCRIA

7. Which letter-cluster will replace the question mark (?) to complete the given series?

SEJW, QGMT, OIPQ, ?, KMVK

(a) MKTN
(b) MKTM
(c) MKMT
(d) MKSN

8. In a certain code language, 'HUSBAND' is written as 'DNABSUH' and 'CLEARLY' is written as 'YLRAELC. How will 'HARBOUR' be written in that language?

(a) RUOBRHA
(b) ORUBRAH
(c) ORUBHRA
(d) RUOBRAH

9. Select the option figure which is embedded in the given figure. (Rotation is NOT allowed)

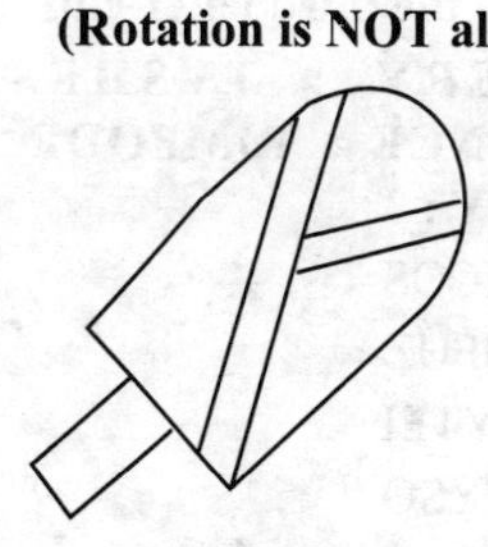

(a) 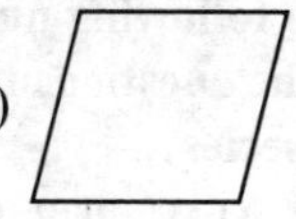

(b) 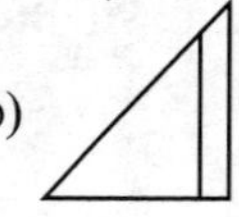

(c) 

(d) 

10. Which two signs should be interchanged to make the below equation mathematically correct?

24 + 36 – 81 × 9 ÷ 2 = 42

(a) 1. and –
(b) × and +
(c) ÷ and ×
(d) + and –

11. Which option represents the correct order of the given words as they would appear in the English dictionary?

1. Jacket
2. Japanese
3. Jabbed
4. Jackpot
5. Janitor

(a) 3,1,2,5,4
(b) 3,1,4,5,2
(c) 3,5,2,1,4
(d) 3,2,1,4,5

12. Select the option that is related to the fifth letter-cluster in the same way as the second letter-cluster is related to the first letter-cluster and the fourth letter-cluster is related to the third letter-cluster.

SURGERY : TVSHFSZ :: SILENCE : TJMFODF :: SOCIETY : ?

(a) YTEICOS
(b) TPDJFUZ
(c) COSYTEI
(d) CIETYSO

13. Which of the following numbers will replace the question mark (?) in the given series?

1483, 2369, ?, 4141, 5027, 5913

(a) 3255
(b) 2869
(c) 3119
(d) 3189

14. Which of the following terms will replace the question mark (?) in the given series?

RHWC, QKVF, ?, OQTL, NTSO

(a) PMUJ
(b) PNUI
(c) QNUI
(d) ONUJ

15. Select the figure from among the given options that can replace the question mark (?) in the following series.

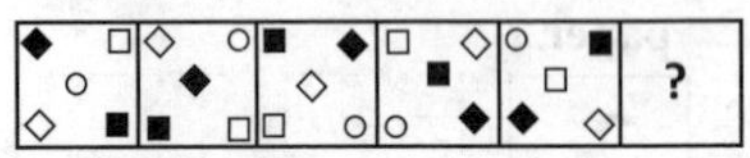

(a) 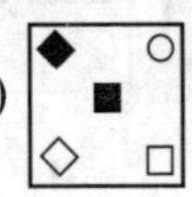

(b) 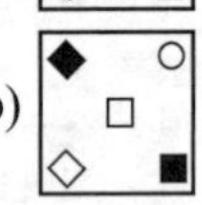

(c) 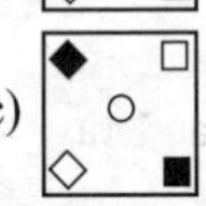

(d) 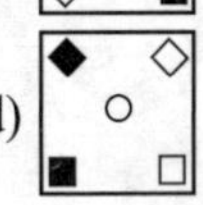

16. Three Statements are given followed by Three conclusions numbered I, II and III.

Assuming the statements to be true, even if they seem to be at variance with commonly known facts, decide which of the conclusions logically follow(s) from the statements.

Statements:

Some trees are fish.

All fishes are goats. No goat is a flower.

Conclusions:

1. Some trees are goats.

II. Some fishes are not flowers.

III. Some flowers are not goats. X

(a) Only conclusion I follows.
(b) Only conclusion II follows.
(c) Only conclusion III follows.
(d) All conclusions follow.

17. Select the correct combination of mathematical signs to sequentially replace the % signs and to balance the given equation.

42% 7 % 5% 10 % 3

(a) ÷, ×, =, ×
(b) ×, =, –, ÷
(c) ÷, ×, =, –
(d) ×, ÷, =, –

18. Which of the following numbers will replace the question mark (?) in the given series?

1, 2, 2, 4, 3, 6, 4, 8, ?

(a) 7 (b) 10
(c) 5 (d) 9

19. Select the set in which the numbers are related in the same way as are the numbers of the following sets.

(NOTE: Operations should be performed on the whole numbers, without breaking down the numbers into its constituent digits. E.g. 13 - Operations on 13 such as adding/subtracting/multiplying etc. to 13 can be performed. Breaking down 13 into 1 and 3 and then performing mathematical operations on 1 and 3 is not allowed)

(17, 136, 40)

(11, 198, 90)

(a) (12,108, 45)
(b) (9,135, 70)
(c) (24,96, 25)
(d) (12, 228, 105)

20. A@ B means A is B's sister
A & B means A is B's Brother
A # B means A is B's wife
A ^ B means A is B's mother
A + B means A is B's father

If Z & P + N ^ Q # S & V+ E @ L. Then which of the following statements is not correct?

(a) V is L's father
(b) Q is E's mother
(c) P is Q's maternal grandfather
(d) N is S's mother-in-law

Part-B General Knowledge and General Awareness

21. Startup India was launched under the ________.

(a) Ministry of Skill Development and Entrepreneurship
(b) Ministry of Social Justice and Empowerment
(c) Ministry of Labour and Employment
(d) Ministry of Commerce and Industry

22. It is used in making gunny bags, mats, ropes, yarn, carpets and other artefacts. Which crop is being spoken about here?

(a) jute
(b) banana
(c) coconut
(d) palm

23. Who among the following has received Rajiv Gandhi Puraskar, Indira Priyadarshini Samman and Rotary International Award?

(a) N. Rajam
(b) Mahaboob Subhani
(c) Zia Mohiuddin Dagar
(d) Shovana Narayan

24. Which of the following is NOT related with the primary sector of economy?

(a) Forestry
(b) Dairy
(c) Fishing
(d) Banking

25. The intervention of the government whether to expand demand or reduce it constitutes the ________ function.

(a) customisation
(b) initiation
(c) stabilisation
(d) creation

26. Sattriya, is the classical dance form of which of the following states?

(a) Tamil Nadu
(b) Uttar Pradesh
(c) Maharashtra
(d) Assam

27. The longest written constitution of the world in which country.

(a) Neatherland
(b) South Africa
(c) Unites State of America
(d) India

28. What makes the imported goods more expensive?

(a) Superior Quality
(b) Custom Made goods
(c) Tariffs
(d) Rarity in nature

29. Which Shiv Sena leader from India was elected as Member of Rajya Sabha from Maharashtra in July 2022?

(a) Sanjay Raut
(b) Vinayak Raut
(c) Uddhav Thackeray
(d) Aaditya Thackeray

30. Which of the following is not a Cricketer?

(a) Saina Nehwal
(b) Sachin Tendulkar
(c) Javagal Srinath
(d) Rahul Dravid

31. In which region did the Swadeshi Movement have the strongest impact on people?

(a) Bengal
(b) Kashmir
(c) Berar
(d) United Provinces

32. In a badminton singles game, if both the players are on 29 points then at what point will one of them win the game?

(a) 31st point
(b) Match will be drawn
(c) 30th point
(d) 32nd point

33. The term of the Lok Sabha, unless dissolved is ________ from the date appointed for its first meeting.

(a) 6 years (b) 5 Years
(c) 3 Years (d) 4 years

34. What is the white precipitate formed in the reaction of sodium sulphate and barium chloride?

(a) Barium hydroxide
(b) Sodium chloride
(c) Sodium oxide
(d) Barium sulphate

35. Ravikirti composed prashasti of which of following Chalukya rulers?

(a) Mangalesha |
(b) Pulakeshin II
(c) Kirtivaraman II
(d) Vikramaditya IV

36. Loo is a characteristic feature of which season?

(a) Summer
(b) Winter
(c) Spring
(d) Autumn

37. How many balanced meals of average size each day should adolescents have?

(a) three (b) six
(c) one (d) two

38. As per the Census 2011, what was the literacy rate in India?

(a) 74.04%
(b) 88.23%
(c) 65.27%
(d) 69.90%

39. Buddha Purnima, celebrated by the devotees of Gautam Buddha, is known as Saga Dawa in which of the following states?

(a) Andhra Pradesh
(b) Maharashtra
(c) Sikkim
(d) Assam

40. Who was appointed as the first female Director General of the Council of Scientific and Industrial Research (CSIR) in August 2022?

(a) Navjit Kaur Brar
(b) Apeksha Fernandes
(c) Nallathamby Kalaiselvi
(d) Savitri Jindal

Part-C : Elementary Mathematics

41. The selling price of an article is $\frac{1}{3}$ times of its cost price. The gain percentage is:

(a) $32\frac{1}{2}$ (b) $32\frac{1}{3}$

(a) $33\frac{1}{3}$ (b) $33\frac{2}{3}$

42. The product of 2 numbers is 6750 and their LCM is 450. If difference between the numbers is equal to their HCF, then find the smaller number.

(a) 150 (b) 75

(c) 120 (d) 90

43. X gets on a lift at the ground floor which goes up at speed of 30 floors per minute whereas Y gets on another lift at the same time on the 50th floor which goes down at the speed of 45 floors per minute. At which floor will their paths cross?(lifts are moving without stopping at any floor)

(a) 18th (b) 25th

(c) 24th (d) 20th

44. Two athletes A and B are running on a circular track of length 1800 m from the same starting point at the same starting time, at the speeds of 9 m/s and 6 m/s, respectively. At how many distinct points will they meet while running in opposite directions?

(a) 15 (b) 3

(c) 1 (d) 5

45. Mehul buys a car for ₹ 560000. He renovates it and eventually sells it for ₹ 640000.

The percent increase in the price of the car is:

(a) 80/9 percent

(b) 100/7 percent

(c) 60/7 percent

(d) 50/3 percent

46. If the length of the longest diagonal of a cube is $6\sqrt{3}$ cm, then find the volume of the cube.

(a) 126 cm^3

(b) 612 cm^3

(c) 216 cm^3

(d) 261 cm^3

47. The total amount after 3 quarters would be ₹13,310. If the rate of interest is 40% per annum and compounding is performed quarterly, determine the present value (in ₹).

(a) 13000

(b) 11000

(c) 10000

(d) 9000

48. Akash travels the distance from his home to school in three equal parts on his bicycle at a speed of 5 km/h, 10 km/h and 15 km/h, respectively. What is the average speed of Akash going from his home to school?

(a) 10 km/h

(b) $9\frac{1}{11}$ km/h

(c) $8\frac{2}{11}$

(d) 11 km/h

49. ₹12,600 is divided among 15 labourers. There are 7 men, 3 women and 5 boys. If each woman receives three times as much as each boy, and each man receives seven times as much as each boy, the share of each woman is ____.

(a) ₹ 1,800

(b) ₹ 1,200

(c) ₹ 600

(d) ₹ 900

50. Find the compound interest on a sum of ₹7,50,000 at the rate of 6% per annum to be compounded half yearly at the end of 2 years. (Approximate to the nearest integer.)

(a) ₹5,676 (b) ₹5,978

(c) ₹6,275 (d) ₹6,933

51. The marked price of a fan is 25% more than its cost price. If a discount of 12% is given on the marked price, then the gain per cent is:

(a) 1.8% (b) 9%

(c) 7% (d) 10%

52. If 3 : 5 = x : 75, then what is the value of x?

(a) 42 (b) 45

(c) 50 (d) 30

53. Aarav and Durga together can do a piece of work in 33 days. They worked together for 15 days and then Aarav left the work and Durga alone finished the remaining work in 30 days. Find the number of days in which Aarav alone can do the total work.

(a) 145/2 days

(b) 135/2 days

(c) 155/2 days

(d) 165/2 days

54. If a person buys 15 pencils for ₹12, and sells 12 pencils for ₹15, find the gain or loss percentage.

(a) Gain of 65.25%

(b) Loss of 56.25%

(c) Gain of 56.25%

(d) Loss of 56.52%

55. There is 16 percent discount on a dozen pairs of trousers marked at ₹ 5000. How many pair of trousers can be bought with ₹ 2100?

(a) 5 (b) 7

(c) 4 (d) 6

56. A number is decreased from 200 to 150. Find the decrease percentage.

(a) 25% (b) 51%

(c) 43% (d) 32%

57. A cylinder has a diameter of 14 cm, and its curved surface area is 220 cm^2. The volume of the cylinder is:

(a) 670 cm^3 (b) 770 cm^3

(c) 707 cm^3 (d) 620 cm^3

58. A train is running at a speed of 129 km/h on a straight railway track, and a small car on a parallel road is running at a speed of 60 km/h. How long (in seconds, rounded off to the nearest integer) will the train take to cross the car completely if the train is 943 m long and they are running in the same direction?

Ignore the length of the car as compared to the length of the train.

(a) 49 (b) 59
(c) 39 (d) 29

59. 12 women and 16 men can do a piece of work in 11 days. If each woman takes twice the time taken by a man to do the work, in how many days will 16 men do the same work?

(a) $\frac{117}{8}$ days

(b) $\frac{115}{8}$ days

(c) $\frac{125}{8}$ days

(b) $\frac{121}{8}$ days

60. Which of the given pairs form a co-prime numbers pair?

(a) (21, 42)
(b) (9,63)
(c) (36, 15)
(d) (11,21)

Part-D : English

61. Select the INCORRECTLY spelt word.

(a) Grammar
(b) Swindle
(c) Kindergarten
(d) Imaginery

62. Select the most appropriate option that can substitute the underlined segment in the given sentence.

I still enjoyed the week <u>despite of the weather</u>.

(a) despite with the weather
(b) despite for the weather
(c) despite to the weather
(d) despite the weather

63. Select the most appropriate meaning of the given idiom.

An axe to grind

(a) Personal and selfish reason
(b) Extra effort for solving problems
(c) Handling sharp items
(d) To act justly

64. Select the most appropriate option to fill in the blanks and make the sentence meaningful.

My _____ gives me fresh coffee every _____.

(a) made; morning
(b) made; mouming
(c) maid; mourning
(d) maid; morning

65. Select the most appropriate synonym of the given word.

Exciting

(a) Dreary
(b) Electrifying
(c) Moral
(d) Vengeful

66. Select the most appropriate ANTONYM of the given word.

Eager

(a) Indifferent
(b) Sharp
(c) Great
(d) Greedy

67. Select the INCORRECTLY spelt word.

(a) Argue
(b) Lapse
(c) Spoil
(d) Blinc

68. Select the most appropriate ANTONYM of the given word.

Invincible

(a) Vulnerable
(b) Powerful
(c) Safe
(d) Secure

69. Select the most appropriate option that can substitute the underlined segment in the given sentence. If there is no need to substitute it, select 'No substitution required'.

The fire fighters were able <u>to put out</u> the fire in the industrial unit.

(a) to put off
(b) putting out
(c) No substitution required
(d) putting off

70. Select the most appropriate option to fill in the blank.

Differences among the various groups do not _____ well for the future of the peace treaty.

(a) auger
(b) ogre
(c) oar
(d) augur

71. Select the most appropriate option that can substitute the underlined segment in the given sentence. If there is no need to substitute it, select 'No substitution'. The District Collector, Mr Kaushalendra Kumar, <u>are visiting the site</u> for inspection.

(a) No substitution
(b) is visiting the site
(c) is visiting cite
(d) are visiting site

72. Select the most appropriate meaning of the given idiom.

Get the picture

(a) To control something
(b) To understand what's happening
(c) To buy something
(d) To watch with own eyes

73. Select the most appropriate synonym of the given word.

Conquer

(a) Attach (b) Separate
(c) Surrender (d) Defeat

74. Select the option that expresses the given sentence in past perfect tense.

A. The participants practised a lot for play.

B. The participants had practised a lot for play.

C. The participants had been practising a lot for play.

D. The participants were practising a lot for play.

(a) C (b) A

(c) B (d) D

75. Select the most appropriate ANTONYM of the given word.

Freedom

(a) Bondage:

(b) Scarcity

(c) Starvation

(d) Courage

Comprehension:

In the following passage, some words have been deleted. Read the passage carefully and select the most appropriate option to fill in each blank.

Delhi National Zoological Park, which opened in 1959, is (1)________ next to the well-known Old Fort. One of the top zoos in the entire Asian continent, it stands out for its (2)________ to give the animals and the birds housed there a habitat that is as close to natural as possible. With a total area of 214 acres, it is perfect for picnics, (3)________ The National Zoological Gardens in New Delhi are home to over 2,000 different animal and bird (4)______. These animals and birds, which originate from many areas such as Africa, America, Australia, etc., (5)______ a home at this zoo. The Mughal Kos Minar serves as the Delhi Zoo's entrance.

76. Select the most appropriate option to fill in blank number 1.

(a) vacated

(b) waited

(c) located

(d) queued

77. Select the most appropriate option to fill in blank number 2.

(a) effects

(b) efforts

(c) affects

(d) escalations

78. Select the most appropriate option to fill in blank number 3.

(a) explicitly

(b) especially

(c) exactly

(d) variably

79. Select the most appropriate option to fill in blank number 4.

(a) kingdoms

(b) varieties

(c) species

(d) beings

80. Select the most appropriate option to fill in blank number 5.

(a) finding

(b) find

(c) found

(d) finds

Answers

1. (b) The mirror image will be option (b).

2. (a)

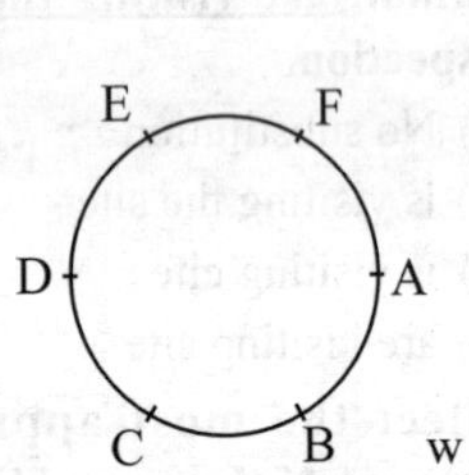

B is sitting next to A & C. Hence, option (a) is correct.

3. (c)

S R T W

↓ ↓ ↓ ↓

↑ ↑ ↑ ↑

U Q P V

P is in front of T. Hence, option (c) is correct.

4. (a) The unfolded from of paper will be option (a).

5. (b)

K S W : N U X :: A G P : D I Q

11 19 23 : 14 21 24 :: 1 7 16 : 4 9 17

+3 +2 +1 +3 +2 +1

:: E O V ?

:: 5 15 22 ______

+3 +2 +1

∴ The required answer is H Q W. Hence, option (b) is correct.

6. (b)

F A V O U R

6 1 22 18 21 18

R U O V A F

18 21 18 22 1 6

M I R A C L E

E L C A R I M

Hence, option (b) is correct

7. (d)

S E K W, Q G M T, O I P Q,

19 5 10 23 17 7 13 20 15 9 16 17

___?___, K M V K,

13 11 19 14 11 13 22 11

Hence, M K S N of option (d) is correct answer.

8. (b)

H U S B A N D

D N A B S U H

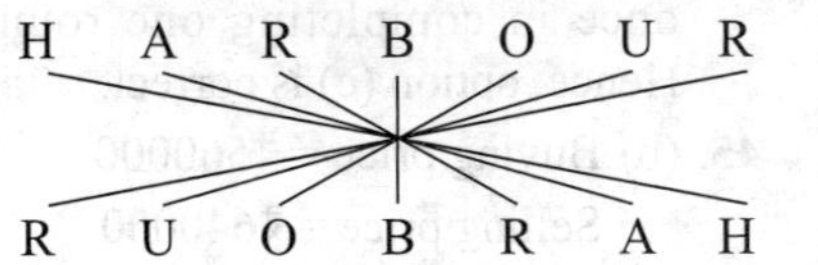

Hence, option (d) is correct.

9. (c) Option (c) is clearly seen embedded in the given figure.

10. (c) 24 + 36 – 81 × 9 ÷ 2 = 42

24 + 36 – 81 ÷ 9 × 2

= 60 – 18 = 42 = RHS

Hence, interchanging ÷ to × we get, option (c) is correct.

11. (b) Option (b) is correct order as per dictionary.

12. (b)

19 21 18 7 5 18 25
S U R G E R Y

19 15 3 9 5 20 25
S O C I E T Y
↓
T P D J F U Z

T V S H F S Z
20 22 19 8 6 11 26

Hence, option (b) is correct.

13. (a)

+886 +886 +886 +886
1483, 2369, ?, 4141, 5027, 5113

Option (a) 3255 is the correct answer.

14. (b)

18 8 23 3   17 11 22 6
R H W C   Q K V F

?   15 17 20 12
P N U I   O Q T L

Hence, required answer is P N U I or option (b).

15. (d) From figure, it is clear tht that correct answer in option (d).

16. (d)

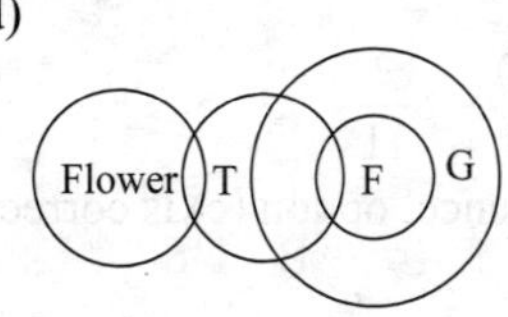

Hence, all conclusion follows. Hence, option (d) is correct.

17. (a) 42 % 7 % 5 % 10 % 3

42 ÷ 7 × 5 = 10 × 3

Hence, option (a) is correct.

18. (b)

+1 +1 +1 +1
1, 2, 2, 4, 3, 6, 4, 8, _?_, 10
+2 +2 +2 +2

Hence, option (c) is the correct answers.

19. (a)

(17, 136, 40)   17×8   40/5 = 8

(11, 198, 90)   11×8   90/5 = 8

∴ (12, 108, 45)   12×9   45/5 = 9

Hence, option (a) is correct.

20. (a)

[Z] ↔ [P] → [N] → (N) → (Q)

= [S] ↔ [V] → [E]

21. (d) Startup India was launched by Prime Minister Shri. Narendra Modi on 16th January 2016. Startup India was launched under the Ministry of Commerce and Industry.

22. (a) Jute is used to make gunny bags and carpets.

23. (d) Shovana Narayan was awarded with the 'Padma Shri' award for excellence and outstanding contribution to dance in 1992. Besides, she has also been awarded with Rajiv Gandhi Puraskar, Indira Priyadarshini Samman, and Rotary International Award and Japan's Oisca Award.

24. (d) Banking does not belong to the primary sector. It belongs to the tertiary sector or service sector. Fishing, mining, and dairying belong to the primary sector which is a basic sector.

25. (c) The intervention of the government, whether to expand demand or reduce it, constitutes the (c) stabilisation function.

26. (d) Sattriya dance form dates back to the 15th century AD and had originated in the monasteries of Assam by the great Vaishnava saint.

27. (d) The Constitution of India was legally adopted on 26th January 1950. The document provides guidelines to the government to work in accordance with its principles. The Indian Constitution is the longest written constitution in the World.

28. (d) Tariff: It is a tax that is imposed on imported products. This tax makes imported products more costly and discourages their use. The purpose of quotas and tariffs is to restrict imports and therefore, protect domestic industries from foreign competition.

29. (a) Sanjay Rajaram Raut is an Indian politician from Shiv Sena (Uddhav Balasaheb Thackeray) party. He is a member of the Parliament of India representing Maharashtra in the Rajya Sabha, the upper house of the Indian Parliament.

30. (--) Saina Nehwal in not a cricketer. She is a badminton player.

31. (a) The demonstrations were held in the whole of Bengal and people were asked to use Swadeshi product and boycott British products. Later along with a boycott of British products the people started boycotting the British services like postal service, courts, schools and colleges etc.

32. (c) A point is scored on every serve and awarded to whichever side wins the rally. The winning side gets the next serve. If the score is 20-20, a side must win by two clear points to win the game. If it reaches 29-29, the first to get their 30th point wins.

33. (b) The term of the Lok Sabha, unless dissolved, is five years from the date appointed for its first meeting.

34. (d) When barium chloride combines with sodium sulfate in the form of their aqueous solution a white precipitate of barium sulphate is formed which is insoluble in water. The reaction also creates sodium chloride (salt) which remains dissolved in water and cannot be seen.

35. (b) Ravikirti was the court poet of 'Pulakeshin II'.

Pulakeshin II was the most famous ruler of the Chalukya dynasty who reigned from 610 to 642 CE.

The most notable military achievement of Pulakeshin II was his victory over the powerful emperor Harshavardhana, who ruled over much of Northern India. The famous Aihole inscription written in classical Sanskrit was composed by Ravikirti.

36. (a) Loo is a strong, gusty, hot, and dry wind that blows during daytime over north and northwestern India. These winds raise the temperature of the region, and exposure to these winds can even prove fatal.

37. (a) Eat 3 meals a day, with healthy snacks. Increase fiber in the diet and decrease the use of salt. Drink water. Try to avoid drinks that are high in sugar.

38. (a) As per the census of 2011, the literacy rate of India is 74.04%. Literacy rate among the males is 82.14% and among females is 65.46%.

39. (c) Saga Dawa or the Triple Blessed Festival is an auspicious month for the Sikkimese Buddhists with prayers held throughout the month in various monasteries. On the full moon of this 4th month of the Tibetan calendar [celebrated as Buddha Purnima in the rest of India] is the main celebration.

40. (d) Senior scientist Nallathamby Kalaiselvi was on 6 August 2022 appointed as the first woman Director General of the Council of Scientific & Industrial Research (CSIR).

41. (b) $SP = \frac{1}{3} CP$

$\therefore$ Loss = CP – SP

$= CP - \frac{1}{3} CP = \frac{2}{3} CP$

$\therefore \% \text{ loss} = \frac{2\ CP}{3\ CP} \times 100$

$= \frac{200}{3} = 66\frac{2}{3}\%$

42. (b) Product of two numbers

= LCM × HCF

$\Rightarrow 6750 = 450 \times HCF$

$\Rightarrow HCF = \frac{6750}{450} = 15$

$\therefore$ Also, the difference of two numbers = HCF

$\Rightarrow N_1 - N_2 = 15 \quad ...(i)$

$N_1N_2 = 6750$

$\Rightarrow (N_1 - N_2)^2 = (15)^2$

$\Rightarrow N_1^2 + N_2^2 - 2N_1N_2 = 225$

$\Rightarrow N_1^2 + N_2^2 - 2N_1N_2 = 225 + 4N_1N_2$

$\Rightarrow (N_1 + N_2)^2 = 225 + 4 \times 6750$

$= 27225$

$\Rightarrow N_1 - N_2 = 165 \quad ...(ii)$

Solving (i) & (ii) we get,

$2N_1 = 180$

$\Rightarrow N_1 = 90, N_2 = 75$

Hence, option (b) is correct.

43. (d) Let they cross at (x^{th}) floor after (t) time

Since (t) is equal for both

$\therefore \frac{\frac{x}{30\text{ floor}}}{60\text{ sec}} = \frac{(50-x)}{\left[\frac{45}{60}\right]}$

$\Rightarrow \frac{60}{30} = \frac{60(50-x)}{45}$

$\Rightarrow \frac{x}{6} = \frac{50-x}{9}$

$\Rightarrow 9x = 300 - 6x$

$\Rightarrow 15x = 300$

$\Rightarrow x = 20$

$\therefore$ They will cross at 20th floor from bottom. Hence, option (d) is correct.

44. (c) When they run in opposite direction, their relative speed is 9 + 6 = 15 m/sec.

$\therefore$ Time taken to meet first $= \frac{1800}{15}$

= 120 sec. Hence, they will meet once in completing one round. Hence, option (c) is correct.

45. (b) Buying price = ₹560000

Selling price = ₹640000

% increase in price

$= \frac{80000}{560000} \times 100 = \frac{100}{7}\%$

Hence, option (b) is correct.

46. (c) Diagonal of a cube $= \sqrt{3}$ a

$= 6\sqrt{3}$ cm

$\Rightarrow \sqrt{3}\,a = 6\sqrt{3}$

$\Rightarrow a = 6$ cm

$\therefore$ Volume of cube $= a^3 = 6^3 = 216\ cm^3$.

Hence, option (c) is correct.

47. (c) 40% Rate

Quality = 10%

Time = 3 quarter

$\therefore \frac{10}{100}$

$\Rightarrow 10 \rightarrow 11$

10 11

10 11

$\Rightarrow 1000 \quad 1331$

$\Rightarrow$ If amount ₹1331, Principal = ₹1000

$\therefore$ If amount ₹13310, $P = \frac{1000}{1331} \times 13310$

$\Rightarrow P = 10000$

Hence, option (c) is correct.

48. (c) Let total distance from school to home = x km

$\text{Average speed} = \frac{\text{Total Distance}}{\text{Total Time}}$

$\Rightarrow \frac{x}{\frac{x}{3\times5} + \frac{x}{3\times10} + \frac{x}{3\times15}}$

$= \frac{x}{\frac{x}{15} + \frac{x}{30} + \frac{x}{45}} = \frac{x}{\frac{6x+3x+2x}{90}}$

$= \frac{90}{11} = 8\frac{2}{11}$

Hence, option (c) is correct.

49. (c) Total money = ₹12600

15 labourers i.e. 7 Men + 3 Women + 5 Boys

Let share of boys be x

According to question, each share ratio

W	B	M
3x	x	7x

Total share received by W + B + M

$= [(3x \times 3) + (x \times 3) + (7x \times 7)]$

or $9x + 5x + 49x = 63x$

or $63x = 12600$

or $x = \frac{12600}{63}$

or $x = 200$

$\therefore$ Share of each women $= 3x$

$= 3 \times 200 = 600$

Hence, option (c) is correct.

50. (d) P = 750000

R = 6%

T = 2 years

Half yearly compounded

$\therefore R = \frac{3}{100}$ T = 4

$\Rightarrow$ P	A	CI
$\Rightarrow$ 100	103	3
100	103	3
100	103	3
100	103	3

$\Rightarrow$ If $P = (100)^4 \rightarrow A = (103)^4$

$\therefore P = 75 \times 10^4$ $CI = (103)^4 - (100)^4$

$\Rightarrow$ Required CI

$= \frac{112550881 - 100000000}{100} \times 750000$

$= \frac{941316075}{10000} =$ ₹94131

Hence, option (d) is correct.

51. (d) CP = 100

MP = 125

D% = 12%

$SP = \frac{88 \times 125}{100} =$ ₹110

$\Rightarrow$ Gain% $= \frac{110 - 125}{100} \times 100 = 10\%$

Hence, option (d) is correct.

52. (b) $3 : 5 = x : 75$

$\Rightarrow \frac{3}{5} = \frac{x}{75}$

$\Rightarrow x = \frac{75 \times 3}{5} = 45$

Hence, option (b) is correct.

53. (b) Aarav + Durga = 33 days

1 day work of Aarav and Durga $= \frac{1}{33}$

15 days work $= \frac{15}{33}$

Work left $= 1 - \frac{15}{33} = \frac{18}{33}$

Time of Durga for finish left work = 30 days

$\therefore$ Durga's efficiency $= \frac{18}{33 \times 30}$

$= \frac{1}{55}$

$\therefore$ Durga can do the work alone in 55 days

$\therefore$ Aarav can do it also in

$\frac{1}{\text{Aarav's efficiency}}$

$= \frac{5 - 3}{165} = \frac{2}{165}$

Aarav's alone take time $= \frac{165}{2}$ days

Hence, option (d) is correct.

54. (d)

	No. of items	Price
CP	15	12
SP	12	15

CP = 225 SP = 144

Loss% $= \frac{225 - 144}{225} \times 100$

= 36%

Hence, option (d) is correct.

55. (d) 16% discount

12 pairs = ₹5000 (Marked Price)

$\therefore$ S.P. $= \frac{84 \times 5000}{100} = 4200$

12 pairs $\rightarrow$ ₹4200

or for ₹2100 $\rightarrow \frac{12}{4200} \times 2100$

= 6 pairs

Hence, option (d) is correct.

56. (a)

200 – 150

Decrease in % $= \frac{50}{200} \times 100 = 25\%$

Hence, option (a) is correct.

57. (b) Curved surface area of cylinder $= 2\pi rh$

$\therefore 2\pi rh = 220$

$r = \frac{14}{2} = 7$ cm

$\Rightarrow 2 \times \frac{22}{7} \times 7 \times h = 220$

$\Rightarrow h = \frac{220}{44} = \frac{20}{4} = 5$ cm

$\therefore$ volume $= \pi r^2 h$

$= \frac{22}{7} \times 7 \times 7 \times 5$

$= 110 \times 7 = 770$ cm^3

Hence, option (b) is correct.

58. (a) Length of train = 943 m

Speed of train = 129 km/hr

Speed of car = 60 km/hr

$\therefore$ Relative speed = (129 – 60)

= 69 km/hr

$\therefore$ Time taken $= \frac{943 \times 18}{69 \times 5}$

$= \frac{41 \times 18}{3 \times 5} = 49.2$ seconds

Hence option (a) is correct.

59. (d) 12W + 16M

2W = 1M

$\Rightarrow$ 12W + 32 W = 11 Days

$\Rightarrow$ 45W = 11 Days

$\Rightarrow 12 \times \frac{1}{2}M + 16M = 11$ Days

$\Rightarrow$ 22M = 11 Days

$\therefore$ T.W. = 22 × 11

$\therefore$ M = 16

Then $T = \frac{22 \times 11}{16} = \frac{121}{8}$ days

Hence, option (d) is correct.

60. (d) Co-prime numbers are those number which have their HCF as 1

$\therefore$ (11, 21) are co-prime which have 1 as their HCF.

Hence, option (d) is correct.

61. (d) The INCORRECTLY spelled word is (d) Imaginery. The correct spelling is "Imaginary."

62. (d) The most appropriate option to substitute the underlined segment in the given sentence is (d) despite the weather. So, the corrected sentence would be: "I still enjoyed the week despite the weather."

63. (a) The most appropriate meaning of the idiom "An axe to grind" is (a) Personal and selfish reason. This idiom refers to someone who has a hidden agenda or a personal motive behind their actions or statements.

64. (d) The most appropriate option to fill in the blanks and make the sentence meaningful is:

My maid gives me fresh coffee every morning.

So, the correct option is (d) maid; morning.

65. (b) The most appropriate synonym for the word "Exciting" is (b) Electrifying.

66. (a) The most appropriate antonym for the word "Eager" is (a) Indifferent.

67. (d) The INCORRECTLY spelled word is (d) Blinc. The correct spelling is "Blink."

68. (a) The most appropriate antonym of the word "Invincible" is "Vulnerable."

69. (a) The most appropriate option to substitute the underlined segment in the given sentence is: (a) to put off So, the corrected sentence would be: "The firefighters were able to put off the fire in the industrial unit."

70. (d) The most appropriate option to fill in the blank is: (d) augur

So, the sentence would be: "Differences among the various groups do not augur well for the future of the peace treaty."

71. (b) The most appropriate option to substitute the underlined segment in the given sentence is:

(b) is visiting the site

So, the corrected sentence would be: "The District Collector, Mr. Kaushalendra Kumar, is visiting the site for inspection."

72. (b) The most appropriate meaning of the idiom "Get the picture" is (b) To understand what's happening.

73. (d) The most appropriate synonym for the word "Conquer" is (d) Defeat.

74. (c) The correct option that expresses the given sentence in past perfect tense is:

C. The participants had been practising a lot for play.

75. (a) The most appropriate antonym of the word "Freedom" is (a) Bondage.

76. (c) LOCATED

77. (b) EFFORTS

78. (b) ESPECIALLY

79. (c) SPECIES

80. (c) FOUND

❑❑❑

SSC Constable (GD)
Solved Paper-2022

Exam Date 11-01-2023

Part-A: General Intelligence and Reasoning

1. Six people U, V, W, X, Y, and Z are sitting in a circle facing opposite to the centre. U is sitting third to the right of Y. W is sitting to the immediate left of U. W is sitting third to the left of V. Z is not sitting next to U. Who is sitting between W and Y?

(a) Z (b) X
(c) U (d) V

2. Which option represents the correct order of the given words as they would appear in the English dictionary?

1. kind 2. kite
3. knit 4. king
5. kindle

(a) 1,5,4,2,3
(b) 1,4,2,5,3
(c) 1,5,2,4,3
(d) 1,4,5,2,3

3. Which letter-cluster will replace the question mark (?) to complete the given series?

XCMQ, YDNR, ?, AFPT, BGQU

(a) ZEOR (b) ZEPS
(c) ZEUS (d) ZEOS

4. Three Statements are given followed by Three conclusions numbered I, II and III. Assuming the statements to be true, even if they seem to be at variance with commonly known facts, decide which of the conclusions logically follow(s) from the statements.

Statements:
All bags are rubber.
Some rubber are chairs. All chairs are tables. Conclusions:
I. Some rubber are bags.
II. Some chairs are rubber.
III. Some chairs are tables.

(a) Both conclusions I and III follow.
(b) Both conclusions I and II follow.
(c) All conclusions follow.
(d) Both conclusions II and III follow.

5. Which of the mathematical signs should be interchanged in the below equation to make it mathematically correct?

$144 - 12 + 18 \times 6 \div 24 = 96$

(a) – and ÷
(b) – and x
(c) × and ÷
(d) – and +

6. 'A + B' means 'B is the brother of A'
'A–B' means 'B is the sister of A'
'A % B' means 'B is the daughter of A'
'A & B' means 'B is the wife of A'
If A & B % C + D E, then how is E related to A?

(a) Mother
(b) Wife
(c) Daughter
(d) Sister

7. Seven friends are sitting around a circular table facing the centre. T is an immediate neighbour of K and U. S is sitting immediate right of K. W is an immediate neighbour of U and M. Who is sitting third to the left of K?

(a) W (b) M
(c) U (d) T

8. Which number will replace the question mark (?) in the following series?

6, 24, 60, 120, ?

(a) 150 (b) 180
(c) 135 (d) 210

9. Three different positions of the same dice are shown. Find the number on the face opposite the face showing '2'.

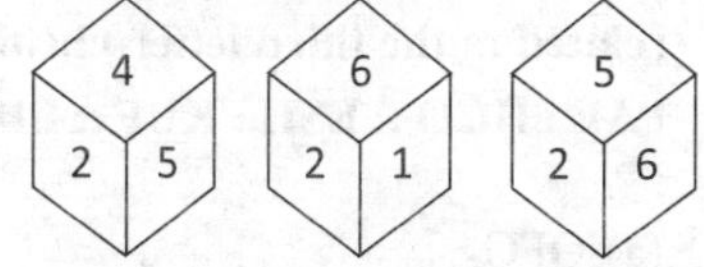

(a) 5 (b) 1
(c) 4 (d) 3

10. Select the figure that will come next in the following series.

(a) 

(b) 

(c) 

(d) 

11. Select the option that is related to the third word in the same way as the second word is related to the

first word. (The words must be considered as meaningful English words and must not be related to each other based on the number of letters/number of consonants/ vowels in the word.)

Kite : Claw :: Horse : ?

(a) Strong
(b) Fast
(c) Power
(d) Hoof

12. In a certain code language, 'GHOST' is written as 'JCRNW and 'FIRED' is written as 'IDUZG'. How will 'RIFLE' be written in the same code language?

(a) UDIGH
(b) VEJFH
(c) PDBGH
(d) VIDBH

13. Select the option that is related to the fifth letter-cluster in the same way as the second letter-cluster is related to the first letter-cluster and the fourth letter-cluster is related to the third letter-cluster.

PAE : HCQ :: ESH : KUF :: FDN : ?

(a) QFG
(b) KFG
(c) KGP
(d) PFH

14. Which letter-cluster will replace the question mark (?) to complete the given series?

QJKE, SHIG, UFGI, ?, YBCM

(a) WCFM
(b) VEFL
(c) VDEN
(d) WDEK

15. Select the correct mirror image of the given combination when the mirror is placed at 'PQ' as shown below.

(a) 
(b) 
(c) 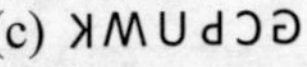
(d) 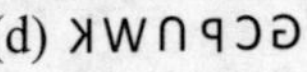

16. In a certain code language, 'SLOWLY' is written as 'TMNXMZ' and 'FRIEND' is written as' GSHDOE'. How will 'BORING' be written in that language?

(a) CPSNOH
(b) CNSHOH
(c) CNSJOH
(d) CNSHOF

17. Select the option figure which is embedded in the given figure. (Rotation is NOT allowed)

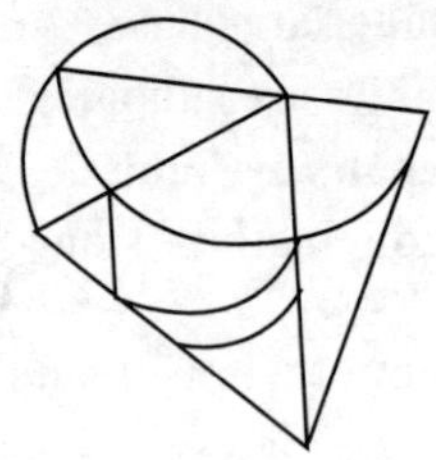

(a) 

(b) 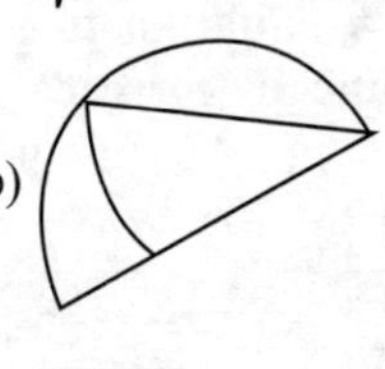

(c) 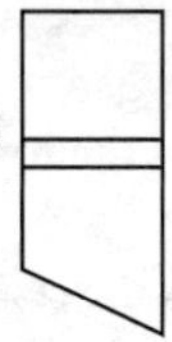

(d) 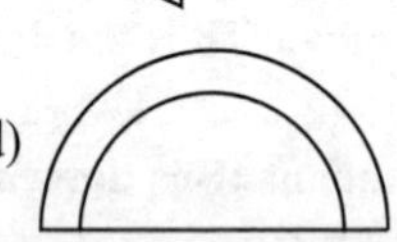

18. Which of the following numbers will replace the question mark (?) in the given series?

62498, 61874, ?, 60644, 60038, 59438

(a) 61256
(b) 61656
(c) 60544
(d) 60446

19. Select the set in which the numbers are related in the same way as are the numbers of the following sets.

(NOTE: Operations should be performed on the whole numbers, without breaking down the numbers into its constituent digits. E.g. 13 Operations on 13 such as adding/ subtracting/multiplying etc. to 13 can be performed. Breaking down 13 into 1 and 3 and then performing mathematical operations on 1 and 3 is not allowed)

(11, 78, 15)

(12, 90, 18)

(a) (12, 89, 17)
(b) (11, 91, 19)
(c) (13, 96, 19)
(d) (10, 54, 17)

20. Select the correct combination of mathematical signs to sequentially replace the * signs and to balance the given equation.

10 * 18 * 19 * 2* 1* 217

(a) ×, +, ×, +, =
(b) ×, +, ×, – =
(c) ×, +, –, –, =
(d) +, +, ×, –, =

Part-B General Knowledge and General Awareness

21. Government of India has approved a new Central Sector Scheme entitled "National Beekeeping & Honey Mission (NBHM)" which is associated to revolution.

(a) savoury
(b) sweet
(c) honey
(d) golden

22. ________are a narrow belt of high altitude (above 12,000 m) westerly winds in the troposphere. Their speed varies from about 110 km/h in summer to about 184 km/h in winter.

(a) Jet Streams (b) Whirlwind
(c) Derecho (d) Hurricane

23. After independence, India launched its First Five Year Plan in ______.
(a) 1952 (b) 1953
(c) 1950 (d) 1951

24. Which Indian dancer among the following was the Youngest recipient of Padma Vibhushan in 2003?
(a) Uday Shankar
(b) Sonal Mansingh
(c) Pandit Birju Maharaj
(d) Kelucharan Mohapatra

25. What is the chemical formula of Calcium Carbonate?
(a) $CaSO_4$ (b) $CaCO_3$
(c) $CaCO_2$ (d) CaO

26. Which vitamin is also known as Thiamin?
(a) Vitamin B2
(b) Vitamin B3
(c) Vitamin B1
(d) Vitamin B12

27. Who took oath as the Governor of Meghalaya in October 2022?
(a) Banwarilal Purohit
(b) Tathagata Roy
(c) Satya Pal Malik
(d) B. D. Mishra

28. Gandhi-Irwin pact was signed in which year?
(a) 1931 (b) 1935
(c) 1929 (d) 1933

29. A budget document, which relates to the revenue receipts and revenue expenditure of the government for a particular financial year, is called _____.
(a) Revenue budget
(b) Zero budget
(c) Logt-term budget
(d) Capital budget

30. The last article of the Constitution of India has been given the number _______. (as on May 2022).
(a) 380 (b) 390
(c) 395 (d) 385

31. As of November 2022, who is the Union Minister for Education in India?
(a) Dharmendra Pradhan
(b) Mansukh Mandaviya
(c) Anurag Thakur
(d) Kiren Rijiju

32. Which union territory has the highest sex ratio as per the 2011 Census?
(a) Lakshadweep
(b) Puducherry
(c) Daman & Diu
(d) Chandigarh

33. _______ is celebrated as Gujarati New Year in India.
(a) Bestu Varas
(b) Vishu
(c) Losar
(d) Losoong

34. Primary raw material for sugar industry is_______.
(a) chemical sweeteners
(b) sweet potato
(c) apple
(d) sugar cane

35. Which among the following classical dance forms was introduced in the 16th century by Vaishnava saint Mahapurusha Sankaradeva?
(a) Kuchipudi
(b) Sattriya
(c) Odissi
(d) Manipuri

36. In which city is the Mohun Bagan Athletic club situated?
(a) Jaipur
(b) Kolkata
(c) Lucknow
(d) Bulandshahr

37. Who hosted the FIFA World Cup 2022?
(a) Brazil
(b) Qatar
(c) Spain
(d) Germany

38. Removal of president of the country from the office is known as ________.
(a) Impeachment
(b) Termination of Services
(c) Resignation
(d) Voluntary Retirement from services

39. Who among the following Greek rulers sent Megasthenes to the court of Chandragupta Maurya?
(a) Seleucus Nicator
(b) Amyntas II
(c) Amyntas III
(d) Phillip II

40. To whom does the right of inheritance extend?
(a) Barren land
(b) Land pollution
(c) Division of land
(d) Land subsidence

Part-C : Elementary Mathematics

41. Manish bought an air conditioner for Rs.46,875, its value is depreciating at the rate of 8% yearly. What will be the price of the air conditioner after 3 years?
(a) ₹ 33,786
(b) ₹ 32,245
(c) ₹ 36,501
(d) ₹ 35,602

42. A person covers a distance of 240 km in 6 hrs on the first day, 360 km in 8 hrs on second day and 450 km in 6 hrs on third day. Find the average distance covered per hour in 3 days.
(a) 52.5 kms
(b) 50.5 kms
(c) 51 kms
(d) 48 kms

43. An increase of 25 percent in the price of onions enables a woman to buy 5 kg less for Rs. 200. The increased price of onions per kg is:
(a) ₹ 5 per kg

(b) ₹ 8 per kg
(c) ₹ 10 per kg
(d) ₹ 15 per kg

44. A person travels in a car for 600 km at an average speed of 50 km/h and 100 km at 100 km/h, and finally reaches his destination by travelling 50 km at a speed of 25 km/h. Determine the average speed during the whole journey.
(a) 50 km/h
(b) 75 km/h
(c) 58.33 km/h
(d) 25 km/h

45. There are 90 female members and 60 male members in a club. If the average age of female members is 35 years, and the average age of male members is 45 years, then find the average age (in years) of the whole club?
(a) 39 (b) 36
(c) 40 (d) 47

46. The difference between the two numbers is 15% of their sum. Find the ratio of the smaller number to the larger number.
(a) $\frac{13}{17}$ (b) $\frac{17}{13}$
(c) $\frac{17}{23}$ (d) $\frac{23}{17}$

47. The radius of a cone is 5 cm and its slant height is 16 cm. It's total surface area (in cm^2) will be:
(a) 330 (b) 300
(c) 310 (d) 320

48. Ruby bought 20 buttons for ₹ 1. How many buttons she must sell for ₹ 1 in order to get a profit of 25%?
(a) 15 (b) 17
(c) 14 (d) 16

49. In a proportion, the product of the 1st and 4th term is 70 and that of 2nd and 3rd term is 3.5x. The value of x is.
(a) 21 (b) 35
(c) 2 (d) 20

50. A and B together can do a piece of the work in 50 hours, B and C together can do the same work in 75 hours and A and C together can do the same in 25 hours. Find the time in which A, B, and C together will complete the task.
(a) 400/11 hours
(b) 150/11 hours
(c) 131/11 hours
(d) 300/11 hours

51. Find the difference between the greatest and the smallest 4-digit numbers exactly divisible by 36 and 48.
(a) 8928
(b) 8892
(c) 8298
(d) 8982

52. If machine A and B can produce 1100 units in 9 h and 12 h respectively. In how many hours can machine A and B working together at these constant rates produce 1100 units?
(a) $\frac{36}{7}$ (b) $\frac{37}{7}$
(c) $\frac{39}{7}$ (b) $\frac{38}{7}$

53. Robin travels one-fourth of the distance at 20 km/h, another one-fourth at 10 km/h, and the remaining distance at 80 km/h. Find Robin's average speed for the entire distance (correct to 2 decimal places)?
(a) 25 km/h
(b) 22.86 km/h
(c) 20 km/h
(d) 18.2 km/h

54. The marked price of an item was Rs. 100000, but the shopkeeper offered a double discount of 20 percent and 10 percent. At what price did he finally sell the item?
(a) ₹ 72000
(b) ₹ 80000
(c) ₹ 70000
(d) ₹ 82000

55. If 2^{305} + 303 is divided by 9, then the remainder is:
(a) 2 (b) 4
(c) 6 (d) 1

56. A chair is bought for ₹800 and sold for ₹1,100. Find the gain percentage.
(a) 40%
(b) 30%
(c) 37.5%
(d) 32.3%

57. The curved surface area of right circular cylinder of height 14 cm is 110 cm^2. What is the base diameter of the cylinder?
(Use $\pi = \frac{22}{7}$)
(a) 2.7 cm
(b) 2.4 cm
(c) 2.5 cm
(d) 2.6 cm

58. The marked price on an item was ₹ 2000/- but the shopkeeper offered a discount of 20 percent. How much did he finally sell the item for?
(a) ₹ 1400
(b) ₹ 1200
(c) ₹ 1500
(d) ₹ 1600

59. In how many years will ₹800 amount to ₹926.10 at 10% per annum, compounded half-yearly?
(a) 3 (b) 2
(c) 2.5 (d) 1.5

60. If a + b = 25 and a – b = 7, then determine the mean proportion of a and b.
(a) 12 (b) 15
(c) 6 (d) 9

Part-D : English

61. Select the most appropriate ANTONYM of the given word.
Compassionate
(a) Likeable
(b) Merciful
(c) Cruel
(d) Fashionable

62. Select the most appropriate synonym for the underlined word in the given sentence.

An oxygen cylinder is used to deliver oxygen through the patient's nasal orifice.

(a) origin
(c) ornate
(c) ordained
(d) opening

63. Select the most appropriate ANTONYM of the given word.

Feeble

(a) Anxious
(b) Weak
(c) Sturdy
(d) Curious

64. The sentence below is divided into four segments. Select the option that has an error of tense.

I has been/visiting my family and relatives/during the winter vacation.

(a) during the winter vacation
(b) family and relatives
(c) visiting my
(d) I has been

65. Select the most appropriate option that can substitute the underlined segment in the given sentence.

My uncle has an extremely large bungalow which has six bedrooms, five bathrooms and four living rooms.

(a) enormous
(b) meagre
(c) great
(d) oversize

66. Select the most appropriate meaning of the underlined idiom in the given sentence.

Siraj-ud Daula's defeat can be attributed to a snake in the grass.

(a) A devoted attendant
(b) A disloyal soldier
(c) A deceitful person
(d) A coiled serpent

67. Select the most appropriate option to fill in the blank.

He is an absolutely ______ man.

(a) chased
(b) chaste
(c) chest
(d) crazed

68. Select the most appropriate ANTONYM of the bracketed word to fill in the blank.

The medicine was so _______ (sweet) that a man had to choose sugar along with it.

(a) rancid
(b) sour
(c) stale
(d) fetid

69. Select the option in which all the words are spelt correctly.

(a) The sage preached that we are accountable to God in this life.
(b) The sage preached that we are akountable to God in this life.
(c) The sage preached that we are accuntable to God in this life.
(d) The sage preached that we are acountable to God in this life.

70. Select the most appropriate option to fill in the blank.

He indeed is intelligent who ______ this and succeeds in making all work truly great.

(a) was noticed
(b) noticed
(c) notices
(d) noticing

71. Select the INCORRECTLY spelt word.

(a) Skulptor
(b) Miraculous
(c) Vision
(d) Succeed

72. Select the most appropriate synonym of the given word.

Ideal

(a) Excellent
(b) Hefty
(c) Bad
(d) Intact

73. Select the most appropriate option that can substitute the underlined segment in the given sentence. If there is no need to substitute it, select 'No substitution'.

I visited the hospital to enquire about eyes surgery.

(a) enquire about eye surgery
(b) enquire for eyes surgery
(c) enquired about eye surgery
(d) No substitution

74. Select the most appropriate meaning of the given idiom.

To call in question

(a) Show indifference
(b) Take a resolute stand
(c) Challenge
(d) Dislike the arrangement

75. Complete the sentence using correct pair of words from the options given.

My brother __________ apples during his fast.

(a) ate; eight
(b) eight; eight
(c) ate; ate
(d) eight; ate

Comprehension:

In the following passage, some words have been deleted. Read the passage carefully and select the most appropriate option to fill in each blank.

One certain benefit of online communication either through email or even communicating through WhatsApp nowadays is that there is a (1) ______ dependence on paper. It is said that to make a ton of paper 17 trees have to be cut down. With the already existing demand for paper to meet (2) ______ needs, it would be horrendous to keep (3)______ the demand for paper worldwide. Online communication is a boon as many documents are now sent by mail through PDF, Microsoft Word or the JPEG format. This means that there is certainly a (4)______ in the use of paper due to online communication. Many people read online newspapers nowadays, which means there is a decline

18, 2022, and was contested by the men's national teams of 32 countries.

38. (a) The President may be removed before his tenure through impeachment for violating the Constitution of India by the Parliament of India. The process may begin in either of the two houses of the Parliament. A House starts by levelling charges against the President.

39. (a) Megasthenes was a Greek ambassador of Seleucus I Nicator in the court of King Chandragupta Maurya. Seleucus I, the Hellenistic king, sent Megasthenes as an ambassador to the court of King Chandragupta Maurya in India.

40. (*)

41. (c) CP of air conditioner = ₹46875

Depreciation = 8%

Price after 3 years = ?

$\therefore$ Let CP = ₹100,

Value after 1 year = 92

After 2 years $= 92 \times \frac{92}{100}$

After 3 years $= \frac{92 \times 92 \times 92}{100}$

$\therefore 100 \quad \rightarrow \quad \frac{92 \times 92 \times 92}{100}$

$₹46875 \rightarrow$

$$\frac{92 \times 92 \times 92 \times 46875}{100 \times 100 \times 100}$$

= ₹36501

Hence, option (c) is correct.

42. (a) Total distance = Average speed × Total time

or Average speed $= \frac{\text{Total distance}}{\text{Total time}}$

$$= \frac{240+360+450}{\frac{240}{6}+\frac{360}{8}+\frac{450}{6}}$$

$$= \frac{1050}{40+45+75}$$

$$= \frac{1050}{160} = 6.5625 \text{ km/hr}$$

Total time = (6 + 8 + 6) = 20 hr

Total distance = 1050

$\therefore$ Average distance/time

$$= \frac{1050}{20} = 52.5 \text{ km}$$

Hence, option (a) is correct.

43. (c) Let price of onion be ₹x/kg

Then purchase in ₹200

$$\frac{200}{x} \text{kg}$$

If price increases by 25%, new price = 1.25x/kg

New quantity purchased $= \frac{200}{1.25x}$

$$\frac{200}{x} - \frac{20000}{125x} = 5$$

$$\Rightarrow \frac{200}{x} - \frac{160}{x} = 5$$

$$\Rightarrow x = \frac{40}{5} = 8$$

Original price = ₹8/kg

New price = 1.25 × 8 = ₹10/kg

Hence, option (c) is correct.

44. (a) Average speed $= \frac{\text{Total distance}}{\text{Total time}}$

$$= \frac{600+100+50}{\frac{600}{50}+\frac{100}{100}+\frac{50}{25}}$$

$$= \frac{750}{12+1+2}$$

$$= \frac{750}{15} = 50 \text{ km/hr}$$

Hence, option (a) is correct.

45. (a) Female members = 90

Male members = 60

Average age of female = 35

$\therefore$ Total age of female = 90 × 35

Average age of male = 45

$\therefore$ Total age of male = 45 × 60

$\therefore$ Total Average age

$$= \frac{90 \times 35 + 60 \times 35}{150}$$

$$= \frac{5850}{150} = 39$$

Hence, option (a) is correct.

46. (c) Let the two numbers be x & y

$\therefore x - y = 15\%(x + y)$

$$\Rightarrow x - y = \frac{15x + 15y}{100}$$

$$\Rightarrow 100x - 100y = 15x + 15y$$

$$\Rightarrow 85x = 115y$$

$$\Rightarrow \frac{y}{x} = \frac{85}{115} = \frac{17}{23}$$

Hence, option (c) is correct.

47. (a) Radius of cone = 5 cm

length (slant height) = 16

$h = \sqrt{16^2 - 5^2} = \sqrt{256 - 25} = \sqrt{231}$

Total surface area of cone

$= \pi rl + \pi r^2$

$= \pi r(l + r)$

$= \frac{22}{7} \times 5[16 + 5]$

$= \frac{22}{7} \times 5 \times 21 = 22 \times 15$

$= 330 \text{ cm}^2$

Hence, option (a) is correct.

48. (d) CP of 1 buttom $= ₹\frac{1}{20}$

Profit = 25%

$$\therefore \text{SP} = \frac{125}{100} \times \frac{1}{20} = \frac{1}{16}$$

16 buttons for ₹1 for 25% gain.

Hence, option (d) is correct.

49. (d) 3.5x = 70 (Given)

$$\Rightarrow x = \frac{700}{35} = 20$$

Hence, option (d) is correct.

50. (d) A + B = 50 hrs.

B + C = 75 hrs.

A + C = 25 hrs.

Total work = 150 hrs.

(A + B)'s efficiency = 3

(B + C)'s efficiency = 2

(A + C)'s efficiency = 6

$\therefore$ (A + B + C)'s Efficiency $= \frac{11}{2}$

Hence, time taken by (A + B + C)

together $= \frac{150}{11} \times 2$

$= \frac{300}{11}$ hrs. Hence, option (d) is correct.

51. (a) Smallest four digit numbers = 1000

Smallest four digit numbers divisible by 36 & 48 will be divisible by their LCM

or LCM of 36 & 48 = 144

dividing 1000 by 144 we get if 8 added to 1000 we get completely divisible number by 144

i.e. 1008

Similarly, largest 4 digit number = 9999

Dividing 9999 by 144 we get, 63 to be subtracted from 9999

(9999 – 63) = 9936

∴ Difference between highest and lowest four digit numbers divisible by 144 are [9936 – 1008]

= 8928.

Hence, option (a) is correct.

52. (a) A's work = 1100 units in 9 hrs

$\therefore$ A's efficiency $= \frac{1100}{9}$

B's work = 1100 units in 12 hrs

$\therefore$ B's efficiency $= \frac{1100}{12}$

$\therefore$ (A + B)'s efficiency

$$= \left[\frac{1100}{9} + \frac{1100}{12}\right]$$

Time taken

$$= \left[\frac{1100}{1100 \times 4 + 1100 \times 3}\right] \times 36$$

$$= \frac{1100}{7700} \times 36 = \frac{36}{7}$$

Hence, option (a) is correct.

53. (b) Let total distance be x

$$T_1 = \frac{x}{4 \times 20}, T_2 = \frac{x}{4 \times 10},$$

$$T_3 = \frac{x}{2 \times 80}$$

$\therefore$ Average speed

$$= \frac{x}{\frac{ü}{80} + \frac{}{40} + \frac{}{160}}$$

$$= \frac{x}{\frac{2x + 4x + x}{160}} = \frac{160 \times x}{7x}$$

= 22.86 km/hr.

Hence, option (b) is correct.

54. (a) Marked price = ₹100000

Discount = 20% & 10%

$$= 20 + 10 - \frac{20 \times 10}{100} = 28\%$$

$$\therefore SP = \frac{72 \times 100000}{100} = ₹72000$$

Hence, option (a) is correct.

55. (a) If $2^{305} + 303$ divided by 9 then

$\frac{2^{305} \times 303}{9}$ as per remainder theorem $\frac{2^1}{9}$ (Remainder 2), $\frac{2^2}{9}$ (Remainder 4), $\frac{2^3}{9}$ (Remainder 8), $\frac{2^4}{9}$ (Remainder 7), $\frac{2^5}{9}$ (Remainder 5), $\frac{2^6}{9}$ (Remainder 1)

Thus, every 6th multiple of 2 will leave remainder 1 on dividing by 9.

$$\therefore \frac{2^{300}\,2^5 + 303}{9} = \frac{(1 \times 5 + 303)}{9}$$

$$= \frac{308}{9} \text{ (Remainder = 2)}$$

Hence, option (a) is correct.

56. (c) CP of chair = ₹800

SP of chair = ₹1100

Gain = (1100 – 800) = ₹300

$$\text{Gain\%} = \frac{300}{800} \times 100$$

= 37.5%

Hence, option (c) is correct.

57. (c) Curved surface area of cylinder = 2πrh

2πrh = 110 (given)

$$\Rightarrow 2 \times \frac{22}{7} \times 14 \times r = 110$$

$$\Rightarrow r = \frac{110}{2 \times 22 \times 2}$$

$$\therefore \text{Diameter} = 2r = \frac{110}{2 \times 22 \times 2}$$

= 2.5 cm

Hence, option (c) is correct.

58. (d) Marked Price = ₹2000

Discount = 20%

$$SP = \frac{80 \times 2000}{100} = ₹1600$$

Hence, option (d) is correct.

59. (d)

$$\frac{9261}{8000} = \left[1 + \frac{5}{100}\right]^{\left(\frac{2t}{2}\right)}$$

$$\Rightarrow \frac{9261}{8000} = \left[\frac{21}{20}\right]^{\left(\frac{2t}{2}\right)}$$

$$\Rightarrow \left[\frac{21}{20}\right]^3 = \left[\frac{21}{20}\right]^{2t}$$

$$\Rightarrow T = \frac{3}{2} = 1.5 \text{ years}$$

Hence, option (d) is correct.

60. (a) $a + b = 25$

$a - b = 7$

a = 16 b = 9

Mean proportional = $\sqrt{ab}$

$= \sqrt{16 \times 9}$

= 4 × 3 = 12

Hence, option (a) is correct.

61. (c) Compassion involves feelings of sympathy and sadness for the suffering of others, and a desire to help or to alleviate the suffering.

Out of the options provided, the most appropriate antonym of "compassionate" is: 'Cruel'.

62. (d) The underlined word in the sentence is 'orifice.'

In English, 'orifice' refers to an opening, as of a pipe or tube, or one in the body, such as a nostril or the mouth.

Given the choices, the most appropriate synonym for 'orifice' in this context is: 'Opening'.

63. (c) The correct answer is "sturdy". The word 'Feeble' means lacking bodily strength. The antonyms of the word 'Feeble' are "strong, mighty, powerful". From the antonym of the given word, we can say that the word 'sturdy' is opposite in meaning.

64. (d) The segment of the sentence that contains an error of tense is: 'I has been'.

In English, the present perfect continuous tense is formed using "has been" or "have been" along with the present participle (verb-ing).

65. (a) The underlined segment in the sentence is 'extremely large'.

In English, 'extremely large' refers to something that is of a great size, more than usual or more than average.

Given the choices, the most appropriate substitution for 'extremely large' in this context is: 'Enormous'.

'Enormous' in English refers to something very large in size, quantity, or extent.

66. (c) The phrase 'snake in the grass' originates from the literal image of a dangerous snake hiding in tall grass.

Given the choices, the most appropriate meaning of 'a snake in the grass' in this context is: 'A deceitful person'.

'A deceitful person' in English refers to someone who deliberately causes others to believe something that is not true, for their own personal advantage.

67. (b) The correct word to fill in the blank in the sentence "He is an absolutely ______ man." is: 'Chaste'.

In English, "chaste" is an adjective that refers to someone who is morally clean and pure, particularly in a sexual context.

68. (b) Considering the given options, the most appropriate antonym of "sweet" to fill in the blank in this context would be: 'Sour'.

69. (a) The sage preached that we are accountable to God in this life.

In English, the word "accountable" is spelled with two "c"s and one "t". It means responsible or answerable. This spelling is correctly used in the first sentence.

70. (b)

71. (a) The incorrectly spelled word among the options is: 'Skulptor'

The correct spelling of this word is "Sculptor".

72. (a) The given word is "Ideal".

"Ideal" in English refers to a standard of perfection or excellence; something that is considered perfect and serves as a model for others.

Considering the given options, the most appropriate synonym for "Ideal" in this context would be: 'Excellent'.

"Excellent" in English refers to something that is extremely good or outstanding, very similar to an ideal standard.

73. (a) The correct answer is 'Option 1'. The most appropriate option to substitute the underlined segment in the given sentence 'I visited the hospital to enquire about eyes surgery.' is: 'enquire about eye surgery'. The correct phrase is "eye surgery," not "eyes surgery."

74. (c) The correct answer is 'Option 3' i.e. 'Challenge'. Key Points. The idiom "To call in question" is given. "To call in question" is an English idiom that means to doubt, challenge, or dispute the truth or validity of something.

75. (a) The correct pair of words to complete the sentence "My brother ______ apples during his fast." is: 'ate; eight'.

"ate; eight" is the correct answer as it maintains the correct grammar and meaning in the sentence.

"Ate" is the past tense of "eat" and "eight" is a number indicating the quantity of apples consumed.

76. (c) less

77. (b) various

78. (d) depriving

79. (b) reduction

80. (c) newspaper

❑❑❑

SSC Constable (GD)

Solved Paper-2022

Exam Date 10-01-2023

Part-A: General Intelligence and Reasoning

1. Select the correct mirror image of the given figure when the mirror is placed at MN as shown below.

(a) 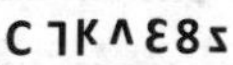

(b) 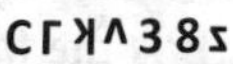

(c) 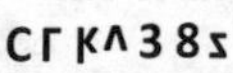

(d) 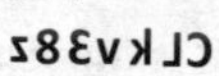

2. Which figure should replace the question mark (?) if the series were to be continued?

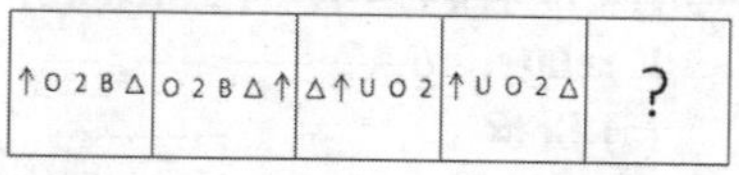

(a) 

(b) 

(c) 

(d) 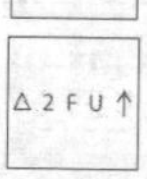

3. Select the option that is related to the fifth letter-cluster in the same way as the second letter-cluster is related to the first letter-cluster and the fourth letter-cluster is related to the third letter-cluster.

YOUR : XPEJ :: TONE: SPLW :: BANK : ?

(a) XYOP
(b) CBOL
(c) ABLQ
(d) YZMP

4. Select the option that is related to the fifth letter-cluster in the same way as the second letter-cluster is related to the first letter-cluster and the fourth letter-cluster is related to the third letter-cluster.

COMFORT : OCFMTRO :: CONTROL : OCTNLOR :: DIGITAL : ?

(a) IDIGLAT
(b) GITALDI
(c) GIDLATI
(d) LATIGID

5. In a certain code language, 'cart light' is coded as 'straw handle', 'plug light' is coded as 'toes handle', and 'cart plug' is coded as 'toes straw'. What is the code word for 'cart'?

(a) plug
(b) straw
(c) handle
(d) toes

6. Which of the following numbers will replace the question mark (?) in the given series?

1, 6, 31, 156, ?, 3906

(a) 781
(b) 2125
(c) 985
(d) 1225

7. Which two signs should be interchanged to make the below equation mathematically correct?

$72 \times 6 + 18 \div 5 - 9 = 93$

(a) × and +
(b) + and –
(c) ÷ and –
(d) × and ÷

8. Which of the following numbers will replace the question mark (?) in the given series?

33, 47, 44, 58, 56, 70, 69, ?

(a) 80
(b) 82
(c) 84
(d) 83

9. Select the set in which the numbers are related in the same way as are the numbers of the following set. (NOTE: Operations should be performed on the whole numbers, without breaking down the numbers into its constituent digits. E.g. 13 – Operations on 13 such as adding /subtracting/ multiplying etc. to 13 can be performed. Breaking down 13 into 1 and 3 and then performing mathematical operations on 1 and 3 is NOT allowed)

(20, 30, 450)

(35, 25, 540)

(a) (9. 17, 264)
(b) (20, 9, 297)
(c) (7, 18, 225)
(d) (8, 15, 227)

10. In a certain code language, FORCE is coded as 47, and GREEN is coded as 49. How will FLAVOUR be coded in that language?

(a) 98
(b) 92
(c) 95
(d) 100

11. Six people are sitting around a circular table facing the centre. Kaya is the immediate neighbour

of Jaya and Tara. Sonal is the immediate neighbour of Priya and Swati. Sonal is sitting immediate right of Priya, Tara and Swati are not sitting immediately next to each other. Who is sitting to the immediate left of Priya?

(a) Tara
(b) Kaya
(c) Jaya
(d) Swati

12. Two different positions of the same dice are shown having alphabets P to U. Find the alphabet on the face opposite the face showing U.

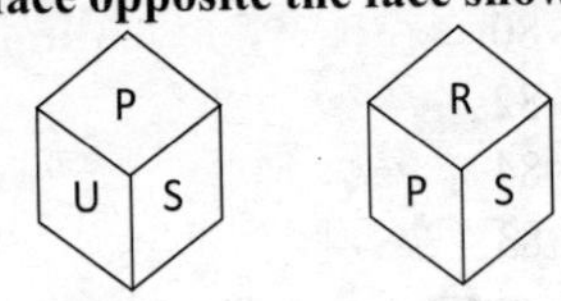

(a) Q
(b) S
(c) T
(d) R

13. Six colleagues A, B, C, D, E and F are having lunch together on a circular table at equal distance, facing the centre of the circle. D is the immediate neighbour of E and B while C is the immediate neighbour of A and F. If A is to the immediate left of E, then who is on the immediate left of C?

(a) D
(b) F
(c) B
(d) E

14. Which of the following terms will replace the question mark (?) in the given series?

EZF, GXH, KTL, QNR, ?

(a) WEY
(b) YGY
(c) YFZ
(d) XFZ

15. Select the option figure which is embedded in the given figure. (Rotation is NOT allowed)

(a) 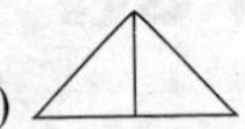

(b) 

(c) 

(d) 

16. Which two signs should be interchanged to make the below equation mathematically correct?

$42 + 16 \div 7 - 36 \times 16 = 76$

(a) + and –
(b) ÷ and x
(c) × and +
(d) ÷ and +

17. Which letter-cluster will replace the question mark (?) to complete the given series?

ZACF, WXZC, ?, QRTW, NOQT

(a) XUVZ
(b) XUYZ
(c) VWZC
(d) TUWZ

18. In this question, three statements are given, followed by two conclusions numbered I and II. Assuming the statements to be true, even if they seem to be at variance with commonly known facts, decide which of the conclusions logically follows/ follow from the statements.

Statements:

All bottles are bags.

Some bags are pencils.

Some pencils are sharpeners.

Conclusions:

I. Some sharpeners are bottles.

II. Some bottles are pencils.

(a) Both conclusions I and II follow.
(b) Neither conclusion I nor II follows.
(c) Only conclusion II follows.
(d) Only conclusion I follows.

19. Which option represents the correct order of the given words as they would appear in the English dictionary?

1. manner
2. manage
3. masculine
4. magic
5. matter

(a) 1.2.4.3,5
(b) 1,4,3,2,5
(c) 4.2.1.3.5
(d) 4.1.2,5,3

20. 'A + B' means 'B is the father of A'

'A # B' means 'B is the sister of A'

'A @ B' means 'B is the brother of A'

If A @ B # C + D + E, then how is E related to A?

(a) Son
(b) Father
(c) Father's father
(d) Father's brother

Part-B General Knowledge and General Awareness

21. Jagoi is a major style of which of the following forms of Indian classical dance?

(a) Sattriya
(b) Kathak
(c) Manipuri
(d) Odissi

22. Identify a way to reduce the pollution caused due to burning of fossil fuels

(a) By lowering the temperature of burning
(b) By increasing the efficiency of the combustion process

(c) By increasing the number of carbon molecules
(d) By decreasing the latent heat

23. Tapan Kumar Pattanayak won the Sangeet natak Akademi Award in which dance form?
(a) Kuchipudi
(b) Chhau
(c) Sattriyal
(d) Odissi

24. Who was the first Indian to conquer the English Channel from Dover to Calais in 1958, and also the only man to swim the oceans of the five continents in one calendar year in 1966?
(a) Mihir Sen
(b) Ramanathan Krishnan
(c) Ajit Patel
(d) Khashaba Jadhav

25. Rs. 2000 banknote of Mahatma Gandhi (New) Series has motif on its back.
(a) Rani Ki Vav
(b) Mangalyaan
(c) Sun Temple, Konark
(d) Red Fort

26. Who commissioned India's first indigenous aircraft carrier INS Vikrant in Kochi in September 2022?
(a) Rajnath Singh
(b) Amit Shah
(c) Jyotiraditya Scindia
(d) Narendra Modi

27. Which latitude line passes through the middle of India influencing the climate of the country?
(a) Equator
(b) Tropic of Capricorn
(c) Tropic of Cancer
(d) Antarctic Circle

28. During the reign of which of the following Mauryan kings, the Kalinga War was fought?
(a) Bindusara
(b) Ashoka
(c) Chandragupta
(d) Dasaratha

29. When was the first complete Census conducted in India?
(a) 1882
(b) 1880
(c) 1887
(d) 1881

30. Who has been appointed as the "State Brand Ambassador" of Uttarakhand government in August 2022?
(a) Dinesh Karthik
(b) Rishabh Pant
(c) Akshay Kumar
(d) Rohit Shetty

31. The President of India is elected by ________.
(a) Only the Members of State Legislative Assemblies
(a) Only the elected members of both Houses of Parliament
(c) Only the members' of Council of States
(d) The Elected Members of both Houses of Parliament and State Legislative Assemblies.

32. Which of the following is the thanksgiving festival of Maharashtra, where bulls are honoured as they are considered indispensable to farming?
(a) Makar Sankranti
(b) Pola Festival
(c) Gudi Padwa
(d) Kala Ghoda Arts Festival

33. Original text of the Indian Constitution contained ________ articles.
(a) 376
(b) 395
(c) 386
(d) 440

34. Which of the following was one of the main objectives of the Seventh Five-Year Plan?
(a) Increase in Infrastructure
(b) Increase in production of Food Grains
(c) Elimination of poverty
(d) Improve the standard of living

35. Moss and Marchantia comes under which of the following?
(a) Algae
(b) Gymnosperms
(c) Pteridophytes
(d) Bryophytes

36. Revenue receipts are ________ as they do not lead to a claim of the government.
(a) capital receipts
(b) reinforceable
(c) redeemable
(d) non-redeemable

37. During emergency which fundamental rights cannot be suspended?
(a) Article 14-15
(b) Article 20-21
(c) Article 18-19
(d) Article 16-17

38. In which among the following states, Arabica coffee grown in India?
(a) Assam
(b) Uttarakhand
(c) West Bengal
(d) Karnataka

39. ________ falls under the Ministry of textiles.
(a) Samarth Scheme
(b) Ambekar Social Innovation & Incubation Mission
(c) MPLADS (Members of Parliament Local Area Development Scheme)
(d) Merchandise Export From India Scheme

40. Which State won the Vijay Hazare Trophy in 2017-18?
(a) Uttar Pradesh
(b) Kerala
(c) Maharashtra
(d) Karnataka

Part-C : Elementary Mathematics

41. A shopkeeper allows a discount of 40% on his articles and still makes a profit of 20%. How much

cost price does shopkeeper pay for an article whose marked price is ₹2,400?
(a) ₹1,728
(b) ₹1,200
(c) ₹1,440
(d) ₹1,152

42. A man covers a certain distance by scooter at 64 km/h and he returns to the starting place riding a bicycle at 16 km/h. Find the average speed for the whole journey.
(a) 25.6 km/h
(b) 26.5 km/h
(c) 40 km/h
(d) 51.2 km/h

43. 5 women can complete a work in 8 days, while 8 children take 10 days to complete the same work. How many days will 2 women and 4 children take to complete the work?
(a) 10
(b) 12
(c) 40
(d) 8

44. The diameter of a right circular cylinder is 14 cm and height is 2 cm. The sum of its curved surface area and the total surface area is: (use $\pi = 22/7$)
(a) 484 cm^2
(b) 308 cm^2
(c) 176 cm^2
(d) 968 cm^2

45. What is the fourth proportional to $\sqrt{6}, \sqrt{8}$ and $\sqrt{21}$?
(a) $3\sqrt{7}$
(b) $2\sqrt{7}$
(c) $8\sqrt{7}$
(d) $5\sqrt{7}$

46. A can paint a painting in 12 days. B can paint the same in 8 days. C can paint the same in 10 days. Find the (approximate) number of days in which the painting can be painted by A if he is accompanied by both B and C together on alternate days and A starts painting on the first day alone.
(a) 4.4 days
(b) 5.4 days
(c) 7.2 days
(d) 8.5 days

47. The population of bears in a city has been growing at 3% every year. If the present population of bears in the city is 21,218, what was the population of bears two years ago?
(a) 18000
(b) 19000
(c) 18500
(d) 20000

48. The income of a person is ₹95,000 and his expenditure is ₹75,000. If his income is increased by 18% and the expenditure by 12%, then what will be the percentage increase in his saving?
(a) 40.6%
(b) 40.8%
(c) 40.4%
(d) 40.5%

49. Mohan is selling a table at ₹2,832. If his profit is 18%, then what is the cost price of the table?
(a) ₹ 2,480
(b) ₹ 2,500
(c) ₹ 2,440
(d) ₹ 2,400

50. In how much time (in years) would ₹80,000 amount to ₹1,17,128 at 10% per annum rate of interest, compounded yearly?
(a) 4 years
(b) 2 years
(c) 2.5 years
(d) 3.5 years

51. 5 bells start commencing together at 9 AM. They ring at the intervals of 12 seconds, 18 seconds, 24 seconds, 36 seconds and 45 seconds. At what time do the bells ring together again?
(a) 9:10 AM
(b) 9:06 AM
(c) 9:08 AM
(d) 9:05 AM

52. A spends 45% of his salary on food and donates 5% of his salary on old age homes. If he spends ₹ 28,500 on food and old age homes, then what will be the salary of A?
(a) ₹ 52,000
(b) ₹ 57,000
(c) ₹ 50,000
(d) ₹ 55,000

53. A cone of radius 9 cm and height 15 cm is melted and made into a cylinder of height 45 cm. The diameter of the cylinder is:
(a) 3 cm
(b) 5 cm
(c) 10 cm
(d) 6 cm

54. A person rides bicycle on four different ways to reach the destination. Determine the average speed during this whole journey.

Way	Speed (km/h)	Distance (km)
A	5	20
B	3	15
C	2	10
D	4	24

(a) $4.5\frac{km}{hr}$
(b) $3.45\frac{km}{hr}$
(c) $5.5\frac{km}{hr}$
(a) $2.45\frac{km}{hr}$

55. Divya bought a car for ₹3,50,000 and sold it for ₹4,35,000. What is her percentage profit (correct up to one decimal place)?
(a) 23.3%
(a) 24.3%
(a) 21.5%
(d) 20.7%

56. If $(5x - 2y) : (x - 2y) = 9 : 17$, then find the value of $\frac{9x}{13y}$

(a) $\frac{72}{421}$

(b) $\frac{151}{1731}$

(c) $\frac{36}{247}$

(d) $\frac{144}{1001}$

57. A car covered 240 km in 5 h. If it travels with half of its usual speed, then how much more time will be taken to cover the same distance?

(a) 3 h

(b) 5h

(c) 10 h

(d) 4 h

58. X bought 40 pencils for a total of ₹ 180 and bought 2 dozens of pens for ₹ 180. Find the difference between the price of one pen and one pencil.

(a) ₹ 3.5

(b) ₹ 3

(c) ₹ 2

(d) ₹ 2.5

59. How many prime numbers are there between 40 and 50?

(a) 4

(b) 5

(c) 3

(d) 2

60. A dealer allowed a discount of 20 percent on marked price of ₹ 72000 on an article and incurred a loss of 10 percent. What discount should he allow on the marked price, so that he gains ₹ 440 on the article?

(a) 10.5 percent

(b) 8.5 percent

(c) 9.5 percent

(d) 11.5 percent

Part-D : English

61. Identify the correctly spelt sentence.

(a) The events arranged or organised in order of time are known as chronoligal order.

(b) The events arranged or organised in order of time are known as chronological order.

(c) The events arranged or organised in order of time are known as chronologikal order.

(d) The events arranged or organised in order of time are known as chronoloigal order.

62. Select the most appropriate ANTONYM of the given word.

Timid

(a) Diffident

(b) Shy

(c) Bold

(d) Fearful

63. Select the most appropriate synonym of the given word.

Blast

(a) Blow up

(b) Recall

(c) Plead

(d) Share

64. Select the most appropriate option that can substitute the underlined segment in the given sentence.

I <u>regarded</u> my brother on passing his graduation examination.

(a) congratulated

(b) disparaged

(c) flattered

(d) kowtowed

65. Select the most appropriate ANTONYM of the given word.

Liability

(a) Resource

(b) Responsibility

(c) Asset

(d) Strike

66. Select the most appropriate homophone to fill in the blank.

In many road accidents people break their bones mainly because their vehicle ________ fails.

(a) brake

(b) broke

(c) brow

(d) bleak

67. Select the correct word for the blanks in the given sentence.

Sivakashi is famous for its ______ box industry, and I am unable to find a ______ for my purple dress.

(a) sweat

(b) match

(c) chatter

(d) bread

68. Select the most appropriate option to fill in the blank.

Truthfully speaking, the victories of peace and harmony have a more ______ impact on human civilisation than the so-called victories of war.

(a) Superior

(b) Transient

(c) Lasting

(d) Greater

69. Select the most appropriate option to substitute the underlined segment in the given sentence.

Purchasing furniture at a low cost <u>could not involve abandoning</u> design or quality.

(a) should not entail sacrificing

(b) did not provoke compromising

(c) have not done regretting

(d) cannot force forgetting

70. Select the most appropriate synonym of the given word.

Colloquial

(a) Lexical

(b) Conversational

(c) Prosodic

(d) Linguistic

71. Select the option that expresses the given sentence in future tense form.

There are multiple facilities available for reaching the island.

(a) There will be multiple facilities available for reaching the island.

(b) There have been multiple facilities available for reaching the island.

(c) There had been multiple facilities available for reaching the island.

(d) There were multiple facilities available for reaching the island.

72. Select the INCORRECTLY spelt word.

(a) Maladjusted

(b) Stakeholder

(c) Permenent

(d) Longitude

73. Select the most appropriate ANTONYM of the given word.

Rancid

(a) Rotten

(b) Urgent

(c) Fresh

(d) Rough

74. Select the most appropriate meaning of the given idiom.

At your beck and call

(a) To have absolute control over someone

(b) To call someone respectfully

(c) To have no control over someone

(d) To call someone and then deny

75. Select the most appropriate meaning of the given idiom.

A night owl

(a) Someone who has good eyesight

(b) Someone who works very hard

(c) Someone who never works

(d) A person who prefers to be awake late at night

Comprehension:

In the following passage, some words have been deleted. Read the passage carefully and select the most appropriate option to fill in each blank.

The companies in the present era (1) ______ priority, during recruitment, to the candidates who have Emotional Intelligence. EI is the ability to understand, analyse and control emotions. Possessing very high EI creates a (2) ______ impact on a person's life. People who have EI always maintain emotional stability even in difficult situations. They can be nice even in socially awkward situations. As they are very good at controlling emotions, they make others feel (3) ______. It is proven that it will make leaders more effective as they understand the feelings of teammates. It allows one (4) ______ impactfully with others. Stress and conflict can be handled so easily. As it allows great empathy towards others, they can be very good at interpersonal relationship. These people strengthen the relationship (5) ______ the people with their interaction and coordination both in personal and professional life. Companies are well aware of the benefits with the employees who have EI.

76. Select the most appropriate option to fill in blank number 1.

(a) has been giving

(b) have been given

(c) are giving

(d) is giving

77. Select the most appropriate option to fill in blank number 2.

(a) creative

(b) positive

(c) colonial

(d) memorable

78. Select the most appropriate option to fill in blank number 3.

(a) comfortable

(b) tolerable

(c) favourable

(d) manageable

79. Select the most appropriate option to fill in blank number 4.

(a) communicate

(b) to communicating

(c) to be communicated

(c) to communicate

80. Select the most appropriate option to fill in blank number 5.

(a) in reference with

(b) between

(c) along with

(d) among

Answers

1. (a) The required mirror image is option (a).

2. (b) From the given figures, it is clear that option (b) is correct.

3. (c)

25 15 21 18 : 24 16 5 10

Y O U R : X P E J

−1 +1 −16 −10

:: 20 15 14 5 : 19 16 12 23

:: T O N E : S P L W

−1 +1 −2 +28

:: B A N K : A B L Q

:: 2 1 14 11 :

26 − 14 = 12 28 − 11 = 17

Hence, option (c) is correct.

4. (a) C O M F O R T

O C F M T R O

D I G I T A L

I D I G L A T

Hence, option (a) is correct.

5. (a) Cart light → Straw Handle → Handle = light

Cart Plug → Toes straw → Cart → Streaw

Hence, option (b) is correct.

6. (a) 1, 6, 31, 156, ?, 3906

$1 \times 5 + 1, \quad 6 \times 5 + 1, \quad 31 \times 5 + 1,$

$156 \times 5 + 1, \quad 6 \times 5 + 1, = 780 + 1$

$= 781$

Hence, option (a) is correct.

7. (d) $72 \times 6 + 18 \div 5 - 9 = 93$

$72 \div 6 + 18 \times 5 - 9$

$= 12 + 90 - 9 = 93 = \text{RHS}$

Hence, interchange $\times \rightarrow \div$

$\therefore$ Option (d) is correct.

8. (d)

33, 47, 44, 58, 56, 70, 69, _?_ 83

+11 +11 +12 +12 +13 +13 +14

Hence, option (d) is correct.

9. (c)

(20, 30, 450) $[20 + 30] \times 9 = 450$

(35, 25, 540) $[35 + 25] \times 9 = 540$

$[7 + 18] \times 9 = 225$

Hence, option (c) is correct answer.

10. (c)

F O R C E

$6 + 15 + 18 + 3 + 5 = 45$

G R E E N

$7 + 18 + 5 + 5 + 14 = 49$

F L A V O U R

$6 + 12 + 1 + 22 + 15 + 21 + 18 = 95$

Hence, option (c) is correct.

11. (a)

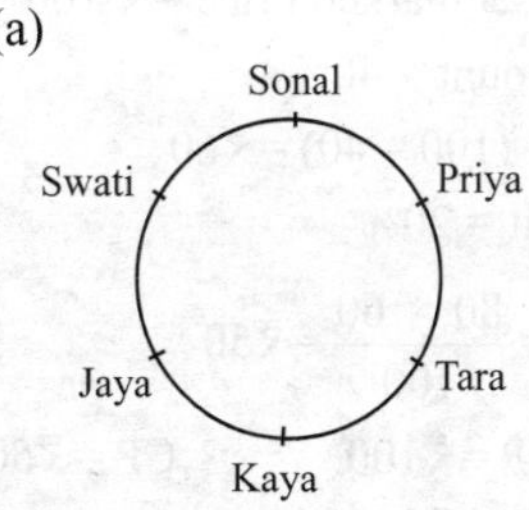

Tara is sitting immediate left of Priya.

Hence, option (a) is correct answer.

12. (d) PS | PS | is common

So, letter opposites are U & R

Hence, option (d) is correct.

13. (b)

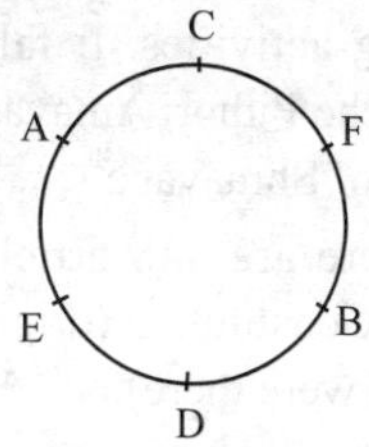

F is on immediate left of C

Hence, option (b) is correct.

14. (a)

+2 +4 +6 +8

E Z F, G X H, K T L, Q N R, Y F Z

5 26 6, 7 24 8 11 20 12 17 14 18

+2 −2 +4 −4 +6 −6 +8 −8

Hence, YFZ or option (c) is correct.

15. (d) From the given figures we can find that option (d) is correct.

16. (c)

$42 + 16 \div 7 - 36 \times 16 = 76$

$\text{LHS} = (42 + 16 \div 7 - 36 \times 16)$

$= 42 \times 16 \div 7 - 36 + 16$

$= 42 \times \frac{16}{7} - 36 + 16$

$= 96 - 36 + 16$

$= 112 - 36$

$= 76 = \text{RHS}$

Hence, option (c) is correct.

17. (d)

26 1 3 6 23 24 26 3 20 21 23 26 17 18 20 23

Z A C F W X Z C T U W Z Q R T W

−3 −3 −3 −3 −3 −3 −3 −3 −3 −3 −3 −3

Hence, option (d) is correct.

18. (b)

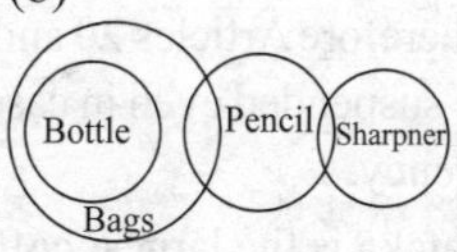

or

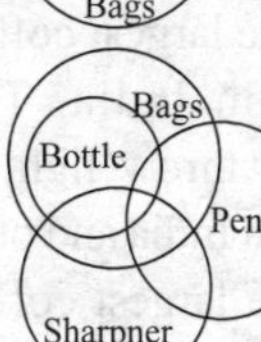

Hence, option (b) is correct.

19. (c) From the given words, the correct sequence is

magic, manage, manner, masculine, matter.

i.e. (4, 2, 1, 3, 5) or option (c) is correct.

20. (c) A @ B # C + D + E

A ⟷ [B] ⟷ (C) ⟵ [D] ⟵ [E]

E is father of A's Father.

Hence, option (c) is correct.

21. (c) Jagoi is a major style of Manipuri, which is one of the forms of Indian classical dance. Manipuri dance originated in the northeastern state of Manipur and is known for its graceful movements, delicate hand gestures, and vibrant costumes.

22. (c) Increasing the efficiency of the combustion process can indeed help reduce the pollution caused by burning fossil fuels.

23. (b) Tapan Kumar Pattanayak won the Sangeet natak Akademi Award for Chhau.Chhau dance is a traditional Indian dance form that originated in the eastern states of Jharkhand, West Bengal, and Odisha.

24. (a) Mihir Sen was the first Indian to conquer the English Channel from Dover to Calais in 1958.He was also the first Asian to achieve this feat. In 1966, he became the only person to swim the oceans of the five continents in one calendar year.

25. (b) The motif of the Mangalyaan on the reverse of Rs 2000 note depicts the country's first venture into the interplanetary space.

26. (d) India's first aircraft carrier INS Vikrant commissioned into the Navy by Narendra Modi at an event in Kochi on September 2. The commissioning of the indigenously-built aircraft carrier INS Vikrant will contribute in ensuring peace and stability in the Indo-Pacific region, besides enhancing the country's overall maritime capabilities. The aircraft carrier, built at a cost of around Rs 20,000 crore, successfully completed the fourth and final phase of the sea trials last month.

27. (c) The Tropic of Cancer is like an imaginary line which is found at an angle of 23.50 degrees North from the Equator and this passes through the middle of India. It also affects the climate of some states in India.

28. (b) The Kalinga war was fought between Ashoka and Raja Anantha Padmanabha in the year 261 BCE.

29. (d) While it has been undertaken every 10 years, beginning in 1872 under british Viceroy Lord Mayo, the first complete census was taken in 1881. Post 1949, it has been conducted by the Registrar General and Census Commissioner of India under the Ministry of Home Affairs, Government of India.

30. (c) Actor Akshay Kumar has been appointed as the brand ambassador of Uttarakhand on 7 February 2022. CM Dhami presented Akshay with a traditional cap of the state, a shawl, and a painting of all the gates of the four pilgrimage sites -- Badrinath, Kedarnath, Gangotri, and Yamunotri.

31. (d) The President is elected not directly by the people but by members of electoral college consisting of:

1. the elected members of both the Houses of Parliament;

2. the elected members of the legislative assemblies of the states; and

3. the elected members of the legislative assemblies of the Union Territories of Delhi and Puducherry.

32. (b) The correct answer is Pola Festival. Pola Festival is a thanksgiving festival celebrated by farmers in Maharashtra and Chhattisgarh, to acknowledge the importance of bulls and oxen, who are a crucial part of agriculture and farming activities. It falls on the day of the Pithori Amavasya in the month of Shraavana.

33. (b) There are 448 articles in the Indian Constitution (originally 395 articles were there).

34. (b) Seventh Five-Year Plan-Its duration was from 1985 to 1990, under the leadership of Rajiv Gandhi. The objectives of this plan include the establishment of a self-sufficient economy, opportunities for productive employment, and up-gradation of technology.The Plan aimed at accelerating food grain production, increasing employment opportunities & raising productivity with a focus on 'food, work & productivity.

35. (d) "Moss" and "Marchantia" are both types of plants belonging to the division Bryophyta. Bryophyta is one of the divisions or phyla of non-vascular plants, which also include liverworts (such as Marchantia) and hornworts.

36. (d) Revenue receipts are receipts of the government which are non-redeemable. Revenue receipts are again classified into tax and non-tax revenues.

37. (b) After the 44th Amendment Act, it was agreed by the Court that in any case no person can be stripped of his right to life and personal liberty. Therefore Articles 20 and 21 cannot be suspended even in case of an emergency.

38. (d) Karnataka is the largest coffee-producing state in India. This article will briefly throw light on coffee production in India and other crops grown in the largest coffee-producing state of India.After Karnataka, the next state which accounts for the highest share of coffee production in India is Kerala.

Kerala produces around 21% of India's coffee.

Both Karnataka and Kerala together account for around 90% of the total coffee produced in India.

The third highest coffee-producing state in India is Tamil Nadu which accounts for 5% of the total coffee produced in India.

Coffee is also grown in Northeastern India, Odisha, and Andhra Pradesh.

The most well-known species of coffee grown in India are Robusta and Arabica.

Arabica coffee species was introduced in the Baba Budan Giri hill ranges of Karnataka in the 17th century.

39. (a) The Ministry of Textiles has implemented the Samarth Scheme, an initiative to build capacity in India's textile sector. Launched in 2017, the scheme is known as the Scheme for Capacity Building in the Textile Sector (SCBTS).

40. (d) The 2017–18 Vijay Hazare Trophy was the 16th season of the Vijay Hazare Trophy, a List A cricket tournament in India.

It was contested by the 28 domestic cricket teams of India.

In the first semi-final, Karnataka beat Maharashtra by 9 wickets to advance to the final.

41. (b) Let marked price = ₹ 100

Discount = 40%

∴ SP = (100 – 40) = ₹60

Profit = 20%

$$\therefore \text{CP} = \frac{80 \times 60}{100} = ₹50$$

∴ If MP = ₹100 CP = ₹50

∴ If MP = ₹2400

$$\text{CP} = \frac{50 \times 2400}{100} = ₹1200$$

Hence, option (b) is correct.

42. (a) Average speed $= \frac{2v_1v_2}{v_1 + v_2}$

$$= \frac{2 \times 64 \times 16}{64 + 16}$$

$=\frac{2 \times 64 \times 16}{80}$

$=\frac{128}{5}=25.6$ km/hr

Hence, option (a) is correct.

43. (a) 5Women can complete work in 8 days

8 children in 10 days

Total work = 5 × 8 = 40

Time taken by 2 Women and 4 children to complete 40 work

$=\frac{40}{(2W+4C)/\text{day work}}$ (i)

$=\frac{80}{8}=10$ days.

5W × 8 = 8C × 10 (ii)

1W = 2C

∴ 2 × 2C + 4C = 8C

or $\frac{40}{4}=10$ days

Hence, option (a) is correct.

44. (a) Diameter of Cylinder = 14 cm

∴ Radius $=\frac{14}{2}=7$ cm

Height = 2 cm.

Curved surface area = 2πrl ...(i)

Total surface area = 2πr(h + r) ...(ii)

Sum of (i) and (ii), we get

2πrh + 2πr(h + r)

= 2πr(h + h + r) = 2πr(2h + r)

$=2\times\frac{22}{7}\times 7\times(2\times 2+7)$

= 2 × 22 × (11) = 44 × 11 = 484 cm

Hence, option (a) is correct.

45. (b) Let 4th population be x

$\therefore \sqrt{6}:\sqrt{8}::\sqrt{21}:x$

$\Rightarrow x=\frac{\sqrt{8}\times\sqrt{21}}{\sqrt{6}}=\sqrt{28}=2\sqrt{7}$

Hence, option (b) is correct.

46. (b) A = 12 days, B = 8 days, C = 10 days

T.W. = 120

$A_{Eff.}=10$ $B_{Eff.}=15$ $C_{Eff.}=12$

A's one day work = 10

Work left = 120 – 10 = 110

(A + B)'s one day work = (10 + 15) = 25

(B + C)'s one day work = 27

(A + B + C)'s one day work = 37

Work completed in 2 days = 10 + 37 = 47

Work done on 3rd day = 10 (by A also)

Work done on 4th day = 37

Work done on 5th day = 10

Total work left for 6th day

= 120 – [47 + 10 + 37 + 10]

= 120 – 104

= 16

∴ Time taken on 6th day $=\frac{16}{37}$

= 4 days

∴ Total time taken = (5 + 4) days

= 5.4 days

Hence, option (b) is correct.

47. (d) Rate = 3%

$$\begin{array}{ll} \therefore\ 100 & 103 \\ \times\ 100 & \times 103 \\ \hline 10000 & 10609 \end{array}$$

∴ If present population is 10609 then population 2 years back = 10000

∴ If present population 21218 then population 2 years back

$=\frac{10000}{10609}\times 21218=20000$

Hence, option (d) is the correct answer.

48. (d) Income = ₹95000

Expenditure = ₹75000

Saving = ₹20000

New income $=\frac{118\times 95000}{100}$

= ₹112100

New expenditure $=\frac{112\times 75000}{100}$

= ₹84000

New saving = ₹28100

Increase in saving

$=\frac{(28100-20000)}{20000}\times 100$

= 40.5%

49. (d) SP = ₹2832

Profit = 18%

CP = ?

CP = 100

% Profit = 18%

SP = 118

$\Rightarrow CP=\frac{2832\times 100}{118}=₹2400$

Hence, option (d) is correct.

50. (a) 10% Rate

$\Rightarrow 117128=80000\left(1+\frac{R}{100}\right)^T$

$\Rightarrow \frac{117128}{80000}=\left(1+\frac{10}{100}\right)^T$

$\Rightarrow \left(\frac{14641}{10000}\right)=\left(\frac{11}{10}\right)^T$

$\Rightarrow \left(\frac{11}{10}\right)^4=\left(\frac{11}{10}\right)^T$

⇒ T = 4 years

Hence, option (a) is correct.

51. (b) LCM of 12, 18, 24, 36, 45 is

$$\begin{array}{r|l} 3 & 12, 18, 24, 36, 45 \\ \hline 3 & 4, 6, 8, 12, 15 \\ \hline 2 & 4, 2, 8, 4, 5 \\ \hline 2 & 2, 1, 4, 2, 5 \\ \hline & 1, 1, 2, 1, 5 \end{array}$$

3 × 3 × 2 × 2 × 2 × 5 = 360

The bells will ring together after 360 seconds or 6 minutes.

∴ After 9:00 AM they will ring together at 9:06 AM. Hence, option (b) is correct.

52. (b) 45% salary on food, 5% on old age.

Total spent = 50% of salary

= ₹28500

∴ Salary = ₹28500 × 2 = ₹57000

Hence, option (b) is correct.

53. (d) Volume of cone $=\frac{1}{3}\pi r_1^2 h_1$

Volume of cylinder $=\pi r_2^2 h_2$

$\Rightarrow \frac{1}{3}\times\pi\times r_1^2\times h_1=\pi\times r_2^2\times h_2$

$\Rightarrow \frac{9\times 9}{3}\times 18 = r_2^2 \times 45$

$\Rightarrow r_2 = 3cm$

Diameter of cylinder = 2 × 3 = 6 cm.

Hence, option (d) is correct.

54. (b) Average speed

$= \frac{\text{Total Distance}}{\text{Total Time}}$

$= \frac{20+15+10+24}{\frac{20}{5}+\frac{35}{3}+\frac{10}{2}+\frac{24}{4}}$

$= \frac{69}{4+5+5+6}$

$= \frac{69}{20} = 3.45$ km/hr

55. (b) CP of Car = ₹350000

SP of Car = ₹435000

Profit = [435000 – 350000]

= ₹ 85000

$\text{Profit\%} = \frac{85000}{350000}\times 100$

$= \frac{170}{7} = 24.28\%$

≈ 24.3%

Hence, option (b) is correct.

56. (c) $\frac{5x-2y}{x-2y} = \frac{9}{17}$

$\Rightarrow 85x - 34y = 9x - 18y$

$\Rightarrow 76x = 16y$

$\Rightarrow x = \frac{16y}{76} = \frac{8y}{38} = \frac{4y}{19}$

$\therefore \frac{9x}{13y} = \frac{9\times 4\times \cancel{y}}{13\times 19\times \cancel{y}} = \frac{36}{247}$

Hence, option (c) is correct.

57. (b) Distance = 240 km

Time = 5 hrs

$\text{Speed} = \frac{240}{5} = 48$ km/hr

$\text{If speed} = \frac{48}{2} = 24$ km/hr

$\text{Time taken} = \frac{240}{24} = 10$ hrs.

∴ It will take 5 hrs of extra time to cover same distance.

Hence, option (b) is correct.

58. (b) CP of 40 pencils for ₹180

$\text{1 pencil cost} = \frac{180}{40}$

= ₹4.50/pencil

CP of 24 pens ₹180

$\text{CP of 1 pen } \frac{180}{24} = \frac{45}{6}$

$= \frac{15}{2} =$ ₹7.50/pen

Difference between price of 1 pen / pencil = (7.50 – 4.50) = ₹3

Hence, option (b) is correct.

59. (c) Prime numbers between 40 and 50 are 41, 43 & 47 i.e. 3

Hence, option (c) is correct answers.

60. (a) Marked Price = ₹72000

Discount = 20%

$SP = \frac{80\times 72000}{100} =$ ₹57600

Loss = 10%

$\therefore CP = \frac{57600}{90}\times 100 =$ ₹64000

Now again if

Gain = ₹440

SP = ₹64440

$\text{Discount\%} = \frac{(72000-64440)}{72000}\times 100$

$= \frac{7560}{720} = 10.5\%$

Hence, option (a) is correct.

61. (b) Correctly spelt word is -The events arranged or organised in order of time are known as chronological order.

62. (c) Antonyms of the word 'timid' are 'brave', 'bold', 'confident', 'courageous'.

63. (a) Blast means a powerful explosion or a sudden release of energy. Blow up means to cause an explosion or to destroy something with an explosion.

64. (a) The most appropriate option that can substitute the word "regarded" in the given sentence is "congratulated." This word means to express joy, pleasure, or acknowledgment to someone for an achievement or success.

65. (c) The correct answer is 'Option c' i.e. 'Asset'. The most appropriate antonym of the word "Liability" is "Asset.

66. (a) Brake: This is the correct homophone that fits the context of the sentence. The sentence talks about road accidents and how people break their bones.

67. (b) The correct sentence is: 'Sivakashi is famous for its matchbox industry, and I am unable to find a match for my purple dress.

68. (c) The correct sentence is: 'Truthfully speaking, the victories of peace and harmony have a more Lasting impact on human civilization than the so-called victories of war'.

69. (a) The most appropriate option to substitute the segment 'could not involve abandoning' in the given sentence 'should not entail sacrificing'.The word 'entail' is similar to 'involve', and 'sacrificing' is akin to 'abandoning'.

70. (b) The word 'Colloquial' refers to language used in ordinary or familiar conversation; it's not formal or literary.The synonym 'Conversational' also denotes language that is used in informal conversation.

71. (a) The given sentence is in present tense, and it talks about the availability of multiple facilities for reaching the island.

When we want to express this in future tense, we use the auxiliary verb "will" before the verb "be" to indicate that the action will happen in the future.

The correct tense structure for this sentence in the future tense is: "There + will + be + (noun or adjective)".

72. (c) INCORRECTLY spelt word is Permenent. It should be permanent.

73. (c) The correct answer is 'Option c' i.e. 'Fresh'. 'Fresh' is the opposite of 'Rancid', making it the correct antonym.

74. (a) The phrase 'At your beck and call' means to be always ready to obey or serve someone, to be continually available to satisfy someone's demands.(It implies a situation where you have absolute control over someone, as they are always ready to respond to your demands.

75. (d) The term 'night owl' is commonly used to describe a person who naturally tends to stay awake till late at night and is most active during this time.

It doesn't necessarily mean they work during this time.

They may simply prefer to be awake and engage in various activities.

76. (c) are giving

77. (b) positive

78. (a) comfortable

79. (c) to communicate

80. (d) among

❑❑❑

SSC Constable (GD)
Solved Paper-2021

Part-A: General Intelligence and Reasoning

1. Which two signs need to be interchanged to make the following equation correct?

16 + 32 × 128 ÷ 9 – 17 = – 4

(a) × and –
(b) ÷ and +
(c) × and ÷
(d) ÷ and –

2. Three different positions of the same dice are shown. Select the number that will be on the face opposite to the one having '4'.

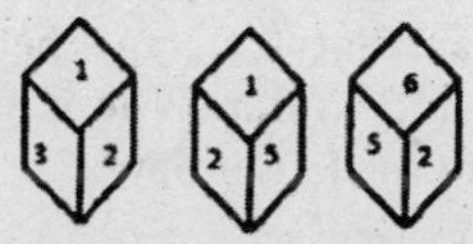

(a) 6 (b) 2
(c) 1 (d) 3

3. Select the Venn diagram that best represents the relationship between the following classes.

Manunals, Zebra, Animals

(a) 

(b) 

(c) 

(d) 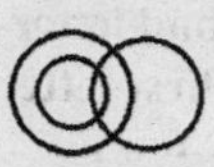

4. In a certain code language, "SINGER' is written as 'TKROUX'. How will 'ROOKIE' be written in that language?

(a) SQSRYK
(b) SQRSYK
(c) SQRRYK
(d) SQSSYK

5. The sequence of folding a piece of paper and the manner in which the folded paper has been cut is shown in the following figures. How would this paper look when unfolded?

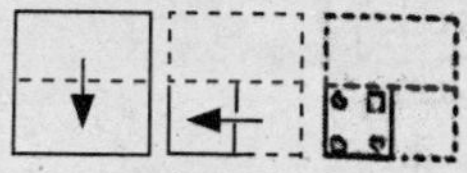

(a) 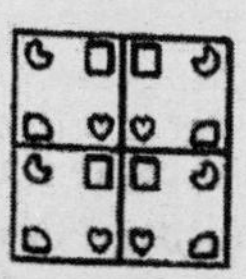

(b) 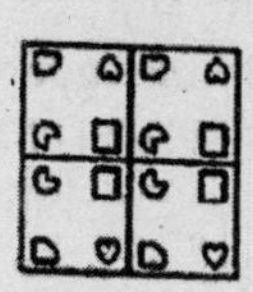

(c) 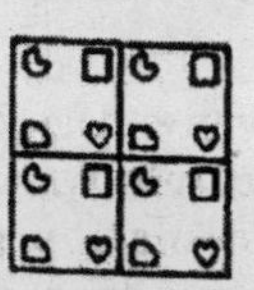

(d) 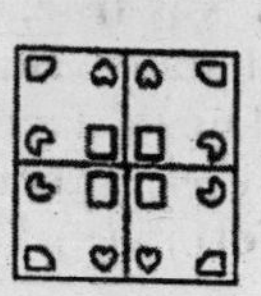

6. Study the given pattern carefully and select the number that can replace the question mark (?) in it.

81 33 56

364

54 11 ?

(a) 9
(b) 28
(c) 27
(d) 14

7. C is the brother of B and D is the grandfather of E. B is the daughter-in-law of D and A is the father of E. How is C related to E?

(a) Paternal Aunt
(b) Maternal aunt
(c) Maternal uncle
(d) Paternal Uncle

8. Which figure will replace the question mark (?) in the following figure series?

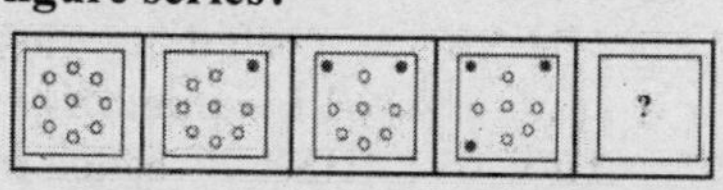

(a) 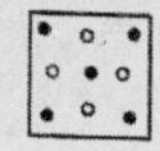

(b) 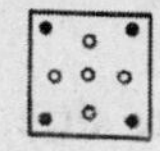

(c) 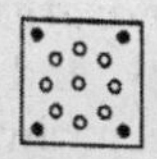

(d) 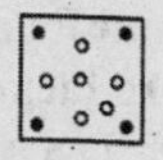

9. Select the option that is related to the third number in the same way as the second number is related to the first number.

77: 11 :: 259: ?

(a) 31
(b) 43
(c) 29
(d) 37

10. Select the letter-cluster from among the given options that can

replace the question mark (?) in the following series.

BKR, DNV, FQZ, ?, JWH

(a) HSC
(b) THE
(c) HUD
(d) HTD

11. A number is subtracted from 4 times of it and then, the number obtained is added to its (the resultant's) next number. If this gives the answer as 91, what was the original number?

(a) 17 (b) 13
(c) 14 (d) 15

12. Select the number from among the given options that can replace the question mark (?) in the following series.

15, 45, 75, 105, ?

(a) 120
(b) 135
(c) 125
(d) 130

13. In a certain code language, 'DESK' Is coded as '@#+%' and 'RAIN' is coded as '$–×'. How will 'RISK'be coded in that language?

(a) $*+%
(b) +–+%
(c) #+%@
(d) S#%×

14. Twelve friends are sitting in two parallel lines. There are 6 people sitting in each row and facing a person of the other row. In row 1, A, B, C, D, E and F are seated and all of them are facing north. In row 2, O, P, Q, R, S and T are seated and all of them are facing south but not necessarily in the same order. C, is third to the right of B. C is not an immediate neighbour to either E or A. P is third to the left of S. Neither P nor S are sitting at the extreme ends of any row. F, faces O, who is second to the right of T, and T is not an immediate neighbour to S. Only two people are sitting between Q and T. A, is not facing R. Which of the following pairs are sitting at the extreme ends?

(a) SB, PC
(b) RB, TC
(c) RE, TC
(d) SA, PD

15. Select the option in which the given figure is embedded (rotation is NOT allowed).

(a) 

(b) 

(c) 

(d) 

16. In a certain code language, COACH is coded as 90, and POST is coded as 210. How will NOISE be coded in that language?

(a) 158
(b) 124
(c) 168
(d) 186

17. Read the given statements and conclusions carefully. Assuming that the information given in the statements is true, even if it appears to be at variance with commonly known facts, decide which of the given conclusions logically follow(s) from the statements.

Statements:

All M. Tech students are engineers.

All LLM students are lawyers,

Conclusions:

I. All lawyers are LLM students.

II. All engineers are M. Tech students.

(a) Both conclusions I and II follow.
(b) Only conclusion II follows.
(c) Only conclusion I follows.
(d) Neither conclusion I nor II follows.

18 'Nephrologist' is related to 'Kidney' in the same way as 'Cardiologist' is related to '_________'.

(a) Pancreas
(b) Lungs
(c) Heart
(d) Gall bladder

19. Select the number from among the given options that can replace the question mark (?) in the following series.

14, 33, 71, 147, 299, ?

(a) 612
(b) 493
(c) 593
(d) 603

20. Neeta, Vinita, Satya, Kamini, Divya and Alpa are sitting around a circular table facing the centre of the table. Alpa is to the immediate right of Vinita. Kamini is between Neeta and Satya. Divya is between Neeta and Vinita. Who is sitting third to the left of Satya?

(a) Divya
(b) Neeta
(c) Vinita
(d) Alpa

21. Four letter-clusters have been given. Out of which three are alike in some manner and one is different. Select the letter-cluster that is different.

(a) DGJMP
(b) TWZCF
(c) PSVYB
(d) NQTWA

22. Select the option that is related to the third letter-cluster in the same way as the second letter-cluster is related to the first letter-cluster.

RKM : VFS :: PSQ:?

(a) SNW
(b) TMW
(c) TNW
(d) SNX

23. Select the combination of letters that when sequentially placed in the blanks of the given series will complete the series.

G__PK___DF___KGD___K

(a) DFGDFP
(b) DPDFKF
(c) DFGPFP
(d) DFGDFK

24. Select the correct mirror image of the given combination when the mirror is placed to its right side.

F R 4 P W 5

(a) 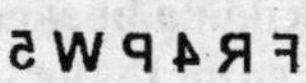

(b) 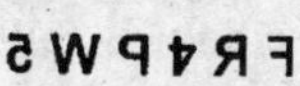

(c) 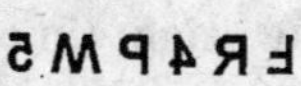

(d) 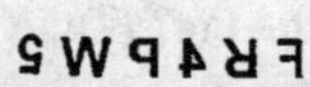

25. Select the correct option that indicates the arrangement of the given words in the order in which they appear in an English dictionary.

1. **Uneventful**
2. **Uneconomical**
3. **Unexplained**
4. **Unexpected**
5. **Unemployment**

(a) 2, 5, 3, 4, 1
(b) 2, 5, 1, 3, 4
(c) 2, 5, 1, 4, 3
(d) 3, 5, 1, 4, 2

Part-B Gerneral Knowledge and Gerneral Awareness

26. Politician writer M Veerappa Moily was awarded the Sahitya Akademi Award 2020 for his poetry titled 'Sri Bahubali Ahimsadigvijayam' in ______

(a) Tamil
(b) Telugu
(c) Kannada
(d) Malayalam

27. Which of the following diseases is caused by the deficiency of haemoglobin?

(a) Malaria
(b) Anemia
(c) Rabies
(d) Cholera

28. Which of the following taxes was introduced in India to achieve the goal of 'One Nation, One Tax, One Market'?

(a) Goods and Services Tax
(b) Union Excise Duty
(c) Custom Duty
(d) Security Transaction Tax

29. Which of the following awards did Virat Kohli win in December 2020?

(a) ICC Men's Test Cricketer of the Decade
(b) ICC Men's T20 Cricketer of the Decade
(c) ICC Men's ODI Cricketer of the Decade
(d) 1CC Spirit of Cricket Award of the Decade

30. When did the Hindu Succession Act abandon the rule of primogeniture in India?

(a) 1956
(b) 1950
(c) 1946
(d) 1960

31. Which of the following statements is INCORRECT?

(a) Food from the stomach passes into the small intestine.
(b) Complete digestion of carbohydrates, proteins and fats takes place in the small intestine.
(c) Saliva contains an enzyme called salivary lipase that breaks down starch into simple sugar.
(d) Food enters the stomach through the oesophagus (esophagus).

32. Which of the following parts of the human body contains gustatory receptors?

(a) Eyes
(b) Nose
(c) Tongue
(d) Skin

33. Farmers in some parts of Indla celebrate the Pola festival by worshiping their______

(a) farm tools
(b) ancestors
(c) farms
(d) bullocks

34. Who among the following laid the foundation of independent Awadh dynasty?

(a) Chin Qilich Khan
(b) Marthanda Varma
(c) Saadat Khan
(d) Haider Ali

35. Which among the following is the longest river in the Thar Desert?

(a) Jhelum
(b) Chambal
(c) Son
(d) Luni

36. The '________' is an initiative of the National Bamboo Mission and the Government e-Marketplace (GeM) to showcase bamboo products.

(a) Indian Gold Collection
(b) Indian Bamboo Collection
(c) Green Wood Collection
(d) Green Gold Collection

37. The fifth storey of Qutub Minar was built during the reign of:

(a) Iltutmish
(b) Mohammad-bin-Tughlaq
(c) Firoz Shah Tughlaq
(d) Razia Sultana

38. In which year was the Indian Industrial and Commercial Congress formed by Indian merchants and industrialists to organise their business interests?

(a) 1934
(b) 1909
(c) 1920
(d) 1945

39. Which of the following words in the Preamble to the Constitution describes India as a country having complete political freedom and being the supreme authority?

(a) Sovereign
(b) Democratic
(c) Socialist
(d) Secular

40. Which of the following persons was NOT amongst the female judges sworn in as judges of the Supreme Court of India on 31st August 2021?
(a) Justice Indira Banerjee
(b) Justice BV Nagarathna
(c) Justice Bela M Trivedi
(d) Justice Hima Kohli

41. Vikramshila Gangetic Dolphin Wildlife Sanctuary is located in which of the following states?
(a) Chhattisgarh
(b) Bihar
(c) Uttar Pradesh
(d) Goa

42. _______is a risk management strategy employed to offset losses in investments by taking an opposite position in a related asset.
(a) Scalability
(b) Hedging
(c) Amortization
(d) Collateral

43. In which state was the Indo-Dutch centre of excellence (CoE) for vegetables and flowers opened in November 2020?
(a) Kerala
(b) Punjab
(c) Telangana
(d) Gujarat

44. The founder of Yes Bank is:
(a) Rajesh Kapoor
(b) Rahul Kumar
(c) Prashant Kumar
(d) Rana Kapoor

45. Which of the following is a temple in Mangaluru, dedicated to an avatar of Lord Shiva?
(a) Mukteshvara Temple
(b) Ananta Vasudeva Temple
(c) Kadri Manjunatha Temple
(d) Gundicha Temple

46. 'The Commonwealth of Cricket: A Lifelong Love Affair with the Most Subtle and Sophisticated Game known to Humankind' is a book written by _______.
(a) Vinod Rai
(b) Vikram Limaye
(c) Diana Edulji
(d) Ramachandra Guha

47. Sutirtha Mukherjee is an Indian______.
(a) golfer
(b) table tennis player
(c) badminton player
(d) swimmer

48. The inaugural Olympic Congress was organised in the year 1894 in:
(a) Stockholm
(b) Oslo
(c) Paris
(d) London

49. Who among the following was elected as the speaker of the Bihar Assembly in November 2020?
(a) Prem Kumar
(b) Vijay Kumar Sinha
(c) Awadh Bihari Choudhary
(d) Jitan Ram Manjhi

50. Article 76 of the Constitution of India is associated with:
(a) Election Commission
(b) Supreme Court
(c) Attorney General of India
(d) Administrative Tribunals

Part-C : Elementary Mathematics

51. The difference betveen the compound interest and the simple interest on a certain sum at 8% per aninum for 2 years is ₹ 144. What is the amount (in ₹)?
(a) 20,500
(b) 24,500
(c) 40,000
(d) 22,500

52. The value of $75 \div 30 - \frac{3}{4}$ of $\left(\frac{5}{7} \div \frac{9}{14}\right) - \left(3\frac{1}{3} - 1\frac{2}{3}\right)$ is:
(a) 0
(b) 10
(c) 1
(d) 5

53. After applying successive discounts of 10% and 5% on the marked price of an article, it was sold for ₹3,420. Fiad the marked price of the article.
(a) ₹15,000
(b) ₹54,400
(c) ₹16,000
(d) ₹14.000

54. 12 spherical balls of radius 10 cm are dropped in a bucket which is full of water up to the brim. The water flowed out is collected in a cylindrical jar of radius 20 cm. What is the beight (in cm) of the water in the jar? (Take $\pi = \frac{22}{7}$)
(a) 45
(b) 32
(c) 40
(d) 18

55. Raghu and Raman start together to walk a certain equal distance at a speed of 10 km/h and 8 km/h, respectively. Raghu arrives 20 minutes before Raman arrives. Find the distance between the start and the end point.
(a) 25 km
(b) 28 km
(c) 24 km
(d) 20 km

56. The sum of two numbers m and n is 84 (m > n) and their difference is 6. What is the ratio of the two numbers?
(a) 4:3
(b) 17:15
(c) 9:8
(d) 15:13

57. Soni and Gita together can complete a Job in 8 h We can and Arti alone can complete the job In 12 h. In how many hours can Gita alone complete the job?
(a) 48
(b) 12
(c) 24
(d) 14

58. The speed of a train is 110 km/h. It is increased by 20% and then runs at uniform speed The train driver sees the 'Slow Down' sign. so he reduces the speed of the train by 40% of the speed at that moment. What is the final speed (in km/h, correct to one decimal place) of the train?

(a) 69.2
(b) 75.5
(c) 66.5
(d) 79.2

59. The average weight of 24 persons in a group is 72 kg. If 3 persons with average weight 78 kg leave the group and 4 persons of average weight 75 kg join the group, then what will be the average weight (in kg) of the persons in the group now?

(a) 66.5
(b) 71.76
(c) 67.74
(d) 67.8

60. Let x be a number between 1420 and 1780 such that when x is divided by 10, 15, 24 and 32, the remainder in each case is 7. The sum of the digits of x is:

(a) 22
(b) 13
(c) 16
(d) 19

61. The least number of square tiles required to pave the floor of a room with dimensions IS metres and 12 metres will be:

(a) 20
(b) 16
(c) 15
(d) 60

62. A can do a certain piece of work in 20 days. B is 25% more efficient than A, and C is 20% more efficient than B. A and C work together for 5 days. B alone will complete the remaining work in:

(a) 9 days
(b) 8 days
(c) 6 days
(d) 5 days

63. By selling an article for ₹170. a man loses 15%. What per cent will be gain or lose, if he sells it for ₹206.40?

(a) Loss, 1.6%
(b) Loss, 3.2%
(c) Gain, 3.2%
(d) Gain, 1.6%

64. Seema is younger than Reema by 8 years. If 4 years back, their ages were in the ratio 1: 2, then the age (in years) of Seema after 6 years from now will be:

(a) 24
(b) 18
(c) 20
(d) 12

65. A trader sells an item for 7805 after offering a discount of 12.5% on its marked price. Had he not offered the discount, he would have earned a profit of 15%. What is the cost price (in ₹) of the item?

(a) 780
(b) 700
(c) 800
(d) 750

66. The speed of a boat in still water is 10 km/h. The time taken by the boat to go 35 km downstream is 1.25 times the time taken by it to go 14 km upstream. How much time (in hours) will it take to go 60 km downstream?

(a) 3
(b) 3.5
(c) 4
(d) 4.5

67. The nurked price of an article is 3450. It is sold for 7267.30, after offering three successive discounts of 10%, and 20%. What is the value of x?

(a) 16.5
(b) 17.5
(c) 18
(d) 19

68. P sold a lamp to Q at a profit of 20%. Later, Q sold the same lamp to P at a profit of 30%, thereby making a profit of ₹108. How much (in ₹) did P pay originally for the lamp?

(a) 300
(b) 330
(c) 320
(d) 280

69. A number is decreased by 25% and then increased by 25%6. The net percentage increase or decrease is:

(a) 2.5% decrease
(b) $6\frac{1}{4}$% decrease
(c) $3\frac{2}{3}$% increase
(d) 4% decrease

70. A certain sum amounts to ₹8,640 in 2 years at simple interest and to ₹9,720 in 3 years. The sum (in ₹) and the rate of interest p.a. respectively, are:

(a) ₹6,450 and 15%
(b) ₹6,450 and $16\frac{2}{3}$%
(c) ₹6,480 and $16\frac{2}{3}$%
(d) ₹6,480 and 15%

71. The ratio of the incomes of A and B is 4:5 and the ratio of their expenditures is 2:3. If A and B save ₹7,200 and ₹600, respectively, then the income (in ₹) of A is:

(a) 19,200
(b) 20,000
(c) 24,000
(d) 18,000

72. The average weight of 56 students in a group is 55 kg. If 12 students of average weight 60 kg leave and 6 students of average weight 52.5 kg join the group, then the average weight of the remaining students in the group decreases by:

(a) 2 kg
(b) 1.8 kg
(c) 1.5 kg
(d) 2.5 kg

73. The value *of* [6 + 3 of 7 – 5] ÷ 2 *of* 11 is:
(a) 22
(b) 11
(c) 1
(d) 121

74. Three solid metallic cubes of sides 6 cm. 8 cm, and 10 cm, respectively, were melted to form a new solid cube. Find the side (in cm) of the new solid cube.
(a) 9
(b) 12
(c) 8
(d) 12.5

75. The difference between the compound interest and the simple interest on a certain sum at 5% per annum for 2 years is ₹152. What is the amount (in ₹)?
(a) 50,500
(b) 60,000
(c) 60,800
(d) 10,500

Part-D : English

76. Select the option that can be used as a one-word substitute for the given group of words,
An object through which we cannot see at all
(a) Opaque
(b) Translucent
(c) Transparent
(d) Crystal

77. Select the most appropriate option to fill in the blank.
The socio-economic policy has been the_____ of much debate.
(a) subject
(b) talk
(c) object
(d) concept

78. Select the option that can be used as a one-word substitute for the given group of words.
Imitate someone's action or words in order to entertain or ridicule
(a) Copy
(b) Mimic
(c) Repeat
(d) Duplicate

79. Select the most appropriate meaning of the given Idiom.
To beat around the bush
(a) To explain something in detail
(b) To avoid noticing someone
(c) To discuss the main topic
(d) To avoid the main issue

80. Select the option that will improve the underlined part of the given sentence. In case no improvement is needed, select 'No improvement required'.
The movie theatre is <u>a excited</u> place where people can relax and enjoy the experience.
(a) exciting
(b) the excited
(c) No improvement required
(d) an exciting

81. Select the INCORRECTLY spelt word.
(a) Omission
(b) Remission
(c) Recession
(d) Precission

82. Select the most appropriate meaning of the given idiom.
Drop names
(a) Delete someone's name from a list
(b) Show disrespect to someone's name
(c) Assume a false name
(d) Name famous people to impress others

83. Select the INCORRECTLY spelt word.
(a) Collection
(b) Complaint
(c) Coressponding
(d) Consolidation

84. Select the most appropriate synonym of the given word.
Defy
(a) Disobey
(b) Destroy
(c) Abide
(d) React

85. Select the most appropriate synonym of the given word.
Stun
(a) Shock
(b) Trick
(c) Joke
(d) Jest

86. Select the option that can be used as a one-word substitute for the given group of words.
Release someone from a duty or obligation
(a) Banish
(b) Expel
(c) Dismiss
(d) Exonerate

87. Select the option that will improve the underlined part of the sentence. In case no improvement is needed, select 'No improvement required'.
The decision to become a doctor <u>is completely hers</u>.
(a) No improvement required
(b) are completely her
(c) is complete her's
(d) is completely her

88. The following sentence has been split into four segments. Identify the segment that contains a grammatical error.
The president forced / to leave the country / when the people rose up against / the government.
(a) when the people rose up against
(b) the government
(c) to leave the country
(d) The president forced

89. The following sentence has been split into four segments. Identify the segment that contains a grammatical error.
The education of girls / is a primary concern for the country, / so it should be started early, / isn't it?

(a) The education of giris
(b) so it should be started early X
(c) is a primary concern for the country
(d) isn't it

90. Select the most appropriate ANTONYM of the given word.

Alert

(a) Aware
(b) Active
(c) Ready
(d) Careless

91. Select the most appropriate option to fill in the blank.

Teams from all over India ______ in the talent show.

(a) participated
(b) prohibited
(c) produced
(d) provided

92. The following sentence has been split into four segments. Identify the segment that contains a grammatical error.

The lady was furious / to see that no one / were wearing masks / on the road near the shop.

(a) The lady was furious
(b) on the road near the shop
(c) were wearing masks
(d) to see that no one

93. Select the option that will improve the underlined part of the given sentence. In case no improvement is needed, select 'No Improvement required'.

<u>Unless we sat</u> in an incorrect posture, we may strain our back.

(a) Until we sit
(b) If we sit
(c) Although we are sitting
(d) No improvement required

94. Select the most appropriate ANTONYM of the given word.

Vulnerable

(a) Secure
(b) Breakable
(c) Tender
(d) Sensitive

95. Select the most appropriate option to fill in the blank.

For a member to borrow money from the association, three ______ need to be met.

(a) points
(b) accounts
(c) restrictions
(d) conditions

Comprehension:

In the following passage, some words have been deleted. Read the passage carefully and select the most appropriate option to fill in each blank.

You should elect me as Class President as I think that everyone's (1)___ matters. I am a confident speaker and have won prizes (2)________ public speaking. I will make sure that the school council (3)______ to us. When people come to me with problems, I (4)______listen carefully. I never judge people who come to me for (5)______. You can count on me for help.

96. Select the most appropriate option to fill in blank no. 1.

(a) reaction
(b) estimate
(c) theorem
(d) opinion

97. Select the most appropriate option to fill in blank no. 2.

(a) on
(b) for
(c) by
(d) of

98. Select the most appropriate option to fill in blank no. 3.

(a) accepts
(b) hears
(c) believes
(d) listens

99. Select the most appropriate option to fill in blank no. 4.

(a) barely
(b) always
(c) seldom
(d) never

100. Select the most appropriate option to fill in blank no. 5.

(a) advice
(b) news
(c) lesson
(d) caution

Answers

1. (c) After interchanging "×" & "÷" the given eqn. can be solved

L.H.S. $\Rightarrow 16 \times 32 \div 128 + 9 - 17$

$\Rightarrow 16 \times 32 \times \frac{1}{128} + 9 - 17$

$\Rightarrow 4 + 9 - 17$

$= -4 =$ R.H.S. Option (c)

2. (b) 

(i) (ii) (iii)

Comparing (i) & (ii), we get 3 = 5

Comparing (ii) & (iii), we get 1 = 6

i.e., 4 = 2 Ans Option (b)

3. (a) Zebra comes under animals & all animals can be mammals so option (a) is correct.

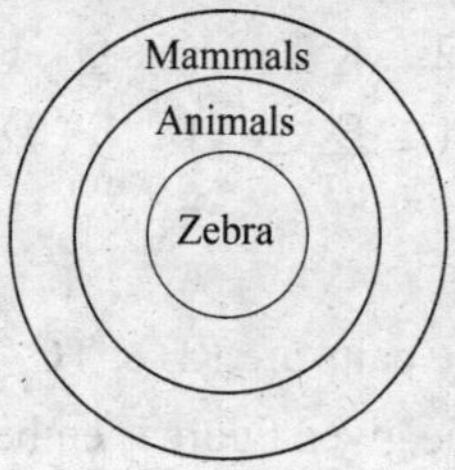

4. (d)

S I N G E R

$\downarrow 1$ ×2 $\downarrow 2$ ×2 $\downarrow 4$ ×2 $\downarrow 8$ ×2 $\downarrow 16$ ×2 $\downarrow 32$

T K R O U X

Similarly

R O O K I E

$\downarrow 1$ ×2 $\downarrow 2$ ×2 $\downarrow 4$ ×2 $\downarrow 8$ ×2 $\downarrow 16$ ×2 $\downarrow 32$

S Q S S Y K

Option (d)

5. (d) After unfolding the given figure will look like i.e, Option (d).

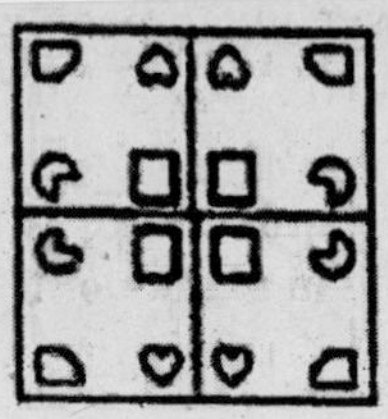

7. (c)

⊞ → Male ⊟ → Female

1D$^+$
|
C$^+$ — B$^-$ ↔ A$^+$
|
E

As per family free C is the maternal uncle of E.

8. (b)Next figure as per series is Option no. (b)

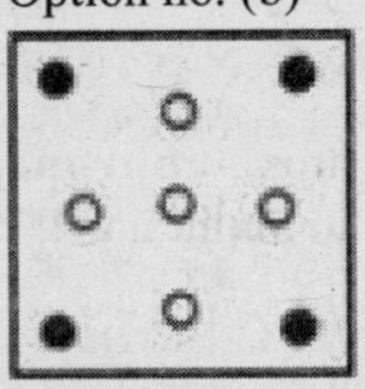

9. (d)77 : 11 :: 259 : ?

$11 \times 7 = 77$

Similarly

$x \times 7 = 259$

$x = 37$

10. (d)

B	K	R
+2↓	+3↓	+4↓
D	N	V
+2↓	+3↓	+4↓
F	Q	Z
+2↓	+3↓	+4↓
H	T	D
+2↓	+3↓	+4↓
J	W	H

11. (d)Let the no. be x

4 times the no = $4x$

Resultant = $4x - x = 3x$

As per question $3x + (3x + 1) = 91$

$6x = 90$

$x = \frac{90}{6}$

$= 15$

12. (b)

15 →(+30) 45 →(+30) 75 →(+30) 105 →(+30) ?

i.e, ? = 105 + 30 = 135

13. (a) D E S K = @ # + %

R A I N = $ – X *

So as per code of the given alphabet

R I S K = $ × + %

14. (c)A, B, C, D, E & F facing North & O, P, Q, R, S, Q T facing South

Step 1: C is 3rd to the right of B & not as immediate neighbour of either E or A

Row 2:....................................(↓)

Row 1: .... B............... C(↑)

E_x
A

Step 2: P is 3rd to the left of S & Neither P nor S are sitting at extreme end of the row.

Row 2: .... S .... P (↓)

Row 1: .... B .... C (↑)

E_x
A

Step 3: F faces O, who is 2nd to the right of T, and T is not as immediate neighbour to S

Row 2: .... S .... O P T (↓)

Row 1: ....B F .... C (↑)

E_x
A

Step 4: Only two people are sitting between Q & T. A, is not facing R.

Row 2: R S Q O P T (↓)

Row 1: E A B F D C (↑)

E_x
A

So the pairs are RE & TC

15. (b)The given figure is embedded in Option no (b) ... i.e.

16. (d)

C O A C H

3 + 15 + 1 + 3 + 8 = 30 × 3 = 90

P O S T

16 + 15 + 19 + 20 = 70 × 3 = 210

Similarly

N O I S E

14 + 15 + 9 + 19 + 5 = 62 × 3

= 186

17. (d)

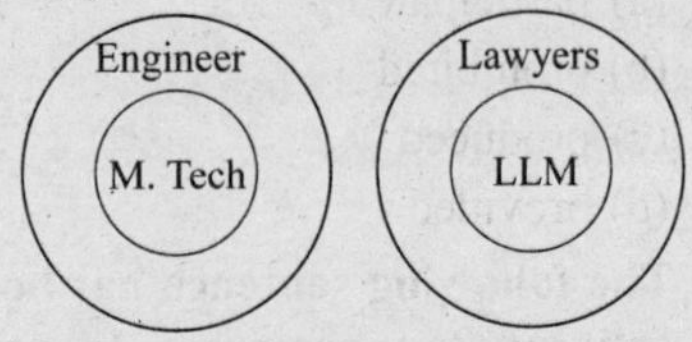

As per logical diagram.

Neither Conclusion (I) nor II follows.

18. (c)The person who study about kidney is known as Nephrologist. Similarly the person who study about heart is known as Cardiologist.

19. (d)

14, →(× 2+5) 33, →(× 2+5) 71, →(× 2+5) 147, →(× 2+5) 299, →(× 2+5) ?

? = 299 × 2 + 5 = 598 + 5 = 603

20. (a) **Step 1:** Alpa is immediate right of Vinita

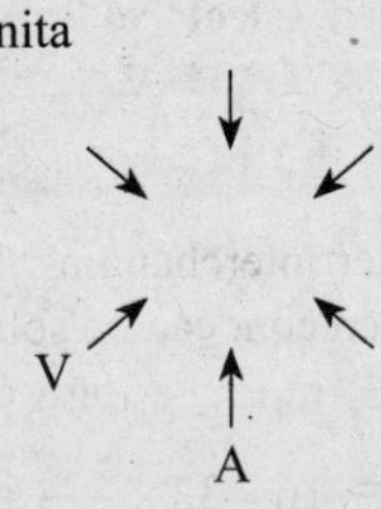

Step 2: Divya is between Neeta & Vanita

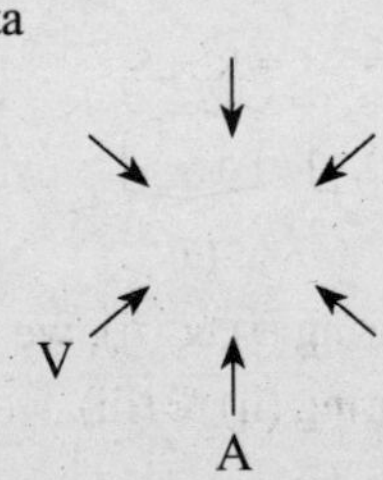

Step 3: Kamini is between Neeta & Satya

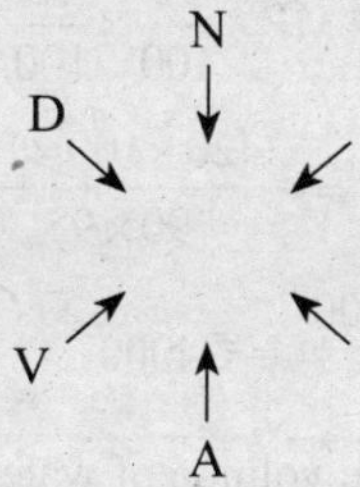

So, Divya sit 3rd to the left of Satya.

21. (d) +3 +3 +3 +3

(a) $D \xrightarrow{+3} G \xrightarrow{+3} J \xrightarrow{+3} M \xrightarrow{+3} P$

(b) $T \xrightarrow{+3} W \xrightarrow{+3} Z \xrightarrow{+3} C \xrightarrow{+3} F$

(c) $P \xrightarrow{+3} S \xrightarrow{+3} V \xrightarrow{+3} Y \xrightarrow{+3} B$

(4) $N \xrightarrow{+3} Q \xrightarrow{+3} T \xrightarrow{+3} W \xrightarrow{+4} A$

So, Option (d) is odd one out.

22. (c)

RKM : VFS : : PSQ : ?

R	K	M
+4↓	–5↓	+6↓
V	F	S

Similarly

P	S	Q
+4↓	–5↓	+6↓
T	N	W

23. (c)

G$\underline{D}\underline{F}$PK $\underline{G}$DF$\underline{P}$K GD$\underline{F}\underline{P}$K

24. (a)The Mirror image of the given figure is Option no. (a)

25. (c)

The words are arranged as per dictionary order

(i) Uneconomical

(ii) Unemployment

(iii) Uneventful

(iv) Unexpected

(v) Unexplained

26. (c) Politician writer M. Virappa Moilley was awarded THE SAHITYA Academy award 2020 for his poetry titled 'Sri Bahubali Ahimsadigvijayamh in Kannada language.

The award, which includes a casket containing an engraved copper plaque, a shawl and an amount of ₹ 1,00,000, was presented at the award presentation function.

27. (b) Among the given options, Anemia is caused by the deficiency of haemoglobin.

28. (a) GST is one indirect tax for the whole nation, which will make India one unified common market. GST is a single tax on the supply of goods and services, right from the manufacturer to the consumer.

29. (c) Virat Kohli won ICC Men's ODI Cricketer of the Decade. Who remains the fastest to score 10000 ODI runs, has put in numerous sensational performances with the bat in the fifty-overs cricket in the last 10 years, making him one of the finest batsmen going around.

30. (a) In 1956, the Hindu Succession Act abandoned the rule of primogeniture in India.

31. (c) The given statement in option c is not correct.

32. (c) Among the given options, tongue is the part of the human body that contains gustatory receptors.

33. (d) Farmers in some Parts of India celebrate the Pola festival by worshipping their Bullocks. Pola is a thanksgiving festival celebrated by farmers Maharashtra and Chhattisgarh, to acknowledge the importance of bulls and oxen, Who are a crucial part of agriculture and farming activities. It falls on the day of the Pithori Amavasya (the new moon day) in the month of Shraavana (usually in August). During Pola, farmers don't work their bulls in the farmland, and the day is a school holiday in the rural parts of Maharashtra.

34. (c) Awadh Oudh, is a region and proposed state in the modern Indian state of Uttar Pradesh which was before independence known as the United Provinces of Agra and Oudh.

Awadh is bounded by the Ganges Doab to the southwest, Rohilkhand to the northwest, Nepal to the north, and Bhojpur-Purvanchal to the east. Its inhabitants are referred to as Awadhis.

It was established as one of the twelve original subahs (top-level imperial provinces) under 16th-century Mughal emperor Akbar and became a hereditary tributary polity around 1722, with Faizabad as its initial capital and Saadat Ali Khan as its first Subadar Nawab and progenitor of a dynasty of Nawabs of Awadh.

35. (d) The Luni is the longest river in the Thar Desert. It originates in the Pushkar valley of the Aravalli Range, near Ajmer, passes through the southeastern portion of the Thar Desert, and ends in the marshy lands of Rann of Kutch in Gujarat, after travelling a distance of 495 km.

36. (d) the government of India has dedicated a window 'The Green Gold Collection' on the GeM (Government e-Marketplace) portal for the marketing of Bamboo Goods.

37. (c) Qutab-ud-din Aibak, the first Muslim ruler of Delhi, commenced the construction of the Qutab Minar in 1200 AD, but could only finish the basement. His successor, Iltutmush, added three more storeys, and in 1368, Firoz Shah Tughlak constructed the fifth and the last storey.

38. (c) In 1920 the Indian Industrial and Commercial Congress formed by Indian merchants and industrialists to organize their business interests.

39. (a) The Preamble of the Indian constitution declares India to be a "Sovereign" country, implying that India has its own supreme law and is not subject to the laws of any other state or nation. Furthermore, India is free of any external interference in its own affairs.

40. (a)

41. (a) The Vikramshila Gangetic Dolphin Sanctuary (VGDS), from Sultanganj to Kahalganj on the Ganga in Bihar is the only dolphin sanctuary in the country. Experts have pegged the population of the Ganges dolphin in VGDS from 150 to 200. National Waterway-1 connecting Haldia to Varanasi passes through the Vikramshila Gangetic Dolphin Sanctuary.

42. (b) Hedging is a risk of management strategy employed to offset losses in investments by taking an opposite position in a related asset.

43. (a) Kerala is the correct answer.

44. (d) Yes Bank is an Indian bank headquartered in Mumbai, India and was founded by Rana Kapoor and Ashok Kapoor in 2004.

45. (c) Kadri Manjunathal temple is a temple in mangaluru, dedicated to an avatar of Lord Shiva.

46. (d) The Commonwealth of Cricket: A lifelong love affair with the most subtle and sophisticated game known to humankind is a book by Ramachandra Guha.

47. (b) Sutirtha Mukherjee is an Indian table tennis player.

48. (c) The inaugural Olympic Congress was organized in the year 1894 in Paris. It was this Congress which founded and established the IOC and laid the groundwork for its statutes. The process of revival of the Olympic Games also began at the Paris Congress of 1894.

49. (b) Vijay Kumar Sinha was elected as the speaker of the Bihar Assembly in November 2020.

50. (c) According to Article 76 of the Indian Constitution, the Attorney General (AG) of India is the highest law officer in the country and a Union Executive member. Article 76 deals with the Attorney General of India.

51. (d) Compound interest (CI)

$$= P\left[\left(1+\frac{r}{100}\right)^n - 1\right]$$

where P is principal, r is rate of interest (annual) and n is number of years

Simple interest $(SI) = A - P$, where A is amount

$$= \frac{PRT}{100}$$, where R is annual rate of interest and T is time in years.

Here, $P = ?$ $R = 8\%$, $\frac{n}{T} = 2$ yrs

$$144 = P\left\{\left[\left(1+\frac{8}{100}\right)^2 - 1\right] - \frac{8\times 2}{100}\right\}$$

$$= P\left\{\left[\left(\frac{27}{25}\right)^2 - 1\right] - \frac{16}{100}\right\}$$

$$= P\left\{\frac{104}{625} - \frac{4}{25}\right\}$$

$$P = \frac{144\times 625}{4} = ₹\,22500$$

52. (a) Here, we apply BODMAS rule

$$75 \div 30 - \frac{3}{4} \text{ of } \left(\frac{5}{7} \div \frac{2}{14}\right) - \left(3\frac{1}{3} - 1\frac{2}{3}\right)$$

$$= 75 \div 30 - \frac{3}{4} \text{ of } \left(\frac{10}{9}\right) - \left(+\frac{5}{3}\right)$$

$$= 75 \div 30 - \left(\frac{5}{6}\right) - \frac{5}{3}$$

$$= 75 \times \frac{1}{30} - \frac{5}{6} - \frac{5}{3}$$

$$= \frac{5}{2} - \left(\frac{5}{6} + \frac{5}{3}\right)$$

$$= \frac{5}{2} - \frac{5}{2} = 0$$

53. (d) Let the Marked Price be MP.

On applying first discount of 10%,

Price becomes $MP \times \frac{90}{100}$

One applying second discount of 5% price becomes $MP \times \frac{90}{100} \times \frac{95}{100}$

But this price is 3420 (Given)

Hence $MP \times \frac{90}{100} \times \frac{95}{100} = 3420$

$$\Rightarrow MP = \frac{3420\times 100\times 100}{90\times 95}$$

$$= \frac{20000}{5} = ₹\,4000$$

54. (c) The volume of water displaced by the spherical balls will be same as volume of water collected in cylindrical jar.

Volume of one spherical ball

$$= \frac{4}{3}\pi r^3 = \frac{4}{3}\pi(10)^3$$

Volume of twelve spherical balls

$$= 12 \times \frac{4}{3}\pi(10)^3$$

Volume of cylindrical column in jar $= \pi R^2 h$, where R is radius of cylinder and h the height of water column

Hence, $12 \times \frac{4}{3}\pi(10)^3 = \pi(20)^2 h$

$$\Rightarrow \pi(d)(10)^2 h = 12 \times \frac{4}{3}\pi(10)^2(10)$$

$$\Rightarrow h = \frac{120}{3} = 40 \text{ cm}$$

55. (d) Let the distance be D km.

Speed of Raghu be x i.e. 10m/h

Speed of Raman be y i.e. 8 km/h

Time taken by Raghu to cover the distance $= \frac{D}{10}$

Time taken by Ranam to cover the Distance $= \frac{D}{8}$

$\{Speed = \frac{Distance}{Time}\}$

So Time $= \frac{Distance}{Speed}$

Given, Raghu takes 30 min $\left(\frac{1}{2}h\right)$ less time than Raman to cover the distance

So, $\frac{D}{8}-\frac{D}{10}=\frac{1}{2}$

$\Rightarrow D\left(\frac{2}{80}\right)=\frac{1}{2}$

$\frac{D}{40}=\frac{1}{2}$

$D=\frac{40}{2}=20$ km

56. (d) Given $m+n=84$

Also, $m-n=6\ (\because m>n)$

Solving, $m+n=84$

$m-n=6$

(+) (+) (+)

$2m=(90)$

$\Rightarrow m=\frac{90}{2}=45$

$m+n=90$; so $n=84-45=39$

Required ratio $=m:n$

$=45:39=15:13$

57. (c) Let, Soni and Gita take individually x and y hours to complete the work

Then Soni's 1 hour work $=\frac{1}{x}$, and

Gita's 1 hour work $=\frac{1}{y}$

Further $\frac{1}{x}+\frac{1}{y}=\frac{1}{8}$

But given Soni alone can complete the job in 12 h, hence $x=12$

So, $\frac{1}{12}+\frac{1}{y}=\frac{1}{8}$

$\Rightarrow \frac{1}{y}=\frac{1}{8}-\frac{1}{12}=\frac{4}{96}$

$\Rightarrow y=24$ h

58. (d) Initially, speed of the train = 110 km/h

On increasing by 20%, it becomes

$=110\times\frac{120}{100}$

= 132 km/h

Now, the train is run at this speed for some time.

On seeing the 'down sign', the train driver reduces speed by 40%

Then, new speed becomes

$132\times\frac{60}{100}=79.2$ km/h

59. (b) Given average weight of 24 persons = 72 kg

So, $\frac{\text{Total wt. of 24 persons}}{24}=72$

$\Rightarrow$ Total weight of 24 persons

$=72\times24$

= 1728 kg

when 3 persons with average wt. 78 kg leave Reduction in becomes by amount 78×3 *i.e.* 234 kg

Also 4 persons with average wt. 75 kg join

Increment in wt. is by amount 75×4 *ie.* 300 kg

Now remainder weight

$=1728-234+300$

= 1794 kg

Remainder people $=24-3+4$

= 25 persons

Average wt. of the new group

$=\frac{1794}{25}=71.76$ kg

60. (c) Since the given/required number leaves remainder 7 on dividing by 10, –11, 15, 24, and 32 each

The number on dividing by the LCM of these number will leave remainder 7 too.

LCM of these numbers is 120

Now on dividing 1420 by 120, weight 100 as remember.

This means, if we add. 27 to the remainder, or for that matter, 27 to 1420, the new remainder would come out as 7.

Hence the required number is 1420 + 27 *ie.* 1447 Its sum of digits is 1 + 4 + 4 + 7 = 16

61. (a) The dimension of the room is 15 m and 12 m

Its area = *lb*

$=(15)(12)=180\text{ m}^2$

The least number of tiles that will be required under the given condition required the square tiles with dimensions as of 15 and 12, which is 3 cm

Now, Area of one such tile = 9 cm^2 (3×3)

Required number of tiles $=\frac{180}{9}$

= 20

62. (d) A can complete a work in 20 days

A's one day work $=\frac{1}{20}$

B is 25% more efficient than B, so B will complete work in 15 days

B's one day work $=\frac{1}{15}$

C is 20% more efficient than B, so can complete the work in 12 days

C's one day work $=\frac{1}{12}$

A and C work for 5 days.

Their five day work is

$\left(\frac{1}{20}+\frac{1}{12}\right)\times5=\frac{2}{3}$

Remaining work $=1-\frac{2}{3}=\frac{1}{3}$

B will complete the remaining work in x days 15 (say) Then,

$\frac{1}{15}\times x=\frac{1}{3}$

$\Rightarrow x=\frac{15}{3}=5$

63. (c) Case I $SP_1=₹\ 170$

Loss = 15%

$CP=SP_1\times\frac{100}{100-\text{loss}}$

$=170\times\frac{100}{85}=₹\ 200$

Case II, $SP_2=₹\ 206.40$ CP/CP_2 $=₹\ 200$

As $SP>CP_1$ It is a case of gain

Gain = selling price – cost price

$=206.40-200=6.40$

Gain% $=\frac{\text{Gain}}{\text{CP}}\times100$

$=\frac{6.40}{200}\times100=3.2\%$

64. (b) Let age of Reema be x yrs, then age of Seema is x–8 yrs (given)

Four years back, age of Reema = $x - 4$ yrs and age of Seema = $x - 12$ yrs $[x - 8 - 4]$

Given, that $\frac{x-12}{x-4} = \frac{1}{2}$

Solving, $2x - 24 = x - 4$

$\Rightarrow x = 20$ yrs

So $y = x - 8$ *ie.* 12 yrs

Age of Seema after 6 yrs = 12 + 6 = 18 yrs

65. (c) We know Profit% $= \frac{\text{Profit}}{\text{CP}} \times 100$

So, in case II $15 = \frac{\text{SP} - \text{CP}}{\text{CP}} \times 100$

$= \frac{805 - \text{CP}}{\text{CP}} \times 100$

15 CP = (805 × 100) – (100 CP)

115 CP = 805 × 100

$\Rightarrow \text{CP} = \frac{805}{115} = ₹\,700$

Hence in case, if CP_1 was the cost price of the article.

then, If he had not offered the discount, then cost price would have escalated by another ₹ $\frac{12.5}{100} \times 800$ *ie.* ₹ 100

So CP at that time would have been ₹ (700 + 100) *ie.* ₹ 800

66. (d) Let u km/h be speed of boat in still water and v km/h be the speed of stream

Then upstream speed of boat $= (u - v)$ km/h and

Then upstream speed of boat $= (u + v)$ km/h

Here, $u = 10$ km/h

$\text{Speed} = \frac{\text{Distance}}{\text{Time}}$

While going down stream, time taken, $T_D = \frac{35}{10 + v}$

While going upstream, time taken, $T_u = \frac{14}{10 - v}$

As per the question,

$\frac{35}{10+v} = 1.25\left(\frac{14}{10-v}\right)$

$= \frac{5}{4}\left(\frac{14}{10-v}\right)$

$\Rightarrow 20 - 2v = 10 + v$

$\Rightarrow v = \frac{10}{3}$ km/h

Time taken to go 60 km downstream

$= \frac{60}{10 + \frac{10}{3}} = \frac{60 \times 3}{40} = 4.5\text{h}$

67. (b) Let Market Price be MP

Once after 1st discount $= \frac{90}{100}$ MP

Once after 2nd discount

$= \left(\frac{100 - x}{100}\right) \times \frac{90}{100}$ MP

Once after 3rd discount

$= \left(\frac{80}{100}\right)\left(\frac{100 - x}{100}\right) \times \frac{90}{100}$ MP

Given

$\left(\frac{80}{100}\right)\left(\frac{100 - x}{100}\right)\left(\frac{90}{100}\right) \times 450$

$= 267.30$

$\Rightarrow \frac{4}{5} \times \frac{100 - x}{100} \times \frac{9}{10} \times 90 = 267.30$

$\Rightarrow 100 - x = \frac{267.30 \times 1000}{4 \times 9 \times 90}$

$= \frac{2970}{36} = 82.5$

$\Rightarrow x = 17.5\%$

68. SP for P is CP for Q. Profit for P = 20%

$20 = \frac{(\text{S.P} - \text{CP})}{\text{CP [for P]}} \times 100$

$= \frac{y - x}{x} \times 100$ [say]

Case II

$30 = \frac{108}{\text{SP (for Q)}} \times 100$

$\text{SP (for Q)} = \frac{108 \times 100}{30} = ₹\,360$

69. (b) Let the number of x

On decreasing by 25%, it becomes

$= \frac{75}{100}x$

Then, on increasing by 25, it becomes

$= \frac{125}{100} \times \frac{75}{100}x$

$= \frac{15}{16}x$

Comparing it with original number x, we see that the new number has decreased

$\text{decrease} = x - \frac{15}{16}x = \frac{x}{16}$

Percentage decrease $= \frac{\frac{x}{16}}{x} \times 100$

$= \frac{1}{16} \times 100 = 6\frac{1}{4}\%$

70. (c) Amount $(A) = P + SI$ and,

Simple Interest $(SI) = \frac{PRT}{100}$, where,

P is principal, R is annual rate of interest, and T is time in years

Here, $A = ₹\,8640$, $T_1 = 2$yrs ;

$A_2 = ₹\,9720$, $T_2 = 3$yrs ;

$P = ?, P = ?$

Case I, $8640 = P + \frac{PR \times 2}{100}$ ...(1)

Case II, $9720 = P + \frac{PR \times 3}{100}$ ...(2)

$1080 = \frac{PR}{100}(3 - 2) = \frac{PR}{100}$

$\Rightarrow PR = ₹\,108000$

Putting this value in either equation (say Equ. 1)

$8640 = P + \frac{108000 \times 2}{100}$

$P = 8640 - 2160 = ₹\,6480$

Now, $R = \frac{108000}{P} = \frac{108000}{6480}$

$= 16\frac{2}{3}\%$

71. (a) Income = Expenditure + Savings

Let incomes of A and B be $4x$ and $5x$ respectively and their expenditure be $2y$ and $3y$ respectively.

Then, their savings are $4x - 2y$ and $5x - 3y$ respectively

Now, $4x - 2y = 7200$ and $5x - 3y = 6000$ (Given)

Solving them

$4x - 2y = 7200$ ...(1)

$5x - 3y = 6000$ ...(2)

or $12x - 6y = 21600$ ...(3)

$+ 10x - 6y = + 12000$ ...(4)

$- \quad + \quad -$

$2x = 9600$

$\Rightarrow x = ₹ 4800$

Now income of A $= 4x = 4 \times 4800$

$= ₹ 19200$

72. (c) Average weight (wt.) of 56 students = 55 kg

So $\frac{\text{Total wt of 56 students}}{56} = 55$

$\Rightarrow$ Total wt of 56 students = 3080 kg

Now, 12 students with average wt. 60 kg leave

Their total wt $= 12 \times 60 = 720$ kg

Also 6 students with average wt. 52.5 kg join

Their total wt $= 6 \times 52.5 = 315$ kg

Now in the new situation,

total students $= 56 - 12 + 6 = 50$

total weight $= 3080 - 720 + 315 = 2675$ kg

Average weight of this new group

$= \frac{2675}{50} = 53.5$ kg

This new average wt is lesser than earlier one by $55 - 53.5$ *i.e.* 1.5 kg

73. (c) Applying BODMAS Rule

$[6 + 3 \text{ of } 7 - 5] \div 2 \text{ of } 11$

$= [6 + 21 - 5] \div 22$

$= [22] \div 22$

$= 22 \div 22$

$= 1$

74. In such case volume of the new object formed is same as combined volume of the melted and fused objects.

Now volume of cube = $(\text{side})^3$

Volumes of given cubes are $(6)^3$, $(8)^3$ and $(10)^3$, respectively *ie.* 216, 512 and 1000 cm^3, respectively

Let a be the volume of the solid cube formed after fusion.

Then $216 + 512 + 1000 = (a)^3$

$\Rightarrow 1728 = a^3$

$a^3 = 1728$

$a = \sqrt[3]{1728}$

$= 12$ cm

75. Compound interest CI

$= P\left[\left(1+\frac{r}{100}\right)^n - 1\right]$

Simple interest $= \frac{prt}{100}$

where P is principal, r is rate of interest (annual), $\frac{n}{t}$ is time in years

Here, $P = ?$, $r = 5\%$, $\frac{n}{t} = 2$ yrs

$\Rightarrow 152 = P\left[\left(1+\frac{r}{100}\right)^n - 1\right] - \frac{prt}{100}$

$= P\left\{\left[\left(1+\frac{r}{100}\right)^n - 1\right] - \frac{rt}{100}\right\}$

$= P\left\{\left[\left(1+\frac{5}{100}\right)^2 - 1\right] - \frac{5\times 2}{100}\right\}$

$= P\left\{\left[\left(\frac{21}{20}\right)^2 - 1\right] - \frac{1}{10}\right\}$

$= P\left\{\frac{441}{400} - \frac{1}{10}\right\}$

$= P\left\{\frac{1}{400}\right\}$

$\Rightarrow P = 152 \times 400 = ₹ 60,800$

76. (a) Opaque objects are one through which rays cannot pass at all, such as, stone, metal block, etc. Transparent objects, on the other hand are those through which light completely passes, for example, glass. Translucent objects are those that allow partial passage of light through them. For example, butter paper. A piece of a homogeneous solid substance having a natural geometric regular form is called a crystal.

77. A debate is a discussion/discourse that revolves around a subject or issue. In this sentence, the subject/issue is the socio-economic policy. Word 'talk' itself is indicative of a discussion and so, it is inappropriate. 'Object' means an 'article' and refers to a physical entity, and concept is the part that helps in understanding of a topic. Both these words also, clearly, are unsuitable.

78. (a) Infact, the word 'mimicry', which means imitating voice of different people is the noun form of the given verb word. Word 'copy' is quite similar in meaning to word 'mimic', with major difference being that it doesn't involve the elements of entertainment/ridicule. Repeat is a physical act of again and again undergoing the same task. 'Duplicate' is a replica of something, which is quite similar to the original in physical form.

79. (d) The origin of 'to beat around the bush' idiom is associated with hunting. In medieval times, hunters hired men to beat the area around bushes with sticks in order to flush out game taking cover underneath. Thus, areas/objects, other than the target, were groped/explored in this course. Likely, when someone talks about other issues, skirting the main issue, this idiom finds application.

80. (d) In this case, movie theatre is a particular spot. Hence, some or the other article is required to be used. Therefore, option isn't correct. Now, not any specific movie theater is being talked about. Hence, definite article 'the' will not be used, and Option b is also not correct. Use of 'a' before 'excited' is incorrect since 'exited' begins with a vowel. As such, option d is the correct Option amongst the given ones.

81. (d) 'Omission' is derived from word 'omit' and means leaving something per chance. 'Remission' means cancellation of a debt, charge, or penalty. Recession originates from word recede, which means waning, quantity/intensity becoming less. 'Precission' is incorrectly spelt. The actual word is precision which means, accuracy.

82. (d) The idiom means mentioning name (s) of important or famous people as if they were personal friends. The purpose is usually to receive preferential treatment.

83. (c) 'Collection' means a group of some object, which may or may not fall under a classification. 'Compliant' means to register grievance against somebody orally or in writing. 'Consolidation' means collection/augmentation in the nature of strengthening. Word 'corresponding' should be actually 'corresponding', which means specifically related to an item/ object.

84. (a) Word 'defy' is going against command or orders of someone. In this regard, it has similar meaning to the word 'disobey'. The other three words are far from meaning of the given since 'destroy' means to perish something; 'abide' means 'to follow' or subscribe to a person's opinion; and 'react' means 'to respond', either in favour or against.

85. (a) 'Ston' word gives the feeling of astonishment and a highly unlikely surprise. 'Trick' means a sort of deception, which may be either done jovially or with bed intentions. 'Joke' means a narration/act with the intention of raising humor. 'Jest' means a 'joking or mocking remark; Though similar to the word 'joke', word jest signifies intention of downplaying someone.

86. (d) Word 'banish' means to send away from a country or place as an official punishment, word 'expel' also has similar meaning, and it means 'evicting someone'. 'Dismissal' is also of almost similar meaning as it means 'asking/ ordering someone to leave a place'. Thus, the first three options, more or less, are vary close to each other in meaning. Exonerate connotes 'relief'. Which may even be from a punishment.

87. (a) Option b is incorrect since it is a case of subject-verb disagreement. Decision is singular and 'are' is used for more than two items. Option c is also incorrect since it gives an impression of possessive case, while possession isn't implied here. Option d, likewise, is also incorrect since it means 'decision' in itself is 'her', which is not intended to be conveyed actually.

88. (d) Option a in its present from is giving the impression that the president forced someone to leave the country, whereas, in actuality, verb 'forced' doesn't clearly signal here that who was forced as per the statement. The 'subject' isn't clear from the reading. If this part is made 'The president was forced', then the sentence assumes clarity. Since then, it would mean that in the wake of an uprising in the country against the president, he was forced to flee the place.

89. (d) It is a case of use of question tag, which are constrictions in which an interrogative element is added to a declarative or an imperative clause. The resulting speech act comprises an assertion paired with a request for confirmation. Modal verbs such as could, should or would is the same question tag. Hence, in this case, question tag should be, 'shouldn't it, rather than isn't it.

90. (d) 'Alert' signifies' 'being cautions', i.e. to be ready for an eventuality. Careless, on the other hand, means uncaring for the result and acting lazily all along. Both these words, obviously, are mutual opposites. The other three words in their meaning are close to the word alert as all of them are indicative of one being prepared for the possible actions.

91. (a) Here, as show is being organised. Obviously, people/ teams are expected to be a part of it or complete in it and showcase their performance, which one does by participation: 'prohibited' is strictly inapplicable as it means 'stop anyone from doing something'. Also 'team', are a group of animate entities, which aren't expected to be produced. Hence, Option c is a misfit. Option d doesn't make any sense in the context.

92. (c) In the part b of the sentence, we see use of phrasal noun 'no one' which connotes singularity. Part c of the sentence, makes use of word 'were', which is used for plural entities. Thus, it is a case of subject-verb disagreement. Word 'were', thus, infact, needs to be replaced by 'was'.

93. (b) 'Until' gives a sense of time, i.e. till the time. However, its use would be grossly wrong since the resultant meaning looks clumsy. 'Although' is used in cases where the consequence didn't align with the possible outcome. So, this preposition too is incorrect. 'If' is used in cases where the purpose is to have an effect of morning or to make aware of the possible adverse effect. This sense is conveyed, thus, by Option b. Hence, it is the correct answer.

94. 'Vulnerable' imparts a sense of weakness; something which can be easily breached. In that sense, word 'secure' is rightly its antonym, as it, means 'safe by all means'. The other three options, namely breakable, tender, and sensitive are similar in meaning to each other and in a sense more closely related in meaning to word 'secure' as 'breakable' means 'fragile', 'tender' mean 'soft', and 'sensitive' means 'easily hurt'.

95. (d) In the given case, a situation is given, namely, for a person/member to borrow from the association. Obviously, money can't be lent to everybody, but to select few, who meet certain parameters, i.e., conditions. Word 'points' is under in its meaning here; word 'account' can be seen to hardly meet the sense to be conveyed, and 'restrictions' is largely inappropriate since these would rather inhibit borrowing.

96. (d) As a class president, a person is required to give weightage to what everyone think. Hence, this word 'opinion' is the most appropriate. 'Reactions' can be positive or negative, and so, they wouldn't facilitate positive decision making all the tone. 'Estimate' is a word that is used more in accounting work, etc. and so, it isn't appropriate too. Similarly, word 'theorem' is used mostly in mathematical concepts, and it also isn't suitable.

97. (b) The person/president-elect (proposed) intends, to convey that he has won prices earlier. Naturally, this must have been so in response to an act, which is indicated by word 'for'. Option a, b and c are grossly inapplicable here because of their meanings.

98. (d) Verbs 'accepts', 'hears', and 'believes' never take preposition 'to' after them as these are all intransitive verbs. Hence, these all need to be rejected. 'Listen to' someone means to 'pay attention to'/'pay head to' someone's else's words. The speaker wants to say that as a future president, he will make sure that their voice is given due attention by the council.

99. (b) Use of word 'hardly', 'seldom', and 'never' in the present context would make the sentence preposterous. It would make it laughable. Since if one comes to a leader with a problem, he/she can hardly afford to dismiss the request/grievance. Option b supplies correct word as, the person/speaker, in capacity of school president, would be always attending all in mitigating their hardships.

100. (a) People are not supposed to turn up to leader for any news or for a lesson. Similarly, Option d, i.e. word 'caution' isn't appropriate by any means. People come to leader mostly for advice and here, the speaker wants to convey that he doesn't judge people on these grounds. He goes on to add that on account of his these qualities, the addresses can bank upon him.

SSC Constable (GD)
Solved Paper-2019

Part-A: General Intelligence and Reasoning

1. Study the diagram below and identify the region representing girls who are employed but unmarried.

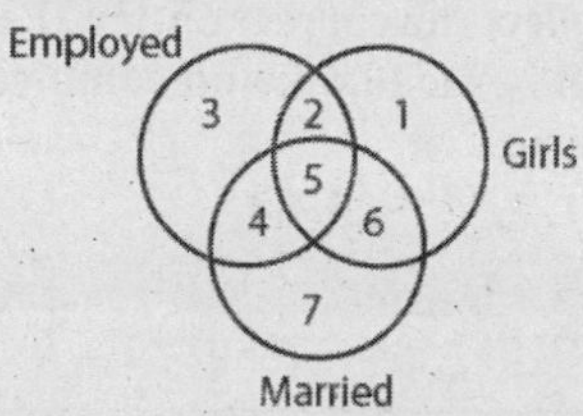

(a) 2 (b) 4
(c) 1 (d) 5

2. A, B, C, D and E are sitting in a row. C is between D and A, E is neither at the end, nor next to D and is to the left of B who is last. Who is to the right of D?

(a) B (b) E
(c) A (d) C

3. The statements below are followed by two conclusions labeled I and II. Assuming that the information in the statements is true, even if it appears to be at variance with generally established facts, decide which conclusions logically and definitely follows from the information given in the statements.

Statement 1 : All shells are skins.

Statement 2 : No skins are cats.

Conclusion I : No shells are cats.

Conclusion II: Some skins are shells.

(a) Neither I lior II follows
(b) Only conclusion I follows
(c) Both I and II follow
(d) Only conclusion II follows

4. Choose the option which completes the given figure series

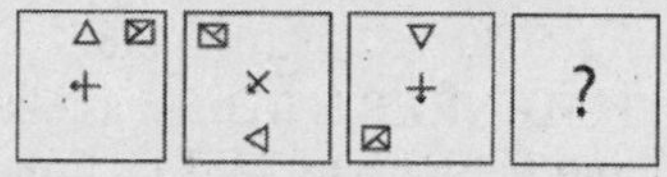

(a) 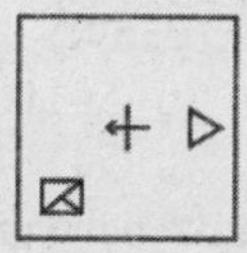 (b) 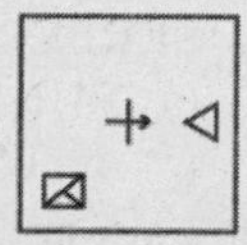

(c) 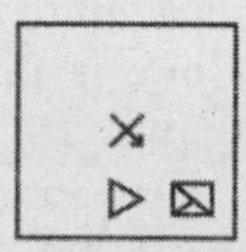 (d) 

5. Four words have been given, out of which three are alike in some manner, while one is different. Choose the odd one.

(a) Scarf (b) Sweater
(c) Sunglass (d) Gloves

6. Four letter clusters have been given, out of which three are alike in some manner, while one is different. Choose the odd one

(a) RSU (b) YAC
(c) LNP (d) CEG

7. A, O, M, H, K and U are sitting in a circle facing the centre. A is NOT sitting next to M or U, U is to the right of H, K is to the left of M, who is opposite O. Who is to the right of O?

(a) H (b) A
(c) K (d) U

8. Choose the option figure in which the problem figure is hidden/ embedded.

(a)  (b) 

(c)  (d) 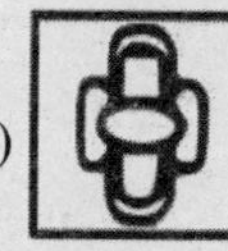

9. Select the correct option that will fill in the blank and complete the series.

1024, ?, 1600, 2000, 2500, 3125

(a) 1350 (b) 1440
(c) 1280 (d) 1125

10. In the following questions a piece of paper is folded in the manner shown in the question figures. Select the figure out of the answer choices showing the unfolded pattern after the punches (cut).

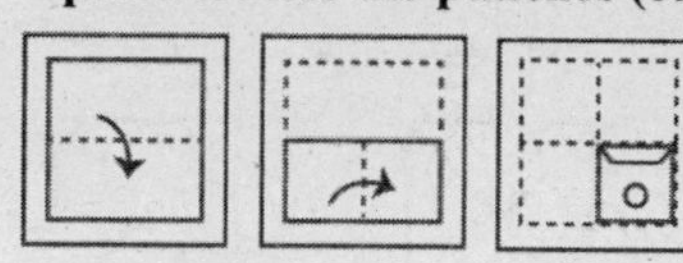

(a) 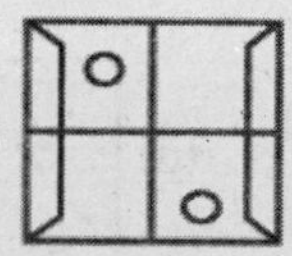 (b) 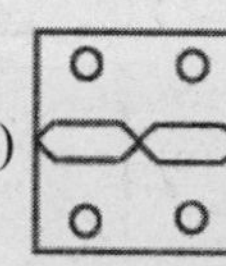

(c) 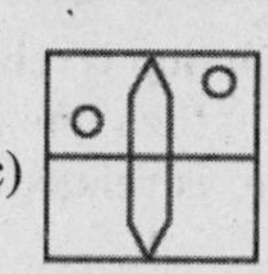 (d) 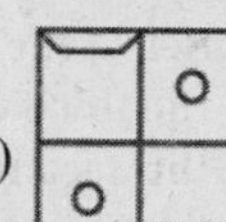

11. Choose the option that most closely resembles the mirror image of the given figure when mirror is placed at right side.

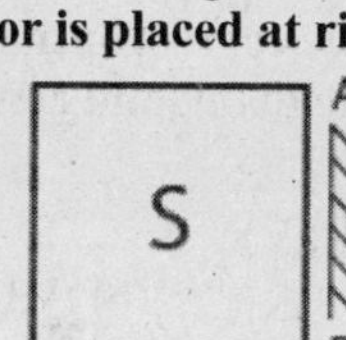

(a)  (b) 

(c)  (d) 

12. Some boys are sitting in a row facing north. Ganesh is 7th on the left of Akshit. Vinay, who is 20th in the row from left, is 7th on the right of Akshit. If Kamal, who is third on the right of Ganesh, Kamal is 20th in the row from right, how many boys are there in the row?

(a) 26 (b) 28
(c) 31 (d) 30

13. Select the option that is related to the third term in the same way as the second term is related to the first term.

Pen : Write :: Knife : ....

(a) Cut (b) Shoot
(c) Blood (d) Vegetable

14. Which of the following answer figure will complete the given figure?

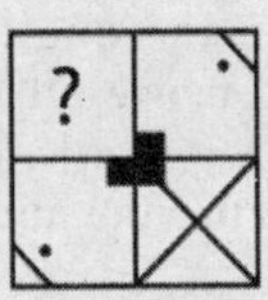

(a)  (b) 

(c)  (d) 

15. Select the option that is related to the third term in the same way as the second term is related to the first term.

TSQ : JHG :: LTM : ?

(a) FBC (b) ACD
(c) UVO (d) NGO

16. Select the correct option that will fill in the blank and complete the series.

LM, QR, VW, ...

(a) UK (b) AB
(c) AD (d) SM

17. Select the correct combination of mathematical signs to replace '*' signs and to balance the given equation:

96*2*20*2*174

(a) × – + = (b) ÷ × + =
(c) – + × = (d) + + ÷ =

18. Select the option that is related to the third term in the same way as the second term is related to the first term.

4896 : 3785 :: 7852 : ?

(a) 4519 (b) 6741
(c) 5630 (d) 3438

19. If MUNREB is written as 628146 and IESRES as 345145, how will SERBER be written?

(a) 541641 (b) 541164
(c) 451146 (d) 541146

20. Four options have been given out of which three are alike in some manner, while one is different. Choose the odd one.

(a) 97 (b) 135
(c) 167 (d) 199

21. Select the option that is related to the third term in the same way as the second term is related to the first term.

Telephone : Communication :: Radio : ....

(a) Broadcast (b) Story
(c) Art (d) Character

22. In the question two statements are given, followed by three conclusions, I, II and III. Assuming that the information in the statements is true, even if it appears to be at variance with generally established facts, decide which conclusions logically and definitely follows from the information given in the Statements.

Statement 1 : All tigers are cats.

Statement 2 : All cats are felines.

Conclusion I : Some felines are tigers.

Conclusion II: All tigers are felines.

Conclusion III : Some felines are cats.

(a) Only conclusion III follows
(b) All conclusions I, II and III follows
(c) Only conclusion I and III follows
(d) Only conclusion I follows

23. Find the missing number from the below options.

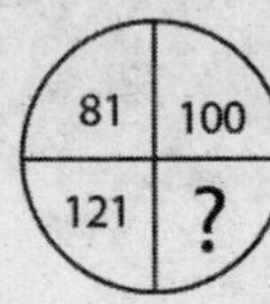

(a) 225 (b) 144
(c) 256 (d) 169

24. In a certain code, COLD is coded as GSPH, then how is NOT coded in the same way?

(a) RSX (b) XRS
(c) RSY (d) XSR

25. Select the correct option that will fill in the blank and complete the series.

–1, 2, 7, ?, 23, 34

(a) 13 (b) 19
(c) 14 (d) 15

Part-B Gerneral Knowledge and Gerneral Awareness

26. Which of the following was the first Law Minister of Independent India?

(a) Jawaharlal Nehru
(b) Abul Kalam Azad
(c) Bhimrao Ramji Ambedkar
(d) Asaf Ali

27. Photosynthesis in plants converts light energy to .... energy.

(a) thermal (b) chemical
C kinetic (d) physical

28. The major gap in the Western Ghats is at:

(a) Palghat (b) Mangalore
(c) Madurai (d) Manipal

29. The 'Ghumura' dance is from the state of:

(a) Punjab (b) Odisha
(c) Tamil Nadu (d) Kerala

30. 'Matki' is a form of dance from the state of:

(a) Kerala
(b) Gujarat
(c) Madhya Pradesh
(d) West Bengal

31. The Chola Empire of the South emerged in the:
(a) 9th century BC
(b) 19th century AD
(c) 9th century AD
(d) 17th century AD

32. In the 2016 Olympics men's singles badminton title was won by:
(a) Lee Chong Wei
(b) Kidambi Srikanth
(c) Chen Long
(d) Lin Dan

33. The British ruled India for nearly:
(a) 50 years (b) 200 years
(c) 100 years (d) 500 years

34. Where did the Chipko movement first start in India?
(a) Tamil Nadu (b) Maharashtra
(c) Karnataka (d) Uttar Pradesh

35. A person who advocates separation of the state from religious institutions is called a ....
(a) Communalist
(b) Secularist
(c) Socialist
(d) Feminist

36. The Prime Minister who led India during the 1965 war with Pakistan is:
(a) Morarji Desai
(b) Indira Gandhi
(c) Lai Bahadur Shastri
(d) Jawaharlal Nehru

37. Which is one of the factors of subsistence used to measure the Poverty Line in India?
(a) Equality
(b) Education
(c) Internet
(d) Transportation

38. The men's title of the 2018 Australian Open Tennis Championship, ... was won by.
(a) Rafael Nadal
(b) Roger Federer
(c) Stan Warwinka
(d) Andy Murray

39. The 2017 Sahitya Academy award for Bengali was won by:
(a) Himanshu Bose
(b) Afsar Ahmed
(c) Ramesh Megh
(d) David Bhattacharya

40. The Goods and Services Tax allowed India to become:
(a) An East and a West market
(b) A common market
(c) A set of separate markets
(d) A South and a North market

41. Which of the following is not a Metamorphic rock?
(a) Gnesis (b) Marble
(c) Slate (d) Limestone

42. The Aga Khan palace is located in the state of:
(a) Maharashtra
(b) Uttar Pradesh
(c) Kerala
(d) Madhya Pradesh

43. A stain of curry on a white cloth become reddish brown when soap is used because the soapis:
(a) Neutral in nature
(b) Acidic in nature
(c) Alkaline in nature
(d) Basic in nature

44. Which is the deepest lake in the world?
(a) Lake Tanganyika
(b) Lake Vostok
(c) Lake Baikal
(d) Lake Superior

45. An ecosystem consists of:
(a) Chemical and physical components
(b) Biotic and abiotic components
(c) Physical and social components
(d) Biotic and antibiotic components

46. Leguminous plants replenish the soil by the presence of
(a) Firmicutes (b) Spirochaete
(c) Rhizobium (d) Aquificae

47. The process of .... is used to increase shelf life of milk by destroying disease causing micro-organisms.
(a) pasteurisation
(b) evaporation
(c) condensation
(d) hydrogenation

48. The railway budget is:
(a) Part of the Central budget
(b) Part of the States budget
(c) Separate from the Central as well as State budget
(d) Separate from the Central budget

49. The reign of the .... dynasty has been described as the golden age of Indian civilization.
(a) Porus (b) Harsha
(c) Buddha (d) Gupta

50. In which year was The Reserve Bank of India was established?
(a) 1926 (b) 1947
(c) 1950 (d) 1952

Part-C : Elementary Mathematics

51. The cost price of 27 articles is same as the selling price of 18 articles. What is the profit percent?
(a) 40% (b) 50%
(c) 30% (d) 25%

52. A train 400 m long passes a pole in 20 seconds. What is the speed of the train?
(a) 70km/hr (b) 72 km/hr
(c) 68 km/hr (d) 64 km/hr

53. A discount of 20% in the price of rice enables X to buy 5 kg more rice for ₹100. What is the reduced price of rice per kg?
(a) ₹ 3 (b) ₹ 2
(c) ₹ 1 (d) ₹ 4

54. A and B can together complete a task 40 days. They worked together for 30 days and then left. A finished the remaining task in next 22 days. In how many days A alone can finish the task?
(a) 48 days (b) 88 days
(c) 30 days (d) 40 days

55. A hollow copper pipe is 22 cm long and its external diameter is 28 cm. If the thickness of the pipe is 3 cm and iron weighs 8.5 g/cm^3, then the weight of the pipe is closest to:

(a) 34 kg (b) 44 kg
(c) 14 kg (d) 24 kg

56. The least number that should be added to 2,397 so that the sum is exactly divisible by 3, 4, 5 and 6 ?
(a) 6 (b) 4
(c) 5 (d) 3

57. The median of 31, 25, 17, 23, 45 and 59 is:
(a) 23 (b) 25
(c) 31 (d) 28

58. Excluding stoppages, the speed of a bus is 70 kmph and including stoppages, it is 56 kmph. For how many minutes does the bus stop per hour?
(a) 10 min (b) 8 min
(c) 15 min (d) 12 min

59. A and B can complete a task in 40 days and 16 days respectively. A started the task alone and then after 12 days B joined him till the completion of the task. How long did the task last after B joined the task?
(a) 8 days (b) 6 days
(c) 14 days (d) 12 days

60. A sum of money amounted to ₹ 720 in 2 years and ₹ 792 in 3 years when interest is compounded annually. The annual rate of interest, (in %) is:
(a) 5% (b) 7.50%
(c) 7% (d) 10%

61. In X's opinion, his weight is greater than 60 kg but less than 68 kg, Y doesn't agree with him and says that X's weight is more than 62 kg but less than 70 kg. The mother of X believes that the weight of X is greater than 64 kg. If all of them are correct in their estimation, then what is the average of different probable weights of X if the weight is an integer?
(a) 68 kg (b) 67 kg
(c) 66 kg (d) 65 kg

62. The ratio of the number of boys and girls in a college is 6 : 7. If the percentage increase in the number of boys and girls be 20% and 10% respectively, what will be the new ratio?
(a) 72:77 (b) 35:36
(c) 36:35 (d) 77:72

63. A right triangle with sides 5 cm, 12 cm and 13 cm is rotated about the side 12 cm to form a cone. The volume of the cone so formed is:
(a) 81π cm^3 (b) 100π cm^3
(c) 91π cm^3 (d) 110π cm^3

64. The value of $64 \div 2 \times (9 \div 3) \times 3 \div 9 - 32$ is:
(a) 1 (b) 0
(c) –1 (d) 2

65. The average weight of 8 people increases by 2.5 kg when a new person comes in place of one of them weighing 75 kg. What is the weight of the new person?
(a) 95 kg (b) 75 kg
(c) 85 kg (d) 65 kg

66. How much time will it take for an amount of ₹ 360 to yield ₹ 72 as interest at 5% p.a. of simple interest?
(a) 3 years (b) 4 years
(c) 2.5 years (d) 3.5 years

67. The pie charts show the market share of companies in the rice market in 2017 and 2018. The value of sales of Company A in 2017 was ₹ 40 lakhs. If its sales grew by 25% in 2018, what was approximate value of sales of company B in 2018?

DISTRIBUTION OF SALES IN 2017

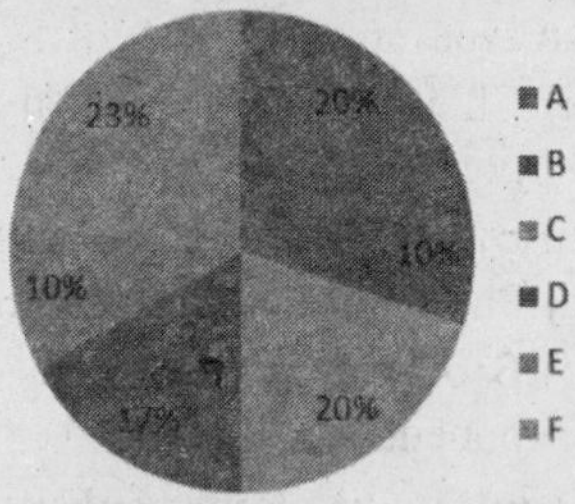

DISTRIBUTION OF SALES IN 2018

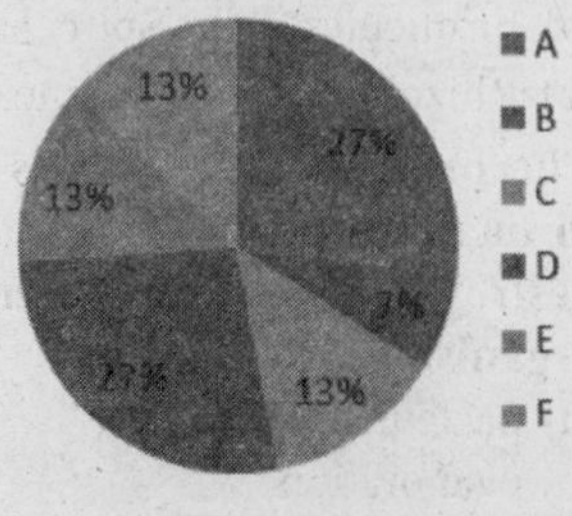

(a) ₹ 12.56 lakhs
(b) ₹ 13.96 lakhs
(c) ₹ 12.96 lakhs
(d) ₹ 13.56 lakhs

68. The value of $24 \div 4 \times (3 + 3) \div 2$ is:
(a) 22 (b) 24
(c) 20 (d) 18

69. 120 men consume 720 kg of rice in 30 days. In how many days can 90 men consume 270 kg?
(a) 18 (b) 12
(c) 9 (d) 15

70. Two students appeared for an examination. One student who scored 20 marks more than the other, his score was 60% of the sum of their marks. What was his score?
(a) 80 (b) 20
(c) 40 (d) 60

71. The line graph shows the scores of a batsman in 6 consecutive matches. What is the range of his scores?

Score in Each Match

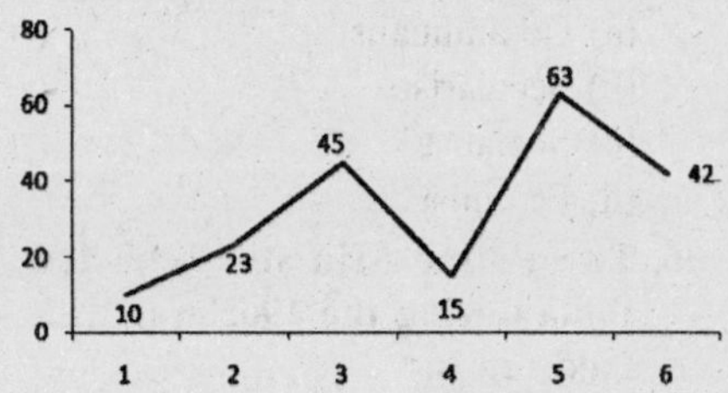

(a) 53 (b) 43
(c) 41 (d) 51

72. An article was sold for ₹ 4,000. Had a discount of 10% was being offered, the profit would have been 20%. The cost price of the article was:
(a) ₹ 3, 200 (b) ₹ 3, 310
(c) ₹ 3, 000 (d) ₹ 3, 600

73. The slant height of a right circular cone is 15 m and its height is 9 m. The area of its curved surface, is:
(a) 169π m^2 (b) 172π m^2
(c) 165π m^2 (d) 180π m^2

74. The bar graph shows the number of paintings sold by an art gallery in each month from January to June. How many paintings does it need to sell in July for the 7 month average to be 90?

Number of Paintings Sold

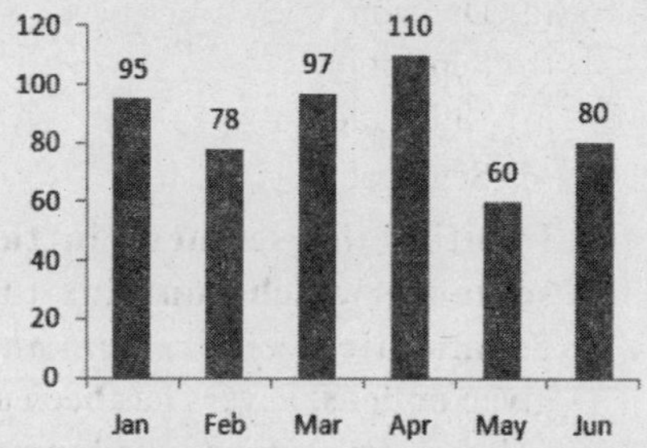

(a) 115 (b) 85
(c) 90 (d) 110

75. In bag there are coins of 25 paisa, 50 paisa and 1 rupee in the ratio of 3 : 4 : 5. If there are in all ₹31, then how many 1 rupee coins are there in the bag?

(a) 12 (b) 16
(c) 24 (d) 20

Part-D : English

Direction (Q. 76–77): Select the most appropriate option to substitute the underlined segment in the given sentence. If there is no need to substitute it, select No substitution required.

76. When the vegetation is altered, the animal life also changed.

(a) No substitution required
(b) also changes
(c) changed
(d) is changing

77. The greed of human beings leads to over utilization of natural resources.

(a) leads for
(b) No substitution required
(c) lead to
(d) leading to

78. Select the meaning of the given idiom.

Piece of cake

(a) Something very difficult
(b) Something very tasty
(c) Something very easy
(d) Something very soft

79. Select the most appropriate option to substitute the underlined segment in the given sentence. If there is no need to substitute it, select No substitution required.

The term flora is use for denote plants of a particular region or period.

(a) used denoting
(b) denoting
(c) used to denote
(d) No substitution required

80. Select the meaning of the given idiom.

A snake in the grass

(a) Cowardly and brutal
(b) Low and mean
(c) An unreliable person
(d) A hidden enemy

81. Select the most appropriate word to fill in the blank.

We should take .... measures to prevent recurrence of such incidents.

(a) substitute (b) effective
(c) casual (d) properly

82. Select the antonym of the given word.

ILLICIT

(a) Illegal (b) Unlawful
(c) Lawful (d) Illegitimate

83. Select the word which means the same as the group of words given.

A sentimental longing or wistful affection for a period in the past

(a) Harmony (b) Affliction
(c) Nostalgia (d) Paradise

84. Select the antonym of the given word.

ABUNDANT

(a) Ample (b) Plentiful
(c) Copious (d) Scarce

85. Select the most appropriate word to fill in the blank.

Dense mangroves are common-varieties with roots submerged .... water.

(a) beside (b) over
(c) under (d) behind

Direction (Q. 86–90): In the following passage some words have been deleted. Fill in the blanks with the help of the alternatives given. Select the most appropriate option for each number.

Passage

Can you (86) .... a world without human beings? Who but humans (87) .... have utilized the resources and created a (88) .... and cultural environment? The people living in a country are important to (89) .... the economy and the society. They (90) .... are the greatest resource.

86. (a) realize (b) figure
(c) devise (d) imagine

87. (a) would (b) could
(c) can (d) will

88. (a) social (b) communal
(c) general (d) familiar

89. (a) evolve (b) develop
(c) mature (d) establish

90. (a) itself (b) themselves
(c) yourselves (d) ourselves

Directions: For the following Questions answer them individually.

91. Select the word which means the same as the group of words given.

Violation of something holy or sacred

(a) Ritual (b) Ceremony
(c) Sacrilege (d) Pious

92. Select the synonym of the given word.

ISOLATION

(a) Association
(b) Communication
(c) Separation
(d) Integration

93. Identify the segment in the sentence which contains the grammatical error from the given options. Concern above rising pollution led to the launch of various action plans.

(a) Concern above
(b) launch of
(c) led to
(d) action plans

94. Select the wrongly spelt word.

(a) Ninety (b) Neither
(c) Noticeable (d) Neccessary

95. Select the most appropriate word to fill in the blank.

The house remained .... for a long time.

(a) evicted (b) empty
(c) vacant (d) blank

96. Select the wrongly spelt word.

(a) Sacrifice (b) Sanctity
(c) Schedule (d) Salry

97. Identify the segment in the sentence which contains the grammatical error from the given options. Most of the fresh water lake in India are in the Himalayan region.

(a) Most of the
(b) in India
(c) are in
(d) fresh water lake

98. Select the most appropriate word to fill in the blank.

The elephants are the most majestic animals .... the mammals.

(a) as
(b) between
(c) among
(d) over

99. Select the synonym of the given word.

INTEGRATION

(a) Division
(b) Separation
(c) Unification
(d) Segregation

100. Identify the segment in the sentence which contains the grammatical error from the given options. Rivers has been of primary importance for human settlements since ancient times.

(a) of primary importance
(b) Rivers has been
(c) since ancient times.
(d) for human settlements

Answers

1. (a)	**2.** (d)	**3.** (c)	**4.** (c)	**5.** (c)	**6.** (a)	**7.** (b)	**8.** (a)	**9.** (c)	**10.** (b)
11. (c)	**12.** (b)	**13.** (a)	**14.** (a)	**15.** (d)	**16.** (b)	**17.** (a)	**18.** (b)	**19.** (a)	**20.** (b)
21. (a)	**22.** (b)	**23.** (b)	**24.** (a)	**25.** (c)	**26.** (c)	**27.** (b)	**28.** (a)	**29.** (b)	**30.** (c)
31. (c)	**32.** (c)	**33.** (b)	**34.** (d)	**35.** (b)	**36.** (c)	**37.** (b)	**38.** (b)	**39.** (b)	**40.** (b)
41. (d)	**42.** (a)	**43.** (d)	**44.** (c)	**45.** (b)	**46.** (c)	**47.** (a)	**48.** (a)	**49.** (d)	**50.** (a)
51. (b)	**52.** (b)	**53.** (d)	**54.** (b)	**55.** (b)	**56.** (d)	**57.** (d)	**58.** (d)	**59.** (a)	**60.** (d)
61. (c)	**62.** (a)	**63.** (b)	**64.** (b)	**65.** (a)	**66.** (b)	**67.** (c)	**68.** (d)	**69.** (d)	**70.** (d)
71. (a)	**72.** (c)	**73.** (d)	**74.** (d)	**75.** (d)	**76.** (b)	**77.** (b)	**78.** (c)	**79.** (c)	**80.** (d)
81. (b)	**82.** (c)	**83.** (c)	**84.** (d)	**85.** (c)	**86.** (d)	**87.** (b)	**88.** (a)	**89.** (b)	**90.** (b)
91. (c)	**92.** (c)	**93.** (a)	**94.** (d)	**95.** (c)	**96.** (d)	**97.** (d)	**98.** (c)	**99.** (c)	**100.** (b)

SSC Constable (GD)
Solved Paper-2015

Part-A : General Intelligence and Reasoning

1. Which answer figure will complete the pattern in the question figure ?

Question Figure:

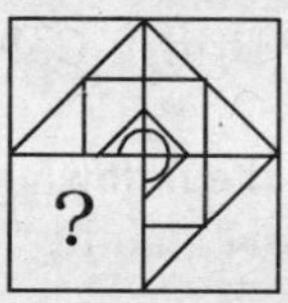

Answer Figures:

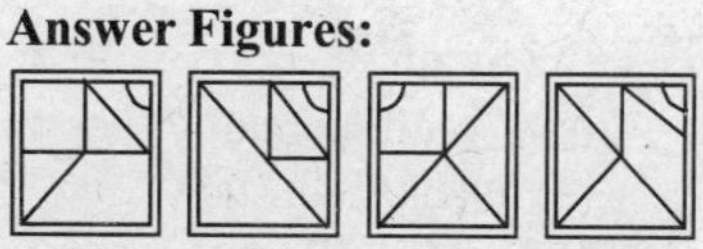

(a) (b) (c) (d)

Directions (Q. 2-5) : Select the related word/letters/ number from the given alternatives.

2. FRENCH : FRANCE :: DUTCH : ?
(a) FIJI (b) NORWAY
(c) HOLLAND (d) SWEDEN

3. BOOK : LIBRARY :: TREE : ?
(a) SHADE (b) FRUIT
(c) FOREST (d) FURNITURE

4. DIMO : DMIO :: JUVR : ?
(a) JRVU (b) JVRU
(c) JVUR (d) JUVR

5. 4 : 19 :: 7 : ?
(a) 52 (b) 68
(c) 49 (d) 28

6. If STOVE is coded as EVOTS and CANDLE is coded as ELDNAC then REPORT is coded as:
(a) SFQPSU (b) QDONQS
(c) TROPER (d) PORTRE

Directions (7 – 9) : Find the odd word/ letters/number from the given alternatives.

7. (a) 22 (b) 18
(c) 12 (d) 15

8. (a) UQ (b) JG
(c) RN (d) NJ

9. (a) SMS (b) Speed post
(c) Letter (d) Money order

10. If ÷ stands for ×, × stands for –, – stands for + and + stands for ÷, then 48 + 6 – 12 ÷ 2 + 10 = ?
(Do chronologically and not according to BODMAS rule.)
(a) 9 (b) 14
(c) 16 (d) 4

11. Select the answer figure in which the question figure is hidden.

Question Figure :

Answer Figures :

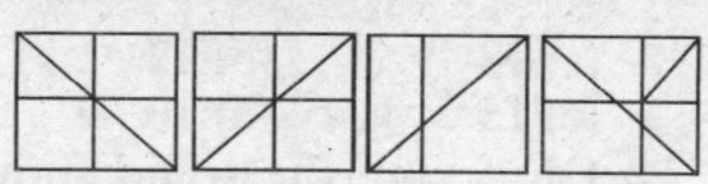

(a) (b) (c) (d)

12. Which one of the given responses would be a meaningful order of the following :
1.Child,
2. Profession,
3. Marriage,
4. Infant,
5. Education
(a) 1, 3, 5, 2, 4
(b) 5, 4, 1, 3, 2
(c) 2, 1, 4, 3, 5
(d) 4, 1, 5, 2, 3

13. Which of the answer figure is exactly the mirror image of the given figure?

Question Figure :

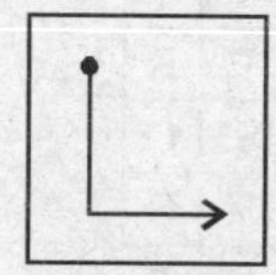

Answer Figures :

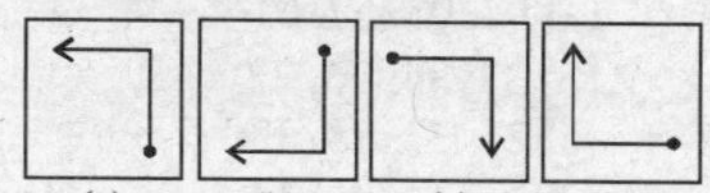

(a) (b) (c) (d)

14. A florist had 133 roses, she sold $\frac{5}{7}$ of them. How many roses had she left ?
(a) 58 (b) 38
(c) 57 (d) 19

15. Which of the answer figure indicates the best relationship between Milk, Goat, Cow, Hen ?

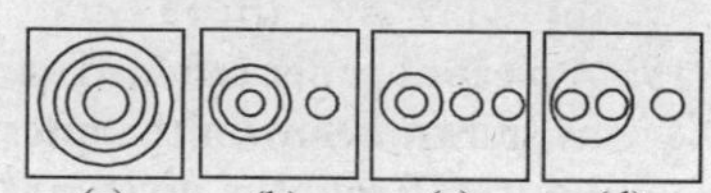

(a) (b) (c) (d)

16. A word is represented by only one set of numbers as given in any one of the alternatives. The sets of numbers given in the alternatives are represented by two classes of alphabets as in two matrices given below. The columns and rows of matrix I are numbered from 0 to 4 and that of matrix II are numbered from 5 to 9. A letter from these matrices can be represented first by its row and next by its column, e.g., 'D' can be represented by 00, 12 etc., and 'P' can be represented by 56, 68 etc. Similarly, you have to identify the set for the word 'FIRE'.

MATRIX - I

	0	1	2	3	4
0	D	E	F	I	N
1	I	N	D	E	F
2	E	F	I	N	D
3	N	D	E	F	I
4	F	I	N	D	E

MATRIX - II

	5	6	7	8	9
5	O	P	R	S	T
6	S	T	O	P	R
7	P	R	S	T	O
8	T	O	P	R	S
9	R	S	T	O	P

(a) 02, 03, 57, 01
(b) 33, 34, 76, 22
(c) 21, 22, 88, 33
(d) 14, 10, 69, 14

Directions (17 – 18) : A series is given with one-term missing. Choose the correct alternative from the given ones that will complete the series.

17. 0.15, 0.3, ?, 1.2, 2.4

(a) 0.6 (b) 0.9
(c) 0.06 (d) 4.8

18. BCD, DBC, EFG, ?, HIJ

(a) IJH (b) GEF
(c) EGF (d) FEG

19. A piece of paper is folded and cut as shown below in the question figures. From the given answer figures, indicate how it will appear when opened.

Question Figures :

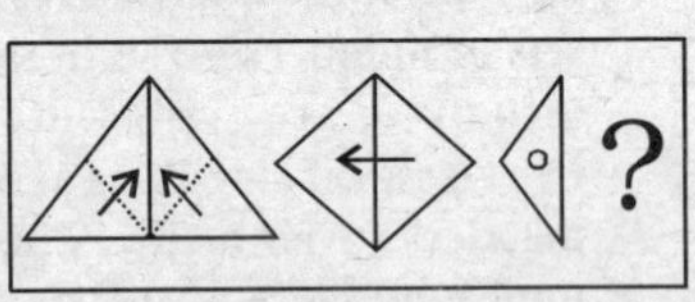

Answer Figures :

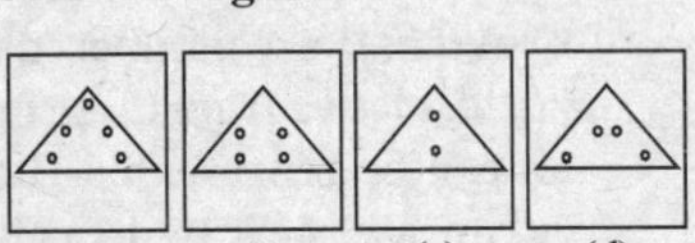

(a) (b) (c) (d)

20. From the given alternative words, select the word which cannot be formed using the letters of the given word.

INTERDEPENDENT

(a) DEPEND (b) REPENT
(c) RETREAT (d) DEEPEN

21. Directions : Two statements are given followed by two Conclusions/Assumptions I and II. You have to consider the statement to be true, even if it seems to be at variance from commonly known facts. You have to decide which of the given conclusions/assumptions can definitely be drawn from the given statement. Indicate your answer.

Statements:

1. All children are students.
2. All students are players.

Conclusions:

I. All cricketers are students.
II. All children are players.

(a) Only conclusion I follows.
(b) Neither conclusion I nor II follows.
(c) Both conclusions I and II follow.
(d) Only conclusion II follows.

22. Five friends are sitting in a row facing South. Here Mohan is between Balu and Raju and Raju is to the immediate right of Praveen and Amith is to the right of Balu. Who is in extreme right end ?

(a) Praveen (b) Amith
(c) Balu (d) Mohan

23. If 2 = 0, 3 = 3, 4 = 6, 5 = 9, then7 = ?

(a) 18 (b) 12
(c) 15 (d) 16

24. Observing the trend find the missing number.

5	4	3
6	7	8
4	2	?
34	30	30

(a) 6 (b) 3
(c) 5 (d) 10

25. Which of the answer figures can be formed using the question figure?

Question Figure :

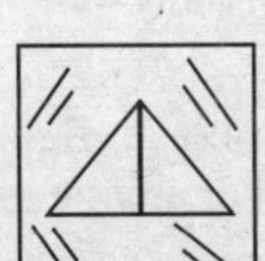

Answer Figures :

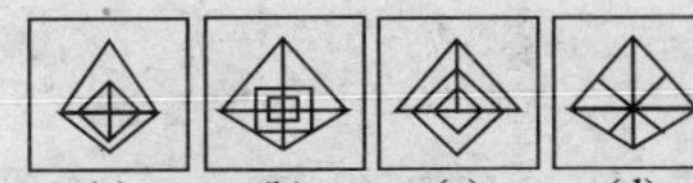

(a) (b) (c) (d)

Part-B : General Knowledge and General Awareness

26. Dadabhai Naoroji has described his theory of 'Drain of Wealth' in the book.

(a) Poverty and Un-British Rule in India
(b) British Rule and its Consequences
(c) Exploitative Nature of British Rule in India
(d) Nature of British Colonial Rule

27. Which one of the following is a non-dimensional quantity?

(a) Gas constant
(b) Strain
(c) Co-efficient of viscocity
(d) Plank's constant

28. Who was the author of Telugu Work Amuktamalyada?

(a) Harihara (b) Devaraya
(c) Krishnadevaraya
(d) Bukka

29. In B.C.G. Vaccine the word 'C' stands for :

(a) Calmette (b) Cough
(c) Chlorine (d) Cadmium

30. The Cash Reserve Ratio is a tool of :

(a) Monetary policy
(b) Tax policy
(c) Agricultural policy
(d) Fiscal policy

31. Who of the Delhi sultans pursued the policy of 'blood and iron' ?

(a) Alauddin Khilji
(b) Ghiyasuddin Tughlaq
(c) Balban
(d) Iltutmish

32. The presence of pollutants in the environment is usually expressed in ppm, where ppm stands for:

(a) particles per mole
(b) purity per microgram
(c) pollutant prevent measures
(d) parts per million

33. Chemical composition of heavy water is :
(a) H_2O_2 (b) H_2O
(c) HDO (d) D_2O

34. The Headquarters of World Trade Organisation (WTO) is situated in:
(a) New Delhi
(b) Geneva, Switzerland
(c) London, UK
(d) Washington, USA

35. Which one of the following is an autotroph?
(a) Butterfly
(b) Algae
(c) Grasshopper
(d) Mushroom

36. The term 'URL' used in Internet technology stands for :
(a) Uniform Resource Locater
(b) Unique Resource Locater
(c) Uniform Remote Locater
(d) Unique Remote Locater

37. Economics classifies the man-made instrument of production as :
(a) organization
(b) capital
(c) equipment
(d) labour

38. Oxide of sulphur present in the atmosphere are washed down by rains to cause :
(a) Depletion of fossil fuel reserves
(b) Eutrophication in lakes
(c) Lowering of pH of soil
(d) Industrial smog formation

39. When water freezes its density:
(a) Decreases
(b) Becomes Zero
(c) Remains constant
(d) Increases

40. How does agriculture promote the Indian industrial development ?
(a) By opening up market for industrial products
(b) By providing food and clothing to labourers
(c) By supplying raw materials
(d) All of the given options

41. Which of the following countries has brought out a stamp on Mother Teresa to celebrate her birth anniversary?
(a) India (b) USA
(c) UK (d) Pakistan

42. The headquaters of United Nations Organization is located at:
(a) Rome (b) Geneva
(c) Washington (d) New York

43. The first President of independent India was:
(a) Dr S. Radha Krishnan
(b) J.L. Nehru
(c) Sardar Patel
(d) Dr Rajendra Prasad

44. The acid which fails to liberate carbon dioxide from sodium bicarbonate is :
(a) Acetic acid
(b) Formic acid
(c) Carbonic acid
(d) Sulphuric acid

45. Democracy is a "government in which everyone has a share" was the opinion of :
(a) Jeovans
(b) Seeley
(c) Plato
(d) Abraham Lincoln

46. The greatness of Shershah lies in his :
(a) Secular attitude
(b) Victories against Humayun
(c) Superior generalship
(d) Administrative reforms

47. Name the first Indian to be banned for using anabolic steroid in Olympic games :
(a) Pratima Kumari
(b) Aswini Akunji
(c) T. Sanmancha Chanu
(d) Sumitha Laha

48. When was the office of District Collector created ?
(a) 1786 (b) 1772
(c) 1771 (d) 1773

49. Who established the 'Sharda Sadan', a school for Indian Widows in colonial India ?
(a) Mahadev Govind Ranade
(b) Sarojini Naidu
(c) Dayanand Saraswati
(d) Pandita Ramabai

50. The smallest ocean is :
(a) Atlantic (b) Pacific
(c) Indian (d) Arctic

Part-C : Elementary Mathematics

51. Average income of 'A' and 'B' is ₹ 200 and average income of 'C' and 'D' is ₹ 250. The average income of A, B, C and D is
(a) ₹ 106.25 (b) ₹ 125
(c) ₹ 200 (d) ₹ 225

52. A certain sum amounts to ₹ 1725 at 15% per annum at simple interest and ₹ 1800 in the same time at 20% per annum at simple interest. Find the sum.
(a) ₹ 1650 (b) ₹ 1500
(c) ₹ 1700 (d) ₹ 1200

Directions (53 – 54) : Study the following data and answer the questions. The score of students of a class are given as follows:

IQ Score	No. of Students
80-90	6
90-100	9
100-110	16
110-120	13
120-130	4
130-140	2

53. Number of students whose IQ score is 140 is
(a) undeterminable from given data
(b) 2
(c) 1
(d) 0

54. The number of students whose IQ score is 100 and more is.
(a) 29 (b) 35
(c) 36 (d) 46

55. The ratio of ages of two persons is 5 : 9 and the age of one of them is greater than the other by 40 years. The sum of their ages in year is
(a) 180 (b) 140
(c) 150 (d) 160

56. Raja can do a piece of work in 20 days while Ramesh can finish it in 25 days. Ramesh started working and Raja joined him after 10 days. The whole work is completed in

(a) 18 days (b) $16\frac{2}{3}$ days
(c) 20 days (d) 15 days

57. In a college election a candidate secured 62% of the votes and is elected by a margin of 144 votes. The total number of votes polled is :
(a) 925 (b) 600
(c) 1200 (d) 800

58. The mean proportion of 1.21 and 0.09 is
(a) 3.3 (b) 0.33
(c) 3.03 (d) 0.033

59. A student starting from his house walks at a speed of $2\frac{1}{2}$ km/hour and reaches his school 6 minutes late. Next day starting at the same time he increases his speed by 1 km/hour and reaches 6 minutes early. The distance between the school and his house is
(a) 4 km (b) $3\frac{1}{2}$ km
(c) $1\frac{3}{4}$ km (d) 6 km

60. A seller increases the cost price of an article by 30% and fixed the marked price as ₹ 286. But during sale he gave 10% discount to the purchaser. Percentage of profit will be
(a) 17 (b) 15
(c) 10 (d) 20

61. A solid right prism made of iron has cross section of a triangle of sides 5 cm, 10 cm, 13 cm and of height 10 cm. If one cubic cm of iron weights 7 g, then the weight of the prism is (approximately)
(a) 1570.8 gram
(b) 1371.32 gram
(c) 1470.8 gram
(d) 1100.68 gram

62. A sum of ₹ 800 becomes ₹ 956 in 3 years at a certain rate of simple interest. If the rate of interest is increased by 4%, what amount will the same sum become in 3 years ?
(a) ₹ 1025 (b) ₹ 1042
(c) ₹ 1052 (d) ₹ 1024

63. A batsman makes a score of 87 runs in the 17th innings and thus increased his average by 3. Find his average after 17th innings.
(a) 39 (b) 87
(c) 90 (d) 84

64. An item was sold for ₹ 3600 at 25% discount. Its marked price was
(a) ₹ 2880 (b) ₹ 2700
(c) ₹ 4800 (d) ₹ 4500

65. A fruit merchant makes a profit of 25% by selling mangoes at a certain price. If he charges ₹ 1 more on each mango, he would gain 50%. At first the price of one mango was
(a) ₹ 5 (b) ₹ 7
(c) ₹ 4 (d) ₹ 6

66. A dealer marks his goods 20% above cost price and allows a discount of 10% to his customers. His gain percentage is
(a) 6% (b) 9%
(c) 7% (d) 8%

67. If the cost of an article is ₹ P after two successive reductions of 20% and 25%, the original price of the article was
(a) ₹ $\frac{5P}{3}$ (b) ₹ $\frac{4P}{5}$
(c) ₹ $\frac{3P}{5}$ (d) ₹ $\frac{5P}{4}$

68. 16 men are able to complete a piece of work in 12 days working 14 hours a day. How long will 28 men, working 12 hours a day, take to complete the work ?
(a) 10 days (b) 7 days
(c) 8 days (d) 6 days

69. A plane can cover 6000 km in 8 hours. If the speed is increased by 250 kmph, then the time taken by the plane to cover 9000 km is
(a) 8 hours (b) 6 hours
(c) 5 hours (d) 9 hours

70. The average of 1,3,5,7,9, 11,........to 25 terms is
(a) 125 (b) 25
(c) 625 (d) 50

71. 1008 divided by which single digit number gives a perfect square ?
(a) 9 (b) 4
(c) 8 (d) 7

72. The value of $\sqrt{0.000441}$ is equal to
(a) 0.21 (b) 0.00021
(c) 0.0021 (d) 0.021

73. A shopkeeper, in order to clear his old stock of T.V. sets, offers 12% discount on the T.V. sets. If the marked price of a T.V. set is ₹ 6500, the selling price of the T.V. set is:
(a) ₹ 5700 (b) ₹ 5720
(c) ₹ 5400 (d) ₹ 6000

74. A right circular cone of height 20 cm and base radius 15 cm is melted and cast into smaller cones of equal sizes of height 5 cm and base radius 1.5 cm. The number of cones cast are
(a) 300 (b) 150
(c) 400 (d) 100

75. The smallest number by which 243000 be divided so that the quotient is a perfect cube is
(a) 3 (b) 27
(c) 9 (d) 1

Part-D : English

Directions (76 – 79) : In the following questions, sentences are given with blanks to be filled in with an appropriate word(s). Four alternatives are suggested for each question. Choose the correct alternative out of the four as your answer.

76. Your ______ nature will aid you in attaining success in every venture you undertake.
(a) rotund
(b) persevering
(c) lackadaisical
(d) catalytic

77. This is our house and that is ______.

(a) theirs (b) their
(c) them (d) their's

78. The publisher is bringing ______ a revised edition of this book.
(a) round (b) out
(c) about (d) up

79. She had to _______ illness in order to avoid going to the party meeting.
(a) feint (b) feign
(c) faint (d) fain

Directions (80 – 82) : In each of the following questions, four alternatives are given for the Idiom/Phrase printed in *italic* in the sentence. Choose the alternative which best expresses the meaning of the Idiom/Phrase as your answer.

80. I have *taken fancy to* this car.
(a) given imaginative touches
(b) revised
(c) developed liking for
(d) improved

81. *Carry out*
(a) bring
(b) continue
(c) complete something
(d) to take in

82. He *beats about the bush*.
(a) talks sensibly
(b) talks continuously
(c) speak well
(d) does not talk specifically

Directions (83 – 85) : In the following questions, a part of the sentence is *italic*. Below are given alternatives to the *italic* part which may improve the sentence. Choose the correct alternative. In case no improvement is needed, choose "No Improvement".

83. Covering thirty kilometres in thirty minutes *are not a great distance* using a brand new car.
(a) aren't a great distance
(b) is no distance
(c) No improvement
(d) is not a great distance

84. Years ago, I met a man *which* was President and Chairman of the board of a company.
(a) Whom
(b) No improvement
(c) Who
(d) Whose

85. Where *are you coming from*?
(a) No improvement
(b) do you come from
(c) were you from
(d) you are coming from

Directions (86 – 88) : In the following questions, choose the word opposite in meaning to the given word.

86. Harmonious
(a) Sonorous
(b) Discordant
(c) Concordant
(d) Balanced

87. Fragile
(a) Weak (b) Brittle
(c) Strong (d) Discard

88. Superficial
(a) Genuine (b) Natural
(c) Artificial (d) Amicable

Directions (89 – 91) : In the following questions, four words are given in each question, out of which only one word is correctly spelt. Find the correctly spelt word as your answer.

89. (a) juvinnile (b) juvenille
(c) juvenile (d) juvinile

90. (a) knowledgeable
(b) knoledgeable
(c) knowledgable
(d) knowledgeble

91. (a) deterriorate
(b) deteriorrate
(c) deteriorate
(d) detariorate

Directions (92 – 94) : In the following questions, out of the four alternatives, choose the one which best expresses the meaning of the given word.

92. Felicitated
(a) admired
(b) adored
(c) encouraged
(d) congratulated

93. Honour
(a) determination
(b) courage
(c) respect
(d) discipline

94. Rectify
(a) clarify (b) condone
(c) correct (d) regularise

Directions (95 – 97) : In the following questions, some parts of the sentences have errors and some are correct. Find out which part of a sentence has an error. The number of that part is the answer. If a sentence is free from error, your answer is No error.

95. The kitchen need painting badly and I must get it done.
(a) need painting badly
(b) The kitchen
(c) No error
(d) and I must get it done

96. If I will play my best I can win any day against anybody.
(a) against anybody
(b) I can win any day
(c) No error
(d) If I will play my best

97. He finds fault at everything I do.
(a) No error (b) at everything
(c) I do (d) He finds fault

Directions (98 – 100) : In the following questions, out of the four alternatives, choose the one which can be substituted for the given words/sentences.

98. Put side by side
(a) Juxtapose (b) Impose
(c) Propose (d) Depose

99. One who cannot be corrected
(a) ineligible
(b) indolent
(c) indefatigable
(d) incorrigible

100. Chief or Commander of army
(a) Lieutenant (b) Major
(c) General (d) Colonel

Answers with Explanations

1. (b)

2. (c) The natives of France are called French. Similarly, the natives of Holland are called Dutch.

3. (c) Library is a building or room in which collections of books, newspapers, journals etc. are kept. Similarly, forest is a large area of land thickly covered with trees, bushes etc.

4. (c) D I M O → D M I O

Similarly,

J U V R → J V U R

5. (a) $4 \times 4 + 3 = 19$

Similarly, $7 \times 7 + 3 = 52$

6. (c) The letters have been written in reverse order in the code.

S T O V E ⇒ E V O T S

C A N D L E ⇒ E L D N A C

Similarly, R E P O R T ⇒ T R O P E R

7. (a) Except 22, all other numbers are multiples of 3.

$3 \times 6 = 18$

$3 \times 4 = 12$

$3 \times 5 = 15$

But, $3 \times 7 + 1 = 22$

8. (b) $U \xrightarrow{-4} Q$

$J \xrightarrow{-3} G$

$R \xrightarrow{-4} N$

$N \xrightarrow{-4} J$

9. (a) SMS (Short Messaging Service) is sent through a mobile phone, while all others are sent through post office.

10. (d)

÷ ⇒ ×	× ⇒ −
− ⇒ +	+ ⇒ ÷

$48 + 6 - 12 \div 2 + 10 = ?$

$\Rightarrow ? = 48 \div 6 + 12 \times 2 \div 10$

$\Rightarrow ? = 8 + 12 \times \frac{2}{10}$

$\Rightarrow ? = 20 \times \frac{2}{10} = 4$

11. (c)

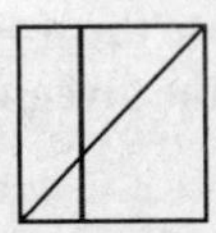

12. (d) Meaningful order of words :

4. Infant
↓
1. Child
↓
5. Education
↓
2. Profession
↓
3. Marriage

13. (b)

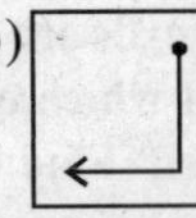

14. (b) Florist sold $= 133 \times \frac{5}{7}$

$= 95$ roses

Remaining roses

$= 133 - 95 = 38$

15. (d) Hen is different from both goat and cow. Goat is different from cow, but both are milching animals.

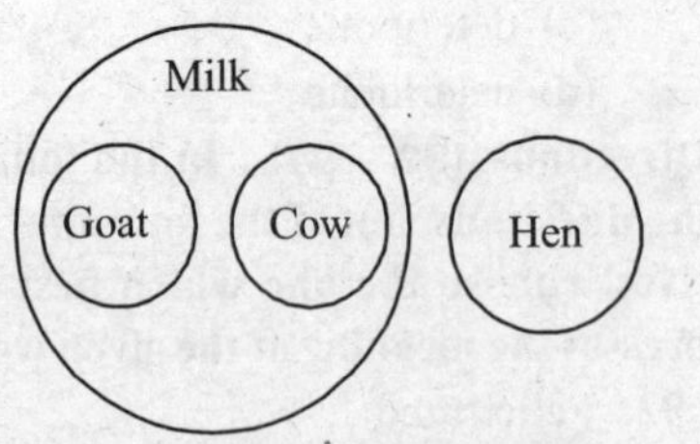

16. (a) F ⇒ 02, 14, 21, 33, 40

I ⇒ 03, 10, 22, 34, 41

R ⇒ 57, 69, 76, 88, 95

E ⇒ 01, 13, 20, 32, 44

Option	F	I	R	E
(1)	02	03	57	01
(2)	33	34	76	22
(3)	21	22	88	33
(4)	14	10	69	14

17. (a) $0.15 + 0.15 = 0.30$

$0.30 + 0.30 = 0.60$

$0.60 + 0.60 = 1.20$

$1.20 + 1.20 = 2.40$

18. (b)

$B \xrightarrow{+2} D \xrightarrow{+1} E \xrightarrow{+2} G \xrightarrow{+1} H$

$C \xrightarrow{-1} B \xrightarrow{+4} F \xrightarrow{-1} E \xrightarrow{+4} I$

$D \xrightarrow{-1} C \xrightarrow{+4} G \xrightarrow{-1} F \xrightarrow{+4} J$

19. (d)

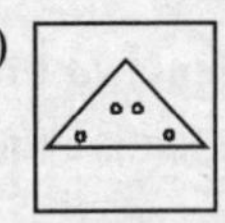

20. (c) There is no 'A' letter in the given word. Therefore, the word RETREAT cannot be formed.

INTER[DEPEND]ENT ⇒ DEPEND

INTE[R]D[EPEN]DE[NT] ⇒ REPENT

INTER[DEPEN]D[E]NT ⇒ DEEPEN

21. (d) Both the Premises are Universal Affirmative (A-type).

All children are students.

All students are players.

A + A ⇒ A - type of Conclusion

"All children are players".

This is Conclusion II.

22. (b)

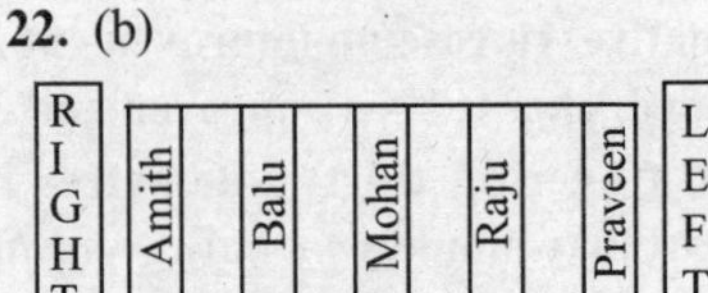

23. (b) $2 \times 2 - 4 = 0$

$3 \times 2 - 3 = 3$

$4 \times 2 - 2 = 6$

$5 \times 2 - 1 = 9$

$7 \times 2 - 2 = 12$

24. (a) First Column
$5 \times 6 + 4 = 34$
Second Column
$4 \times 7 + 2 = 30$
Third Column
$3 \times 8 + ? = 30$
$\Rightarrow ? = 30 - 24 = 6$

25. (c)

26. (a) Dadabhai Naoroji's book 'Poverty and Un-British Rule in India' brought attention to the draining of India's wealth into Britain. Further in his book, he stated the loss of 200-300 million pounds of revenue to Britain. Dadabhai Naoroji considered it as a major evil of British in India.

27. (b) A dimensionless quantity is simply a quantity that has no units and therefore no dimensions. A ratio between two numbers is a non-dimensional or dimensionless quantity. Strain which is defined as change in dimension over original dimension has no dimensional formula. So it is a dimensionless quantity.

28. (c) Krishnadevaraya (1509–1530), the greatest emperor of the Vijayanagara Empire, composed Amuktamalyada. Considered a masterpiece in Telugu literature, the epic poem is believed to have been written and dedicated to Lord Venkateswara. The administration of the empire was carried on along the lines indicated in his Amuktamalyada.

29. (a) The acronym BCG stands for Bacillus Calmette–Guérin, a vaccine against tuberculosis and for the treatment of some bladder cancers. It is prepared from a strain of the attenuated (virulence-reduced) live bovine tuberculosis bacillus, Mycobacterium bovis. It is on the World Health Organization's List of Essential Medicines.

30. (a) Cash Reserve Ratio (CRR) is a specified minimum fraction of the total deposits of customers, which commercial banks have to hold as reserves either in cash or as deposits with the central bank. CRR is a crucial monetary policy tool and is used for controlling money supply in an economy.

31. (c) Balban, who was the ninth sultan of the Mamluk dynasty of Delhi, adopted the policy of Blood and Iron to tackle the law and order situation in the area around Delhi and in the Ganga-Yamuna doab. The Mewatis had become so bold as to plunder people upto the outskirts of Delhi. As a result of his policy of blood and iron, robbers were mercilessly pursued and put to death.

32. (d) PPM is an abbreviation of Parts Per Million. It is commonly used as a measure of small levels of pollutants in air, water, body fluids, etc. Parts per million is the mass ratio between the pollutant component and the solution.

33. (d) The chemical composition of Heavy water (deuterium oxide) is $2H_2O$ or D_2O. It is a form of water that contains a larger than normal amount of the hydrogen isotope deuterium (^2H or D, also known as heavy hydrogen), rather than the common hydrogen-1 isotope (^1H or H, also called protium) that makes up most of the hydrogen in regular water.

34. (b) The World Trade Organization (WTO) headquartered at Centre William Rappard, Geneva, Switzerland. It is an intergovernmental organization which regulates international trade. The WTO officially commenced on 1 January 1995 under the Marrakesh Agreement.

35. (b) An autotroph is an organism that can produce its own food using light, water, carbon dioxide, or other chemicals. Plants are the most familiar type of autotroph, but there are many different kinds of autotrophic organisms. Algae, which live in water and whose larger forms are known as seaweed, is autotrophic.

36. (a) URL is an acronym for Uniform Resource Locator. Commonly referred to as a web address, URL is a reference to a web resource that specifies its location on a computer network and a mechanism for retrieving it.

37. (b) Some economists have classified factors into two categories, land and labour (or nature and man) on the ground that they are the only original or primary factors. It is said that capital has no independent origin and is merely the outcome of combined efforts of land and labour. However, other economists include all man-made instruments for production in the category of Capital. It includes machines, tool, factories, buildings, canals, roads, raw materials, etc., which play vital role in production.

38. (a) The oxide of Sulphur (Sulphur Dioxide) is washed down on earth as acid rain. It makes the soil acidic by lowering its pH; this affects plants and animals adversely. Acid rain contains H+, SO_4^{2-} ions which when added to the soil leaches the nutrients from the soil. Acid rain renders the river or even ocean water acidic, thereby affecting marine animals adversely. Changes in pH of fresh water affect the reproduction and survival of many species or fish.

39. (a) Water at ordinary temperatures contracts and increases in density as it is cooled, like most substances. But at about 4°C it reaches a maximum density and then decreases in density as it approaches the freezing point. This is referred to as anomalous property of water.

40. (d) According to Prof. Kindleberger, Todaro, Lewis and Nurkse etc., agriculture makes its contribution to economic development in several ways as following:

- By providing food and raw material to non-agricultural sectors of the economy,
- By creating demand for goods produced in non-agricultural sectors, by the rural people on the strength of the purchasing power, earned by them on selling the marketable surplus,
- By providing investable surplus in the form of savings and taxes to be invested in non-agricultural sector,
- By earning valuable foreign exchange through the export of agricultural products, etc.

41. (b) The United States (US) Postal Service, on 26 August 2010, honoured India's Nobel peace prize winner Mother Teresa by releasing a postage stamp on her birth centenary. Her portrait by award winning American artist Thomas Blackshear II also featured on it. In 1996, the then president Bill Clinton and the US Congress awarded Mother Teresa honorary US citizenship.

42. (d) The headquarters of the United Nations is a complex in New York City. The complex has served as the official headquarters of the United Nations since its completion in 1952. It is located in the Turtle Bay neighbourhood of Manhattan (New York).

43. (d) Rajendra Prasad was the first President of the Republic of India. He held the office from 26 January 1950 to 12 May 1962. Prasad was the only president to serve two terms in office. Upon independence in 1947, Prasad was elected president of the Constituent Assembly of India, which prepared the Constitution of India and served as its provisional parliament.

44. (d) Sodium bicarbonate and organic acid (Formic acid, Acetic acid, Carbonic acid, etc.) react vigorously to liberate carbon dioxide. For example, Sodium bicarbonate ($NaHCO_3$) when treated with acetic acid reacts vigorously to liberate carbon dioxide.

$$NaHCO_3 + CH_3COOH \rightarrow CH_3COONa + H_2O + CO_2$$

45. (b) The notion that democracy is a form of government is widely held and has been supported by a host of writers. According to Seeley, "democracy is a government in which everyone has a share". Seeley points towards the pure form of democracy.

46. (d) Sher Shah Suri is mainly remembered for his administrative reforms which was modified and expanded by later rulers. He established a sound and strong administrative system by dividing his empire into 42 Sarkars each of which was subdivided into Parganas. Besides he introduced proper land revenue system and carried out currency reforms. He was an enlightened despotism.

47. (b) Six Indian women athletes, including Asian Games double gold medallist Ashwini Akkunji, were given one-year suspensions after testing positive for banned anabolic steroids in December 2011. India's 400 metre runners Akkunji, Jauna Murmu, Mandeep Kaur, Priyanka Panwar, Sini Jose and Tiana Mary Thomas had tested positive for methandienone.

48. (b) The office of District Collector was created in 1772 by Warren Hastings, the then Governor-General of India. The post was abolished in 1773, but restored in 1781. The district continued to be the unit of administration after India gained independence in 1947.

49. (d) Pandita Ramabai, an Indian social reformer, established 'Sharda Sadan' at Bombay in 1889 with an objective to provide shelter to the 'destitute high caste widows.' She also established the Mukti Mission in Pune, as a refuge for young widows deserted and abused by their families and 'Krupa Sadan,' a home for "fallen" women, who had been cast out of society.

50. (d) The Arctic Ocean is the smallest of the world's five ocean basins. With an area of about 5.4 million square miles, the Arctic Ocean is about 1.5 times as big as the United States. It is bordered by Greenland, Canada, Norway, Alaska, and Russia. It is almost completely covered with ice for the majority of the year.

51. (d) Total income of A and B

= ₹ (2 × 200) = ₹ 400

Total income of C and D

= ₹ (2 × 250) = ₹ 500

∴ Required average

$= \frac{400+500}{4} = \frac{900}{4}$

= ₹ 225

52. (b) Let the principal be ₹ x.

$\text{S.I.} = \frac{\text{Principal} \times \text{Time} \times \text{Rate}}{100}$

According to the question,

$x + \frac{x \times 15 \times 1}{100} = 1725$

$\Rightarrow \frac{115x}{100} = 1725$

$\Rightarrow x = \frac{1725 \times 100}{115}$

= ₹ 1500

53. (a) IQ score ⇒ 130–140 ⇒ 2

IQ score of 140 is undeterminable

54. (b) Number of students whose IQ score is 100 and more = 16 + 13 + 4 + 2 = 35.

55. (b) Age of first person = $5x$ years

Age of second person = $9x$ years

According to the question,

$9x - 5x = 40 \Rightarrow 4x = 40$

$\Rightarrow x = 10$

∴ Sum of their ages

$= 5x + 9x = 14x = 14 \times 10 =$ 140 years

56. (b) Work done by Raja and Ramesh in 1 day

$= \frac{1}{20} + \frac{1}{25} = \frac{5+4}{100} = \frac{9}{100}$

Work done by Ramesh in 10 days $= \frac{10}{25} = \frac{2}{5}$

Remaining work $= 1 - \frac{2}{5} = \frac{3}{5}$

∴ This part is done by Raja and Ramesh.

∴ Time taken

$= \frac{3}{5} \times \frac{100}{9} = \frac{20}{3} = 6\frac{2}{3}$ days

∴ Required time

$= 10 + 6\frac{2}{3} = 16\frac{2}{3}$ days

57. (b) Total number of votes polled $= x$ (let)

According to the question,

$\frac{x \times 62}{100} - \frac{x \times (100-62)}{100} = 144$

$\Rightarrow \frac{62x}{100} - \frac{38x}{100} = 144$

$\Rightarrow \frac{24x}{100} = 144$

$\Rightarrow 24x = 144 \times 100$

$\Rightarrow x = \frac{144 \times 100}{24} = 600$

58. (b) $\frac{1 \cdot 21}{x} = \frac{x}{0.09}$, Where, x = mean proportion

$\Rightarrow x^2 = 1.21 \times 0.09$

$\Rightarrow x^2 = 1.1 \times 1.1 \times 0.3 \times 0.3$

$\Rightarrow x = 1.1 \times 0.3 = 0.33$

59. (c) Distance between school and house $= x$ km (let)

$\text{Time} = \frac{\text{Distance}}{\text{Speed}}$

According to the question,

$\frac{x}{\frac{5}{2}} - \frac{x}{\frac{7}{2}} = \frac{6+6}{60} = \frac{1}{5}$

(Difference of time = 6 + 6 = 12 minutes)

$\Rightarrow \frac{2x}{5} - \frac{2x}{7} = \frac{1}{5}$

$\Rightarrow \frac{14x - 10x}{35} = \frac{1}{5}$

$\Rightarrow \frac{4x}{35} = \frac{1}{5} \Rightarrow 4x = \frac{35}{5} = 7$

$\Rightarrow x = \frac{7}{4} = 1\frac{3}{4}$ km.

60. (a) C.P. of article

$= ₹ \left(\frac{100}{130} \times 286\right) = ₹ 220$

$\text{S.P. of article} = \frac{286 \times 90}{100}$

= ₹ 257.40

∴ Profit

= ₹ (257.40 – 220) = ₹ 37.40

∴ Profit percent

$= \frac{37.40 \times 100}{220} = 17\%$

61. (a) The base of a prism is a triangular.

Semi-perimeter of triangle(s)

$= \frac{5+10+13}{2} = \frac{28}{2} = 14$ cm.

∴ Area of triangle

$= \sqrt{s(s-a)(s-b)(s-c)}$

$= \sqrt{14(14-5)(14-10)(14-13)}$

$= \sqrt{14 \times 9 \times 4 \times 1}$

$= 6\sqrt{14}$ sq. cm.

∴ Volume of prism

= Area of base × height

$= 6\sqrt{14} \times 10$

$= 60\sqrt{14}$ cu.cm.

= 60 × 3.742 = 224.52 cu.cm.

∴ Weight of the prism

= (224.52 × 7) gram

= 1571.64 gram

62. (c) S.I. = 956 – 800 = ₹ 156

$\therefore$ Rate = $\frac{\text{S.I.}\times 100}{\text{Principal} \times \text{Time}}$

$= \frac{156 \times 100}{800 \times 3} = 6.5\%$

New rate = (6.5 + 4)%

= 10.5%

$\therefore$ S.I.

$= \frac{\text{Principal} \times \text{Time} \times \text{Rate}}{100}$

$= \frac{800 \times 3 \times 10.5}{100} =$ ₹ 252

$\therefore$ Amount = ₹ (800 + 252)

= ₹ 1052

63. (a) Average of runs in 16 innings

= 87 – 17 × 3 = 87 – 51 = 36

$\therefore$ Required average

= 36 + 3 = 39 runs

64. (c) C.P. of article = ₹ x (let).

According to the question,

$\frac{x \times 75}{100} = 3600$

$\Rightarrow x = \frac{3600 \times 100}{75} =$ ₹ 4800

65. (a) Original price of 1 mango = ₹ x (let).

$\therefore$ C.P. of 1 mango $= \frac{100x}{125}$

= ₹ $\frac{4x}{5}$

According to the question,

$x + 1 = \frac{4x}{5} \times \frac{150}{100}$

$\Rightarrow x + 1 = \frac{6x}{5} \Rightarrow \frac{6x}{5} - x = 1$

$\Rightarrow \frac{x}{5} = 1 \Rightarrow x =$ ₹ 5

66. (d) Let the C.P. of article be ₹ 100.

$\therefore$ Marked price = ₹ 120

According to the question,

After a discount of 10%,

S.P. = $\frac{120 \times 90}{100}$ = ₹ 108

$\therefore$ Profit = 108 – 100 = ₹ 8

$\therefore$ Profit percent = 8

67. (a) Price of article = ₹ x (let)

According to the question,

$P = \frac{x(100-20)}{100} \times \frac{100-25}{100}$

$\Rightarrow P = x \times \frac{80}{100} \times \frac{75}{100}$

$\Rightarrow P = x \times \frac{4}{5} \times \frac{3}{4} = \frac{3x}{5}$

$\Rightarrow x =$ ₹ $\frac{5}{3}P$

68. (c)

Men	Working hours	Days
16 ↑	14 ↑	12
28	12	x ↓

$\therefore \left.\begin{matrix} 28:16 \\ 12:14 \end{matrix}\right\} :: 12 : x$

$\Rightarrow 28 \times 12 \times x = 16 \times 14 \times 12$

$\Rightarrow x = \frac{16 \times 14 \times 12}{28 \times 12} = 8$ days

69. (d) Speed of plane = $\frac{\text{Distance}}{\text{Time}}$

$= \frac{6000}{8} = 750$ kmph

New speed = (750 + 250) kmph = 1000 kmph

$\therefore$ Required time = $\frac{9000}{1000}$

= 9 hours

70. (b) Sum of first n odd natural numbers = n^2

$\therefore$ Their average = $\frac{n^2}{n} = n$

$\therefore$ Required average = 25, because n = 25.

71. (d)

2	1008
2	504
2	252
2	126
3	63
3	21
	7

$\therefore 1008 = 2 \times 2 \times 2 \times 2 \times 3 \times 3 \times 7$

$= 2^2 \times 2^2 \times 3^2 \times 7$

$\therefore$ Required answer = 7

72. (d) $\sqrt{0.000441} = \sqrt{\frac{441}{1000000}}$

$= \frac{21}{1000} = 0.021$

73. (b) Rate of discount = 12%

$\therefore$ S.P. of TV set

= 6500 × (100 – 12)%

$= \frac{6500 \times 88}{100} =$ ₹ 5720

74. (c) Volume of cone = $\frac{1}{3}\pi r^2 h$

$= \frac{1}{3} \times \pi \times 15 \times 15 \times 20$

$= 1500\pi$ cu.cm.

$\therefore$ Volume of a smaller cone

$= \frac{1}{3}\pi \times 1.5 \times 1.5 \times 5$

$= 3.75\pi$ cu.cm.

$\therefore$ Number of smaller cones

$= \frac{1500\pi}{3.75\pi} = 400$

75. (c) 243000 = 243 × 1000

$= 3 \times 3 \times 3 \times 3 \times 3 \times 10 \times 10 \times 10$

$= 3^3 \times 3^2 \times 10^3$

$\therefore$ Required number = $3^2 = 9$

76. (b) **Persevering (Adjective)** = showing determination to achieve a particular aim despite difficulties.

77. (d) Here possessive case (their's) should be used.

78. (b) **Bring out** = to produce something; to publish something.

79. (b) **Feign (Verb)** = to pretend that you have a particular feeling or that you are ill/sick/tired etc.

80. (c) **Take fancy** = to attract or please somebody; to start liking somebody/something often without an obvious reason.

81. (c) **Carry out** = to do and complete a task.

82. (d) **Beat about the bush** = to talk about something for a long time without coming to the main point.

83. (d) It is a measure of certain distance/time. Hence, singular verb should be used.

84. (c) For a person, relative pronoun 'who' should be used.

85. (b) Here, present simple should be used.
Where do you come from? = Where do you live?

86. (b) **Harmonious (Adjective)** = friendly; peaceful and without any disagreement.
Discordant (Adjective) = not in agreement

87. (c) **Fragile (Adjective)** = easily broken or damaged; weak and uncertain; easily destroyed or spoilt.

88. (a) **Superficial (Adjective)** = appearing to be true, real or important; artificial; cursory.
Genuine (Adjective) = real; exactly what it appears to be.

89. (c) **Juvenile** = connected with young people who are not yet adults.

90. (d) **Knowledgeable** = well informed.

91. (c) **Deteriorate** = to become worse.

92. (d) **Felicitate (Verb)** = congratulate.

93. (c) **Honour (Verb/Noun)** = respect; great respect and admiration for somebody.

94. (c) **Rectify (Verb)** = to put right something that is wrong; correct.

95. (a) Here, subject is singular. Hence, badly needs painting .... should be used.

96. (d) As the structure and sense suggest, in the conditional clause, Present Simple i.e., If I play my best ..... should be used.

97. (b) It is preposition related error.
Find fault with somebody/something = to look for and discover mistakes.

98. (a) **99.** (d)

100. (c) **General** = highest in rank; chief.

SSC Constable (GD)

Solved Paper-2013

Part-A : General Intelligence and Reasoning

Directions (Q. 1-4) : In the following questions, select the related word/letter/number from the given alternatives.

1. Postman : Letter :: Teacher : ?
(a) Knowledge (b) Experience
(c) Idea (d) Wisdom

2. Sad : Cry :: Angry : ?
(a) Cheer (b) Roar
(c) Voice (d) Shout

3. CFBZ : ZBFC :: XYVW : ?
(a) WYXV (b) WXVY
(c) WVYX (d) XYVW

4. 4 : 16 :: 9 ?
(a) 64 (b) 22
(c) 100 (d) 36

Directions (Q. 5-7) : In the following questions, find out the odd word/letter/number from the given alternatives.

5. (a) Volt (b) Watt
(c) Ampere (d) Kilogram

6. (a) ZSLE (b) YRKD
(c) XQJC (d) WIPB

7. (a) 25 (b) 36
(c) 78 (d) 144

8. Which one of the given responses would be a meaningful order of the following words?
1. Lips 2. Eyes
3. Nose 4. Ears
5. Forehead
(a) 1, 2, 3, 4, 5 (b) 5, 4, 3, 2, 1
(c) 5, 2, 4, 3, 1 (d) 1, 3, 4, 2, 5

Directions (Q. 9-11) : In the following questions, a series is given with one term/two terms missing. Choose the correct alternative from the given options that will complete the series.

9. C, I, N, R, U, ?
(a) W (b) X
(c) V (d) Y

10.

2	4	8	7
4	2	?	8
8	6	2	?
7	8	2	2

(a) 2 and 6 (b) 6 and 2
(c) 8 and 3 (d) 4 and 9

11. 11, 18, 27, ?
(a) 38 (b) 40
(c) 42 (d) 44

12. How many rotations will the hour-hand of a clock complete in 72 h?
(a) 3 (b) 9
(c) 12 (d) 6

13. From the given alternatives, select the word which cannot be formed using the letters given in the word LAWYER
(a) YEAR (b) WEAR
(c) EAR (d) JAW

14. If QUESTION is coded as 56214379, then how can you code QUEENS?
(a) 562291 (b) 926251
(c) 599621 (d) 926651

15. Select the correct combination of the mathematical signs to replace * signs and to balance the given equation.
(81 * 9) * 8 * 7 * 79
(a) + − × = (b) ÷ − + =
(c) × − ÷ = (d) ÷ × + =

16. If CAT = 24 and DOG = 26, then TIGER is equal to :
(a) 59 (b) 67
(c) 72 (d) 48

17. Hari faces towards East. Turning to his right, he walks 50 m and then turning to his left, he walks 50 m. After this, he turns to his right and walks 50 m. Again, he turns to his right and walks 100 m. Finally, he turns to his right and walks 100 m. In which direction is he from his starting point now?
(a) East (b) West
(c) North (d) South

18. How many triangles are thre in the given figure?

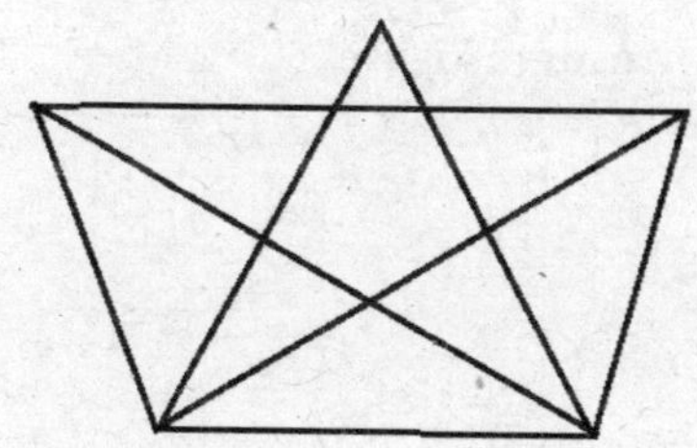

(a) 16 (b) 19
(c) 10 (d) 24

19. Which of the following diagrams best depicts the relationship among Reptiles, Dinosaurs, Turtles?

(a) 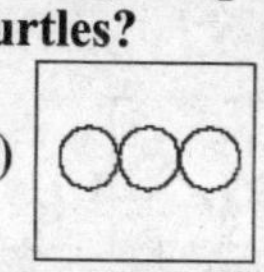 (b) 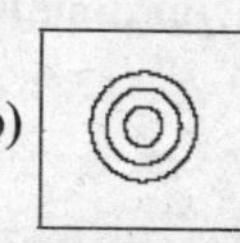

(c) 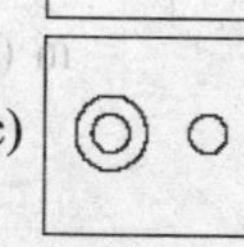 (d) 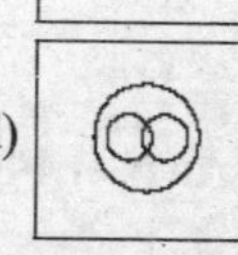

20. A statement is given, followed by two Conclusions I and II. You have to consider the statement to be true even, if it seems to be at variance from commonly known facts. You have to decide which of the given conclusions, if any follow from the given statement.

Statement:

The Government of India has recently announced several concessions and offered attractive package tours to foreign visitors.

Conclusions:

I. Now more number of foreign tourists will visit India.

II. The Government of India seems to be serious in attracting tourists.

(a) Only Conclusion I follows
(b) Only Conclusion II follows
(c) Neither Conclusion I nor II follows
(d) Both Conclusions I and II follow

21. Which answer figure will complete the pattern in the question figure?

Question Figure:

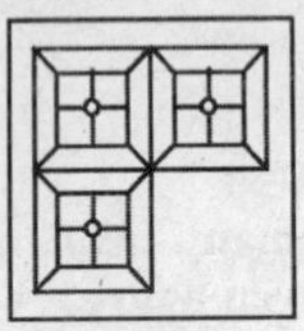

Answers Figures :

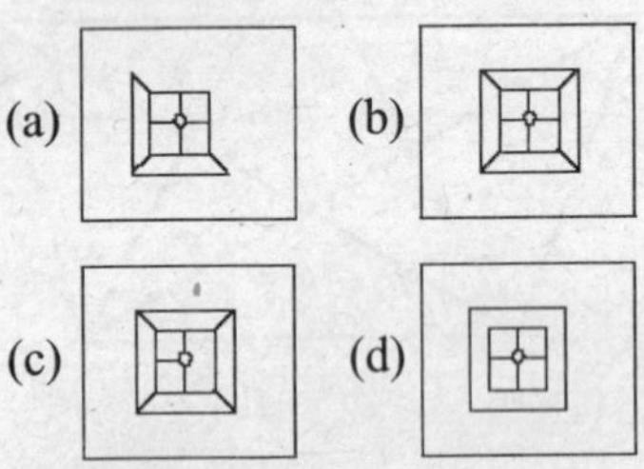

22. From the given answer figures, select the one in which the question figure is hidden/embedded.

Question Figure:

Answer Figures:

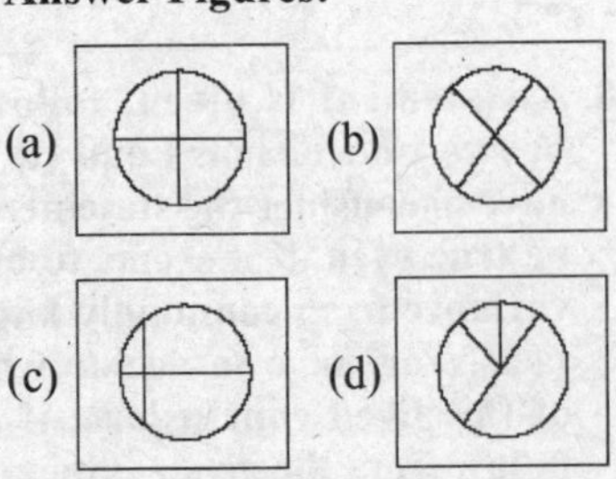

23. A piece of paper is folded and cut as shown below in the question figures. From the given answer figures, indicate how it will appear when opened?

Question Figures:

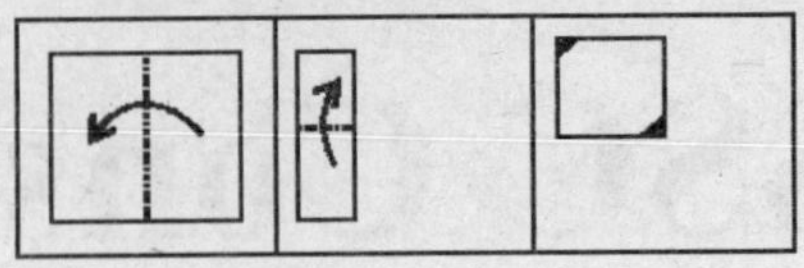

Answer Figures:

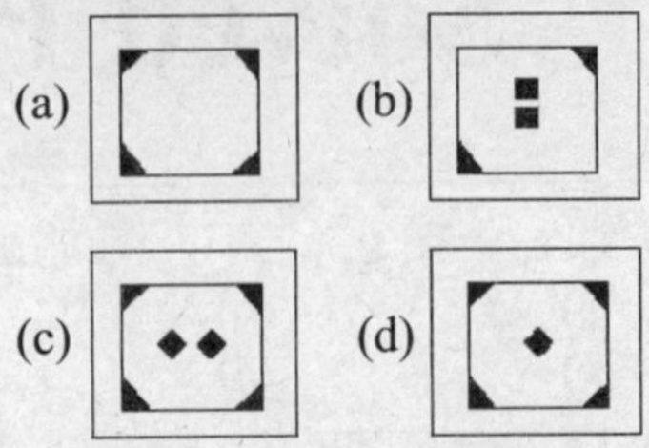

24. If a mirror is placed on the line MN, then which of the answer figures is the correct image of the given question figure?

Question Figure:

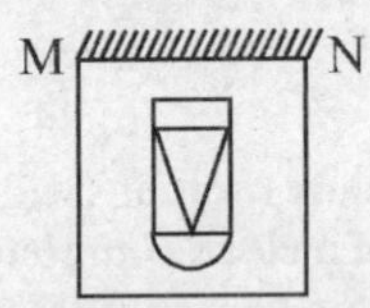

Answer Figures:

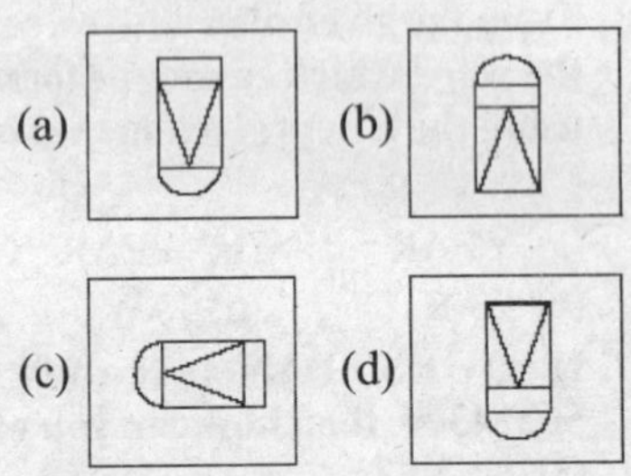

25. A word is represented by only one set of numbers given in anyone of the alternatives. The sets of numbers given in the alternatives are represented by two classes of alphabets as in the two matrices given below. The columns and rows of Matrix I are numbered from 0 to 4 and that of Matrix II are numbered from 5 to 9. A letter from these matrices can be represented first by its row next by its column e.g. 'A' can be represented by 00, 13 etc., and 'K' can be represented by 55, 68, etc. Similarly, you have to identify the set of the given word 'DEMO'.

Matrix I

	0	1	2	3	4
0	A	B	C	D	E
1	E	D	B	A	C
2	B	E	A	C	D
3	D	C	E	B	A
4	C	A	D	E	B

Matrix II

	5	6	7	8	9
5	K	L	M	N	O
6	O	N	I	K	M
7	I	O	K	M	N
8	N	M	O	I	K
9	M	K	N	O	L

(a) 24, 32, 57, 65
(b) 11, 21, 69, 13
(c) 24, 32, 78, 03
(d) 42, 32, 78, 554

Part-B : General Knowledge and General Awareness

26. Labour is considered as a king under :

(a) Socialism
(b) Capitalism
(c) Communism
(d) Mixed Economy

27. Which one of the following denotes an enterprise?

(a) Physical capital
(b) Working capital
(c) Human capital
(d) Fixed capital

28. The Constitution makes provision for the creation of new All India Services only if :

(a) Lok Sabha passes a resolution of this effect by a majority of 2/3 of its members present and voting
(b) Rajya Sabha passes a resolution to this effect by a majority of 2/3 of its members present and voting
(c) President issues an ordinance to this effect
(d) President permits the Prime Minister to do so

29. Political liberty implies :

(a) the right of the citizen to free movement
(b) the right of the citizen to free speech

(c) the right of the citizen to follow his/her religion
(d) the right of the citizen to participate in the administration of the state

30. Privilege to some people in a society on the basis of their caste is an infringement of :
(a) Economic justice
(b) Social justice
(c) Legal justice
(d) Political justice

31. Who was the 23rd Tirthankara of Jainism?
(a) Rishabhdeva
(b) Parsavanatha
(c) Neminath
(d) Mahavira

32. Which of the following was not a centre of learning in ancient India?
(a) Taxila (b) Nalanda
(c) Kaushambi (d) Vikramshila

33. The famous Bourbon dynasty ruled over :
(a) England (b) Austria
(c) France (d) Prussia

34. Which one of the following languages belongs to the Austric group?
(a) Marathi (b) Ladakhi
(c) Khasi (d) Tamil

35. Which one of the following is not a biosphere reserve?
(a) Great Nicobar 1989
(b) Sunderbans 1989
(c) Nanda Devi 1988
(d) Gulf of Kachchh 2008

36. Which atom is not found in proteins?
(a) Carbon (b) Nitrogen
(c) Phosphorus (d) Sulphur

37. Organization formed by individuals of a species is :
(a) Community (b) Population
(c) Race (d) Ecosystem

38. Plague is transmitted by :
(a) House fly (b) Tsetse fly
(c) Rat flea (d) Mosquito

39. A nuclear reaction must be balanced in terms of :
(a) mass and volume
(b) energy and weight
(c) number of electrons
(d) mass and energy

40. The chemical used in a photographic plate is :
(a) barium chloride
(b) silver bromide
(c) silver nitrate
(d) silver chloride

41. For taking the clinical photograph of bones, we use :
(a) UV rays (b) IR rays
(c) X rays (d) Cosmic rays

42. A watch spring when wound up acquires :
(a) mechanical energy
(b) kinetic energy
(c) potential energy
(d) light energy

43. Impact printers :
(a) Strike a ribbon against the paper to produce character images
(b) include ink jet and thermal devices
(c) are more expensive than laser printers
(d) use optical technology

44. Central Zoo Authority is located in :
(a) New Delhi (b) Chennai
(c) Kolkata (d) Dehradun

45. First permanent research station established by India in South polar region in Antarctica is :
(a) Maitri
(b) Dakshin Gangotri
(c) Bharti
(d) Himadri

46. The first mathematical calculator was designed by :
(a) Napier (b) Leibnitz
(c) Fischer (d) Pingale

47. Chairperson of UPA's Think Tank (National Advisory Council) is :
(a) Jayanthi Natarajan
(b) Sonia Gandhi
(c) Priyanka Gandhi
(d) Montek S. Ahluwalia

48. The Malabar coast in India is towards :
(a) Port Blair
(b) Eastern Ghats
(c) Western Ghats
(d) Indira Point

49. Who was awarded 'Indira Gandhi Award' for National Integration Posthumously?
(a) Rajiv Gandhi
(b) Abdul Gaffar
(c) Shyam Benegal
(d) Vipin Hazarika

50. The 'Pragya Award' is given to authors of books written in :
(a) Bengali (b) Hindi
(c) Sanskrit (d) Marathi

Part-C : Elementary Mathematics

51. The corret value of $(0.01) - (0.01)^2$ is :
(a) 0.0101 (b) 0.1001
(c) 0.0011 (d) 0.0001

52. A least number of 4 digits when increased by 5 is completely divisible by 12, 15, 20 and 35. The number is :
(a) 1275 (b) 1265
(c) 1235 (d) 1255

53. Identify the missing number in the sequence
3, 6, 11, 18, *
(a) 29 (b) 27
(c) 22 (d) 30

54. 8 men can paint a house in 5 days. How many men will be required to paint the same house in 4 days?
(a) 9 (b) 10
(c) 11 (d) 7

55. A and B together can do a work in 15 days. B alone can do the same work in 60 days. Then, the time taken by A alone to do the work (in days) is
(a) 30 (b) 45
(c) 20 (d) 60

56. If the edge of a cube is increased by 100%, then the surface area of the cube is increased by :
(a) 100% (b) 200%
(c) 300% (d) 400%

57. The area of the shaded region in the given figure is :

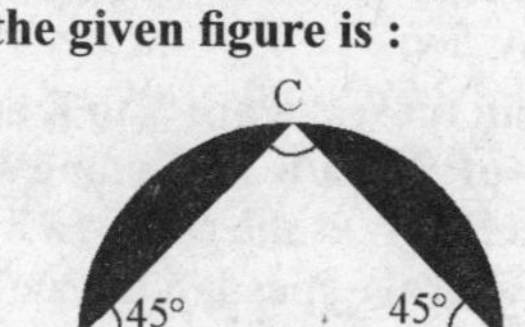

(a) $a^2(\pi - 1)$ sq units
(b) $\frac{a^2}{2}(\pi - 2)$ sq units
(c) $a^2(\pi - 2)$ sq units
(d) $\frac{a^2}{2}(\pi - 1)$ sq units

58. A book seller gives 12% discount on the printed price. What does a customer pay for a book with a printed price of ₹ 75?
(a) ₹ 66 (b) ₹ 64
(c) ₹ 70 (d) ₹ 63

59. If marked price is ₹ 180 and price after discount is ₹ 153, then the rate of discount is :
(a) 21% (b) 19%
(c) 17% (d) 15%

60. The single discount equivalent to two successive discounts of 10% and 20% is equal to :
(a) 30% (b) 28%
(c) 10% (d) 38%

61. 22 carat gold is mixed with 18 carat gold in the ratio 1 : 2 to get *x* carat gold. Then, the value of *x* is :
(a) 20 (b) $15\frac{2}{3}$
(c) 14 (d) $19\frac{1}{3}$

62. *x* varies directly with the product of *y* and *z*. When *y* = 45 and *z* = 20, *x* = 200. When *y* = 90, *z* = 30, then *x* is :
(a) 200 (b) 900
(c) 600 (d) 2700

63. The average of the first 9 positive even numbers is :
(a) 12 (b) 9
(c) 10 (d) 10.5

64. The average age of a class of 20 boys is 12 yr. What will the average age of the class, if 5 new boys join the class whose average is 7 yr?
(a) 10 yr (b) 11 yr
(c) 10.5 yr (d) 11.5 yr

65. A man travels from A to B at the rate of 7 km/h and come back from B to A at the rate of 5 km/h. The average speed of the man for the whole journey is :
(a) $6\frac{1}{2}$ km/h (b) 6 km/h
(c) $5\frac{5}{6}$ km/h (d) $5\frac{1}{6}$ km/h

66. The ratio of cost price and selling price is 20:25. The profit percent is :
(a) 25 (b) 20
(c) 125 (d) 80

67. A trader purchased a radio at $\frac{6}{7}$th of its marked price and sold it at $14\frac{2}{7}$% more than its marked price. His gain is :
(a) $15\frac{1}{7}$% (b) $28\frac{4}{7}$%
(c) $33\frac{1}{3}$% (d) None of these

68. If 90% of *x* is 315 km, then the value of *x* is :
(a) 325 km (b) 350 km
(c) 405 km (d) 340 km

69. Mr A spents 78% of his monthly income and saves the rest. If his annual saving is ₹ 22440, then his monthly income (in ₹) is :
(a) 7800 (b) 8500
(c) 9700 (d) 10125

70. The ratio between the rates of walking of A and B is 2 : 3. If the time taken by B to cover a certain distance is 36 min. then the time taken by A to cover that distance is :
(a) 24 min (b) 54 min
(c) 48 min (d) 36 min

71. A train 100 m long running at 36 km/h, takes 25 s to pass a bridge. The length of the bridge is :
(a) 100 m (b) 80 m
(c) 150 m (d) 360 m

72. Find the difference between SI and CI on ₹ 2000 in 2 yr at 6% per annum.
(a) ₹ 7.30 (b) ₹ 7.10
(c) ₹ 7.00 (d) ₹ 7.20

73. Anil lent ₹ 1000 to Sourav for 4 yr and ₹ 3000 to Vinod for 2 yr. If he received ₹ 900 as simple interest altogether, the rate of interest is :
(a) 5% (b) 7%
(c) 8% (d) 9%

Directions (Q. 74–75) : The following graph shows the number of people owning two wheelers in 7 different towns. Study the graph and answer the questions.

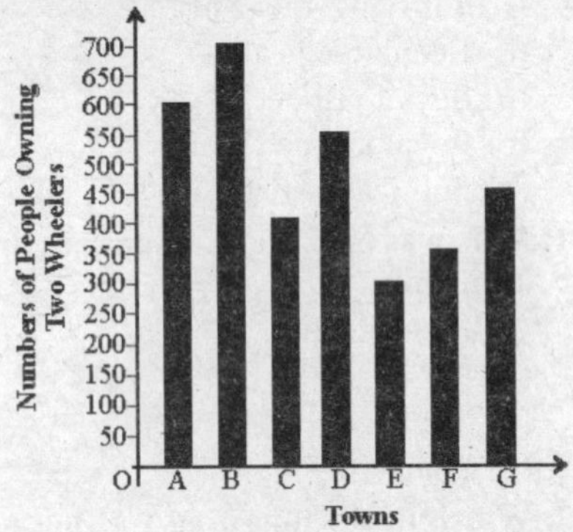

74. The town which has twice as many vehicles as Town E is :
(a) Town A (b) Town C
(c) Town B (d) Town D

75. The number of towns that have at the most 400 vehicles is :
(a) 4 (b) 3
(c) 2 (d) 1

Part-D : English Language

Directions (Q. 76-78) : In the following questions, some parts of the sentences have errors and some are correct. Find out which part of a sentence has an error. If the sentence is error free, your answer is (d).

76. No sooner (a)/ had he said it (b)/ when he realised his fault. (c)/ No error (d)

77. Human nature is more or less (a)/ the same in India (b)/ likewise in Europe. (c)/ No error (d)

78. By accidentally (a)/ he befriends an elephant trained in a circus (b)/ and with his help reaches Mumba (c)/ No error (d).

Directions (Q. 79-82) : In the following questions, sentences are given with blanks to be filled with an appropriate word(s). Four alternatives are suggested for each question. Choose the correct alternative out of the four.

79. Rita .... her cooking last night.
(a) does not do (b) did not do
(c) will not do (d) would not do

80. I have known her .... the end of the World War-II.

(a) from (b) since
(c) during (d) towards

81. His appointment may .... some new life into the committee.

(a) increase (b) inject
(c) infect (d) insure

82. The pages of the book .... by Ravi were lying on the floor.

(a) torn off (b) torn away
(c) torn of (d) torn in

Directions (Q. 83-85) : In the following questions, out of the four alternatives, choose the one which best expresses the meaning of the given word.

83. Determination :

(a) Looseness (b) Vacillating
(c) Deterioration (d) Firmness

84. Amend :

(a) Increase (b) Improve
(c) Simplify (d) Reduce

85. Obstruction :

(a) Encouragement
(b) Disapproval
(c) Hindrance
(d) Assistance

Directions (Q. 86-88) : In the following questions, choose the word opposite in meaning to the given word.

86. Healthy :

(a) Vigorous (b) Monotonous
(c) Sick (d) Disorderly

87. Accord :

(a) Command
(b) Obey
(c) Disagreement
(d) Communicate

88. Inconsistent :

(a) Irregular (b) Erratic
(c) Regular (d) Indifferent

Directions (Q. 89-91) : In the following questions, four alternatives are given for the Idiom/Phrase underlined in the sentence. Choose the alternative which best expresses the meaning of the Idiom/Phrase.

89. A true friend is always ready to stand by with you even in difficult times.

(a) stand for
(b) stand up
(c) to support
(d) standing beside

90. Sunny turned a deaf ear to his friend's pleas.

(a) listened to (b) disregarded
(c) agreed to (d) obeyed

91. Sweepers are seen once in a blue moon in our locality.

(a) rarely seen
(b) never seen
(c) regularly seen
(d) seen once during a lunar eclipse

Directions (Q. 92-94) : In the following questions, part of the sentence is underlined. Below are given alternatives of the underlined sentence. Choose the correct alternative. In case no improvement is needed, your answer is (d).

92. I don't hardly think it will rain.

(a) hardly think
(b) don't think hardly
(c) hardly don't think
(d) No improvement

93. Two negatives destroy one another.

(a) each other
(b) themselves
(c) with one another
(d) No improvement

94. I asked him why is he so angry upon me?

(a) is he so angry with me
(b) he is so angry with me
(c) he was so angry with me
(d) No imoprovement

Directions (Q. 95-97) : In the following questions, out of the four alternatives, choose the one which can be substituted for the given words/ sentences.

95. One who pays rent to the landlord.

(a) Termagant (b) Trojan
(c) Tenant (d) Payee

96. Two pieces of bread spread with butter or any other food :

(a) Stand dune (b) Loaves
(c) Bun (d) Sandwich

97. Without change of tone or pitch.

(a) Monotone (b) One tone
(c) Single tone (d) First tone

Directions (Q. 98-100) : In the following questions words are given in each questions, out of which only one word is correctly spelt. Find the correctly spelt word :

98. (a) Renaissance (b) Renaisance
(c) Renassance (d) Renaissancee

99. (a) Fictiteous (b) Fictisious
(c) Fictitieous (d) Fictitious

100. (a) Annoyence (b) Annayonce
(c) Annoyance (d) Anoyance

Answers with Explanations

1. (a) As postman delivers the letters, similarly the teacher gives knowledge to the students.

2. (d) Somebody cries in sad situation, similarly somebody shouts when he is angry.

3. (c)

As,

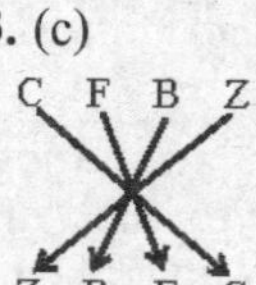

Similarly,

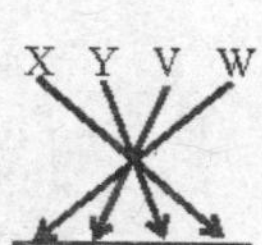

4. (d) As,

$(2)^2 = 4$ and $(2 \times 2)^2 = 16$

Similarly,

$(3)^2 = 9$ and $(3 \times 2)^2 = 36$

5. (d) Except kilogram, all units are related to current.

6. (d) Except the letters group WIPB, all are in certain sequence as follow.

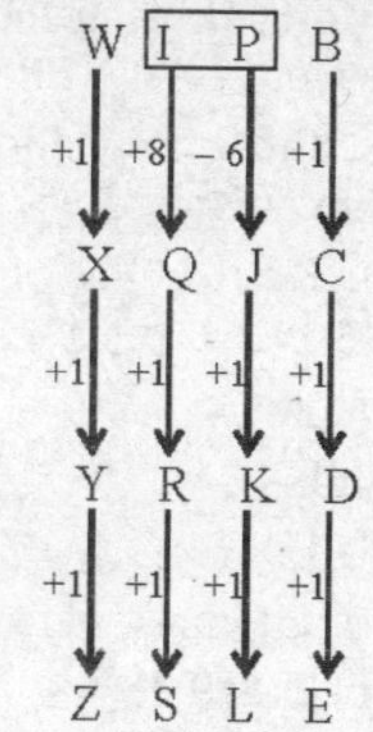

7. (c) Except 78, all are square numbers.

8. (c) The meaningful order is,

Forehead → Eyes → Ears → Nose → Lips
(5) (2) (4) (3) (1)

9. (a)

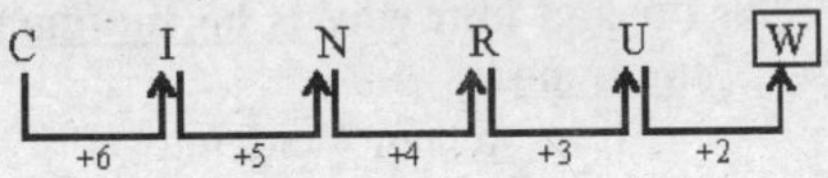

So, the missing term is W.

10. (b) Here, the sum of first row is equal to the first column, the sum of second row is equal to the second column, the sum of third row is equal to the third column and the same way is followed in fourth row and fourth column.

i.e., $2+4+8+7=21$ (First row)

$\Rightarrow 2+4+8+7=21$ (First column)

$4+2+x_1+8=4+2+6+8$

$14+x_1=20$

$x_1=6$

and $8+6+2+x_2=8+x_1+2+2$

$16+x_2=12+6$

(Putting the value of x_1)

$x_2=18-16$

$x_2=2$

So, the missing terms are 6 and 2.

11. (a)

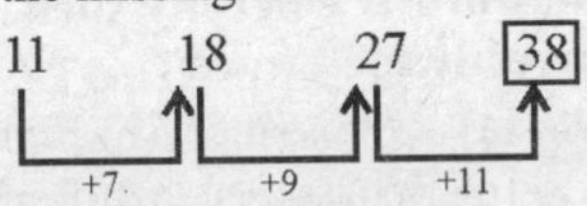

So, the missing term is 38.

12. (d) ∴ One rotation the hour-hand of a clock complete in 12 h.

∴ 6 rotations the hour-hand of a clock complete in

$= 12 \times 6 \text{ h} = 72 \text{ h}$.

13. (d) Due to the letter 'J' Jaw cannot be formed using the letters in the word LAWYER.

14. (a) As, the given code for the following word

Q U E S T I O N
↓ ↓ ↓ ↓ ↓ ↓ ↓ ↓
5 6 2 14 3 7 9

Similarly,

Q U E E N S
↓ ↓ ↓ ↓ ↓ ↓
5 6 2 2 9 1

15. (d) Using the signs of option (d)

$(81 * 9) * 8 * 7 * 79$

$\Rightarrow (81 \div 9) \times 8 + 7 = 79$

$\Rightarrow 9 \times 8 + 7 = 79$

$\Rightarrow 72 + 7 = 79$

$\Rightarrow 79 = 79$

16. (a) As

C A T
↓ ↓ ↓ = 3 + 1 + 20 = 24
3 1 20

and D O G = 4 + 15 – 7 = 26
↓ ↓ ↓
4 15 7

Similarly,

T I G E R = 20 + 9 + 7 + 5 + 18 = 59
↓ ↓ ↓ ↓ ↓
20 9 7 5 18

17. (b)

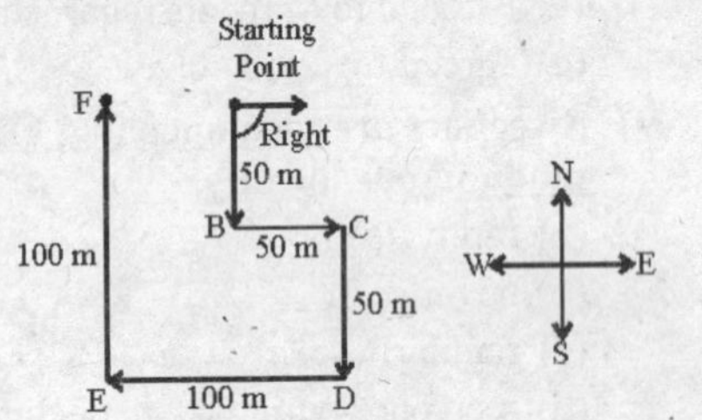

As per the given instruction Hari is in West to his starting point.

18. (d)

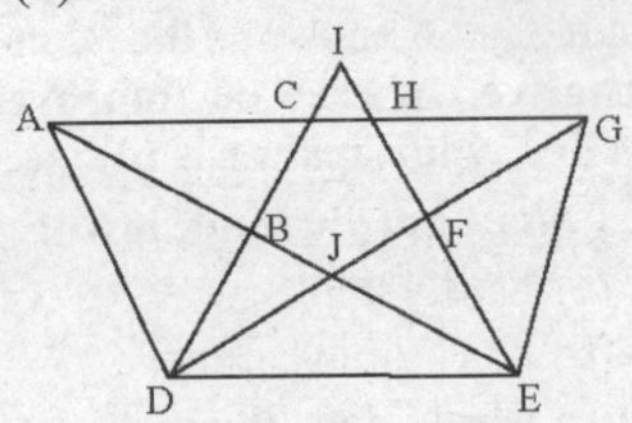

Single triangles ACB, ADB, CIH, HGF, GFF, JFE, JDE and DBJ

Double triangles ADC, AJD, DBE, DEF, HGE, and JGE

Triple triangles ADE, DGE DIE, EBI, AGJ, CDG and AEH.

Total number of triangle = (8 + 6 + 7 + 3) = 24

19. (c) The relationship among reptiles, dinosaurs and turtles is given below.

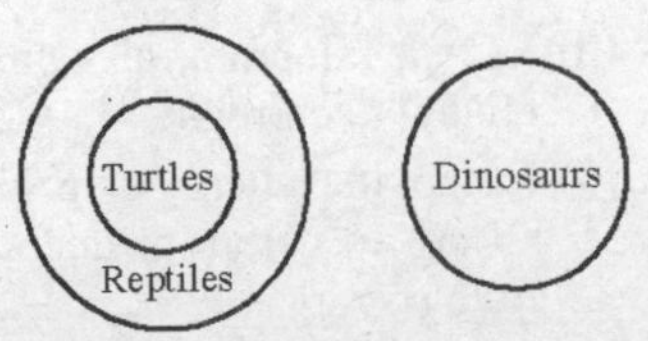

20. (a) According to the statement, offered and concession are given to only foreign visitors. So, only Conclusion I follows.

21. (b) The answer figure (b) will complete the pattern in the question figure.

22. (d) **23.** (d) **24.** (a)

25. (a) According to the given Matrices I and II.

D = 24, E = 32, M = 57, O = 65

So, the option (a) is correct.

26. (c) Communism is a theoretical economic system characterized by the collective ownership of property and by the organization of labour for the common advantage of all members.

27. (b) Working capital is a financial metric which represents operating liquidity available to a business, organization or other entity, including government entity.

28. (b) Article 312 empower Parliament to create new All India Services, if Rajya Sabha passes a resolution to this effect by a majority of 2/3 of its member present and voting.

29. (d) Political liberty implies the right of the citizen to participate in the administration of the state.

30. (b) Social justice means absense of discrimination on the grounds of caste, religion, colour, creed, sex or language. It is ensured by abolishing any title to honour (Art 18) and untouchability (Art 17).

31. (b) The 23rd Tirthankara of Jainism, Parsvanatha was the son of king Ashavasena of Varanasi.

32. (c) Kaushambi was the capital of Vatsa Mahajanpadas.

33. (c) The house of Bourbon is a European royal house of French origin, a branch of the capetian dynasty Bourbon kings first ruled Navarre and France in the 16th century.

34. (c) The Austric languages of India belong to the Austro Asiatic sub-family, which are represented by languages of

Munda Orkol group, spoken in the Central Eastern and North Eastern India and languages of the Non Khmer group like Khasi and Nicobarese.

35. (d) The Indian Government has established 18 biosphere of India which protect larger areas on natural habitat and often include one of more natural parks and or reserve along buffer zones that are open to some economic user. Gulf of Kachchh is not a biosphere reserve.

36. (c) The term protein was cointed by Mulder in 1818. These are composed of carbon, hydrogen, oxygen nitrogen and sulphur proteins are polymers of amino acids.

37. (b) A population is a summation of all the organisms of the same group or species, who live in the same geopraphical area and have the capability of interbreeding.

38. (c) Plague is a human disease caused by Bacteria. It is transmitted by Rat flea.

39. (d) A nuclear reaction must be balanced in terms of mass and energy. The mass number and total energy before the reaction must equal the total energy before the reaction must equal the total energy after the reaction.

40. (b) Silver Bromide (AgBr) is a water insoluble salt well known for its unusual sensitivity to light. This property has allowed silver halides to become the basis of modern photographic materials.

41. (c) X rays are a form of elctromagnetic radiation most X rays have a wavelength in the range of 0.1Å to 100 Å.

42. (c) A watch spring when wound up acquires potential energy.

43. (a) Impact printers create an image by using some mechanism to physically press and inked ribbon against the paper, causing the ink to be deposited on the paper in the shape desired.

44. (a) The Central Zoo Authority has been constituted under the Wildlife (protection) Act. The main objective of the authority is to complement the national effort in conservation of wildlife.

45. (b) Dakshin Gangotri was the first permanent Indian Researh Station in Antarctica. It was established during the third Indian Expedition to Antarctica in 1982–83.

46. (a) Napier's bones is an abacus invened by John Napier for calculation of products and quotients of numbers.

47. (b) The National Advisory Council (NAC) of India is an advisory body set up to advise the Prime Minister of India. It is not a constitutional body created by the first United Progressive Alliance (UPA) Government. Sonia Gandhi has been as Chairperson for much of the tenure of the UPA.

48. (c) The Malabar coast in India is towards Western Ghats. It is between Mangalore and Kanyakumari.

49. (a) The Indira Gandhi Award for National Integration is given annually starting from 1985 to distinguished persons/institutions for promoting national integration Rajiv Gandhi. Beant Singh and Shankar Dayal Sharma Awarded Indira Gandhi Award posthumously.

50. (b) 'The Pragya Award' is given to authors of books written in Hindi by the Rajasthan Hindi Granth Akademi.

51. (a) $0.01 + (0.01)^2 = 0.01 + 0.0001 + 0.0101$

52. (b) A least number of 4 digits = 1000

LCM of 12, 15, 20, 35 = 420

The required number is

$420 + n = 5$

$= 420 \times 3 + 5$

$= 1260 + 5 = 1265$

53. (b)

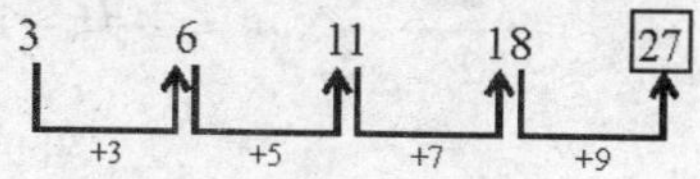

54. (b) $M_1 = 81, D_1 = 5, M_2 = x, D_2 = 4$

Using the formula,

$$\frac{M_1D_1}{W_1} = \frac{M_2D_2}{W_2}$$

$$\Rightarrow \frac{8 \times 5}{1} = \frac{x \times 4}{1} \Rightarrow x = 10$$

55. (c) $(A + B)$'s 1 day's work $= \frac{1}{15}$

B's 1 day's work $= \frac{1}{60}$

$\therefore$ A's 1 day's work

$$= \left(\frac{1}{15} - \frac{1}{60}\right) = \frac{1}{20}$$

$\therefore$ A alone do the work in 20 days.

56. (c) The required surface area increased

$$= \left[\left(\frac{100 + x}{100}\right)^2 - 1\right] \times 100\%$$

$$= \left[\left(\frac{100 + 100}{100}\right)^2 - 1\right] \times 100\%$$

$$= \left[\left(\frac{200}{100}\right)^2 - 1\right] \times 100\%$$

$= [(2)^2 - 1] \times 100\%$

$= (4 - 1) \times 100\%$

$= 300\%$

57.

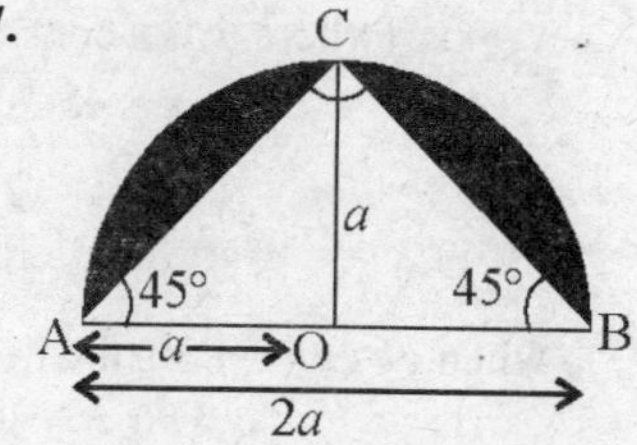

The required Area = Area of the semicircle – Area of ΔABC

$$= \frac{\pi r^2}{2} - \frac{1}{2} \times \text{Base} \times \text{Height}$$

$$= \frac{\pi \times (a)^2}{2} - \frac{1}{2} \times (a + a) \times a$$

$$= \frac{\pi a^2}{2} - \frac{1}{2} \times a^2 = \frac{a^2}{2}(\pi - 2)$$

sq units

58. Required price = 88% of 75

$$= \frac{75 \times 88}{100}$$

$= ₹ 66$

59. (d) Discount = ₹ (180 – 153) = ₹ 27

∴ Rate of discount

$$= \frac{(27 \times 100)}{100}\% = 15\%$$

60. (b) Required discount

$$= \left(a + b - \frac{a \times b}{100}\right)\%$$

$$= \left(10 + 20 - \frac{10 \times 20}{100}\right)\%$$

= (30 –2)% = 28%

61. (d) Using the rule of alligation,

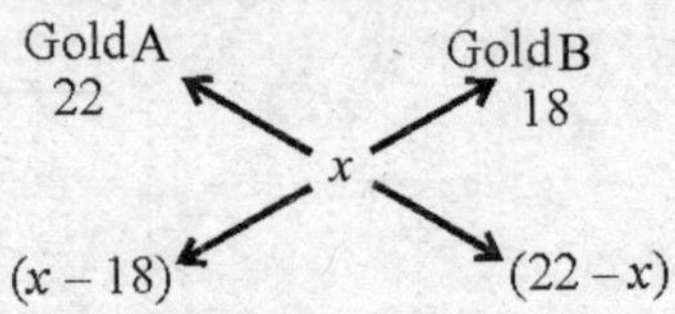

$$\frac{x - 18}{22 - x} = \frac{1}{2}$$

$$\Rightarrow \quad 2x - 36 = 22 - x$$

$$\Rightarrow \quad 3x = 58$$

$$\therefore \quad x = 19\frac{1}{3}$$

62. (c) According to the question,

$x = yz$

$x = kyz$ (where, k is a constant.)

$$\therefore \quad 200 = k \times 45 \times 20$$

$$\therefore \quad k = \frac{200}{900} = \frac{2}{9}$$

when $y = 90$, $z = 30$, then $x = k$,

$y = 90$, $z = 30$

$$= \frac{2}{9} \times 90 \times 30 = 20 \times 30 = 600$$

63. (c) The average of the first n positive even number $= n + 1$

So, the required average

= (9 + 1) = 10

64. (b) Required average

$$= \frac{20 \times 12 + 5 \times 7}{20 + 5} = \frac{240 + 35}{25}$$

$$= \frac{275}{25} = 11 \text{ yr}$$

65. (c) The average speed of man

$$= \left(\frac{2ab}{a + b}\right)\text{km} = \frac{2 \times 7 \times 5}{7 + 5}$$

$$= \frac{70}{12} = 5\frac{5}{6} \text{ km/h}$$

66. (a) $\frac{CP}{SP} = \frac{20}{25}$ (given)

Let CP = $20x$ and SP = $25x$

∴ The required profit percent

$$= \left(\frac{SP - CP}{CP} \times 100\right)\%$$

$$= \left(\frac{25x - 20x}{20x} \times 100\right)\% = 25\%$$

67. (c) Let the marked price is ₹ 700

Then, CP $= 700 \times \frac{6}{7} =$ ₹ 600

and SP $= 700 + 700 \times \frac{100}{7} \times \frac{1}{100}$

= (700 + 100) = ₹ 800

So the required gain

$$= \left(\frac{SP - CP}{CP} \times 100\right)\%$$

$$= \left(\frac{800 - 600}{600} \times 100\right)\%$$

$$= \frac{200 \times 100}{600}\% = \frac{100}{3}\%$$

$$= 33\frac{1}{3}\%$$

68. (b) 90% of $x = 315$

$$\Rightarrow x \times \frac{90}{100} = 315$$

$$\Rightarrow \quad x = \frac{315 \times 100}{90} = 350 \text{ km}$$

69. (b) Let the monthly income of Mr. A = ₹ x

Saving of Mr. A = (100 – 78)% of x = 22% of x

$$\therefore 22\% \text{ of } x = \frac{22440}{12}$$

(Monthly saving)

$$\therefore 100\% \text{ of } x = \frac{1870 \times 100}{22}$$

= ₹ 8500

70. (b) Ratio between the rates of walking of A : B = 2 : 3

∴ Ratio of rates of their time taken = 3 : 2 (Raciprocal of speed)

∴ Time taken by A $= \left(\frac{36 \times 3}{2}\right)$ min

= 54 min

So, the time taken by A to cover that much distance is 54 min.

71. (c) Let the length of bridge be x metres

Speed of train = 36 km/h

$$= \left(36 \times \frac{5}{18}\right) \text{ m/s} = 10 \text{ m/s}$$

Total distance = Length of train + Length of bridge = $(100 + x)$ m

Time taken = 25x

$$\therefore \text{ Speed} = \frac{\text{Distance}}{\text{Time}}$$

$$\Rightarrow \quad 10 = \frac{100 + x}{25}$$

$$\Rightarrow \quad 250 = 100 + x$$

$$\therefore \quad x = 250 - 100$$

$= 150$ m

72. (d) Using the formula I_0

$$= p \times \left(\frac{r}{100}\right)^2$$

Here, $p =$ ₹ 2000, $r = 6\%$

$$\therefore \quad I_0 = 2000 \times \left(\frac{r}{100}\right)^2$$

$$= 2000 \times \frac{36}{10000}$$

= ₹ 7.20

73. (d) Let the rate of interest be r% yearly

Then,

$$\Rightarrow \quad 900 = \frac{p_1 r_1 r}{100} + \frac{p_2 r_2 r}{100}$$

$$\Rightarrow \quad 900 = \frac{1000 \times 4 \times r}{100} + \frac{3000 \times 2 \times r}{100}$$

$$\Rightarrow \quad 900 = 40r + 60r$$

$$\Rightarrow \quad r = \frac{900}{100}\% = 9\%$$

74. (a) Vehicles of E = 3
Twice of vehicles E
= 3 × 200 = 600
So, the Town A has twice as many vehicles as Town E.

75. (b) The number of towns that have not more then at the most 400 are 3 i.e. C. E. F.

76. (c) Use 'then' instead of 'when' because the sentence which starts from 'No sooner' is always followed by than.

77. (c) Replace 'likewise' with 'as' because the same is followed by relative pronoun 'that' or 'as'.

78. (d) No error

79. (b) Use 'did not do' here because from the use of 'last night the sentence' indicates about past.

80. (b) Use 'since' because since is used with the present perfect or past perfect tence to denote a time in the past until a later past time or until now.

81. (a) Use 'increase' here. Increase refers to raise.

82. (a) Use "torn off" which refers to separate something by tearing.

83. (d) Determination means 'certainty' firmness has also the same meaning as determination.

84. (b) Amend means 'modify'. Improve has also the same meaning as amend.

85. (c) Obstruction means 'interruption' Hindrance has also the same meaning as obstruction.

86. (c) Sick is an opposite word for healthy here.

87. (c) Disagreement is an opposite word for accord.

88. (c) Inconsistent means uncertain. Here regular is correct opposite word for inconsistent.

89. (c) The phrase 'stand by' means 'to support'.

90. (b) The idiom 'turned a deaf ear to' means disregarded.

91. (a) The idiom 'seen once in a blue moon' means 'rarely seen'.

92. (a) Use hardly think in place of don't hardly think.

93. (a) Use each other in place of one another.

94. (c) Use he was so angry with me instead of is he so angry upon me.

95. (c) Tenant pays rent to the land-lord.

96. (d) Sandwich is two pieces bread spread with butter or any other food.

97. (a) Without change of tone or pitch is called monotone.

98. (a) Renaissance is correctly spelt word.

99. (d) Fictitious is correctly spelt word.

100. (c) Annoyance is correctly spelt word.

SSC Constable(GD)

Practice Set-1

PART-A
GENERAL INTELLIGENCE AND REASONING

Directions (Q. No. 1-4) : Select the related word/letters/number from the given alternatives.

1. School : Teacher : : Hospital : ?
(a) Clerk (b) Doctor
(c) Student (d) Patient

2. JY : 35 : : RT : ?
(a) 48 (b) 38
(c) 35 (d) 24

3. AD : N : : BD : ?
(a) P (b) X
(c) Y (d) Z

4. 97 : 2 : : 84 : ?
(a) 4 (b) 3
(c) 6 (d) 5

Directions (Q. No. 5-7) : Select the odd word/letters/number/number pair from the given alternatives.

5. (a) Niece (b) Nephew
(c) Aunt (d) Sister

6. (a) AE (b) IM
(c) UA (d) GK

7. (a) 17 (b) 23
(c) 29 (d) 33

8. (a) 7214 (b) 3618
(c) 3519 (d) 9436

Directions (Q. No. 9-11) :A series is given with one term missing. Choose the correct alternative from the given ones that will complete the series.

9. ?, HI, OP, WX
(a) AB (b) BC
(c) DE (d) EF

10. 144, 256, 400, ?
(a) 441 (b) 576
(c) 625 (d) 289

11. 5, 7.5, 12.5, 22.5, ?
(a) 42.5 (b) 42
(c) 44 (d) 43.5

12. In the following question, two statements are given each followed by two conclusions I and II. You have to consider the statements to be true even if they seem to be at variance from commonly known facts. You have to decide which of the given conclusions, if any, follows from the given statements.

Statements:
(I) All shawls are carpets.
(II) No carpet is a pullover.

Conclusion:
(I) No shawls are pullovers.
(II) All carpets are shawls.

(a) Conclusion I follows
(b) Conclusion II follows
(c) Neither I nor II follows
(d) Both I and II follows

13. Vineet is taller than Raman but shorter than Jyoti. Sumit is the shortest. Deepak is taller than Sumit but shorter than Raman. Who is the tallest?
(a) Jyoti (b) Raman
(c) Vineet (d) Deepak

14. Arrange the given words in the sequence in which they occur in the dictionary.
i. Rainbow **ii. Rancour**
iii. Rattle **iv. Rainy**
(a) i, iii, ii, iv (b) i, iv, ii, iii
(c) i, iv, iii, ii (d) ii, i, iv, iii

15. In a certain code language, "BORROW" is written as "769965" and "BOMB" is written as "7647". How is "WOMB" written in that code language?
(a) 5647 (b) 5467
(c) 5677 (d) 5776

16. In the following question, select the missing number from the given series.

5	15	10
4	17	9
10	?	10

(a) 11 (b) 12
(c) 15 (d) 10

17. If "A" denotes "multiplied by", "B" denotes "subtracted from", "C" denotes "added to" and "D" denotes "divided by", then
7 B 17 C 88 D 11 A 6 = ?
(a) 27 (b) 28
(c) 38 (d) 26

18. Which set of letters when sequentially placed at the gaps in the given letter series shall complete it?
A _ B C _ B B C _ B B _
(a) BAAC (b) BBBC
(c) BABA (d) ABBC

19. Rahul moves 5 km towards south and then takes a left turn to move 5 km more. Again, he takes a left turn and moves 10 km and finally, he moves 5 km towards west. In which direction is he now from his initial position?
(a) West (b) East
(c) South (d) North

20. Johnny's father is the brother-in-law of Nisha's only sister. How is Johnny related to Nisha?
(a) Son (b) Grandson
(c) Father (d) Cousin

21. If a mirror is placed on the line MN, there which of the answer figures is the right image of the given figure ?

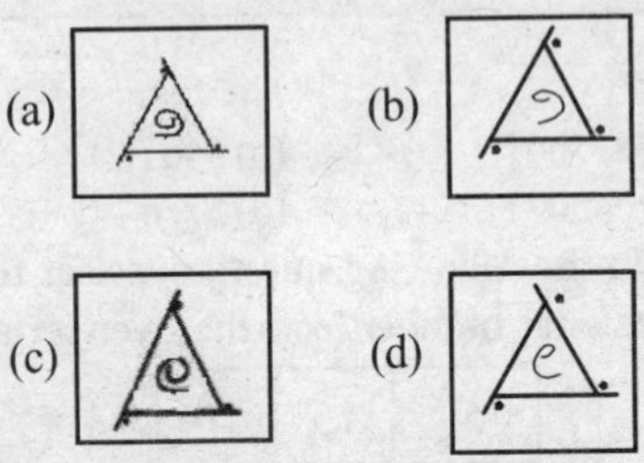

22. The diagram that identifies best representation of the relationship among the given classes.
Doctor, Smoker, Indian, Non-Smoker

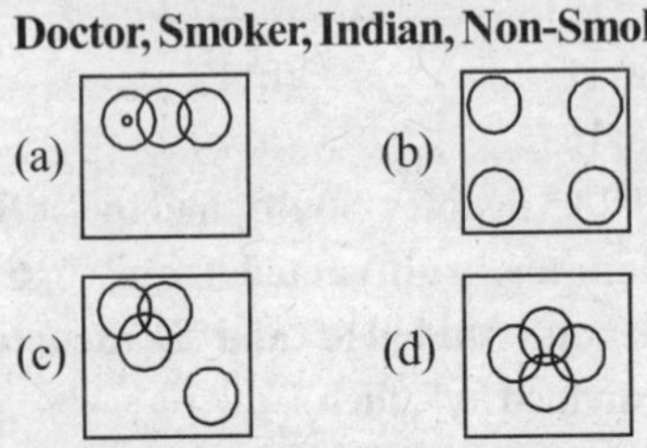

23. A piece of paper is folded and punched as shown below in the question figures. From the given answer figures, indicate how it will appear when opened.

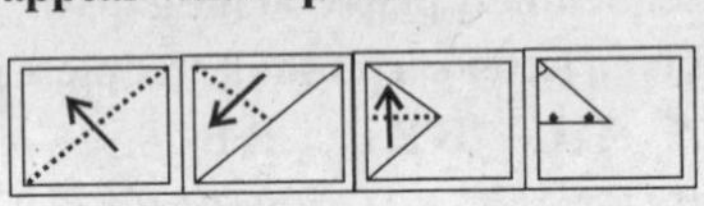

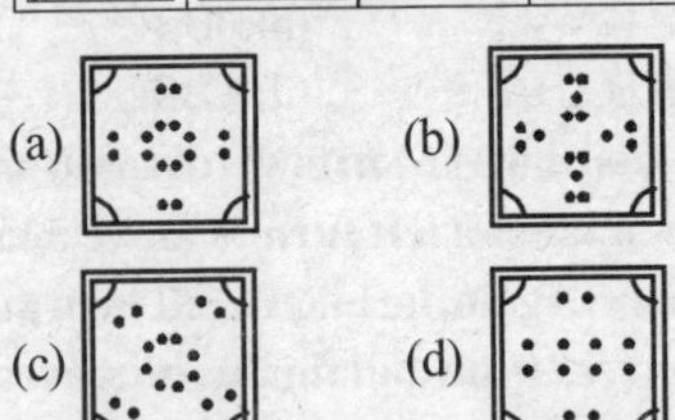

24. From the given answer figures, select the one in which the question figure is hidden/embedded.
Question figure :

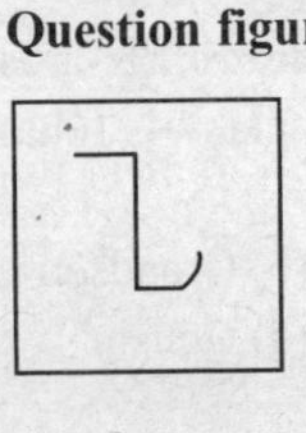

Answer figures :

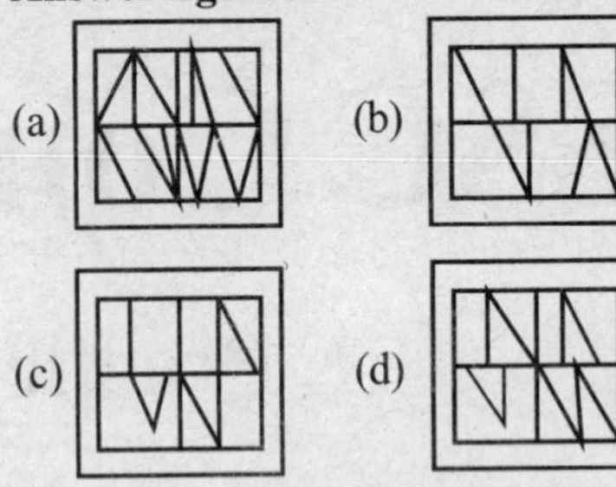

25. A word is represented by only one set of number as given in any one of the alternatives. The sets of numbers given in the alternative, are represented by two classes of alphabets as shown in the given two matrices. The columns and rows of Matrix-I are numbered from 0 to 4 and that of Matrix-II are numberd from 5 to 9. A letter from these matrices can be represented first by its row and next by its column, for example, 'N' can be represented by 21, 43 etc. and 'R' can be represented by 66, 57 etc., Similarly, you have to identify the set for the word 'JOIN'.

Matrix-I

	0	1	2	3	4
0	J	H	J	K	A
1	E	J	O	J	O
2	J	N	P	O	S
3	T	F	O	H	D
4	Q	O	W	N	F

Matrix-II

	5	6	7	8	9
5	X	Z	R	P	A
6	Z	R	I	I	S
7	I	C	F	K	N
8	N	I	G	N	M
9	M	V	N	P	N

(a) 00,43,32,79 (b) 02,67,14,57
(c) 11,32,66,79 (d) 20,23,86,97

PART-B
GENERAL KNOWLEDGE AND GENERAL AWARENESS

26. Who built the Buddhist monuments at Sanchi ?
(a) Mughal dynasty
(b) Maurya dynasty
(c) Gupta dynasty
(d) Chola dynasty

27. Gulzar won Oscars for the movie 'Slumdog Millionaire' in the category of
(a) Best sound mixing
(b) Best original score
(c) Best original song
(d) Best foreign language film

28. Which of the following is a primary function of haemoglobin?
(a) Utilisation of energy
(b) Prevention of anaemia
(c) Destruction of bacteria
(d) To transport oxygen

29. Vascular bundles are absent in
(a) Bryophyta (b) Pteridophyta
(c) Gymnosperms (d) Angiosperms

30. Sauria lacertidae is the scientific name of
(a) crocodile
(b) hippopotamus
(c) lizard
(d) house fly

31. In Chemistry, soap is a salt of
(a) fatty acid
(b) glycol
(c) phosphorus
(d) ammonium carbonate

32. A .... is a pair of forces, equal in magnitude, oppositely directed, and displaced by perpendicular distance or moment.
(a) bond (b) couple
(c) pair (d) duo

33. Which of these is not an Operating System?
(a) Android (b) iOS
(c) HTML (d) Symbian

34. Chapchar Kut is a festival of which State?
(a) Manipur (b) Nagaland
(c) Mizoram (d) Meghalaya

35. Who built the Taj Mahal?
(a) Humayun (b) Shah Jahan
(c) Babar (d) Jahangir

36. In which stage of the business cycle the inventory stock will be the highest ?
(a) Boom (b) Depression
(c) Recession (d) Recovery

37. Which type of pathogen causes the water-borne disease SARS (Severe Acute Respiratory Syndrome)?
(a) Viras
(b) Parasitic
(c) Protozoan
(d) Bacterial

38. Excessive richness of nutrients in a lake or other body of water is called
(a) Biomagnification
(b) Global Warming
(c) Salination
(d) Eutrophication

39. Which of the following is a Direct tax ?
(a) Excise duty
(b) Customs duty
(c) Service tax
(d) Wealth tax

40. The boundary line between India and Pakistan is called
(a) McMahon line (b) Maginot line
(c) Radcliffe line (d) Sir Creek

41. Which city is located on the banks of the river Mahanadi?
(a) Bengaluru (b) Cuttack
(c) Badrinath (d) Kota

42. When was the battle of Haldighati fought?
(a) 1776 (b) 1676
(c) 1576 (d) 1476

43. In 1498, which Portuguese explorer discovered a new sea route from Europe to India?
(a) Vasco da Gama
(b) Christopher Columbus
(c) Sir Francis Drake
(d) John Cabot

44. Who invented Aspirin?
(a) Ruth Handler
(b) John Harington
(c) Rowland Hill
(d) Felix Hoffmann

45. A larger force on a rotating body results in larger
(a) mass
(b) torque
(c) axis of rotation
(d) centre of mass

46. What is the unit of the physical quantity, magnetic flux density?
(a) Siemens (b) Weber
(c) Henry (d) Tesla

47. Article-24 of the Indian Constitution 'Prohibition of employment of children in factories, etc. deals with
(a) fundamental rights of the Indian Citizen
(b) Union government
(c) State government
(d) Directive principles of State policy

48. Article-134A of the Indian Constitution 'Certificate for appeal to the Supreme Court' deals with
(a) State government
(b) Union government
(c) Fundamental rights of the Indian citizen
(d) Directive principles of State policy

49. Highest number of test hundreds is scored by
(a) Jacques Kallis
(b) Sachin Tendulkar
(c) Ricky Ponting
(d) Brian Lara

50. Who is the author of 'Can Love Happen Twice'?
(a) Keshav Aneel
(b) Ravinder Singh
(c) Sudeep Nagarkar
(d) Aravind Adiga

PART-C

ELEMENTARY MATHEMATICS

51. If 3.352 – (9.759 – x) – 19.64 = 7.052, then what is the value of x?
(a) –6.181 (b) 13.581
(c) 33.099 (d) 39.803

52. Square of $(7-4x)$ is :
(a) $16x^2-28x+49$ (b) $49-28x-16x^2$
(c) $49-56x-16x^2$ (d) $16x^2-56x+49$

53. On a certain principal if the simple interest for two years is ₹ 3000 and compound interest for two years is ₹ 3225, what is the rate of interest?
(a) 7.5 percent (b) 30 percent
(c) 15 percent (d) 22.5 percent

54. At 10% discount the selling price of a toaster is ₹ 18000, what is the selling price if the discount is 37.5%?
(a) ₹ 7812.5 (b) ₹ 12500
(c) ₹ 8593.75 (d) ₹ 15468.75

55. An engineering student has to secure 24% marks to pass. He gets 61 and fails by 29 marks. What is the maximum marks for that exam?
(a) 375 marks (b) 400 marks
(c) 425 marks (d) 450 marks

56. The third proportional of two numbers 9 and 15 is :
(a) 21 (b) 30
(c) 25 (d) 45

57. What will be the roots of the quadratic equation $x^2-25x+156=0$?
(a) 12, 13 (b) 25, 1
(c) 9, 16 (d) 31, 6

58. If a cone of radius 3.5 cm and height 9.6 cm is melted and constructed into a cylinder of the same radius, what will be the height of this cylinder? (Take $\pi = 22/7$)
(a) 3.2 cm (b) 6.4 cm
(c) 1.6 cm (d) 4.8 cm

59. A shopkeeper by selling 9 Rolex watches, earns a profit equal to the selling price of 4 Rolex watches. His profit percentage is :
(a) 44.4 percent (b) 88.8 percent
(c) 80 percent (d) 8.8 percent

60. A circle is inscribed in a square. If the length of the diagonal of the square is $14\sqrt{2}$ cm, what is the area (in sq. cm.) of the circle?
(a) 308 (b) 462
(c) 154 (d) 616

61. In ΔPQR, S and T are points on side PQ and PR respectively. ST is parallel to QR. If S divides PQ in the ratio 4:1 and length of QR is 15 cm, what is the length of ST?
(a) 3 cm (b) 5 cm
(c) 12 cm (d) 10 cm

62. If $1/(1+\cos A)+1/(1-\cos A)=x$, then value of x is :
(a) $2\sec^2 A$ (b) 2 cosecA
(c) $2\operatorname{cosec}^2 A$ (d) 2 secA

63. Of the 3 numbers whose average is 64, the first number is 1/3 times the sum of other 2. The first number is —
(a) 72 (b) 32
(c) 96 (d) 48

64. Ajit is two times as good a workman as Badrinath and therefore is able to finish a job in 30 days less than Badrinath. Working together, they can do it in :
(a) 10 days (b) 30 days
(c) 15 days (d) 20 days

65. The length of the diagonal of a square is 10 cm. What is the area of this square?
(a) 50 sq cm (b) 100 sq cm
(c) 200 sq cm (d) 25 sq cm

66. A car travels a certain distance at 32 km/h and comes back at 68 km/h. What is the average speed for total journey?
(a) 50 km/hr (b) 37.04 km/hr
(c) 43.52 km/hr (d) 56.48 km/hr

67. What is the compound interest (in ₹) for 1 year on a sum of ₹ 20000 at the rate of 40% per annum compounded half yearly ?
(a) 8000 (b) 8650
(c) 8750 (d) 8800

68. A train of length 100 metre crosses another train of length 150 metre running on a parallel track in the opposite direction in 9 seconds. If the speed of train having length 150 metre is 40 km/hr, then what is the speed (in km/hr) of the other train ?
(a) 30 (b) 48
(c) 50 (d) 60

69. The present population of a town is 26010. It increases annually at the rate of 2%. What was the population of town two years ago ?
(a) 25000 (b) 25100
(c) 25200 (d) 25500

70. While selling an article for ₹ 18450, a person suffered a loss of 50%. At what price he sould have sold the article (in ₹) to earn a profit of 50%?
(a) 13837 (b) 52000
(c) 55350 (d) 56775

71. The average of three consecutive even numbers is A. If next five even numbers are added, what is the average of these eight numbers ?
(a) A+3 (b) A+4
(c) A+5 (d) A+7

72. A man has 3 sons, 2 daughters and a wife. They divided a sum of ₹ 19000 among themselves such that each daughter got 1.5 times the amount received by each son and his wife received ₹ 600 less than each son. What is the total amount (in ₹) received by the three sons together ?
(a) 2800 (b) 3600
(c) 5600 (d) 8400

Directions (73-75) : The table given below represents the marks obtained by 5 students in 4 different subjects. Each student was given marks out of 100 in each of the given subjects.

Student	English	Mathematics	Science	Hindi
1	87	96	90	81
2	74	99	94	89
3	89	99	99	92
4	62	89	96	91
5	95	92	92	86

73. In which subject the total marks of all the students is highest ?
(a) English
(b) Mathematics
(c) Science
(d) Hindi

74. Which student scored the maximum marks in all the 4 subjects taken together ?
(a) Student 1
(b) Student 2
(c) Student 3
(d) Student 5

75. A new subject is added in which all the students have scored 100 marks. If total marks are calculated as sum of the marks of highest 4 subjects, then who will be second in terms of total marks ?
(a) Student 3 (b) Students 2
(c) Student 5 (d) Students 4

PART-D
ENGLISH

Directions (Q.Nos. 76-77): In the following questions, some part of the sentence may have errors. Find out which part of the sentence has an error and select the appropriate option. If a sentence is free from error, select 'No Error'.

76. While he went beside (a)/ with our decisions, we were (b)/ never sure he totally agreed. (c)/ No error (d)

77. The after morning (a)/ she woke to the first ray of (b)/ light through the window. (c) No error (d)

Directions (Q.Nos. 78-79): In the following questions, the sentence given with blank to be filled in with an appropriate word (s). Select the correct alternative out of the four and indicate it by selecting the appropriate option.

78. The psychopath gets a .... sense of enjoyment from torturing animals.
(a) perverse (b) agreeable
(c) happy (d) resonable

79. When Jaspal got angry, he started to .... his feelings with his hands.
(a) participate (b) immolate
(c) intoxicate (d) gesticulate

Directions (Q.Nos. 80-83): In the following questions, out of the four alternatives, select the word similar in meaning to the word given.

80. Fossilise
(a) Amalgamate (b) Dissolve
(c) Flex (d) Liquefy

81. Depict
(a) Conceal (b) Distort
(c) Characterise (d) Suppress

82. Differ
(a) Alter (b) Concur
(c) Digress (d) Vary

83. Salve
(a) Cerate (b) Liniment
(c) Remedy (d) Blockage

Directions (Q.Nos. 84-85) : In the following questions, out of the four alternatives, select the alternative which best expresses the meaning of the idiom/phrase.

84. Gnash your teeth
(a) Express rage
(b) Brush your teeth
(c) Laugh hysterically
(d) Take a big bite

85. Let something slip through one's fingers
(a) Lose a wedding ring
(b) Not be able to understand a difficult concept
(c) Let go of certain unpleasant things
(d) to waste an opportunity to achieve something

Directions (Q.Nos. 86-87): In the following questions, out of the four alternatives, select the alternative which will improve the bracketed part of the sentence. In case no improvement is needed, select 'no improvement'.

86. What would you like (to do it) for your birthday?
(a) to do
(b) doing
(c) does
(d) No improvement

87. You must (be mistake).
(a) be mistakenly
(b) be mistaken
(c) be mistook
(d) No improvement

Directions (Q.Nos. 88-89): In the following questions, out of the four alternatives, select the alternative which is the best substitute of the words/ sentence.

88. Complete with regard to every detail
(a) Thorough (b) Lackadaisical
(c) Lax (d) Cursory

89. The faculty or power of using one's will
(a) Antagonism (b) Aversion
(c) Rejection (d) Volition

Directions (Q.Nos. 90-91): In the following questions, four words are given out of which one word is correctly spelt, select the correctly spelt word.

90. (a) Jukstapose (b) Jaxtapuse
(c) Juxtapose (d) Jaxtapose

91. (a) Musemant (b) Ammusement
(c) Ammusemant (d) Amusement

Directions (Q.Nos. 92-93) : Each of these questions below consists of a set of labelled sentences. First part of the sentence is fixed, and other parts are jumbled. Out of the four options given, select the most logical order of the sentences to form a coherent paragraph.

92. Evidently it was too (X) of a deadly-looking cobra or (Y) two we saw no reptiles (Z) dry for game, and with the exception
(a) YZX (b) YXZ
(c) XZY (d) ZXY

93. Some of these (X) height of more than (Y) 2000 feet above the sea (Z) rocks rise to the
(a) YZX (b) ZXY
(c) YXZ (d) XZY

94. In the following question, a sentence has been given in Active/Passive voice. Out of the four alternatives suggested, select the one which best expresses the same sentence in Passive/Active voice. I will wash the car every Sunday.
(a) The car is washed by me every Sunday.
(b) Every Sunday by me the car is to be washed.
(c) Every Sunday by myself the car is to be washed.
(d) The car will be washed by me every Sunday.

95. In the following question, a sentence has been given in Direct/Indirect speech. Out of the four alternatives suggested, select the one which best expresses the same sentence in Indirect/Direct speech. The watchman said, thief ! thief ! catch him!
(a) The watchman shouted to the crowd to catch the thief.
(b) The watchman shouted to the crowd, thief, thief, catch him.
(c) The watchman shouted to the crowd, catch the thief.
(d) The watchman shouted to the crowd, catch him.

Directions (Q.Nos. 96-100): A passage is given with five questions following it. Read the passage carefully and choose the best answer to each question out of the four alternatives.

There's more than the 101-seater dining table at the Falaknuma palace that is awe inspiring. The library done in rosewood and mahogany is a place that will force anyone to pause, if only to admire the fine original polish, the furniture and the walnut carved high roof. The last is supposedly and imitation of the one at Windsor Castle. The library is almost the size of a large banquet hall and acts as the passage to other parts of the palace including the dining area. For years the palace had no librarian because they couldn't find the right person to do justice to the treasure trove of books collected by the Nizam's family over several decades. That is until they found Asif Husain Arastu who belongs to the family that owned the famous AA Husain book store in Abids. So when his friend and historian Anuradha Naik pointed out the palace's requirement at the library, Husain was delighted. On his very first day as the librarian at the magnificent Taj Falaknuma place, Asif Husain found a reference book on 'How to paint grass' by Alfred East.

96. Which of the following is false about Arastu?
(a) He was a descendent of the Nizam's family.
(b) He was the librarian at the Falaknuma Palace.
(c) He owned a book store.
(d) He was a friend of Anuradha Naik.

97. The roof the the library has carvings made of which wood?
(a) Rosewood (b) Mahogany
(c) Sandalwood (d) Walnut

98. Name the author of the book that Hussain found on his first day as the librarian?
(a) Alfred East
(b) Anuradha Naik
(c) Mark Twain
(d) Charles Dickens

99. The books at the library were collected by
(a) Hyderabad University
(b) Anuradha Naik
(c) The Nizam's Family
(d) Asif Husain Arastu

100. Which part of the palace is an imitation of the Windsor Palace?
(a) 101-seater dining table
(b) The library's roof
(c) The banquet hall
(d) The library's furniture

Answers with Explanations

1. (b) As, teacher is related to school. Similarly, doctor is related to hospital.

2. (b) As,

J Y
10 $25 \rightarrow (10+25)=35$
Similarly,
R T
18 $20 \rightarrow (18+20)=38$
Finally, the missing term is 38.

3. (b) As,

A $D \rightarrow N$
1 4 14
Similarly,
B $D \rightarrow X$
2 4 24
Finally, the missing term is 24.

4. (a) As, $97 \rightarrow (9-7) \rightarrow 2$
Similarly, $84 \rightarrow (8-4) \rightarrow 4$
Finally, the missing number is 4.

5. (b) Nephew is odd word from the group niece, aunt and sister.

6. (c) A →(+4) E, I →(+4) M, U →(+20) A, G →(+4) K
Finally UA is odd word.

7. (d) 17, 23 and 29 are prime numbers and 33 is composite number.

8. (c) 3519 is odd number and 7214, 3816 and 9436 are even numbers.

9. (b)
+6 +7 +8
B C H I O P W X
2 3 8 9 15 16 23 24
+6 +7 +8
Finally, the missing term is BC.

10. (b) $144=(12)^2 \rightarrow 12$
$256=(16)^2 \rightarrow (12+4)=16$
$400=(20)^2 \rightarrow (16+4)=20$
Similarly,
$576=(24)^2 \rightarrow (20+4)=24$
Finally, the missing term is 576.

11. (a)
5 →(+2.5) 7.5 →(+5) 12.5 →(+10) 22.5 →(+20) 42.5
Finally, the missing term is 42.5.

12. (a) According to statements, option (a) is correct.

13. (a) According to question, the sequence is :
Jyoti > Vineet > Raman > Deepak > Sumit.

14. (b) According to dictionary, the arrangement of words is
(i) Rainbow, (iv) Rainy, (ii) Rancour, (iii) Rattle.

15. (a) If,

B	O	R	R	O	W
↓	↓	↓	↓	↓	↓
7	6	9	9	6	5

and

B	O	M	B
↓	↓	↓	↓
7	6	4	7

Then,

W	O	M	B
↓	↓	↓	↓
5	6	4	7

Finally, **WOMB** is written in code language as 5647.

16. (d) $5+15+10=30$
$\Rightarrow 4+17+9=30$
$\Rightarrow 10+?+10=30$
$\Rightarrow ?+20=30$
$\therefore ?=(30-20)=10$

17. (c) Given expression = 7 B 17 C 88 D 11 A 6
$=7-17+88\div 11\times 6$
$=7-17+8\times 6$
$=7-17+48$
$=55-17=38$

18. (a) A[B]BC/[A]BBC/[A]BB[C]
The series ABBC ABBC ABBC
So, the set of letters BAAC completes the series.

19. (d)

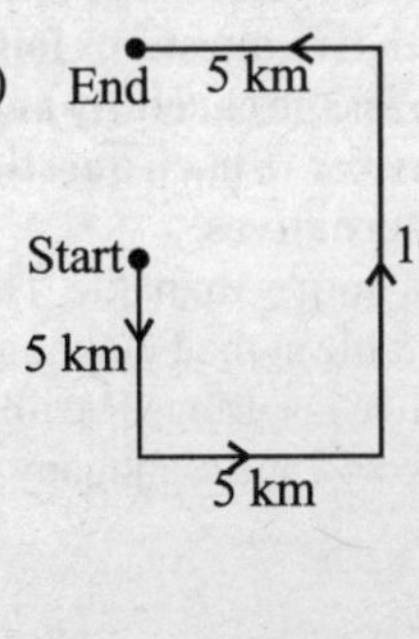

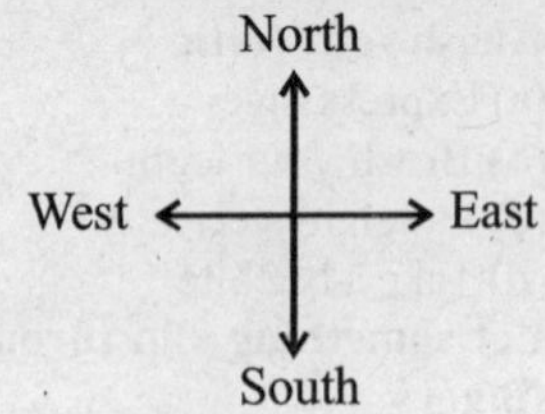

So, Rahul is now in north direction from his initial position.

20. (a) According to question, Johnny is son of Nisha.

21. (b)

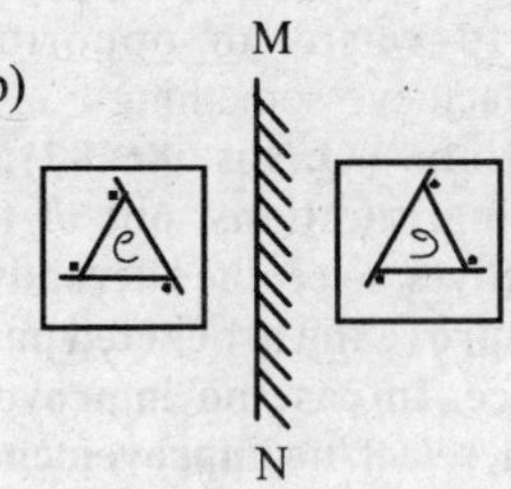

22. (d) The Indian can be doctor and doctor can be smoker or not. So the best relationship among these is:

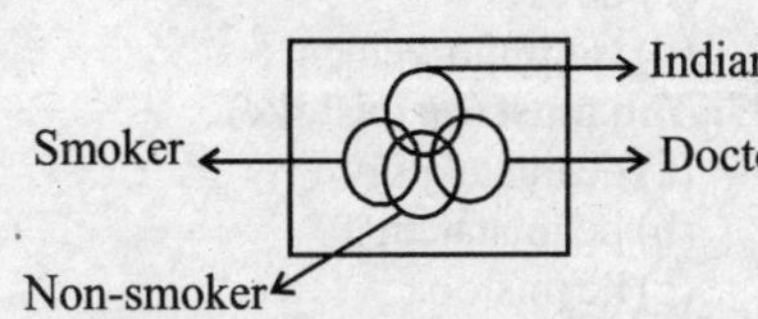

23. (a) A piece of paper is folded and punched, when opened it will appear as given below:

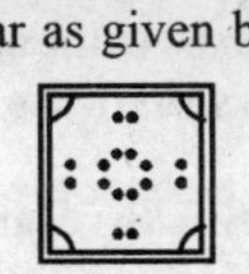

24. (a)

25. (d) J = 00, 02, 11, 13, (20)
O = 12, 14, (23), 32, 41
I = 67, 68, 75, (86)
N = 21, 43, 79, 85, 88, (97) 99
For JOIN, the set of word is, 20, 23, 86, 97

26. (b) The 'Great Stupa' at Sanchi is the oldest structure and was originally commissioned by the emperor Ashoka the Great in the 3rd century BCE. Ashoka belonged to the Mauryan Empire and most of the Buddhist monuments were build during this period only.

27. (c) Gulzar won Oscars in the category of Best Original Song for the song 'Jai Ho' in movie named Slumdog Millionaire.

28. (d) The major function of haemoglobin is to transport oxygen from the lungs to the body's tissues and then transport carbon dioxide out of the tissue back to the lungs.

29. (a) Bryophyta, traditional name for any nonvascular seedless plant. In contrast to vascular plants, the bryophyte sporophyte usually lacks a complex vascular system and produces only one spore-containing organ (sporangium) rather than many.

30. (c)

Scientific Name	**Animal**
Sauria lacertidae	Lizard
Crocodylus niloticus	Crocodile
Hippopotamus amphibious	Hippopotamus
Musca domestica	House fly

31. (a) Soap is produced by a saponification or basic hydrolysis reaction of fat or oil. Currently, sodium carbonate or sodium hydroxide is used to neutralise the fatty acid and convert it to the salt.

32. (b)

33. (c) Operating System is the low-level software that supports a computer's basic functions, such as scheduling tasks and controlling peripherals. Hypertext Markup Language (HTML), a standardised system for tagging text files to achieve font, colour, graphic, and hyperlink effects on World Wide Web pages. All others are operating systems.

34. (c) The Chapchar Kut is a festival of Mizoram, India. It is celebrated during March after completion of their most arduous task of Jhum operation i.e., jungle-clearing (clearing of the remnants of burning). It is a spring festival celebrated with great fervor and gaiety.

35. (b)

36. (b) In Economics, a depression is a sustained, long-term downturn in economic activity in one or more economies. The value of money depreciates in this phase which leads to increase in Inventory stock.

37. (a) SARS is caused by a member of the coronavirus family of viruses (the same family that can cause the common cold). It is believed that the 2003 epidemic started when the virus spread from small mammals in China. When someone with SARS coughs or sneezes, infected droplets spray into the air.

38. (d) Eutrophication refers to the excessive richness of nutrients in a lake or other body of water, frequently due to run-off from the land, which causes a dense growth of plant life. Biomagnification, also known as bioamplification or biological magnification, is the increasing concentration of a substance, such as a toxic chemical, in the tissues of organisms at successively higher levels in a food chain. Global Warming is the increase of Earth's average surface temperature due to effect of greenhouse gases, such as carbon dioxide emissions from burning fossil fuels or from deforestation, which trap heat that would otherwise escape from Earth.

39. (d) A tax, such as income tax, which is levied on the income or profits of the person who pays it, rather than on goods or services is called as direct tax. Key examples of direct taxes are Income tax, Wealth tax, Corporation tax.

40. (c) The Radcliffe Line was published on August 17, 1947 as a boundary demarcation line between India and Pakistan upon the Partition of India. It was named after its architect, Sir Cyril Radcliffe, who as chairman of the Border Commissions. McMahon line is between India and China. Sir Creek is a 96 km tidal estuary on the border of India and Pakistan. The Creek, which opens up into the Arabian Sea, divides the Gujarat State of India from the Sindh province of Pakistan. The Maginot Line named after the French Minister of War Andre Maginot, was a line of concrete fortifications, obstacles, and weapon installations built by France in the 1930s to deter invasion by Germany. Constructed on the Fench side of its borders with Switzerland, Germany, and Luxembourg.

41. (b)

City	**River**
Bengaluru	Vrishabhavathi
Cuttack	Mahanadi
Badrinath	Alaknanda
Kota	Chambal

42. (c) The Battle of Haldighati was fought in Haldighati, Rajasthan on June 18 or 21, 1576 for around four hours between Rana of Mewar, Maharana Pratap and Mughal Emperor Akbar's forces led by Man Singh I.

43. (a) The discovery of the sea route to India is the description sometimes used in Europe and among the Portuguese for the first recorded trip made directly from Europe to India via the Atlantic Ocean. It was undertaken under the command of Portuguese explorer Vasco da Gama during the reign of King Manuel I in 1497-1499.

44. (d) Felix Hoffmann, a German chemist, produced a stable form of acetylsalicylic acid, more commonly known as aspirin, in 1897. Aspiring is used to reduce fever and relieve mild to moderate pain from conditions such as muscle aches, toothaches, common cold, and headaches. Aspirin is known as a salicylate and a nonsteroidal anti-inflammatory durg (NSAID).

45. (b)

46. (d)

Physical Quantity	**Unit**
Electyrical Conductance	Siemens
Magnetic flux	Weber
Inductance	Henry
Magnetic flux Density	Tesla

47. (a) Article-24 mandates that no child below age of 14 years shall be employed to work any factory or mine or engaged in any other hazardous employment. Article-(12-35) deals with the fundamental rights of the citizen of India.

48. (b)

49. (b) Sachin Tendulkar has scored 100 centuries (100 or more runs) in Test matches and One Day International (ODI) matches, organised by the International Cricket Council. His total of 51 centuries in Test matches and 49 in ODIs is a world record for highest number of centuries by a batsman.

50. (b)

51. (c) $3.352-9.759+x-19.64=7.052$

$\Rightarrow 3.352+x-29.399=7.052$

$\Rightarrow x=7.052-3.352+9.759+19.64$

$=33.099$

52. (d) Square of $(7-4x)$

$=(7-4x)^2=(7)^2+(-4x)^2+2\times 7\times(-4x)$

$=49+16x^2-56x$

$=16x^2-56x+49$

53. (c) Let principal be x in time t at rate of R.

By tricky formula

Difference in S.I. and C.I.,

$$I_D=\frac{R\times I_S}{200},$$

where I_S = Simple Interest

$$3225-3000=\frac{R\times 3000}{200}$$

$$\Rightarrow \quad R=\frac{225\times 200}{3000}$$

$$\Rightarrow \quad R=\frac{75\times 2}{10}$$

$$\Rightarrow \quad R=\frac{15\times 2}{2}\Rightarrow R=15\%$$

54. (b) Discount is always given on marked price, let it be x.

$$\text{S.P.}=\frac{x\times 90}{100}$$

$$90x=100\times 18000$$

$$x=\frac{100\times 18000}{90}=₹20{,}000$$

S.P. on 37.5% discount

$$=\frac{x\times(100-37.5)}{100}$$

$$=\frac{20{,}000\times 62.5}{100}$$

$$=200\times 62.5=₹12{,}500.0$$

55. (a) Let total marks be x

According to question,

$$\Rightarrow \frac{x\times 24}{100}=(61+29)$$

$$\Rightarrow x=\frac{90\times 100}{24}=\frac{15\times 100}{4}$$

$$=15\times 25$$

$\therefore$ $x=375$ marks.

56. (c) Let third proportion be x

$9:15::15:x$

Then, according to questions,

$$\frac{9}{15}=\frac{15}{x}$$

$$9x=15\times 15$$

$$x=\frac{15\times 15}{9}=5\times 5=25$$

Hence, third proportion is 25.

57. (a)
$$x^2-25x+156=0$$
$$\Rightarrow x^2-12x-13x+156=0$$
$$\Rightarrow x(x-12)-13(x-12)=0$$
$$\Rightarrow (x-12)(x-13)=0$$
$$\Rightarrow x-12=0 \text{ or } x-13=0$$
$$x=12, \text{ or } x=13$$

Hence, the roots are 12, 13.

58. (a) Volume of cylinder = Volume of cone

$$\pi R^2H=\frac{1}{3}\pi r^2 h$$

$$\Rightarrow \quad \pi\times 3.5\times 3.5\times H$$

$$=\frac{1}{3}\times\pi\times 3.5\times 3.5\times 9.6$$

$$H=\frac{1}{3}\times 9.6=3.2\text{ cm}$$

Hence, the height of cylinder is 3.2 cm.

59. (c) Let S.P. of one Rolex watch be ₹ x

S.P. of 9 watches = ₹ $9x$.

$$(SP-CP)=\text{Profit}$$
$$(9x-CP)=4x$$
$$(9x-4x)=CP$$
$$C.P.=5x$$

$$\text{Profit percent}=\frac{4x\times 100}{5x}=80\%$$

60. (c) Let side of a square be x

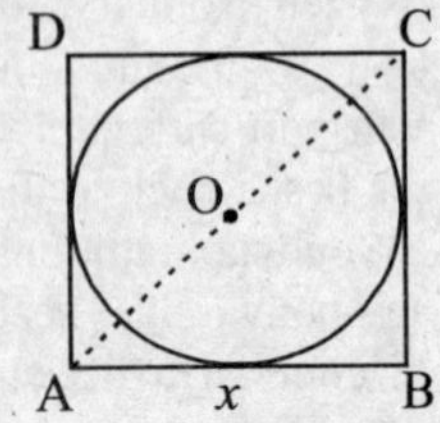

$$AB^2+BC^2=AC^2$$

$$x^2+x^2=\left(14\sqrt{2}\right)^2$$

$$2x^2=196\times 2$$

$$x^2=196$$

$$x=14\text{ cm}$$

Because, the circle is touching both sides of a square so radius

$$=\frac{14}{2}=7\text{ cm}$$

Area of circle $=\pi r^2$

$$=\frac{22}{7}\times 7\times 7=154\text{ cm}^2$$

61. (c) Let sides be $4x$ and x

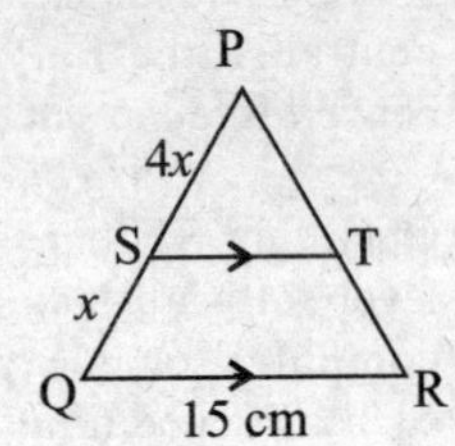

$$\frac{PQ}{PS}=\frac{QR}{ST}\Rightarrow\frac{5x}{4}=\frac{15}{ST}$$

$$ST=\frac{15\times 4}{5}=12\text{ cm}$$

62. (c)
$$\frac{1}{1+\cos A}+\frac{1}{(1-\cos A)}=x$$

$$\Rightarrow \frac{1-\cos A+1+\cos A}{(1+\cos A)(1-\cos A)}=x$$

$$\Rightarrow \frac{2}{1-\cos^2 A}=x$$

$\Rightarrow\ x = \dfrac{2}{\sin^2 A} = 2\ \text{cosec}^2 A$

63. (d) Let three numbers be x_1, x_2 and x_3

Total sum of three numbers

$x_1 + x_2 + x_3 = 64 \times 3 = 192$ ...(i)

$\Rightarrow\ x_1 = \dfrac{1}{3}(x_2 + x_3)$

$\Rightarrow\ 3x_1 = x_2 + x_3$ ...(ii)

On putting, $x_2 + x_3 = 3x_1$ in (i)

$\Rightarrow\ x_1 + 3x_1 = 192$

$\Rightarrow\ 4x_1 = 192$

$\therefore\ x_1 = \dfrac{192}{4} = 48$

64. (d) Ajit is able to finish a job in 30 days

He is able to work in 1 day

$= \dfrac{1}{30}$ part

Badrinath will complete it in 60 days.

Badrinath will complete it in

1 day $= \dfrac{1}{60}$ part

Both will complete in 1 day

$= \dfrac{1}{30} + \dfrac{1}{60}$ part

$= \dfrac{2+1}{60} = \dfrac{3}{60} = \dfrac{1}{20}$ part

Hence, time taken by both = 20 days

65. (a) Let side of a square be x

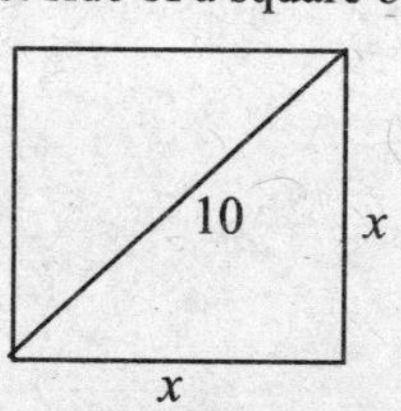

Length of a diagonal = 10

According to questions

$(10)^2 = x^2 + x^2$

$2x^2 = 100$

$\Rightarrow\ x^2 = \dfrac{100}{2} = 50$

Area of square = $x^2 = 50$

Hence, area of square is 50 cm².

66. (c) Average speed of a car

$= \left(\dfrac{2ab}{a+b}\right)$ km/hr

Here, $a = 32$ km/hr,

$b = 68$ km/hr

$= \dfrac{2 \times 32 \times 68}{32 + 68}$

$= \dfrac{2 \times 32 \times 68}{100}$

$= 43.52$ km/h

67. (d) Rate of interest = 20% per half yearly

Equivalent rate for 1 year

$= \left(20 + 20 + \dfrac{20 \times 20}{100}\right)\% = 44\%$

$\therefore$ C.I. $= \dfrac{20000 \times 44}{100} =$ ₹ 8800

68. (d) Speed of first train 150 metre long = 40 kmph

Speed of second train = x *kmph*

Total length of both trains

= (100 + 150) metre

= 250 metre $= \dfrac{1}{4}$ km.

According to the question,

$\dfrac{\text{Total length of trains}}{\text{Relative speed}} = \text{Time}$

$\Rightarrow\ \dfrac{\frac{1}{4}}{x+40} = \dfrac{9}{3600} = \dfrac{1}{400}$

$\Rightarrow\ 4(x+40) = 400$

$\Rightarrow\ x + 40 = 100$

$\Rightarrow\ x = 100 - 40 = 60$ kmph.

69. (a) The population of city 2 years ago

$= \dfrac{P}{\left(1 + \dfrac{R}{100}\right)^2}$

$= \dfrac{26010}{\left(1 + \dfrac{2}{100}\right)^2} = \dfrac{26010}{\left(1 + \dfrac{1}{50}\right)^2}$

$= \dfrac{26010}{\left(\dfrac{51}{50}\right)^2} = \dfrac{26010 \times 50 \times 50}{51 \times 51}$

$= 25000$

70. (c) C.P. of article = ₹$\left(\dfrac{100}{50} \times 18450\right)$

= ₹ 36900

To gain 50%, S.P. of article

= ₹$\dfrac{(36900 \times 150)}{100}$ = ₹ 55350

71. (c) New average will increase by 5.

i.e., New average = A + 5

Illustration :

$\dfrac{2+4+6}{3} = \dfrac{12}{3} = 4;$

$\dfrac{2+4+6+8}{4} = \dfrac{20}{4} = 5;$

$\dfrac{2+4+6+8+10}{5} = \dfrac{30}{5} = 6.$

72. (d) Let each son's share be = ₹ x

Each daughter's share = ₹ $1.5x$

Wife's share = ₹ $(x - 600)$

According to the question,

$3x + 2 \times 1.5x + x - 600 = 19000$

$\Rightarrow\ 3x + 3x + x = 19000 + 600 = 19600$

$\Rightarrow\ 7x = 19600$

$\Rightarrow\ x = \dfrac{19600}{7} =$ ₹ 2800

$\therefore$ Total share of three sons

= ₹ (3 × 2800) = ₹ 8400

73. (b) Marks obtained by all students in Math

= 96 + 99 + 99 + 89 + 92 = 475

In Science = 90 + 94 + 99 + 96 + 92 = 471

74. (c) Total marks of student 3 = 89 + 99 + 99 + 92 = 379

75. (b) Sum of four maximum marks of

Student-3 = 100 + 99 + 99 + 92 = 390

Student-2 = 100 + 99 + 94 + 89 = 382

Student-5 = 100 + 95 + 92 + 92 = 379

Student-4 = 100 + 96 + 91 + 89 = 376

76. (a) Besides will be used in place of beside as besides means 'apart from or beyond' while beside means 'next to'.

77. (a) 'after' will be replaced by 'next' as after does not make any sense and next is used here for the coming morning.

78. (a) 'perverse' is the correct word fill in the blank as it makes the correct sense and it means behaving on a way that is unreasonable or unacceptable.

79. (d)

80. (a) 'Fossilise' and 'amalgamate' are the synonyms as both the words mean 'to make or become solid or integrate.'

81. (c) 'Depict' and 'characterise' are the synonyms as both the words mean 'portray in words or describe.'

82. (b) 'Concur' will be the opposite in meaning to the word 'differ' as differ means 'disagree' while 'concur' means agree.

83. (d) 'Blockage' will be the opposite in meaning to the word 'salve' as it means 'to ease or comfort' while 'blockage' means 'to hamper or clog'.

84. (a) 'Gnash your teeth' means to complain angrily and noisily about something, so 'express rage' is the correct answer.

85. (d) 'Let something slip through one's fingers' means to waste an opportunity to achieve something, so the given option (d) is correct.

86. (a) 'to do' should be used in place of 'to do it' in the sentence to make it grammatically correct.

87. (b) 'be mistaken' will be used in place of 'be mistake' as it is a Passive Voice so third form of Verb 'mistake' will be used to make it grammatically correct.

88. (a) 'Thorough' will be the correct word as a substitute of 'complete with regard to every detail'.

89. (d) 'Volition' is the correct word which can be the substitute of 'the faculty or power of using one's will'.

90. (c)

91. (d)

92. (d) 'ZXY' will be the correct sequence. (Evidently it was too dry for game, and with the exception of a deadly looking cobra or two we saw no reptiles.)

93. (b)

94. (d)

95. (a) 'The watchman shouted to the crowd to catch the thief' is the correct indirect speech of the given sentence.

96. (a)

97. (d)

98. (a)

99. (c)

100. (b)

SSC Constable(GD)

Practice Set-2

PART-A
GENERAL INTELLIGENCE AND REASONING

Directions (Q. No. 1-4) : Select the related word/letters/number from the given alternatives.

1. Iraq : Dinar :: Korea: ?
(a) Pound (b) Yen
(c) Dollar (d) Won

2. AOE : ? : : GMA : IUO
(a) MXI (b) MWS
(c) MWI (d) MXJ

3. DeF : Ihg : : wxY : ?
(a) bAZ (b) Baz
(c) BaZ (d) baz

4. 81 : 121 : : 49 : ?
(a) 81 (b) 62
(c) 52 (d) 100

Directions (Q. No. 5-7) : Select the odd word/letters/number/number pair from the given alternatives.

5. (a) BEH (b) DGJ
(c) HKN (d) MNO

6. (a) 5210 (b) 8432
(c) 8648 (d) 7240

7. (a) 81 (b) 125
(c) 64 (d) 198

Directions (Q. Nos. 8-10) : A series is given with one term missing. Choose the correct alternative from the given ones that will complete the series.

8. ijk, mno, lmn, pqr, opq,?
(a) stv (b) suv
(c) stu (d) stt

9. AZ, BY, CX,?
(a) CW (b) DW
(c) DX (d) DY

10. 23, 32, 42, 53, 65, ?
(a) 78 (b) 88
(c) 58 (d) 98

11. In the following question, two statements are given each followed by two conclusions I and II. You have to consider the statements to be true even if they seem to be at variance from commonly known facts. You have to decide which of the given conclusions, if any follows from the given statements.

Statements :
(I) Life is a journey with few known people, few partially known and mostly strangers.
(II) In a journey, the importance of destination is as equal as the pathway of reaching that destination.

Conclusions :
(I) Importance of people in life is considerable, as they are our journey mates.
(II) Life teaches us many lessons to face various known and unknown difficulties.

(a) Only conclusion II follows
(b) Conclusion I and II both follow
(c) Neither I nor II follow
(d) Only conclusion I follows

12. B is older than C but not as old as D. E is not as old as B. Who is the oldest of all?
(a) B (b) E
(c) C (d) D

13. Arrange the given words in the sequence in which they occur in the dictionary.
i. Stable **ii. Stranger**
iii. Stability **iv. Struggle**
(a) iii, ii, i, iv (b) iii, i, ii, iv
(c) iii, iv, i, ii (d) iv, i, ii, iii

14. In a certain code language "TITANIC" is written as "7371835" and "SEMATIC" is written as "6241735". How will "MAINTAIN" be written in that code language?
(a) 41387138 (b) 43187138
(c) 41837138 (d) 41783138

15. In the following qustions, select the missing number from the given series.

6	5	4
7	6	5
5	7	6
37	23	?

(a) 10 (b) 12
(c) 13 (d) 14

16. After interchanging + & × and 12 &18, which of the following equations will hold true?
(a) $(9+1)\times 18 = 60$
(b) $(18+6)\times 12 = 90$
(c) $(12+18)\times 12 = 72$
(d) $(12+6)\times 18 = 36$

17. In the following question, which one set of letters when sequentially placed at the gaps in the given letter series shall complete it?
ab_bc_bb__abb_c
(a) babcb (b) bbaaa
(c) aabbc (d) abcbc

18. I am facing north. I turn left and walk 30 m. Then I turn right and walk 20 m, then I turn left and walk 10 m and then turning right and walk 50 m. Then I turn left and walk 50 m. In which direction am I from the starting point?
(a) North (b) South
(c) North-west (d) North-east

19. Raju introduces Yash by saying, "He is the husband of the granddaughter of my grandmother's husband". How is Yash related to Raju?
(a) Nephew
(b) Father
(c) Brother
(d) Brother-in-law

20. Identify the diagram that best represents the relationship among the given classes.
Kitchen, Utensils, Glass

(a) 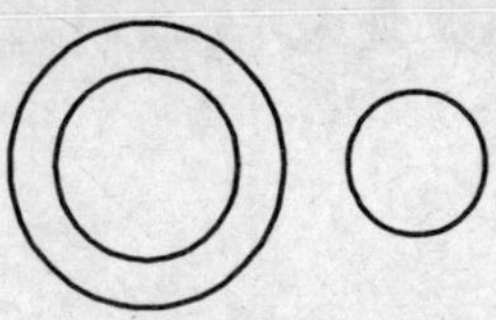

(b) 

(c) 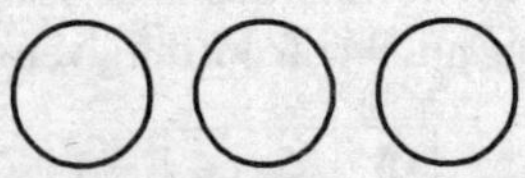

(d) 

21. If a mirror is placed on the line XY, then which of the answer figure is the right image of the given figure ?
Question Figure :

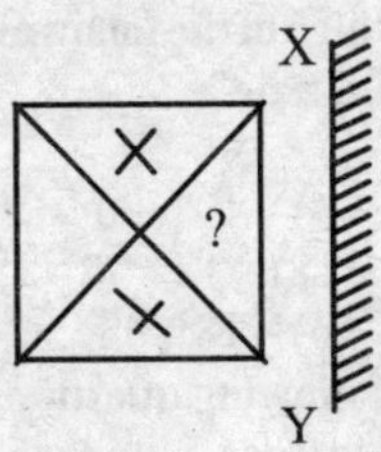

Answer Figures :

(a) 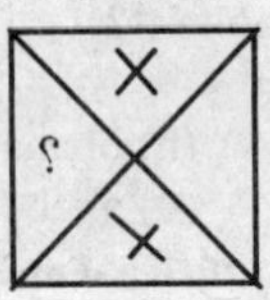

(b) 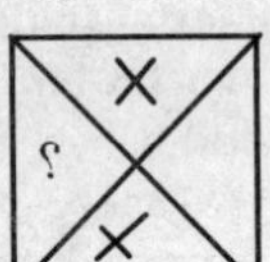

(c) 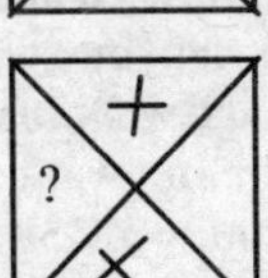

(d) 

22. A piece of paper is folded and punched as shown below in the question figures. From the given answer figures, indicate how it will appear when opened.
Question Figures :

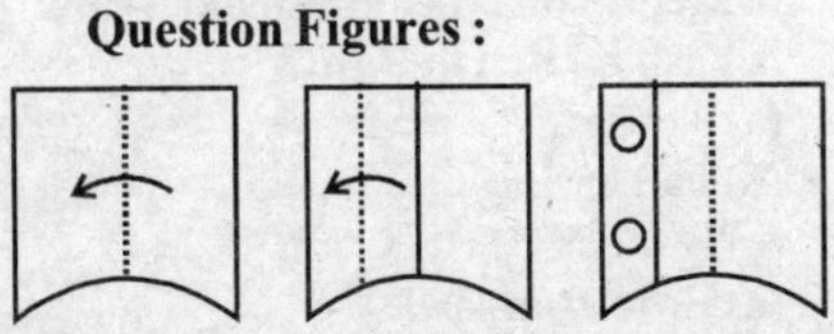

Answer Figures :

(a) 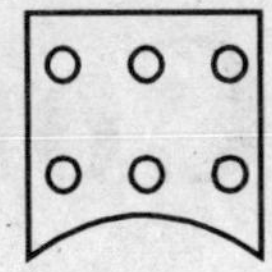

(b) 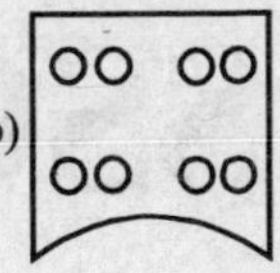

(c) 

(d) 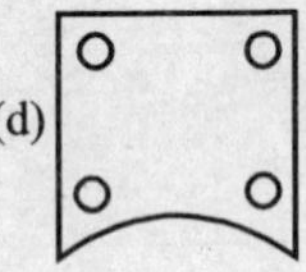

23. Three positions of a cube are shown below. What will come opposite to face containing '1' ?

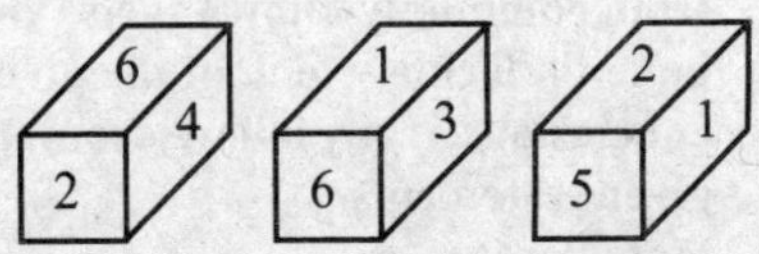

(a) 2 (b) 3
(c) 4 (d) 6

24. Which answer figure will complete the pattern in the question figure ?
Question Figure :

Answer Figures :

(a) 

(b) 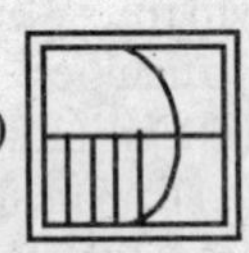

(c) 

(d) 

25. A word is represented by only one set of number as given any one of the alternatives. The sets of numbers given in the alternatives are represented by two classes of alphabets as shown in the given two matrices. The column and rows of Matrix-I are numbered from 0 to 4 and that of Matrix-II are numbered from 5 to 9. A letter by its column, for example, 'M' can be represented by 10, 03 etc. and 'H' can be represented by 55, 78 etc. Similarly, you have to identify the set for the word 'MATHS'.

Matrix-I

	0	1	2	3	4
0	T	S	N	M	E
1	M	T	S	N	E
2	S	E	M	T	N
3	N	M	E	S	T
4	E	N	T	S	M

Matrix-II

	5	6	7	8	9
5	H	G	I	P	A
6	G	H	A	I	P
7	A	I	G	H	I
8	I	P	H	A	G
9	P	A	P	G	H

(a) 03, 59, 11, 78, 43
(b) 10, 67, 22, 55, 01
(c) 22, 75, 00, 66, 21
(d) 44, 88, 23, 98, 20

PART-B
GENERAL KNOWLEDGE AND GENERAL AWARENESS

26. Chemical formula of washing soda is
(a) $Na_2SO_4.10H_2O$ (b) $NaHCO_3$
(c) $Na_2CO_3.10H_2O$ (d) $Ca(OH)_2$

27. Hydrochloric acid is also known as
(a) Galic acid (b) Picric acid
(c) Muriatic acid (d) Chloric acid

28. Khangchendzonga National Park is located at
(a) Uttar Pradesh
(b) West Bengal
(c) Sikkim
(d) Jammu and Kashmir

29. Biosphere Reserve of India Nanda Devi is located in the state of
(a) Uttarakhand
(b) Sikkim
(c) Meghalaya
(d) Himachal Pradesh

30. In a desert region, soil erosion can be checked by
(a) Contour ploughing
(b) Using farm manure
(c) Tree plantation/Afforestaion
(d) Crop rotation

31. The first oil refinery in India was set up at
(a) Barauni
(b) Vishakhapatnam
(c) Digboi
(d) Mumbai

32. The chemical name of baking soda is
(a) Sodium carbonate
(b) Sodium bicarbonate
(c) Sodium chloride
(d) Sodium nitrate

33. The name of the train "Shatabdi Express" refers to the centenary of
(a) Mahatma Gandhi
(b) Indian National Congress
(c) India's War of Independence
(d) Jawaharlal Nehru

34. Which one of the following is not a rabi crop ?
(a) Mustard (b) Rice
(c) Wheat (d) Gram

35. The driest part of India is
(a) Western Rajasthan
(b) Jammu and Kashmir
(c) Gujarat
(d) Madhya Pradesh

36. "Mumbai High" is associated with
(a) Steel (b) Petroleum
(c) Mausoleum (d) Jute

37. Which one of the following goods has only exchange value ?
(a) Diamond (b) Television
(c) Computer (d) Rice

38. The power to decide an Election Petition for the State is vested in the
(a) Parliament
(b) Supreme Court
(c) High Courts
(d) Election Commission

39. How many items are there in the Union List ?
(a) 52 (b) 66
(c) 97 (d) 99

40. What is the maximum gap permissible between two sessions of Parliament ?
(a) One month
(b) Three months
(c) Six months
(d) Twelve months

41. When were the Fundamental Duties incorporated in the Constitution ?
(a) 1975 (b) 1976
(c) 1977 (d) 1979

42. The number of Nationalised Banks in India is
(a) 14 (b) 21
(c) 20 (d) 22

43. Rift Valley is formed
(a) between two anticlines
(b) between two faults
(c) erosion of synclinal basin
(d) due to volcanic eruption

44. Lake formed by Aswan Dam in Africa is
(a) Chad (b) Victoria
(c) Nasser (d) Tanganyika

45. How many judges are there in Supreme Court ?
(a) 25 (b) 26
(c) 30 (d) 31

46. During the reign of Bindusara there was unrest at
(a) Ujjayani
(b) Pushkalavati
(c) Taxila
(d) Rajagriha

47. Widening of a river valley takes place due to
(a) Corrosion
(b) Lateral erosion
(c) Corrasion
(d) Hydraulic action

48. Water of coconut is
(a) liquid nucellus
(b) liquid mesocarp
(c) liquid endocarp
(d) degenerated liquid endosperm

49. Bulbils takes part in
(a) Sexual reproduction
(b) Vegetative reproduction
(c) Food storage
(d) Respiration

50. Fish is a first class protein as it contains
(a) essential amino-acids
(b) non-essential amino acids
(c) all essential fatty acids
(d) no amino acid

PART-C
ELEMENTARY MATHEMATICS

51. Coefficient of x^2 in $4x^3 - 2x^2 + 2x - 3$ is:
(a) 6 (b) –2
(c) 3 (d) –3

52. If a merchant offers a discount of 40% on the list price, then he makes a loss of 10%. What % profit or % loss will he make if he sells at a discount of 20% on the list price?
(a) 4 percent loss
(b) 14 percent profit
(c) 5.5 percent loss
(d) 20 percent profit

53. The mean of marks secured by 60 students in division A of class X is 66, 45 students of division B is 62 and that of 75 students of division C is 60. Find the mean of marks of the students of three divisions of class X.
(a) 61.8 (b) 62.5
(c) 61.1 (d) 63.9

54. On dividing $221a^2b^2$ by $13b^2$, we get :
(a) $17a^2$ (b) $17b^2$
(c) $13a^2b^2$ (d) 13

55. A missile travels at 1116 km/h. How many metres does it travel in one second?
(a) 360 metres (b) 368 metres
(c) 310 metres (d) 348 metres

56. If the radius of a circle is increased by 31% its area increases by :
(a) 62 percent
(b) 31 percent
(c) 35.805 percent
(d) 71.61 percent

57. A bank offers 20% compound interest per half year. A customer deposits ₹ 6,000 each on 1st January and 1st July of a year. At the end of the year, the amount he would have gained by way of interest is—
(a) ₹ 7680 (b) ₹ 3840
(c) ₹ 1920 (d) ₹ 960

58. The third proportional of two numbers 4 and 28 is :
(a) 52 (b) 56
(c) 84 (d) 196

59. Mummy can bake 75 cakes in 15 hours, Mummy and Sister together can bake 120 cakes in 20 hours. How many cakes sister can bake in 30 hours?
(a) 45 (b) 30
(c) 60 (d) 10

60. A rice trader buys 20 quintals of rice for ₹ 8,580. However, 22% rice is lost in transportation. At what rate should he sell to earn 20% profit?
(a) ₹ 278.8 per quintal
(b) ₹ 514.8 per quintal
(c) ₹ 660 per quintal
(d) ₹ 654.2 per quintal

61. What is the equation of the line which has 3/1 and –4/7 as x and y intercept respectively?
(a) $8x - 21y = -12$
(b) $8x + 21y = 14$
(c) $8x - 21y = 12$
(d) $8x + 21y = -14$

62. A tetrahedron has 4 vertices. How many edges does it have?
(a) 8 (b) 12
(c) 6 (d) 10

63. The circumference of a circle is equal to the perimeter of an equilateral triangle. If the radius of the circle is 14cm what is the length of the side of the equilateral triangle?
(a) 88 cm (b) 88/3 cm
(c) 88/√3 cm (d) 88√3 cm

64. If the curved surface area of a right circular cone is 10010 sq cm and its radius is 35 cm, find its volume?
(a) 6930 cubic cm
(b) 13860 cubic cm
(c) 3465 cubic cm
(d) 27720 cubic cm

65. sin (A + B) – sin (A – B) is equal to
(a) 2sinAcosB (b) 2cosAcosB
(c) 2cosAsinB (d) 2sinAsinB

66. The simple interest on a sum of money for 10 years is ₹ 3130. If the principal becomes 5 times after 5 years, what will be the total interest (in ₹) obtained after 10 years ?
(a) 6260 (b) 7825
(c) 9390 (d) 15650

67. Aman and Kapil start from Delhi and Gwalior respectively towards each other at the same time. They meet at Mathura and then take 196 minutes and 225 minutes respectively to reach Gwalior and Delhi. If speed of Aman is 30 km/hr, what is the speed (in km/hr) of Kapil ?
(a) 28 (b) 30
(c) $\frac{225}{7}$ (d) $\frac{392}{15}$

68. The number of trees in a town is 17640. If the number of trees increases annually at the rate of 5%, how many trees were there 2 years ago ?
(a) 14000 (b) 15000
(c) 16000 (d) 19450

69. Average age of team having 12 players is 23 years. If the age of the coach is also included, then the average age increases by 2 years. What is the age (in years) of the coach ?
(a) 41 (b) 47
(c) 49 (d) 51

70. The length, breadth and height of a cuboid are in the ratio 19 : 11 : 13. If length is 30 cm more than height, then what is the volume in (cm^3) of this cuboid ?
(a) 81510 (b) 89665
(c) 195300 (d) 339625

71. An article is listed at ₹ 2375. A man purchases it at two successive discounts of 50% and 25% and spends ₹ 165 on repairing of article. If he sells the article at a profit of 62.5%, what is the selling price (in ₹) of the article ?
(a) 1467.6 (b) 1492.6
(c) 1715.39 (d) 1467.6

72. Nirmit can do $\frac{2}{3}$rd of a job in 18 days. Kashish is twice as efficient as Nirmit. In how many days will Kashish complete the job ?
(a) $\frac{29}{4}$ (b) $\frac{27}{2}$
(c) $\frac{31}{2}$ (d) $\frac{13}{2}$

Directions (Q. 73-75) : The table given below shows the percentage of literate people in 6 cities. This table also shows the ratio of males to females among literate poeple.

City	% of literate People	Males : Females
1	80	4 : 5
2	85	7 : 4
3	78	3 : 2
4	63	1 : 1
5	92	9 : 7
6	58	2 : 3

% of literate people of any city = (Literate people of the city/Total population of the city) × 100

73. If the total population of city 4 is 600000, then how many literate people are there in city 4?
(a) 480000 (b) 378000
(c) 468000 (d) 348000

74. Total population of city 6 is 200000 and the total population of city-2 is 220000. What is the respective ratio of literate males of city 2 and literate females of city 6?
(a) 348 : 595 (b) 255 : 199
(c) 595 : 348 (d) 199 : 255

75. If there are 259210 literate females in city 5, what is the total population of city 5?
(a) 644000 (b) 354200
(c) 690000 (d) 483000

PART-D
ENGLISH

76. In the following question, out of the four alternatives, choose the word which best expresses the meaning of the given word.
ENIGMA
(a) Attractive (b) Riddle
(c) Flare-up (d) Dream

77. In the following question, out of the four alternatives, choose the word which is opposite in meaning to the given word.
INERTIA
(a) Stupor (b) Vigour
(c) Languor (d) Inertness

78. Four words are given, out of which only one word is spelt correctly. Choose the correctly spelt word.
(a) Pious (b) Pios
(c) Pieos (d) Piuos

Directions (Q. 79–81) : In the following questions, one part of the sentence may have an error. Find out which part of the sentence has an error and choose the option corresponding to it. If the sentence is free from error, choose the "No error" option.

79. Each child (a)/ was given a (b)/red beautiful balloon. (c)/ No error (d)

80. She has had the best medical facilities available (a)/ but she will not be cured (b)/ unless she does not have a strong desire to live. (c)/ No error (d)

81. As if aware of my condition (a)/ the infuriated bird suddenly doubled back on its course (b)/ and charged straight after me. (c)/ No error (d)

Directions (Q. 82–84): The sentences given with blanks are to be filled with an

appropriate word(s). Four alternatives are suggested for each question. For each question, choose the correct alternative.

82. The passengers were afraid but the captain _______ them that there was no danger.

(a) suggested (b) pleaded
(c) advise (d) assured

83. I insisted _______ his leaving the place.

(a) on (b) about
(c) in (d) with

84. Please don't _______ me when I'm speaking.

(a) interrupted (b) interrupts
(c) interrupt (d) interrupting

Directions (Q. 85–87): In each of the questions, four alternatives are given for the Idiom/Phrase. Choose the alternative which best expresses the meaning of the Idiom/Phrase.

85. Beat around the bush

(a) Walk around the forest
(b) Clean the bushy areas
(c) Avoiding the main topic
(d) Play around the forest

86. Make room

(a) Clean the room
(b) Make space
(c) Attain the room
(d) Make a clean sweep

87. Mend your ways

(a) Happy with one's behaviour
(b) Sad with one's behaviour
(c) Destroy one's behaviour
(d) Improve one's behaviour

Directions (Q. 88–90): In the following questions, out of the four alternatives, choose the one which can be substituted for the given words/sentences.

88. A record of one's own life written by oneself

(a) History
(b) Biography
(c) Bibliography
(d) Autobiography

89. Belong to the same period

(a) Comrades
(b) Contemporaries
(c) Compromises
(d) Renegades

90. One who listens secretly to private conversation

(a) Eavesdropper (b) Encroacher
(c) Eaves bearer (d) Listener

Directions (Q. 91–95): In each of the following questions, a sentence/a part of the sentence is printed in Italic. Four alternatives are given to the bold part which will improve the sentence. Choose the correct alternative corresponding to it. In case no improvement is needed, choose the option corresponding to "No improvement".

91. You must complete this work *up to Sunday.*

(a) within Sunday
(b) by Sunday
(c) on to Sunday
(d) No improvement

92. *Hole* wheat bread is good for health.

(a) Whole
(b) Healthy
(c) Holed
(d) No improvement

93. She has no pen to *write.*

(a) write with
(b) write at
(c) write in
(d) No improvement

94. He dislikes the word, *isn't he*?

(a) doesn't he?
(b) didn't he ?
(c) does he?
(d) No improvement

95. He is one of *those who likes to help others.*

(a) those persons who like to help others
(b) those who like to help the other
(c) those who like to help others
(d) No improvement

Directions (Q. 96–100) : A passage is given with 5 questions following it. Read the passage carefully and choose the best answer to each question out of the four alternatives.

Crude mineral oil comes out of the earth as a thick brown or black liquid with strong smell. It is a complex mixture of many different substances, each with its own individual qualities. Most of them are combinations of hydrogen and carbon in varying proportions. Such hydrocarbons are also found in other forms such as bitumen, asphalt and natural gas. Mineral oil originates from the carcasses of tiny animals and from plants that live in the sea. Over million of years, these dead creatures form large deposits under sea-bed and ocean currents cover them with a blanket of sand and silt. As this material hardens, it becomes sedimentary rock and effectively shuts out the oxygen, thus preventing the complete decomposition of the marine deposits underneath. The layers of sedimentary rocks become thicker, and heavier. Their pressure produces heat, which transforms the tiny carcasses into crude oil in a process that is still going on today.

96. How does crude oil come out of the earth?

(a) Thick brown or black liquid with mild smell
(b) Thick red brown liquid with strong smell
(c) Mixture of different colours
(d) Thick brown or black liquid with a strong smell

97. What is crude mineral oil?

(a) Complex mixture of many different substances
(b) Simple mixture of natural gas
(c) Plain white oil
(d) It is bitumen

98. From where does mineral oil originate?

(a) Complex mixture of substances
(b) Carcasses of tiny animals and plants that live in the sea
(c) From lakes
(d) Only from plants

99. The time taken for the marine deposits to harden into rocks is

(a) a few centuries
(b) millions of years
(c) a few decades
(d) thousands of years

100. Sedimentary rocks lead to the formation of oil deposits because

(a) their pressure produces heat and turns deposits of animal carcasses and plants into oil
(b) it turns heavy and shuts out the oxygen
(c) it becomes hard and forms into rocks to squeeze oil
(d) it becomes light and soft and applies pressure to produce oil

Answers

1. (d) As, Iraq's currency is Dinar. Similarly, Korea's currency is won.

2. (c) As, 

Similarly, 

Finally the missing term is MWI.

3. (b) As, Similarly,

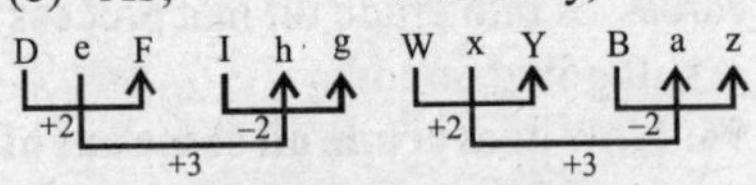

Finally the missing term is Baz.

4. (a) As, $81 \rightarrow 121$

$9+2=11 \Rightarrow (11)^2=121$

Similarly,

$49 \rightarrow 81$

$7+2=9 \Rightarrow (9)^2=81$

Finally the missing number is 81.

5. (d)

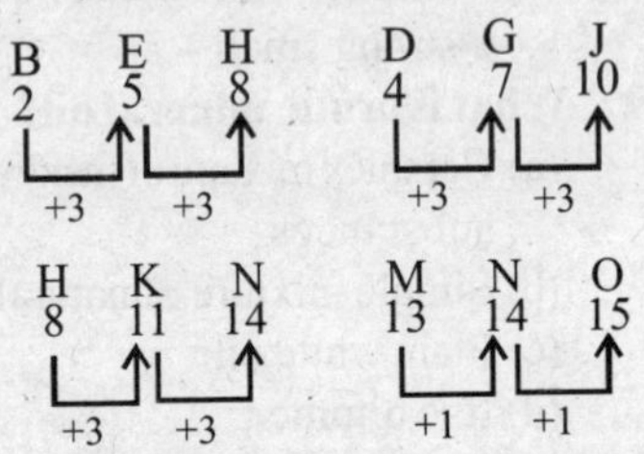

Finally the odd word pair is MNO.

6. (d) $5210=5\times2=10$

$8432=8\times4=32$

$8648=8\times 6=48$

$7240=7\times 2=14$

Finally the odd number is 7240.

7. (d) $81=(9)^2$

$125=(5)^3$

$64=(4)^3$

$198=(14)^2+2$

Finally the odd number is 198.

8. (c)

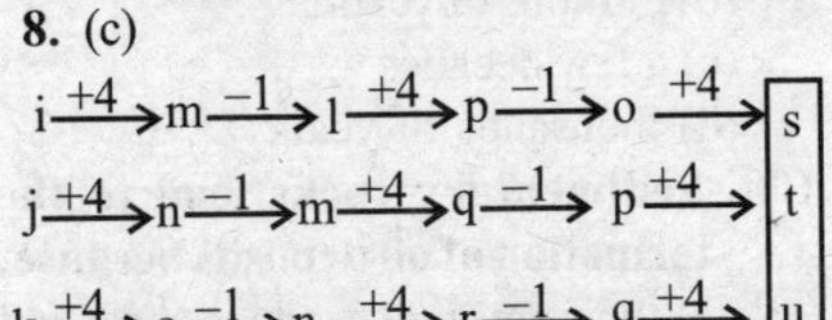

Finally the missing term is stu.

9. (b)

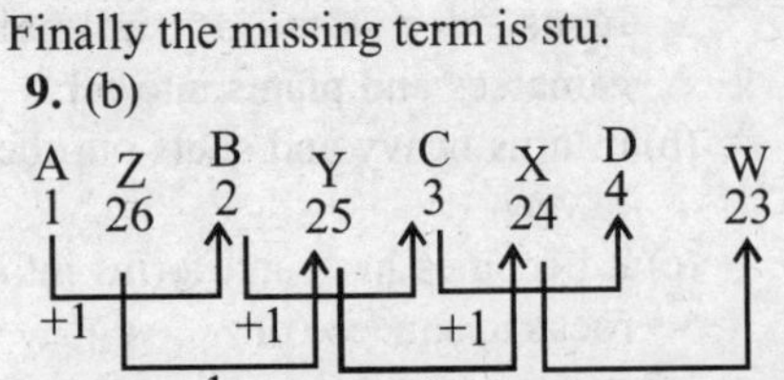

Finally the missing term is DW.

10. (a) The sequence of the series is :

$23+9=32$

$32+10=42$

$42+11=53$

$53+12=65$

$65+13=78$

Finally the missing term is 78.

11. (d) According to statements, only conclusion I follows.

12. (d) According to question, the sequence is :

$D>B>C>E$

Finally D is oldest of all.

13. (b) According to dictionary. The arrangement of the words is given below—

(iii) Stability

(i) Stable

(ii) Stranger

(iv) Struggle

Finally (iii), (i), (ii), (iv) is right sequence.

14. (a) As, And

T I T A N I C → 7 3 7 1 8 3 5

S E M A T I C → 6 2 4 1 7 3 5

Similarly

∴ M A I N T A I N → 4 1 3 8 7 1 3 8

15. (d) As, $6\times7-5=37$

and

$5\times6-7=23$

similarly

$4\times5-6=14$

Finally the missing number is 14.

16. (b) $+ \longrightarrow \times$

$\times \longrightarrow +$

$18 \longrightarrow 12$

$12 \longrightarrow 18$

$\Rightarrow (18+6)\times12=90$

$\Rightarrow (12\times6)+18=90$

$\Rightarrow (72+18)=90$

$\Rightarrow 90=90$

17. (a) ab[b]bc[a]bb[b][c]abb[b]c

The series becomes abbbc abbbc abbbc

Finally the set of letters is babcb.

18. (c)

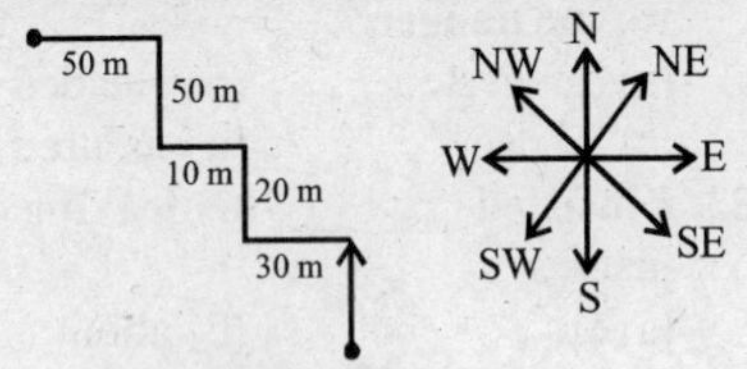

Finally 9 am in North-west direction from the starting point.

19. (d)

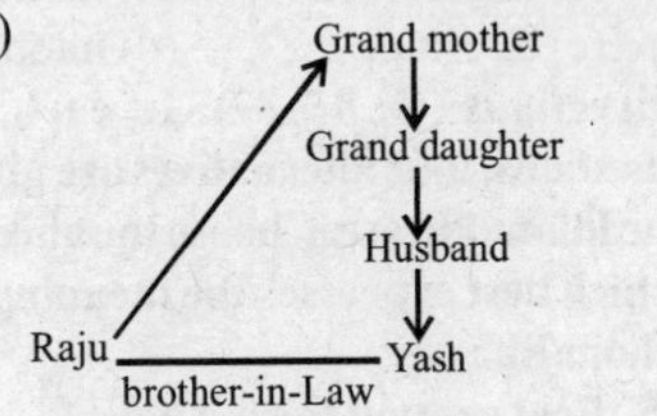

Finally Yash is Brother-in-law of Raju.

20. (b) Kitchen, Utensils, glass are complements of each other because, utensils and glass are in kitchen. So the best representeation among them is given below—

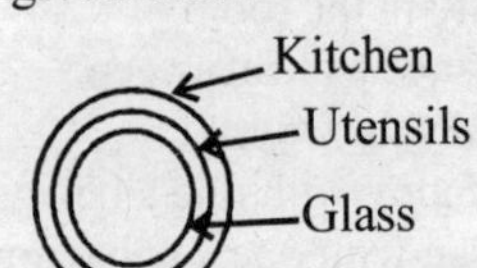

21. (b)

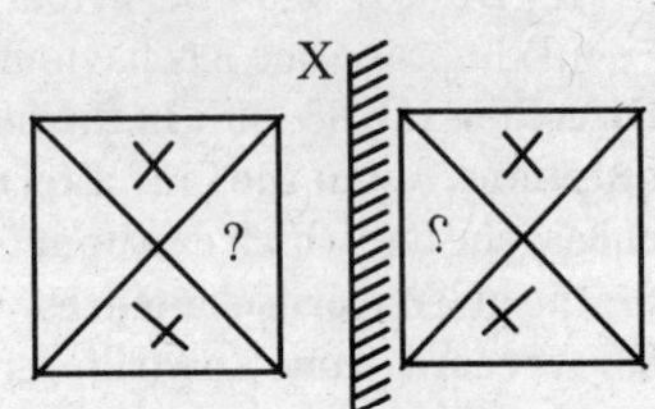

The right mirror image of the given image is 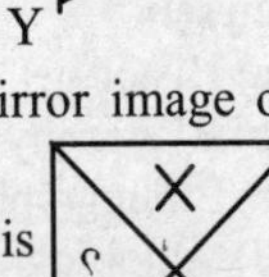

22. (b) A piece of paper is folded and punched. when opened it will appear as given below—

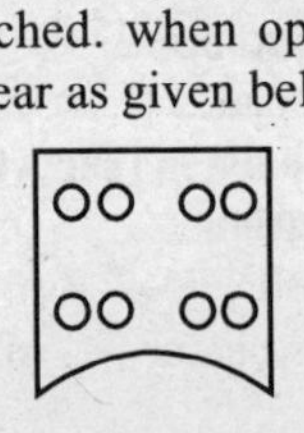

23. (c) The numbers 2, 3, 5 and 6 lie on the faces adjacent to number 1. Therefore, 4 lies opposite 1.

24. (d) Answer figure (d) will complete the pattern of the question figure.

25. (a) M = (03), 10, 22, 31, 44
A = (59), 67, 75, 88, 96
T = 00, (11), 23, 34, 42
H = 55, 66, (78), 87, 99
S = 01, 12, 20, 33, (43)
For 'MATHS' the set of number is 03, 59, 11, 78, 43.

26. (c) Washing Soda is essentially Sodium Carbonate, a sodium salt of carbonic acid (soluble in water). The molecular formula of washing soda is $Na_2CO_3.10H_2O$. It is used as an agent to soften hard water. It reacts with the calcium and magnesium bonds present in the water, enabling the detergent to work.

27. (c) Hydrochloric acid was historically called acidum salis, muriatic acid, and spirits of salt because it was produced from rock salt and green vitriol and later from the chemically similar substances common salt and sulfuric acid. Hydrochloric acid is found naturally in gastric acid.

28. (c) Khangchendzonga National Park is located in Sikkim. The park gets its name from the mountain Khangchendzonga which is 8,586 metres tall, the third-highest peak in the world. The park is known for animals like musk deer, snow leopard and Himalayan Thar.

29. (a) The Nanda Devi National Park (Biosphere Reserve) is situated around the peak of Nanda Devi, in Uttarakhand. It was established in 1982. Along with the adjoining Valley of Flowers National Park, it was inscribed a World Heritage Site by UNESCO in 1988.

30. (c) Afforestation holds the key for preventing soil erosion in desert regions and further desertification. Trees or even small plants bind soil to their roots, thereby checking their loosening. Some other measures include: introduction of improved dry farming practices and animal husbandry and plantations for fuel and fodder.

31. (c) Digboi in Tinsukia district of Assam has the distinction of having the oldest oil refinery of India and Asia as well. It was here that the first commercially viable well in India, well No.1, was successfully drilled in September 1889 and first modern refinery in India was built and commissioned in December 1901 by Assam Oil Company Ltd.

32. (b) Sodium bicarbonate ($NaHCO_3$) is also known as baking soda. It is a chemical leavening agent which is added to baked goods before cooking to produce carbon dioxide and cause them to 'rise'.

33. (d) The word "Shatabdi" means centenary in Sanskrit, Hindi and several Indian languages. The first Shatabdi train was started in 1988 to commemorate the centenary of Pandit Jawahar Lal Nehru's Birthday (the First Prime Minister of India) by Madhav Rao Scindia, minister for railways. It operated from New Delhi to Jhansi, later extended to Bhopal.

34. (b) Rabi refers to agricultural crops sown in winter and harvested in the spring. Examples of Rabi Crops: Wheat, Gram, Pea, Mustard, Linseed, Barley. Rice is a Kharif crop, cultivated and harvested during the rainy (monsoon) season in the South Asia.

35. (a) Western Rajasthan is the driest region in India. Jaisalmer in western Rajasthan is the driest place which receives the lowest rainfall (less than 10 cm). It is due to its distance from the monsoon winds of the Bay of Bengal and location in the sub-tropical high pressure belt.

36. (b) Bombay High, also known as Mumbai High, is an offshore oilfield 162 kilometres off the coast of Mumbai about 75 m of water. The oil operations are run by India's Oil and Natural Gas Corporation (ONGC).

37. (a) Adam Smith argued that although water has no value in exchange it has considerable value in use, while a diamond has no value in use but considerable value in exchange. It is known as Paradox of value. This distinction was associated with a belief that only physical things could have a value and that labour was the source of all value.

38. (c) Section 80-A of the Representation of the People Act, 1951 provides that the High Court shall be the authority for presentment of election petitions under Article 329(b) of the Constitution. This was incorporated by an amendment in the year 1966 (Act 47 of 1966).

39. (c) The Union List or List-I is a list of 100 items (though last item is numbered 97) given in Part XI of the Constitution of India on which Parliament has exclusive power to legislate. Out of the 100 items on the list, one is no longer in force.

40. (c) The Constitution empowers the President to summon each House at such intervals that there should not be more than 6-month's gap between the two sessions. Hence the Parliament must meet at least twice a year. In India, the parliament conducts three sessions each year.

41. (b) The Forty Second Constitution Amendment Act, 1976 has incorporated ten Fundamental

Duties in Article 51(a) of the Constitution of India. This was done in accordance with the recommendation of the Sardar Swaran Singh Committee. India adopted Fundamental Duties from the Constitution of erstwhile USSR.

42. (c) On July 19, 1969, 14 commercial banks were nationalized, which got presidential approval on August 9, 1969. In 1980, in order to provide government more power and command over credit delivery, six more commercial banks in India were nationalized.

43. (b) A rift valley is a linear shaped lowland between several highlands or mountain ranges created by the action of a geologic rift or fault. It is formed by the subsidence of a segment of the Earth's crust between dip-slip, or normal, faults.

44. (c) Lake Nasser was created by the construction of the Aswan High Dam in Southern Egypt across the waters of the Nile between 1958 and 1971. The largest man-made lake in the world, Lake Nasser has a major role in Egypt's fishing industry.

45. (d) As originally enacted, the Constitution of India provided for a Supreme Court with a Chief Justice and 7 judges. As the work of the Court has increased, the present sanctioned strength has swelled to 31.

46. (c) During the reign of Bindusara, Chandragupta Maurya's son and successor, there was unrest at Taxila in the north-western province of Sindh. He sent Asoka (his son) to quell the uprising. Taxila was a highly volatile place because of the Indo-Greek presence and mismanagement of Governor Susima.

47. (b) Lateral or sideways erosion widens the river valley; while, Vertical or downward erosion deepens the river valley. Due to continued lateral erosion, the river valley increasingly becomes broader and shallower. The valley slopes are also eroded by weathering and mass wasting and by the development of tributary valleys.

48. (d) Coconut water, the clear liquid inside young green coconuts (fruits of the coconut palm), is liquid endosperm. In early development, it serves as a suspension for the endosperm of the coconut during their nuclear phase of development. It contains sugars, vitamins, minerals, proteins, free amino acids and growth promoting factors.

49. (b) Bulbil is a small bulblike organ of vegetative reproduction growing in leaf axils or on flower stalks of plants such as the onion and tiger lily. It is a reproductive organ that takes part in vegetative reproduction. The bulbils drop from the parent plant on to the ground, give out adventitious roots and develop into new plants.

50. (a) Animal proteins derived from meat and fish are called first class proteins. A first class protein is one which contains all 8 essential amino acids (which cannot be made by the body). They are also called complete proteins. Plant proteins are called second class proteins.

51. (b) $4x^3 - 2x^2 + 2x - 3$

Coefficient of $x^2 = -2$

52. (d) **By Tricky formulae :**

$$\text{Profit}\% = \left[(\text{Profit} - \text{P}\%)\left(\frac{100-y}{100-x}\right) - 100\right]$$

$$\text{Profit}\% = \left[(100-10)\left(\frac{100-20}{100-40}\right) - 100\right]$$

$$= \left(90 \times \frac{80}{60} - 100\right)$$

$= (120 - 100) = 20\%$

Here + sign indicates that the merchant will get 20% profit.

53. (b) Mean Marks

$$= \frac{60\times 66 + 45\times 62 + 75\times 60}{60+45+75}$$

$$= \frac{3960+2790+4500}{180}$$

$$= \frac{11250}{180} = 62.5$$

54. (a) $\dfrac{221a^2b^2}{13b^2} = 17a^2$

55. (c) Speed of missile = 1116 km/h

$$= \frac{1116\times 1000}{3600} \text{ m/sec}$$

$$= 1116 \times \frac{5}{18} = \frac{124\times 5}{2}$$

$= 62 \times 5 = 310$ metres/sec.

Missile will travel 310 metres in 1 second.

56. (d) **By Tricky formulae :**

Area increased of a circle

$$= \left[2a + \frac{a^2}{100}\right]\%$$

$$= \left[2\times 31 + \frac{31\times 31}{100}\right]\%$$

$= (62 + 9.61)\% = 71.61\%$

57. (b) Amount

$$= \text{P}\left(1 + \frac{20}{100}\right)^2 + \frac{\text{P}\times 40\times 1}{100\times 2}$$

$$= 6000 \times \frac{36}{25} + \frac{6000\times 40}{100\times 2}$$

$$= \frac{6000\times 36\times 4}{100} + \frac{240000}{200}$$

$= 60 \times 144 + 1200$

Amount $= (8640 + 1200) = 9840$

Compound Interest = (9840 − 6000) = ₹ 3840.

58. (d) Let numbers be x

$4 : 28 :: 28 : x$

$\Rightarrow \frac{4}{28} = \frac{28}{x}$

$\Rightarrow x = \frac{28 \times 28}{4}$

$\Rightarrow x = 7 \times 28 = 196$

59. (b) Mummy can cook cakes in

1 hour $= \frac{75}{15} = 5$ cakes

Mummy and sister can cook in 1 hour

$= \frac{120}{2} = 6$ cakes

Sister can cook in 1 hour
$= (6-5) = 1$ cake

Sister can cook in 30 hours
$= 1 \times 30 = 30$ cakes

60. (c) Cost price of 20 quintal rice
= ₹ 8580

Left rice $= 20 \times \frac{78}{100}$

$= \frac{1560}{100} = 15.60$ quintal

The trader wants 20% profit,

SP $= \left(\frac{120}{100} \times 8580\right)$

$= 858 \times 12 =$ ₹ 10296

Rate/quintal of rice $= \frac{10296}{15.60}$

$= \frac{102960}{156} =$ ₹ 660 per quintal

61. (c) Here $a = 3/2$ and $b = -\frac{4}{7}$

Equation of intercept

$\frac{x}{a} + \frac{y}{b} = 1$

$\Rightarrow \frac{x}{3/2} + \frac{y}{-4/7} = 1$

$\Rightarrow \frac{2x}{3} - \frac{7y}{4} = 1$

$\Rightarrow \frac{8x - 21y}{12} = 1$

$8x - 21y = 12$

62. (c) Formula F + V = E + 2

$\Rightarrow (4+4) = E + 2$

$\Rightarrow (8-2) = E$

$\Rightarrow E = 6$

There are 6 edges in it.

63. (b) According to question,

$2\pi r = 3a$

$\Rightarrow 2 \times \frac{22}{7} \times 14 = 3a$

$\Rightarrow \frac{88}{3} = a$

$\Rightarrow$ Side $(a) = \frac{88}{3}$ cm

64. (b) πrl = C.S.A. of a cone

$\Rightarrow \frac{22}{7} \times 35 \times l = 10010$

$\Rightarrow l = \frac{10010}{110} = 91$cm

$h = \sqrt{l^2 - r^2} = \sqrt{91^2 - 35^2}$

$= \sqrt{(91+35)(91-35)}$

$= \sqrt{126 \times 56}$

$= \sqrt{4 \times 4 \times 3 \times 3 \times 7 \times 7}$

$\Rightarrow h = 4 \times 3 \times 7 = 84$ cm

$\Rightarrow V = \frac{1}{3}\pi r^2 h$

$= \frac{1}{3} \times \frac{22}{7} \times 35 \times 35 \times 84$

$= 13860$ cubic cm

65. (c) sin (A + B) – sin (A – B)
= SinA.cosB + cosAsinB
– sinAcosB + cosA. sinB
= 2 sinB.cosA

66. (c) S.I. for first 5 years

$=$ ₹ $\left(\frac{3130}{10} \times 5\right) =$ ₹ 1565

After 5 years, principal becomes five times of itself.

$\therefore$ S.I. for 10 years = ₹ (1565 + 5 × 1565)
= ₹ (1565 + 7825) = ₹ 9390

67. (a) According to the question.

$\frac{v_1}{v_2} = \sqrt{\frac{T_2}{T_1}}$

$\Rightarrow \frac{30}{v_2} = \sqrt{\frac{225}{196}} = \frac{15}{14}$

$\Rightarrow 15 v_2 = 30 \times 14$

$\Rightarrow v_2 = \frac{30 \times 14}{15} = 28$ kmph.

68. (c) Number of trees 2 years ago

$= \frac{P}{\left(1 + \frac{R}{100}\right)^n}$

$= \frac{17640}{\left(1 + \frac{5}{100}\right)^2} = \frac{17640}{\left(1 + \frac{1}{20}\right)^2}$

$= \frac{17640}{\left(\frac{21}{20}\right)^2} = \frac{17640 \times 20 \times 20}{21 \times 21}$

$= 16000$

69. (c) Age of coach = 23 + total increase
$= (23 + 2 \times 13)$ years = 49 years

70. (d) Height of cuboid $= x$ cm.

$\therefore$ Its length $= (x + 30)$ cm.

According to the question.

$\frac{x+30}{x} = \frac{19}{13}$

$\Rightarrow 19x = 13x + 390$

$\Rightarrow 6x = 390$

$\Rightarrow x = \frac{390}{6} = 65$ cm.

Length $= (65 + 30)$ cm $= 95$ cm.

$\therefore$ Breadth $= (\frac{95}{19} \times 11)$ cm $= 55$ cm.

$\therefore$ Volume of cuboid = (95 × 55 × 65) cu. cm
= 339625 cu. cm.

71. (c) Single equivalent discount of two successive discount

$= \left(x + y - \frac{xy}{100}\right)\%$

$= \left(50 + 25 - \frac{50 \times 25}{100}\right)\%$

$= (75 - 12.5)\% = 62.5\%$

$\therefore$ C.P. of article = (100 − 62.5)% of 2375

$=$ ₹ $\left(\frac{2375 \times 37.5}{100}\right) =$ ₹ 890.625

Actual cost = ₹ (890.625 + 165)
= ₹ 1055.625

To gain 62.5% required S.P.

$= ₹\left(\frac{1055.625 \times 162.5}{100}\right)$

$= ₹ 1715.39$

72. (b) Time taken by Nirmit in doing $\frac{2}{3}$rd work = 18 days

$\therefore$ Time taken by Nirmit in doing 1 work $= \frac{18 \times 3}{2} = 27$ days

Kashish is twice as efficient as Nirmit.

$\therefore$ Time taken by Kashish $= \frac{27}{2}$

$= 13\frac{1}{2}$ days

73. (b) Literate people in city-4

$= \frac{600000 \times 63}{100} = 378000$

74. (c) Literate males in city-2

$= 220000 \times \frac{85}{100} \times \frac{7}{11} = 119000$

Literate females in city-6

$= 200000 \times \frac{58}{100} \times \frac{3}{5} = 69600$

$\therefore$ Required ratio = 119000 : 69600 = 595 : 348

75. (a) Literate males in city-5

$= \frac{9}{7} \times 259210 = 333270$

$\therefore$ Literate population = 333270 + 259210 = 592480

$\therefore$ Population of City-5

$= \frac{592480}{92} \times 100 = 644000$

76. (b) Enigma (Noun) = a person, thing or situation that is mysterious and difficult to understand: mystery; puzzle; riddle.

77. (b) Inertia (Noun) = lack of energy; lack of desire or ability to move or change.
Vigour (Noun) = energy, force or enthusiasm; vitality.

78. (a)

79. (c) It is position of words related error. Hence, beautiful red balloon...... should be used here.

80. (c) Here, unless should be followed by positive sentence i.e., unless she does have/unless she has a strong desire to live.
Unless is used to say that something can only happen or be true in a particular situation.

81. (c) Charge (Verb) = to rush forward and attack.
We charged at the enemy.
Hence, and charged straight at me should be used here.

82. (d) Assure (Verb) = to guarantee; to tell somebody that something is definitely going to happen.

83. (a) Insist = to demand earnestly.

84. (c) Structure of Imperative sentence Imperative:
Do/does + not + WI (infinitive without to)
Hence, interrupt (= intervene) .... should be used here.

85. (c) Beat around the bush = to talk about something for a long time without coming to the main point.

86. (b) Make room = make space
Look at the sentence :
How can we make room for all the furniture ?

87. (d) Mend your ways = to stop behaving badly.

88. (d) **89.** (b)

90. (a)

91. (b) By ⇒ not later than the time mentioned
Hence, by Sunday should be used.

92. (a) Hole = hollow space
Whole = full, complete

93. (a) Here, corresponding preposition should follow.

94. (a) The sentence is in Present Simple.
Hence, doesn't he ? should be used as question tag.

95. (c) Here, antecedent of relative pronoun 'whose' is 'those' (Plural). Hence, Plural Verb i.e. those who like to help others .... should be used here.

96. (d) Look at the first sentence:
Crude mineral oil comes out of the earth as a thick ....

97. (a) Look at the second sentence :
It is a complex mixture of........

98. (b) Look at the sentence:
Mineral oil originates from the carcasses of.......... .

99. (b) Look at the sentence:
Over million of years, these dead creatures ....

100. (a) It is obvious from the last sentence.

General Intelligence and Reasoning

1 ANALOGY

Analogy basically means "resemblance of one object to another in certain aspects." The aim of analogy is to test the candidate's ability to discover the relationship between the question pair and then to find the required pair of words which is most similar to that relationship.

In this chapter, a question consists of words related to each other based on some logic and it is required to find a word/pair of words analogous to those given in the question

To solve these questions, following two simple steps are to be followed

Step I The candidate is required to identify the relationship between the pair of numbers/letters/words given.

Step II Find out the other pair such that the relationship between the third and the fourth numbers/letters/words is similar to the relationship that exists between the first and second numbers/letters/words.

Some Important Relationships

Synonyms Relationship

Dwelling	:	Abode	**Vacant**	:	Empty
Ban	:	Prohibition	**House**	:	Home
Idea	:	Notion	**Contact**	:	Meet
Endless	:	Eternal	**Escape**	:	Abscond
Kind	:	Benevolent	**Enormous**	:	Huge
Synthetic	:	Artificial	**Encumber**	:	Burden
Substitute	:	Replace	**Dissipate**	:	Squander

Part and Whole Relationship

Fan	:	Blade	**Bicycle**	:	Pedal
Cart	:	Wheel	**Pen**	:	Nib
Circle	:	Arc	**Class**	:	Student
House	:	Room	**Car**	:	Steering

Antonyms Relationship

Meet	:	Avoid	**Never**	:	Always
Scarcity	:	Abundance	**Weak**	:	Robust
Deep	:	Shallow	**Advance**	:	Retreat
Cordial	:	Hostile	**Slim**	:	Bulky
Chaos	:	Peace	**Affirm**	:	Deny
Gradual	:	Abrupt	**Stale**	:	Fresh
Final	:	Initial	**Create**	:	Destroy
Notice	:	Ignore	**Rejoice**	:	Mourn

Product and Raw Material Relationship

Jaggery	:	Sugarcane	**Book**	:	Paper
Paper	:	Pulp	**Road**	:	Asphalt
Shoes	:	Leather	**Rubber**	:	Latex
Jewellery	:	Gold	**Prism**	:	Glass
Cloth	:	Fibre	**Furniture**	:	Wood
Omelette	:	Egg	**Linen**	:	Flax
Sack	:	Jute	**Wall**	:	Brick

Individual and Group Relationship

Sheep	:	Flock	**Goods**	:	Stock
Fish	:	Shoal	**Soldiers**	:	Army
Termites	:	Colony	**Pupils**	:	Class
Riders	:	Cavalcade	**Singer**	:	Chorus
Grapes	:	Bunch	**Sailors**	:	Crew
Bees	:	Swarm	**Players**	:	Team
Robbers	:	Gang	**Flowers**	:	Bouquet

Worker and Tool Relationship

Surgeon	:	Scalpel	**Tailor**	:	Needle
Labourer	:	Spade	**Author**	:	Pen
Blacksmith	:	Anvil	**Soldier**	:	Gun
Farmer	:	Plough	**Sculptor**	:	Chisel
Warrior	:	Sword	**Woodcutter**	:	Axe
Mason	:	Plumb line	**Carpenter**	:	Saw

Worker and Product Relationship

Poet	:	Poem	**Cobbler**	:	Shoes
Producer	:	Film	**Editor**	:	Newspaper
Choreographer	:	Ballet	**Tailor**	:	Clothes
Dramatist	:	Play	**Chef**	:	Food
Farmer	:	Crop	**Sculptor**	:	Bust

Letter Based Analogy

Before discussing such type of relationship in analogy, students are suggested to remember the following things

Forward Letter Positions (Left to Right)

A	B	C	D	E	F	G	H	I	J	K
L	M	N	O	P	Q	R	S	T	U	V
W	X	Y	Z							
1	2	3	4	5	6	7	8	9	10	11
12	13	14	15	16	17	18	19	20	21	22
23	24	25	26							

Backward Letter Positions (Right to Left)

A	B	C	D	E	F	G	H	I	J	K
L	M	N	O	P	Q	R	S	T	U	V
W	X	Y	Z							
26	25	24	23	22	21	20	19	18	17	16
15	14	13	12	11	10	9	8	7	6	5
4	3	2	1							

Opposite Letters

A	B	C	D	E	F	G	H	I	J	K	L	M
Z	Y	X	W	V	U	T	S	R	Q	P	O	N

Number Based Relationship

Such relationship is based on arithmetical oprations like addition, multiplication, subtraction, dividions of numbers etc. This can be better understood with the formats of the questions as given below

Solved Examples

Example 1: 'Melt' is related to 'Liquid' in the same way as 'Freeze's is related to

(a) Ice (b) Crystal
(c) Water (d) Cubes

Solution (a): The term 'Melt' is associated with 'Liquid' because after melting the ice, we obtain liquid. Similarly, the state of 'Water' after freezing is 'Ice'.

Example 2: 'Doctor' is related to 'Stethoscope' in the same way as 'Painter' is related to

(a) Painting (b) Brush
(c) Exhibition (d) Art

Solution (b): 'Stethoscope' is used by a 'Doctor' as a tool to performs his work. Similarly, a 'Painter' uses a 'Brush' as a tool to perform his work.

Example 3: Apple : Fruit :: Potato : ?

(a) Flower (b) Fruit
(c) Sweet (d) Root

Solution (d): 'Apple' is a 'Fruit' and similarly 'Potato' is a modified 'Root'.

Example 4: Eye : See :: Leg : ?

(a) Write
(b) Breath
(c) Walk
(d) Hear

Solution (c):'Eye' is the part of body which is used to 'See' and in the same way 'Leg' is the part of body which is used to 'Walk'.

Directions (5-6) Find the correct number/numbers for from the given alternatives.

Example 5: 4 : 8 :: 16 : ?

(a) 28 (b) 18
(c) 20 (d) 32

Solution (d): As, 4 → 8 (×2)

Similarly, 16 → 32 (×2)

∴ ? = 32

Example 6: 386 : 383 :: 517 : ?

(a) 514
(b) 571
(c) 715
(d) 512

Solution (a): As, 386 – 3 = 383, Similarly, 517 – 3 = 514

Exercise

1. 'Hate' is related to 'Love' in the same way as 'Create' is related to
(a) Make (b) Renovate
(c) Destroy (d) Build
2. 'Bull' is related to 'Cow' in the same way as 'Horse' is related to
(a) Animal (b) Mare
(c) Stable (d) Ment
3. 'Sports' is related to 'Logo' in the same way as 'Nation' is related to
(a) Emblem (b) Animal
(c) Ruler (d) Anthem
4. 'Data Processing' is related to 'Raw Data' in the same way as 'University' is related to
(a) Teacher (b) Building
(c) Students (d) Principal
5. 'Braille' is related to 'Blindness' in the same way as 'Sign language' is related to
(a) Exceptional (b) Touch
(c) Deafness (d) Presentation
6. 'Boat' is related to 'Oar' in the same way as 'Bicycle' is related to
(a) Road (b) Wheel
(c) Seat (d) Paddle
7. 'Match' is related to 'Victory' in the same way as 'Examination' is related to

(a) Write (b) Appear
(c) Success (d) Attempt

8. 'Flower' is related to 'Essence' in the same way as 'oven' is related to
(a) Vapour (b) Fire
(c) Heat (d) Steam

9. 'Clock' is related to 'Time' in the same way as 'Metre' is related to
(a) Speed (b) Distance
(c) Wrist (d) Sand

10. 'Museum' is related to 'Curator' in the same way as 'Prison' is related to
(a) Warden (b) Monitor
(c) Manager (d) jailor

11. 'Hour' is related to 'Second' in the same way as 'Tertiary' is related to
(a) Ordinary (b) Secondary
(c) Primary (d) Intermediary

12. 'Fire is related to 'Ashes' in the same way as 'Explosion' is related to
(a) Sound (b) Debris
(c) Explosive (d) Flame

13. 'Parliament' is related to 'Great Britain' in the same way as 'Congress' is related to
(a) Japan (b) India
(c) USA (d) Netherlands

14. 'Ignite' is to 'Combustion' as Trigger' is to
(a) Gun (b) War
(c) Projectile (d) Reaction

15. 'Disease' is related to 'Medicine' in the same way as 'Famine' is related to
(a) Drought (b) River
(c) Waterfall (d) Rainfall

Directions (16-35) In each of the following questions, there is a certain relationship between two given words on one side of (::) and one word is given on another side (::) while another word is to be found from the given alternatives, having the same relation with this word as the words of the given pair bear. Choose the correct alternative.

16. King : Throne :: Judge : ?
(a) Lawyer (b) Bench
(c) Court (d) Trial

17. Lion : Roar :: Ass : ?
(a) Bark (b) Trumpet
(c) Howl (d) Bray

18. Lamb : Frisk :: Mouse : ?
(a) Trot (b) Scamper
(c) Gallop (d) Flit

19. Truthfulness : Liar :: Loyalty : ?
(a) Worker (b) Traitor
(c) Diligent (d) Faithful

20. House : Door :: Compound : ?
(a) Gate (b) Fence
(c) Foundation (d) Wall

21. Hongkong : Chine :: Vatican : ?
(a) France (b) Mexico
(c) Canada (d) Rome

22. Giant : Dwarf :: Genius : ?
(a) Wicked (b) Gentle
(c) Idiot (d) Tiny

23. Aryabhatta : Mathematician : Varahamihira : ?
(a) Physician (b) Astronomer
(c) Scientist (d) Architect

24. Sheep : Mutton :: Deer : ?
(a) Veal (b) Meat
(c) Flesh (d) Venison

25. Tea : Leaves :: Coffee : ?
(a) Plant (b) Leaves
(c) Seeds (d) Stimulant

26. Deep : Shallow :: Sharp : ?
(a) Knife (b) Blade
(c) Blunt (d) Ocean

27. Horse : Stable :: Man : ?
(a) Woman (b) Den
(c) Clothes (d) House

28. Peat : Lignite :: Bituminous : ?
(a) Granite (b) Basalt
(c) Anthracite (d) Coke

29. Cougar : South America :: Okapi : ?
(a) India
(b) Central Africa
(c) North America
(d) Pakistan

30. Love : Friend :: Hate : ?
(a) Hatred (b) Brother
(c) Enemy (d) Companion

31. Circle : Arc :: Square : ?
(a) Line (b) Triangle
(c) Sphere (d) Rectangle

32. Brinjal : Vegetable :: Orange : ?
(a) Fruit (b) Stem
(c) Leaf (d) Root

33. Contamination : Food :: Infection :?
(a) Germs (b) Disease
(c) Body (d) Microbes

34. Pleasure : Sorrow :: Right : ?
(a) Wrong (b) Wonderful
(c) Happy (d) Sure

35. Aluminium : Bauxite :: Iron : ?
(a) Pyrite (b) Magnesite
(c) Pynolosite (d) Haematitle

Directions (36-50) In each of the following questions, there is some relationship between the two terms to the left of (::) and the same relationship holds between the two terms to its right. Also, in each question, one term either to the right of (::) or to the left of it is missing. This terms is given as one of the alternatives given below each question. Find out this terms.

36. CLOSE : DNRWJ :: OPEN : ?
(a) PRJO (b) RPJB
(c) PRHR (d) RZWR

37. EGIK : LJHF :: SUWY : ?
(a) ZXVT (b) TVXZ
(c) LNPR (d) MOQS

38. ACEG : IKMO :: PRTV : ?
(a) QRUW (b) JLMP
(c) WXAC (d) XZBD

39. acme : mace :: face : ?
(a) cefa (b) cfae
(c) cfea (d) afce

40. BJNT : CIOS :: DHPV : ?
(a) EGQU (b) ELQW
(c) ELPV (d) EIOU

41. ABCDE : FGHIJ :: PQRST : ?
(a) TSRQP (b) UVWXY
(c) KLMNO (d) EDCBA

42. NO : RS :: TU : ?
(a) XY (b) YX
(c) ZY (d) YZ

43. HCM : FAK :: SGD : ?
(a) QEB (b) QIB
(c) ESQ (d) GES

44. BCFE : HILK :: NORQ : ?
(a) TXWU (b) TXUW
(c) TUXW (d) TVWX

45. FILM : ADGH :: MILK : ?
(a) ADGF (b) HDGE
(c) HDGF (d) HEGF

46. ABCD : WXYZ :: EFGH : ?
(a) STUV (b) STOU
(c) STUE (d) TSUV

47. AB : ZY :: CD : ?
(a) VU (b) WX
(c) UV (d) XW

48. ACE : BDF :: MOQ : ?
(a) BMW (b) NQP
(c) NPR (d) BEF

49. SHOE : NCJZ :: REWA : ?
(a) WBJF (b) CITY
(c) CAYR (d) MZRW
(e) None of these

50. FLOWER : REWOLF : FRUITS : ?
(a) STRUIF (b) STUIRF
(c) STIURF (d) STUIFR

Directions (51-70) In each of the following questions, there is a certain relationship between two given

numbers on one side of (::) and one number is given on another side of (::) where another number is to be found from the given alternatives, having the same relationship with this number as the numbers of the given pair bear. Choose the best alternative.

51. 14 : 9 :: 26 : ?
(a) 12 (b) 13
(c) 15 (d) 31

52. 100 : 121 :: 144 : ?
(a) 160 (b) 93
(c) 169 (d) 426

53. 3 : 27 :: 4 : ?
(a) 16 (b) 64
(c) 32 (d) 28

54. 7544 : 5322 :: 4673 : ?
(a) 2367 (b) 2451
(c) 2531 (d) 4472

55. 63 : 21 :: 27 : ?
(a) 6 (b) 9
(c) 1 (d) 3

56. 25 : 625 :: 35 : ?
(a) 1575 (b) 1205
(c) 875 (d) 635

57. 1234 : 40 :: 6789 : ?
(a) 20 (b) 30
(c) 40 (d) 50

58. 08 : 66 :: ? : 38
(a) 2 (b) 6
(c) 12 (d) 19

59. 583 : 488 :: 293 : ?
(a) 581 (b) 291
(c) 378 (d) 487

60. 85 : 40 :: 77 : ?
(a) 14 (b) 48
(c) 49 (d) 50

61. 64 : 144 :: 256 : ?
(a) 16 (b) 32
(c) 400 (d) 336

62. 01 : 36 :: 2 : ?
(a) 69 (b) 49
(c) 81 (d) 70

63. 11 : 132 :: ?
(a) 15 : 250 (b) 10 : 100
(c) 9 : 90 (d) 13 : 169

64. 08 : 28 :: 15 : ?
(a) 63 (b) 65
(c) 126 (d) 124

65. $\frac{1}{9}:\frac{1}{81},\frac{1}{13}:?$
(a) $\frac{1}{127}$ (b) $\frac{1}{169}$
(c) $\frac{1}{125}$ (d) $\frac{1}{120}$

66. 4 : 9 :: 8 : ?
(a) 2 (b) 13
(c) 31 (d) 10

67. 1, 2, 4, 7 : 3, 4, 6, 9 :: ? : 2, 3, 5, 8
(a) 0, 1, 3, 6 (b) 2, 4, 5, 8
(c) 1, 3, 4, 7 (d) 3, 5, 6, 8

68. 17 : 34 :: ? : 10
(a) 11 (b) 8
(c) 5 (d) 15

69. 20 : 11 :: 102 : ?
(a) 49 (b) 52
(c) 61 (d) 98

70. 6 : 35 :: 7 : ?
(a) 48
(b) 42
(c) 34
(d) 13

Answers with Explanations

1. (c) As 'Hate' is opposite of 'Love, similarly 'Create' is opposite of 'Destroy.

2. (b) Male female relationship exists in this case.

3. (a) The symbol 'Logo' is related to 'Sports'. Likewise 'Emblem' is related to a 'Nation'.

4. (c) 'Date Processing' is the process of using 'Raw Data' to shape it in the final product. Likewise 'University' is the place which shapes the 'Students' for their career.

5. (c) 'Braille' is the technique of reading and writing for the blind persons. Similarly, 'Sign language' is the technique of reading and writing for deaf persons.

6. (d) 'Oar' is a device used to push a 'Boat'. Likewise 'Paddle' is used to push the 'Bicycle'.

7. (c) One of the outcomes of a 'Match' is 'Victory'. Likewise 'Success' is one of the outcomes of 'Examination'.

8. (c) Second denotes the trait for which first is used.

9. (b) As a 'Clock' measures 'Time', similarly 'Distance' is measured in 'Metres'.

10. (d) Person incharge of a 'Museum' is known as 'Curator'. Likewise person incharge of a 'Prison' is called 'Jailor'.

11. (c) 'Hour' is the third position after 'Second' in time measurement. Likewise 'Tertiary' is the third position after 'Primary' in the order of ranking.

12. (b) 'Fire reduces anything to 'Ashes' in the same way as 'Explosion' reduces anything to 'Debris'.

13. (c) The supreme law making authority of 'Great Britian' is known as 'Parliament'. In the same way, law making supreme body of 'USA' is known as 'Conaress'.

14. (d) 'Ignite' leads to 'Combustion' and 'Trigger' leads to violent 'Reaction'.

15. (d) As 'Disease' can be cured by taking proper 'Medicine', similarly famine can be avoided by adequate 'Rainfall'.

16. (b) As 'King is related to 'Judge', in the same way 'Throne' is related to 'Bench'.

17. (d) 'Roar' is the sound produced by 'Lion', similarly 'Bray' is the sound produced by 'Ass'.

18. (b) 'Frisk' is the name given to the movement of 'Lamb'. Similarly 'Scamper' is the name given to the movement of 'Mouse'.

19. (b) Former cannot be expected from the latter.

20. (a) 'Doors' are entry to a 'House' or we can get into the house through door. In the same way, gates are entry to a compound or we can get into a compound through 'Gate'.

21. (d) As, 'Hongkong' is in 'China', in the same way 'Vatican is situated in Rome.

22. (c) 'Dwarf' is the antonym of 'Giant', in the same way 'Genious' is the antonym of 'idiot'.

23. (a) 'Aryabhatta' was the famous 'Mathematician' of the ancient period, in the same way 'Varahamihira, was a famous 'Physician' of ancient period.

24. (d) As 'Mutton' is the meat of 'Sheep', similarly, 'Venison' is the meat of 'Deer'.

25. (c) Latter is the original form of the former.

26. (c) 'Deep' is opposite to 'Shallow', in the same way 'Sharp' is opposite to 'Blunt'.

27. (d) A 'Horse' lives in 'Stable', similarly a 'Man' lives in a 'House'.

28. (c) All represent the different forms of coal.

29. (b) As, 'Cougar' (a type of lion) is found in 'South America', similarly, Okapi is found in Central Africa.

30. (c) Former is received from the latter.

31. (a) As 'Arc is a part of 'Circle', in the same way 'Line' is a part of 'Square'.

32. (a) 'Brinjal' is a 'Vegetable', in the same way 'Orange' is a 'Fruit'.

33. (c) 'Food' gets affected by 'Contramination', in the same way 'Body' gets affected by 'Infection.'

34. (a) 'Pleasure' is opposite of 'Sorrow', in the same way 'Right' is opposite of 'Wrong'.

35. (d) Latter represents the ore of the former.

36. (c) As,

3 12 15 19 5
C L O S E
+1 +2 +3 +4 +5
D N R W J
4 14 18 23 10

Similarly, 15 16 5 14
O P E N
+1 +2 +3 +4
P R H R
16 18 8 18

37. (a) As, E G I K → L J H F (+1, +1, +1, +1)

Similarly,

S U W Y ← Z X V T (+1, +1, +1, +1)

38. (d) As,

1 3 5 7
A C E G
+8 +8 +8 +8
I K M O
9 11 13 15

Similarly,

16 18 20 22
P R T V
+8 +8 +8 +8
X Z B D
24 26 2 4

39. (b) As, a c m e → m a c e
1 2 3 4 3 1 2 4

40. (a) As,

2 10 14 20
B J N T
+1 –1 +1 –1
C I O S
3 9 15 19

Similarly,

4 8 16 22
D H P V
+1 –1 +1 –1
E G Q U
5 7 17 21

41. (b) ABCDE : FGHIJ :: PQRST : UVWXY

Letters of 'second' part are consecutive of 'first' part.

42. (a) As,

14 15
N O
+4 –4
R S
18 19

Similarly, 20 21
T U
+4 +4
X Y
24 25

43. (a) As,

8 3 13 → 6 1 11
H C M F A K
(–2, –2, –2)

Similarly,

19 7 4 → 17 5 2
S G D Q E B
(–2, –2, –2)

44. (c) As,

2 3 6 5
B C F E
+6 +6 +6 +6
H I L K
8 9 12 11

Similarly,

14 15 18 17
N O R Q
+6 +6 +6 +6
T U X W
20 21 24 23

45. (c) As,

6 9 12 13
F I L M
–5 –5 –5 –5
A D G H
1 4 7 8

Similarly, 13 9 12 11
M I L K
–5 –5 –5 –5
H D G F
8 4 7 6

46. (a) As,

A B C D → W X Y Z
(Opposite letter, Opposite letter, Opposite letter, Opposite letter)

Similarly,

E F G H ⟶ S T U V

(E–V, F–U, G–T, H–S: Opposite letter)

47. (d) As opposite letters of AB are ZY, similarly, opposite letters of CD are XW.

48. (c) As, A C E → (+1, +1, +1) → B D F

Similarly,

M O Q → (+1, +1, +1) → N P R

49. (d) As, S H O E → (–5, –5, –5, –5) → N C J Z

Similarly,

R E W A → (–5, –5, –5, –5) → M Z R V

50. (c) As,

F L O W E R ⟶ R E W O L F

Similarly,

F R U I T S ⟶ S T I U R F

As by reversing the letters of the word FLOWER, we get REWOLF, similarly, FRUITS can be written as STIURF.

51. (c) As, $(9 \times 2) = 18$ and $(18 - 4) = 14$

Similarly, $(15 \times 2) = 30$ and $(30 - 4) = 26$

$\therefore$? = 15

52. (c) As, $100 : 121$ or $10^2 : 11^2$

$144 : 169 \Rightarrow 12^2 : 13^2$

53. (b) As, cube of 3 is 27.

54. (b) As, 7544 : 5322 (– 2222)

Similarly,

4673 : 2451 (– 2222)

55. (b) As, $63 \div 3 = 21$ similarly,

$27 \div 3 = \boxed{9}$

56. (d) As, $25 : 625 \rightarrow 25$ is common in both and 6 is added before it.

Similarly $35 : \boxed{635} \rightarrow 35$ is common in both and 6 is added before it.

57. (b) As, 1234 : 10

$1 + 2 + 3 + 4 = 10$

Similarly, 6789 : 30

$6 + 7 + 8 + 9 = 30$

58. (b) As, $66 - 2 = 64 \rightarrow \sqrt{64} = 8$

Similarly, $38 - 2 = 36 \rightarrow \sqrt{36} = 6$

59. (c) Taking option (c),

As sum of digits of $583 = 5 + 8 + 3 = 16$

and sum of digits of $488 = 4 + 8 + 8 = 20$

Similarly, sum of digits of $293 = 2 + 9 + 3 = 14$

and Sum of digits of $\boxed{378} = 3 + 7 + 8 = 18$

Here, difference of both are

$(20 - 16)$

$= (18 - 14) = 4$

60. (c) As, 85 : $\boxed{40}$ (8×5)

Similarly, 77 : $\boxed{49}$ (7×7)

Similarly, $27 \div 3 = 9$

61. (c) As, $8^2 = 64$

and $(8 + 4)^2 = 12^2 = 144$

Similarly, $16^2 = 256$

and $(16 + 4)^2 = 20^2 = \boxed{400}$

62. (b) According to the statement,

Here, $(1 + 5)^2 = 36$

Similarly, $(2 + 5)^2 = 49$

63. (c) As, $11 \times (11 + 1) = 11 \times 12 = 132$

Similarly, $9 \times (9 + 1) = 9 \times 10 = 90$

64. (b) As, $08 \times 02 = 16$ and 16

$= 2 \times 8 = 28$

Similarly, $15 \times 02 = 30$ and

$6 \times 5 = 65$

65. (c) As, $\left(\frac{1}{9}\right)^2 = \frac{1}{81}$

Similarly, $\left(\frac{1}{13}\right)^2 = \frac{1}{169}$

66. (b) As, 4 : 9 (+5)

Similarly, 8 : 13 (+5)

67. (a) As, 1 2 4 7 → (+2, +2, +2, +2) → 3 4 6 9

Similarly, 0 1 3 6 → (+2, +2, +2, +2) → 2 3 5 8

68. (c) As, 17 : 34 (×2)

Similarly, 5 : 10 (×2)

69. (b) As, 20 : 11 (÷2+1)

Similarly, 102 : 52 (÷2+1)

70. (a) As, 6 : 35 ((6–1)(6+1))

Similarly, 7 : 48 ((7–1)(7+1))

2 CLASSIFICATION

Classification is the process of grouping various objects on the basis of their common properties like shape, size, category, colour, trait etc., and finding the odd object from the group.

Different type of questions covered in this chapter are as follow

- Choosing the Odd Word
- Choosing the Odd Pair of Words
- Choosing the Odd Letter/Group
- Choosing the Odd Number/Pair/Group.

In this chapter, the questions contain a set of different items and it is asked to find the odd item out of the given ones.

All the items except one, follow a certain rule or pattern or they possesses some common quality or characteristics between them and one which is odd does not possesses the common quality or characteristics.

Choosing the odd Letter/Group

Under this classification, a single letter or group/ pair of letters are given in each of four or five options. Three or four of them are similar to each other in same manner while one is different and this is to be chosen by the candidate as the answer.

But before movind on the different types of letters classification, we must know the following.

Forward Letter Positions (Left to Right)

A	B	C	D	E	F	G	H	I	J	K	L	M	N	O	P	Q	R	S	T	U	V	W	X	Y	Z
1	2	3	4	5	6	7	8	9	10	11	12	13	14	15	16	17	18	19	20	21	22	23	24	25	26

Backward Letter Positions (Right to Left)

A	B	C	D	E	F	G	H	I	J	K	L	M	N	O	P	Q	R	S	T	U	V	W	X	Y	Z
26	25	24	23	22	21	20	19	18	17	16	15	14	13	12	11	10	9	8	7	6	5	4	3	2	1

Opposite Letters

A	B	C	D	E	F	G	H	I	J	K	L	M
Z	Y	X	W	V	U	T	S	R	Q	P	O	N

Chossing the odd Number/Pair/Group

In this type of questions, certain pairs/groups of numbers are given out of which all except one may have the same property or may be related to each other according to the same rule. The candidate is required to choose the odd pair/group.

Solved Examples

Example 1: Find the odd word.

(a) Commander (b) Major

(c) Brigadier (d) Captain

Sol. (a) All except 'Commander' are ranks of army.

Example 2: Find the odd word

(a) Pen (b) Book

(c) Page (d) Pencil

Sol. (b) All except 'Book' are used for writing work.

Example 3: Find the odd group of letters.

(a) AOE

(b) EUI

(c) OUT

(d) IEM

Sol. (c) All except 'OUT' have a difference of four position.

1	15	5	5	21	9	15	21	20	9	5	13
A	O	E	E	U	I	O	U	T	I	E	M
+4			+4			+5			+4		

Example 4: Find the odd number.

(a) 1444

(b) 1553

(c) 8590

(d) 1984

Sol. (b) All except '1553' are even numbers.

Exercise

Directions (1-20): In the following question, three or four alternative are same in a certain way out of four or five and so form a group. Find the odd word that does not belong to the group.

1. (a) Cello (b) Guitar (c) Flute (d) Violin
2. (a) Sweetness (b) Elegant (c) Bright (d) Beautiful
3. (a) Mile (b) Centimetre (c) Litre (d) Yard
4. (a) Chop (b) Slit (c) Chirp (d) Slice
5. (a) Goat (b) Dog (c) Sheep (d) Cow
6. (a) Iron (b) Mercury (c) Silver (d) Gold
7. (a) Zinc (b) Bronze (c) Silver (d) platinum
8. (a) Ink (b) Paper (c) Office (d) Pen
9. (a) Father (b) Mother (c) Friend (d) Brother
10. (a) Red (b) Blue (c) Yellow (d) Black
11. (a) Kanpur (b) Lucknow (c) Lahore (d) patna
12. (a) Ample (b) Copious (c) Plentiful (d) Abundance
13. (a) Temple (b) Mosque (c) Theatre (d) Church
14. (a) Sweet (b) Sour (c) Salty (d) Tasteless
15. (a) Violin (b) Sitar (c) Sitar (d) Flute
16. (a) Bengaluru (b) Patna (c) Bhagalpur (d) Ranchi
17. (a) Carpenter (b) Goldsmith (c) Blacksmith (d) Driver
18. (a) Circle (b) Triangle (c) Rectangle (d) Square
19. (a) Bat (b) Parrot (c) Crow (d) Pigeon
20. (a) Cube (b) Square (c) Cuboid (d) Sphere

Directions (21-40) : In each of the following questions, some groups of letters are given, all for which except one, share a common similarity while one is different. Select the odd one.

21. (a) MKHE (b) MIDA (c) KHEB (d) WTQN
22. (a) YXVU (b) ORQP (c) KJHG (d) MLJI
23. (a) EHG (b) JML (c) PSR (d) UYX
24. (a) KJG (b) ZYV (c) NMK (d) FEB
25. (a) CDFE (b) JKLM (c) STVU (d) WXZY
26. (a) XWU (b) QPM (c) KJH (d) DCA
27. (a) MOR (b) GIL (c) SUX (d) VXZ
28. (a) HKI (b) UXV (c) CFD (d) MQN
29. (a) BdEg (b) PrSu (c) KmNp (d) TwXz
30. (a) CdaB (b) VwtU (c) Lmjk (d) RsqP
31. (a) MrW (b) ChN (c) KpU (d) BgL
32. (a) ZYAB (b) TSGH (c) ONLM (d) UTFH
33. (a) ELS (b) HOV (c) CJQ (d) KRX
34. (a) BEA (b) PSO (c) WZV (d) RTQ
35. (a) GDF (b) VRT (c) KHJ (d) NKM
36. (a) DACB (b) EBCD (c) SPQR (d) XUVM
37. (a) O (b) I (c) E (d) B
38. (a) ACE (b) FHJ (c) KLN (d) NPR
39. (a) BDH (b) CFL (c) EJU (d) DHP
40. (a) ADGPT (b) ACERK (c) ABDEQ (d) ADIPY

Directions (40-60) In each of the following questions, four/five options are given. Out of these, three/four are alike in a particular way but remaining one is different. Find the odd one from the given options which is different from others.

41. (a) 121 (b) 169 (c) 225 (d) 289
42. (a) 119 (b) 154 (c) 85 (d) 51
43. (a) 64 (b) 208 (c) 316 (d) 118
44. (a) 143 (b) 171 (c) 117 (d) 195
45. (a) 17 (b) 44 (c) 29 (d) 13
46. (a) 12 (b) 24 (c) 42 (d) 32
47. (a) 12 (b) 28 (c) 52 (d) 96
48. (a) 26 (b) 34 (c) 72 (d) 46
49. (a) 11 (b) 17 (c) 45 (d) 37
50. (a) 729 (b) 123 (c) 423 (d) 621
51. (a) 63 (b) 126 (c) 215 (d) 342
52. (a) 272 (b) 210 (c) 240 (d) 304
53. (a) 144 (b) 169 (c) 288 (d) 324
54. (a) 120 (b) 72 (c) 108 (d) 98
55. (a) 28 (b) 42 (c) 35 (d) 65

56. (a) 25 (b) 9
(c) 16 (d) 18

57. (a) 4867 (b) 5555
(c) 6243 (d) 6655

58. (a) 4 (b) 64
(c) 225 (d) 47

59. (a) 13 (b) 17
(c) 19 (d) 27

60. (a) 13
(b) 43
(c) 63
(d) 23

Answers with Explanations

1. (c) All are music instruments excepts flute. All have string to play the music but flute does not have.

2. (a) All except sweetness are related with beauty but sweetness is related with taste.

3. (c) All others are units to measure distance.

4. (c) Except 'Chirp' all other are related to cutting.

5. (b) Only 'Dog' is different because dog does not eat grass.

6. (b) All others are Solid metals.

7. (b) 'Bronze' is an alloy, rest are metals.

8. (c) All others are stationery.

9. (c) All others are family members.

10. (d) All others are primary colours.

11. (c) All others are Indian cities.

12. (d) Except 'Abundance' all mean sufficient amount but abundance is used for more than sufficient amount.

13. (c) All others are worship places.

14. (d) All others are type of taste.

15. (d) All others are string instruments.

16. (c) All others are capital cities of Indian states.

17. (d) Except 'Driver', all three can make article in their specialisation but only 'Driver' serves his work.

18. (a) All others are made of straight lines.

19. (a) Except 'Bat' all other are birds.

20. (b) All others are three-dimensional bodies

21. (b) The pattern used for classification is placement of alphabets in the order (– 3, – 3, – 3). Since, option (b) does not follow the pattern, it is odd in the group.

22. (b) Except ORQP all others have the same gap between the adjacent letters.

Y X V U (–1, –2, –1) O R Q P (+3, –1, –1)

K J H G (–1, –2, –1) M L J I (–1, –2, –1)

Clearly, ORQP is different from other options.

23. (d) In all other groups, there is a gap of one letter between first and third letters.

24. (c) In all other groups, there is a gap of two letter as in alphabet between the second and the third letters.

25. (b)

C D F E (–1, +2, –1) J K L M (+1, +1, +1)

S T V U (+1, +2, –1) W X Z Y (+1, +2, –1)

Clearly, 'JKLM' is different from the others.

26. (b) In all other groups, there is a gap of one letter as in alphabet between the second and third letters.

27. (d) In all other groups, there is a gap of two letter between second and third letters as in the alphabet.

28. (d) In all other groups, there is a gap of one letter between second and third letters as in the alphabet.

29. (d) In all other groups, there is a gap of one letter between first and second letters as in the alphabet.

30. (d) In all other groups, third and fourth letters are consecutive alphabet.

31. (b) In all other groups, first and third letters are equidistant from the middle letters as in the original alphabet.

32. (d)

Z Y (–1) A B (+1) T S (–1) G H (+1)

O N (–1) L M (+1) U T (–1) F H (+2)

Clearly, option (d) is different from the others.

33. (d) In all other groups, letters adjacent to the middle one are equidistant from it in the alphabet.

34. (d) In all other groups, there is a gap of two letters between first and second letters as in the alphabet.

35. (b) In all other groups, first and third letters are consecutive letters of the alphabet.

36. (a)

D $\xrightarrow{-3}$ A $\xrightarrow{+2}$ C $\xrightarrow{-1}$ B

E $\xrightarrow{-3}$ B $\xrightarrow{+1}$ C $\xrightarrow{+1}$ D

S $\xrightarrow{-3}$ P $\xrightarrow{+1}$ Q $\xrightarrow{+1}$ R

X $\xrightarrow{-3}$ U $\xrightarrow{+1}$ V $\xrightarrow{+1}$ W

37. (d) Except B, all are the vowels.

38. (c)

A C E (+2, +2) F H J (+2, +2)

K L N (+1, +2) N P R (+2, +2)

All except 'KLN' have a difference of two positions between first and second, second and third.

39. (c) Clearly, 'EJU' is different from the other options because the second difference is twice the first difference.

B D H (+2, +4) C E L (+3, +6)

E J U (+5, +11) D H P (+4, +8)

40. (a) All others have two vowels.

41. (c) All others are squares of prime numbers.

42. (b) All others are divisible by 17.

43. (a) This is the only square in the group.

44. (b) All others are divisible by 13.

45. (b) Except '44', all are prime numbers.

46. (d) All others are divisible by 3.

47. (d) All others have only 3 factors

$12 = 2 \times 2 \times 3$, $28 = 2 \times 2 \times 7$,

$52 = 2 \times 2 \times 13$

$68 = 2 \times 2 \times 17$, $96 = 2 \times 2 \times 2 \times 2 \times 2 \times 3$

48. (c) All others have only 2 factors with prime numbers.

$26 = 2 \times 13$, $34 = 2 \times 17$, $72 = 2 \times 2 \times 2 \times 3 \times 3$, $46 = 2 \times 23$,

$38 = 2 \times 19$

49. (c) All others are prime numbers.

50. (a) Only '729' is a perfect cube.

51. (b) All others are one less than the cube of a number.

52. (c) $\therefore 272 = 2 + 7 + 2 = 11$

$210 = 2 + 1 + 0 = 3$

$240 = 2 + 4 + 0 = 6$

$304 = 3 + 0 + 4 = 7$

The sum of digit of all numbers except 240 is a prime number, where as sum of digits of the number 240 is a non-prime. Hence, it is different from all others.

53. (c) All others are perfect square of natural number.

54. (d) All others are divisible by 12.

55. (d) All others are divisible by 7.

56. (d) All except '18' are square of natural numbers.

$(5)^2 = 25$, $(3)^2 = 9$, $(4)^2 = 16$

57. (d) $4867 \rightarrow 4 + 8 + 6 + 7 = 25$, which is divisible by 5.

$5555 \rightarrow 5 + 5 + 5 + 5 + 5 =$ which is divisible by 5.

$6243 \rightarrow 6 + 2 + 4 + 3 = 15$, which is divisible by 5.

$6655 \rightarrow 6 + 6 + 5 + 5 = 22$, which is not divisible by 5.

58. (d) All others are complete squares.

59. (d) All others are prime numbers.

60. (c) All others are prime numbers.

3 SERIES TEST

Series is a sequential order of letters, numbers or both arranged such a way that each term in the series is obtained according to some specific rules. These rules can be based on mathematical operations, place of letters in alphabetical order etc.

Different type of questions covered in this chapter are as follows

- Number Series
- Letter Series
- Alpha-Numeric Series
- Continuous Pattern Series

In questions on series, a specified sequence/order of letters, numbers or a combination of both is given where one of the term (letter/number/letter and number) of the series is missing either at the end of the series or in between the series.

The candidate is required to identify the pattern involved in the formation of series and accordingly find the missing term to complete the series. Also, there may be some questions where one of the term in the series is incorrect and the candidate is required to find out that term of the series by identifying the pattern involved in the formation of series.

There is no set pattern and each question may follow a different pattern or sequential arrangement of letters or digits, which you have to detect using your common sense and reasoning ability.

1. Finding Missing Number

In such types of questions, a series of numbers is given with one number/term missing from its place. The candidate is required to recognise the pattern involved in the formation of series and find the missing number accordingly.

Various different patterns are involved in the formation of series. Now, let us discuss some most common patterns involved in the formation of series.

Example 1: What comes in place of question mark (?) in the following number series?

2, 3, 5, 8, 12, 17, ?

(a) 23 (b) 19
(c) 18 (d) 25

Solution (a): In the given series, the different between two consecutive numbers is in increasing order i.e., 1, 2, 3, 4, 5 and 6, respectively.

2 3 5 8 12 17 [23]

+1 +2 +3 +4 +5 +6

2. Finding the Wrong Number

In this type of questions, a series of numbers is given which follow a certain pattern and one of its term is incorrect and does not fit into the series. The candidate is required to identify the pattern involved in the formation of series and then find out that number which does not follow the specific pattern of the series. This particular number is the wrong term in the series and is your required answer.

Example 2: In the following number series, only one number is wrong. Find out the wrong number.

9050, 5675, 3478, 2147, 1418, 1077, 950

(a) 3478 (b) 1418
(c) 5675 (d) 1077

Solution (d): The pattern is as follows:

1075

9050 5675 3478 2147 1418 [1077] 950

$-(15)^3$ $-(13)^3$ $-(11)^3$ $-(9)^3$ $-(7)^3$ $-(5)^3$

Hence, 1077 is wrong number and should be replaced by 1075.

3. Finding the missing letter

Letter series is a sequence of letters taken from English alphabet and such sequence follows a certain logical pattern. In terms of letter series, certain logical pattern means that every next element of the series is obtained according to a certain change. In this series, candidates are required to find out the next letter in the series or the missing letter in the series or letter which is wrong in the series.

To solve problems of this kind candidates are required to find the rules followed in the series and determine the pattern of the series.

Example 3: Replace the question mark (?) in the series given below.

B, B, A, D, Z, F, Y, H, X, ?

(a) J (b) N
(c) M (d) O

Solution (b) This series has two parts. In first part, every next term is obtained by subtracting 1 from the corresponding position of its previous letter. While in second part, every next term is obtained by adding 2 to the corresponding position of its previous term (letter).

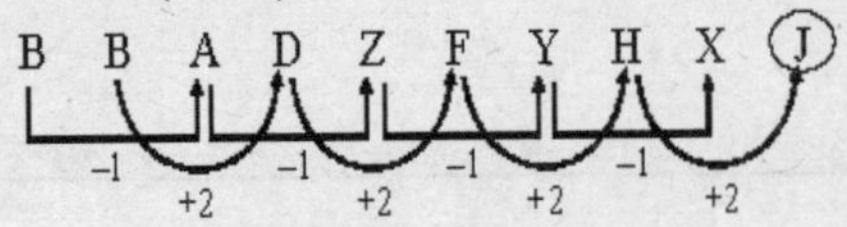

4. Finding the group of missing letter

Continuous pattern series generally consists of small letters of English alphabet where the letters are arranged following a certain pattern. However, some letters are missing from the series. The candidate is required to identify the pattern and accordingly find the proper sequence of these missing letters from the given alternatives.

Directions: Find the missing term in the following series.

Example 4: _aa_ba_bb_ab_aab

(a) aaabb
(b) babab
(c) bbaab
(d) None of these

Solution (c) The series is as follows baab/baab/baab/baab

Solved Examples

Example 1: What comes in place of question mark (?) in the following number series?

95, 94, 92, 89, 85, 80, ?

(a) 74 (b) 69
(c) 75 (d) 77

Solution (a) Here, the difference between two consecutive elements is in increasing order.

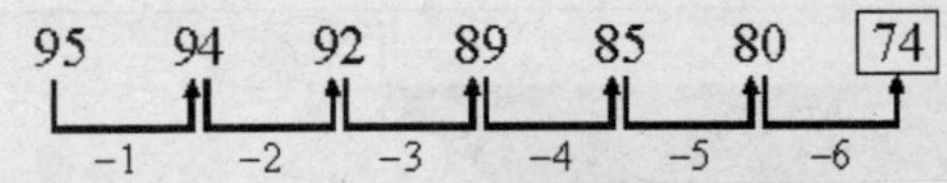

Example 2. What comes in place of question mark (?) in the series given below?

4, 8, 12, 16, 20, ?

(a) 18 (b) 21
(c) 19 (d) 24

Solution (b) In the given series, the difference between two consecutive elements is same i.e., 4.

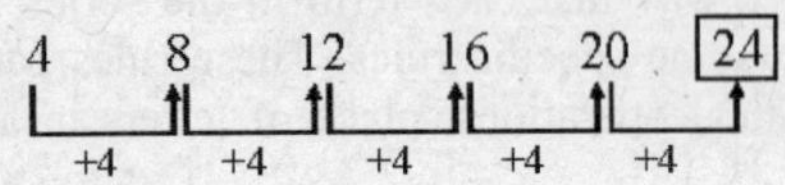

Example 3: Replace the question mark (?) In the following series with appropriate letter.

P, M, J, G, D, ?

(a) A (b) C
(c) B (d) E

Solution (a) Every next term is obtained by subtracting 3 from the corresponding position of its previous term (letter).

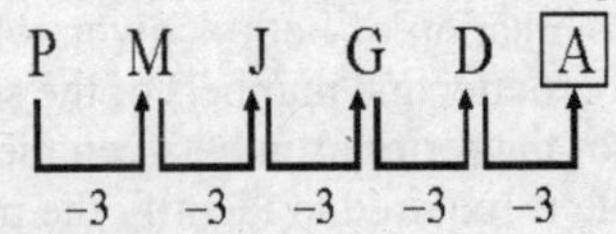

∴ Missing letter = A

Example 4: a_bc_c_abb_bca_

(a) abbba (b) accba
(c) cccbc (d) cbbac

Solution (b) The series is as follows aabcc/ccabb/bbcaa

∴ Required answer = accba

Exercise

Directions (1-15) Find the missing number in the series given below.

1. 16, 22, 34, 58, 106, ?, 394
(a) 178 (b) 175
(c) 288 (d) 202

2. 10, 33, 102, 309, ?
(a) 1030 (b) 1050
(c) 928 (d) 930

3. 121, 112, ?, 97, 91, 86
(a) 102 (b) 108
(c) 99 (d) 104

4. 875, 874, 866, 839, 775, 650, 434, ?
(a) 322 (b) 281
(c) 91 (d) 18

5. 3, 5, 7, ?, 13, 17, 19, 23
(a) 9 (b) 11
(c) 8 (d) 10

6. 823543, 46656, 3125, 256, ?, 4, 1
(a) 28 (b) 27
(c) 36 (d) 49

7. 14, 16, 35, 109, 441, ?
(a) 2651 (b) 2205
(c) 2315 (d) 2211

8. 4, 18, ?, 100, 180, 294.
(a) 32 (b) 36
(c) 48 (d) 40

9. 3, 22, ?, 673, 2696, 8093
(a) 133 (b) 155
(c) 156 (d) 134

10. 6, 42, ?, 1260, 5040, 15120, 30240
(a) 546
(b) 424
(c) 252
(d) 328

11. 17, 43, 81, 131, ?
(a) 375 (b) 468
(c) 300 (d) 193

12. 30, 68, 130, 222, ?, 520, 738
(a) 420 (b) 350
(c) 250 (d) 280

13. 19, 429, 32, 57, 52, 392, 46, ?
(a) 56 (b) 18
(c) 9 (d) 3

14. 15, 17, 20, 22, 27, 29, ?, ?
(a) 31, 38 (b) 36, 38
(c) 36, 43 (d) 38, 45

15. 90, 61, 52, 63, 94, ?, 18
(a) 72
(b) 46
(c) 54
(d) 81

Directions (16-29): In each of these questions, a number series is given. In each series, only one number is wrong. Find out the wrong number.

16. 6 7 9 13 26 37 69
(a) 7 (b) 26
(c) 69 (d) 37

17. 87, 54, 28, 13, 5, 2, 2
(a) 28 (b) 54
(c) 13 (d) 2

18. 22, 37, 52, 67, 84, 97
(a) 52 (b) 84
(c) 97 (d) 67

19. 6072, 1008, 200, 48, 14, 5, 3
(a) 1008 (b) 200
(c) 48 (d) 14

20. 10, 13, 26, 37, 51, 85, 154
(a) 10 (b) 26
(c) 51 (d) 154

21. 895, 870, 821, 740, 619, 445, 225
(a) 870 (b) 821
(c) 740 (d) 445

22. 4, 3, 9, 34, 96, 219, 435
(a) 4 (b) 9
(c) 34 (d) 435

23. 1, 2, 6, 21, 86, 445, 2676
(a) 2 (b) 6
(c) 21 (d) 86

24. 644, 328, 164, 84, 44, 24, 14
(a) 328 (b) 164
(c) 84 (d) 44

25. 157.5 45 15 6 3 2 1
(a) 1 (b) 2
(c) 6 (d) 157.5

26. 2, 6, 24, 96, 285, 568, 567
(a) 6 (b) 24
(c) 96 (d) 285

27. 4, 5, 14, 39, 103, 169, 290
(a) 5 (b) 14
(c) 39 (d) 103

28. 2, 3, 6,15, 37.5, 157.5, 630
(a) 3 (b) 6
(c) 15 (d) 37.5

29. 2, 5, 11, 27, 58, 121, 248
(a) 5 (b) 11
(c) 27 (d) 58

Directions (30-44): What comes in place of question mark (?) in the series given below?

30. AZ, BY, CX, ?
(a) EW (b) EU
(c) GH (d) DW

31. AC, FH, K?, PR, UW
(a) L (b) J
(c) M (d) N

32. AMN, BOP, CQR, ?
(a) BAS (b) DST
(c) EQP (d) FRS

33. AIBJCK??
(a) EM (b) EL
(c) DL (d) DM

34. NZ, OY, PX, QW, RV, ?
(a) FS (b) SU
(c) UF (d) TU

35. AMV, BNW, COX, ?, EQZ
(a) DMO (b) DPY
(c) DYP (d) DLZ

36. XWA, VTC, SPF, OKJ, ?
(a) JDN (b) JEO
(c) LPN (d) JDP

37. BEAG, DGCI, FIEK, ?
(a) HMIE (b) HKGM
(c) HGKJ (d) HKLI

38. bc, cde, de, efg, fg, ?
(a) ghi (b) fgh
(c) hij (d) ijk

39. BDF, HJL, NPR, ?
(a) OQS (b) TUV
(c) TVX (d) UVW

40. ABCD, BCDA, CDAB, ?, ABCD
(a) BADC (b) DABC
(c) DBAC (d) DACB

41. YVP, WTN, URL, ?
(a) VSP (b) SRJ
(c) SPJ (d) TQL

42. PQRS, QPRS, RPQS, ?
(a) SQPR (b) RPQS
(c) QSPR (d) SQPR

43. TSMD, TSDM, TMDS, ?
(a) TSDM (b) SDTM
(c) TMDS (d) SDMT

44. AFI, JOR, MRU, ?
(a) GJN (b) HMP
(c) PMO (d) RJL

Directions (45-50): In each of the following questions, continuous pattern series is given. Some of the letters of the series are missing. These missing letters are given in that order as one of the four alternatives below the series. Find out the correct alternatives.

45. ab_cabb_caa_bccab_cab_cc
(a) abbcc (b) baabc
(c) bcbbb (d) bcaac

46. adb_ac_da_cddcb_dbc_cbda
(a) bccba (b) cbbaa
(c) ccbba (d) bbcad

47. c_bba_cab_ac_ab_ac
(a) b, c, b, a, c
(b) c, a, b, c, b
(c) a, c, c, b, c
(d) a, c, b, c, b

48. bc_bca_cab_ab_a_ca
(a) abcab (b) cabac
(c) abccb (d) cabca

49. mc_m_a_ca_ca_c_mc
(a) acmmma
(b) camcam
(c) aaacmm
(d) acmmmc

50. a_a_abab_ba
(a) abab (b) baab
(c) abba (d) bbab

Answers with Explanations

1. (d) Here, series moves with the addition of 6, 12, 24, 48, 96 and 192, respectively. Hence, the missing number is 202.

2. (d) The pattern is as follows

10 → 33 → 102 → 309 → [930]
(×3+3) (×3+3) (×3+3) (×3+3)

3. (d) Here, series is written in descending order with a difference of 9, 8, 7, 6 and 5, respectively. Hence, the missing number will be 104.

4. (c) Keep subtracting the next larger perfect cube i.e, 1, 8, 27, 64, 125, 216, 343.

∴ ? = (434 – 343) = 91

5. (b) The given series is the series of prime numbers.

3, 5, 7, 11, 13, 17, 19, 23

∴ ? = 11

6. (b) The sequence is 7^7, 6^6, 5^5, 4^4, 3^3, 2^2, 1^1

∴ ? = 3^3 = 9

7. (d) The pattern is as follows

14 16 35 109 441 [2211]

×1+2 ×2+3 ×3+4 ×4+5 ×5+6

8. (c) The pattern of series is as follows:

4 18 [48] 100 180 294

$2^2\times1$ $3^2\times2$ $4^2\times3$ $5^2\times4$ $6^2\times5$ $7^2\times6$

9. (d) The pattern is as follows

3 22 [134] 673 2696 8093

×7+1 ×6+2 ×5+3 ×4+4 ×3+5

10. (c) The pattern is as follows:

6 42 [252] 1260 5040 15120 30240

×7 ×6 ×5 ×4 ×3 ×2

11. (d) The pattern is as follows:

17 43 81 131 [193]

+26 +38 +50 +62

+12 +12 +12

12. (b) The pattern is as follows:

30 68 130 222 [350] 520 738

+38 +62 +92 +128 +170 +218

+24 +36 +36 +42 +48

+6 +6 +6 +6

13. (d) Here, the series is a palindromic sequence where the series looks similar when seen from either end.

14. (b) The pattern is as follows:

15 17 20 22 27 29 [36] [38]

+2 +3 +2 +5 +2 +7 +2

15. (b) When the digits of the numbers are reversed these are the perfect squares 09, 16, 25, 36, 49, 64, 81, consecutive

∴ ? = Reverse of 64 = 46

16. (b) The pattern is as follows:

[21]

6 7 9 13 26 37 69

+1 +2 +4 +8 +16 +32

Hence, 21 should come in place of 26 in the series.

17. (b) Series moves from the right end with addition of 0, 3, 8, 15, 24 and 35 i.e, with a difference of numbers, which are one less than the square of successive natural numbers. Therefore, number 54 should be replaced by 52.

18. (b) The pattern is as follows:

[82]

22 37 52 67 84 97

+15 +15 +15 +15 +15

So, 84 is the incorrect term, it should be 82.

19. (a) The pattern is as follows :

1010

6072 [1008] 200 48 14 5 3

+6–2 +5–2 +4–2 +3–2 +2–2 +1–2

Hence, number 1008 is wrong and should be replaced by 1010.

20. (c) The pattern is as follows:

+16 +32 [+96]

10 13 26 37 51 85 154

[58]

+24 +48

Hence, number 51 is wrong and should be replaced by 58.

21. (d) The pattern is as follows:

450

895 870 821 740 619 [445] 225

$-(5)^2$ $-(7)^2$ $-(9)^2$ $-(11)^2$ $-(13)^2$ $-(15)^2$

Hence, number 445 is wrong and should be replaced by 450.

22. (d) The pattern is as follows:

[433]

4 3 9 34 96 219 435

$+1^3-2$ $+2^3-2$ $+3^3-2$ $+4^3-2$ $+5^3-2$ $+6^3-2$

From above, we can say that 435 is wrong in the given series. 433 should come in place of 435.

Hence, number 11 is wrong and should be replaced by 12.

23. (d) The pattern is as follows:

88

1 2 6 21 [86] 445 2676

×1+1 ×2+2 ×3+3 ×4+4 ×5+5 ×6+6

Hence, number 86 is wrong and should be replaced by 88.

24. (a) The pattern is as follows:

324

644 [328] 164 84 44 24 14

÷2+2 ÷2+2 ÷2+2 ÷2+2 ÷2+2 ÷2+2

Hence, number 328 is wrong and should be replaced by 324.

25. (a) The pattern is as follows:

[2]

157.5 45 15 6 3 2 1

÷3.5 ÷3 ÷2.5 ÷2 ÷1.5 ÷1

From above, 2 should come in place of 1 in given series.

26. (b) The pattern is as follows:

25 3

2 6 [24] 96 285 568 567

×6–6 ×5–5 ×4–4 ×3–3 ×2–2 ×1–1

Hence, number 24 is wrong and should be replaced by 25.

27. (d) The pattern is as follows:

88

4 5 14 39 [103] 169 290

$+(1)^2$ $+(3)^2$ $+(5)^2$ $+(7)^2$ $+(9)^2$ $+(11)^2$

Hence, number 103 is wrong and should be replaced by 88.

28. (d) The pattern is as follows:

45

2 3 6 15 [37.5] 157.5 630

×1.5 ×2 ×2.5 ×3 ×3.5 ×4

Hence, number 37.5 is wrong and should be replaced by 45.

29. (b) The pattern is as follows:

12

2 5 [11] 27 58 121 248

×2+1 ×2+2 ×2+3 ×2+4 ×2+5 ×2+6

30. (d) The pattern is as follows:

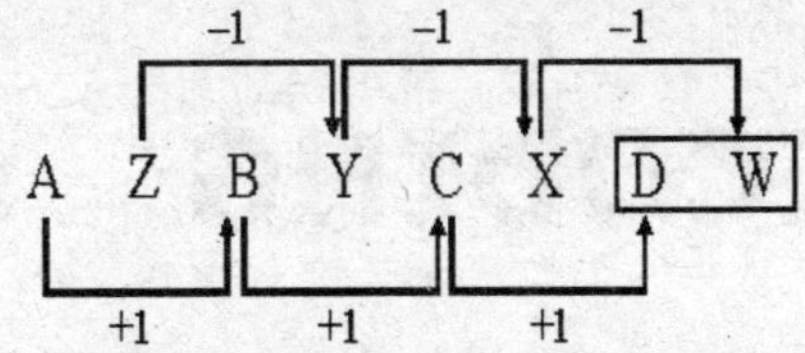

31. (c) The pattern is as follows:

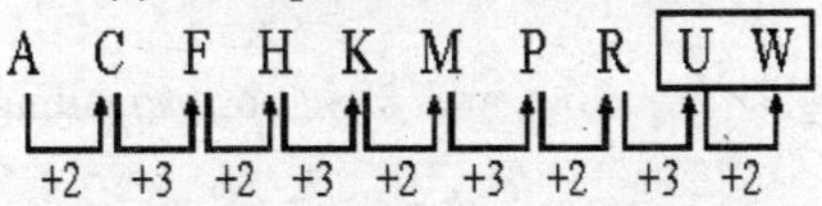

32. (b) The pattern is as follows:

$A \xrightarrow{+1} B \xrightarrow{+1} C \xrightarrow{+1} D$

$M \xrightarrow{+2} O \xrightarrow{+2} Q \xrightarrow{+2} S$

$N \xrightarrow{+2} P \xrightarrow{+2} R \xrightarrow{+2} T$

33. (c) The pattern is as follows:

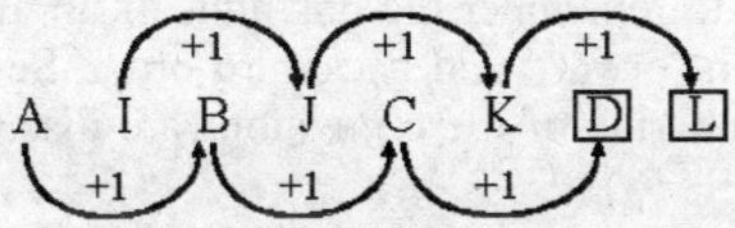

34. (b) Here, the pattern is as follows:

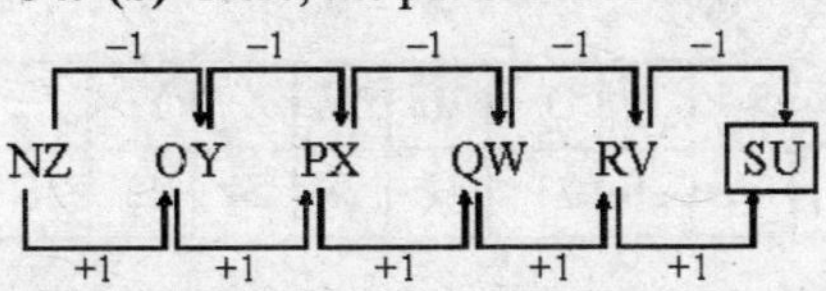

35. (b) The pattern is as follows:

$A \xrightarrow{+1} B, \xrightarrow{+1} C \xrightarrow{+1} D \xrightarrow{+1} E$

$M \xrightarrow{+1} N \xrightarrow{+1} O \xrightarrow{+1} P \xrightarrow{+1} Q$

$V \xrightarrow{+1} W \xrightarrow{+1} X \xrightarrow{+1} Y \xrightarrow{+1} Z$

∴ = DPY

36. (b) The pattern is as follows:

$X \xrightarrow{-2} V \xrightarrow{-3} S \xrightarrow{-4} O \xrightarrow{-5} J$

$W \xrightarrow{-3} T \xrightarrow{-4} P \xrightarrow{-5} K \xrightarrow{-6} E$

$A \xrightarrow{+2} C \xrightarrow{+3} F \xrightarrow{+4} J \xrightarrow{+5} O$

37. (b) The pattern is as follows:

$B \xrightarrow{+2} D \xrightarrow{+2} F \xrightarrow{+2} H$

$E \xrightarrow{+2} G \xrightarrow{+2} I \xrightarrow{+2} K$

$A \xrightarrow{+2} C \xrightarrow{+2} E \xrightarrow{+2} G$

$G \xrightarrow{+2} I \xrightarrow{+2} K \xrightarrow{+2} M$

38. (a) There are two interwoven series here.

bc, de, fg, (Each next term is formed by next two letters) cde, efg, ghi (last letter of the previous term starts the new term and next two letters are included in the same term).

∴ ? = ghi

39. (c) The pattern is as follows:

$B \xrightarrow{+6} H \xrightarrow{+6} N \xrightarrow{+6}$ T

$D \xrightarrow{+6} J \xrightarrow{+6} P \xrightarrow{+6}$ V

$F \xrightarrow{+6} L \xrightarrow{+6} R \xrightarrow{+6}$ X

40. (b) In the following series, the next term is obtained by shifting the first letter of the previous term to the last place.

∴ = DABC

41. (c) The pattern is as follows

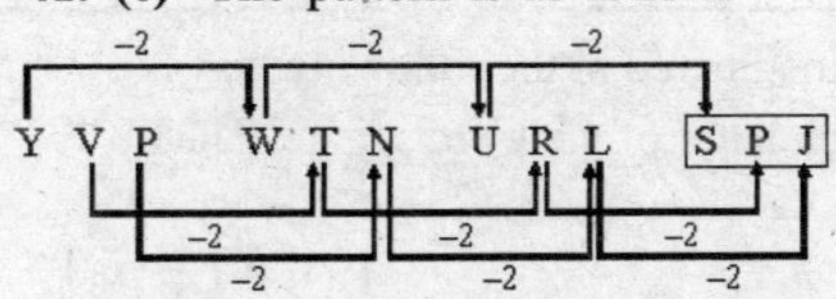

42. (a) From element first to second first two letters get reversed, from second to third, first three letters get reversed and from third to last, all the four letters get reversed.

∴ Required answer = SQPR

43. (d) From element first to second last two letter are written in reverse order, from element second to third, last three letters are written in reverse order and from element third to fourth, all the four letters are written in reverse order.

∴ Required answer = SDMT

44. (b) The pattern followed in each term is

First letter + = Second letter and second letter + = Third letter

As,

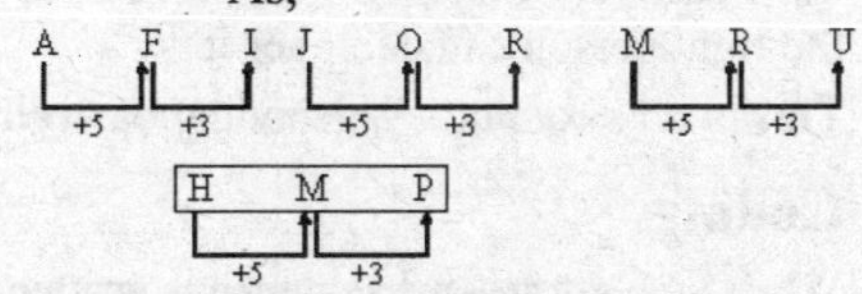

45. (c) Series pattern: abbcabbcc/aabbcc/abbcabbcc

∴ Required answer = bcbbb

46. (b) In the above series, the letters are equidistant from the beginning and the end.

adbcacbdabcddcbadbcacbda

hence, the missing letter are cbbaa.

47. (d) Series pattern: cab/bac/cab/bac/cab/bac

∴ Required answer = acbcb

48. (c) Series pattern: bc/abc/abc/abc/abc/abca

∴ Required = abccb

49. (a) Series pattern: mca/mca/mca/mca/mca/mc

∴ Required answer = acmma

50. (d) Here, in the series letters ab are repeated.

ab/ab/ab/ab/ab/ab = bbab

∴ ? = bbab

4 CODING DECODING

Coding-Decoding is process of transmitting an information from one place to other using some suitable codes, so that it might reach to other person safety. Coding & decoding of an information is done with various rules or patterns, so that only the right person can decipher it.

This process of coding-decoding basically involves.

Coding

When any letter/word/sentence is written or said in such a language which hides the actual meaning of that particular letter/ word/ sentence from others except the desired person.

Decoding

It helps in tracing out the actual meaning of a coded letter/word/sentence. Generally, coding is done on the basic of the letters of English alphabet and their corresponding positions.

In these questions, a word (basic word) is coded in a particular way and candidates are asked to code other words in the same way. As the matter of fact, there exists no uniform and particular type of category of these questions according to which we could classify questions of coding-decoding. However, keeping in view the candidate's convenience, we have classified different types of questions with illustrations and explanations under different headings.

To solve the questions based on coding-decoding, first of all it is necessary to remember the positions of all alphabetical letters, both in forward and backward order. Several ways for easy remembering of these positions are discussed here.

Forward Order Position of letters (Left to Right)

A	B	C	D	E	F	G	H	I	J	K	L	M	N	O	P	Q	R	S	T	U	V	W	X	Y	Z
1	2	3	4	5	6	7	8	9	10	11	12	13	14	15	16	17	18	19	20	21	22	23	24	25	26

Forward order position of letters can be remembered in the following ways

(*i*) Here is a gap of four letters between each letter of the word group 'EJOTY'.

Letter ⟶ E J O T Y

↓ ↓ ↓ ↓ ↓

Position order ⟶ 5 10 15 20 25

(*ii*) Here is a gap of two letters between each letter of the word group 'CFILORUX'.

Letter ⟶ C F I L O R U X

↓ ↓ ↓ ↓ ↓ ↓ ↓ ↓

Position order ⟶ 3 6 9 12 15 18 21 24

Backward Letter Positions (Right to Left)

A	B	C	D	E	F	G	H	I	J	K	L	M	N	O	P	Q	R	S	T	U	V	W	X	Y	Z
26	25	24	23	22	21	20	19	18	17	16	15	14	13	12	11	10	9	8	7	6	5	4	3	2	1

Students find it difficult to remember backward order position but, if they keep forward order positions of letters in their mind, they can easily calculate the backward order of letters in the following way

⇒ Backward order position of any letter = 27 – Forward order position of that letter

∴ Backward order position of A = 27 – Forward order position of A = 27 – 1 = 26

Opposite Letters

These are called opposite letters as the forward order corresponding position of an opposite letter is as same as the backward order corresponding position of its opposite letter.

1 2 3 4 5 6 7 8 9 10 11 12 13

↕ ↕ ↕ ↕ ↕ ↕ ↕ ↕ ↕ ↕ ↕ ↕ ↕

A B C D E F G H I J K L M

26	25	24	23	22	21	20	19	18	17	16	15	14
↕	↕	↕	↕	↕	↕	↕	↕	↕	↕	↕	↕	↕
Z	Y	X	W	V	U	T	S	R	Q	P	O	N

A and Z is a pair of opposite letters.

Now, it is clear from the above presentation that two letters are called opposite to each other, if sum of their corresponding positions is equal to 27.

⇒ Opposite position of any letter = 27 – Corresponding position of that letter

∴ Opposite position of A = 27 – Corresponding position of A = 27 – 1 = 26 = Z

Solved Examples

Example 1: If in a certain code language 'TREND' is written as 'USFOE', the how will 'ENTRY' be written in that code?

(a) GNUSZ (b) FOUSZ
(c) FUDSZ (d) FOUZS

Solution (b) As,

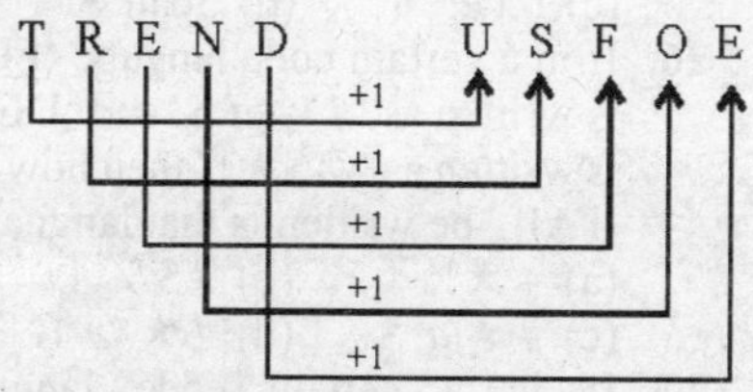

Similarly,

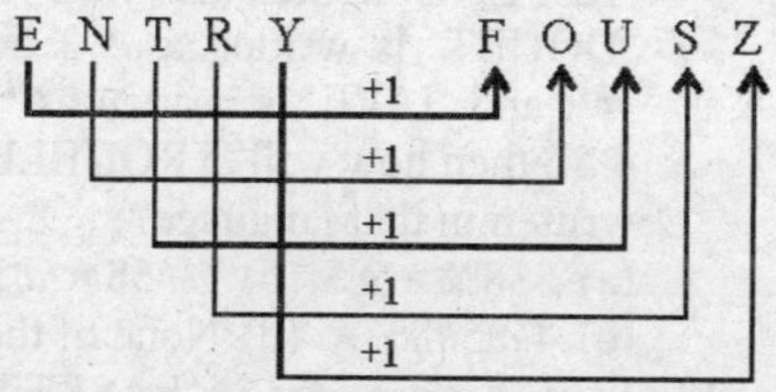

Example 2: If in a certain code language 'PUT' is written as '57', then how will 'BAT' be written in that language?

(a) 25 (b) 60
(c) 55 (d) 23

Solution (d) As,

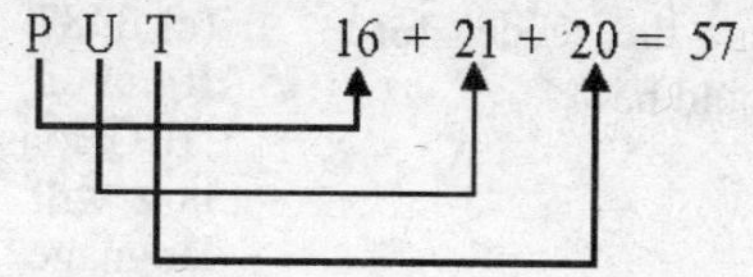

Similarly,

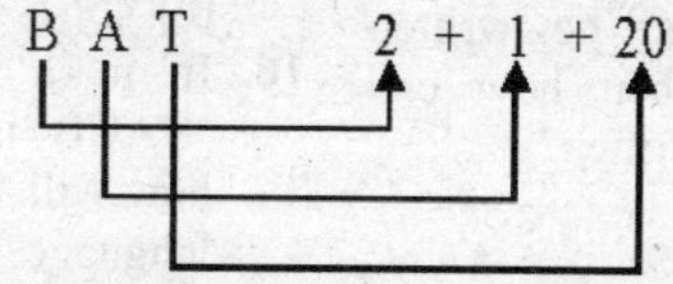

∴ BAT = 23

Example 3: In a certain code 'GONE' is written as 5 % 2 # and 'MEDAL' is written as 4#3 $@, then how will 'GOLD' be written in that code?

(a) 5 @ % 3 (b) 5 % @ 3
(c) 5 # @ 3 (d) 5 % # 3

Solution (b) As, G O N E → 5 % 2 #

and M E D A L → 4 # 3 $ @

Similarly G O L D → 5 % @ 3

Example 4: If 'blue' means 'green', 'green' means 'white', white 'means' 'yellow', 'yellow' means 'black' 'black' means 'red' and 'red' means 'brown', then what is the colour of 'milk'?

(a) Black (b) White
(c) Yellow (d) Green

Solution (c) Colour of 'milk' is 'white' but here 'white' means 'yellow'. Hence, colour of 'milk' is yellow.

Exercise

1. If in a certain code language 'CHOLINE' is written as 'OCIHLEN', then how will 'SURGEON' be written in that language?
(a) RSUEGNO
(b) RSEGUNO
(c) RESUGNO
(d) RSEUGNO

2. If 'SWAMINATHAN' is coded as 'NAHTANIMAWS' in a certain code language, then how would you code 'SIRNAME' in that language?
(a) EMAMSIR
(b) EMARNIS
(c) EMNARIS
(d) EMANRIS

3. IF 'VEHEMENT' is written as 'VEHETNEM', then how 'mournful' be written in that code language?
(a) MOURLUFN
(b) MOUNULER
(c) OURMNFUL
(d) URNFULMO

4. In a certain code language, 'COMPUTRONE' is written as 'PMOCTUENOR'. How is 'advantages' written in that same code?
(a) ADVANSEGAS
(b) ADVTANSEAG
(c) AVDANTAGES
(d) AVDTNSEGA

5. In a certain language, 'EXECUTIVE' is coded as 'TCLEUXVEE', then how is MAUSOLEUM' coded in that same language?
(a) LSEUOAUMM
(b) AUUCOSLMM
(c) AUEUOSEMM
(d) SLUEOAUMM

6. If 'CARPET' is coded as 'TCEAPR', then the code for 'NATIONAL' would be
(a) NLATNOIA
(b) LANOITAN
(c) LNAANTOI
(d) LNOINTAA

7. If NEUROTIC' can be written as 'TICRONEU' then how can 'PSYCHOTIC' be written?
(a) TICOCHPSY
(b) TICCHOPSY
(c) TICCOHPSY
(d) TICHCOPSY

8. If in a certain code language 'PERSON' is coded as 'STXWJU', then how will 'MOTHER' be coded in that language?
(a) RTYUJM (b) RTYJMU
(c) WJMYTR (d) RTYMUJ

9. In a certain code, 'FLOWERS' is written as 'EKNVDQR'. How will 'SUPREME' be written in that code?
(a) TQDROLD (b) RTODQLD
(c) TQDDROL (d) RTOQDLD

10. If in a certain code language 'TRIVENDRUM' is written as 'VTKXGPFTWO', then how will 'ERNAKULAM' be written in that language?
(a) GTPCMWNOC
(b) GTPCMWNCO
(c) GTPCMNWCO
(d) GTPMCWNCO

11. If in a certain code language 'EARTH' is written as 'JVTCG', then how will 'GLOBE' be written in that language?
(a) GDQNI (b) GDQIN
(c) GDNIQ (d) GDIQN

12. If in a certain code language 'SAND' is written as 'VDQG' 'BIRD' is written as 'ELUG', then how will 'LOVE' be written in that language?
(a) PRYG (b) ORTG
(c) NPUH (d) ORYH

13. If in a certain code language 'RAMAN' is coded as '18113114', then how will 'KAPILA' be coded in that language?
(a) 111196112 (b) 111169112
(c) 111169121 (d) 116119121

14. If in a certain code language 'BHAI' is written as '2819', then how will 'CDGH' be written in that language?
(a) 8437 (b) 7348
(c) 3487 (d) 3478

15. If in a certain code language 'HIGH' is written as '/8978', then how will 'DEAF' be written in that language?
(a) 5416 (b) 4516
(c) 4561 (d) 4156

16. If in a certain code language 'HACB' is written as '8132', then how will 'DEFA' be written in that language?
(a) 4651 (b) 4561
(c) 4156 (d) 5641

17. If ion a certain code language 'PAPER' is written as '16116518', then how will 'BRINJL' be writen in that language?
(a) 2189141012
(b) 2189141021
(c) 23189140112
(d) 2389411021

18. If in a code language letters, of the word 'CAMEL' are coded as '25106', then word 'LION' is coded as '6793' and the word 'TIRE' is coded as '4780'. How will the letters of the word 'ELITE' be coded in that language?
(a) 06740 (b) 06470
(c) 60476 (d) 06704

19. If in a certain code language 'TALK' is written as '2121312', then how will 'PATNA' be coded int hat language?
(a) 17212152 (b) 17221251
(c) 17221125 (d) 17221152

20. If in a certain code language 'GRADUATE' is written as '2092623626722', then how will 'ARIHANT' be written in that language?
(a) 269181926137
(b) 269181926173
(c) 269811926137
(d) 269181962137

21. If in a certain code language 'PERFECT' is written as '116', then how will 'COMPACT' be written in that code?
(a) 85 (b) 111
(c) 98 (d) 118

22. If in a certain code language 'TRUE' is written as '8316', then how will 'TAP' be written in that language?
(a) 3120 (b) 2002
(c) 2015 (d) 1122

23. If in a certain code language 'SON' is written as '81213' 'life' is written as '15182122', then how will 'never' be written in that language?
(a) 13225229 (b) 22135229
(c) 13225292 (d) 13222529

24. If in a certain code language 'STAR' is written as '5 $ 2 ★', 'TORE' is written as '$ 3 2 @', then how will 'OATS' be written in that language?
(a) 3 5 ★ $ (b) 3 5 $★
(c) 3 $ 5 ★ (d) 3 5 ★ $

25. If in a certain code language 'GONE' is written as '5 @' © 9' and 'SEAL' is written as '6 9 % ★', then how will 'LOGS' be written in that language?
(a) ★ ©56 (b) ★ ©96
(c) 65 @ ★ (d) 56@ ★

26. If in a certain code languge 'FIRE' is written as '# % @ $' and 'DEAL' is written as '© $★↑' then how will 'FAIL' be written is that language?
(a) # ★% ↑ (b) # $ % ↑
(c) # ★@ $ (d) # ★ © ↑

27. If in a certain code language 'ROPE' is written as '% 5 7 $', 'DOUBT' is written as ' 3 5 # 8 ★', and 'LIVE' is written as '@ 2 4 $', then how will 'TROUBLE' be written in that language?
(a) 5$8%★@$ (b) %#58★@$
(c) 4@5#8%★ (d) None of these

28. In a certain code, 'BASKET' is written as '5$3%#1' and 'TRIED' is written as '14 2 # ★'. How is 'SKIRT' written in that code?
(a) 3 %1 4★ (b) 3 1 4 %★
(c) 3 % # 4 1 (d) 3 # 4 % 1

29. If in a certain language 'HEART' is written as '@8531', 'FEAST' is written as '#8541', then how will 'FARTHEST' be written in that language?
(a) @ 8543#18 (b) #5314@81
(c) # 531@841 (d) 4531@845

30. If 'bucket' is known as 'tub', 'tub' is known as 'glass', 'glass' is known as 'saucer', 'saucer' is known as 'spoon', then which utensil will be used for drinking water?
(a) Tub (b) Saucer
(c) Glass (d) Spoon

31. If 'HINDI' is called 'ENGLISH'; 'ENGLISH' is called 'URDU'; 'URDU' is called 'HISTORY';

'HISTORY' is called 'ECONOMICS'; 'ECONOMICS' is called 'BIOLOGY', then in which subject we read the story of Mughal Kind Shahjahan?
(a) History (b) English
(c) Urdu (d) Economics

32. If 'blue' is called 'green', 'green' is called 'white', 'white' is called 'red', 'red' is called 'black' then what is the colour or clear sky?
(a) Blue (b) Green
(c) White (d) Black

33. If in a certain code language 'Sachin is great' is written as 'ga ma ra', 'is he poor' is written as 'ta sa ga', then find the code for' is?
(a) ta
(b) ma
(c) ga
(d) ra

34. If in a certain code language 'fruits are sweet' is written as 'pa ma la' and 'you are sweet' is written as 'pa ma ta', then find the code for 'fruits'.
(a) ta (b) ma
(c) pa (d) la

35. If in a certain code language 'pick and choose' is written as 'ko ho po' and 'pick up and come' is written as 'to no ko po', then how will 'pick be written in that language?
(a) ko
(b) po
(c) ko or po
(d) Cannot be determined

Answers with Explanations

1. (d) As,

1 2 3 4 5 6 7 → 3 1 5 2 4 7 6
C H O L I N E → O C I H L E N

Similarly,

1 2 3 4 5 6 7 → 3 1 5 2 4 7 6
SURGEON → RSEUGNO

2. (c) As,

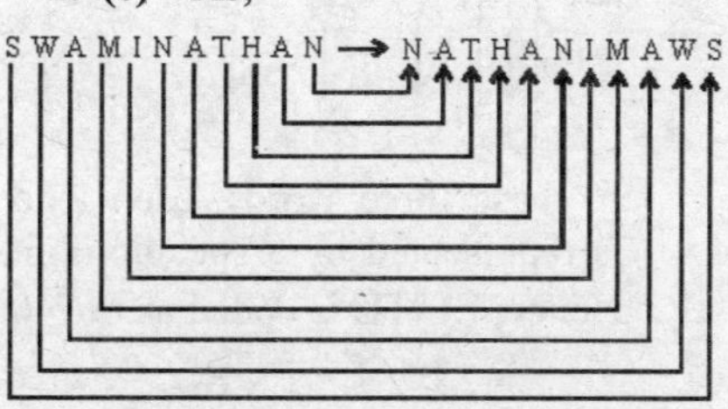

Similarly

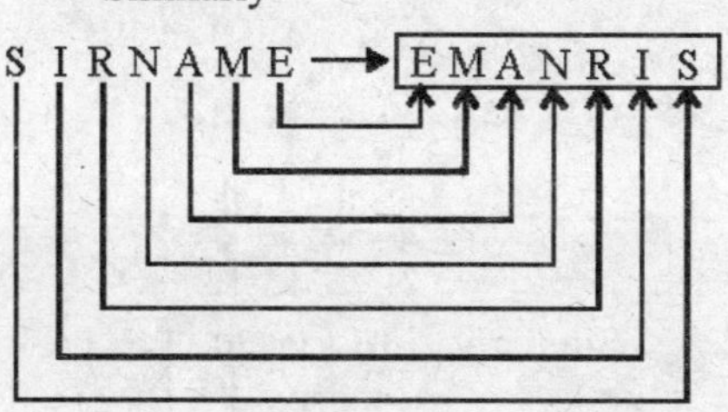

3. (a) As,

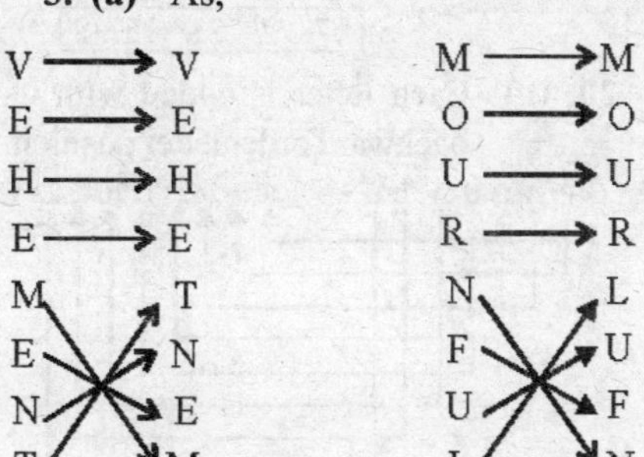

4. (d) As

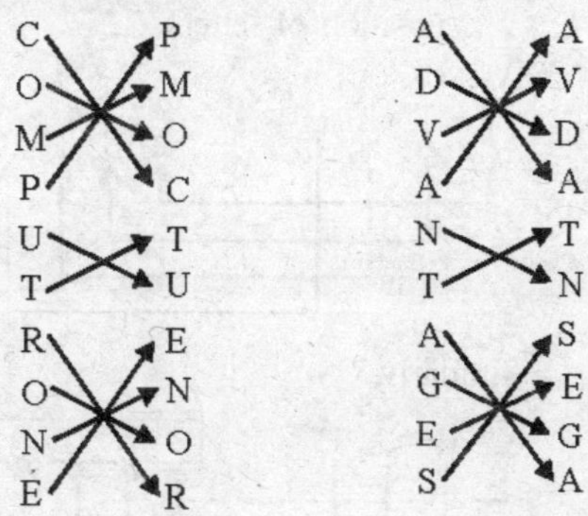

5. (A) As,

E X E C U T I V E
1 2 3 4 5 6 7 8 9
↓
T C I E U X V E E
6 4 7 3 5 2 8 1 9

Similarly,

M A U S O L E U M
1 2 3 4 5 6 7 8 9
↓
L S E U O A U M M
6 4 7 3 5 2 8 1 9

6. (c) Letters of the basic word are written in the coded word in such a way that last and first letters, second last and second letters, third last and third letters and so on are written together in the coded word.

7. (c) As,

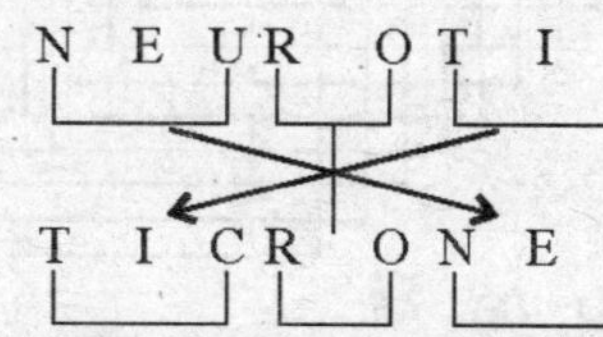

Similarly,

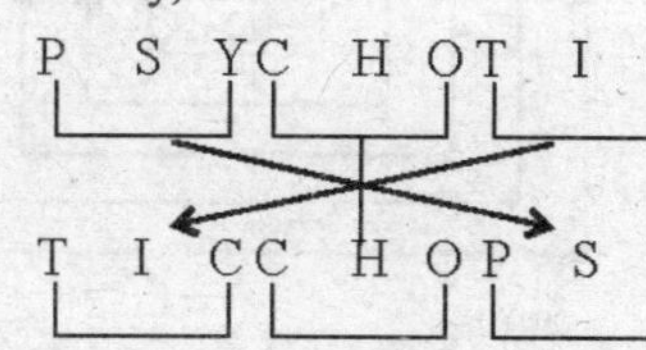

8. (c) As,

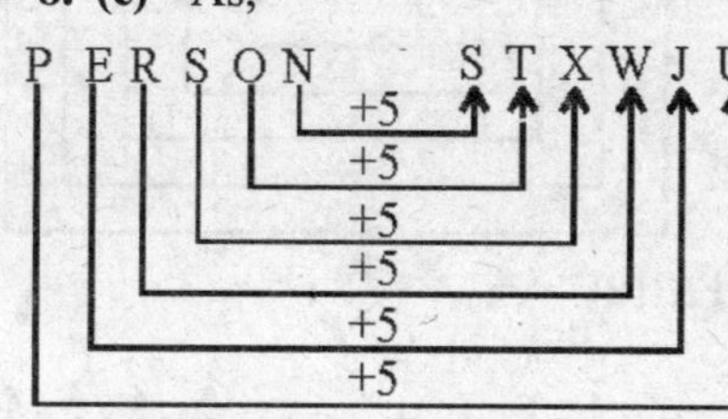

Similarly,

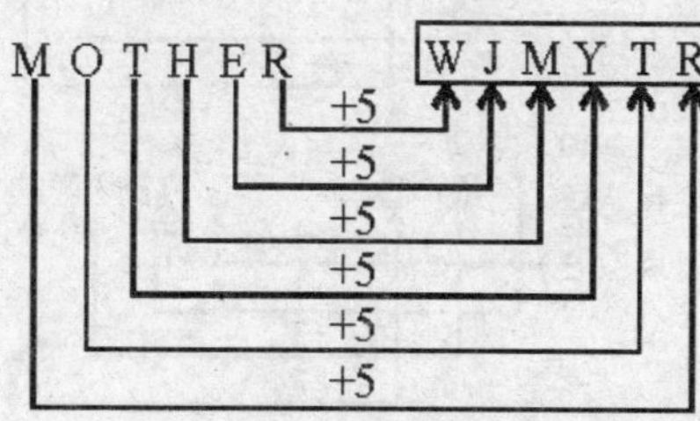

9. (d) As,

6	12	15	23	5	18	19
F	L	O	W	E	R	S
↓–1	↓–1	↓–1	↓–1	↓–1	↓–1	↓–1
E	K	N	V	D	Q	R
5	11	14	22	4	17	18

Similarly,

19 21 16 18 5 13 5
S U P R E M E
–1 –1 –1 –1 –1 –1 –1
R T O Q D L D
18 20 15 17 4 12 4

10. (b) As,

T R I V E N D R U M → V T K X G P F T W O (+2 each)

Similarly,

E R B A J Y K A M → G T P C M W N C O (+2 each)

11. (a) As,

E A R T H → J V T C G (+2 each)

Similarly,

G L O B E → G D Q N I (+2 each)

12. (d) As,

S A N D → V D Q G (+3 each)

and

B I R D → E L U G (+3 each)

Similarly,

L O V E → O R Y H (+3 each)

13. (c) Coded with corresponding positions of letters.

As,

R A M A N → 18 1 13 1 14

Similarly,

K A P I L A → 11 1 16 9 12 1

14. (d) Coded with corresponding position of letters.

As,

B A H I → 2 8 1 9

Similarly,

C D G H → 3 4 7 9

15. (b) Coded with corresponding position of letters.

As,

H I G H → 8 9 7 8

Similarly

D E A F → 4 5 1 6

16. (b) Coded with corresponding position of letters.

As,

H A C B → 8 1 3 2

Similarly,

D E F A → 4 5 6 1

17. (a) Coded with corresponding position of letters.

As,

P A P E R → 16 1 16 5 18

Similarly,

B R I N J L → 2 18 9 14 10 12

18. (a) As,

C A M E L L I O N
↓ ↓ ↓ ↓ ↓ ↓ ↓ ↓ ↓
2 5 1 0 6 6 7 9 3

and

T I R E
↓ ↓ ↓ ↓
4 7 8 0

In these three words, each letter is represented by a specific digit. Hence, ELITE is coded as 06740.

E L I T E
↓ ↓ ↓ ↓ ↓
0 6 7 4 0

19. (d) As,

20 1 12 11
T A L K
+1 +1 +1 +1
21 2 13 12

Similarly,

16 1 20 14 1
P A T N A
+1 +1 +1 +1 +1
17 2 21 15 2

20. (a) Each letter is coded with its backward order letter position.

G R A D U A T E → 20 9 26 23 6 26 7 22

Similarly,

A R I H A N T → 26 9 18 19 26 13 7

21. (d) Backward order corresponding positions of letters are added.

As,

P E R F E C T → 11 + 22 + 9 + 21 + 22 + 24 + 7 = 116

Similarly

C O M P E C T → 24 + 12 + 14 + 11 + 26 + 24 + 7 = 118

22. (b) Backward order letter positions are multiplied.

As,

T R U E → 7 × 9 × 6 × 22 = 8316

Similarly,

T A P → 7 × 26 × 11 = 2002

23. (a) Letter are coded with their backward order letter positions.

As, S O N → 8 12 13

and L I F E → 15 18 21 22

Similarly,

N E V E R → 13 22 5 22 9

24. (b) As,

S T A R → 5 $ ★ 2 and T O R E → $ 3 2 @

Similarly O A T S → 3 ★ $ 5

25. (d) As, G O N E → 5 @ © 9 and

S E A L → 6 9 % ★

Similarly L O G S → ★ @ 5 6

26. (a) As, F I R E → # % @ $ and

E E L L → © $ ★ ↑

Similarly F A I L → # ★ % ↑

27. (d) As,

R O P E D O U B T → % 5 7 $ 3 5 # 8 ★

and

L I V E → @ 2 4 $

Similarly T R O U B L E → ★ % 5 # 8 @ $

28. (a) As, B A S K E T → 5 $ 3 % # 1

and

T R I E D → 1 4 ★ # 2

Similarly, S K I R T → 3 % ★ 4 1

29. (c) As, H E A R T → @ 8 5 3 1

and

F E A S T → # 8 5 4 1

Similarly, F A R T H E S T → # 5 3 1 @ 8 4 1

30. (b) 'Glass' is used for drinking water and here 'glass is called as 'saucer'. Hence, in this case saucer is used for drinking 'water.

31. (d) In 'History', we read the story of Shahjahan' but here History is called 'Economics'. Hence, in this case, we read about Shahjanhan in **Economics**.

32. (b) The colour of clear sky is 'blue' but here 'blue' is called 'green'. Hence, i this case colour of clear sky is 'green'.

33. (c) Sachin is great → ga ma ra ... (i)

is he poor → ta sa ga ... (ii)

From Eqs. (i) and (ii)

is ⇒ ga

34. (d) fruits are sweet → pa ma la .... (i)

you are sweet → pa ma ta ...(ii)

From Eqs. (i) and (ii)

'are sweet' ⇒ pa ma

∴ fruits ⇒ la

35. (c) pick and choose → ko ho po ...(i)

pick up and come → to no ko po ...(ii)

From Eqs. (i) and (ii),

pick and ⇒ ko po

pick ⇒ ko or po

5 LOGICAL SEQUENCE OF WORDS AND DICTIONARY ORDER

Logical Arrangement is the meaningful arrangement of words in accordance will the natural laws and universally accepted concepts.

In these types of problems, a sequence is to be formed with the given number of words in such a way that the particular arrangement of the words gives a logical step by step completion of some process or activity. In these questions, four/five/six words are given which are related to each other in some or other way. The candidate is required to find out the proper logical arrangement of the words from the given alternatives.

Several types of problems based on logical arrangement of words, asked in various competitive exams, are categorised as follows.

Solved Examples

Example 1. Arrange the following words in a meaningful order.

1. Reading　　2. Composing
3. Writing　　4. Printing

(a) 1, 3, 4, 2　　(b) 2, 3, 4, 1
(c) 3, 1, 2, 4　　(d) 3, 2, 4, 1

Sol. (d) The given words represent the various stages in the process of publishing. Firstly, the matter is written, followed by composition of that written matter. Then, this composed matter is printed followed by reading. So, the correct order is $3 \rightarrow 2 \rightarrow 4 \rightarrow 1$.

Example 2. Arrange the following words in a logical sequence.

1. Application　　2. Selection
3. Exam　　4. Interview
5. Advertisement

(a) 1, 2, 3, 5, 4　　(b) 5, 1, 3, 4, 2
(c) 5, 3, 1, 4, 2　　(d) 4, 5, 1, 2, 3

Sol. (b) For a job,

Advertisement is the 1st stage — 5

Application is the 2nd stage — 1

Exam is the 3rd stage — 3

Interview is the 4th stage — 4

Selection is the final stage — 2

$\therefore$ Correct sequence = 5, 1, 3, 4, 2

Example 3. Arrange the following words according to English dictionary.

1. Hepatitis　　2. Cholera
3. Peptidoglycan　　4. Chitin

(a) 2, 3, 1, 4　　(b) 4, 2, 1, 3
(c) 4, 1, 3, 2　　(d) 3, 1, 4, 2

Sol. (b)According to English dictionary, Chitin comes first, followed by Cholera which in turn is followed by Hepatitis and the last will be Peptidoglycan. So, the correct sequential order of words is $4 \rightarrow 2 \rightarrow 1 \rightarrow 3$ i.e.,

Chitin → Cholera → Hepatitis → Peptidoglycan

Example 4. Arrange the following words according to English dictionary.

1. Episode　　2. Epistle
3. Episcope　　4. Epigraph

(a) 1, 2, 3, 4　　(b) 4, 2, 1, 3
(c) 3, 2, 1, 4　　(d) 4, 3, 1, 2

Sol. (d)As per the English dictionary, the correct sequential order of words is

Epigraph → Episcope → Episode → Epistle i.e.,

$4 \rightarrow 3 \rightarrow 1 \rightarrow 2$

Example 5. Arrange the following words in a logical sequence.

1. Country　　2. Furniture
3. Forest　　4. Wood
5. Trees

(a) 1, 2, 4, 3, 5　　(b) 1, 5, 3, 2, 4
(c) 4, 2, 3, 5, 1　　(d) 4, 2, 5, 3, 1

Sol. (d)

Wood → Furniture → Trees → Forest → Country

This order is given in option (d) i.e., 4, 2, 5, 3, 1

Exercise

1. Arrange the given words in the sequence in which they occur in the dictionary.

i. Misleader
ii. Monarchy
iii. Mobil
iv. Manage
v. Movies

(a) i, iv, iii, ii, v
(b) iv, i, iii, v, ii
(c) i, iii, ii, v, iv
(d) iv, i, iii, ii, v

2. Arrange the given words in the sequence in which they occur in the dictionary.
i. Heredity ii. Hesitate
iii. Heavy iv. Herald
(a) iii, iv, i, ii
(b) i, iv, iii, iv
(c) ii, iii, i, iv
(d) iv, iii, ii, i

3. Arrange the given words in the sequence in which they occur in the dictionary.
i. Terrace ii. Tenant
iii. Tea iv. Tomorrow
(a) iii, ii, i, iv
(b) i, ii, iii, iv
(c) iv, i, ii, iii
(d) i, iii, ii, iv

4. Arrange the given words in the sequence in which they occur in the dictionary.
i Pitiful ii Plague
iii Pitiless iv Plaque
v. Plankton
(a) iii, i, ii, v, iv
(b) i, iii, iv, v, ii
(c) i, iii, ii, iv, v
(d) i, iii, ii, v, iv

5. Arrange the given words in the sequence in which they occur in the dictionary.
i. Prandial ii. Preach
iii. Priam iv. Price
v. Pseudo
(a) iii, iv, v, i, ii
(b) i, v, iv, ii, iii
(c) i, ii, iii, iv, v
(d) v, iii, iv, i, ii

6. Arrange the given words in the sequence in which they occur in the dictionary.
i. Cooperate
ii. Cultivate
iii. Culmination
iv. Corporate
(a) iv, ii, i, iii
(b) ii, i, iii, iv
(c) ii, iii, i, iv
(d) i, iv, iii, ii

7. Arrange the given words in the sequence in which they occur in the dictionary.
i. Closing ii. Closure
iii. Closer iv. Closable
(a) ii, i, iii, iv
(b) iv, iii, i, ii
(c) iv, i, ii, iii
(d) iv, iii, ii, i

8. Arrange the given words in the sequence in which they occur in the dictionary.
i. Regulate ii. Remedy
iii. Reassemble iv. Research
(a) iii, i, ii, iv
(b) i, ii, iii, iv
(c) iv, ii, i, iii
(d) i, iii, iv, ii

9. Arrange the given words in the sequence in which they occur in the dictionary.
i. Hunger ii. Horse
iii. Hungry iv. Handmade
(a) iv, ii, i, iii
(b) iii, iv, ii, i
(c) iv, iii, i, ii
(d) i, iv, ii, iii

10. Arrange the given words in the sequence in which they occur in the dictionary.
i. Carrier ii. Capability
iii. Cause iv. Course
(a) ii, i, iii, iv
(b) i, ii, iii, iv
(c) ii, iii, i, iv
(d) ii, iv, i, iii

11. Arrange the given words in the sequence in which they occur in the dictionary.
i. Savage ii. Sausage
iii. Savour iv. Saviour
(a) iii, iv, i, ii
(b) ii, i, iv, iii
(c) ii, iii, i, iv
(d) iii, iv, ii, i

12. Arrange the given words in the sequence in which they occur in the dictionary.
i. Serious,
ii. Senior,
iii. Senate,
iv. Statesman.
(a) iii, ii, i, iv
(b) i, ii, iii, iv
(c) iv, i, ii, iii
(d) i, iii, ii, iv

13. Arrange the given words in the sequence in which they occur in the dictionary.
i. Agent
ii. Argentine
iii. Assiduous
iv. Accentuate
(a) iii, ii, i, iv
(b) iv, iii, i, ii
(c) iv, ii, i, iii
(d) iv, i, ii, iii

14. Arrange the given words in the sequence in which they occur in the dictionary.
i. Treasure ii. Treat
iii. Tremor iv. Trestle
(a) i, ii, iii, iv
(b) iv, iii, i, ii
(c) ii, iii, i, iv
(d) iv, iii, ii, i

15. Arrange the given words in the sequence in which they occur in the dictionary.
i. Cease
ii. Consecutive
iii. Constructive
iv. Cement
(a) iii, i, iv, ii
(b) i, iv, ii, iii
(c) i, iv, iii, ii
(d) iv, i, ii, iii

16. Arrange the given words in the sequence in which they occur in the dictionary.
i. Temerity ii. Temporary
iii. Tempered iv. Temperature
(a) i, iv, iii, ii
(b) iii, ii, iv, i
(c) i, ii, iii, iv
(d) iv, iii, i, ii

17. Arrange the given words in the sequence in which they occur in the dictionary.
i. Rainbow ii. Rancour
iii. Rattle iv. Rainy

(a) i, iii, ii, iv
(b) i, iv, ii, iii
(c) i, iv, iii, ii
(d) ii, i, iv, iii

18. Arrange the given words in the sequence in which they occur in the dictionary.
i Treadmill
ii Treason
iii Treacherous
iv Tread
(a) ii, iii, iv, i
(b) iii, iv, ii, i
(c) iii, iv, i, ii
(d) i, ii, iii, iv

19. Arrange the given words in the sequence in which they occur in the dictionary.
i Forehead ii Forensic
iii Forest iv Foremost
(a) i, iv, ii, iii
(b) iii, ii, iv, i
(c) i, ii, iii, iv
(d) i, iv, iii, ii

20. Arrange the given words in the sequence in which they occur in the dictionary.
i. Permanence
ii. Permanent
iii. Permafrost
iv. Permeability
(a) ii, iii, iv, i
(b) iii, ii, i, iv
(c) iv, ii, i, iii
(d) iii, i, ii, iv

21. Arrange the given words in the sequence in which they occur in the dictionary.
i. Catadrome ii. Catagenesis
iii. Catabolic iv. Catabolism
(a) ii, iii, iv, i
(b) iii, iv, i, ii
(c) iii, iv, ii, i
(d) i, ii, iii, iv

22. Arrange the given words in the sequence in which they occur in the dictionary.
i. Foresay ii. Foreseize
iii. Foreseeable iv. Foresail
(a) i, iii, iv, ii
(b) i, iii, ii, iv
(c) iii, i, ii, iv
(d) iv, i, iii, ii

23. Arrange the given words in the sequence in which they occur in the dictionary.
i. Shortage
ii. Shore
iii. Shamelessly
iv. Shadiness
v. Shallow
(a) iii, iv, v ii, i
(b) iv, iii, ii, v, i
(c) iv, v, iii, ii, i
(d) iii, iv, ii, i, v

24. Arrange the given words in the sequence in which they occur in the dictionary.
i Application
ii Approve
iii Appeal
iv Astonishing
(a) ii, iii, iv, i
(b) iii, ii, i, iv
(c) iii, i, ii, iv
(d) i, ii, iii, iv

25. Arrange the given words in the sequence in which they occur in the dictionary.
i. Monopoly
ii. Manifesto
iii. Manifold
iv. Mankind.
(a) ii, iii, iv, i
(b) iii, ii, iv, i
(c) i, iii, iv, ii
(d) i, iv, iii, ii

26. Arrange the given words in the sequence in which they occur in the dictionary.
i. Nature
ii. Nest
iii. Numeric
iv. News
(a) iii, i, ii, iv
(b) iv, ii, iii, i
(c) i, ii, iv, iii
(d) i, ii, iii, iv

27. Arrange the given words in the sequence in which they occur in the dictionary.
i. Drama ii. Dramatical
iii. Dramaticismiv. Dramality
v Dramatise
(a) i, iv, ii, iii, v
(b) i, iv, ii, v, iii
(c) i, iv, v, iii, ii
(d) iv, i, v, iii, ii

Answers with Explanations

1. (d) According to dictionary, the sequence of words is:
(iv) Manage, (i) Misleader, (iii) Mobil, (ii) Monarchy, (v) Movies.

2. (a) According to dictionary the arrangement of words is given below:
(iii) Heavy, (iv) Herald, (i) Heredity, (ii) Hesitake,

3. (a) According to dictionary, the arrangement of words is given below:
(iii) Tea, (ii) Tenant, (i) Terrace, (iv) Tomorrow

4. (d) According to dictionary, arrangement of words is,
(i) Pitiful, (iii) pitiless, (ii) plague, (v) plankton, (iv) plaque.

5. (c) According to dictionary the arrangement of words is given below:
(i) Prandial, (ii) Preach, (iii) Priam, (iv) Price, (v) Pseudo

6. (d) According to dictionary, the arrangement of words is given as:
(i) Cooperate, (iv) Corporate, (iii) Culmination, (ii) Cultivate.

7. (b) According to dictionary, the arrangement of words is:
(iv) Closable, (iii) Closer, (i) Closing, (ii) Closure.

8. (a) According to dictionary, the arrangement of the words is,
(iii) Reassemble, (i) Regulate, (ii) Remedy, (iv) Research.

9. (a) According to dictionary, the arrangement of given words is,
(iv) Handmade, (ii) Horse, (i) Hunger, (iii) Hungry.

10. (a) According to dictionary, the arrangement of words is,

(ii) Capability, (i) Carrier, (iii) Cause, (iv) Course

11. (b) According to dictionary, the arrangement of the words is: (ii) Sausage, (i) Savage, (iv) Saviour, (iii) Savour.

12. (a) According to dictionary, arrangement of given words is: (iii) Senate, (ii) Senior, (i) Serious, (iv) Statesman.

13. (d) According to dictionary, the arrangement of the words is: (iv) Accentuate, (i) Agent, (ii) Argentine, (iii) Assiduous

14. (a) According to dictionary, Arrangement of words is:
(i) Treasure (ii) Treat (iii) Tremor (iv) Trestle

15. (b) According to dictionary, the arrangement of words is: (i) Cease (iv) Cement (ii) Consecutive (iii) Constructive

16. (a) According to dictionary, the arrangement of words is:
(i) Temerity (iv) Temperature (iii) Tempered (ii) Temporary

17. (b) According to dictionary, the arrangement of words is
(i) Rainbow, (iv) Rainy, (ii) Rancour, (iii) Rattle.

18. (c) According to dictionary, the sequence of words is, (iii) Treacherous (iv) Tread (i) Treadmill (ii) Treason

19. (a) According to dictionary, the sequence of the words is: (i) Forehead, (iv) Foremost, (ii) Forensic, (iii) Forest

20. (d) According to dictionary, the sequence is:
(iii) Permafrost (i) Permanence (ii) Permanent, (iv) Permeability.

21. (b) According to dictionary, the sequence of the words is: (iii) Catabolic, (iv) Catabolism, (i) Catadrome, (ii) Catagenesis.

22. (d) According to dictionary, the arrangement of the given words is,
(iv) Foresail, (i) Foresay, (iii) Foreseeable, (ii) Foreseize.

23. (c) According to dictionary, the arrangement of the words is given below:
(iv) Shadiness, (v) Shallow, (iii) Shamelessly, (ii) Shore, (i) Shortage

24. (c) According to dictionary, the sequence of words is:
(iii) Appeal, (i) Application, (ii) Approve, (iv) Astonishing.

25. (a) According to dictionary, the sequence of words is,
(ii) Manifesto (iii) Manifold (iv) Mankind (i) Monopoly

26. (c) The correct order is:
(i) Nature (ii) Nest (iv) News (iii) Numeric

27. (a) According to dictionary, the arrangement of given words is,
(a) Drama (iv) Dramality (ii) Dramatical (iii) Dramaticism (v) Dramatise.

6 DIRECTION SENSE TEST

Direction is a measurement of position of one thing with respect to another thing or a reference point. Distance between two points is a measurement of the shortest distance, i.e., the displacement between the two points.

The Shortest distance between two points many be different from the total distance covered in going from one point to the other.

The problems based on direction and distance have instructions regarding the movement of a person or an object from a starting point (also called origin) upto and end point (also called destination).

These instructions generally provide magnitude as well as direction of the movement. These questions are designed to test the candidate's ability to sense direction.

Questions on direction and distance are simpler than other questions, if the student possesses the right knowledge of the directions.

Prime Direction

There are four prime directions as shown below

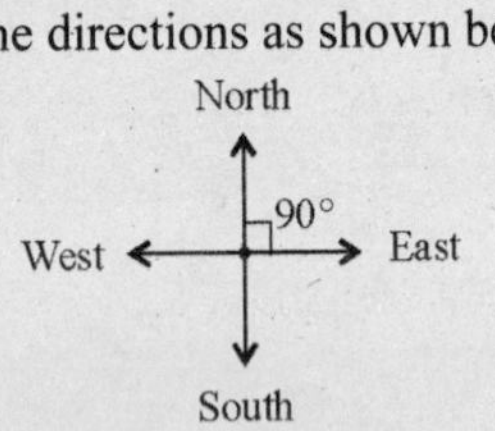

1. North 2. Sourh 3. East 4. West

The angle between any two prime directions is 90°.

Subdirections/Cardinal Directions

A direction between two main or prime directions is known as a subdirection/cardinal direction.

There are four subdirections as given below

1. North-East (NE) 2. South-East (SE)
3. South-West (SW) 4. North-West (NW)

The angle between any two adjacent subdirection is 90°:

Representation of Directions

The various directions discussed above are represented on paper as shown below

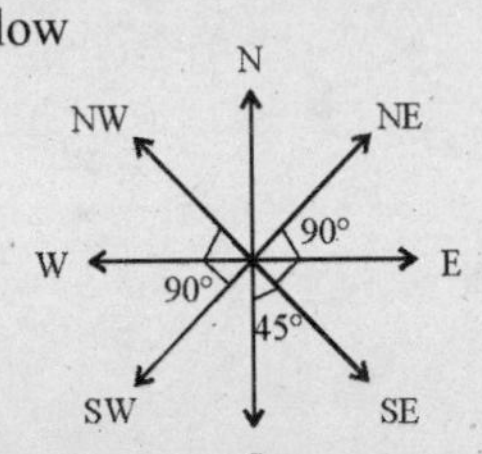

Angle formed between a prime direction and a subdirection is 45°.

Solved Examples

Example 1. Vipul goes Northward 10 m. He turns left and walks 30 m, then again turns left and walks 50 m, then how much distance Vipula travelled?

(a) 60 m (b) 20 m
(d) 10 m (d) 90 m

Sol. (d) According to the question, the direction diagram is drawn as

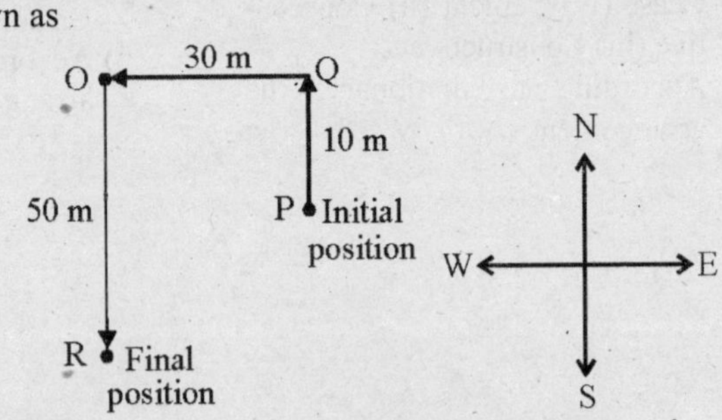

Total distance = PQ + QO + OR = 10 + 30 + 50

= 90 m

Example 2. Shiv goes 4 km straight from his school. He turns to his right and walks 3 km. He again moves 2 km after turning right to reach his house. If his house is located in South-East from his school, then in which direction Shiv started moving initially from his school?

(a) North-East (b) West
(d) East (d) North

Sol. (c) According to the information stated in the question, direction diagram can be drawn as follows

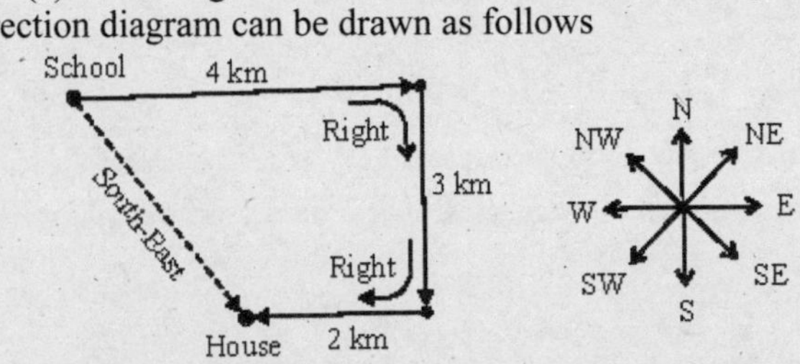

Clearly, he started moving towards East initially.

Example 3. Vijay starts waking straight towards East. After walking 75 m he turns to the left and walks 25 m straight. Again he turns to the left and walks a distance of 40 m straight. Again he turns to the left and walks a distance of 25 m. How far is he from the starting point?

(a) 140 m (b) 115 m
(d) 50 m (d) 35 m

Sol. (d) According to the question, the direction diagram is as shown below

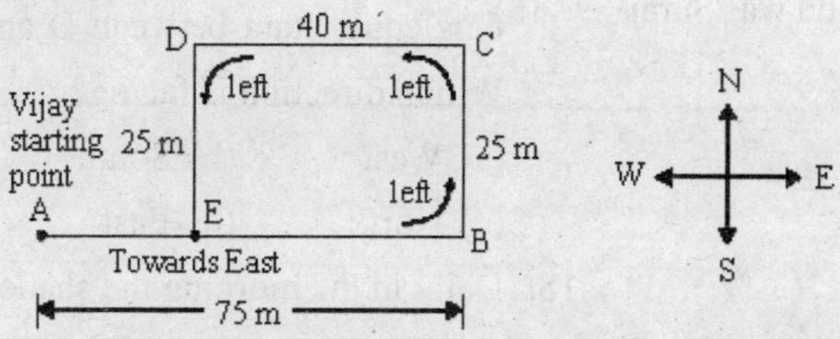

$\therefore$ Distance between starting and ending point,
AE = AB = AB – EB = 75 – 40 = 35 m

Example 4. Raghu is at point A. He walks 3 k m to the North and then turns to his left. He walks 4 km in this direction. He turns left again and walks 6 km. If he wishes to reach point A again, in which direction should he be walking and what distance will he have to cover?

(a) South-East, 5 km (b) South-East, 4 km
(c) North-East, 5 km (d) North-East, 4 km

Sol. (c) According to the question, the direction diagram is as follows

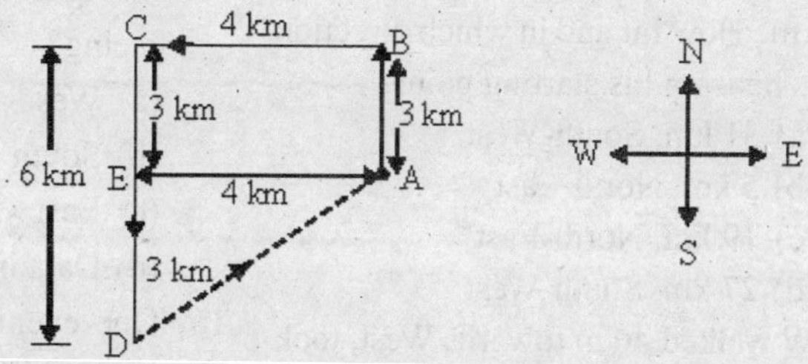

By Pythagoras theorem,
$(AD)^2 = (AE)^2 + (DE)^2 = (4)^2 + (3)^2 = 16 + 9$
$\Rightarrow (AD)^2\ 25 \Rightarrow AD = 5$ km

Clearly, Raghu should walk 5 km in North-direction to reach the point A again.

Exercise

1. Laxman went 15 km to the West from house, then turned left and walked 20 km. He, then turned East and walked 25 km and finally turning left covered 20 km. How far is he now from his house?
(a) 15 km (b) 20 km
(c) 25 km (d) 10 km

2. Molly travelled from point A to point B which is 5 ft. He, then travelled 6 ft to his right and then turned to left and went 4 ft. Finally, he again went 6 ft to his left. How far is he from the point B now?
(a) 10 ft (b) 6 ft
(c) 5 ft (d) 4 ft

3. In an open ground, Rakesh walks 20 m towards North, turns left and goes 40. He turns to his left again to walks 50 km. How far is he from starting point?
(a) 110 m (b) 70 m
(c) 50 m (d) 40 m

4. Kamal of facing South. He turns 135° in the anti-clockwise direction and then 18° in the clockwise direction. What direction is he facing now?
(a) North (b) South-West
(c) East (d) South-West

5. A person walks 1 mile to West, turns left and walks 1 mile and turns left and walks 1 mile and again turns left and walks 1 mile. What is the direction he is facing now?
(a) North (b) South
(c) East (d) West

6. I was facing East from where I turned to my left and walked 12 ft, then I turned towards right and walked 6 ft. After that I walked 6 ft in South direction and at last I walked 6 ft in the West. Then, in which direction am I standing from the original point?
(a) West (b) East
(c) South (d) North

7. A policeman left his police post and proceeded South 4 km on hearing a loud sound from point A. On reaching the place, he heard another sound and proceeded 4 km to his left to the point B. From B he proceeded left to reach another place C, 4 km away. In which direction, he has to go to reach his police post?
(a) North (b) South
(c) East (d) West

8. B is to the South-West of A, C is to the East of B and South-East of A and D is to the North of C in line with B and A. In which direction of A is D located?
(a) North (b) East
(c) South-East (d) North-East

9. A boy first goes in South direction, then he turns towards left and travels for some distance. After that he turns right and moves certain distance. At last he turns left and travels again for some distance. Now, in which direction is he moving?
(a) South (b) West
(c) East (d) North

10. If East is replaced by South-East, then West will be replaced by which of the following direction?
(a) North-East (b) North
(c) East (d) North-West

11. Neeraj wants to go to school from his house. First of all he goes to the crossing, from here he turns to right and reaches the bus stand. Bus stand is opposite to the library. In which direction is school locate?
(a) North
(b) East
(c) Cannot be determined
(d) West

12. Town D is towards East of town F. Town B is towards North of town D. Town H is towards South of town B. Towards which direction is town H from town F?
(a) East
(b) South-East
(c) North-East
(d) Data inadequate

13. A person moves 15 km in East direction, then turns towards North and moves 4 km. From here he turns towards West and travels 12 km. How far and in which direction is he from his starting point?
(a) 31 km, South-West
(b) 5 km, North-East
(c) 19 km, North-East
(d) 27 km, South-West

14. W walked 40 m towards West, took a left turn and walked 30 m. He, then took a right turn and walked 20 m. He again took a right turn and walked 30 m. How far was he from the starting point?
(a) 70 m
(b) 60 m
(c) 90 m
(d) Cannot be determined

15. One morning after sunrise, Suraj was standing facing a pole. The shallow of the pole fell exactly to his right. Which direction was Suraj facing?
(a) West
(b) South
(c) East
(d) Data inadequate

16. One evening. Raja started to walk towards the Sun. After walking a while, he turned to his right and again to his right. After walking a while, he again turned right. In which direction is he facing?
(a) South (b) East
(c) West (d) North

17. Five boys A, B, C, D and E are sitting in a park in a circle. A is facing South-West, D is facing South-East, B and E are right opposite A and D respectively and C is equidistant between D and B. Which direction is facing?
(a) West (b) South
(c) North (d) East

18. Daily in the morning the shadow of Gol Gumbaz falls on Bara Kaman and in the evening the shadow of bara Kaman falls on gol Gumbaz exactly. So in which direction in Gol Gumbaz to Bara Kaman?
(a) Eastern side
(b) Western side
(c) Northern side
(d) Southern side

Answers with Explanations

1. (d) According to the question, the direction diagram will be as follows

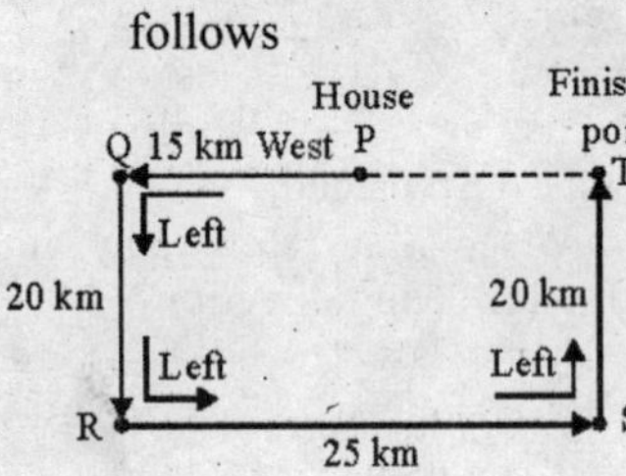

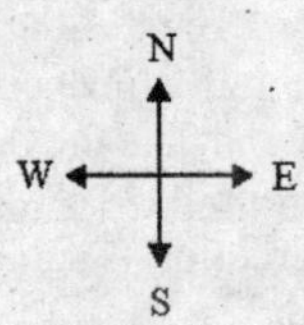

PQ = 15 km
QR = TS = 20 km
RS = 25 km
∴ Required distance,
PT = QT − QP = RS − QP
= 25 − 15 = 10 km

2. (d) According to the question, the direction diagram will be as follows

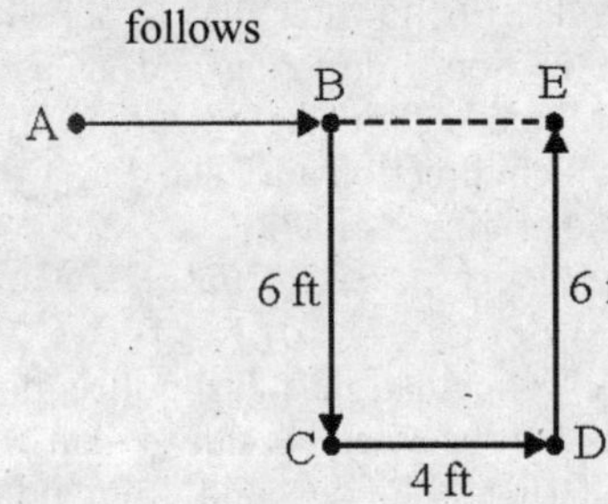

A = Initial point
E = Finishing point
AB = 5 ft
BC = DE = 6 ft
BE = CD = 4 ft
∴ Required distance, BE = 4 ft

3. (c) According to the question, the direction diagram is as follows

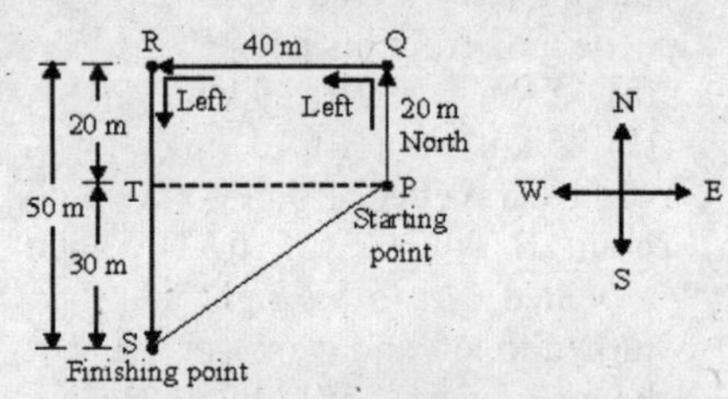

Here, PQ = RT = 20 m, QR = TP = 40 m
and RS = 50 m
Now, TS = RS − RT = 50 − 20 = 30 m
∴ Required distance,

$$PS = \sqrt{(TP)^2 + (TS)^2}$$
$$= \sqrt{(40)^2 + (30)^2}$$
$$= \sqrt{1600 + 900}$$
$$= \sqrt{2500} = 50 \text{ m}$$

4. (b) According to the question, the direction diagram will be as follows

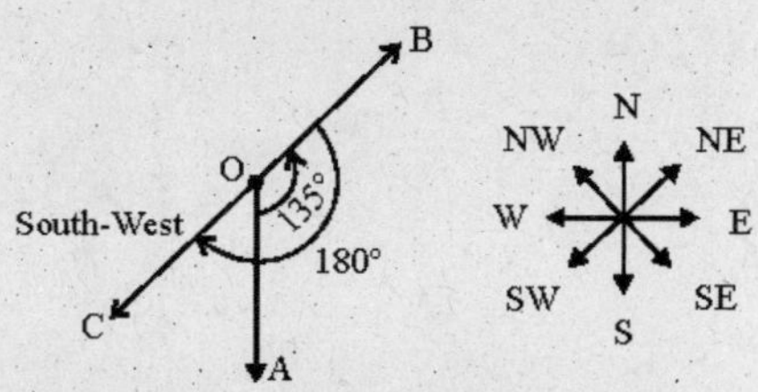

Clearly, Kamal is facing south-west.

5. (c) According to the question, the direction diagram will be as follows

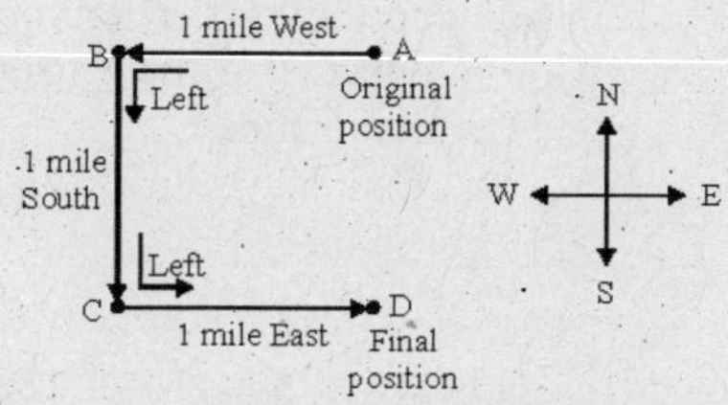

Clearly, person is facing East.

6. (d) According to the question, the direction diagram will be as follows

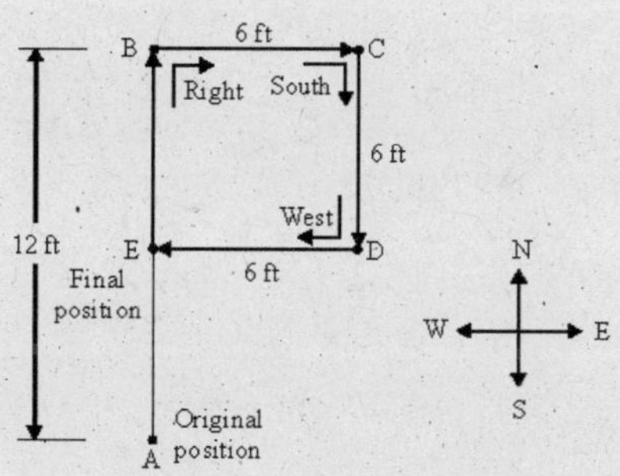

Clearly E is to the North of A.

7. (d) According to the question, the direction diagram will be as follows

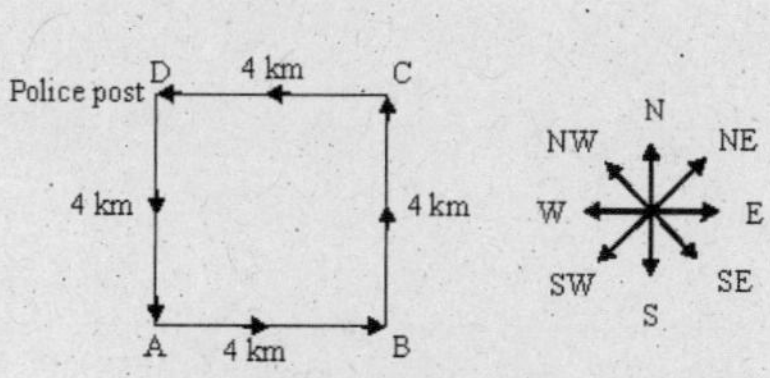

Clearly, from C the policeman will have to go towards West to reach police post at D.

8. (d) According to the question, the direction diagram will be as follows

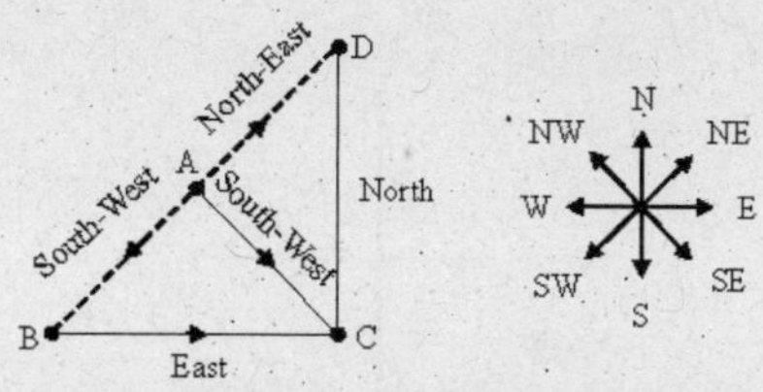

Clearly, D is the North-East of A.

9. (c) According to the question, the direction diagram will be as follows

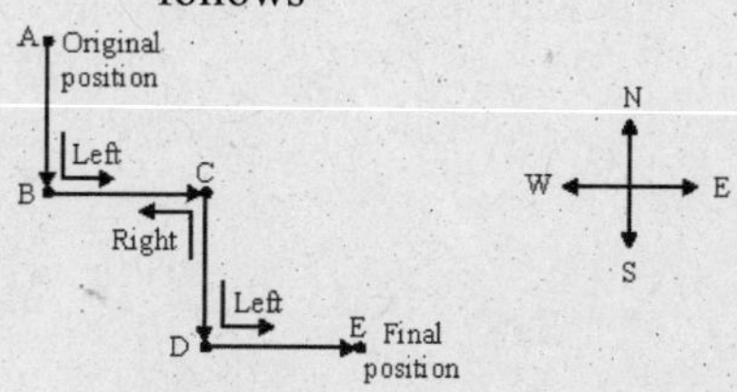

Clearly, boy is moving towards East.

10. (d) According to the question, the diagram will be as follows

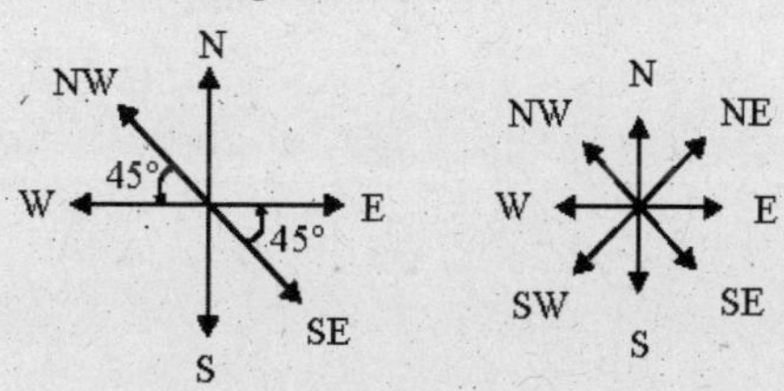

Clearly, West will be replaced by North-West.

11. (c) Neither initial nor final direction is given. Hence, the direction cannot be determined.

12. (d) According to the question, the direction diagram is as follows

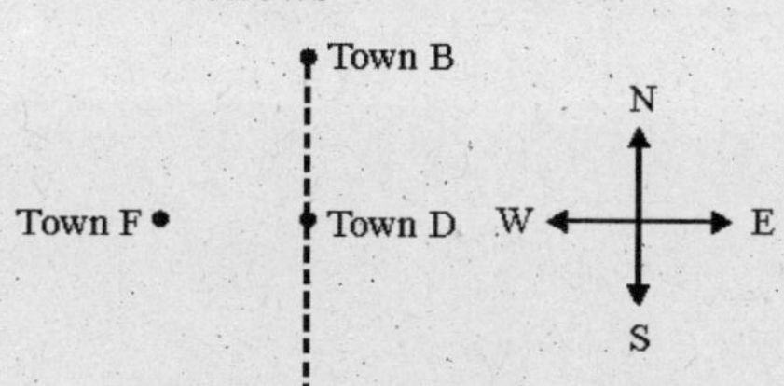

Now, H may lie anywhere on the dotted line. Hence, direction of H with respect to F cannot be determined definitely as data given is inadequate.

13. (b) According to the question, the direction diagram is as follows

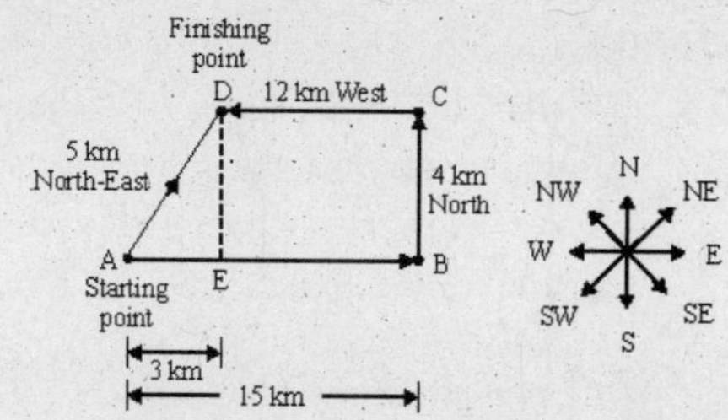

$AB = 15$ m

$BC = DE = 4$ km

$CD = EB = 12$ km

$AE = AB - CD$

$= 15 - 12 = 3$ km

∴ Required distance,

$$AD = \sqrt{(DE)^2 + (AE)^2} = \sqrt{4^2 + 3^2}$$

$$= \sqrt{16+9} = 5 \text{ km}$$

Hence, D is 5 km North-East from the starting point A.

14. (b) According to the question, the direction diagram will be as follows

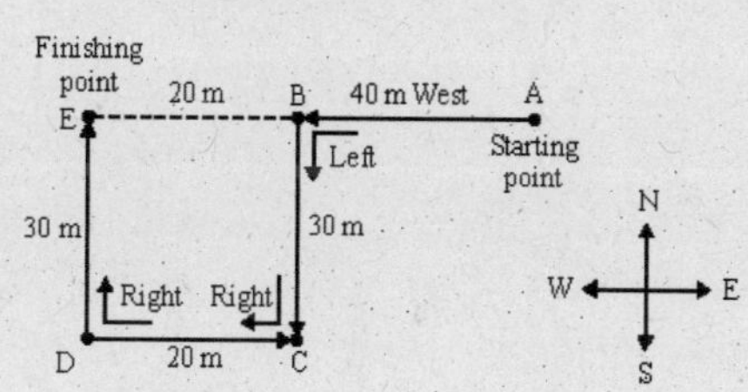

$AB = 40$ m

$BC = DE = 30$ m

$CD = BE = 20$ m

∴ Required distance $AE = AB + BE$

$= 40 + 20 = 60$ m

15. (b) Sun rises in the East in the morning. So, in the morning the shadow falls towards the West. Now, pole's shadow falls in to Suraj's right. So, he is standing facing South.

16. (a)

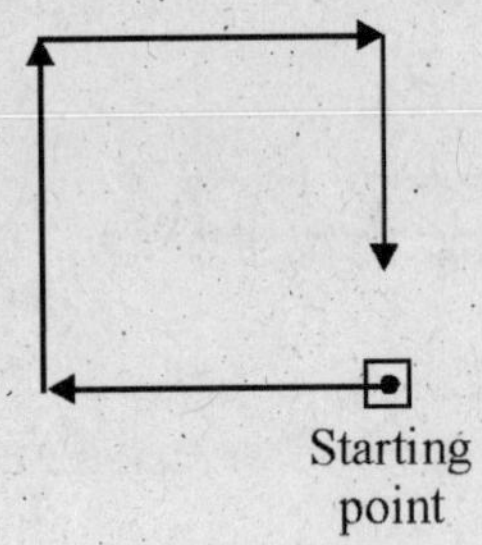

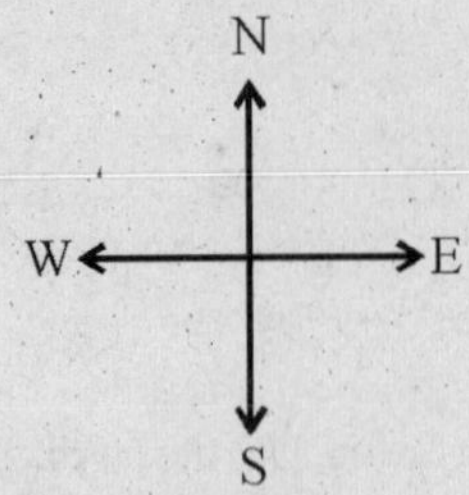

It is clear from the diagram the Raja is now facing towards South.

17. (d)

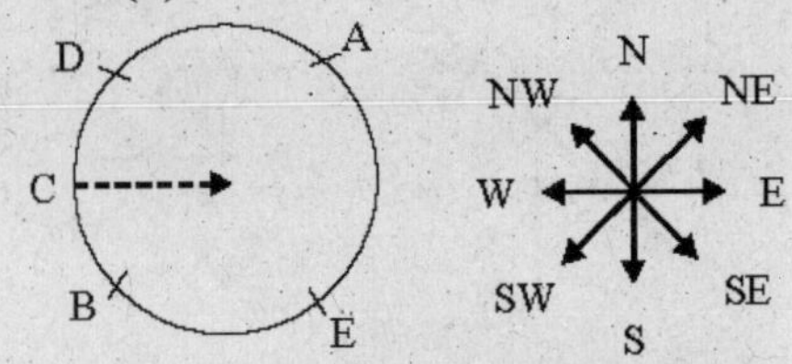

Clearly, C is facing towards East.

18. (a) In the morning an object casts its shadow to the West. And in the evening an object casts its shadow to the East. Therefore, Gol Gumbaz is to the Eastern side of Bara Kaman.

7 BLOOD RELATION

Blood relation between two individuals is defined as a relation between them by the virtue of their birth rather than by their marriage or any other reasons.

Blood relation questions involve analysis of information showing the blood relationship among members of the family. In this a chain of relationships is given in the form of information and on the basis of this information, relation between any two members of the chain is asked from the candidate. Candidates are supposed to be familiar with the knowledge of different relationships in the family.

Solved Examples

Example 1. Rajesh is the brother of Ankit. Shano is the sister of Shubham. Ankit is the son of Shano. How is Rajesh related to Shano?

(a) Father (b) Brother
(d) Son (d) Nephew

Sol. (c) Let us draw the family diagram from the given information, as follows

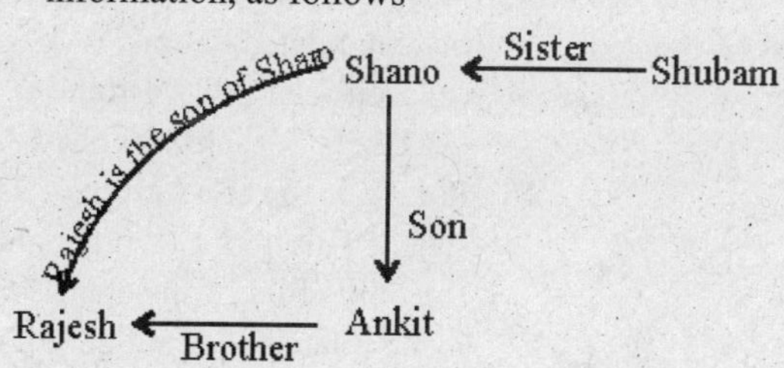

Now, it is clear that Rajesh is the son of Shano.

Example 2. Pointing to a lady a man said, "The son of her only brother is the brother of my wife." How is the lady related to the man?

(a) Mother's sister
(b) Grandmother
(d) Mother-in-law
(d) Sister of father-in-law

Sol. (d) Let us draw the family diagram from the given information as follows

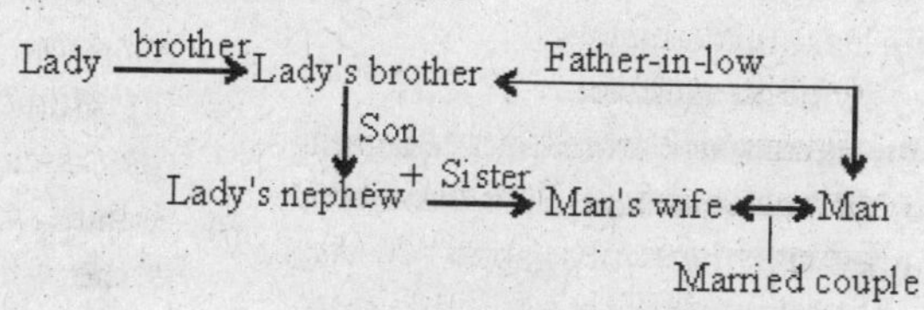

Now, it is clear that the lady is the sister of man's father-in-law.

Example 3. If A is B's sister, C is B's mother, D is C's father and E is D's mother, then how is A related to D?

(a) Granddaughter
(b) Daughter
(d) Aunt
(d) Father

Sol. (a) Let us draw a family diagram from the given information, as follows

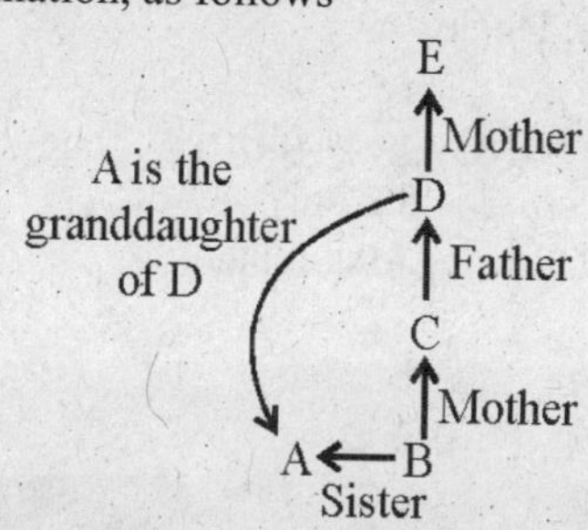

Now, it is clear that A is the granddaughter of D.

Exercise

1. Pointing towards a photograph, Ram said, "She is the mother of my brother's son's wife's sister". How is the lady in the photograph related to Ram's brother?
(a) Sister
(b) Daughter-in-law
(c) Daughter
(d) None of these

2. Introducing a man, a woman said, "His wife is the only daughter of my mother." How is the women related with the man?
(a) Sister-in-law
(b) Wife
(c) Aunt
(d) Mother-in-law

3. Pointing to a lady Simon said, "She is the daughter of the only sister of my father." How is lady related to Simon?
(a) Mother (b) Aunt
(c) Sister (d) Cousin sister

4. Introducing Asha to guests, Bhaskar said, "Her father is the only son of

my father". How is Asha related to Bhaskar?
(a) Niece
(b) Grand daughter
(c) Mother
(d) Daughter

5. Pointing towards a girl, Mihir said, "She is the only daughter of only child of my grandfather". How is the girl related to Mihir?
(a) Daughter
(b) Niece
(c) Sister
(d) Data inadequate
(e) None of these

6. Fatima while introducing Mustafa to her husband said, "His brother's father is the only son of my grandfather". How is Fatima related to Mustafa?
(a) Aunt (b) Sister
(c) Niece (d) Mother

7. Pointing to a woman in the photograph, Rajesh said, "The only daughter of her grandfather is my wife". How is Rajesh related to that woman?
(a) Uncle
(b) Father
(c) Maternal Uncle
(d) Brother

8. Introducing Alka to guests, Brijesh said, "Her father is the only son of my father". How is Alka related to Brijesh?
(a) Daughter (b) Mother
(c) Sister (d) Niece

9. Neelam, who is Rohit's daughter, says to Indu, Your mother Reeta is the younger sister of my father, who is third child of Sohanji". How is Sohanji related to Indu?
(a) Maternal uncle
(b) Father
(c) Grandfather
(d) Father-in-law

10. C is the mother of A and B. If D is the husband of B, then what is C to D?
(a) Mother
(b) Aunt
(c) Mother-in-law
(d) Sister

11. Sohan said to Mohan, "This girl is the wife of the grandson of my mother". How is Sohan related to this girl?
(a) Grandfather
(b) Father
(c) Husband
(d) Father-in-law

12. P's father is Q's son. M is the parental uncle of P and N is the brother of Q. How is M related to N?
(a) Nephew
(b) Cousin
(c) Data inadequate
(d) None of these

13. Kamal told Vimal, "Yesterday I defeated the only brother of the daughter of my grandmother." Whom did Kamal defeated?
(a) Father
(b) Son
(c) Brother
(d) Father-in-law

14. A and B are brothers, C and D are sisters. A's son is D's brother, then how is B related to C?
(a) Father (b) Brother
(c) Grandfather (d) Uncle

15. D is the son-in-law of B, who is the brother-in-law of A, who is the brother of C. How is A related to B?
(a) Father
(b) Son
(c) Data inadequate
(d) None of these

16. Pointing to a lady, Chouhan said, 'She is the only daughter of my father-in-law's wife. How is this lady related to Chouhan?
(a) Mother (b) Wife
(c) Cousin (d) Sister

17. A man showed a boy next to him and said, "He is the son of my wife's sister-in-law but I am the only child of my parents." How is my son related to him?
(a) Cousin (b) Brother
(c) Uncle (d) Nephew

18. Pointing towards a girl, Anurag says, "This girl is the daughter of the only child of my father". What is the related of Anurag's wife with the girl?
(a) Sister (b) Aunt
(c) Daughter (d) Mother

Answers with Explanations

1. (d) Let us draw the family diagram

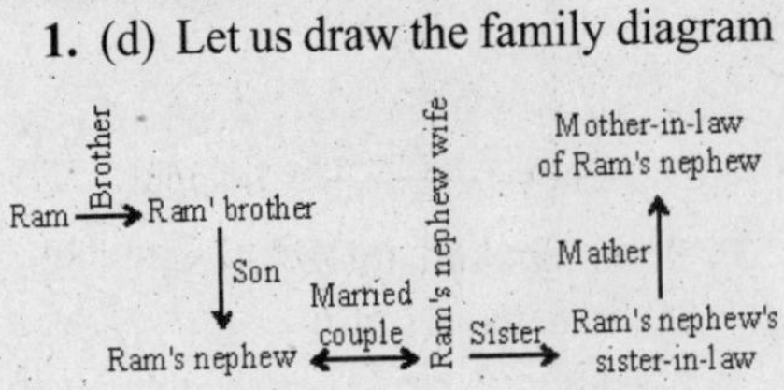

Hence, it is clear that the lady in the photograph is mother-in-law of Ram's diagram.

2. (b) Let us draw the family diagram

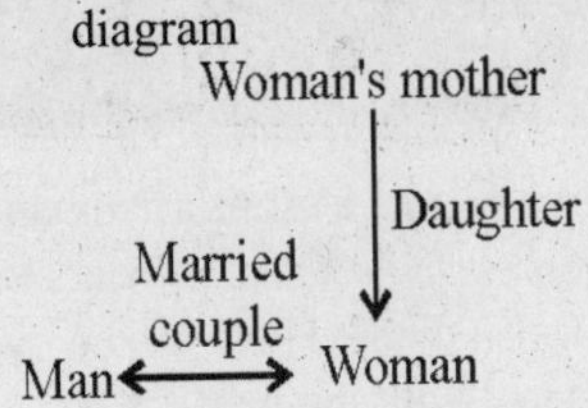

So, it is clear that woman is the wife of that man.

3. (d)

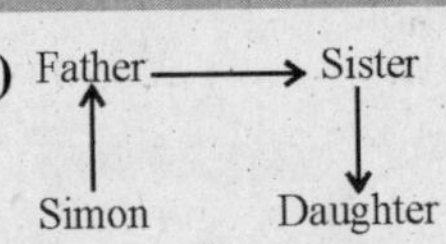

Thus, the lady is cousin sister of Simon.

4. (d)

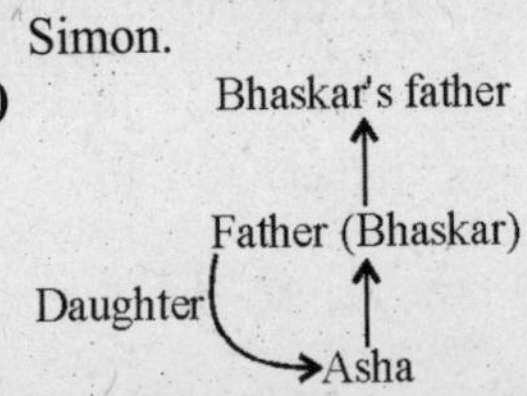

Only son of Bhaskar's father is Bhaskar himself. Therefore Asha's father is Bhaskar. Hence, Asha is the daughter of Bhaskar.

5. (c) Let us draw the family diagram

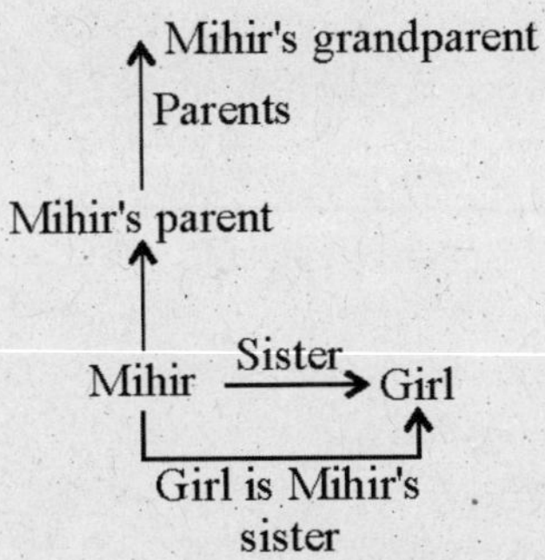

Clearly, only child of Mihir's grandfather is Mihir's father/ mother and only daughter of Mihir's sister.

6. (b) Let us draw the family diagram

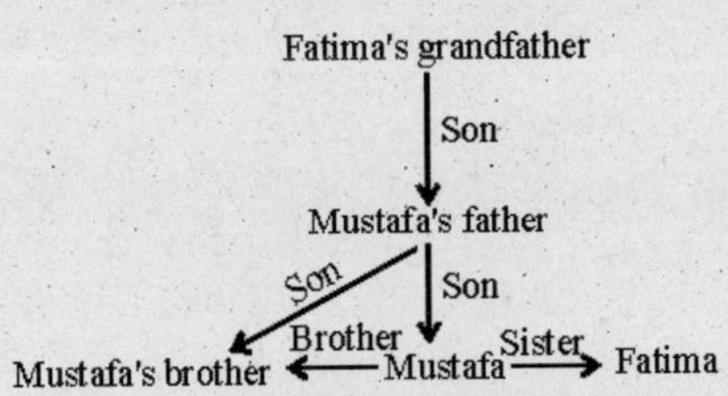

So, it is clear that Fatima is the sister of Mustafa.

7. (b)

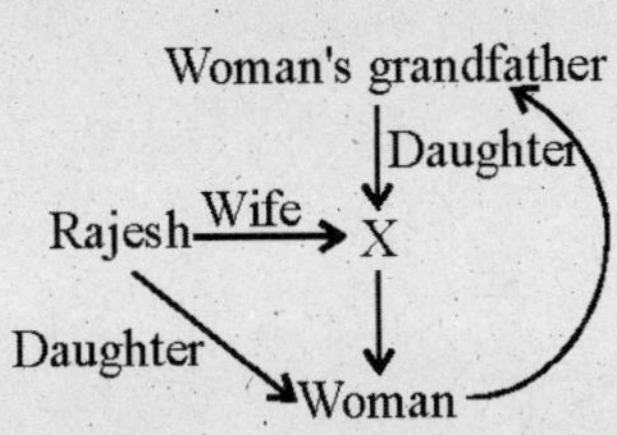

So, Rajesh is father of that woman.

8. (a) Let us draw the family diagram

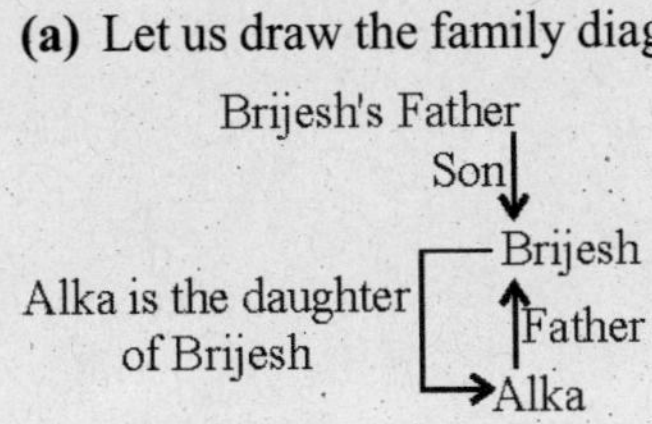

Clearly, the only son of Brijesh's father is Brijesh himself. This means Brijesh is the father of Alka. Hence, Alka is the daughter of Brijesh.

9. (c) Following family diagram can be drawn based on the given information.

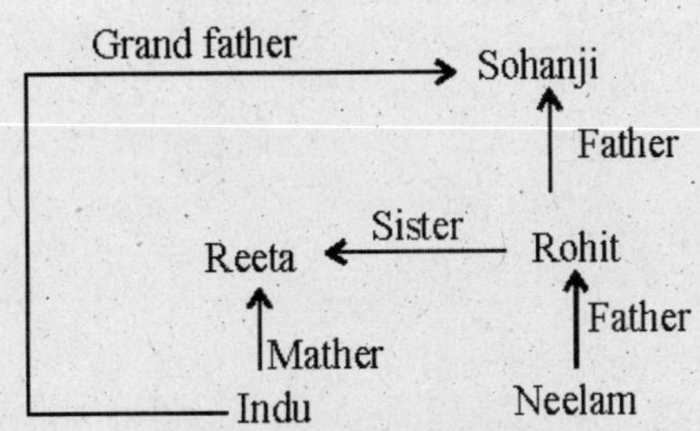

Now, it is clear the Sohanji is the grandfather of Indu.

10. (c)

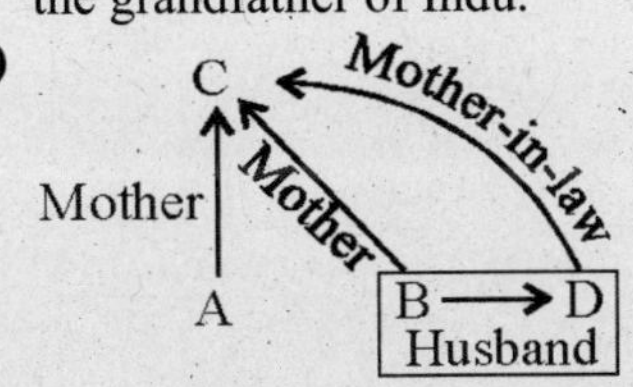

So, C is mother-in-law of D.

11. (d) Let us draw the family diagram

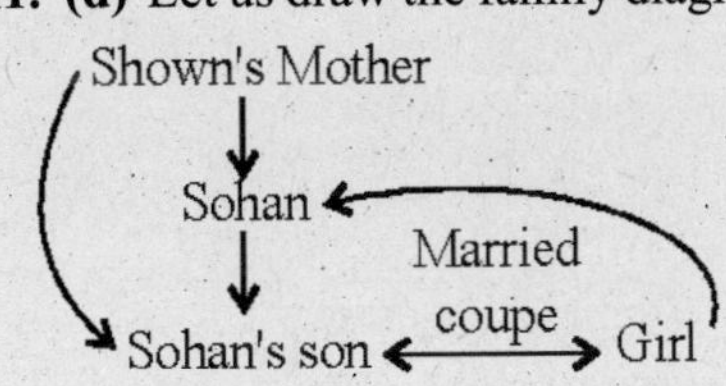

So, Sohan is father-in-law of that girl.

12. (a) M ⇒ Paternal uncle of P

N ⇒ Brother of Q

P's father ⇒ Q's son

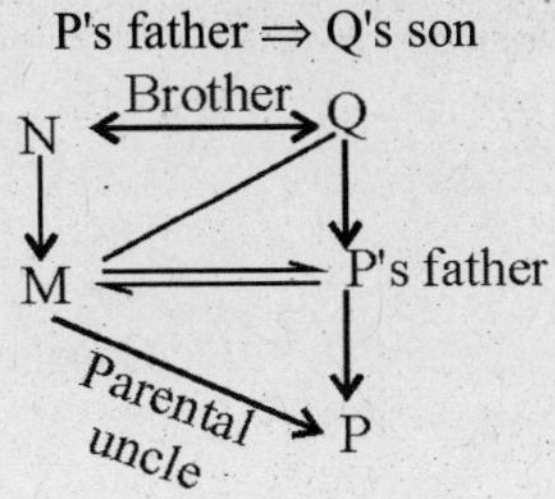

Clearly, N is brother of Q and M is brother of P's father who is Q's son.

So, M is nephew of N.

13. (a) Let us draw the family diagram

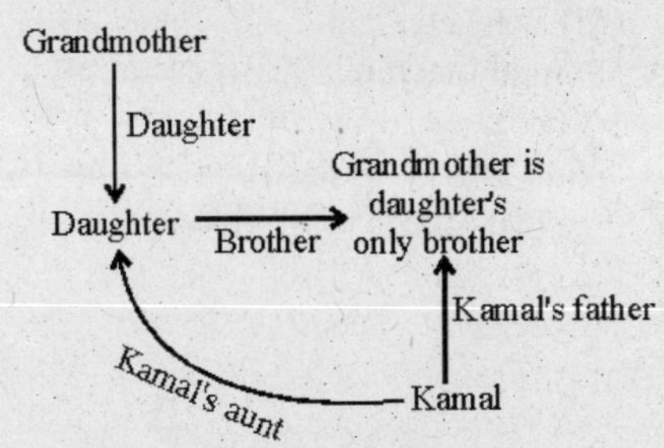

Hence, Kamal has defeated his father.

14. (d) A and B are brothers.

C and D are sisters.

A's son is D's brother

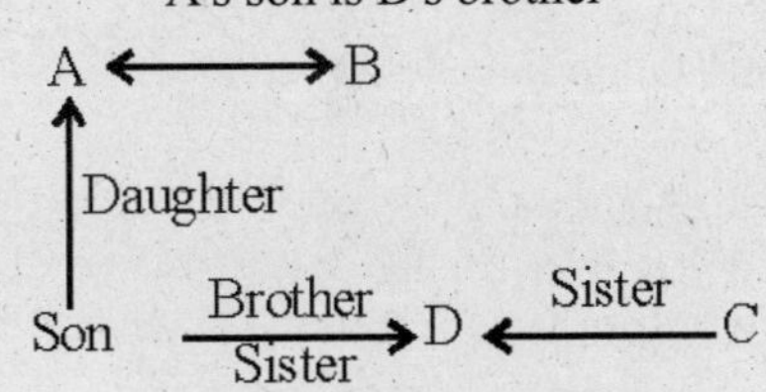

Hence, B is the uncle of C.

15. (d) Brother-in-law

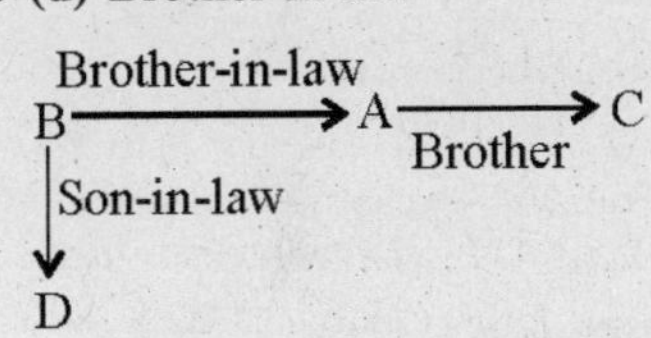

Clearly, A is also the brother-in-law of B.

16. (b) Let us draw family diagram

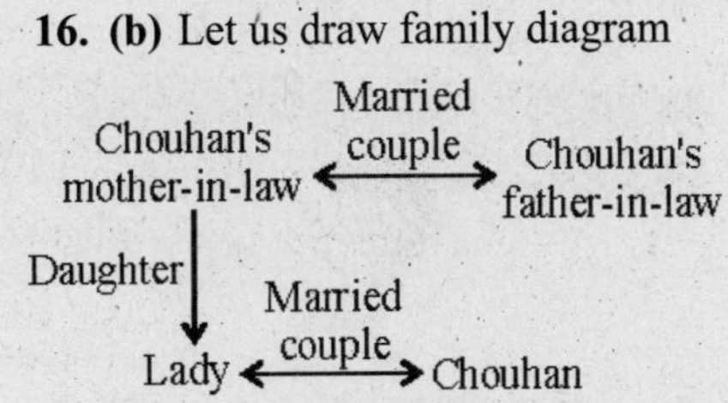

So, lady is wife of Chouhan.

17. (a) Let us draw the family diagram

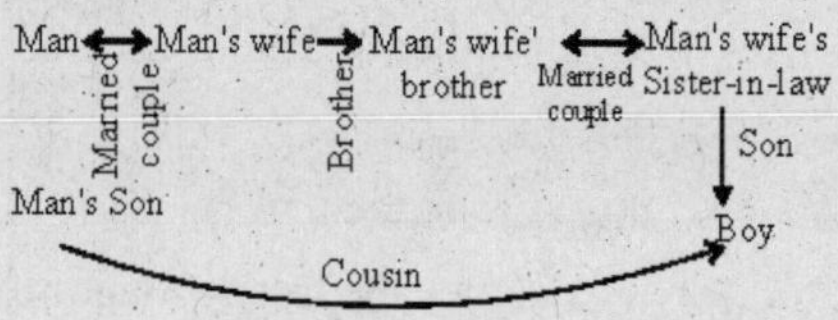

Hence, man's son is the cousin of that boy.

18. (d) Let us draw the family tree

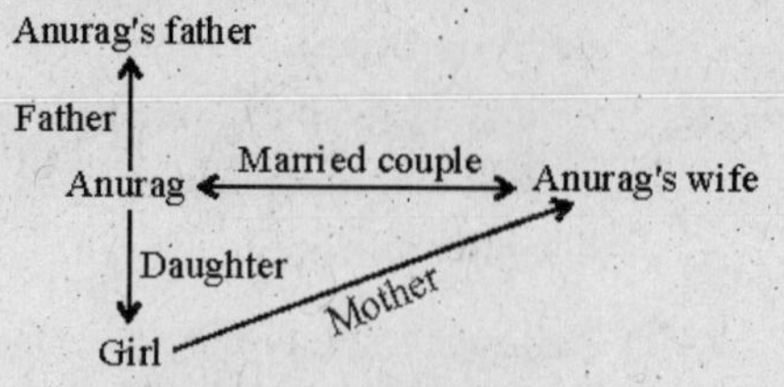

The daughter of only child of Anurag's father will be daughter of Anurag. Thus, Anurag's wife will be the mother of this girl.

8 RANKING TEST

This chapter broadly deals with the problems related to the arrangement of persons/objects is ascending/descending order (based on different parameters like height, weight, merit, position etc.), determining the position of a person/ object in a row/queue and the problems related to the time sequence test wherein the candidate has to find out a particular day based on some given conditions.

Solved Examples

Example 1. In a queue of girls, Akanksha is 9th from left and Mona is 17th from right. If the positions of Akansha and Mona are it interchanged, then nee position of Akansha is 15th from left. Find the number of girls between Mona and Akansha.

(a) 4 (b) 5

(c) 6 (d) 7

Solution (b)

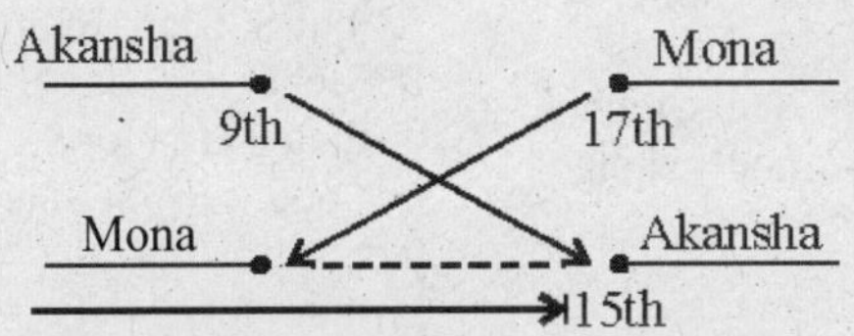

Total number of persons between Mona and Akansha $= 15 - 9 - 1 = 5$

Example 2. Radha remembers that her father's birthday is after but before 21st of March, while her brother Mahesh remembers that his father's birthday is before 22nd but after 19th of March. On which date is the birthday of their father?

(a) 19th (b) 20th

(d) 21th (d) Cannot be determined

Solution (b) According to Possibility of Date

Radha 17, 18, 19, 20

Mahesh 20, 21

Here, 20 th is common to both.

So, their father's birthday is on 20th March.

Example 3. In a row of students, Anil is 7th from the left while Jack is 18th from right. Both of them interchange their position such that Anil becomes 21st from the left. How many people are there in the row?

(a) 38 (b) 39

(d) 40 (d) None of these

Solution (a)

Anil's original position from left = 7th

Jack's original position from right = 18th

Anil's position from left after interchange = 21st

Since, Anil exchanged his seat with Jack, it means Jack's original position is 21st from the left.

$\therefore$ Total number of people = (Initial/position of Jack from the right + Initial position of Jack from the left) – 1

$= 18 + 21 = 38$

Exercise

1. In a row of girls, Kamya is fifth from the left and Preeti is sixth from the right. When they exchange their positions, then kamya becomes thirteenth from the left. What will be Preeti's position from the right?
   (a) 7th (b) 17th
   (c) 11th (d) 18th
2. 37 boys are standing in a row facing the school building. Ashwini is 15th from the left end. If he is shifted six places to the right, what is his position from the right end?
   (a) 16th (b) 21st
   (c) 20th (d) None of these
3. In a row of boys, Jeevan is 7th from the start and 11th from the end. In another row of boys, Vikash is 10th from the start and 12th from the end. How many boys are there in both the rows together?
   (a) 38
   (b) 40
   (c) 32
   (d) Cannot be determined
4. Kavi ranked 9th from the top and 38th from the bottom in a class. How many students are there in the class?
   (a) 45 (b) 42
   (c) 46 (d) 44
5. Rashmi is 14th from the right end in a row of 40 girls. What is her position from the left end?
   (a) 25th (b) 27th
   (c) 21st (d) None of these
6. Lakshmi is elder than Meenu. Leela is elder than Meenu but younger than Lakshmi. Latha is younger than both Meenu and Hari but Hari is younger than meenu. Who is the youngest?
   (a) Lakshmi (b) Meenu
   (c) Leela (d) Latha
7. In a cricket team, Dhoni is taller than Virat but not as tall as Raina, Rohit is shorter than Dhoni but

taller than shikhar. Who among them is the shortest?
(a) Dhoni
(b) Virat
(c) Shikhar
(d) Cannot be determined

8. P, Q, R and S are four males. P is the eldest in the group but he is not the poorest, R is the riches but not the eldest, Q is elder than S but he is not elder than P or R, P is riches than Q but he is not richer than S. How the four persons can be arranged in decreasing order of their age and money?
(a) PQRS, RPSQ
(b) PRQS, RSPQ
(c) PRQS, RSQP
(d) PRSQ, RSPQ

9. The age of Ram is twice the age of Shyam and half the age of Sohan, Shyam is elder than Mohan. Who is the eldest?
(a) Mohan (b) Ram
(c) Sohan (d) Shyam

10. The age of Amit is same as Sumit because they are twins, Richa is younger than Sumit, Richa is younger than Jyotsana but elder than Saurabh, Sumit is younger than Jyotsana. Who is elder than Mohan. Who is the eldest?
(a) Amit (b) Jyotsana
(c) Richa (d) Saurabh

11. Shailendra is shorter than keshav but taller than Rakesh, Madhav is the tallest. Aashish is a little shorter than Keshav and little taller than Shailendra. If they stand in the order of increasing heights, who will be the second?
(a) Aashish (b) Shailendra
(c) Rakesh (d) Madhav

12. Anil is taller than Sunny and Sunny is shorter than Baby Anil is taller than Bose whose height is less than Sunny Baby is shorter than Anil. Who is the shortest among them?
(a) Anil (b) Baby
(c) Sunny (d) Bose

13. Seema's younger brother Sohan in older than Seeta. Sweta is younger than Deepti but elder than Seema. Who is the eldest?
(a) Seema (b) Sweta
(c) Seeta (d) Deepti

14. Mohan correctly remember that his father's birthday is before 20th January but after 16th January whereas his sister correctly remembers that their father's birthday is after 18th January but before 23rd January. On which date in January is definitely their father's birthday?
(a) 18th
(b) 19th
(c) 20th
(d) Data inadequate

15. Meena correctly remembers that her father's birthday is after 18th May but before 22nd May. Her brother correctly remembers that their father's birthday is before 24th May but after 20th May. On which date in May was definitely their father's birthday?
(a) 20th
(b) 19th
(c) 18th
(d) None of these

16. Rajat correctly remembers that his mother's birthday is not after 18th of June. His sister correctly remembers that their mother's birthday is before 20th June but after 17th June. On which day in April was definitely their mother's birthday?
(a) 17th
(b) 19th
(c) 18th
(d) 17th or 18th

17. Pratap correctly remembers that his mother's birthday is before 23rd April but after 19th April, whereas his sister correctly remembers that their mother's birthday is not on or after 22nd April. On which day in April is definitely their's mother's birthday?
(a) 20th
(b) 21st
(c) 20th or 21st
(d) Cannot be determined

18. Sammer remembers that his brother's birthday is after fifteenth but before 18th of February whereas his sister Kanika remembers that her brother's birthday is after 16th but before 19th of Februrary. On which day in February is Sammer's brother's birthday?
(a) 15th February
(b) 18th February
(c) 17th February
(d) None of these

19. Ayush remembers that Sanjay's birthday is certainly after January 12 but not later than 16th January. If Mehar remembers that Sanjay's birthday is before 17th of Jan but not before 13th Jan. On which of the following day was Sanjay's birthday?
(a) 14th
(b) 15th
(c) 16th
(d) Either 14th or 15th

20. In a row of girls, Veena is 12th from the start and 19th from the end. In another row of girls, Sunita is 14th from the start and 20th from the end. How many girls are there in both the rows together?
(a) 72
(b) 65
(c) 63
(d) 61

Answers with Explanations

1. (b) Kamya's new position is 13th from left. But it is the same as Preeti's earlier position which is 6th from the right.

The row consists of $(12+1+5)$
$= 18$ girls

Now, Preeti's new position is Kamya's earlier position which is 5th from the left.

$\therefore$ Preeti's new position from the right
$= 18 - 5 + 1$
$= 13 + 1 = 14$

2. (d) Now, position of Ashwini
$= (15 + 6)$
$= 21$st from left

$\therefore$ Ashwini's position from right
$= (37 + 1 - 21) = 17$th

3. (a) Total number of boys
= (Number of boys in Jeevan's row) + (Number of boys in Vikash's row)
= (6 + 1 + 10) + (9 + 1 + 11) = (17 + 21) = 38

4. (c) Required number = (38 + 9 – 1) = 47 – 1 = 46

5. (b) Required position = (40 + 1 – 14) = 27th

6. (d) According to the question,
Lakshmi > Meenu
Lakshmi > Leela > Meenu
Meenu > Hari > Latha
On arranging the above data, we get
Lakshmi > Leela > Meenu > Hari > Latha
Hence, Latha is the youngest.

7. (d) The data is inadequate because it is not given that who between Virat and Shikhar is taller. Hence, answer cannot be determined.

8. (b) Decreasing order (agewise)
P > R > Q > S
Decreasing order (moneywise)
R > S > P > Q

9. (c) Let the age of Shyam = x yr
Then, age of Ram = $2x$ yr
and age of Sohan = $4x$ yr
$\therefore$ $4x > 2x > x$
On arranging the above data, we get
$\therefore$ Sohan > Ram > Shyam > Mohan
So, Sohan is the eldest.

10. (b) Amit = Sumit, Sumit > Richa
Jyotsana > Richa > Saurabh
Jyotsana > Sumit
On arranging the above data, we get
$\therefore$ Jyotsana > Sumit = amit > Richa > Saurabh.
So, Jyotsana is eldest among them

11. (b) According to the question,
K > S > R
Madhav is the tallest.
K > A > S
On arranging the above data, we get
$\therefore$ M > K > A > S > R
or
R < S < A < K < M
↓ ↓ ↓ ↓ ↓
1 2 3 4 5

K=Keshav
S=Shailendra
R=Rakesh
M=Madhav
A=Aashish

Hence, Shailendra will be the second.

12. (d) According to the question,
Anil > Sunny
Baby > Sunny
Anil > Sunny > Bose
Anil > Baby
On arranging the above data, we get
Anil > Baby > Sunny > Bose
So, shortest person in Bose.

13. (d) According to the question, sequence is as follows
Deepti > Sweta > Seema > Sohan > Seeta
So, Deepti is the eldest.

14. (b) Days by Mohan, [17th, 18th or 19th] January.
Days by his sister, [19th, 20th, 21st or 22nd] January.
Required day is 19th January as it is common in both the groups.

15. (d) Days by Meena, 19th 20th or 21st May.
Days by her brother, 21st, 22nd or 23rd May.
Clearly, 21st may is common in both the groups and hence it is the required day.

16. (c) Days by Rajat, June 18 or earlier.
Days by his sister, June 18 or June 19.
Clearly, June 18 is the required day.

17. (c) Days by Pratap = [20, 21 or 22] in April.
Days by his sister. not on or after 22 April
Clearly, then answer is = [20 or 21] in April

18. (c) Days by Sameer [16, 17] in February
Days by Kanika [17, 18] in February
17th February is common in both the groups.
Clearly, the correct date is 17th February.

19. (d) Days by Ayush, [13, 14,15] in January
Days by Mehar, [14,15 , 16] in January
Clearly, 14th and 15th January are common in both the groups.
Hence, the correct answer is either 14th or 15th January.

20. (c) In first row. Veena is 12th from start and 19th from end.
Then, total number of girls = (12 + 19 – 1) = 30
In second row, Sunita is 14th from start and 20th from the end.
The, total number of girls = (14 + 20 – 1) = 33
$\therefore$ Total number of girls = 30 + 33 = 63

9 MATHEMATICAL OPERATIONS

Questions on mathematical operations are designed to test a candidate's skill in mathematical operations. The four fandamental operations— addition (+), subtraction (–), multiplication (×) and division (÷) and also statements such as 'less than', 'greater than', 'equal to', 'not equal to', etc. are represented by symbols different from the usual ones. The candidate has to substitute the real signs and solve the questions accordingly to get the answer. There are three types of questions based on mathematical operations are usually asked in competitive examinations.

1. **Problem-Solving by substitution :** In this type of questions, you have substitutes for various mathematical symbols or numerals followed by a question involving calculation of an expression the correct/incorrect equation. While solving a mathematical expression proceed according to the rule BODMAS—*i.e.,*

   B → Brackets
   O → Of
   D → Division
   M → Multiplication
   A → Addition
   S → Subtration

2. **Interchanging the signs and numbers :** In this type of questions, certain signs or numbers interchange between each other. The candidate is required to change the given signs or change the given numbers with each other.
3. **Deriving the appropriate conclusion :** In this type of questions, certain relationship between different sets of elements is given (in terms of >, <, =) using either the real symbols or substituted symbols.

Solved Examples

Example 1. If '+' means '–', '×' means '÷', '÷' means '+' and '–' means '×', then which of the following will be the value of the expression

$252 \times 9 - 5 + 32 \div 92$?

(a) 152 (b) 175
(c) 150 (d) 200

Solution (d): Putting the proper signs in the given expression, we get

$252 + 9 \times 5 - 32 + 92$
$= 28 \times 5 - 32 + 92$
$= 140 - 32 + 92 = 200$

Example 2. If 6 ★ 5 = 31, 7 ★ 8 = 57, 3 ★ 4 = 13, then 9 ★ 10 = ?

(a) 90 (b) 91
(c) 60 (d) 75

Solution (b):

As, 6 ★ 5 = 6 × 5 + 1 = 31
7 ★ 8 = 7 × 8 + 1 = 57
and, 3 ★ 4 = 3 × 4 + 1 = 13
Similarly, 9 ★ 10 = 9 × 10 + 1 = 91

Example 3. If P denotes 'multiplied by', T denotes 'subtracted from'. M denotes 'added to' and B denotes 'divided by', then 28B7P8T6M4 = ?

(a) –30 (b) 30
(c) 32 (d) 61

Solution (b): Using the correct symbols, we have:

Given expression $= 28 \div 7 \times 8 - 6 + 4$
$= 4 \times 8 - 6 + 4$
$= 32 - 6 + 4 = 36 - 6 = 30$

Example 4. If `+' means `X', '–' means '÷' 'X' means '+' and '÷', mean '–' then $10 \times 18 - 9 + 3 \div 1$ is equal to

(a) 16 (b) 15
(c) 17 (d) 18

Solution (b): Lives Equation

$= 10 \times 18 - 9 + 3 \div 1$
According to question
$= 10 + 18 \div 9 \times 3 - 1$
$= 10 + 2 \times 3 \div 1 = 15$

Exercise

Directions (Q. 1-24): Choose the correct option in each of the following questions:

1. If ÷ means ×, × means +, + means – and – means ÷, find the value of $16 \times 3 + 5 - 2 \div 4$:

   (a) 9
   (b) 10
   (c) 19
   (d) None of these

2. If × means +, + means ÷, – means × and ÷ means –, then $8 \times 7 - 8 + 40 \div 2 = ?$

   (a) 1 (b) $7\frac{2}{5}$
   (c) $8\frac{3}{5}$ (d) 44

3. If Q means 'add to', J means 'multiply by', T means 'subtract from' and K means 'divide by', then 30 K 2 Q 3 J 6 T 5 = ?
(a) 18 (b) 28
(c) 31 (d) 103

4. If P denotes 'multiplied by', T denotes 'subtracted from', M denotes 'added to' and B denotes 'divided by', then :
28 B 7 P 8 T 6 M 4 = ?
(a) $-\frac{3}{2}$ (b) 30
(c) 32 (d) 34

5. If 'when' means '×', 'you' means '÷', 'come' means '–' and 'will' means '+', then what will be the value of "8 when 12 will 16 you 2 come 10" ?
(a) 45 (b) 94
(c) 96 (d) 112

6. If + means ×, × means –, ÷ means + and – means ÷ , then which of the following gives the result of 175 – 25 ÷ 5 + 20 × 3 + 10 ?
(a) 77 (b) 160
(c) 240 (d) 2370

7. If '+' means '×', '–' means '÷', '×' means '–' and '÷' means '+', then the value of 9 + 8 ÷ 8 – 4 × 9 is :
(a) 56 (b) 65
(c) 66 (d) 55

8. If '–' means '×', '×' means '+', '+' means '÷' and '÷' means '–', then the vaule of 14 – 10 × 4 – 16 + 8 is :
(a) 241 (b) 124
(c) 142 (d) 412

9. If '+' means '×', '–' means '÷', '×' means '–' and '÷' means '+', then the vaule of 32 ÷ 8 – 4 × 12 + 4 is :
(a) – 14 (b) – 41
(c) – 40 (d) – 12

10. If 'A' means '+', 'B' means '–', 'C' means '×' and 'D' means '÷', then :
18 C 14 A 6 B 16 D 4 is equal to :
(a) 63 (b) 288
(c) 254 (d) 1208

11. If '÷' means '–', '–' means '+', '+' means '×' and '×' means '÷', then what is the value of 3 ÷ 4 × 2 – 1 + 5 = ?
(a) 4 (b) 5
(c) 6 (d) 7

12. If '+' means '÷', '×' means '–', '÷' means '×' and '–' means '+', then what is the value of given expression ?
25 + 5 × 10 ÷ 2 + 5
(a) 10 (b) 0
(c) 5 (d) 15

13. If 'R' means '÷', 'Q' means '×', 'P' means '+' then 18 R 9 P 2 Q 8 = ?
(a) 18 (b) 16
(c) 28 (d) 30

14. If 'P' denotes '÷', 'Q' denotes '×', 'R'denotes '+' and S denotes '–', then 18 Q 12 P 4 R 5 S 6 :
(a) 53 (b) 59
(c) 63 (d) 65

15. If × stands for addition, < stands for subtraction, + stands for division, > stands for multiplication, – stands for equation, ÷ stands for greater than, and = stands for less than, state which of the following is true?
(a) 5 > 8 + 4 – 10 < 4 × 8
(b) 3 × 4 > 2 – 9 + 3 < 3
(c) 5 × 3 < 3 ÷ 8 + 4 × 10
(d) 3 × 2 < 4 ÷ 16 > 2 + 4

16. If 55 + 66 = 33 and 22 + 99 = 33, what is 44 + 88?
(a) 36 (b) 38
(c) 40 (d) 33

17. Which of the following interchange of signs would make the given equation correct?
2 × 3 + 6 – 12 ÷ 4 = 17
(a) × and + (b) + and –
(c) + and ÷ (d) – and ÷

18. B stands for addition, G stands for subtraction, E stands for multiplication, C stands for sivision, D stands for equal to, A stands for greater than, R stands for less than. In each of the four alternatives only one expression is correct according to the letter symbol. Identify that expression.
(a) 15 C 3 B 2 A 6 E 2
(b) 15 B 2 G 5 A 4 G 4
(c) 15 C 3 B 2 D 6 B 1
(d) 15 B 3 D 4 E 6

19. If 2 27 = 4 ★ 7 ,32 = 6 ★, then 7 ★ 6 =?
(a) 73 (b) 37
(c) 67 (d) 42

20. Select the correct combination of Mathematical signs to replace ★ signs and to balance the given equation.
15 17 ★ 6 ★ 3 ★ 24 ★
(a) – ÷ + = (b) + ÷ – =
(c) + × = ÷ (d) – × = +

21. Which of the following interchanges of numbers would make the given equation correct?
8 × 20 ÷ 3 + 9 – 5 = 38
(a) 3, 9 (b) 3, 8
(c) 8, 9 (d) 3, 5

22. Put the correct mathematical signs in the following equation from the given alternatives :
33 ? 11 ? 3 ? 6 ? = 115
(a) –, ×, + (b) +, –, ×
(c) ×, ÷, – (d) ÷ , ×, ×

23. In the following problem, = stands for ÷ ,+ stands for –, × stands for =, – stands for >, > stands for +, < stands for ×, ÷ standsfor <. when these new symbols are substituted, only one will be wrong. Identify the wrong one
(a) 4 < 2 + 5 + 8 × 5
(b) 4 = 2 + 5 > 8 × 5
(c) 4 < 2 > 5 + 8 × 5
(d) 4 > 2 < 5 + 8 – 5

24. Select the correct combination of mathematical signs to replace signs and to balance the given equation.
8 0 = 2 ★ 96 ★ 6 ★
(a) × ÷ – (b) × – ÷
(c) – × ÷ (d) ÷ – ×

Answers with Explanations

1. (a) Using the correct symbols, we have
Given expression
= 16 + 3 – 5 ÷ 2 × 4
$= 19 - \frac{5}{2} \times 4$
= 19 – 10 = 9

2. (b) Using the correct symbols, we have
Given expression
= 8 + 7 × 8 ÷ 40 – 2

$= 8 + 7 \times \frac{1}{5} - 2$

$= 6 + \frac{7}{5} = \frac{37}{5} = 7\frac{2}{5}$

3. (b) Using the correct symbols, we have
Given expression
$= 30 \div 2 + 3 \times 6 - 5$
$= 15 + 18 - 5 = 28$

4. (b) Using the correct symbols, we have
Given expression
$= 28 \div 7 \times 8 - 6 + 4$
$= 4 \times 8 - 6 + 4$
$= 32 - 6 + 4 = 36 - 6 = 30$

5. (b) Using the correct symbols, we have
Given expression
$= 8 \times 12 + 16 \div 2 - 10$
$= 96 + 8 - 10$
$= 104 - 10 = 94$

6. (a) Using the proper signs in the given expression, we get
$175 \div 25 + 5 \times 20 - 3 \times 10$
$= 7 + 5 \times 20 - 3 \times 10$
$= 7 + 100 - 30 = 107 - 30 = 77$

7. (b) Using proper symbols, we get
$= 9 \times 8 + 8 \div 4 - 9$
$= 72 + 2 - 9 = 65$

8. (c) Using proper symbols, we get:
$= 14 \times 10 + 4 - 16 \div 8$
$= 140 + 4 - 2 = 142$

9. (a) Using proper operations, we get:
$= 32 + 8 \div 4 - 12 \times 4$
$= 32 + 2 - 12 \times 4$
$= 32 + 2 - 48 = -14$

10. (c) Using proper signs, we get :
$= 18 \times 14 + 6 - 16 \div 4$
$= 252 + 6 - 4 = 254$

11. (c) Using the proper symbols, we have:
$3 \div 4 \times 2 - 1 + 5$
$= 3 - 4 \div 2 + 1 \times 5$
$= 3 - 2 + 1 \times 5 = 6$

12. (b) Using the correct symbols, we have:
$25 + 5 \times 10 \div 2 - 15$
$= 25 \div 5 - 10 \times 2 + 15$
$= 5 - 20 + 15 = 0$

13. (a) Using the correct symbols, we have :
18 R 9 P 2 Q 8
$= 18 \div 9 + 2 \times 8$
$= 2 + 2 \times 8 = 18$

14. (a) Using the correct symbols, we have:
18 Q 12 P 4 R 5 S 6
$= 18 \times 12 \div 4 + 5 - 6$
$= 18 \times 3 + 5 - 6$
$= 54 + 5 - 6$
$= 59 - 6 = 53$

15. (a) According to given information,
from option (a),
$5 > 8 + 4 = 10 < 4 \times 8$
$\Rightarrow 5 \times 8 \div 4 < 10 - 4 + 8$
$\Rightarrow 5 \times 2 < 18 - 4 \Rightarrow 10 < 14$
from option (b),
$3 \times 4 > 2 - 9 + 3 < 3$
$\Rightarrow 3 + 4 \times 2 = 9 \div 3 - 3$
$\Rightarrow 3 + 8 = 3 - 3$
$\Rightarrow 11 \neq 0$
from option (c),
$5 \times 3 < 3 \div 8 + 4 \times 10$
$\Rightarrow 5 + 3 - 3 > 8 \div 4 + 10$
$\Rightarrow 8 - 3 > 2 + 10$
$\Rightarrow 5 \ngtr 12$
from option (d),
$3 \times 2 < 4 \div 16 > 2 \times 4$
$\Rightarrow 3 + 2 - 4 > 16 \times 2 \div 4$
$\Rightarrow 5 - 4 > \frac{16 \times 2}{4} \Rightarrow 1 \ngtr 8$

16. (a) $55 + 66 \Rightarrow 5 + 6 = 11, 11 \times 3 = 33$
$22 + 99 \Rightarrow 2 + 9 = 11, 11 \times 3 = 33$
Similarly $44 + 88 \Rightarrow 4 + 8 = 12, 12 \times 3 = 36$

17. (a) $2 \times 3 + 6 - 12 \div 4 = 17$
$\Rightarrow 2 + 3 \times 6 - 12 \div 4 = 17$
$\Rightarrow 2 + 18 - 3 = 17$

18. (b) From Option (a)
15 C 3 B 2 A 6 E 2
$\Rightarrow 15 \div 3 + 2 > 6 \times 2$
$\Rightarrow 5 + 2 \ngtr 12$
from Option (b)
15 B 2 G 5 A 4 G 4
$\Rightarrow 15 + 2 - 5 > 4 - 4$
$\Rightarrow 12 > 0$
from Option (c)
15 C 3 B 2 D 6 B 10
$\Rightarrow 15 \div 3 + 2 = 6 + 10$
$\Rightarrow 5 + 2 = 16$
$\Rightarrow 7 = 16$
from Option (d)
15 B 3 D 4 E 6
$\Rightarrow 15 + 3 = 4 \times 6$
$\Rightarrow 18 \neq 24$

19. (b) $2 \star 6 \longrightarrow 3\;2$, $7 \star 4 \longrightarrow 2\;7$ ($\div 2$)

Therefore, $7 \star 6 \longrightarrow 3\;7$ ($\div 2$)

20. (b) $15 \star 24 \star 3 \star 6 \star 17$
$\Rightarrow 15 + 24 \div 3 - 6 = 17$
$\Rightarrow 15 + 8 - 6 = 17$

21. (d) $8 \times 20 \div 3 + 9 - 5 = 38$
$\Rightarrow 8 \times 20 \div 5 + 9 - 3 = 38$
$\Rightarrow 8 \times 4 + 9 - 3 = 38$
$\Rightarrow 32 + 6 = 38$

22. (c) $33 \times 11 \div 3 - 6 = 115$
$\Rightarrow \frac{363}{3} - 6 = 115$
$\Rightarrow 121 - 6 = 115$

23. (a) From option (a)
$4 < 2 + 5 + 8 \times 5$
$\Rightarrow 4 \times 2 - 5 - 8 = 5$
$\Rightarrow 8 - 5 - 8 \neq 5$
from option (b)
$4 = 2 + 5 > 8 \times 5$
$\Rightarrow 4 \div 2 - 5 + 8 = 5$
$\Rightarrow 2 - 5 + 8 = 5$
from option (c)
$4 < 2 > 5 + 8 \times 5$
$\Rightarrow 4 \times 2 + 5 - 8 = 5$
$\Rightarrow 8 + 5 - 8 = 5$
from Option (d)
$4 > 2 < 5 + 8 - 5$
$\Rightarrow 4 + 2 \times 5 - 8 > 5$
$\Rightarrow 4 + 10 - 8 > 5 \Rightarrow 6 > 5$

24. (b) $8 \star 6 \star 96 \star 2 = 0$
$\Rightarrow 8 \times 6 - 96 \div 2 = 0$
$\Rightarrow 48 - 48 = 0$

10 MISSING NUMBERS

Under this segment of reasoning, numbers or letters or both are represented through one or more figures (geometrical; or any other figure). Such numbers or letters are arranged inside the figure according to a certain pattern (i.e., based on particular logic and/or mathematical calculations) but in such arrangement one character is missing which is denoted by question mark (?). The candidate is required to find out the character that the can replace the question mark (?) satisfying the logic and calculations.

Solved Examples

Directions : (Example Nos. 1-3) Find the missing character from the given alternatives.

Example 1.

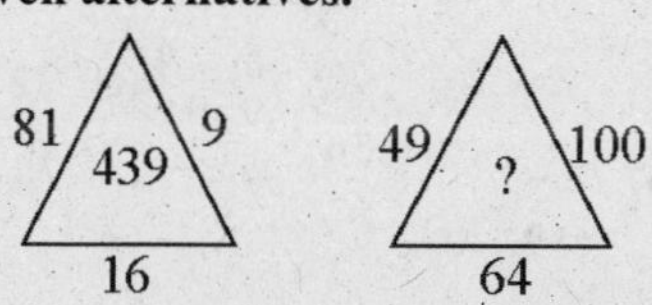

(a) 8710 (b) 1078
(c) 8107 (d) 789

Solution (c) Numbers placed along the sides of the triangle are the squares of the numbers at the centre of the triangle, as shown below

$(4)^2 = 16, (3)^2 = 9, (9)^2 = 81$

Similarly, $\sqrt{64} = 8, \sqrt{100} = 10, \sqrt{49} = 7$

So, the missing number = $\boxed{8107}$

Example 2.

4	5	6
2	3	7
1	8	3
21	98	?

(a) 85 (b) 94
(c) 104 (d) 49

Solution (b)

As, $(4)^2 + (2)^2 + (1)^2 = 21$

$(5)^2 + (3)^2 + (8)^2 = 98$

Similarly, $(6)^2 + (7)^2 + (3)^2 = 94$

Example 3.

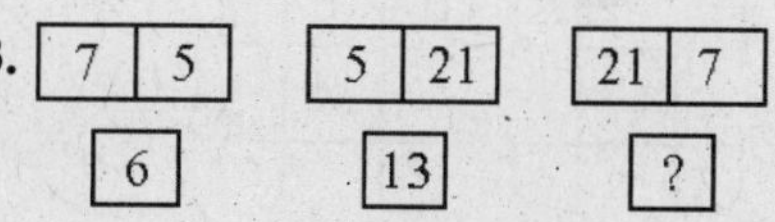

(a) 4 (b) 8
(c) 20 (d) 14

Solution (d)

As, $\frac{7+5}{2} = 6$ and $\frac{5+21}{2} = 13$

Similarly, missing number = $\frac{7+21}{2} = \boxed{14}$

Exercise

Directions (Q. Nos. 1-20): In each of the following questions, a set of figures carrying certain characters is given. Assuming that the characters in each set follow a similar pattern, find the missing character in each case.

1.

17	8	5	5
13	7	5	4
6	12	6	3
10	6	4	?

(a) 4 (b) 5
(c) 6 (d) 7

2.

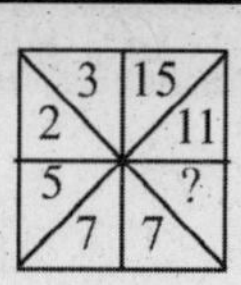

(a) 5 (b) 12
(c) 13 (d) 26

3.

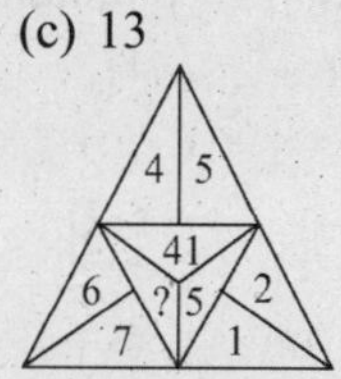

(a) 16 (b) 9
(c) 85 (d) 112

4.

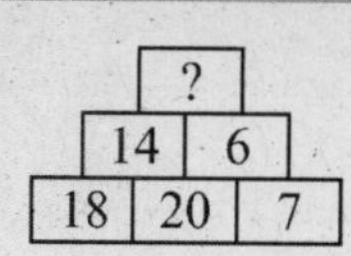

(a) 24 (b) 25
(c) 28 (d) 20

5.

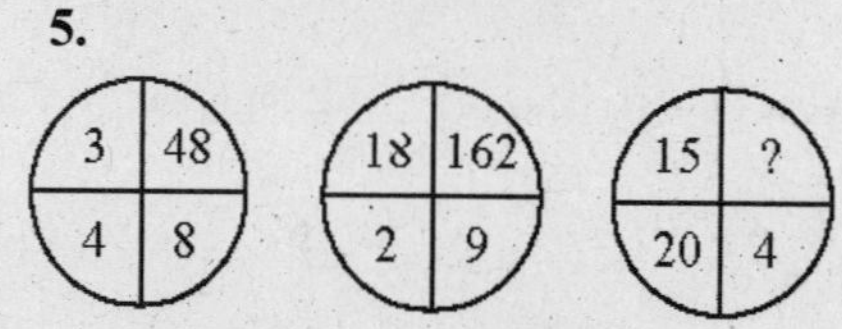

(a) 600 (b) 550
(c) 435 (d) 172

6.

7	6	9
2	8	4
4	3	?
36	42	26

(a) 5 (b) 2
(c) 3 (d) 4

7.

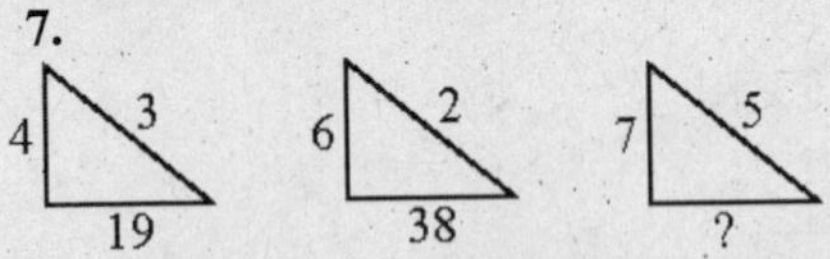

(a) 55 (b) 51
(c) 54 (d) 58

8.

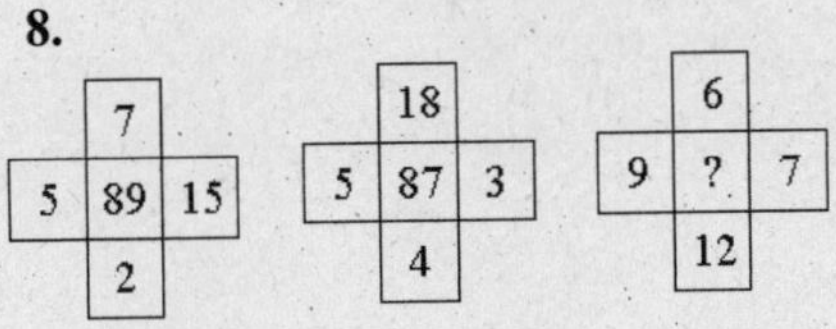

(a) 135 (b) 85
(c) 195 (d) 95

9.

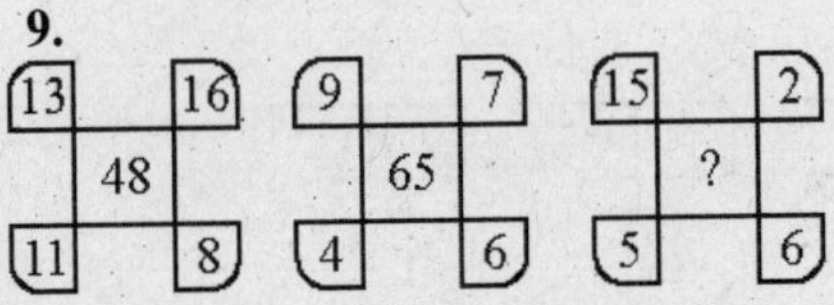

(a) 90 (b) 87
(c) 53 (d) 80

10.

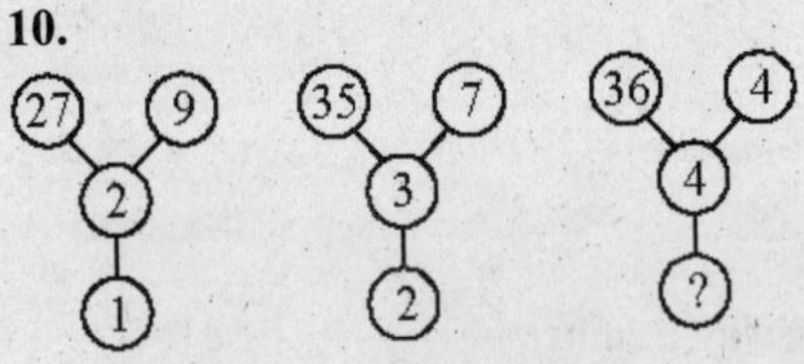

(a) 3 (b) 4
(c) 5 (d) 6

11.

(a) 77 (b) 36
(c) 99 (d) 63

12.

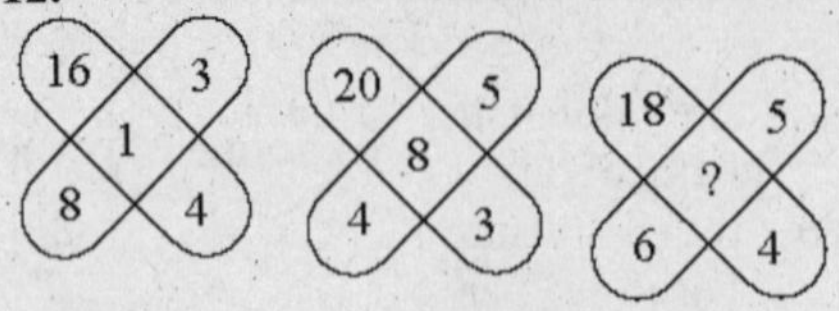

(a) 3 (b) 10
(c) 15 (d) 60

13.

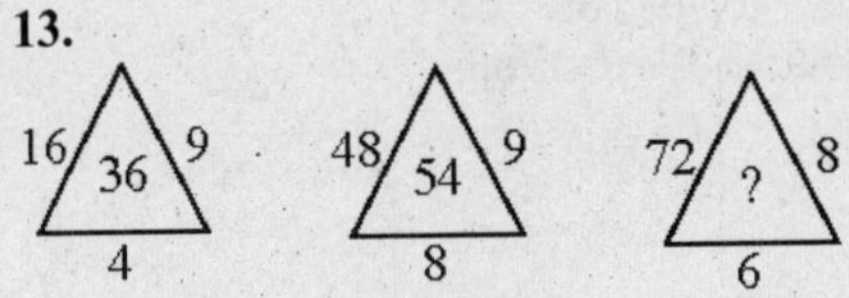

(a) 96 (b) 76
(c) 48 (d) 32

14.

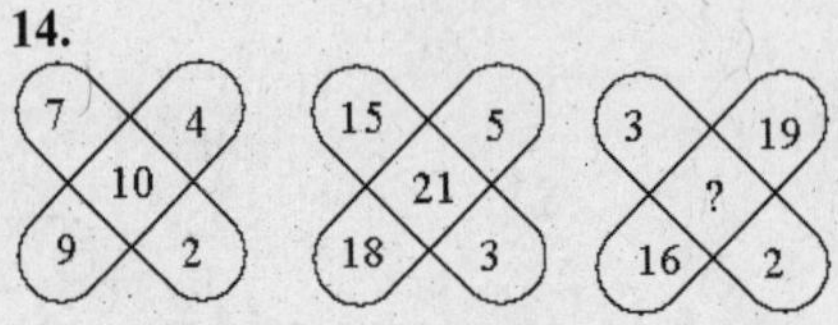

(a) 25 (b) 88
(c) 9 (d) 17

15.

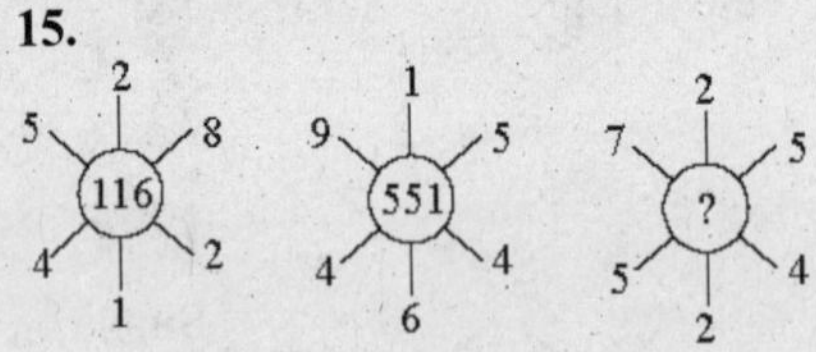

(a) 287 (b) 215
(c) 201 (d) 275

16.

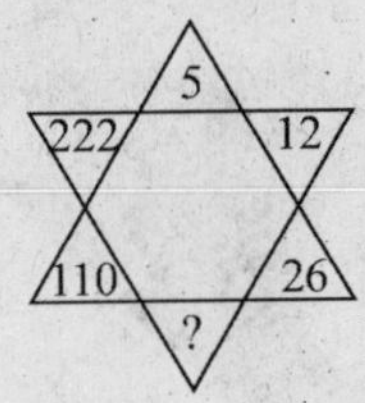

(a) 54 (b) 51
(c) 48 (d) 44

17.

9	5	6
5	7	?
3	4	5
135	140	150

(a) 4 (b) 5
(c) 8 (d) 10

18.

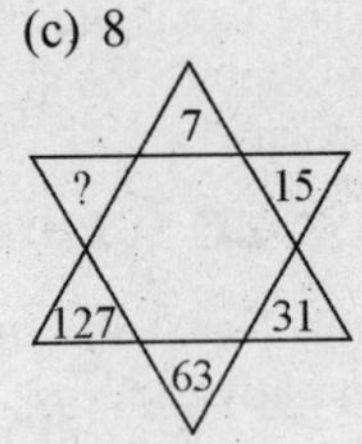

(a) 190 (b) 221
(c) 236 (d) 255

19. 63 7 9
20 5 6
20 4 ?

(a) 8 (b) 3
(c) 5 (d) 2

20.

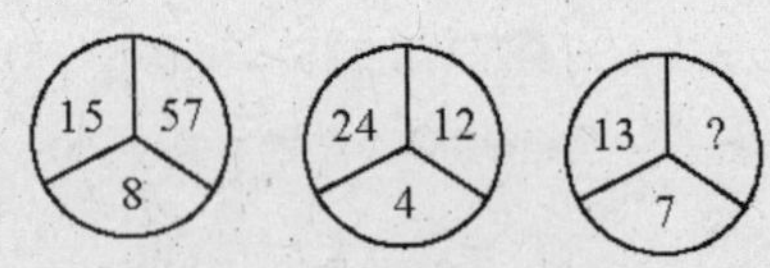

(a) 14 (b) 55
(c) 23 (d) 50

Answers with Explanations

1. (a) Here, in Row 1 : $\frac{17+8}{5}=5$

In Row 2 : $\frac{13+7}{5}=4$

In Row 3 : $\frac{6+12}{6}=3$

In Row 4 : $\frac{10+6}{4}=\boxed{4}$

2. (a) As, $(3 \times 2)+1=7$
$(5 \times 2)+1=11$
and $(7 \times 2)+1=15$

Similarly, $?=2 \times 2+1=\boxed{5}$

3. (c) The pattern in the question is
$4^2+5^2=16+25=41$,
$2^2+1^2=4+1=5$
$7^2+6^2=49+36=\boxed{85}$

4. (b) Here, the pattern is as follows
$14+6=20$
Similarly, $18+7=\boxed{25}$

5. (a) Moving in anti-clockwise direction in each of the figures, we have
$\frac{3\times4\times8}{2}=48$
and $\frac{18\times2\times9}{2}=162$
Similarly, $\frac{15\times20\times4}{2}=\boxed{600}$

6. (b) As, $7+2=9$; $9 \times 4=36$
$6+8=14$; $14 \times 3=42$

Similarly, $9 + 4 = 13$ and $13 \times 2 = 26$

Hence, number 2 will come in place of question mark.

7. (c) As, $4^2 + 3 = 19$

and $6^2 + 2 = 38$

Similarly $7^2 + 5 = \boxed{54}$

Hence, option (c) is the correct answer.

8. (a) As, $(7 \times 2) + (5 \times 15) = 89$

and $(18 \times 4) + (5 \times 3) = 87$

Similarly $(6 \times 12) + (9 \times 7) = \boxed{135}$

9. (d) As, $(13 - 11) \times (16 + 8) = 48$

and $(9 - 4) \times (7 + 6) = 65$

Similarly $(15 - 5) \times (2 + 6) = \boxed{80}$

10. (c) As, $27 \div 9 - 2 = 3 - 2 = 1$

and $35 \div 7 - 3 = 5 - 3 = 2$

Similarly, $36 \div 4 - 4 = 9 - 4 = \frac{60}{2} = \boxed{5}$

11. (b) As, $3 + 6 + 7 + 4 = 20$

and $8 + 5 + 4 + 6 = 23$

Similarly, $? = 11 + 9 + 7 + 9 = \boxed{36}$

12. (a) As, $16 - (3 + 4 + 8) = 1$

and $20 - (5 + 3 + 4) = 8$

Similarly, $18 - (5 + 4 + 6) = \boxed{3}$

13. (a) As, $(16 \times 9) \div 4 = 36$

and $(48 \times 9) \div 8 = 54$

Similarly, $(72 \times 8) \div 6 = \boxed{96}$

Hence, number 96 will come in place of question mark.

14. (a) As, $(7 \times 4) - (9 \times 2) = 10$

and $(15 \times 5) - (18 \times 3) = 21$

Similarly, $(19 \times 3) - (16 \times 2) = \boxed{25}$

15. (c) As, $528 - 412 = 116$

and $915 - 364 = 551$

Similarly, $725 - 524 = \boxed{201}$

16. (a) Pattern given in figure is as follows

$5 \times 2 + 2 = 12$, $12 \times 2 + 2 = 26$

$26 \times 2 + 2 = \boxed{54}$, $54 \times 2 + 2 = 110$

So, the missing number is 54

17. (b) The pattern is as follows

$9 \times 5 \times 3 = 135$

$5 \times 7 \times 4 = 140$

Similarly, $6 \times \boxed{5} \times 5 = 150$

Hence, number 5 will come in place of question mark.

18. (d) The pattern in clockwise direction is

$(7 \times 2) + 1 = 15$

$(15 \times 2) + 1 = 31$

$(31 \times 2) + 1 = 63$

$(63 \times 2) + 1 = 127$

$\therefore ? = (127 \times 2) + 1 = \boxed{255}$

19. (c) As, $7 \times 9 = 63$ and $5 \times 6 = 30$

Similarly, $4 \times ? = 20 \Rightarrow ? = \frac{20}{4} = \boxed{5}$

20. (d) As, $\frac{15+57}{9} = 8$ and $\frac{24+12}{9} = 4$

Similarly, $\frac{13+?}{9} = 7$

$\therefore ? + (7 \times 9) - 13 = 63 - 13 = \boxed{50}$

11 MATRIX

In this chapter a single matrix or a couple of matrices is given with numbers and letters written inside matrix or matrices. Students are required to identify the code for the given word on the basis of codes formed from matrix/matrices. Following example will give a proper understanding of the topic.

Solved Example

Example 1. A word is represented by only one set of numbers as given in any one of the alternatives. The sets of numbers given in the alternatives are represented by two classes of alphabets as shown in the given two matrices. The columns and rows of Matrix-I are numbered from 0 to 4 and that of Matrix-II are numbered from 5 to 9. A letter from these matrices can be represented first by its row and next by its column, for example, 'P' can be represented by 00, 14 etc., and 'A' can be represented by 56, 79 etc. similarly you have to identify the set for the word 'ROSE'.

Matrix-I

	0	1	2	3	4
0	P	U	L	S	E
1	U	L	S	E	P
2	L	S	E	P	U
3	S	E	P	U	L
4	E	P	U	L	S

Matrix-II

	5	6	7	8	9
5	R	A	D	I	O
6	A	D	I	O	R
7	D	I	O	R	A
8	I	O	R	A	D
9	O	R	A	D	I

(a) 55, 95, 44, 42

(b) 96, 95, 44, 40

(c) 69, 86, 21, 43

(d) 87, 95, 44, 43

Sol. (b) From the given matrices,

Matrix-I

	0	1	2	3	4
0	P	U	L	Ⓢ	Ⓔ
1	U	L	Ⓢ	Ⓔ	P
2	L	Ⓢ	Ⓔ	P	U
3	Ⓢ	Ⓔ	P	U	L
4	Ⓔ	P	U	L	Ⓢ

Matrix-II

	5	6	7	8	9
5	Ⓡ	A	D	I	Ⓞ
6	A	D	I	Ⓞ	Ⓡ
7	D	I	Ⓞ	Ⓡ	A
8	I	Ⓞ	Ⓡ	A	D
9	Ⓞ	Ⓡ	A	D	I

Codes for respective words are :

R ⇒ 55, 69, 78, 87, 96

O ⇒ 59, 68, 77, 86, 95

S ⇒ 03, 12, 21, 30, 44

E ⇒ 04, 13, 22, 31, 40

Comparing from options

∴ ROSE ⇒ 96, 95, 44, 40

Exercise

1. A word is represented by only one set of numbers as given in any one of the alternatives. The sets of numbers given in the alternatives are represented by two classes of alphabets as shown in the given two matrices. The columns and rows of Matrix-I are numbered from 0 to 4 and that of Matrix-II are numbered from 5 to 9. A letter from these matrices can be represented first by its row and next by its column, for example, 'N' can be represented by 21, 67 etc., and 'R' can be represented by 57, 66 etc. Similarly, you have to identify the set for the word 'GRIM'.

Matrix-I

	0	1	2	3	4
0	Q	R	A	N	B
1	W	I	N	H	L
2	E	N	S	G	O
3	N	Y	G	O	M
4	M	T	O	F	A

Matrix-II

	5	6	7	8	9
5	Z	M	R	I	Q
6	X	R	N	W	A
7	C	S	Y	E	U
8	S	N	T	M	S
9	G	B	E	R	U

(a) 23, 57, 11, 88

(b) 32, 66, 58, 67

(c) 95, 02, 11, 86
(d) 23, 11, 57, 88

2. A word is represented by only one set of numbers as given in any one of the alternatives. The sets of numbers given in the alternatives are represented by two classes of alphabets as shown in the given two matrices. The columns and rows of Matrix-I are numbered from 0 to 4 and that of Matrix-II are numbered from 5 to 9. A letter from these matrices can be represented first by its row and next by its column, for example, 'U' can be represented by 10, 33 etc. and 'N' can be represented by 75, 89 etc. Similarly, you have to identify the set for the word 'BOARD'.

Matrix-I

	0	1	2	3	4
0	R	B	U	P	A
1	U	A	R	B	P
2	P	R	U	A	B
3	A	P	B	U	R
4	B	U	A	R	P

Matrix-II

	5	6	7	8	9
5	D	N	S	H	O
6	S	D	O	N	H
7	N	O	H	D	S
8	H	S	D	O	N
9	O	H	N	S	D

(a) 32, 76, 04, 21, 55
(b) 01, 66, 11, 43, 99
(c) 40, 59, 41, 00, 66
(d) 30, 67, 42, 34, 78

3. A word is represented by only one set of numbers as given in any one of the alternatives. The sets of numbers given in the alternatives are represented by two classes of alphabets as shown in the given two matrices. The columns and rows of Matrix-I are numbered from 0 to 4 and that of Matrix-II are numbered from 5 to 9. A letter from these matrices can be represented first by its row and next by its column, for example, 'F' can be represented first by its row and next by its column, for example, 'F' can be represented by 32, 42 ect. and 'M' can be represented by 68, 88 etc. Similarly, you have to identify the set for the word 'SNOW'.

Matrix-I

	0	1	2	3	4
0	1	N	U	H	E
1	U	I	N	L	L
2	W	G	I	N	E
3	W	W	F	I	U
4	W	W	F	N	E

Matrix-II

	5	6	7	8	9
5	I	S	D	R	O
6	O	I	I	M	S
7	O	S	G	I	O
8	D	M	T	M	I
9	S	D	D	M	S

(a) 76, 43, 59, 21
(b) 95, 23, 79, 10
(c) 99, 01, 57, 30
(d) 69, 12, 65, 20

4. A word is represented by only one set of numbers as given in any one of the alternatives. The sets of numbers given in the alternatives are reprsented by two classes of alphabets as shown in two matrices given below. The columns and rows of Matrix-I are numbered from 0 to 4 and that of Matrix-II are numbered from 5 to 9. A letter from these matrices can be represented first by its row and next by its column, e.g. 'B' can be represented by 21, 32 etc. 'W' can be represented by 97, 89 etc. Similarly, you have to identify the set for the word 'SAINT'.

Matrix-I

	0	1	2	3	4
0	S	L	K	J	J
1	B	S	F	F	G
2	I	B	S	H	H
3	D	I	B	S	C
4	E	E	I	B	C

Matrix-II

	5	6	7	8	9
5	O	A	N	Q	Q
6	T	O	A	N	R
7	U	T	O	A	N
8	V	P	T	O	W
9	P	V	W	T	O

(a) 00, 56, 20, 68, 76
(b) 11, 67, 31, 57, 12
(c) 22, 78, 20, 02, 44
(d) 33, 67, 42, 00, 99

5. A word is represented by only one set of numbers as given in any one of the alternatives. The sets of numbers given in the alternatives are represented by two classes of alphabets as shown in the given two matrices. The columns and rows of Matrix-I are numbered from 0 to 4 and that of Matrix-II are numbered from 5 to 9. A letter from these matrices can be represented first by its row and next by its column, for example, 'M' can be represented by 10, 03 ect, and 'H' can be represented by 55, 78 etc. Similarly, you have to identify the set for the word 'MATHS'.

Matrix - I

	0	1	2	3	4
0	T	S	N	M	E
1	M	T	S	N	E
2	S	E	M	T	N
3	N	M	E	S	T
4	E	N	T	S	M

Matrix - II

	5	6	7	8	9
5	H	G	I	P	A
6	G	H	A	I	P
7	A	I	G	H	I
8	I	P	H	A	G
9	P	A	P	G	H

(a) 03, 59, 11, 78, 43
(b) 10, 67, 22, 55, 01
(c) 22, 75, 00, 66, 21
(d) 44, 88, 23, 98, 20

6. A word is represented by only one set of numbers as given in any one of the alternatives. The sets of numbers given in the alternatives are represented by two classes of alphabets as shown in the given two matrices. The columns and rows of Matrix-I are numbered from 0 to 4 and that of matrix-II are numbered from 5 to 9. A letter from these matrices can be represented first by its row and next by its column, for example, 'C' can be represented by 21, 43, etc. and 'U' can be represented by 75, 98 etc. Similarly, you have to identify the set for the word 'LUNCH'.

Matrix-I

	0	1	2	3	4
0	H	L	M	O	C
1	C	M	O	L	H
2	M	C	L	H	M
3	O	H	C	M	O
4	L	O	H	C	L

Matrix-II

	5	6	7	8	9
5	B	U	S	G	N
6	S	B	U	N	G
7	U	S	N	B	G
8	G	N	B	S	U
9	N	S	G	U	B

(a) 40, 56, 68, 21, 31
(b) 01, 67, 95, 11, 23
(c) 22, 75, 86, 03, 24
(d) 32, 98, 77, 43, 14

7. A word is represented by only one set of numbers as given in any one of the alternatives. The sets of numbers given in the alternatives are represented by two classes of alphabets as shown in the given two matries. the columns and rows of Matrix-l are numbered from 0 to 4 and that of Matrix-ll are numbered from 5 to 9. A letter from these matrices can be represented first by its row and next by its column, for example, 'V' can be represented by 21, 33 etc. and 'I' can be represented by 75, 97 etc. Similarly. you have to identify the set for the word 'WHALE'.

Matrix - I

	0	1	2	3	4
0	U	W	V	A	L
1	A	U	W	L	V
2	L	V	U	W	A
3	U	A	L	V	W
4	W	U	V	A	L

Matrix - II

	5	6	7	8	9
5	E	H	U	I	V
6	V	U	H	E	I
7	I	E	U	H	V
8	U	I	E	V	H
9	H	V	I	U	E

(a) 23, 56, 10, 43, 68
(b) 34, 67, 24, 04, 55
(c) 40, 76, 03, 44, 99
(d) 01, 78, 31, 34, 76

8. A word is represented by only one set of numbers as given in any one of the alternatives. The sets of numbers given in the alternatives are represented by two classes of alphabets as shown in the given two matrices. The columns and rows of Matrix-I are numbered from 0 to 4 and that of Matrix-II are numbered from 5 to 9. A letter from these matrices can be represented first by its row and next by its column, for example, N can be represented by 21, 67, etc., and R can be represented by 66, 57, etc. Similarly, you have to identify the set for the word RAIN.

Matrix-I

	0	1	2	3	4
0	T	R	A	N	I
1	W	U	N	H	L
2	I	N	S	G	O
3	N	Y	P	O	E
4	H	T	O	I	A

Matrix-II

	5	6	7	8	9
5	T	A	R	I	H
6	X	R	N	W	B
7	C	S	Y	E	R
8	S	N	T	M	S
9	I	A	E	R	H

(a) 66, 96, 20, 87
(b) 79, 58, 44, 21
(c) 98, 56, 12, 58
(d) 01, 44, 58, 67

9. A word is represented by only one set of numbers as given in any one of the alternatives. The sets of numbers given in the alternatives are represented by two classes of alphabets as shown in the given two matrices. The columns and rows of Matrix-I are numbered from 0 to 4 and that of Matrix-II are numbered from 5 to 9. A letter from these matrices can be represented first by its row and next by its column, for example, 'N' can be represented by 21, 43, etc., and 'R' can be represented by 66, 57, etc. Similarly, you have to identify the set for the word 'BRIDE'

Matrix-I

	0	1	2	3	4
0	A	B	D	E	N
1	N	E	D	A	B
2	E	N	A	B	D
3	B	D	E	N	A
4	D	A	B	N	E

Matrix-II

	5	6	7	8	9
5	O	S	R	P	I
6	S	R	O	I	P
7	R	I	P	S	O
8	P	O	I	R	S
9	I	P	S	O	R

(a) 42, 75, 68, 24, 34
(b) 96, 88, 68, 24, 32
(c) 30, 88, 68, 24, 32
(d) 30, 76, 66, 24, 32

10. A word is represented by only one set of numbers as given in any one of the alternatives. The sets of numbers given in the alternatives are represented by two classes of alphabets as shown in the given two matrices. The columns and rows of Matrix-I are numbered from 0 to 4 and that of Matrix-II are numbered from 5 to 9. A letter from these matrices can be represented first by its row and next by its column, for example, 'N' can be represented by 21, 43 etc. and 'R' can be represented by 66, 57 etc. Similarly, you have to identify the set for the word 'GEAR'.

Matrix-I

	0	1	2	3	4
0	A	S	E	G	A
1	Q	D	H	L	S
2	W	N	T	K	D
3	H	D	Y	A	F
4	R	G	A	N	G

Matrix-II

	5	6	7	8	9
5	E	T	R	R	F
6	G	R	P	L	R
7	I	O	U	R	M
8	D	F	R	K	Q
9	S	R	W	D	E

(a) 03, 99, 57, 77
(b) 44, 55, 42, 66
(c) 41, 00, 02, 78
(d) 65, 02, 00, 43

11. A word is represented by only one set of numbers as given in any one of the alternatives. The sets of numbers given in the alternatives are represented by two classes of alphabets as shown in the given two matrices. The columns and rows of Matrix-I are numbered from 0 to 4 and that of Matrix-II are numbered from 5 to 9. A letter from these matrices can be represented first by its row and next by its column, for example, 'N' can be represented by 21, 67 etc. and 'R' can be represented by 66, 57 etc. Similarly, you have to identify the set for the word 'PUMP'.

Matrix-I

	0	1	2	3	4
0	P	R	A	N	B
1	W	U	N	H	L
2	E	N	S	G	O
3	N	Y	P	O	M
4	M	T	O	F	A

Matrix-II

	5	6	7	8	9
5	Z	M	R	I	Q
6	X	R	N	W	P
7	C	S	Y	E	U
8	S	N	P	M	S
9	P	B	E	R	P

(a) 23, 57, 11, 88
(b) 69, 11, 40, 99
(c) 32, 02, 11, 87
(d) 00, 99, 87, 32

12. A word is represented by only one set of numbers as given in any one of the alternatives. The sets of numbers given in the alternatives are represented by two classes of alphabets as shown in the given two matrices. The columns and rows of Matrix-I are numbered from 0 to 4 and that of Matrix-II are numbered from 5 to 9. A letter from these matrices can be represented first by its row and next by its column, for example, 'D' can be represented by 20, 44 etc., and 'T' can be represented by 57, 76 etc. Similarly, you have to identify the set for the word 'MOUSE'.

Matrix-I

	0	1	2	3	4
0	D	E	R	U	M
1	M	R	E	D	U
2	D	M	U	R	E
3	U	D	M	E	R
4	E	U	R	M	D

Matrix- II

	5	6	7	8	9
5	S	N	T	A	O
6	T	S	A	O	N
7	O	T	N	S	A
8	A	O	S	N	T
9	N	A	O	T	S

(a) 21, 59, 03, 99, 40
(b) 32, 68, 13, 66, 01
(c) 04, 75, 41, 86, 12
(d) 43, 86, 30, 55, 32

13. A word is represented by only one set of numbers as given in any one of the alternatives. The sets of numbers given in the alternatives are represented by two classes of alphabets as shown in the given two matrices. The columns and rows of Matrix-I are numbered from 0 to 4 and that of Matrix-II are numbered from 5 to 9. A letter from these matrices can be represented first by its row and next by its column, for example, 'F' can be represented by 32, 42 etc. and 'M' can be represented by 88, 68 etc. Similarly, you have to identify the set for the word TURN.

Matrix - I

	0	1	2	3	4
0	A	N	U	H	E
1	U	A	N	L	L
2	U	G	A	N	E
3	U	L	F	A	U
4	U	L	F	N	E

Matrix - II

	5	6	7	8	9
5	I	S	T	R	O
6	R	I	T	M	S
7	R	S	G	R	O
8	T	S	T	M	R
9	S	T	T	M	S

(a) 67, 20, 76, 43
(b) 57, 01, 65, 12
(c) 85, 30, 89, 23
(d) 97, 02, 78, 22

14. A word is represented by only one set of numbers as given in any one of the alternatives. The sets of numbers given in the alternatives are represented by two classes of alphabets as shown in the given two matrices. The columns and rows of Matrix-I are numbered from 0 to 4 and that of Matrix-II are numbered from 5 to 9. A letters from these matrices can be represented first by its row and next by its column, for example, 'G' can be represented by 76, 67, etc. and 'S' can be represented by 21, 32 etc. Similarly, you have to identify the set for the word 'BOARD'.

Matrix - I

	0	1	2	3	4
0	E	D	T	U	O
1	A	E	T	O	U
2	A	S	O	D	V
3	P	A	S	O	V
4	P	A	T	S	O

Matrix - II

	5	6	7	8	9
5	Q	Q	R	Y	Y
6	J	B	G	R	C
7	I	G	B	C	R
8	D	I	F	B	C
9	H	H	H	F	B

(a) 66, 04, 12, 85, 23
(b) 77, 13, 20, 57, 85
(c) 88, 44, 31, 57, 01
(d) 98, 44, 41, 68, 85

15. A word is represented by only one set of numbers as given in any one of the alternatives. The sets of numbers given in the alternatives are represented by two classes of alphabets as shown in the given two matrices. The columns and rows of Matrix-I are numbered from 0 to 4 and that of Matrix-II are numbered from 5 to 9. A letter from these matrics can be represented first by its row and next by its column, for example, 'W' can be represented by 21, 23 etc. and 'J' can be represented by 79, 97 etc. Similarly, you have to identify the set for the word 'GERM'.

Matrix - I

	0	1	2	3	4
0	M	A	R	E	G
1	G	E	M	Q	H
2	U	W	R	W	P
3	G	V	A	P	O
4	M	A	R	Y	I

Matrix - II

	5	6	7	8	9
5	V	M	P	G	M
6	R	P	E	D	U
7	P	M	G	E	J
8	N	R	E	A	K
9	M	U	J	S	L

(a) 10, 11, 02, 59
(b) 04, 87, 31, 76
(c) 30, 67, 44, 40
(d) 77, 96, 12, 95

Answers with Explanations

1. (a) For GRIM,
G = (23), 32, 95
R = 01, (57), 66, 98
I = (11), 58
M = 34, 40, 56, (88)
Finally, we get the set of numbers 23, 57, 11, 88.

2. (a) For BOARD
B = 01, 13, 24, (32), 40
O = 59, 67, (76), 88, 95
A = (04), 11, 23, 30, 42
R = 00, 12, (21), 34, 43
D = (55), 66, 78, 87, 99
The set of numbers 32, 76, 04, 21, 55 is suitable for the word 'BOARD'.

3. (d) S = 56, (69), 76, 99
N = 01, (12), 23, 43
O = 59, (65), 75, 79
W = (20), 30, 31, 40, 41
For 'SNOW' the set of numbers is 69, 12, 65, 20.

4. (a) S = (00), 11, 22, 33
A = (56), 67, 78,
I = (20), 31, 42
N = 57, (68), 79
T = 65, (76), 87, 98
For 'SAINT' the set of letters is 00, 56, 20, 68, 76.

5. (a) M = (03), 10, 22, 31, 44
A = (59), 67, 75, 88, 96
T = 00, (11), 23, 34, 42
H = 55, 66, (78), 87, 99
S = 01, 12, 20, 33, (43)
For 'MATHS' the set of numbers is 03, 59, 11, 78, 43.

6. (a) L = 01, 13, 22, (40), 44
U = (56), 67, 75, 89, 98
N = 59, (68), 77. 86, 95
C = 04, 10, (21), 32, 43
H = 00, 14, 23, (31), 42
For 'LUNCH' the set of numbers is 40, 56, 68, 21, 31.

7. (b) W = 01, 12, 23, (34), 40
H = 56, (67), 78, 89, 95
A = 03, 10, (24), 31, 43
L = (04), 13, 20, 32, 44
E = (55), 68, 76, 87, 99
For 'WHALE' the set of numbers is 34, 67, 24, 04, 55.

8. (d) R = 01, 57, 66, 79, 98

A = 02, 44, 56, 96

I = 04, 20, 43, 58, 95

N = 03, 12, 21, 30, 67, 86

For 'RAIN' the set of numbers is 01, 44, 58, 67.

9. (c) B = 01, 14, 23, 30 42

R = 57, 66, 75, 88, 99

I = 59, 68, 76, 87, 95

D = 02, 12, 24, 31, 40

E = 03, 11, 20, 32, 44

For BRIDE, the set of numbers is 30, 88, 68, 24, 32.

10. (b) G = 03, 41, 44, 65

E = 02, 55, 99

A = 00, 04, 33, 42

R = 40, 57, 58, 66, 69, 78, 87, 96

For 'GEAR' the set of numbers is 44, 55, 42, 66.

11. (b) P = 00, 32, 69, 87, 95, 99

U = 11, 79

M = 34, 40, 56, 88

P = 00, 32, 69, 87, 95, 99

For 'PUMP' the set of numbers is 69, 11, 40, 99.

12. (a) M = 04, 10, 21, 32, 43

O = 59, 68, 75, 86, 97

U = 03, 14, 22, 30, 41

S = 55, 66, 78, 87, 99

E = 01, 12, 24, 33, 40

For 'MOUSE' the set of numbers is 21, 59, 03, 99, 40.

13. (c) T = 57, 67, 85, 87, 96, 97

U = 02, 10, 20, 30, 34, 40

R = 58, 65, 75, 78, 89

N = 01, 12, 23, 43

For 'TURN' the set of numbers is 85, 30, 89, 23.

14. (b) B = 66, 77, 88, 99

O = 04, 13, 22, 33, 44

A = 10, 20, 31, 41

R = 57 68, 79

D = 01, 23, 85

For 'BOARD' the set of numbers is 77, 13, 20, 57, 85.

15. (a) G = 04, 10, 30, 58, 77

E = 03, 11, 67, 78, 87

R = 02, 22, 42, 65, 86

M = 00, 12, 40, 56, 59, 76, 95

For 'GERM' the set of numbers is 10, 11, 02, 59.

12 VENN DIAGRAM

A venn diagram is a representation method for all possible relation that can exists between given group of elements in single figure.

Logical venn diagram depicts the process of representing the thing/objects/persons/departments/organistation/events etc, through diagrammatic medium by the use of figures such as square, circle, rectangle, parallelogram, trapezium, triangle etc. The representation of various similarity and dissimilarity of the object through the diagram provides a better insight to the candidate, regarding the role and area of representation of various objects.

Based on the variety of questions that are asked in competitive exams, we have classified these logical venn diagrammes into two types as follows:

Type 1: Identification of Relation based Venn Diagram

The most common type of question that we encounter in logical venn diagram are based on circular venn diagram. The questions asked from this type contain, a group of some elements (things) and also some diagram. Here, a candidate is required to find out the diagram which classify the given group currently or illutrates the relation between them.

The main motive of asking these types of questions is to analyse the candidate's ability to relate a certian given group of items and illutrate it diagrammatically.

Type 2: Analysis Based venn Diagram

In these types of questions, generally a venn diagram comparing of different geomatrical figures is given. Each geometrical figure in the diagram represents a certain class. The candidate is required to study and analyse the figure carefully and then answer the given question based on it.

Solved Examples

Example 1. Which one of the following diagrams best depicts the relationship between Kanpur, Varanasi and Meerut?

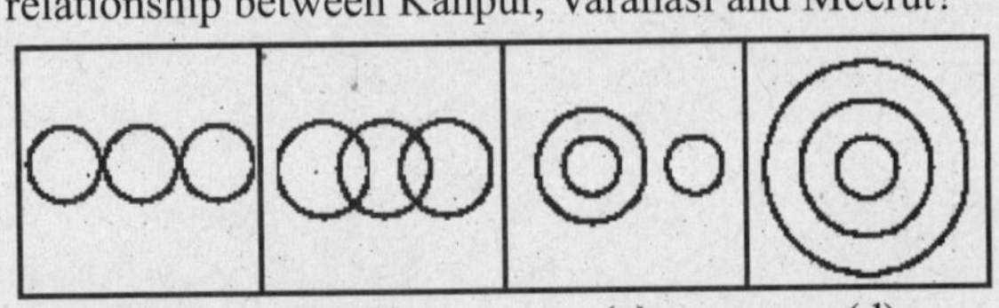

(a) (b) (c) (d)

Sol. (a) Kanpur, Varanasi and Meerut all are cities of Uttar Pradesh but they are entirely different from one another. This can be expressed by option (a).

Example 2. Which of the following diagrams best depicts the relationship between Married, Women and Techers?

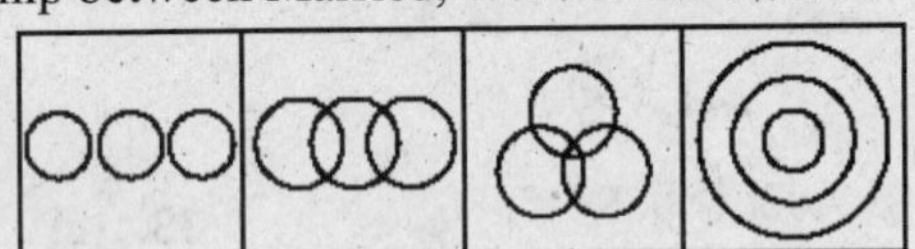

(a) (b) (c) (d)

Sol. (c) Some women are teachers. Some women are married. Some teachers are married. Some married women are teachers. This can be expressed as given in option (c).

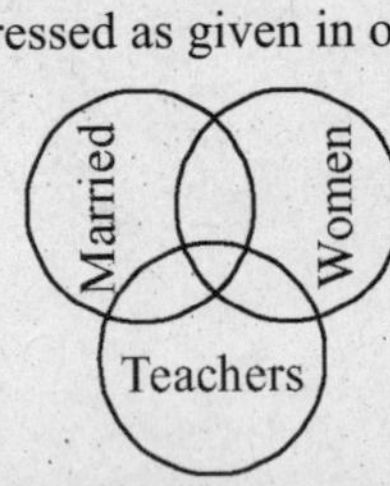

Example 3. In the given diagram, square represents doctors, triangle represents lady and circle represents surgeon. Which of the following letters represents those ladies who are doctors and surgeon both?

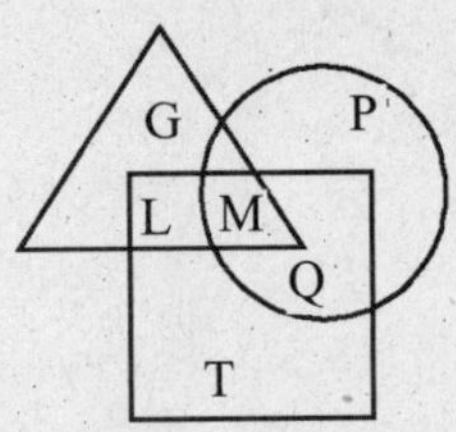

(a) M
(b) G
(c) Q
(d) P

Sol. (a) It is clear from the diagram that M is Common in all the three figures i.e., square, traingle and circle. It means that required letter is M.

Exercise

1. Which one of the following diagrams best represents the relationship between Snake, Lizard and Reptiles?

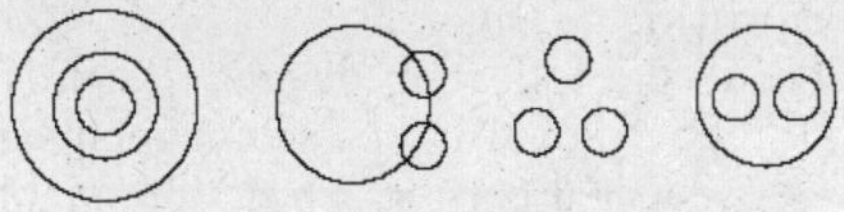

(a) (b) (c) (d)

2. Which of the following diagrams represents the correct relationship between Harbivours, Tigers and Animals?

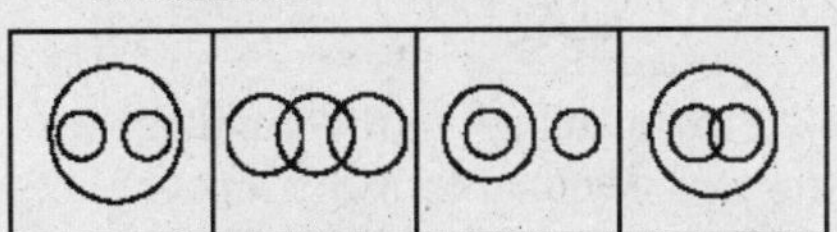

(a) (b) (c) (d)

3. Choose the correct relationship depicting diagram for Smokers, Lawyers, Non-smokers.

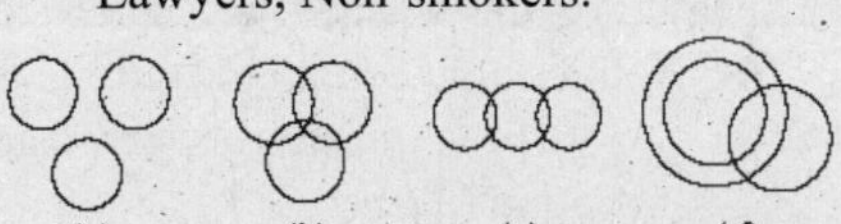

(a) (b) (c) (d)

4. Which one of the following diagrms best depicts the relationship among Earth, Sea Sun?

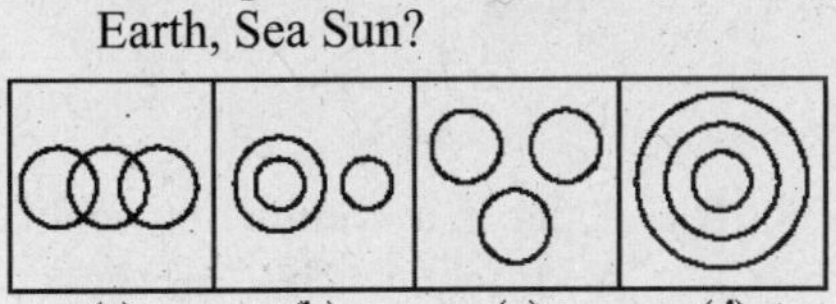

(a) (b) (c) (d)

5. Which of the following diagram represents a relationship between players and footballers?

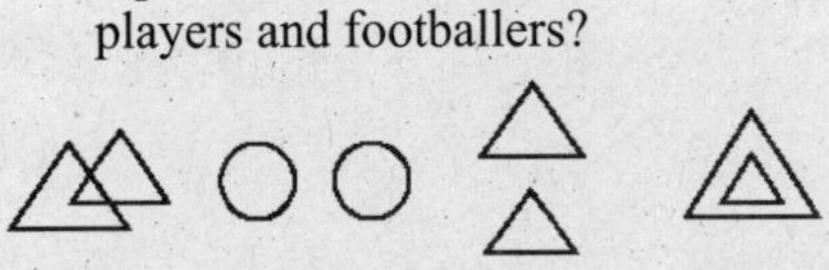

(a) (b) (c) (d)

6. Which of the following diagrams represents pens and pencils?

(a) (b) (c) (d)

7. Which one of the following diagrams represents the correct relationship among Teachers, Educated, Employed?

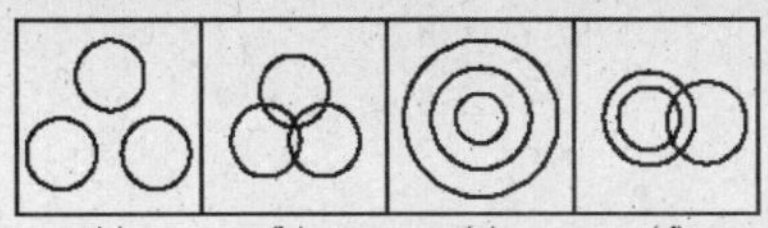

(a) (b) (c) (d)

8. Identify the diagram that best represents the relationship among the classes given below. Police, Thief, Criminal.

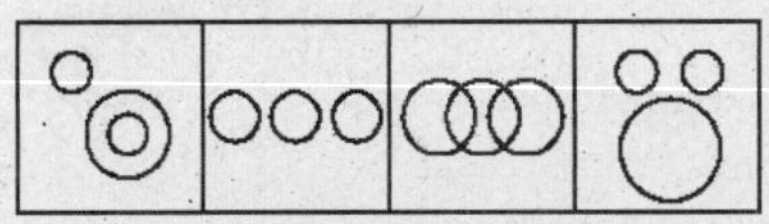

(a) (b) (c) (d)

9. Identify the diagram that best represents the relationship among the classes given below.

(a) (b) (c) (d)

10. Which of the following diagrams best represents a relationship among Criminal, Theif and Pick pocketer?

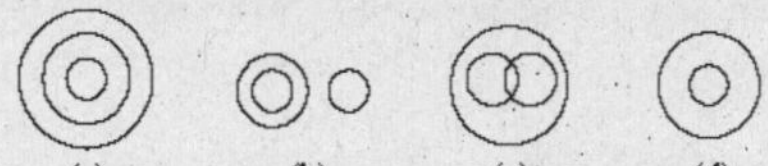

(a) (b) (c) (d)

11. Which of the following diagrams best represents the relationship among Pradesh, Kanpur, Jaipur?

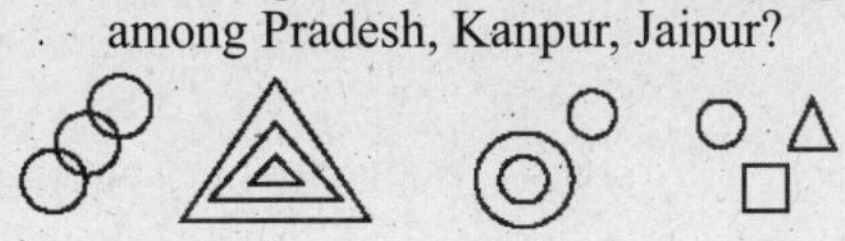

(a) (b) (c) (d)

12. Identify the diagram that best represents the relationship among the classes given below. Soprtman, Cricketers, Batsman

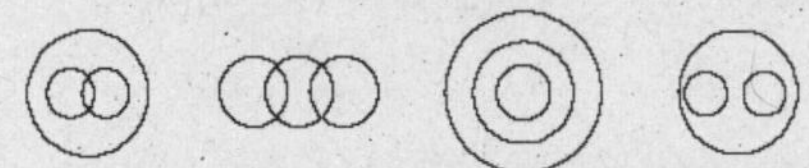

(a) (b) (c) (d)

13. Identify the diagram that best represents the relationship among the classes given below. Liquid, Milk, River, Water

(a) (b) (c) (d)

14. Which of the following diagrams represents the relation between Currency, Rupee and Dollar?

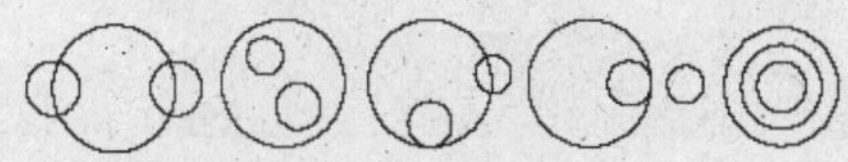

(a) (b) (c) (d) (e)

15. Which one of the following diagrams best depicts the relationship among Elephant, Wolves and Animals?

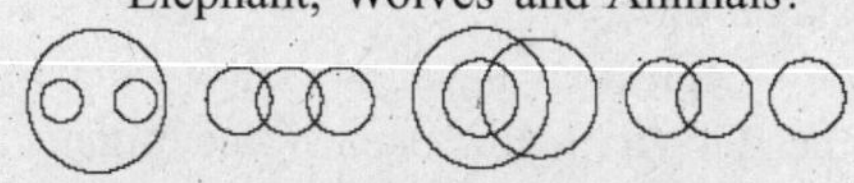

(a) (b) (c) (d)

16. Which diagram correctly represents the relationship between Politicians, Poets and Women?

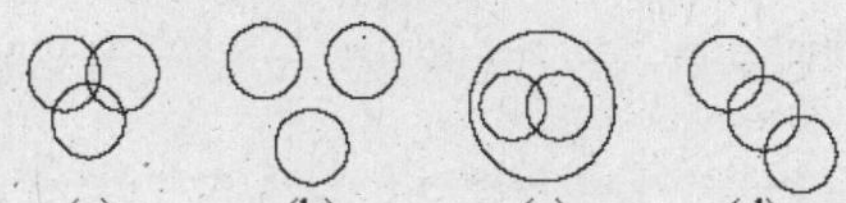

(a) (b) (c) (d)

17. See the following diagram carefully to answer the question that follows

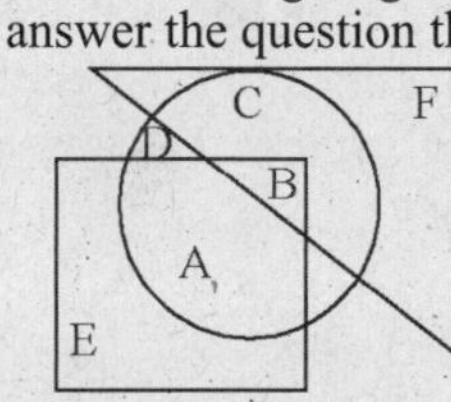

Which of the following statements is correct according to the diagram given above?

(a) A and B lie in all the three figures
(b) E, A, B and C lie in all the three figures
(c) F, C, D, B and A lie in all the three figures
(d) Only B lies in all the three figures

18. See the given diagram and then find out the youth who does job but not educated.

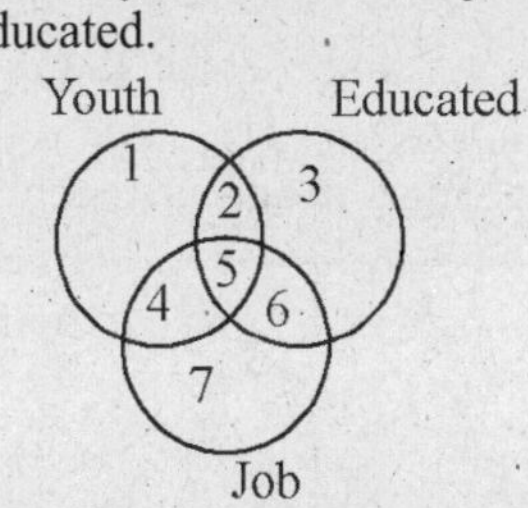

(a) 5 (b) 4
(c) 6 (d) 7

19. Identify the region that represents students who study Biology and Computer but not Mathematics.

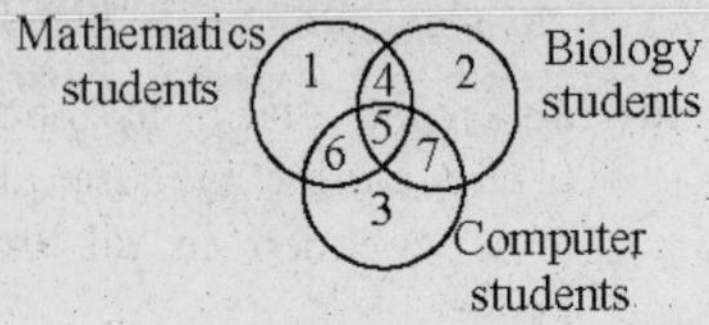

(a) 6
(b) 2
(c) 7
(d) 4

20. Given below are three figures which represent Graduates, Post-graduates, Officers, Which part represents all the Officers who are graguates and post-graduates?

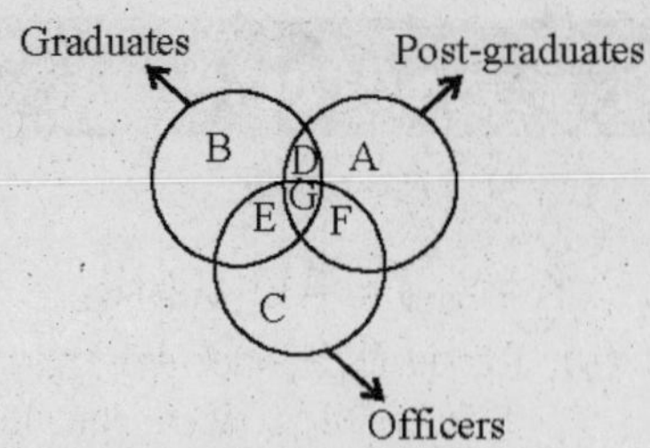

(a) G (b) D
(c) B (d) C

21. The diagram represents the students who are singer, dancers and poets

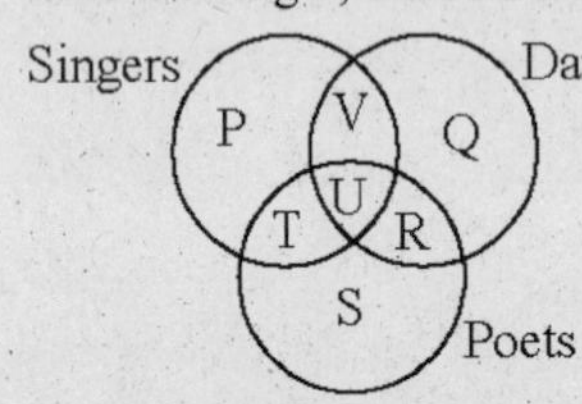

Study the above diagram identify the region which represents the students who are both poets and singers but not dancers
(a) P + T + S
(b) T
(c) T + U + R + S
(d) P + T + U + S

22. In the following diagram, identify the region that represents appointed educated persons whose job is not permanent.

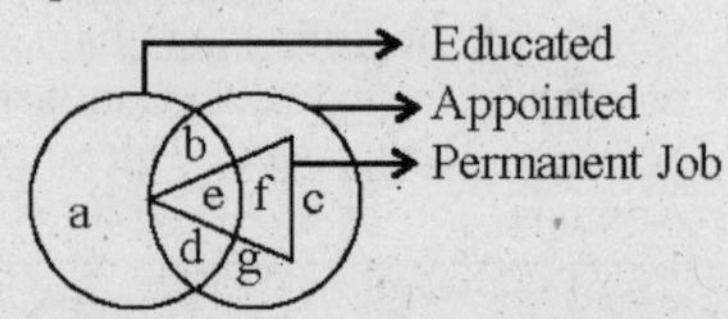

(a) b and g (b) a and ds
(c) a and c (d) b and d

Answers with Explanations

1. (d) Snake and lizard are entirely different but both belong to the class of reptiles. This can be expressed as given in option (d).

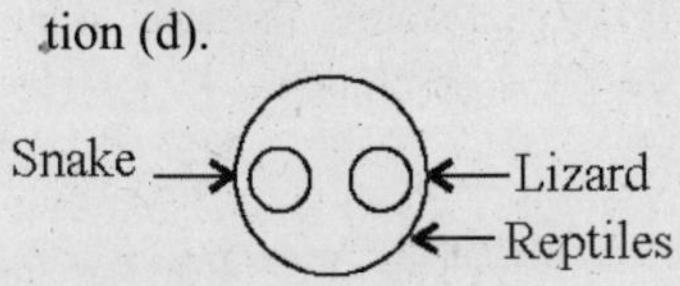

2. (a) Tigers are animals but not herbivorous. This can be expressed as given in option (a).

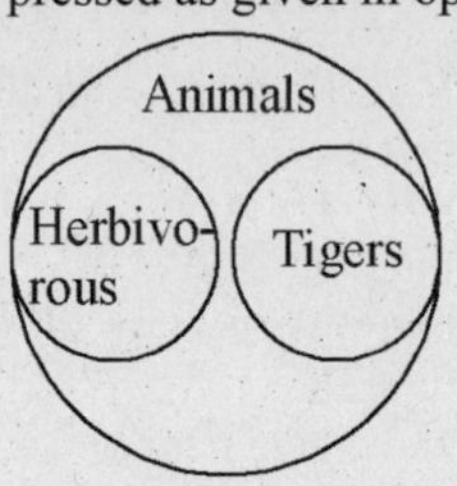

3. (c) Some lawyers may be smokers while some lawyers may non-smokers. But all the smokers and non-smokers are not be lawyers. This can be expressed as given in option (c).

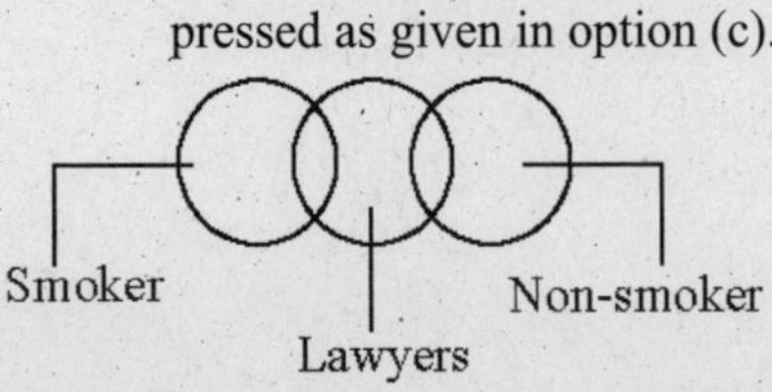

4. (a) Sea is a part of the Earth but Sun is present outside the Earth. This relation can be expressed as given in option (b).

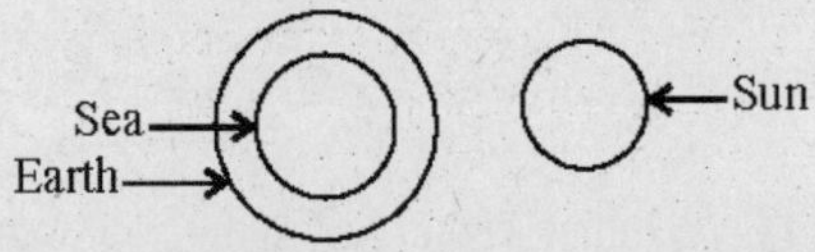

5. (c) Pen and pencil both are used for writing but they are entirely different. This cam be expressed as given in option (c).

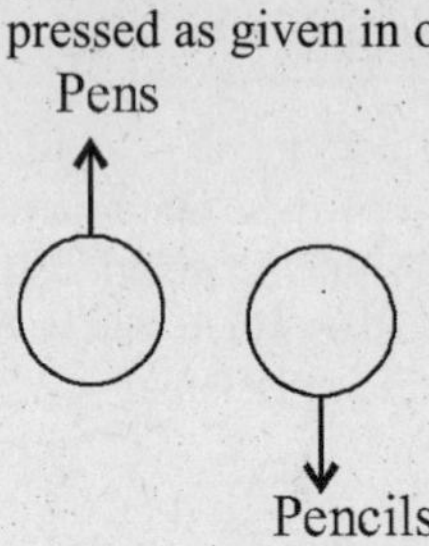

6. (d) All footballers are players. It means the class of footballers exists completely inside the class of players. This can be expressed as given in option (d).

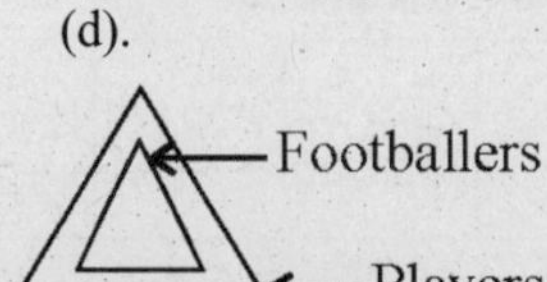

7. (a) All the teachers are educated but some are employed. This can be expressed as given in option (d).

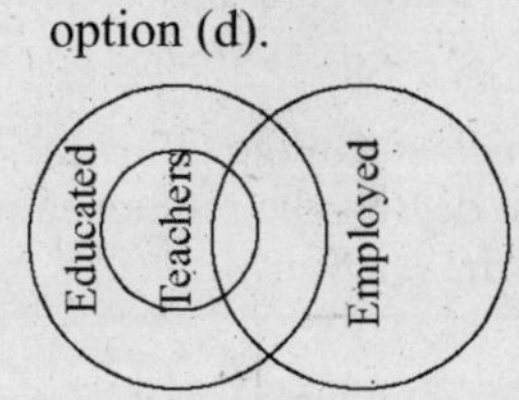

8. (a) Thief is a criminal but police is different. This can be expressed as given in option (a).

9. (b) Tea and coffee are different type of drink.

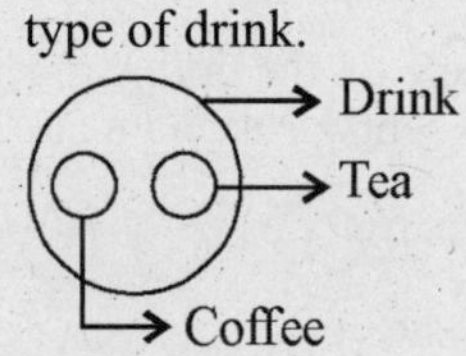

10. (c) Some thieves are pick pockets and they both come under the category of criminals. This can be expressed as given in option (c).

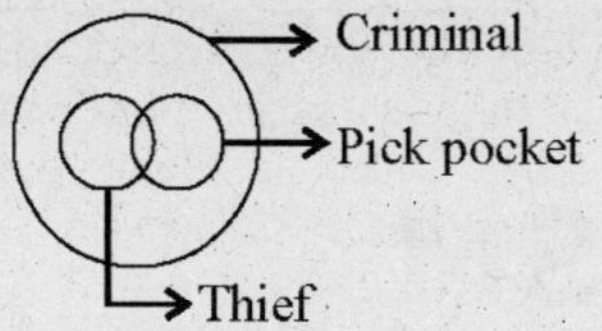

11. (c) Kanpur is a city in the state of Uttar Pradesh while Jaipur is entirely different as is a city in Rajasthan. This can be expressed as given in option (c).

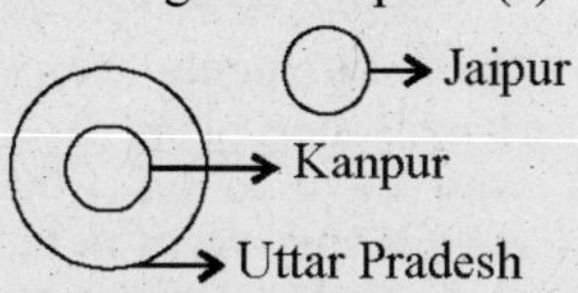

12. (c) A batsman is a cricketer and circketer are sportmen.

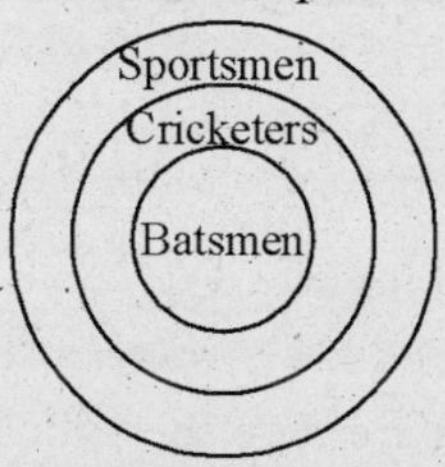

13. (a) 'Milk' and 'River water' both are liquids. This can be expressed as given in option (a).

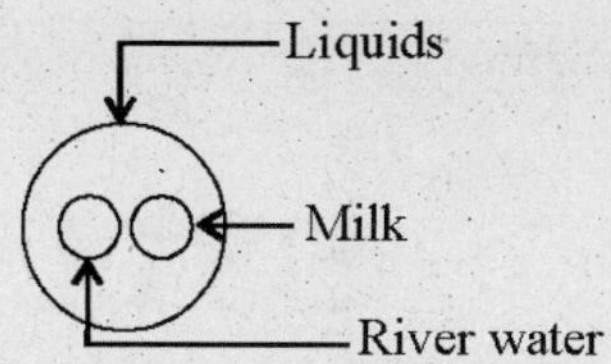

14. (b) Rupee and doller are entirely different from each other but come under the category currency. This can be expressed as given in option (b).

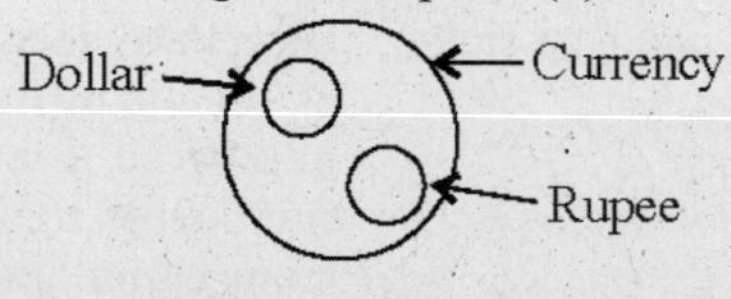

15. (a) Wolves and elephants both are animals but are different form each other. This can be expressed as given in option (a).

16. (a) Some women are poets. Some women are politicians. Some women politicians are poets. This can be expressed as given as given in option (a).

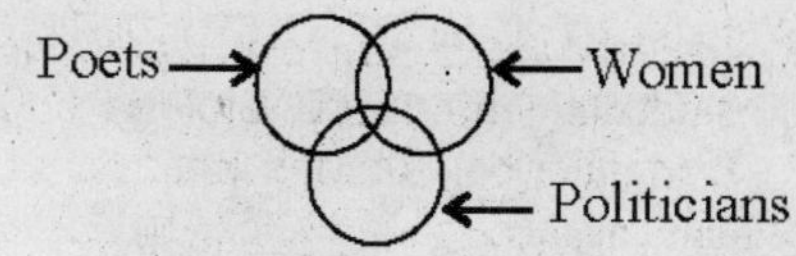

17. (d) Statement given in option (d) is correct because only B is common in all three figures.

18. (b) The region 4 is common to youth and job but not educated.

19. (c) The region which represents students who study Biology and Computer but not Mathmetics is '7'.

20. (a) The part of figure representing offices, who are graduated and post-graduates is common to all three circles i.e., G.

21. (b) Region T is common to the both singers and poets but not dancers.

22. (d) According to the diagram, region b and d represent appointment educated persons whose job is not permanent.

13 SYLLOGISM

Syllogism is the process whereby the ideas of a man are logically expressed. It is the Science of thought as expressed in language. In this chapter questions are based on some statements and their conclusions.

There are four types of logical Propositions:

(i) Universal affirmative
(ii) Universal negative
(iii) Particular affirmative
(iv) Particular negative

1. **Universal affirmative**—The foundational premise beginning with All is classed as universal affirmative.

   ***Example :* All men are scholars.**

   Given example belongs to universal affirmative. But its opposite *i.e.* all scholars are men is not true.

2. **Universal negative**—When a proposition begins with no then such a foundational premise is categorised as universal negative.

   ***Example :* No coffee is drinkable.**

3. **Particular affirmative**—If a proposition commences with Some then such a particular statement is grouped under Particular affirmative.

   ***Exemple :* Some note-books are books. Opposite of this proposition is also possible. As some books are note-books.**

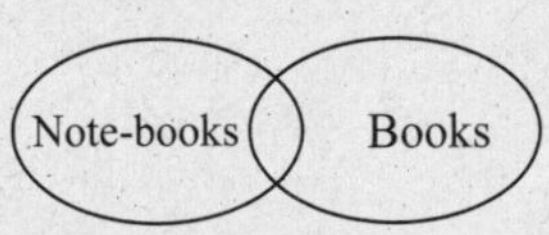

4. **Particular negative**—When a proposition starts with some not then such a foundational premise is kept under the category of Particular negative.

   ***Example :* Some boys are not wild.**

   If two conclusions belong to any of the given combination they will be referred to as special case. In this case the answer will be followed by either......... or.......... .

Solved Examples

Directions (Ex. 1-4) : Two statements are given in each of the following questions, followed by two conclusions numbered I and II. You have to take the given two statements to be true even if they seem to be at variance from commonly known facts. Read the conclusions and then decide which of the given conclusions logically follows from the two given statements, disregarding known facts. Give answer:

(a) if only conclusion I follows.
(b) if only conclusion II follows.
(c) if neither I nor II follows.
(d) if both conclusions I and II follow.

Example 1.

Statements : I. All fish are tortoise.
II. No tortoise is a crocodile.

Conclusions : I. No crocodile is a fish.
II. No fish is a crocodile.

Solution (c):

According to question,

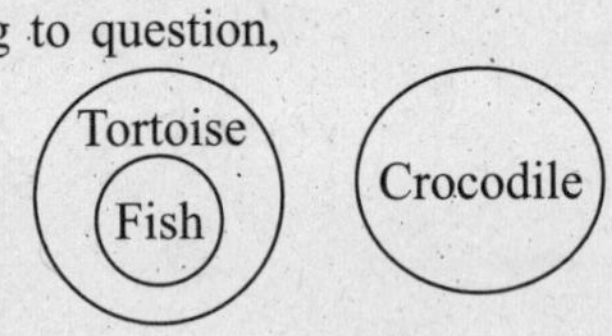

Clearly, no crocodile is fish and no fish is a crocodile.

Example 2.

Statements : I. Some engineers are actors.
II. Some actors are scientists.

Conclusions : I. All scientist are engireers.
II. All scientists are actors.

Solution (c): According to question,

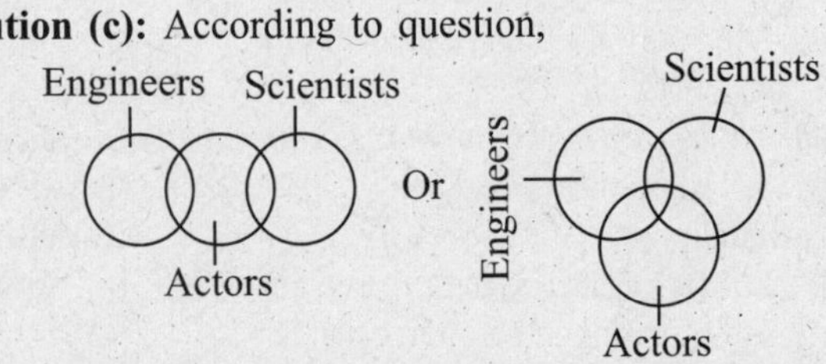

In fact no mutual relationship is established between Particular premises.

Example 3.

Statements : I. All men are dogs.
II. All dogs are cats.

Conclusions : I. All men are cats.
II. All cats are men.

Solution (a):

According to question,

Clearly all men are cats.

Example 4.

Statements : I. All trucks fly.
II. Some scooters fly.

Conclusions : I. All trucks are Scooters.
II. Some Scooters do not fly.

Solution (b):

According to question,

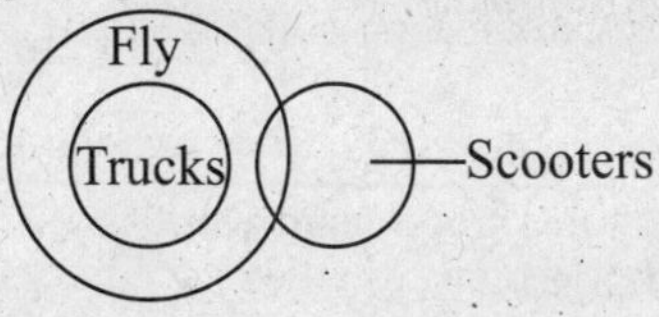

Exercise

Directions (Q. Nos. 1 - 15): Two statements are given in each of the following questions, followed by two conclusions numbered I and II. You have to take the given two statements to be true even, if they seem to be at variance from commonly known facts. Read the conclusions and then decide which of the given conclusions logically follows from the two given statements, disregarding known facts.

Give answer:

(a) if only Conclusion I follows
(b) if only Conclusion II follows
(c) if neither Conclusion I nor II follows
(d) if both Conclusions I and II follow

1. Statements
I. All leaders are good team workers.
II. All good team workers are good orators.
Conclusions
I. Some good team workers are leaders.
II. All good orators are leaders.

2. Statements
I. All terrorists are human.
II. All humans are bad.
Conclusions
I. All terrorists are bad.
II. No human can be a terrorist.

3. Statements
I. Some teachers are followers.
II. Some followers are famous.
Conclusions
I. Some teachers are famous.
II. Some followers are teachers.

4. Statements
I. All fish are tortoise.
II. No tortoise is a crocodile.
Conclusions
I. No crocodile is a fish.
II. No fish is a crocodile.

5. Statements
I. All trucks fly.
II. Some scooters fly.
Conclusions
I. All trucks are scooters.
II. Some scooters do not fly.

6. Statements
I. All writers are lawyers.
II. All readers are lawyers.
Conclusions
I. Some lawyers are readers.
II. Some readers are writers.

7. Statements
I. All players are doctors.
II. Some doctors are actors.
Conclusions
I. Some doctors are players as well as actors.
II. All actos are doctors.

8. Statements
I. Some hens are cows.
II. All cows are horses.
Conclusions
I. Some horses are hens.
II. Some hens are horses.

9. Statements
I. All skaters are good swimmers.
II. All good swimmers are runners.
Conclusions
I. Some runners are skaters.
II. Some skaters are good swimmers.

10. Statements
I. Some buses are four wheelers.
II. All four wheelers are vans
Conclusions
I. Some vans are buses.
II. Some buses are vans.

11. Statements Some gears are wheels.
All wheels are brakes.
Conclusions
I. No brake is gear.
II. Atleast some gears are brakes.

12. Statements
No month is a year.
No year is a second.
Conclusions
I. All months are seconds.
II. No second is month.

13. Statements
No plane is hill.
Some hills are towns.
Conclusions
I. No town is plane.
II. Some towns are plane.

14. Statements
All metals are liquids.
All liquids are gases.
Conclusions
I. All metals are gases.
II. Atleast some gases are liquids.

15. Statements
Some cities are towns.
Some villages are cities.
Conclusions
I. Atleast some villages are towns.
II. No village is a town.

Answers with Explanations

1. (a)

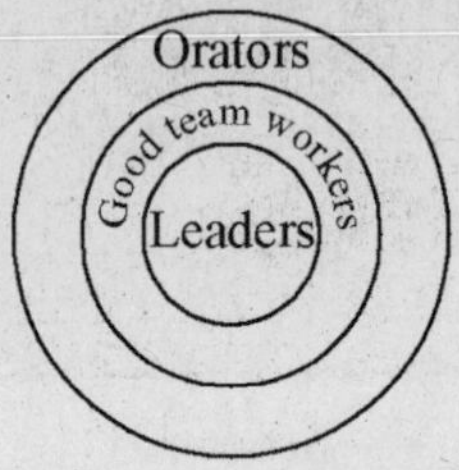

Clearly, some good team workers are leaders.

2. (a)

Clearly, all terrorists are bad.

3. (b)

Clearly, only some followers are teachers.

4. (d)

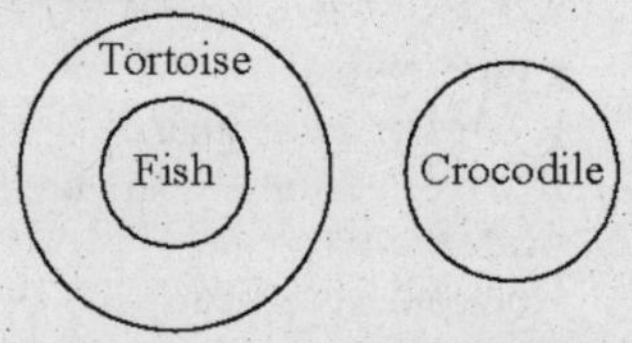

Clearly, no crocodile is fish and no fish is a crocodile.

5. (b)

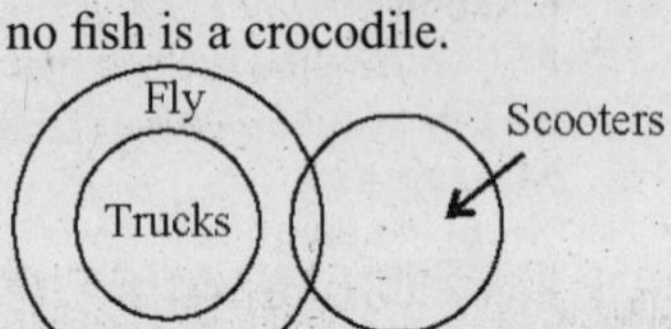

Clearly, some scooters do not fly.

6. (a)

So, only conclusion I follows.

7. (a)

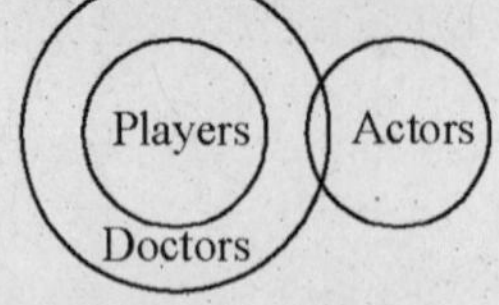

From above, it is clear that only Conclusion I follows.

8. (d)

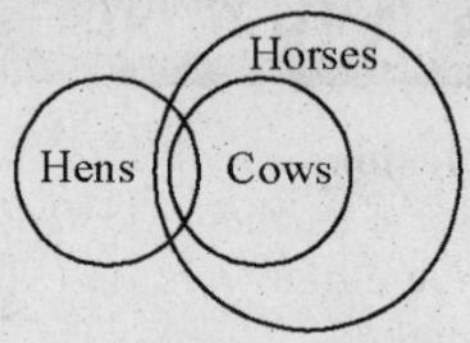

Clearly, both Conclusion I and II follow.

9. (a)

Hence, only Clnclusion I follows.

10. (d) As per the question,

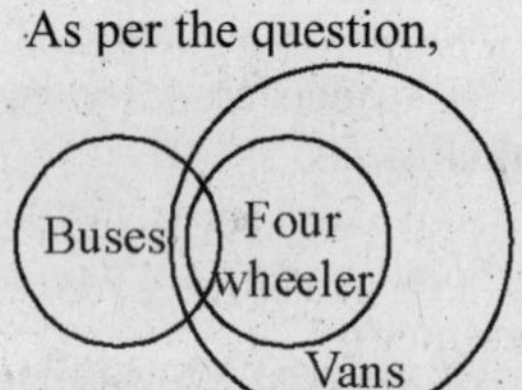

Hence, both Conclusions I and II follow.

11. (b)

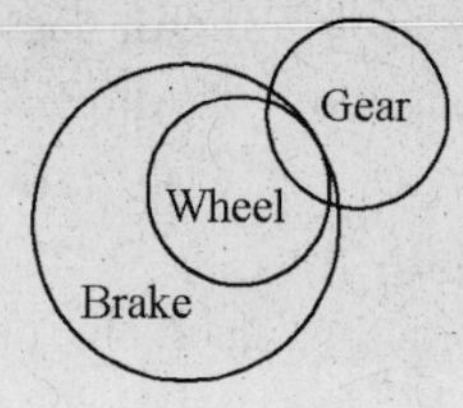

So, only Conclusion II follows.

12. (b)

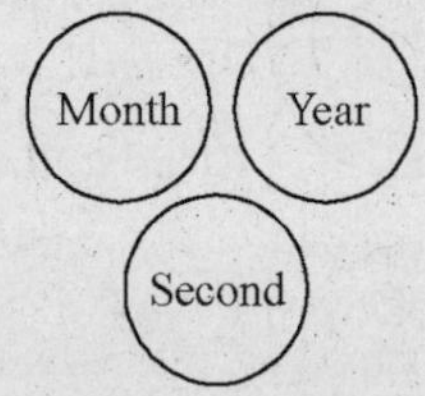

So, only Conclusion II follows.

13. (d)

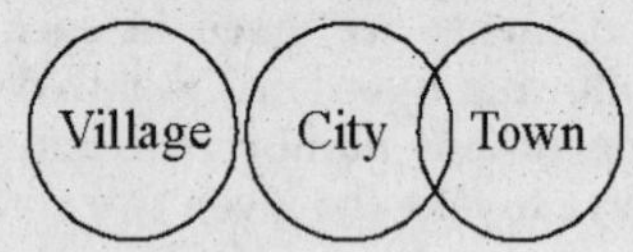

So, neither Conclusions I nor II follow.

14. (a)

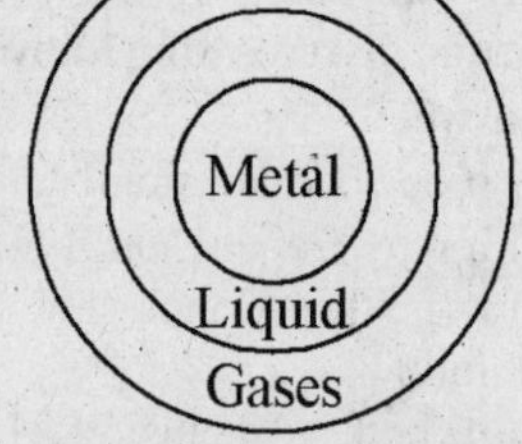

So, both Conclusions I and II follow.

15. (a)

So, only Conclusion II follows.

14 STATEMENTS AND CONCLUSIONS

Problems based on Drawing Inference the candidate's ability to interpret the statement. Consequent effect of a statement has to be analysed before reaching the correct conclusion.

This chapter is a mere extension of the previous chapter's statement and assumptions. Here candidates are required to approach the questions for solution from a different angle. This approach basically emphasises the need for being more systematic and logical in drawing inferences.

These types of questions are based on a link between statement and conclusion, but the link should be logical. In these questions a statement or a passage is given which is followed by two conclusions. You have to find out the correct conclusion. The conclusion should be reasonable or sensible.

Solved Examples

Directions (Examples 1 to 2) : A statement is followed by two conclusions I and II. You have to consider the statement to be true even if it seems to be at variance with commonly known facts. You have to decide which of the given conclusions can definitely be drawn from the given statement. Indicate your answers.

Example 1.

Statement : Honesty and hard work lead to economic improvement of an individual.

Conclusions : I. There is a direct relation between honesty and economic improvement.

II. Hard work and honesty always pay dividends.

(a) If only conclusion I follows.

(b) If only conclusion II follows.

(c) Both I and II follow.

(d) Neither I nor II follows.

Solution (A): Only conclusion I follows. The use of term always makes second statement invalid.

Example 2.

Statement : The use of non-conventional source of energy will eliminate the energy crisis in the world.

Conclusions : I. Modern technology is gradually replacing the con-ventional sources of energy.

II. The excessive exploitation of enviorn-ment has led to the deplation of conve-ntional sources of energy.

(a) If only conclusion I follows.

(b) If only conclusion II follows.

(c) If neither I nor II follows.

(d) If both I and II follow.

Solution (c): The statement speaks of a suggestion regarding benefits of the use of non-conventional source of energy. It is not given whether non-conventional methods are replacing conventional methods. Hence conclusion I does not follow. Conclusion II also does not follow as it is not in the light of the statement.

Exercise

Directions (Q. Nos. 1-15): The questions given below have a statement followed by two conclusions I and II. Consider the statement and the following conclusions. Decide which of the conclusions follows from the statement.

Give answer:

(a) if Conclusion I follows

(b) if Conclusion II follows

(c) if neither Conclusion I nor II follows

(d) if both Conclusions I and II follow

1. **Statement** According to a recent report, a glass of wine daily for women with breast cancer could boost the success rate of treatment.

Conclusions

I. Women taking a glass of wine daily will never suffer from breast cancer.

II. A glass of wine will cure the women suffering from breast cancer.

2. **Statement** National integration is necessary because there are diversities in India.

Conclusions

I. India is a country of people with diverse cultures, different languages and different social and economic setups.

II. Ours is a disintegrated nation.

3. **Statement** A Brahmin priest is expected to be able to recite atleast one of the Vedas.

Conclusions

I. Any person who can recite the Vedas is a Brahmin.

II. Reciting the Vedas is a Brahmin's obligation.

4. Statement Though in terms of number of schools, the educational system has very much expanded but most of them are not sufficiently equipped and not able to touch the high water mark in education.

Conclusions

I. We should provide good teachers and equipments to existing schools now onwards.

II. Now, it is not necessary to open new schools.

5. Statement In India, emphasis should be given more on agriculture, engineering and technological fields rather than on basic and pure science.

Conclusions

I. India has achieved sufficient development in the field of basic and pure science.

II. In the past, the production sector of economy was neglected.

6. Statement The majority of Indian labourers belong to unorganised sector and most of them earn very low.

Conclusions

I. The labourers belonging to organised sector have better benefits and stability.

II. Some labourers belonging to unorganised sectors have regular and certain income.

7. Statement According to a prediction our planet would not be able to support the human population for long, as population grows at geometric rate while food supply grows at arithmetic rate.

Conclusions

I. Unchecked growth in population is going to put strain on our food supply.

II. Earth is facing the threats of famine in future due to growing population.

8. Statement A real friend is one who walks in when the rest of the world walks out.

Conclusions

I. A true friend, stays with us through rough weather while the fair weather friends leave us in the lurch.

II. Adversity is the test of true friendship.

9. Statement The Chief Minister emphasised the point that the government will try its best for the development of these people.

Conclusions

I. The former government had not tried seriously for the development of these people.

II. This government will not try seriously for the development of urban poor.

10. Statement Company can understand the problems of its customers by direct marketing where it gets a chance to correct those problems. Thus, the customer becomes reliable buyers.

Conclusions

I. Responsible companies earn profit by direct marketing.

II. Direct marketing is the only key to succeed in business.

11. Statement Company 'X' has a record in making cameras with quality and modernisation to ensure that you do not lose even a single shot despite bad weather.

Conclusions

I. No other company has any recognition in camera industry.

II. Any common man can take good photographs using camera 'X'.

12. Statement The greatest need in India today is not for sophisticated gadgets but for programmes which will provide employment to a large number of people.

Conclusions

I. There is an adequate number of sophisticated gadgets in India.

II. Emphasis is being laid on procuring sophisticated gadgets.

13. Statement Company 'X' has marked its product; "Go ahead and purchase it, if price and quality are your considerations."

Conclusions

I. The product must be good in quality.

II. The price of the product must be reasonable.

14. Statement In case of the outstanding candidates, the condition of previous experience of social work may be waived by the Admission Committee for MA (Social work).

Conclusions

I. Some of the students for MA (Social work) will have previous experience of social work.

II. Some of the students for MA (Social work) will not have previous experience of social work.

15. Statement It is almost impossible to survive and prosper in this world without sacrificing Ethics and Morality.

Conclusions

I. World appreciates some concepts but may not uphold it.

II. Concept of Ethics and Morality are not 'practicable in life.

Answers with Explanations

1. (b) From the statement, we can clearly say that 'A glass of wine will cure the woman suffering from breast cancer'.

2. (a) From the statement, we clearly say that 'India is country of people with diverse cultures, different languages and different social and economic setups'.

3. (c) Neither Conclusion I nor II follows.

4. (a) Clearly, opening a number of schools will not serve the very purpose of education unless these schools are provided with good teachers and equipments. But solution given in Conclusion II is not the right solution of the problem. Hence, only Conclusion I follows.

5. (b) Clearly, more emphasis should be laid on productivity instead of sciences but it does not mean that country has achieved sufficient progress in science. Hence, only Conclusion II follows.

6. (b) Clearly, most of the labourers belonging to unorganised sector earn very low and uncertain income, it means that there are some labourers who earn regular and certain income. Hence, only Conclusion II follows.

7. (d) Both conclusions follow.

8. (d) Both conclusions follow.

9. (c) It cannot be say that the present government did not do anything seriously about the development of rural or urban poor nor does it mean that present government will not do anything for the development of other sectors except, of rural or urban poor Hence, neither Conclusion I nor II follows.

10. (a) The word 'only in Conclusion II makes it doubtful. Conclusion I is direct result of the statement as statement speaks of the merits of direct marketing.

11. (c) Clearly, companies other than 'X' may also have recognition in camera industry. So, Conclusion I does not follows. Also Conclusion II does not follows as according to statement, the quality of camera, not of the cameraman. Hence, neither Conclusion I nor II follows.

12. (d) The statement says that greatest need in India is not for sophisticated gadgets but for programmes but this does not mean that there is an adequate number of sophisticated gadgets. Secondly, there is a need for programmes but it cannot be concluded that emphasis is being laid on procuring sophisticated gadgets. Hence, none of the conclusion follows.

13. (d) It is clear from the statement that a product of company 'X' has good quality and is also available at a reasonable price. Hence, both the conclusions follow.

14. (d) Both the conclusions follow. The waiver is incorporated because some of the students for MA will have previous experience and some of the students will not have previous experience of social work.

15. (d) Conclusions I and II convey almost the same meaning that principles related to Ethics and Morality seem to be good but are not practicable in real life. Hence, both the conclusions follow.

15 BEST REASON TEST

In Best Reason test some statements or events are given. After that four alternatives are given. From the amongst, one alternative is the best. The candidate is required to choose the most suitable option/alternative. In answering these types of questions, the candidate should have the best knowledge of science, geography and daily visual events.

Solved Examples

Example 1. Fire brigade buses are of red colour because:

(a) red colour indicates the sign of danger.
(b) red colour is officially recommended by the department.
(c) they should look prominent then other buses.
(d) red colour is durable.

Answer: (c) Buses are of various kinds of colours, but fire brigade buses are only of red colours. Here red colour indicates the particularisation of the fire brigade buses are rejection of all other buses.

Exercise

Directions (Q. 1-18) : In each of the following questions four possible alternatives are given. The candidates are required to find out the most suitable alternative.

1. Children like to read comics because–
(a) they teach morals.
(b) it is the cheapest means of recreation.
(c) they make the children laugh.
(d) they contain amusing pictures.

2. An educated friend is useful because–
(a) he is more intelligent than others.
(b) he is a perfect friend.
(c) he can earn by getting job.
(d) he can have more understanding than others.

3. Ice floats on water because–
(a) it is transparent.
(b) it is spongy
(c) its weight is less than the weight of water of equal volume.
(d) it is a substance which melts quickly.

4. Generally, the patients of tuberculosis go to the hill stations because–
(a) it is pleasurable to enjoy the natural environment.
(b) cold weather is favourable for the patients of tuberculosis.
(c) they are advised by the physician to do so.
(d) atmospheric pressure decreases there with the height from sea level.

5. Wet clothes dry more quickly on a dry day than on a rainy day because–
(a) breeze blows rapidly during the dry days.
(b) the sun does not rise in a rainy day.
(c) wet clothes absorb the moisture of air on a rainy day.
(d) the air is more moist on a rainy day than on a dry day.

6. People wear goggles because–
(a) they protect their eyes from dazzling light.
(b) they conceal their eyes.
(c) they look handsome.
(d) they see better by it.

7. Policeman wears a uniform because–
(a) it is provided by government free of cost.
(b) it scares the criminals.
(c) he can be easily recognised.
(d) it keeps his smart.

8. People use rubber soles in their shoes because–
(a) they are fashionable.
(b) rubber is more porous than leather.
(c) they produce less sound.
(d) they are durable.

9. Ladies wear ornament so that–
(a) they can conceal their defects.
(b) they can prevent theft of their ornament.
(c) they may feel to be lucky.
(d) they look beautiful.

10. Every nation must maintain an army because–
(a) it will be helpful in reducing the population of the nation.
(b) it is essential for defence of the nation.
(c) it will increase the strength of the people.
(d) it will be helpful in expansion the impire.

11. Children should avoid smoking because–
(a) it is a bad habit.
(b) elders advise them not to do so.
(c) it is an unnecessary expenditure.
(d) it is injurious to health.

12. Platinum is more costly than silver because it is–
(a) heavier
(b) whiter
(c) rarely found
(d) harder

13. In summer, people want to wear light-coloured dress because–
(a) in this dress they look every smart.
(b) they will be safe against the excess of heat.
(c) the light-coloured material is cheap.
(d) the light-coloured dress absorbs the external heat.

14. Farmers are manure in their fields becuase–
(a) it kills the germs of the soil.
(b) it helps in maintaining the fertility of the soil.
(c) the government adviser to do so.
(d) it is their traditional practice.

15. Science research scholars wear options because–
(a) aprons mark them out as members of that department.
(b) aprons indicate a sign of scholarship.
(c) aprons keep them smart.
(d) aprons keep their dresses safe.

16. A deaf is always dumb because–
(a) he is born so.
(b) ear is internally connected to throat.
(c) deaf and dumb are synonyms.
(d) speaking is learnt by hearing from others.

17. Nowadays many young people use high-healed shoes because–
(a) these shoes increase the heights of the young people.
(b) it comes under fashion
(c) it is safer for them to wear these types of shoes.
(d) they practice to balance their bodies after wearing such shoes.

18. A reporter says that the number of bus accidents is more than that of car accidents, the number of car accidents is less than that of truck accidents, the number of truck accident is less then that of bus accidents. Which of the following conclusions can be drawn by the report?
(a) There are more buses on the road than trucks.
(b) Truck drivers are very careless.
(c) There are more trucks than cars on the road.

Answers

1. (d)	**2.** (d)	**3.** (c)	**4.** (c)	**5.** (d)	**6.** (a)	**7.** (c)	**8.** (b)	**9.** (d)
10. (b)	**11.** (d)	**12.** (c)	**13.** (b)	**14.** (b)	**15.** (d)	**16.** (d)	**17.** (b)	**18.** (d)

16 COUNTING FIGURES

The chapter on analytical reasoning involves the problems relating to the counting of geometrical figures in a given complex figure. These figures are divided into many different figures by various lines. The candidate has to find out the number of particular figures in the picture.

SOLVED EXAMPLES

Example 1. How many triangles are possible from the figure given below?

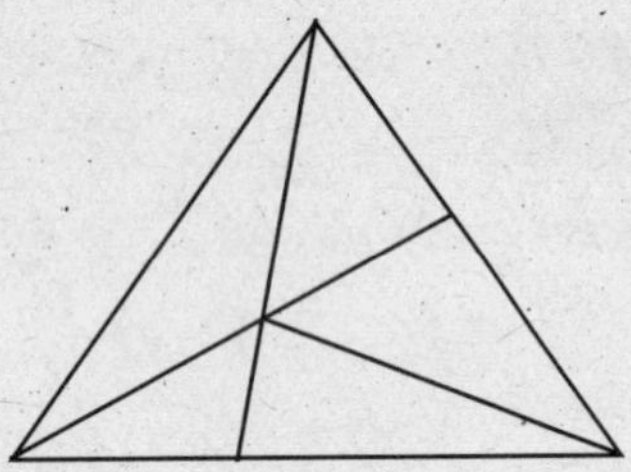

(a) 10 (b) 12
(c) 14 (d) 16

Solution: (b) It will be easier to find out the answer if various points of the given figure are named.

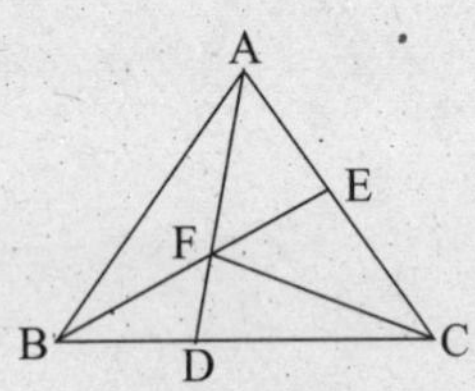

By inspection we see that the following triangles are possible :

ABC, ABD, ADE, ABE, BEC, ABF, BFD, CFD, CEF, AFE, AFC, BFC.

Thus, we see that there are 12 triangles in the given figure.

Example 2. How many triangles are possible from the figure given below?

(a) 16 (b) 22
(c) 28 (d) 32

Solution: (c) We shall label the figure as shown.

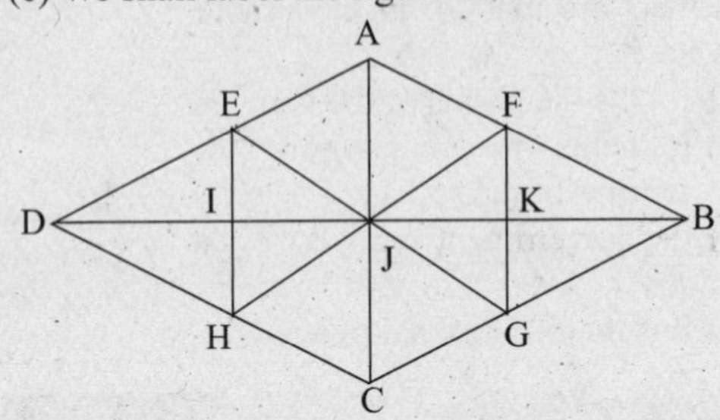

The simplest triangles are AFJ, FJK, FKB, BKG, JKG, JGC, HJC, HIJ, DIH, DEI, EIJ and AEJ *i.e.,* 12 in number.

The triangles composed of two components each are: JFB, FBG, BJG, JFG, DEJ, EJH, DJH and DEH *i.e.,* 8 in number.

The triangles composed of three components each are AJB, JBC, DJC and ADJ *i.e.,* 4 in number.

The triangles composed of six components each are DAB, ABC, BCD and ADC *i.e.,* 4 in number.

Thus, there are 12 + 8 + 4 + 4 = 28 triangles in the figure.

Example 3. How many triangles are there in the following figure?

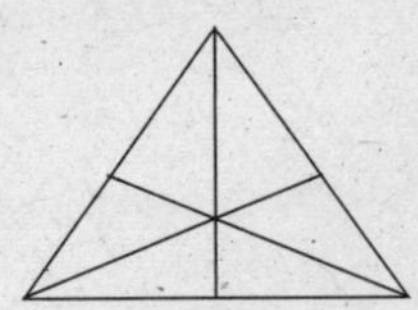

(a) 16 (b) 13
(c) 9 (d) 7

Solution: (a), The figure may be labelled as shown :

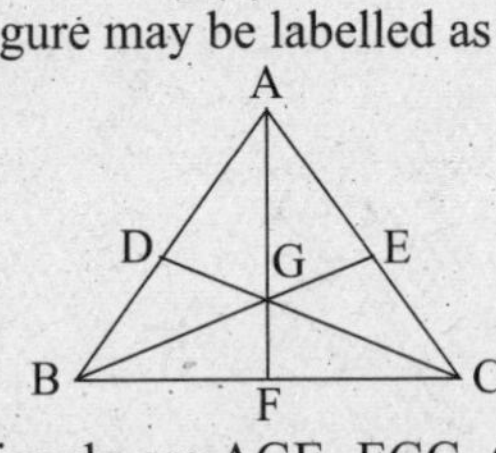

The simplest triangle are AGE, EGC, GFC, BGF, DGB and ADG *i.e.* 6 in number.

The triangles composed of two components each are AGC, BGC and ABG *i.e.* 3 in number.

The triangles composed of three components each are AFC, BEC, BDC, ABF, ABE and DAC *i.e.* 6 in number.

There is only one triangle *i.e.* ABC composed of six components.

Therefore, there are 6 + 3 + 6 + 1 = 16 triangles in the given figure.

Exercise

1. How many triangles are there in the given figure?

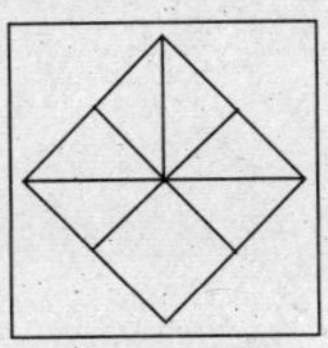

(a) 7 (b) 10
(c) 8 (d) 9

2. Find out the number of squares in the given pattern:

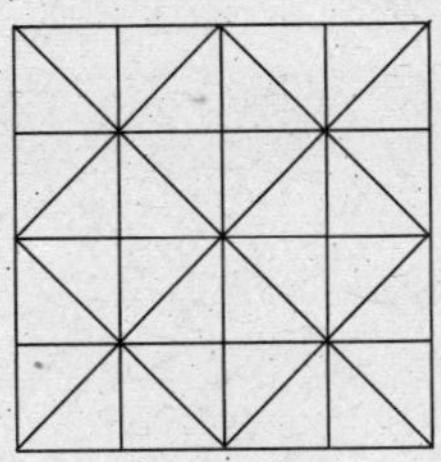

(a) 26 (b) 30
(c) 35 (d) 38

3. How many triangles are there in the following figure?

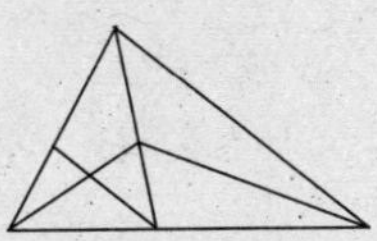

(a) 11 (b) 13
(c) 9 (d) 15

4. How many triangles are there in the following figure?

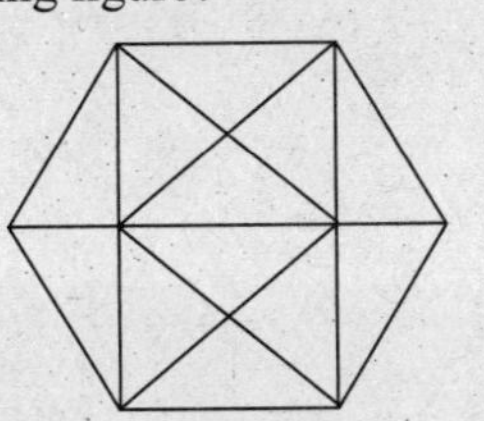

(a) 20 (b) 24
(c) 28 (d) 32

5. How many triangles are there in the following figure?

(a) 29 (b) 27
(c) 23 (d) 30

6. How many triangles are there in the given figure?

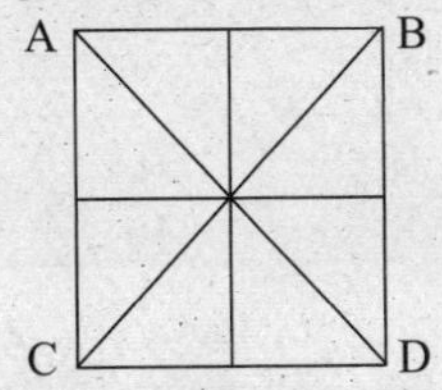

(a) 16 (b) 14
(c) 8 (d) 12

Directions (Qs. 7 to 8) : In each of the following questions, count the number of triangles and squares in the given figure :

7.

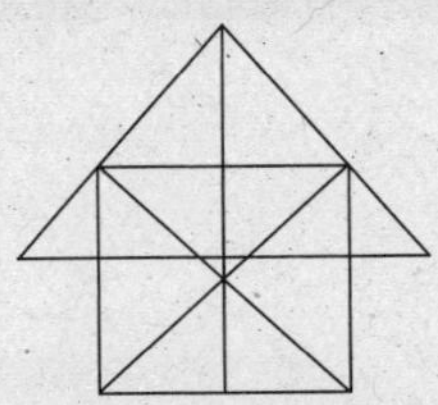

(a) 28 triangles, 6 squares
(b) 26 triangles, 6 squares
(c) 28 triangles, 5 squares
(d) 26 triangles, 5 squares

8.

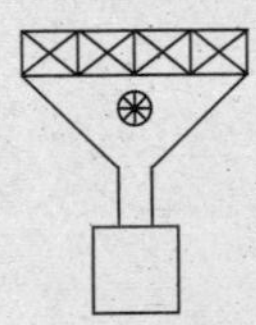

(a) 38 triangles, 8 squares
(b) 36 triangles, 10 squares
(c) 38 triangles, 6 squares
(d) 36 triangles, 8 squares

9. In the given figure, if the centres of all the circles are joined by horizontal and vertical lines, then find the number of squares that can be formed.

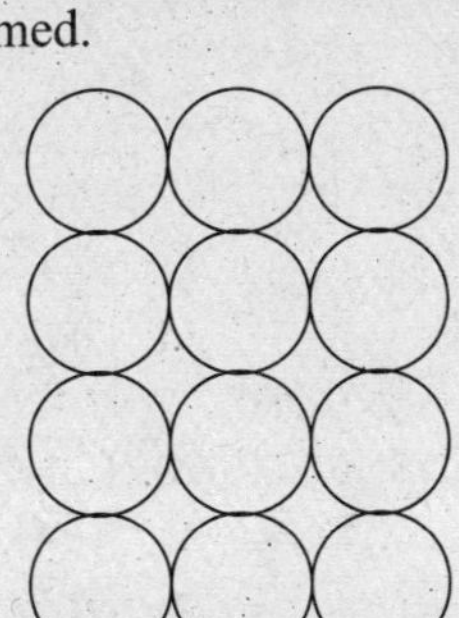

(a) 6 (b) 7
(c) 8 (d) 9

10. How many triangles are there in the given figure?

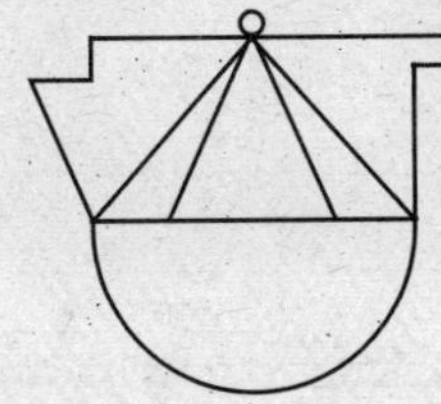

(a) 6 (b) 8
(c) 10 (d) 4

11. Find the minimum number of straight lines to make the figure given below :

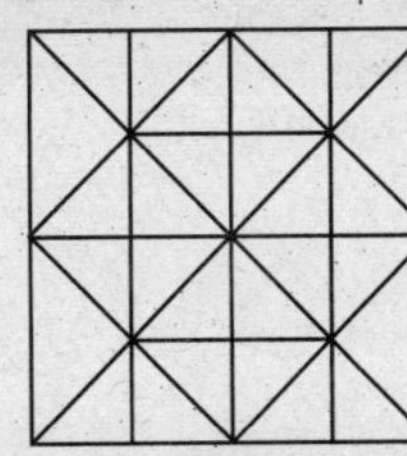

(a) 11 (b) 14
(c) 16 (d) 17

12. How many hexagons (six-sided figures) can you find here?

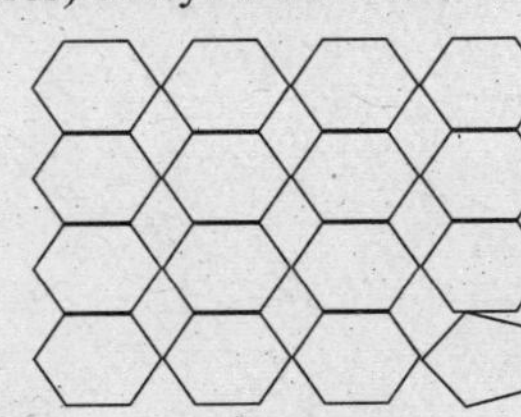

(a) 21 (b) 22
(c) 20 (d) 18

13. How many rectangles are there in the given figure?

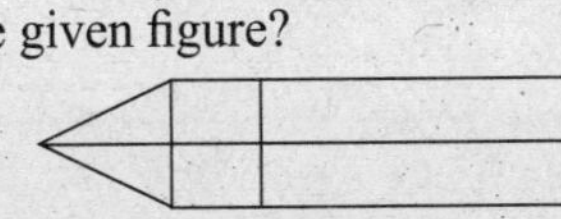

(a) 7 (b) 8
(c) 6 (d) 9

14. What is the number of triangles in the figure given below?

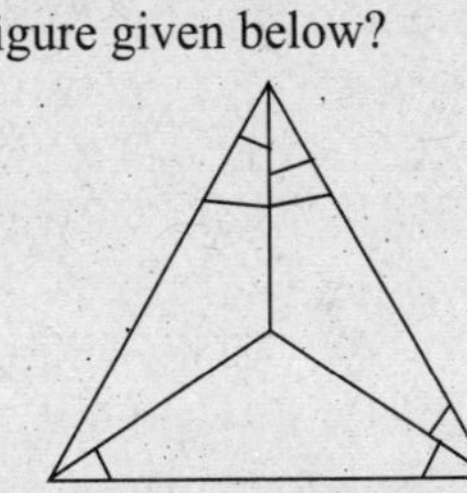

(a) 7 (b) 8
(c) 13 (d) 11

15. What is the number of Parallelograms in the figure given below?

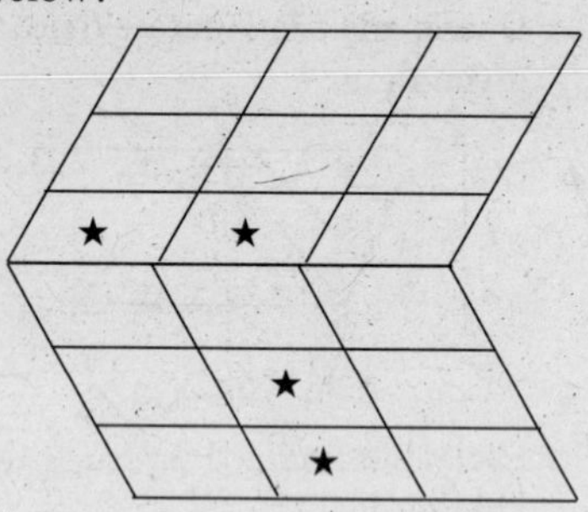

(a) 38 (b) 25
(c) 28 (d) 35

16. What is the number of triangles in the figure given below?

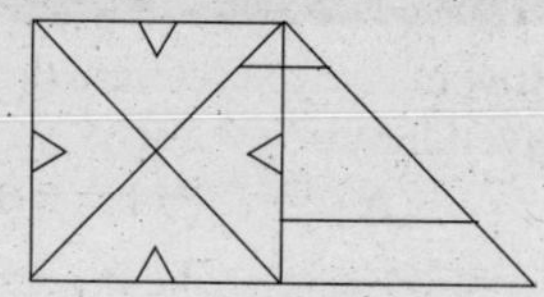

(a) 18 (b) 19
(c) 20 (d) 17

17. How many squares are there in the figure given below?

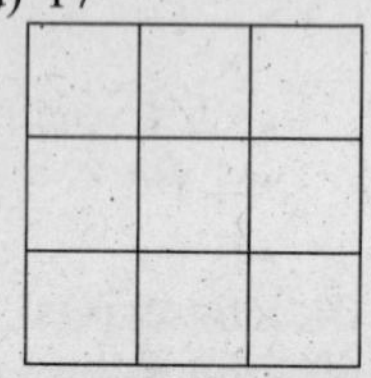

(a) 11 (b) 14
(c) 13 (d) 16

18. What is the number of triangles in the figure given below?

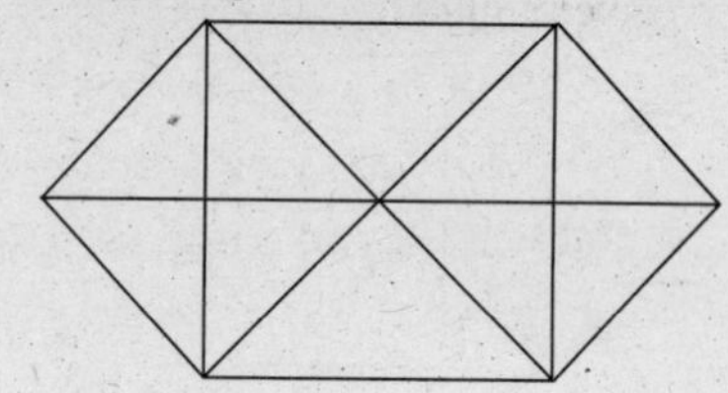

(a) 20
(b) 22
(c) 26
(d) 29

Answers with Explanations

1. (b)

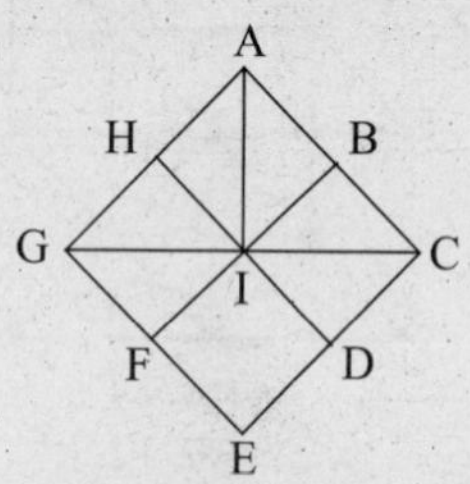

The triangles are : ATH, AIB, BIC, CID, GIH, GIF, ECG, ACG, AIG, AIC.

Thus, there are 10 tringles.

2. (c)

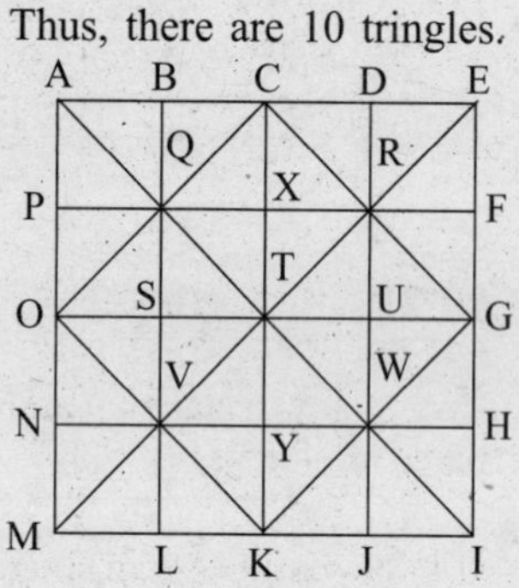

The squares are :

ABQP, BCXQ, CDRX, DEFR, PQSO, QXTS, XRUT, RFGU, OSVN, STYV, TUWY, UGHW, NVLM, VYKL, YWJK, WHIJ, ACTO, CEGT, OTKM, TGIK, BDUS, SUJL, QRWV, PXYN, WFHY, OQTV, VTWK, QCRT, TRGW, OCGK, AEIM, ADWN, BEHV, PRJM, QFIL.

There are 35 squares.

3. (b)

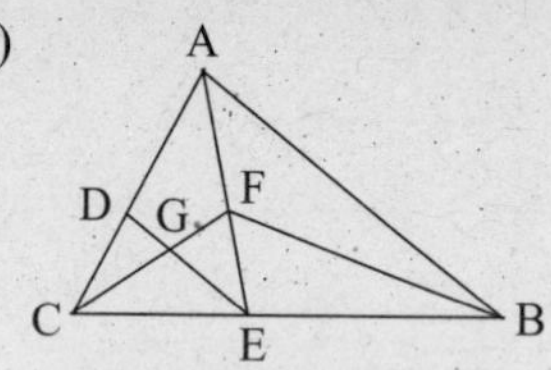

Triangles formed are as :

1. ABF 2. BFE 3. EFG
4. CEG 5. CDG 6. ABE
7. BCF 8. CEF 9. CDE
10. ACE 11. ADE 12. ABC
13. ACF

4. (c)

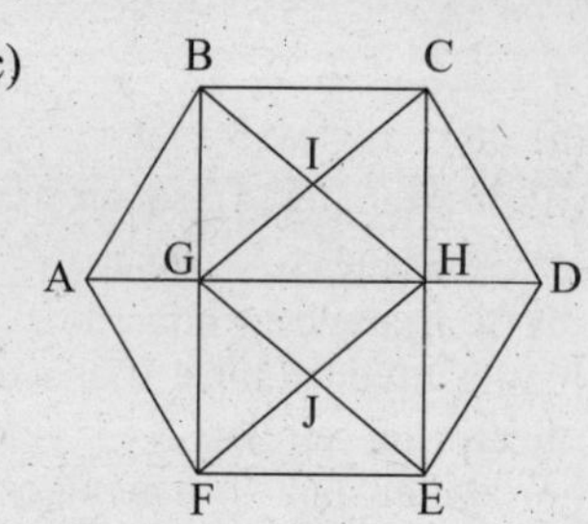

Triangles are :

1. ABG 2. AGF 3. CHD
4. DEH 5. BGI 6. BCI
7. HCI 8. HGI 9. GHJ
10. EHJ 11. EFJ 12. FGJ
13. ABF 14. CDF 15. BCG
16. BCH 17. CGH 18. BGH
19. EGH 20. EFH 21. EFG
22. FGH 23. ABH 24. AFH
25. CDG 26. DEG 27. BFH
28. CEG

5. (b)

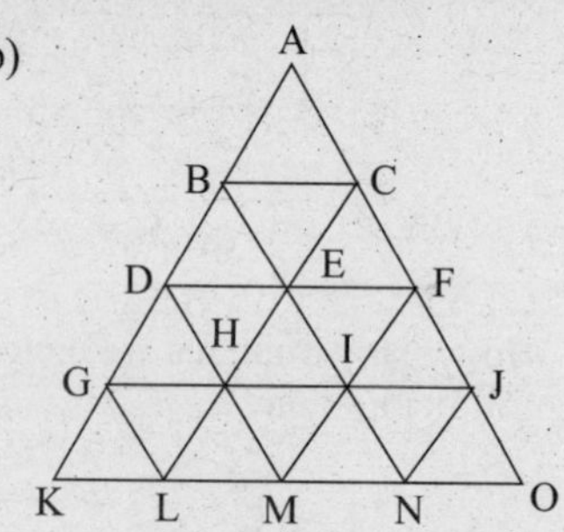

Triangles are:

1. ABC 2. BDE 3. BCE
4. CEF 5. DEH 6. EHI
7. EFI 8. FIJ 9. DGH
10. GKL 11. HLM 12. HIM
13. IMN 14. IJN 15. JNO
16. ADF 17. DFM 18. DKM
19. ELN 20. FMO 21. AGJ
22. AKO 23. BGI 24. CHJ
25. CLO 26. BNK 27. GHL

6. (a)

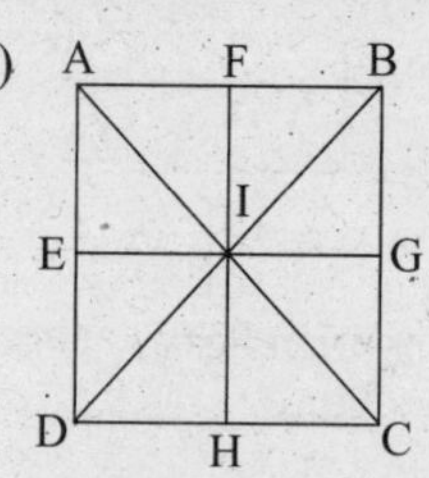

Triangles are :

1. AFI 2. BFI 3. BGI
4. CGI 5. CHI 6. DHI
7. DEI 8. AEI 9. ABI
10. BCI 11. CDI 12. ADI
13. ABC 14. BCD 15. ACD
16. ABD

7. (d) No. of Δ of single component = 10

No. of Δ of double components = 9

No. of Δ of three components = 2

No. of Δ of four components = 3

No. of Δ of six components = 2

∴ Total number of triangles = 26

Now, No. of □ of two components = 2

No. of □ of three components = 2

No. of □ of ten components = 1

∴ Total number of squares = 5

8. (a) No. of Δ of single component = 16

No. of Δ of double components = 16

No. of Δ of four components = 6

∴ Total number of triangles = 38

Now, No. of □ of single component = 1

No. of □ of two components = 3

No. of □ of four components = 4

∴ Total number of squares = 8

9. (c) The figure may be labelled as shown.

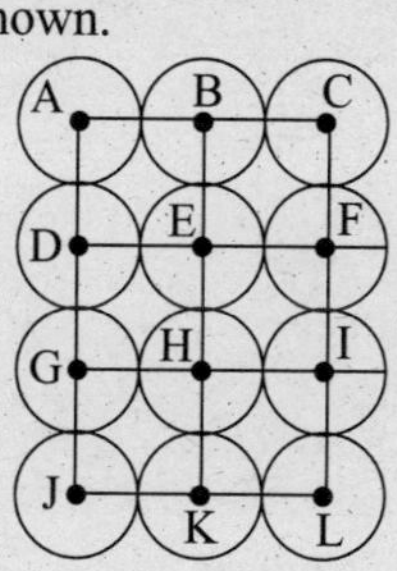

The squares are :

ABED, BCFE, DEHG, EFIH, GHKJ, HILK, ACIG, DFLJ.

∴ Total number of squares = 8

10. (a) No. of Δ of single component = 3

No. of Δ of double components = 2

No. of Δ of three components = 1

∴ Total number of triangles = 6

11. (c) 16 straight lines.

12. (a) No. of ⬡ of single component = 15

No. of ⬡ of four components = 6

∴ Total number of hexagons = 21

13. (d) No. of ▭ of single component = 4

No. of ▭ of double components = 4

No. of ▭ of four components = 1

∴ Total number of rectangles = 9

14. (d)

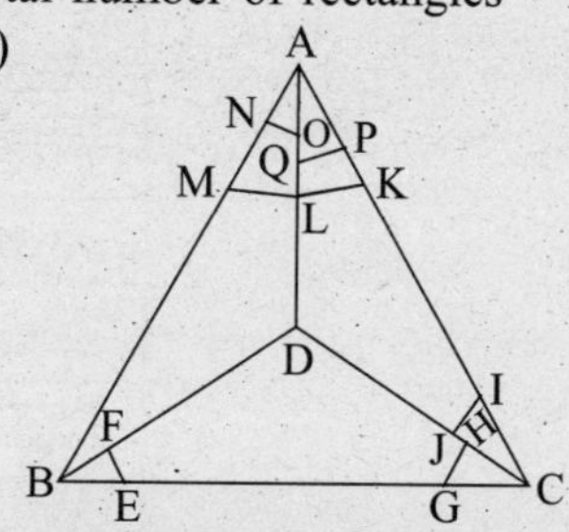

The triangles in the figure are as given below:

ABC, ADB, ADC, DBC, BFE, CHG, CHJ, ANO, APQ, AML, ALK.

15. (c)

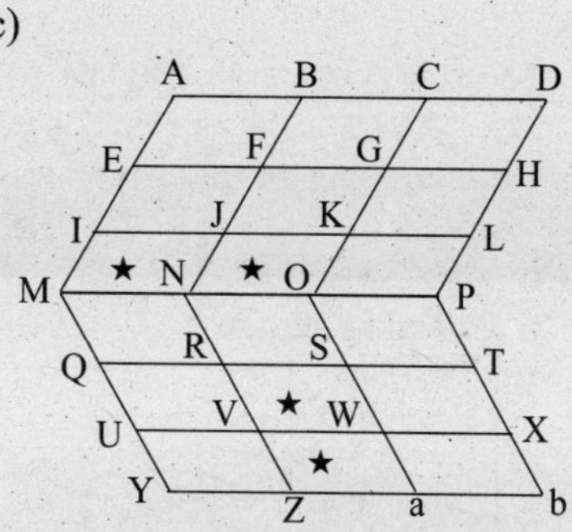

The parallelograms in the figure as given below :

ABEF, BCGF, CDHG, EFJI, IJNM, JKON, KLPO, ADPM, ACKI, BDLJ, EGOM, FHPN, MPbY, MNRQ, NOSR, OPTS, QRVU, RSWV, STXW, UVZY, VWaZ, WXba, MOWU, NPXW, YaSa, RTbZ, FJKG, GHLK.

16. (a)

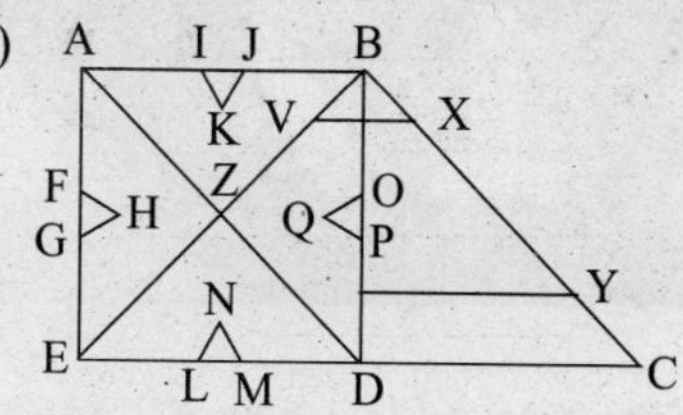

Triangles in the figure are given below :

ABE, AED, BED, BAD, AZE, EZD, ZBD, ABZ, IJK, FHG, LMN, OPQ, BDC, EBC, BVU, BUX, VBX, BPY.

17. (b)

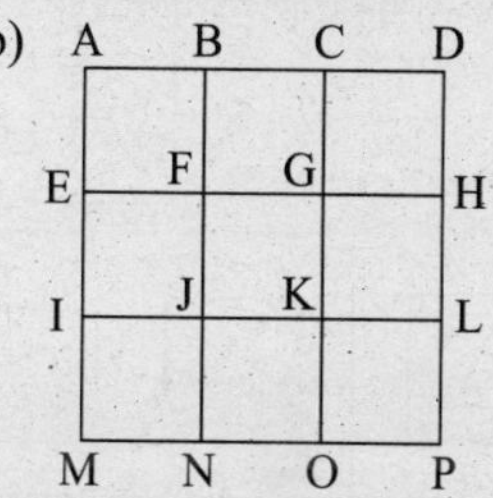

The squares in the figure are given below :

ABEF, BCGF, CDHG, EFJI, EGKJ, GHLK, IJNM, JKON, KLPO, ADPM, ACKI, BDLJ, MOGE, NPHF.

18. (b)

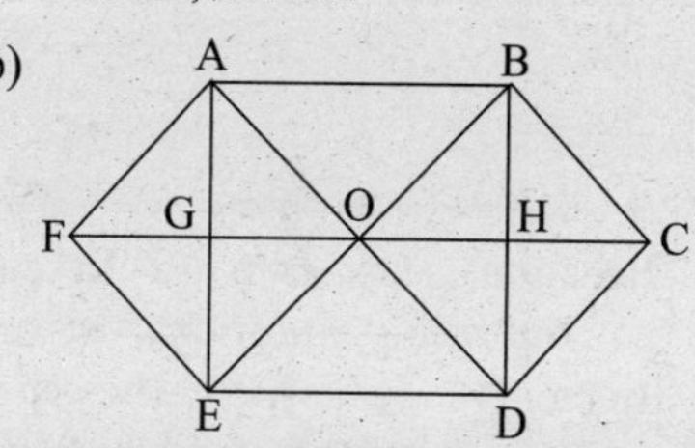

Triangles in the figure are given below :

FOE, OAB, BHC, GAF, ABE, BOD, OED, OAF, DHC, GEF, AED, BCD, ODC, OBH, OAG, EDB, AEO, OBC, OHD, OGE, DBA, AFE.

17 FORMATION OF FIGURES

Such types of questions in this chapter are based on formation of a figure from various given parts/fragmentation of a figure into simple parts. Choosing the patterns with identical components and rearrangement of pattern.

Example 1. In the following question find out which of the figures (a), (b), (c), (d) can be formed from the pieces given in the problem figure.

Problem figure :

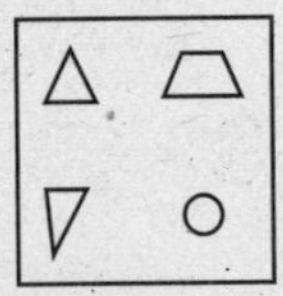

Answer figures :

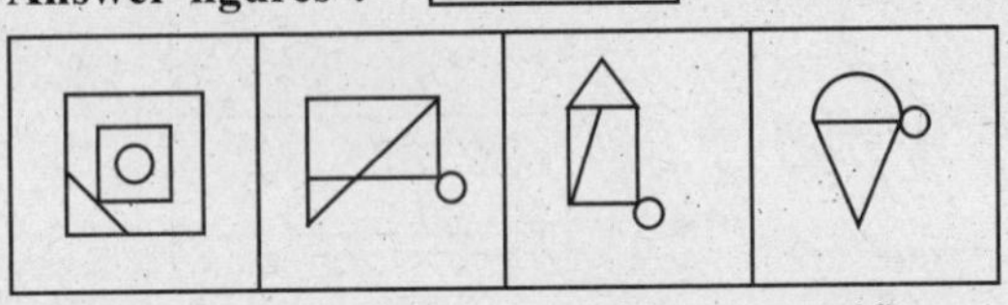

(a) (b) (c) (d)

Solution: (c) Using all components given in problem figure, we can arrange them as

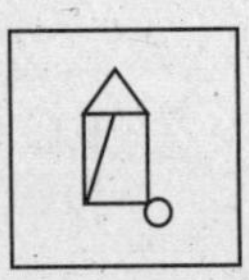

Example 2. In the following question find out which of the figures (a), (b), (c), (d) can be formed from the Pieces given in the problem figure.

Problem figure :

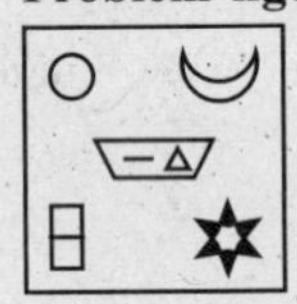

Answer figures :

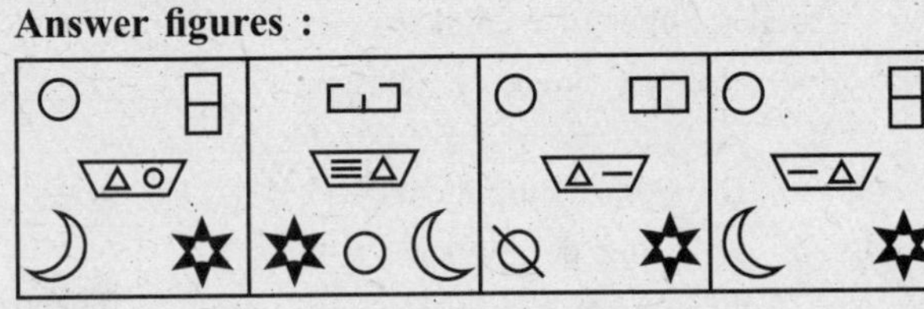

(a) (b) (c) (d)

Solution: (d) Using all components given in problem figure we can arrange them as

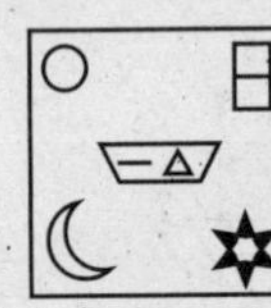

Exercise

Directions (Qs. 1 to 6): In each of the following questions, select the alternative in which the specified components of the problem figure are found.

1. **Question figure :**

Answer figures :

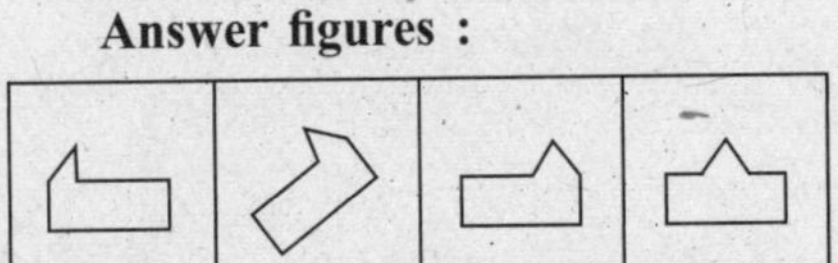

(a) (b) (c) (d)

2. **Question figure :**

Answer figures :

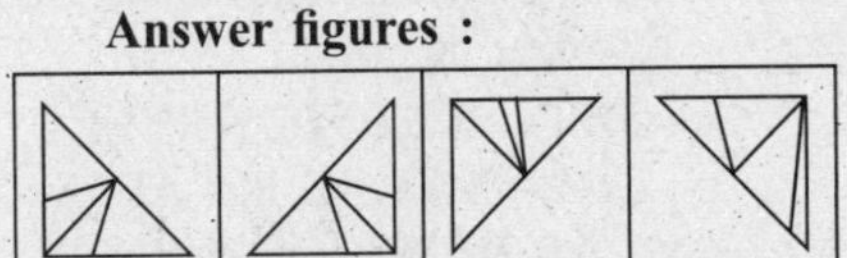

(a) (b) (c) (d)

3. **Question figure :**

Answer figures :

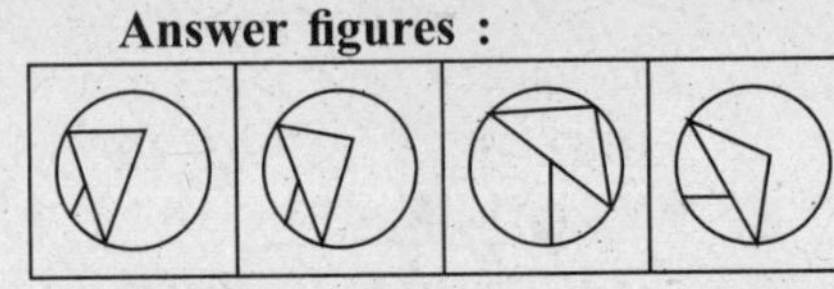

(a) (b) (c) (d)

4. **Question figure :**

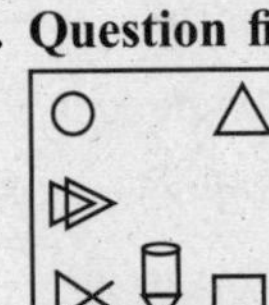

Answer figures :

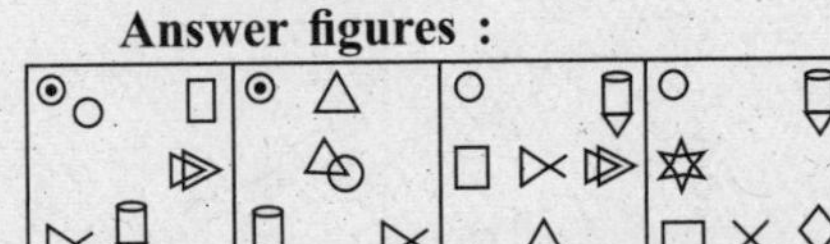

(a) (b) (c) (d)

5. Question figure :

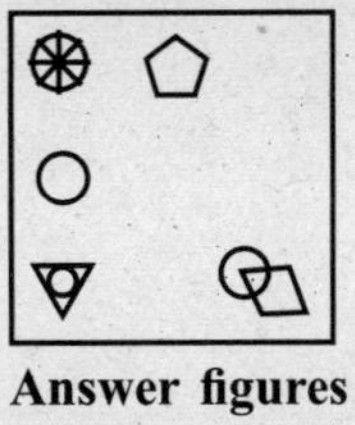

Answer figures :

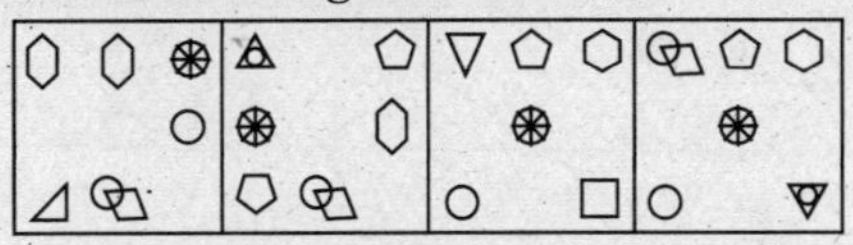

(a) (b) (c) (d)

6. Question figure :

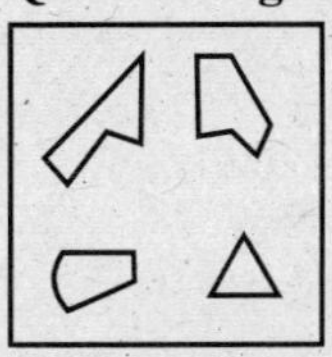

Answer figures :

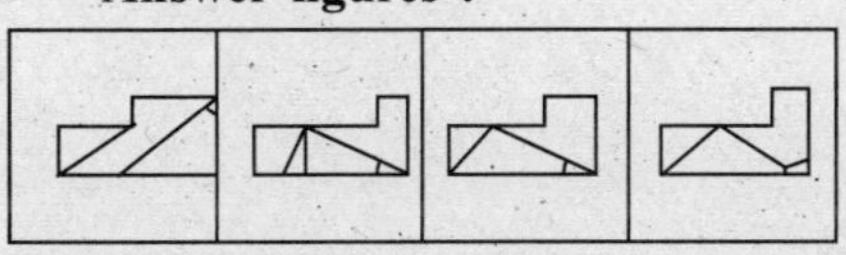

(a) (b) (c) (d)

Directions (Qs. 7 to 8) : In the following questions, among the four answer figures, which figure can be formed from the cut-pieces given below in the question figure?

7. Question figure :

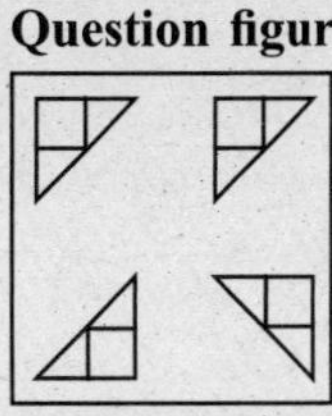

Answer figures :

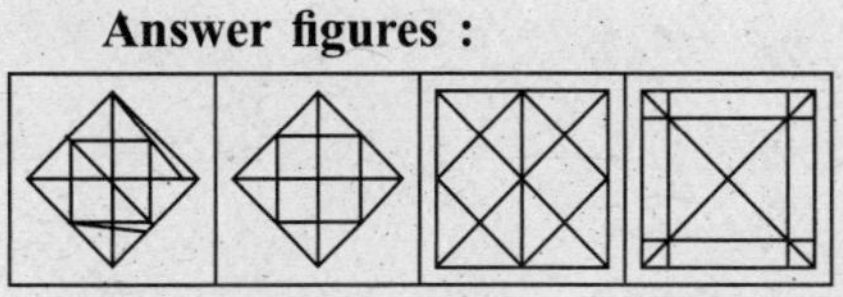

(a) (b) (c) (d)

8. Question figure :

Answer figures :

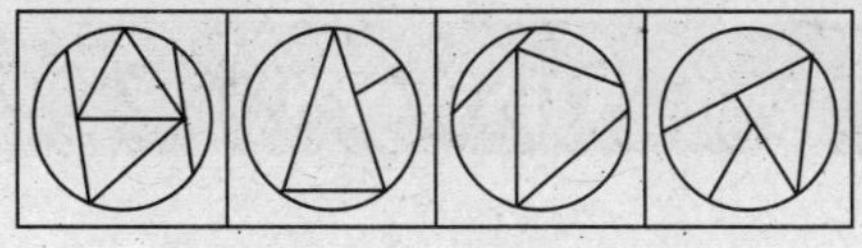

(a) (b) (c) (d)

9. Which of the answer figures is not made up of only the components of the key figure (question figure)?

Question figure :

Answer figures :

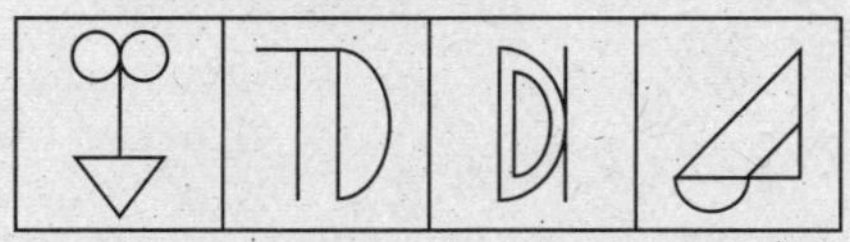

(a) (b) (c) (d)

10. A circular paper is folded and punched as shown below. From the responses given find out how it will appear when unfolded?

Question figure :

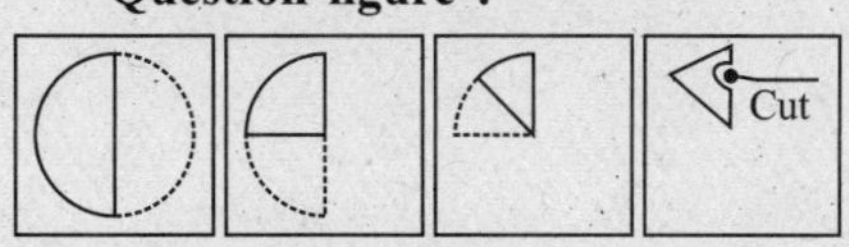

Answer figures :

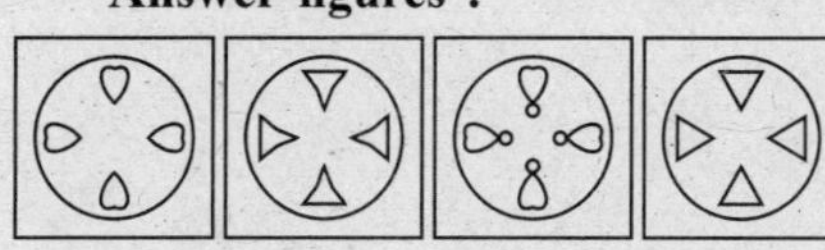

(a) (b) (c) (d)

11. In the following question, find out how will the question figure look like after rotation of 180º?

Question figure :

Answer figures :

(a) (b) (c) (d)

12. Which of the answer figures includes the separate components found in the question figure?

Question figure :

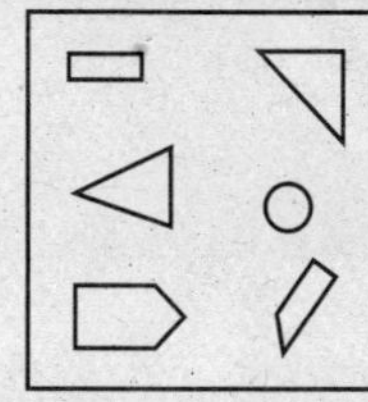

Answer figures :

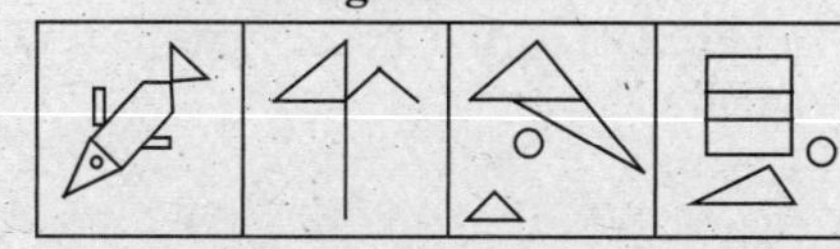

(a) (b) (c) (d)

13. Which answer figure includes all the components given in the question figure?

Question figure :

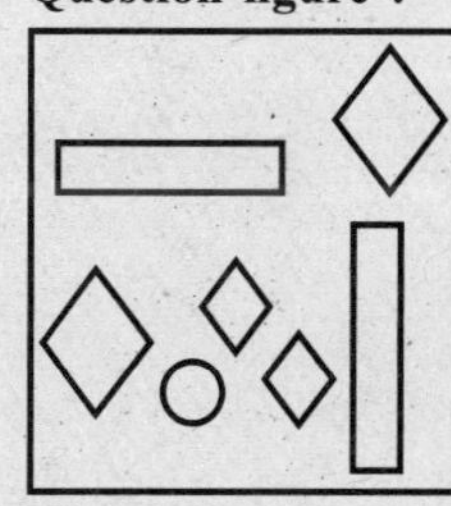

Answer figures :

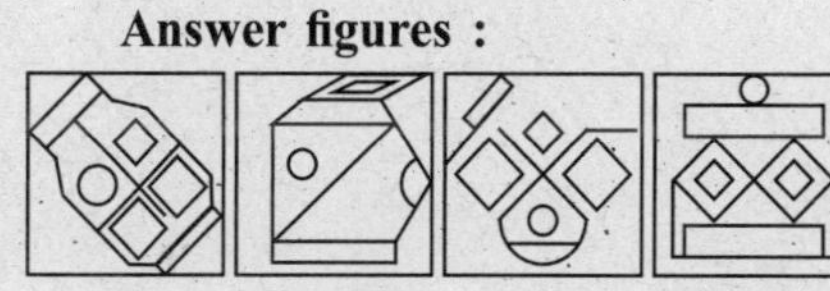

(a) (b) (c) (d)

14. Identify the answer figures from which the pieces given in question figure have been cut.

Question figure :

Answer figures :

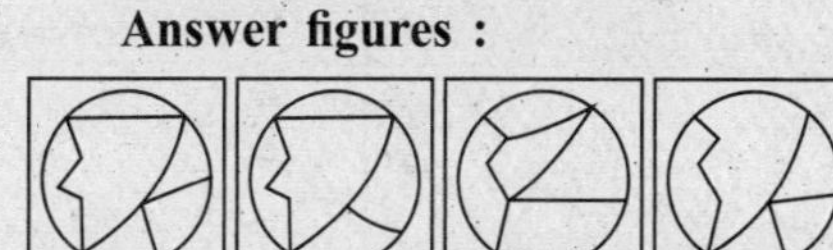

(a) (b) (c) (d)

Answers

1. (b)	**2.** (a)	**3.** (b)	**4.** (c)	**5.** (b)	**6.** (c)	**7.** (b)
8. (d)	**9.** (a)	**10.** (a)	11. (b)	**12.** (a)	**13.** (d)	**14.** (b)

18 MIRROR IMAGE

Mirror image is the image or the reflection of an object into a mirror when that object is placed near it.

In case of standard form of mirror i.e., when the mirror is placed vertically, the object gets laterally inverted. In other words, the **Left Hand Side** (LHS) and **Right Hand Side** (RHS) of an object interchange their places while top and bottom remain the same.

Objective having different mirror images

Mostly the mirror image of a figure is different from the original figure which is because of the dissimilarity in the left and right halves of the figure. This can be better understood with the help of the examples given below.

Solved Examples

Direction: (Example Nos. 1-2) : In the following, choose the correct mirror image of the figure given from amongst the four alternatives (a), (b), (c) and (d), when mirror is placed on the line AB.

Example 1. Question Figure

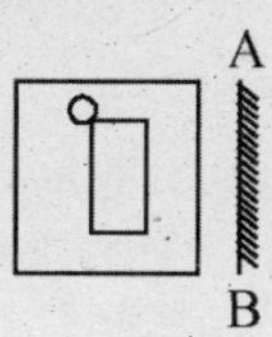

Answer Figures

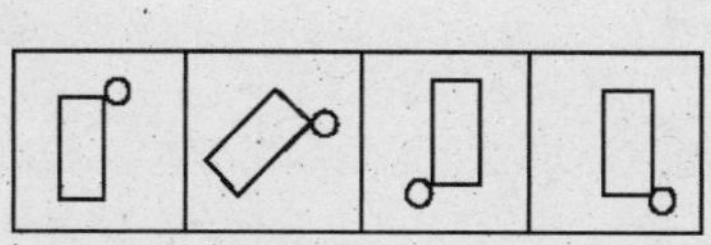

(a) (b) (c) (d)

Solution (a): Here, the mirror is placed vertically at AB on the RHS of the question figure. Hence, only the figure given in answer figure (a), would be obtained as the correct mirror image.

Example 2. Question Figure

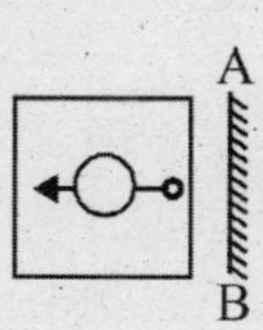

Answer Figures

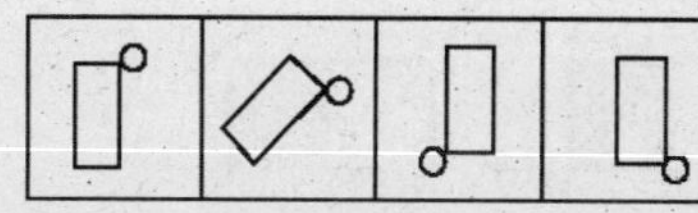

(a) (b) (c) (d)

Solution (c): Here, the mirror is placed vertically at AB on the RHS of the question figure. Hence, only the figure given in answer figure (c), would be obtained as the correct mirror image.

Directions Example Nos. (3-4) : In each of the following questions, choose the correct mirror image from the alternatives (a), (b), (c) and (d) when mirror is placed along the line AB.

Example 3. Question Figure

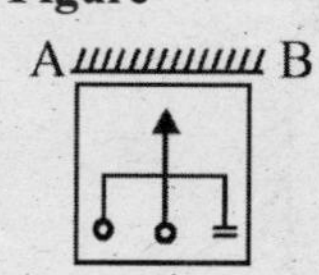

Answer Figures

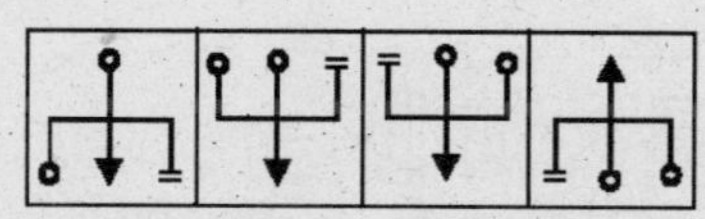

(a) (b) (c) (d)

Solution (b): Here, the mirror is placed horizontally at AB on the top of the question figure. Hence, only the figure given in answer figure (b), would be obtained as the correct mirror image.

Example 4. Question Figure

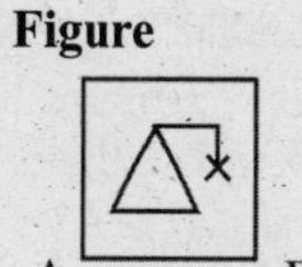

Answer Figures

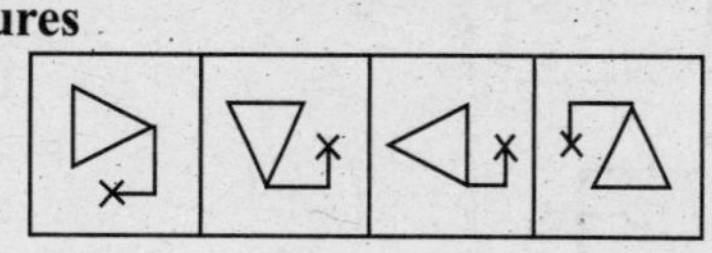

(a) (b) (c) (d)

Solution (b): Here, the mirror is placed horizontally at AB on the bottom of the question figure. Hence, only answer figure (b) is the vertically inverted form of question figure in which top and bottom interchange places while LHS and RHS remain the same.

Exercise

1. If a mirror is placed on the line MN, then which of the answer figures is the right image of the given figure ?

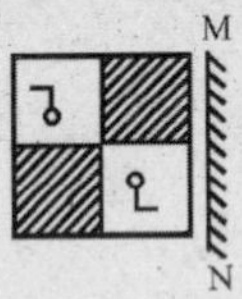

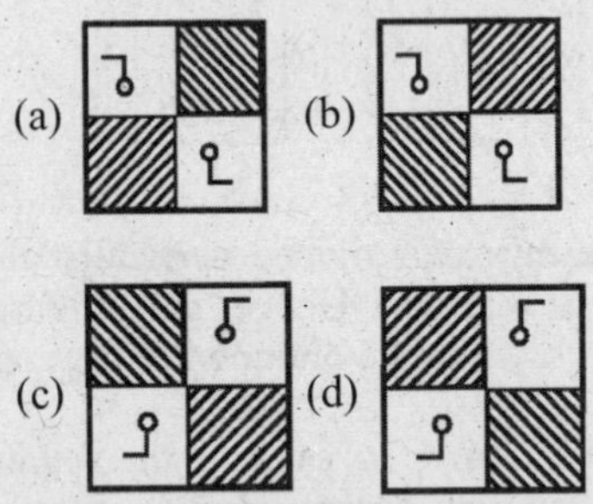

2. If a mirror is placed on the line MN, then which of the answer figures is the right image of the given figure?

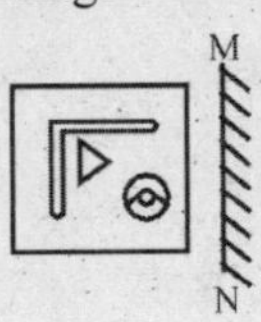

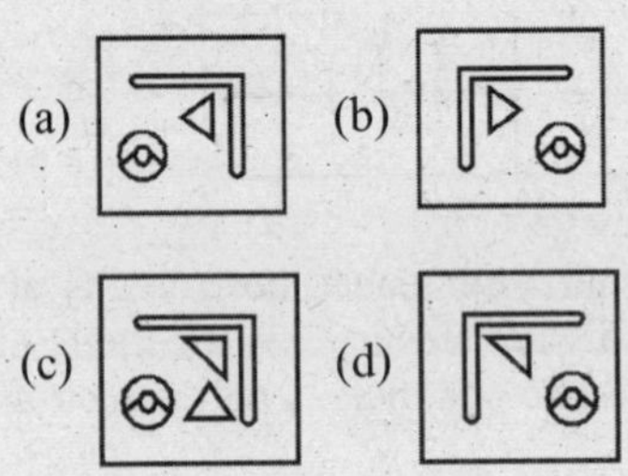

3. If a mirror is placed on the line MN, then which of the answer figures is the right image of the given figure?

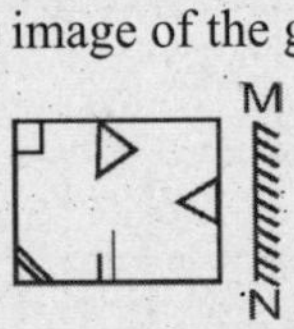

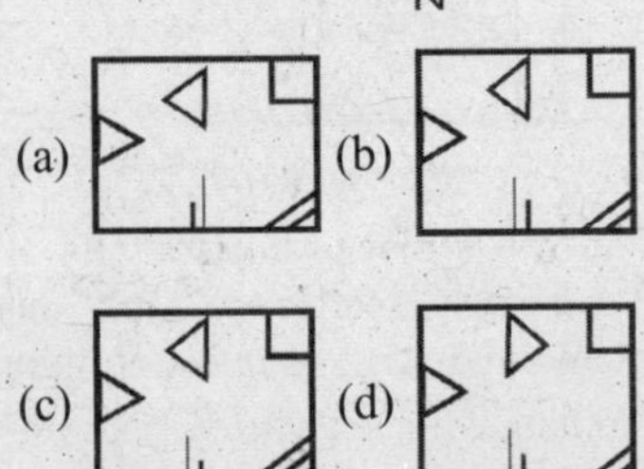

4. If a mirror is placed on the line MN, then which of the anwer figures is the right image of the given figure?

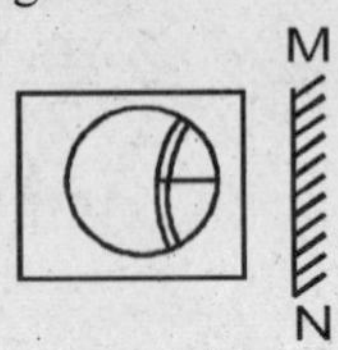

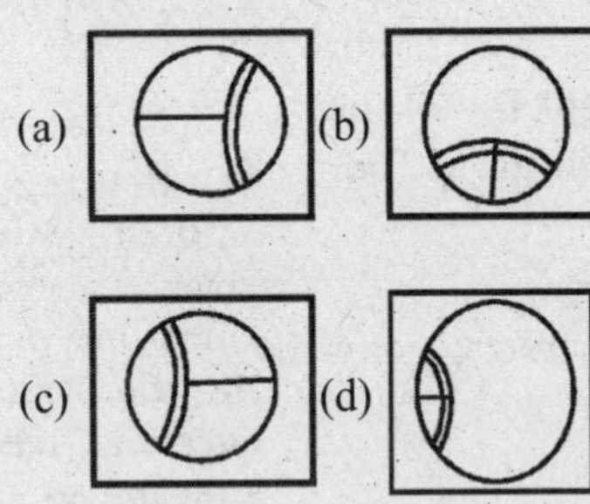

5. If a mirror is placed on the line XY, then which of the answer figures is the right image of the given figure?

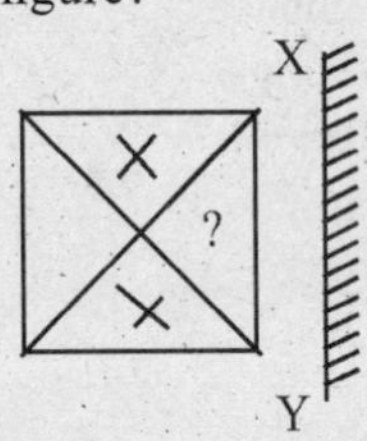

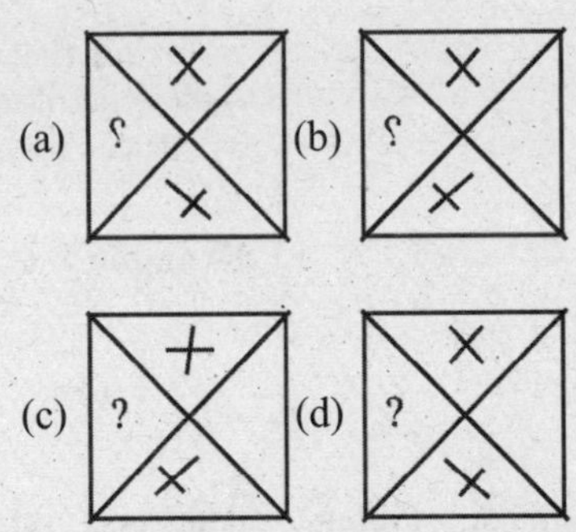

6. If a mirror is placed on the line MN, then which of the answer figures is the right image of the given figure ?

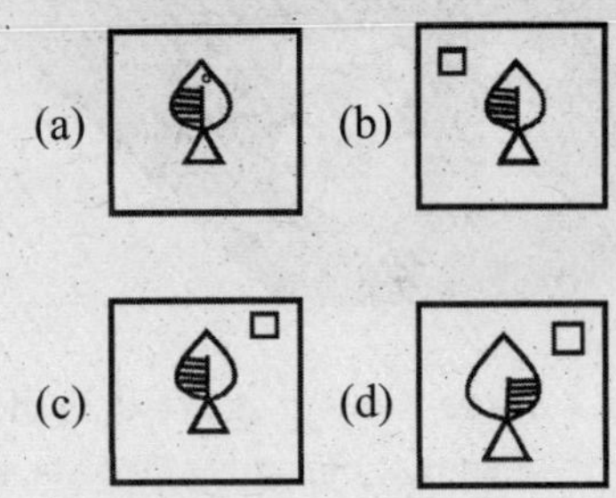

7. If a mirror is placed on the line MN, then which of the answer figures is the right image of the given figure?

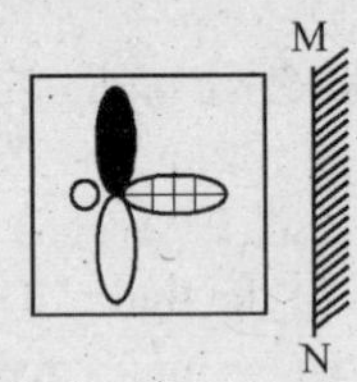

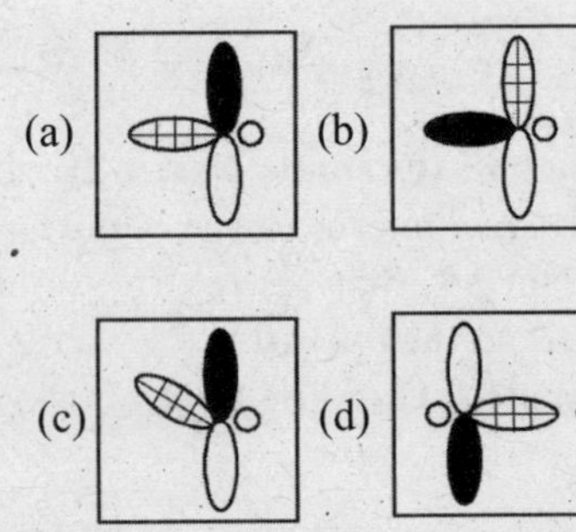

8. If a mirror is placed on the line MN, then which of the answer figures is the right image of the given figure?

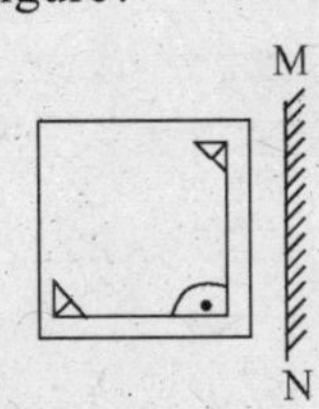

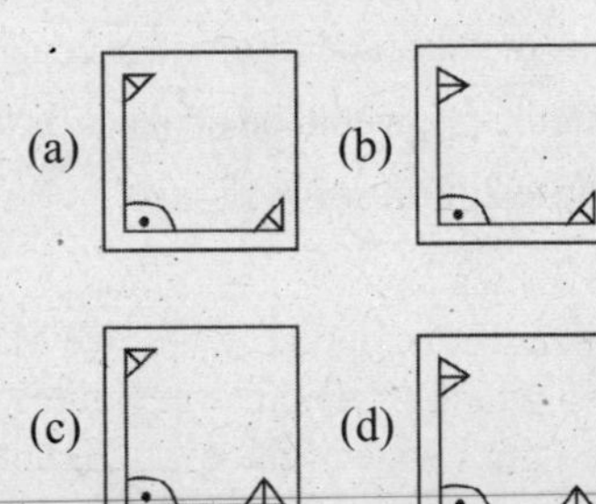

9. If a mirror is placed on the line MN, then which of the answer figures is the right image of the given figures?

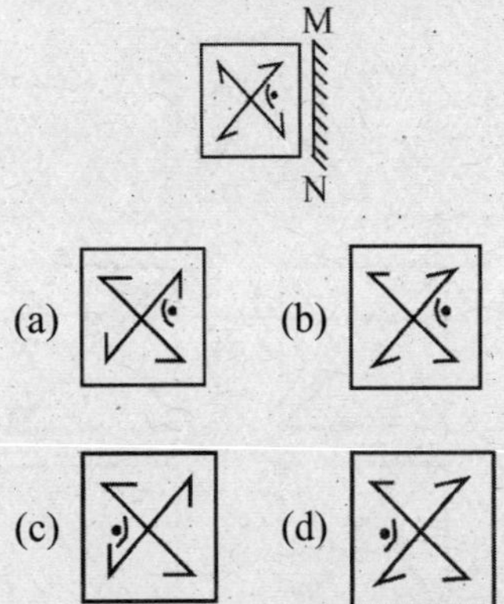

10. If a mirror is placed on the line MN, then which of the answer figures is the right image of the given figure?

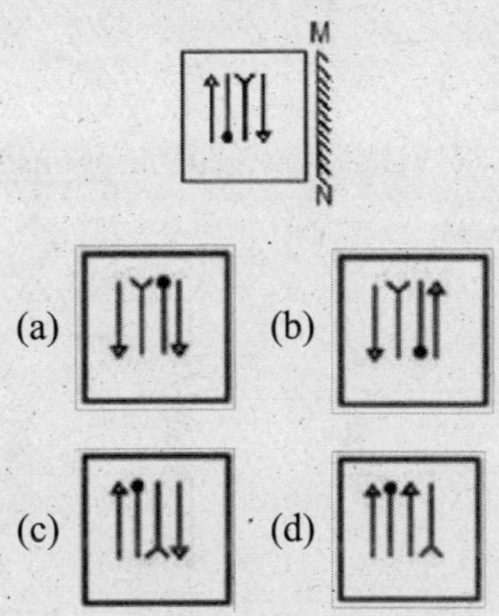

11. If a mirror is placed on the line XY, then which of the answer figures is the right image of the given figure?

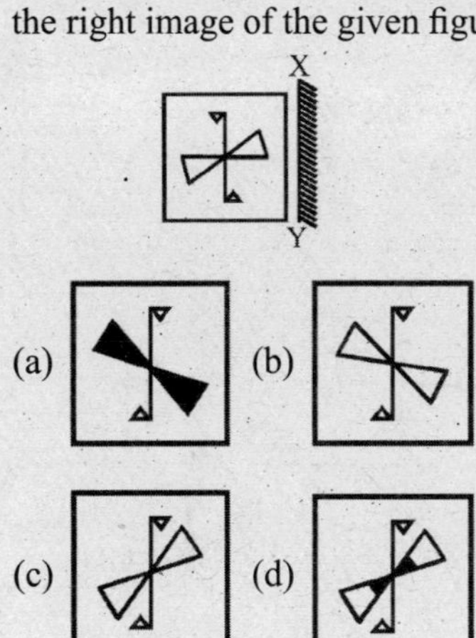

12. If a mirror is placed on the line MN, then which of the answer figures is the right image of the given figure ?

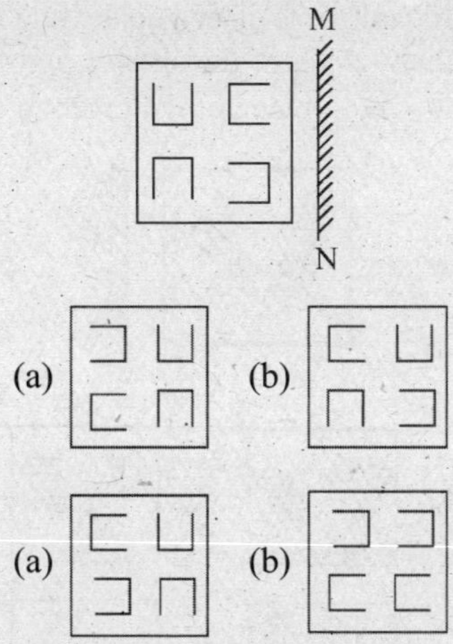

13. If a mirror is placed on the line MN, then which of the answer figures is the right image of the given figure?

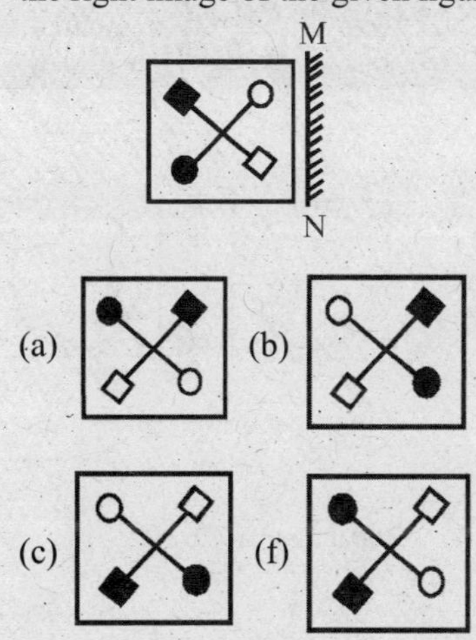

14. If a mirror is placed on the line MN, then which of the answer figures is the right image of the given figure?

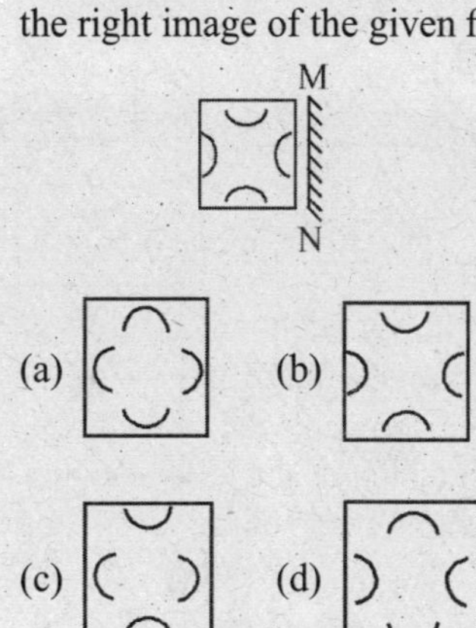

15. If a mirror is placed on the line MN, then which of the answer figures is the right image of the given figure?

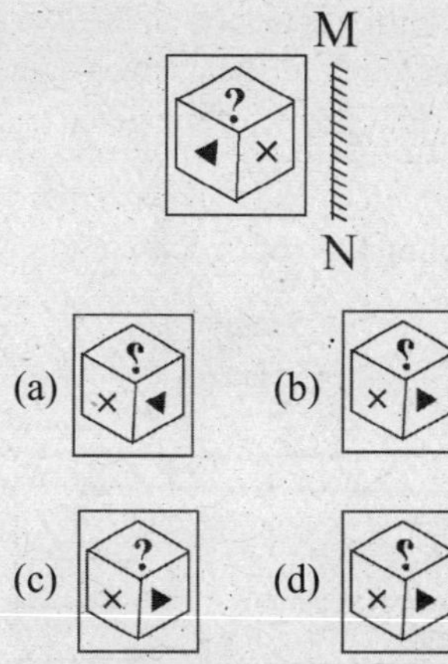

16. If a mirror is placed on the line MN, then which of the answer figures is the right image of the given figure?

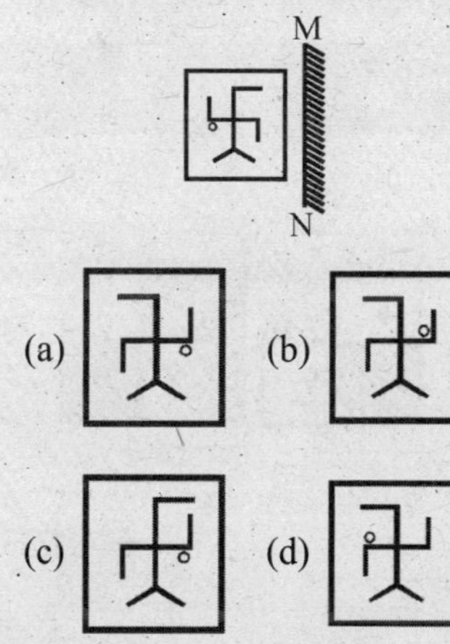

17. If a mirror is placed on the line MN, then which of the answer figures is the right image of the given figure?

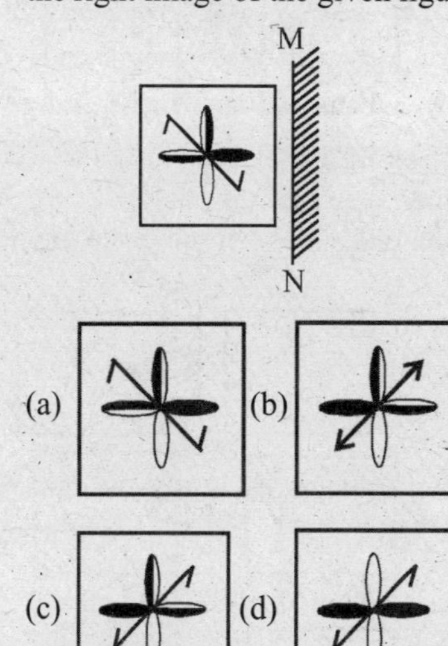

18. If a mirror is placed on the line MN, then which of the answer figures is the right image of the given figure?

(a)  (b) 

(c)  (d) 

19. If a mirror is placed on the line MN, then which of the answer figures is the right image of the given figure?

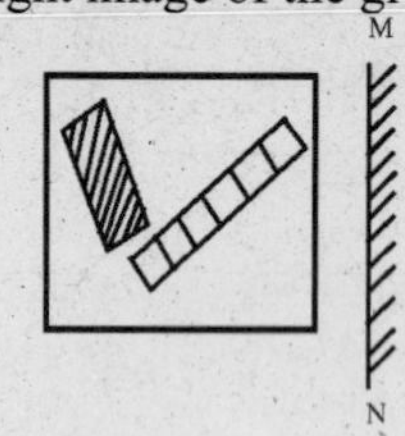

(a)  (b) 

(c)  (d) 

20. If a mirror is placed on the line MN, then which of the answer figures is the right image of the given figure?

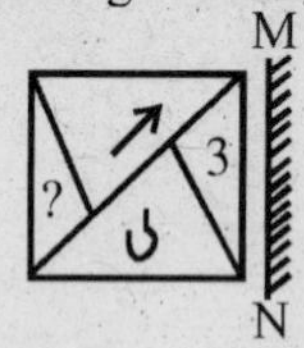

(a) 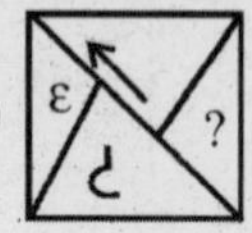 (b) 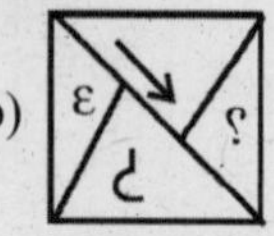

(c) 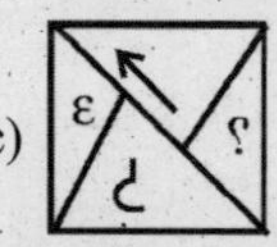 (d) 

Answers with Explanations

1. (c) 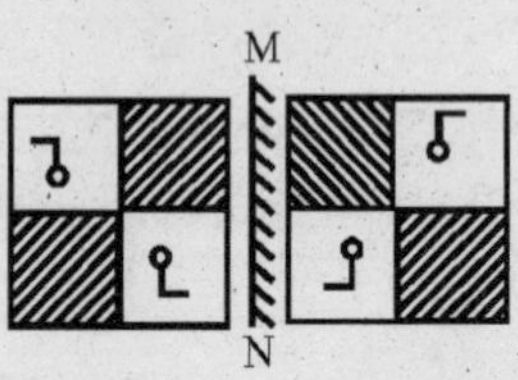

Finally, the right mirror image of given figure is 

2. (a) 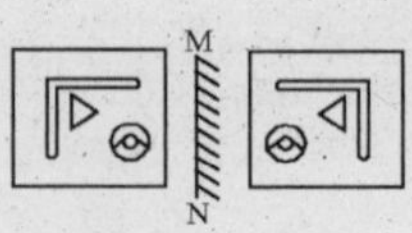

Finally, the right image is .

3. (b) 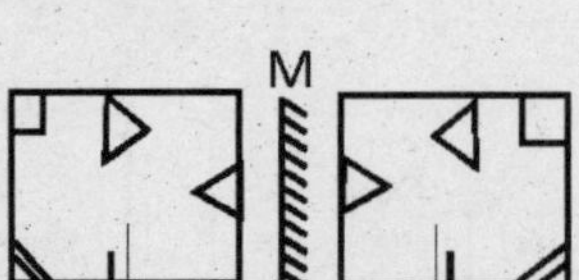

Finally, the right mirror image of the given figure is 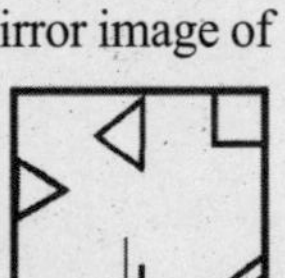

4. (d) 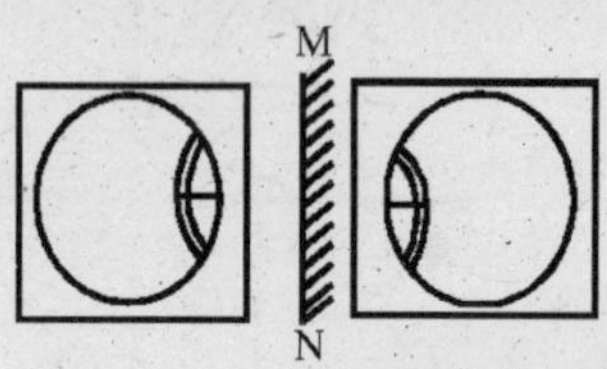

Finally, the right mirror image of the given figure is 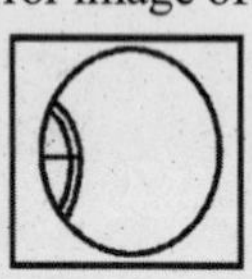

5. (b) 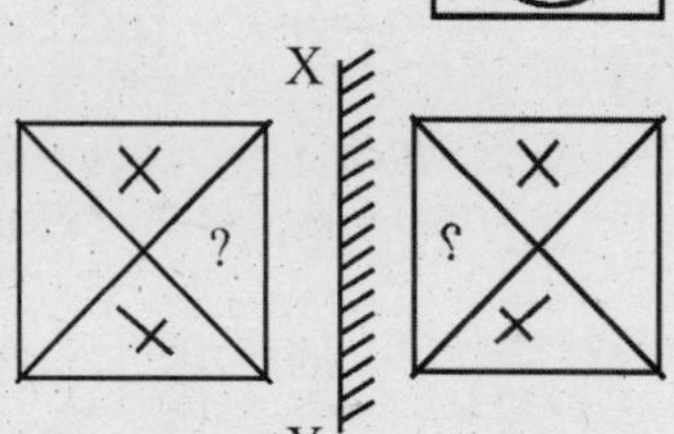

The right mirror image of the given figure is 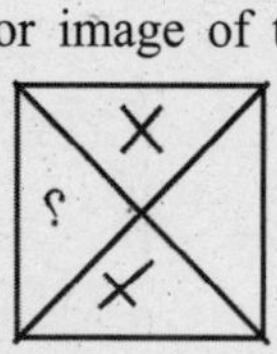

6. (b) 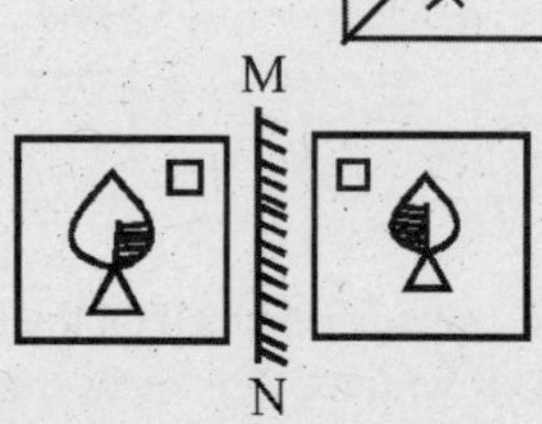

Finally the right mirror image of the given figure is .

7. (c) 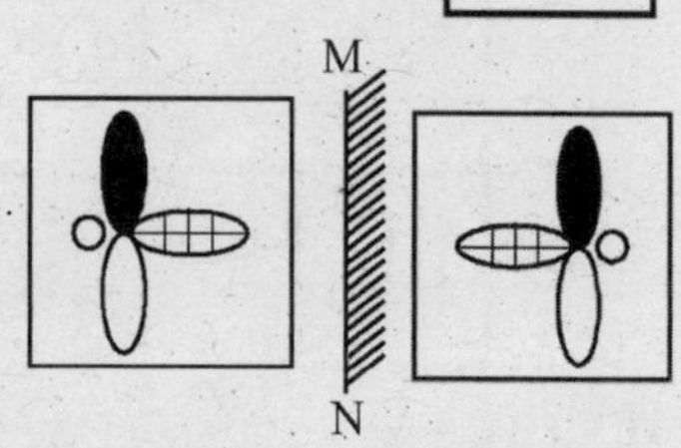

Finally, the right mirror image of the given figure is 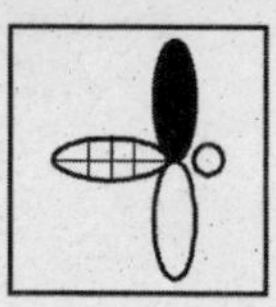

8. (a) 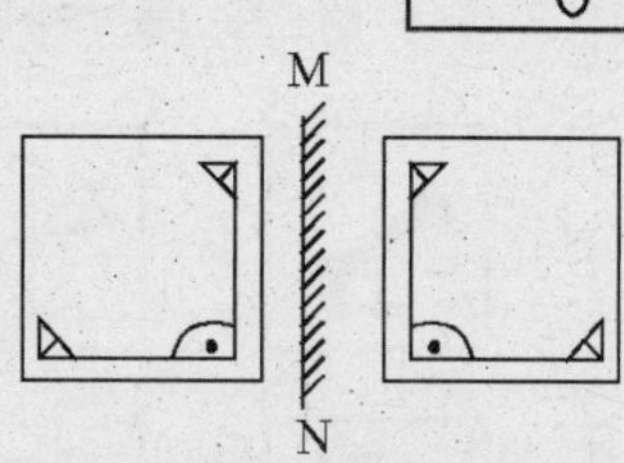

Finally, the right image of the given figure is 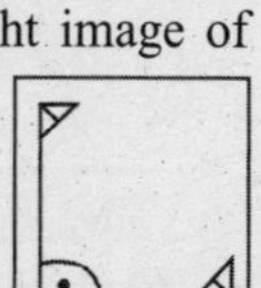

9. (c) 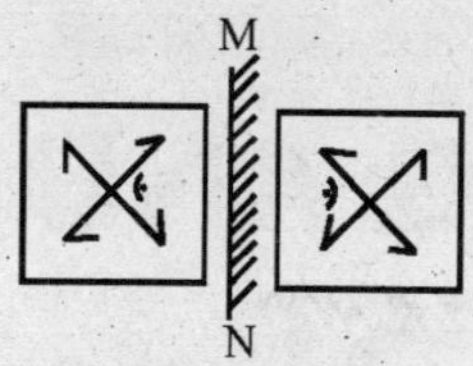

Finally, the right image of the given figure is 

10. (b) 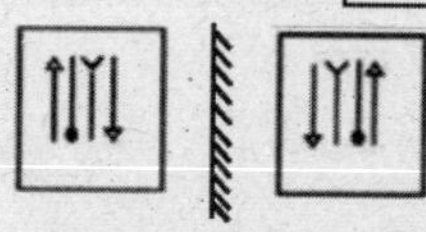

Finally, the mirror image of the given figure is .

11. (b) 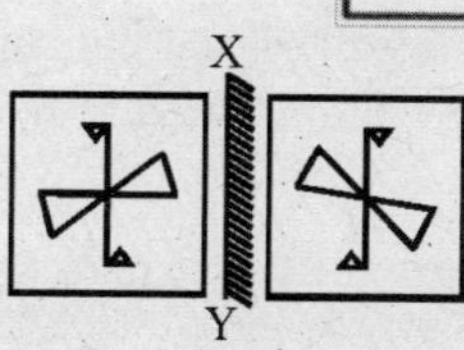

Finally, the right mirror image of the given figure is 

12. (a) 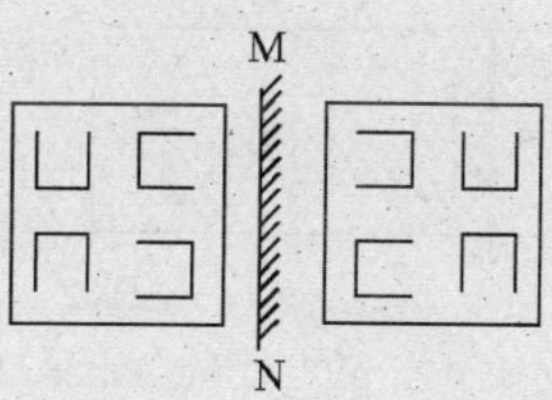

Finally, the right image of the given figure is 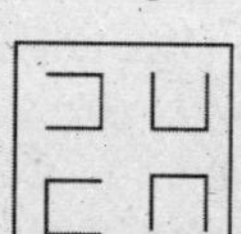

13. (b) 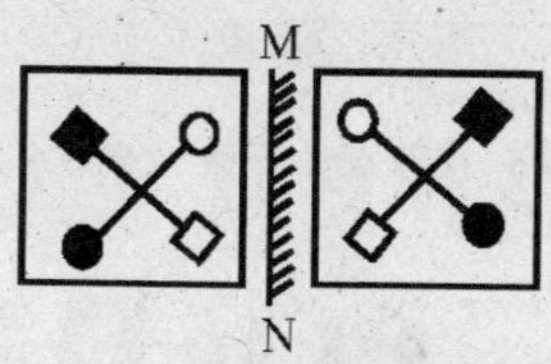

Finally, the right image of the given figure is .

14. (b) 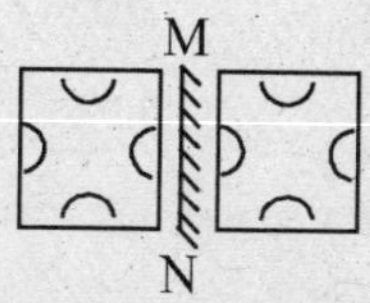

Finally the right mirror image of the given figure is 

15. (d) 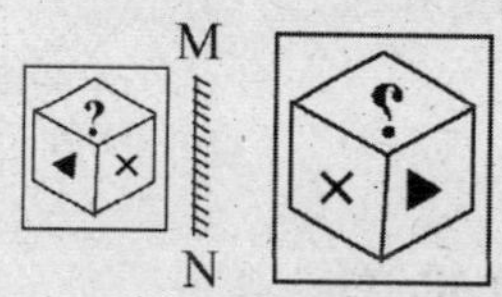

Finally, the right mirror image of the given figure is 

16. (a) 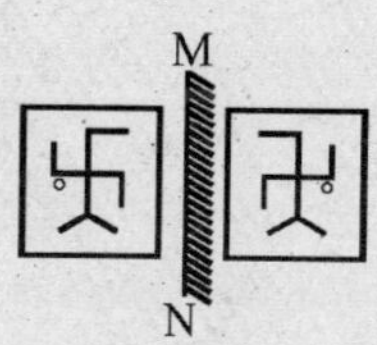

Finally, the right image of the given figure is 

17. (c) 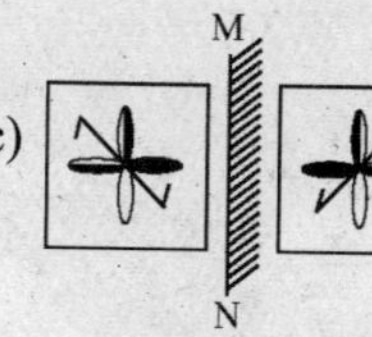

Finally, 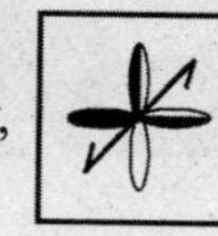 is the right mirror figure.

18. (b) 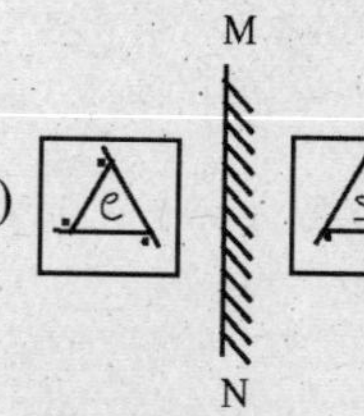

 is the right mirror image.

19. (b) 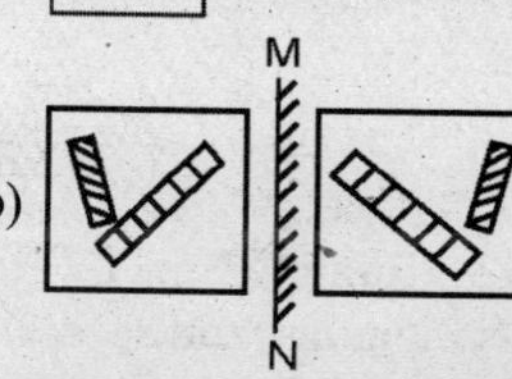

Finally, the right image of the given figure is 

20. (c) 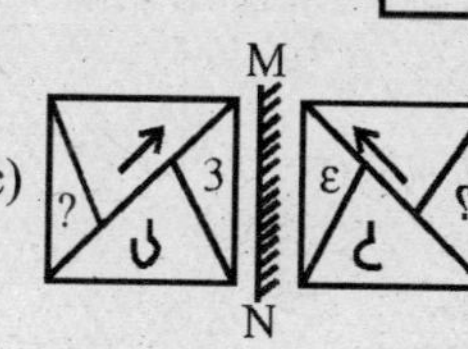

 is the right image of the given figure.

19 PAPER CUTTING AND FOLDING TEST

In questions based on paper cutting, one or more question figures are given showing the manner in which a piece of paper is folded, where a dotted line is the reference line along which the paper has to be folded and the arrow indicates the direction of the fold. Then the paper is punched (cut) from a particular section. Such cuts may be based on varying patterns appear on the paper when the paper is unfolded after cutting. The candidates are required to see the question figure(s) carefully and then identify the unfolded paper having correct cutting pattern out of the four answer choices given in the form of figures.

Solved Examples

Direction : (Example Nos. 1-2) : A paper sheet is folded in a particular manner and several punches (cuts) are made. When unfolded the paper sheet looks like the question figure (X). From the given options select the one that follows the manner in which the paper is folded and punched.

Example 1. Question Figure

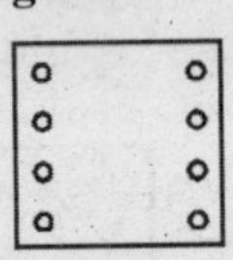

X

Answer Figures

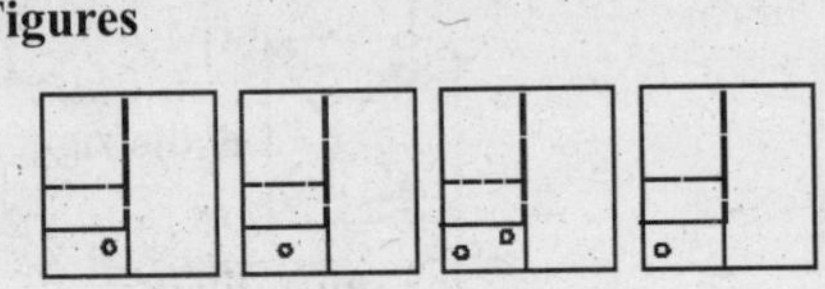

(a) (b) (c) (d)

Solution (d): When we fold figure (X), then it looks like answer figure (d).

Example 2. Question Figure

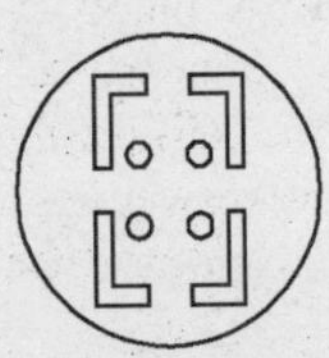

X

Answer Figures

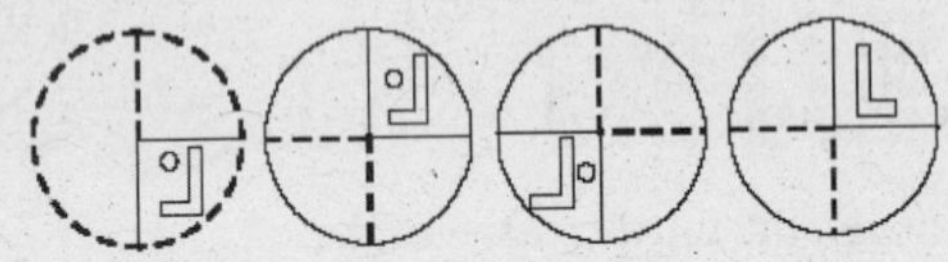

(a) (b) (c) (d)

Solution (a): When we fold question figure (X), then it looks like answer figure (a).

Example 3. A piece of paper is folded and cut as shown below in the question figures. From the given answer figures, indicate how it will appear when opened.

Question Figures

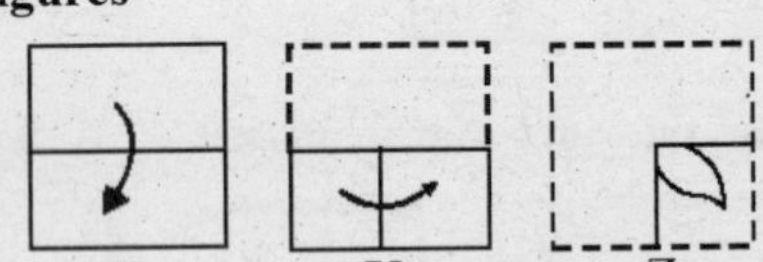

X Y Z

Answer Figures

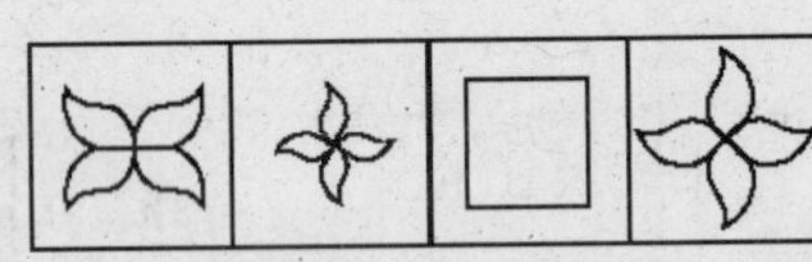

(a) (b) (c) (d)

Solution (a): It is clear that in figure (X), the paper has been folded from the upper half to lower half, in figure (Y), the paper has been folded from left to right making it one fourth of the original size.

Now, as given in figure (Z), the cut is marked. The design of the cut will appear in answer figure (a), when it is unfolded. Hence, answer figure (a) represents the correct unfolded shape of the paper after the cut.

Example 4. The three question figures marked X, Y and Z show the manner in which a paper is folded step by step and then cut. From the answer figures (a), (b), (c) and (d), select the one, showing the unfolded shape of the paper after the cut.

Question Figures

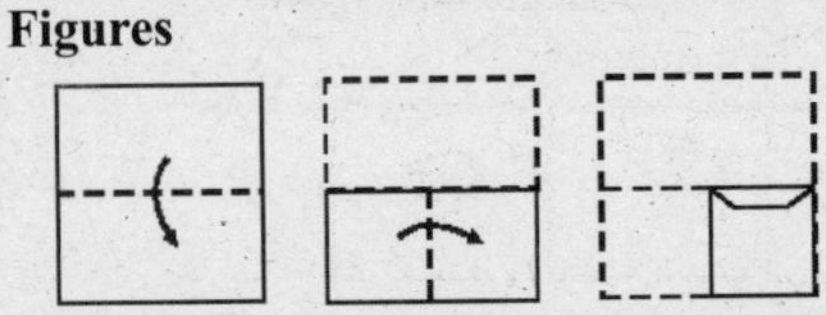

X Y Z

Answer Figures

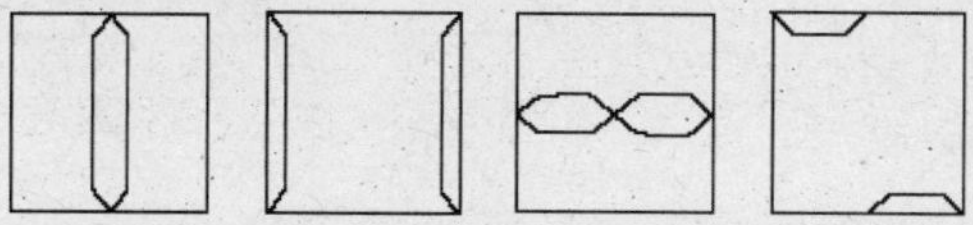

(a) (b) (c) (d)

Solution (c): It is clear that in figure (X), the paper has been folded from the upper half to lower half. In figure (Y), the paper has been folded from left to right making it one-fourth of the original size. Now, as given (Z), the cut is made in such a way that the design of the cut will appear along the central line of the page, when it is unfolded. Hence, answer figure (c) represents the correct unfolded shape of the paper after the cut.

Exercise

1. A piece of paper is folded and punched as shown below in the question figures. From the given answer figures, indicate how it will appear when opened.

(a)  (b) 

(c)  (d) 

2. A piece of paper is folded and punched as shown below in the question figures. From the given answer figures, indicate how it will appear when opened.

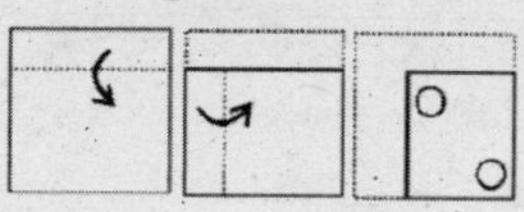

(a) 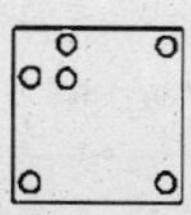 (b) 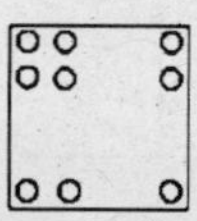

(c) 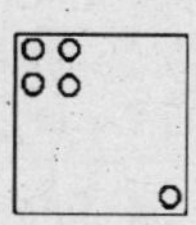 (d) 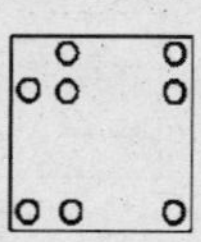

3. A piece of paper is folded and punched as shown below in the question figures. From the given answer figures, indicate how it will appear when opened.

(a)  (b) 

(c) 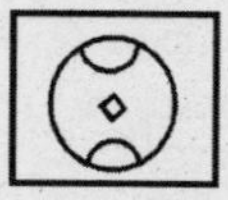 (d) 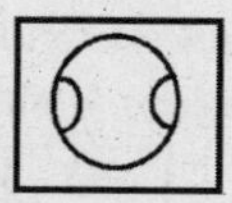

4. A piece of paper is folded and punched as shown below in the question fugures. From the given answer figures, indicate how it will appear when opened.

(a)  (b) 

(c)  (d) 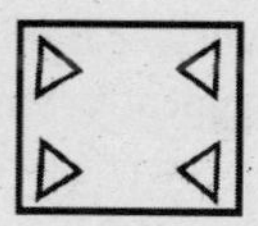

5. A piece of paper is folded and punched as shown below in the question figures. From the given answer figures, indicate how it will appear when opened.

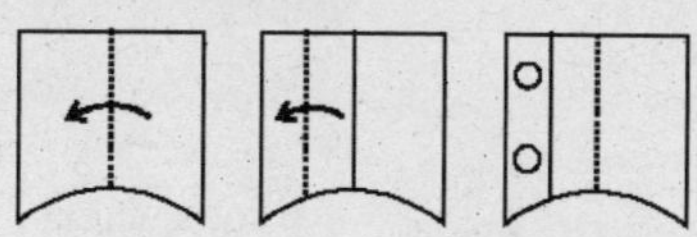

(a)  (b) 

(c)  (d) 

6. A piece of paper is folded and punched as shown below in the question figures. From the given answer figures, indicate how it will appear when opened.

(a)  (b) 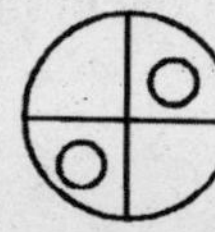

(c)  (d) 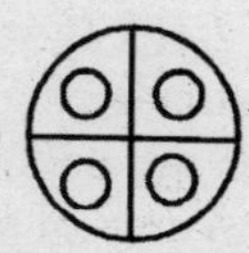

7. A piece of paper is folded and punched as shown below in the question figures. From the given answer figures, indicate how it will appear when opened.

(a) 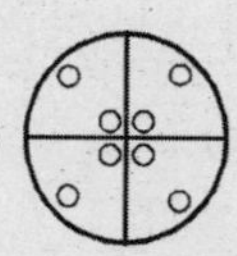 (b) 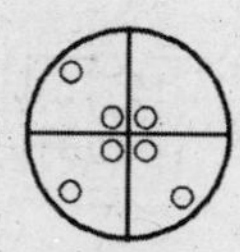

(c) 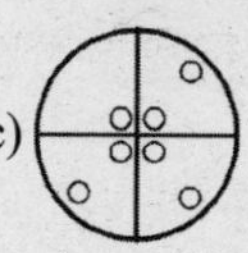 (d) 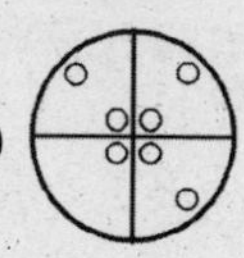

8. A piece of paper is folded and punched as shown below in the question figures. From the given answer figures, indicate how it will appear when opened.

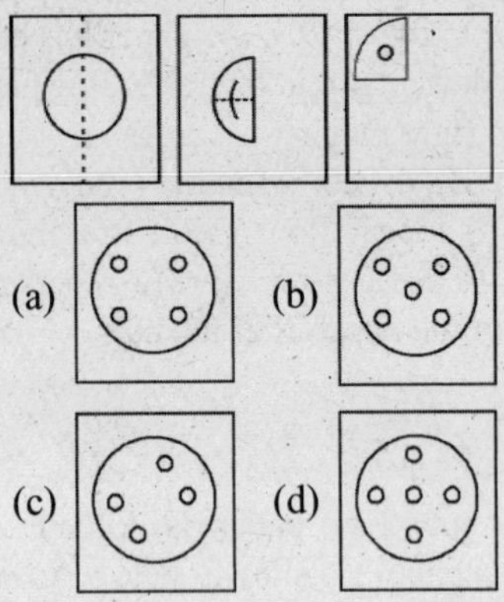

9. A piece of paper is folded and punched as shown below in the question figures. From the given answer figures, indicate how it will appear when opened.

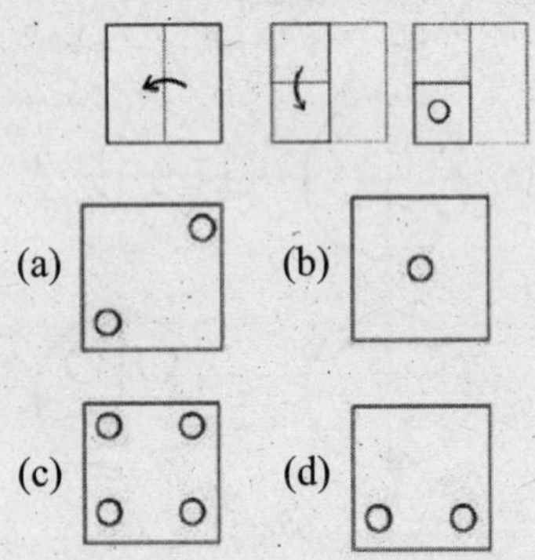

10. A piece of paper is folded and punched as shown below in the question figures. From the given answer figures, indicate how it will appear when opened.

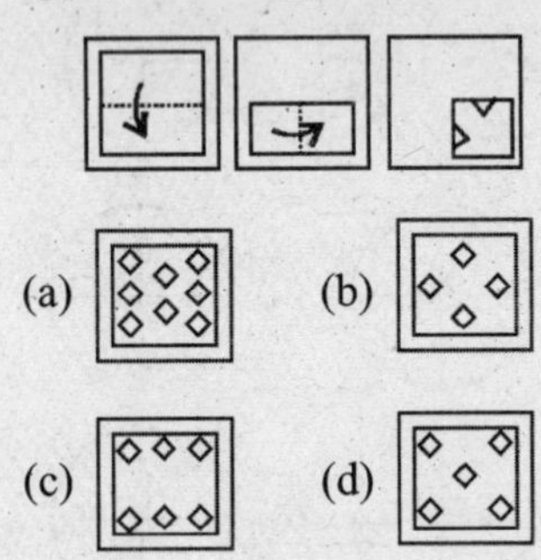

11. A piece of paper is folded and punched as shown below in the question figures. From the given answer figures, indicate how it will appear when opened.

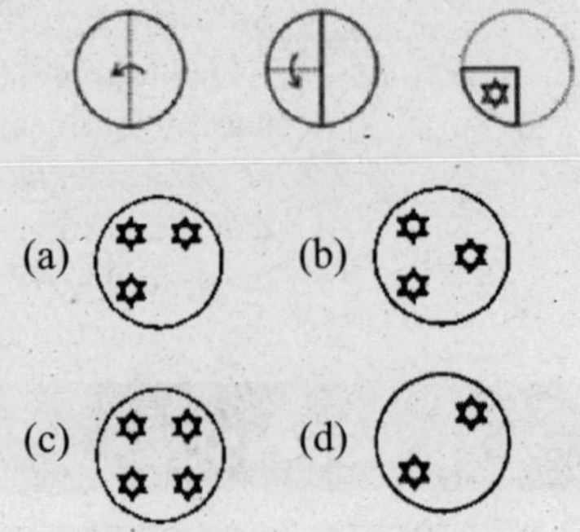

12. A piece of paper is folded and punched as shown below in the question figures. From the given answer figures, indicate how it will appear when opened.

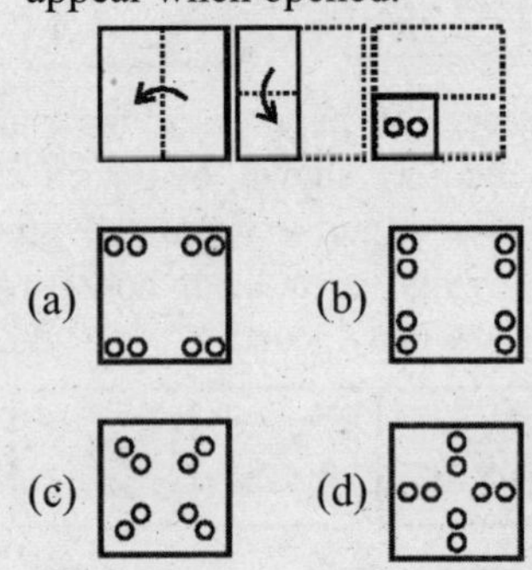

13. A piece of paper is folded and punched as shown below in the question figures. From the given answer figures, indicate how it will appear when opened.

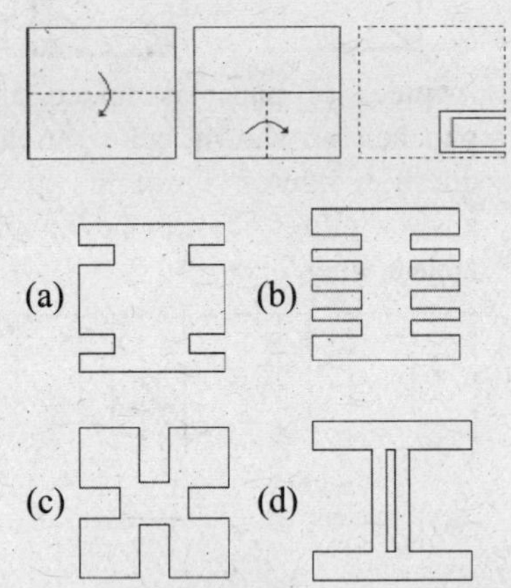

14. A piece of paper is folded and punched as shown below in the question figures. From the given answer figures, indicate how it will appear when opened.

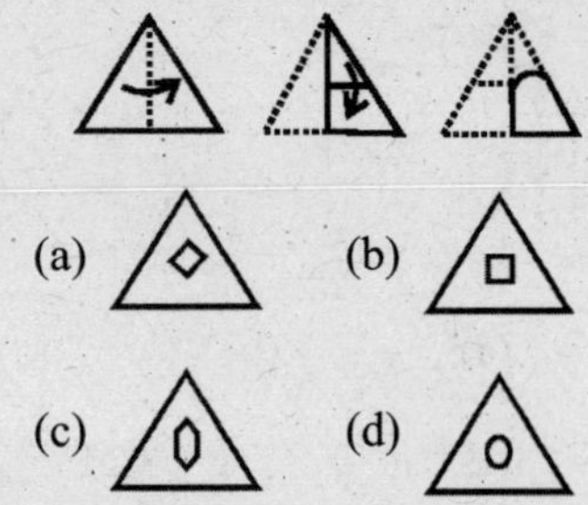

15. A piece of paper is folded and punched as shown below in the question figures. From the given answer figures, indicate how it will appear when opened.

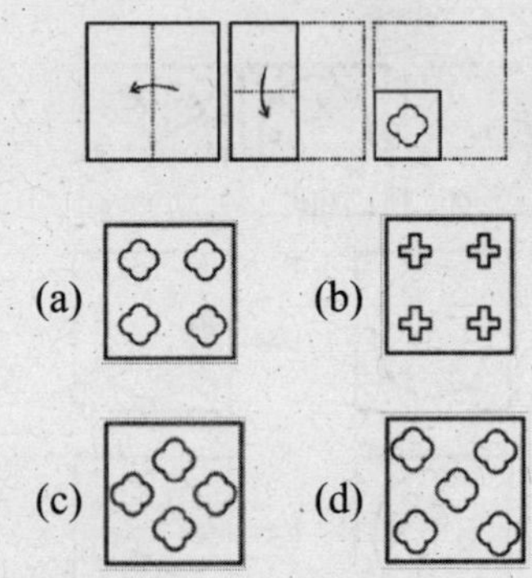

16. A piece of paper is folded and punched as shown below in the question figures, From the given answer figures, indicate how it will appear when opened.

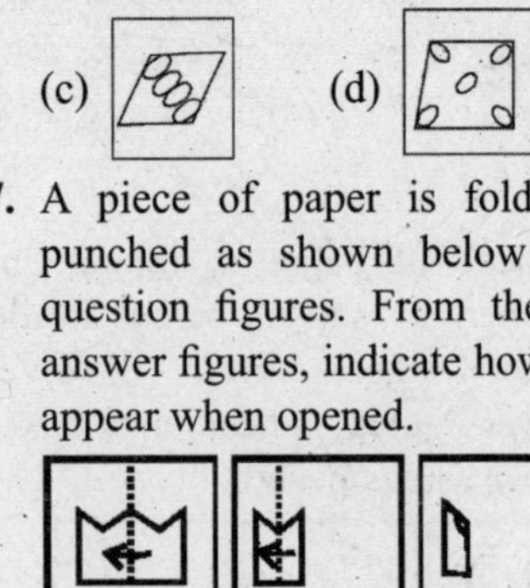

17. A piece of paper is folded and punched as shown below in the question figures. From the given answer figures, indicate how it will appear when opened.

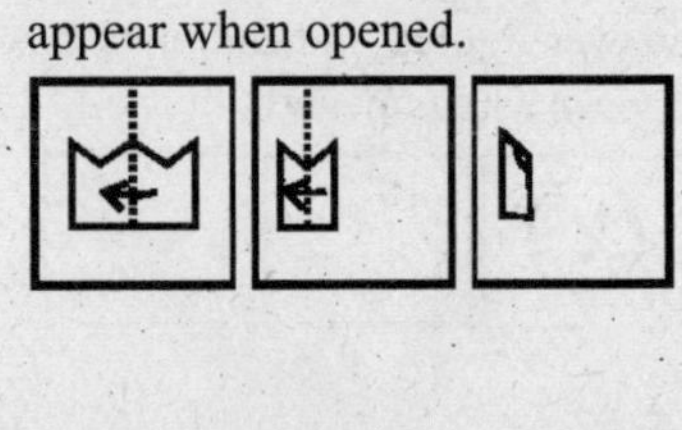

(a)  (b) 

(c)  (d) 

18. A piece of paper is folded and punched as shown below in the question figures. From the given answer figures, indicate how it will appear when opened.

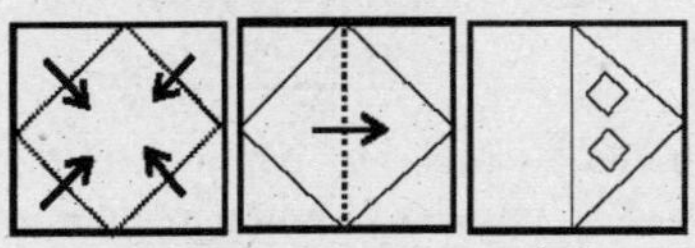

(a)  (b) 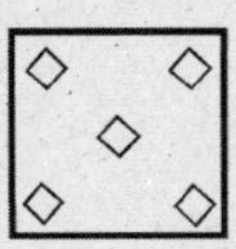

(c) 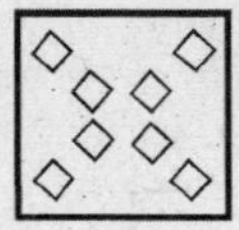 (d) 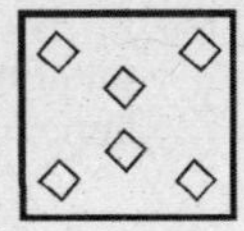

19. A piece of paper is folded and punched as shown below in the question figures. From the given answer figures, indicate how it will appear when opened.

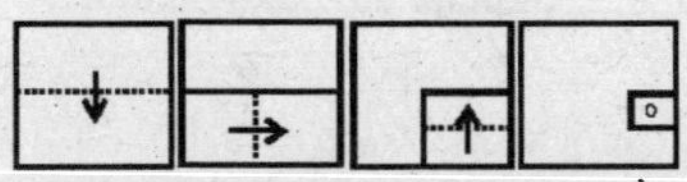

(a) 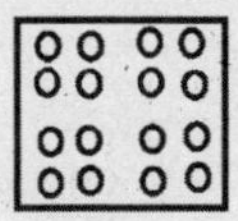 (b) 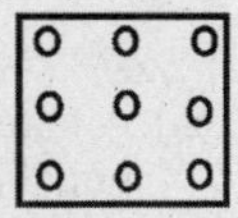

(c) 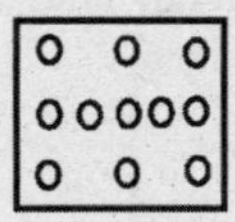 (d) 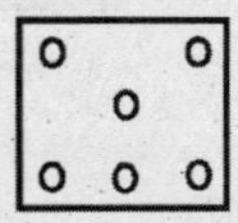

20. A piece of paper is folded and punched as shown below in the question figures. From the given answer figures, indicate how it will appear when opened.

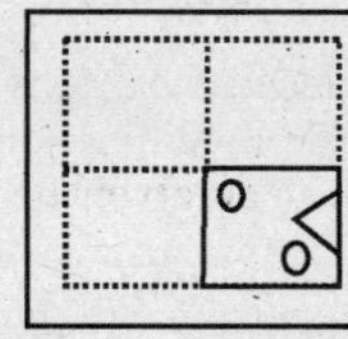

(a) 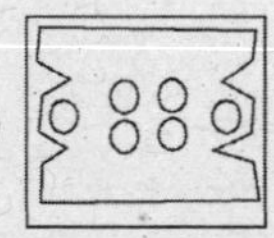 (b) 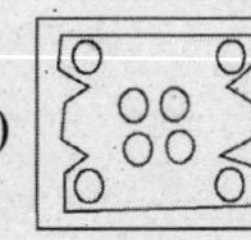

(c) 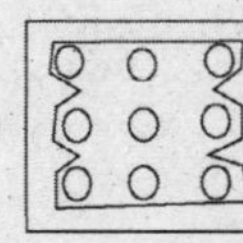 (d) 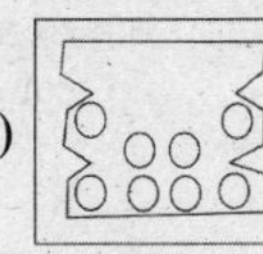

Answers with Explanations

1. (b) A piece of paper is folded and punched. When opened, it will appear as given below :

2. (c) A piece of paper is folded and punched. When opened, it will appear as given below :

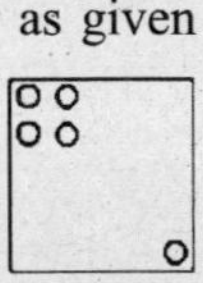

3. (b) A piece of paper is folded and punched. When opened, it will appear as:

4. (a) A piece of paper is folded and punched. When opened, it will appear as given below :

5. (b) A piece of paper is folded and punched. When opened it will appear as :

6. (d) A piece of paper is folded and punched. When opened it will appear as given below :

7. (a) A piece of paper is folded and punched. When opened it will appear as given below :

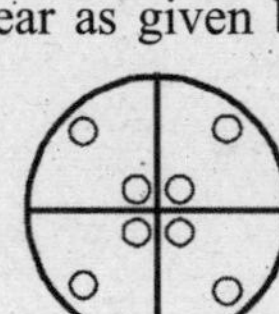

8. (a) A piece of paper is folded and punched. When opened it will appear as given below :

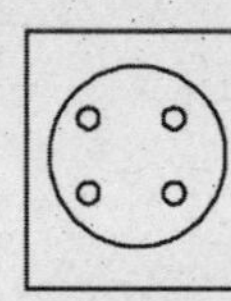

9. (c) A piece of paper is folded and punched. When opened, it will appear as given below :

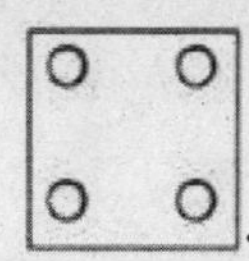

10. (b) A piece of paper is folded and punched.
When opened it will appear as given below :

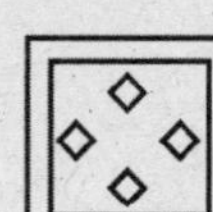

11. (c) A Piece of paper is folded and punched. When opened it will appear as given below :

12. (a) A piece of paper is folded and punched. When opened it will appear as given below :

13. (a) A piece of paper is folded and punched. When opened, it will appear as given below :

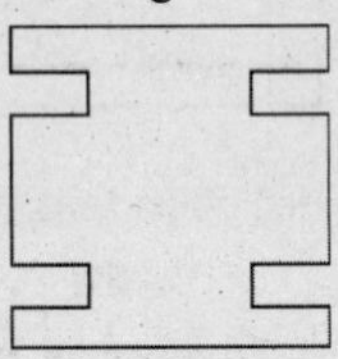

14. (a) A piece of paper is folded and punched. When opened it will appear as given below :

15. (a) A piece of paper is folded and punched. When opened, it will appear as given below :

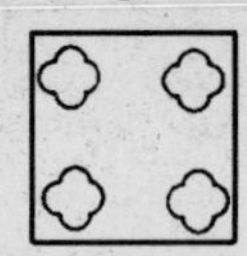

16. (a) A piece of paper is folded and punched. When opened it will appear as :

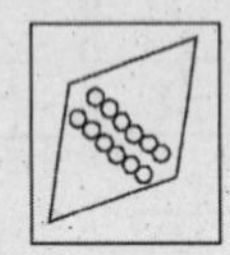

17. (b) A piece of paper is folded and punched. When opened it will appear as given below :

18. (c) According to question, a piece of paper is folded and punched, when opened it will appear as shown below:

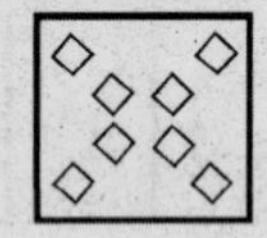

19. (a) After a piece of paper is folded and punched and opened it will appear as shown below :

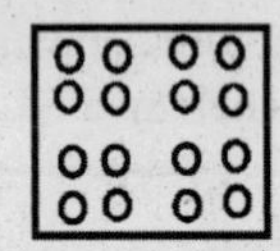

20. (b) A piece of paper is folded and punched. When opened it will appear as given below :

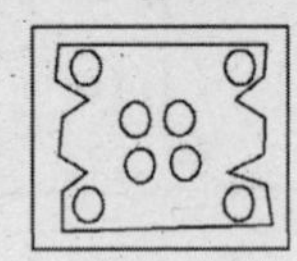

20 HIDDEN AND EMBEDDED FIGURE

"Hidden or Embedded" as the name suggests is a brain teasing exercise of figures hidden within other figure. These questions are asked under Non Verbal/Visual Reasoning branch of Reasoning Section.

Type 1: In such questions, a figure X is given, followed by 4 option figures. Candidate has to analyze the given options to find the hidden figure.

The option having X as embedded figure will be considered as the correct answer.

Let's try to understand this with the help of an example.

Example 1. Figure is embedded in any one of the given options. Mark the figure that contains X as answer.

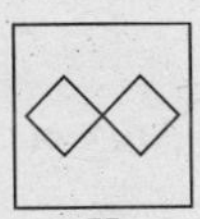

X

Answer Figures

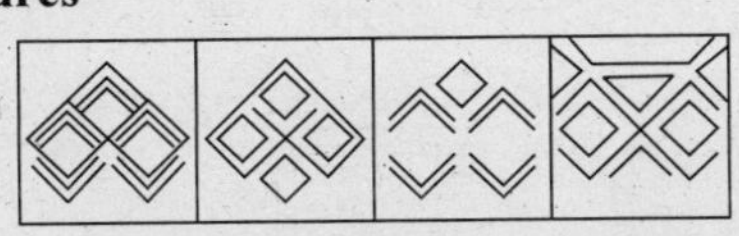

(a) (b) (c) (d)

Solution (a)

Explanation: If we see this figure this way

The figure X is found to be embedded under the given option (a).

Type 2: In such questions, a figure X is given, followed by 4 option figures. Candidate has to analyze the given options to find which of the given options is not there in the given question.

The option having X as embedded figure in given question will be considered as answer.

Example 2. Figure is embedded in any one of the given options. Mark the figure that contains X as answer.

X

Answer Figures

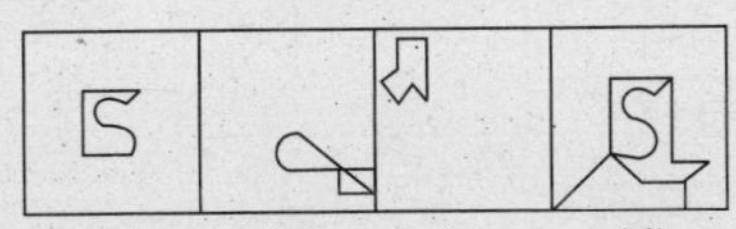

(a) (b) (c) (d)

Solution (c)

Explanation: All the given options except (c) can be found in the given figure.

Exercise

Direction (Q. No. 1-10): In each of the following questions, find the answer figure in which question figure is embedded.

1. Question Figure

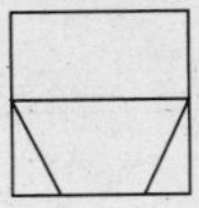

Answer Figures

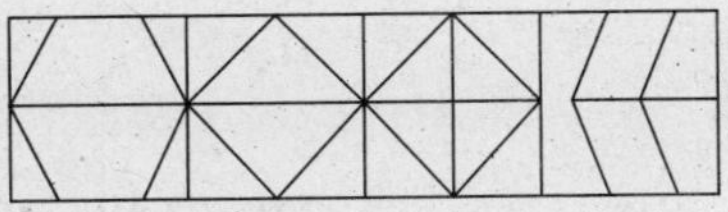

(a) (b) (c) (d)

2. Question Figure

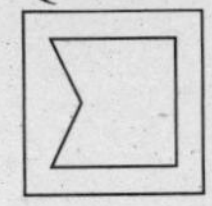

Answer Figures

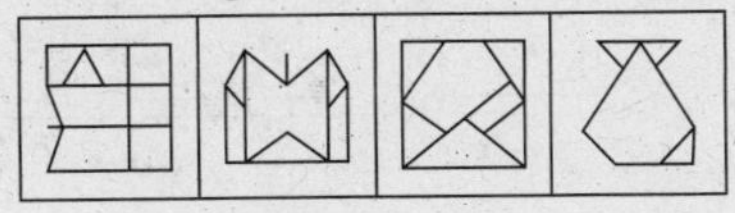

(a) (b) (c) (d)

3. Question Figure

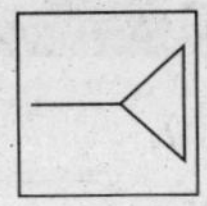

Answer Figures

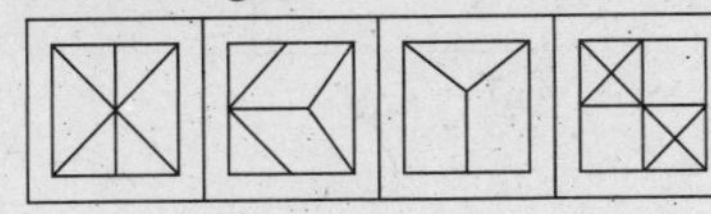

(a) (b) (c) (d)

4. Question Figure

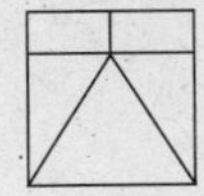

Answer Figures

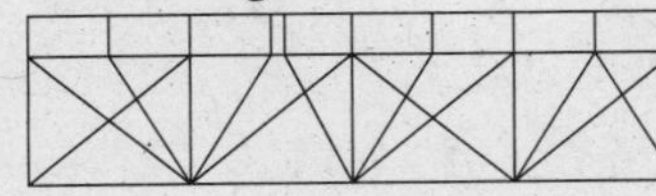

(a) (b) (c) (d)

5. Question Figure

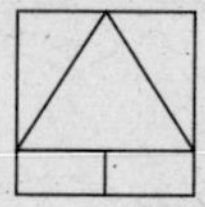

Answer Figures

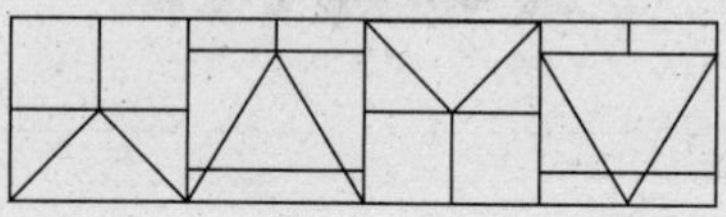

(a) (b) (c) (d)

6. Question Figure

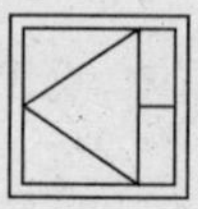

Answer Figures

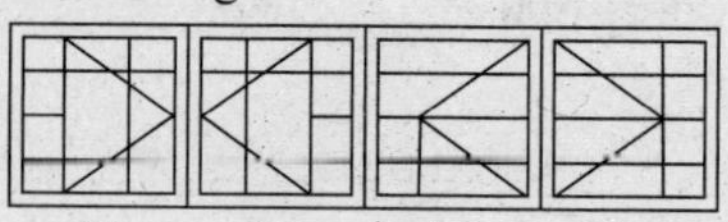

(a) (b) (c) (d)

7. Question Figure

Answer Figures

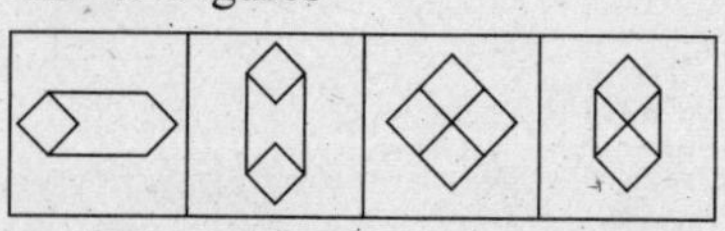

(a) (b) (c) (d)

8. Question Figure

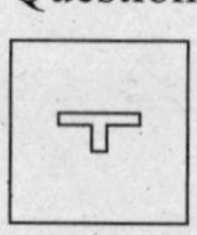

Answer Figures

(a) (b) (c) (d)

9. Question Figure

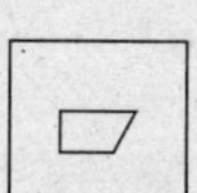

Answer Figures

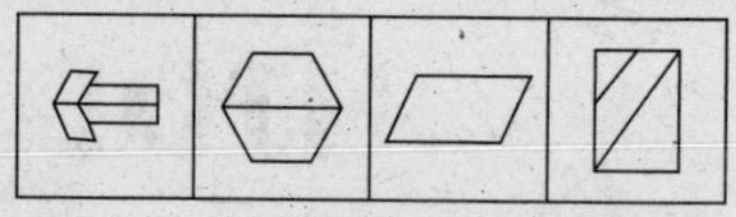

(a) (b) (c) (d)

10. Question Figure

Answer Figures

(a) (b) (c) (d)

Direction (Q. No. 11-17): In each of the following questions, choose the answer figure which is embedded in the question figure.

11. Question Figure

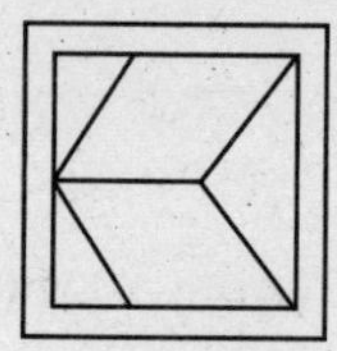

Answer Figures

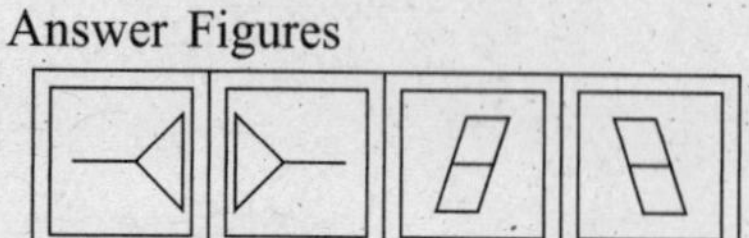

(a) (b) (c) (d)

12. Question Figure

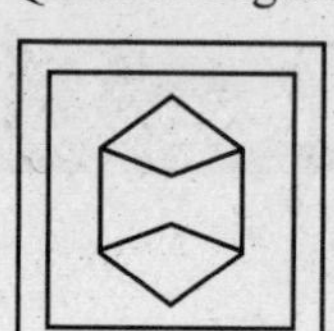

Answer Figures

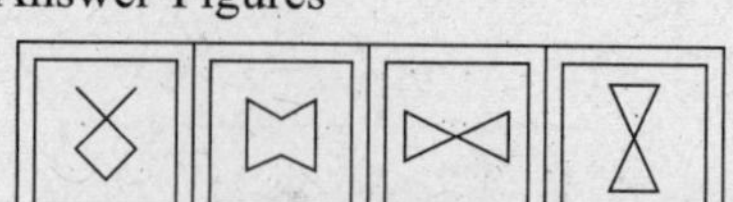

(a) (b) (c) (d)

13. Question Figure

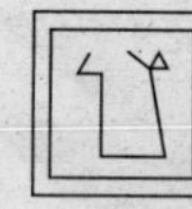

Answer Figures

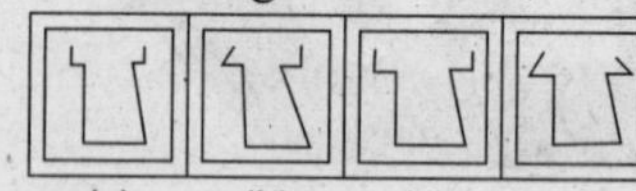

(a) (b) (c) (d)

14. Question Figure

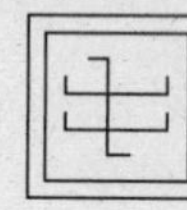

Answer Figures

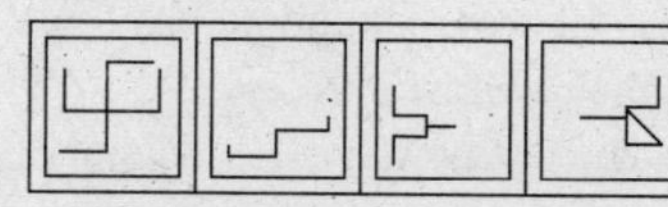

(a) (b) (c) (d)

15. Question Figure

Answer Figures

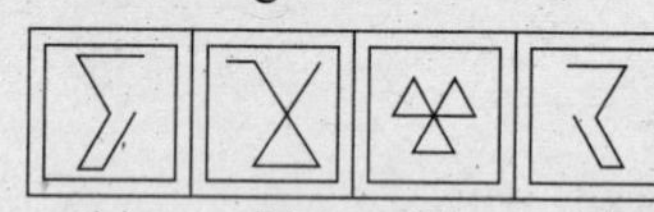

(a) (b) (c) (d)

16. Question Figure

Answer Figures

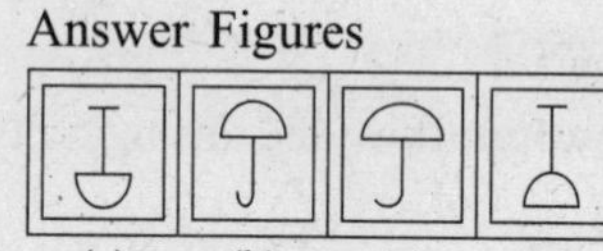

(a) (b) (c) (d)

17. Question Figure

Answer Figures

(a) (b) (c) (d)

Answers

1. (a) **2.** (a) **3.** (b) **4.** (d) **5.** (d) **6.** (b) **7.** (b) **8.** (a) **9.** (a) **10.** (a)
11. (a) **12.** (b) **13.** (d) **14.** (b) **15.** (a) **16.** (c) **17.** (d)

21 CUBES AND DICES

Cubes and Dices are basically two different concepts but always taken care under a common head as both the figures are 3D. These figures have common type of questions that can be solved using a common concept.

Let's try to figure it one by one.

Cubes and Cuboids

In a cube or cuboid, there are six faces. Cube has equal length, breadth and height whereas varying dimensions are there in cuboids.

Number of units in a cube = $(side)^3$, whereas

Number of units in a cuboid = $(l \times b \times h)$.

Let's try to figure out various types of questions asked under this topic.

Example: A cube of each side 4 cm has been painted black, red and green on pairs of opposite faces. It is then cut into small cubes of each side 1 cm. Then -

1. How many small cubes will be there?
2. How many small cubes will have three painted faces?
3. How many small cubes will have atleast two faces painted?
4. How many small cubes will have atleast one face painted?
5. How many small cubes will be only painted green?
6. How many small cubes will be only painted red?
7. How many small cubes will be only painted black?
8. How many small cubes will have only two faces painted black and red?
9. How many small cubes will have only two faces painted red and green?
10. How many small cubes will have one face painted?
11. How many small cubes will have only two faces painted black and green and all other faces unpainted?
12. How many small cubes will have no face painted?
13. How many small cubes will have only two faces painted?

Solution: The solution will be given as follows:

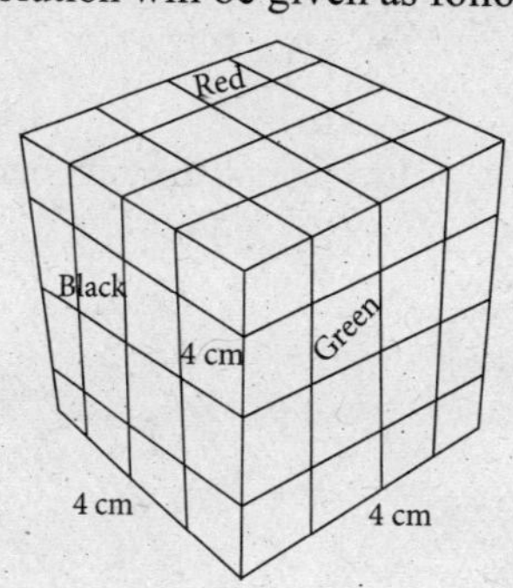

1. Total number of cubes = $(side)^3 = (4)^3 = 64$
2. Number of small cubes having three faces painted – Only the cubes at the corner will have all the three faces painted. Hence, the number of cubes will be 8.
3. Number of small cubes having at least two faces painted = (Number of cubes having 2 faces painted + 3 faces painted) = 24 + 8 = 32
4. Sides having atleast one side painted = Number of cubes having (1 face painted + 2 faces painted +3 faces painted) = 24 + 24 + 8 = 56
5. No of cubes having only green paint = 4 + 4 = 8
6. No. of cubes having only red paint = 4 + 4 = 8
7. No. of cubes having only black paint = 4 + 4 = 8
8. Number of cubes having two faces painted red and black = 4 + 4 = 8
9. Number of cubes having two faces painted red and green = 4 + 4 = 8
10. Number of cubes having only one face painted – Since there are 6 faces in big cube and each of the face of big cube there will be four such small cubes. Hence in all there will be 6 × 4 = 24 cubes
11. Number of cubes having two faces painted green and black = 4 + 4 = 8.

    These blocks will have no other paint.
12. No. of small cubes having no face painted = $(x - 2)^3 = (4 - 2)^3 = 8$
13. No. of cubes having only two faces painted = Total number of edges are 12, hence the no. of small cubes with two faces painted = 12 × 2 = 24.

DICES

Dice is also a type of cube with numbers 1 to 6 mentioned on each face. Only one number is written on one face. Sometimes faces are colored and black dots from 1 to 6 are marked.

Understanding the Concept

Under the concept, candidate has to answer the Question based on variation of numbers on various faces.

There are few set of rules to solve such type of questions.

Let there be a cube with sides as follows– ABCG, GCDE, DEFH, BCDH, AGEF and ABHF.

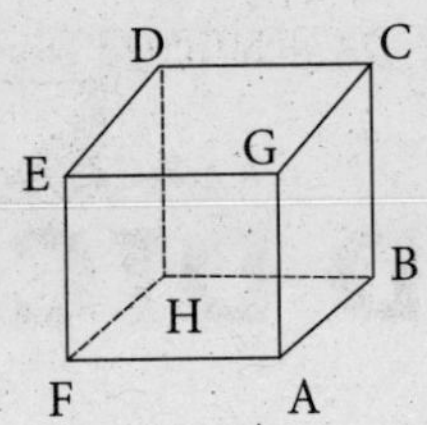

Rule 1: Two opposite faces cannot be adjacent.

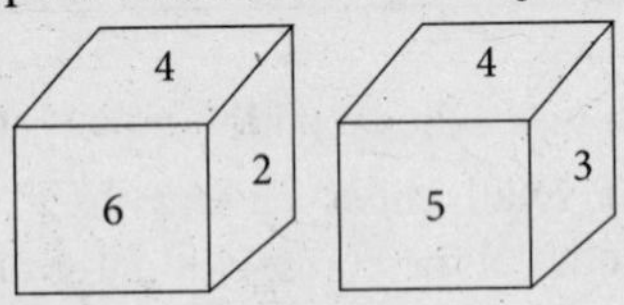

Rule 2: If two different positions of dice are shown and one of the two column faces is in same position then the remaining faces will be opposite to each other.

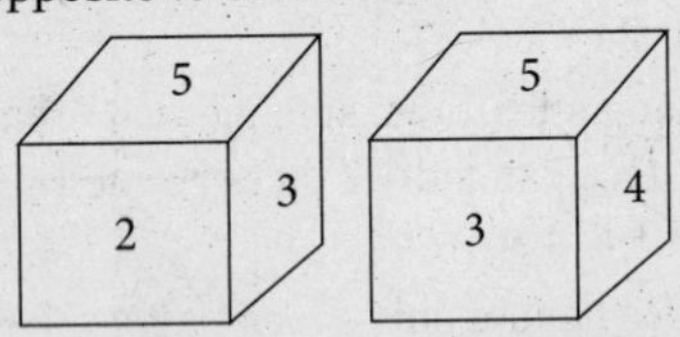

Rule 3: If in two different positions of dice, the position of the common face be same, then each of the opposite faces of remaining faces will be in same position.

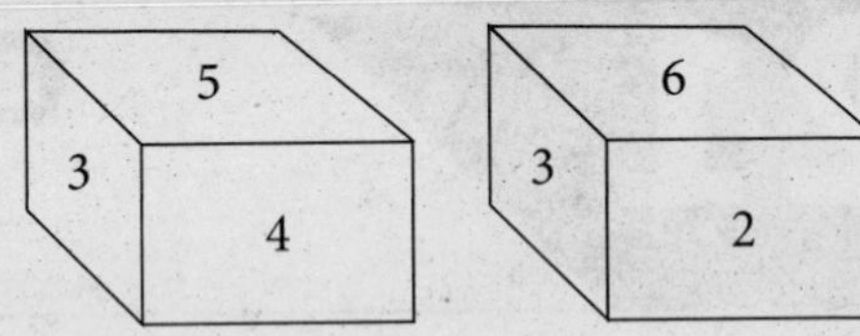

Rule 4: If in two positions of dice, the position of the common faces be not the same, then opposite face of the common face will be that which is not shown on any face of the two positions. Hence, the opposite faces of the remaining faces will not be the same.

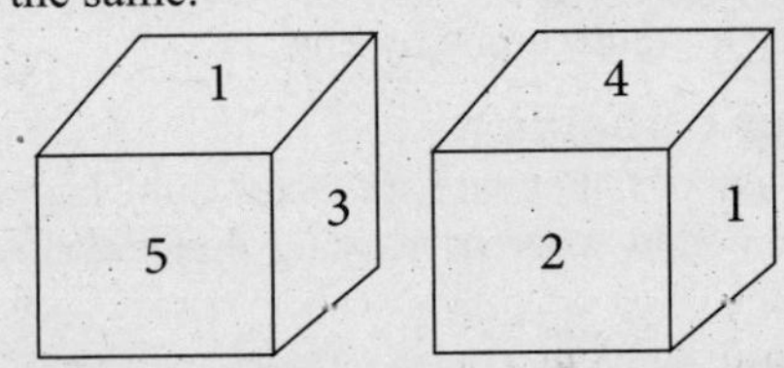

Let's concrete these concepts with the help of some Practice Questions.

Exercise

1. How many edges a cube/cuboid has?
(a) 4 (b) 12
(c) 16 (d) 10

2. A cube/cuboid has always
(a) 8 corners (b) 6 faces
(c) 12 edges (d) All of these

3. How many pair of opposite faces a cube/cuboid has?
(a) 4 (b) 2
(c) 5 (d) None of these

4. How many adjacent faces, each face of a cube has?
(a) 2 (b) 4
(c) 6 (d) 8

5. How many faces are hidden in a cube?
(a) 4 (b) 1
(c) 2 (d) 3

6. How many edges are invisible in a cube?
(a) 5 (b) 4
(c) 2 (d) 3

7. How many hidden corners are there in a cube?
(a) 3 (b) 6
(c) 1 (d) 5

8. Which of the following statements is true?
(a) Length, breadth and height of cube are equal
(b) A cube is a three dimensional body
(c) A cube has 12 edges out of which only 9 are visible at a time
(d) All of the above

9. How many smaller cubes of 1 cm side can be formed with a solid cube of 3 cm side?
(a) 3 (b) 6
(c) 9 (d) 27

10. How many times will a solid cube of 4 cm side be cut to obtain smaller cubes of 2 cm side?
(a) 2 (b) 3
(c) 5 (d) 7

11. Count the number of blocks in the given figure.

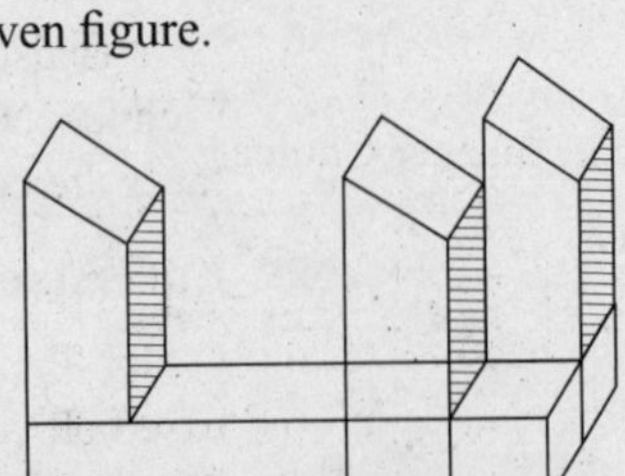

(a) 6 (b) 7
(c) 8 (d) 9

12. How may cubes are there in the diagram?

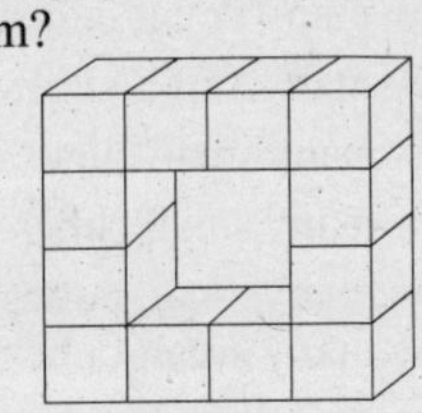

(a) 16 (b) 12
(c) 10 (d) 8

13. Count the number of cubes in the given figure.

(a) 8 (b) 9
(c) 12 (d) 15

14. Count the number of cubes in the given figure.

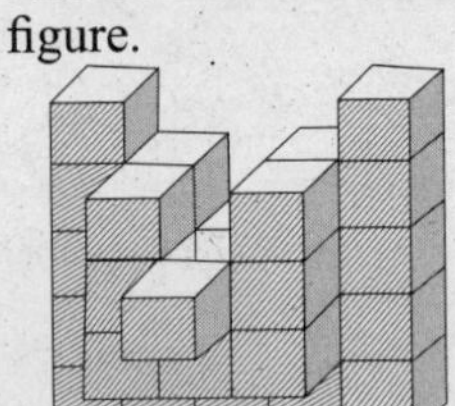

(a) 25 (b) 30
(c) 35 (d) 40

15. How many cubes are there in the group?

(a) 10 (b) 16
(c) 18 (d) 20

16. The four-different positions of a dice are given below:

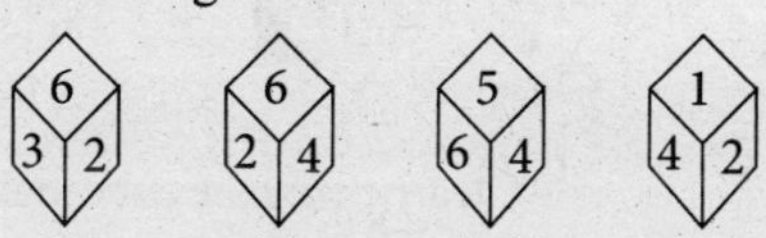

(i) (ii) (iii) (iv)

Which number is on the face opposite 6?

(a) 1
(b) 2
(c) 3
(d) 4

17. How many dots are there on the dice face opposite the one with three dots?

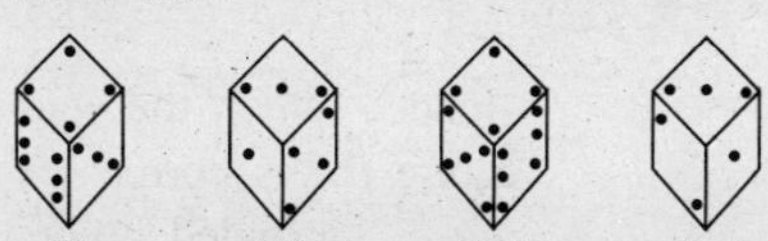

(i) (ii) (iii) (iv)

(a) 2
(b) 4
(c) 5
(d) 6

18. What number is opposite 3, if four different positions of a dice are as shown below?

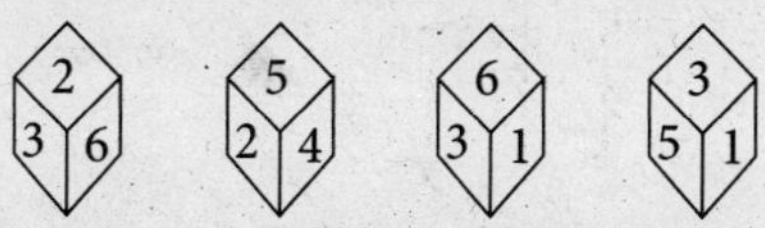

(i) (ii) (iii) (iv)

(a) 6
(b) 4
(c) 3
(d) 2

19. Shown below are four different positions of the same dice. Find the number on the face opposite the face showing 6.

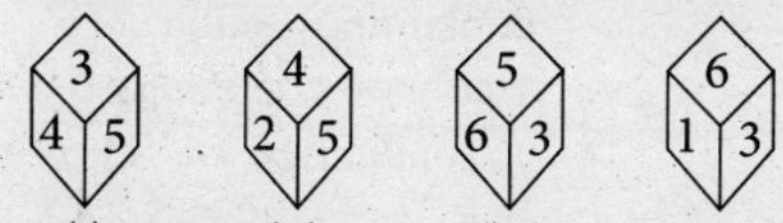

(i) (ii) (iii) (iv)

(a) 1
(b) 2
(c) 4
(d) 5

20. Which number is on the face opposite 4, if the four different positions of a dice are as shown in the figures given below?

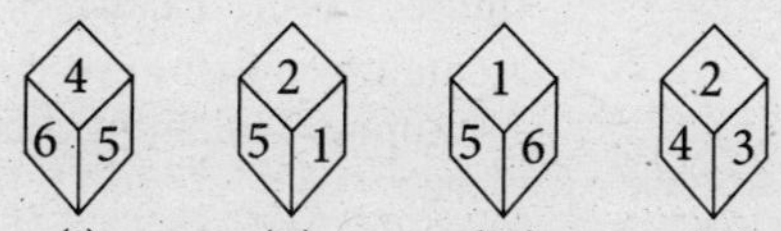

(i) (ii) (iii) (iv)

(a) 5
(b) 3
(c) 2
(d) 1

Directions (Q. No. 21-24) In each question given below, an unfolded dice is given in the left side while in the right side, four answer choices are given in the form of complete dices. You are required to select the correct answer choice(s) which is/are formed by folding the unfolded dice.

21. Unfolded Dice

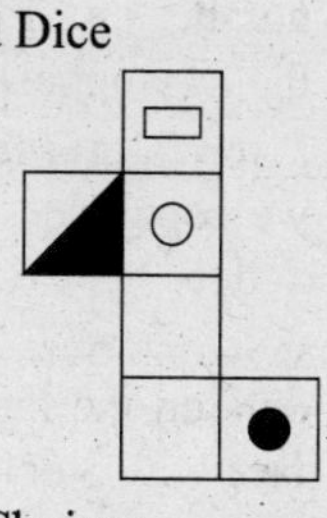

Answer Choices

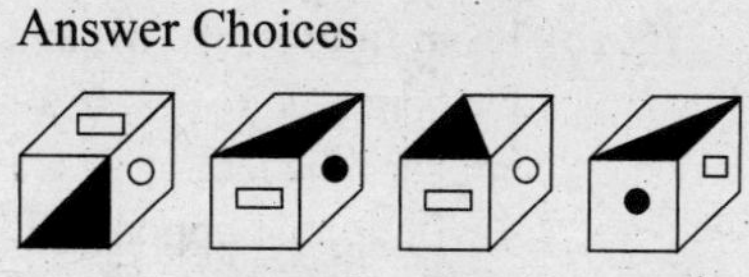

(a) (b) (c) (d)

22. Unfolded Dice

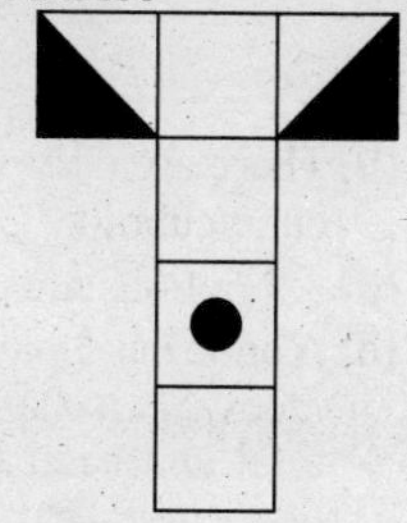

Answer Choices

(a) (b) (c) (d)

23. Unfolded Dice

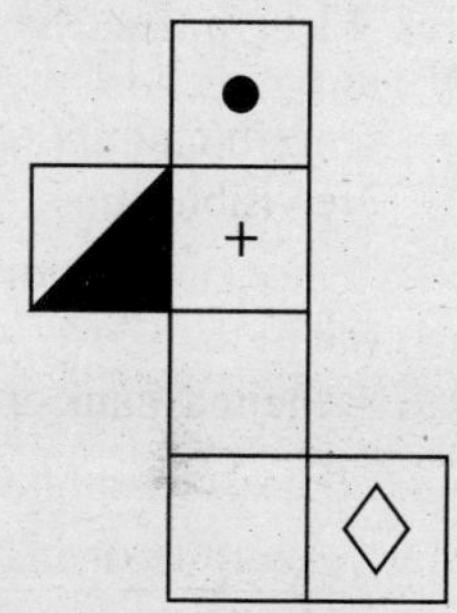

Answer Choices

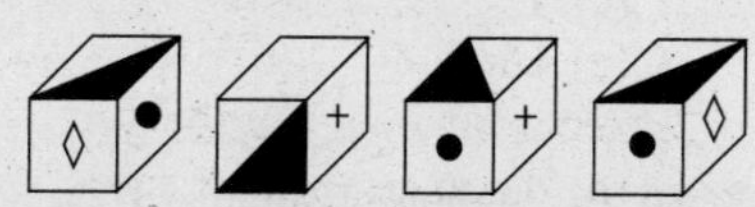

(a) (b) (c) (d)

24. Unfolded Dice

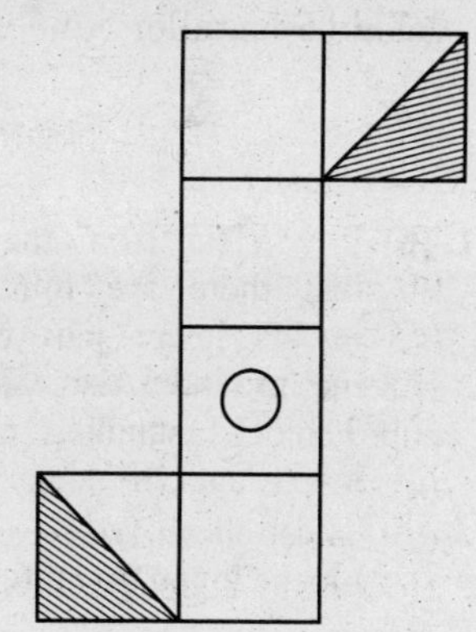

Answer Choices

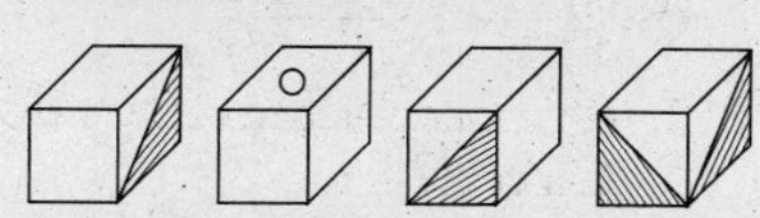

(a) (b) (c) (d)

Answers with Explanations

1. **(b)** There are only 12 edges in a cube/cuboid.
2. **(d)** All options are correct.
3. **(d)** A cube has 3 pair of opposite faces as it has 6 faces in total and each face has one opposite face.
4. **(b)** There are only 4 adjacent faces for each face of a cube.
5. **(d)** Hidden faces = 3.
6. **(d)** A cube has 12 edges out of which 9 are visible.

   $\therefore$ Invisible edges = 12 – 9 = 3
7. **(c)** When a cube is seen from any direction, then at a time a maximum of only 7 corners are visible out of 8.

   Hence, only 1 corner is hidden.
8. **(d)** All of the above.
9. **(d)** Required number of smaller cubes

$$= \frac{\text{Volume of bigger cube}}{\text{Volume of smaller cube}}$$

$$= \frac{(3)^3}{1^3} = (3)^3 = 27$$

10. **(b)** Required number of times

$$= \left(\frac{\text{Side of bigger cube}}{\text{Side of smaller cube}} - 1\right) \times 3$$

$$= \left(\frac{4}{2} - 1\right) \times 3 = (2 - 1) \times 3 = 3$$

11. **(b)** It is clear from the figure, that there are four blocks in the lower part close to the ground. Also, there are 3 blocks standing over the lower layer of blocks.

    Thus, there are 4 + 3 = 7 blocks in the given figure.
12. **(b)**

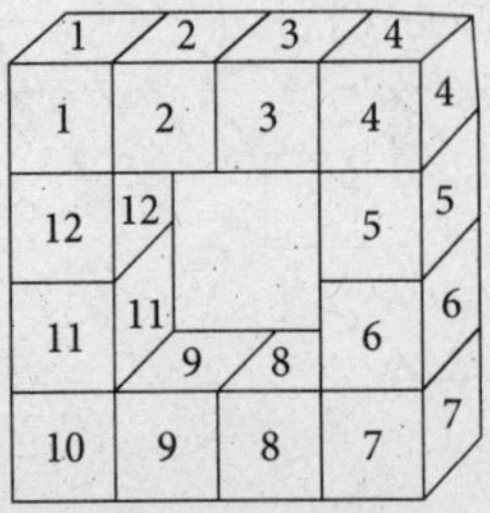

So, there are 12 cubes in the given figure, which are illustrated above.

13. **(d)** From the given question figure, it is clear that 4 columns containing 1 cube each

    1 column containing 3 cubes

    $\therefore$ Total cubes $= (4\times1)+(1\times3)+(4\times2) = 4+3+8 = 15$
14. **(b)** From the given question figure, it is clear that

    13 rows containing 1 cube each

    7 rows containing 2 cubes each

    1 row containing 3 cubes

    $\therefore$ Total cubes $= (13\times1)+(7\times2)+(1\times3) = 13+14+3 = 30$
15. **(d)** From the given question figure, it is clear that

    1 column containing 4 cubes

    2 columns containing 3 cubes each

    3 columns containing 2 cubes each

    4 columns containing 1 cube each

    $\therefore$ Total cubes $= (1\times4)+(2\times3)+(3\times2)+(4\times1) = 4+6+6+4 = 20$
16. **(a)** From figures (i), (ii) and (iii), we conclude that the numbers 2, 3, 4 and 5 appear adjacent to 6.

    Clearly, the remaining number i.e., 1 will appear on the face opposite 6.
17. **(c)** From figures (i), (ii) and (iv), we conclude that 6, 4, 1 and 2 dots appear adjacent to 3 dots. Clearly, there will be 5 dots on the face opposite the face with 3 dots.
18. **(b)** From figures (i), (iii) and (iv), we conclude that 2, 6, 1 and 5 appear adjacent to 3. Clearly, 4 will appear opposite 3.
19. **(c)** From figures (i), (ii) and (iii), we conclude that 3, 4, 2 and 6 lie adjacent to 5. Therefore, 1 must lie opposite 5.

    From figures (i), (iii) and (iv), we conclude that 4, 5, 6 and 1 lie adjacent to 3. Therefore, 2 must lie opposite 3. Now, we have 1 opposite 5 and 2 opposite 3. Hence, 4 must lie opposite 6.
20. **(d)** From figures (i) and (iv) we conclude that 6, 5, 2 and 3 lie adjacent to 4. It follows that 1 lies opposite 4.
21. **(a)** According to the question,

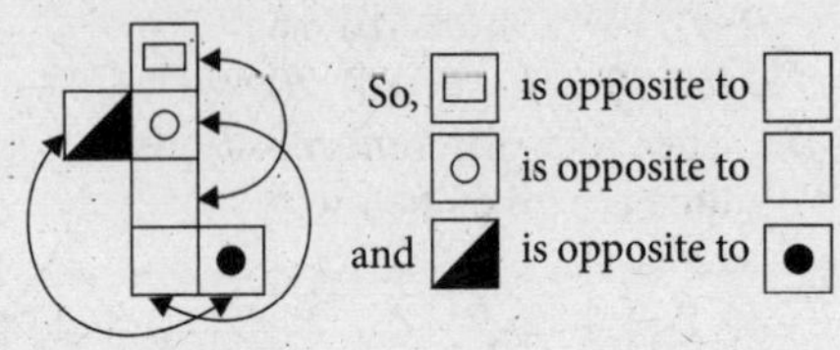

Clearly, only the cube in figure (a) is correct because when unfolded dice will be folded, this figure will be formed.

22. **(b)** According to the question,

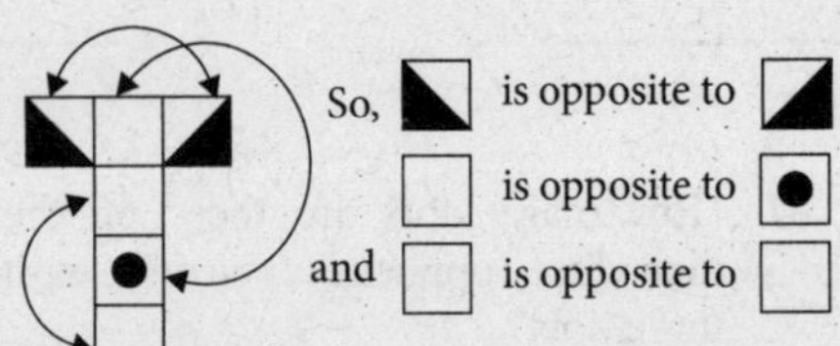

Hence, only the cube in figure (b) is correct because when unfolded dice will be folded, only this figure will be formed.

23. **(b)** As per the question,

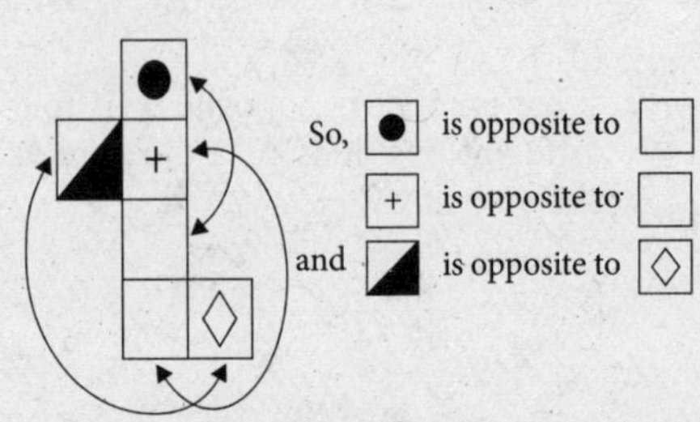

Hence, option (b) will be the correct answer.

24. (b) According to the question,

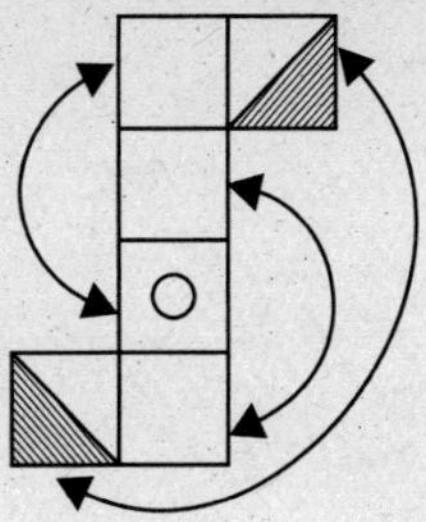

and

 is opposite to 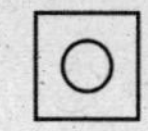

 is opposite to 

Clearly, option (b) is the correct answer.

General Knowledge and General Awareness

1 INDIAN HISTORY

ANCIENT INDIA

Indus Valley Civilisation

- The most accepted period–2500 BC-1750 BC (by Carbon-14 dating).
- **John Marshall** was the first scholar to use the term 'Indus Valley Civilisation'.
- The Indus Valley Civilisation belongs to Proto-historic Period (Chalcolithic Age/Bronze Age).
- **Dayaram Sahni** first discovered Harappa Civilisation in 1921.
- **R.D. Banerjee** discovered Mohenjodaro or **Mound of the Dead** in 1922.

Vedic Culture (1500 BC-600 BC)

- Boghazkai inscription (Asia Minor, Turkey) proves Central Asian Theory as their homeland.
- The group that came to India first settled in the present Frontier Province and the Punjab–then called **Sapta Sindhu**, i.e. region of seven rivers.
- Vedic literature comprises four literary productions: (1) The Samhitas or Vedas; (2) The Brahmanas; (3) The Aranyakas; (4) The Upanishads.
- There are four Vedas–Rigveda, Samaveda, Yajurveda and Atharvaveda. The first three Vedas are jointly called Vedatrayi, i.e. trio of Vedas.

RigVeda

- The oldest religious text in the world.
- Collection of hymns, composed around 1700 BC, contains 1,028 hymns and is divided into 10 mandalas.
- The third mandala contains the **Gayatri Mantra**.

Samaveda (Book of Chants)

It is a collection of melodies. It contains Dhrupad Raga.

YajurVeda

The beliefs and rituals of non-Aryans are written in it.

AtharvaVeda

It is a book of **magical formula.**

The Upanishads

They define the doctrine of Karma, Atman (soul), Brahma (God), and origin of Universe. There are 108 Upanishads.

Vedangs

- They are the limbs of the Vedas. These are treaties of Science and Arts.
- **There are six Vedangs:**
  i. Shiksha (Phonetics)
  ii. Kalpa Sutras (Rituals)
  iii. Vyakarana (Grammar)
  iv. Nirukta (Etymology)
  v. Chhanda (Metrics)
  vi. Jyotisha (Astronomy)
- Panini wrote Ashtadhyayi (4th century BC) on Vyakarana.

Upavedas

There are four Upavedas:

- **Ayurveda** (Upaveda of the Atharvaveda)
- **Dhanurveda** (Upaveda of the Rigveda)
- **Gandharvaveda** (Upaveda of the Samaveda)
- **Sthapatyaveda** (Upaveda of the Yajurveda)

Puranas

There are 18 famous 'Puranas'. **Matsya Purana** is the oldest Puranic text.

Sutras

Sutra literature is divided into three classes:

i. Srauta Sutra–Dealing with large public sacrifices
ii. Griha Sutra–Dealing with rituals connected with birth, naming, marriage
iii. Dharma Sutra–Explain social and local customs

Smritis also known as

- **Dharma Shastra** are the law books.
- **Manav Dharma Shastra or Manusmirti** is the oldest and most famous.

Epic

There are mainly two **Mahakavyas** (Epics):

i. **The Ramayana (Valmiki):** It is known as **Adi Kavya** (the oldest epic of the world). At present, it consists of 24,000 shlokas.
ii. **The Mahabharata (Ved Vyasa):** The longest epic of the world. At present, it consists of 1,00,000 shlokas, i.e., verses in 18 Parvans, i.e., chapters, plus the Harivamsa supplement.

RigVedic/Early Vedic Period (1500–1000 BC)

Geographical Area

- Rigveda is the only source of knowledge for this period.
- Early Vedic people had knowledge of rivers Yamuna, Saraswati (Nanditara) and Ganga, Ocean mentioned as Samudra (referred to collection of water and not sea), snow mountains (Himvat) and desert land (Dhawa).
- **The Purohita** or domestic priest was the first ranking official.
- Rigveda speaks of assemblies, such as the **Sabha, Samiti, Vidath and Gana**.
- Sabha was committee of few privileged and important individuals.

Society

- The Rig-vedic society comprised four varnas, namely **Brahmana, Kshatriya, Vaishya** and **Shudra**. This classification of society was based on the professions or occupations of the individuals.
- Child marriage was not in vogue.
- The cow was already deemed **Aghanya**, i.e. not to be killed.

➢ Alcoholic drinks, **Sura** and **Soma** were also consumed.

Religion

➢ **Indra, Agni** and **Varuna** were the most popular deities of Rigvedic Aryans. **Savitri was the god of light.** The famous Gayatri Mantra is addressed to her.

➢ Their religion primarily consisted of the worship of gods but **Yajna** or sacrifice became more important.

Later Vedic Period (1000 BC-600 BC)

With reference to the territorial divisions, the later Vedas give three broad divisions of India, viz. **Aryavarta** (Northern India), **Madhyadesa** (Central India) and **Dakshinapath** (Southern India).

Magadha Empire

➢ The period from 6th century BC to 4th century BC saw the struggle for supremacy among four mahajanapadas–Magadha, Kosala, Vatsa and Avanti.

➢ The founder of Magadha was **Jarasandha** and **Brihadratha**.

Nanda Dynasty (344 BC-323 BC)

Mahapadmananda

➢ The Shishunaga dynasty was overthrown by **Mahapadma**.

➢ It is considered to be the first non-Kshatriya dynasty and ruled for 100 years.

➢ He conquered **Kosala** and **Kalinga**.

Dhanananda

➢ The last king Dhanananda is possibly identical with the **Agrammes** or **Xandrames** of the Greek texts.

➢ It was during the rule of Dhanananda that the invasion of Alexander took place in north-west India in 326 BC.

➢ The Nanda dynasty came to an end about 322–21 BC and was supplanted by another dynasty known as Mauryas, with **Chandragupta Maurya** as the founder.

Religious Movements (600 BC-400 BC)

Buddhism: Buddha's Life

Gautama Buddha, founder of Buddhism, was born in 563 BC (widely accepted), on the Vaishakha Purnima day at **Lumbinivana** in **Kapilvastu** (now situated in the foothills of Nepal) in the **Sakya Kshatriya** clan.

Major Events of Buddha's Life

Events	Symbols
Janma (Birth)	Lotus and Bull
Mahabhinishkramana (Renunciation)	Horse
Nirvana (Sambodhi Enlightenment)	Bodhi tree
Dharmachakra Paravartan First Sermon	Wheel
Mahaparinirvana (Death)	Stupa

Teachings of Buddha

(a) His four Noble Truths:

1. The world is full of sorrows.
2. The cause of sorrow is desire, Dwadash Nidan/Pratitya Samutpada.
3. If desires are conquered, all sorrows can be removed, Nirvana.
4. This can be achieved by following the eight-fold path, Ashtangika Marga.

(b) Eight-fold Path:

(Ashtangika marga)

- Right understanding
- Right thought
- Right speech
- Right action
- Right livelihood
- Right effort
- Right mindfulness
- Right concentration.

(c) Three Jewels (Triratnas):

- Buddha
- Dhamma
- Sangha

Buddhist Sangha

It consisted of monks (Bhikshus or Shramanas) and nuns, who acted as a torchbearer of the dhamma. The worshippers were called upasakas.

Jainism

➢ It was founded by Rishabhnath.

➢ According to Jain tradition, there were 24 **Tirthankaras** the first being Rishabhadeva/Adinatha and the last being Mahavira.

➢ The name of two Jain Tirthankaras–**Rishabha** and **Arishtanemi** are found in the **Rigveda**.

Doctrines of Jainism

➢ **Triratnas, i.e., Three Gems of Jainism**

1. **Samyak Shradha/Vishwas (right faith):** It is the belief in Tirthankaras.
2. **Samyak Gyan (right knowledge):** It is the knowledge of the Jain creed.
3. **Samyak Karma/Acharana (right action/conduct):** It is the practice of the five vows of **Jainism**.

Five Carinal Principles

- Non-injury (Ahimsa).
- Non-lying (Satya).
- Non-stealing (Asteya).
- Non-possession (Aparigraha).
- Observing continence (Brahmacharya).

➢ The first four principles were given by Parshvnath while fifth was added by Lord Mahavira.

Jain Literature

➢ The sacred literature of the Svetambaras is written in a **Prakrit**.

➢ The important Jain texts are: (i) **Kalpasutra** (in Sanskrit)–Bhadrabahu, (ii) **Bhadrabahu Charita**, (iii) **Parishishta Parvan** (an appendix of **Trishashthi-shalaka Purush**) –Hemchandra.

Jain Councils

➢ First Jain council was held at Pataliputra in the fourth century BC under the leadership of Stulabahu.

➢ Second Jain council was at Vallabhi in Gujarat in third century under the leadership of Aryaskandil Nagarjuna Suri.

➢ Third Jain council was held at Vallabhi in 5th century A.D. under the leadership of Devardhi Kshama Sramana.

Origin of the Mauryas

Chandragupta Maurya (322 BC-298 BC)

➢ Also called **Sandrocottus/ Androcottus** by the Greek scholars.

➢ He dethroned the last Nanda ruler Dhanananda and founded the Mauryan dynasty with capital at Patliputra.

➢ Chandragupta defeated Seleucus I Nicator, the general of Alexander in North-West India in 305 BC.

➢ Seleucus sent a Greek Ambassador, **Megasthenes**, to the court of Chandragupta Maurya.

- Chandragupta embraced Jainism and went to Chandragiri Hill, at Shravanbelagola with Bhadrabahu, where he died of slow starvation (Salekhan).
- Chandragupta was the first Indian ruler to unite the whole North India.

Ashoka (273 BC-232 BC)

- He was the greatest Mauryan ruler whose empire extended to the whole of sub-continent except extreme south. It included Afghanistan, Baluchistan, Kashmir and valleys of Nepal.
- According to Buddhist tradition, Ashoka usurped the throne after killing his 99 brothers and spared **Tissa**, the youngest one.
- Ashoka had himself formally crowned in 269 BC.
- Ashoka fought the **Kalinga War** in 261 BC in the 9th year of his coronation.
- He embraced Buddhism under **Upagupta**.
- He sent his son Mahendra and daughter Sanghamitra to Ceylon as Buddhist missionaries with a sapling of original peepal tree.
- He inaugurated **Dhamma Yatras** from the 11th year of his reign by visiting Bodh Gaya; also appointed Dhamma Mahamatras (officer of righteousness to spread the message of Dhamma).

Ashoka's Dhamma

Its broad objective was to preserve the social order it ordained that people should obey their parents, pay respect to Brahmans and Buddhist monks show mercy to slaves and servants.

Later Mauryas
(232 BC-185 BC)

The last Mauryan ruler, **Brihadratha**, was assassinated in 185 BC by his commander-in-chief, **Pushyamitra Sunga**.

Post-Maurya/Pre-Gupta Period (185 BC-319 AD)

The Sunga Dynasty (185 BC to 73 BC)

- Sunga Dynasty was established by **Pushyamitra Sunga**, a Brahmin Commander-in-Chief of the last Mauryan ruler named Brihadratha in 185 BC.
- He is considered to be the persecutor of Buddhism.
- Pushyamitra was succeeded by his son **Agnimitra**, the hero of Kalidasa's drama **Malavikagnimitra**.
- **Patanjali**, author of the **Mahabhasya** was the priest of two Ashvamedha Yaggas, performed by Pushyamitra Sunga.
- The famous book on Hindu law **Manusmriti** was compiled during this period.

Kanva Dynasty (73 BC-28 BC)

- In 73 BC, Devabhuti, the last ruler of the Sunga dynasty, was murdered by his minister **Vasudeva**, who usurped the throne and founded the Kanva dynasty.
- The last ruler, Susarman, was killed by Andhra King, Simuka.

Satavahana Dynasty (60 BC-225 AD)

Capital–Pratishthan-Paithan (Maharashtra)

- **Simuka** (60 BC-37 BC) was the founder of the Satavahana Dynasty.
- **Gautamiputra Satakarni** revived the Satavahana power and defeated the Saka Ksatrap Snehapana. He was the greatest Satavahana ruler.
- **Pulamayi III** was the last Satavahana ruler.
- **Stupas:** The most famous of these attributed to the Satavahana period are **Amravati**, a sculptural treasure house, and **Nagarjunakonda**.
- The official language of the Satvahanas was **Prakrit**.

Foreign Successors of Mauryas

The Sakas (1st Century BC-4th Century AD)

- The **Sakas**, also known as **Scythians**, replaced the Indo-Greeks in India.
- The most famous Saka ruler in India was **Rudradaman** (130 AD).
- In about 58 BC, the king of Ujjain, Vikramaditya is supposed to have fought effectively against the Sakas. An era called **Vikrama Samvat** is reckoned from 58 BC.

The Kushanas (1st Century AD-3rd Century AD)

- Kushanas replaced the Greeks and Parthians.
- Their capitals were at **Peshawar (Purushapura)** and **Mathura**.
- The most famous Kushana ruler was Kanishka, also known as 'Second Ashoka'. He started an era in 78 AD which is now known as the **Saka Era** and is used by the Government of India.
- Kanishka was a great patron of Mahayana Buddhism. In his reign, **4th Buddhist Council** was held in **Kundalavana, Kashmir** where the doctrines of the Mahayana form of Buddhism were finalised.
- The Kushanas controlled the famous **silk route**.
- The Kushanas were the first rulers in India to issue gold coins on a wide scale.
- In the royal court of Kanishka, a host of scholars found patronage. **Parsva, Vasumitra, Asvaghosha, Nagarjuna, Charaka** and **Mathara** were some of them.
- Kushana Empire gave rise to Gandhara and Mathura Schools of Art.
- Vatsyayana wrote **Kamasutra** in this period.

Gupta Period (319 AD-540 AD)

- This period is referred to as the Classical Age or Golden Age of ancient India.
- Sri Gupta was the founder of the Gupta dynasty. Sri Gupta was followed by his son Ghatotkacha and he was followed by his son Chandragupta. Both used the simple title of Maharaja.

Chandragupta I (319AD-334 AD)

- He was the first Gupta ruler to assume the title of **Maharajadhiraja**.
- He started the **Gupta Era** in 319AD-320 AD.

Samudragupta (335AD-380 AD)

- Samudragupta was the greatest king of the Gupta dynasty.
- Samudragupta's military campaigns justify description of him as the **Napoleon of India** by **V.A. Smith**.

Chandragupta (II) (380AD-414 AD)

- **Chandragupta II conquered Western Malwa and Gujarat, from the Shaka Kshatrapas Rudrasena III.**
- He issued silver coins in the memory of victory over Sakas. He was the first Gupta ruler to issue silver coins and adopted the titles **Sakari** and **Vikramaditya**.

- It was in Chandragupta's time that the Chinese pilgrim **Fahien** visited India.

Navratna (Nine Gems) of Chandragupta II

1. Kalidasa (Poetry: Ritusamhara, Meghadutam Abhijnan Shakuntalam).
2. Amarsinh (Amarsinh Kosha)
3. Dhanvantri (Navanitakam medicine text)
4. Varahamihira (Pancha Siddhantika)
5. Vararuchi
6. Ghatakarna
7. Kahapranak
8. Velabhatta
9. Shanku

Kumaragupta I (415AD-455AD)

He founded the **Nalanda Mahavihara** which developed into a great centre of learning.

Skandagupta (455AD-467 AD)

- He repulsed the ferocious Hunas' attacks twice. The heroic feat entitled him the title **Vikramaditya** (Bhitari Pillar Inscription).
- During his period, Sudarshana Lake was repaired and its embankments were rebuilt.

Contribution of Gupta Rulers

- **City Administration:** Paura was the council responsible for city administration.
- **Army Military:** Chariots receded into the background and **cavalry** came to the forefront.
- **Senabhakta:** It was a form of tax.
- **Revenue:** Land revenue was the chief source of states' income.
- **Judiciary:** For the first time, civil and criminal laws were clearly defined and demarcated.
- **Coinage:** Guptas issued the largest number of gold coins, which were called **Dinaras** in their inscriptions. Silver coins were called **Rupayakas**.

MEDIEVAL INDIA

Delhi Sultanate (1206 AD-1526 AD)

- First Muslim invasion by Mohammad bin Qasim (712 AD).
- First Turkish Invasion by Mahmud Ghaznavi (998 AD-1030 AD): Sultan Mahmud of Ghazni. In 1025, he attacked and raided the most celebrated Hindu temple of Somnath.

Mahmud of Ghazni

- He patronised three persons, contemporary to him: **Firdausi** (court poet), **Al Beruni** (scholar) and **Utbi** (court historian).
- Al Beruni wrote Kitab-ul-Hind.
- Mahmud is said to have made **17 raids** into India. A decisive battle between Mahmud and Anandpala was fought in 1008AD-1009 AD at **Waihind** during his sixth expedition.
- In 1194 AD, Jaichand of Kannauj was also defeated at the **Battle of Chandawar**.
- **Second Turk Invasion-Mohammad Ghori's invasion (1175 AD-1206 AD):** Mohammad Ghori invaded India and laid the foundation of the Muslim domination in India. He may be considered the founder of Muslim rule in India.

The Slave Dynasty (1206 AD-1290 AD)

Qutubuddin Aibak (1206 AD-1210 AD)

- A Turkish slave by origin after the death of Ghori, Aibak founded the Slave Dynasty in 1206 AD. For his generosity, he was given the title of **Lakh Baksh** (giver of lakhs).
- He died in 1210 AD while playing **Chaugan** or polo.
- He constructed two mosques, **Quwwat-ul-Islam** in Delhi and **Adhai din ka Jhonpra** in Ajmer. He also began the construction of **Qutub Minar**, in honour of famous Sufi Saint, **Khwaja Qutubuddin Bakhtiyar Kaki**.

Aram Shah (1210 AD)

After Qutubuddin's death, his son Aram Shah succeeded him.

Razia Sultan (1236 AD-1240 AD)

She was the first and Muslim woman ruler of Medieval India.

Balban (1266 AD-1287 AD)

- He himself was a member of Chalisa or Chahalgani but he broke the power of Chahalgani and restored the prestige of the crown.
- He created a strong centralised army and established the military department **Diwan-i-Arz**. He ordered the separation of military affairs from finance department (Diwan-i-Wazarat).

The Khilji Dynasty (1290 AD-1320 AD)

Jalaluddin Khilji

- He was the first ruler of Delhi Sultanate to clearly put forward the view that the state should be based on the willing support of the governed and that since the large majority of the people in India were Hindus, the state in India could not be a truly Islamic State.
- The most important aspect of his reign was invasion of Devagiri in 1294 AD by his nephew and son-in-law Alauddin Khilji.

Alauddin Khilji (1296 AD-1316AD)

- He came to the throne by treacherously murdering his uncle and father-in-law Jalaluddin Khilji.
- He was the first Turkish Sultan who separated religion from politics.

The Tughlaq Dynasty (1320 AD-1414 AD)

Ghiyasuddin Tughlaq

- Ghazi Malik or Ghiyasuddin Tughlaq was the founder of Tughlaq dynasty.
- He was the first sultan of Delhi who took up the title of Ghazi or **slayer of the infidels**.
- **Construction of canals** and formulation of a **famine policy**.
- Started the barter system or sharing of crops.
- He built the city of **Tughlaqabad** near Delhi and made it his capital.
- Sufi saint, Shaikh Nizam-ud-din Aulia said Delhi is far away in regard to him.
- He died in 1325 AD, after a fall from a high-raised pavilion.

Mohammad Bin Tughlaq (1325AD-1351AD)

- Prince **Jauan**, son of Ghiyasuddin Tughlaq, ascended the throne in 1325 AD.

- Transfered the Capital (1327 AD) from Delhi to Devagiri, which was thus named Daulatabad.
- The famous Moroccan traveller Ibn Batuta came to Delhi in 1334 AD and acted as the Qazi of the capital for eight years. He recorded the contemporary Indian science in his **Safranamah** (Rahela).

Firoz Shah Tughlaq (1351 AD-1388 AD)

- He decreed that whenever a noble died, his son should be allowed to succeed to his position.
- It was during the time of Firoz that **Jizya** became a separate tax. Firoz refused to exempt the Brahmanas from payment of Jizya.
- He was a great builder. The cities of Fatehabad, Hisar, Jaunpur and Firozabad stand to his credit.
- Barani, the historian, was in his court. He wrote **Tarikh-i-Feroshahi** and **Fatwa-i-Jahangiri**.

Timur's Invasion (1398 AD-1399 AD)
Timur, the lame, a Turkish Chief invaded India in 1398 during the reign of **Muhammad Shah Tughlaq**, the last ruler of Tughlaq dynasty. Timur returned to Central Asia, leaving a nominee named Khizr Khan to rule in Punjab.

The Lodhi Dynasty (1451 AD-1526 AD)

Bahlol Lodhi (1451 AD-1488 AD)

- Founder of Lodhi dynasty in India.
- Never sat on throne, used to sit on carpets along with Anines.

Sikandar Lodhi (1489 AD-1517AD)

- Noblest of the three Lodhi rulers, real name was **Nizam Khan** (son of Bahlol Lodhi).
- He built a new city named Agra, and made it his capital.
- He was a poet and wrote verses in Persian under the pet name **Gularukh**.

Ibrahim Lodhi (1517 AD-1526AD)

- He was the last king of the Lodhi dynasty and the last sultan of Delhi.
- He was defeated and killed at the hands of Babur in the **First Battle of Panipat in 1526 AD**.

Amir Khusro

- He was a Persian poet (1253 AD-1325 AD) associated with royal courts of more than seven rulers of the Delhi Sultanate.
- He was also a musician, he invented sitar.
- He innovated **Khayal** (a style of singing).
- In his book **Tarikh-i-Alai**, he gave an account of conquest of Alauddin Khilji.
- He also lived in the court of Ghiyasuddin Tughlaq and wrote **Tughlaqnamah**.
- Khusro is also known as **Tuti-i-Hind** or 'Parrot of India'.

Vijayanagar and Other Kingdoms

Vijayanagar Empire (1336 AD-1580 AD)

- Vijayanagar kingdom and the city were founded by Harihar and Bukka.
- They were brought to the centre by Muhammad-bin-Tughlaq, converted to Islam and were sent to South to control rebellion but motivated by a Bhakti saint Vidyaranya, they established Vijayanagar kingdom in 1336 AD.
- Vijayanagar period can be divided into four distinct dynasties, viz. Sangam, Saluva, Tuluva and Aravidu.

Bahamani Kingdom

- The Bahamani kingdom of Deccan was founded by **Hasan Gangu**. The capital was Gulbarga. Hasan Gangu took the title of Alauddin Hasan Bahaman Shah and became the first king of Bahaman in 1347AD.
- The last ruler of Bahamani kingdom was **Kalim Ullah Shah**.
- **Nizam Shahis of Ahmadnagar**. Founder–Ahmad Nizam Shah, later annexed by Shahjahan.
- **Muhammad Quli Qutab Shah** was the greatest of all. He founded the city of **Hyderabad**. He built the famous **Charminar**. The kingdom was annexed by Aurangzeb (1687 AD).

Mughal Period (1526 AD-1540AD and 1555 AD-1857 AD)

Babur (1526 AD-1530 AD)

- The foundation of the Mughal rule in India was laid by Babur in 1526 AD.
- Babur defeated **Ibrahim Lodhi** in the **First Battle of Panipat** on April 21, 1526 AD and established the Mughal dynasty.
- In 1527 AD, he defeated **Rana Sanga** of Mewar at **Khanwa**.
- In 1528 AD, he defeated **Medini Rai** of **Chaneri** at **Chanderi**.
- In 1529 AD, he defeated Muhammad Lodhi (uncle of Ibrahim Lodhi) at **Ghaghra**.
- He wrote his autobiography **Tuzuk-i-Baburi** in Turki language.

Humayun (1530 AD-1540 AD and 1555 AD-1556 AD)

- His first campaign was against **Kalinjar**.
- **Battle of Chausa** (1539 AD) was fought between **Sher Shah** and **Humayun's** army. **Humayun** was badly defeated and escaped. He was saved by **Nizam**.
- **Battle of Kannauj (Bilgrama) (1540 AD):** Humayun was again defeated by Sher Shah.
- **Bairam Khan**, his most faithful officer, helped him. After the battle of Machhiwara against the Afghans and battle of Sirhind against Sikandar Shah, Humayun's second coronation was organised.
- His sister, **Gulbadan Begum** wrote his biography **Humayunama.**

Sher Shah Suri and the Afghan Empire (1540 AD-1555 AD)

- His real name was **Farid**.
- He usurped the throne as 'Hazarat-i-Ala'.
- **Battle of Chausa:** In 1539 AD, he captured Chausa from Humayun. He assumed the title of Sher Shah as the emperor.
- **Malik-Mohammed Jayasi** wrote **Padmavat** (Hindi) during his reign.

Akbar (1556 AD-1605 AD)

- Akbar, the eldest son of Humayun, ascended the throne under the title of **Jalaluddin Muhammad Akbar Badshah Ghazi** at the young age of 14 at **Kalanaur, Punjab** and his tutor **Bairam Khan** was appointed as the regent.
- **Second Battle of Panipat (5th November, 1556)** was fought between **Hemu** (the Hindu General of Muhammad Adil Shah) and **Bairam Khan** (the regent of Akbar). **Hemu** was defeated, captured and slained by **Bairam Khan**.

- He also ended the interference from **Peticoat Government** (1560 AD-1562 AD) represented by **Maham Anaga** and **Adham Khan Junta**.
- The **Battle of Haldighati** (1576 AD) was fought between **Rana Pratap** of Mewar and Mughal army led by **Man Singh** of Amer. Rana Pratap was defeated.
- Akbar proclaimed a new religion, Din-i-Ilahi, in 1581 AD.
- Birbal was the only Hindu who followed this new religion Din-i-Ilahi. However, it did not become popular.
- Tulsidas **(Ramcharitmanas)** also lived during Akbar's period.
- Abul Fazal wrote ***Akbarnama***, the appendix of which was called **Ain-i-Akbari**.

Navratnas in Akbar's Court

1. **Abul Fazal**
2. **Faizi**
3. **Tansen**
4. **Birbal**
5. **Raja Todar Mal**
6. **Raja Man Singh I**
7. **Abdul Rahim Khan-I-Khana**
8. **Fakir Aziao-Din**
9. **Mulla Do-Piyaza**

Jahangir (1605 AD-1627 AD)

- Salim, son of Akbar, came to the throne after Akbar's death in 1605 AD.
- In 1608 AD, **Captain William Hawkins**, a representative of East India Company, came to Jahangir's court. **Sir Thomas Roe**, an ambassador of King James I of England, also came to his court. Jahangir granted permission to the English to establish a trading port at Surat.
- He wrote his memories **Tuzuk-i-Jahangiri** in Persian.

Shahjahan (1628 AD-1658 AD)

- His real name was **Khurram**. He was the youngest prince to be appointed as governor of Deccan at the age of 15.
- His beloved wife **Mumtaj Mahal** (original name **Arzumand Bano**) died in 1631 AD. To perpetuate her memory, he built the Taj Mahal at Agra in 1632 AD-1653 AD.
- The **Red Fort**, **Jama Masjid** and **Taj Mahal** are some of the magnificent structures built during his reign.
- Shahjahan was imprisoned by his son Aurangzeb in the Agra Fort, where he died in captivity in 1666 AD. He was buried in the Taj (Agra).

Aurangzeb (1658 AD-1707 AD)

- After the victory of Samugath, Aurangzeb was crowned at Delhi under the title Alamgir.
- Aurangzeb compiled **Fatwa-i-Alamgiri**.
- He was called **Zinda Pir**, the living saint.
- **Jat** revolted under **Gokla Rajaram and Churaman**.

Marathas

Shivaji (1627 AD – 1680 AD)

- He had established an independent Maratha Kingdom.
- In 1674, he was formally crowned as the Chhatrapati
- He promoted the usage of Marathi and Sanskrit.

Sambhaji (1680 AD-1689 AD)

He provided protection and support to **Akbar II**, the rebellious son of Aurangzeb.

Rajaram (1689 AD-1700 AD)

Rajaram created the new post of **Pratinidhi**, thus taking the total number of ministers to nine (Pratinidhi + Ashtapradhan).

The Peshwas (1713 AD-1880 AD)

Balaji Vishwanath (1713 AD-1720 AD)

- Shahu honoured him with title of 'Sena Karta' in 1708 AD and made him his Peshwa in 1713 AD.
- He concluded an agreement with the Sayyed brothers, by which the Mughal emperor, Farrukhsiyar recognised Shahu as the King of Swarajya.

Baji Rao (1720 AD-1740 AD)

- Maratha power reached its zenith under him.
- He conquered Salsette and Bassein in 1733 AD. He also defeated the Nizam-ul-Mulk near Bhopal and concluded the treaty of **Durai Sarai**, by which he got Malwa and Bundelkhand (1737 AD).

Balaji Baji Rao Nana Sahib (1740 AD-1761 AD)

In the third Battle of Panipat in 1761 AD between the Marathas and Ahmad Shah Abdali, Viswas Rao, the son of Nana Sahib, died.

The Advent of Europeans

Portuguese

- The Cape route was discovered from Europe to India by **Vasco da Gama**.
- He reached the port of Calicut on May 17, 1498 AD and was received by the Hindu ruler of Calicut (known by the title of **Zamorin**).
- The first Governor of Portuguese in India was Francisco Almcida (1509 AD). He introduced "The Policy of Blue Water".
- First Portuguese factory was established at Calicut.

Dutch

- The Dutch East India Company established factories in India at Masulipatnam in 1605 AD, Pulicat (1610 AD), Surat (1616 AD), Bimlipatam (1641 AD), Karaikal (1645 AD), Chinsura, Kasimbazar, Patna, Balasore, Nagapatam and Cochin.
- The Dutch conceded to British after their defeat in the Battle of Sedera in 1759 AD.

English

The Governor and company of merchants of London trading into the East Indies, popularly known as the English East India Company, were formed in 1600 AD.

British East India Company

- The first factory was built in Surat (1608 AD). Surat was replaced by Bombay and made the headquarters on the West coast in 1687 AD.
- In 1717 AD, John Surman obtained royal farman from the Mughal emperor Farrukhsiyar. This farman is also called the Magna Carta of the British rule in India as it gave large concessions to the company.

MODERN INDIA

Expansion of British Power

Bengal

- **Battle of Plassey:** On 23rd June, 1757 AD, English won the battle against Siraj-ud-Daula, and compelled the Nawab to concede all the demands.
- **Battle of Buxar:** Mir Qusim formed an alliance with Nawab of Awadh, Shuja-ud-Daula, and Mughal Emperor Shah Alam-II and fought with the British army at Buxar on 22nd October, 1764 AD.

Impact of Victory of Plassey and Buxar

- Victory of Plassey laid the foundation of British rule in India and made them a powerful factor in Bengal politics.
- Victory of Buxar established English supremacy over whole of North India as the emperor of Hindustan was defeated.

Treaty of Allahabad (August 1765 AD)

English got the Diwani right (right to collect revenue) of Bengal, Bihar and Orissa and gave Rupees 26 lakh.

Drain of Wealth

'Drain of Wealth' theory refers to an importation of national product of India, which was not available for consumption to its people.

Indian Renaissance

Arya Samaj

- The first Arya Samaj unit was founded by Swami Dayanand Saraswati in 1875 AD in Bombay.
- He looked on the Vedas as 'India's Rock and Ages'. His mottos were **Go back to Vedas** and **India for the Indians**.

Ramakrishna Mission

It was established by Swami Vivekananda to carry on relief and social work after death of his **Guru Rama Krishna Paramahansa** in 1897 AD.

Swami Vivekananda

- His original name was **Narendranath Dutt**.
- He attended the Parliament of Religions held at Chicago in 1893 AD and published two papers, **Prabhudhha Bharat** in English and **Udbodhana** in Bengali.
- He was considered as the spiritual father of the modern nationalist movement.

Veda Samaj

It is called Brahmo Samaj of South. It was started by Sridharalu Naidu.

The Prarthana Sabha

- It was founded in 1867 AD by M.G. Ranade.
- Prominent leaders were Dr. Atmaram Pandurang and R.G. Bhandarkar and N.G. Chandavarkar.

Young Bengal Movement

- It was founded by **Henry Louis** and **Vivian Derozio**.
- They believed in truth, freedom and religion. It supported women's education.

Indian Reform Association

It was founded by **Keshab Chandra Sen** in Calcutta in 1870 AD.

Theosophical Society

The Theosophical Society India was founded by **Annie Besant**. She founded Central Hindu College in 1898 AD, which became Banaras Hindu University in 1916 AD.

Deccan Education Society

- Founded by **M.G. Ranade, V.G. Chibdonkar** and **G.G. Agarkar** in Pune in 1884 AD.
- The society founded the **Ferguson College**.

The Servants of India Society

Founded by **Gopal Krishna Gokhale** in Bombay in 1905 AD.

Poona Seva Sadan

Founded by G.K. Devdhar and Ramabai Pande in Pune.

Nishkam Karma Math

- Founded by **Dhondo Keshav Karve** in Pune.
- Founded India's first Women's University in Pune in 1916.

The Bharat Stri Mandal

Founded by **Saralabala Devi Chaudharani** in Calcutta. It was the first All India Women Organisation.

The Indian Women's Association

Founded by **Annie Besant** in Madras (1917 AD).

Khudai Khidmatgar Movement

Started by **Khan Abdul Gaffar Khan** in NWFP (1929 AD).

Atmaram Panduran (1823 AD-1898 AD)

Atmaram Pandurang founded **Prarthana Samaj** in 1867 AD in Bombay.

The Revolt of 1857 AD

Occurred during the reign of Governor-General Lord Canning.

Causes of the Revolt

- **Political: Nana Sahib** was refused pension, as he was the adopted son of Peshwa Baji Rao II. Avadh was annexed in 1856. On charges of mal-administration, Satara, Jhansi, Nagpur and Sambhalpur were annexed owing to Doctrine of Lapse.
- **Economic:** Heavy taxation, forcibly evictions, discriminatory tariff policy against Indian products.
- **Socio-religious:** Abolition of sati in 1829 AD; legalisation of widow remarriage in 1856 AD, etc.
- **Military:** Discrimination with Indian soldiers.
- **Immediate cause:** The introduction of Enfield rifles, whose cartridges were said to have a greased cover made of beef and pork, sparked off the revolt.

> **Rani Laxmi Bai**
>
> Rani Laxmi Bai, nicknamed Manu was married to Raja Gangadhar Rao in 1842. The couple adopted a child in 1853 but Lord Dalhousie wished to annex Jhansi under the Doctrine of Lapse. Rani did not surrender and died fighting at Kalpi near Jhansi during the revolt of 1857.

Impact of the Revolt of 1857 AD

1. In August 1857 AD, the British Parliament passed an Act which put an end to the rule of the Company. The control of the British Government in India was transferred to the British Crown.
2. The British Governor-General of India was now also given the title of Viceroy.
3. After the revolt, the British pursued the policy of **divide and rule**.

Indian National Movement

Indian National Congress (I.N.C.)

- The Indian National Union was formed in 1884 AD by A.O. Hume.

- The first session of the Indian National Congress was held at **Gokuldas Tejpal Sanskrit College** in Bombay under the presidentship of **W.C. Bannerji**.

Facts

Ist President of INC	W. C. Bannerji
Ist Woman President	Annie Besant
Ist Muslim President	Badruddin Tyabji
Ist English President	George Yuke
Gandhi became President	1924, Belgaum

The Partition of Bengal (1905) and Boycott and Swadeshi Movement (1905AD-1908 AD)

- The Partition of Bengal came into effect on 16th October, 1905 AD.
- On 7th August, 1905 AD, a resolution to boycott British goods was adopted at a meeting of the INC held in Calcutta.
- **Tilak** took the movement to different parts of India, especially in Pune and Bombay. **Ajit Singh** and **Lala Lajpat Rai** spread the Swadeshi message in Punjab and other parts of Northern India. **Syed Haider Raza** set up to agenda in Delhi. **Chidambaram Pillai** took the movement to Madras Presidency.

Formation of the Muslim League

- Set up in 1906 AD, under the leadership of Aga Khan, Nawab Salimullah of Dhaka and Nawab Mohsin-ul-Mulk.
- The extremists were led by **Bal Gangadhar Tilak**, **Lala Lajpat Rai** and **Bipin Chandra Pal** and the moderates were led by **Gopal Krishna Gokhale**.

Indian Council Act of 1909 AD or Morley-Minto Reforms

- Separate electorate introduced for Muslims.
- Non-officials to be elected indirectly. Thus, election introduced for the first time.

Ghadar Party (1913 AD)

- Formed by Lala Har Dayal, Tarak Nath Das and Sohan Singh Bhakna.
- Indian revolutionary in the United States of America and Canada had established the **Ghadar (Rebellion) Party** in 1913 AD.

Home Rule Movement (1916 AD)

The Home Rule League was pioneered on the lines of a similar movement in Ireland. The Muslim League also supported the movement.

Tilak's Home Rule Movement

The Congress Session at Allahabad in December 1921 decided to launch a **Civil Disobedience Movement**.

The Gandhian Era (1917 AD-1947 AD)

Mahatma Gandhi (1869 AD-1948AD): Chronological Overview

In India: (1915 AD-1948 AD)

- **1915 AD:** Arrived in Bombay (India) on 9th January 1915 AD; Foundation of Satyagraha. Ashram at Kocharab near Ahmedabad (20th May). In 1917 AD, Ashram was shifted at the banks of Sabarmati.
- **1917 AD:** Gandhi entered active politics with **Champaran campaign**. Champaran Satyagraha was his first Civil Disobedience Movement in India.
- **1948 AD:** Mahatma Gandhi was shot dead by **Nathu Ram Godse** while on his way to the evening prayer meeting at **Birla House, New Delhi** (30th January, 1948 AD).

Main Events During the Gandhian Era

Rowlatt Act (1919 AD)

Mahatma Gandhi decided to fight against this act and he gave a call of Satyagraha on 6th April, 1919 AD. He was arrested on 8th April, 1919 AD.

Jallianwala Bagh Massacre (13th April, 1919 AD)

The arrest of **Dr. Saifuddin Kitchlu** and **Dr. Satyapal** on 10th April, 1919 AD, under the Rowlatt Act in connection with Satyagraha caused serious unrest in Punjab. A public meeting was held on 13th April, 1919 AD in a park called **Jallianwala Bagh** in **Amritsar**. As soon as the meeting started, **General Reginald Dyer** ordered indiscriminate heavy firing.

☞ **Note: Sardar Udham Singh**, an Indian patriot from Punjab, shot down General Reginald Dyer in London in 1940 AD.

Khilafat Movement (1920 AD-1922 AD)

The Ali Brothers–Mohammad Ali and **Shaukat Ali**–launched an anti-British movement in 1920 AD–the movement for the restoration of the Khilafat Movement. **Maulana Abul Kalam Azad** also led the movement. It was supported by **Mahatma** Gandhi and INC.

Non-cooperation Movement (1920 AD-1922 AD)

At the **Calcutta session** in September 1920 AD, the Congress resolved in favour of the Non-cooperation Movement and defined **Swaraj** as its ultimate aim (according to Gandhiji).

There was an attack on a local police station by angry peasants at **Chauri Chaura** in Gorakhpur district on 5th February, 1922 AD. Mahatma Gandhi, shocked by Chauri Chaura incident, withdrew the Non-Cooperation Movement on 12th February, 1922 AD.

The Swarajists

- In December 1922 AD, C.R. Das and Motilal Nehru formed Congress Khilafat Swarajya Party with C.R. Das as the President and Motilal Nehru as the Secretary.
- Madan Mohan Malaviya and Lala Lajpat Rai founded the **Independent Congress Party** later in 1933 AD. It was recognised as the Congress Nationalist Party.

Simon Commission (1927 AD)

- In 1927 AD, the British Government appointed the **Indian Statutory Commission** known popularly by its chairman Simon.
- The **Muslim League** and **Hindu Mahasabha** decided to support the Congress.
- At Lahore, Lala Lajpat Rai was severely beaten in a lathicharge and he succumbed to his injuries.

Nehru Report (1928 AD)

- Nehru report was tabled in 1928 AD by **Motilal Nehru**.
- It remains memorable as the first major Indian effort to draft a constitutional framework for India.

Dandi March/Salt Satyagraha (1930 AD)

- Along with 78 followers, Mahatma Gandhi started his famous march from **Sabarmati Ashram** on 12th March, 1930 AD for the small village **Dandi** to break the Salt Law.
- Under the leadership of Abdul Gaffar Khan, popularly known as **The Frontier Gandhi**, the Pathans organised the society of **Khudai Khidmatgars** (servants of God) known popularly as **Red Shirts**.

The Government of India Act, 1935

The Simon Commission report submitted in 1930 AD formed the basis for the Government of India Act, 1935. The Act: (i) introduced provincial autonomy; (ii) abolished dyarchy in the provinces; (iii) made ministers responsible to the legislative and federation at the centre. The Act of 1935 was unanimously rejected by the Congress.

Pakistan Resolution/Lahore Resolution (24th March, 1940 AD)

The Lahore Session of the Muslim League was held on 24th March, 1940 AD. Pakistan Resolution was passed.

August Offer/Linlithgow Offer (8th August, 1940 AD)

On this day, **Viceroy Linlithgow** came out with certain proposals known as **August Offer** declaring that the goal of the British Government was to establish **Dominion Status** in India.

Individual Civil Disobedience/ Individual Satyagraha (October 1940 AD-December 1941 AD)

The Congress Working Committee decided to individually fight disobedience on 17th October, 1940 AD. **Vinoba Bhave** was the first Satyagrahi, followed soon by many more, including **Nehru** and **Patel**.

Cripps Mission (1942 AD)

The British Government's refusal of accepting immediately the Congress demand was the cause of failure of the mission.

Quit India Movement (1942 AD)

- The All India Congress Committee met at **Bombay** on 8th August, 1942 AD. It passed the famous **Quit India** resolution and proposed to the starting of a non-violent mass struggle under **Gandhiji's leadership**.
- It is also called **Vardha Proposal** and **Leaderless Revolt**.
- His message was **'Do or Die'**.

Demand for Pakistan

- In 1930 AD, Mohammad Iqbal, for the first time, suggested that the frontier province, Sind, Baluchistan and Kashmir be made the Muslim state within the federation.
- Chaudhry Rehmat Ali coined the term **'Pakstan'** (later **'Pakistan'**).
- **Pakistan Resolution:** The Muslim League first passed the proposal of separate Pakistan in its Lahore Session in 1940 AD (called Jinnah's two-nation theory).

The Indian National Army and Subhash Chandra Bose

- The idea of Indian National Army (INA) was first conceived in Malaya by **Mohan Singh**, an Indian officer of the British Indian Army.
- In March 1942, a conference of India was held in Tokyo and **Indian Independence League** was formed.
- Subhash Chandra Bose escaped to Berlin in 1941 AD and set up **Indian League** there.
- He formed **Forward Bloc** in 1939 AD.

INA Trials

12th November, 1945 was celebrated as the INA Day.

Cabinet Mission (March-June, 1946 AD)

The Cabinet Mission, which included **Lord Pathick Lawrence Stafford Cripps** and **AV. Alexander** visited India and met the representatives of different political parties. The Mission envisaged the establishment of a Constituent Assembly to frame the constitution as well as an interim government.

Direct Action Campaign (16th August, 1946 AD): The Muslim League launched a direct action campaign on 16th August, 1946 AD, which resulted in widespread communal riots in the country.

Interim Government

- Interim Government was headed by **Jawahar Lal Nehru**.
- The **Constituent Assembly** begins its session on **9th December, 1946 AD** and Dr. Rajendra Prasad was elected its President.
- **Mountbatten** would replace Wavell as the Viceroy.

Mountbatten Plan (3rd June, 1947 AD)

- **3rd June Plan:** In case of partition, two dominions and two Constituent Assemblies would be created. The plan declared that power would be handed over by 15th August, 1947 AD.
- Mountbatten's formula was to divide India but retain maximum unity.

India Independence Act, 1947 AD

- On 18th July, 1947 AD, the British Parliament ratified the Mountbatten Plan as the **Independence of India Act, 1947**.
- The Act provided creation of two independent dominions of India and Pakistan.
- On 15th August, 1947, India got independence. Jinnah became the first Governor-General of Pakistan. India requested Mountbatten to continue as the Governor-General of India.

Governor-Generals and Viceroys

Robert Clive

Governor of Bengal during 1757 AD-1760 AD and again 1765 AD-1767 AD and established Dual Government in Bengal from 1765 AD-1772 AD.

Warren Hastings (1774 AD-1785 AD)

- He became Governor of Bengal in 1772 AD and first Governor-General of Bengal in 1773 AD.
- Established India's first Supreme Court in Calcutta.

Lord Cornwallis (1786 AD-1793 AD)

- He introduced Izaredari System in 1773 AD.
- He started the **permanent settlement of Bengal**.
- He created the post of **District Judge.** He is called Father of Civil Services in India.

Lord Wellesley (1798 AD-1803 AD)

- Introduced the system of Subsidiary alliance. Madras Presidency was formed during his tenure.
- In 1800 AD, he set up Fort William College in Calcutta. He was famous as Bengal Tiger.
- He brought the censorship of Press Act, 1799 AD.

Lord Minto (1807 AD-1813 AD)

- Treaty of Amritsar (1809 AD) with Ranjit Singh.
- Charter Act of 1813 AD ended the monopoly of East India Company in India.

Lord Hastings (1813 AD-1823 AD)

- Adopted the policy of intervention and war.
- Introduced the Ryotwari settlement in Madras by Thomas Munro, the Governor.

Lord William Bentinck (1828 AD-1834 AD)

- Regarded as the 'Father of Modern Western Education in India'.

- Abolition of Sati in 1829 AD.
- Suppression of Thugi (1830 AD).
- Deposition of Raja of Mysore and annexation of his territories (1831 AD).
- He was the First Governor-General of India.

Lord Ellenborough (1842 AD-1844 AD)

Abolished slavery (1843 AD).

Lord Dalhousie (1848 AD-1856 AD)

- Abolished Titles and pensions, Widow Remarriage Act (1856 AD).
- Started the first railway line in 1853 AD; Started electric telegraph service. Laid the basis of the modern Postal System (1854 AD); A separate public works department was set up for the first time.

Lord Canning (1856 AD-1858AD)

- The last Governor General of East India Company
- He withdrew Doctrine of Lapse.

Lord Canning (1858 AD-1862AD)

The Indian Councils Act of 1861 AD was passed; Indian Penal Code of Criminal Procedure (1859 AD) was passed; The Indian High Court Act (1861 AD) was enacted; Income-tax was introduced for the first time in 1858 AD; The Universities of Calcutta, Bombay and Madras founded in 1857 AD.

Sir Johan Lawrence (1864 AD-1869 AD):

High Courts were established at Calcutta Bombay and Madras in 1865 AD.

Lord Mayo (1869 AD-1872 AD)

- He established the Department of Agriculture and Commerce.
- In 1872 AD, first Census was done in India.
- He was the only **Viceroy to be murdered** in office by a convict in the Andaman in 1872 AD.

Lord Lytton (1876 AD-1880 AD)

- Most infamous Governor-General; Arranged the Grand Darbar in Delhi; Royal Title Act (1876 AD) and Queen Victoria was declared as the Kaisari Hind.
- The infamous **Vernacular Press Act** (1878 AD) and lowered the maximum age of ICS from 21 to 19 years.

Lord Ripon (1880 AD-1884 AD)

- He was famously known as "Father of Local Self-Government".
- First Official Census in India (1881 AD).
- Appointed **Hunter Commission** for education reforms in 1882AD.

Lord Dufferin (1884 AD-1888AD)

- Formation of **Indian National Congress** (INC) in 1885 AD.
- Dufferin called INC as 'microscopic minority'.

Lord Curzon (1899 AD-1905AD)

- Appointed a Police Commission in 1902 AD under Andrew Frazer.
- Indian Universities Act passed in 1904 AD.
- Famine Commission under MacDonnell.

Lord Minto II (1905 AD-1910AD)

Swadeshi Movement (1905 AD-1908 AD); Foundation of the Muslim League, 1906 AD; Surat session and split in the Congress (1907 AD).

Lord Hardinge (1910 AD-1916AD)

- Annulment of the Partition of Bengal (1911), Transfer of capital from Calcutta to Delhi (1911); Delhi Darbar and Coronation of King George V and Queen Mary (1911).
- In 1911, Bihar and Orissa separated from Bengal and, became a new state.

Lord Chelmsford (1916 AD-1921 AD)

Home Rule Movement launched by Tilak and Annie Besant (1916); Lucknow Pact between Congress and Muslim League (1916); Arrival of Mahatma Gandhi in India (1915); Champaran Satyagraha (1917); Repressive Rowlatt Act (1919); Jallianwala Bagh Massacre (April 13, 1919). Khilafat Movement (1920–1922); Non-Cooperation Movement (1920–1922).

Lord Reading (1921 AD-1926AD)

- Rowlatt Act was repealed along with Press Act of 1910.
- Chauri-Chaura incident and withdrawal of Non-Cooperation Movement.
- Formation of Swaraj Party by CR Das and Motilal Nehru (1923).
- Kakori Train Conspiracy (1925).
- Lee Commission (1924) for public services.
- **RSS** founded in 1925.

Lord Irwin (1926 AD-1931 AD)

- Simon Commission visited India in 1928.
- Nehru Report, 1928.
- Lahore Session of the Congress, (1929) and Poorna Swaraj, declaration.
- Civil Disobedience Movement, 1930 started with.
- **Dandi March** (12 March 1930).
- Gandhi-Irwin Pact, 5 March 1931.
- Jawaharlal Nehru and Subhash Chandra Bose founded **Independence of India League.**

Lord Willingdon (1931 AD-1936AD)

Civil Disobedience Movement (1932); Announcement of MacDonald. Communal Award (1932); Foundation of Congress Socialist Party–CSP (1934); Burma Separated from India (1935), All India Kisan Sabha (1936).

Lord Linlithgow (1934 AD-1944AD)

- First General Election (1936–37) Congress Ministries.
- Deliverance day by Muslim League 1939.
- Lahore Resolution of Muslim League (1940) demand of Pakistan.
- August Offer, 1940.
- Cripps Mission, 1942.
- Quit India Movement, 1942.
- "Divide and Quit" at the Karachi Session (1940).
- In Haripura Session (1939) of Congress complete Independence was declared.

Governor Generals of Free India (1947 AD-1950 AD)

Lord Mountbatten (1947–1948)

The first Governor General of free Indian); Murder of Gandhi (Jan. 30, 1948).

C. Rajagopalachari (June 1948–January 25, 1950)

The last Governor General of free India; The only Indian Governor General.

Exercise

1. In which Indian Religion, there are 24 Tirthankaras?
(a) Jainism (b) Buddhism
(c) Hinduism (d) Sikhism
2. The oldest rock-cut architecture is found in ____.
(a) Rajasthan (b) Bihar
(c) Karnataka (d) Mizoram
3. Rashtrapati Bhavan was built in ____.
(a) 1852 (b) 1910
(c) 1947 (d) 1986
4. Santhara is a religious ritual of ____ community.
(a) Sikhs (b) Jews
(c) Jain (d) Buddhists
5. Battle of Haldighati was fought in the year ____.
(a) 1764 (b) 1526
(c) 1576 (d) 1857
6. Group of Monuments at Hampi is in ____.
(a) Karnataka
(b) Madhya Pradesh
(c) Maharashtra
(d) Rajasthan
7. Chang Lo is a folk dance of ____.
(a) Arunachal Pradesh
(b) Punjab
(c) Assam
(d) Nagaland
8. Chanakya was the chief advisor of ____.
(a) Babur
(b) Chandragupta Maurya
(c) Akbar
(d) Kautilya
9. Battle of Haldighati in 1576 was fought between Akbar and ____.
(a) Sher Shah
(b) Maharana Pratap
(c) Hemu Vikramaditya
(d) Nader Shah
10. Gandhi Irwin pact happened in which year?
(a) 1905 (b) 1931
(c) 1947 (d) 1942
11. In 1739, who defeated the Mughal army at the Battle of Karnal?
(a) Nader Shah
(b) Genghis Khan
(c) Hemu Vikramaditya
(d) Bajirao I
12. The Red Fort (Delhi) was built by ____.
(a) Babur (b) British
(c) Shah Jahan (d) Aurangzeb
13. Whom did Akbar defeat in the 2nd battle of Panipat in 1556?
(a) Genghis Khan
(b) Nader Shah
(c) Hemu Vikramaditya
(d) Bajirao I
14. Aurangzeb, the Mughal Emperor died in?
(a) 1507 (b) 1607
(c) 1707 (d) 1807
15. Shiva cave is located in ____.
(a) Ajanta Caves
(b) Ellora Caves
(c) Elephanta Caves
(d) Badami Caves
16. Rock Shelters of Bhimbetka is in ____
(a) Maharashtra
(b) Himachal Pradesh
(c) Karnataka
(d) Madhya Pradesh
17. Before its Independence, Bangladesh was part of ____
(a) India
(b) China
(c) Pakistan
(d) United Kingdom
18. Humayun was born in the year ____.
(a) 1508 (b) 1608
(c) 1708 (d) 1808
19. Ashoka converted to which religion after the Kalinga war?
(a) Jainism (b) Buddhism
(c) Christianity (d) Judaism
20. Gandhi Ji started the Non-Cooperation Movement in ____.
(a) 1880 (b) 1900
(c) 1920 (d) 1940
21. Chhatrapati Shivaji Terminus station was designed by
(a) Frederick William Stevens
(b) Santiago Calatrava
(c) Fazlur Rahman Khan
(d) Frei Otto
22. Chhatrapati Sambhaji (1680-1688 AD) was the ruler of which dynasty?
(a) Maratha (b) Nanda
(c) Haryanka (d) Maurya
23. Birbal was an advisor in the court of ____.
(a) Babur (b) Akbar
(c) Aurangzeb (d) Jahangir
24. Humayun's Tomb is located in ____.
(a) Delhi (b) Agra
(c) Gwalior (d) Jaipur
25. The decision to effect the Partition of Bengal was announced in 1905 by
(a) Lord William Bentinck
(b) Lord Mountbatten
(c) Warren Hastings
(d) Lord Curzon
26. Who set up the Sabarmati Ashram in Ahmedabad?
(a) Subhash Chandra Bose
(b) Mohandas Gandhi
(c) Jawaharlal Nehru
(d) Sarojini Naidu
27. ____ is a depiction of the Hindu God Shiva as the cosmic dancer who performs his divine dance called Tandavam.
(a) Murugan (b) Nataraja
(c) Vishnu (d) Venkateshwar
28. Which among the following games was very popular in ancient India?
(a) Chess (b) Cricket
(c) Hockey (d) Football
29. Ashoka The Great (273-232 B.C.) was the ruler of which dynasty?
(a) Mewar (b) Mughal
(c) Maurya (d) Peshwas
30. Indus Valley Civilization was a ____ age civilization.
(a) Silver (b) Tin
(c) Gold (d) Bronze
31. To whom did Akbar gave the title Mian?
(a) Raja Todar Mal
(b) Man Singh I
(c) Birbal
(d) Tansen
32. Churches and Convents of Goa were built by
(a) British (b) Dutch
(c) Portuguese (d) Mughals
33. Ghatotkacha (who ruled in the years 290-305 B.C.) was a king from which dynasty?
(a) Gupta Dynasty
(b) Kanva Dynasty
(c) Shunga Dynasty
(d) Maurya Dynasty

34. Who are credited to a large extent for ending the Mughal rule in India?
(a) Mauryas (b) Cholas
(c) Guptas (d) Marathas

35. Ajanta Caves is in ____
(a) Maharashtra
(b) Himachal Pradesh
(c) Karnataka
(d) Madhya Pradesh

36. In 1617 the British East India Company was given permission by ____ to trade in India.
(a) Babur (b) Akbar
(c) Aurangzeb (d) Jahangir

37. Who built the Group of Monuments at Pattadakal?
(a) Chola Kings
(b) Pallava Kings
(c) Chera Kings
(d) Chalukya Kings

38. The Kalinga war was fought in ____.
(a) 161 BC (b) 261 BC
(c) 361 BC (d) 461 BC

39. Tipu Sultan was also known as the Lion of____.
(a) Bangalore (b) Delhi
(c) Kochi (d) Mysore

40. Who built the Buddhist Monuments at Sanchi?
(a) Mughal Dynasty
(b) Maurya Dynasty
(c) Gupta Dynasty
(d) Chola Dynasty

41. When was the battle of Haldighati fought?
(a) 1776 (b) 1676
(c) 1576 (d) 1476

42. In 1498, which Portuguese explorer discovered a new sea route from Europe to India?
(a) Vasco da Gama
(b) Christopher Columbus
(c) Sir Francis Drake
(d) John Cabot

43. Buland Darwaza is the main entrance to the palace at ____.
(a) Amer Fort
(b) Gwalior Fort
(c) Fatehpur Sikri
(d) Agra Fort

44. Who was the first ruler of Pala dynasty?
(a) Gopala
(b) Vivyanathan
(c) Dharmapala
(d) Bhaskaran

45. Which empire is regarded as the Golden Age of Hinduism?
(a) Maurya (b) Mughal
(c) Gupta (d) Chola

46. ____ is a collection of architectural astronomical instruments, built by Maharaja Jai Singh II.
(a) Jantar Mantar, Delhi
(b) Group of Monuments at Hampi
(c) Group of Monuments at Pattadakal
(d) Nalanda, Bihar

47. Tripitakas are sacred books of ____.
(a) Sikhs (b) Jews
(c) Buddhists (d) Muslims

48. Bahadur Shah I (1707-1712 AD) was the ruler of which dynasty?
(a) Nanda (b) Maurya
(c) Mughal (d) Haryanka

49. Khas Mahal and the Shish Mahal are built in which World Heritage Monument?
(a) Humayun's Tomb
(b) Mahabodhi Temple Complex
(c) Qutub Minar
(d) Agra Fort

50. Diwane-i-khas is in which of these monuments?
(a) Humayun's Tomb
(b) Mahabodhi Temple Complex
(c) Qutub Minar
(d) Red Fort Complex

51. During the Independence Movement, Subhash Chandra Bose revamped the Indian National____.
(a) Navy (b) Army
(c) Defence (d) Air Force

52. Aurangzeb was the son of ____.
(a) Babur (b) Humayun
(c) Akbar (d) Shah Jahan

53. Who built the Group of Monuments at Mahabalipuram?
(a) Chola Kings
(b) Pallava Kings
(c) Chera Kings
(d) Chalukya Kings

54. Bimbisara was the king of which dynasty?
(a) Haryanka (b) Maurya
(c) Shunga (d) Nanda

55. World War I started in the year
(a) 1914 (b) 1919
(c) 1939 (d) 1945

56. Moti Masjid is situated in which of these World Heritage Sites?
(a) Humayun's Tomb
(b) Mahabodhi Temple Complex
(c) Qutub Minar
(d) Red Fort Complex

57. Who was the trusted General of the Mughal emperor Akbar?
(a) Raja Todar Mal
(b) Man Singh I
(c) Birbal
(d) Tansen

58. Who was the trusted General of the Mughal emperor Akbar?
(a) Raja Todar Mal
(b) Man Singh I
(c) Birbal
(d) Tansen

59. Mausoleum (Dargah) of Salim Chishti is situated in ____.
(a) Humayun's Tomb
(b) Fatehpur Sikri
(c) Gwlior Fort
(d) Agra Fort

60. Qutub Minar is located in ____.
(a) Delhi (b) Ghaziabad
(c) Noida (d) Gurugram

61. Bajirao I (1720-1740 AD) was the ruler of which dynasty?
(a) Nanda (b) Peshwas
(c) Haryanka (d) Maurya

62. Which of these railway stations is a World Heritage Site?
(a) Kharagpur Railway Station
(b) Howrah Station
(c) Chhatrapati Shivaji Terminus
(d) Kanpur Central

63. Akbar's regime, ____was the military head.
(a) Sultan Ahmed Fawad
(b) Suri Moja
(c) Mir Khaas
(d) Mir Bakshi

64. Who pioneered the guerrilla warfare methods?
(a) Babur
(b) Akbar
(c) Shivaji
(d) Bajirao Peshwa

65. Ajanta Caves in Maharashtra have rock-cut cave monuments of which religion?
(a) Sikhism (b) Buddhism
(c) Christianity (d) Hinduism

66. Whose reign in Indian History is called the Golden Age of India?
(a) Mughal Empire
(b) Maratha Empire
(c) Gupta Empire
(d) Maurya Empire

67. Who was the second woman to become the president of the Indian National Congress in 1925 and the first Indian woman to do so?
(a) Vijaylakshmi Pandit
(b) Sarojini Naidu
(c) Padmaja Naidu
(d) Fathima Bibi

68. Which caves is a cultural mix of religious arts of Buddhism, Hinduism and Jainism?
(a) Ajanta (b) Ellora
(c) Elephanta (d) Badami

69. Which World Heritage Monument has been acclaimed as the "Necropolis of the Mughal dynasty"?
(a) Humayun's Tomb
(b) Mahabodhi Temple Complex
(c) Qutub Minar
(d) Red Fort Complex

70. Who was first Viceroy and Governor-General of pre-independence era?
(a) Warren Hastings
(b) Lord William Bentinck
(c) Lord Mountbatten
(d) Lord Canning

71. Jahangir was the son of ____.
(a) Babur (b) Humayun
(c) Akbar (d) Shah Jahan

72. ____ caves are a network of sculpted caves located in Mumbai Harbour.
(a) Ajanta (b) Ellora
(c) Elephanta (d) Badami

73. The Renaissance is a period in Europe, from the ____.
(a) 18th to the 20th century
(b) 14th to the 17th century
(c) 11th to the 13th century
(d) 7th to the 10th century

74. Aurangzeb (1658-1707 AD) was the ruler of which dynasty?
(a) Nanda (b) Mughal
(c) Maurya (d) Haryanka

75. Which world heritage site comprises of the tomb of Iltutmish?
(a) Humayun's Tomb
(b) Mahabodhi Temple Complex
(c) Qutub Minar
(d) Red Fort Complex

76. Khajuraho Group of monuments are attributed to which dynasty?
(a) Chandela (b) Mughal
(c) Maurya (d) Shunga

77. Which world heritage site comprises of the Alai Darwaza Gate?
(a) Humayun's Tomb
(b) Mahabodhi Temple Complex
(c) Qutub Minar
(d) Red Fort Complex

78. Babur (1526-1530 AD) was the ruler of which dynasty?
(a) Mughal (b) Nanda
(c) Maurya (d) Haryanka

79. Who built Jodhpur Fort?
(a) Guru Ramdas
(b) Shah Jahan
(c) Rao Jodhaji
(d) Mahatma Gandhi

80. Battle of Panipat was fought in the year ____
(a) 1764 (b) 1757
(c) 1526 (d) 1857

81. Noor Jahan was wife of which Mughal Emperor?
(a) Akbar (b) Aurangzeb
(c) Jahangir (d) Shah Jahan

82. Battle of Tarain was fought in the year ____?
(a) 1526 (b) 1757
(c) 1191 (d) 1857

83. Garden inside the Taj Mahal is known as ____
(a) Mughal Garden
(b) Taj Bageecha
(c) Taj Mahal Garden
(d) Mahal Bageecha

84. Who started the Home Rule League?
(a) Bal Gangadhar Tilak
(b) Rajendra Prasad
(c) Mahatma Gandhi
(d) Jawahar Lal Nehru

85. The name by which Ashoka is generally referred to in his inscription is ____?
(a) Chakravarti (b) Dharmadeva
(c) Priyadarshi (d) Dharmakrit

86. Which temple is built in the form of the chariot of Surya, the Sun God with 24 wheels?
(a) Soorya Narayana Temple
(b) Dakshinaraka Temple
(c) Surya Pahar Temple
(d) Konark Sun Temple

87. The battle of Tarain was fought between Prithviraj Chauhan and __.
(a) Mahmood Gaznabi
(b) Muhammad Ghori
(c) Babar
(d) Humayun

88. Isfahan, the Persian Capital is said to have provided the inspiration to build which of these monuments?
(a) Humayun's Tomb
(b) Mahabodhi Temple Complex
(c) Qutub Minar
(d) Red Fort Complex

89. Akbar (1556-1605 AD) was the ruler of which dynasty?
(a) Nanda (b) Maurya
(c) Mughal (d) Haryanka

90. The Bibi Ka Maqbara is a tomb located in ____. It was built by Azam Shah, son of Aurangzeb, in 1678.
(a) Hyderabad (b) Aurangabad
(c) Lucknow (d) Allahabad

91. Battle of Kanauj was fought in the year ____?
(a) 1764 (b) 1526
(c) 1540 (d) 1857

92. Ashoka was an emperor of the ____ Dynasty.
(a) Mughal (b) Chola
(c) Maurya (d) Gupta

93. Which Mughal emperor imprisoned his father and executed his brother?
(a) Babur (b) Humayun
(c) Aurangzeb (d) Shah Alam II

94. Humayun's Tomb was built by ____.
(a) Humayun
(b) Hamida Banu Begum
(c) Babur
(d) Akbar

95. Who built Sabarmati Ashram?
(a) Guru Ramdas
(b) Shah Jahan
(c) Rao Jodhaji
(d) Mahatma Gandhi

96. From which monument, Gautama Buddha propagated his divine knowledge of Buddhism to the world?
(a) Humayun's Tomb
(b) Mahabodhi Temple Complex
(c) Qutub Minar
(d) Red Fort Complex

97. Jahangir was born in the year ____.
(a) 1569 (b) 1669
(c) 1769 (d) 1869

98. Bahadur Shah (First) was born in the year ____.
(a) 1543 (b) 1643
(c) 1743 (d) 1843

Answers

1. (a)	**2.** (b)	**3.** (b)	**4.** (c)	**5.** (c)	**6.** (a)	**7.** (d)	**8.** (b)	**9.** (b)	**10.** (b)
11. (a)	**12.** (c)	**13.** (c)	**14.** (c)	**15.** (c)	**16.** (d)	**17.** (c)	**18.** (a)	**19.** (b)	**20.** (c)
21. (a)	**22.** (a)	**23.** (b)	**24.** (a)	**25.** (d)	**26.** (b)	**27.** (b)	**28.** (a)	**29.** (c)	**30.** (d)
31. (d)	**32.** (c)	**33.** (a)	**34.** (d)	**35.** (a)	**36.** (d)	**37.** (d)	**38.** (b)	**39.** (d)	**40.** (b)
41. (c)	**42.** (a)	**43.** (c)	**44.** (c)	**45.** (b)	**46.** (b)	**47.** (a)	**48.** (c)	**49.** (d)	**50.** (d)
51. (b)	**52.** (d)	**53.** (b)	**54.** (a)	**55.** (a)	**56.** (d)	**57.** (b)	**58.** (b)	**59.** (b)	**60.** (a)
61. (b)	**62.** (c)	**63.** (d)	**64.** (c)	**65.** (b)	**66.** (c)	**67.** (b)	**68.** (b)	**69.** (a)	**70.** (d)
71. (c)	**72.** (c)	**73.** (b)	**74.** (b)	**75.** (c)	**76.** (a)	**77.** (c)	**78.** (a)	**79.** (c)	**80.** (c)
81. (c)	**82.** (c)	**83.** (a)	**84.** (a)	**85.** (c)	**86.** (d)	**87.** (b)	**88.** (d)	**89.** (c)	**90.** (b)
91. (c)	**92.** (c)	**93.** (c)	**94.** (b)	**95.** (d)	**96.** (a)	**97.** (a)	**98.** (b)		

2 GEOGRAPHY

Universe

- The universe comprises billions of galaxies. The galaxies are made up of millions of stars held together by the force of gravity and these stars account for most of the masses of the galaxy.

Stars

- Stars are made of hot burning gases.
- They emit light of their own and are very large and very hot.
- Light takes about 4.3 years to reach us from the next nearest star **Proxima Centauri**.

The Sun

- It is the nearest star to the earth.
- Its diameter is 14 lakh km.
- It is composed of 71% Hydrogen, 26.5% helium and 2.5% other elements.

The Earth

- The Earth is 23½° tilted on its axis and, thus, makes 66½° angle.
- It takes 23 hours 56 minutes and 4.091 seconds to rotate on its axis.
- Earth is known as the **"watery planet"** or the **"blue planet"**.
- Earth is the only known planet which provides sustenance of life on it.

The Moon

- The Moon is the only satellite of the earth.
- It has diameter of 3475 km and its circumference is 10864 km while its orbit is elliptical.

Specifics of the Planets	
Biggest planet	Jupiter
Biggest Satellite	Ganymede
Blue planet	Earth
Green planet	Uranus
Brightest planet	Venus
Brightest star (outside solar system)	Sirius (Dog Star)
Closest star of solar system	Proxima Centauri
Coldest planet	Neptune
Evening star	Venus
Farthest planet from Sun	Neptune
Planet with maximum number of satellites	Jupiter
Hottest planet	Venus
Densest planet	Earth
Morning star	Venus
Nearest planet to Earth	Venus
Nearest planet to Sun	Mercury
Red planet	Mars
Smallest planet	Mercury
Earth twin	Venus

Meteors and Meteorites

- Meteors and Meteorites are also called shooting stars.
- When meteors are large and do not burn up completely, they land on the earth's surface and are known as **Meteorites**.

Biosphere

The part of the earth where life exists is called the **Biosphere** ('bios' means 'life').

Lithosphere

- The uppermost layer of the earth's crust which is capable of supporting life is called Lithosphere.
- The Lithosphere (or land) covers two-sevenths or 29.22% of the total surface area of the earth.

Hydrosphere

Hydrosphere (or sea) covers 70.70% of the total surface area of the earth.

Latitude

Latitude is the angular distance of a point on the earth surface from the centre of earth, measured in degree. These lines are called parallels of latitude and on the globe they are circles.

Longitude

- Longitude is the angular distance of a point on the earth surface along the equator, east or west from the **Prime Meridian.**
- Prime Meridian is the semi-circle from pole to pole, from which all the other meridians radiate Eastwards and Westwards up to 180°.
- 180° meridian **(International Date Line)** is exactly opposite to the Prime Meridian. Such points are called anti-pedal points.

Local Time (LT) and Time Zones

- The Indian Government has accepted the meridian of 82.5 degree east for standard time, which is 5 hrs. 30 mins. ahead of the Greenwich Mean Time.
- Russia has as many as 11 time zones.
- Both USA and Canada have five time zones.

The Date Line and Universal Time (UT)

- It is the 180 degree meridian running over the Pacific Ocean, deviating at Aleutian Island, Fiji, Samoa and Gilbert Island.

The international date line has been established most of it following the 180th meridian–where by common agreement, whenever we cross it the date advances one day (going west) or goes back one day (going east).

- The line passes the **Bering Strait** between Alaska and Siberia.

Longest day in the Northern hemisphere	21 June
Shortest day in the Northern hemisphere	22 December
Equal day and night in the Northern hemisphere	21 March and 23 September
Longest day in the Southern hemisphere	22 December
Shortest day in Southern hemisphere	21 June
Equal day and night in the Southern hemisphere	21 March and 23 September

Earthquakes

- The sudden tremors or shaking of the earth's crust is called an **earthquake.**
- **'Seismology'** deals with the study of earthquake.
- **'Richter scale'** and **'Mercalli scale'** are the instruments to measure record the magnitude and the **intensity** of an earthquake respectively.

Atmosphere

The atmosphere extends to about 1000 km from the surface of the earth. But 99% of the total mass of the atmosphere is found within 32 km.

Composition of the Atmosphere

(i) Nitrogen–78%, (ii) Oxygen–21%, (iii) Argon–0.93%, (iv) Carbon dioxide–0.03%, (v) Neon–0.0018%, (vi) Helium–0.0005%, (vii). Ozone–0.006%, (viii) Hydrogen–0.0005%.

Structure of the Atmosphere

There are five distinct layers of the atmosphere– (a) Troposphere, (b) Stratosphere, (c) Mesosphere, (d) Thermosphere, and (e) Exosphere.

Measurement and Units of Atmospheric Pressure

- The **mercury barometer** is the standard instrument for measuring atmospheric pressure.
- **Standard sea level pressure is 76 km of 29.92 inches on this scale.**
- Orica atmospheric pressure (76 cm of mercury) = 760 mm of Hg = 1013.25 millibars (mb).

Winds

- Wind is the movement of air caused by the uneven heating of the earth by the sun.
- The air moves from high pressure to low pressure.
- The imaginary line joining the points having same pressure is called **isobars.**

Humidity

- Humidity of air refers to the contents of the water vapour present in the air at a particular time and place.
- Humidity is measured by an instrument called hygrometer.

Forests

They are of the following types:

(a) **Tropical Evergreen Rain Forests:** The leaves of trees in such forests are very wide. Examples: Red wood, palm, etc.

(b) **Tropical Semi-Deciduous Forests:** Such forests receive rainfall less than 150 cms. Saagwan, saal, bamboo, etc. are found in such forests.

(c) **Tundra Forests:** Such forests are covered with snow. Only Mosses, a few sledges and Lichens grow here in the summer.

Famous Grassland of the world

Grassland		Countries
Steppe	–	Eurasis
Prairie	–	U.S.A.
Pampas	–	Argentina
Veld	–	South Africa
Downs	–	Australia

Some Important Facts

World Continents

Continents	Biggest Country	Highest Peak	Longest River
Asia	China	Mt. Everest (8850 m)	Yangtze Kiang
Africa	Sudan	Mt. Kilimanjaro (5895 m)	Nile
Australia	Australia	Mt. Kosciuszko (2228 m)	Darling
Antarctica		Vinson Massif (5140 m)	
North America	Canada	Mt. Mckinley (6194 m)	Mississippi Missouri
South America	Brazil	Mt. Aconcagua (6960 m)	Amazon
Europe	Russia	Mt. Elbrus (5642 m)	Ob

Major Rivers of the World

River	Origin	Length (m)	Falls in
Nile	Victoria Lake	6,650	Mediterranean Sea
Amazon	Andes (Peru)	6,428	Atlantic Ocean
Yangtze	Tibetan Kiang Plateau	6,300	China Sea
Mississippi Missouri	Itaska Lake (USA)	6,275	Gulf of Mexico (USA)
Yenisei	Tannu-Ola Mts.	5,539	Arctic Ocean
Huang Ho	Kunlun Mts.	5,464	Gulf of Chibli
Ob	Altai Mts.	5,410	Russia Gulf of Ob
Congo	Lualaba and Luapula rivers	4,700	Atlantic Ocean
Amur	North-east	4,444	China Sea of Okhotsk
Lena	Baikal Mts.	4,400	Laptev Sea
Mekong	Tibetan Highlands	4,350	South China Sea
Mackenzie	Great Slave Lake	4,241	Beaufort Sea
Niger	Guinea	4,200	Gulf of Guinea

Major Lakes of the World

Highest Lake	Lake Titicaca in Bolivia
Largest Saline Water Lake	Lake Caspian Sea
Deepest Lake	Lake Baikal in Siberia
Largest Lake	Caspian Sea
Largest Fresh Water Lake	Lake Superior
India's Largest Lake	Chilka Lake in Orissa

Oceans of the World

Oceans	Area (sq.km)	Greatest Depth
Pacific	16,62,40,000	Mariana Trench
Atlantic	8,65,60,000	Puerto Rico Trench
Indian	7,34,30,000	Java Trench
Arctic	1,32,30,000	–
Antarctic/Southern	2,03,30,000	South Sandwich Trench

Important Cities on River Banks (World)

City	River	Country
Amsterdam	Amsel	Netherlands
Ankara	Kazil	Turkey
Bangkok	Chao Praya	Thailand
Basra	Eupharates and Tigris	Iraq
Baghdad	Tigris	Iraq
Berlin	Spree	Germany
Bonn	Rhine	Germany
Budapest	Danube	Hungary
Bristol	Avon	UK
Buenos Aires	Laplata	Argentina
Chittagong	Majyani	Bangladesh
Canton	Si-Kiang	China
Cairo	Nile	Egypt
Chung King	Yang-tse-king	China
Cologne	Rhine	Germany
Dresden	Elbe	Germany
Hamburg	Elbe	Germany
Kabul	Kabul	Afghanistan
Karachi	Indus	Pakistan
Khartoum	Confluence of Blue and White Nile	Sudan
Lahore	Ravi	Pakistan
Leningrad	Neva	Russia
Lisbon	Tagus	Portugal
London	Thames	England
Moscow	Moskva	Russia
Montreal	St. Lawrence	Canada
New Orleans	Mississipi	USA
New York	Hudson	USA
Ottawa	Ottawa	Canada
Paris	Seine	France
Perth	Swan	Australia
Prague	Vitava	Czech Republic
Rome	Tiber	Italy
Rotterdam	New Mass	The Netherlands

Stalingrad	Volga	Russia
Sidney	Darling	Australia
Tokyo	Arakava	Japan
Vienna	Danube	Austria
Warsaw	Vistula	Poland
Washington DC	Potomac	USA
Yangoon	Irrawaddy	Myanmar

Important Boundaries

Durand Line	Pakistan and Afghanistan
MacMohan Line	India and China
Radcliffe Line	India and Pakistan
Maginot Line	France and Germany
Oder Niesse Line	Germany and Poland
Hindenberg Line	Poland and Germany (at the time of First World War)
38th Parallel	North and South Korea
49th Parallel	USA and Canada

Geography of India

The Indian Subcontinent

Mainland of the Indian Subcontinent, comprising India, Pakistan, Bangladesh, Nepal, and Bhutan extends between 8°4'N and 37°9'N latitudes and between 68°7'E and 97°15'E longitudes.

Size and Extent of Subcontinent

- From North to South this subcontinent stretches over 3,200 km and from east to west it is 3,000 km. 82°30' E meridian helps in calculating the Indian Standard Time (IST) which is 5 hours 30 minutes ahead of the Greenwich Mean Time (GMT).
- This very meridian (82½°E) dictates time in Sri Lanka and Nepal also.

Political Divisions of India

India is divided into 29 States and 7 Union Territories.

Basic information

- Latitudinal extent: 8°4' North to 37°6' North.
- Longitudinal extent: 68°7' East to 97°25' East.
- North south extent: 3214 km.
- East west extent: 2933 km.
- Land frontiers: 15200 km.
- Total coastline: 7516.6 km.
- Number of states: 29.
- Number of union territories: 7.
- Land neighbours (7): Pakistan, Afghanistan, China, Nepal, Bhutan, Bangladesh and Myanmar.
- State with longest coastline: Gujarat.
- Active volcano: Barren Island in Andaman and nicobar.
- Southernmost point; Indira point in great Nicobar.
- Southernmost tip main land: Kanyakumari.
- Northernmost point: Indira Col.
- Westenmost point: West of ghaur mota in Gujarat
- Easternmost point: Kibithu in Arunachal Pradesh.
- The Tropic of Cancer (23½° N) passes through the middle of the country. The location of the country is in the northern and the eastern hemispheres.

Indian states situated on the border

Country	Indian States
Pakistan (4)	Gujarat, Rajasthan, Punjab and Jammu and Kashmir
Afghanistan (1)	Jammu and Kashmir
China (5)	Jammu and Kashmir, Uttrakhand, Himachal Pradesh, Sikkim and Arunachal Pradesh
Nepal (5)	Uttar Pradesh, Uttrakhand, Bihar, West Bengal, Sikkim
Bhutan (4)	Sikkim, West Bengal, Assam and Arunachal Pradesh
Bangladesh (5)	West Bengal, Assam, Meghalaya, Tripura and Mizoram

Size of India (In Terms of Area and Population)

- India is the **seventh largest country** (in terms of area) in the world.
- India ranks as the **second largest country** in terms of population (next to China only).
- India contains about one-sixth of the total population of the world.

Physical Features

- Indian subcontinent can be divided into following physical divisions:
  - The Great Mountain wall of the North.
  - The Great Northern Plains.
  - The Great Peninsular Plateau.
  - The Coastal Plains.
  - The Great Indian Desert.
  - The Island Groups.

Himalayas

- Himalayas are young fold mountains of tertiary period, which were folded over Tethys Sea due to inter-continental collision.
- They stretch from the Indus River in the West to the Brahmaputra River in the East.
- The Himalayas, the highest mountain wall of the world, are situated on the northern boundary of India like an arc.
- Mount Everest, the highest peak in the world, lies in these mountains in Nepal.
- The total length is about 2500 km with verying width 240 to 320 km and a total area of 5000 km^2.

Divisions of the Himalayas

The Himalayas consist of three parallel mountain ranges: (i) The Greater Himalayas (ii) The Lesser Himalayas and (iii) The Outer Himalayas.

Location	Important Passes
Jammu and Kashmir	Burzi-La, Joji-La Karakorm Banihal Rohtang
Himachal Pradesh	Bara La, Cha-La, Shipki-La
Uttarakhand	Niti-La, Lipu-Lekh-La
Sikkim	Jelep-La, Nathu-La
Arunachal Pradesh	Bomdi-La

The Great Peninsular Plateau

- It is composed of old cystallin igneous and metamorphic rocks.
- It covers a total of 16000 km^2.
- Narmada which flows through a rift valley divides the region into two parts— the central highland in the north and the deccan plateau in the south.

Eastern Ghats

It comprises the discontinuous and low hills that are highly eroded by the rivers such as the Mahanadi, the Godavari, the Krishna, the Cauvery, etc.

Western Ghats

Western Ghats are locally known by different names such as Sahyadri in Maharashtra, Nilgiri hills in Karnataka and Tamil Nadu and Annamalai hills, Cardamom hills in Kerala.

The Coastal Plains

Narrow steeps of flat land on eastern and western coasts are known as the East Coastal Plain and the West Coastal Plain respectively.

The Great Indian Desert

- It lies to the west of the Aravali range.
- It is in the rain shadow area of the Bay of Bengal current.

Important River Valley Projects of India

Bhakra Nangal Project	On Satluj in Punjab. Highest in India. Height 226m. Reservoir is called Gobind Sagar Lake.
Mandi Project	On Beas in H.P.
Chambal Valley Project	On Chambal in M.P. and Rajasthan. 3 dams are there: Gandhi Sagar dam, Rana Pratap Sagar dam and Jawahar Sagar dam
Damodar Valley Project	On Damodar in Jharkhand. Based on Tennessee Valley Project, USA
Hirakud Project	On Mahanadi in Orissa. World's longest dam: 4,801 m
Rihand Project	On Son in Mirzapur. Reservoir is called Govind Vallabh Pant Reservoir
Kosi Project	On Kosi in N. Bihar
Mayurakshi Project	On Mayurakshi in W.B.
Kakrapara Project	On Tapi in Gujarat
Nizamsagar Project	On Manjra in A.P.
Nagarjuna Sagar Project	On Krishna in A.P.
Tungabhadra Project	On Tungabhadra in A.P. and Karnataka
Shivasamudram Project	On Cauvery in Karnataka
Tata Hydel Scheme	On Bhima in Maharashtra
Sharavathi Hydel Project	On Jog Falls in Karnataka
Farakka Project	On Ganga in W.B. Apart from power and irrigation, it helps to remove silt for easy navigation
Ukai Project	On Tapti in Gujarat
Mahi Project	On Mahi in Gujarat
Salal Project	On Chenab in J and K
Mata Tila Multipurpose Project	On Betwa in U.P. & M.P.
Thein Project	On Ravi, Punjab
Pong Dam	On Beas, Punjab

Climate of india

Climatic Diversity in the Indian Subcontinent

India has tropical monsoon type of climate. It is greatly influenced by the presence of Himalayas in the North as they block the cold masses from Central Asia.

El Nino and La Nina

El Nino is a narrow warm current, which occasionally appears off the coast of Peru in December by temporarily replacing the cold Peru Current. La Nina is the reverse of El-Nino. It is a harbinger of heavy monsoon showers in India.

Agriculture in India

- About 65–70% of the total population of the country is dependent on agriculture.
- Agriculture with its allied activities accounts for 45% of our national income.

There are three crop seasons in India:

- **Kharif:** Sown in June/July, harvested in September/October, e.g., rice, jowar, bajra, ragi, maize, cotton and jute.
- **Rabi:** Sown in October/December, harvested in April/May, e.g., wheat, barley, peas, rapeseed, mustard grains.
- **Zyad:** They are raised between April/June, e.g., melons, watermelons, cucumbers, *toris*, leafy and other vegetables.

Sources of Irrigation in India

There are various sources of irrigation which are:

(a) **Wells and Tubewells:** 46% of total irrigation.
(b) **Canals:** 39% of total irrigation.
(c) **Tanks:** 8% of total irrigation.
(d) **Other sources:** 7% of total irrigation (Dongs, Kuhls, Springs etc.).

National Highways

- They are constructed and maintained by the Central Government.
- The National Highways has 71,772 km length comprising only 2% of the total length of roads, carries about 40% of the total traffic of India.
- NH7 is the longest National Highway in India.
- NH47 is the shortest highway in the Indian highway network.

State Highways

- They are constructed and maintained by the State Government.
- Maharashtra has the maximum length of roads.

Rail Transport

- The total route covered is approximately 63000 km.
- Indian Railway was nationalised in 1950.
- The management and governance of the Indian Railways is in the hands of the Railway Board.
- Railways have been divided into 17 zones.
- India has the second largest railway network in Asia and the fourth largest in the World after the USA, Russia and China.

Air Transport

- JRD Tata was the first person to take a solo flight from Mumbai to Karachi in 1931.
- In 1935, the 'Tata Airlines' started its operation between Mumbai and Thiruvananthapuram and in 1937 between Mumbai and Delhi.
- Airways in India started in 1911.

Water Transport

- The Central Water Tribunal was established in 1887.
- Its headquarters is in Kolkata.

Internal Waterways

- India has got about 14,544 km of navigable waterways which comprise rivers, canals, backwaters, creeks, etc.
- The Inland Waterways Authority of India (IWAI) came into existence on 27 October, 1986.

Ports in India

- India has about 190 ports, with 13 major and the rest intermediate and minor.
- Largest port of India is Jawaharlal Nehru Port in Mumbai.

Important Indian Towns on Rivers

Town	River
Mathura	Yamuna
Delhi	Yamuna
Agra	Yamuna
Badrinath	Alaknanda
Kanpur	Ganga
Kota	Chambal
Ahmedabad	Sabarmati
Bareilly	Ram Ganga
Ayodhya	Saryu
Lucknow	Gomti
Srinagar	Jhelum
Varanasi	Ganga
Patna	Ganga
Ujjain	Kshipra
Jamshedpur	Swarnarekha
Surat	Tapti
Curnool	Tungabhadra
Vijayvada	Krishna
Nasik	Godavari
Hyderabad	Musi
Tiruchirapalli	Cauvery
Cuttack	Mahanadi
Sambalpur	Mahanadi
Kolkata	Hooghly
Guwahati	Brahmaputra
Dibrugarh	Brahmaputra

Nuclear Power Stations in India

Tarapur	Maharashtra
Kalpakkam	Tamil Nadu, called Indira Gandhi Centre for Atomic Research
Narora	U. P.
Rawatbhata	Kota, Rajasthan
Kaiga	Karnataka
Kakrapar	Gujarat
Kudankulam	Tamil Nadu

Major Thermal Power Plants in India

Neyveli	Tamil Nadu
Korba	Chhattisgarh
Obra	U. P.
Harduaganj	U. P.
Rihand	U. P.
Singrauli	U. P.
Parichha	U. P.
Talcher	Odisha
Farakka	W. Bengal
Satpura	M. P.
Ramagundam	A. P.
Vindhyanchal	M. P.

Exercise

1. The Paithan (Jayakwadi) Hydro-electric project, completed with the help of Japan, is on the river
   (a) Ganga (b) Cauvery
   (c) Narmada (d) Godavari
2. The percentage of irrigated land in India is about
   (a) 45 (b) 65
   (c) 35 (d) 25
3. The southernmost point of peninsular India, that is, Kanyakumari, is
   (a) north of Tropic of Cancer
   (b) south of the Equator
   (c) south of the Capricorn
   (d) north of the Equator
4. The pass located at the southern end of the Nilgiri Hills in south India is called
   (a) the Palghat gap
   (b) the Bhorghat pass

(c) the Thalgat pass
(d) the Bolan pass

5. Which of the following factors are responsible for the rapid growth of sugar production in south India as compared to north India?
I.Higher per acre field of sugarcane
II.Higher sucrose content of sugarcane
III. Lower labour cost
IV. Longer crushing period
(a) I and II (b) I, II and III
(c) I, III and IV (d) I, II and IV

6. Which of the following rivers does not flow into the Arabian Sea?
(a) Tungabhadra
(b) Sabarmati
(c) Mandovi
(d) Narmada

7. Which of the following is the highest peak of Satpura Range?
(a) Gurushikhar
(b) Dhupgarh
(c) Pachmarhi
(d) Mahendragiri

8. Consider the following Mangrove areas:
1.Bhitarkanika
2.Pichavaram
3.Coondapur
Which among the above is/are situated on the Eastern Coast of India?
(a) Only 1 (b) 1 and 2
(c) 1 and 3 (d) 1, 2 and 3

9. Tropic of Cancer passes through which of the following group of Indian States:
(a) Gujarat, MP, Chhattisgarh, Manipur
(b) Rajasthan, Jharkhand, West Bengal, Mizoram
(c) UP, MP, Bihar, Jharkhand
(d) Maharashtra, Chhattisgarh, Odisha, Andhra Pradesh

10. The land frontier of India is about 15200 KM. Which of the following countries shares the largest border length with India:
(a) Bangladesh (b) Pakistan
(c) China (d) Nepal

11. The lacustrine deposits of Kashmir called 'Karewas' are known for :
(a) Saffron Cultivation
(b) Terrace farming
(c) Apple Orchards
(d) Jhum Cultivation

12. Which of the following Mountain passes forms the 'tri-junction' of India,China and Myanmar?
(a) Nathu La (b) Jelep La
(c) Bomdi La (d) Diphu

13. Which of the following mountain ranges form a dividing line between the Ganges Plain and the Deccan Plateau?
(a) Aravalli (b) Vindhya
(c) Satpura (d) Ajanta

14. The famous hill-station 'Kodaikanal' lies in:
(a) Nilgiri hills
(b) Palani hills
(c) Cardamom hills
(d) Javadi hills

15. The Andaman and Nicobar Islands are submerged parts of mountain range called:
(a) Arakan Yoma
(b)Pegu Yoma
(c) Askai Chin
(d) Tien Shan

16. Which of the following Indian States/UT has the maximum percentage of mangrove cover in the country?
(a) Gujarat
(b) Wcst Bengal
(c) Andaman and Nicobar
(d) Odisha

17. Asia's largest tulip garden is located in which state?
(a) Jammu & Kashmir
(b) Assam
(c) Sikkim
(d) Uttarakhand

18. Barak valley in Assam is famous for which among the following?
(a) Petroleum Production
(b) Tea Cultivation
(c) Bamboo Industry
(d) Cottage Industries

19. Which among the following spreads from Sasaram and Rohtas in Western Bihar to Chittaurgarh in Rajasthan?
(a) Aravali System
(b) Vindhyan System
(c) Dharwar System
(d) Cudappah System

20. The famous "Chatham Saw Mill" is located in which among the following states / union territories of India?
(a) Daman & Diu
(b) Goa
(c) Andaman & Nicobar Islands
(d) Laskhadweep

21. Area wise, which among the following is the largest physiographic unit of India?
(a) Himalayan Mountains
(b) Thar Desert
(c) Deccan Plateau
(d) Great Plains of North India

22. Heritage power project Sonapani mini-hydel power project is located in which state?
(a) Meghalaya
(b) Mizoram
(c) Nagaland
(d) Arunachal Pradesh

23. At which among the following places, Brahamputra takes a U-turn at the time of entering into India?
(a) Kula Kangri
(b) Lunpo Gangri
(c) Namcha Barwa
(d) Noijin Kangsang

24. Jarawas and Sentinelese tribes are found in which among the following state/Union Territory of India?
(a) Andaman & Nicobar Islands
(b) Madhya Pradesh
(c) Lakshadweep
(d) Arunachal Pradesh

25. Tumkur, where Geological Survey of India has found indications of Gold Reserves, is located in which among the following states?
(a) Andhra Pradesh
(b) Karnataka
(c) Tamil nadu
(d) Maharatsra

26. From which of the following countries India does NOT import Uranium?
(a) Kazakhstan (b) Namibia
(c) Brazil (d) Mongolia

27. Which of the following states is/are not a part of Western Ghats?
(a) Gujarat
(b) Tamil Nadu
(c) Andhra Pradesh
(d) Both (b) and (c)

28. The percentage of earth surface covered by India is
(a) 2.4 (b) 3.4
(c) 4.4 (d) 5.4

29. Which among the following is/are the major factor/factors responsible for the monsoon type of climate in India?

I. Location
II. Thermal contrast
III. Upper air circulation
IV. Inter-tropical convergence zone
(a) I
(b) II, III
(c) II, III and IV
(d) I, II, III and IV

30. The present forest area of India, according to satellite data, is
(a) increasing
(b) decreasing
(c) static
(d) decreasing in open forest area but increasing in closed forest area

31. The India's highest annual rainfall is reported at
(a) Namchi, Sikkim
(b) Churu, Rajasthan
(c) Mawsynram, Meghalaya
(d) Chamba, Himachal Pradesh

32. The refineries are Mathura, Digboi and Panipat are set up by
(a) Indian Oil Corporation Ltd.
(b) Hindustan Petroleum Corporation Ltd.
(c) Bharat Petroleum Corporation Ltd.
(d) Crude Distillation unit of Madras Refineries Ltd.

33. The year ____ is called a Great Divide in the demographic history of India.
(a) 1901 (b) 1921
(c) 1941 (d) 1951

34. The only private sector refinery set up by Reliance Petroleum Ltd. is located at
(a) Guwahati (b) Jamnagar
(c) Mumbai (d) Chennai

35. The only state in India that produces saffron is
(a) Assam
(b) Himachal Pradesh
(c) Jammu and Kashmir
(d) Meghalaya

36. Three important rivers of the Indian subcontinent have their sources near the Mansarover Lake in the Great Himalayas. These rivers are
(a) Indus, Jhelum and Sutlej
(b) Brahmaputra, Sutlej and Yamuna
(c) Brahmaputra, Indus and Sutlej
(d) Jhelum, Sutlej and Yamuna

37. The zonal soil type of peninsular India belongs to
(a) red soils (b) yellow soils
(c) black soils (d) older alluvium

38. Which of the following groups of rivers originate from the Himachal mountains?
(a) Beas, Ravi and Chenab
(b) Ravi, Chenab and Jhelum
(c) Sutlej, Beas and Ravi
(d) Sutlej, Ravi and Jhelum

39. Which of the following groups of states has the largest deposits of iron ore?
(a) Andhra Pradesh and Karnataka
(b) Bihar and Orissa
(c) Madhya Pradesh and Maharashtra
(d) West Bengal and Assam

40. Which of the following union territories of India has the highest density of population per sq km?
(a) Pondicherry (b) Lakshadweep
(c) Delhi (d) Chandigarh

41. Which atomic power station in India is built completely indigenously?
(a) Kalpakkam
(b) Narora
(c) Rawat Bhata
(d) Tarapore

42. The south-west monsoon contributes ____ of the total rain in India.
(a) 86% (b) 50%
(c) 22% (d) 100%

43. Which of the following groups of rivers have their source of origin in Tibet?
(a) Brahmaputra, Ganges and Sutlej
(b) Ganges, Sutlej and Yamuna
(c) Brahmaputra, Indus and Sutlej
(d) Chenab, Ravi and Sutlej

44. Which of the following measures are effective for soil conservation in India?
I. Avoiding crop rotation
II. Afforestation
III. Encouraging the use of chemical fertilizers
IV. Limiting shifting cultivation
(a) I and II (b) II and IV
(c) III and IV (d) I, II and III

45. Which of the following crops needs maximum water per hectare?
(a) Barley (b) Maize
(c) Sugarcane (d) Wheat

46. The watershed between India and Myanmar is formed by
(a) the Naga hills
(b) the Garo hills
(c) Khasi hills
(d) the Jaintia hills

47. The originating in the Himalayan mountain complex consists of how many distinct drainage systems of the Indian Subcontinent?
(a) Two (b) Three
(c) Four (d) Five

48. Which of the following crops is regarded as a plantation crop?
(a) Coconut (b) Cotton
(c) Sugarcane (d) Rice

49. Which of the following countries leads in the production of aluminium and its products in the world?
(a) Australia (b) France
(c) India (d) USA

50. The natural region which holds the Indian subcontinent is
(a) equatorial climate change region
(b) hot deset
(c) monsoon
(d) mediterranean

51. The most ideal region for the cultivation of cotton in India is
(a) the Brahmaputra valley
(b) the Indo-Gangetic valley
(c) the Deccan plateau
(d) the Rann of Kutch

52. The number of major ports in India is
(a) 5 (b) 8
(c) 13 (d) 15

53. Which of the following is a peninsular river of India?
(a) Gandak (b) Kosi
(c) Krishna (d) Sutlej

54. Which of the following is the most important raw material for generation of power in India?
(a) Coal
(b) Mineral Oil
(c) Natural Gas
(d) Uranium

55. When it is noon IST at Allahabad in India, the time at Greenwich, London, will be
(a) midnight ,GMT
(b) 1730 hours
(c) 0630 hours
(d) None of the above

56. Which country has the largest coast line?
(a) USA (b) Australia
(c) Canada (d) India

57. The river Godavari is often referred to as Vridha Ganga because
(a) it is the older river of India
(b) of its large size and extent among the peninsular rivers
(c) there are a fairly large number of pilgrimage centres situated on its banks
(d) its length is nearly the same as that of the river Ganges

58. The scarcity or crop failure of which of the following can cause a serious edible oil crisis in India?
(a) coconut (b) Groundnut
(c) Linseed (d) Mustard

59. The pennines (Europe), Appalachians (America) and the Aravallis (India) are examples of
(a) old mountains
(b) young mountains
(c) fold mountains
(d) block mountains

60. The Jhamarkotra mines of Rajasthan are best known for which among the following minerals?
(a) Mica
(b) Zinc
(c) Rock Phosphate
(d) Lime Stone

61. 'Gir Kesar' , which has been given the Geographical Indication (GI) tag, is a famous variety of which among the following?
(a) Saffron (b) Pepper
(c) Mango (d) Sweat

62. The Kandaleru Dam is located in which state?
(a) Kerala
(b) Maharashtra
(c) Andhra Pradesh
(d) Goa

63. Pagladia Dam Project is located in which state?
(a) Arunachal Pradesh
(b) Sikkim
(c) Assam
(d) West Bengal

64. Prior to Census 2011, in which among the following census highest Sex Ratio was recorded in India?
(a) Census 1941
(b) Census 1951
(c) Census 1961
(d) Census 1971

65. Which among the following rivers is known as Yarlung Tsangpo in Tibet?
(a) Indus (b) Yamuna
(c) Ganges (d) Brahamputra

66. Which among the following was steel plant of India is sometimes called India's First Swadeshi Steel Plant?
(a) Bengal Iron Works Company
(b) TISCO
(c) IISCO
(d) Bokaro Steel Plant

67. In which of the following states, India's maximum number of mines producing minerals (excluding minor minerals, petroleum (crude), natural gas and atomic minerals) are located?
(a) Gujarat
(b) Andhra Pradesh
(c) Jharkhand
(d) Madhya Pradesh

68. Which among the following coal producer of India is outside the Coal India Ltd?
(a) Southern Eastern Coalfields (Bilaspur)
(b) Bharat Coking Coal (Dhanbad)
(c) Mahanandi Coalfields (Sambalpur)
(d) Singerani Collieries Company (Telangana)

69. An Inland water transit and trade protocol exists between India and which among the following neighbors?
(a) Sri Lanka (b) Bangladesh
(c) Pakistan (d) Myanmar

70. Which among the following is the largest district of Maharashtra in terms of Area?
(a) Aurangabad
(b) Ahamednagar
(c) Sindhudurg
(d) Latur

71. Which among the following is not a member country of the Mekong Ganga Cooperation?
(a) India
(b) Bangladesh
(c) Thailand
(d) Vietnam

72. Which among the following is a geology award given annually by Indian Geophysical Union?
(a) Dr. BC Roy Award
(b) Siva Prasad Barooah National Award
(c) M. S. Krishanan Award
(d) Karmaveer Puraskaar

73. Which among the following is the only place in India, where Chinese Fishing Nets are used outside China?
(a) Pondicherry
(b) Kochi
(c) Kolkata
(d) Bhubneshwar

74. Saddam Beach is located in which state?
(a) Tamil Nadu
(b) Kerala
(c) Maharastra
(d) Karnataka

75. Which of the following variety of Marble is found in India?
(a) Makrana
(b) Bhainslana
(c) Phrygia
(d) Carrara

76. In which year , Dakshin Gangotri, India's first settlement in Antarctica got buried in Ice?
(a) 1980 (b) 1985
(c) 1987 (d) 1989

77. Temi Tea Garden is located in which state?
(a) Meghalaya (b) Sikkim
(c) Assam
(d) West Bengal

78. Damodar and Sone river valley and Rajmahal hills in the eastern India are depository of the______?
(a) Cuddappa System Rocks
(b) Dharwar System Rocks
(c) Gondwana System Rocks
(d) Vindhyan System Rocks

79. Port Pipavav, which is the first private sector port in India, is located in which of the following states?
(a) West Bengal
(b) Maharashtra
(c) Gujarat
(d) Andhra Pradesh

80. Which among the following boards is defunct now?
(a) Tea Board of India
(b) Rubber Board
(c) National Biotechnology Board
(d) None of them

81. Which among the following is the latest refinery established?
(a) Digboi (b) Panipat
(c) Trombay (d) Vishakapatnam

82. "Ambassa" was in news as the Geological Survey of India has found huge reserves of coal. In which state Ambasa is located?
(a) Meghalaya (b) Tripura
(c) Assam (d) Nagaland

83. Which among the following is sometimes known as "Third Pole"?
(a) Hudson Highlands
(b) Rocky Mountains
(c) Severny Island ice cap
(d) Siachen Glacier

84. Indian Institute of Crop Processing Technology is located in?
(a) Madurai (b) Thanjaur
(c) Kochi (d) Ooty

85. Which of the following city of Tamil Nadu is known as world's largest producer and most important trading center of turmeric in Asia?
(a) Athoor (b) Karaikudi
(c) Thanjavur (d) Erode

86. Multi-modal International Cargo Hub and Airport (MIHAN) project is in which of the following cities?
(a) Mangalore (b) Hyderabad
(c) Pune (d) Nagpur

87. Which of the following states has largest coastline?
(a) Gujarat
(b) Andhra Pradesh
(c) Maharastra
(d) Tamilnadu

88. Which among the following part of Bombay (now Mumbai) is known as Old Woman's Island?
(a) Parel (b) Worli
(c) Colaba (d) Mazgaon

89. The Jakham Dam is located in which state?
(a) Madhya Pradesh
(b) Gujarat
(c) Rajasthan
(d) Uttar Pradesh

90. Which among the following group of states represents one third of India's cattle population?
(a) Uttar Pradesh, Bihar, Maharastra
(b) Punjab, Orissa, Rajasthan
(c) Karnataka, Rajasthan, Andhra Pradesh
(d) Madhya Pradesh, West Bengal,Uttar Pradesh

91. Which among the following tribe has the largest population in India?
(a) Bhils (b) Meenas
(c) Gonds (d) Sahariyas

92. Bring out the inly mentioned location:
(a) Pasteur Institute of India: Coonoor
(b) National TB Training Institute - Bangalore
(c) Central leprosy Training & Research institute - Chengalpattu
(d) Kasturba Health Society - Ahamadabad

93. Which among the following is sometimes known as "Third Pole"?
(a) Hudson Highlands
(b) Rocky Mountains
(c) Severny Island ice cap
(d) Siachen Glacier

94. "Ambassa" was in news as the Geological Survey of India has found huge reserves of coal. In which state Ambasa is located?
(a) Meghalaya (b) Tripura
(c) Assam (d) Nagaland

95. Which among the following is not matched correctly:
(a) Steel Authority of India Ltd (SAIL) : New Delhi
(b) MECON Ltd. : Ranchi
(c) Hindustan Steel Works Construction Ltd (HSCL) : Kolkata
(d) Ferro Scrap Nigam Ltd.(FSNL) : Bokaro

96. Which among the following is the latest refinery established?
(a) Digboi (b) Panipat
(c) Trombay (d) Vishakapatnam

Answers

1. (d)
2. (c)
3. (d)
4. (a)
5. (d)
6. (a)
7. (b)
8. (b)
9. (b)
10. (a)
11. (a)
12. (d)
13. (b)
14. (b)
15. (a)
16. (b)
17. (a)
18. (b)
19. (b)
20. (c)
21. (c)
22. (a)
23. (c)
24. (a)
25. (b)
26. (c)
27. (c)
28. (a)
29. (d)
30. (b)
31. (c)
32. (a)
33. (b)
34. (b)
35. (c)
36. (c)
37. (a)
38. (a)
39. (b)
40. (c)
41. (a)
42. (a)
43. (c)
44. (b)
45. (c)
46. (a)
47. (b)
48. (a)
49. (d)
50. (c)
51. (c)

52. (c)
53. (c)
54. (a)
55. (c)
56. (c)
57. (b)
58. (b)
59. (a)
60. (c)
61. (c)
62. (c)
63. (c)
64. (c)
65. (d)
66. (d)
67. (b)
68. (d)
69. (b)
70. (b)
71. (b)
72. (c)
73. (b)
74. (b)
75. (a)
76. (d)
77. (b)
78. (c)
79. (c)
80. (c)
81. (b)
82. (b)
83. (d)
84. (b)
85. (d)
86. (d)
87. (a)
88. (c)
89. (c)
90. (d)
91. (a)
92. (d)
93. (d)
94. (b)
95. (d)
96. (b)

3 INDIAN POLITY AND CONSTITUTION

Constitution

Constitution is the foundational law of a country which ordains the fundamental principles on which the government (or the governance) of that country is based. With the exception of the United Kingdom, almost all democratic countries possess a written constitution.

Evolution of Indian Constitution

The first Constitution of India framed and given to themselves by the people of India was adopted by the Constituent Assembly on 26 November 1949. It came into full effect from 26 January 1950. The Constitution as originally adopted had 22 parts, 395 articles and 8 schedules.

Constituent Assembly and Making of the Constitution

- The Cabinet Mission envisaged the establishment of a Constituent Assembly to frame a Constitution for the country. Members of the Constituent Assembly were elected by the Provincial Legislative Assemblies.
- After the partition of India, number of members of the Constituent Assembly came to 299, of whom 284 were actually present on 26 November 1949 and signed on the finally approved Constitution of India Assembly, which had been elected for undivided India, held its first meeting on December 9, 1946, and reassembled on August 14, 1947, as the sovereign Constituent Assembly for the dominion of India.
- It took **two years, eleven months and eighteen days** for the Constituent Assembly to finalise the Constitution.
- The Assembly appointed the Drafting Committee with Dr. B.R. Ambedkar as the Chairman on August 29, 1947.
- The members of the Drafting Committee were N. Gopalaswamy Ayyangar, Alladi Krishnaswamy Ayya, K.M. Munshi, Mohd. Saadullah, B.L. Mitter (later replaced by N. Madhava Rao), and Dr. D.P. Khaitan (replaced on death by T.T. Krishnamachari).
- **Dr. Sachidanand Sinha** was the first President of the Constituent Assembly.
- **Dr. Rajendra Prasad** was elected as the President of the Assembly.

Enactment of the Constitution

On November 26, 1949, Constitution was adopted, containing Preamble and 395 Articles, 18 Parts and 8 Schedules. The Constitution in its current form consists of a Preamble, 24 Parts, 448 Articles and 12 Schedules.

Enforcement of the Constitution

The Constitution came into force on January 26, 1950.

Salient features of the constitution

- Parliamentary Government
- India has a parliamentary system of government both at the centre and at the states. The president is the head of the union of India and the Governors are head of the states but they act on the advice of the council of ministers. They have nominal powers.
- **Federal system with unitary features:** Our constitution contains federal features of government like division of powers written constitution, independent judiciary and bicameralism but a large number of unitary features like a strong center, single citizenship flexibility of constitution, integrated judiciary emergency provisions etc.
- Independent Judiciary
- Secular state
- Emergency provisions

Schedules of the Indian Constitution

1st Schedule: 29 States and 7 Union Territories with Territorial demarcations.

2nd Schedule: Part 'A' Salary and emoluments of the President and Governors of States.

Part 'B' Omitted.

Part 'C' Salary and emoluments of the Speaker/Deputy Speaker or Chairman/Vice-Chairman of the Lok Sabha, Rajya Sabha and State Legislative Assemblies or Councils.

Part 'D' Salary and emoluments of the judge of the Supreme Court and High Courts.

Part 'E' Salary and emoluments of the Comptroller and Auditor General of India.

3rd Schedule: Forms of oath and affirmations of members of legislatures, ministers and judges.

4th Schedule: Allocation of seats to States and Union Territories in the Rajya Sabha.

5th Schedule: Administration and control of Scheduled Areas and STs.

6th Schedule: Administration of Tribal Areas of North-Eastern States.

7th Schedule: Distribution of power between the Union and the State Government. (Union List, State List and Concurrent List).

8th Schedule: Description of 22 languages recognised by the constitution.

9th Schedule: Validation of certain Acts and Regulations.

10th Schedule: Provisions as to disqualification on ground of defection (Anti-defection Law introduced by the 52nd Constitutional Amendment Act).

11th Schedule: Power, authority and responsibilities of Panchayats, 29 subjects over which the Panchayats have jurisdiction (refer to the 73rd Constitutional Amendment Act).

12th Schedule: Powers, authority and responsibilities of Municipalities, 18 subjects over which the

Municipalities have jurisdiction (refer to the 74th Constitutional Amendment Act).

The Preamble

➢ **Text of the Preamble:** "We, the People of India having solemnly resolved to constitute India into a **Sovereign Socialist Secular Democratic Republic** and to secure to all citizens **Justice**, social, economic and political; **Liberty** of thought, expression, belief, faith and worship, **Equality** of status and of opportunity; and to promote among them all **Fraternity** assuring the dignity of the individual and the unity and integrity of the Nation in our Constituent Assembly on this twenty-sixth day of November, 1949, do hereby adopt, enact and give to ourselves this constitution."

➢ The Preamble to the Indian Constitution is based on the **Objectives Resolution** drafted and moved by Pandit Nehru and adopted by the Constituent Assembly.

➢ The Preamble is **not enforceable in a court of law**.

➢ The Preamble has been amended only once so far, in 1976, by 42nd Constitutional Amendment Act, which added three new words **Socialist, Secular** and **Integrity.** This amendment was held to be valid.

Fundamental Rights

➢ The Fundamental Rights have been described in **Articles 12-35**, Part III of Indian Constitution.

➢ Right to Freedom articles 19-22.

➢ Right against Exploitation Articles 23-24

➢ Right to Freedom of religion Articles 25-28

➢ Cultural and Educational Rights Articles 29-30

➢ Right to Constitutional Remedies Article-32

➢ The Writs

➢ Right to Information

Fundamental Duties

In 1976, the FDs of citizens were added by 42nd **Constitutional Amendment Act** on the basis of Swaran Singh Committee Report.

List of Fundamental Duties

According to **Article 51A**, it shall be the duty of every citizen of India:

➢ To abide by the Constitution and respect its ideals and institutions, the National Flag and the National Anthem;

➢ To cherish and follow the noble ideals that inspired the national struggle for freedom;

➢ To uphold and protect the sovereignty, unity and integrity of India;

➢ To promote harmony and the spirit of common brotherhood amongst all the people of India transcending religious, linguistic and regional or sectional diversities and to renounce practices derogatory to the dignity of women;

➢ To defend the country and render national service, when called upon to do so;

➢ To value and preserve the rich heritage of the country's composite culture;

➢ To protect and improve the natural environment including forests, lakes, rivers and wildlife and to have compassion for living creatures;

➢ To develop scientific temper, humanism and the spirit of inquiry and reform;

➢ To safeguard public property and to abjure violence;

➢ To strive toward excellence in all spheres of individual and collective activity so that the nation constantly rises to higher levels of endeavour and achievement; and

➢ To provide opportunities for education to his child or ward between the age of 6 to 14 years. This duty was added by the 86th Constitutional Amendment Act, 2002.

Executive of the Union

The President

➢ President is the head of the Union Executive.

➢ The President of India is indirectly elected by an electoral college, in accordance with the system of proportional representation by means of the single transferable vote.

➢ The Electoral College for the president consists of:

- The elected members of both Houses of Parliament;
- The elected members of the Legislative Assemblies of the states; and
- The elected members of the Legislative Assemblies of Union Territories of Delhi and Pondicherry (now Puducherry).

Term of the President

Under Article 56, the President shall hold office for a term of five year from the date on which he enters upon his office.

Presidents of India

S.No.	Name	Period
1.	Rajendra Prasad	26 Jan. 1950 to 13 May 1962
2.	Sarvapalli Radhakrishnan	13 May 1962 to 13 May 1967
3.	Zakir Hussain	13 May 1967 to 3 May 1969
4.	Varahagiri Venkata Giri	3 May 1969 to 20 July 1969
5.	Muhammad Hidayatullah	20 July 1969 to 24 Aug. 1969
6.	Varahagiri Venkata Giri	24 Aug. 1969 to 24 Aug. 1974
7.	Fakhruddin Ali Ahmed	24 Aug. 1974 to 11 Feb. 1977
8.	Basappa Danappa Jatti	11 Feb. 1977 to 25 July 1977
9.	Neelam Sanjiva Reddy	25 July 1977 to 25 July 1982
10.	Giani Zail Singh	25 July 1982 to 25 July 1987
11.	Ramaswamy Venkataraman	25 July 1987 to 25 July 1992
12.	Shankar Dayal Sharma	25 July 1992 to 25 July 1997

13.	Kocheril Raman Narayanan	25 July 1997 to 25 July 2002
14.	A.P.J. Abdul Kalam	25 July 2002 to 25 July 2007
15.	Pratibha Patil	25 July 2007 to 25 July 2012
16.	Pranab Mukherjee	25 July 2012 to 25 July 2017
17.	Ramnath Kobind	25 July 2017 to till date

The Vice-President

- Vice-President is indirectly elected by means of single transferable vote.
- State Legislatures do not take part in the election of Vice-President.
- Electoral College of Vice-President consists of elected and nominated members of both the Houses of Parliament.
- All disputes regarding election of Vice-President are adjudicated by the Supreme Court.

Term of Office Under Article 67

- Holds office for a **term of 5 years** from the date on which he enters upon his office.
- Can be removed by a resolution of the Rajya Sabha passed by an absolute majority and agreed by the Lok Sabha [Article 67 (b)].

The Prime Minister and the Union Council of Ministers

Prime Minister

Prime Minister is the head of the government while President is the head of the State of the Republic of India.

Article 75 says that the Prime Minister shall be appointed by the President.

Oath, Term and Salary

The **term of the Prime Minister is not fixed** and he holds office during the pleasure of the President. However, this does not mean that the President can dismiss the Prime Minister at any time. So long as the Prime Minister enjoys the majority support in the Lok Sabha, he cannot be dismissed by the President. However, if he loses the confidence of the Lok Sabha, he must resign or the President can dismiss him.

Prime Ministers of India

S.No.	Name	Period
1.	Jawahar Lal Nehru	15 Aug. 1947 to 27 May 1964
2.	Gulzarilal Nanda	27 May 1964 to 9 June 1964
3.	Lal Bahadur Shastri	09 June 1964 to 11 Jan. 1966
4.	Gulzarilal Nanda	11 Jan. 1966 to 24 Jan. 1966
5.	Indira Gandhi	24 Jan. 1966 to 24 March 1977
6.	Morarji Desai	24 March 1977 to 28 July 1979
7.	Charan Singh	28 July 1979 to 14 Jan. 1980
8.	Indira Gandhi	14 Jan. 1980 to 31 Oct. 1984
9.	Rajiv Gandhi	31 Oct. 1984 to 2 Dec. 1989
10.	Vishwanath Pratap Singh	2 Dec.1989 to 10 Nov. 1990
11.	Chandra Shekhar	10 Nov. 1990 to 21 June 1991
12.	P.V. Narasimha Rao	21 June 1991 to 16 May 1996
13.	Atal Behari Vajpayee	16 May 1996 to 1 June 1996
14.	H.D. Deve Gowda	1 June 1996 to 21 April 1997
15.	Atal Behari Vajpayee	19 March 1998 to 22 May 2004
16.	Dr. Manmohan Singh	22 May 2004 to 26 May 2014
17.	Narendra Modi	26 May 2014 to till date

Appointment of Ministers

Ministers are appointed by the President on the advice of the Prime Minister.

Oath and Salary of Ministers

President administers the oath to the Ministers.

Responsibility of Ministers

Under Article 75, the CoMs is collectively responsible to Lok Sabha for all their acts.

Deputy Prime Minister

The post of Deputy Prime Minister is not mentioned in the Constitution.

List of Deputy Prime Ministers

Name	Tenure
Sardar Vallabhbhai Patel	1947–1950
Morarji Desai	1967–1969
Charan Singh and Jagjiven Ram	1979–1979
Y. B. Chavan	1979–1980
Devi Lal	1989–1990
Devi Lal	1990–1991
L. K. Advani	2002–2004

The Attorney General of India

- The Attorney General is the first Law Officer of the Government of India.

- The Attorney General for India is appointed by the President and holds office during the pleasure of the President. He must have the same qualifications as required to be a Judge of the Supreme Court.
- The Attorney General for India is not a member of the Cabinet. But he has the right to speak in the Houses of Parliament or in any Committee thereof, but he has no right to vote.
- He is entitled to the privileges of a Member of Parliament. In the performance of his official duties, the Attorney General has the right of audience in all Courts in the territory of India.

The Comptroller and Auditor General of India

- Though appointed by the President, the Comptroller and Auditor General can be grounded of proved misbehaviour or incapacity.
- His salary and conditions of service are laid down by Parliament and cannot be varied to his disadvantage during his term of office.
- The term of office of the Comptroller and Auditor General (CAG) is 6 years from the date on which he assumes office.
- CAG vacates office on attaining the age of 65 years even without completing the 6-year term. He can resign by writing under his hand, addressed to the President of India.
- His salary is equal to that of a Judge of the Supreme Court.

The Parliament of India

- The Parliament of India consists of the President, the Lok Sabha and the Rajya Sabha (Article 79).
- Out of seven UTs only two (Delhi and Puducherry) have representation in the Rajya Sabha.

Rajya Sabha [Article 80]

- Rajya Sabha is a permanent body and **not subject to dissolution.** Its maximum strength is 250. The total membership of the present Rajya Sabha is 245 however one-third members retire every second year. Their seats are filled up by fresh elections and presidential nomination at the beginning of every third year.
- There are no seats reserved for SCs and STs in Rajya Sabha.
- Representation of People Act (1951) provided the term of office of a member of the Rajya Sabha shall be **six years.**

Lok Sabha [Article 81]

- Its maximum strength is 550 + 2 members of its Anglo-Indian Community, which includes 530 members from States and 20 from Union Territories. Present strength of Lok Sabha is 545.
- The representatives of the States are directly elected by the people of the States on the basis of adult suffrage.
- Every citizen who is not less than 18 years of age and is not otherwise disqualified is entitled to vote at such election.
- The normal term of the Lok Sabha is 5 years, but it may be dissolved earlier by the President.
- The normal term of Lok Sabha can be extended by an Act passed by Parliament itself during Emergency.
- The extension cannot be made for a period exceeding one year at a time.
- Such extension cannot continue beyond a period of six months after the proclamation of Emergency ceases to operate.
- Parliament must meet at least twice a year and not more than six months shall elapse between two sessions of Parliament.

Speaker and Deputy Speaker of The Lok Sabha

- He is elected by Lok Sabha from amongst its members, as soon as, after the first meeting.
- He remains in his office during the life of the Lok Sabha. He vacates office earlier in any of the following cases:
- If he ceases to be member of Lok Sabha;
- If he resigns by writing to the Deputy Speaker; and
- If he is removed by a resolution passed by a majority of all the members of the Lok Sabha. Such a resolution can be moved only after giving 14 days advance notice.

Deputy Speaker

Anthasayanam Ayyangar was the First Deputy Speaker of Lok Sabha.

Special Power of Rajya Sabha

Due to its federal character, the Rajya Sabha has been given two exclusive or special powers that are not enjoyed by the Lok Sabha.

1. It can authorise the Parliament to make a law on a subject enumerated in the State List (Article 249).
2. It can authorise the Parliament to create new all-India Service (Common for both the Centre and States (Article 312).

Chairman and Deputy Chairman of the Rajya Sabha

- Vice-President of India is ex-officio Chairman of the Rajya Sabha and functions as the Presiding Officer of that House so long as he does not officiate as the President.
- The Chairman may be removed from his office only if he is **removed** from the office of the Vice-President.

Executive of the States: the Governor

- The Governor is the Constitutional Head of the State and the same Governor can act as Governor of more than one State (Articles 153 and 154).
- Under **Article 155,** the Governor is appointed by the President. **Article 156** states that the Governor holds office during the pleasure of the President.

Tenure of Governor Under Article 156

(a) The Governor shall hold office during the pleasure of the President;
(b) He may resign by writing under the hand addressed to the President;
(c) He holds office for a period of 5 years.
(d) There is no bar to a person being appointed Governor more than once.

Chief Minister's (CM) Appointment

Article 164, says that Chief Minister shall be appointed by the Governor of the State.

Oath, Term and Salary

- Oath of the office of Chief Minister is administered by the Governor to person appointed for this purpose.

- A person, who is not a member of State Legislature can be appointed but he has to get himself elected within 6 months otherwise he is removed.
- The **term of the CM is not fixed** and he holds office during the pleasure of the Governor.
- He cannot be dismissed by the Governor as long as he enjoys the majority support in the Legislative Assembly. But, if he loses the confidence of the Assembly, he must resign or the Governor can dismiss him.

The Supreme Court

- **Article 124** states the establishment and constitution of Supreme Court.
- Every Judge of the Supreme Court, after consulting the Chief Justice of the Supreme Court, is appointed by the President of India.
- At present, the Supreme Court consists of 31 Judges (one CJI and 30 Judges).

Tenure of Judges

The Constitution makes the following provisions:

- Holds office **until he attains the age of 65 years**.
- Resign his office by writing to the President.
- Removed from his office by the President on the recommendation of the Parliament.

Constitutional Bench

A bench consisting of at least 5 judges constituted by the CJI to hear a case involving a substantial question of law.

The High Court

- Accordingly, the President determines the strength of a High Court from time-to-time depending upon its workload.
- The territorial jurisdiction of a High Court is co-terminus with the territory of a State.

Finance Commission

- The Constitution provides for the establishment of a Finance Commission (Articles 272, 273, 275, and 280) by the President.
- The Finance Commission consists of a Chairman and four other members.
- According to the qualifications prescribed by the Parliament, the Chairman is selected among persons who have had experience in public affairs.
- The Commission submits its recommendations to the President which are generally accepted by the Central Government. The recommendations of the Commission are applicable for a period of five years.

Public Service Commissions

- A Joint Public Service Commission can be created by Parliament in pursuance of a resolution passed by the State Legislatures concerned.
- The Union Public Service Commission can serve the needs of a State, if so requested by the Governor of that State and approved by the President.
- Appointment, determination of number of members of the Commission and their conditions of service is done by:
  - The President in the case of the Union or a Joint Commission, and
  - The Governor of State in the case of a State Commission.
- Half of the members of Commission should be persons who have held office under the Government of India or of a State for at least 10 years (Article 316).
- The term of service of a member of a Commission is 6 years from the date of his entering upon office, or until the age of retirement, whichever is earlier.
- Age of retirement for a member of UPSC is **65 years**.
- Age of retirement for a member of PSC of a State or a Joint Commission is **62 years**.
- Services of a member of a Public Service Commission can be terminated by:
  - Resignation in writing addressed to the President (to the Governor in the case of a State Commission).
  - Removal by the President.
- The expenses of the Commission are charged on the Consolidated Fund of India or of the Sate (as the case may be).
- The Chairman of the UPSC is ineligible for further employment either under the Government of India or under the Government of a State.
- The Chairman of a State Public Service Commission is eligible for appointment as the Chairman or member of the Union Public Service Commission or as the Chairman of any other State Public Service Commission, but not for any other employment either under the Government of India or under the Government of a State.
- A member of a State Public Service Commission is eligible for appointment as the Chairman of a State Public Service Commission and Chairman or member of UPSC, but not for any other employment either under the Government of India or under the Government of a State.

Election Commission

- The Election Commission was established in accordance with the Constitution on 25 January 1950.
- The Election Commission consists of a Chief Election Commissioner and two other Election Commissioners.
- President can determine the number of Election Commissioners.

Chief Election Commissioner (CEC)

- The President appoints the Chief Election Commissioner, who has tenure of 6 years, or up to the age of 65 years, whichever is earlier.
- The CEC enjoys the same status and receives the same salary and perks as available to Judges of the Supreme Court.
- The Chief Election Commissioner can be removed from his office only in a manner and on the grounds prescribed for removal of Judge of the Supreme Court.
- Other Election Commissioners can be removed by the President on the recommendation of the Chief Election Commissioner.

Exercise

1. The minimum age for being eligible to become the Prime Minister of India is
   (a) 21 years (b) 25 years
   (c) 30 years (d) 35 years
2. Which one of the following is not mentioned in the Indian constitution?
   (a) Election Commission
   (b) Planning Commission
   (c) Public Service Commission
   (d) Finance Commission
3. When was the constituent assembly established to frame the constitution of India?
   (a) 10th June, 1946
   (b) 6th December, 1946
   (c) 26th November, 1949
   (d) 26th December,1949
4. The number of articles in the Indian constitution at the time of its ad was
   (a) 350 (b) 360
   (c) 390 (d) 395
5. When was the President's succession act enacted?
   (a) 1955 (b) 1959
   (c) 1964 (d) 1969
6. In a parliamentary system, the executive is responsible to
   (a) the legislature
   (b) the judiciary
   (c) the people
   (d) none of these
7. Who enjoys the right to impose reasonable restrictions on the Fundamental Rights?
   (a) The President
   (b) The Supreme Court
   (c) The Parliament
   (d) The Lok Sabha
8. How many times the President has declared the financial emergency?
   (a) once (b) twice
   (c) thrice (d) never
9. Who decides the disputes regarding the election of the President?
   (a) The Speaker
   (b) The Supreme Court
   (c) The Election Commission
   (d) The Parliament
10. How many seats are reserved for Union Territories in the Lok Sabha?
    (a) 10 seats (b) 15 seats
    (c) 20 seats (d) 30 seats
11. Who is legally competent to declare war?
    (a) The President
    (b) The Prime Minister
    (c) The Lok Sabha
    (d) The Parliament
12. Fundamental duties were introduced in the Indian constitution by the
    (a) 40th Amendment
    (b) 42nd Amendment
    (c) 43rd Amendment
    (d) 44th Amendment
13. Directive principles of state policy are directly concerned with
    (a) Fundamental rights
    (b) Fundamental duties
    (c) Gandhian principles
    (d) Preamble
14. What is the Maximum age prescribed for election as President of India?
    (a) 58 years (b) 60 years
    (c) 62 years (d) no such limit
15. The President of India can declare emergency
    (a) on his own
    (b) on the recommendations of the council of Ministers
    (c) on the recommendations of the Prime Minister
    (d) on the recommendations of the Parliament
16. The preamble to the Indian constitution was amended by the
    (a) 24th Amendment
    (b) 36th Amendment
    (c) 42nd Amendment
    (d) 44th Amendment
17. Who is the chairman of the thirteenth finance commission of India?
    (a) K.C. Pant
    (b) Y.B. Chawan
    (c) A. M.Khusro
    (d) Vijay Kelkar
18. Who has the right to convince the joint session of the two houses of Parliament in India?
    (a) The Prime Minister
    (b) The President
    (c) The Vice-President
    (d) None of them
19. The Chief source of political power in India is
    (a) the people
    (b) the constitution
    (c) the parliament
    (d) the parliament and the state legislatures
20. The Prime Minister is the
    (a) Head of the State
    (b) Head of the Government
    (c) Head of the State and the head of the Government
    (d) None of these
21. Under which High Court Andaman & Nicobar Islands come?
    (a) Madras High Court
    (b) Kerala High Court
    (c) Andhra Pradesh High Court
    (d) Calcutta High Court
22. Which article accords special status to Jammu & Kashmir?
    (a) 356 (b) 360
    (c) 372 (d) 370
23. The union territories of India are administered by the
    (a) President
    (b) Prime Minister
    (c) Defence Minister
    (d) Chief Minister
24. Untouchability comes under which fundamental rights in the Indian constitution?
    (a) Right to freedom
    (b) Right to equality
    (c) Right against exploitation
    (d) Right to freedom of religion
25. Organisation of village panchayats are in corporated under which head in the Indian constitution?
    (a) Fundamental rights
    (b) Citizenship
    (c) Directive principles of the state
    (d) Fundamental duties
26. The Chief Justice of the Supreme Court is appointed by
    (a) The President
    (b) The Prime Minister
    (c) The Parliament
    (d) The Law Minister
27. Who will act as the President of India when the offices of both the President and the Vice-President are vacant?
    (a) The Chief Election Commissioner
    (b) The Prime Minister

(c) The Chief Justice of India
(d) The Speaker of Lok Sabha

28. Who has the right to convene the joint session of the two houses of parliament in India?
(a) The Prime Minister
(b) The President
(c) The Vice-President
(d) None of them

29. The planning commission was created in
(a) 1950 A.D (b) 1952 A.D
(c) 1953 A.D (d) 1954 A.D

30. The first citizen of India is the
(a) President
(b) Vice-President
(c) Prime Minister
(d) Speaker

31. The emergency provisions of Indians constitution were borrowed from
(a) Government of India Act, 1935
(b) Soviet Union
(c) Constitution of USA
(d) Weimer constitution of Germany

32. After great labour, the constitution was ready on
(a) 26th December, 1949
(b) 26th January, 1950
(c) 26th November, 1949
(d) 30th November, 1949

33. Indian constitution is often called
(a) Lawyer's paradise
(b) Dictatorial constitution
(c) Evolved constitution
(d) Enacted constitution

34. At present the right to property is merely a
(a) legal right (b) moral right
(c) natural right (d) none of these

35. The term of the office of the President is
(a) 2 years (b) 4 years
(c) 6 years (d) 5 years

36. Lower house of the Indian Parliament is known as
(a) Lok Sabha (b) Rajya Sabha
(c) Assembly (d) Council

37. The highest appeal court in a state is
(a) Session court
(b) Supreme court
(c) Magistrate court
(d) High court

38. Who was the permanent chairman of the constituent assembly?
(a) Dr.Rajendra Prasad
(b) Dr.Ambedkar
(c) Pandit Jawaharlal Nehru
(d) Mahatma Gandhi

39. Freedom of religion is included in articles?
(a) 25-27 (b) 25-28
(c) 26-29 (d) 24-27

40. Which one of the following statements is not correct?
(a) Equal representation is given to states in Rajya Sabha
(b) The Central Government is very strong
(c) Both the Center and the States can legislate on concurrent list
(d) Residuary powers are with the centre

41. Indian upper house is known as
(a) the house of people
(b) the council of states
(c) parliament
(d) none of these

42. The first civil service commission in India was set up on the basis of recommendation of
(a) Aichison Commission
(b) Lee Commission
(c) Simon Commission
(d) Planning Commission

43. The constitution provides for the setting up of the Finance Commission every
(a) year (b) third year
(c) fifth year (d) seventh year

44. The constitution of India was adopted by the
(a) Constituent Assembly
(b) First Parliament
(c) Lok Sabha
(d) Drafting Committee

45. Normally the Parliament can legislate on the subjects enumerated in
(a) the union list
(b) the concurrent list
(c) the state list
(d) the union as well as the concurrent list

46. The constitution of India vests the executive authority of the union in the
(a) President
(b) Council of Ministers
(c) President and Parliament
(d) Prime Minister

47. According to the constitution the upper house of the state legislative can be created or abolished by
(a) The State Legislative Assembly
(b) The Parliament of India
(c) The Governor of the State
(d) Presidential order

48. Which state legislative assembly has the maximum strength?
(a) Andhra Pradesh
(b) West Bengal
(c) Uttar Pradesh
(d) Maharashtra

49. Which one of the following categories of members are not included in the legislative council?
(a) Members elected by Municipalities, District Boards and other local authorities in the state.
(b) Representatives of temple, churches and mosques.
(c) Representatives of persons engaged in teaching in institutions not lower in standard than secondary school
(d) Members nominated by the Governor from amongst persons having special knowledge of literature, science, art, cooperative movements and social service

50. Who had played key role in the formation of Lokpal Bill in India?
(a) Baba Amte
(b) Anna Hajare
(c) Vipin Hazarika
(d) Kiran Bedi

51. The Residuary powers of legislation under Indian Constitution rests with
(a) President (b) Prime Minister
(c) Parliament (d) States

52. Appointments for all India Services are made by
(a) UPSC
(b) President
(c) Prime Minister
(d) Parliament

53. Right to Constitutional Remedies comes under ________
(a) Legal rights
(b) Fundamental rights
(c) Human rights
(d) Natural rights

54. he Comptroller and Auditor-General of India submits his report relating to the accounts of the Union to the ________.
(a) Finance Minister
(b) Prime Minister

(c) President
(d) Chief Justice of the Supreme Court

55. In a Parliamentary form of Government ________
(a) The Legislature is responsible to the Judiciary
(b) The Executive is responsible to the Legislature.
(c) The Legislature is responsible to the Executive
(d) The Judiciary is responsible to the Legislature

56. Which of the following statements is correct about the President of India ?
(a) Addresses first session of Parliament after each General Election.
(b) Addresses first session of Parliament at the beginning of each year
(c) Addresses every session of Parliament
(d) Never addresses Parliament

57. Right to Privacy comes under ____
(a) Article 19 (b) Article 20
(c) Article 21 (d) Article 18

58. What is the meaning of "Public Interest Litigation"?
(a) Anything of public interest
(b) A case brought by victim to court, involving public interest.
(c) A case brought by anyone to court involving public interest.
(d) A directive issued by Supreme Court involving public interest

59. Who appoints and dismisses the gazetted officials of the Union Government?
(a) The President of India
(b) The Prime Minister of India
(c) The Home Minister of India
(d) The Finance Minister of India

60. Which of the following is a name of US Parliament?
(a) Diet
(b) Senate
(c) Congress
(d) House of Commons

61. Which of the following is not provided in the constitution ?
(a) Election Commission
(b) Finance Commission
(c) Public Service Commission
(d) Planning Commission

62. The Comptroller and Auditor General of India does not audit the receipts and expenditure of
(a) Central Government
(b) Local Bodies
(c) State Government
(d) Government Companies

63. The minimum number of members that must be present to hold the meeting of the Lok Sabha is
(a) One-fourth of the total membership
(b) One-tenth of the total membership
(c) Fifty percent strength of the Lok Sabha
(d) At least hundred members

64. In India which of the following taxes is levied by the State governments?
(a) Excise duty on liquor
(b) Capital gains tax
(c) Customs tax
(d) Corporation tax

65. After hour, a motion moved by a Member of Parliament to draw the attention of Executive for discussing a definite matter of public importance is
(a) Privilege motion
(b) Calling attention Motion
(c) Adjournment motion
(d) No-confidence motion

66. The Chairman of the Public Accounts Committee of the Parliament is appointed by the
(a) President of India
(b) Prime Minister of India
(c) Speaker of Lok Sabha
(d) Chairman of Rajya Sabha

67. Which of the following constitutional Amendment Act, deals with the Elementary Education as a Fundamental Right?
(a) 84th Amendment Act
(b) 85th Amendment Act
(c) 86th Amendment Act
(d) 87th Amendment Act

68. In which way the President can assign any of the functions of the Union Government to the State Government ?
(a) In his discretion
(b) In consultation with the Chief Justice of India
(c) In consultation with the Government of the State
(d) In consultation with the State Governor

69. In the 42nd Constitutional Amendment 1976, which word was added to the Preamble?
(a) Democratic (b) Equality
(c) Secular (d) Socialist

70. Chief Ministers of States are members of ________
(a) NITI Commission(Aayog)
(b) Finance Commission
(c) National Development Council
(d) Election Commission

71. The Comptroller and Auditor General is closely connected with which of the following Committees of Parliament?
(a) The Estimates Committee
(b) The Committee on Public Undertakings
(c) The Public Accounts Committee
(d) All of these

72. The Speaker of Lok Sabha addresses his letter of resignation to the
(a) President of India
(b) Prime Minister
(c) Deputy Speaker of Lok Sabha
(d) The Chief Justice of India

73. The power of the Supreme Court of India to decide disputes between the Centre and the States falls under its
(a) Advisory jurisdiction
(b) Original jurisdiction
(c) Appellate jurisdiction
(d) Jurisprudence

74. If a budget is defeated in the legislature of a state then
(a) The Finance Minister alone has to resign
(b) The Finance Minister concerned has to be suspended
(c) The council of Ministers along with the Chief Minister has to resign
(d) Re-election have to be ordered

75. Lok Sabha Secretariat comes under the direct control of
(a) Ministry of Home Affairs
(b) Ministry of Parliamentary Affairs
(c) Speaker of Lok Sabha
(d) President

76. The word "Secular" was added to the Preamble of the Constitution of India by which Constitutional Amendment?

(a) 41st Constitutional Amendment
(b) 42nd Constitutional Amendment
(c) 43rd Constitutional Amendment
(d) 44th Constitutional Amendment

77. What is the minimum age for membership to Rajya Sabha ?
(a) 20 years (b) 25 years
(c) 30 years (d) 35 years

78. The minimum age limit for the membership of the Vidhan Parishad is _____.
(a) 21 years (b) 25 years
(c) 30 years (d) 35 years

79. The Preventive Detention Act curtailed
(a) Right to Freedom
(b) Right to Equality
(c) Right to Property
(d) Education Right

80. Ideas of welfare state are contained in
(a) Fundamental Rights
(b) Directive Principles of State Policy
(c) Preamble of the Constitution
(d) Part VII

81. Who has the right to decide whether a Bill is a money bill or not?
(a) Speaker of Lok Sabha
(b) Prime Minister
(c) President
(d) Finance Minister

82. The discretionary powers of a Governor is limited in
(a) Appointment of Chief Minister
(b) Dismissal of the Ministry
(c) Dissolution of the Legislative Assembly
(d) Assent to Bills

83. Who is the first law officer of the country?
(a) Chief Justice of India
(b) Attorney General
(c) Law Minister
(d) Solicitor General

84. The Residuary powers of legislation under Indian Constitution rests with
(a) President (b) Prime Minister
(c) Parliament (d) States

85. Appointments for all India Services are made by
(a) UPSC
(b) President
(c) Prime Minister
(d) Parliament

86. Right to Constitutional Remedies comes under _____
(a) Legal rights
(b) Fundamental rights
(c) Human rights
(d) Natural rights

87. The Comptroller and Auditor-General of India submits his report relating to the accounts of the Union to the _____.
(a) Finance Minister
(b) Prime Minister
(c) President
(d) Chief Justice of the Supreme Court

88. Whose recommendation is mandatory to impeach the President of India from his office before the completion of his/her term?
(a) The Prime Minister
(b) The Speaker of the Lok Sabha
(c) The Chief Justice of India
(d) The two houses of the parliament

89. How many types of writ are there in the Indian Constitution?
(a) 5 (b) 4
(c) 3 (d) 2

90. How many Fundamental Duties are mentioned in Indian constitution?
(a) Five (b) Seven
(c) Nine (d) Eleven

91. Part IV of Constitution of India deals with which of the following?
(a) The Union
(b) The States
(c) Fundamental Rights
(d) Directive Principles of State Policy

92. In Indian Constitution, the method of election of President has been taken from which country?
(a) Britain (b) USA
(c) Ireland (d) Australia

93. What is the literal meaning of the term "Quo-Warranto"?
(a) We command
(b) To forbid
(c) By what authority (or) warrant
(d) None of these

94. Who administers the oath of the President of India?
(a) Governor General of India
(b) Chief Justice of India
(c) Prime Minister of India
(d) Vice President of India

95. Who among the following gave monistic theory of sovereignty?
(a) Austin (b) Darwin
(c) Aristotle (d) Marx

96. Which of the following are constituents of Indian Parliament?
(i) The President
(ii) The Council of States (Rajya Sabha)
(iii) The House of the People (Lok Sabha)
(a) (ii) and (iii)
(b) (i) and (ii)
(c) (i) and (iii)
(d) (i), (ii) and (iii)

97. Who among the following is the executive head of state in India?
(a) Prime Minister
(b) President
(c) Cabinet Secretary
(d) Finance Secretary

98. Which of the following has the supreme command of the Indian Defence Forces?
(a) Prime Minister of India
(b) Defence Minister of India
(c) Council of Ministers of India
(d) President of India

99. Anti-defection law is given in which schedule of Indian constitution?
(a) Second Schedule
(b) Tenth Schedule
(c) Third Schedule
(d) Fourth Schedule

100. Who appoints Governor of a state in India?
(a) Prime Minister of India
(b) Council of Minister
(c) Judge of Supreme Court
(d) President of India

101. What is the literal meaning of 'Certiorari'?
(a) We command
(b) To have the body of
(c) To forbid
(d) To be certified (or) to be informed

102. Who among the following is not a member of any of the two houses of our country?
(a) Prime Minister
(b) Finance Minister
(c) President
(d) Railway Minister

103. Which article of Indian constitution has the provision for National Emergency?
(a) Article 350 (b) Article 352
(c) Article 312 (d) Article 280

104. Fundamental duties are mentioned in which of the following part of Indian Constitution?
(a) Part II (b) Part III
(c) Part V (d) Part IV A

105. What is the minimum age for becoming a Governor of state in India?
(a) 30 years (b) 25 years
(c) 35 years (d) 45 years

106. Which of the following is a feature of federal Government?
(a) Supremacy of Parliament
(b) Supremacy of Judiciary
(c) Division of powers between federal and state Government
(d) Single citizenship

107. Under which article, President of India can proclaim financial emergency?
(a) Article 32 (b) Article 349
(c) Article 360 (d) Article 355

108. Under which article, President of India can proclaim Constitutional Emergency?
(a) Article 32 (b) Article 349
(c) Article 356 (d) Article 360

109. How many members of upper house (Rajya Sabha) can be nominated by President of India?
(a) 10 (b) 12
(c) 14 (d) 16

110. Which of the following is justiciable in nature?
(a) Fundamental Duties
(b) Directive principles of state policy
(c) Fundamental Rights
(d) None of these

111. Which of the following Amendments is also known as the 'Mini Constitution' of India?
(a) 7th Amendment
(b) 42nd Amendment
(c) 44th Amendment
(d) 74th Amendment

112. Which of the following right has been removed from fundamental rights and converted to a simple legal right?
(a) Right to life and personal liberty
(b) Right to property
(c) Right to education
(d) Right to freedom of religion

113. Which of the following does not come under Fundamental Duty?
(a) To safeguard public property
(b) To protect and improve the natural environment
(c) To promote harmony
(d) To protect freedom of speech and expression

114. Comptroller and Auditor General of India is appointed for how many years?
(a) 2 (b) 4
(c) 6 (d) 5

115. Who is the custodian of Contingency Fund of India?
(a) The Prime Minister
(b) Judge of Supreme Court
(c) The President
(d) The Finance Minister

116. Which of the following Country doesn't have a written Constitution?
(a) United Kingdom
(b) Australia
(c) United States of America
(d) Bangladesh

117. In the Indian Parliamentary System, 'Vote on Account' is valid for how many months (except the year of elections)?
(a) 2 months (b) 3 months
(c) 6 months (d) 9 months

118. India has taken the concept of 'Judicial Review' from which country's constitution?
(a) United States
(b) United Kingdom
(c) Canada
(d) Ireland

119. How many times a person can be elected as the President of India?
(a) One time (b) Two times
(c) Three times (d) There is no limit

120. Which article was referred to as the 'the heart and soul' of the constitution by Dr. B. R. Ambedkar?
(a) Article 4 (b) Article 32
(c) Article 28 (d) Article 30

121. Which of the following provision needs a special majority in Parliament?
(a) Change in Fundamental Rights
(b) Creation of New States
(c) Abolition of Legislative Councils in State
(d) Rules and Procedures in Parliament

122. Which of the following is not a fundamental duty?
(a) To abide by constitution and respect the National Flag
(b) To promote harmony and brotherhood
(c) To uphold and protect the sovereignty
(d) Abolition of titles except military and academic

123. Which article can be used by The President of India to declare financial emergency?
(a) Article 32 (b) Article 349
(c) Article 360 (d) Article 365

124. ______ means that the Supreme Court will reconsider the case and the legal issues involved in it.
(a) Original Jurisdiction
(b) Writ Jurisdiction
(c) Appellate Jurisdiction
(d) Advisory Jurisdiction

125. Which amendment of the Constitution of India increased the age of retirement of High Court judges from 60 to 62 years?
(a) 10th (b) 12th
(c) 15th (d) 245th

126. In which of the following cases did the Supreme Court rule that Constitutional Amendments were also laws under Article 13 of the Constitution of India, which could be declared void for being inconsistent with Fundamental Rights?
(a) Keshavanand Bharati Case
(b) Golaknath Case
(c) Minerva Mills Case
(d) Maneka Gandhi Case

127. Which of the following statement(s) is/are not correct for the Ninth Schedule of the Constitution of India?
1. It was inserted by the first amendment in 1951.
2. It includes those laws which are beyond the purview of judicial review.
3. It was inserted by the 42nd Amendment.
4. The laws in the Ninth Schedule are primarily those which pertain to the matters of national security.

Select the correct answer using the code given below :
(a) 1 and 2 (b) 2 and 3
(c) 3 and 4 (d) 3 only

Answers

1. (b)	2. (b)	3. (b)	4. (d)	5. (a)	6. (c)	7. (a)	8. (d)	9. (b)	10. (c)
11. (a)	12. (b)	13. (c)	14. (d)	15. (b)	16. (c)	17. (d)	18. (b)	19. (b)	20. (a)
21. (d)	22. (d)	23. (a)	24. (b)	25. (c)	26. (a)	27. (c)	28. (b)	29. (a)	30. (a)
31. (d)	32. (c)	33. (d)	34. (a)	35. (d)	36. (a)	37. (d)	38. (a)	39. (b)	40. (a)
41. (b)	42. (a)	43. (c)	44. (a)	45. (d)	46. (a)	47. (b)	48. (c)	49. (b)	50. (b)
51. (c)	52. (b)	53. (b)	54. (c)	55. (b)	56. (a)	57. (c)	58. (b)	59. (a)	60. (c)
61. (d)	62. (b)	63. (b)	64. (a)	65. (c)	66. (c)	67. (c)	68. (d)	69. (c)	70. (c)
71. (c)	72. (c)	73. (b)	74. (c)	75. (c)	76. (b)	77. (c)	78. (c)	79. (a)	80. (b)
81. (a)	82. (d)	83. (b)	84. (c)	85. (b)	86. (b)	87. (c)	88. (d)	89. (a)	90. (d)
91. (d)	92. (c)	93. (c)	94. (b)	95. (a)	96. (d)	97. (b)	98. (d)	99. (b)	100. (d)
101. (d)	102. (c)	103. (b)	104. (d)	105. (c)	106. (c)	107. (c)	108. (c)	109. (b)	110. (c)
111. (b)	112. (b)	113. (d)	114. (c)	115. (c)	116. (a)	117. (a)	118. (a)	119. (d)	120. (b)
121. (a)	122. (d)	123. (c)	124. (c)	125. (c)	126. (b)	127. (c)			

4 INDIAN ECONOMY

Characteristics of Indian Economy

Main characteristics of Indian economy are:

i. **Agrarian Economy:** In an Agrarian economy, agriculture dominance prevails in both the Gross National Product (GNP) and employment.

ii. **Mixed Economy:** It is an economy, where both public and private sector co-exist.

iii. **Developing Economy:** Following features show that Indian economy is a developing economy:

(a) Low per capita income.
(b) Occupational pattern is primary producing.
(c) Heavy population pressure.
(d) Prevalence of chronic unemployment and under-employment.
(e) Steadily improving rate of capital formation.
(f) Low capital per head.
(g) Unequal distribution of wealth/assets.

Broad Sectors of Indian Economy

- **Primary Sector:** Agriculture forestry, fishing.
- **Secondary Sector:** Mining, manufacturing, electricity gas and water supply, construction.
- **Tertiary Sector:** (also called service sector) Business, transport, telecommunication, banking, insurance, real estate, community and personnel services.

Agriculture and Land Development

Agriculture is the mainstay of the Indian Economy.

Major Crops of India

Types of Crops	Meaning	Major Crops
Foodgrains	Crops that are used for human consumption	Rice, Wheat, Maize, Millets, Pulses and oil seeds
Commercial Crops	Crops which are grown for sale either in raw form or in semi processed form	Cotton, Jute, Sugarcane, Tobacco and oil seeds
Plantation Crops	Crops which are grown on plantations covering large estates	Tea, Coffee, Coconut and Rubber
Horticulture	Sections of agriculture in which fruits and vegetables are grown	Fruits and vegetables

Economic Planning

The Planning Commission was constituted in India in 1950 as a non-constitutional and advisory corporation.

Niti Aayog

- NITI Aayog or National Institution for Transforming India Aayog is the replacement of Planning Commission of India.
- National Institution for Transforming India (NITI) Aayog has been created in accordance to the announcement made by the Prime Minister, Narendra Modi on 15 August, 2014.
- PM is the chairperson of this Niti Aayog.

Major Functions

- An administration paradigm in which the Government is an 'enabler' rather than a 'provider of the first and last resort'.
- Progress from 'food security' to focus on a mix of agricultural production, as well as actual returns that farmers get from their produce.
- To ensure, on areas that are specifically referred to it, that the interests of national security are incorporated in economic strategy and policy.

National Development Council

- National Development Council was constituted on 6 August 1952.
- The Prime Minister is the ex-officio Chairman and the Secretary of Planning Commission is the ex-officio Secretary of this council.
- Chief Ministers of all the states and the members of Planning Commission are the members of National Development Council (NDC). It is an extra-constitutional body.

The Indian Capital Market

- The capital market in India includes: (i) Government Securities (Gilt-edged market); (ii) Industrial Securities Market; (iii) Development financial institutions like IFCI, IDBI, ICICI, SFCs, IIBI, UTI, etc.; and (iv) financial intermediaries like merchant banks.
- Merchant bank, mutual fund, leasing companies, risk capital companies, etc. collect and invest public money into the capital market.
- Unit Trust of India (UTI) is the biggest Mutual Fund Institution of India.

Stock Exchange

- The stock exchanges is the market for buying and selling of stocks, shares, securities, bonds and debentures, etc.
- Under the Securities Contract (Regulation) Act of 1956, the Government of India has so far recognised

23 stock exchanges. Bombay is the premier exchange in the country.

Banking in India

- The Finance Ministry issues currency notes and coins of rupee one, all other currency notes are issued by the Reserve Bank of India.
- The public sector banks account for more than 92% of the entire banking business in India occupying a dominant position in the commercial banking. The State Bank of India and its associate banks along with another 19 banks are the public sector banks.

Establishment of Various Financial Institutions

1.	Reserve Bank of India	1934
2.	Industrial Finance Corporation of India	1948
3.	ICICI	1955
4.	SBI	1955. Nationalised
5.	Life Insurance Corporation (LIC)	1956
6.	Industrial Development Bank of India (IDBI)	1964
7.	Unit Trust of India (UTI)	1964
8.	HUDCO	1970
9.	General Insurance Corporation (GIC)	1972
10.	NABARD	1982
11.	SEBI (Replaced Controller of Capital Issue)	1988. Functional in 1992
12.	Small Industries Development Bank of India (SIDBI)	1990. Subsidiary of IDBI
13.	IRDA	1999

Scheduled and Non-scheduled Banks

- The scheduled banks are those which are entered in the second schedule of the RBI Act, 1934.
- The commercial banks (India and foreign), regional rural banks and state co-operative banks are scheduled banks. Non-scheduled banks are those which are not included in the second schedule of the RBI Act, 1934.

Reserve Bank of India (RBI)

- RBI was set up on the basis of Hilton Young Commission recommendation in April 1935, with the enactment of RBI Act, 1934. Its first Governor was C.D. Deshmukh.
- The headquarters of RBI is in **Mumbai**.

The quantitative credit control consists of:

- **Bank Rate:** It is also called the rediscount rate. It is the rate, at which the RBI gives finance to commercial banks.
- **Cash Reserve Ratio** (CRR): The RBI (Amendment) Bill, 2006, empowers RBI to prescribe CRR–Cash that banks deposit with the RBI without any floor rate or ceiling rate.
- **Statutory Liquidity Ratio** (SLR): It is the ratio of liquid asset, which all commercial Banks have to keep in the form of cash, gold and **unencumbered** approved securities equal to not more than 40% of their total demand and time deposit liabilities (range is 25-40%).
- **Repo Rate:** It is the rate, at which RBI lends short-term money to the bank against securities.
- **Reverse Repo Rate:** It is the rate, at which banks park short-term excess liquidity with the RBI.
- **Open Market Operations** (OMOs): Under OMOs, the RBI sells G-securities in the market.

Regional Rural Banks

The Regional Rural Banks (RRBs), the newest form of banks, have come into existence since middle of 1970s (sponsored by individual nationalised commercial banks) with the objective of developing rural economy by providing, crediting and depositing facilities for agriculture and other productive activities of all kinds in rural areas.

Co-operative Banks

Co-operative banks are so-called because they are organised under the provisions of the Co-operative Credit Societies law of the states. The major beneficiary of the Co-operative Banking is the agricultural sector in particular and the rural sector in general. The first such bank was established in 1904.

Development Banks

- **Industrial Development Bank of India** (IDBI), established in 1964.
- **Industrial Finance Corporation of India** (IFCI), established in 1948.
- **Industrial Credit and Investment Corporation of India Limited** (ICICI), established in 1991.
- **Small Industries Development Bank of India (SIDBI),** established in 1988.
- **Export-Import Bank of India** (Exim Bank), established in 1982.
- National Housing Bank (NHB) started operations in 1988.
- **NABARD** (National Bank for Agriculture and Rural Development) was established in 1982.

Insurance

- Insurance industry includes two sectors–Life Insurance and General Insurance. Life Insurance in India was introduced by Britishers. A British firm in 1818 established the Oriental Life Insurance Company at Calcutta now Kolkata.
- Life Insurance Corporation (LIC) of India was established in September 1956. General Insurance Corporation (GIC) was established in November 1972.

Insurance Regulatory and Development Authority (IRDA)

- IRDA was set up on April 19, 2000 under the IRDA Act, 1999.
- IRDA comprises of a chairman, three whole-time members and four part-time members.

Tax System

- A compulsory contribution given by a citizen or organisation to the government is called Tax.
- There are two types of taxes: 1. Direct Taxes and 2. Indirect Taxes.
- **Direct Taxes:** The taxes levied by the Central Government on income and wealth are important direct taxes. The important taxes levied on incomes are–corporation tax and income tax. Taxes levied on wealth are wealth tax, gift tax, etc.
- **Indirect Taxes:** The main forms of indirect taxes are customs and excise duties and sales tax. The Central Government is empowered to levy customs and excise duties (except on alcoholic liquors and narcotics) where sales tax is the exclusive jurisdiction of the State Governments.
- **Progressive Tax:** A tax that takes away a higher proportion of one's income as the income rises is known as progressive tax. Indian Income Tax is a progressive and direct tax.
- **GST:** GST would be applicable on "supply" of goods or services as against the present concept of tax on the manufacture of goods or on sale of goods or on provision of services. GST would be based on the principle of destination based consumption taxation as against the present principle of origin-based taxation. It would be a dual GST with the Centre and the States simultaneously levying it on a common base. The GST to be levied by the Centre would be called Central GST (central tax-CGST) and that to be levied by the States [including Union territories with legislature] would be called State GST (state tax-SGST). Union territories without legislature would levy Union territory GST (union territory tax-UTGST).

Industry

Industry sector comprises mining, manufacturing, electricity and gas and construction.

Public Sector

In terms of ownership, public sector enterprise (PSE) comprises all undertakings that are owned by the government, or the public, whereas private sector comprises enterprises that are owned by private persons.

Maharatna

In 2009, the government established the **Maharatna** status, which raised the PSEs investment ceiling from ₹ 1,000 crores to ₹ 5,000 crores.

List of Maharatnas

- Oil and Natural Gas Corporation (ONGC)
- Bharat Heavy Electricals Limited (BHEL)
- Gas Authority of India Limited (GAIL)
- Steel Authority India Limited (SAIL)
- Indian Oil Corporation (IOC)
- National Thermal Power Corporation (NTPC)
- Coal India Limited (CIL)
- Bharat Petroleum Corporation Limited.

List of Navratnas

- Bharat Electronics Limited
- Hindustan Aeronautics Limited
- Hindustan Petroleum Corporation Limited
- Mahanagar Telephone Nigam Limited
- National Aluminium Company Limited
- National Mineral Development Corporation
- Neyveli Lignite Corporation Limited
- Oil India Limited
- Power Finance Corporation Limited
- Power Grid Corporation of India Limited
- Rashtriya Ispat Nigam Limited
- Rural Electrification Corporation Limited
- Shipping Carnation of India Limited
- Container Corporation of India Ltd.
- Engineers India Ltd.
- National Building Construction Corporation Ltd.

Navratna

To qualify as a Navratna Company:

- The company must obtain a score of 60 (of the total 100).
- The score is based on six parameters, which included net profit to net worth, total manpower cost to total cost of production, Profit before Depreciation, Interest and Taxes (PBDIT) to capital employed, PBDIT to turnover, earning per share and inter-sectoral performance.
- The company must first be a Miniratna-I and must have four independent directors on its board.
- The Navratna status empowers a company to invest upto ₹ 1,000 crores on 15% of their net worth overseas without government approval.
- At present, there are **16 Navratnas**.

Small Scale Industries

Their importance can be explained as:

i. Employment Generation.
ii. Equitable Distribution.
iii. Mobilisation of Small Savings.
iv. Exports contribution.
v. Environment-friendly.

Large Scale Industries

Iron and Steel Industry

- First steel industry at Kulti, West Bengal–Bengal Iron Works Company was established in 1870.
- First large scale steel plant–TISCO at Jamshedpur (1907) was followed at by IISCO at Burnpur (1919).
- India is the fourth largest producer of crude steel in the world.
- India is the largest producer of sponge iron since 2002.
- Steel Authority of India Limited (SAIL) was established in 1974.

Cotton and Synthetic Textile Industry

It is the largest industry in India. The first Indian modernised cotton cloth mill was established in 1818 at fort Gloster near Kolkata but this was unsuccessful.

Jute Industry

Jute industry was started in 1855 at Resra and India is the largest producer and second largest exporter of jute in the world.

Gems and Jewellery

According to the data released by the World Gold Council (WGC), India is the largest consumer of gold.

Paper Industry

The first paper mill in India was set up at Sreerampur, West Bengal, in the year of 1862.

Silk Industry

- India is the second largest (after China) silk manufacturer.
- The majority of silk is produced mainly in Bhoodan Pochampally (also known as silk city), Kanchipuram, Dharamvaram and Mysore.

Sugar Industry

- India is the largest producer of sugar in the world with a 22% share.

- It is the second largest agro-based industry in the country.
- Dual price mechanism with partial control is applied to sugar industry.

Cement Industry

India is the second largest producer of cement in the world.

Petrochemical Industry

The real thrust to this industry came with the establishment of Indian Petrochemical Corporation Limited at Baroda.

Fertilizer Industry

- The first fertiliser industry was set up in 1906, in **Ranipet** near Chennai.
- India is the third largest producer of fertilizer after China and USA and second largest consumer after China.
- Urea is the only fertilizer under statutory price control.

Automotive Industry

- India is the **second** largest manufacturer of motorcycle and fifth largest manufacturer of commercial vehicles in the world.
- India is the largest manufacturer of tractors in the world.
- Automobile Industry was delicensed in July 1991 with the announcement of the New Industrial Policy.

Steel

- Iron and Steel Industry took birth in India in the year 1870 when Bengal Iron Works Company established its plant at Kulti, West Bengal.
- Large scale iron and steel production was started in 1907 by TISCO established at Jamshedpur (Jharkhand).
- As per the data from International Iron and Steel Institute (IISI) India is the **7th largest producer of steel** in the world.
- At present India is the 9th largest **Crude Steel** producing country in the world.
- Today, India is the largest producer of sponge iron in the world.

Balance of Payments

- BoP comprises current account, capital account and omissions and changes in foreign exchange reserves.
- Under current account transactions are classified into merchandise (exports and imports) and invisibles.
- **Balance of Payment Crisis:** It means that exports exceed imports in value.
- The main component of capital account includes foreign investment, loans and banking capital.

Special Economic Zone (SEZ)

- Asia's first Export Processing Zone (EPZ) was set up in Kandla, India in 1965.
- The first SEZ policy was announced in April 2000.
- SEZ Act, 2005, was enacted with from 10 February 2005.

Exercise

1. The term 'mixed economy' denotes:
   (a) existence of both rural and urban sectors
   (b) existence of both private and public sectors
   (c) existence of both heavy and small industries
   (d) existence of both developed and underdeveloped sectors
2. In an economy, the sectors are classified into public and private on the basis of:
   (a) employment condition
   (b) nature of economic activities
   (c) ownership of enterprises
   (d) use of raw materials
3. The 'Dual Economy' is a mixture of:
   (a) traditional agriculture sector and modern industrial sector
   (b) industrial ownership of the manufacturing sector
   (c) state ownership of the means of production in corporation of foreign organisation
   (d) industrial sector and trading of goods obtained through imports
   (e) none of these
4. Which sector of Indian Economy has shown remarkable expansion during the last decade?
   (a) Primary Sector
   (b) Secondary Sector
   (c) Tertiary Sector
   (d) Mining Sector
5. When development in economy takes place, the share of tertiary sector in National Income:
   (a) first falls and then rises
   (b) first rises and then falls
   (c) keeps on increasing
   (d) remains constant
6. It will be true to classify India as:
   (a) A food-deficit economy
   (b) A labour-surplus economy
   (c) A trade-surplus economy
   (d) A capital-surplus economy
7. Mixed economy means:
   (a) When agriculture and industry are given equal importance
   (b) When public sector exists alongwith the private sector in national economy
   (c) Where globalization is transferred with heavy dose of Swadeshi in national economy
   (d) Where the centre and the State are equal partners in economic planning and development
8. The Indian Economy is characterised by:
   1. Pre-dominance of Agriculture
   2. Pre-dominance of Industry
   3. Low Per Capita Income
   4. Massive Unemployment

   Select your answer from the code given below:

   Codes:
   (a) 1 and 2 only
   (b) 1, 2 and 3 only
   (c) 2, 3 and 4 only
   (d) 1, 3 and 4 only
9. In India, planned economy is based on:
   (a) Gandhian System
   (b) Socialist System
   (c) Capitalist System
   (d) Mixed Economy System

10. Economic liberalisation in India started with:
(a) substantial changes in industrial licensing policy
(b) the convertibility of Indian rupee
(c) doing away with procedural formalities for foreign direct investment
(d) significant reduction in tax rates

11. A firm sells new shares worth ₹ 1000 direct to individuals. This transaction will cause:
(a) Gross National Product to rise by ₹ 1000
(b) Gross Domestic Product to rise by ₹ 1000
(c) National Income to rise by ₹ 1000
(d) No impact on Gross National Product

12. Which is not included in the private income arising in a country?
(a) Factor income from net domestic product
(b) Net factor income from abroad
(c) Current transfer from Government
(d) Current payments on foreign loans

13. In India, agriculture income is calculated by:
(a) Output method
(b) Input method
(c) Expenditure method
(d) Commodity method

14. Who coined the term 'Hindu rate of growth' for Indian Economy?
(a) A.K. Sen
(b) Kirit S. Parikh
(c) Raj Krishna
(d) Montek Singh Ahluwalla

15. Under which plan did the Government introduce an agriculture strategy which gave rise to Green Revolution ?
(a) Second Five Year Plan
(b) Third Five Year Plan
(c) Fourth Five Year Plan
(d) Sixth Five Year Plan

16. The Second Five Year Plan was based on:
(a) Mahalanobis Model
(b) Vakil and Brahmanada's Wage — Goods Model
(c) Harrod-Domar Growth Model
(d) Solow Growth Model

17. The Planning Commission of India is:
(a) A constitutional body
(b) An independent and autonomous body
(c) A Statutory body
(d) A non-statutory body

18. Mahalanobis Model has been associated with which Five Year Plan?
(a) First Five Year Plan
(b) Second Five Year Plan
(c) Third Five Year Plan
(d) Fourth Five Year Plan

19. Which plan gave emphasis on removal of poverty for the first time?
(a) Fourth (b) Fifth
(c) Sixth (d) Seventh

20. The period of the Eleventh Five Year Plan is:
(a) 2005 to 2010
(b) 2006 to 2011
(c) 2007 to 2012
(d) 2008 to 2013

21. The Planning Commission of India was constituted in the year:
(a) 1942 (b) 1947
(c) 1950 (d) 1955

22. Which one of the following is NOT correct?
(a) First Five Year Plan: 1951 – 56
(b) Second Five Year Plan: 1956 – 61
(c) Third Five Year Plan: 1961 – 66
(d) Fourth Five Year Plan: 1966 – 71

23. In the post-independence period, economic reformers were first introduced in India under:
(a) Janata Party Government (1977)
(b) Indira Gandhi Government (1980)
(c) Rajiv Gandhi Government (1985)
(d) P.V. Narasimha Rao Government (1990)

24. Only one of the following can be the ex-officio Chairman of the Planning Commission. He is the:
(a) Minister for Planning and Development
(b) Home Minister
(c) Prime Minister
(d) Finance Minister

25. GDP at factor cost is:
(a) GDP minus indirect taxes plus subsidies
(b) GNP minus depreciation allowance
(c) NNP plus depreciation allowances
(d) GDP minus subsidies plus indirect taxes

26. Per Capita Income is obtained by dividing National Income by:
(a) Total population of the country
(b) Total working population
(c) Area of the country
(d) Volume of the capital used

27. Which one of the following is a development expenditure?
(a) Irrigation expenditure
(b) Civil administration
(c) Debt services
(d) Grant-in-Aid

28. Gross Domestic Product (GDP) is defined as the value of all:
(a) goods produced in an economy in a year
(b) goods and services in an economy in a year
(c) final goods produced in an economy in a year
(d) final goods and services product in an economy in a year

29. Depreciation is equal to:
(a) Gross National Product – Net National Product
(b) Net National Product – Gross National Product
(c) Gross National Product – Personal Income
(d) Personal Income – Personal Income

30. Which one of the following is NOT a method of measurement of National Income?
(a) Value Added Method
(b) Income Method
(c) Expenditure Method
(d) Investment Method

31. Net National Product (NNP) of a country is:
(a) GDP minus depreciation allowances
(b) GDP plus net income from abroad
(c) GNP minus net income from abroad
(d) GNP minus depreciation allowances

32. National Income is based on the:
(a) total revenue of the State
(b) production of goods and services

(c) net profit earned and expenditure made by the State
(d) the sum of all factions of income

33. Which of the following is definitely a major indication of the State of the economy of a country?
(a) Rate of GDP growth
(b) Rate of inflation
(c) Number of Banks in a country
(d) Stock of foodgrains in a country

34. Which of the following can be called as a part of the Service Sector?
(a) Textile Mills
(b) Banking
(c) Coal Mines
(d) Agriculture

35. Many a times we read a term in financial newspapers 'GDP'. What is the full form of the same?
(a) Gross Domestic Product
(b) Global Domestic Ratio
(c) Global Depository Receipts
(d) None of these

36. Which sector of Indian Economy contributes largest to the Gross National Product?
(a) Primary Sector
(b) Secondary Sector
(c) Tertiary Sector
(d) Public Sector

37. National Income estimates in India are prepared by:
(a) Planning Commission
(b) Reserve Bank of India
(c) Central Statistical Organisation
(d) Indian Statistical Institute

38. Per Capita Income of country is derived from:
(a) National Income
(b) Population
(c) National Income and Population both
(d) None of these

39. The main source of National Income in India is:
(a) Service Sector
(b) Agriculture
(c) Industrial Sector
(d) Trade Sector

40. The base year for computation of National Income in India is:
(a) 1990 - 91
(b) 1993 - 94
(c) 1999 - 2000
(d) 2000 - 01

41. In India, Hindu Rate of Growth is associated with which of the following?
(a) Birth rate\
(b) Population
(c) Per Capita Income
(d) National Income

Answers

1. (b)	**2.** (c)	**3.** (a)	**4.** (c)	**5.** (c)	**6.** (b)	**7.** (b)	**8.** (d)	**9.** (b)	**10.** (a)
11. (d)	**12.** (d)	**13.** (a)	**14.** (c)	**15.** (b)	**16.** (a)	**17.** (d)	**18.** (b)	**19.** (b)	**20.** (c)
21. (c)	**22.** (d)	**23.** (d)	**24.** (c)	**25.** (a)	**26.** (a)	**27.** (a)	**28.** (d)	**29.** (a)	**30.** (d)
31. (d)	**32.** (b)	**33.** (a)	**34.** (b)	**35.** (a)	**36.** (c)	**37.** (c)	**38.** (c)	**39.** (a)	**40.** (b)
41. (d)									

5 GENERAL SCIENCE

PHYSICS

Unit
The chosen standard used for measuring a physical quantity is called unit.

System of Units
Units depend on choice. Each choice of units leads to a new system (set) of units.

The internationally accepted systems are (i) CGS system; (ii) EPS System; (iii) FPS System; and (iv) SI Units.

SI Base Units

Base quantity	Unit	Symbol
Length	metre	m
Mass	kilogram	kg
Time	second	s
Electric current	ampere	A
Thermodynamic temperature	kelvin	K
Amount of substance	mole	mol
Luminous intensity	candela	cd
Supplementary Physical Quantity	**Supplementary Unit**	**Symbol**
Plane angle	radian	rad.
Solid angle	steradian	Sr

Standard Units

viscocity	pascal second
Power	dioptre
Inductance	henry
Loudness	phon
Magnetic inductance	tesla
Magnetic flux	weber
Electric charge	farad, coulomb

Scalar Quantities
Physical quantities which have magnitude only and no direction are called scalar quantities.

Example: Mass, Speed, Volume, etc.

Vector Quantities
Physical quantities which have magnitude and direction both and which obey triangle law are called vector quantities.

Example: Displacement, Velocity, etc.

Kinematics

Distance
Distance is the length of actual path covered by a moving object in a given time interval.

- Distance is a scalar quantity whereas displacement is a vector quantity both having the same unit (metre).

Displacement
- The difference between the final and the initial position of an object is called displacement. It may be positive, negative or zero.
- It is a vector quantity. Its unit is metre.
- The magnitude of displacement may or may not be equal to the path length traversed by an object.

Speed
- The **average speed** of particle for a given interval of time is defined as the ratio of total distance travelled to the total time taken.

$$\text{Average speed} = \frac{\text{Total distance travelled}}{\text{Total time taken}}$$

- Displacement may be positive, negative or zero whereas distance is always positive.
- Distance travelled by the moving object in unit time interval is called speed. It is scalar quantity and its SI unit is metre/second (m/s). Velocity of a moving object is defined as the displacement of the object in the unit time interval. It is a vector quantity and its SI unit is metre/second.
- Acceleration of an object is defined as the rate of change of velocity of the object. It is a vector quantity and its SI unit is metre/second^2 (m/s^2). If velocity decreases with time then acceleration is negative and is called retardation.

$$\text{Velocity} = \frac{\text{Displacement}}{\text{time}}$$

Uniform Velocity
- An object is said to be moving with uniform velocity if it undergoes equal displacements in equal intervals of time.

Angular Velocity
The angle subtended by the line joining the object from the origin of circle in unit time interval is called angular velocity.

Relative Velocity
- When two bodies are moving in the straight line, the speed (or velocity) of one with respect to another is known as its relative speed (or velocity).

Important Prefixes to Units

tera (T) 10^{12}	giga (G) 10^{9}	Mega (M)10^{6}
kilo (K) 10^{3}	hecto (h) 10^{2}	deka (da) 10
deci (d) 10^{-1}	centi (C) 10^{-2}	mili (m) 10^{-3}
Micro (μ) 10^{-6}	nano (n) 10^{-9}	Pilo (P) 10^{-12}
Femp (f) 10^{-15}	atto (a) 10^{-18}	

Acceleration

- It is the rate of change of velocity. Its SI unit is m/s^2. It is a vector quantity.
- When the velocity of a body increases with time then its acceleration is negative and is called retardation or deceleration.

Motion

If the position of an object changes with time, it is said to be in motion. A particle at rest does not have the speed and acceleration, while a particle in motion has its speed and also may have some acceleration.

Projectile Motion

- When a particle is so projected that it makes certain angle with horizontal then the motion of the particle is said to be projectile.
- Path of projectile is a parabola.
- To achieve maximum range the body should be projected at an angle of 45°.
- When a body is dropped freely from the top of the tower and another body is projected horizontally from the same point, both will reach the ground at the same time.
- If we throw two balls of different masses in horizontal direction then they will again reach on earth at the same time because both the balls will have zero velocity in vertical direction.

Circular motion

- When an object moves along a circular path, then its motion is called circular motion e.g., motion of a top etc.
- If an object moves a long a circular path with uniform speed, its motion is called uniform circular motion.
- It is accelerated even if speed of the body is constant. The motion of satellite is an acclerated motion.

Newton's first law of motion

- Everybody maintains its initial state of rest or of motion with uniform speed on a straight line unless an external force acts on it.
- First law is also called law of Galileo or law of inertia.

Inertia

Inertia is the property of a body by virtue of which the body opposes change in its initial state of rest or motion with uniform speed on a straight line.

Some Examples of Inertia

- When a car or train starts suddenly, the passengers bend backward.
- When a running horse stops suddenly, the rider bends forward.
- When a coat/blanket is beaten by a stick, the dust particles are removed.
- First law gives the definition of force.

Force

Force is that external cause which when acts to a body changes or tries to change the initial state of the body. Momentum is the property of a moving body and is defined as the product of mass and velocity of the body. It is a vector quantity. Its SI unit is kg m/s.

Newton's Second Law of Motion

- The rate of change in momentum of a body is directly proportional to the applied force on the body and takes place in the direction of force.
- Newton's second law gives the magnitude of force.
- Newton's first law is contained in the second law.

Newton's Third Law of Motion

To every action, there is an equal and opposite reaction.

Centripetal Force

A body performing circular motion is acted upon by a force which is always directed towards the centre of the circle. This force is called centripetal force.

Cyclist bends his body towards the centre on a turn while turning to obtain the required centripetal force.

Centrifugal Force

In applying the Newton's laws of motion, we have to consider some forces which cannot be assigned to any object in the surrounding. These forces are called pseudo force or inertial force. Centrifugal force is also called a Pseudo force. It is always equal and opposite to centripetal force.

Cream separator, centrifugal driver, etc. work on the principle of centrifugal force.

Moment of Force

- The rotational effect of a force on a body about an axis of rotation is described in terms of moment of force.
- The centre of gravity of a body is that point, through which the entire weight of body acts.
- The weight of a body acts through centre of gravity in the downward direction.

Work, Energy and Power

Work

- When a body is displaced by applying a force on it, then work is said to be done.

Positive Work Done

- Positive work means that force is parallel to displacement.

Negative Work Done

- Negative work means that force is opposite to displacement.

Zero Work Done

- If the force is perpendicular to the displacement and if either the force or the displacement is zero, work done is zero.

Energy

- It is defined as capacity of doing work.
- Its unit is joule in SI and erg in CGS system.
- Capacity of doing work by a body is called its energy.
- Energy is a scalar quantity and its SI unit is joule.
- Energy developed in a body due to work done is called mechanical energy.

PE of a body in the gravitational field of earth is *mgh*.
where m = mass, g = acceleration due to gravity, h = height of the body from surface of the earth.

Kinetic Energy

- If a body of mass m is moving with velocity v, then kinetic energy

$$KE = \frac{1}{2}mv^2 = \frac{P^2}{2m}$$

where p is the linear momentum.

- When momentum is doubled, kinetic energy becomes four times.
- If a body is moving in horizontal circle then its kinetic energy is same at all points, but if it is moving in vertical circle, then the kinetic energy is different at different points.

Potential Energy

- It is the energy possessed by a body by virtue of its position.
- Suppose a body is raised to a height h above the surface of the earth, then potential energy of body = mgh.
- When a body is falling downwards, then its potential energy goes on changing to kinetic energy.

Transformation of Energy

- In a heat engine, heat energy changes into mechanical energy.
- In the electric bulb, the electric energy is converted into light energy.
- In burning coal, oil, etc., the chemical energy changes to heat energy.
- In solar cell, solar energy changes into electrical energy.
- In playing sitar, mechanical energy changes into sound energy.
- In microphone, sound energy changes into electrical energy.
- In loud speaker, electrical energy changes into sound energy.
- In battery, chemical energy changes into mechanical energy.
- In electric motor, electrical energy changes into mechanical energy.

Power

- Rate of doing work is called power.
- SI unit of power is watt named as a respect to the scientist James Watt or Joule Per second and it is scalar quantity.

  1 W = 1 J/s

  1 kW = 10^3 W

  1 MW = 10^6 W

  1 Watt/s (W–s) = 1 J
- Horse power is a practical unit of power. 1 H.P. = 746 watt.

Power is the rate at which work is done. It is the work/time ratio. Mathematically, it is computed using the following equation:

$$\text{Power} = \frac{\text{Work done}}{\text{Time taken}}$$

$$P = \frac{W}{T}$$

Gravitation

Definition

Every body attracts another body by a force called force of gravitation.

Gravitational Force

- Mathematically, it is represented as: $F = G\dfrac{Mm}{r^2}$

Where, F is gravitational force, G is gravitational constant, M is the mass of first particle, m is the mass of second particle and r is the distance between them.

- This is called Newton's Universal Law of Gravitation.
- The value of G is 6.67×10^{-11} N m²/kg².

Newton's Law of Gravitation

The force of gravitational attraction between two-point bodies is directly proportional to the product of their masses and inversely proportional to the square of the distance between them.

Gravity

- The acceleration due to gravity is the rate of increase of velocity of a body falling freely towards the earth. It is represented by

$$g = \frac{GM_e}{R_e^2}$$

where $\mathbf{M_e}$ is the mass of the earth and $\mathbf{R_e}$ is the radius of the earth.

- The value of g at the surface of earth is 9.8 m/s².
- The value of g on the Moon is 1/6th of that on the earth.

Variation in the Value of Gravity

- When we go above the surface of the earth, the acceleration due to gravity goes on decreasing.
- When we go below the surface of the earth, the acceleration due to gravity goes on decreasing and becomes zero at the centre of the earth.
- On increasing the rotational motion of earth, the value of g decreases.
- Decreasing the rotational motion of earth, the value of g increases.
- When we go from the equator towards the poles, the value of g goes on increasing.
- If earth stops its rotation about its own axis then at the equator the value of g increases and consequently the weight of body lying there increases.

Variation in g

i. Value of g decreases with height or depth from earth's surface.
ii. g is maximum at poles.
iii. g is minimum at equator.
iv. g decreases due to rotation of earth.
v. g decreases if angular speed of earth increases and increases if angular speed of earth decreases.

- If angular speed of earth becomes 17 times its present value, a body on the equator becomes weightless.

Centre of Gravity

- The centre of gravity of a body is that point at which the whole weight of the body appears to act.
- The gravitational force of earth (gravity) is called acceleration due to gravity (denoted as g) and its value is 9.8 m/s².
- Acceleration due to gravity is independent of shape, size and mass of the body.

Weight

- The weight of a body is the force with which it is attracted towards the centre of Earth.
- It is measured by a spring balance.
- It is not constant and it changes from place to place.

Pressure

- Pressure is defined as force acting normally on unit area on the surface. SI unit of pressure is N/m² also called Pascal (Pa). Pressure is a scalar quantity.

$$\text{Pressure} = \frac{\text{Normal force}}{\text{Area}}$$

- Atmospheric pressure of 1 atm = 1.01 × 10^{-5} N/m^2 = 760 torr

Atmospheric Pressure

Atmospheric pressure is that pressure which is exerted by a mercury column of 76 cm length at 0°C at 45° latitude at sea-level.

- Atmospheric pressure decreases with altitude (height from earth surface). This is why (i) It is difficult to cook on the mountain. (ii) The fountain pen of a passenger leaks in an aeroplane at a height.
- Atmospheric pressure is measured by barometer.
- Sudden fall in barometric reading is the indication of storm.
- Slow fall in barometric reading is the indication of rain.
- Slow rise in the barometric reading is the indication of clear weathers.

Pressure in liquid

Force exerted on unit area of wall or base of the container by the molecules of liquid is the pressure of liquid.

i. In a static liquid at same horizontal level, pressure is same at all points.
ii. Pressure at a point in a static liquid has same value in all directions.
iii. Pressure at a point in a liquid is proportional to the depth of the point from the free surface.
iv. Pressure at a point in a liquid is proportional to the density of the liquid.

Density

- The density of a substance (ρ) is defined as the ratio of its mass (M) to its volume (V).

$$\text{i.e. Density} = \frac{\text{Mass}}{\text{Volume}}$$

- Density of water is maximum at 4°C.
- The **relative density** is defined as the ratio of the density of the substance to the density of water at 4°C.
- Ice floats on water surface as its density (0.92 g/cm^3) is lesser than the density of water (1g/cm^3).
- If ice floating in water in a vessel melts, the level of water in the vessel does not change.
- The density of sea water is more than that of normal water. This explains why it is easier to swim in sea water.

Motion

Simple Harmonic Motion (SHM)

If a particle repeats its motion about a fixed point after a regular time interval in such a way that at any moment the acceleration of the particle is directly proportional to its displacement from the fixed point at the moment and is always directed towards the fixed point at that moment and is always directed towards the fixed point then the motion of the particle is called simple harmonic motion. The fixed point is called mean point or equilibrium point.

Characteristics of SHM

When a particle executing SHM passes through the mean position:

i. No force acts on the particle.
ii. Acceleration of the particle is zero.
iii. Velocity is maximum.
iv. Kinetic energy is maximum.
v. Potential energy is zero.

When a particle executing SHM is at the extreme end, then:

i. Acceleration of the particle is maximum.
ii. Restoring force acting on particle is maximum.
iii. Velocity of particle is zero.
iv. Kinetic energy of a particle is zero.
v. Potential energy is maximum.

Periodic Motion

Any motion which repeats itself after regular interval of time is called periodic or harmonic motion.

Oscillatory Motion

- If a particle repeats its motion after a regular time interval about a fixed point, motion is said to be oscillatory or vibratory.
- Motion of piston in an automobile engine and motion of balance wheel of a watch are the examples of oscillatory motion.

Time Period

Time taken in one complete oscillation is called time period.

Frequency is the number of oscillations completed by oscillating body in unit time interval. Its SI unit is Hertz.

Simple Pendulum

- It is a heavy point mass suspended from a rigid support by means of an elastic inextensible string.
- Time period of simple pendulum $= T = 2\pi\sqrt{\frac{l}{g}}$
- Where l is the length of simple pendulum and g is the acceleration due to gravity.
- If a simple pendulum is suspended in a lift descending down with acceleration, then time period of pendulum will increase. If lift is ascending, then time period of pendulum will decrease.
- If a lift falling freely under gravity, then the time period of the Pendulum will be infinite.

Wave

- A wave is a disturbance which propagates energy from one place to the other without the transport of matter.
- These are of two types:
  i. Mechanical waves
  ii. Electromagnetic waves

Mechanical Waves

- The waves which require material medium (solid, liquid or gas) for their propagation are called mechanical waves or elastic waves.

These are of two types:

i. Longitudinal waves
ii. Transverse waves

Longitudinal Waves: If the particles of the medium vibrate in the direction of propagation of wave, the wave is called longitudinal wave. Waves on springs or sound waves in air are examples of longitudinal waves.

Transverse Waves: If the particles of the medium vibrate perpendicular to the direction of propagation of wave, the wave is called transverse wave.

Waves on strings under tension, waves on the surface of water are examples of transverse waves.

Electromagnetic waves

- The waves which do not require medium for their propagation, i.e. which can propagate even though the vacuum are called non-mechanical waves. Light and heat are the examples of non-mechanical wave. In fact all the electromagnetic waves are non-mechanical.

- All the electromagnetic waves consist of photons.
- The wavelength range of electromagnetic waves is 10^{-4} m to 10^{4} m.

Properties of Electromagnetic Waves

Following waves are not electromagnetic:

i. Cathode rays
ii. Canal rays
iii. Sound waves
iv. Ultrasonic waves

Note: Electromagnetic waves of wavelength range 10^{-3} m to 10^{-2} m are called microwaves.

Sound Wave

- It is longitudinal mechanical.
- The longitudinal mechanical waves which lie in the range 20 Hz to 20,000 Hz are called **audible** or **sound waves.**
- The longitudinal mechanical waves having frequencies less than 20 Hz are called **infrasonic**. These are produced by earthquakes, volcanic, eruption, Ocean waves, elephants, and whales.
- The longitudinal mechanical waves having frequencies greater than 2000 Hz are called **ultrasonic waves.**

Applications of Ultrasonic Waves

1. For sending signals.
2. For measuring the depth of sea.
3. For cleaning clothes, aeroplanes and machinery parts of clocks.
4. For removing lamp-shoot from the chimney of factories.
5. In sterilising of a liquid.
6. In ultrasonography.

Speed of Sound

- In a medium, the speed of sound basically depends upon elasticity and density of medium.
- When sound enters from one medium to another medium, its speed and wavelength changes but frequency remains unchanged.
- In a medium the speed of sound is independent of frequency.
- Speed of sound is maximum in solids and minimum in gases.
- The speed of sound is more in humid air than in dry air because the density of humid air is less than the density of dry air.
- The unit of loudness is decibel (dB).

Effect of pressure on speed of sound: The speed of sound is independent of pressure.

Effect of temperature on speed of sound: The speed of sound increases with the increase of temperature of the medium.

Intensity of Sound

Area Code	Kind of area	Intensity during the day (decibel)	Intensity at night (decibel)
A	Industrial area	75	70
B	Commercial area	65	55
C	Residential area	55	45
D	Peaceful area	50	40

Effect of humidity on speed of sound: The speed of sound is more in humid air than in dry because the density of humid air is less than the density of dry air.

Heat

Heat is that form of energy which flows from one body to other body due to difference of temperature between the bodies. The amount of heat contained in a body depends upon the mass of the body.

- It is due to the kinetic energy of the molecules constituting the body.
- Its units are calorie (cal), kilocalorie (kcal) or joule (J).
- 1 cal = 4.18 Joule, 1 kcal = 1000 cal

Temperature

Temperature is that physical cause which decides the direction of flow of heat from one body to other body. Heat energy always flows from body at higher temperature to body at lower temperature.

- The normal temperature of a human body is 37°C or 98.4 °F.
- Triple point is the state at which all the three states of matter co-exist. The triple point of water is 273.16 K.

The device which measures the temperature of a body is called thermometer.

Thermometers

Scale	Minimum Temperature	Maximum Temperature (Boiling Point)
Centigrade or celsius	0°C	100°C
Fahrenheit	32°F	212°F
Reumer	0°R	80°R

Transmission of Heat

Conduction

In this process, heat is transferred from one place to other place by the successive vibrations of the particles of the medium without bodily movement of the particles of the medium. In solids, heat transfer takes place by conduction.

Convection

In this process, heat is transferred by the actual movement of particles from one place to other place. Due to movement of particles, a current of particles sets up, which is called convection current. In liquids and gases, heat transfer takes place by convection.

- Earth's atmosphere is heated by convection.

Radiation

In this method, transfer of heat takes place with the speed of light without affecting the intervening medium.

Fusion

The process by which a substance is changed from solid state to liquid state is called fusion. Fusion takes place at a fixed temperature called melting point (MP).

Freezing

The process by which a substance is changed from liquid state to solid state is called freezing. Freezing takes at a fixed temperature called freezing point (FP). For a substance MP = FP.

- Melting point of substances which contract in the process of fusion (as ice) decreases with the increase in pressure. Melting point of substances which expand in the process of fusion (as wax) increases with the increase in pressure.
- With the addition of impurity (as salt in ice), melting point of a substance decreases.

Vapourisation

The process by which a substance is changed from liquid state to vapour state is called vapourisation.

Evaporation

The process of vapourisation which takes place only from the exposed surface of liquid and that at all temperatures is called evaporation.

Evaporation causes cooling. This is why water in an earthen pot gets cooled in summer.

Boiling

The process of vapourisation which takes place at a fixed temperature and from whole part of liquid is called boiling. The temperature at which boiling takes place is called **boiling point**.

Condensation

The process by which a substance is changed from vapour state to liquid state is called condensation.

- Boiling point of a liquid increases with the increase in pressure.
- Boiling point of a liquid increases with the addition of impurity.

Light

Light is a form of energy which is propagated as electromagnetic waves. In the spectrum of electromagnetic waves it lies between ultra-violet and infra-red region and has wavelength between 3900 Å to 7800 Å.

- Electromagnetic waves are transverse, hence light is transverse wave.
- Wave nature of light explains rectilinear propagation, reflection, refraction, interference, diffraction and polarisation of light.
- Clearly light behaves as wave and particle both.
- Speed of light is maximum in vacuum and air (3×10^8 m/s).
- It is a transverse wave.
- It takes 8 min 19 s to reach on the earth from the sun.
- The light reflected from moon takes 1.28 s to reach earth.

Refractive Index

Refractive Index of a medium is defined as the ratio of speed or light in vacuum to the speed of light in the medium.

- Velocity of light is larger in a medium which has small refractive index.
- Light takes 8 minute 19 second (499 second) to reach from sun to the earth.
- The light reflected from moon takes 1.28 second to reach earth.

Luminous Bodies

Those objects which emit light by themselves are called luminous bodies.

Non-luminous Bodies

Those objects which do not emit light by themselves but are visible by the light falling on them emitted by the luminous bodies are called non-luminous bodies.

A material can be classified as:

i. **Transparent:** The bodies which allow most of the incident light to pass through them are called transparent bodies, e.g., glass and water.
ii. **Translucent:** The bodies which allow a part of incident light to pass through them are called translucent bodies, e.g., pied paper.
iii. **Opaque:** The substances which do not allow the incident light to pass through them are called opaque bodies, e.g., mirror, metal, wood, etc.

Reflection of Light

- The return of light into the same medium after striking a surface is called reflection.

There are two laws of reflection.

i. The angle of incidence is always equal to angle of reflection.
ii. The incident ray, normal and reflected ray, all lie in the same plane.

Reflection From Plane Mirror

i. The image is virtual and laterally inverted.
ii. The size of image is equal to that of object.
iii. The distance of image from the mirror is equal to distance of object from the mirror.
iv. If an object moves towards (or away from) a plane mirror with speed u, relative to the object, the image moves towards (or away) with a speed of $2v$.
v. If a plane mirror is rotated by an angle θ, keeping the incident ray fixed, the reflected ray is rotated by an angle 2θ.
vi. To see his full image in a plane mirror, a person requires a mirror of at least half of his height.

☞ **Note:** Image formed by a convex mirror is always virtual, erect and diminished.

Reflection at spherical surface

- Spherical mirrors are the mirrors in which reflecting surface side is spherical.

There are two types of spherical mirrors:

i. convex mirror
ii. concave mirror

Mirror formula is given by $\frac{1}{v}+\frac{1}{u}=\frac{1}{f}$

u = Object distance
v = Image distance
f = Focal length of the mirror.

Uses of Concave Mirror

i. As a shaving glass.
ii. As a reflector for the headlights of a vehicle, search light.
iii. In ophthalmoscope to examine eye, ear, nose by doctors.
iv. In solar cookers.

Uses of Convex Mirror

i. As a rear view mirror in vehicles because it provides the maximum rear field of view and image formed is always erect.
ii. In sodium reflector lamp.

Image formation by concave mirror

Position of object	Position of image	Size of image	Nature of image
At infinity	At F	Highly diminished	Real and inverted
Between infinity and C	Between F and C	Diminished	"
At C	At C	Same size	"
Between F and C	Between infinity and C	Enlarged	"
At F	At infinity	Highly enlarged	"
Between F and P	Behind the mirror	Enlarged	Virtual and erect

Where (C) is centre of curvature
P is pole of the mirror
F is focus.

Image formation by convex mirror

Position of object	Position of image	Size of image	Nature of image
At infinity	At F	Highly dimished	Erect and virtual
Between infinity and Pole	Between F and P	Diminished	Erect and virtual

Refraction of Light

When a ray of light propagating in a medium enters the other medium, it deviates from its path. This phenomenon of change in the direction of propagation of light at the boundary, when it passes from one medium to other medium, is called refraction of light.

When a ray of light enters from rarer medium to denser medium from water to glass) it deviates towards the normal drawn on the boundry of two media at the incident point. Similarly, in passiing from denser to rarer medium, a ray deviates away from the normal. If light is incident normally on the boundary, i.e. parallel to normal, it enters the second medium undeviated.

Laws of Refraction

i. Incident ray, refracted ray and normal drawn at incident point always lie in the same plane.
ii. **Snell's law:** For a given colour of light, the ratio of sine of angle of incidence to the sine of angle of refraction is a constant.

- The refractive index of a medium decreases with the increase in wavelength of light.
- The refractive index of a medium decreases with an increase in temperature.
- When a ray of light enters from one medium to other medium, its frequency and phase do not change but wavelength and velocity changes.

Some Illustrations of Refraction

i. Bending of a linear object when it is partially dipped in a liquid inclined to the surface of the liquid.
ii. Twinkling of stars.
iii. Oval shape of sun in the morning and evening.
iv. An object in a denser medium, when seen from a rarer medium, appears to be at a smaller distance.

- **Due to refraction,** rivers appear shallow, coin in a beaker filled with water appears raised, pencil in the beaker appears broken.
- At sunset and sunrise, due to refraction, **sun appears above horizon** while it is actually below horizon.
- The duration of day appears to be increased by nearly 4 minute to **atmospheric refraction.**
- Writing on a **paper appears lifted** when a glass slab is placed over the paper.
- The refractive index of a medium is maximum for violet colour of light and minimum for red colour of light.
- Refractive index decreases with rise in the temperature.

Critical angle: In case of propagation of light from denser to rarer medium through a plane boundary, critical angle is the angle of incidence for which angle of refraction is 90°.

Total Internal Reflection of Light

- If the angle of incidence in denser medium is greater than critical angle (*C*), then the ray is reflected back into the first rarer medium, this phenomenon is called **total internal reflection**.
- In a desert, the phenomenon of **mirage** occurs due to total internal reflection.

Illustrations of Total Internal Reflection

i. Sparkling of diamond.
ii. Mirage and looming.
iii. Shining of air bubble in water.
iv. Increase in duration of sun's visibility.
v. Shining of a smoked ball or a metal ball on which lamp stool deposited when dipped in water.
vi. Optical Fibre.

Applications

i. For transmitting optical signals and the two dimensional picture.
ii. For transmitting electrical signals by first converting them to light.
iii. For visualising the internal sites of the body by doctors in endoscopy.

Refraction of Light through Lens

- When a lens is thicker at the middle than at the edges, it is called convex lens or a converging lens. When the lens is thicker at edge than in the middle, it is called as concave lens or diverging lens.

lenses

- Lens is a transparent medium bounded by two curved surfaces. Lenses are of two types:

i. Concave or divergent lens.
ii. Convex or convergent lens

$$\text{Magnification } (m) = \frac{\text{Lenght (height) of image}}{\text{Length (height) of object}} = \frac{v}{u}$$

Image Formation by a Convex Lens

Position of object	Position of image	Size of image	Nature of image
At infinity	At F_2	Highly diminished	Real and inverted
Beyond 2 F_1	Between F_2 and 2 F_2	Diminished	Real and inverted
At 2 F_1	At 2 F_2	Same size	Real and inverted
Between 2 F_1 and F_1	Beyond 2 F_2	Enlarged	Real and inverted
At F_1	At infinity	Highly enlarged	Real and inverted
Between F_1 and lens	Behind the object on the same side of the object	Enlarged	Virtual and erect

Power of a Lens

Power of a lens is its capacity to deviate a ray. It is measured as the reciprocal of the focal length in metres. Unit of power is dioptre (D).

- Power of a convex lens is positive and that of a concave lens is negative.
- If two lenses are placed in contact, then the power of combination is equal to the sum of powers of individual lenses.

Dispersion of Light

When a ray of white light (or a composite light) is passed through a prism, it gets splitted into its constituent colours. This phenomenon is called dispersion of light. The coloured pattern obtained on a screen after dispersion of light is called spectrum.

- The dispersion of light is due to different deviation suffered by different colours of light. The deviation is maximum for violet colour and minimum for red colour of light. The different colours appeared in the spectrum are in the following order: violet, Indigo, Blue, Green, Yellow, Orange and red (VIBGYOR).
- The dispersion of light is due to different velocities of light of different colours in a medium. As a result, the refractive index of a medium is different for different colours of light.
- The velocity of light in a medium is maximum for that colour for which refractive index is minimum.

Rainbow

Rainbow is formed due to dispersion of sun light by the suspended water droplets.

- Primary rainbow is formed due to two refractions and one total internal reflection of light falling on the raindrops.
- Secondary rainbow is formed due to two refractions and two internal reflections of light falling on raindrops.

Human Eye

- Least distance of distinct vision is 25 cm.

Defects of Human Eye and the Remedies

1. **Myopia or short sightedness:** A person suffering from myopia can see the near objects clearly while far objects are not clear.

   Remedy: Diverging lens is used.
2. **Hyperopia or hypermetropia or longsightedness:** A person suffering from hypermetropia can see the distant objects clearly but not the near objects.

   Remedy: A converging lens is used.
3. **Presbyopia:** This defect is generally found in elderly person. Due to stiffening of ciliary muscles, eye looses much of its accommodating power. As a result, the distant as well as the nearby objects cannot be seen.

   Remedy: For its remedy, two separate lenses or a bifocal lens are/is used.
4. **Astigmatism:** This defect arises due to difference in the radius of curvature of cornea in the different planes. As a result rays from an object in one plane are brought to focus by eye in another plane. For its remedy cylindrical lens is used.

Electricity

Charge

Charge is the basic property associated with matter due to which it produces and experiences electric and magnetic effects.

- It is something that a body attains when it loses or gains the electrons.
- Its S.I. unit is coulomb C.
- Electricity is associated with the charge.
- Similar charges repel each other and opposite charges attract each other.
- The proton possesses positive charge (+ e) and electron possesses an equal negative charge (– e).
- Charging of bodies takes place due to transfer of electrons from one body to other body.
- Human body and earth act like a conductor. Silver is the best conductor.
- The surface density of charge at a point on the surface of conductor depends upon the shape of conductor and presence of other conductors or insulators near the given conductor.
- The surface density of charge at any part of the conductor is inversely proportional to the radius of curvature of the surface of that part.

This is why surface density of charge is maximum at the pointed parts of the conductor.

Conductor

Conductors are those materials which allow electricity (charge) to pass through them.

Examples: (a) Metals like silver, iron, copper, (b) Earth (especially the most part) acts like a huge conductor.

Insulator or Dielectric: Insulators are those materials which do not allow electricity to flow through them.

Examples: Wood, paper.

> **Coulomb's Law**
> According to Coulomb's law, the attraction or repulsion between two point charges at rest is directly proportional to the product of the magnitudes of the charges and inversely proportional to the square of the distance between them.

Electric Field

- The region around an electric charge in which the electric effect can be experienced is called the electric field.
- Electric field intensity inside a charged hollow conductor is zero.

Electric Field Intensity

Electric field intensity at a point in an electric field is the force experienced by a unit positive charge placed at that point.

Electric Field of hollow conductor: Electric field intensity inside a charged hollow conductor is zero. Charge given to such a conductor (or conductor of any shape) remains on its surface only.

This explains why a hollow conductor acts as an electrostatic shield. For this reason it is safer to sit in a car or bus during lightning.

Electric Potential: Electric potential at a point in an electric field is the work done in bringing a unit positive charge from infinity to that point. SI unit of electric potential is volt.

Potential Difference: Work done in bringing a unit positive charge from one point to other point is the potential difference between the two points. Its SI unit is volt and it is a scalar quantity.

Electric Capacity

Electric capacity of a conductor is defined as the charge required to increase the potential of the conductor by unity. Its SI unit is farad (F).

Electric Current

Electric current is defined as the rate of flow of charge or charge flowing per unit time interval. Its direction is the direction of flow of positive charge. Its SI unit is ampere (A).

Resistance: The opposition offered by a conductor to the flow of current through it is called resistance. Its SI unit is ohm.

Ohm's Law

If physical conditions like temperature, intensity of light, etc. remains unchanged then electric current flowing through a conductor is directly proportional to the potential difference across its ends.

Ohmic Resistance: The resistances of such conductors which obey Ohm's law are called ohmic resistances. For example, resistance of melanin wire.

Non-ohmic Resistance: The resistances of such materials which do not obey ohm's law are called non-ohmic resistances.

Example: Resistance of diode valve, resistance of triode valve.

Conductance

Reciprocal of resistance of a conductor is called its conductance.

Its SI unit is ohm^{-1} (also called mho or siemen.)

- The resistance of a conductor is directly proportional to its length and inversely proportional to its cross sectional area.

Specific conductance or conductivity: The reciprocal of resistivity of a conductor is called its conductivity (s). Its SI unit is mho m^{-1} or siemen metre (sm^{-1}).

- In series combination, the equivalent resistance is equal to the sum of the resistances of individual conductors. ($R = R_1 + R_2 + ...R_n$)
- In parallel combination, the reciprocal of equivalent resistance is equal to the sum of the reciprocal of individual resistances.
- **Specific resistance** or **Resistivity** depends only on the material of conductor and its temperature. Resistivity increases with temperature.
- If a wire is stretched or doubled on itself, its resistance will change, but its specific resistance will remain unaffected.

Electric Power

The rate at which electrical energy is consumed in a circuit is called electric power. Its SI unit is watt.

1 kilowatt hour = 3.6×10^6 joule

Ammeter

Ammeter is a device which is used to measure electric current in a circuit. It is connected in series in the circuit.

- The resistance of an ideal ammeter is zero.

Voltmeter

Voltmeter is a device used to measure the potential difference between two points in a circuit. It is connected in parallel to the circuit.

- The resistance of an ideal voltmeter is infinite.

Electric Fuse

Electric fuse is a protective device used in series with an electric appliance to save it from being damaged due to high current. In general, it is a small conducting wire of alloy of copper, tin and lead, having low melting point.

- Pure fuse is made up of tin.

Galvanometer

Galvanometer is a device used to detect and measure electric current in a circuit.

Magnetism

- Magnet is a piece of iron or other material that can attract iron containing objects and that points north and south when suspended.

Directive Property

When a magnet is freely suspended, it aligns itself in the geographical north-south direction.

- Natural magnet is oxide of iron.
- The magnets made by artificial methods are called artificial magnets or manmade magnets. They may be of different types like bar magnet, horse shoe magnet, Robinson's ball ended magnet, magnetic needle, electromagnet, etc.
- The two points near the two ends of a magnet where the attracting capacity is maximum are called magnetic poles.
- The imaginary line joining the two poles of a magnet is called magnetic axis of the magnet.
- Similar poles repel each other and dissimilar poles attract each other.

➢ When magnetic substance is placed near a magnet, it gets magnetised due to induction.

Magnetic Field

Region in space around a magnet where the magnet has its magnetic effect is called magnetic field of the magnet.

Intensity of Magnetic Field or Magnetic Flux Density

Magnetic flux density of a point in a magnetic field is the force experienced by a north pole of unit strength placed at that point.

Its SI unit is Newton/ampere-metre Weber/metre or tesla (T).

Magnetic Lines of Force

The magnetic lines of force are imaginary current which represent a magnetic field graphically.

Magnetic Substance

i. **Diamagnetic substance:** Diamagnetic substances are such substances which, when placed in a magnetic field, acquire feeble magnetism opposite to the direction of the magnetic field.

Examples: Bismuth, Zinc, Copper.

ii. **Paramagnetic Substance:** Paramagnetic substances are such substances which when placed in a magnetic field acquire a feedback magnetised in the direction of field.

Examples: Iron, Cobalt.

Curie Temperature

As temperature increases, the magnetic property of ferromagnetic substance decreases and above a certain temperature the substance changes into paramagnetic substance. This temperature is called Curie temperature.

➢ Permanent magnets are made of steel, cobalt steel, alcomax or alnico.

➢ Electromagnets, cores of transformers, telephoediaphragms and motors are made of soft iron, mu-metal and stalloy.

Terrestrial Magnetism

Our earth behaves as a powerful magnet whose south pole is near the geographical North Pole and whose North Pole is near the geographical South Pole.

i. **Declination:** The acute angle between magnetic meridian and geographical meridian at a place is called the angle of declination at that place.

ii. **Dip or Inclination:** Dip is the angle which the resultant earth's magnetic field at a place makes with the horizontal. At poles and equator, dip is 90° and 0° respectively.

List of Scientific Instruments

Instrument	Use
Altimeter	It measures altitudes and is used in aircrafts.
Ammeter	It measures strength of electric current (in amperes).
Anemometer	It measures force and velocity of wind.
AudioPhone	It is used for improving imperfect sense of hearing.
Audiometer	It measures intensity of sound.
Barometer	It measures atmospheric pressure.
Binocular	It is used to view distant objects.
Bolometer	It measures heat radiation.
Barograph	It is used for continuous recording of atmospheric pressure.
Cinematography	It is an instrument used in cinema-making to throw on screen and enlarged image of photograph.
Crescograph	It measures the growth in plants.
Cyclotron	A charged particle accelerator which can accelerate charged particles to high energies.
Calorimeter	It measures quantity of heat.
Carburetor	It is used in an internal combustion engine for charging air with petrol vapour.
Cardiogram	It traces movements of the heart, recorded on a cardiograph.
Chronometer	It determines longitude of a place kept onboard ship.
Dynamometer	It measures electrical power.
Dynamo	It converts mechanical energy into electrical energy.
Endoscope	It examines internal parts of the body.
Eudiometer	Glass tube for measuring volume changes in chemical reactions between gases.
Electrometer	It measures electricity.

Electroscope	It detects presence of an electric charge.
Fathometer	It measures the depth of the ocean.
Galvanometer	It measures the electric current of low magnitude.
Hydrometer	It measures the specific gravity of liquids.
Hygrometer	It measures humidity in air.
Hydrophone	It measures sound under water.
Kymograph	It graphically records physiological movements (blood pressure and heartbeat).
Lactometer	It determines the purity of milk.
Manometer	It measures the pressure of gases.
Mariner's Compass	It is an instrument used by the sailors to determine the direction.
Microphone	It converts the sound waves into electrical vibrations and to magnify the sound.
Microscope	It is used to obtain magnified view of small objects.
Photometer	The instrument compares the luminous intensity of the source of light.
Periscope	It is used to view objects above sea level (used in submarines).
Potentiometer	It is used for comparing electromotive force of cells.
Odometer	An instrument by which the distance covered by wheeled vehicles is measured.
Pyrometer	It measures very high temperature.
Radar	It is used for detecting the direction and range of an approaching plane by means of radio microwaves.
Radiometer	It measures the emission of radiant energy.
Refractometer	It measures refractive index.
Saccharimeter	It measures the amount of sugar in the solution.
Seismograph	It measures the intensity of earthquake shocks.
Speedometer	It is an instrument placed in a vehicle to record its speed.
Sphygmomanometer	It measures blood pressure.
Spherometer	It measures the curvatures of surfaces.
Stereoscope	It is used to view two dimensional pictures.
Sextant	This is used by navigators to find the latitude of a place by measuring the elevation above the horizon of the sun or another star.
Spectrometer	It is an instrument for measuring the energy distribution of a particular type of radiation.
Stethoscope	An instrument which is used by the doctors to hear and analyze heart and lung sounds.
Tachometer	An instrument used in measuring speeds of aeroplanes and motorboats.
Telescope	It views distant objects in space.
Thermometer	This instrument is used for the measurement of temperatures.
Thermostat	It regulates the temperature at a particular point.

Invention and Discovery

Inventions/ Discoveries	Name of the Scientist/Person
Archimedean Screw	Archimedes
Atom	Neils Bohr
Atomic Number	Mosley
Atomic Physics	Enrico Fermi
Atomic Structure	Bohr and Rutherford
Atomic Theory	Dalton

Automatic Gearbox	Hermann Fottinger
Adding Machine	Pascal
Aeroplane	Wright brothers
Air Brake	George Westinghouse
Air Pump	Otto von Guericke
Airship (rigid)	G. Ferdinand von Zeppelin
Aniline Dyes	Hoffman
Antiseptic Surgery	Lord Joseph Lister
Arc Lamp	C. F. Brush
Automobile	Daimler
Automobiles using gasoline	Karl Benz
Avogadro's Hypothesis	Avogadro
Bacteriology	Robert Koch
Bakelite	Leo H Baekeland
Balloon	Jacques and Joseph Montgolfier
Ball-Point Pen	John J. Loud
Barometer	Evangelista Torricelli
Beri-Beri	Eijkman
Bicycle	Kirkpatrick Macmillan
Bicycle Tyre	J.B. Dunlop
Bacteriophage	Max Delbruck
Bifocal Lens	Benjamin Franklin
Binomial Nomenclature	Carl Linnaeus
Biogenetic Principle	Ernst Haeckel
Bismuth	Valentine
Bomb	Edward Teller
Boson	S.N.Bose
Boyle's law	Boyle
Braille	Louis Braille
Breaking up the Nucleus of an atom	Rutherford
Cinema	A.L. and J.L. Lumiere
Centrigrade scale	A. Celsius
Chemical Structure	August Kekule
Chemotherapy	Paul Ehrlich
Chloroform	James Harrison and James Young Simpson
Cholera Bacillus	Robert Koch
Calculating Machine	Pascal
Camera	George Eastman
Carburettor	Gottlieb Daimler
Cell Doctrine	Rudolf Virchow
Celluloid	A. Parker
Cement	Joseph Aspdin
Chromosomal Theory of Heredity	Thomas Hunt Morgan
Chronometer	John Harrison

Cine Camera	Friese-Greene
Cinematography	Thomas Alva Edison
Classical Field Theory	Michael Faraday
Clock (machanical)	Hsing and Ling-Tsan
Clock (pendulum)	C. Hugyens
Coloured Photography	Lippman
Computer	Charles Babbage
Cosmic Rays	R.A.Millikan
Crescograph	J.C.Bose
Crystal Dynamics	C.V.Raman
Cyclotron	Lawrence
Deuterium (Heavy Water)	H.C. Urey
Diesel Engine	Rudolf Diesel
Diesel Oil Engine	Rudolf Diesel
Difference Engine	Charles Babbage
Electrons	J.J. Thomson
Solar System	Copernicus (1540)
Specific Gravity	Archimedes
Dynamite	Alfred B. Nobel
Dynamo	Michael Faraday
Effect of Pressure on Trough Bodies	Meghnad Saha
Eightfold Way	Murray Gell-Mann
Electric Battery	Alessandro Volta
Electrical Waves	Heitz
Electricity	Faraday
Electromagnet	William Sturgeon
Electromagnetic Field	James Clerk Maxwell
Electromagnetic Theory	Maxwell
Electron	Joseph J. Thomson
Electron Theory	Bohr
Electronic Computer	Dr. Alan M. Turing
Elevator	Elisha G. Otis
Energy of the Sun	Hans Bethe
'Equal' sign (=)	Robert Recorde
Ethology	Konrad Lorenz
Eugenics	Francis Galton
Fahrenheit Scale	Fahrenheit
Film and Goods Photographic	Kodak
Electric Flat Iron	H.W. Seeley
Electric Furnace	William Siemens
Electric Generator	Michael Faraday
Electric Guitar	Adolph Rickenbacker
Electric iron	H.W. Seeley
Electric Lamp	Thomas Alva Edison
Electric Measurement	Gauss

Electric Motor (AC)	Nikola Tesla
Electric Razor	Jacob Schick
Film (with sound)	Dr. Lee de Forest
Fundamental Laws of Electric Attraction	Coulomb
Galvanometer	Andre-Marie Ampere
Gas Lighting	William Murdoch
Gasoline Engine	Karl Benz
Genetic Code	Frederick Sanger
Glider	Sir George Caley
Gramophone	Thomas Alva Edison
Gun Powder	Rogei Bacon
Heavens	William Herschel
Heavy Hydrogen	Urey
Helicopter	Broquett
Heliocentric Universe	Nicolaus Copernicus
Helium Gas	Lockyer
Hovercraft	Christopher Cockerell
Hydrogen	Cavendish
Hydrophobia	Louis Pasteur
Intelligence Test	Binet
Internal Combustion Engine	Otto
Jeans	Levi Strauss
Jet Engine	Sir Frank Whittle
Jet Propulsion	Frank Whittle
Kala-azar Fever	U.N. Brahmachari
Kaleidoscope	David Brewster
Laboratory Gas Burner	Robert Wilhelm von Bunsen
I.Q. Test	Alfred Binet
In Number Theory	Ramanujam
Incandescent Bulb	Edison
Induction Coil	Rohm Korff
Induction of Electric Current	Faraday
Insulin	F. Banting
Laughing Gas	Priestley
Law of Electrolysis	Faraday
Law of Gases	Gay Lussac
Laws of Electrical Resistance	Ohm
Laws of Gravitation	Newton
Laws of Heredity	Gregory Mandel
Laws of Inheritance	Gregory Mendel
Laws of Motion	Newton
Laws of Multiple Proportion	Dalton
Laws of Natural Selections	Darwin
Logarithms	John Napier

Machine Gun	Dr. Richard Gatling
Malarial Parasite	Ronald Ross
Match (safety)	J.E. Lurdstrom
Mathematical Astro-physics	Chandrasekhar
Mathematical Genius	Carl Gauss (Karl Friedrich Gauss)
Mauve Dye	Perkin
Measurement of Electrical Energy	Joule, James Prescoft
Mechanical Equivalent of Heat	Joules
Mercury Thermometer	Fahrenheit
Meson	Hideki Yakawa
Microphone	Johann Phillip Reis, Alexander Graham Bell, Elisha Gray, Amos E. Dolbear, and Thomas Edison
Microscopic Anatomy	Marcello Malpighi
Lift	E.g., Otis
Lift (Elevators)	Otis
Lightning Conductor	Benjamin Franklin
Line of Demarcation (Ship)	Plimsoll
Liquid Oxygen	Dewar
Locomotive	Richard Trevithick
Logarithmic Tables	John Napier
Motor Car (Petrol)	Karl Butler
Movie Projector	Thomas Alva Edison
Neon Gas	Ramsay, Travers
Neon Lamp	G. Claude
Neurophysiology	Charles Sherrington
Neutron	Chadwick
New Anatomy	Andreas Vesalius

CHEMISTRY

Matter and its states

- It exists in five states viz, solid, liquid, gas, plasma, Bose-Einstein condensate, out of which the former three are commonly seen.
- Anything that occupies space, possesses mass and can be felt by any one or more of our senses is called **matter**.

States of Matter

Solid State

A solid possesses definite shape and definite volume which means that it cannot be compressed on applying pressure.

Liquid State

A liquid possesses definite volume but no definite shape.

Gases

- These have neither definite volume nor definite shape.
- Solid, liquid and gases are inter-convertible by changing the conditions of temperature and pressure.
- **Fluorescent tube** contains helium (He) gas and neon sign bulb contains neon (Ne) gas.

Bose-Einstein condensate

- In 1924–25, Satyendra Nath Bose and Albert Einstein gave the information about Bose-Einstein condensate.
- It is a state of matter of a lower density gas of boson cooled up to temperature which is very close to absolute zero or –273.15°C. Infact, it is a fifth state of matter.
- **Pure substances:** A single substance (or matter) which cannot be separated into other kinds of matter by any physical process is called pure substance.

Elements

- They contain only single type of atoms.
- Elements which are liquid at room temperature are mercury (Hg) and bromine (Br_2).
- Examples (of elements) are diamond, graphite, sulphur (S_8), phosphorus (P_4), ozone (O_3), oxygen (O_2), etc.
- Elements have the following order of abundance in earth crust, Oxygen > silicon > aluminium (metal) > iron > calcium.

- Elements have the following order of abundance in human body: Oxygen > carbon > hydrogen > nitrogen.

Extraction Process for Various Elements

Frasch process	Sulphur
Acheson process	Graphite
Hall Herault	Aluminium
Ostwald process	Nitric acid
Bayer process	Extraction of aluminium from ore
Bessemer process	Steel from molten pig iron
Patio process	Silver
Dow process	Bromine
Pidgeion process	Magnesium
Fischer Tropsch process	Gasoline
Azeotropic distillation	Absolute alcohol

Metals

Metals are solids (exception mercury which is liquid at room temperature) are normally hard. They have lustre, high MP and BP and also with increase in temperature due to vibration of positive ions at their Lattice points.

Non-metals

Non-metals are the elements with properties opposite to those of the metals. They are found in all states of matter. They do not possess lustre (exception is iodine). They are poor conductors of electricity (exception is graphite) and they are not malleable and ductile.

Metalloids

Metalloids are the elements which have common properties of both metals and non-metals.

Compounds

Compounds are pure substances that are composed of two or more different elements in fixed proportion by mass.

- These contain more than one kind of atom.
- Their examples are silica (SiO_2), water (H_2O), sugar ($C_{12}H_{22}O_{11}$), salt (NaCl), etc.

Organic Compounds

The compounds obtained from living sources are called organic compounds. **Examples** are carbohyrates, proteins, oils, fats, etc.

Inorganic Compounds

The compounds obtained from non-living sources such as rocks and minerals are called inorganic compounds. **Examples** are common salt, marble, washing soda, etc.

Mixtures

A material obtained by mixing two or more substances in any indefinite proportion is called a mixture. **Examples** are milk, sea water, petrol, paint, glass, cement, wood, etc.

(a) Homogeneous Mixture

A mixture is said to be homogeneous if it does have a uniform composition throughout.

Example: Salt-solution, sugar solution, etc.

(b) Heterogeneous Mixture

A mixture is said to be heterogeneous if it does not have a uniform composition throughout and has visible boundaries of separation between the various constituents.

Example: A mixture of sulphur and sand, a mixture of iron fillings and sand, etc.

Separation of mixtures

Sublimation

In this process, a solid substance passes direct into its vapours on application of heat. The vapours when cooled, give back the original substance.

Filtration

This is a process for quick and complete removal of suspended solid particles from a liquid, by passing the suspension through a filter paper.

Evaporation

If a solution of solid substance in a liquid is heated, the liquid gets converted into its vapours and slowly goes off completely. This process is called evaporation.

Crystallisation

This method is mostly used for separation and purification of solid substances. In this process, the impure solid or mixture is heated with suitable solvent to its boiling point and the hot solution is filtered. The clear filtrate is cooled slowly to room temperature. When pure solid crystallises out, this is separated by filtration and dried.

Distillation

It is a process of converting a liquid into its vapour by heating and then condensing the vapour again into the same liquid by cooling. Thus, distillation involves vapourisation and condensation both.

(A) Vacuum Distillation

- It is also known as distillation under reduced pressures.

(B) Steam Distillation

- It is used to separate a steam volatile compound from non-volatile or non-steam volatile compounds.

(C) Fractional Distillation

- This process is similar to the distillation process except that a fractionating column is used to separate two or more volatile liquids which have different boiling points.

Concept of Change in State

(a) **Melting Point:** The temperature at which solid and the liquid forms of the substance exist at equilibrium or both forms have same vapour pressure is called melting point.

(b) **Boiling Point:** The temperature at which the vapour pressure of a liquid becomes equal to the atmospheric pressure is called boiling point.

(c) **Freezing Point:** The temperature at which a substance is changed from liquid state to solid state is called freezing point.

(d) **Vapour Pressure:** The pressure exerted by the vapours of liquid in equilibrium with liquid at a given temperature is called vapour pressure. Vapour pressure depends on (i) its nature and (ii) temperature.

Higher the vapour pressure, lesser will be the magnitude of intermolecular forces present in molecules. Vapour pressure of a liquid increases with increase in temperature.

Atomic Structure

Atom

The smallest particle of an element is called an atom. The atom of the hydrogen is the smallest and lightest.

Characteristics of Atoms

Atomic Number (Z)

- It is equal to the number of protons.
- It is equal to the number of electrons in netural atom.

Mass Number (A)

- It is equal to the sum of number of protons and number of neutrons.
- It is written as a superscript to the right of the symbol of the atom e.g., C^{12} here 12 is the mass number of carbon (C).

Molecule

A molecule is the smallest particle of a compound that can have a stable and independent existence.

Mole

A mole is a collection of 6.023×10^{23} particles.

Avogadro's Number

The number 6.023×10^{23} is called Avogadro's number.

Atomic Mass

It is the ratio of mass of one atom of the element to the part of the mass of one atom of Carbon-12.

Molecular Mass

It indicates how many times one molecule of a substance is heavier in comparison to the mass of the atom of Carbon-12.

Electron

i. Electron had been discovered by J.J. Thomson.
ii. The name of electron was given by Stoney.
iii. An electron was obtained from Cathode rays experiment.

- Its antiparticle is positron.
- It has mass 9.1×10^{-19} kg or 0.00054 u.
- It has charge -1.6×10^{-19} C (by Millikan oil drop experiment).

Proton

i. A proton had been discovered by Goldstein.
ii. A proton was named by Rutherford.
iii. A proton was obtained from anode rays experiment.

- It is positively charged.
- It is present in the nucleus.
- It has charge $+1.6 \times 10^{-19}$ C and mass 1.672×10^{-27} kg or 1.00727 u.

Neutron

i. A neutron had been discovered by James Chadwick.
ii. Charge on neutron is zero.
iii. A neutron was obtained from radioactivity phenomenon.

- It has zero charge and mass 1.674×10^{-17} kg or 1.00867 u.
- It is present inside the nucleus. Its antiparticle is antineutrino.

Atomic number (Z): The number of proton or electron in an atom of the element is called atomic number. It is denoted by **Z**.

Proton, Neutron and Electron Data

Particle	Relative Charge	Relative/C	Charge/kgs	Mass
Protons	1	+1	$+1.6\times10^{-19}$	$1.67\times10\times^{-27}$
Neutrons	1	neutral	0	1.67×10^{-27}
Electrons	0.0005	–1	-1.6×10^{-19}	9.11×10^{-31}

Nucleus

- It contains protons and neutrons which are collectively called nucleons.
- **Mass number (A):** The sum of number of protons and neutrons in an atom of the elements is called mass number. It is denoted by **A**.
- **Isotopes:** These are atoms of the elements having the same atomic number but different mass number.
- Hydrogen (H-1) is the lightest isotope and lead-208 is the heaviest isotope (with mass 207.974).
- **Thomson's model of an atom:** According to Thomson, an atom is treated as sphere of radius 10^{-8} cm in which positively charged particles are uniformly distributed and negatively charged electrons are embedded through them. This is also called Plum-Pudding model of an atom or watermelon model of an atom.

Cathode Rays

- These rays were discovered by J.J. Thomson.
- These rays originate from cathode and travels in a straight line towards anode.

Anode Rays

- These rays were discovered by Goldstein (also called positive rays).
- These rays do not originate from anode.
- These are positively charged and have velocity less than cathode rays.
- **Hydrogen** is the only atom in which neutrons are not present.
- According to **de-Broglie**, all particles have wave nature.

Radioactivity

- It was discovered by **Henry Becquerel** but term radioactivity was given by **Madam Curie**. It is the process of spontaneous disintegration of nucleus and is measured by Geiger counter.
- It involves emission of α, β and γ rays/particles and has units Curie, Becquerel, Rutherford.

Alpha (α) Particle

- These are positively charged helium nuclei $(2He_4)^{2+}$.
- An α-emission reduces the atomic mass by 4 and atomic number by 2.

Beta (β) Particle

- These are negatively charged electrons $({}^{-1}e_0)$.
- A β-emission increases the atomic number by one with no change in atomic mass.

Gamma (γ) Rays

- These are electromagnetic radiations and have very high penetrating power.
- Their emission increases does not affect the position of nuclei in the Periodic Table.

Nuclear Reactor

- It is a device that is used to produce electricity and permits a controlled chain nuclear fission.
- It contains fuels e.g., $_{92}U^{235}$, moderator (e.g., graphite and heavy water, D_2O) to slow down neutrons and control rods (made up of boron steel or cadmium) to absorb neutrons.
- It may also contain liquid sodium as coolant.

Half-Life Period

- It is the time in which a radioactive substance remains half of its original amount.

Uses of RadioIcsotopes

1. **Iodine-131** is employed to study the structure and activity of thyroid gland.
2. **Iodine-123** is used in external radiation therapy for the treatment of cancer.
3. **Cobalt-60** is used in external radiation therapy for the treatment of cancer.
4. **Sodium-24** is injected along with salt solution to trace the flow of blood.
5. **Phosphorus-32** is used for leukemia therapy.
6. **Carbon-14** is used to study the kinetics of photosynthesis.

Radiocarbon Dating

- It is used in determining the age of carbon bearing materials such as wood, animal fossils, etc.

Uranium Dating

- It is used to determine the age of earth, minerals and rocks.

Periodic Classification of Elements

Father of Periodic Table is **Mendeleev**.

Periodic Table

- It is a tabular display of the chemical elements, organised on the basis of their properties.

Mendeleev's Periodic Table (1869)

- It is based upon the Mendeleev's periodic law, which states, "Properties of the elements are the periodic function of their atomic masses."

Modern Periodic Law: Modern periodic law was given by Moseley.

According to Moseley: "The physical and chemical properties of the elements are the periodic function of their atomic numbers."

Modern Periodic Table

It is just graphical representation of Aufbau principle. It is based on the electronic configuration of elements and contains 118 elements.

Modern periodic table is classified as:

i. *s*-block; iii. *d*-block;
ii. *p*-block; iv. *f*-block.

S-Block

- It contains group 1 and 2, i.e., hydrogen and alkali metals (Li, Na, K, Rb, Cs, Fr) and alkatine earth metals (Be, Mg, Ca, Sr, Ba, Ra). General electronic configuration of these elements is ns^{0-2}.
- These elements are soft metals, electropositive.

P-Block

- It comprises the last six groups (13–18).
- General electronic configuration of this block elements is $ns^2 np^{1-6}$.
- It is only block which contain metals, non-metals and metalloids.

D-Block

- It comprises 10 groups (3 to 12). These elements are called transition elements.
- General electronic configuration of d-block elements is $(n-1)d^{1-10} ns^{1-2}$.
- Hg, Zn, Cu, Sc etc. are d-block elements but not the transtion elements.

F-Block

- There are two series in this block 4 F and 5F series. 4F series elements are called lanthanides and 5F series elements are called actinides.
- General electronic configuration of this block elements is $(n-2)F^{1-14} (n-1) d^{1-10} ns^{1-2}$.

Chemical Bonding

The force that holds together the different atoms in a molecule is called chemical bond.

Ions

- These are of two types: cations and anions. **Cations** are formed by the loss of electrons and carry positive charge. **Anions** are formed by the gain of electrons and carry negative charge.

Ionic bond or (Electrovalent bond)

A bond formed by the complete transfer of ions or more electrons from one atom to other atom is called ionic bond.

Covalent bond

A bond formed between two same or different atoms by mutual contribution and sharing of electrons is called covalent bond.

Co-ordinate bond (or Dative bond): Co-ordinate bond is a special type of covalent bond in which one atom donates electrons of other atom. The bonding between donor to acceptor atom is called **co-ordinate bond**.

Valency

- It is the number of electrons taking part in bonding (i.e., bond formation).

Chemical Reaction

- The process in which substances (reactants) react to form new compunds (products) is known as chemical reaction.

Types of Reactions

Decomposition reactions: In these reactions, compound either of its own or upon heating decomposes to give two or more components out of which at least one is in the elemental state.

$$2\,KClO_3 \xrightarrow{\Delta} 2KCl + 3O_2$$

Potassium Chlorate — Potassium Chloride — Oxygen

Addition reactions: In such reactions, two or more substances combine to give a single substance.

Substitution reactions: In such reactions, an atom or a group of atoms of a molecule is replaced by another atom or group of atoms.

Combination reactions: In combination reactions, compounds are formed as a result of the chemical combination of two or more elements.

$$CaO + H_2O \longrightarrow Ca(OH)_2$$

Calcium Oxide — Water — Calcium Hydroxide

Displacement reactions: In these reactions, an atom/ion present in a compound gets replaced by an atom/ion of another element.

$$CuSO_4 + Fe \longrightarrow FeSO_4 + Cu$$

Copper Sulphate — Ferrous Sulphate

Disproportionation reactions: The chemical reaction in which only one substance is oxidised as well as reduced simultaneously is called disproportionation reaction.

Dissociation reactions: These are those reversible reactions in which a molecule dissociates into two or more simple molecules.

$$2HI \rightleftharpoons H_2 + I_2$$

Hydrogen iodide — Hydrogen — Iodine

Catalysis

- It was discovered by Berzelius.
- It is a term used for the reactions/processes which occur in the presence of certain substances that increase the rate of the reaction without being consumed. Such substances are called **catalysts**.

Uses of Catalysts

S. No.	Process	Catalyst
1.	Manufacture of Ghee from vegetable oils	Nickel
2.	Conversion of milk into curd	Lactase
3.	Decon's process for manufacture of chlorine	Cupric Chloride
4.	Conversion of sucrose into glucose and fructose	Invertase enzyme
5.	Contact process for manufacture of sulphuric acid	Pt Powder
6.	Conversion of proteins into peptide	Pepsin enzyme
7.	Conversion of glucose into ethyl alcohol	Zymase enzyme
8.	Formation of vinegar from cane sugar	Mesoderm acetate
9.	Conversion of starch into maltose	Diastase enzyme

Acids, Bases and Salts

Acid

An acid is a substance which

i. Is sour to taste.
ii. Turns blue litmus paper into red.
iii. Contains replaceable hydrogen.
iv. Gives hydrogen ion (H^+) in aqueous solution.
v. Can donate a proton.
vi. Can accept an electron.

Basicity of an acid: The number of removable hydrogen ions from an acid is called basicity of that acid.

Uses of HCl

i. Used as bathroom cleaner.
ii. As a pickling agent before galvanization.
iii. In the tanning of leather.
iv. In the dying and textile industry.
v. In the manufacture of gelatin from bones.

Uses of HNO_3

i. In the manufacture of explosives like TNT (Trinitrotoluene), TNB (Trinitrobenzene), Picric acid (Trinitrophenol), etc.
ii. Found in rain water (first shower).
iii. In the manufacture of rayon.

Uses of Sulphuric acid (H_2SO_4)

i. In lead storage battery.
ii. In the manufacturing of HCl.
iii. In the manufacturing of Alum.
iv. In the manufacturing of fertilisers, drugs, detergents and explosives.

Use of Boric Acid: It is used as an antiseptic.

Uses of Phosphoric Acid

i. Its calcium salt makes our bones.
ii. It forms phosphatic fertilisers.

Use of Ascorbic Acid: Source of vitamin C.

Use of Citric Acid: Flavouring agent and food preservative.

Use of Acetic Acid: Flavouring agent and food preservative.

Uses of Tartaric acid

i. Souring agent for pickles.
ii. A component of baking powder (sodium bicarbonate + tartaric acid).

Bases

A Base is a substance which:

i. Is bitter in taste.
ii. Turns red litmus paper into blue.
iii. Gives hydroxyl ions (OH^-) in aqueous solution.
iv. Can accept proton.
v. Can donate electrons.

- Oxides and hydroxides of metals are bases.
- Water soluble bases are called alkali.
- All alkalies are bases but all bases are not alkalies because all bases not soluble in water.

Acidity of a base: The number of removable hydroxyl (OH^-) ions from a base is called acidity of a base.

The pH scale: pH of a solution is the negative logarithm of the concentration of hydrogen ions on mole per litre.

Indicators

- These are the substances which give different colours in acid and base solution.

pH Value

- It is a measure of acidity or basicity of a solution.
- It is defined as the negative logarithm of the concentration in (mol/L) of hydrogen ions which it contains.
- It is seven for neutral solution, greater than seven for basic solution and less than seven for acidic solution.

Salts

- These are the product of neutralisation reaction between an acid and a base.

Washing Soda

- It is chemically sodium carbonate decahydrate ($Na_2CO_3.10H_2O$) and is used in glass, soap and paper industries and for removing permanent hardness of water.

Baking Soda

- It is sodium hydrogen carbonate ($NaHCO_3$). It is a mild non-corrosive base.
- When mixed with a mild edible acid such as tartaric acid it is called baking powder and is used to make bread or cake soft and spongy.

- It is used as mild antiseptic for skin infections, in soda-acids and as fire extinguishers.

Bleaching Powder

- It is chemically Ca (OCl)Cl or $CaOCl_2$.
- It is used for disinfecting drinking water.

Plaster of Paris

- It is chemically calcium sulphate hemihydrate.
- It is used to plaster fractured bones, for making toys, materials for decoration and for making surfaces smooth.

Copper Sulphate

- Copper sulphate when anhydrous, is white and when associated with water of crystallisation (i.e. $CuSO_4 . 5H_2O$), is blue, so it is called **blue vitriol**. It is used to test the presence of water.

Lime

- It is chemically calcium oxide and also called quicklime.
- It is used in the manufacture of glass, cement, etc. and for drying ammonia and alcohol.

Potassium Nitrate

- It is used as fertilizer in gun powder in matchsticks, etc.
- Ant or bee sting contains methanoic or **formic acid**.

Behaviour of Gases

Boyle's Law

At constant temperature, the volume of a definite mass of a gas is inversely proportional to pressure.

Charles' Law

- At constant pressure volume of a fixed mass of a gas is directly proportional to its absolute temperature.
- **Applications of Charles' Law**: Bursting of hydrogen balloon, making of chapatti.

Gay-Lussac's Law

At constant volume, the pressure of given mass of a gas is directly proportional to the temperature in Kelvin.

The Combined Gas Law or Ideal Gas Equation

- It is a gas law which combines Charles law, Boyle's law and Gay-Lussac's law.

Avogadro's Gas Law

At constant temperature and pressure the volume of a gas is directly proportional to the number of molecules.

Ideal Gas Equation

$PV = nRT$ is called ideal gas equation, where

P = Pressure
V = Volume
n = Number of mole
T = Temperature in Kelvin.

Diffusion of gases: The process of intermixing of gases irrespective of the density relationship and without the effect of external agency is called diffusion of gases.

Graham's Law of Diffusion

- According to this law, "the rate of diffusion of a gas is inversely proportional to the square root of its density."

Ideal and Real Gases

- Ideal gases follow gas laws in all conditions of temperature and pressure.
- **Critical temperature** is the temperature above which a gas cannot be liquefied.
- **Dalton's law of partial pressure:** It states that, if two or more gases which do not react chemically are enclosed in a vessel, the total pressure, of all gases of the gaseous mixture is equal to the sum of the partial pressures of all gases which exert pressure when enclosed separately in the same vessel at constant temperature.

Carbon and its Compounds

Allotropy

The substances which have same chemical properties, but different physical properties are called allotropes and this property is called allotropy.

Example: Allotropes of Carbon are diamond, graphite and charcoal.

Diamond

i. It is the purest form of carbon.
ii. It is hardest natural known substance.
iii. It is transparent and its specific gravity is 3.52.
iv. It is a bad conductor of electricity and heat.
v. It has very high refractive index of 2.415.
vi. It is chemically inert and on heating above 15000°C, it gets transformed into graphite.
vii. It has high MP and density.
viii. Black diamond called **Carbonado** contains traces of graphite.

Graphite (Plumbago or Black Lead)

i. It is soft, greasy, dark grayish colored crystalline solid.
ii. It is good conductor of heat and electricity.
iii. It is chemically more reactive than diamond.
iv. Its layer structure is headed by weak van der Waal's forces.

Fullerenes

- It (C60) looks like a soccer ball (or bucky-ball).

Graphene

- Graphene is an allotrope of carbon.

Carbon Monoxide (CO)

- It is formed by incomplete combustion. It is a colourless, odourless gas.

Organic Compounds

- These are the compounds of mainly carbon and hydrogen or compounds of carbon and hydrogen with other elements like phosphorus, oxygen, nitrogen, sulphur, halogens, etc.
- Urea is the first synthesised organic compound (by Wöhler).
- **Acetic acid** was the first organic compound synthesised in the laboratory from its elements.

Hydrocarbons

Compounds made of carbon and hydrogen atoms only, are called hydrocarbons. The natural source of hydrocarbons is petroleum.

1. **Saturated hydrocarbons:** The hydrocarbons in which carbon atoms are singly bonded are called saturated hydrocarbons. Saturated hydrocarbons are also called alkanes or paraffins.
   General formula of alkane $-C_nH_{2n+2}$.
2. **Unsaturated hydrocarbons:** The hydrocarbons in which carbon atoms are either doubly or triply bonded are called unsaturated hydrocarbons. Doubly bonded (carbon atoms) hydrocarbons are called alkenes. The general formula of alkene is C_nH_{2n}.

Triply-bonded carbon: Hydrocarbons containing at lease one carbon–carbon triple bond between two carbon atoms are called alkynes. The general formula of alkynes is C_nH_{2n-2}.

Aromatic Hydrocarbons

These are homocyclic compounds which contain at least one benzene ring in which carbon atoms are linked to one another by alternate single and double bonds.

Isomerism: Two or more compounds having same molecular formula but different physical and chemical properties are called isomers and this phenomenon is called isomerism.

Polymerisation: The simple molecules which combine to form a macro molecule called polymer. The process by which the simple molecules (monomers) are converted into polymer is called polymerisation.

Natural occurring polymers are protein, nucleic acid, cellulose, starch, etc.

Uses of Some Important Organic Compounds

- **Methane (CH_4)** is used to manufacture printer ink, methyl alcohol and to obtain light and energy.
- **Ethylene (C_2H_4)** is used to prepare mustard gas (war gas) and for ripening of fruits.
- **Glycol ($C_2H_6O_2$)** is used as an antifreeze mixture in car radiator and to prevent the freezing of fuel in spacecrafts.
- **Acetylene (C_2H_2)** is used to generate light, weld metals as oxy-acetylene flame and to prepare synthetic rubber (neoprene).
- **Methyl Alcohol (CH_3OH)** is used as a fuel with petrol, used to synthesise varnish and polish, used to denature ethanol.
- **Chloroform ($CHCl_3$)** is used as an anesthetic and to preserve substances obtained from plants and animals. It converts into poisonous phosgene ($COCl_2$), when exposed to sunlight. So, it is kept in dark bottles.
- **Glycerin ($C_3H_8O_3$)** is used as a preservative for fruits and juices, in leather industry and in coagulation of rubber.
- **Acetic acid (CH_3COOH)** is used in vinegar, medicines, and as a solvent.
- **Oxalic acid ($C_2H_2O_4$)** is used in printing of clothes, in photography and in the synthesis of coal tar.
- **Glucose ($C_6H_{12}O_6$)** is used for the synthesis of alcohol and as a preservative for fruit juice.
- **Benzene (C_6H_6)** is used as a solvent for oil fat and in drycleaning. Sodium benzoate is a food preservative.
- **Toluene ($C_6H_5CH_3$)** is used to synthesis explosive TNT, for drycleaning and for the synthesis of medicines like chloramine.
- **Phenol (C_6H_5OH)** is used to synthesis explosive, 2,4,6-trinitrophenol (picric acid) and bakelite.
- **Ethyl Alcohol (C_2H_5OH)** is used for drinking, in medicine to prepare tincture and as insecticide, and as a fuel with petrol.

Fuels

A substance that can supply energy either alone or by reacting with another substance is known as fuel. Heat produced by fuel is measured in Calories. An ideal fuel should:

i. Have high calorific value.
ii. Be cheap and easily available.
iii. Be easily stored and transport.
iv. Be regulated and controlled.
v. Have low ignition temperature.

The quantity of fuel is expressed in the form of calorific value.

Calorific Value

- It is defined as the heat obtained when 1 g of a fuel is burned in excess of oxygen and is expressed in kcal/g.
- **Hydrogen** is the fuel of future.
- Alcohol, when mixed with petrol, is called power alcohol. It is an alternative source of energy.
- For the **combustion of substance**, its ignition temperature should be low.

Flame

- It is the hot part of fire and has three parts:

1. **Innermost region**
   - It is black because of the presence of unburned carbon particles.
   - It has the lowest temperature.
2. **Middle region**
   - It is yellow luminous due to partial combustion of fuel.
3. **Outermost Region**
   - It is blue (non-luminous) due to complete combustion of fuel.
   - It is the hottest part of flame.

Metallurgy

The process of extracting metal in pure form from its ore is known as metallurgy.

Metals: These are the elements which are hard, lustrous, ductile, malleable, sonorous and conductor of heat and electricity in their solid as well as molten state. These evolve hydrogen gas when react with water and acids. Mercury (metal) is liquid at room temperature. Ti is called strategic metal.

Minerals: The compound of a metal found in nature is called a mineral.

Ores: Those minerals from which metal can be economically and easily extracted are called ores.

All ores are minerals but all minerals are not ores.

Gangue (or matrix): The ore is generally associated with earthy impurities like sand, rocks and limestone known as gangue or matrix.

Flux: A substance added to ore to remove impurities is called flux. There are two types of flux–(i) acidic flux, (ii) basic flux.

Slag: Combination of gangue with flux in ores forms a fusible material which is called slag.

Concentration: The process of removal of gangue from the ore is known as concentration of ore.

Calcination: It is the process of heating the concentrated ore in absence or in limited supply of air, below its melting point.

Roasting: Roasting is a process in which ore is heated usually in the presence of air, at temperatures below its melting point.

Smelting: The reduction of oxide ore with carbon at high temperature is known as smelting.

Corrosion

- It is the process of oxidative deterioration of a metal surface by the action of environment to form unwanted corrosion.
- Corrosion of iron is called rusting.
- It is prevented by the following methods:
  - By electroplating
  - By surface coating
  - By alloying
  - By galvanisation of iron

Alloys

- These are mixtures of two metals or a metal and a non-metal.

S. No.	Alloys	Constituents
1.	Brass	Copper (80%) & Zinc (20%)
2.	Bronze	Copper (90%) & Tin (1%)
3.	German Silver	Copper (60%), Zinc (20%) & Nickel (20%)
4.	Duralumin	Aluminium & Copper
5.	Alnico	Aluminium, Nickel, Cobalt & Iron
6.	Magnalium	Aluminium (95%) & Magnesium (5%)
7.	Babbitt Metal	Tin, Antimony, Copper & Lead. Used in ball bearings to reduce friction.
8.	Invar	Iron & Nickel. Used in precision instruments
9.	Bell metal	Copper & tin
10.	Gun Metal	Copper, Tin & Zinc
11.	Monel Metal	Nickel (67%), Copper & Iron
12.	Pewter	Tin (80-90%), Copper & Lead
13.	Solder	Tin, Lead & Antimony

Compounds of Metals and Non-Metals and Their Uses

1. **Ferrous sulphate** ($FeSO_4$). $4H_2O$: In dye industry, and Mohr's salt.
2. **Iodine** (I_2): (i) As antiseptic, (ii) In making tincture of iodine.
3. **Bromine** (Br_2): (i) In dye industry (ii) As a laboratory reagent.
4. **Chlorine** (Cl_2): In the formation of (i) Mustard gas (ii) Bleaching.
5. **Sulphuric acid** (H_2SO_4): (i) As a reagent (ii) In purification of petroleum (iii) In lead storage battery.
6. **Sulphur** (S): Antiseptics, vulcanization of rubber, gun powder, medicine.
7. **Phosphorus (P)** : (i) Red Phosphorus refrigerant, in match industry, etc. (ii) White Phosphorus–Rat killing Medicine.
8. **Carbon dioxide** (CO_2): Soda water, Fire extinguisher.
9. **Graphite:** As electrodes.
10. **Alum** [$K_2SO_4Al_2$ $(SO_4)_3.H_2O$]: (i) Purification of water (ii) Leather industry.
11. **Mercuric Chloride** ($HgCl_2$): Calomel, Insecticides (Corrosive sublimate).
12. **Mercuric oxide (HgO):** Ointment, poison.
13. **Zinc Sulphide (ZnS):** White pigment.
14. **Zinc Sulphate (White vitriol)** ($ZnSO_4{:}7H_2O$): Lithopone, Eye ointment.
15. **Zinc Chloride ($ZnCl_2$):** Textile industry.
16. **Zinc oxide (ZnO):** Ointment.
17. **Plaster of Paris** [$(CaSO_4)_2$. $2H_2$/ $CaSO_4\frac{1}{2}H_2O$)]: Statue, Surgery.
18. **Calcium sulphate ($CaSO_4$. $2H_2O$):** Cement industry.
19. **Calcium carbonate ($CaCO_3$):** Lime and toothpaste.
20. **Cupric oxide (CuO):** Blue and green glass, purification of petroleum.
21. **Cuprous Oxide (Cu_2O):** Red Glass, pesticides.
22. **Copper (Cu):** Electrical wire.
23. **Sodium nitrate ($NaNO_3$):** Fertilizer.
24. **Sodium Sulphate (Glauber's salt) ($Na_2SO_4.10H_2O$):** Medicine, cheap glass.
25. **Sodium bicarbonate (Baking soda) ($NaHCO_3$):** Fire extinguisher, bakery, reagent.
26. **Sodium Carbonate (Washing soda):** (i) Glass industry, (ii) Paper industry, (iii) Removal of permanent hardness of water, (iv) Washing.
27. **Heavy Water (D_2O):** Nuclear reactor.
28. **Liquid Hydrogen:** Rocket fuel.

Elements/Compounds and Their Uses

Xenon	High-speed photographic tubes. Electric valves and T.V. tubes
Krypton	Incandescent bulb. Airfield lights because of characteristic red colour.
Lithium	Deoxidizer and to remove unwanted gases during the manufacture of metals.
Beryllium X-ray	(Transparent) window. Moderator in nuclear reactions around the core.
Neon	Neon lights. Cryogenics
Hopsalite	Mixture of oxides of manganese, cobalt, copper and silver-Antipollution
Ammonia	Refrigerant, fertilisers
Yttrium	Used in TVs to produce red colour
Bismuth	Mixed with iron to make it malleable
Sodium	Street lamp

Gadolinium	CDs. Aluminium is sometimes used to coat the disc
Cesium	Atomic clocks
Tellurium	Tint glass (one-way visibility used in cars)
Technetium	Superconductor at–262 degree Celsius
Paraformaldehyde	Common disinfectant and contraceptives
Potassium Dichromate	Used in breath analyser for detecting alcohol. Safe limit is 0.1%.

Non-Metal

- In Modern Periodic Table, there are 24 non-metals.
- Electronegative elements are non-metals.
- Non-metals are bad conductors of heat and electricity except graphite, Bi and Ge are semi-conductors.
- Protium is the only one isotope in Periodic Table having zero neutrons.
- Deuterium oxide is known as heavy water and used in nuclear reactor as moderator.
- Liquid hydrogen is used as rocket fuel.
- Hydrogen is known as range element because it may kept in group I and group VIIA.
- These may be solid, liquid or gas (bromine is the only liquid non-metal).
- These are soft, non-lustrous, brittle, non-sonorous and non-conductor of heat and electricity.
- These form oxides with oxygen which are generally acidic.

Helium

- It is noble gas.
- It is used for filling balloons and other lighter aircraft.
- Helium (He), when mixed with O_2, is used by deep-sea divers for breathing and for respiratory patients.

Neon

- It is used in neon signs.

Argon

- It is used to generate inert atmosphere for welding and to fill incandescent light bulbs.

Xenon

- It is called stranger gas.

Water (H_2O)

Hard water–Less froth with soap.
Soft water–More froth with soap.

Oxygen

Ozone (O_3) is the allotrope of Oxygen.

Nitrogen

78% by volume in atmosphere, liquid nitrogen is used for refrigeration. Ammonia is an important compound of N_2 which is prepared by Haber's process.

Ammonia

- As refrigerant, in the manufacture of HNO_3.
- In fertilizer like urea, ammonium sulphate, etc.
- In the manufacture of Na_2CO_3 and $NaHCO_3$.
- In preparation of ammonium salt.
- In preparation of explosive.
- In preparation of artificial silk.
- Nitrogen fixation in leguminous plants.

Phosphorous

- An important constituent of animals and plants. It is present in bones and DNA.

Halogens

- **Fluorine** is used in the preparation of UF_6 and SF_6 for energy production and as dielectric constant, respectively.
- By using HF, chlorofluorocarbon compound and polytetrafluoroethylene can be synthesised.
- Chlorofluorocarbon is known as Freon and is used as refrigerant and aerosol.
- Non-stick utensils are made up of teflon.
- **Chlorine** is used to prepare PVC, insecticides herbicides, etc.
- **Bromine** is used in ethylene bromide synthesis which is mixed with leaded petrol.

Inert Gases

- They belong to 18th group of Periodic Table. For example, He, Ne, Ar, Kr, Xe, Rn.
- Except Rn, all inert gases are present in atmosphere.
- Argon is used in Arc. welding and electric bulbs.
- Helium is light and non-inflammable so, used in balloon, weather indicator, etc.
- Neon is used in discharge tube glow light.

Some Important Explosives

- **Dynamite:** It was discovered by Alfred Nobel in 1863. It is prepared by absorption of raw dust with nitro-glycerin. In modern dynamite, Sodium Nitrate is used in place of Nitro-glycerin.
- **Tri Nitro Phenol (TNP):** It is also known as picric acid.
- **R.D.X.** is highly explosive known as plasticiser in which aluminium powder is mixed to increase the temperature and the speed of fire.

Man-made substances

- **Fertilisers:** The substances added to the soil to make up the deficiency of essential elements are known as fertilisers, these are either natural or synthetic (chemical).
  Among the chemical fertilisers, the two important categories are:
- **Phosphate fertilisers:** The most abundant phosphate is rock phosphate $[3Ca_3(PO_4)_2]$, which is mostly consumed by the fertiliser industry in the manufacture of 'superphosphate of lime', 'triple superphosphate' and 'altrophs'–a combined phosphatic and nitrogenous fertiliser.
  Nitrogenous Fertilizers: Plants need nitrogen for rapid growth and increase in their protein content. For this reason, nitrogenous fertilizers are of some more importance. The chief nitrogenous fertilizers are ammonium sulphate, calcium cyanamide, sodium nitrate, ammonium nitrate, urea, and ammonium phosphate.
- **Dyes:** Coloured substances used for colouring textiles, foodstuffs, silk, wool, etc. are called dyes.
- **Cement:** It is a complex material containing the silicates of calcium and aluminium. A paste of sand, cement and water is called mortar.

A mixture of stone chips (gravel), cement and water is known as concrete. Concrete with steel bars and wires is called reinforced concrete. It is used for constructing roads, bridges and pillars.

- **Glass:** It is an amorphous or transparent solid, also called **supercooled liquid**. It mainly contains silica (SiO_2).

Different kinds of glass are as follows:

1. **Soda or soft glass** is sodium calcium silicate used for making bottles, window panes, etc.
2. **Potash glass or hard glass** contains potassium. It is used for making chemical apparatus: beakers, flasks, funnel, etc.
3. **Crown glass** contains potassium oxide, barium oxide, boric oxide, and silica. It is used for optical apparatus.
4. **Flint glass** contains lead oxide and is used in optical instruments like lenses, prisms.
5. **Crook's glass** contains cesium oxide. It is used for spectacles as it absorbs UV rays.
6. **Jena glass** contains B_2O_3 and alumina. It is used for making laboratory bottles, for keeping acids and alkalies.
7. **Milky glass** is prepared by adding tin oxide, calcium phosphate or cryolite to the melt glass.
8. Glass laminates is made by fixing polymer sheets between layers of glass. It is used to make window and screens of cars, trains and aircraft. Specially manufactured glass laminates are used as bulletproof material.

   It has the following composition: calcium oxide (CaO) = 50–60%, silica (SiO_2) = 20–25%, alumina (Al_2O_3) = 5–10%; magnesium oxide (MgO) = 2–3%.

   It is manufactured from limestone and clay.

- **Paint:** A chemical that contains a pigment as a vehicle and a thinner.

White pigment: Zinc oxide, white lead and titanium dioxide. The pigment mixed with a vehicle, which is an oil like ***linseed* or *soyabean*** oil a ***polymer.*** A thinner is a solvent such as ***turpentine oil* or *kerosene.***

Luminous paints: Glow when exposed to light.

- **Soaps:** These are sodium and potassium salts of higher fatty acids.
- **Detergents:** These are sodium or potassium salts of long chain alkyl or aryl sulphonates or sulphates.
- These are also called **soapless soap**.
- **Antibiotic:** Medicinal compounds produced by moulds and bacteria, capable of destroying or preventing the growth of bacteria in animal systems.
- **Antibody:** Kinds of substances formed in the blood, tending to inhibit or destroy harmful bacteria, etc.
- **Antidote:** Medicine used against a poison.
- **Antigen:** Substance capable of stimulating formation of antibodies.
- **Antipyretics** are used to reduce body temperature during high fever, e.g., paracetamol, aspirin, phenacetin, analgin, and novalgin.
- **Tranquilizers** are used to treat stress, mild, and severe mental disease.
- **Antiseptic:** Prevent the growth of microorganisms or kill them but are not harmful to living tissues, e.g., dettol and savlon.
- **Analgesics:** Painkillers are called analgesics, e.g., aspirin, paracetamol and morphine.
- **Antimalarials** are used to treat malaria, e.g., chloroquin.
- **Sulphadrugs:** Alternatives of antibiotics, sulphanilamide, sulphadiazine sulphagunamidine.
- **Antacid:** Substances which remove the excess acid and raise the pH to appropriate level in scotch are called antacids.
- **Antacids** are used as a remedy for acidity.
- **Pesticides** are used to destroy the organisms that harm the crop.

These are of the following types.

1. **Insecticides**, e.g., DDT, aluminium phosphate, gammexane.
2. **Fungicide**, e.g., Bordeaux mixture.
3. **Herbicides**, e.g., benzepam, benzadox.
4. **Rodenticides**, e.g., aluminium phosphide.

- **Chloroform:** A sweetish, colourless liquid. It is used as a solvent and anaesthetic.
- **Saccharin:** A white crystalline solid which is 550 times sweeter than sugar, but does not have any food value. It is used by diabetic patients
- **DDT:** Dichlorodiphenyltricholoro ethane is a white powder used as an insecticide.

Propellants

Liquid propellants	Liquid hydrogen, liquid ammonia, hydrazine, nitromethane, methyl nitrate, hydrogen peroxide
Solid propellants	Polybutadiene, acrylic acid, nitroglycerine + nitrocellulose
Hybrid propellants	N_2O_4 + Acrylic rubber

Dyes

Nitro dyes	Less important as the colours are not fast
Azo dyes	Azo (-N=N-) group is chromophore
Triphenylmethane dye	Malachite green
Direct dyes	Mautius yellow, Naphthol yellow, Congo red, etc.
Mordant dyes	Alizarin
Vat dyes	Indigo

BIOLOGY

Classification of Organisms

Classification means to categorise organisms into different groups.

1. Monera

It includes all prokaryotic organisms like bacteria, cynobacteria and archiobacteria.

2. Protista

This kingdom includes unicellular form usually found in parasitic and saprophytic forms. Euglena has both heterotrophic and autotrophic modes of nutrition.

3. Fungi

This kingdom includes non-green plants. It has saprophytic nutrition and growing on dead and decaying organic matter.

Example: Mushroom, Mucor, Albugo, etc.

4. Plantae

This kingdom includes all plants except some algae, diatoms, fungi and ember of monera and protista.

5. Animalia

Almost all animals come under this kingdom except protozoan.

Study of Cell

- **Cell:** The **Cell** is the basic structural and functional unit of all known living organisms. It is the smallest unit of life and is often called the building block of life.
- The largest known cells are unfertilized **ostrich egg** cells.
- The smallest cell is of **PPLO** (*Mycoplasma gallisepticum*).
- Human nerve cell is the **longest animal cell.**
- Largest unicellular plant is Acetabularia (10 cm) and animal is *Amoeba,* (1mm).
- The largest human cell is the **female ovum** and the smallest human cell is the **red blood cell.**
- **Robert Hooke** coined the term *cell.*
- The first living cell was discovered by **Leeuwenhoek.**
- The longest cell is *Neuron.*
- The biggest cell is egg of *Ostrich.*

Types of Cells

i. **Prokaryotic Cells:** These are primitive cells, lacking a nucleus and most of the other cell organelles.

ii. **Eukaryotic Cells:** These have nucleus and membrane bound cell organelles.

Difference Between Eukaryotic Cells and Prokaryotic Cells

Cell organelle	Eukaryotic	Prokaryotic
Nucleus	Present	Absent
Number of chromosomes	More than one	One–but not true chromosome: Plasmids
Cell Type	Usually multicellular	Usually unicellular (some cyanobacteria may be multicellular)
True Membrane-bound Nucleus	Present	Absent
Example	Animals and plants	Bacteria and archaea
Genetic Recombination	Meiosis and fusion of gametes	Partial, undirectional transfers, DNA
Lysosomes and peroxisomes	Present	Absent
Microtubules	Present	Absent or rare
Endoplasmic reticulum	Present	Absent
Mitochondria	Present	Absent
Cytoskeleton	Present	May be absent
DNA wrapping on proteins	Eukaryotes wrap their DNA around proteins called histones	Multiple proteins act together to fold and condense prokaryotic DNA. Folded DNA is then organized into a variety of conformations that are supercoiled and wound around tetramers of the HU protein.
Ribosomes	Larger	Smaller
Vesicles	Present	Present
Golgi apparatus	Present	Absent
Chloroplasts	Present (in plants)	Absent; chlorophyll scattered in the cytoplasm
Flagella	Microscopic in size; membrane bound; usually arranged as nine doublets surrounding two singlets	Submicroscopic in size, composed of only one fiber
Permeability of nuclear membrane	Selective	Not present
Plasma membrane with steroid	Yes	Usually no
Cell wall	Only in plant cells and fungi (chemically simpler)	Usually chemically complexed
Vacuoles	Present	Present
Cell size	10-100 μm	1-10 μm

Main Features of the Cell Theory

1. All organisms are composed of cell.
2. Each cell arises from pre-existing cell.
3. Every organism starts its life from single cell.

Parts of cell and their functions

1. **Cell wall:** In plant cell there is a rigid cell wall which is non-living and freely permeable. It is made up of cellulose and chitin. It provides shape and rigidity to the cell.
2. **Cell membrane:** It is also known as plasma membrane which form the outer covering of animal cell. In plant cell it is found within cell wall.
   Function: It regulates movement of molecules inside and outside of the cell.
3. **Protoplasm:** The whole fluid present inside plasma-membrane is protoplasm.
   (A) **Cytoplasm:** The fluid found outside the nuclear membrane.
   (B) **Nucleoplasm:** The fluid found inside the nuclear membrane.

Mitochondria

- It is a semi-autonomous organelle and called **powerhouse of the cell** because in it stepwise oxidation of fuel occurs which results in release of chemical energy. This energy is stored in the form of ATP.

Endoplasmic Reticulum

- These are hollow membranous system having ribosomes (thus called Rough ER) or no ribosomes (thus called Smooth ER). Rough Endoplasmic Reticulum is the site of protein synthesis, while Smooth Endoplasmic Reticulum is the site of synthesis of steroids and detoxification.

Golgi Apparatus

- Play important role in secretion, transportation and acrosome formation.

Plastid

Only found in plant cells.

(a) **Chloroplasts:** These are green pigment found in green planted involved in photosynthesis. So, it is known as *'Kitchen of the cell'*.
Function: Chloroplast provides green colour to plant and take part photosynthesis.

(b) **Chromoplast** provides various colours to the plant.

(c) **Leucoplast** is colourless. It stores the food in the form of starch, lipid or protein.

Functions:

i. It helps in osmoregulation. It stores toxic metabolic water.
ii. It controls all the activities of a cell. So, it is also known as the 'control-room' of a cell. Chromatin transmits hereditary characters from parents to their offspring.

The red colour of tomatoes is due to the presence of lycopene pigment, i.e., chromophore.

The colour of **carrot** is due to carotene.

Ribosomes

It is made up of ribonucleic acid (RNA).

Functions

i. Take part in protein synthesis.
ii. It helps in intracellular digestion. The enzyme found in lysosome may digest the entire cell. So it is also known as suicidal bag.
iii. Help in the formation of spindle fibre during cell division.

Chromosome

- Chromosome is thread-like structure, found in the nucleus. Bead-like structure found on chromosome is called **genes,** which are made up of DNA and are the carrier of genetic information from generation-to-generation. In some viruses, RNA is the genetic material called **retrovirus.**
- Eukaryotic cells possess many chromosomes.

Organism	Number of pairs of chromosomes
Dog	39 = 78
Human	23 = 46
Monkey	21 = 42
Onion	8 = 16

Difference between plant and animal cell

Plant cell	Animal cell
It has cell wall.	Cell wall is usually absent.
Plastids are found.	Plastids are usually absent.
A big vacuole is present.	Vacuole is absent or very small in size

Lysosomes

- These are sometimes called **suicidal bags of the cell.**

Centrosomes

- Participate in the formation of spindle during cell division and cilia.

Vacuoles

- These are non-living reservoirs, bounded by a membrane called **tonoplast.**
- It stores toxic metabolic waste and helps in osmoregulation.

Nucleus

- It was discovered by **Robert Brown.**
- Nucleus is rich in protein and RNA. Chromatin is the **controlling centre of a cell.**

Nucleic Acids

- These contain the genetic instructions used in the development and functioning of all known **living organisms.**
- These are of two types DNA and RNA.

Deoxyribonucleic Acid (DNA)

- It is a long polymer made from repeating units called **nucleotides.**
- Each nucleotide consists of a nucleoside and a phosphate group, joined together by ester bonds.
- It has four bases, e.g., adenine, guanine, cytosine and thymine.
- DNA was discovered by **James D Watson** and Francis Crick, who got Nobel Prize for this discovery.

DNA Synthesise RNA

☞ **Note: DNA:** DNA is mainly found in nucleus in small amount it is also found in mitochondria and chloroplast.

Gene: Gene is hereditary unit which is made by a segment of DNA found on the chromosome.

Ribonucleic Acid (RNA): RNA is single stranded nucleic acid made up to phosphate, ribose sugar and nitrogenous base uracil, adenine, guanine and cytosine. It is found in nucleus as well as cytoplasm.

Function: Synthesis of protein.

Comparison of DNA and RNA

Comparison	DNA	RNA
Name	Deoxyribonucleic acid	Ribonucleic acid
Function	Long-term storage of genetic information; transmission of genetic information to make other cells and new organisms.	Used to transfer the genetic code from the nucleus to the ribosomes to make proteins. RNA is used to transmit genetic information in some organisms and may have been the molecule used to store genetic blueprints in primitive organisms.
Structural Features	B-form double helix. DNA is a double-stranded molecule consisting of a long chain of nucleotides.	A-form helix. RNA usually is a single-strand helix consisting of shorter chains of nucleotides.
Composition of Bases and Sugars	Deoxyribose sugar Phosphate backbone Adenine, guanine, cytosine, thymine bases	Ribose sugar Phosphate backbone Adenine, guanine, cytosine, uracil bases
Propagation	DNA is self-replicating.	RNA is synthesized from DNA on an as-needed basis.
Base-pairing	AT (adenine-thymine) GC (guanine-cytosine)	AU (adenine-uracil) GC (guanine-cytosine)
Reactivity	The C-H bonds in DNA make it fairly stable, plus the body destroys enzymes that would attack DNA. The small grooves in the helix also serve as protection, providing minimal space for enzymes to attach.	The O-H bond in the ribose of RNA makes the molecule more reactive, compared with DNA. RNA is not stable under alkaline conditions, plus the large grooves in the molecule make it susceptible to enzyme attack. RNA is constantly produced, used, degraded, and recycled.
Ultraviolet Damage	DNA is susceptible to UV damage.	Compared with DNA, RNA is relatively resistant to UV damage.

Cell cycle

It is the sequence of events in which cell duplicates its genetic material, synthesises the other constituents of the cell and ultimately divide into two daughter cells.

Cell Division

The process in which cells increase in their number is called cell division.

(A) **Mitosis:** Mitosis cell division occurs in somatic cells which take part in growth, repair and development. In an unicellular organism, asexual reproduction takes place by this type of cell division.

(B) **Meiosis:** Meiosis cell division occurs in a reproductive cell. This type of division takes place during the formation of haploid gamete, i.e, over a sperm.

ZOOLOGY

Animal Tissue

i. **Epithelial Tissue:** Epithelial tissue cover the external surface of the body and internal free surface of many organs.
Example: skin, intestine, gland.

ii. **Connective Tissue:** These tissues connect and bind different tissues and organs.
Example: Adipose tissue found beneath the skin. Ligament is made up of fibrous connective tissue, cartilage, bone and blood.

☞ **Note:** Blood is only tissue which is found in the form of fluid.

iii. **Muscular Tissue:** This is also known as contractile tissue. All the muscles of the body are made up of this tissue.

(a) **Unstriped:** This muscle tissue is found on the walls of those parts which are not controlled by will.

(b) **Striped:** These muscles are found in the parts of the body that move voluntarily.

(c) **Cardiac:** These muscles are found only on the walls of the heart.

The largest muscle of the human body is Gluteus Maximus.

The smallest muscle of the human body is Stapedius.

iv. **Nervous Tissue:** This tissue is also called sensitive tissue.

Human Blood

- The quantity of blood in the human's body is 7% of the total weight.
- Blood is fluid connective tissue and composed of blood corpuscles, plasma and platelets.
- It is slightly alkaline in nature (pH 7.4).
- Its volume in an adult is 5.8 L.
- People who live at high altitudes have more blood than those who live in low regions. This extra blood supplies additional oxygen to body cells.
- During blood clotting fibrinogen changes into fibrin by thrombin which is obtained from thromboplastin in the presence of Ca^{2+}.
- Female contains half litre of blood less in comparison to male.

Blood Consists of Two Parts

(A) Plasma; and (B) Blood corpuscles.

(A) **Plasma:** This is the liquid part of blood. 60% of the blood is plasma. Its 90% part is water, 7% protein, 0.9% salt and 0.1% is glucose.

- **Function of plasma:** Transportation of digested food, hormones, excretory product, etc. from the body takes place through plasma.
- **Serum:** When Fibrinogen and protein is extracted out of plasma the remaining plasma is called serum.

(B) **Blood corpuscles:** This is the remaining 40% part of the blood.

i. **Red Blood Corpuscles (RBC):** Red Blood Corpuscles (RBC) in mammal is biconcave.
   - There is no nucleus in it. Exception–Camel and Lama. RBC is formed in Bone marrow.
   - Its life span is from 20 days to 120 days.
   - Its destruction takes place in liver and spleen. Therefore, liver is the grave of RBC.
   - It contains haemoglobin, in which haeme iron containing compound found and due to this the colour of blood is red.
   - The main function of RBC is to carry oxygen to all cells of the body bring back the carbon dioxide.

ii. **White Blood Corpuscles (WBC) or Leucocytes:**
   - Its formation takes place in Bone marrow, lymph node and sometimes in liver and spleen.
   - Its life span is from 1 to 2 days.
   - Nucleus is present in the White Blood Corpuscles.
   - Its main function is to protect the body from the disease. The ratio of RBC and WBC is 600 : 1.

iii. **Blood Platelets or Thrombocytes:** It is found only in the blood of human and other mammals.
   - There is no nucleus in it.
   - Its formation takes place in Bone marrow.
   - Its life span is from 3 to 5 days.
   - It dies in the Spleen.
   - Its main function is to help in clotting of blood.

Functions of Blood

i. To control the temperature of the body and to protect the body from diseases.
ii. Clotting of blood.
iii. Transportation of O_2, CO_2, digested food, conduction of hormones, etc.
iv. To help in establishing coordination among different parts.

➢ The main reason behind the difference in blood of human is the glycoprotein which is found in Red Blood Corpuscles called antigens. Antigens are of two types: Antigen A and Antigen B.

➢ On the basis of presence of Antigen or Glycoprotein, there are four group of blood in human:

(a) That contains Antigen A–Blood Group A.
(b) That contains Antigen B–Blood Group B.
(c) That contains both the Antigens A and B–Blood Group AB.
(d) That contains neither of the Antigens–Blood Group O.

An opposite type of protein is found in blood plasma. This is called antibody. This is also of two types–Antibody 'a' and Antibody 'b'.

Blood Transfusion: Antigen 'A' and antibody 'a', Antigen 'B' and antibody 'b' cannot live together. In case of so happened these get most sticky, such spoils the blood. This is called agglutination of blood.

Blood Group **O** is called **Universal Donor** because it does not contain any antigen.

Blood Group **AB** is called **Universal Receptor** because it does not contain any antibody.

If in the blood of people it is found, their blood is said to be Rh-positive and if in the blood of people it is not found, their blood is said to be Rh-negative.

At the time of blood transfusion, Rh-factor is also tested. Rh-positive is given to Rh-positive blood and Rh-negative is given to Rh-negative blood only.

Possible Combinations of Blood Groups

Male	Female	Blood group of Children not possible
A	A	B & AB
A	B	–
A	AB	O
A	O	B or AB
B	B	A, AB
B	AB	O
B	O	A, AB
AB	AB	O
AB	O	O, AB
O	O	A, B, AB

Blood Pressure (BP)

➢ The pressure created by the blood on the walls of the blood vessels due to the repeated pumping of heart is called **blood pressure**. It is measured by **sphygmomanometer.**

➢ Blood pressure in a normal person is 120/80 mm Hg.

➢ If a person has persistent high blood pressure then it is called hypertension and persistent high blood pressure is 150/90 mm Hg.

➢ **Hypotension** is condition of low blood pressure, *i.e.,* persistent 100/50 mm Hg.

➢ Electrocardiograph (ECG) is used to check proper working of heart.

System of the Human Body

Epidermis

➢ The top layer of skin made up of epithelial cells and does not contain blood vessels.

Dermis

➢ It gives elasticity to the integument, allowing stretching and conferring flexibility, while resisting distortions, wrinkling and sagging.

Hypodermis

➢ It is made up of adipose tissue.

Teeth

➢ With the help of teeth the food is chewed. Teeth are of four types

i. Incisors
ii. Canines
iii. Premolars
iv. Molars

➢ Hardest part in the body is tooth enamel.

Tongue

- Saliva, secreted by the salivary glands, is mixed with the chewed food by the tongue.
- Complete digestion process takes place in following four steps:
  - i. Ingestion of Food
  - ii. Digestion in Mouth.
  - iii. Digestion in Stomach.
  - iv. Digestion in Intestine.
- The food passes down through the oesophagus into stomach.
- Now food is mixed with gastric juice and hydrochloric acid which disinfect the food and creates acidic medium.
- Pepsin digests proteins and converts them into peptones.
- Renin coverts milk into curd.
- The digested food now is called chyme.
  1. **Ingestion:** Taking the food into the mouth is called ingestion.
  2. **Digestion:** Conversion of non-absorbable food into absorbable form. The digestion of the food is started in the mouth.
- Saliva is secreted by salivary gland in mouth in which two types of enzymes are found, ptyalin and maltase. They convert starch into simple sugar and make it digestible.
- From the mouth the food goes into stomach through foodpipe.
- No digestion takes place in foodpipe.

Digestion in Stomach

- The food lies approximately for four hours in the stomach.
- Hydrochloric acid secreted from the Oxyntic cells of the stomach kill all the bacteria coming with food and accelerate the reaction of enzymes.
- The enzymes in the gastric juice of stomach are–Pepsin and Renin.
- Pepsin breaks down the protein into peptones.
- Renin breaks down the caseinogen into casein.

Small Intestine

Digestion in Intestine

Food passes into ileum and mixes with intestinal juice, where:

- Maltase converts into glucose.
- Lactose converts into glucose and galactose.
- Sucrose converts into glucose and fructose.
- Trypsin digests the peptides into amino acids.
- Food now is called chyle.

The main organs participating in digestion:

Liver: This is the largest gland of the human body. Its weight is approximately 1.5–2 kilogram.

- Bile is secreted through liver only.
- Liver converts excess of amino acid into ammonia by deamination. The ammonia is further converted into urea by ornithine cycle. Urea comes out from body through kidney.
- Liver converts some quantity of protein into glucose during defecation of carbohydrate.
- Liver regulates the quantity of glucose in the blood.
- In case of decrease of fat in food liver converts some of the parts of carbohydrates into fat.
- The production of fibrinogen protein takes place by liver which helps in clotting of blood.
- The production of Heparin protein takes place in liver which prevent the clotting of blood inside the body.
- The liver reserves some quantity of iron, copper and vitamin.
- It helps in regulating the body temperature.
- Liver is an important clue in investigating a person's death that is been due to poison in food.

Gall Bladder: Gall bladder is a pear shaped sac, in which the bile coming out of liver is stored.

- Bile is a yellowish-green coloured alkaline liquid, whose pH value is 7.7.
- The quantity of water is 85% and the quantity of bile pigment is 12% in water.

The main functions of bile are as under:

- i. It makes the medium of food alkaline so that pancreatic juice can work.
- ii. It kills the harmful bacteria coming with food.
- iii. It emulsifies the fats.
- iv. It accelerates the bowel movement of intestine by which digestive juices in the food mix well.
- v. It is helpful in the absorption of vitamin K and other vitamins mixed in fats.

In case of obstruction in bile duct, liver cells stop taking bilirubin form. As a result, bilirubin spreads throughout the body. This is called jaundice.

Pancreas: This is the second largest gland of the human body. It acts simultaneously as endocrine and exocrine type of gland.

Islets of Langerhans: This is a part of the pancreas.

- **Insulin:** It is secreted by β-Cells of Islets of Langerhans which is a part of pancreas.
  It controls the process of making glycogen from glucose.
  Diabetes is caused due to the deficiency of insulin.
- Excessive flow of insulin causes Hypoglycemia in which one loses the producing capacity and vision deterioration.
  Glucagon: It re-converts the glycogen into glucose.

CIRCULATORY SYSTEM

The discovery of blood circulation was done by William Harvey.

Heart

It remains safe in the pericardial membrane.

Heart of the human is made up of four chambers.

- The chamber which receives the blood from body tissues is called **auricles** and the chambers of heart which pump blood to body tissues are called **ventricles.**
- There is a thin two layered sac around the heart known as **pericardium,** filled with a watery fluid called pericardial fluid, which allows frictionless movements of heart and protects it from mechanical shocks.
- The blood vessel: carrying the blood from the body towards the heart is called vein.
- In the vein there is impure blood i.e. carbon dioxide mixed blood with the exception is pulmonary vein, which always carry pure blood.

- Pulmonary vein carrying the blood from lungs to left auricle. It has pure blood.
- The blood vessel carrying the blood from the heart towards the body is called artery.
- In artery there is pure blood i.e. oxygen mixed blood. Its exception is pulmonary artery.
- Pulmonary artery carries the blood from right ventricle to lungs. It contains impure blood.
- The artery carrying blood to the muscles of the heart are called coronary arteries. Any type of hindrance in it cause heart attack.

Course of circulation: Mammals have double circulation. It is because blood have to cross two times from heart before circulating throughout body.

- To pump out blood, the heart chamber undergoes alternate contraction called **systole** and relaxation called **diastole.**
- Arteries carry **pure blood** from the heart while veins carry **impure blood** to the heart.
- Human heartbeat is myogenic in nature, i.e., initiated by a patch of modified heart muscles itself without requiring an external stimulation. This patch is called **SA node** (sino-auricular node) or **pacemaker.**
- The normal **rate of heartbeat** of a newborn baby is about 140 per minute.
- When SA-node becomes defective, i.e., it does not generate cardiac impulse, it can be cured by surgical grafting of an artificial pacemaker (an electric device) in the chest of the patient. It stimulates the heart electrically at regular intervals.

EXCRETORY SYSTEM

Kidney

- It is bean-shaped, chocolate brown structure lying in the abdomen, one on each side of the vertebral column just below the diaphragm.
- The left kidney is placed in little higher than the right kidney (but reverse in rabbit).
- These form the urine and controls osmotic pressure within the organism with respect to external environment.
- Nephrons are the functional and structural unit of kidney. They contain Bowman's capsule and Henle's loop.
- The process of filtration of liquids into the cavity of Bowman's capsule is called ultrafiltration.
- The main function of the kidneys is purification of blood plasma, i.e. to excrete the unwanted nitrogenous waste substances through urination.
- In the kidneys average 125 ml per minute blood is filtered.

Ureters

- These bring the urine downwards and open into urinary bladder.

Urinary Bladder

- It temporarily stores the urine.

Urethra

- In females, this tube is small and serves as a passage of urine only.
- In males, it is long and functions as a common passage for urine and spermatic fluids.

Urine

- It is pale yellow coloured fluid due to presence of urochrome pigment.
- It is acidic in nature (pH 6.0) and is slightly heavier than water.
- **Chemical composition of urine**: Water is 95-96%, urea is 2% and some other substances like uric acid, creatinine, etc. are 2-3%.
- Kidney stone is calcium oxalate.
  i. **Skin:** Oil glands and sweat glands found in the skin secrete sebum and sweat.
  ii. **Liver:** Liver cells play the main role in excretion by converting and more amino acids and ammonia of blood into urea.
  iii. **Lungs:** The lungs excrete two types of gaseous substances–carbon dioxide and water vapour.

Hemodialysis: Process of removal of excess urea from the blood of patient using artificial kidney.

CENTRAL NERVOUS SYSTEM

- Nervous system is found only in animals and absent in plants.
- Part of the nervous system which keeps control on the whole body and on nervous system itself is called Central Nervous System. The Central Nervous System of human is made up of two parts–Brain and Spinal Cord.
- Brain is covered by a membrane called meninges. It is situated in a bony box called cranium which protects it from external injury.

Brain

- Brain lies in the cranium of skull.
- The functions of brain parts are as follows:
  i. **Cerebrum** leads to consciousness, storage of memory of information.
  ii. **Thalamus** deals with pain, pressure and temperature.
  iii. **Hypothalamus** deals with water balance in body, behavioural patterns of sex, sleep, stress emotions, etc. It also regulates pituitary hormones and metabolism of fat, carbohydrate and water.
  iv. **Midbrain** deals with visual analysis, etc.
  v. **Cerebellum** controls coordination of accurate movements and balancing.
  vi. Medulla oblongata is long connecting part of brain to spinal cord. It deals with control of heartbeats, blood vessels, breathing, salivary secretion and most of reflex and involuntary (uncontrolled) movements.

Spinal Cord

The posterior region of the medulla oblongata is the spinal cord. Its main functions are:

(a) Coordination and control of reflex actions i.e. it works as the centre of the reflex actions.
(b) It carries the waves coming out of the brain.

SKELETAL SYSTEM

(i) Axial Skeleton (80 Bones)

- It includes skull, vertebral column and bones of chest.
- Vertebral column is responsible for the upright position of the human body.

(ii) Appendicular Skeleton (126 Bones)

- Their functions are to make locomotion possible and to protect the major organs of locomotion, digestion, excretion, and reproduction.

i. **Skull:** There are 29 bones in it.
ii. **Vertebral Column:** The vertebral column of the human is made up of 33 vertebrae.

Functions of the Skeletal System

i. To provide a definite shape to the body.
ii. To provide protection to soft parts of the body.
iii. To provide a base to the muscles for joining.
iv. To help in respiration and nutrition.
v. To form Red Blood Corpuscles.

- The total number of bones in a human's body–206
- The total number of bones during childhood–300
- The largest bone of the body–Femur (bone of thigh).
- The smallest bone of the body–Stapes (bone of ear).

☞ **Note:** The muscles and bones are joined together by tendon. The muscle which joins bone to bone is called ligament.

Classification of Hormones

Amines	Peptide hormones	Steroids/sterols	Lipids
Adrenaline	Acth Or Corticotropin	Cortisol	Prostaglandins
Dopamine	Vasopressin	Aldosterone	Leukotrienes
Noradrenaline	Calcitonin	Testosterone	Prostacyclin
Melatonin	Corticotropin-Releasing Hormone (Crh)	Androstenedione	Thromboxane
Serotonin	Erythropoietin (Epo)	Oestrogen	
Thyroxine	Follicle-Stimulating Hormone (Fsh)	Estradiol	
Triiodothyronine	Gastrin	Progesterone	
	Glucagon	Progestins	
	Gonadotropin-Releasing Hormone (Gnrh)	Calcitriol	
	Growth Hormone-Releasing Hormone (GHRH)	(Sterol)	
	Insulin		
	Leptin		
	Luteinizing Hormone (LH)		
	Oxytocin		
	Parathyroid Hormone (PTH)		
	Prolactin (PRL)		

RESPIRATORY SYSTEM

- Respiration is a catabolic process in which the respired oxygen is used in the oxidation of food resulting in the release of energy.

Human Respiratory System

- Overall passage of air in humans is as follows:

Nostrils–Pharynx–Larynx–Trachea–Bronchi–Bronchioles–Alveoli–Cells–Blood.

External Respiration

- It involves inspiration and expiration of air.
- **Inspiration** is the process of intake of air. During inspiration, muscles of the diaphragm contract and diaphragm flatten. The lower ribs are raised upward and outwards, the chest cavity enlarges, the air pressure in the lungs is decreased, air rushes into the lungs.
- **Expiration** is breathing out of air. During expiration, relaxation of muscles of the ribs and diaphragm takes place. Diaphragm again becomes dome-shaped. Chest cavity is reduced and air is forced outward through nose and trachea.

Internal Respiration (Oxidation of Food)

- It is a complex process in which food is broken down to release energy. It is a biochemical phase takes place inside the cell.
- Transportation of oxygen takes place by haemoglobin of blood, whereas transportation of only 10-20% carbon dioxide takes place by haemoglobin of blood.
- Respiration being a catalytic process also **reduces the weight** of the body.

Glucose is oxidised by oxygen reached into the cell. This process is called cellular respiration.

SENSE ORGANS

Eye

It consists of three parts.

1. Sclerotic Layer

- Cornea
- Conjunctiva

2. Choroid Layer

It is the middle layer and consists of:

i. **Pupil:** It changes size as the amount of light changes.
ii. Ciliary body.
iii. **Iris:** It controls the amount of light that enters the eye by changing the size of the pupil.

iv. Lens is a biconvex transparent circular solid part located just behind the iris.

3. Retina

- Light sensitive tissue that lines the back of the eye.
- The image formed on retina is real and inverted.
- Rods are highly sensitive to dim light and contain a reddish purple pigment called rhodopsin.
- Cones are sensitive to bright light, hence differentiate the colours.
- The **fovea centralis** is the area of sharpest vision.
- The **blind spot:** no image is formed in this region.

Eye Defects

- Nearsightedness (Myopia)
- Farsightedness (Hypermetropia)
- Astigmatism
- Presbyopia
- Conjunctivitis

Ear

- Human ear can list in the sound of 60-80 decibel.
- Defects of ear are: **Otalgia ear-ache** (Pain in ear); **Otitis media** (acute infection of middle ear), **labyrinthine** disease (malfunction of inner ear).

Nose (Olfactory Organ)

Olfactory cells

- Dogs have an acute olfactory sense.

NUTRIENTS

- These are metals, non-metals and their salts other than the four elements–carbon, hydrogen, nitrogen and oxygen and constitute about 4% of total body weight.
- Milk, eggs, meat, fruit, food, vegetables, etc. are the sources of minerals.

Nutrition is one of the basic functions of life in which intake of food, digestion, absorption, assimilation are included.

Carbohydrates

Carbohydrates are organic compounds in which the ratio of Carbon, Hydrogen and Oxygen is 1: 2: 1.

Carbohydrates are classified into three major groups:

(a) **Monosaccharides:** These are the simple sugar made up of single polyhydroxy or ketone unit. Most abundant monosaccharides found in nature are glucose. Triose, tetrose, pentoses, heptoses are the type of monosaccharides.

(b) **Oligosaccharides:** When 2 to 10 monosaccharides join together they form oligosaccharides. Maltose, sucrose, lactose are disaccharides made up of two monosaccharides.

(c) **Polysaccharides:** These are the compounds of sugar which are formed due to joining large number of monosaccharide. Some examples of polysaccharides are starch, glycogen, cellulose, chitin, etc.

Functions of Carbohydrates

1. Carbohydrate works as fuel during the process of respiration, glucose break into CO_2 and H_2O with the release of energy. One gram of glucose gives 4.2 kilo calories energy.
2. Nucleic acids are polymers of nucleosides and nucleotides and contain pentose sugar.
3. Lactose of milk is formed from glucose and galactose.
4. Glucose is used for the formation of fat and amino acid.
5. Carbon skeleton of monosaccharides is used in the formation of fatty acid, chitin, cellulose, etc.

Sources of Carbohydrates

Wheat, rice, maize, sweet potato and other plant and animals are the sources of carbohydrate.

Proteins

- This is a complex organic compound made up of 20 types of amino acids.
- Nitrogen is present in protein in addition to C, H and O.
- Twenty-two types of protein is necessary for human body, out of which 12 are synthesized by body itself and remaining 10 are obtained by food are called essential amino acid.
- These are the compounds of carbon (C), hydrogen (H), oxygen (O), nitrogen (N) and sulphur (S). These form 15% part of human body.
- Their main sources are groundnuts, soyabean, pulses, fish, etc.

Functions of Proteins

1. It takes part in the formation of cells, protoplasm and tissues.
2. These are important for physical growth. Physical growth hampers by their deficiency. Lack of proteins causes Kwashiorkor and Marasmus diseases in children.
3. In case of necessity they provide energy to the body.
4. They control the development of genetic characters.
5. These are helpful in conduction also.

Kwashiorkor: In this disease hands and legs of children get slimmed and the stomach comes out.

Marasmus: In this disease muscles of children are loosened.

Fats

- Fat is an ester of glycerol and fatty acid.
- Normally fat remains as solid at 20°C temperature, but if it is in liquid form at this temperature, this is called oil.
- 9.3 kilocalorie energy is liberated from 1 gram fat.
- These are also the compounds of carbon (C), hydrogen (H) and oxygen (O).
- Fatty acids are of two types. Saturated and Unsaturated. Saturated fatty acids are found in coconut oil and palm oil, while unsaturated fatty acids are found in fish oil and vegetable oil.
- Excess of saturated fats raises the level of blood cholesterol and may cause arteriosclerosis (hardening of arteries). This may lead to heart attack.

Main Functions of Fat

1. It provides energy to the body.
2. It remains under the skin and prevents the loss of heat from the body.
3. It makes the food material tasty.
4. It protects different parts of the body from injury.

- Due to the lack of fat skin gets dried, weight of the body decreases and the development of the body checked.
- Due to the excessiveness of fat the body gets fatty, heart disease takes place and blood pressure increases.

Roughage

- Roughage is another term for dietary fibre, e.g., natural food, *dalia*, etc.
- Helps in retaining water in the body.

Vitamins

It was first invented by FG Hopkins. However, the term vitamin was coined by **C Funk.**

- They provide no calories, they only regulate chemical reactions occurring in the metabolism of the body.
  - i. **Vitamin soluble in water:** Vitamin-B and Vitamin-C.
  - ii. **Vitamin soluble in fat:** Vitamin-A, Vitamin-D, Vitamin-E and Vitamin-K.
- Cobalt is found in Vitamin-B12.
- Synthesis of vitamins cannot be done by the cells and it is fulfilled by the vitamin foods.
- However, synthesis of Vitamin-D and K takes place in our body.
- Synthesis of Vitamin-D takes place by the ultraviolet rays present in the sunlight through cholesterol (ergesterol) of skin.
- Vitamin-K is synthesized in our colon by the bacteria and from there it is absorbed.

Vitamin	Chemical Name	Solubility	Deficiency Disease	Food Sources
Vitamin A	Retinol	Fat	Night blindness	Orange, ripe, yellow fruits, leafy vegetables, carrots, pumpkin, fish, soymilk, milk
Vitamin B_1	Thiamine	Water	Beriberi	Pork, oatmeal, brown rice, vegetables, potatoes, liver, eggs
Vitamin B_2	Riboflavin	Water	Ariboflavinosis, Glossitis	Dairy product, bananas, popcorn, green beans
Vitamin B_3	Niacin, Nicotinomide	Water	Pellagra	Meat, fish, eggs, mushrooms, seeds, nuts
Vitamin B_5	Pantothenic	Water	Parestheria	Meat, broccoli, avocados
Vitamin B_6	Pyridoxine	Water	Anemia	Meat, true nuts, bananas
Vitamin B_7	Priotin	Water	Dematitis, enteritis	Raw egg yolk, liver, peanuts, leafy green vegetables
Vitamin B_g	Folic acid	Water	Megalobastic anemia	Leafy vegetables, pasta, bread, coreal.
Vitamin B_{12}	Cyanocobalamin	Water	Pernicious anemia	Meat, poultry, fish, eggs, milk
Vitamin C	Ascorbic acid	Water	Scurvy	Many fruits and vegetables
Vitamin D	Cholecalciferol	Fat	Rickets	Fish, eggs, liver, mushrooms
Vitamin E	Tocopherols	Fat	Sterility in males and miscarriage in females	Many fruits and vegetables, nuts and seeds
Vitamin K	Phylloquinone	Fat	Bleeding disthesis	Leafy green vegetables, egg yolks

Minerals

These control the metabolism of body.

Water

65-75% weight of the body is water.

Main Functions of Water

1. Water controls the temperature of our body by sweating and vaporizing.
2. It is the important way of excretion of the waste substances from the body.
3. Most of the organic chemical reactions in our body are performed through hydrolysis.

Diseases

Diseases Caused by Protozoa:

i. **Diarrhoea:** The reason of this disease is the presence of internal protozoa, namely *Entamoeba histolytica* which is spread through houseflies.

ii. **Filaria:** This disease is caused by *Wuchereia baoncrofti*. This is circulated by the stings of *culex* mosquitoes. This disease is also known as Elephantiasis.

Diseases Caused by Fungus

i. **Asthma:** This spore of the fungi, namely *Aspergillus fumigate* reaches the lungs of the human and constitutes a net-like formation, thus obstructs the function of lungs. This is an infectious disease.

ii. **Athlete's foot:** This disease is caused by the fungi namely *Tenia pedes*.

iii. **Scabies:** This disease is caused by the fungi, namely *Acarus scably*.

iv. **Baldness:** This is caused by the fungi, namely *Taenia capitis*.

v. **Ringworm:** This disease spreads through the fungi namely *Trycophyton lerucosum*. This is an infectious disease.

Deficiency Diseases

Deficiency	Diseases	Comments
Vitamin A (retinol)	Xeropthalmia Dermatosis	Lachrimal glands stop producing tears leading to blindness.
(Vitamin B_1) Thiamine	Beri-Beri	Extreme weakness, swelling, pain in legs, loss of appetite, enlarged heart, headache and shortness of breath.
(Vitamin B_2) Riboflavin	Ariboflavinosis	Blurred vision, burning of the eye and tongue, cracking of skin at angle of mouth.
(Vitamin B_3) Niacin (Nicotinamide)	Pellagra,Glossits	Tip and lateral margins of tongue, mouth and gums become red, swollen and develop ulcers
(Vitamin B_5) Pentothenic Acid	Achromotrichia	
Pyridoxine (Vitamin B_6)	Abnormal Protein Metabolism	
(Vitamin B_7) Pantothenic Acid Biotin	Dermatitis, enteritis and anaemia	
(Vitamin B_9) Folic and Folinic Acid	Megaloblast and Birth defects	
(Vitamin B_{12}) Cyanocobalamin	Pernicious or Megaloblastic Anaemia	Reduction of Haemoglobin due to disturbance in the formation of RBC.
Vitamin C (Ascorbic acid)	Scurvy	Pain in joints, loss of weight, gums become spongy and bleed Teeth loose and fragile.
Vitamin D (Cholecalciferol)	Rickets Osteomalacia	Occurs in Children. Softness and deformities of bones Bones susceptible to fracture.
Vitamin E (Tocopherol)		
Vitamin K (Phylloquinone)		
Potassium	Hypokalaemia	Rise in heart beat rate Kidney damage.
Sodium	Hyponatraemia	Low blood pressure.
Proteins	Kwashiorkor	Potbelly due to retention of water by the cells (Oedema).

Diseases caused by Microorganisms

Virus	Bacteria	Protozoas	Fungi	Worms
Small Pox	Sore throat	Malaria	Ringworm	Taeniasis
Chicken Pox	Diphtheria	Amoebic dysentery	Athlete's Foot	Schistosomiasis
Common Cold	Pneumonia	Trypanosomiasis	Madura Foot	Bilharziasis
Influenza/Flu	Tuberculosis	Oriental Sore	Dhobie Itch	Ancylostomiasis
Measles	Plague	Kala Azar		Hookworm
Mumps	Tetanus	Giardiasis		Ascariasis
Encephalitis	Typhoid	Diarrhoea		Enterobiasis
Poliomyelitis	Cholera	Vaginitis		Pinworm disease
Rabies	Bacillary Dysentery			Filariasis
Dengue	Whooping Cough			Elephantiasis
Herpes	Gonorrhoea			
AIDS	Leprosy Botulism			

Hormones

Gland	Hormone	Effect
Pituitary/Hypophysis Anterior Lobe	Growth Hormone or Somatotrophic Hormone (STH)	Growth of long bones, muscles.
	Thyroid Stimulating Hormone (TSH)	
	Adrenocorticotrophic Hormone (ACTH)	Influences the production of corticosteroids by adrenal cortex involved in defending body against physiological stress.
	Follicle-stimulating Hormone (FSH)	Growth and maturation of follicles in the ovary, production of female sex hormone estrogen and maturation of spermatozoa in males..
	Luteinizing Hormone (LH)	Stimulates interstitial cells in the testis to produce testosterone. Causes ovulation. Release of estrogen & formulation of corpus luteum in female.
	Prolactin or Luteotrophic Hormone (LH)	Helps to maintain pregnancy. Stimulate mammary glands to secrete milk.
Middle Lobe	Melanophore-stimulating Hormone (MSH)	Associated with melaonophyte which gives skin its colour.
Posterior Lobe	Vasopressin or Anti-diuretic Hormone	Controls water reabsorption in the kidney tubule.
	Oxytocin	Causes uterine contractions and active expulsion of milk during and after birth.
Hypothalamus	Releasing Hormone (RH) for each anterior pituitary hormone: GH-RH, TSH-RH, ACTH-RH, FSH-RH and likewise	Production of all the anterior pituitary hormones is controlled by messages from the hypothalamus via hypophyseal portal vessels.
Thyroid	Thyroxine/Calcitonin	BMR influences heat production, Calcium level in blood.
Parathyroids	Parathormone	Raises blood calcium level.
Adrenals	Aldosterone	Regulates sodium and potassium levels in the blood to control blood pressure.
	Hydrocortisone	Plays key role in stress response; increases blood glucose levels and mobilises fat stores; reduces inflammation.
	Epinephrine or Adrenalin	Increases blood pressure, heart and metabolic rate, and blood sugar levels; dilates blood vessels. Also released during exercise
	Norepinephrine/Noradrenalin	Increases blood pressure and heart rate; constricts blood vessels.
Thymus	Thymosin	Development of white blood cells.
Pancreas	Insulin Glucagon	Controls blood sugar level. Increase the blood sugar level
Ovaries	Estrogen	Secondary sexual characteristics.
	Progesterone	Prepares Endometrium (inner lining of Uterus) and maintains it during pregnancy.

Exercise

1. Which programming language is developed by James A Gosling?
(a) ASP.Net (b) Java
(c) PHP (d) C#
2. Kaleidoscope was invented by ______.
(a) John Barber
(b) Tim Berners-Lee
(c) Alan Blumlein
(d) David Brewster
3. The nitrogenous waste of Human Beings is
(a) Ammonia
(b) Urea
(c) Ammonium Nitrate
(d) Uric Acid
4. Haustoria or sucking roots are found in which of the following?

(a) Wheat (b) Mango
(c) Chestnut (d) Cuscuta

5. Equs Asinus is the scientific name of
(a) Donkey (b) Cow
(c) Deer (d) Kangaroo

6. ______ is an anaesthetic agent.
(a) Acetylene
(b) Glycol
(c) Diethylether
(d) Ethylene

7. ______ is used for making chemical apparatus like beakers, flasks etc.
(a) Potash glass
(b) Hard glass
(c) Soda glass
(d) Jena glass

8. When ice floats on water, its _____ part remains outside the water.
(a) 0.5 (b) 0.3
(c) 0.1 (d) 1

9. Instrument for measuring low temperatures is called
(a) Diagometer
(b) Cryometer
(c) Chromatoptometer
(d) Cymometer

10. Which drug is used as an Anti-Anxiety drug?
(a) Warfarin (b) Diazepam
(c) Latanoprost (d) Hydralazine

11. *Ficus benghalensis* is the scientific name of ______.
(a) Banyan (b) Pineapple
(c) Babul (d) Tulsi

12. *Equus burchellii* is the scientific name of _______.
(a) Horse (b) Zebra
(c) Buffalo (d) Ass

13. Atomic number of which of the following elements is greater than that of Copper?
(a) Iron (b) Chromium
(c) Zinc (d) Manganese

14. Vacuum Tubes were used by _____ Generation of Computers.
(a) First (b) Second
(c) Third (d) Fourth

15. Which of the following is false with reference to a photo-voltaic cell?
(a) It is another name for solar cell
(b) It can be used as infra-red detectors
(c) It can store light energy in the form of electrical energy
(d) It converts electric energy into light energy

16. Methane, an air pollutant is produced _______
(a) by action of ultraviolet light on nitrogenous compounds.
(b) as a by-product of manufacturing ammoniacal fertilizers.
(c) by burning of coal in insufficient air.
(d) by digestion of food by animals.

17. Which drug is used as an Anti-biotic?
(a) Metformin
(b) Ranitidine
(c) Azithromycin
(d) Ibuprofen

18. *Tamarindus indica* is the scientific name of ________.
(a) Neem (b) Pineapple
(c) Tamarind (d) Chiku

19. In eukaryotic cells synthesis of RNA takes place in the ________.
(a) mitochondria
(b) centrioles
(c) ribosomes
(d) nucleus

20. The modern periodic table consists of 18 groups and 7 periods. What is the atomic number of the element placed in the 2nd group and the 4th period?
(a) 20 (b) 22
(c) 18 (d) 10

21. Which of the following elements has the lowest melting point?
(a) Zinc (b) Titanium
(c) Sulphur (d) Fluorine

22. In Computers, what does ALU stand for?
(a) Advanced Logic Unit
(b) Accelerated Logic Unit
(c) Arithmetic Logic Unit
(d) Asymmetric Logic Unit

23. _____ is caused by parasites of the Plasmodium genus.
(a) Dysentery
(b) Malaria
(c) Chickenpox
(d) Herpes

24. Who invented Aerosol can?
(a) Erik Rotheim
(b) Erik Mathew
(c) Erik Tim
(d) Eric Flayer

25. A transformer can do all of the following except
(a) step-up a/c voltage
(b) step-up a/c current
(c) step-up a/c power
(d) step-down a/c voltage

26. What is the unit of the physical quantity "Magnetic field strength"?
(a) joule per meter
(b) newton per meter
(c) kelvin per meter
(d) ampere per meter

27. *Acinonyx jubatus* is the scientific name of
(a) Bear (b) Horse
(c) Cheetah (d) Zebra

28. Atomic number of which of the following elements is greater than that of Zinc?
(a) Copper (b) Iron
(c) Chromium (d) Bromine

29. Commonly used abbreviation SEO in computer science stands for?
(a) System Engine Optimization
(b) Search Engine Optimization
(c) Structured Engine Optimization
(d) Single Engine Optimization

30. Who invented Java Script, the programming language?
(a) Brendan Eich
(b) Willem Einthoven
(c) George Eastman
(d) Emil Erlenmeyer

31. ________ of a material is defined as the minimum amount of the work necessary to remove a free electron from the surface of the material.
(a) The electro-repulsive force
(b) The coulomb factor
(c) The power factor
(d) The work function

32. Human beings' hearing range is
(a) 50 to 50,000 Hz
(b) 40 to 40,000 Hz
(c) 30 to 30,000 Hz
(d) 20 to 20,000 Hz

33. Which drug is used as a Thyroid Hormone?
(a) Metformin
(b) Ketoconazole
(c) Promethazine
(d) Levothyroxine

34. Which of the following constitute to form a gene?
(a) Polynucleotides
(b) Hydrocarbons
(c) Lipoproteins
(d) Lipids

35. Atomic number of which of the following elements is greater than that of Iron?

(a) Manganese
(b) Cobalt
(c) Calcium
(d) Chromium

36. A series of instructions written by a programmer according to a given set of rules or conventions is called_____.
(a) Syntax (b) a Byte
(c) a Set (d) Macro

37. Who invented LCD Projector?
(a) Gene Dolgoff
(b) Brendan Eich
(c) Douglas Engelbart
(d) Federico Faggin

38. A cannon ball is fired. The motion of this ball is an example of______.
(a) straight line motion
(b) projectile motion
(c) hyperbolic motion
(d) horizontal motion

39. What is the unit of the physical quantity, Magnetic flux?
(a) farad (b) weber
(c) tesla (d) henry

40. Vertebrates belongs to the phylum
(a) Arthropoda (b) Annelida
(c) Cnidaria (d) Chordata

41. What is washing soda?
(a) Aluminium bicarbonate
(b) Sodium bicarbonate
(c) Aluminium sulphate
(d) Sodium carbonate

42. _____is a drug or substance that makes you feel relaxed and makes your body work and react more slowly.
(a) Antidote
(b) Analgesic
(c) Antihistamine
(d) Depressant

43. *Carica papaya* is the scientific name of
(a) Peepal (b) Papaya
(c) Tamarind (d) Drumstick

44. Muscles get tired when there is shortfall of
(a) Lactic acid (b) Na^+ ions
(c) ATP (d) Sulphates

45. The chemical formula of Ammonium nitrate is
(a) $(NHB)_2NO_3$ (b) NH_4NO_3
(c) $NH_4(NOC)_2$ (d) NH_2NO_3

46. Which of the following elements has the lowest melting point?
(a) Xenon (b) Iodine
(c) Barium (d) Magnesium

47. Who invented Induction Coil?
(a) Edwin Howard Armstrong
(b) John Barber
(c) Edwin Beard Budding
(d) Nicholas Callan

48. Find the power of a convex lens if the image formed is at a distance of 16 cm from the lens when the object is placed on the other side of the lens at 2 cm from the optical centre.
(a) –3.75 diopters
(b) –11.25 diopters
(c) 3.75 diopters
(d) 11.25 diopters

49. What is the unit of the physical quantity "Inductance"?
(a) weber (b) farad
(c) henry (d) tesla

50. ______ is a drug that doctors give to people to make them calm or help them sleep.
(a) Barbiturate
(b) Antidepressant
(c) Antihistamine
(d) Beta-Blocker

51. *Artocarpus integra* is the scientific name of ________.
(a) Guava (b) Pineapple
(c) Silver Oak (d) Jackfruit

52. Which organ stores fat soluble vitamins?
(a) Blood (b) Skin
(c) Liver (d) Pancreas

53. Fe has 26 protons in its nucleus. What are the number of electrons in Fe_2^+ (II) ion?
(a) 24 (b) 26
(c) 28 (d) 13

54. Which of the following elements has the lowest melting point?
(a) Titanium (b) Sulphur
(c) Argon (d) Zinc

55. ALU is a part of a computer is. ______
(a) Application (b) ROM
(c) RAM (d) Processor

56. Who invented the 3-D printer?
(a) Nick Holonyak
(b) Elias Howe
(c) Chuck Hull
(d) Christiaan Huygens

57. Alpha particles are ________
(a) twice the mass of beta particles.
(b) negatively charged.
(c) just like helium nuclei.
(d) lower in ionizing power as compared to gamma rays.

58. Unit of impedance is. ________
(a) ohm (b) henry
(c) tesla (d) hertz

59. Which disease is caused due to deficiency of Iodine?
(a) Rickets
(b) Scurvy
(c) Goitre
(d) Growth retardation

60. *Grevillea robusta* is the scientific name of
(a) Peepal (b) Teak
(c) Silver Oak (d) Jack fruit

61. The Modern Periodic Table consists of 18 groups and 7 periods. What is the atomic number of the element placed in the 3rd group and the 4th period?
(a) 23 (b) 21
(c) 19 (d) 11

62. Which of the following elements has the lowest melting point?
(a) Oxygen (b) Gold
(c) Silver (d) Manganese

63. Who is known as father of computer?
(a) Charles Babbage
(b) Tim Berners Lee
(c) Douglas Carl Engelbart
(d) Sabeer Bhatia

64. Who discovered X-Ray?
(a) Wilhelm Rontgen
(b) William Lee
(c) X Rollswick
(d) I Thompson

65. Find the power of a convex lens if the image formed is at a distance of 25 cm from the lens when the object is placed on the other side of the lens at 12 cm from the optical centre?
(a) – 4.33 diopters
(b) 12.33 diopters
(c) – 12.33 diopters
(d) 4.33 diopters

66. What is the unit of the physical quantity 'Entropy'?
(a) watt per kelvin
(b) newton per kelvin
(c) pascal per kelvin
(d) joule per kelvin

67. Kidney stones are composed of
(a) Calcium Oxalate
(b) Sodium Chloride
(c) Magnesium Nitrate
(d) Calcium Bicarbonate

68. Which of the following is not true about Angiosperms?
(a) Dominant phase is gametophytes
(b) Vascular bundles are present
(c) Spores are heterospores
(d) Seeds are covered

69. All of the following are excretory (waste) products of animals, except
(a) Uric Acid
(b) Ammonia
(c) Carbohydrates
(d) Urea

70. RNA is a polymeric molecule. What does RNA stand for?
(a) Rado Nuclear Acid
(b) Ribo Nucleic Acid
(c) Rhino Nuclear Acid
(d) Resto Nucleus Acid

71. The common name of dichlorodifluoromethane is
(a) galena (b) freon
(c) gypsum (d) borax

72. ______ performs tasks such as inserting, updating, or deleting data occurrences.
(a) Data definition language
(b) Data manipulation language
(c) Query language
(d) OQL

73. Who invented the computer mouse?
(a) Gene Dolgoff
(b) Brendan Eich
(c) Douglas Engelbart
(d) Federico Faggin

74. ______ states that internal energy is a function of state and the increase in internal energy is equal to the sum of the heat supplied to system and work done by the system.
(a) First law of thermodynamics
(b) Hooke's Law
(c) The coulomb's law
(d) Faraday's Law

75. What is the direction of torque?
(a) Perpendicular to the direction of applied force
(b) Same as the direction of applied force
(c) Opposite to the direction of applied force
(d) Parallel to the radius

76. Which organ does detoxification and produces chemicals needed for digestion?
(a) Salivary glands
(b) Pancreas
(c) Thyroid gland
(d) Liver

77. $NaHCO_3$ is chemical formula for
(a) Borax (b) Vinegar
(c) Lime (d) Baking soda

78. Which of the following elements has the lowest melting point?
(a) Chromium (b) Hydrogen
(c) Zinc (d) Silver

79. C Programming language was developed by
(a) Charles Babbage
(b) Larry Wall
(c) James Gosling
(d) Dennis Ritchie

80. Instrument for measuring blueness of the sky or ocean is called
(a) Bathymeter (b) Ceraunograph
(c) Cyanometer (d) Barometer

81. Farad is unit of ________.
(a) Capacitance
(b) Reactance
(c) Electric charge
(d) Electric conductance

82. Which drug is used to cure Incontinence?
(a) Oxybutynin
(b) Ranitidine
(c) Azithromycin
(d) Levothyroxine

83. In which part of the cell are proteins made?
(a) reticulum
(b) Golgi apparatus
(c) ribosomes
(d) lysosome

84. Polio is a disease caused by which of the following?
(a) Bacteria (b) Mosquito
(c) Virus (d) Cockroach

85. Chemical formula of Ammonia is
(a) PH_3 (b) NO_2
(c) AlN (d) NH_3

86. Which of the following elements has the lowest melting point?
(a) Oxygen (b) Platinum
(c) Sodium (d) Tin

87. Find the power of a convex lens if the image formed is at a distance of 20 cm from the lens when the object is placed on the other side of the lens at 25 cm from the optical centre.
(a) 1 diopters (b) –9 diopters
(c) 9 diopters (d) –1 diopters

88. What is the unit of the physical quantity "Capacitance"?
(a) weber (b) farad
(c) tesla (d) ohm

89. The outer white part of the eye that protects the inner structures is
(a) Iris (b) Sclera
(c) Retina (d) Cornea

90. Proteins are made up of ________.
(a) Amino acids
(b) Fatty acids
(c) Glucose
(d) Nucleotides

91. The Modern Periodic Table consists of 18 groups and 7 periods. What is the atomic number of the element placed in the 4th group and the 4th period?
(a) 24 (b) 20
(c) 22 (d) 12

92. A Gigabyte equals all of the following, except ________.
(a) 1000 megabytes
(b) trillion bytes
(c) Million kilobytes
(d) 1 thousandth of a terabyte

93. Who discovered Catalysis?
(a) Messcureni (b) Berzelius
(c) Hooke (d) Garner

94. Find the power of a convex lens if the image formed is at a distance of 20 cm from the lens when the object is placed on the other side of the lens at 60 cm from the optical centre.
(a) 3.33 diopters
(b) 6.67 diopters
(c) – 6.67 diopters
(d) – 3.33 diopters

95. What is the unit of the physical quantity "Heat capacity"?
(a) watt per kelvin
(b) joule per kelvin
(c) newton per kelvin
(d) pascal per kelvin

96. *Moringa oleifera* is the scientific name of________.
(a) Banyan (b) Gulmohar
(c) Amla (d) Drumstick

97. ________ is a drug that makes your heart work more slowly, used for treating high blood pressure.
(a) Contraceptive
(b) Beta-Blocker
(c) Depressant
(d) Enema

98. *Ocimum tenuiflorum* is the scientific name of________.
(a) Neem (b) Mango
(c) Babul (d) Tulsi

99. Which gland secretes bile, a digestive fluid?
(a) pancreas (b) liver
(c) thyroid (d) testes

100. The chemical formula of ammonium chloride is ________.
(a) $(NHD)_2Cl$ (b) NH_4Cl_3
(c) NH_4Cl_2 (d) NH_4Cl

101. Which of the following elements has the lowest melting point?
(a) Iron (b) Nitrogen
(c) Iodine (d) Lead

102. In Internet, what is the full form of TCP ?
(a) Transfer Control Program
(b) Transfer Control Protocol
(c) Transmission Control Program
(d) Transmission Control Protocol

103. Pyrolusite is an ore/mineral of ________.
(a) Mercury
(b) Manganese
(c) Molybdenum
(d) Lead

104. Who invented Internet Protocol?
(a) Vint Cerf
(b) David Chaum
(c) Georges Claude
(d) Josephine Cochrane

105. Find the power of a convex lens if the image formed is at a distance of 10 cm from the lens when the object is placed on the other side of the lens at 40 cm from the optical centre.
(a) 12.5 diopters
(b) 7.5 diopters
(c) – 12.5 diopters
(d) – 7.5 diopters

106. Filament of electric bulb is made of ________.
(a) Magnesium (b) Lead
(c) Tin (d) Tungsten

107. The amount of blood filtered together by both the kidneys in a 70 kg adult male human in a minute is
(a) 1100 ml (b) 100 ml
(c) 1500 ml (d) 500 ml

108. Which feature of a plant helps to distinguish a monocot from a dicot?
(a) pollination (b) venation
(c) vernation (d) aestivation

109. The Mutation Theory was proposed by ________.
(a) Charles Lyell
(b) William Smith
(c) Hugo De Vries
(d) Harrison Schmitt

110. Which of the following elements has the lowest melting point?
(a) Helium (b) Potassium
(c) Tungsten (d) Sulphur

111. Atomic number of which of the following elements is greater than that of Phosphorus?
(a) Aluminium (b) Silicon
(c) Chlorine (d) Magnesium

112. The designers of the Internet Protocol defined an IP address as a ________ bit number.
(a) 8 (b) 16
(c) 32 (d) 64

113. Which type of pathogen causes the water-borne disease Hepatitis-A?
(a) Parasitic (b) Viral
(c) Protozoan (d) Bacterial

114. ________ is a natural electrical phenomenon characterized by the appearance of streamers of reddish or greenish light in the sky, especially near the northern or southern magnetic pole.
(a) Acaulis (b) Alatus
(c) Albopictus (d) Aurora

115. Who invented Laser?
(a) William Friese-Greene
(b) Arthur Fry
(c) Gordon Gould
(d) Otto von Guericke

116. What is the SI unit of Torque?
(a) newton/meter
(b) newton meter
(c) newton second
(d) newton/meter squared

117. What is the unit of the physical quantity, Illuminance?
(a) siemens (b) tesla
(c) lux (d) weber

118. *Arboreal ateles* is the scientific name of________.
(a) Squirrel (b) Sparrow
(c) Lizard (d) Spider monkey

119. The chemical formula of Ammonia is ________
(a) NH (b) NH_4
(c) NH_2 (d) NH_3

120. Who discovered Fullerene (an allotrope of carbon)?
(a) K Scheele
(b) Richard Smalley
(c) Faraday
(d) Heisenberg

121. ________ perform Internet Protocol blocking to protect networks from unauthorized access.
(a) Firewalls (b) Proxy Servers
(c) Routers (d) VoIP

122. Which type of pathogen causes the waterborne disease Salmonellosis?
(a) Algal (b) Parasitic
(c) Bacterial (d) Viral

123. Which of the following is not a Halon gas ?
(a) methane
(b) Carbon tetrachloride
(c) iodomethane
(d) bromomethane

124. If a body moves with a uniform speed in a circular motion, then ________
(a) its acceleration is increasing
(b) its acceleration is zero
(c) its velocity is changing
(d) its velocity is uniform

125. ________ is the fourth state of matter.
(a) Plasma (b) Steam
(c) Gas (d) Matteroid

126. Blood leaving the liver and moving towards thc heart has a higher concentration of________
(a) Lipids
(b) Urea
(c) Bile Pigments
(d) Carbon dioxide

127. Bulb is a modification of which part of a plant?
(a) The root (b) The stem
(c) The radicle (d) The fruit

128. Which of the following carries blood away from the heart to different body parts?
(a) Arteries (b) Nerves
(c) Capillaries (d) Veins

129. Chemical formula of water is ________.
(a) O_2H (b) OH
(c) HO (d) H_2O

130. Atomic number of which of the following elements is greater than that of Aluminium?
(a) Phosphorus (b) Neon
(c) Magnesium (d) Sodium

131. Which of these is not a web browser?
(a) Chrome (b) Firefox
(c) Safari (d) Linux

132. Who invented dishwasher?
(a) Vint Cerf
(b) David Chaum
(c) Georges Claude
(d) Josephine Cochrane

133. ________states that the induced e.m.f. is directly proportional to the rate of change of magnetic flux linkage or rate of cutting of magnetic flux linkage..
(a) Lenz's Law (b) Hooke's Law
(c) Ohm's Law (d) Faraday's Law

134. If the vector sum of torques acting on a system is zero, then the object is in ________
(a) static equilibrium
(b) translatory equilibrium
(c) linear equilibrium
(d) rotational equilibrium

135. BCG vaccine is given to protect from which of the following?
(a) Jaundice
(b) Anaemia
(c) Tuberculosis
(d) Polio

136. Parallel venation is found in ________.
(a) plants which are monocots
(b) plants which have a dicot stem
(c) plants with leaves similar to Tulsi
(d) plants with tap roots

137. The hardest part of the body is ________
(a) Bones (b) Tooth Enamel
(c) Skull (d) Spinal Cord

138. The Chemical formula of Ammonium sulphate is
(a) NH_4SO_4 (b) $(NHD)_2SO_3$
(c) NH_4SO_3 (d) $(NHD)_2SO_4$

139. The common name of lead (II) sulphide is
(a) borax (b) epsom salt
(c) galena (d) brimstone

140. SMTP in computer science stands for?
(a) Simple Markup Transfer Protocol
(b) Systems Mail Transfer Protocol
(c) Simple Mail Transfer Protocol
(d) Systems Memory Transfer Protocol

141. Which type of pathogen causes the waterborne disease, E. coli Infection?
(a) Protozoan (b) Parasitic
(c) Bacterial (d) Viral

142. ________is a measure of the actual amount of water vapour in a particular sample of air: measured as a partial pressure.
(a) Specific Humidity
(b) Absolute Humidity
(c) Relative Humidity
(d) Dew Point

143. Who Invented Lawnmower?
(a) Edwin Howard Armstrong
(b) John Barber
(c) Edwin Beard Budding
(d) Nicholas Callan

144. ________is defined as the force acting per unit current per unit length on a wire placed at right angles to the magnetic field.
(a) Magnetic susceptibility
(b) Magnetic flux density
(c) Magnetic flux
(d) Magnetic pulse

145. If an object moves in a purely rotatory motion, then each constituent particle of the body moves in a circle, the centre of which is located on a line is called ________
(a) the axis of rotation
(b) the line of rotation
(c) the spinning rod
(d) the fixed line

146. Which of the following is a primary function of haemoglobin?
(a) Utilization of energy
(b) Prevention of anaemia
(c) Destruction of bacteria
(d) To transport oxygen

147. Vascular bundles are absent in______.
(a) Bryophyta
(b) Pteridophyta
(c) Gymnosperms
(d) Angiosperms

148. *Sauria lacertidae* is the scientific name of________.
(a) Crocodile (b) Hippopotamus
(c) Lizard (d) Housefly

149. In chemistry, soap is a salt of a ______.
(a) Fatty acid
(b) Glycol
(c) Phosphorus
(d) Ammonium Carbonate

150. A ________ is a pair of forces, equal in magnitude, oppositely directed, and displaced by perpendicular distance or moment.
(a) bond (b) couple
(c) pair (d) duo

151. Which of these is not an Operating System?
(a) Android (b) iOS
(c) HTML (d) Symbian

152. Which type of pathogen causes the water-borne disease SARS (Severe Acute Respiratory Syndrome)?
(a) Viral (b) Parasitic
(c) Protozoan (d) Bacterial

153. Excessive richness of nutrients in a lake or other body of water is called _____.
(a) Biomagnification
(b) Global Warming
(c) Salination
(d) Eutrophication

154. Who Invented Aspirin?
(a) Ruth Handler
(b) John Harington
(c) Rowland Hill
(d) Felix Hoffmann

155. A larger force on a rotating body results in larger _____.
(a) mass
(b) torque

(c) axis of rotation
(d) centre of mass

156. What is the unit of the physical quantity, Magnetic flux density?
(a) siemens (b) weber
(c) henry (d) tesla

157. The fat digesting enzyme Lipase is secreted by which of the following?
(a) Kidneys
(b) Pancreas
(c) Large Intestine
(d) Liver

158. The arrangement of leaves on an axis or stem is called
(a) phyllotaxy (b) vernation
(c) venation (d) phytotaxy

159. The study of Cells is also known as
(a) Cytology (b) Physiology
(c) Nucleology (d) Cellology

160. The Chemical formula of Urea is
(a) $(NH_4)_2CO_2$ (b) $(NH_2)CO$
(c) $(NH_4)_2CO$ (d) $(NH_2)_2CO$

161. Atomic number of which of the following elements is greater than that of Magnesium?
(a) Neon (b) Fluorine
(c) Sodium (d) Aluminium

162. TCP in computer science stands for?
(a) Transmission Control Protocol
(b) Total Control Protocol
(c) Technology Control Protocol
(d) Transfer Control Protocol

163. Who invented water turbine?
(a) Enrico Fermi
(b) Adolf Gaston Eugen Fick
(c) Sandford Fleming
(d) Benoit Fourneyron

164. _______ of a wave is the rate of transfer of energy per unit area perpendicular to the direction of travel of the wave.
(a) Interference (b) Rectification
(c) Intensity (d) Diffraction

165. Motion of a train is an example of ______.
(a) Rotatory motion
(b) Spin motion
(c) Projectile motion
(d) Translatory motion

166. Deficiency of which vitamin causes night blindness?
(a) Vitamin K (b) Vitamin C
(c) Vitamin B_1 (d) Vitamin A

167. The flower with the world's largest bloom is _____.
(a) Pando
(b) Posidonia
(c) *Rafflesia arnoldii*
(d) *Helianthus annuus*

168. The scientist who proposed the cell theory was
(a) Schleiden and Schwann
(b) Lamarck
(c) Treviranus
(d) Whittaker and Stanley

169. ______ decreases the rate of setting of cement.
(a) Alumina
(b) Silica
(c) Gypsum
(d) Magnesium oxide

170. Alkenes were earlier known as ______.
(a) Paraffins (b) Titoffins
(c) Olefins (d) Meloffins

171. A language used to control the tasks of the computer itself, such as starting other programs, is _____.
(a) Command Language
(b) Machine Language
(c) Markup Language
(d) Style Sheet Language

Answers

1. (b)	**2.** (d)	**3.** (b)	**4.** (d)	**5.** (a)	**6.** (c)	**7.** (b)	**8.** (c)	**9.** (d)	**10.** (b)
11. (a)	**12.** (b)	**13.** (c)	**14.** (a)	**15.** (d)	**16.** (d)	**17.** (c)	**18.** (c)	**19.** (d)	**20.** (a)
21. (d)	**22.** (c)	**23.** (b)	**24.** (a)	**25.** (c)	**26.** (d)	**27.** (c)	**28.** (d)	**29.** (b)	**30.** (a)
31. (d)	**32.** (d)	**33.** (d)	**34.** (a)	**35.** (b)	**36.** (a)	**37.** (a)	**38.** (b)	**39.** (b)	**40.** (d)
41. (d)	**42.** (d)	**43.** (b)	**44.** (c)	**45.** (b)	**46.** (a)	**47.** (d)	**48.** (d)	**49.** (c)	**50.** (a)
51. (d)	**52.** (c)	**53.** (a)	**54.** (c)	**55.** (d)	**56.** (c)	**57.** (c)	**58.** (a)	**59.** (c)	**60.** (c)
61. (b)	**62.** (a)	**63.** (a)	**64.** (a)	**65.** (b)	**66.** (d)	**67.** (a)	**68.** (a)	**69.** (c)	**70.** (b)
71. (b)	**72.** (b)	**73.** (c)	**74.** (a)	**75.** (a)	**76.** (d)	**77.** (d)	**78.** (b)	**79.** (d)	**80.** (c)
81. (a)	**82.** (a)	**83.** (c)	**84.** (c)	**85.** (d)	**86.** (a)	**87.** (c)	**88.** (b)	**89.** (b)	**90.** (a)
91. (c).	**92.** (b)	**93.** (b)	**94.** (b)	**95.** (b)	**96.** (d)	**97.** (b)	**98.** (d)	**99.** (b)	**100.** (d)
101. (b)	**102.** (d)	**103.** (b)	**104.** (a)	**105.** (a)	**106.** (d)	**107.** (a)	**108.** (b)	**109.** (c)	**110.** (a)
111. (c)	**112.** (c)	**113.** (b)	**114.** (d)	**115.** (c)	**116.** (b)	**117.** (c)	**118.** (d)	**119.** (d)	**120.** (b)
121. (a)	**122.** (c)	**123.** (a)	**124.** (c)	**125.** (a)	**126.** (c)	**127.** (b)	**128.** (a)	**129.** (d)	**130.** (a)
131. (d)	**132.** (d)	**133.** (d)	**134.** (d)	**135.** (c)	**136.** (a)	**137.** (b)	**138.** (d)	**139.** (c)	**140.** (c)
141. (c)	**142.** (b)	**143.** (c)	**144.** (b)	**145.** (a)	**146.** (d)	**147.** (a)	**148.** (c)	**149.** (a)	**150.** (b)
151. (c)	**152.** (a)	**153.** (d)	**154.** (d)	**155.** (b)	**156.** (d)	**157.** (b)	**158.** (a)	**159.** (a)	**160.** (d)
161. (d)	**162.** (a)	**163.** (d)	**164.** (c)	**165.** (d)	**166.** (d)	**167.** (c)	**168.** (a)	**169.** (c)	**170.** (c)
171. (a)									

Elementary Mathematics

1 NUMBERS AND FRACTIONS

- **Numeral:** In Hindu Arabic system, we use ten symbols, numeral 0, 1, 2, 3, 4, 5, 6, 7, 8 and 9. We call them digits.

  A number is denoted by a group of digits, called numeral.
- **Place value:** In a numeral 176524, we have

  Place value of 4 = $(4 \times 1) = 4$

  Place value of 2 = $(2 \times 10) = 20$

  Place value of 5 = $(5 \times 100) = 500$

  Place value of 6 = $(6 \times 1000) = 6000$

  Place value of 7 = $(7 \times 10000) = 70000$

  Place value of 1 = $(1 \times 100000) = 100000$
- **Face value:** The face value of a digit in a numeral is the value of the digit itself. Wherever it may be in the place value chart.

  In the numeral 17625, the face value of 5 is 5, the face value of 2 is 2, the face value of 6 is 6 and so on.

Types of numbers:

(i) **Natural numbers :** The counting numbers are called natural numbers.

Thus, N = {1, 2, 3, 4, 5, 6, 7 ...} is the set of natural numbers.

(ii) **Whole numbers :** All natural numbers together with zero (0) form the set W of all whole numbers.

W = {0, 1, 2, 3, 4, 5, 6, 7 ...} is the set of all whole numbers.

Note:

- Every natural number is a whole number.
- 0 is a whole number which is not a natural number.

(iii) **Integers:** All natural numbers, negatives of natural number and 0, together form the set I of all integers.

Thus, I = {.... – 4, – 3, – 2, –1, 0, 1, 2, 3, 4, ...}, I is the set of all negative and positive integers.

(iv) **Even numbers:** A number divisible by 2 is called an even number.

Thus, {2, 4, 6, 8, 10, 12, 14, 16 ...} is the set of all even numbers.

(v) **Odd numbers:** A number not divisible by 2 is called an odd number.

Thus, {1, 3, 5, 7, 9, 11, 13, 15....} is the set of odd numbers.

(vi) **Prime numbers:** A number greater than 1 having exactly two factors, namely 1 and itself is called a prime number.

(vii) **Rational numbers:** A number of the form $\frac{p}{q}$ is called Rational number, (where p and q are integers and $q \neq 0$)

Thus, $\frac{3}{4}, \frac{5}{6}, \frac{6}{7}$ etc. are rational numbers.

(viii) **Irrational numbers:** A number which is not of the form of $\frac{p}{q}$ is called irrational number (where p and q are integers and ($q \neq 0$)

Thus $\sqrt{3}, \sqrt{5}, \pi$ etc. are Irrational numbers.

(ix) **Composite numbers :** Numbers greater than 1 which are not prime, are called composite numbers.

Thus, 4, 6, 8, 9, 10 and 12 etc. are composite numbers.

Note: (i) 1 is neither prime nor composite.

(ii) 2 is the only even number which is prime.

(x) **Co-prime:** Two natural numbers a and b are said to be co-prime if their HCF is 1.

Thus, (2, 3), (4, 5), (7, 9) etc. are pairs of co-primes.

Division on numbers: Dividend, Divisor, Quotient and Remainder.

Let a number a is divided by another number b and we get quotient q and remainder r.

Then, Dividend = Divisor × Quotient + Remainder

$[a = bq + r]$ where $(a \leq r < b)$

Test of divisibility:

(i) **Divisibility by 2:** A number is divisible by 2 if its units digit is any of 0, 2, 4, 6 and 8.

Example: 342, 4616, 52316 etc.

(ii) **Divisibility by 3:** A number is divisible by 3 if the sum of its digits is divisible by 3.

Example: 96342, 462372 etc.

(iii) **Divisibility by 4:** A number is divisible by 4 if the number formed by the last two digits is divisible by 4.

Example: 1728, 16520, 17624 etc.

(iv) **Divisibility by 5:** A number is divisible by 5, if its unit's digit is either 0 or 5.

Example: 625, 15725, 100000 etc.

(v) **Divisibility by 6:** A number is divisible by 6 if it is divisible by both 2 and 3.

Example: 6432, 74936 etc.

(vi) **Divisibility by 8:** A number is divisible by 8, if the number formed by the last three digits of the given number is divisible by 8.

Example: 175248, 976488 etc.

(vii) **Divisibility by 9:** A number is divisible by 9, if the sum of its digits is divisible by 9.

Example: 6372, 5943276 etc.

(viii) **Divisibility by 10:** A number is divisible by 10, if it ends with zero.

Example: 17650, 1000, 18980, 16550 etc.

(ix) **Divisibility by 11:** A number is divisible by 11, if the difference of the sum of its digits at odd places and the sum of its digits at even places, either or a number divisible by 11.

Example: The number 14641 is divisible by 11, since:

(Sum of digits at odd places) – (sum of digits at even places) $= (1+6+1)-(4+4) = 8-8 = 0$

So, number 14641 is divisible by 11.

(x) **Divisiblity by 12:** A number is divisible by 12, if it is divisible by 4 and 3.

Example: 43524, 34632 etc.

Fractions: A fraction is the part of a whole. Mathematically, we define fractions as the numbers of the form $\frac{a}{b}$, where a and b are whole numbers and $b \neq 0$.

Thus, a fraction consists of a top number and a bottom number, separated by a dividing line. The top number is called the numerator and bottom number is called denominator.

Example: $\frac{3}{4}, \frac{5}{6}, \frac{6}{7}$ and $\frac{9}{11}$ etc.

Kinds of Fractions:

(i) **Like fractions:** Fractions having same denominators are called like fractions.

Example: $\frac{7}{5}, \frac{3}{5}, \frac{9}{5}$ etc.

(ii) **Unlike fractions:** Fractions having the different denominators are called unlike fractions.

Example: $\frac{1}{3}, \frac{4}{5}, \frac{6}{7}$ etc.

(iii) **Proper Fractions:** A fraction whose numerator is less than its denominator, is called proper fraction.

Example: $\frac{1}{5}, \frac{4}{6}, \frac{6}{11}$ etc.

(iv) **Improper fractions:** A fraction whose numerator is greater than or equal to its denominator is called an improper fraction.

Example: $\frac{7}{5}, \frac{11}{9}, \frac{8}{7}$ etc.

(v) **Complex fractions:** A fraction whose one or both the terms are fractions, is called a complex fraction.

(vi) **Example:** $\left(\frac{4/3}{7}\right), \left(\frac{4/3}{7/5}\right)$ etc.

Decimal fractions: Fractions in which denominators are powers of 10 are known as decimal fractions.

Example: $\frac{1}{10^2}, \frac{1}{10^3}, \frac{1}{10^4}$ etc.

Recurring Decimal: If in a decimal fraction, a figure or a set of figures is repeated continuously, then such a number is called recurring decimal.

Examples : (i) $\frac{1}{9} = 0.1111... = 0.\overline{1}$

(ii) $\frac{50}{3} = 16.666.... = 16.\overline{6}$

- **Pure recurring decimal:** A decimal fraction in which all the figures after the decimal points are repeated, is called a pure recurring decimal.
- **Mixed recurring decimal:** A decimal fraction in which some figures do not repeat and some of these are repeated, is called mixed recurring decimal.

Examples : (i) $0.12444... = 0.12\overline{4}$

(ii) $0.1424242..... = 0.1\overline{42}$

- **Converting a mixed recurring decimal into vulgar fraction:** If the numerator take the difference between the number formed by all the digits after decimal points (taking repeated digits only once) and that formed by the digits which are not repeated. In the denominator, take the number formed by as many nines as there are repeating digits followed by as many zeros as is the number of non repeating digits.

Examples :

(i) $0.1\overline{7} = \frac{17-1}{90} = \frac{16}{90} = \frac{8}{45}$

(ii) $0.1\overline{52} = \frac{152-52}{990} = \frac{100}{990} = \frac{10}{99}$

Some Important Results on Addition :

(i) Sum of first n natural numbers $= \frac{n(n+1)}{2}$

(ii) Sum of the first n even numbers $= n(n+1)$

(iii) Sum of the first n odd numbers $= n^2$

(iv) Sum of the squares of first, n natural numbers

$= \frac{n(n+1)(2n+1)}{6}$

(v) Sum of the cubes of first n natural numbers

$= \left[\frac{n(n+1)^2}{4}\right]$

Some Important Results on Division:

(i) $(x^n - a^n)$ is divisible by $(x - a)$ for all values of n.

(ii) $(x^n - a^n)$ is divisible by $(x + a)$ for all values of n.

(iii) $(x^n + a^n)$ is divisible by $(x + a)$ for all values of n.

Solved Examples

Example 1: Find the sum of first 12 natural numbers.

Sol. Sum of first 'n' natural numbers = $\frac{n(n+1)}{2}$

(Here $n = 12$)

$\therefore$ Required sum = $\frac{12(12+1)}{2} = 78$

Example 2: If 590 * 9 is exactly divisible by 9. Find the digit in place of *.

Sol. 590 * 9 = (5 + 9 + 0 + * + 9) = (23 + *) must be divisible by 9.

$\therefore$ * = 4 ($\because$ smallest number which is divisible by 9 nearest to 23 is 27)

Example 3: $\frac{3}{4}$ of a number exceeds its $\frac{2}{3}$ by 6. Find the number.

Sol. Let the required number be x.

Then, $\frac{3}{4}x - \frac{2}{3}x = 6$

$\Rightarrow \frac{9x - 8x}{12} = 6$

$\Rightarrow x = 72$

Example 4: Find the difference between $\frac{13}{15}$ of ₹ 675 and $\frac{9}{16}$ of ₹ 656.

Sol. $\frac{13}{15}$ of ₹ 675 = $\left(\frac{13}{15} \times 675\right)$ = ₹ 585

$\frac{9}{16}$ of ₹ 656 = $\left(\frac{9}{16} \times 656\right)$ = ₹ 369

Required difference = ₹ (585 – 369)
= ₹ 216

Exercise

1. Reduce 2530/1430 to lowest terms.
(a) 47/17
(b) 23/13
(c) 47/19
(d) 29/17

2. What should be the missing digit so that the number 347_547 becomes exactly divisible by 11?
(a) 5
(b) 3
(c) 9
(d) 2

3. If 9/4th of 7/2 of a number is 126, then 7/2th of that number is ....
(a) 56
(b) 284
(c) 72
(d) 26

4. The ten's digit of a 2 digit number is greater than the units digit by 4. If we subtract 36 from the number, the new number obtained is a number formed by interchange of the digits. Find the number.
(a) 37
(b) 18
(c) 81
(d) 73

5. (91 + 92 + 93 + ... + 110) is equal to
(a) 4020
(b) 2010
(c) 6030
(d) 8040

6. The ten's digit of a 2-digit number is greater than the units digit by 7. If we subtract 63 from the number, the new number obtained is a number formed by interchange of the digits. Find the number.
(a) 81
(b) 18
(c) 62
(d) 26

7. What is the value of (81 + 82 + 83 + ... +130)?
(a) 5275
(b) 10550
(c) 15825
(d) 21100

8. What is the value of 5/9 + 7/8 ?
(a) 103/72
(b) 97/42
(c) 12/17
(d) 15/13

9. The sum of the digits of a 2-digit number is 11. If we add 45 to the number, the new number obtained is a number formed by interchange of the digits. What is the number ?
(a) 83 (b) 38
(c) 64 (d) 46

10. Two fractions are such that their product is 9/10 and sum is 77/40. What are the two fractions ?
(a) 2/5, 9/4
(b) 1/5, 9/2
(c) 4/5, 9/8
(d) 2/5, 9/4

11. The simplest form of 3774/2958 is:
(a) 43/19
(b) 37/29
(c) 31/13
(d) 31/23

12. The simplest form of 3565/1495 is :
(a) 31/13
(b) 43/19
(c) 23/13
(d) 31/23

13. The sum of thrice a number and twice its reciprocal is 97/4. What is the number ?
(a) 9 (b) 10
(c) 8 (d) 7

14. What is the value of 99992×100008 ?
(a) 9999999936
(b) 9999899936
(c) 9999999836
(d) 9999999926

15. Two fractions are such that their product is 4 and sum is 68/15. Find the two fractions.
(a) 6/15, 10/3
(b) 6/5, 10/3
(c) 7/2, 8/7
(d) 10/7, 14/5

16. When 0.363636.....is converted into a fraction, then the result is ....
(a) 7/11
(b) 4/11
(c) 14/33
(d) 8/33

17. $2 \times [0.3(1.3+3.7)]$ of $0.8 = ?$
(a) 1.9
(b) 0.72
(c) 2.16
(d) 2.4

18. If 7/8th of 5/4th of a number is 315, then 5/9th of that number is ....
(a) 123
(b) 81
(c) 140
(d) 160

19. Which of the following numbers is not a prime number?
(a) 731
(b) 227
(c) 347
(d) 461

20. The largest 5 digit number exactly divisible by 95 is :
(a) 99936
(b) 99935
(c) 99940
(d) 99933

21. When 0.090909.....is converted into a fraction, then the result is :
(a) 1/3
(b) 1/11
(c) 2/33
(d) 6/11

22. If 6/7th of 8/5th of a number is 192, then 3/4th of that number is ....
(a) 105
(b) 77
(c) 36
(d) 80

23. If the number 583_437 is completely divisible by 9, then the smallest whole number in the place of the blank digit will be :
(a) 4
(b) 5
(c) 3
(d) 6

24. The sum of a non-zero number and thrice its reciprocal is 52/7. Find the number.
(a) 8
(b) 9
(c) 7
(d) 6

25. What should be the missing digit so that the number 275_476 becomes exactly divisible by 11?
(a) 6 (b) 4
(c) 2 (d) 3

26. Product of digits of a 2 digit number is 72. If we add 9 to the number, the new number obtained is a number formed by interchange of the digits. Find the number.
(a) 98
(b) 89
(c) 78
(d) 87

27. What smallest number should be added to 2957 so that the sum is completely divisible by17 ?
(a) 9
(b) 2
(c) 3
(d) 1

28. The ten's digit of a 2-digit number is greater than the units digit by 2. If we subtract 18 from the number, the new number obtained is a number formed by interchange of the digits. Find the number.
(a) 75
(b) 64
(c) 53
(d) 86

29. If Gaganjyot's salary is 7/6 times of Hafiz's and Sayed's is 8/7 times of Hafiz's,what is the ratio of Gaganjyot's salary of Sayed's salary ?
(a) 49 : 48
(b) 3 : 4
(c) 4 : 3
(d) 48 : 49

30. What is the value of (91 + 92 + 93 +........+140) ?
(a) 5775 (b) 11550
(c) 17325 (d) 23100

Answers with Explanations

1. (b) $\frac{2530}{1430} = \frac{253 \div 11}{143 \div 11} = \frac{23}{13}$

2. (b) Let missing digit be x

Sum of odd place – sum of even place = 0, 11, 22, ...

$(3+7+5+7)-(4+x+4)$

$= 0, 11, \quad 22, ... \; 22-(8+x)$

$= 0, 11, 22$

$\Rightarrow 22-8-x = 11$

$\Rightarrow 14-x = 11$

$\Rightarrow 14-11 = x$

Hence, x = 3, which is exactly divisible by 11.

3. (a) Let the number be x

$\frac{9}{4}$ of $\frac{7}{2}$ of $x = 126$

$\frac{9}{4} \times \frac{7}{2} x = 126$

$\frac{63}{8} x = 126$

$x = \frac{126 \times 8}{63} = \frac{14 \times 8}{7} = 16$

$\frac{7}{2} x = \frac{7}{2} \times 16 = 56$

4. (d) Let two digit number be $10x + y$

According to question

In case I,

$x = y + 4$

$x - y = 4$

In case II

$10x + y - 36 = 10y + x$

$a(x - y) = 36$

$x - y = 4$

By solving, $x = 7$, and $y = 3$

We get the number $= 10 \times 7 + 3$

$= 73$

5. (b) $(91 + 92 + 93 + ... + 110)$

$= (1 + 2 + 3 ... + 110)$

$- (1 + 2 + 3 + ...90)$

where $n_1 = 110$ amd $n_2 = 90$

$$= \frac{n_1(n_1+1)}{2} - \frac{n_2(n_2+1)}{2}$$

$$\frac{110 \times 111}{2} - \frac{90 \times 91}{2}$$

$= 55 \times 111 - 45 \times 91$

$= 6105 - 4095 = 2010$

6. (a) Let the number be $10x + y$

$x = y + 7$

$x - y = 7$

$10x + y - 63 = 10y + x$

$9(x - y) = 63$

$x - y = 7$

We assume based on given options

$x = 8$ and $y = 1$

Hence, the number is 81.

7. (a) $(81 + 82 + 83 + ... + 130)$

$= (1 + 2 + 3 + 4 + ... + 130)$

$- (1 + 2 + 3 + 80)$

$$= \frac{n_1(n_1+1)}{2} - \frac{n_2(n_2+1)}{2}$$

$$\frac{130(130+1)}{2} - \frac{80(80+1)}{2}$$

$= 65 \times 131 - 40 \times 81$

$= 8515 - 3240$

$= 5275$

8. (a) The value of $\frac{5}{9} + \frac{7}{8}$

$$= \frac{40 + 63}{72} = \frac{103}{72}$$

9. (b) Let the number be $10x + y$

In case I

$x + y = 11$ ...(i)

$10x + y + 45 = 10y + x$

In case II

$10x + y - 10y - x = -45$

$9(x - y) = -45$

$x - y = -5$ ...(ii)

Solving equation (i) and (ii), we get

$x = 3$ and $y = 8$

Hence, the number

$= 30 + 8 = 38.$

10. (c) Let x and y be two fractions

In case-I

$$xy = \frac{9}{10} \quad ...(i)$$

In case-II

$$x + y = \frac{77}{40} \quad ...(ii)$$

Solving equations (i) and (ii), we get

$$x + y = \frac{77}{40}$$

$$\frac{9}{10y} + y = \frac{77}{40}$$

$40y^2 - 77y + 36 = 0$

$(8y - 9)(5y - 4) = 0$

$$y = \frac{9}{8}, \text{ or } y = \frac{4}{5}$$

$$x = \frac{4}{5} \text{ or } x = \frac{9}{8}$$

11. (b) The simplest form of 3774/2958

$$= \frac{1887}{1479} = \frac{37}{29}$$

12. (a) The fraction is $\frac{3565}{1495}$

$\therefore$ The simplest form $= \frac{31}{13}$

13. (c) Let the number be x

$\therefore$ According to question,

$$3x + \frac{2}{x} = \frac{97}{4}$$

$$\frac{3x^2 + 2}{x} = \frac{97}{4}$$

$12x^2 + 8 = 97x$

$12x^2 - 97x + 8 = 0$

$12x^2 - 96x - x + 8 = 0$

$12x(x - 8) - 1(x - 8) = 0$

$(x - 8)(12x - 1) = 0$

$x - 8 = 0$ and $12x - 1 = 0$

$$x = 8, \; x = \frac{1}{12}$$

$\therefore$ Hence, the number is 8.

14. (a) The expression,

$99992 \times 100008 = 9999999936$

15. (b) Let the two fractions are x and y respectively. According to question,

$x \times y = 4$ ...(i)

and $x + y = \frac{68}{15}$ ...(ii)

From eq^n (i) $x \times y = 4$

$$y = \frac{4}{x}$$

Putting value of y in eq^n (ii)

$$x + \frac{4}{x} = \frac{68}{15}$$

$$\frac{x^2 + 4}{x} = \frac{68}{15}$$

$15x^2 + 60 = 68x$

$15x^2 - 68x + 60 = 0$

$$15x^2 - \left(\frac{6}{5} + \frac{10}{3}\right)x + 60 = 0$$

$$15x^2 - \frac{6}{5}x - \frac{10}{3}x + 60 = 0$$

$$\left(x - \frac{6}{5}\right)\left(x - \frac{10}{3}\right) = 0$$

$$x - \frac{6}{5} = 0 \text{ and } x - \frac{10}{3} = 0$$

$$x = \frac{6}{5} = 0, \; x = \frac{10}{3}$$

Finally the two fractions are $\frac{6}{5}$ and $\frac{10}{3}$ respectively.

16. (b) $x = 0{\cdot}363636$ ....

$x = 0{\cdot}\overline{36}$ ...(i)

$100x = 36{\cdot}\overline{36}$ ...(ii)

Subtracting equation (i) from (ii)

$99x = 36$

$$x = \frac{36}{99} = \frac{4}{11}.$$

17. (d) $2 \times [0{\cdot}3(1{\cdot}3 + 3{\cdot}7)]$ of $0{\cdot}8 = ?$

$? = 2 \times [0{\cdot}3(5)] \times 0{\cdot}8$

$= 2 \times 1{\cdot}5 \times 0{\cdot}8$

$= 2{\cdot}4.$

18. (d) Let the number be x

$$\frac{7}{8} \times \frac{5}{4} \text{ of } x = 315$$

$$\frac{35}{32}x = 315$$

$$x = \frac{315 \times 32}{35} = 288$$

Now, $\frac{5}{9}$ of 288 $= \frac{5}{9} \times 288 = 160.$

19. (a) 731 is not a prime number.

20. (c) The largest 5 digit number = 99999

$$95\overline{)99999}(1052$$
$$\begin{array}{r} 95\downarrow\downarrow \\ \hline 499 \\ 475\downarrow \\ \hline 249 \\ 190 \\ \hline 59 \end{array}$$

Hence, divisible by 95 = 99999 – 59
= 99940

21. (b) $x = 0.090909............ = 0.09$

$100x = 9.09$

Subtracting (i) from (ii), we get

$99x = 9$

$$x = \frac{9}{99} = \frac{1}{11}$$

22. (a) Let the number be x

$$\frac{x \times 6}{7} \times \frac{8}{5} = 192$$

$$x = \frac{192 \times 35}{6 \times 8} = \frac{24}{6} \times 35 = 140$$

$$\frac{3}{4} \text{ of } x = \frac{3}{4} \times 140 = 3 \times 35 = 105$$

23. (d) 583 – 437 is completely divisible by 9.

583 m 437

Sum of digits of this number must be divided by 9

$5 + 8 + 3 + m + 4 + 3 + 7 = 36$

$m + 30 = 36$

$m = 36 - 30 = 6$

Hence, the digit is 6 to be divisible by 9.

24. (c) Let the number be x

$$x + \frac{3}{x} = \frac{52}{7}$$

$$\frac{x^2 + 3}{x} = \frac{52}{7}$$

$$7x^2 + 21 = 52x$$
$$7x^2 - 52x + 21 = 0$$
$$7x^2 - 49x - 3x + x = 0$$
$$7x(x - 7) - 3(x - 7) = 0$$
$$(x - 7)(7x - 3) = 0$$
$$x - 7 = 0 \text{ or } 7x - 3 = 0$$
$$x = 7 \text{ or } x = \frac{3}{7}$$

Hence, the required number is 7.

25. (d) 275 – 476 is exactly divisible by 11

2 7 5 x 4 7 6 is exactly divisible by 11

$(2 + 5 + 4 + 6) - (7 + x + 7) = 0, 11,$
$22\ 17 - (14 + x)$

$17 - 14 - x = 0$

$\Rightarrow \quad 3 = x$

$\Rightarrow \quad x = 3$

Hence, the missing digit is 3.

26. (b) Let the number be $10x + y$ where x and y are digits,

In case – I

$xy = 72$ ...(i)

In case –II

$10x + y + 9 = 10y + x$

$9(x - y) = -9$

$x - y = -1$ ...(ii)

On putting $x = y - 1$ in eq. (i), we get

$$(y - 1)y = 72$$
$$y^2 - y - 72 = 0$$
$$y^2 - 9y + 84 - 72 = 0$$
$$y(y - 9) + 8(y - 9) = 0$$
$$(y - 9)(y + 8) = 0$$
$$y = 9, \text{ or } y = -8$$
$$y = 9, x = 8$$

Hence, the number = $10 \times 8 + 9$
$= 80 + 9 = 89$

27. (d)

$$17\overline{)2957}(173$$
$$\begin{array}{r} 17\downarrow \\ \hline 125 \\ 119\downarrow \\ \hline 67 \\ 51 \\ \hline 16 \end{array}$$

$17 - 16 = 1$

$\therefore$ 1 should be added to divide completely.

28. (d) Let two digit number be $10x + y$

In case –I

$x = y + 2$

$x - y = 2$ ...(i)

In case –II

$10x + y - 18 = 10y + x$

$9x - 9y = 18$

$9(x - y) = 18$

$\Rightarrow \quad x - y = 2$ ...(ii)

solving by hit and trial method

$x = 8, y = 6$

Hence, the number will be 86.

29. (a) Gaganjyot's salary = $\frac{7}{6}$ of Hafiz

Sayed's salary = $\frac{8}{7}$ of Hafiz

$$\text{Required ratio} = \frac{7}{6} \Big/ \frac{8}{7} = \frac{7 \times 7}{6 \times 8}$$

$$= \frac{49}{48} = 49 : 48$$

30. (a) We know that

$$1 + 2 + 3 + ... n = \frac{n(n+1)}{2}$$

$\therefore$ The value of $(91 + 92 + ...140) - (1 + 2 + ... 90)$

$$= \frac{140(140+1)}{2} - \frac{90(90+1)}{2}$$

$$= \frac{140 \times 141}{2} - \frac{90 \times 91}{2}$$

$= 70 \times 141 - 45 \times 91$

$= 9870 - 4095 = 5775$

2 LCM AND HCF OF NUMBERS

- **Factors and multiples:** If a number 'p' divides another number 'q' exactly, we say that 'p' is a factor of 'q' and 'q' is a multiple of 'p'.

  Thus, a factor of a number is an exact divisor of that number and, a number is said to be a multiple of any of its factors.

  Example: Since, 5 divides 25 exactly, so, 5 is a factor of 25 and 25 is a multiple of 5.
- **Least Common Multiple (L.C.M.):** The least number which is exactly divisible by each one of the given numbers is called their L.C.M.

Methods of finding L.C.M.

(i) **Prime factorisation method:** Resolve each of the given numbers into a product of prime factors. LCM is the product of terms of highest power of all factors.

Example: Find the LCM of 60, 108 and 162.

Sol. $60 = 2 \times 2 \times 3 \times 5 = 2^2 \times 3^1 \times 5^1$

$108 = 2 \times 2 \times 3 \times 3 \times 3 = 2^2 \times 3^3$

$162 = 2 \times 3 \times 3 \times 3 \times 3 = 2 \times 3^4$

$\therefore$ LCM $= 2^2 \times 3^4 \times 5 = 1620$

(ii) **Common division method:** Arrange the given number in a row in any order. Divide by a number which divides exactly at last two of the given numbers and carry forward the number which are not divisible repeat the above process till no two of the numbers are divisible by the same number, other than 1. The product of the divisor and the undivided numbers is the required LCM of the given numbers.

Exmaple: Find the LCM of 48 and 120.

Sol.

2	48
2	24
2	12
2	6
3	3
	1

2	120
2	60
2	30
3	15
5	5
	1

$\therefore$ LCM $= 2 \times 2 \times 2 \times 2 \times 3 \times 5 = 240$

- **Highest Common Factor (HCF or GCD):** The HCF or GCD of two or more numbers is the greatest number that divides each one of them exactly.

  Example: HCF of 12, 16, 20, 24, 32 is 4

Methods of finding HCF

(i) **Prime factorisation method:** Express each one of the given numbers as the product of prime factors. The product of terms containing least powers of common prime factors gives the HCF of the given numbers.

Example: Find the HCF of 270 and 504.

Sol. $270 = 2 \times 3 \times 3 \times 3 \times 5$

$= 3^3 \times 2^1 \times 5^1$

$504 = 2 \times 2 \times 2 \times 3 \times 3 \times 7$

$= 2^3 \times 3^2 \times 7$

$\therefore$ HCF $= 2 \times 3^2 = (2 \times 9) = 18$

(ii) **Long division method:** Suppose we have to find the HCF of two given numbers. Divide the longer number by smaller one. Now, divide the divisor by the remainder. Repeat the process till the remainder is zero. The last divisor is called the HCF of numbers.

HCF of three numbers = HCF of [(HCF of any two) and the third]

Example: Find the HCF of 496 and 872

Sol.

```
496 ) 872 ( 1
      496
      ---
      376 ) 496 ( 1
            376
            ---
            120 ) 376 ( 3
                  360
                  ---
                   16 ) 120 ( 7
                        112
                        ---
                          8 ) 16 ( 2
                              16
                              --
                              X
```

$\therefore$ HCF of 496 and 872 = 8

Note: Two natural numbers are called co-prime numbers, if their HCF is 1.

Relation between HCF and LCM of two numbers

(i) Product of two given numbers

= Product of their HCF and LCM

(ii) LCM of number

$$= \frac{\text{Product of two given numbers}}{\text{HCF of the numbers}}$$

(iii) HCF of the number

$$= \frac{\text{Product of two given numbers}}{\text{LCM of the numbers}}$$

HCF and LCM of fractions

(i) HCF of given fractions

$$= \frac{\text{HCF of numerators}}{\text{LCM of demominators}}$$

(ii) LCM of given fractions

$$= \frac{\text{LCM of numerators}}{\text{HCF of denominators}}$$

Some Important Tricky Formulae

(i) To find the greatest number that will exactly divide x, y and z, then,
Required number = HCF of x, y and z

(ii) To find the greatest number that will divide x, y and z leaving remainders r_1, r_2 and r_3 respectivley, then
Required number = HCF of $(x - r_1)$, $(y - r_2)$ and $(z - r_3)$

(iii) To find the least number which is exactly divisible by x, y and z, then Required number = LCM of x, y and z.

(iv) To find the greatest number that will divide x, y and z leaving the same remainder 'r' in each case then,
Required number = HCF of $(x - r)$, $(y - r)$ and $(z - r)$.

Solved Examples

Example 1: Find the least number which when divided by 8, 18, 24, and 30 leaves the same remainder 6 in each case.

Sol. Required number

2	8,	18,	24,	30
2	4,	9,	12,	15
3	2,	9,	6,	15
3	2,	3,	2,	5
2	2,	1,	2,	5
	1,	1,	1,	5

= (LCM of 8, 18, 24 and 30) + 6
= $(2 \times 2 \times 2 \times 3 \times 3 \times 5) + 6$
= (360 + 6)
= 366

Example 2: Find the greatest number that exactly divides 714, 1666 and 3570.

Sol. Required greatest number = HCF of 714, 1666 and 3570 = 238

```
714)1666(2
    1428
    ----
     238)714(3
         714
         ---
          X

238)3570(15
    238
    ----
    1190
    1190
    ----
      X
```

Example 3: Find the length of the longest rope which can be used to measure exactly the lengths 7m, 3m 85 cm and 12m 95 cm.

Sol. The given length are

7m = 700 cm
3m 85 cm = 385 cm
12 m 95 cm = 1295 cm

∴ Length of the rope = HCF of 700, 385 and 1295 = 35 cm

```
385)700(1
    385
    ---
    315)385(1
        315
        ---
         70)315(4
            280
            ---
             35)70(2
                70
                --
                 X

35)1295(37
   105
   ---
   245
   245
   ---
    X
```

Example 4: Find the HCF of $\frac{3}{2}, \frac{6}{7}$ and $\frac{5}{14}$.

Sol. HCF of $\frac{3}{2}, \frac{6}{7}$ and $\frac{5}{14} = \frac{\text{HCF of 3, 6, and 5}}{\text{LCM of 2, 7, 14}} = \frac{1}{14}$

Exercise

1. The H.C.F. of two numbers is 16. Which one of the following can never be their L.C.M?
(a) 32 (b) 80
(c) 46 (d) 60

2. The L.C.M. of two numbers is 495 and their H.C.F is 5. If the sum of the numbers is 10, then their difference is:
(a) 10
(b) 46
(c) 70
(d) 90

3. The H.C.F. of two numbers is 11 and their L.C.M. is 7700. If one of the numbers is 275, then the other is:
(a) 279 (b) 283
(c) 308 (d) 318

4. Three numbers are in the ratio of 5 : 6 : 7 and their L.C.M. is 360. Their H.C.F. is :
(a) 20 (b) 80
(c) 120 (d) 200

5. The L.C.M. of two numbers is 48. The numbers are in the ratio 3 : 4. The sum of the numbers is:
(a) 28
(b) 80
(c) 120
(d) 200

6. Three numbers which are co-prime to each other are such that the product of the first two is 551 and that of the last two is 1073. The sum of the three numbers is:
(a) 75
(b) 81
(c) 85
(d) 89

7. The sum of two number is 528 and their H.C.F. is 33. The number of pairs of numbers satisfying the above conditions is:
(a) 4
(b) 6
(c) 8
(d) 12

8. The sum of two numbers is 216 and their H.C.F. is 27. The numbers are:
(a) 81, 135
(b) 81, 189
(c) 108, 108
(d) 37, 179

9. The ratio of two numbers is 5 : 6 and their H.C.F. is 12. Their L.C.M. is:
(a) 60
(b) 72
(c) 180
(d) 360

10. Three numbers are in the ratio 2 : 3 : 4 and their H.C.F. is 12. The numbers are :
(a) 24, 36, 48
(b) 10, 15, 20
(c) 20, 25, 30
(d) 12, 24, 36

11. The G.C.D. of 1.08, 0.36 amd 0.9 is:
(a) 0.03
(b) 0.9
(c) 0.18
(d) 0.108

12. The L.C.M. of 148 and 185 is:
(a) 740
(b) 1480
(c) 940
(d) 1880

13. Find the lowest common multiple of 36, 54 and 60.
(a) 340
(b) 240
(c) 440
(d) 540

14. The least number by which 72 must be multiplied in order to produce a multiple of 112, is:
(a) 6
(b) 12
(c) 14
(d) 18

15. What least number must be subtracted from 427398 so that remaining number is divisible by 15?
(a) 3
(b) 13
(c) 11
(d) 12

Answers with Explanations

1. (d) H.C.F. of two numbers divides their L.C.M. exactly.

2. (a) Let the numbers be x and $(10-x)$
Then, $x(10-x) = 5 \times 495$
$\Rightarrow x^2 - 10x - 2475 = 0$
$\Rightarrow (x-55)(x+45) = 0$
$\Rightarrow x = -55$ or $x = 45$
$\therefore$ The numbers are 45 and 55
Required difference $= (55-45) = 10$

3. (c) Other number
$= \left(\frac{11 \times 7700}{275}\right) = 308$

4. (a) Let the numbers be $5x$, and $6x$ and $7x$. Then, their L.C.M. $= 18x$,
So. $18x = 3600$ or $x = 20$
$\therefore$ The numbers are (5×20), (6×20) and (7×20)
Hence, required H.C.F. $= 20$

5. (a) Let the numbers be $3x$ and $4x$
Then, their L.C.M. $= 12x$
So, $12x = 48$ or $x = 4$
$\therefore$ The numbers are 12 and 16

6. (c) Since the numbers are co-prime, they contain only 1 as the common factor. Also, the given two products have the middle number in common.
Let middle term be x
So, 1st number $= \left(\frac{551}{29}\right) = 19$
Third number $= \left(\frac{1073}{29}\right) = 37$
$\therefore$ Required sum $= (19+29+37) = 85$

7. (a) Let the required numbers be 33a and 33b.
Then,
$33a + 33b = 528 \Rightarrow a + b = 16$.
Now coprimes with sum 16 are (1, 15) (3, 13), (5, 11) and (7, 9)
$\therefore$ Required numbers are $(33 \times 1, 33 \times 15), (33 \times 3, 33 \times 13), (33 \times 5, 33 \times 11), (33 \times 7, 33 \times 9)$.
The number of such pairs is 4.

8. (a) Let the required numbers be $27a$ and $27b$.
$27a + 27b = 216$
$\Rightarrow a + b = 8$.
Now co-prime with sum 8 are (1, 7) and (3, 5)
$\therefore$ Required numbers are $(27 \times 1, 27 \times 7)$ and $(27 \times 3, 27 \times 5)$ i.e., (27, 189) and (81, 135). Out of these the answer pair is (81, 135).

9. (d) Let the numbers be $5x$ and $6x$. Then, their H.C.F. $= x$. So, $x = 12$, So, the numbers are 60 and 72.

10. (a) Let the required numbers be $2x$, $3x$ and $4x$. Then their H.C.F $= x$. So, $x = 12$.

11. (c) Given numbers are 1.08, 0.36 and 0.90
HCF of 108, 36 and 90 is 18
$\therefore$ H.C.F of given numbers $= 0.18$

12. (c) LCM of 148 and 185
$= 2 \times 2 \times 5 \times 37 = 940$

2	148	185
2	74	185
37	37	185
	1	5

13. (d) LCM of 36, 54 and 60
$= 2 \times 2 \times 3 \times 3 \times 3 \times 5 = 540$

2	36	54	60
2	18	27	30
3	9	27	15
3	3	9	5
	1	3	5

14. (c) Required number is divisible by 72 as well as by 112, if it is divisible by their LCM, which is 1008.

15. (a) On dividing 427398 by 15,
we get remainder = 3

$\therefore$ Required number to be subtracted = 3

3 SIMPLIFICATION

Simplification: The process which is used to solve complex mathematical operations of any expression like addition, multiplication, division, brackets etc. is called simplification.

Generally, by using 'BODMAS' Rule we can simplify any expression.

B → Bracket
O → of
D → Division
M → Multiplication
A → Addition
S → Subtraction

Note (i): After removing the bar, the brackets must be removed, strictly in the order ( ), { }, [ ]

(ii) After removing the brackets, we must use the following operations strictly in the order given below, (*i*) of (*ii*) division (*iii*) multiplication (*iv*) addition and (*v*) subtraction.

Some Important Algebraic Identities:

(i) $(a+b)^2 = (a^2 + 2ab + b^2)$

(ii) $(a - b)^2 = (a^2 - 2ab + b^2)$

(iii) $(a + b)^2 - (a - b)^2 = 4ab$

(iv) $(a + b)^2 (a - b)^2 = (a^2 + b^2)$

(v) $(a^2 - b^2) = (a + b)(a - b)$

(vi) $(a^3 + b^3) = (a + b)(a^2 - ab + b^2)$

(vii) $(a^3 - b^3) = (a - b)(a^2 + ab + b^2)$

(viii) $(a + b)^3 = a^3 + b^3 + 3ab(a + b)$

(ix) $(a + b + c)^2 = a^2 + b^2 + c^2 + 2(ab + bc + ca)$

(x) $(a - b - c)^2 = a^2 + b^2 + c^2 - 2(ab - bc + ca)$

(xi) If $a + b + c = 0$ $(a \neq b \neq c)$

$a^2 + b^2 + c^2 - ab - bc - ca = 0$ (*i.e.* $a = b = c$)

$a^3 + b^3 + c^3 - 3abc = (a + b + c)$
$(a^2 + b^2 + c^2 - ab - bc - ca)$

$a^3 + b^3 + c^3 - 3abc = 0$ $(\because a+b+c=0)$

Solved Examples

Example 1: If $x^3 + y^3 = 50$ and $(x + y) = 10$, then find the value of $\left(\frac{1}{x}+\frac{1}{y}\right)$.

Sol. $(x + y)^3 = (10)^3 = 1000$

$\Rightarrow x^3 + y^3 + 3xy(x + y) = 1000$

$\Rightarrow 50 + 3xy \times 10 = 1000$

$\Rightarrow 30xy = 950 \Rightarrow xy = \frac{950}{30} = \frac{95}{3}$

$\therefore \frac{x+y}{xy} = \left(\frac{1}{x}+\frac{1}{y}\right) = \frac{10}{\frac{95}{3}} = \frac{30}{95}$

Example 2: Find the value of $2+\cfrac{1}{1+\cfrac{1}{3+\cfrac{1}{4}}}$

Sol. Given expression $= 2+\cfrac{1}{1+\cfrac{1}{3+\cfrac{1}{4}}}$

$$2+\cfrac{1}{1+\cfrac{1}{3+\cfrac{1}{4}}} = 2+\cfrac{1}{1+\cfrac{4}{13}} = 2+\cfrac{1}{\cfrac{17}{13}}$$

$$= \left(2+\frac{13}{17}\right) = \frac{47}{17}$$

Example 3: I paid $\frac{3}{5}$ of a bill. If ₹ 600 of the bill is still due, what was the amount of the bill?

Sol. Let the amount of the bill be ₹ x

Paid bill = ₹ $\frac{3}{5}x$

Bill due = ₹ $\left(x-\frac{3}{5}x\right)$ = ₹ $\frac{2}{5}x$ $\frac{2}{5}x = 600$

$\Rightarrow x = \left(\frac{600\times 5}{2}\right) = 1500$

$\therefore$ Total amount = ₹ 1500

Example 4: Amit read $\frac{3}{8}$*th* of a book on one day, $\frac{4}{5}$*th* of the remainder on another day. If there were 30 pages how many pages did the book contain?

Sol. Let the book contains x pages

Part Read on one day = $\frac{3}{8}x$

Remaining part = $\left(x-\frac{3}{8}x\right) = \frac{5}{8}x$

∴ Read on the next day

$= \left(\frac{4}{5}\times\frac{5}{8}x\right) = \frac{x}{2}$

According to question,

$\frac{3}{8}x+\frac{x}{2}-x = 30$

$x-\frac{3}{8}x-\frac{x}{2} = 30$

$\Rightarrow \frac{8x-3x-4x}{8} = 30$

$\Rightarrow x = 240$

Example 5: A total of 324 coins of 20 paise and 25 paise take a sum of ₹70. Find the number of 25 paise coins.

Sol. Let the 25 paise coins be x

Then, 20 paise coins = $(324 - x)$

According to question,

$\frac{x}{4}+\frac{324-x}{5} = 70$

$\Rightarrow 5x + 4(324 - x) = 70 \times 20$

$\Rightarrow 5x - 4x = 1296 = 1400$

$\Rightarrow x = 104$

Example 6: Find the value of

$\left(\frac{1}{1\times4}+\frac{1}{4\times7}+\frac{1}{7\times10}+\frac{1}{10\times13}+\frac{1}{13\times16}\right)$

Sol. Given expression

$= \left(\frac{1}{1\times4}+\frac{1}{4\times7}+\frac{1}{7\times10}+\frac{1}{10\times13}+\frac{1}{13\times16}\right)$

$= \frac{1}{3}\left[\left(1-\frac{1}{4}\right)+\left(\frac{1}{4}-\frac{1}{7}\right)+\left(\frac{1}{7}-\frac{1}{10}\right)+\left(\frac{1}{10}-\frac{1}{13}\right)\right.$

$\left.+\left(\frac{1}{13}-\frac{1}{16}\right)\right]$

$= \frac{1}{3}\left(1-\frac{1}{16}\right) = \left(\frac{1}{3}\times\frac{15}{16}\right) = \frac{5}{16}$

Exercise

1. $\frac{(569+163)^2-(569-163)^2}{569\times163} = ?$

(a) 2

(b) 4

(c) 406

(d) None of these

2. If $3x-4y+z=7$; $2x-z+3y=19$; $x+2y+2z=24$, then what is the value of x, y and z respectively?

(a) 4, 6, 5 (b) 6, 4, 5

(c) 6, 5, 4 (d) 4, 5, 6

3. If $2x+y=17$; $y+2z=15$ and $x+y=9$, then what is the value of $2x+3y+4z$?

(a) 61 (b) 47

(c) 45 (d) 55

4. If $3x-2y=5$ and $\frac{y}{x+y}=\frac{15}{17}$, then what is the value of $x-y$?

(a) $-\frac{39}{2}$ (b) $\frac{49}{2}$

(c) 9 (d) 2

5. If $2x+y=5$ and $3x-4y=2$, then the value of $(x+y)^2$ is:

(a) 9 (b) 5

(c) 3 (d) 4

6. If $2p+3q=18$ and $2p-q=2$, then $2p+q=?$

(a) 6 (b) 7

(c) 10 (d) 20

7. If $a+b=5$ and $3a+2b=20$, then $(3a-b)$ will be:

(a) 5 (b) 25

(c) 15 (d) 35

8. Which of the following values of x and y satisfy the following equations I and II?

(I) $2x+y=15$ (II) $3x-y=25$

(a) −8, 1 (b) −8, −1

(c) 8, −1 (d) 8, 1

9. If $4x+5y=83$ and $\frac{4x}{3y}=\frac{21}{33}$, then $x+y=?$

(a) 4 (b) 8

(c) 7 (d) 18

10. Find x if $\frac{x}{3}-\frac{x}{4}=5$.

(a) −60 (b) −100

(c) 100 (d) 60

11. If $a=6+x$ and $b=2x+15$, then for what value of x, a is twice of b?

(a) 8 (b) −8

(c) ½ (d) 2

12. If $\frac{37}{13}=2+\cfrac{1}{x+\cfrac{1}{y+\cfrac{1}{z}}}$, where x, y, z are natural numbers, then x, y, z are :

(a) 1, 2, 5 (b) 1, 5, 2

(c) 5, 2, 11 (d) 11, 2, 5

13. Simplify: $\cfrac{1}{1+\cfrac{\frac{2}{3}}{1+\frac{2}{3}+\cfrac{\frac{8}{9}}{1-\frac{2}{3}}}}$

(a) $\frac{11}{13}$ (b) $\frac{13}{15}$

(c) $\frac{13}{11}$ (d) $\frac{4}{7}$

14. $\dfrac{2}{2+\dfrac{2}{\dfrac{2}{3+\dfrac{2}{3}}}\times 0.39}$ is simplified to:

(a) $\frac{1}{3}$ (b) $\frac{100}{111}$

(c) $\frac{9}{10}$ (d) $\frac{9}{10}$

15. $10-10\times\dfrac{2\frac{1}{5}-1\frac{2}{7}}{2-\dfrac{1}{4\frac{1}{6}}}$ is equal to:

(a) 3 (b) 5

(c) 4 (d) 10

16. If $\dfrac{2+\dfrac{1}{3\frac{4}{5}}}{2+\dfrac{1}{3+\dfrac{1}{1+\dfrac{1}{4}}}}=x$, then the value of x is:

(a) 2 (b) 3

(c) 1 (d) $\frac{8}{7}$

17. The price of rice increases by 40 paise every year, while the price of wheat increases by 15 paise every year. If in 2000, the price of rice was ₹ 4.20 and that of wheat was ₹ 6.30, in which year rice will cost 40 paise more than the wheat?

(a) 2011 (b) 2019

(c) 2012 (d) 2009

18. Raju has 31.25 metres of the cloth and he has to make 16 pieces out of a metre of cloth. How many pieces can he make out of this cloth?

(a) 300 (b) 400

(c) 520 (d) 500

19. If $\frac{169}{0.169}=\frac{16.9}{x}$, then the value of x is:

(a) 0.0169 (b) 1.69

(c) 16.9 (d) 169

20. $(\sqrt{1})^2+(\sqrt{2})^2+(\sqrt{3})^2+(\sqrt{4})^2=?$

(a) 6 (b) 8

(c) 10 (d) 9

21. $0.5\div 0.005=?$

(a) 10

(b) 100

(c) 1000

(d) None of these

22. $0.6\times 0.06=?$

(a) 0.36 (b) 0.0036

(c) 0.036 (d) 3.6

23. $2+\dfrac{1}{2+\dfrac{1}{2}}=?$

(a) $7\frac{1}{2}$ (b) $6\frac{1}{2}$

(c) $2\frac{2}{5}$ (d) $1\frac{1}{3}$

24. $?=1001.101+101.01+11.11$

(a) 1122.221

(b) 1113.221

(c) 1113.23

(d) 1022.312

25. $20\frac{1}{2}+30\frac{1}{3}-15\frac{1}{6}=?$

(a) $34\frac{1}{6}$ (b) $35\frac{2}{3}$

(c) $35\frac{5}{6}$ (d) $45\frac{1}{3}$

26. A person perchased 15 pens and 30 books worth ₹ 825. If the cost of a book is double that of a pen calculate the cost of one book.

(a) ₹ 11 (b) ₹ 22

(c) ₹ 15 (d) ₹ 20

27. $\frac{1}{3}$ of the income of a person is spent over food, $\frac{1}{2}$ toward loan. If the remaining amount is ₹ 2000. Calculate his income.

(a) ₹ 6,000

(b) ₹ 8,000

(c) ₹ 10,000

(d) ₹ 12,000

28. If A gets double the amount of B and B gets $\frac{1}{3}$ the amount of C, what is the share of A, if the total amount is ₹ 3000?

(a) ₹ 1,000

(b) ₹ 1,500

(c) ₹ 500

(d) ₹ 2,000

29. If the numerator of a fraction is increased by 20% and the denominator is decreased by 10%, the value of the fraction becomes $\frac{16}{21}$. The original fraction is–

(a) $\frac{3}{5}$ (b) $\frac{4}{7}$

(c) $\frac{2}{3}$ (d) $\frac{5}{7}$

30. The number that should be added to both numerator and denominator of $\frac{4^2}{9^2}$ so that the fraction becomes $\frac{4}{9}$ is:

(a) 0 (b) 36

(c) 16 (d) 81

31. Six persons went to a hotel for taking their meals. Five of them spent ₹ 32 each on their meals while the sixth person spent ₹ 80 more than the other five persons, then the average expenditure of all the persons is:

(a) ₹ 192

(b) ₹ 240

(c) ₹ 288

(d) ₹ 336

Answers with Explanations

1. (b) Expression

$$= \frac{(569+163)^2-(569-163)^2}{569\times 163}$$

Let $a=569$ and $b=163$

$\therefore$ Expression

$$= \frac{(a+b)^2-(a-b)^2}{ab} = \frac{4ab}{ab} = 4$$

2. (b)
$3x-4y+z=7$ ...(i)
$2x+3y-z=19$ ...(ii)
$x+2y+2z=24$ ...(iii)

Adding (i) and (ii), we get: $5x-y=26.$

Subtracting (i) from (ii) and adding to (iii), we get:

$97=36$ or $y=4$

Putting $y=4$ in (iv), we get:

$5x=30$ or $x=6$

Putting $x=6$, $y=4$ in (iii), we get:

$2z=10$ or $z=5.$

3. (b)
$2x+y=17$ ...(i)
$y+2z=15$ ...(ii)
$x+y=9$ ...(iii)

Solving equations (i), (ii) and (iii) we get : $x=8$ $y=1$ and $z=7$.

$\therefore$ $2x+3y+4z=2\times 8+3\times 1+4\times 7=47$

4. (a) $3x-2y=5$ ...(i)

and $\frac{y}{x-y}=\frac{15}{17}$

$\Rightarrow$ $17y=15x-15y$

$\Rightarrow$ $15x-2y=0$ ...(ii)

Solving these equations we get $x=3$,

$y=\frac{45}{2}$

Which gives $x+y=3-\frac{45}{2}=-\frac{39}{2}$

5. (a)
$2x+y=5$ ...(i)
and $3x-4y=2$ ...(ii)

Multiplying (i) by 4 and adding (ii) to it, we get : $11x=22$ or $x=2$.

Putting $x=2$ in (i), we get : $y=1$

So, $2xy=2\times 2\times 1=4.$

$(x+y)^2=x^2+y^2+2xy$

$4+1+4=9$

6. (c) $(2p+3q)+(2p-q)=18+2$

$\Rightarrow$ $4p+2q=20$

$\Rightarrow$ $2(2p+q)=20$

$\Rightarrow$ $2p+q=10$

7. (d)
$a+b=5$ ...(i)
and $3a+2b=20$ ...(ii)

Multiplying (i) by 2 and subtracting from (ii), we get: $a=10.$

Putting a = 10 in (i), we get :

$b=-5$

$\therefore$ $(3a-b)=3\times 10-(-5)=30+5=35.$

8. (c)
$2x+y=15$ ...(i)
and $3x-y=25$ ...(ii)

Solving (i) and (ii), we get:

$x=8, y=-1$

9. (d) $\frac{4x}{3y}=\frac{21}{33}$

$\Rightarrow$ $\frac{x}{y}=\left(\frac{21}{22}\times\frac{2}{3}\right)=\frac{7}{11}\Rightarrow x=\frac{7}{11}y$

$= 4x+5y=83$

$\Rightarrow$ $4\times\frac{7}{11}y+5y=83$

$\frac{28}{11}y+5y=83$

$\Rightarrow$ $83y=83\times 11\Rightarrow y=11$

$\therefore$ $x=\frac{7}{11}y=\left(\frac{7}{11}\times 11\right)=7$

So $x+y=11+7=18$

10. (d) $\frac{x}{3}-\frac{x}{4}=5\Rightarrow\frac{4x-3x}{12}=5$

$x=60$

11. (b)
$2(2x+15)=6+x$
$4x+30=6+x$
$3x=24$
$x=-8$

12. (b) $2+\cfrac{1}{x+\cfrac{1}{y+\cfrac{1}{z}}}=\frac{37}{13}$

$=2\frac{11}{13}=2+\frac{11}{13}$

$\Rightarrow$ $\cfrac{1}{x+\cfrac{1}{y+\cfrac{1}{z}}}=\frac{11}{13}$

$\Rightarrow$ $\cfrac{1}{x+\cfrac{1}{y+\cfrac{1}{z}}}=\frac{11}{13}$

$\Rightarrow$ $x+\cfrac{1}{y+\cfrac{1}{z}}=1+\frac{2}{11}$

$\Rightarrow x=1,\ y+\frac{1}{z}$

$=\frac{11}{2}=5\frac{1}{2}=5+\frac{1}{2}$

$\Rightarrow x=1,\ y=5,\ z=2$

13. (b) Given exp.

$$=\cfrac{1}{1+\cfrac{\frac{2}{3}}{\cfrac{5}{3}+\cfrac{\frac{8}{9}}{(1/3)}}}=\cfrac{1}{1+\cfrac{2/3}{\frac{5}{3}+\frac{8}{9}\times 3}}$$

$$=\cfrac{1}{1+\cfrac{2/3}{(13/3)}}=\cfrac{1}{1+\frac{2}{13}}=\frac{13}{15}$$

14. (b) Given exp.

$$=\cfrac{2}{2+\cfrac{2}{3+\cfrac{2}{(11/3)}}\times 0.39}=\cfrac{2}{2+\cfrac{2}{3+\frac{6}{11}}\times 0.39}$$

$$=\cfrac{2}{2+\cfrac{2}{(39/11)}\times 0.39}$$

$$=\cfrac{2}{2+\frac{22}{39}\times\frac{39}{100}}=\cfrac{2}{2+\frac{22}{100}}=\cfrac{2}{2+\frac{11}{50}}$$

$$= \frac{2}{(111/50)} = \frac{100}{111}$$

15. (c) Given exp.

$$= 10 - 10 \times \frac{\frac{11}{5} - \frac{9}{7}}{2 - \frac{1}{(25/6)}} = 8 - 8 \times \frac{\frac{32}{35}}{2 - \frac{6}{35}}$$

$$= 10 - 10 \times \frac{32}{35} \times \frac{35}{64} = 8 - 4 = 4.$$

16. (c)

$$x = \frac{2 + \frac{1}{(19/5)}}{2 + \frac{1}{3 + \frac{1}{(5/4)}}} = \frac{2 + \frac{5}{29}}{2 + \frac{1}{3 + \frac{4}{5}}} = \frac{2 + \frac{5}{19}}{2 + \frac{1}{(19/5)}}$$

$$= \frac{2 + \frac{5}{19}}{2 + \frac{5}{19}} = 1$$

17. (a) Suppose Rice x will cost 30 paise more than wheat after a years. Then,

$(4.20 + 0.30a) - (6.30 + 0.15a) = 0.40$

$\Leftrightarrow 0.15a = 0.40 + 2.10$

$$\Leftrightarrow a = \frac{2.50}{0.25} = \frac{250}{25} = 10$$

$\therefore$ x will cost 40 paise more than y 10 years after 2001 i.e., in 2011.

18. (d) Length of each piece

$$= \left(\frac{1}{16}\right) \text{m} = 0.0625 \text{ m}$$

$\therefore$ Required number of pieces

$$= \left(\frac{31.25}{0.0625}\right) = \left(\frac{3125 \times 100}{625}\right) = 500$$

19. (a)

$$\frac{169}{0.169} = \frac{16.9}{x} \Leftrightarrow \frac{169 \times 100}{169} = \frac{16.9}{x}$$

$$\Leftrightarrow x = \frac{16.9}{1000} = 0.0169$$

20. (c) $? = (\sqrt{1})^2 + (\sqrt{2})^2 + (\sqrt{3})^2 + (\sqrt{4})^2$

$= (1 + 2 + 3 + 4)$

$= 10$

21. (b) $? = 0.5 \div 0.005 = \frac{0.5}{0.005} = 100$

22. (c) $? = 0.6 \times 0.06 = 0.036$

23. (c) $? = 2 + \frac{1}{2 + \frac{1}{2}} = 2 + \frac{2}{5}$

$$= \frac{12}{5} = 2\frac{2}{5}$$

24. (a) $? = 1001.101 + 101.01 + 11.11$

$? = 1122.221$

25. (b) $? = 20\frac{1}{2} + 30\frac{1}{3} - 15\frac{1}{6}$

$$= 20 + \frac{1}{2} + 30 + \frac{1}{3} - 15 - \frac{1}{6}$$

$$= (20 + 30 - 15) + \frac{1}{2} + \frac{1}{3} - \frac{1}{6}$$

$$= \left(35 + \frac{4}{6}\right) = 35\frac{2}{3}$$

26. (b) Let the cost of one pen be ₹ x

$\therefore$ Cost of one book = ₹ $2x$

Then, $15x + 30x = 825$

$\Rightarrow$ $15x + 60x = 825$

$\therefore$ $75x = 825$

$\Rightarrow$ $x = 11$

$\therefore$ Cost of one book = ₹ (2×11)

= ₹ 22

27. (d) Let the total income of person be ₹ x

$\therefore$ Expenditure on food = ₹ $\frac{x}{3}$

Expenditure on loan = ₹ $\frac{x}{2}$

According to question,

$$\frac{x}{3} + \frac{x}{2} + 2000 = x$$

$$\Rightarrow \quad x - \frac{x}{3} - \frac{x}{2} = 2000$$

$$\Rightarrow \quad \frac{x}{6} = 2000$$

$\Rightarrow$ $x =$ ₹ 12000

28. (b) Let C gets ₹ x

Then, B gets = ₹ $\frac{x}{3}$ and A gets ₹ $\frac{2}{3}x$

According to question,

$$x + \frac{x}{3} + \frac{2}{3}x = 3000$$

$$\Rightarrow \quad \frac{6}{3}x = 3000$$

$\Rightarrow$ $x =$ ₹ 1,500

29. (b) Let the numerator of fraction be x and denominator be y.

Then, original fraction = $\frac{x}{y}$.

$$\therefore \quad \frac{12x}{90y} = \frac{16}{21}$$

$$\Rightarrow \quad \frac{4x}{3y} = \frac{16}{21}$$

$$\Rightarrow \quad \frac{x}{y} = \frac{16 \times 3}{21 \times 4} = \frac{4}{7}$$

30. (b) Let the required number be x.

Then, $\frac{16 + x}{81 + x} = \frac{4}{9}$

$\Rightarrow$ $144 + 9x = 324 + 4x$

$\Rightarrow$ $5x = 180$

$\Rightarrow$ $x = 36$

31. (c) Let the total expenditure be ₹ x

Then, according to question

$$x - 5 \times 32 = \frac{x}{6} + 80$$

$$\Rightarrow \quad x - \frac{x}{6} = 80 + 160$$

$$\Rightarrow \quad \frac{5}{6}x = 240$$

$$\Rightarrow \quad x = \left(\frac{240 \times 6}{5}\right) = ₹\ 288$$

4 AVERAGE

Average: The sum of all the observations divided by total number of observations is called Average.

$$\therefore \boxed{\text{Average} = \frac{\text{Sum of all observations}}{\text{Number of observations}}}$$

Sum of all observations
= Average × No. of observations.

Some Important General Formulae:

(i) The average of consecutive natural numbers up to n is $\left(\frac{n+1}{2}\right)$

(ii) The average of odd numbers from 1 to n

$$= \left(\frac{\text{Last odd number} + 1}{2}\right)$$

(iii) The average of even numbers from 1 to n

$$= \left(\frac{\text{Last even number} + 2}{2}\right)$$

(iv) The average of first n consecutive even numbers $= (n+1)$

(v) The average of first n consecutive odd numbers $= n$

(vi) The average of squares of natural numbers upto n is $\frac{(n+1)(2n+1)}{6}$

(vii) The average of cubes of natural numbers up to n

$$= \left[\frac{n(n+1)^2}{4}\right]$$

(viii) The average of squares of natural numbers up to n is $\left[\frac{(n+1)(2n+1)}{6}\right]$

(ix) The average of squares of first n consecutive even numbers

$$= \left[\frac{2(n+1)(2n+1)}{3}\right]$$

(x) The average of squares of consecutive even numbers up to n

$$= \left[\frac{(n+1)(n+2)}{3}\right]$$

(xi) If a person travels a distance at speed of x km/hr and the same distance at a speed of y km/hr, then the average speed during the whole Journey $= \left(\frac{xy}{x+y}\right)$ km/hr

(xii) If a batsman completed 'n' innings and his average is 'x' runs. He must make in his next innings so as to raise his average to 'y' then

Required number of runs

$$= [n(y-x)+y]$$

(xiii) If a batsman in his nth innings makes a score of 'x' and thereby increases his average by 'y', then

Average after 'n' innings

$$= [x - y(n-1)]$$

(xiv) If the average of 'n' quantities is equal to 'x' and when a quantity is removed, the average becomes 'y', then.

Value of remnant quantity

$$= [n(x-y)+y]$$

(xv) If the average of 'n' quantities is equal to 'x' and when a new quantity is added, the average becomes 'y', then

Value of new quantity

$$= [n(y-x)+y]$$

(xvi) If the average age of 'x' boys is 'a' and the average age of 'y' boys out of them (x boys) is 'b', then

Average age of the rest of the boys $= \left[\frac{ax-by}{x-y}\right]$

(xvii) If the average of 'x' quantities is 'a' and the average of 'y' quantities is 'b', then

Average of all quantities together $= \left[\frac{ax+by}{x+y}\right]$

Solved Examples

Example 1: The average of 6 numbers is 8. What is the 7th number so that average becomes 12?

Sol. Let the 7th number be x.

$\therefore$ Sum of 6 numbers = $(6 \times 8) = 48$

$$\therefore \frac{48+x}{7}=12$$

$\Rightarrow 48 + x = 84$

$\Rightarrow x = (84 - 48) = 36$

Example 2: The average of 10 numbers is 12. The average of 6 of then is 8. What is the average of remaining four numbers?

Sol. Sum of 10 numbers = $(10 \times 12) = 120$

Sum of 6 numbers = $(6 \times 8) = 48$

$\therefore$ Average of remaining four numbers $= \frac{120-48}{4}$

$$= \frac{72}{4}=18$$

Example 3: Find the average of squares of first 17 consecutive even numbers.

Sol. Average of squares of first n consecutive even numbers

$$= \frac{2(n+1)(2n+1)}{3}$$

(Here $n = 17$)

$\therefore$ Required average

$$= \frac{2(17+1)(2\times17+1)}{3}$$

$$= \frac{2\times18\times35}{3} = 420$$

Exercise

1. In a class of 56 students there are 21 girls. The average weight of these girls is 56 kg and average weight of the full class is 62.875 kgs. What is the average weight of the boys of the class ?
   (a) 69.75 kg
   (b) 72.5 kg
   (c) 67 kg
   (d) 65 kg
2. The average revenues of 9 consecutive years of a company is ₹ 65 lakhs. If the average of first 5 years is ₹ 60 lakhs and that of last 5 years is ₹ 72 lakhs, find the revenue for the 5th year.
   (a) ₹ 77 lakhs
   (b) ₹ 75 lakhs
   (c) ₹ 73 lakhs
   (d) ₹ 71 lakhs
3. The mean of marks secured by 45 students in division A of class X is 69, 65 students of division B is 65 and that of 50 students of division C is 63. Find the mean of marks of the students of three divisions of Class X.
   (a) 65.5
   (b) 64.8
   (c) 64.1
   (d) 66.9
4. The average revenues of 7 consecutive years of a company is ₹ 83 lakhs. If the average of first 4 years is ₹ 78 lakhs and that of last 4 years is ₹ 90 lakhs, find the revenue for the 4th year.
   (a) ₹ 91 lakhs
   (b) ₹ 93 lakhs
   (c) ₹ 89 lakhs
   (d) ₹ 87 lakhs
5. The mean of marks secured by 60 students in division A of class X is 66, 45 students of division B is 62 and that of 75 students of division C is 60. Find the mean of marks of the students of three divisions of class X.
   (a) 61.8
   (b) 62.5
   (c) 61.1
   (d) 63.9
6. In the first 43 overs of a cricket match, the run rate was 5 runs/over. Calculate the required run rate in the remaining 7 overs to reach the target of 285 runs.
   (a) 10.6
   (b) 11.2
   (c) 10
   (d) 9.4
7. Among three numbers, the first is twice the second and thrice the third. If the average of three numbers is 517, then what is the difference between the first and the third number?
   (a) 564 (b) 759
   (c) 485 (d) 799
8. Of the 3 numbers whose average is 70, the first is 1/9 times the sum of other two. The first number is :
   (a) 32 (b) 21
   (c) 14 (d) 42
9. The average revenues of 11 consecutive years of a company is ₹ 77 lakhs. If the average of first 6 years is ₹ 72 lakhs and that of last 6 years is ₹ 84 lakhs. What is the revenue for the Sixth year.
   (a) ₹ 91 lakhs
   (b) ₹ 87 lakhs
   (c) ₹ 85 lakhs
   (d) ₹ 89 lakhs
10. A factory buys 8 machines. 3 Machine A, 4 Machine B and rest Machine C. Prices of the machines are ₹ 45000, ₹ 25000 and ₹ 35000 respectively. Calculate the average cost (in ₹) of these machines ?
   (a) 33750
   (b) 35000
   (c) 36250
   (d) 32250

11. The brother is elder to his sister by 6 years. Seven years ago the product of their ages was 72. What is the age of the brother ?
(a) 13 years
(b) 12 years
(c) 6 years
(d) 19 years

12. The average marks of 56 students is shown as 60. It includes a wrong entry of 92 marks instead of 29 marks. The correct average is ....
(a) 58.875 marks
(b) 61.125 marks
(c) 63.375 marks
(d) 56.625 marks

13. A factory buys 7 machines. 2 Machine A, 2 Machine B and rest Machine C. Prices of the machines are ₹ 95000, ₹ 75000 and ₹ 43000 respectively. Calculate the average cost of these machines.
(a) 71000
(b) 67000
(c) 75000
(d) 65500

14. The average revenues of 9 consecutive years of a company is ₹ 76 lakhs. If the average of first 5 years is ₹ 71 lakhs and that of last 5 years is ₹ 83 lakhs, find the revenue for the 5th year.
(a) ₹ 88 lakhs
(b) ₹ 84 lakhs
(c) ₹ 86 lakhs
(d) ₹ 82 lakhs

15. The mean of marks secured by 65 students in division A of class X is 54, 30 students of division B is 50 and that of 55 students of division C is 48. Find the mean of marks of the students of three divisions of Class X.
(a) 50.3
(b) 49.6
(c) 51
(d) 52.4

16. The average weight of Shubha, Govinda and Reshma is 65 kg. If the average weight of Shubha and Govinda be 63 kg and that of Govinda and Reshma be 70 kg, then the weight of Govinda is
(a) 41
(b) 71
(c) 88
(d) 46

17. The average revenues of 9 consecutive years of a company is ₹ 68 lakhs. If the average of first 5 years is ₹ 63 lakhs and that of last 5 years is ₹ 75 lakhs, find the revenue for the 5th year.
(a) ₹ 80 lakhs
(b) ₹ 76 lakhs
(c) ₹ 78 lakhs
(d) ₹ 74 lakhs

18. In a class of 65 students there are 39 girls. The average weight of these girls is 60 kg and average weight of the full class is 64 kgs. What is the average weight of the boys of the class?
(a) 69
(b) 66
(c) 68
(d) 70

19. The mean of marks secured by 55 students in division A of class X is 58, 45 students of division B is 54 and that of 75 students of division C is 52. Find the mean of marks of the students of three divisions of Class X.
(a) 53.7
(b) 54.4
(c) 53
(d) 55.8

20. Of the 3 numbers whose average is 64, the first number is 1/3 times the sum of other 2. The first number is—
(a) 72
(b) 32
(c) 96
(d) 48

Answers with Explanations

1. (c) Total weight of 21 girls $= 56 \times 21$
$= 1176$ kg
Total weight of full class
$= 62.875 \times 56 = 3521$ kg
Total weight of $(56 - 21)$
$= 35$ boys
$= 3521 - 1176 = 2345$ kg
Average weight of 35 boys
$$= \frac{2345}{35} = 67 \text{ kg}$$

2. (b) Total revenues of 9 years
$= 65 \times 9 = 585$ lakhs
Total revenues of first 5 years
$= 60 \times 5 = 300$ lakhs
Total revenues of last 5 years
$= 72 \times 5 = 360$ lakhs
Total revenues of 10 years
$= 300 + 360 = 660$ lakhs
Revenues of 5th year
$= 660 - 585$
$=$ ₹ 75 lakhs

3. (a) Mean marks of 3 divisions of class X
$$= \frac{45 \times 69 + 65 \times 65 + 50 \times 63}{160}$$
$$= \frac{3105 + 4225 + 3150}{160}$$
$$= \frac{10480}{160} = 65.5$$

4. (a) Total revenues of 7 years
$= 83 \times 7 = 58$ lakhs
Total revenues of first 4 years
$= 78 \times 4 = 312$ lakhs
Total revenues of last 4 years
$= 90 \times 4 = 360$ lakhs
Total revenues of 8 years
$= 672$ lakhs
Revenues of 4th year
$= 672 - 581 =$ ₹ 91 lakhs

5. (b) Mean Marks
$$= \frac{60 \times 66 + 45 \times 62 + 75 \times 60}{60 + 45 + 75}$$

$= \frac{3960 + 2790 + 4500}{180}$

$= \frac{11250}{180} = 62.5$

6. (c) Total runs in the first 43 overs $= 43 \times 5 = 215$ runs.
Required runs in 7 overs $= 285 - 215 = 70$

Run rate in 7 overs $= \frac{70}{7}$

$= 10$ runs / over

7. (a) Let three numbers be p, q, r
According to question

$p = 2q = 3r$

Average $= \frac{p+q+r}{3}$

$517 = \frac{2q + q + \frac{2}{3}q}{3}$

$= \frac{6q + 3q + 2q}{9}$

$517 = \frac{11}{9}q$

$\frac{517 \times 9}{11} = 47 \times 9 = 423$

$p = 2q = 2 \times 423 = 846$

$r = \frac{2}{3}q = \frac{2}{3} \times 423$

$= 2 \times 141 = 282$

Difference of the first and the third number

$= p - r = 846 - 282 = 564.$

8. (b) Let the first number $= x_1$ and other two numbers $= x_2$ and x_3
According to question,

$\frac{x_1 + x_2 + x_3}{3} = 70$

$x_1 + x_2 + x_3 = 70 \times 3$ ...(i)

and $x_1 = \frac{1}{9}(x_2 + x_3)$ ...(ii)

$\therefore$ From eq^n (i)

$\frac{1}{9}(x_2 + x_3) + x_2 + x_3 = 70 \times 3$

$\frac{10}{9}(x_2 + x_3) = 70 \times 3$

$x_2 + x_3 = \frac{70 \times 3 \times 9}{10} = 189$

From eq^n (ii)

$x_1 = \frac{1}{9} \times 189 = 21$

Finally, the first number is 21.

9. (d) Total revenues of 11 years
$= 77 \times 11$ lakhs
$= 847$ lakhs
Total revenues of 6 years
$= 72 \times 6$ lakhs
$= 432$ lakhs
Total revenues of next 6 years
$= 84 \times 6$ years
$= 504$ lakhs
Average of 6th years
$= (432 + 504) - 847$
$= 936 - 847$
$=$ ₹ 89 lakhs

10. (a) Average Cost

$= \frac{3 \times 45000 + 4 \times 25000 + 1 \times 35000}{8}$

$= \frac{135000 + 100000 + 35000}{8}$

$= \frac{270,000}{8} =$ ₹ 33750.

11. (d) Let age of her sister $= x$
Brother's age $= x + 6$
7 years ego,

$(x - 7)(x + 6 - 7) = 72$

$\Rightarrow (x - 7)(x - 1) = 72$

$\Rightarrow x^2 - 8x + 7 = 72$

$\Rightarrow x^2 - 8x + 7 - 72 = 0$

$\Rightarrow x^2 - 8x - 65 = 0$

$x^2 - 13x + 5x - 65 = 0$

$x(x - 13) + 5(x - 13) = 0$

$(x - 13)(x + 5) = 0$

$x = 13$, or $x + 5 = 0$

$x = -5$ (Invalid)

Brother's Age $= 13 + 6 = 19$ years.

12. (a) Total marks of 56 students
$= 56 \times 60 = 3360$

Correct Average

$= \frac{3360 + 29 - 92}{56}$

$= \frac{3297}{56} = 58{\cdot}875.$

13. (b) Average cost of machines

$= \frac{95000 \times 2 + 75000 \times 2 + 43000 \times 3}{2 + 2 + 3}$

$= \frac{190000 + 150000 + 129000}{7}$

$= \frac{469000}{7} =$ ₹ 67000

14. (c) Total values of 9 years $= 76 \times 9$ lakhs $= 684$ lakhs
Total values of 5 years $= 71 \times 5 = 355$ lakhs
Total values of last 5 years $= 83 \times 5 = 415$ lakhs
Total values of 10 years
$= 770$ lakhs
The values of 5th years
$= (770 - 684)$ lakhs
$=$ ₹ 86 lakhs

15. (c) Mean marks of 3 divisions

$= \frac{m_1x_1 + m_2x_2 + m_3x_3}{m_1 + m_2 + m_3}$

$= \frac{65 \times 54 + 30 \times 50 + 55 \times 48}{65 + 30 + 55}$

$= \frac{3510 + 1500 + 2640}{150}$

$= \frac{7650}{150} = 51$

Hence, the mean marks is 51.

16. (b) Total weight of Shubha, Govinda and Reshma $= 65 \times 3$

S + G + R = 195kg ...(i)

Total weight of Subha Govinda $= 63 \times 2 = 126$kg

S + G = 126kg ...(ii)

Total weight of Govinda and Reshma

$= 2 \times 70 = 140$

$= 140$ kg ...(iii)

S + 2G + R

$= 126 + 140 = 266$kg ...(iv)

Subtracting equation (i) from (iv)

Weight of Govinda $= 266 - 195 = 71$ kg

17. (c) Total revenues of 9 years
$= 9 \times 68 = 612$ lakhs
Total revenues of first 5 years
$= 5 \times 63 = 315$ lakhs
Total revenues of last 5 years
$= 5 \times 75 = 375$ lakhs
The revenues of 5th year
$= 315 + 375 - 612$
$= 690 - 612 = 78$ lakhs
Hence, the volume of 5th year is ₹ 78 lakhs.

18. (d) Total weight of 39 girls
$= 60 \times 39$ kg
$= 2340$ kg
Total weight of full class
$= 64 \times 65$
$= 4160$ kg
Average weight of boys

$$= \frac{4160 - 2340}{26}$$

$$= \frac{1820}{26} = 70 \text{ kg.}$$

19. (b) Mean of Marks

$$= \frac{55 \times 58 + 45 \times 54 + 75 \times 52}{55 + 45 + 75}$$

$$= \frac{3190 + 2430 + 3900}{175}$$

$$= \frac{9520}{175} = 54.4$$

20. (d) Let three numbers be x_1, x_2 and x_3
Total sum of three numbers

$$x_1 + x_2 + x_3 = 64 \times 3 = 192 \quad \text{...(i)}$$

$$x_1 = \frac{1}{3}(x_2 + x_3)$$

$$3x_1 = x_2 + x_3 \quad \text{...(ii)}$$

On putting, $x_2 + x_3 = 3x_1$ in (i)

$$x_1 + 3x_1 = 192$$

$$4x_1 = 192$$

$$x_1 = \frac{192}{4} = 48$$

5 PERCENTAGE

Percent: 'Per cent' means 'per hundred' or 'out of hundred'. We denote it by the symbol %.

Percentage: By a certain percentage, we means that many hundredths.

Examples: (i) $x\% = \frac{x}{100}$

(ii) $10 = \frac{10}{100} = \frac{1}{10}$

Important Points:

- To express a fraction as a per cent, multiply it by 100.

Examples: (i) $\frac{2}{5} = \left(\frac{2}{5} \times 100\right)\% = 40\%$

(ii) $\frac{3}{7} = \left(\frac{3}{7} \times 100\right)\% = \frac{300}{7} = 42\frac{6}{7}\%$

- To convert a percentage into a fraction, we divide it by 100 and remark the % sign.

Examples: (i) $12\% = \frac{12}{100} = \frac{6}{50} = \frac{3}{25}$

(ii) $25\% = \frac{25}{100} = \frac{1}{4}$

- A percentage can be expressed as a ratio with its second term 100 and first term equal to the given percentage.

Examples: (i) $24\% = \frac{24}{100} = \frac{6}{25} = 6:25$

(ii) $18\% = \frac{18}{100} = 9:50$

- To express a given ratio as a per cent, convert the given ratio into a fraction, and then multiply the fraction by 100.

Examples: (i) $4:5 = \left(\frac{4}{5} \times 100\right)\% = 80\%$

(ii) $5:8 = \left(\frac{5}{8} \times 100\right)\% = \frac{125}{2}\% = 62\frac{1}{2}\%$

- To express a given percentage as a decimal, divide it by 100 and then convert it into decimal form.

Examples: (i) $8\% = \frac{8}{100} = \frac{2}{25} = 0.08$

(ii) $20\% = \frac{20}{100} = \frac{1}{5} = 0.2$

- To express a given decimal as a per cent, multiply it by 100.

Examples: (i) 0.25 = (0.25 × 100)% = 25

(ii) 0.02 = (0.02 × 100)% = 2%

Important General Formulae:

1. Let P be the population of a town at present. If it increases at r% per annum, then,

   (i) Population after n years = $P\left(1+\frac{r}{100}\right)^n$

   (ii) Population of town n years ago = $P\left(1-\frac{r}{100}\right)^n$

2. Let the present value of a machine be ₹ P and it depreciate at r% per annum. Then,

   (i) Value of the machine after n years = ₹ $\left[P\left(1+\frac{r}{100}\right)^n\right]$

   (ii) Value of the machine n years ago = ₹ $\left[P\left(1-\frac{r}{100}\right)^n\right]$

3. (i) Increase per cent = $\left(\frac{\text{Increase in value}}{\text{original value}} \times 100\right)\%$

   (ii) Decrease per cent = $\left(\frac{\text{Decrease in value}}{\text{original value}} \times 100\right)\%$

Note: The change in value is always calculated on the original value.

Solved Examples

Example 1: 15% of a number is 40. Find the number.

Sol. Let the required number be x.

Then, $x \times \frac{15}{100} = 40$

$$\Rightarrow x = \left(\frac{40 \times 100}{25}\right) = 160$$

Example 2: An contains 16% Zine. How many kg of the are will be required to get 48% Zine ?

Sol. Let the required by x kg

Then, $\frac{16}{100} \times x = 48$

$$\Rightarrow x = \left(\frac{48 \times 100}{16}\right) \text{kg} = 300 \text{ kg}$$

Example 3: The price of a fen increases from ₹ 860 to ₹ 989. Find the increase percent in its price.

Sol. Increase = ₹ (989 – 860) = ₹ 129

∴ Increase percent

$$= \left(\frac{129}{860} \times 100\right)\% = 15\%$$

Example 4: Find the number which when increased by 10% becomes 660.

Sol. Let the number be x.

$$\therefore \left(x + x \times \frac{10}{100}\right) = 660$$

$$\Rightarrow \left(x + \frac{1}{10}x\right) = 660$$

$\Rightarrow 11x = (660 \times 10)$

$\Rightarrow x = 600$

Exercise

1. A student multiplied a number by 11/13 instead of 13/11. What is the percentage error in the calculation ?
(a) 39.67 percent
(b) 28.4 percent
(c) 14.2 percent
(d) 19.83 percent

2. When a number is increased by 26, it becomes 113% of itself. What is the number?
(a) 200
(b) 312
(c) 390
(d) 234

3. An engineering student has to secure 25% marks to pass. He gets 56 and fails by 34 marks. Find the maximum marks.
(a) 385 marks
(b) 360 marks
(c) 410 marks
(d) 435 marks

4. A student multiplied a number by 6/7 instead of 7/6. What is the percentage error in the calculation?
(a) 36.11 percent
(b) 26.53 percent
(c) 13.27 percent
(d) 18.06 percent

5. When a number is increased by 34, it becomes 117% of itself. What is the number ?
(a) 408
(b) 200
(c) 510
(d) 306

6. Two students appeared for an examination. One of them secured 10 marks more than the other and his marks were 75% of the sum of their marks. The marks obtained by them are :
(a) 52 and 42
(b) 68 and 58
(c) 63 and 53
(d) 15 and 5

7. When a number is increased by 42, it becomes 121% of itself. What is the number ?
(a) 504
(b) 200
(c) 630
(d) 378

8. If 25% of an electricity bill is deducted, ₹ 1788 is still to be paid. How much was the bill ?
(a) ₹ 1430
(b) ₹ 2420
(c) ₹ 1466
(d) ₹ 2384

9. Daily local train ticket costs ₹ 30 and Monthly Pass costs ₹ 670.8. If I buy the Monthly Pass and travel for 26 days in a month than I save ?
(a) 12 percent
(b) 14 percent
(c) 25 percent
(d) 10 percent

10. When a number is increased by 18, it becomes 106% of itself. What is the number ?
(a) 300
(b) 216
(c) 270
(d) 162

11. A man spends 59% of his income and saves the rest. What percentage of his expenditure does he save?
(a) 72.57 percent
(b) 83.19 percent
(c) 89.09 percent
(d) 69.49 percent

12. Two students appeared for an examination. One of them secured 24 marks more than the other and his marks were 65% of the sum of their marks. The marks obtained by them are.
(a) 78 and 54
(b) 85 and 61
(c) 67 and 43
(d) 52 and 28

13. Two numbers are 35% and 50% lesser than a third number. By how much percent is the second number

to be enhanced to make it equal to the first number ?

(a) 23.08 percent

(b) 15 percent

(c) 25 percent

(d) 30 percent

14. Two students appeared for an examination. One of them secured 21 marks more than the other and his marks were 80% of the sum of their marks. The marks obtained by them are

(a) 88 and 67

(b) 89 and 68

(c) 28 and 7

(d) 98 and 77

15. A student multiplied a number by 6/13 instead of 13/6. What is the percentage error in the calculation?

(a) 369.44 percent

(b) 39.35 percent

(c) 184.72 percent

(d) 78.7 percent

16. When a number is increased by 24, it becomes 110% of itself. What is the number?

(a) 288 (b) 360

(c) 216 (d) 240

Answers with Explanations

1. (b) Let the number be x.

$$\% \text{ error} = \frac{\frac{13}{11}x - \frac{11}{13}x}{\frac{13}{11}x} \times 100\%$$

$$= \frac{\frac{48}{11 \times 13}x}{\frac{13}{11}x} \times 100\%$$

$$= \frac{48x \times 11}{11 \times 13 \times 13} \times 100\%$$

$$= \frac{4800}{169}\% = 28.4\%$$

2. (a) Let the number be x

According to question

$$x + 26 = x \times \frac{113}{100}$$

$$100x + 2600 = 113x$$

$$113x - 100x = 2600$$

$$13x = 2600$$

$$x = \frac{2600}{13} = 200$$

3. (b) Let maximum marks be x

$$\frac{25}{100}x = 56 + 34 = 90$$

$$x = \frac{90 \times 100}{25} = 360 \text{ marks}$$

4. (b) Let the number be x

$$\text{Percentage error} = \frac{\frac{7}{6}x - \frac{6}{7}x}{\frac{7}{6}x} \times 100\%$$

$$= \frac{49x - 36x}{\frac{7}{6}x \times 42} \times 100\%$$

$$= \frac{13 \times 6x}{7x \times 42} \times 100\%$$

$$= \frac{1300}{49}\%$$

$$= 26.53\%$$

5. (b) Let the number be x

$$x + 34 = \frac{117}{100} \text{ of } x$$

$$\Rightarrow \frac{117}{100}x - x = 34$$

$$\Rightarrow \frac{17x}{100} = 34$$

$$\Rightarrow x = \frac{3400}{17} = 200$$

6. (d) Let first student get x marks and second $(x + 10)$ marks

$$x = \frac{75}{100}(x + x + 10)$$

$$10 + x = \frac{3}{4}(2x + 10)$$

$$40 + 4x = 6x + 30$$

$$10 = 2x \Rightarrow x = 5$$

Their marks were 5 and 15.

7. (b) Let the number be x.

$\therefore$ According to question,

$$x + 42 = \frac{121}{100} \times x$$

$$\frac{121x}{100} - x = 42$$

$$\frac{21x}{100} = 42$$

$$x = \frac{42 \times 100}{21} = 200$$

Finally, the number is 200.

8. (d) Let the amount of bill be ₹ x.

$$x - \frac{25}{100}x = 1788$$

$$\frac{3x}{4} = 1788$$

$$x = \frac{1788 \times 4}{3} = 2384$$

The bill was ₹ 2384.

9. (b) Cost of ticket for 26 days

= ₹ 30 × 26

= ₹ 780

Cost of monthly pass = 780 – 670·8 = 109·2

$$\text{Saving\%} = \frac{109{\cdot}2 \times 100}{780} = 14\%.$$

10. (a) Let a number be x

$$x + 18 = \frac{106}{100}x$$

$$\frac{106}{100}x - x = 18$$

$$\frac{106x - 100x}{100} = 18$$

$$6x = 18 \times 100$$

$$x = 300.$$

11. (d) Saving % = 100 – 59 = 41%.

% of saving to expenditure to save.

$$= \frac{41 \times 100}{59} = 69{\cdot}49\%.$$

12. (d) Let the number of marks of other student be x

Then one student gets $= x + 24$
According to question

$$x + 24 = \frac{65}{100}(2x + 24)$$

$$= \frac{13}{20}(2x + 24)$$

$20x + 24 \times 20 = 26x + 24 \times 13$
$6x = 7 \times 24$

$$x = \frac{7 \times 24}{6} = 28$$

Marks of other student $= 28 + 24 = 52$

13. (d) Required % $= \frac{(50 - 35)}{50} \times 100\%$

$$= \frac{15 \times 100}{50} = 15 \times 2 = 30\%$$

14. (c) Let one student get x marks another get $(x + 21)$ marks

According to question,

$$x + 21 = \frac{80}{100}(x + x + 21)$$

$$x + 21 = \frac{4}{5}(2x + 21)$$

$5x + 105 = 8x + 84$
$3x = 105 - 84 = 21$

$$x = \frac{21}{3} = 7$$

Marks of another student
$= 21 + 7 = 28$

Hence, their marks are 28 and 7.

15. (d) Let number be x
Percentage error

$$= \frac{\left(\frac{13}{6}x - \frac{6}{13}x\right) \times 100}{13/6x}$$

$$= \frac{\frac{169x - 36x}{78}}{13x/6} \times 100$$

$$= \frac{133 \times 6 \times 100}{78 \times 13}$$

$$= \frac{133 \times 100}{169} = 78.7\%$$

16. (d) Let the number be x
According to question

$$x + 24 = \frac{110}{100}x$$

$$\Rightarrow \quad x + 24 = \frac{11x}{10}$$

$10(x + 24) = 11x$
$11x - 10x = 240$
$x = 240$

6 PROFIT, LOSS AND DISCOUNT

- **Cost price (C.P.):** The price at which an article is purchased is called its cost price.
- **Selling price (S.P.):** The price at which an article is sold is called its selling price.
- If selling price > cost price, there is a gain

  $\therefore$ Gain = (S.P. – C.P.)
- If selling price < cost price, there is a loss

  $\therefore$ Loss = (C.P. – S.P.)

  Note: Loss or gain is always reckoned on cost price.

Important General Formulae:

(i) Gain percent $= \left(\dfrac{\text{Gain}}{\text{cost price}} \times 100\right)\%$

(ii) Loss percent $= \left(\dfrac{\text{loss}}{\text{cost price}} \times 100\right)\%$

(iii) Cost price $= \dfrac{100}{(100 \pm \text{gain or loss\%})} \times \text{selling price}$

(iv) Selling price $= \dfrac{(100 \pm \text{gain or loss\%})}{100} \times \text{cost price}$

Note: Use '+' for gain and '–' for loss.

- **Marked price:** In big shops and departmental stores every article is togged with a card and its price written on it. This is called the marked price of that article, abbreviated as M.P.
- **Discount:** In order to give boost to the sale of item or to clear the old stock, sometimes the shopkeepers offer a certain percentage of rebate on the marked price. This rebate is known as discount.

  Note: Discount is always recognised on the marked price list price.
- **Successive discounts:** Suppose 40% discount is given on the marked price of an article and further a discount of 10% is given on the reduced price. Then, we say that successive discounts of 30% and 20% are given on the article.

(i) Discount = marked price – selling price

(ii) Discount percent $= \dfrac{\text{Discount}}{\text{marked price}} \times 100\%$

(iii) Selling price = marked price – discount

Solved Examples

Example 1: If selling price is doubled, the profit triples. Find the profit percent.

Sol. Let cost price be ₹ x and selling price be ₹ y.

Then, Profit = $(y - x)$

According to question

$$3(y - x) = 2y - x$$
$$\Rightarrow \quad 3y - 3x = 2y - x$$
$$\Rightarrow \quad y = 2x$$
$$\therefore \quad \text{Profit} = (2x - x) = ₹\ x$$
$$\therefore \text{ Profit percent } = \left(\frac{x}{x} \times 100\right)\% = 100\%$$

Example 2: The ratio of cost price and selling price of an article is 20 : 21. What is the profit percent on it?

Sol. Let the cost price be ₹ $20x$ and selling price be ₹ $21x$.

$$\therefore \text{ Profit} = ₹\ (21x - 20x) = ₹\ x$$
$$\therefore \text{ Profit percent } = \left(\frac{x}{20x} \times 100\right)\% = 5\%$$

Example 3: Roni bought a purse for ₹ 500. How much should she sell it to gain 16%?

Sol. Selling price of purse $= \dfrac{(100+16)}{100} \times 500$

$$= \left(\frac{116}{100} \times 500\right) = ₹\ 580$$

Example 4: Cost price of 11 apples is equal to the selling price of 10 apples. Find the profit percent.

Sol. Profit percent

$$= \frac{(11-10)}{10} \times 100\% = \left(\frac{1}{10} \times 100\right)\% = 10\%$$

Exercise

1. Marked price of an item is ₹ 800. On purchase of 1 item discount is 15%, on purchase of 4 items discount is 38%. Rajshri buys 5 items, what is the effective discount.
(a) 33.4 percent (b) 16 percent
(c) 9 percent (d) 17.5 percent
2. Rajesh sells a machine for ₹ 57 lakhs at a loss. Had he sold it for ₹ 67 lakh, his gain would have been 7 times the former loss. Find the cost price of the machine.
(a) ₹ 58.25 lakhs (b) ₹ 65.75 lakhs
(c) ₹ 75.14 lakhs (d) ₹ 50.75 lakhs
3. If 2 pairs of trouser is offered free on purchase of 3 pairs of trousers priced ₹ 900 each what is the effective discount on each pair of trouser?
(a) 40 percent (b) 33.33 percent
(c) 30 percent (d) 20 percent
4. Marked price of an item is ₹ 900. On purchase of 2 items discount is 6%, on purchase of 3 items discount is 12%. Rajani buys 5 items, what is the effective discount?
(a) 17.5 percent (b) 9.6 percent
(c) 35 percent (d) 37 percent
5. When a number is increased by 21, it becomes 114% of itself. What is the number?
(a) 150 (b) 252
(c) 315 (d) 189
6. The total cost of a microwave oven with mixer was ₹ 36750. The mixer was sold at a profit of 32% and the microwave oven at a loss of 22%. If the sale price was the same in both the items, then the cost price of the cheaper item was ....
(a) ₹ 13100 (b) ₹ 18375
(c) ₹ 13650 (d) ₹ 16850
7. A rice trader buys 16 quintals of rice for ₹ 5632. 20% rice is lost in transportation. At what rate should he sell to earn 25% profit?
(a) ₹ 225.2 per quintal
(b) ₹ 550 per quintal
(c) ₹ 440 per quintal
(d) ₹ 563.2 per quintal
8. A rice trader buys 20 quintals of rice for ₹ 8,580. However, 22% rice is lost in transportation. At what rate should he sell to earn 20% profit?
(a) ₹ 278.8 per quintal
(b) ₹ 514.8 per quintal
(c) ₹ 660 per quintal
(d) ₹ 654.2 per quintal
9. 30% discount is offered on an item. By applying a promo code the customer wins 20% cash back. What is the effective discount?
(a) 44 percent (b) 52.8 percent
(c) 50 percent (d) 26 percent
10. A wholesaler sells a watch to a retailer at a gain of 35% and the retailer sells it to a customer at a loss of 25%. If the customer pays ₹ 2379.375, what had it cost the wholesaler?
(a) ₹ 2350 (b) ₹ 2409
(c) ₹ 2928 (d) ₹ 2291
11. The price of an article is cut by 24%, to restore to its original value, the new price must he increased by ....
(a) 24 percent (b) 19.35 percent
(c) 30 percent (d) 31.58 percent
12. If 2 shirts are offered free on purchase of 3 shirts priced ₹ 600 each, then what will be the effective discount on each shirt ?
(a) 30 percent (b) 66.67 percent
(c) 40 percent (d) 25 percent
13. A rice trader buys 12 quintals of rice for ₹ 1,870. 15% rice is lost in transportation. At what rate should he sell to earn 20% profit ?
(a) ₹ 110.3 per quintal
(b) ₹ 187 per quintal
(c) ₹ 220 per quintal
(d) ₹ 224 per quintal
14. If 1 shirt is offered free on purchase of 3 shirts priced ₹ 500 each, then what is the effective discount on each shirt?
(a) 30 percent (b) 33 percent
(c) 20 percent (d) 25 percent
15. The total cost of a washing machine with an electric chimney was ₹ 57,750. The electric chimney was sold at a profit of 34% and the washing machine at a loss of 24%. If the sale price was the same in both the items, then the cost price of the cheaper item was ....
(a) ₹ 26850 (b) ₹ 20900
(c) ₹ 28875 (d) ₹ 25850
16. Ticket for an adult is ₹ 500 and a child is ₹ 200. 1 child goes free with two adults. If a group has 20 adults and 8 children what will be the discount the group get ?
(a) 53.43 percent (b) 13.79 percent
(c) 32.2 percent (d) 35.06 percent
17. 30% discount is offered on an item. By applying a promo code, the customer wins 5% cash back. What is the effective discount ?
(a) 33.5 percent (b) 35.175 percent
(c) 35 percent (d) 6.5 percent
18. A shopkeeper by selling 8 iphones, earns a profit equal to the selling price of 3 iphones. His profit percentage is :
(a) 60 percent (b) 37.5 percent
(c) 75 percent (d) 15 percent
19. A shopkeeper by selling 23 Lotto shoes, earns a profit equal to the selling price of 7 Lotto shoes. His profit percentage is :
(a) 43.75 percent (b) 30.4 percent
(c) 60.8 percent (d) 17.05 percent
20. 30% discount is offered on an item. By applying a promo code the customer wins 10% cash back. What is the effective discount ?
(a) 40.7 percent (b) 40 percent
(c) 37 percent (d) 13 percent
21. Ticket for an adult is ₹ 1200 and a child is ₹ 800 respectively. One child goes free with two adults. If a group has 25 adults and 5 children what is the discount the group gets ?
(a) 17.24 percent (b) 24 percent
(c) 24.41 percent (d) 11.76 percent

22. Rajan sells a machine for ₹ 52 lakhs at a loss. Had he sold it for ₹ 62 lakh, his gain would have been 9 times the former loss. What is the cost price of the machine ?

(a) ₹ 61 lakhs (b) ₹ 53 lakhs
(c) ₹ 67.77 lakhs (d) ₹ 45 lakhs

23. A shopkeeper, sold cocoa seeds at the rate ₹ 1,230 per kg and bears a loss of 5%. Now if he decides to sell it at ₹ 1,353 per kg, what will be the result ?

(a) 4.76 percent gain
(b) 9 percent gain
(c) 4.5 percent loss
(d) 9 percent loss

24. If a merchant offers a discount of 20% on the list price, then he makes a loss of 10%. What % profit or % loss will she make if he sells at a discount of 5% of the list price ?

(a) 6.875 percent profit
(b) 20 percent profit
(c) 14 percent profit
(d) 30 percent loss

25. A trader had 16 quintals of wheat. He sold a part of it at 17% profit and the rest at 27% profit, so that he made a total profit of 21%. How much wheat did he sell at 27% profit?

(a) 960 kg (b) 640 kg
(c) 320 kg (d) 1280 kg

Answers with Explanations

1. (a) S.P. of 1 item $= 800 \times \frac{85}{100} = ₹680$

S.P. of 4 items $= 3200 \times \frac{100-38}{100}$

$= 3200 \times \frac{62}{100} = 1984$

S.P. of 5 items = ₹ 4000

$\therefore$ effective discount %

$= \frac{4000-(1984+680)}{4000} \times 100$

$= \frac{4000-2664}{4000} \times 100$

$= 33.4\%$

2. (a) Let cost price be x of machine

S.P. = 57 lakhs

Loss = CP – SP = $x - 57$

S.P. – C.P. = gain = $7(x-57)$

$67 - x = 7(x-57)$

$67 - x = 7x - 399$

$8x = 67 + 399 = 466$

$x = \frac{466}{8} = ₹ 58.25$ lakhs

3. (a) 3 pairs of trousers + 2 pair + trousers = ₹ 900

5 pairs of trousers = 900

1 pair of trousers $= \frac{900}{5} = ₹ 180$

5 pair of trousers = 300 × 5

= ₹ 1500

Effective discount %

$= \left(\frac{1500-900}{1500}\right) \times 100\%$

$= \frac{600}{1500} \times 100 = 40$ percent

4. (b) C.P. of 2 items

$= \frac{(100-6)}{100} \times 900 \times 2$

$= 94 \times 9 \times 2 = ₹\ 846 \times 2 = ₹1692$

C.P. of 3 items $= \frac{(100-12)}{100} \times 900 \times 3$

$= 88 \times 9 \times 3 = ₹\ 792 \times 3$

$= ₹\ 2376$

Total C.P. of Rajani = 1692 + 2376

= ₹ 4068

Total price with out discount

= 900 × 5 = ₹ 4500

Discount = (4500 – 4068) = ₹ 432

Effective Distance %

$= \frac{432 \times 100}{4500} = 9.6\%$

5. (a) Let the number be x

$x + 21 = \frac{114x}{100}$

$21 = \frac{114x - 100x}{100}$

$14x = 2100$

$x = \frac{2100}{14} = \frac{300}{2} = 150$

6. (c) Let the cost price of mixer be x and microwave be $(36750 - x)$

According to question.

$\frac{(100+32)}{100}x = \frac{(100-22)}{100}(36750-x)$

$132x = 78(36750 - x)$

$132x + 78x = 78 \times 36750$

$210x = 78 \times 36750$

$x = \frac{78 \times 36750}{210}$

$= 78 \times 175 = 13650$

The cost price of mixer is ₹ 13650 and the cost price of microwave = 36750 – 13650 = ₹ 23100

The cost price of the cheaper item mixer is ₹ 13650

7. (b) C.P. of 16 quintal rice = ₹ 5632

Left rice $= \frac{16 \times 80}{100} = 12.8$ quintal

S.P. of rice

$= \frac{5632 \times (100+25)}{100}$

$= \frac{5632 \times 125}{100} = \frac{5632 \times 5}{4}$

$= 1408 \times 5 = ₹\ 7040$

Rate of selling rice $= \frac{7040}{12.8} = ₹\ 550$ per quintal

8. (c) Cost price of 20 quintal rice

= ₹ 8580

left rice $= 20 \times \frac{78}{100} = \frac{1560}{100}$

= 15.60 quintal

The trader wants 20% profit,

$SP = \frac{120}{100} \times 8580$

$= 858 \times 12 = ₹\ 10296$

Rate/quintal of rice

$= \frac{10296}{15.60} = \frac{102960}{156}$

$= ₹ 660$ per quintal

9. (a) Let M.P. be ₹ 100

S.P. of an article

$= \frac{100-30}{100} \times 100 = ₹ 70$

Now again 20% discount is given

Then

$S.P. = \frac{100-20}{100} \times 70 = \frac{80 \times 70}{100} = 56$

Hence, effective discount $= (100-56)\%$

$= 44$ percent

10. (a) $W \xrightarrow{35\%} R \xrightarrow{-25\%} C$

Let C.P. of a wholesaler be x

$S.P. = \frac{100+35}{100}x = \frac{135x}{100}$

$S.P. \text{ for retailer} = \frac{135x}{100} \times \frac{100-25}{100}$

$2379.375 = \frac{135x}{100} \times \frac{3}{4}$

$x = \frac{2379.375 \times 100 \times 4}{3 \times 135}$

$= \frac{237937.5 \times 400}{3 \times 135} = 587.5 \times 4$

$= 2350.0$

Hence, the cost price of a watch is ₹ 2350.

11. (d) Let the cost price of an article be x

After 24% discount

$= x \times \frac{100-24}{100} = \frac{76}{100}x$

Increased price of an article

$= x - \frac{76}{100}x = \frac{24}{100}x$

$\text{Required increased \%} = \frac{\frac{24}{100}x}{\frac{76}{100}x} \times 100\%$

$= \frac{2400}{76} = \frac{600}{19}$

$= 31.58\%$

12. (c) Cost price of each shirt

$= \frac{₹ 600}{3} = ₹ 200$

Cost price of 5 shirts

$= ₹ 200 \times 5 = ₹ 100$

$\text{Profit} = ₹ 1000 - ₹ 600$

$= ₹ 400$

$\text{Effective percent} = \frac{400 \times 100\%}{1000} = 40\%$

13. (c) Left quantity of rice

$= 12 \times \frac{100-15}{100}$

$= \frac{12 \times 85}{100} = \frac{1020}{100}$

$= 10 \cdot 20$ quintals

$S.P. \text{ at } 20\% \text{ profit} = \frac{120}{100} \times 1870$

$= 12 \times 187 = ₹ 2244$

$\text{Selling price per quintal} = \frac{2244}{10 \cdot 20}$

$= \frac{22440}{102}$

$= ₹ 220$ per quintal

14. (d) Selling price of three shirts

$= 3 \times 500 = ₹ 1500$

Selling price of four shirts

$= 4 \times 500 = ₹ 2000$

$\text{Discount} = 2000 - 1500 = 500$

$\text{Effective \%} = \frac{500 \times 100}{2000} = 25\%$

15. (b) Let the cost of washing machine be x and the cost of chimney

$= 57750 - x$

According to question,

$\frac{100-24}{100}x = (57750 - x) \times \frac{134}{100}$

$\frac{76}{100}x = (57750 - x) \times \frac{134}{100}$

$76x = 57750 \times 134 - 134x$

$134x + 76x = 57750 \times 134$

$210x = 57750 \times 134$

$x = \frac{57750 \times 134}{210} = 36850$

Cost of washing machine = ₹ 36850

Cost of chimney = ₹ 57750 − 36850

= ₹ 20900

The chimney is cheaper = ₹ 20900

16. (b) 20 cost of tickets of adults and 8 children with discount

= 16 adults + 8 children + 4 adults

= 8 (2 adults + 1 child) + 4 adults

$= 8 \times (2 \times 500) + 4 \times 500$

$= 8000 + 2000$

$= ₹ 10000$

Without discount cost of tickets

= 20 adults + 8 children

$= 20 \times 500 + 8 \times 200$

$= 10000 + 1600 = ₹ 11600$

$\text{Discount} = 11600 - 10000$

$= ₹ 1600$

$\text{Discount \%} = \frac{1600 \times 100\%}{11600}$

$= \frac{1600}{116} = 13.79\%$

17. (a) After 30% discount on an item the price is 70.

Applying 5% cash back, the price is

$= \frac{70 \times 5}{100} = 3.5$

$\therefore$ The effective discount $= 30 + 3.5$

$= 33.5\%$

18. (a) $\text{Profit} = (8-3) = 5$

$\therefore \text{Profit percentage} = \frac{3 \times 100}{5} = 60\%$

19. (a) Shopkeeper's profit $= (23-7) = 16$

$\text{Profit Percentage} = \frac{7 \times 100}{16} = 43 \cdot 75\%$

20. (c) On 30% discount the price of item,

$= 100 - 30 = 70$

$\therefore$ Applying promo the price of item

$= \frac{70 \times 10}{100} = 7$

Finally the effective discount

$= 30 + 7 = 37\%$.

21. (d) Price of tickets with discount 25 adults + 5 children

(10 adults + 5 children) + 15 adults

$= 10 \times 1200 + 15 \times 1200$

$= 12000 + 18000$

$= ₹ 30000.$

Without Discount

$= 25 \times 1200 + 5 \times 800$

$= 30000 + 4000$

$= ₹ 34000.$

Discount %

$$= \left(\frac{34000 - 30000}{34000}\right) \times 100\%$$

$$= \frac{4000 \times 100}{34000}\% = \frac{200}{17}$$

$= 11{\cdot}76\%$.

22. (b) Let the loss be ₹ x.

Then gain = $9x$

S.P. = C.P. – Loss

C.P. = S.P. + Loss

$= 5200000 + x$ ...(i)

Again S.P. = C.P. + gain

$5200000 = \text{C.P.} + 9x$

C.P. $= 6200000 - 9x$ ...(ii)

From equation (i) and (ii)

$5200000 + x = 6200000 - 9x$

$10x = 6200000 - 5200000$

$= 10{,}00000$

$$x = \frac{1000000}{10} = 100000$$

The cost price of machine

= C.P. + x

$= 5200000 + 100000$

$= 5300000 =$ ₹ 53 Lakhs.

23. (a) Loss on selling of cocoa seeds

$$= ₹\,1230 \times \frac{5}{100}$$

$=$ ₹ $61{\cdot}50$.

C.P. = S.P. + Loss

$= 1230 + 61{\cdot}50$

$=$ ₹ $1291{\cdot}5$.

If he sells for ₹ 1353

S.P. > C.P. he will get profit

Profit = S.P. – C.P.

$= 1353 - 1291{\cdot}50$

$= 61{\cdot}5$

Profit % =

$$\frac{61{\cdot}5 \times 100}{1291{\cdot}5} = \frac{61500}{12915}$$

$= 4{\cdot}76\%$ gain.

24. (a) Let the M.P. of article be x

$$\text{S.P.} = \frac{x \times 80}{100} = \frac{4}{5}x$$

$$\text{S.P.} = \frac{\text{C.P.} \times 90}{100} = \frac{9}{10}\text{C.P.}$$

$$\frac{4}{5}x = \frac{9}{10}\text{C.P.}$$

$$\text{C.P.} = \frac{40}{45}x = \frac{8}{9}x$$

S.P. of 5% discount

$$= \frac{95}{100}x = \frac{19}{20}x$$

S.P. > C.P.

$$\text{Profit\%} = \frac{\left(\frac{19}{20}x - \frac{8}{9}x\right)}{\frac{8}{9}x} \times 100\%$$

$$= \frac{\left(\frac{171x - 160x}{180}\right) \times 100\%}{\frac{8}{9}x}$$

$$= \frac{11x \times 9 \times 100\%}{180 \times 8x} = 6{\cdot}875\%$$

25. (b) Let he sells x quintals at ₹ 17%.

According to question,

$$\frac{x \times 117}{100} + \frac{(16 - x) \times 127}{100}$$

$$= \frac{16 \times 121}{100}$$

$$\frac{117x - 127x}{100} = \frac{16 \times 121}{100} - \frac{16 \times 127}{100}$$

$$\frac{-10x}{100} = -\frac{16 \times 6}{100}$$

$$x = \frac{960}{10} = 9{\cdot}6 \text{ quintals}$$

$= 9{\cdot}60 \times 100$

$= 960$ kg

Quantity sold at 27%

$= 1600 - 960 = 640$ kg

7 RATIO AND PROPORTION

Ratio: The ratio of any number a to any other number b is expressed as $a \div b$ or $\frac{a}{b}$ or $a : b$.

In the ratio $a : b$, we call a as the first term or antecedent and b, the second term or consequent.

Note: The multiplication or division of each term of a ratio by the same non-zero number does not affect the ratio.

Example: $3 : 2 = 6 : 4 = 9 : 6$ etc.

Types of Ratios:

(i) **Compound ratio:** When two or more ratios are multiplied together, they are said to be compound ratio.

Example: If $\frac{a}{b}$ and $\frac{c}{d}$ are ratios, then $\frac{ac}{bd}$ is their compound ratio.

(ii) **Duplicate ratio:** When a ratio is compounded with itself, the resulting ratio is called the duplicate ratio.

Example: $a^2 : b^2$ is duplicate ratio of $a : b$

so, $16 : 9$ is duplicate ratio of $4 : 3$

(iii) **Sub-Duplicate ratio:** If a square root is applied on a ratio, the result is called sub-duplicate ratio.

Example: If $a : b$ is ratio, then the sub-duplicate ratio is $\sqrt{a} : \sqrt{b}$. So, $\sqrt{9} : \sqrt{4}$ is sub-duplicative ratio of $9 : 4$.

(iv) **Triplicate ratio:** If a ratio is compounded three times, it is called triplicate ratio.

So, $a^3 : b^3$ is the triplicate ratio of $a : b$

Example: Triplicate ratio of $4 : 5$ is $(4)^3 : (5)^3 = 64 : 125$.

(v) **Sub-Triplicate ratio:** If cube root is applied on a ratio, then result is called sub-triplicate ratio.

Example: If $a : b$ is ratio, then its sub triplicate ratio is $(a)^{1/3} : (b)^{1/3}$. So, $\sqrt[3]{8} : \sqrt[3]{27}$ is subtriplicate ratio of $8 : 27$.

(vi) **Reciprocal Ratio:** If $a : b$ is a ratio, then $\frac{1}{a} : \frac{1}{b}$ or $b : a$ is its reciprocal ratio.

Proportion: When two ratios are equal, then such an equality of two ratios is called proportion.

If $a : b = c : d$, we write $a : b :: c : d$ and we say that a, b, c, d are in proportion.

Note: a and d are called extremes and b and c are called means terms.

So, Product of means = Product of extremes

Thus, $a : b :: c : d \Rightarrow ad = bc$

- **Fourth proportional:** If $a : b = c : x$, then x is called the fourth proportional to a, b, c

$\therefore \quad ax = bc$

$\Rightarrow \; x = \frac{bc}{a}$

- **Third proportional :** If x is the third proportional to a, b, then

$a : b :: b : x$

$\Rightarrow \; b^2 = ax \Rightarrow b = \sqrt{ax}$

- **Mean proportional :** If x is the mean proportional to a, b, then

$a : x :: x : b$

$\Rightarrow x^2 = ab \Rightarrow x = \sqrt{ab}$

Note: If $a : b :: c : d$, then

$\frac{a+b}{b} = \frac{c+d}{d}$ (Componendo)

$\frac{a-b}{b} = \frac{c-d}{d}$ (Dividendo)

$\frac{a+b}{a-b} = \frac{c+d}{c-d}$ (Componendo and Dividendo)

Solved Examples

Example 1: Two numbers are in the ratio 5 : 6. On adding 5 to the first and 8 to the second, their ratio becomes 3 : 4. Find the numbers.

Sol. Let the required numbers be $5x$ and $6x$ respectively.

Then, $\frac{5x+5}{6x+8}=\frac{3}{4}$

$\Rightarrow 20x + 20 = 18x + 24$

$\Rightarrow 2x = 4 \Rightarrow x = 2$

$\therefore$ Numbers are (5 × 2) and (6 × 2) = 10 and 12

Example 2: If A : B = 4 : 5, B : C = 5 : 6, then find A : C.

Sol. $\frac{A}{C}=\left(\frac{A}{B}\times\frac{B}{C}\right)=\left(\frac{4}{5}\times\frac{5}{6}\right)=\frac{4}{6}=\frac{2}{3}$

$\therefore$ A : C = 2 : 3

Example 3: Express the ratio 125 : 275 in simplest form.

Sol. HCF of 125 and 275 = 25

$125 : 275 = \frac{125\div 25}{275\div 25}=\frac{5}{11}=5:11$

$\therefore$ Simplest form of 125 : 275 is 5 : 11.

Exercise

1. If $a : b$ = 5:8, find the value of $(6a-5b)/(a+2b)$.
(a) 10/21 (b) 21/10
(c) –21/10 (d) –10/21
2. The ratio of present ages of Ratna and Shantanu is 5:4. After 19 years the ratio of their ages will be 10:9. What is Ratna's present age?
(a) 19 (b) 15
(c) 9 (d) 72
3. If $(x+y):(x-y)=11:1$, find value of $(5x+3y)/(x-2y)$.
(a) 45/4 (b) 4/45
(c) – 45/4 (d) – 4/45
4. The third proportional of two numbers 4 and 28 is................... .
(a) 52 (b) 56
(c) 84 (d) 196
5. The sum of the ages of husband and wife at present is 100. Ten years ago the ratio of their ages was 9:7. What is the age of the husband?
(a) 45 years (b) 55 years
(c) 65 years (d) 40 years
6. The ratio of present ages of Ramaya and Saurabh is 8:7. After 10 years the ratio of their ages will be 12:11. What is Ramaya's present age?
(a) 20 (b) 14
(c) 63 (d) 45
7. Find two numbers such that their mean proportional is 12 and third proportional is 768.
(a) 3 and 24 (b) 3 and 48
(c) 6 and 48 (d) 6 and 24
8. Profit of ₹ 187200 has to be divided among three partners Amit, Brijmohan and Chiranjeev in the ratio 1 : 2 : 5. How much does Chiranjeev get ?
(a) ₹ 46800 (b) ₹ 23400
(c) ₹ 117000 (d) ₹ 58500
9. The third proportional of two numbers 7 and 21 is :
(a) 35 (b) 63
(c) 42 (d) 21
10. The sum of the ages of husband and wife at present is 60. Four years ago the ratio of their ages was 7 : 6. What is the age of the husband ?
(a) 28 years (b) 32 years
(c) 42 years (d) 38 years
11. The ratio of present ages of Rangitha and Shaheen is 6 : 5. After 12 years the ratio of their ages will be 7 : 6. What is Rangitha's present age?
(a) 60 (b) 55
(c) 72 (d) 28
12. If Girish's salary is 4/9 times of Harishankar's and Shirish's salary is 5/6 times of Harishankar's, what is the ratio of Girish's salary to Shirish's?
(a) 27:10 (b) 10:27
(c) 8:15 (d) 15:8
13. If $a:b$ = 3:8, find the value of $(5a-3b)/(2a+b)$.
(a) 9/14 (b) 14/9
(c) –9/14 (d) –14/9
14. Find two numbers such that their mean proportional is 8 and third proportional is 64.
(a) 4 and 8 (b) 8 and 16
(c) 8 and 8 (d) 4 and 16
15. The bus fare between two cities is increased in the ratio 5 : 11. Find the increase in the fare, if the original fare is ₹ 275.
(a) ₹ 605 (b) ₹ 121
(c) ₹ 330 (d) ₹ 242
16. The ratio of present ages of Ranjini and Shahid is 5:4. After 13 years the ratio of their ages will be 6:5. What is Ranjini's present age?
(a) 52 (b) 65
(c) 60 (d) 32
17. Find two numbers such that their mean proportional is 16 and third proportional is 1024.
(a) 4 and 32 (b) 4 and 64
(c) 8 and 64 (d) 8 and 32
18. If Giridhar's salary is 5/3 times of Hariraj's and Shaunak's is 2/3 times of Hariraj's, what is the ratio of Giridhar's salary to Shaunak's?
(a) 9 : 10 (b) 10 : 9
(c) 5 : 2 (d) 2 : 5
19. In an army selection process, the ratio of selected to unselected was 3:1. If 60 less had applied and 30 less selected, the ratio of selected to unselected would have been 5:1. How many candidates had applied for the process?
(a) 240 (b) 480
(c) 120 (d) 720
20. The third proportional of two numbers 9 and 15 is :
(a) 21 (b) 30
(c) 25 (d) 45

Answers with Explanations

1. (a) It is given that $a : b = 5 : 8$
$\Rightarrow a/b = 5/8$

Now $\dfrac{6a-5b}{a+2b} = \dfrac{6\frac{a}{b}-5}{\frac{a}{b}+2}$

$= \dfrac{6\times\frac{5}{8}-5}{\frac{5}{8}+2}$

$= \dfrac{(30-40)/8}{(5+16)/8}$

$= \dfrac{10}{21}$

Hence, ratio is 10/21

2. (a) Ratio of present ages of Ratna and shantanu is $5x$ and $4x$

$\dfrac{5x+19}{4x+19} = \dfrac{10}{9}$

$45x + 171 = 40x + 190$

$x = \dfrac{19}{5}$

Ratna's present age

$= 5x = 5 \times \dfrac{19}{5}$

= 19 years

3. (c) $\dfrac{x+y}{x-y} = \dfrac{11}{1}$

By using componendo and dividendo

$\dfrac{2x}{2y} = \dfrac{12}{10} = \dfrac{6}{5}$

$\dfrac{x}{y} = 6/5$

$\dfrac{5x+3y}{x-2y} = \dfrac{\left(5\frac{x}{y}+3\right)}{\left(\frac{x}{y}-2\right)}$

$= \dfrac{\left(5\times\frac{6}{5}+3\right)}{\frac{6}{5}-2}$

$= \dfrac{360+15}{6-10} = \dfrac{45}{-4} = -45/4$

4. (d) Let numbers be $4 : 28 :: 28 : x$

$\dfrac{4}{28} = \dfrac{28}{x}$

$x = \dfrac{28\times 28}{4} = 7\times 28$

$= 196$

5. (b) According to question

$H + W = 100 \Rightarrow H = 100 - W$

$\dfrac{H-10}{W-10} = \dfrac{9}{7}$

$7H - 70 = 9W - 90$

$7(100 - W) - 70 = 9W - 90$ ...(i)

From equation (i)

$700 - 7W - 70 = 9W - 90$

$700 + 90 - 70 = 9W + 7W$

$720 = 16W$

$W = 45$

Age of wife = 45 years

$H = 100 - W = 100 - 45 = 55$ years

Age of husband (H) = 55 years

6. (a) Let ages of Ramaya and Saurabh $= 8x$ and $7x$

According to question,

$\dfrac{8x+10}{7x+10} = \dfrac{12}{11}$

$88x + 110 = 84x + 120$

$4x = 10 \Rightarrow x = 2.5$

Hence, present age of Ramaya $= 8 \times 2.5 = 20$ years.

7. (b) Let two numbers be x and y

$\sqrt{xy} = 12$ (i)

$xy = 144$ (ii)

$x : y :: y : 768$

$\dfrac{x}{y} = \dfrac{y}{768}$

$y^2 = 768x = 768 \times \dfrac{144}{y}$

$y^3 = 768 \times 144$

$y = (16)^{3\times\frac{1}{3}} \times 3^{3\times\frac{1}{3}}$

$y = 16 \times 3 = 48$

$x = \dfrac{144}{y} = \dfrac{144}{48} = 3$

Hence, the numbers are 3 and 48.

8. (c) Given Ratio = 1 : 2 : 5

Sum of ratios = 1 + 2 + 5 = 8

Profit of Chiranjeev

$= \dfrac{5\times 187200}{8} = 5 \times 23400$

= ₹117000

9. (b) Let the third proportional number be x. According to question,

$7 : 21 :: 21 : x$

$7x = 21 \times 21$

$x = \dfrac{21\times 21}{7} = 63$

Finally, third proportional number is 63.

10. (b) Let the age of husband be x years.

The age of wife $= 60 - x$

Four years ago

$\dfrac{x-4}{60-x-4} = \dfrac{7}{6}$

$\dfrac{x-4}{56-x} = \dfrac{7}{6}$

$6x - 24 = 56 \times 7 - 7x$

$13x = 392 + 24$

$x = \dfrac{416}{13} = 32$ years

Age of husband = 32 years.

Age of wife = 60 – 32 = 28 years.

11. (c) Let present ages of Rangitha and Shaheen be $6x$ and $5x$.

According to question,

$\dfrac{6x+12}{5x+12} = \dfrac{7}{6}$

$36x + 72 = 35x + 84$

$36x - 35x = 84 - 72$

$x = 12$

Rangitha's present age = 6 × 12 = 72 years.

12. (c) Let Harishankar's salary be x

Girish's salary $= \dfrac{4}{9}x$

Shirish's salary $= \dfrac{5}{6}x$

Ratio of Girish's salary to Shirish's salary

$$= \frac{\frac{4}{5}x}{\frac{5}{6}x}$$

$$= \frac{4\times6}{5\times5} = \frac{24}{45} = \frac{8}{15}$$

$= 8:15.$

13. (c) $a:b = 3:8$

$\therefore \quad a/b = \frac{3}{8}$

$$\frac{5a-3b}{2a+b} = \frac{5\frac{a}{b}-3}{2\frac{a}{b}+1} = \frac{5\times\frac{3}{8}-3}{2\times\frac{3}{8}+1}$$

$$= \frac{15-24}{6+8} = \frac{-9}{14}$$

14. (d) Let two numbers be x and y

mean $= \sqrt{xy}$

$8 = \sqrt{xy}$

$64 = xy$ ...(i)

$x:y::y:64$

$\frac{x}{y} = \frac{y}{64}$ But, $x = \frac{64}{y}$

$\frac{64}{y^2} = \frac{y}{64}$

$y^3 = 64\times64 = 4\times4\times4\times4\times4\times4$

$\Rightarrow \quad y = 4\times4 = 16$

$\Rightarrow \quad xy = 64$

$\Rightarrow x\times16 = 64$

$\Rightarrow \quad x = \frac{64}{16} = 4$

Hence $x=4, y=16$ are the numbers.

15. (c) According to the question let new fare be x

$5:11 = 275:x$

$\frac{5}{11} = \frac{275}{x}$

$x = \frac{275\times11}{5}$

$= 55\times11 = 605$

Increased bus fare = 605 – 275 = ₹ 330

16. (b) Let present ages of Rajini and Shahid be $5x$ and $4x$.

According to question

$\frac{5x+13}{4x+13} = \frac{6}{5}$

$25x+65 = 24x+78$

$x = 78-65 = 13$

Present age of Rajini

$= 5\times13 = 65$ years

17. (b) Let numbers be x and y.

Mean = 16

$\sqrt{xy} = 16$

$\therefore$ Squaring both sides

$xy = 256$

$x = \frac{256}{y}$

$x:y::y:1024$

$\frac{x}{y} = \frac{y}{1024}$

From (i) and (ii)

$\frac{256/y}{y} = \frac{y}{1024}$

$\frac{256}{y^2} = \frac{y}{1024}$

$y^3 = 1024\times256$

$y = \sqrt[3]{16\times16\times16\times4\times4\times4}$

$y = 16\times4 = 64$

$\because \quad xy = 256$

$x\times64 = 256$

$x = \frac{256}{64} = 4$

Hence, the numbers are 4 and 64.

18. (c) According to question

Let Hariraj's salary be x

Girdhari's salary

$= \frac{5}{3}$ of Hariraj $= \frac{5}{3}x$ ...(i)

Shaunak's salary

$= \frac{2}{3}$ Hariraj $= \frac{2}{3}x$ ...(ii)

Ratio of Girdhari's salary to Shaunak's salary

$= \frac{5}{3}x : \frac{2}{3}x = 5:2$

19. (a) Let the number of candidates selected and unselected be $3x$ and x

No. of candidates applied

$= 3x + x = 4x$

$\frac{4x-60}{x-30} = \frac{5}{1}$

$5x-150 = 4x-60$

$x = 150-60 = 90$

Hence, number of candidates applied

$= 3x-30$

$= 3\times90-30$

$= 270-30 = 240$

20. (c) Let third proportional be x

$9:15::15:x$

$\frac{9}{15} = \frac{15}{x}$

$9x = 15\times15$

$x = \frac{15\times15}{9} = 5\times5 = 25$

Hence, third proportional is 25.

8 TIME AND WORK

- If a worker can finish a work in n days, then the worker's one day's work $= \frac{1}{n}$
- If a worker's 1 day's work $= \frac{1}{n}$, then the worker can finish the work in n days.
- If M_1 men can complete W_1 works in D_1 days and M_2 men can complete W_2 works in D_2 days, then there will be a general formula:

$$M_1D_1W_1 = M_2D_2W_2$$

- If M_1 men can do W_1 works in D_1 days working H_1 hours a day and M_2 men can do W_2 works in D_2 days working H_2 hours a day, then there will be a general formula:

$$\frac{M_1D_1H_1}{W_1} = \frac{M_2D_2H_2}{W_2}$$

Solved Examples

Example 1: Suresh is twice as good a workman as Ramesh and together they finish a piece of work in 18 days. In how many days will Suresh alone finish the work ?

Sol. (Suresh's 1 day's work) : (Ramesh's 1 day's work) = 2 : 1

$\therefore$ Suresh + Ramesh's 1 day's work $= \frac{1}{18}$

Suresh's 1 day's work $= \left(\frac{1}{18} \times \frac{2}{3}\right) = \frac{1}{27}$

Hence, Suresh alone can finish the work in 27 days.

Example 2: A and B together can finish a work in 8 days. A can do the same work on his own in 12 days. How long will B take to do the work by himself ?

Sol. (A + B)'s 1 day's work $= \frac{1}{8}$

A's 1 day's work $= \frac{1}{12}$

$\therefore$ B's 1 day's work $= \left(\frac{1}{8} - \frac{1}{12}\right) = \frac{1}{24}$

$\therefore$ B alone can finish the work in 24 days.

Example 3: To complete a work, P takes 50% more time than Q. If together they take 18 days to complete the work, how much time shall Q take to do it?

Sol. Let Q alone can do the work in x days

$\therefore$ P can do the work in $\frac{3}{2}x$ days.

According to question,

$$\frac{1}{x} + \frac{2}{3x} = \frac{1}{18}$$

$$\Rightarrow \frac{5}{3x} = \frac{1}{18} \Rightarrow x = 30 \text{ days}$$

Exercise

1. A carpenter can build a cupboard in 48 hours. After 12 hours he takes a break. What fraction of the cupboard is yet to be built?
(a) 0.4 (b) 0.5
(c) 0.75 (d) 0.25
2. Makarand works 2 times as fast as Samarjit. If Samarjit can complete a job alone in 27 days, then in how many days can they together finish the job?
(a) 6 days (b) 7 days
(c) 5 days (d) 9 days
3. Murad can do a piece of work in 33 hours. If he is joined by Joel who is 100% more efficient, in what time will they together finish the work?
(a) 4 hours (b) 6 hours
(c) 2 hours (d) 11 hours
4. Mahanath works 2 times as fast as Sahay. If Sahay can complete a job alone in 21 days, then in how many days can they together finish the job ?
(a) 7 days (b) 6 days
(c) 5 days (d) 2 days
5. Jaikishan can do a piece of work in 15 hours. If he is joined by Jhanvi who is 50% more efficient, in what time will they together finish the work ?
(a) 6 hours (b) 12 hours
(c) 3 hours (d) 9 hours
6. Praful has done 1/2 of a job in 30 days, Sarabjit completes the rest of the job in 10 days. In how many days can they together do the job ?
(a) 30 days (b) 45 days
(c) 15 days (d) 60 days

7. A mason can build a wall in 18 hours. After 9 hours he takes a break. What fraction of the wall is yet to be built ?
(a) 0.9 (b) 0.25
(c) 0.5 (d) 0.2

8. Mother can bake 20 cakes in 4 hours, Mother and Dadima together can bake 60 cakes in 10 hours. How many cakes Dadima can bake in 30 hours ?
(a) 30 (b) 75
(c) 60 (d) 25

9. Meghnad can do a piece of work in 45 hours. If he is joined by Jayshri, who is 50% more efficient, in what time will they together finish the work ?
(a) 9 hours (b) 6 hours
(c) 12 hours (d) 18 hours

10. A can do a work in 15 days and B in 20 days. If they work on it together for 6 days, then what fraction of work is left ?
(a) 1/4 (b) 2/9
(c) 1/5 (d) 3/10

11. Aman is 5 times as good a workman as Bhairav and therefore is able to finish a job in 48 days less than Bhairav. Working together, they can do it in :
(a) 20 days (b) 5 days
(c) 25 days (d) 10 days

12. A can do a work in 15 days and B in 9 days. If they work on it together for 5 days, then what fraction of work is left ?
(a) 1/6 (b) 3/7
(c) 1/3 (d) 1/9

13. Akash is 3 times as good a workman as Baldev and therefore is able to finish a job in 40 days less than Baldev. Working together, they can finish it in:
(a) 15 days (b) 60 days
(c) 20 days (d) 10 days

14. A can do a work in 20 days and B in 50 days. If they work on it together for 5 days, then what fraction of work is left ?
(a) 13/20 (b) 1/3
(c) 1/6 (d) 2/9

15. Badki can bake 45 cakes in 9 hours, Badki and Chutki together can bake 80 cakes in 10 hours. How many cakes Chutki can bake in 40 hours?
(a) 125 (b) 10
(c) 120 (d) 20

16. Mandar works 3 times as fast as Samarth. If Samarth can complete a job alone in 28 days, then in how many days can they together finish the job?
(a) 4 days (b) 5 days
(c) 8 days (d) 7 days

17. Painter A can paint a house in 40 days and Painter B can do it in 60 days. With help of C, they did the job in 20 days only. Then, C alone can do the job in :
(a) 120 days (b) 20 days
(c) 225 days (d) 15 days

18. Manjeet can do a work in 18 hours. If he is joined by Jaya who is 100% more efficient, in what time will they together finish the work?
(a) 6 hours (b) 3 hours
(c) 12 hours (d) 24 hours

19. A does 60% of a work in 15 days. He then calls B, and they together finish the remaining work in 5 days. How long B alone would take to do the whole work?
(a) 25 days (b) 20 days
(c) 80 days (d) 24 days

20. Ajit is two times as good a workman as Badrinath and therefore is able to finish a job in 30 days less than Badrinath. Working together, they can do it in :
(a) 10 days (b) 30 days
(c) 15 days (d) 20 days

21. A does 80% of a work in 20 days. Then he calls B and they together finish the remaining work in 4 days. How long B alone would take to do the whole work ?
(a) 12.5 days (b) 100 days
(c) 22.5 days (d) 35 days

Answers with Explanations

1. (c) A cupboard built in 1 hour

$= \frac{1}{48}$ parts

In 12 hours it is built $= \frac{12}{48}$ part

$= \frac{1}{4}$ part

Left part of cupboard $= 1 - \frac{1}{4}$

$= \frac{3}{4} = 0.75$

2. (d) Makarand works = 2 times of Samarjit

Samarjit can complete a job in 27 days

Makarand can complete in 27/2 days

Let both will do it in t days

$\frac{1}{t} = \frac{2}{27} + \frac{1}{27} = \frac{3}{27}$

$\Rightarrow t = \frac{27}{3} = 9$ days

3. (d) Murad can do a piece of work in = 33 hours

Joel can do it in $= \frac{33}{2}$ hours

Let both will finish in t hours

$\frac{1}{t} = \frac{1}{33} + \frac{2}{33} = \frac{1+2}{33}$

$= \frac{3}{33} = \frac{1}{11}$

$t = 11$ hours

4. (a) Sahay can complete a job = 21 days

Mahanath can complete a job

$= \frac{21}{2}$ days

Sahay can do a work in 1 day

$= \frac{1}{21}$

Mahanath can do a work in 1 day

$= \frac{2}{21}$

Both can work in 1 day $= \frac{1}{21} + \frac{2}{21}$

$= \frac{1+2}{21} = \frac{3}{21} = \frac{1}{7}$

Both will complete a work in 7 days.

5. (a) Jaikishan can do a piece of work = 15 days

Jhanvi who is 50% more efficient

$= \frac{15}{150\%} = \frac{15 \times 2}{3} = 10$ days

Work done in 1 day $= \frac{1}{15} + \frac{1}{10}$

$= \frac{2+3}{30} = \frac{5}{30} = \frac{1}{6}$

Time taken by both = 6 days.

6. (c) Full job done by Praful in 60 days

Left job $= 1 - \frac{1}{2} = \frac{1}{2}$

$\frac{1}{2}$ job is completed by Sarabjit

= 10 days

Full job is completed by Sarabjit

$= 10 \times 2 = 20$ days

1 day's job of both

$= \frac{1}{60} + \frac{1}{20} = \frac{1+3}{6}$

$= \frac{4}{60} = \frac{1}{15}$

Time taken by both

$= \frac{1}{\frac{1}{15}}$ days = 15 days

7. (c) A mason can build a wall in 18 hours and after a hour he takes a break.

∴ The fraction of the wall to be

built $= \frac{9}{18} = 0.5$

8. (a) In 1 hr. number of cakes baked by

mother $= \frac{20}{4} = 5$ cakes

In 1 hr., number of cakes baked

by mother and Dadima $= \frac{60}{10} = 5$ cakes

In 1 hr., no. of cakes baked by Dadima = 1 cake

In 30 hrs. No. of cakes baked by Dadima = 30 cakes

9. (d) Work done in 1 hour by Meghnad

$= \frac{1}{45}$ parts

Work done in 1 hour by Jaishree

$= \frac{3}{45 \times 2}$ parts

Work done by both $= \frac{1}{45} + \frac{3}{90}$

$= \frac{3+2}{90} = \frac{5}{90}$

Time taken by both

$= \frac{90}{5} = 18$ hours.

10. (d) A's one day work $= \frac{1}{15}$

B's one day work $= \frac{1}{20}$

(A+B)'s one day work $= \frac{1}{15} + \frac{1}{20}$

$= \frac{4+3}{60} = \frac{7}{60}$

(A+B)'s 6 days work

$= 6 \times \frac{7}{60} = \frac{7}{10}$

Left work $= 1 - \frac{7}{10} = \frac{3}{10}$.

11. (d) Aman = 5 × Bhairav

Let Bhairav takes time = t days

Aman takes = $t - 48$

Bhairav's 1 day work $= \frac{1}{t}$

Aman's 1 day work $= \frac{1}{t-48}$

Both's 1 day work $= \frac{1}{t} + \frac{1}{t-48}$

According to question,

$$\frac{1}{t-48} = \frac{5}{t}$$
$$5t - 240 = t$$
$$4t = 240$$
$$t = 60$$

Both's 1 day's work $= \frac{1}{60} + \frac{1}{12}$

$= \frac{1+5}{60} = \frac{6}{60} = \frac{1}{10}$

Time taken by both $= \frac{1}{1/10}$ days

= 10 days.

12. (d) A's 1 day work $= \frac{1}{15}$

B's 1 day work $= \frac{1}{9}$

(A + B)'s 5 days work

$= 5\left(\frac{1}{15} + \frac{1}{9}\right)$

$= 5\left(\frac{3+5}{45}\right) = \frac{8}{9}$

Left work $= 1 - \frac{8}{9} = \frac{1}{9}$

13. (a) Let Akash Completes a work in = x days

Baldev Completes a work in = $3x$ days

According to question,

$$3x - x = 40$$
$$2x = 40$$
$$x = 20$$

Akash's 1 day work $= \frac{1}{20}$

Baldev's 1 day work $= \frac{1}{60}$

Both's 1 day work $= \frac{1}{20} + \frac{1}{60}$

$= \frac{3+1}{60} = \frac{4}{60}$

Time taken by both = 60/4 = 15days

14. (a) A's one day work $= \frac{1}{20}$

B's one day work $= \frac{1}{50}$

(A + B)'s one day work

$= \frac{1}{20} + \frac{1}{50} = \frac{5+2}{100} = \frac{7}{100}$

(A + B)'s 5 days work $= \frac{7}{100} \times 5 = \frac{7}{20}$

Left work $= 1 - \frac{7}{20}$

$= \frac{20-7}{20} = \frac{13}{20}$

15. (c) Badki can bake cake in 1 hour

$= \frac{45}{9} = 5$

Badki and Chutki can bake cake

in 1 hour $= \frac{80}{10} = 8$

Chutki can bake cake in 1 hour

$= 8 - 5 = 3$

Chutki can bake cake in 40 hours

$= 3 \times 40 = 120$ cakes

16. (d) Mandar= 3 times of Samarth

Samarth completes in 1 day $= \frac{1}{28}$

Mandar completes in 1 day $= \frac{3}{28}$

Both will complete in 1 day

$= \frac{1}{28} + \frac{3}{28} = \frac{4}{28} = \frac{1}{7}$

Time taken by both $= \frac{1}{\frac{1}{7}} = 7$ days.

17. (a) A's one day work of painting

$= \frac{1}{40}$

B's one day work of painting

$= \frac{1}{60}$

(A+B+C)'s one day work of painting $= \frac{1}{20}$

(A+B)'s one day work

$= \frac{1}{40} + \frac{1}{60}$

$= \frac{3+2}{120}$

$= \frac{5}{120} = \frac{1}{24}$

C's one day work $= \frac{1}{20} - \frac{1}{24}$

$= \frac{6-5}{120}$

$= \frac{1}{120}$

Time taken by C to complete whole work $= \frac{1}{1/120} = 120$ days.

18. (a) Manjeet's one day work $= \frac{1}{18}$

Jaya is 100% more efficient.

Jaya will complete whole work in 9 days

Jaya's 1 day work $= \frac{1}{9}$

Both's 1 day work $= \frac{1}{18} + \frac{1}{9}$

$= \left(\frac{1+2}{18}\right) = \frac{3}{18} = \frac{1}{6}$

Time taken to complete work by both

$= \frac{1}{1/6} = 6$ hours.

19. (a) A's 60% of the work is completed in = 15 days

A's whole work is completed by

$= 15 \times \frac{100}{60} = 25$ days

(A + B)'s 40% is completed in = 5 days

(A + B)'s whole work

$= 5 \times \frac{100}{40} = \frac{5 \times 5}{2} = \frac{25}{2}$

(A + B)'s 1 day work $= \frac{2}{25}$

B's one day work

$= \frac{2}{25} - \frac{1}{25} = \frac{1}{25}$

Time taken by B $= \frac{1}{\frac{1}{25}} = 25$ days

20. (d) Ajit is able to finish a job = 30 days

He is able to work in 1 day $= \frac{1}{30}$

Badrinath will complete it in 60 days

Badrinath will complete it in 1 day

$= \frac{1}{60}$

Both will complete in 1 day

$= \frac{1}{30} + \frac{1}{60}$

$= \frac{2+1}{60} = \frac{3}{60} = \frac{1}{20}$

Hence, time taken by both = 20 days

21. (b) A's one day work $= \frac{1}{20}$

Both completes remaining work in 4 days.

Both's one day work $= \frac{1}{4}$

Left work= 100% – 80% = 20%

$= \frac{20}{100} = \frac{1}{5}$

B's one day work

$= \frac{1}{4} - \frac{1}{20} = \frac{5-1}{20} = \frac{4}{20} = \frac{1}{5}$

20% is completed by B in = 5 days

100% work is completed

$= \frac{5 \times 20 \times 100}{100} = 100$ days

9 TIME, SPEED AND DISTANCE

Speed: Speed of an object is the distance covered by it in unit time. Normally it is denoted by km/hr or m/sec.

$$\text{Speed} = \frac{\text{Distance}}{\text{Time}}$$

$$\text{Distance} = \text{Speed} \times \text{Time}$$

$$\text{Time} = \frac{\text{Distance}}{\text{Speed}}$$

Note: (*i*) To convert a speed of km/hr into m/sec, multiply by $\frac{5}{18}$.

(*ii*) To convert a speed of m/sec into km/hr multiply by $\frac{18}{5}$.

Important General Formulae:

- **Average speed:** The speed of a vehicle (or an object) does not always remain uniform over the entire distance covered. It may vary during the period of journey. Thus, for the purpose of calculations we find out the average speed of vehicle (or object) for the whole journey performed, using the formula:

$$\text{Average speed} = \frac{\text{Total distance travelled}}{\text{Total time taken}}$$

- **Relative speed:** The speed of an object with respect to another is called the relative speed.

(*i*) If two objects move in the same direction at speeds of x km/hr and y km/hr, then their relative speed $= (x - y)$ km/hr (where $x > y$)

(*ii*) If two objects move in the opposite directions, then their relative speed $= (x + y)$ km/ hr

- Let a man covers a distance at x km/hr and an equal distance at y km/hr, then average speed during whole journey

$$= \left(\frac{2xy}{x+y}\right) \text{ km/hr}$$

- If the ratio of speed of x and y is $a : b$, then the ratio of times taken by them to cover the same distance is $b : a$.
- Time taken by a train l metres long in passing a signal post, pole or a tree = Time taken by the train to cover l metres.
- Time taken by a train l metres long in passing stationary object of length x meters = Time taken by the train to cover $(l + x)$ metres.
- Time taken by a train l metres long, running at x km/hr to pass a man, running at y km/hr in the direction of the train = Time taken to cover l metres at $x - y$ km/hr.
- Time taken by a train l metres long, running at x km/hr to pass a man, running at y km/hr in the direction opposite of that of the train = Time taken to cover l metre at $x + y$.
- Time taken by faster train of length l_1 metres running at x km/hr to pass the slower train of length l_2 metres running at y km/hr in the same direction = Time taken to cover $(l_1 + l_2)$ metres at $(x - y)$ km/hr.

Solved Examples

Example 1: A train covers a distance of 10 km in 12 minutes. Find the time taken by it to cover the same distance, if its speed were decreased by 5 km/hr.

Sol. Distance covered by train = 10 km

$$\text{time taken} = \left(\frac{12}{60}\right) \text{ hrs} = \frac{1}{5} \text{ hr.}$$

Speed of the train = (10×5) km/hr = 50 km/hr

Decreased speed = $(50 - 5)$ km/hr = 45 km/hr

$\therefore$ Required time = $\left(\frac{10}{45}\times 60\right)$ min

$= 13\frac{1}{3}$ min = 13 min 20 sec.

Example 2: A train 150 m long is running at a speed of 62 km/hr in the same direction in which the man is running at 8 km/hr. How long does it take to pass the man?

Sol. Speed of the train relative to man

= (62 – 8) km/hr = 54 km/hr

$= \left(54\times\frac{5}{18}\right)$ km/hr = 15 km/hr

$\therefore$ Time taken by the train to cross a man

$= \left(150\times\frac{1}{15}\right)$ sec

= 10 sec.

Example 3: A train 425 m long is running at 72 km/hr. If it crosses platform in 50 seconds, find the length of the platform.

Sol. Speed of the train

$= \left(72\times\frac{5}{18}\right)$ m/sec = 20m/sec

Distance covered by the train in 50 sec

= (20 × 50) m = 1000 m

$\therefore$ Length of platform = (1000 – 425) m = 575 m

Exercise

1. A missile travels at 1116 km/h. How many metres does it travel in one second?
(a) 360 metres
(b) 368 metres
(c) 310 metres
(d) 348 metres

2. A man travels 401 kilometres in, partly by rail and partly by steamer. He spends 6 hours more time on steamer. If the velocity of the steamer is 21 km/hr and the velocity of rail is 56 km/hr, how much distance does he cover by steamer?
(a) 241 km (b) 302 km
(c) 201 km (d) 362 km

3. A man travels 800 km in partly by rail and partly by steamer. He spends 7 hours more time on steamer. If the velocity of the steamer is 20 km/hr and the velocity of rail is 55 km/hr, how much distance does he cover by steamer?
(a) 316 km (b) 379 km
(c) 474 km (d) 569 km

4. To travel 672 km, an Express train takes 14 hours more than Rajdhani. If however, the speed of the Express train is doubled, it takes 8 hours less than Rajdhani. The speed of Rajdhani is :
(a) 30.5 km/hr
(b) 14.3 km/hr
(c) 38.7 km/hr
(d) 22.4 km/hr

5. To travel 732 km, an Express train takes 6 hours more than Rajdhani. If the speed of the Express train is doubled, it takes 3 hours less than Rajdhani. The speed of Rajdhani is :
(a) 81.3 km/hr (b) 61 km/hr
(c) 40.7 km/hr (d) 101.7 km/hr

6. To cover a distance of 315 km in 2.8 hours what should be the average speed of the car in metres/second ?
(a) 112.5 m/s (b) 56.25 m/s
(c) 62.5 m/s (d) 31.25 m/s

7. Rizvan walks at 15 km/hr and Ruchitha cycles at 20 km/hr towards each other. What was the distance between them when they started if they meet after 42 minutes ?
(a) 36.8 kms (b) 30.6 kms
(c) 24.5 kms (d) 18.4 kms

8. A car travels a certain distance at 34 km/h and comes back at 66 km/h. What is the average speed for total journey ?
(a) 50 km/hr (b) 39.76 km/hr
(c) 55.12 km/hr (d) 44.88 km/hr

9. 9 hrs after a goods train passed a station, another train travelling at a speed of 72 km/hr following that goods train passed through that station. If after passing the station the train overtakes the goods train in 3 hours, what is the speed of the goods train?
(a) 21.6 km/hr
(b) 27 km/hr
(c) 18 km/hr
(d) 14.4 km/hr

10. To travel 648 km, an Express train takes 12 hours more than Rajdhani. If however, the speed of the Express train is doubled, it takes 6 hours less than Rajdhani. The speed of Rajdhani is ....
(a) 36 km/hr
(b) 18 km/hr
(c) 45 km/hr
(d) 54 km/hr

11. 4 hrs after a goods train passed a station, another train travelling at a speed of 60 km/hr following that goods train passed through that station. If after passing the station the train overtakes the goods train in 8 hours, what is the speed of the goods train?
(a) 40 km/hr
(b) 48 km/hr
(c) 60 km/hr
(d) 32 km/hr

12. Rehman walks at 8 km/hr and Roma cycles at 13 km/hr towards each other. What was the distance between them when they started if they meet after 36 minutes?
(a) 12.6 kms
(b) 18.9 kms
(c) 15.8 kms
(d) 9.5 kms

13. Two cars travel from city A to city B at a speed of 30 and 44 km/hr respectively. If one car takes 3.5 hours lesser time than the other car for the journey, then the distance between city A and city B is :
(a) 330 km
(b) 396 km
(c) 495 km
(d) 264 km

14. A car travels a certain distance at 24 km/h and comes back at 36 km/h. Find the average speed for total journey.
(a) 28.8 km/hr
(b) 30 km/hr
(c) 27.6 km/hr
(d) 31.2 km/hr

15. A man travels 400 km in, partly by rail and partly by steamer. He spends 9 hours more time on steamer. If the velocity of the steamer is 30 km/hr and the velocity of rail is 70 km/hr, how much distance does he cover by steamer?
(a) 309 km
(b) 371 km
(c) 464 km
(d) 556 km

16. Two cars travel from city A to city B at a speed of 36 and 54 km/hr respectively. If one car takes 3.5 hours lesser time than the other car for the journey, then the distance between City A and City B is :
(a) 454 km
(b) 567 km
(c) 302 km
(d) 378 km

17. Two cars travel from city A to city B at a speed of 30 and 48 km/hr respectively. If one car takes 3 hours lesser time than the other car for the journey, then the distance between City A and City B is :
(a) 288 km
(b) 240 km
(c) 360 km
(d) 192 km

18. Two cars travel from city A to city B at a speed of 30 and 36 km/hr respectively. If one car takes 3 hours lesser time than the other car for the journey, then the distance between City A and City B is :
(a) 648 km
(b) 810 km
(c) 432 km
(d) 540 km

Answers with Explanations

1. (c) Speed of missile = 1116 km/h

$$= \frac{1116 \times 1000}{3600}$$

$$= 1116 \times \frac{5}{18} = \frac{124 \times 5}{2}$$

$$= 62 \times 5 = 310 \text{ metres/sec.}$$

Missile will travel 310 metres in 1 second.

2. (c) Let a man take t hours by train and $(t + 6)$ hours by steamer.
Distance $= 56 \times (t) + 21\,(t + 6)$

$$401 = 56t + 21t + 126$$

$$77t = 401 - 126 = 275$$

$$t = \frac{275}{77} = \frac{25}{7}$$

Distance travelled by steamer

$$= 21 \times \left(\frac{25}{7} + 6\right)$$

$$= 21 \times \frac{(25+42)}{7}$$

$$= 3 \times 67$$

$$= 201 \text{ km}$$

3. (a) Let the man travel by rail be t hours and by steamer $(t + 7)$ hours
According to question

$$t \times 55 + (t+7) \times 20 = 800 \text{ km}$$

$$55t + 20t = 800 - 140$$

$$75t = 660$$

$$t = \frac{660}{75}$$

Distance covered by steamer

$$= (t+7) \times 20$$

$$= \left(\frac{660}{75} + 7\right) \times 20$$

$$= \left(\frac{660+525}{75}\right) \times 20$$

$$= \frac{1185}{75} \times 20$$

$$= \frac{1185 \times 4}{15}$$

$$= 79 \times 4 = 316 \text{ km}$$

4. (d) Let speed of Rajdhani train be u at time t, speed of Express train $= 2u$
Speed of Rajdhani u

$$u = \frac{D}{T} = \frac{672}{(t+14)} \quad ...(i)$$

Speed of Express train

$$2u = \frac{672}{t-8} \quad ...(ii)$$

Dividing equation (i) by (ii), we get

$$\frac{1}{2} = \frac{t-8}{t+14}$$

$$t + 14 = 2t - 16$$

$$2t - t = 14 + 16 = 30$$

$$t = 30 \text{ hours}$$

$$\text{Speed of Rajdhani train} = \frac{672}{30}$$

$$= 22{\cdot}4 \text{ km/hr.}$$

5. (b) Let Rajdhani take time $= t$ hours
Express train take time $= (t+6)$ hours
Speed of Express train $= v$
When Speed of Express train $= 2v$
Then time taken $= (t - 3)$

$$\text{Speed} = \frac{\text{Distance}}{\text{Time}}$$

$$v = \left(\frac{732}{t+6}\right) \text{ km/h} \quad ...(i)$$

$$2v = \left(\frac{732}{t-3}\right) \text{ km/h} \quad ...(ii)$$

Dividing equation (i) by (ii),

$$\frac{v}{2v} = \frac{732}{(t+6)} \times \frac{(t-3)}{732} = \frac{t-3}{t+6}$$

$$\frac{1}{2} = \frac{t-3}{t+6}$$

$t+6=2t-6$

$t=6+6=12$ hours

Speed of Rajdhani train

$=\frac{732}{t}=\frac{732}{12}=61$ km/h

6. (d) Speed of car $=\frac{\text{Distance}}{\text{Time}}$

$=\frac{315\text{ km}}{2.8\text{ hr.}}$

$=\frac{3150}{28}=\frac{3150\times1000\text{ m}}{28\times3600\text{ sec}}$

$=\frac{450\times5}{4\times18}=31.25$ m/s

7. (c) Let the distance between Rizwan and Ruchitha be x.

Relative speed $=15+20=35$ km/hr.

$\because$ When they started to walk in opposite, then distance

$=\frac{35\times42}{60}=24.5$ km

8. (d) Average speed of total journey

$=\frac{2ab}{a+b}=\frac{2\times34\times66}{34+66}$

$=\frac{4488}{100}=44.88$ km/hr

9. (c) Let speed of goods train be v km/h

Distance covered in 9 hr $=9\times v=9v$ km

Relative speed = $(72-v)$ km/h of another train

Distance covered by another train $=3(72-v)$ km

According to question

$9v=3(72-v)$

$3v=72-v$

$4v=72$

$v=\frac{72}{4}=18$ km/hr.

10. (d) Let Rajdhani take t-hours.

Express train takes $=(t+12)$ hours

Let Speed of Rajdhani be v

and speed of express train $=2v$

$\frac{648}{v}-\frac{648}{2v}=6$

$648\left(\frac{2-1}{v}\right)=6$

$\frac{1}{2v}=\frac{6}{648}=\frac{1}{108}$

$v=\frac{108}{2}=54$ km/hr.

11. (a) Let speed of the goods train be v.

Total time taken by goods train $=(4+8)=12$ hr

Distance covered by goods train = Distance covered by another train

$12v=8\times60$

$v=\frac{480}{12}=40$ km/hr.

12. (a) Total distance covered

$=8\times\frac{36}{60}+13\times\frac{36}{60}$

$=8\times\frac{3}{5}+13\times\frac{3}{5}$

$=\frac{24+39}{5}=\frac{63}{5}=12\cdot6$ km

13. (a) Let time for slow car be t hours and time for fast car $(t-3.5)$ hours

Distance between two places will be equal

$30t=44(t-3.5)$

or $44(t-3.5)=30t$

$44t-30t=44\times3.5$

$t(44-30)=44\times3.5$

$t=\frac{44\times3.5}{14}=22\times0.5$

$=11$ hours

Distance between A and B $=30t$

$=30\times11=330$ km

14. (a) Average speed $=\frac{2xy}{x+y}$

$=\frac{2\times24\times36}{(24+36)}$

$=\frac{2\times24\times36}{60}$

$=\frac{48\times6}{10}=28\cdot8$ km/hr

15. (a) Let time taken by train be t and by steamer $=(t+9)$

Distance = Speed × Time

$400=70t+30(t+9)$

$400=100t+30\times9$

$400-270=100t$

$130=100t$

by rail $=\frac{130}{10}=1\cdot3$ hours

time taken by steamer $=1\cdot3+9$

$=10\cdot3$ hours

Distance covered by steamer

$=30\times10\cdot3=309$ km

16. (d) Let the time taken by first car be t hours.

Time taken by other car = $(t-3.5)$ hours.

Distance = Speed × Time

But distance will be same in both cases.

Then,

$54(t-3.5)=36t$

$(54-36)t=54\times3.5$

$t=\frac{54\times3.5}{18}=3\times3.5$

$=10.5$

Distance $=36t=36\times10.5=36\times\frac{21}{2}$

$=18\times21=378$ km

17. (b) Let slow speed car takes time $=t$ hours

and fast speed car takes $=(t-3)$ hours

Distance will be same in both cases

$48(t-3)=30t$

$48t-48\times3=30t$

$(48-30)t=48\times3$

$t=\frac{48\times3}{18}=8$ hours

Distance $=30\times8=240$ km.

18. (d) Let first car takes t hours

Then time taken by second car $=(t-3)$

Distance between A and B be x

Both distances would be equal

$30t=36(t-3)$

$30t=36t-108$

$(36-30)t=108$

$6t=108$

$t=\frac{108}{6}=18$ hours

Distance between A and B = 30×18 $=540$ km.

10 SIMPLE AND COMPOUND INTEREST

- **Principal**: The money borrowed or lent out for a certain period of time is called the principal.
- **Interest:** The additional money paid by the borrower in lieu of the money used by him is called interest.
- **Rate:** Interest on ₹ 100 for 1 year is called rate percent per annum (apprenticed as rate percent p.a.)
- **Amount:** Total money paid back to the lender is called amount.

  Amount = Principal + Interest
- **Simple interest:** If interest is reckoned uniformly on the original principal throughout the loan period, then the interest is called simple interest.
- **Compound Interest:** Compound interest arises when interest is added to the principal of deposit of loan, so that from that moment on the interest that has been added also earns interest. This addition of interest to the principal is called compounding.

  The diffierence between the final amount and the original principal is called the compound interest.

$$\therefore \text{ Compound Interest (C.I.)} = P\left[\left(1+\frac{R}{100}\right)^n - 1\right]$$

Important General Formulae

Let Principal = ₹ P, Rate = R% per annum and Time = T years

Then,

(*i*) $\text{S.I.} = \dfrac{P \times R \times T}{100}$ (*ii*) $R = \dfrac{100 \times S.I.}{P \times T}$

(*iii*) $P = \dfrac{100 \times S.I.}{R \times T}$ (*iv*) $T = \dfrac{100 \times S.I.}{P \times R}$

Note: (*i*) While calculating the time period between two given, dates, the day on which the money is borrowed is not considered for interest while the day on which the money is returned, is considered.

(*ii*) For converting the time in days into years, we always divide by 365, whether it is an ordinary year or a leap year.

Let Principal = ₹ P, Rate = R% p.a. and Time = *n* years

(i) When interest is compounded annually,

$$\therefore \text{ Amount} = P\left(1+\frac{R}{100}\right)^n$$

(ii) When interest is compounded half yearly,

$$\therefore \text{ Amount} = P\left(1+\frac{R}{200}\right)^{2n}$$

(iii) When interest is compounded quarterly,

$$\text{Amount} = P\left(1+\frac{R}{400}\right)^{4n}$$

(iv) When time is fraction of a year, say $2\frac{1}{2}$ years,

$$\text{then, Amount} = P\left(1+\frac{R}{100}\right)^2\left(1+\frac{R}{2\times 100}\right)$$

(v) When rate of interest is R_1% during first year, R_2% during 2nd year, R_3% during third year, then

Amount after 3 years

$$= P\left(1+\frac{R_1}{100}\right)\left(1+\frac{R_2}{100}\right)\left(1+\frac{R_3}{100}\right)$$

Solved Examples

Example 1: Find the compound interest on ₹ 2800 for $1\frac{1}{2}$ years at 10% p.a.

Sol. $\text{Compound interest} = P\left[\left(1+\frac{R}{100}\right)^T - 1\right]$

$$= 2800\left[\left(1+\frac{10}{100}\right)^1\left(1+\frac{10}{200}\right)-1\right]$$

$$= 2800\left[\frac{11}{10}\times\frac{21}{20}-1\right]$$

$$= \left(\frac{2800\times31}{200}\right) = ₹\ 434$$

Example 2 : Find the difference between the simple interest and the compound interest on ₹ 5000 at 10% p.a. for 3 years.

Sol. $S.I. = \left(\frac{5000\times10\times3}{100}\right) = ₹\ 1500$

$$C.I. = 5000\left[\left(1+\frac{10}{100}\right)^3 -1\right]$$

$$= 5000\left[\frac{1331-1000}{1000}\right] = ₹\ 1655$$

$\therefore$ Required difference = ₹ (1655 – 1500) = ₹ 155

Example 3: Simple interest on a certain sum is $\frac{4}{9}$ of the sum. Find the rate percent and the time if both are numerically equal.

Sol. Let the sum be ₹ x

Then simple interest = ₹$\frac{4}{9}x$

$$\therefore S.I. = \frac{P\times R\times T}{100}$$

$$\frac{4}{9}x = \frac{x\times R\times R}{100} \qquad (\because T = R)$$

$$\Rightarrow R^2 = \frac{400}{9} \Rightarrow R = \frac{20}{3} = 6\frac{2}{3}\%$$

$\Rightarrow (R = T)$

Example 4: In what time will the simple interest on a certain sum of money at $7\frac{1}{2}\%$ per annum be $\frac{3}{8}$ of itself?

Sol. Let sum be ₹ x

Then simple interest = ₹ $\frac{3}{8}x$

$$\therefore T = \left(\frac{100\times S.I.}{P\times R}\right) = \left(\frac{100\times\frac{3}{8}x}{x\times\frac{15}{2}}\right) \text{ years}$$

$$= \left(\frac{100\times3x\times2}{x\times15\times8}\right) \text{ years} = 5 \text{ years}$$

Exercise

1. A bank offers 5% compound interest per half year. A customer deposits ₹ 3200 each on 1st January and 1st July of a year. At the end of the year, the amount he would have gained by way of interest is:
(a) ₹ 976 (b) ₹ 244
(c) ₹ 488 (d) ₹ 122
2. If the amount received at the end of 2nd and 3rd year at Compound Interest on a certain Principal is ₹ 25088, and ₹ 28098.56 respectively, what is the rate of interest?
(a) 6 percent (b) 24 percent
(c) 12 percent (d) 19 percent
3. A bank offers 20% compound interest per half year. A customer deposits ₹ 6,000 each on 1st January and 1st July of a year. At the end of the year, the amount he would have gained by way of interest is:
(a) ₹ 7680 (b) ₹ 3840
(c) ₹ 1920 (d) ₹ 960
4. Simple interest on a certain sum of money for 3 years at 16% per annum is half the compound interest on ₹ 12000 for 2 years at 10% per annum. The sum placed on simple interest is :
(a) ₹ 5250 (b) ₹ 1325
(c) ₹ 2100 (d) ₹ 2625
5. If the amount received at the end of 2nd and 3rd year at compound interest on a certain principal is ₹ 28090, and ₹ 29775.4 respectively, what is the rate of interest?
(a) 6 percent (b) 3 percent
(c) 12 percent (d) 10 percent
6. The effective annual rate of interest corresponding to a nominal rate of 7% per annum payable half yearly is :
(a) 14 percent
(b) 14.25 percent
(c) 7 percent
(d) 1.72 percent
7. A sum fetched a total simple interest of ₹ 7056 at the rate of 8 percent per year in 7 years. What is the sum ?
(a) ₹ 12600 (b) ₹ 15120
(c) ₹ 10080 (d) ₹ 7560
8. If the amount received at the end of 2nd and 3rd year at Compound Interest on a certain Principal is ₹ 33708, and ₹ 35730.48 respectively, what is the rate of interest ?
(a) 6 percent (b) 3 percent
(c) 12 percent (d) 10 percent
9. If the amount received at the end of 2nd and 3rd year at compound interest on a certain principal is ₹ 16854 and ₹ 17865.24 respectively, what is the rate of interest ?
(a) 3 percent (b) 12 percent
(c) 6 percent (d) 10 percent
10. A bank offers 10% compound interest per half year. A customer deposits ₹ 2000 each on 1st January and 1st July of a year. At the end of the year, the amount he would have gained by way of interest is :
(a) ₹ 1240 (b) ₹ 310
(c) ₹ 155 (d) ₹ 620
11. On a certain Principal if the Simple interest for two years is ₹ 4800 and

Compound interest for the two years is ₹ 5088, what is the rate of Interest?
(a) 6 percent (b) 24 percent
(c) 12 percent (d) 18 percent

12. At what rate of compound interest per annum will as sum of ₹ 20000 become ₹ 23328 in 2 years ?
(a) 8 percent (b) 16 percent
(c) 24 percent (d) 12 percent

13. The difference between simple and compound interests compounded annually on a certain sum of money for 2 years at 9% per annum is ₹ 405. The sum is :
(a) ₹ 50,000 (b) ₹ 1,00,000
(c) ₹ 2,00,000 (d) ₹ 1,50,000

14. A bank offers 15% compound interest per half year. A customer deposits ₹ 8800 each on 1st January and 1st July of a year. At the end of the year, the amount he would have gained by way of interest is.
(a) ₹ 8315 (b) ₹ 2079
(c) ₹ 4158 (d) ₹ 1039

15. A bank offers 15% compound interest per half year. A customer deposits ₹ 2400 each on 1st January and 1st July of a year. At the end of the year, the amount he would have gained by way of interest is :
(a) ₹ 2268 (b) ₹ 1134
(c) ₹ 567 (d) ₹ 283

16. At what rate of compound interest per annum will a sum of ₹ 10000 become ₹ 12321 in 2 years?
(a) 22 percent (b) 11 percent
(c) 7 percent (d) 15 percent

17. A bank offers 5% compound interest per half year. A customer deposits ₹ 6400 each on 1st January and 1st July of a year. At the end of the year, the amount he would have gained by way of interest is:
(a) ₹ 1952 (b) ₹ 488
(c) ₹ 976 (d) ₹ 244

18. Simple interest on a certain sum of money for 3 years at 10% per annum is half the compound interest on ₹ 6000 for 2 years at 10% per annum. The sum placed on simple interest is :
(a) ₹ 4200 (b) ₹ 2100
(c) ₹ 1050 (d) ₹ 1680

19. Simple interest on a certain sum of money for 3 years at 14% per annum is half the compound interest on ₹ 10000 for 2 years at 10% per annum. The sum placed on simple interest is :
(a) ₹ 5000 (b) ₹ 1250
(c) ₹ 2000 (d) ₹ 2500

20. Simple interest on a certain sum of money for 3 years at 18% per annum is half the compound interest on ₹ 9000 for 2 years at 10% per annum. The sum placed on simple interest is :
(a) ₹ 3500 (b) ₹ 875
(c) ₹ 1750 (d) ₹ 1400

Answers with Explanations

1. (c) $A = P\left(1+\frac{R}{100}\right) + \left(\frac{P\times10\times1}{2\times100}\right)$

$$A = 3200\left(1+\frac{5}{100}\right)^2 + \frac{3200\times10\times1}{100\times2}$$

$$= 3200\times\frac{21}{20}\times\frac{21}{20}+160$$

$$= 8\times441+160$$

$$= 3528+160 = 3688$$

Interest = 3688 – 3200 = ₹ 488

2. (c) Let the rate be r, then

$$A = P\left(1+\frac{r}{100}\right)^n$$

$$25088 = P\left(1+\frac{r}{100}\right)^2 \quad ...(i)$$

$$28098.56 = P\left(1+\frac{r}{100}\right)^3 \quad ...(ii)$$

Dividing eq. (ii) by (i)

$$\frac{28098.56}{25088} = \left(1+\frac{r}{100}\right)$$

$$\frac{28098.56-25088}{25088} = \frac{r}{100}$$

$$\frac{r}{100} = \frac{3010.56}{25088}$$

$$r = \frac{201056}{25088} = 12 \text{ percent}$$

3. (b) Amount

$$= P\left(1+\frac{20}{100}\right)^2 + \frac{P\times40\times1}{100\times2}$$

$$= 6000\times\frac{36}{25}+\frac{6000\times40}{100\times2}$$

$$= \frac{6000\times36\times4}{100}+\frac{240000}{200}$$

$$= 60\times144+1200$$

Amount = 8640 + 1200

Amount = 9840

Compound Interest = 9840 – 6000 = ₹ 3840

4. (d) $C.I. = P\left[\left(1+\frac{R}{100}\right)^2-1\right]$

$$= 12000\left[\left(1+\frac{10}{100}\right)^2-1\right]$$

$$= 12000\times\left[\left(\frac{11}{10}\times\frac{11}{10}\right)^2-1\right]$$

$$= 12000\left[\frac{121-100}{100}\right]$$

$$= 12000\times\frac{21}{100}$$

$$= 120\times21 = ₹ 2520$$

But $\frac{1}{2}\times2520 = \frac{P\times16\times3}{100}$

$$P = \frac{1260\times100}{16\times3}$$

$$= \frac{420\times100}{16} = 105\times25 = ₹ 2625$$

5. (a) By using formula

$$A = P\left(1+\frac{R}{100}\right)^n$$

$$28090 = P\left(1+\frac{R}{100}\right)^2 \quad ...(i)$$

$$29775.4 = P\left(1+\frac{R}{100}\right)^3 \quad ...(ii)$$

Dividing equation (ii) by (i), we get

$$\frac{29775.4}{28090} = \frac{\left(1+\frac{R}{100}\right)^3}{\left(1+\frac{R}{100}\right)^2}$$

$$= \left(1+\frac{R}{100}\right)$$

$$\frac{R}{100} = \frac{29775.4-28090}{28090}$$

$$= \frac{1685.4}{28090}$$

$$R = \frac{168540}{28090} = 6\%$$

6. (d) Difference of S.I. and C.I.

$$= P\left[\left(1+\frac{R}{100}\right)^n - 1\right] - \frac{P\times 7\times 1}{100}$$

$$= P\left[\left(1+\frac{3.5}{100}\right)^2 - 1\right] - \frac{7P}{100}$$

$$= P\left[\left(\frac{103.5}{100}\right)^2 - 1\right] - \frac{7P}{100}$$

$$= P\left[\frac{(103.5)^2-(100)^2}{(100)^2} - \frac{7}{100}\right]$$

$$= P\left[\frac{203.5\times 3.5}{(100)^2} - \frac{7}{100}\right]$$

$$= P\left[\frac{712.25-700}{(100)^2}\right] = P\frac{12.25}{(100)^2}$$

Effective% of S.I. and C.I.

$$= \frac{\frac{P\times 12.25}{(100)^2}}{\frac{712.25\,P\times 1}{(100)^2}} \times 100\%$$

$$= \frac{12.25}{712.25}\times 100\%$$

$$= \frac{1225}{71225}\times 100\% = 1.72\%$$

7. (a) Let the sum be X

$\therefore$ According to question,

$$7056 = \frac{X\times 8\times 7}{100}$$

$$\therefore \quad X = \frac{7056\times 100}{8\times 7}$$

$$= ₹\,12600$$

8. (a) Let the rate of interest is 100

$$\therefore \text{interest} = \frac{35730{\cdot}48\times 100}{33708}$$

$$= ₹\,106$$

$\therefore$ rate of interest $= 106 - 100 = 6\%$

9. (c) $A = P\left(1+\frac{R}{100}\right)^n$

$$16854 = P\left(1+\frac{R}{100}\right)^2 \quad ...(i)$$

$$17865{\cdot}24 = P\left(1+\frac{R}{100}\right)^3 \quad ...(ii)$$

Dividing eq. (ii) by (i)

$$\left(1+\frac{R}{100}\right) = \frac{17865{\cdot}24}{16854} = \frac{1786524}{1685400}$$

$$= \frac{446631}{421350}$$

$$R = \frac{446631-421350}{421350}$$

$$= \frac{25281\times 100}{421350} = 6\%.$$

10. (d) Total Amount

$$= 2000\left(1+\frac{10}{100}\right)^2 + \frac{PRT}{100}$$

$$= 2000\times\frac{11\times 11}{10\times 10} + 2000\times\frac{10}{100}\times 1$$

$= 2420 + 200$

Total Amount $= 2620$

Interest $= A - P = 2620 - 2000 = ₹\,620.$

11. (c) Difference of S.I. and C.I.

$5088 - 4800 = 288$

$$288 = \frac{R\times S.I.}{200}$$

$$288 = \frac{R\times 4800}{200}$$

$$R = \frac{288\times 200}{4800} = 6\times 2 = 12\%$$

12. (a) $A = P\left(1+\frac{R}{100}\right)^n$

$$23328 = 20000\left(1+\frac{R}{100}\right)^n$$

$$\Rightarrow \frac{23328}{20000} = \left(1+\frac{R}{100}\right)^n$$

$$\Rightarrow \frac{11664}{10000} = \left(1+\frac{R}{100}\right)^n$$

$$\Rightarrow \left(\frac{108}{100}\right)^2 = \left(1+\frac{R}{100}\right)^n$$

Taking square root both sides

$$\Rightarrow \frac{108}{100} = 1+\frac{R}{100}$$

$$\Rightarrow \left(\frac{108-100}{100}\right) = \frac{R}{100}$$

$$\Rightarrow \frac{8}{100} = \frac{R}{100}$$

$$\therefore \quad R = 8\%$$

13. (a) According to question

$$P\left[\left(1+\frac{R}{100}\right)^n - 1\right] - \frac{PRT}{100} = 405$$

$$P\left[\left(1+\frac{9}{100}\right)^2 - 1 - \frac{9\times 2}{100}\right] = 405$$

$$P\left[\left(\frac{109}{100}\right)^2 - 1 - \frac{18}{100}\right] = 405$$

$$P\left[\frac{11881}{10000} - \frac{118}{100}\right] = 405$$

$$P\left[\frac{11881-11800}{10000}\right] = 405$$

$P\times 81 = 405\times 10000$

$$P = \frac{405\times 10000}{81} = ₹\,50000$$

So, the sum is ₹ 50,000.

14. (c) $A = P\left(1+\frac{R}{100}\right) + \left(\frac{PRT}{100}\right)$

$$A = 8800\left(1+\frac{15}{100}\right)^2 + \frac{8800\times 30\times 1}{100\times 2}$$

$$= 8800\left(\frac{23}{20}\right)^2 + 88\times 15$$

$$= 8800\times\frac{529}{400} + 1320$$

$= 22\times 529 + 1320$

$= 11638 + 1320 = ₹\,12958$

Interest earned $= 12958 - 8800$

$= ₹\ 4158$

15. (b) $A = P\left(1+\frac{R}{100}\right)^n + \frac{PRT}{100}$

$= 2400\left(1+\frac{15}{100}\right)^2 + \frac{2400 \times 30 \times 1}{100 \times 2}$

$= 2400\left(1+\frac{3}{20}\right)^2 + 24 \times 15$

$= 2400 \times \frac{23}{20} \times \frac{23}{20} + 24 \times 15$

$= 6 \times 23 \times 23 + 24 \times 15$

$= 3174 + 360 = ₹\,3534$

Compound interest $= 3534 - 2400$

$= ₹\,1134$

16. (b) C.I. $= A - P = 12321 - 10000 = 2321$

$A = P\left(1+\frac{r}{100}\right)^n$

$\frac{12321}{10000} = \left(1+\frac{r}{100}\right)^2$

$\left(\frac{111}{100}\right)^2 = \left(1+\frac{r}{100}\right)^2$

$\frac{111}{100} - 1 = \frac{r}{100}$

$\frac{11}{10} \times 100 = r$

$\therefore \quad r = 11\%$

17. (c) $A = P\left(1+\frac{r}{100}\right)^n + \frac{PRT}{100}$

$= 6400\left(1+\frac{5}{100}\right)^2 + \frac{6400 \times 10 \times 1}{100 \times 2}$

$= 6400 \times \frac{21}{20} \times \frac{21}{20} + 320$

$= 7056 + 320$

$A = 7376$

C.I. $= A - P = 7376 - 6400$

$= ₹\,976$

18. (b) Let the sum be P

$\frac{P \times 10 \times 3}{100} = \frac{1}{2} \times 6000\left[\left(1+\frac{10}{100}\right)^2 - 1\right]$

$= \frac{1}{2} \times 6000\left[\left(\frac{11}{10} \times \frac{11}{10}\right) - 1\right]$

$\frac{P \times 3}{10} = 3000 \times \frac{21}{100} = ₹\,630$

$P = \frac{630 \times 10}{3}$

$= ₹\,210 \times 10 = 2100$

Hence, the sum is ₹ 2100.

19. (d) Let the sum be P

$\frac{P \times 3 \times 14}{100} = \frac{1}{2} \times 10000\left[\left(1+\frac{10}{100}\right)^2 - 1\right]$

$\frac{P \times 3 \times 14}{100} = \frac{1}{2} \times 10000\left[\frac{11}{10} \times \frac{11}{10} - 1\right]$

$\frac{P \times 42}{100} = \frac{1}{2} \times 100\,[21]$

$P = ₹\,\frac{105000}{42}$

$= \frac{5000}{2} = ₹\,2500$

20. (c) Let the sum be P

$\frac{P \times 18\% \times 3}{100} = \frac{1}{2} \times 9000\left[\left(1+\frac{10}{100}\right)^2 - 1\right]$

$\frac{P \times 18 \times 6}{100} = 9000\left[\left(\frac{11}{10}\right)^2 - 1\right]$

$= 9000\left[\frac{121-100}{100}\right]$

$\frac{P \times 18 \times 6}{100} = 9000 \times \frac{21}{100} = 1890$

$P = \frac{1890 \times 100}{18 \times 6} = 1750$

Hence, the sum is ₹ 1750.

11 MENSURATION

Area: The measure of the surface enclosed by a plane figure it called its area.

Area is measured in square units.

Perimeter: The perimeter of a plane figure is the length of its boundary.

The units of perimeter are same as the units of length.

Important General Formulae

1. **Square**: Let there be a square of each side measuring a units. Then,

   (*i*) Area of the square $= a^2$ sq. units

   or $\frac{1}{2}(d)^2$ sq. units

   (*ii*) Perimeter of the square $= 4a$ units

   (*iii*) Diagonal of the square $= \sqrt{2}a$ units

2. **Rectangle:** Let there be a rectangle with length l units and breadth b units. Then,

   (*i*) Area of the rectangle $= lb$ sq. units

   (*ii*) Perimeter of the rectangle: $2(l + \text{b})$ units

   (*iii*) Diagonal of the rectangle: $\sqrt{l^2 + b^2}$

3. **Area of four walls of a room:** Let there be a room with length l units, breadth b units, and height h units. Then,

   (*i*) Area of four walls $= [2(l + b) \times h]$ sq. units

   (ii) Diagonal of the room $= \sqrt{l^2 + b^2 + h^2}$ units.

4. **Parallelogram:** Let there be a parallelogram with base b units and height h units. Then,

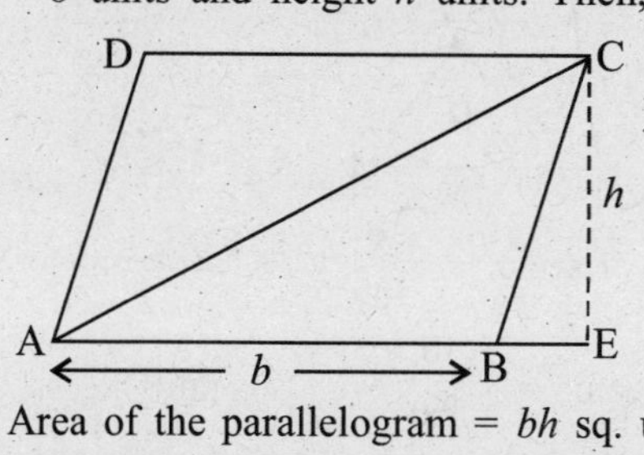

Area of the parallelogram $= bh$ sq. units.

Note: The diagonal of a parallelogram divides it into two triangles, equal in area.

5. **Rhombus:** Let there be a rhombus of diagonals d_1 and d_2 units. Then,

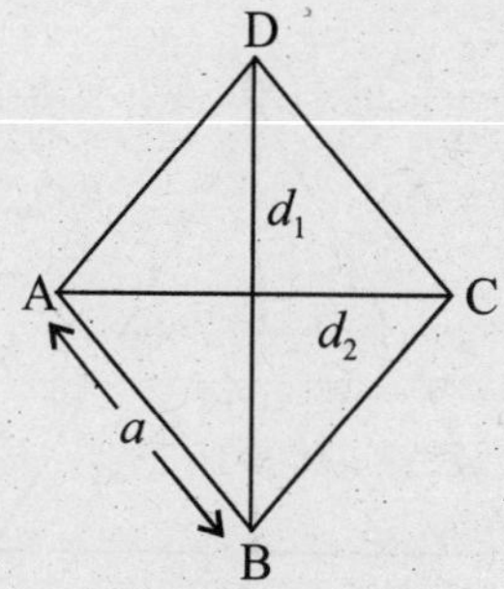

   (*i*) Area of the Rhombus $= \frac{1}{2} d_1 d_2$ sq. units

   (*ii*) Perimeter of the Rhombus $= 4a$ units.

Note: The diagonals of a rhombus bisect each other at right angles.

6. **Trapezium:** Let $ABCD$ be a trapezium in which $AB \parallel DC$.

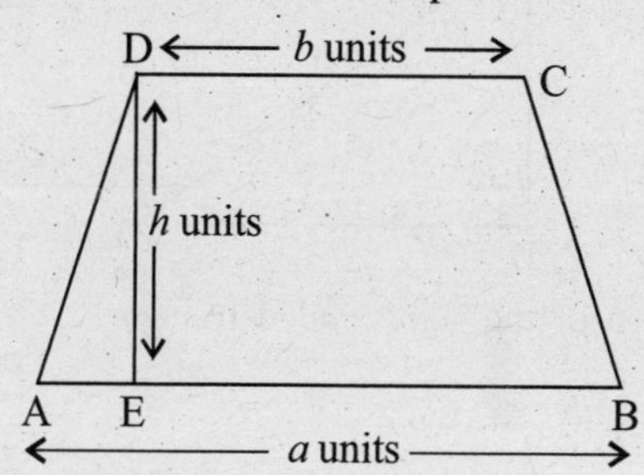

Let $AB = a$ units, $DC = b$ units and $DE = h$ units.

   (*i*) Area of the trapezium $= \frac{1}{2}[(a + b) \times h]$ sq. units.

   (*ii*) Perimeter of the trapezium $= (AE + BE + BC + DC + AD)$ units.

7. **Triangle :** Let a, b, c be the lengths of the sides of a triangle. Then,

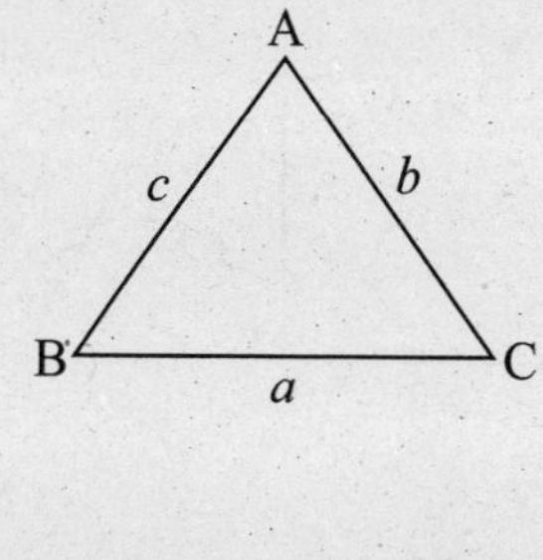

(*i*) Semi perimeter of triangle = $\frac{(a+b+c)}{2}$ units

(*ii*) Area of the triangle = $\sqrt{s(s-a)(s-b)(s-c)}$ sq. units

Note: This is known as Hero's formula.

Let the base of a triangle be b units and its corresponding height be h units. Then,

(*i*) Area of the triangle = $\frac{1}{2}bh$ sq. units.

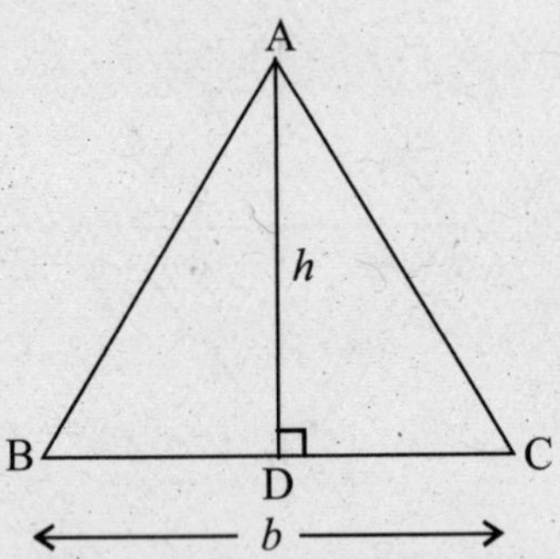

8. **Right angled Triangle:** Let the base of a right angled triangle be b units and its altitude be a units. then,

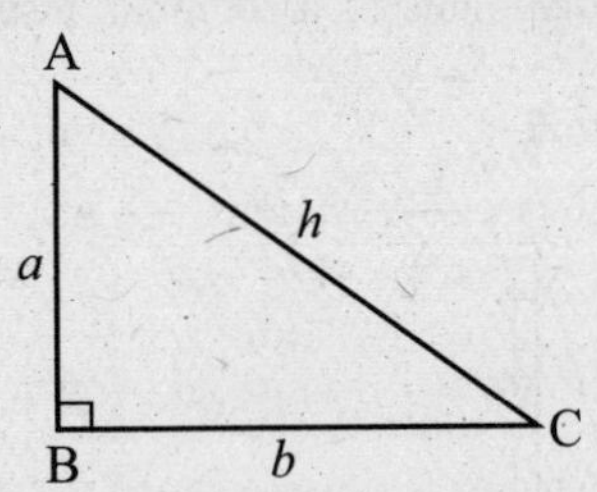

(i) Area of the right angled triangle

$= \frac{1}{2}ab$ sq. units

(ii) Perimeter of right angled triangle = $(a + b + h)$ units.

9. **Equilateral triangle:** Let there be an equilateral triangle of each side measuring a units then,

(*i*) Perimeter of equilateral triangle = $3a$ units

(*ii*) Area of equilateral triangle = $\frac{\sqrt{3}}{4}a^2$ sq. units

Let altitude of equilateral triangle is given. Then,

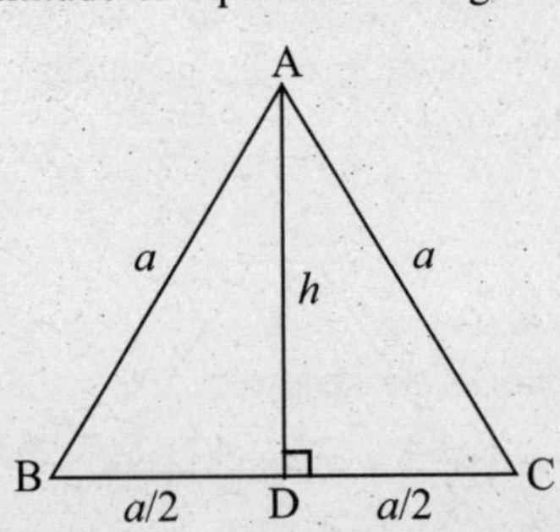

(*i*) Area of equilateral triangle = $\frac{1}{2}ah$ sq. units

(*ii*) Altitude of equilateral triangle = $\frac{\sqrt{3}}{2}a$ units.

10. **Regular Hexagon:** Let there be a regular Hexagon of each side measuring a units. Then

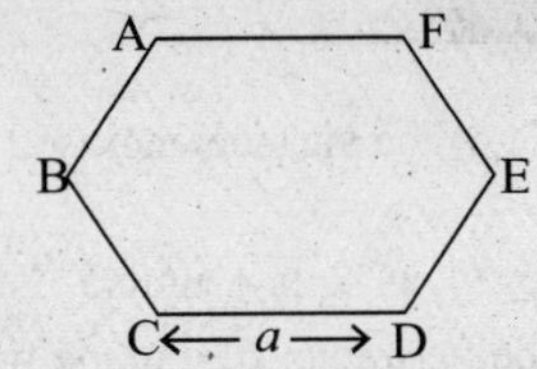

(*i*) Area of regular Hexagon = $\frac{3\sqrt{2}}{2}a^2$ sq. units.

(*ii*) Perimeter of regular Hexagon = $6a$ units.

(*iii*) Sum of the interior angles of a regular Hexagon

$= 2(n-2) \times 90^\circ$

$= 2(6-2) \times 90^\circ$

$= 720^\circ$

11. **Circle:** Let there be a circle of radius r units. Then

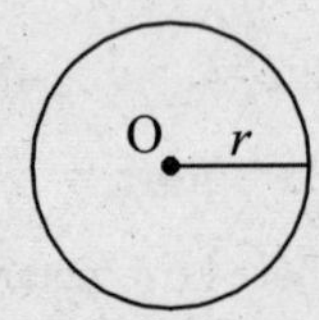

(*i*) Area of circle = πr^2 sq.units

(*ii*) Circumference of circle = $2\pi r$ units = πd units

12. **Semicircle:** Let there be a semicircle of radius r units.

(*i*) Area of semicircle = $\frac{1}{2}\pi r^2$ sq. units

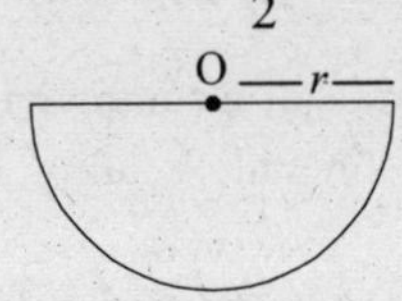

(*ii*) Perimeter of semicircle = $(\pi r + 2r)$ units

13. **Sector of circle**

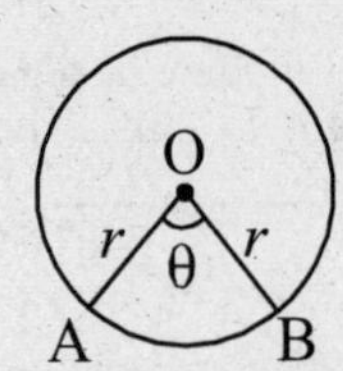

(*i*) Perimeter of sector = $\frac{\theta}{360^\circ}(2\pi r + 2r)$ units

(*ii*) Area of sector = $\left(\frac{\theta}{360^\circ}\pi r^2\right)$ sq. units

14. **Cuboid:** Let length of cuboid be l units, breadth b units and height h units. Then,

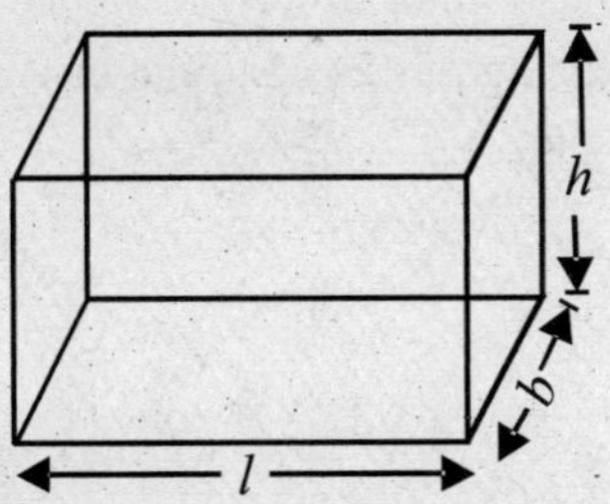

(i) Volume of the cuboid = lbh cubic units.

(ii) Total surface area of the cuboid

$$= 2\,(lb + bh + hl) \text{ sq. units}$$

(iii) Lateral suface area of the cuboid

$$= 2[(l + b) \times h] \text{ sq. units}$$

(iv) Diagonal of the cuboid = $\sqrt{l^2 + b^2 + h^2}$ units

15. **Cube:** Let each side of cube be a units. Then,

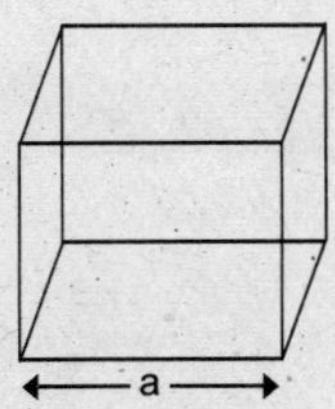

(i) Volume of the cube = a^3 cubic units.

(ii) Diagonal of the cube = $a\sqrt{3}$ units

(iii) Total surface area of the cube = $6a^2$ sq units

(iv) Lateral surface area of the cube = $4a^2$ sq. units

16. **Cylinder :** Let base radius of a cylinder be r units and height h units. Then,

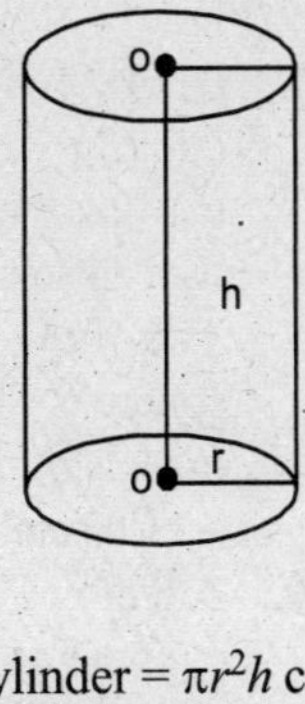

(i) Volume of the cylinder = $\pi r^2 h$ cubic units

(ii) Lateral surface area of the cylinder = $2\pi rh$ sq. units

(iii) Total surface area of the cylinder = $2\pi r(h + r)$ sq. units.

17. **Cone:** Let the base radius of a cone be r units, height h units and slant height l units. Then,

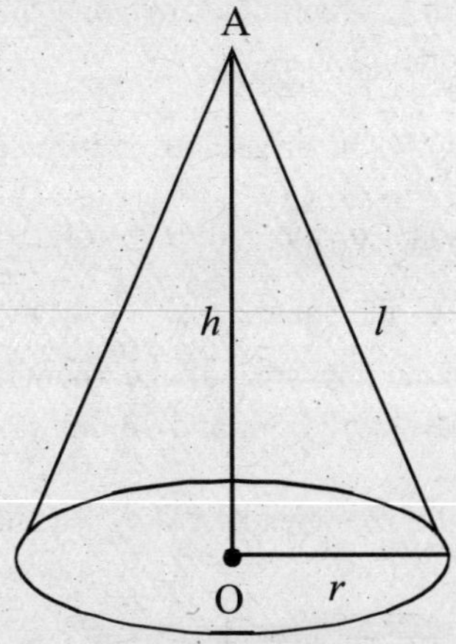

(i) Volume of the cone = $\frac{1}{3}\pi r^2 h$ cubic units.

(ii) Lateral surface area of the cone = πrl sq. units

(iii) Total surface area of the cone = $\pi r(l + r)$ sq. units

(iv) Slant height of the cone (l) = $\sqrt{h^2 + r^2}$ units

18. **Frustum of a Cone:** Let the base radius of frustum of a cone be R units, top radius r units, height h units and slant height l units. Then,

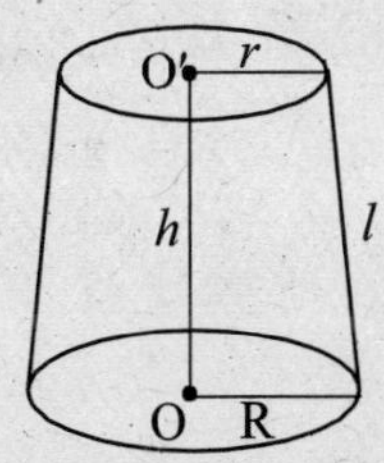

(i) Volume of the frustum of a cone

$$= \frac{\pi h}{3}(R^2 + r^2 + Rr) \text{ cubic units.}$$

(ii) Lateral surface area of the frustum of a cone

$$= \pi l(R + r) \text{ sq. units}$$

(iii) Total surface area of the frustum of a cone

$$= \{\pi R^2 + \pi r^2 + \pi l\,(R + r)\} \text{ sq. units}$$
$$= \pi[R^2 + r^2 + l\,(R + r)] \text{ sq. units.}$$

19. **Sphere:** Let the radius of a sphere is r units

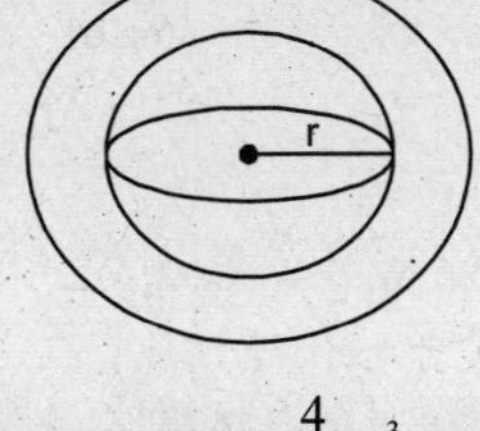

(i) Volume of the sphere = $\frac{4}{3}\pi r^3$ cubic units

(ii) Curved surface area of sphere = $4\pi r^2$ sq. units.

Solved Examples

Example 1: Find the perimeter, diagonal and area of a square having each side 12 m long.

Sol. (*i*) Perimeter of the square = $4a = (4 \times 12)$ m = 48m

(*ii*) Diagonal of the square = $a\sqrt{2} = 12\sqrt{2}$ m

(*iii*) Area of the square = $(12)^2$ sq. m = 144 sq. m

Example 2: Find the area of the rhombus, the length of whose diagonals are 25 cm and 20 cm.

Sol. Area of the rhombus = $\frac{1}{2}d_1d_2$ sq. units

$$= \left(\frac{1}{2}\times 25\times 20\right) \text{cm}^2 = 250 \text{ cm}^2$$

Example 3: The height of a cylinder is 14cm and curved surface area is 352 cm^2. Find the volume of the cylinder.

Sol. Curved surface area of the cylinder = $2\pi rh$

$$\therefore \quad 2\times\frac{22}{7}\times r\times 14 = 352$$

$$\Rightarrow \quad 88r = 352$$

$$\Rightarrow \quad r = 4 \text{ cm}$$

$\therefore$ Volume of the cylinder = $\pi r^2 h$

$$= \left[\frac{22}{7}\times(4)^2\times 14\right]\text{cm}^3$$

$$= 704 \text{ cm}^3$$

Example 4: The volume of a right circular cone is 1232 cm^3 and its vertical height is 24 cm. Find its curved surface area.

Sol. Let the radius be r cm.

$$\therefore \quad \frac{1}{3}\times\frac{22}{7}\times r^2\times 24 = 1232$$

$$\Rightarrow \quad r^2 = 49 \Rightarrow r = 7 \text{ cm}$$

Slant height of the cone (l) = $\sqrt{(7)^2+(24)^2}$

$$= \sqrt{49+576}$$

$$= \sqrt{625} = 25 \text{ cm}$$

$\therefore$ Curved surface area = πrl

$$= \left(\frac{22}{7}\times 7\times 25\right)\text{cm}^2$$

$$= 550 \text{ cm}^2$$

Example 5: If the radius of a sphere is 6 cm, then find its volume.

Sol. Volume of the sphere = $\frac{4}{3}\pi r^3$

$$= \left[\frac{4}{3}\pi\times(6)^3\right]\text{cm}^3$$

$$= \left(\frac{4}{3}\times 216\pi\right)\text{cm}^3$$

$$= 288\,\pi \text{ cm}^3$$

Exercise

1. The radius of a hemisphere is 14 cm, find its volume.
(a) 11498.66 cubic cm
(b) 1916.44 cubic cm
(c) 2874.67 cubic cm
(d) 5749.33 cubic cm

2. One diagonal of a rhombus is half the other. If the length of the side of the rhombus is 20 cm, what is the area of the rhombus?
(a) 320 sq cm (b) 160 sq cm
(c) 240 sq cm (d) 360 sq cm

3. The curved surface area of a hemisphere is 27.72 sq cm and volume is 19.404 cubic cm, find its radius.
(a) 4.2 cm (b) 2.1 cm
(c) 0.7 cm (d) 1.05 cm

4. The circumference of a circle is equal to the perimeter of an equilateral triangle. If the radius of the circle is 14cm what is the length of the side of the equilateral triangle?
(a) 88 cm (b) 88/3 cm
(c) 88/√3 cm (d) 88√3 cm

5. If the curved surface area of a right circular cone is 10010 sq cm and its radius is 35cm, find its volume.
(a) 6930 cubic cm
(b) 13860 cubic cm
(c) 3465 cubic cm
(d) 27720 cubic cm

6. If curved surface area of a cylinder is 1320 sq cm and height is 10 cm, find its radius.
(a) 21 cm (b) 42 cm
(c) 63 cm (d) 10.5 cm

7. A circle is inscribed in a square. If the length of the diagonal of the square is 14√2 cm, what is the area of the circle?
(a) 308 sq cm (b) 462 sq cm
(c) 154 sq cm (d) 616 sq cm

8. The total surface area of a hemi sphere is 41.58 sq cm, find its radius.
(a) 4.2 cm (b) 0.7 cm
(c) 1.05 cm (d) 2.1 cm

9. A tent is to be built in the form of a cylinder of radius 7 m surmounted by a cone of the same radius. If the height of the cylindrical part is 8 m and slant height of the conical part is 12 m, how much canvas will be required to build the tent ? Allow 20% extra canvas for folding and stitching : (Take $\pi = 22/7$).

(a) 1478.4 sq mts
(b) 2217.6 sq mts
(c) 369.6 sq mts
(d) 789.2 sq mts

10. A cylindrical vessel of radius 8 cm is partially filled with water. By how much will the water level rise if a sphere of radius 7 cm is completely immersed in this water ?

(a) 7.15 cm (b) 14.3 cm
(c) 21.45 cm (d) 28.6 cm

11. If the volume of a cylinder is 2156 cubic cm and height is 14 cm, find its radius.

(a) 14 cm (b) 21 cm
(c) 3.5 cm (d) 7 cm

12. A cone is hollowed out of a solid wooden cube of side 7 cm. The diameter and height of the cone is same as the side of the cube. What is the volume of the remaining cube ?

(a) 253.17 cubic cms
(b) 228.84 cubic cms
(c) 143.26 cubic cms
(d) 257.68 cubic cms

13. Of the 3 numbers whose average is 72, the first is 2/7 times the sum of other two. The first number is :

(a) 48 (b) 72
(c) 32 (d) 96

14. If the radius of a circle is increased by 29%, its area increases by :

(a) 58 percent
(b) 29 percent
(c) 33.205 percent
(d) 66.41 percent

15. A cylindrical vessel of height 7 cm and radius 5 cm is completely filled with sand. When this sand is poured out it forms a right circular cone of radius 8 cm what will be the height of this cone ?

(a) 8.2 cm (b) 16.4 cm
(c) 24.6 cm (d) 32.8 cm

16. If curved surface area of a cylinder is 616 sq cm and height is 14 cm, find its radius.

(a) 14 cm (b) 7 cm
(c) 21 cm (d) 3.5 cm.

17. Curved surface area of a cylinder is 660 sq cm. If circumference of its base is 44 cm, find the volume of the cylinder.

(a) 4620 cubic cm
(b) 2310 cubic cm
(c) 6930 cubic cm
(d) 1155 cubic cm

18. The diagonal of a square is equal to the side of an equilateral triangle. If the area of the square is $15\sqrt{3}$ sq cm, what is the area of the equilateral triangle?

(a) $45/\sqrt{2}$ sq cm (b) $45\sqrt{2}$ sq cm
(c) 45 sq cm (d) 45/2 sq cm

19. If the curved surface area of a right circular cone is 3080 sq cm and its slant height is 35 cm, find its total surface area.

(a) 11088 sq cm (b) 1848 sq cm
(c) 5544 sq cm (d) 2772 sq cm

20. The diameter of a circle is equal to the side of the square. What is the area of square if the area of the circle is 49π sq cm. ?

(a) 196 sq cm (b) 154 sq cm
(c) 124 sq cm (d) 98 sq cm

21. The radius of a hemisphere is 7 cm, find its volume.

(a) 718.67 cubic cm
(b) 1437.34 cubic cm
(c) 239.56 cubic cm
(d) 359.34 cubic cm

22. If the radius of a circle is increased by 15% its area increases by :

(a) 30 percent
(b) 32.25 percent
(c) 15 percent
(d) 16.125 percent

23. Curved surface area of a cylinder is 528 sq cm. If circumference of its base is 44 cm, find the height of the cylinder.

(a) 12 cm (b) 24 cm
(c) 36 cm (d) 6 cm

24. If the curved surface area of a right circular cone is 10010 sq cm and its slant height is 91 cm, find its total surface area.

(a) 27720 sq cm (b) 4620 sq cm
(c) 6930 sq cm (d) 13860 sq cm

25. A cone of radius 3.5 cm and height 12 cm is completely filled with water. This water is emptied into an empty cylindrical vessel of radius 7 cm. What will be the height of water in this vessel ?

(a) 2 cm (b) 0.33 cm
(c) 0.5 cm (d) 1 cm

Answers with Explanations

1. (d) It is given that $r = 14$ cm

Volume of hemisphere $= \frac{2}{3}\pi r^3$

$= \frac{2}{3} \times \frac{22}{7} \times 14 \times 14 \times 14$

$= \frac{44}{3} \times 2 \times 196$

$= 5749.33$ cubic cm

2. (a) Two diagonals of a rhombus are d and $d/2$ respectively.

In ΔABO

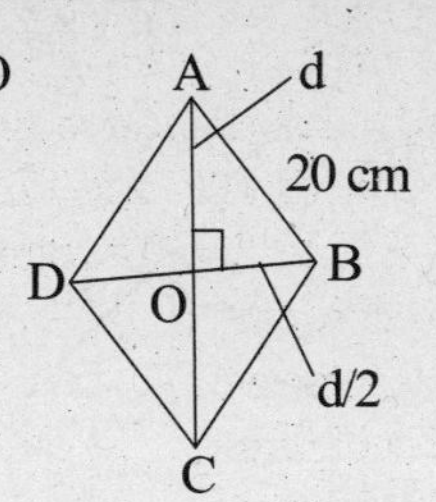

$$\left(\frac{d}{2}\right)^2 + \left(\frac{d}{4}\right)^2 = (20)^2$$

$$\frac{d^2}{4} + \frac{d^2}{16} = 400$$

$$d^2\left(\frac{4+1}{16}\right) = 400$$

$$d^2 = \frac{400 \times 16}{5}$$

$$d = \frac{20 \times 4}{\sqrt{5}} = \frac{80}{\sqrt{5}} = 16\sqrt{5} \text{ cm}$$

$$\text{Area of Rhombus} = \frac{1}{2} d \times \frac{d}{2}$$

$$= \frac{1}{2} \times \frac{80}{\sqrt{5}} \times \frac{40}{\sqrt{5}}$$

$$= \frac{3200}{10}$$

$= 320$ sq. cm.

3. (b) Curved surface area $= 2\pi r^2$

$$27.72 = 2 \times \frac{22}{7} \times r^2$$

$$r^2 = \frac{27.72 \times 7}{44}$$

$$= \frac{2.52 \times 7}{4} = 0.63 \times 7$$

$$r^2 = 0.09 \times 7 \times 7$$

$$r = 0.3 \times 7 = 2.1 \text{ cm}$$

4. (b) According to question

$$2\pi r = 3a$$

$$2 \times \frac{22}{7} \times 14 = 3a$$

$$\frac{88}{3} = a$$

$$\text{Side, } (a) = \frac{88}{3} \text{ cm}$$

5. (*) $\pi rl =$ C.S.A. of a cone

$$\frac{22}{7} \times 35 \times l = 10010$$

$$l = \frac{10010}{110} = 91 \text{cm}$$

$$h = \sqrt{l^2 - r^2} = \sqrt{91^2 - 35^2}$$

$$= \sqrt{(91+35)(91-35)}$$

$$= \sqrt{126 \times 56}$$

$$= \sqrt{4 \times 4 \times 3 \times 3 \times 7 \times 7}$$

$$h = 4 \times 3 \times 7 = 84$$

$$V = \frac{1}{3} \pi r^2 h$$

$$= \frac{1}{3} \times \frac{22}{7} \times 35 \times 35 \times 84$$

$= 107800$ cubic cm

6. (a) C.S.A. of a cylinder $= 2\pi rh$

$$1320 = 2 \times \frac{22}{7} \times r \times 10$$

$$r = \frac{1320 \times 7}{44 \times 10}$$

$$r = 21 \text{ cm}$$

7. (c) Diagonal $= 14\sqrt{2}$ cm

Let sides of a square be x

$$x^2 + x^2 = d^2$$

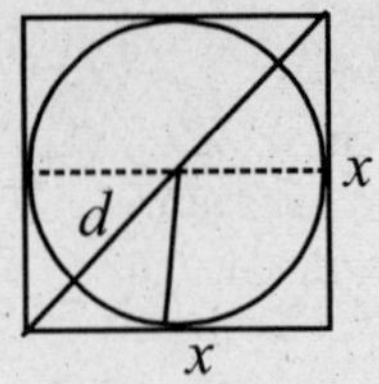

$$2x^2 = \left(14\sqrt{2}\right)^2$$

$$x^2 = \frac{14 \times 14 \times 2}{2}$$

$$x = 14 \text{ cm}$$

Since, circle touches its four sides,

$$r = \frac{x}{2} = \frac{14}{2} = 7 \text{ cm}$$

$$\text{Area of the circle} = \pi r^2$$

$$= \frac{22}{7} \times 7 \times 7$$

$$= 154 \text{ cm}^2$$

8. (d) Total surface area of hemisphere $= 41.58$ sq. cm

$$3\pi r^2 = 41.58$$

$$3 \times \frac{22}{7} r^2 = 41.58$$

$$r^2 = \frac{41.58 \times 7}{3 \times 22}$$

$$r = \sqrt{0.63 \times 7}$$

$$= \sqrt{.09 \times 7 \times 7}$$

$$= 0.3 \times 7 = 2.1 \text{ cm.}$$

9. (d)

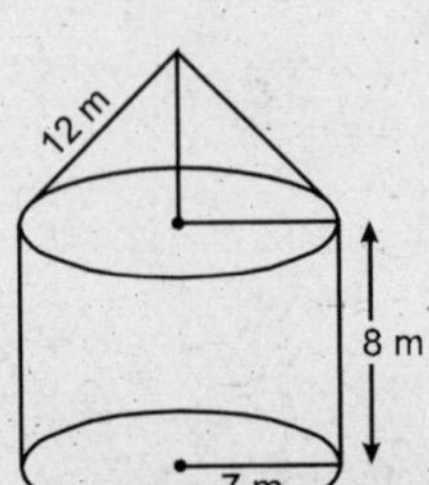

Total area of canvas $= 2\pi rh + \pi rl$

$$l = \sqrt{h^2 + r^2} = \sqrt{144 + 49}$$

$$= \sqrt{193} = 13{\cdot}9 \text{ m}$$

$$= \pi r(2h + l)$$

$$= \frac{22}{7} \times 7\,(2 \times 8 + 13{\cdot}9)$$

$$= 22\,(16 + 13{\cdot}9) = 22 \times 29{\cdot}9$$

$$= 657{\cdot}8 \text{ m}^2$$

Net cloth required

$$= \frac{657{\cdot}8 \times 120}{100}$$

$$= \frac{657{\cdot}8 \times 12}{10} = 789{\cdot}3 \text{ m}^2$$

10. (d) Volume rises in cylinder = Volume of sphere

$$2\pi rh = \frac{4}{3} \pi R^3$$

$$h = \frac{\frac{4}{3} \pi R^3}{2\pi r}$$

$$= \frac{2}{3} \frac{R^3}{r} = \frac{2 \times 7 \times 7 \times 7}{3 \times 8}$$

$$= \frac{343}{12} = 28.6 \text{ cm}$$

Hence, water level will rise in cylinder upto height = 28.6 cm.

11. (d) Volume of a cylinder $= \pi r^2 h$

$$2156 = \frac{22}{7} \times (r^2) \times 14$$

$$r^2 = \frac{2156 \times 7}{22 \times 14} = 49$$

$$r = \sqrt{49}$$

$$r = 7 \text{ cm}$$

Hence, the required radius is 7 cm.

12. (a) Volume of cube = (side)^3

$$= 7 \times 7 \times 7 = 343 \text{ cm}^3$$

$$\text{Volume of cone} = \frac{1}{3} \pi r^2 h$$

$$= \frac{1}{3} \times \frac{22}{7} \times \frac{7}{2} \times \frac{7}{2} \times 7$$

$$= 89.833 \text{ cm}^3$$

$\therefore$ Volume of remaining cube

$$= 343 - 89.833$$

$$= 253.166 = 253.17 \text{ cm}^3$$

13. (a) Let the three numbers be X_1, X_2, X_3 respectively. According to question,

$$\frac{X_1 + X_2 + X_3}{3} = 72$$

$$\therefore X_1 + X_2 + X_3 = 72 \times 3 \quad ...(i)$$

and $$X_1 = \frac{2}{7}(X_2 + X_3)$$

$$X_1 = \frac{2}{7}X_2 + \frac{2}{7}X_3 \quad ...(ii)$$

Putting value of X_1 in equation (i)

$$X_1 + X_2 + X_3 = 72 \times 3$$

$$\Rightarrow \frac{2}{7}X_2 + \frac{2}{7}X_3 + X_2 + X_3 = 72 \times 3$$

$$\Rightarrow \frac{9}{7}X_2 + \frac{9}{7}X_3 = 72 \times 3$$

$$\Rightarrow \frac{9}{7}(X_2 + X_3) = 72 \times 3$$

$$\therefore (X_2 + X_3) = \frac{72 \times 3 \times 7}{9} = 168$$

From eq^n (ii)

$$\Rightarrow X_1 = \frac{2}{7} \times 168 = 48$$

Finally, the first number (X_1) is 48.

14. (d) Let the radius of circle $= r$

$\therefore$ Area of circle $= \pi r^2$

If radius increased by 29%

Then the new radius of the circle

$$= r + \frac{29r}{100} = \frac{129r}{100}$$

$\therefore$ The new area of circle

$$= \pi \times \left(\frac{129r}{100}\right)^2$$

$\therefore$ Area increased

$$= \pi\left(\frac{129r}{100}\right)^2 - \pi r^2$$

$$= \pi r^2\left[\left(\frac{129}{100}\right)^2 - 1\right]$$

$$= \pi r^2\left[\frac{16641}{10000} - 1\right]$$

$$= \pi r^2\left[\frac{6641}{10000}\right]$$

$\therefore$ Area increased in percent

$$= \frac{6641 \times 100}{10000} = 66{\cdot}41\%$$

15. (a) For a cylindrical vessel

height $= 7$ cm

and radius $= 5$ cm

and for a right circular cone

radius $= 8$ cm

height $= H$ cm

$\therefore$ Volume of a right circular cone = Volume of cylindrical vessel

$$\frac{1}{3}\pi r_1^2 h = \pi r_2^2 h$$

$$\frac{1}{3} \times \frac{22}{7} \times (8)^2 \times H = \frac{22}{7} \times (5)^2 \times 7$$

$$\frac{64}{3} \times H = 25 \times 7$$

$$H = \frac{25 \times 7 \times 3}{64}$$

$$= 8.20 \text{ cm}$$

16. (b) Curved surface area of a cylinder $= 616 \text{ cm}^2$

$$2\pi rh = 616$$

$$2 \times \frac{22}{7} \times r \times 14 = 616$$

$$44r \times 2 = 616$$

$$r = \frac{616}{44 \times 2} = \frac{56}{8} = \frac{14}{2}$$

$$r = 7 \text{ cm.}$$

17. (b) Circumference $C = 2\pi r$

$$\Rightarrow 44 = 2 \times \frac{22}{7} \times r$$

$$\Rightarrow r = \frac{44 \times 7}{44} = 7 \text{ cm}$$

Curved surface area $= 2\pi rh$

$$\Rightarrow 660 = 2 \times \frac{22}{7} \times h \times 7$$

$$\Rightarrow \frac{660}{2 \times 22} = h$$

$$h = 15 \text{ cm}$$

Volume of cylinder $= \pi r^2 h$

$$= \frac{22}{7} \times 7 \times 7 \times 15$$

$$= 2310 \text{ cm}^3.$$

18. (d) Let the side of a square be x.

Area of square $= x^2$

$$15\sqrt{3} = x^2$$

$$2 \times 15\sqrt{3} = 2x^2 = d^2$$

$\because$ (diagonal)$^2 = d^2$

$\because d^2 = x^2 + x^2 = 2x^2$

Area of an equilateral triangle.

$$= \frac{\sqrt{3}}{4} \times d^2$$

$$= \frac{\sqrt{3}}{4} \times 30\sqrt{3}$$

$$= \frac{90}{4} = \frac{45}{2} \text{ sq. cm}$$

19. (c) C.S.A. of cone $= \pi rl$

$$3080 = \frac{22}{7} \times r \times 35 = 110r$$

$$r = \frac{3080}{110} = 28$$

$$h^2 = \sqrt{l^2 - r^2}$$

$$= \sqrt{35^2 - 28^2} = 21$$

T.S.A. $= \pi rl + \pi r^2 = \pi r(1 + r)$

$$= \frac{22}{7} \times 28(35 + 28)$$

$$= 88 \times 63 = 5544 \text{ cm}^2$$

20. (a) Let the side of a square be x and radius be r

$$\frac{\text{Area of square}}{\text{Area of circle}} = \frac{(\text{side})^2}{\pi r^2} = \frac{x^2}{\pi r^2}$$

According to given condition

Diameter = side of a square

$$2r = x \Rightarrow 4 = \frac{x^2}{r^2} \; 49\pi$$

$$\text{Area of square} = \frac{49\pi \times 4}{\pi} = 196 \text{ cm}^2$$

21. (a) $r = 7$ cm

Volume of hemisphere

$$= \frac{2}{3}\pi r^3 = \frac{2}{3} \times \frac{22}{7} \times (7 \times 7 \times 7)$$

$$= \frac{2 \times 22 \times 49}{3} = \frac{44 \times 49}{3}$$

$$= \frac{2156}{3} = 718{\cdot}67\text{cm}^3$$

22. (b) If radius is increased 15%

$$\text{Increase \% in area} = \left(2r + \frac{r^2}{100}\right)\%$$

$$= \left(15 \times 2 + \frac{(15)^2}{100}\right)\%$$

$$= \left(30 + \frac{225}{100}\right)\%$$

$$= 30 + 2.25 = 32.25\%$$

23. (a) Curved surface area $= 528 \text{ cm}^2$

Perimeter × height $= 528 \text{ cm}^2$

$$2\pi rh = 528$$

$$44 \times h = 528$$

$$h = \frac{528}{44}$$

$$= \frac{48}{4} = 12 \text{ cm}$$

24. (d) Curved surface area (C.S.A) $= \pi rl$

$$10010 = \frac{22}{7} \times r \times 91 = 22r \times 13$$

$$\therefore \quad r = \frac{10010}{22 \times 13} = \frac{5005}{11 \times 13} = \frac{455}{13} = 35 \text{ cm}$$

Total suface area $= \pi rl + \pi r^2$

$$= 10010 + \frac{22}{7} \times 35 \times 35$$

$$= 10010 + 110 \times 35$$

$$= 10010 + 3850$$

$$= 13860 \text{ sq. cm}$$

25. (d) Volume of cylinder = Volume of cone

$$\pi r_2^2 h_2 = \frac{1}{3} \pi r_1^2 h_1$$

$$3 \times 7 \times 7 \times h_2 = 3{\cdot}5 \times 3{\cdot}5 \times 12$$

$$\Rightarrow \quad h_2 = \frac{3{\cdot}5 \times 3{\cdot}5 \times 12}{7 \times 7 \times 3}$$

$$\Rightarrow \quad h_2 = \frac{0{\cdot}5 \times 0{\cdot}5 \times 12}{3} = 0{\cdot}25 \times 12$$

$$\Rightarrow \quad h_2 = \frac{3{\cdot}00}{3} = 1 \text{cm}$$

12 GEOMETRY

Important Facts and Formulae

- A line is made up of an infinite number of points and it has only length.

  i.e., A line has no end points on either side.

  A **line segment** has two end points. A **ray** has one end point.

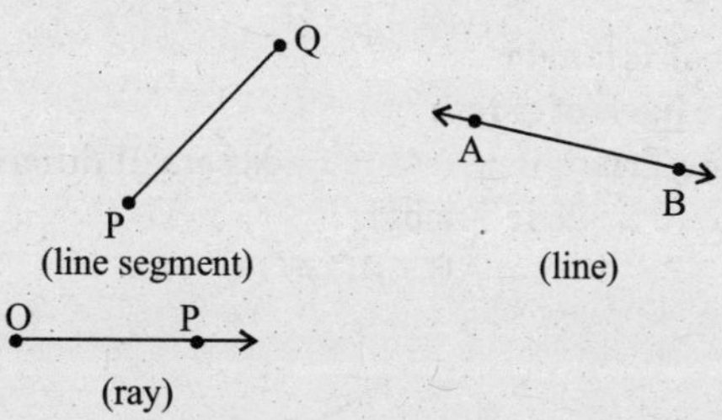

- A line segment PQ is generally denoted by $\overline{PQ}$.
- A line AB is denoted by $\overleftrightarrow{AB}$.
- And the ray OP is denoted by $\overrightarrow{OP}$.
- **Collinear points :** Three or more than three points are said to be collinear if there is a line which contains them all.

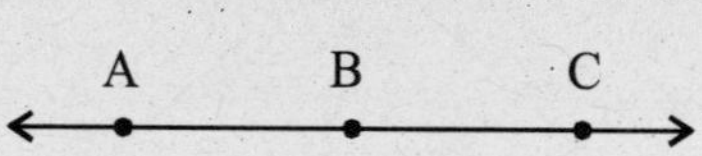

  Here A, B and C are collinear points.

- **Concurrent lines :** Three or more than three lines are said to be concurrent if there is a point which lies on all of them. AB, CD and EF are concurrent lines.

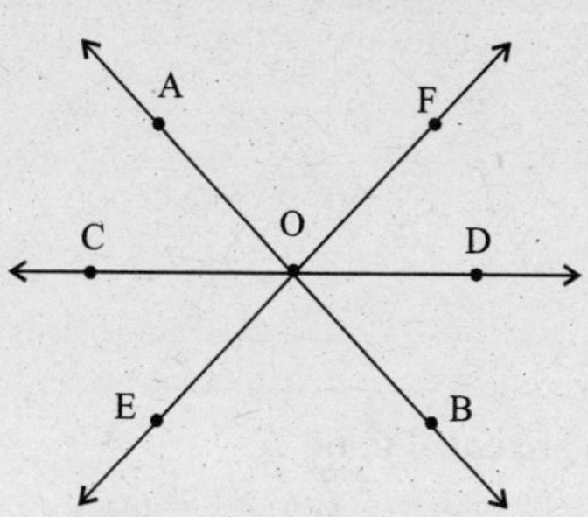

  Recall that an "angle" is formed when lines or line segments meet. *e.g.*,

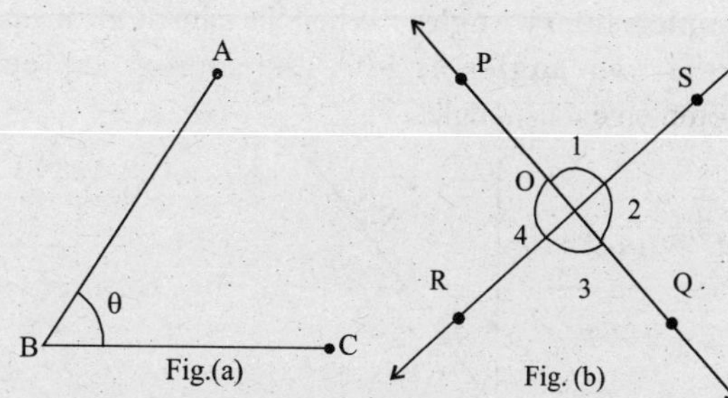

Fig.(a) Fig. (b)

  in figure (a) $\angle\theta$ is formed by AB and BC and in figure (b) $\angle 1$, $\angle 2$, $\angle 3$ and $\angle 4$ are formed by PQ and RS.

- **Adjacent Angles :** Two angles are said to be adjacent if

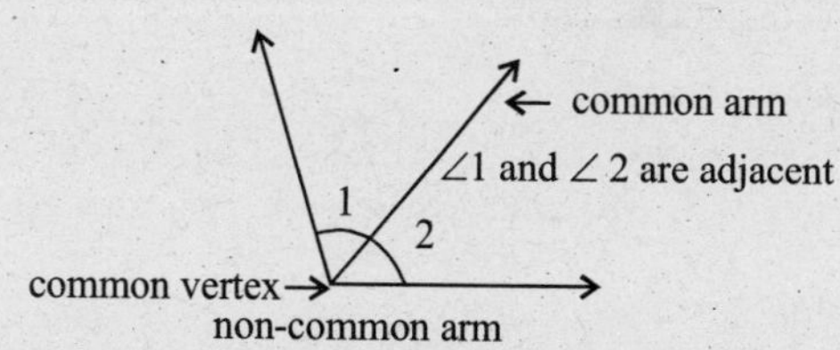

  (i) They have a common vertex;

  (ii) They have a common arm; and

  (iii) The non-common arms are on either side of the common arm.

- **Linear pair :** A linear pair is a pair of adjacent angles whose non-common sides are opposite rays.

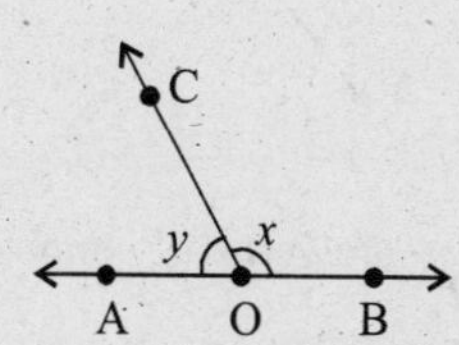

  $\angle x$, $\angle y$ are a linear pair and $\angle x + \angle y = 180°$

  i.e., linear pair angles are supplementary.

- **Parallel Lines :** If two lines have no point in common they are said to be Parallel lines.

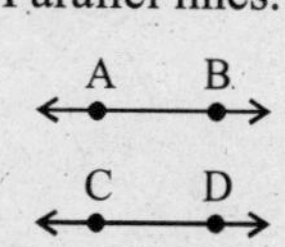

- **Intersecting lines :** If two lines have a point in common, they are said to be intersecting lines. Two lines can intersect at the most at one point.

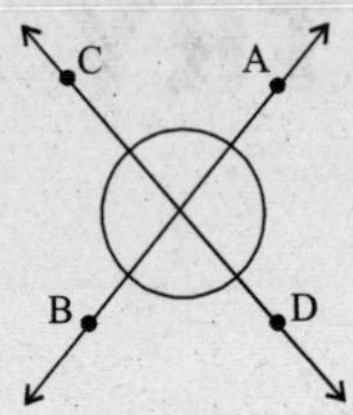

- **Complementary Angles :** When the sum of the measures of the two angles is 90°, the angles are called "Complementary Angles."

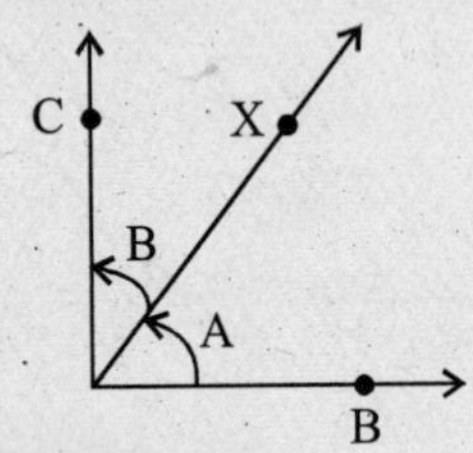

i.e., $\angle A + \angle B = 90°$
or $\angle A = \angle 90° - \angle B$ complement of $\angle A$.

- **Supplementary Angles :** Sum of two angles which are supplementary is 180°.

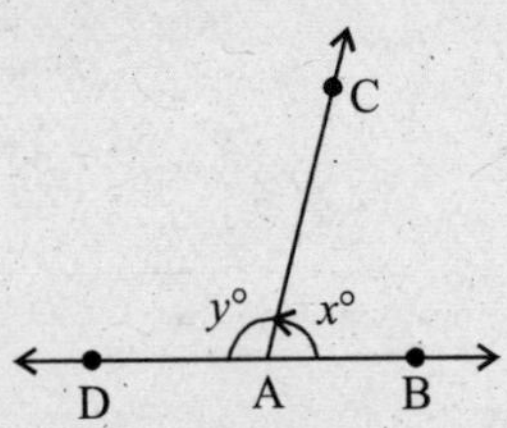

i.e., $\angle x + \angle y = 180°$

- **Vertically opposite Angles :**

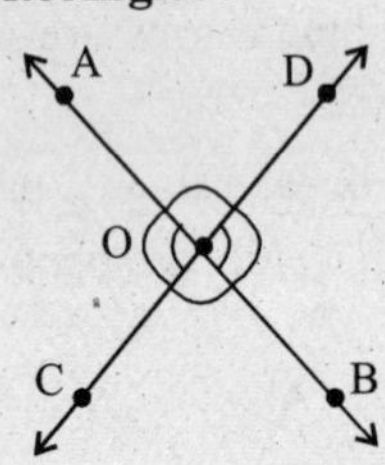

$\left.\begin{array}{l}\angle AOD, \angle BOC \\ \angle AOC, \angle BOD\end{array}\right\}$ are vertically opposite angles

- **Angles made by a transversal line :**

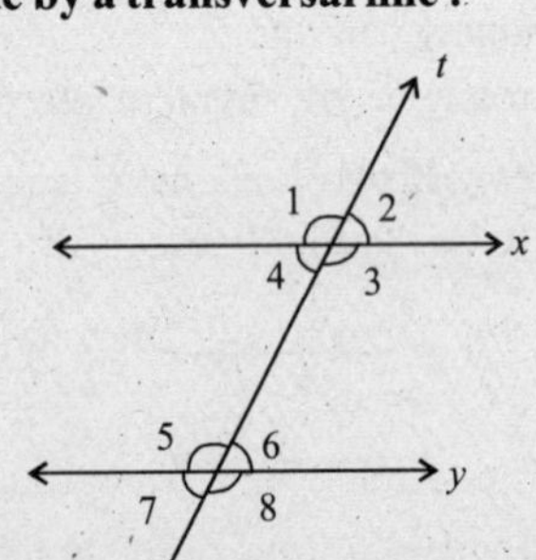

Interior Angles : $\angle 3, \angle 4, \angle 5, \angle 6$
Exterior Angles : $\angle 1, \angle 2, \angle 7, \angle 8$
Pairs of corresponding angles : $\angle 1$ and $\angle 5$, $\angle 2$ and $\angle 6$, $\angle 4$ and $\angle 7$, $\angle 3$ and $\angle 8$
Pairs of alternate interior angles : $\angle 3$ and $\angle 5$, $\angle 4$ and $\angle 6$
Pairs of alternate exterior angles : $\angle 1$ and $\angle 8$, $\angle 2$ and $\angle 7$
Pairs of interior angles on the same side of the transversal : $\angle 3$ and $\angle 6$, $\angle 4$ and $\angle 5$

If two parallel lines are intersected by a transversal then :

1. Each pair of corresponding angles are equal.
2. Each pair of alternate interior angles are equal.
3. Interior angles on the same side of the transversal are supplementary.

Triangles

A plane figure bounded by three lines in a plane is called a triangle.

Types of Triangles :

1. On the basis of sides :

(i) Scalene Triangle : All three sides are of different lengths is called a Scalene Triangle.

$$AB \neq BC \neq CA$$

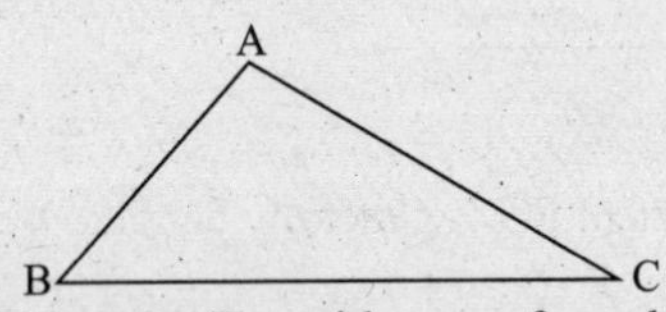

(ii) Isosceles Triangle : Two sides are of equal length, is called an Isosceles Triangle.

$$AB = AC \neq BC$$

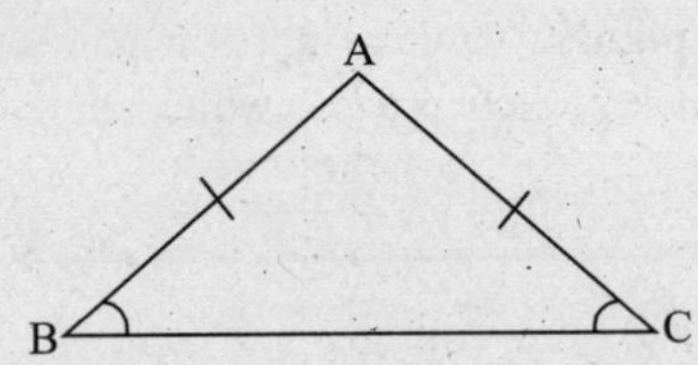

Angles opposite to equal sides are equal.

i.e., $\angle B = \angle C$

(iii) Equilateral Triangle : A triangle having all sides equal is called Equilateral triangle.

$$AB = BC = CA$$

- All angles are equal to 60°

$$\angle A = \angle B = \angle C = 60°$$

2. On the basis of Angles :

(i) Right-angled Triangle : In a triangle, in which one of the angles measures 90° is called a right-angled triangle.

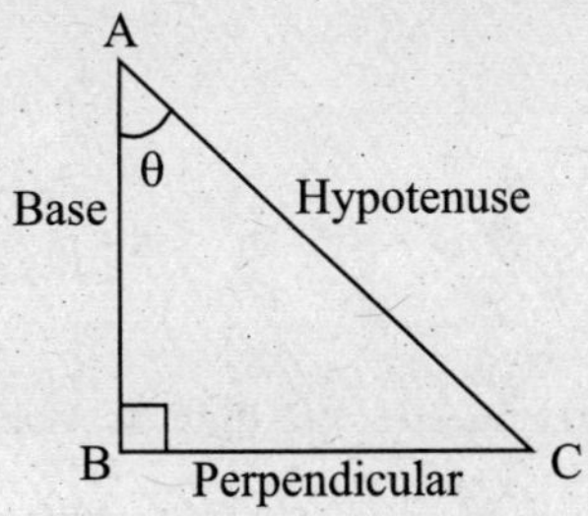

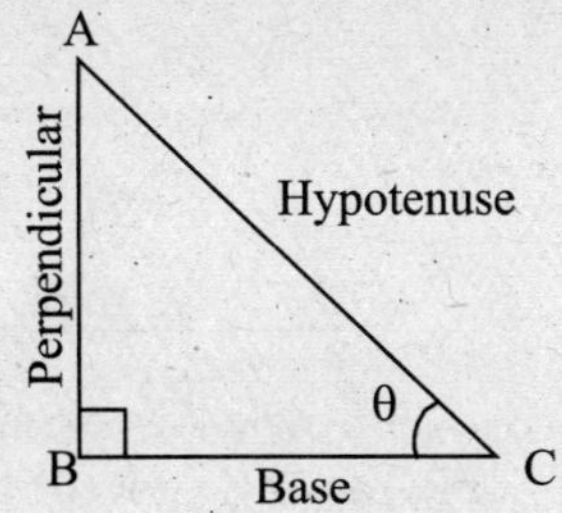

(ii) Acute-angled Triangle : A triangle in which every angle is more than 0° and less than 90° is called an acute-angle triangle.

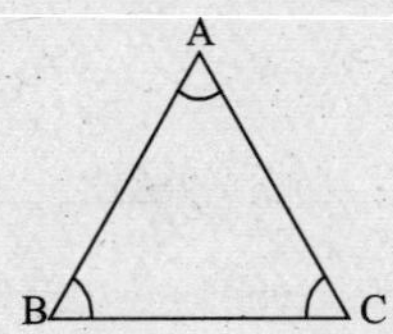

(iii) Obtuse-angled triangle : A triangle in which one of the angles is more than 90° is called an obtuse-angle triangle.

Note : An equilateral triangle is an isosceles triangle but the converse is not true.

Perimeter of a triangle (2s) : The sum of lengths of three sides of a triangle is called its perimeter.

$$2s = a + b + c$$

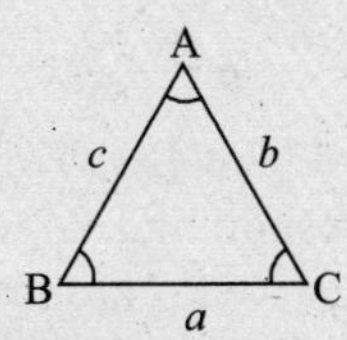

- Angle Sum property of a triangle :

  Theorem 1. The sum of the angles of a Δ is 180°.

  Theorem 2. (Exterior angle Theorem) : If a side of a triangle is produced, the exterior angle so formed is equal to the sum of the two interior opposite angles.

$$\angle ACD = \angle ABC + \angle BAC$$

$$\Rightarrow \quad \angle 4 = \angle 1 + \angle 2$$

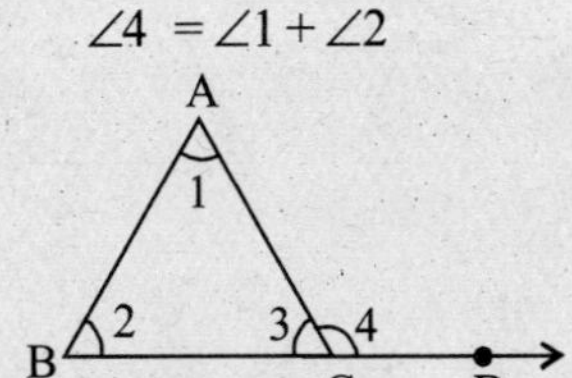

Centres of a Triangles

- **In-Centre of Triangles :** The point of intersection of all the three angle bisectors of a triangle is called its in-centre (I).

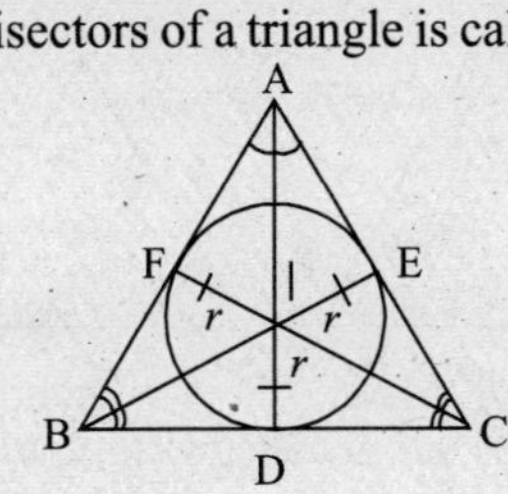

- The distance between In-centre and its all three sides is always equal and called inradius (r).

$$ID = IE = IF = r \text{ (inradius)}$$

$$\text{Inradius } (r) = \frac{\text{Area of a } \Delta \text{ (A)}}{\text{semi perimeters (s)}} = \frac{A}{s}$$

$$\angle BIC = 90 + \frac{1}{2}\angle A \quad \angle AIC = 90 + \frac{1}{2}\angle B$$

$$\angle AIB = 90 + \frac{1}{2}\angle C$$

- **Circumcentre of Triangle :** The point of intersection of the ⊥ bisectors of three sides of a triangle is called its circumcentre.

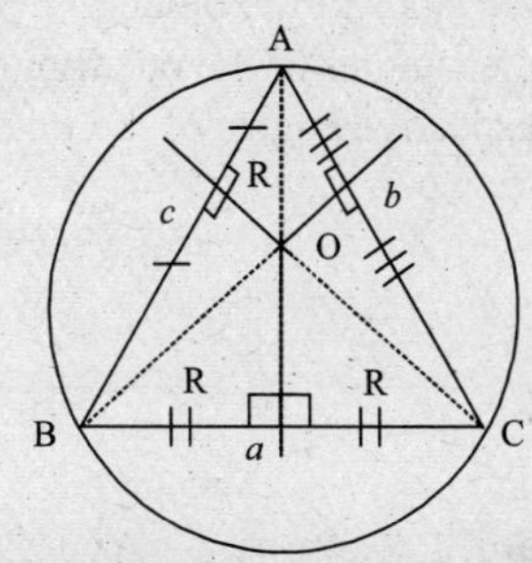

- The distance between circumcentre and its all three vertices are always equal and called circumradius.

$$OA = OB = OC = R$$

(circumradius)

$$\text{Circumradius (R)} = \frac{a.b.c}{4A}$$

$$\angle BOC = 2.\angle A \quad \angle AOC = 2.\angle B$$

$$\angle AOB = 2.\angle C$$

- **Centroid :** It is the point of intersection of all the three medians. It is denoted by G.

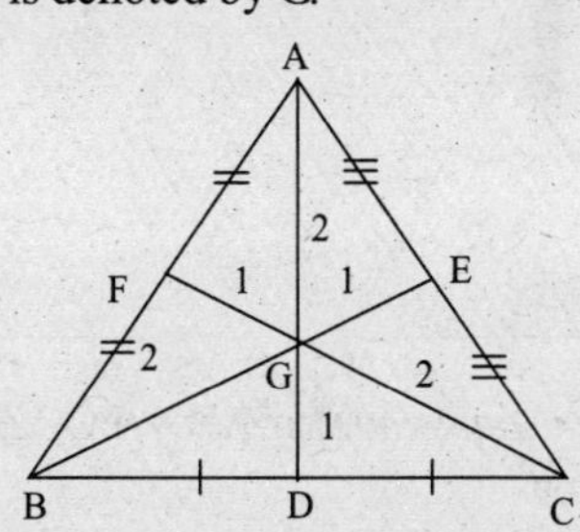

- **Medians :** A line segment joining the mid-point of the side with opposite vertex.
- The centroid (G) divides a median in the ratio of 2 : 1.

$$AG : GD = BG : GE = CG : GF = 2 : 1$$

- A median divides Area of a Δ in exactly two parts.
- **Orthocentre :** It is the point of intersection of all the three altitudes.
- **Altitude :** The altitude of a triangle is a line segment perpendicularly drawn from vertex to the side opposite to

it. The side on which $\perp^r$ is drawn is called its base.

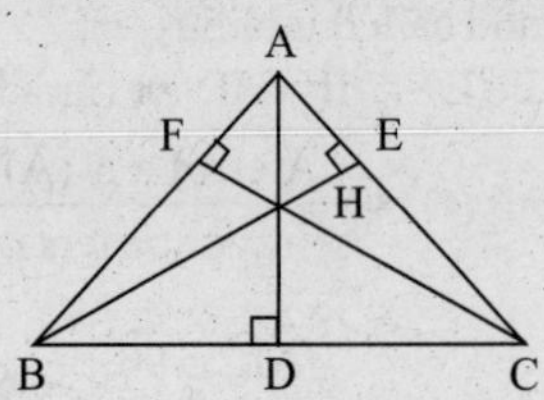

$\angle BHC = 180° - \angle A \quad \angle AHB = 180° - \angle C$

$\angle AHC = 180° - \angle B$

- **Congruency of triangles :** Two triangles are said to be congruent if they are equal in all respects *i.e.*,

1. Each of the three sides of one triangle must be equal to the three respective sides of the other.
2. Each of the three angles of the one triangle must be equal to the three respective angles of the other.

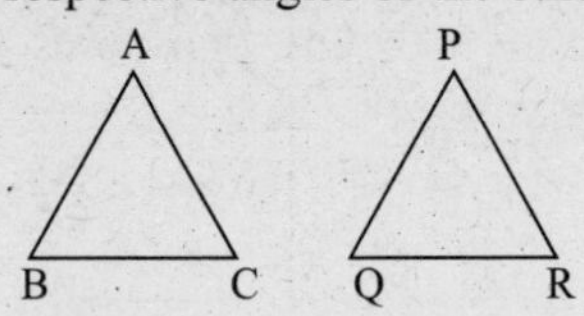

i.e., $\left.\begin{array}{l} AB = PQ \\ AC = PR \\ CB = QR \end{array}\right\}$ and $\left.\begin{array}{l} \angle A = \angle P \\ \angle B = \angle Q \\ \angle C = \angle R \end{array}\right\}$

- **Tests of congruency :** With the help of the following given tests, we can deduce without having detailed information about triangles that whether the given two triangles are congruent or not.

1. S-S-S (Side-Side-Side)

if $AB = PQ, AC = PR, BC = QR$

then $\Delta ABC \cong \Delta PQR$

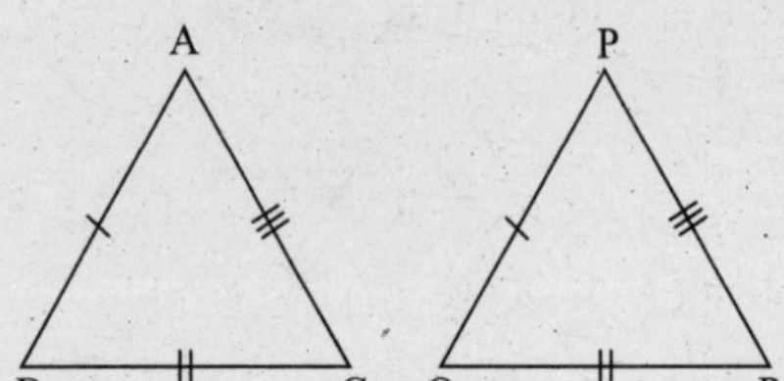

2. S-A-S (Side-Angle-Side) if AB = PQ, $\angle ABC = \angle PQR$, BC = QR then

$\Delta ABC \cong \Delta PQR$

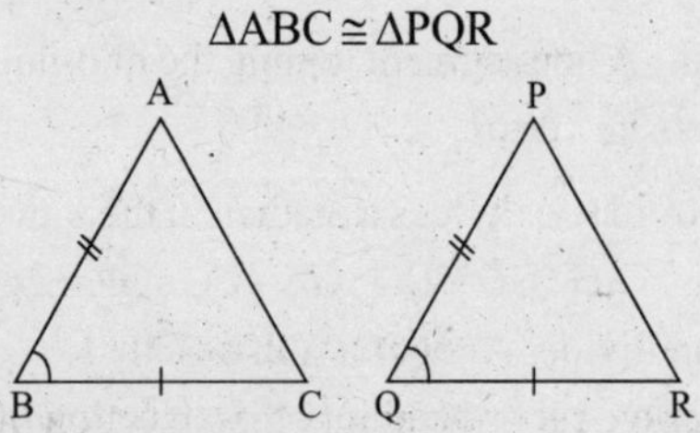

3. A-S-A (Angle-Side-Angle)

if $\angle ABC = \angle PQR, BC = QR$,

$\angle ACB = \angle PQR$ then,

$\Delta ABC \cong \Delta PQR$

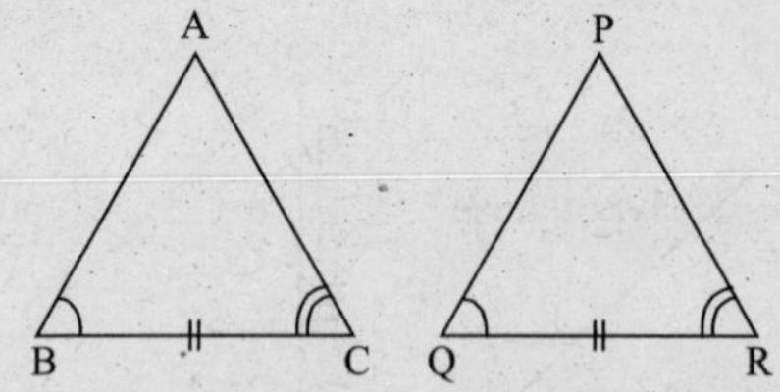

4. A-A-S (Angle-Angle-Side) if $\angle ABC = \angle PQR$, $\angle ACB = \angle PRQ$ and AC = PR (or AB = PQ) then,

$\Delta ABC \cong \Delta PQR$

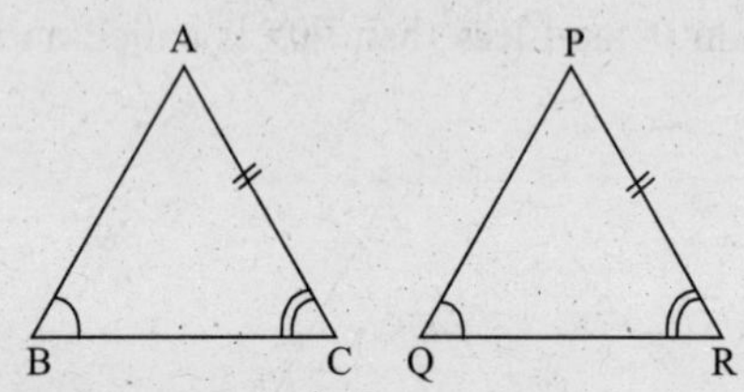

5. R-H-S (Right angle-Hypotenuse-Side)

if $AC = PR, \angle B = \angle Q$ and $BC = QR$

$\therefore \quad \Delta ABC \cong \Delta PQR$

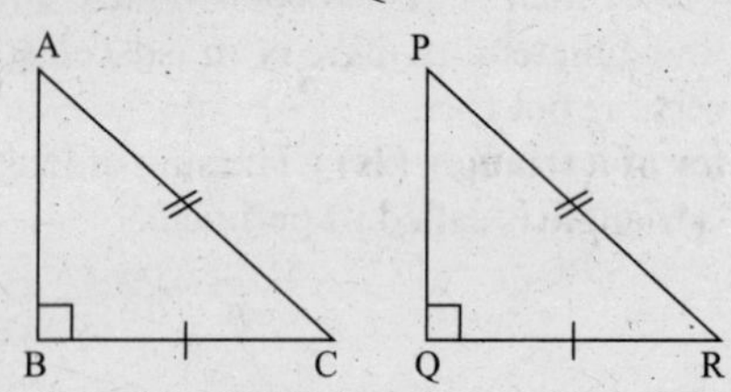

- **Similarity of triangles :** Two triangles are said to be similar if the corresponding angles are congruent and their corresponding sides are in proportion. The symbol for similarity is '~'.

If $\Delta ABC \sim \Delta PQR$ then

$\angle ABC \cong \angle PQR, \angle BCA \cong \angle QRP$

$\angle BAC \cong \angle QPR$

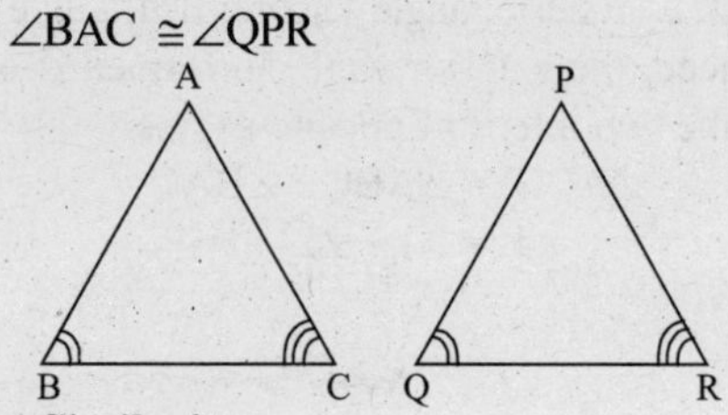

Test for Similarity

1. A-A (Angle-Angle)

if $\angle ABC \cong \angle PQR$

and $\angle ACB \cong \angle PRQ$

then, $\Delta ABC \sim \Delta PQR$

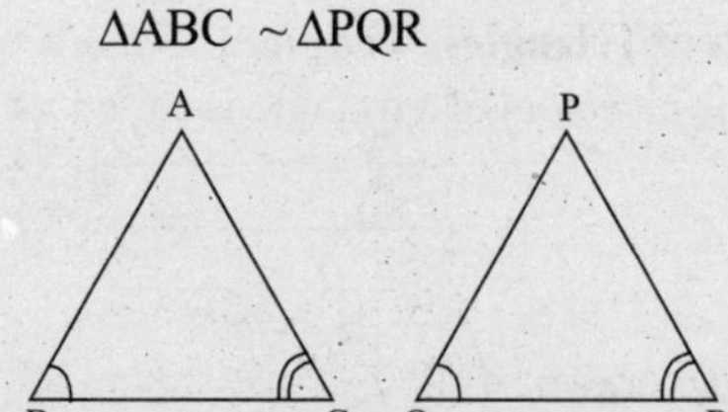

2. S-A-S (Side-Angle-Side)

if $\frac{AB}{PQ} = \frac{BC}{QR}$ and $\angle ABC = \angle PQR$

then, $\Delta ABC \sim \Delta PQR$

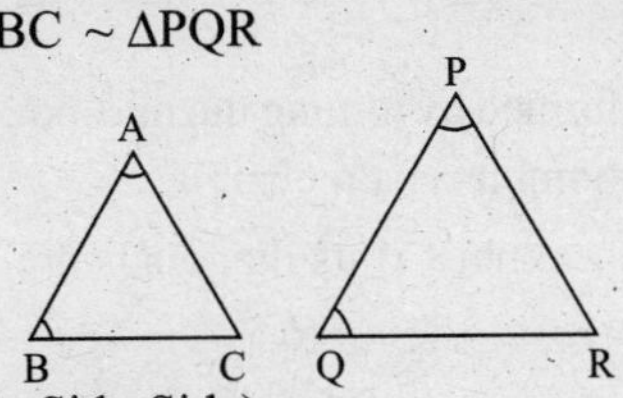

3. S-S-S (Side-Side-Side)

if $\frac{AB}{PQ} = \frac{BC}{QR} = \frac{AC}{PR}$

then, $\Delta ABC \sim \Delta PQR$

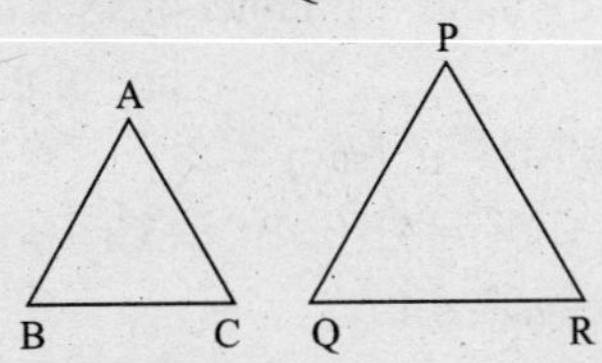

- **Properties of Similar triangles :** If the two triangles are similar, then for the proportional/corresponding sides we have the following results :

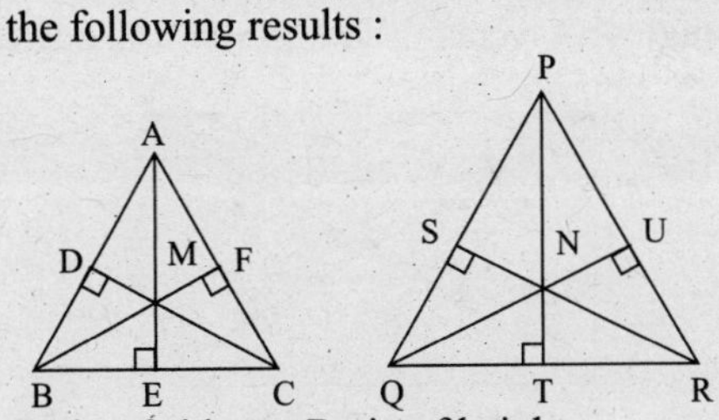

1. Ratio of sides = Ratio of heights (altitudes)
   = Ratio of medians
   = Ratio of angle bisectors
   = Ratio of in radii
   = Ratio of circum radii
2. Ratio of areas = Ratio of squares of corresponding sides, *i.e.*, if $\Delta ABC \sim \Delta PQR$, then

$$\frac{A(\Delta ABC)}{A(\Delta PQR)} = \frac{(AB)^2}{(PQ)^2} = \frac{(BC)^2}{(QR)^2} = \frac{(AC)^2}{(PR)^2}$$

3. In a right angled triangle, the triangles on each side of the altitude drawn from the vertex of the right angle to the hypotenuse are similar to the original triangle and to each other too.

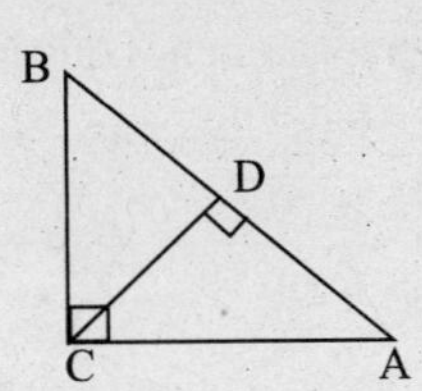

i.e., $\Delta BCA \sim \Delta BDC \sim \Delta CDA$

4. If a line drawn parallel to one side of a triangle intersects the other two sides in distinct points, the other two sides are divided in the same ratio.

i.e., $\frac{AD}{DB} = \frac{AE}{EC}$ & $\frac{AD}{AB} = \frac{AE}{AC} = \frac{DE}{BC}$

and $\Delta ADE \sim \Delta ABC$

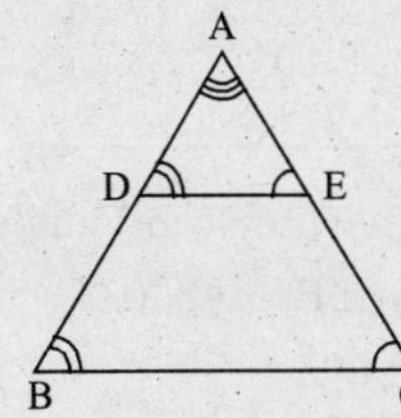

- If D and E are the mid-points of AB and AC & DE || BC then,

$$DE = \frac{1}{2}BC$$

- Vice versa is also true *i.e.*,
  If a line divides any two sides in the same ratio $\left(i.e., \frac{AD}{DB} = \frac{AE}{EC}\right)$ then the line is parallel to third line *i.e.*, DE || BC.

5. Two triangles between the two parallel lines will always be similar.

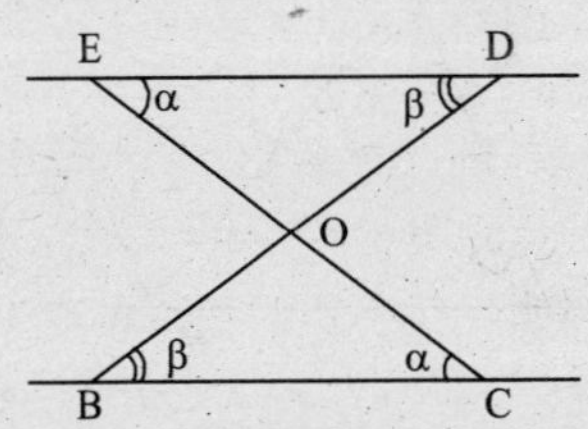

If ED || BC then $\Delta EOD \sim \Delta COB$.

6. If the area of two similar triangles are equal then the triangles are congruent.

If Area of ABC = Area of PQR

$\Delta ABC \sim \Delta PQR$

$\Rightarrow$ $\Delta ABC \cong \Delta PQR$

$\Rightarrow$ If in ΔABC, bisector of external angle A, intersects BC produced to D, then

$$\frac{AB}{AC} = \frac{BD}{CD}$$

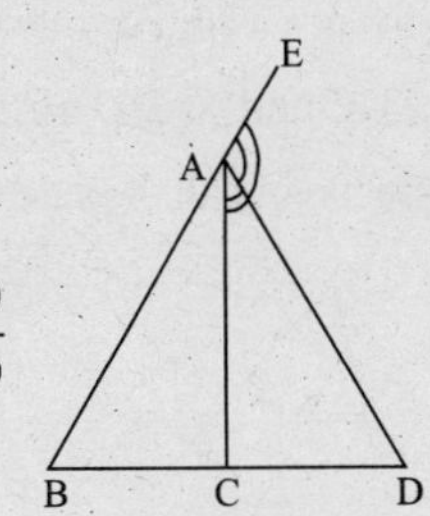

Quadrilaterals

A plane figure bounded by four line segments AB, BC, CD and DA is called a quadrilateral. It is denoted by symbol '□' *i.e.*, □ABCD.

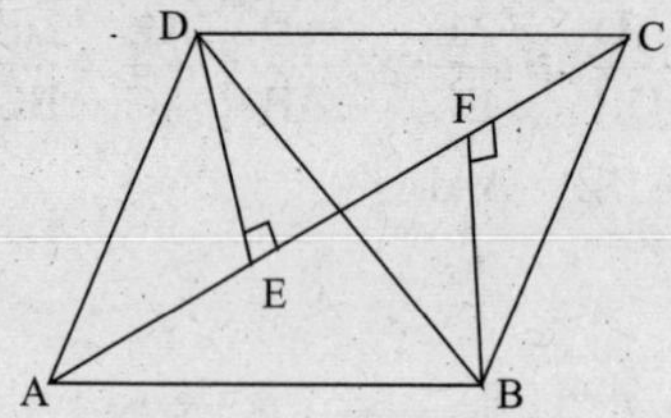

pairs of consecutive (adjacent) angles :

$(\angle A, \angle B), (\angle B, \angle C), (\angle C, \angle D), (\angle D, \angle A)$

pairs of adjacent sides :

(AB, BC), BC, CD), (CD, DA) and (DA, AB).

- **Properties :** Sum of four interior angles is 360° *i.e.*, $\angle A + \angle B + \angle C + \angle D = 360°$.

  The figure formed by joining the mid-points of a quadrilateral is a parallelogram.

$$\text{Area of } \square ABCD = \frac{1}{2} AC \times (DE + BF)$$

Types of Quadrilaterals :

1. Parallelogram (|| gm) : A quadrilateral whose opposite sides are parallel.

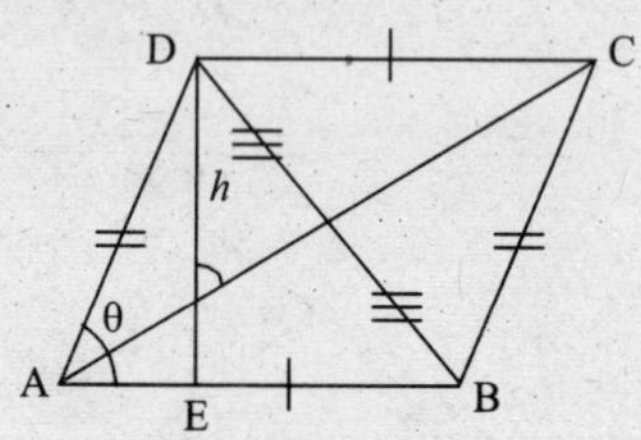

- **Properties :**

1. The opposite sides are equal and parallel.
2. Opposite angles are equal. $(\angle A = \angle C)$ and $(\angle B = \angle D)$
3. Sum of any two adjacent angles is 180°.
4. Diagonals bisect each other.
5. Diagonals need not be equal in length.
6. Diagonals need not bisect at right angle.
7. Each diagonal divides a ||gm into two congruent triangles. *i.e.*, $\Delta ABC \cong \Delta ADC$ and $\Delta ABD \cong \Delta BCD$.

2. Rhombus : A ||gm having all the sides equal is a "rhombus."

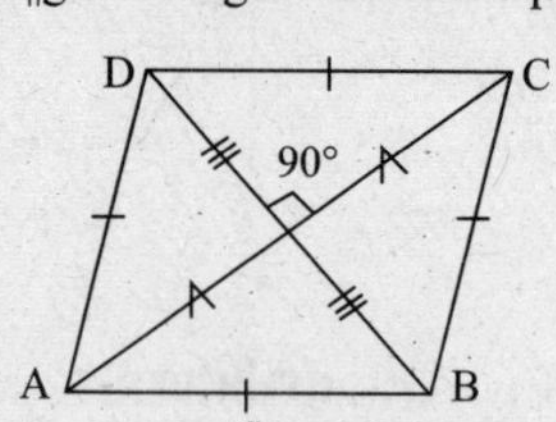

- **Properties :**

1. $AB = BC = CD = DA = a$ (say).
2. Diagonals bisect each other at right angle, but they are not necessarily equal.
3. A rhombus may or may not be a square but all squares are rhombus.
4. The figure formed by joining the mid-points of the adjacent sides of a rhombus is a rectangle.
5. A ||gm is a rhombus if its diagonals are perpendicular to each other.
6. (a) Area of rhombus $= \frac{1}{2} \times$ product of diagonals

   $= \frac{1}{2} \times d_1 d_2$

   (b) Area of rhombus = Product of adjacent sides × sine of the included angle.
7. $AC = d_1$ and $BD = d_2$ (say)

   then $d_1^2 + d_2^2 = AB^2 + BC^2 + CD^2 + DA^2$

   $\Rightarrow d_1^2 + d_2^2 = 4a_2$
8. A rhombus is a square if its diagonals are equal *i.e.*, if $d_1 = d_2 \Rightarrow ABCD$ is a square.

3. Rectangles : A rectangle is a ||gm with all angles 90°.

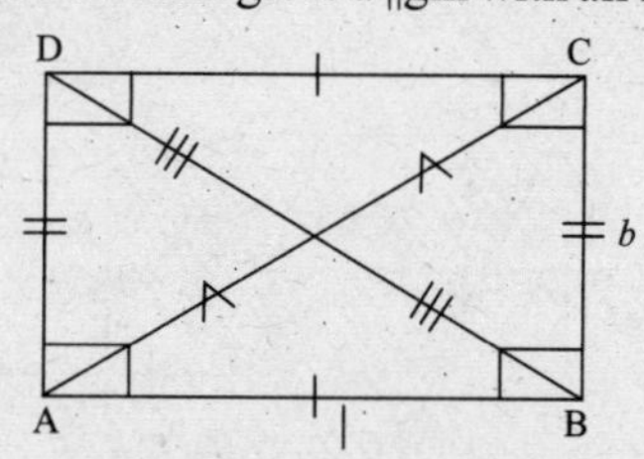

- **Properties :**

1. Diagonals are equal and bisect each other, but not necessarily at right angles.
2. For the given perimeter of rectangles, a square has maximum area.
3. The figure formed by joining the mid-points of the adjacent sides of a rectangle is rhombus.
4. Area of rectangle ABCD = length × breadth

   $= l \times b$
5. Diagonals of a rectangle $= \sqrt{l^2 + b^2}$
6. Bisectors of the angles of a rectangle (a ||gm) form another rectangle.

4. Trapezium : A trapezium is a quadrilateral with only two sides parallel to each other.

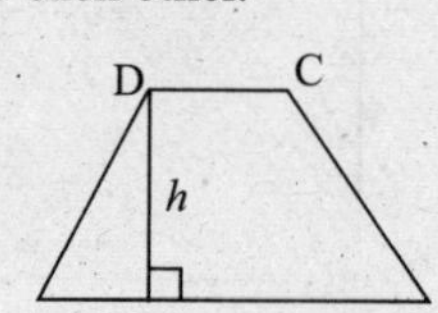

- **Properties :**

1. $\angle A + \angle D = \angle B + \angle C = 180°$.

2. If E and F are the mid-points of two non-parallel sides AB and BC respectively, then

$$\text{Median (EF)} = \frac{1}{2}(\text{AB} + \text{DC})$$

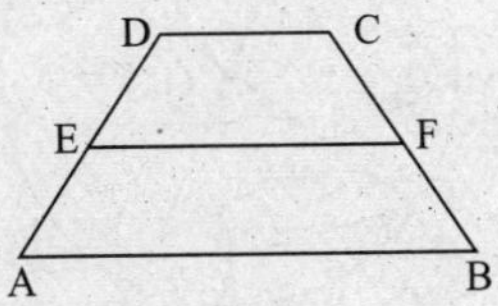

3. Area of trapezium

$$= \frac{1}{2}(\text{sum of parallel sides}) \times \text{height}$$

$$= \frac{1}{2} \times (\text{AB} + \text{CD}) \times \text{DM}$$

$$= \frac{1}{2}(\text{AB} + \text{CD}) \times h$$

4. Sum of square of diagonals = (sum of squares of non-parallel side) + 2(product of || sides)

   i.e., $AC^2 + BD^2 = BC^2 + AD^2 + 2AB.CD$

5. By joining the mid-points of adjacent sides of a trapezium four similar triangles are obtained.

6. $$\frac{AO}{OC} = \frac{BO}{OD}$$

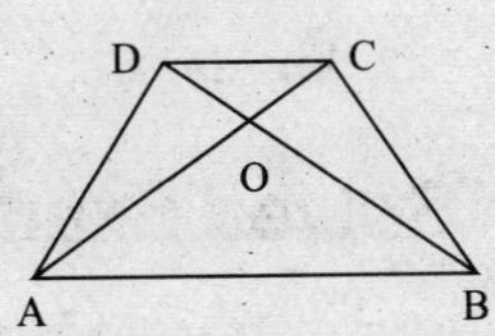

The mid-point Theorem :

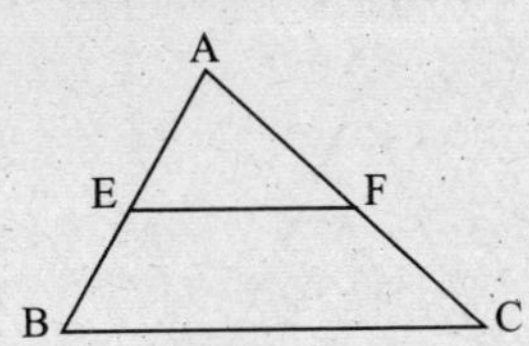

E and F are the mid-points of side AB and AC respectively, then

$$EF = \frac{1}{2}BC \text{ and } EF \parallel BC$$

5. **Square :** A square is a rectangle with adjacent sides equal or a rhombus with each angle 90°.

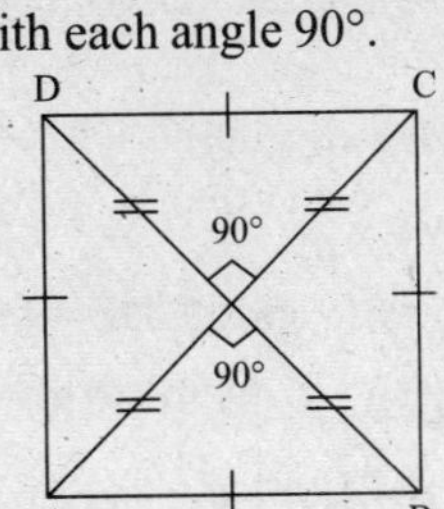

- **Properties :**

1. AB = BC = CD = AD = a (say) & ∠A = ∠B = ∠C = ∠D = 90°.
2. Diagonals are equal and bisect each other at right angle.
3. The figure formed by joining the mid-points of the adjacent sides of a square is a square.
4. Area= $(\text{side})^2 = a^2 = \frac{d^2}{2}$ and

   diagonal $(d) = a\sqrt{2}$

6. **Polygons :** A closed-figure bounded by three or more than three straight lines.

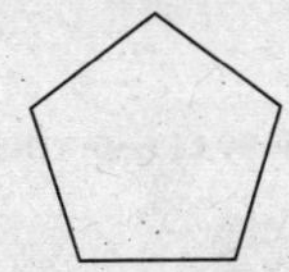

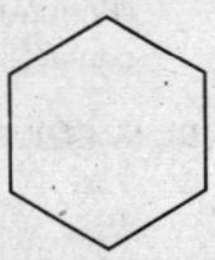

e.g., No of sides	Name
3	Triangle
4	Quadrilateral
5	Pentagon
6	Hexagon
7	Heptagon
8	Octagon
9	Nonagon
10	Decagon

- **Regular Polygons :** A polygon in which all the sides are equal and also the interior angles are equal, is called a 'Regular polygon.'

  If n = total no. of sides of a regular polygon, then

1. Sum of interior angles = $(n-2) \times 180°$
2. Each exterior angle = $\left(\frac{360°}{n}\right)$
3. Sum of all exterior angles = 360°
4. Each interior angle = 180° – exterior angle

   ⇒ interior angle + exterior angle = 180°
5. Number of diagonals = $\frac{n(n-3)}{2}$

Circles

A circle is a set of points on a plane which lie at a fixed distance from a fixed point.

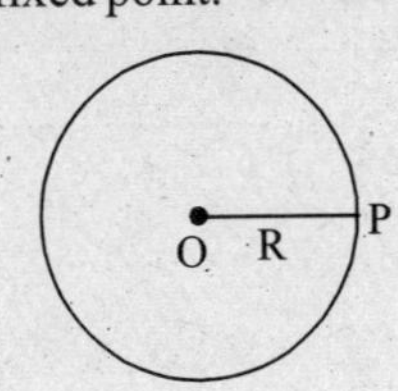

Fixed-point (O) is called "Centre" and R = OP = Radius = Fixed distance.

Tangent : A line meeting a circle in only one point is called a tangent.

Secant : A line which intersects a circle in two distinct points is called a "Secant".

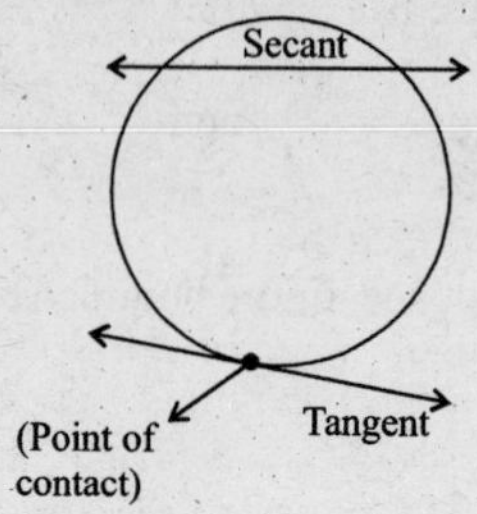

Chord : A line segment whose end-points lie on the circle.

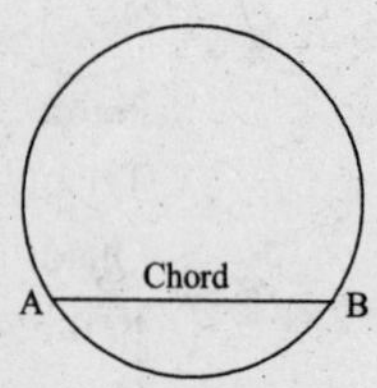

Diameter : A chord which passes through the centre is called the diameter of the circle.

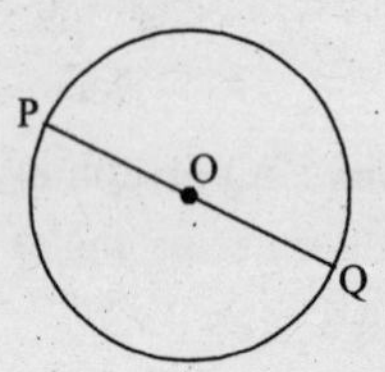

1. The perpendicular from the centre of a circle to a chord bisects the chord.

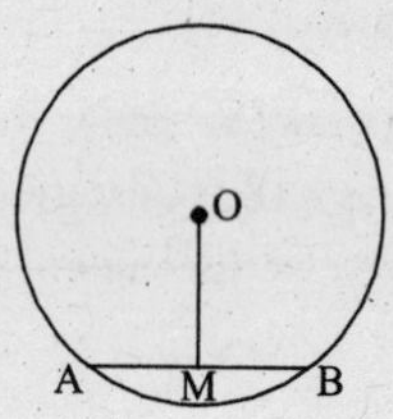

i.e., if OM $\perp$ AB, then AM = BM.

2. **Converse of the above theorem :** The line joining the centre of a circle to the mid point of a chord is perpendicular to the chord.

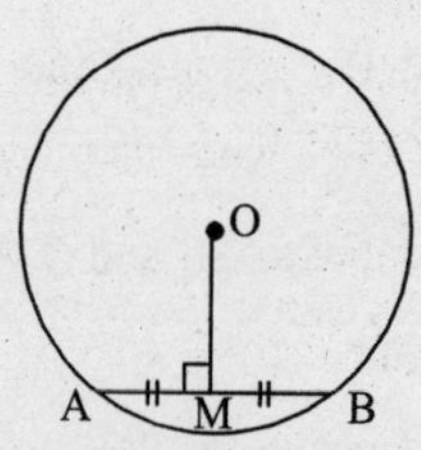

i.e., AM = MB, then OM $\perp$ AB.

3. Equal chords of a circle subtend equal angles at the centre.

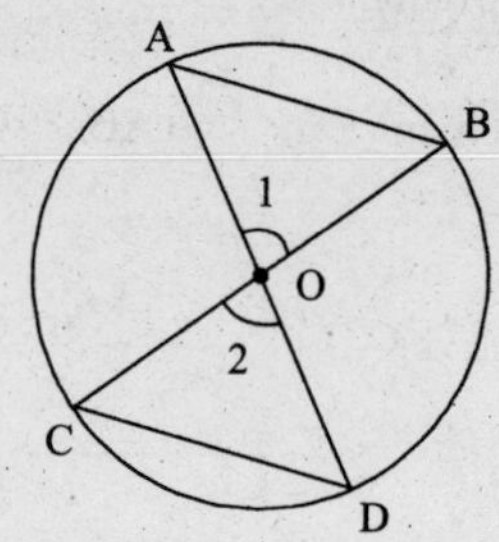

i.e., if AB = CD, then $\angle 1 = \angle 2$.

4. (Converse of the above theorem) angles subtended by two chords at the centre of a circle are equal then the chords are equal.

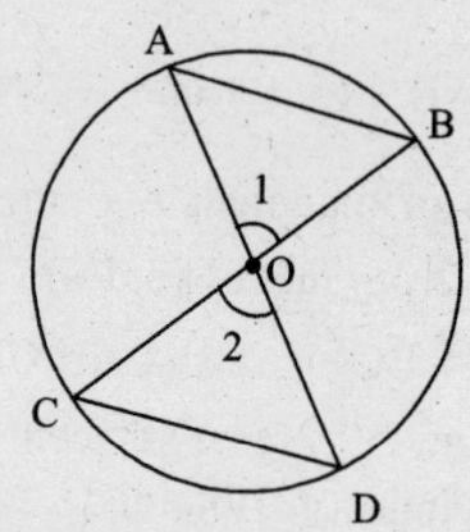

i.e., if $\angle 1 = \angle 2$, then AB = CD.

Solved Examples

Example 1. In the figure given below, AB is parallel to CD. $\angle ABC = 65°$, $\angle CDE = 15°$ and AB = AE

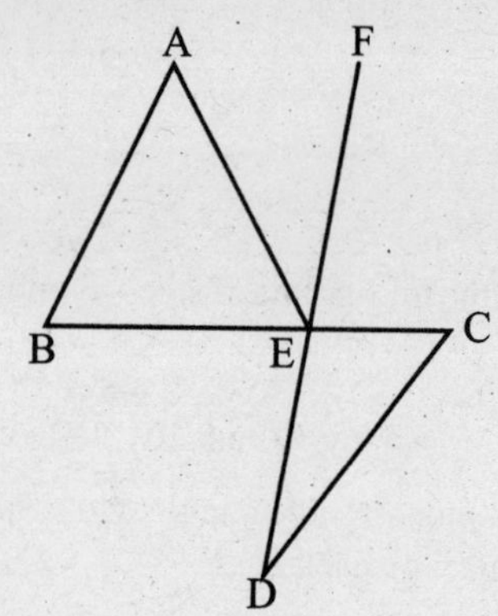

What is the value of $\angle AEF$?

Sol. Given that,

$\angle ABC = 65°$ and $\angle CDE = 15°$

Here, $\angle ABC + \angle TCB = 180°$ ($\because$ AB $\parallel$ CD)

$\therefore \angle TCB = 180° - 65° = 115°$

$\because \angle TCB + \angle DCB = 180°$ (linear pair)

$\therefore \angle DCB = 65°$

Now, in ΔCDE

$\angle CED = 180° - (\angle ECD + \angle EDC)$

$(\because \angle ECD = \angle BCD)$

$= 180° - (65° + 15°) = 100°$

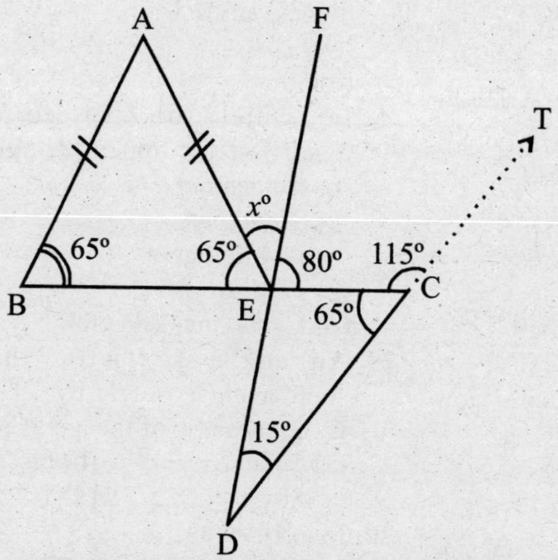

$\because \quad \angle DEC + \angle FEC = 180° \quad$ (linear pair)

$\Rightarrow \quad \angle FEC = 180° - 100° = 80°$

Given that, AB = AE

i. e., Δ ABE an isosceles triangle

$\therefore \quad \angle ABE = \angle AEB = 65°$

$\because \quad \angle AEB + \angle AEF + \angle FEC = 180°$

(straight line)

$\Rightarrow \quad 65° + x° + 80° = 180°$

$\therefore \quad x° = 180° - 145° = 35°$

Example 2. In the figure given below, EC is parallel to AB, $\angle ECD = 70°$ and $\angle BDO = 20°$

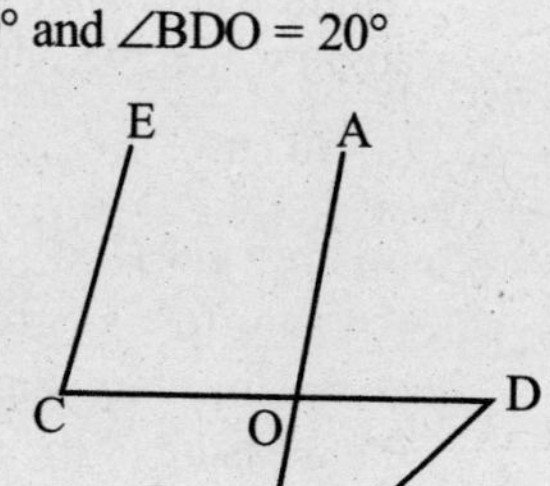

What is the value of $\angle OBD$?

Sol. Given that, EC || AB

$\therefore \quad \angle ECO + \angle AOC = 180°$

$\Rightarrow \angle AOC = 180° - 70° = 110°$

$\therefore \angle BOD = \angle AOC = 110°$ (alternate angle)

Now, in ΔOBD

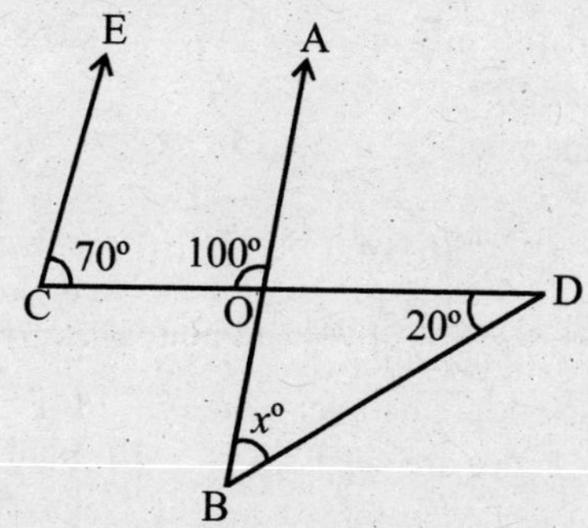

$\angle BOD + \angle ODB + \angle DBO = 180°$

$\therefore \; 110° + 20° + x° = 180° \Rightarrow x° = 50°$

Example3. The ratio of two complementary angle is 1 : 5. What is the difference between the two angles ?

Sol. Given that, $\frac{\alpha}{\beta} = \frac{1}{5} \Rightarrow \alpha = k$ and $\beta = 5k$ (say)

or complementary angles.

$\alpha = 90° - \beta \Rightarrow k = 90° - 5k$

$\Rightarrow k = 15°$

$\therefore \; \alpha = 15°$ and $\beta = 75°$

$\therefore$ Difference between angles $= 75° - 15° = 60°$

Example4.

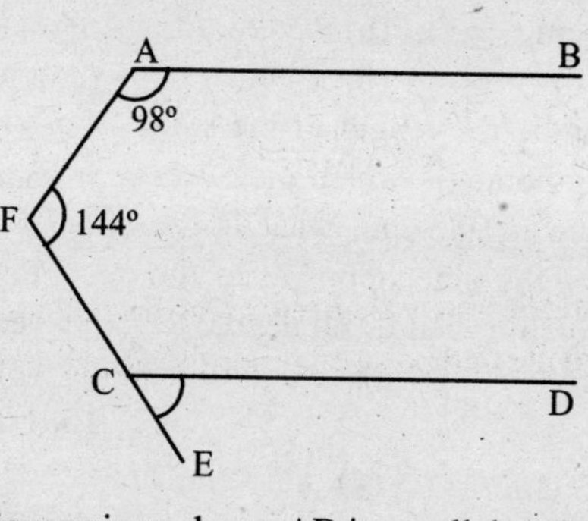

In the figure given above, AB is parallel to CD. If $\angle BAF = 98°$ and $\angle AFC = 144°$, then what is $\angle ECD$ equal to ?

Sol. Draw a line MN parallel to AB and CD.

$\therefore \; \angle AFN = 180° - 98° = 82°$

$\Rightarrow \angle CFN = 144° - 82° = 62°$

$\therefore \; \angle FCD = 180° - 62° = 118°$

$\Rightarrow \angle ECD = 180° - 118° = 62°$

Exercise

1. If the sum of the measures of all the interior angles of polygon is 1800°, find the number of sides of the polygon.
(a) 12 (b) 14
(c) 16 (d) 8

2. In an isosceles trapezium ....
(a) Opposite sides are parallel
(b) Opposite angles are supplementary
(c) Opposite anlges are not equal
(d) Diagonals bisect opposite angles

3. ΔDEF is similar to ΔGHI. Length of DE is 16 cm and length of the corresponding side GH is 25 cm. What is the ratio of areas of ΔDEF : ΔGHI ?
(a) 4 : 5 (b) 16 : 25
(c) 256 : 625 (d) 25 : 16

4. Find the sum of the measures of all the interior angles of a polygon having 10 sides.
(a) 2520° (b) 2880°
(c) 1440° (d) 3240°

5. In ΔABC, D and E are points on side AB and AC respectively. DE is parallel to BC. If lengths of AD, DB and DE are 8 cm, 6 cm and 7.2 cm respectively, find length of BC.
(a) 12.6 cm (b) 9.3 cm
(c) 8.1 cm (d) 5.4 cm

6. In a triangle the length of the side opposite the angle which measures 30 degree is $9\sqrt{3}$ cm, what is the length of the side opposite to the angle which measures 60 degree?
(a) 27 cm (b) 9 cm
(c) $12\sqrt{3}$ cm (d) $\frac{15\sqrt{3}}{2}$ cm

7. ΔABC is similar to ΔPQR. Length of AB is 36 cm and length of the corresponding side PQ is 16 cm. If area of ΔABC is 1296 sq cm, what is the area of ΔPQR ?
(a) 128 sq cm (b) 512 sq cm
(c) 64 sq cm (d) 256 sq cm

8. A hexagonal prism has 18 edges. How many vertices does it have?
(a) 8 (b) 12
(c) 20 (d) 22

9. Δ DEF is similar to Δ GHI. Length of DE is 9 cm and length of the corresponding side GH is 16 cm. What is the ratio of areas of Δ DEF :
(a) 3:4 (b) 9:16
(c) 81:256 (d) 16:9

10. Find the sum of the measures all the interior angles of a polygon having 12 sides.
(a) 1800° (b) 2520°
(c) 2880° (d) 3240°

11. A tetrahedron has 4 vertices. How many edges does it have?
(a) 8 (b) 12
(c) 6 (d) 10

12. In ΔPQR, S and T are points on side PQ and PR respectively. ST is parallel to QR. If S divides PQ in the ratio 4:3 and length of QR is 4.9 cm, find ST?
(a) 5.6 cm (b) 7.2 cm
(c) 2.1 cm (d) 3.6 cm

13. What is the altitude of an equilateral triangle whose side is $12\sqrt{3}$ cm?
(a) 12 cm (b) $15\sqrt{3/2}$ cm
(c) $(9\sqrt{3})/2$ cm (d) 18 cm

14. ΔABC is similar to ΔDEF. Length of AB is 12 cm and length of the corresponding side DE is 8 cm. What is the ratio of perimeter of ΔABC: Perimeter of ΔDEF?
(a) 9 : 4 (b) 4 : 9
(c) 3 : 2 (d) 2 : 3

15. Find the sum of interior angles of a decagon?
(a) 1620° (b) 2520°
(c) 1800° (d) 1440°

16. What is the equation of the line which has $\frac{5}{2}$ and $-\frac{4}{3}$ as x and y intercepts respectively ?
(a) $8x + 15y = 20$
(b) $8x - 15y = 20$
(c) $4x - 15y = 30$
(d) $4x + 15y = 30$

17. The measures of the four angles of a quadrilateral are in the ratio 1 : 2 : 4 : 5. What is the measure of the biggest angle ?
(a) 120° (b) 30°
(c) 60° (d) 150°

18. In which of the following quadrilaterals opposite angles are supplementary ?
(a) Rhombus
(b) Parallelogram
(c) Trapezium
(d) Cyclic quadrilateral

19. An angle is smaller than its supplementary angle by 70°. What is the measure of the angle ?
(a) 125° (b) 55°
(c) 80° (d) 10°

20. In a rhombus ....
(a) Adjacent sides are not equal
(b) Opposite angles are supplementary
(c) Diagonals bisect opposite angles
(d) Consecutive angles are equal

21. In ΔABC, the angle bisector of ∠A cuts BC at E. Find length of AC, if lengths of AB, BE and EC are 9 cm, 3.6 cm and 2.4 cm.
(a) 5.4 cm (b) 8 cm
(c) 4.8 cm (d) 6 cm

22. In a triangle, the length of the opposite side of the angle which measures 45° is $8\sqrt{2}$ cm, what is the length of the side opposite to the angle which measures 90° ?
(a) 16 cm (b) $4\sqrt{3}$ cm
(c) $8\sqrt{3}$ cm (d) $6\sqrt{3}$ cm

23. An angle is greater than its complementary angle by 40°. Find the measure of the angle ?
(a) 25° (b) 65°
(c) 130° (d) 50°

24. In a rhombus ....
(a) opposite angles are supplementary
(b) diagonals form two congruent triangles
(c) diagonals are congruent
(d) diagonals do not bisect opposite angles

25. ΔABC is right angled at B. BD is the altitude. AD is 8 cm and DC is 5 cm. What is the length of BD ?
(a) 25 cm (b) 20 cm
(c) 16 cm (d) 15 cm

26. In a rectangle :
(a) Diagonals bisect opposite angles
(b) Consecutive sides are congruent
(c) All sides are congruent
(d) Diagonals form two congruent triangles

27. In ΔPQR, S and T are points on side PQ and PR respectively. ST is parallel to QR. If S divides PQ in the ratio 1 : 5 and length of QR is 15 cm, find ST ?
(a) 2.4 cm (b) 3.6 cm
(c) 2.5 cm (d) 5.6 cm

28. In ΔABC, the median AD is 8 cm and CB is 16 cm, measure of angle CAB is ....
(a) 90° (b) 30°
(c) 60° (d) 120°

29. An angle is smaller than its supplementary angle by 50°. What is the measure of the angle ?
(a) 115° (b) 60°
(c) 30° (d) 65°

30. Points P and Q lie on side AB and AC of triangle ABC respectively such that segment PQ is parallel to side BC. If the ratio of areas of triangle APQ: triangle ABC is 16:25. Then the ratio of AP:PB is?
(a) 4 : 5 (b) 1 : 4
(c) 5 : 1 (d) 4 : 1

31. Line segment AB is parallel to line segment CD. AD intersects BC in E. If lengths of AE, BC and ED are 12 cm, 12 cm and 18 cm respectively, what is the length of EC?
(a) 4.8 cm (b) 9.3 cm
(c) 8.1 cm (d) 7.2 cm

32. In a triangle the length of the side opposite the angle which measures 60° is 15 cm, what is the length of the side opposite to the angle which measures 90°?
(a) 15 cm (b) $(15\sqrt{3})/2$ cm
(c) $10\sqrt{3}$ cm (d) 10 cm

33. In ΔABC, D and E are points on side AB and AC respectively. DE is parallel to BC. If lengths of AD, DB and DE are 9 cm, 6 cm and 5.4 cm respectively find length of BC?
(a) 3.6 cm (b) 4.8 cm
(c) 11.2 cm (d) 9 cm

34. In a triangle the length of the side opposite the angle which measures 30 degree is 12 cm, what is the length of the side opposite to the angle which measures 60 degree?
(a) 9 cm (b) $12\sqrt{3}$ cm
(c) $(15\sqrt{3})/2$ cm (d) $(9\sqrt{3})/2$ cm

35. Dodecahedron has 20 vertices. How many edges does it have?
(a) 30 (b) 16
(c) 12 (d) 24

36. ΔABC is similar to ΔPQR. Length of AB is 18 cm and length of the corresponding side PQ is 12 cm. If area of ΔABC is 324 sq cm, what is the area of ΔPQR ?
(a) 72 sq cm (b) 144 sq cm
(c) 36 sq cm (d) 487.5 sq cm

37. In ΔDEF, G and H are points on side DE and DF respectively. GH is parallel to EF. If G divides DE in the ratio 1:3 and HF is 7.2 cm, find length of DF.
(a) 2.4 cm (b) 4.8 cm
(c) 3.6 cm (d) 9.6 cm

38. A triangular prism has 9 edges. How many vertices does it have?
(a) 8 (b) 6
(c) 12 (d) 10

39. Find length of the arc whose central angle is 45° and radius of the circle is 28 cm ?
(a) 11 cm (b) 33 cm
(c) 44 cm (d) 22 cm

40. What is the measure of an interior angle of a regular decagon?
(a) 120° (b) 140°
(c) 144° (d) 150°

41. ΔGHI is similar to ΔKLM. If the ratio of Perimeter of ΔGHI : Perimeter of ΔKLM = 9:4 and length of GH is 27 cm what is the length of the corresponding side KL?
(a) 12 cm (b) 9 cm
(c) 24 cm (d) 18 cm

42. What is the measure of an exterior angle of a regular dodecagon?
(a) 45° (b) 40°
(c) 36° (d) 30°

43. Find the sum of the measures all the exterior angles of a decagon.
(a) 720° (b) 2160°
(c) 360° (d) 1800°

44. Points P and Q lie on side AB and AC of triangle ABC respectively such that segment PQ is parallel to side BC. If the ratio of AP : PB is 2 : 5, and area of Δ APQ is 4 sq cm, what is the area of trapezium PQCB?
(a) 49 sq cm (b) 45 sq cm
(c) 25 sq cm (d) 21 sq cm

45. What is the measure of an interior angle of a regular dodecagon?
(a) 120° (b) 140°
(c) 150° (d) 144°

46. In ΔPQR, S and T are points on side PQ and PR respectively. ST is parallel to QR. If S divides PQ in the ratio 4:1 and length of QR is 15 cm,what is the length of ST?
(a) 3 cm (b) 5 cm
(c) 12 cm (d) 10 cm

47. Δ ABC is similar to Δ DEF. Length of AB is 18 cm and length of the corresponding side DE is 10 cm. What is the ratio of perimeter of Δ ABC : perimeter of Δ DEF ?
(a) 5 : 9 (b) 9 : 5
(c) 81 : 25 (d) 25 : 81

48. Find the sum of interior angles of a dodecagon ?
(a) 1620° (b) 1800°
(c) 1440° (d) 1260°

Answers with Explanations

1. (a) Let the number of sides be n in a polygon

$(n-2) \times 180^\circ = 1800^\circ$

$$n-2 = \frac{1800^\circ}{180^\circ} = 10$$

$$n = 10 + 2 = 12$$

Hence, the number of sides is 12.

2. (b) Opposite angles are supplementary.

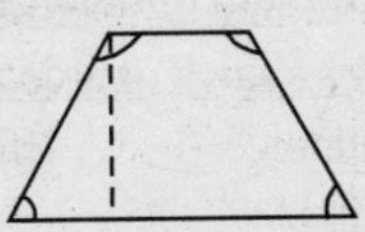

3. (c)

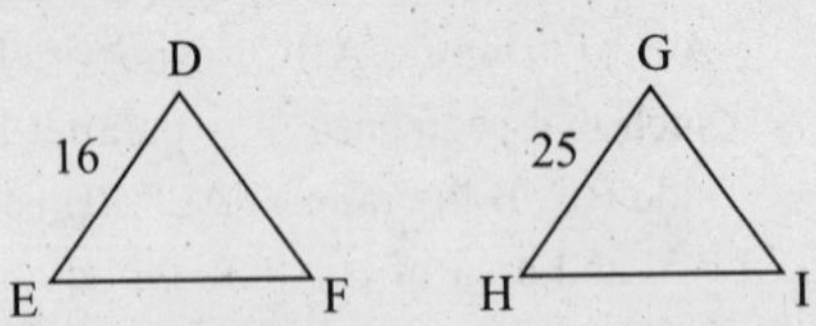

$$\therefore \frac{\text{Area of } \Delta DEF}{\text{Area of } \Delta GHI} = \frac{DE^2}{GH^2}$$

$$= \frac{(16)^2}{(25)^2} = \frac{256}{625}$$

Hence, the ratio of ΔDEF and ΔGHI is 256 : 625.

4. (c) Sum of interior angles

$= (2n-4) \times 90^\circ$

$= (2 \times 10 - 4) \times 90^\circ$

$= (20 - 4) \times 90^\circ$

$= 16 \times 90^\circ$

$= 1440^\circ$

5. (a) In ΔADE and ΔABC both are similar

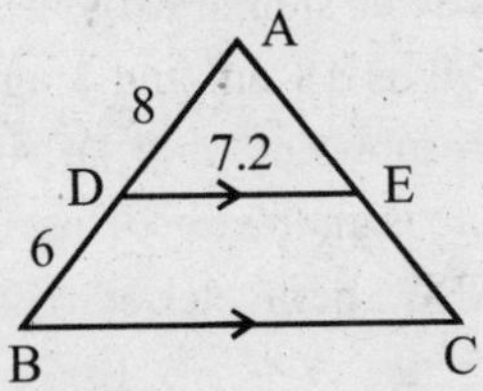

By B.P.T. theorem

$$\frac{AD}{AB} = \frac{DE}{BC}$$

$$\frac{AD}{AD+DB} = \frac{7.2}{BC}$$

$$\frac{8}{8+6} = \frac{7.2}{BC}$$

$$BC = \frac{7.2 \times 14}{8}$$

$$BC = 0.9 \times 14 = 12.6 \text{ cm}$$

6. (a) $\tan 30^\circ = \frac{AC}{BC}$

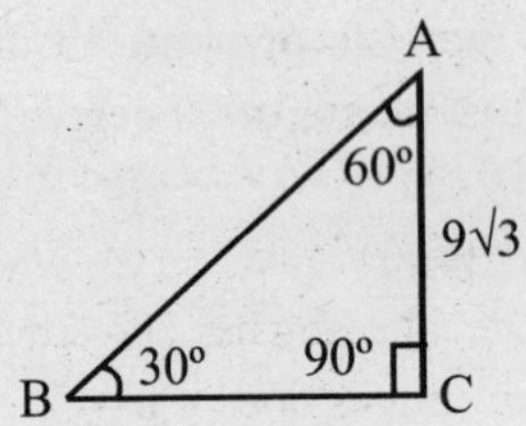

$$\tan 30^\circ = \frac{9\sqrt{3}}{BC} \Rightarrow \frac{1}{\sqrt{3}} = \frac{9\sqrt{3}}{BC}$$

$$BC = 9\sqrt{3} \times \sqrt{3} = 9 \times 3$$

$$BC = 27 \text{ cm}$$

7. (d)

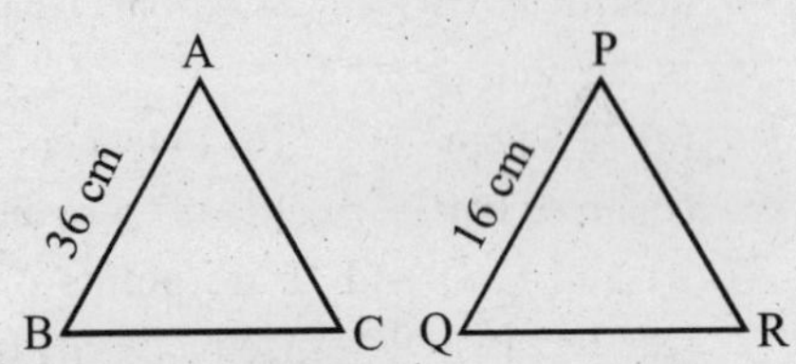

$$\frac{ar(\Delta ABC)}{ar(\Delta PQR)} = \frac{AB^2}{PQ^2} = \frac{(36)^2}{(16)^2}$$

$$\frac{1296}{ar(\Delta PQR)} = \left(\frac{36}{16}\right)^2 = \left(\frac{9}{4}\right)^2$$

$$ar(\Delta PQR) = \frac{16 \times 1296}{81}$$

$$= 16 \times 16$$

$$= 256 \text{ sq cm}$$

8. (b) Hexagonal prism

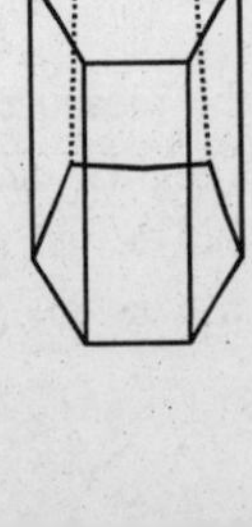

$F + V = E + 2$

$8 + V = 18 + 2$

$V = 20 - 8$

$= 12$

9. (c)

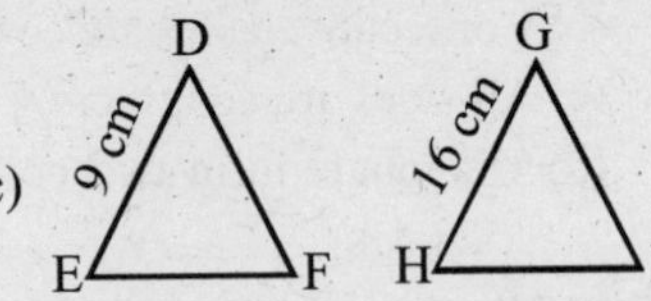

We know that

$$\frac{ar(\Delta DEF)}{ar(\Delta GHI)} = \frac{DE^2}{GH^2}$$

$$= \frac{(9)^2}{(16)^2} = \frac{81}{256}$$

Ratio of areas of triangles

$= 81 : 256$

10. (a) Sum of angles $= (n-2) \times 180^\circ$

$= (12-2) \times 180^\circ$

$= 10 \times 180^\circ$

$= 1800^\circ$

11. (c) $F + V = E + 2$

$4 + 4 = E + 2$

$8 - 2 = E$

$\therefore E = 6$

There are 6 edges in it.

12. (c) Let sides be $4m$ and $3m$,

$$\frac{PQ}{PS} = \frac{PS+QS}{PS} = \frac{QR}{ST}$$

$$\frac{4m+3m}{3m} = \frac{4.9}{ST}$$

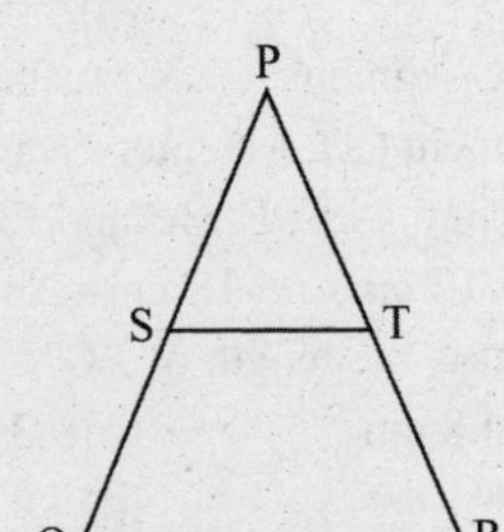

$$\frac{7}{3} = \frac{4.9}{ST}$$

$$ST = \frac{4.9 \times 3}{7} = 0.7 \times 3 = 2.1 \text{ cm}$$

13. (d)

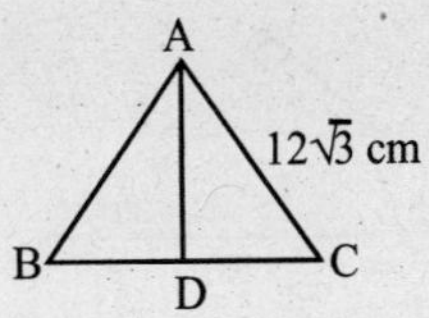

D is the mid point of BC, because in equilateral triangle BC is divided by attitude.

$$DC = \frac{12\sqrt{3}}{2} = 6\sqrt{3}$$

$$AD = \sqrt{(AC)^2 - (DC)^2}$$

$$= \sqrt{(12\sqrt{3})^2 - (6\sqrt{3})^2}$$

$$= \sqrt{144 \times 3 - 36 \times 3}$$

$$= \sqrt{36(4 \times 3 - 3)}$$

$$= \sqrt{36 \times 9} = 6 \times 3 = 18 \text{ cm}$$

14. (c)

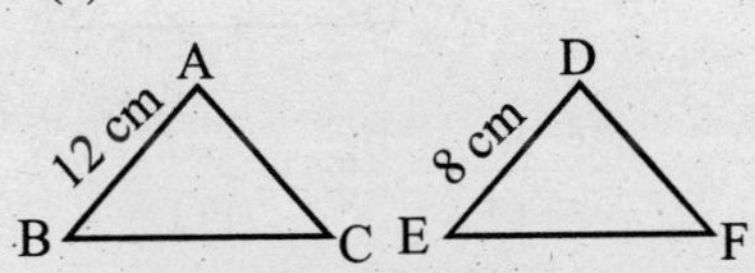

We know that

$$\frac{\text{Perimeter of } \Delta ABC}{\text{Perimeter of } \Delta DEF} = \frac{AB}{DE}$$

$$\frac{\text{Perimeter of } \Delta ABC}{\text{Perimeter of } \Delta DEF} = \frac{12}{8} = \frac{3}{2}$$

Hence, the required ratio is 3 : 2

15. (d) A decagon has 10 sides.
The sum of angles
$= (n-2) \times 180°$
$= (10-2) \times 180°$
$= 8 \times 180°$
$= 1440°$

16. (b) Equation of intercept,

$$\frac{x}{a} + \frac{y}{b} = 1$$

where, $a = \frac{5}{2}, b = \frac{-4}{3}$

$$\frac{x}{\frac{5}{2}} + \frac{y}{\frac{-4}{3}} = 1$$

$$\frac{2x}{5} - \frac{3y}{4} = 1$$

$$\frac{8x - 15y}{20} = 1$$

$$8x - 15y = 20$$

17. (d) Let the angles be x, $2x$, $4x$ and $5x$.
$\because$ Sum of angles of a quadrilateral is 360°

$$x + 2x + 4x + 5x = 360°$$

$$12x = 360°$$

$$x = \frac{360°}{12} = 30°$$

The biggest angle $= 5x = 5 \times 30°$
$= 150°$

18. (d) Cyclic quadrilateral.

19. (b) Let the angle be x
Its supplementary angle $= 180° - x$
According to condition

$\Rightarrow \quad x = 180° - x - 70°$

$\Rightarrow \quad 2x = 110°$

$\therefore \quad x = \frac{110°}{2} = 55°$

20. (c) Diagonals bisect opposite angles.

21. (d) In ΔABE and ΔACE

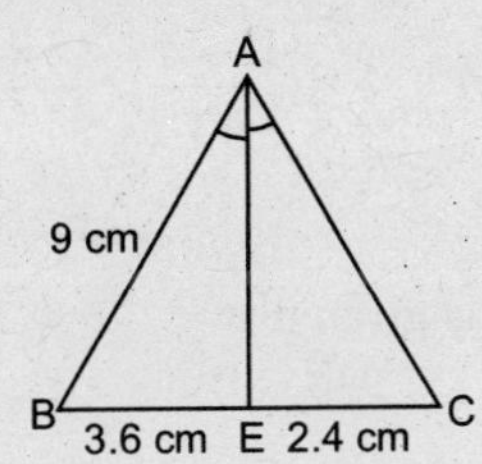

$$\frac{AB}{BE} = \frac{AC}{EC}$$

$$\frac{9}{3{\cdot}6} = \frac{AC}{2{\cdot}4}$$

$$AC = \frac{9 \times 2{\cdot}4}{3{\cdot}6} = \frac{9 \times 24}{36} = 6 \text{ cm}$$

22. (a)

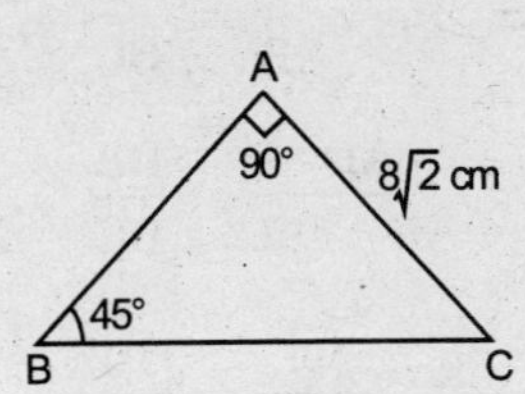

$\angle C = 180° - (90° + 45°) = 45°$
Hence, Opposite side of $\angle C$ is also $AB = AC = 8\sqrt{2}$

$$BC = \sqrt{AB^2 + AC^2}$$

$$= \sqrt{(8\sqrt{2})^2 + (8\sqrt{2})^2}$$

$$= \sqrt{128 + 128}$$

$$= \sqrt{256} = 16.$$

The length of BC is 16 cm.

23. (b) Let the angle be x
Complementary angle $= 90° - x$
According to question,

$\Rightarrow \quad x + x - 40° = 90°$

$\Rightarrow \quad 2x = 90° + 40°$

$\Rightarrow \quad 2x = 130°$

$\therefore \quad x = 65°$

24. (b) Diagonals form two congruent triangles.

25. (b) In ΔABC

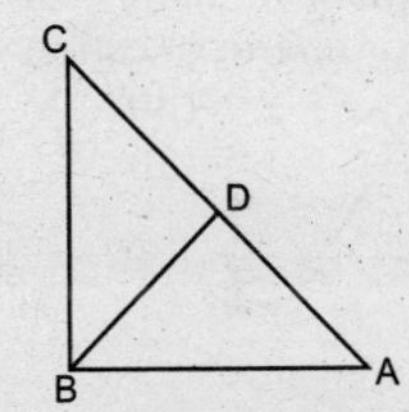

$$2BD = AD \cdot CD$$

$$2BD = 8 \times 5$$

$$BD = \frac{8 \times 5}{2} = 20 \text{ cm}$$

26. (d) In a rectangle diagonals form two congruent triangles.

27. (c)

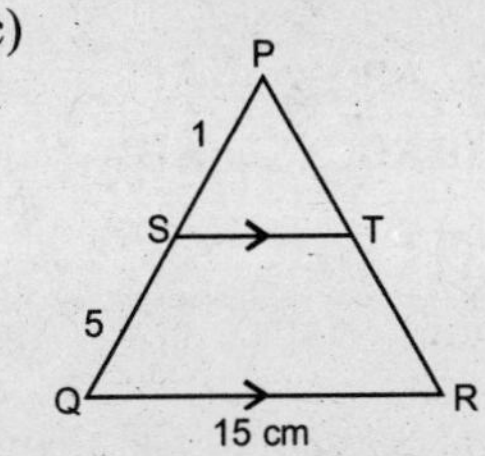

Let the length of PS and SQ be x and $5x$.
Then $PQ = PS + SQ = x + 5x = 6x$

$$\frac{PS}{PQ} = \frac{ST}{QR}$$

$$\frac{x}{6x} = \frac{ST}{15 \text{ cm}}$$

$$ST = \frac{15}{6} = 2{\cdot}5 \text{ cm}.$$

28. (a)

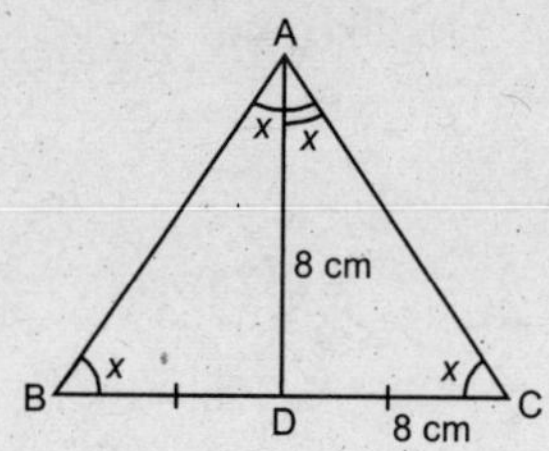

Let $\angle DAC$ be x

$\angle DAC = \angle DCA = x$

[... Equal angles of opposite equal sides]

In ΔABC

$\angle A + \angle B + \angle C = 180°$

[By angle sum property of triangle]

$2x + x + x = 180°$

$4x = 180°$

$x = 45°$

$\angle BAC = 2x = 2 \times 45° = 90°.$

29. (d) Let the angle be $x°$

Supplement angle = $(180° - x)$

According to question

$\Rightarrow \quad x = 180° - x - 50°$

$\Rightarrow \quad 2x = 130°$

$\therefore \quad x = \dfrac{130°}{2} = 65°.$

30. (d)

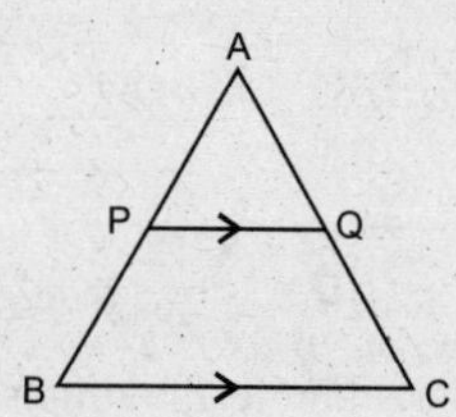

In ΔAPQ and ΔABC

$$\frac{ar(\Delta APQ)}{ar(\Delta ABC)} = \frac{AP^2}{AB^2}$$

$$\frac{16}{25} = \frac{AP^2}{AB^2}$$

$$\frac{AP}{AB} = \sqrt{\frac{16}{25}} = \frac{4}{5}$$

$$\frac{AP}{AP + PB} = \frac{4}{5}$$

$[\therefore AB = AP + PB]$

$5AP = 4AP + 4PB$

$5AP - 4AP = 4PB$

$AP = 4PB$

$$\frac{AP}{PB} = \frac{4}{1}$$

$AP : PB = 4 : 1.$

31. (d)

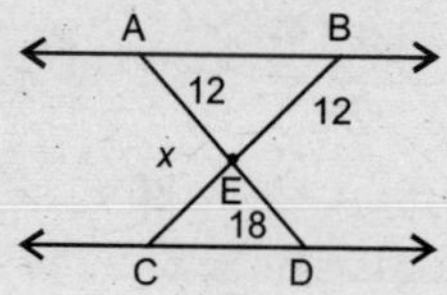

EC = ?

... AB || CD, then By BPT

$$\frac{12 - x}{x} = \frac{12}{18} = \frac{2}{3}$$

$36 - 3x = 2x$

$5x = 36$

$$x = \frac{36}{5} = 7{\cdot}2 \text{ cm.}$$

32. (c)

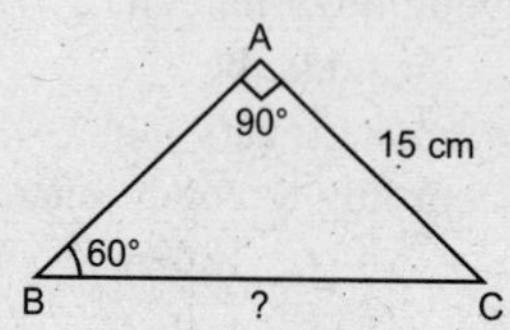

$$\frac{a}{\sin A} = \frac{b}{\sin B}$$

$$\frac{15}{\sin 60°} = \frac{b}{\sin 90°}$$

$$\Rightarrow \quad b = \frac{15 \times 2}{\sqrt{3}} = \frac{15 \times 2\sqrt{3}}{3}$$

$= 10\sqrt{3}$ cm.

33. (d) It is given that

DE || BC

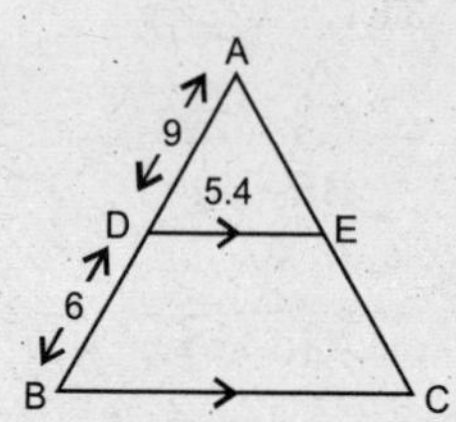

By BPT theorem

$$\Rightarrow \quad \frac{AD}{AB} = \frac{DE}{BC}$$

$$\Rightarrow \quad \frac{AD}{AD + DB} = \frac{DE}{BC}$$

$$\Rightarrow \quad \frac{9}{9 + 6} = \frac{5{\cdot}4}{BC}$$

$$BC = \frac{5{\cdot}4 \times 15}{9} = 0{\cdot}6 \times 15 = 9 \text{ cm.}$$

34. (b)

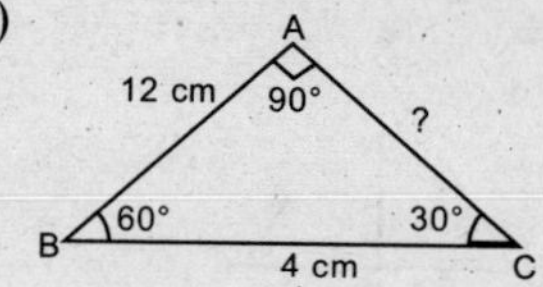

It is a right angle triangle at A

$$\tan 60° = \frac{P}{B} = \frac{AC}{AB} = \frac{AC}{12}$$

$$\sqrt{3} = \frac{AC}{12}$$

$\therefore \quad AC = 12\sqrt{3}$ cm.

35. (a) V = 20, E = ? and F = 12

According to theorem

$V + F = E + 2$

$20 + 12 = E + 2$

$E = 32 - 2 = 30$

36. (b)

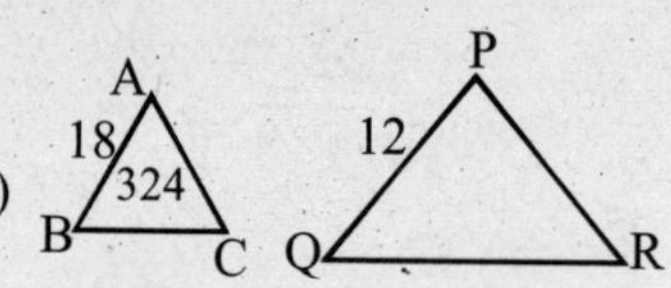

$$\frac{\text{Area of } \Delta ABC}{\text{Area of } \Delta PQR} = \frac{AB^2}{PQ^2}$$

$$= \frac{18 \times 18}{12 \times 12} = \frac{3 \times 3}{2 \times 2} = \frac{9}{4}$$

$$\frac{324}{\text{area of } \Delta PQR} = \frac{9}{4}$$

$$\Rightarrow \quad \text{Area of } \Delta PQR = \frac{324 \times 4}{9}$$

$= 36 \times 4 = 144 \text{ cm}^2$

37. (d) Let DH be x.

In Δ DEF

$$\Rightarrow \quad \frac{DG}{GE} = \frac{DH}{HF}$$

$$\Rightarrow \quad \frac{1}{3} = \frac{x}{7.2}$$

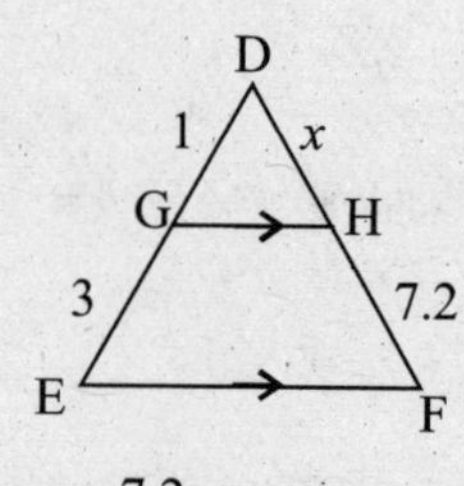

$$\Rightarrow x = \frac{7.2}{3} = 2.4 \text{ cm}$$

$\therefore$ DF = DH + HF = (2.4 + 7.2)

= 9.6 cm

38. (b) There are six vertices at top and bottom.

39. (d) The length of arc $= \frac{2\pi r\theta}{360}$

$= 2\pi r \times \frac{45^\circ}{360^\circ}$

$= 2 \times \frac{22}{7} \times 28 \times \frac{45^\circ}{360^\circ}$

$= 44 \times 4 \times \frac{1}{8} = 22$ cm

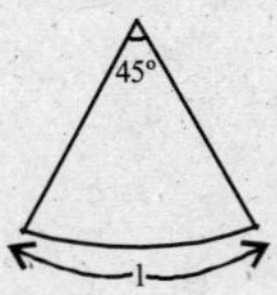

40. (c) Interior angle of a regular decagon

$= \frac{(2n-4)\times 90^\circ}{n}$

$= \frac{(2\times 10-4)\times 90^\circ}{10}$

$= 16 \times 9 = 144^\circ$

41. (a)

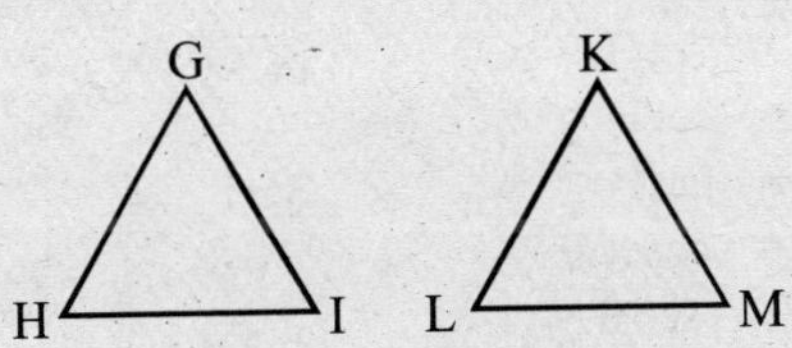

$\frac{\text{Perimeter of } \Delta\, GHI}{\text{Perimeter of } \Delta\, KLM}$

$= \frac{GH}{KL}$

$\Rightarrow \frac{9}{4} = \frac{27}{KL}$

$\therefore KL = \frac{27\times 4}{9} = 12$ cm.

42. (d) Dodecagon has 12 sides

Interior angle

$= \frac{(2n-4)\times 90}{n}$

$= \frac{(2\times 12-4)\times 90^\circ}{12}$

$= \frac{20\times 90^\circ}{12} = 10 \times 15$

$= 150^\circ$

Exterior angle $= 180^\circ - 150^\circ = 30^\circ$

43. (c) Interior angle

$= \frac{(2n-4)\times 90^\circ}{n}$

Where $n = 10$

$= \frac{(2\times 10-4)\times 90^\circ}{10}$

$= \frac{(20-4)\times 90^\circ}{10}$

$= 144^\circ$

Exterior angle $= (180^\circ - 144^\circ) = 36^\circ$

Sum of all exterior angles

$= 10^\circ \times 36^\circ = 360^\circ$

44. (b) AP : PB = 2 : 5

AP : AB = 2 : (5 + 2) = 2 : 7

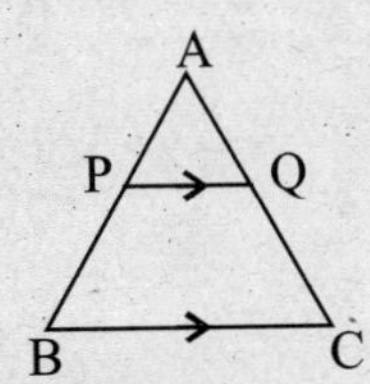

$\frac{\text{Area of } \Delta APQ}{\text{Area of } \Delta ABC} = \frac{AP^2}{AB^2}$

$= \frac{(2)^2}{(7)^2}$

$\frac{\text{Area of } \Delta APQ}{\text{Area of } \Delta ABC} = \frac{4}{49}$

Hence, area of trapezium = ar(ΔABC) – ar(ΔAPQ) = (49 – 4) = 45 sq.cm

45. (c) Interior angles of a regular dodecagon

where $n = 12$

$= \frac{(2n-4)\times 90}{n}$

$= \frac{(2\times 12-4)\times 90}{12}$

$= \frac{20\times 90}{12} = 5 \times 30 = 150^\circ$

So, interior angle is 150°.

46. (c) Let sides be $4x$ and x

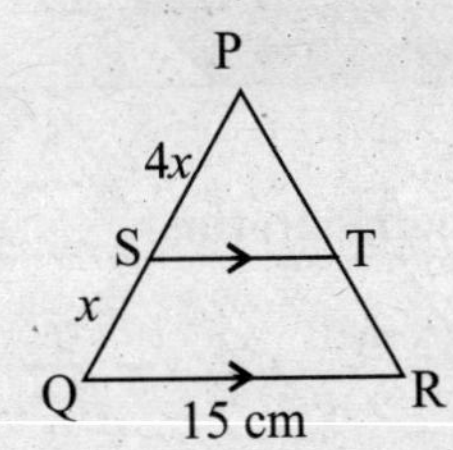

$\frac{PQ}{PS} = \frac{QR}{ST}$

$\Rightarrow \frac{5x}{4x} = \frac{15}{ST}$

$ST = \frac{15\times 4}{5} = 12$ cm

47. (b)

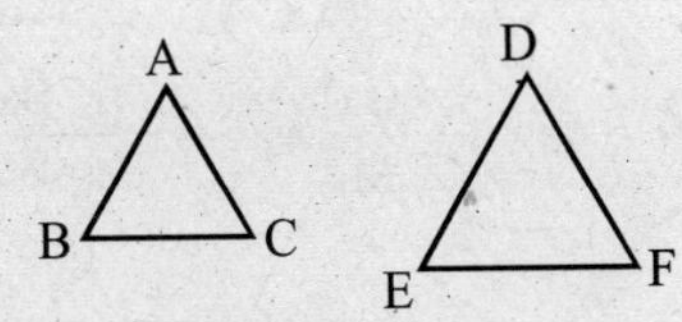

Given AB = 18

DE = 10

Perimeter of two triangles is directly proportional to their sides.

$\frac{\text{Perimeter of } \Delta ABC}{\text{Perimeter of } \Delta DEF} = \frac{AB}{DE}$

$= \frac{18}{10} = \frac{9}{5} = 9:5$

48. (b) A dodecagon has 12 sides, $n = 12$

Sum of interior angles

$= (n-2) \times 180^\circ$

$= (12-2) \times 180^\circ$

$= 10 \times 180^\circ$

$= 1800^\circ$

13 TRIGONOMETRY

Trigonometric Ratios

$$\sin\theta = \frac{MP}{OP} = \frac{y}{r} = \frac{\text{Perpendicular}}{\text{Hypotenuse}}$$

$$\cos\theta = \frac{OM}{OP} = \frac{x}{r} = \frac{\text{Base}}{\text{Hypotenuse}}$$

$$\tan\theta = \frac{MP}{OM} = \frac{y}{x} = \frac{\text{Perpendicular}}{\text{Base}}$$

$$\text{cosec}\,\theta = \frac{OP}{MP} = \frac{r}{y} = \frac{\text{Hypotenuse}}{\text{Perpendicular}}$$

$$\sec\theta = \frac{OP}{OM} = \frac{r}{x} = \frac{\text{Hypotenuse}}{\text{Base}}$$

$$\cot\theta = \frac{OM}{MP} = \frac{x}{y} = \frac{\text{Base}}{\text{Perpendicular}}$$

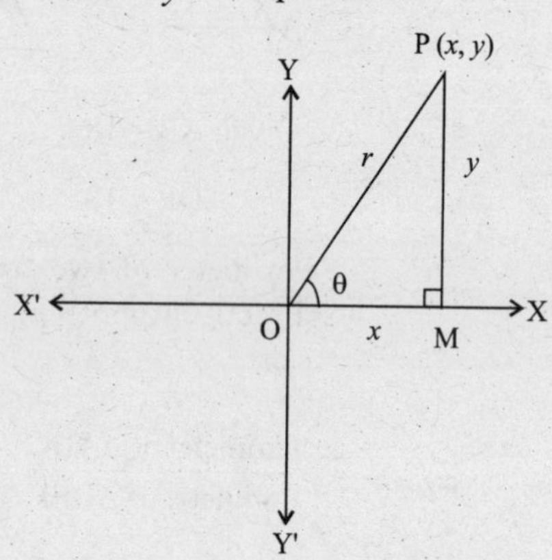

Signs of Trigonometric Ratios :

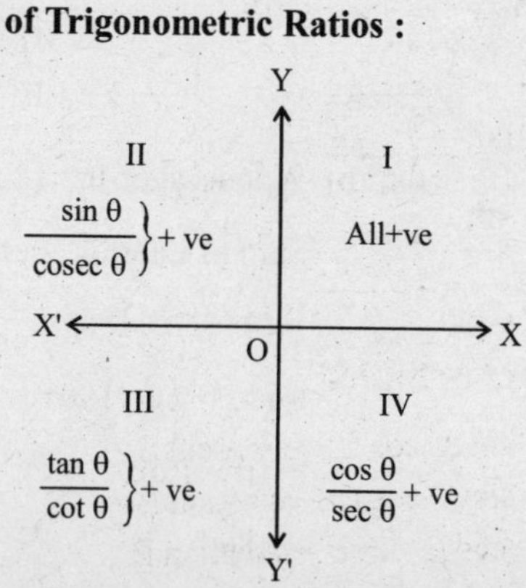

Trigonometric Ratios of Allied Angles :

1. T-ratios of $(-\theta)$ in terms of those of θ :
   (I) $\sin(-\theta) = -\sin\theta$
   (II) $\cos(-\theta) = \cos\theta$
   (III) $\tan(-\theta) = -\tan\theta$
   (IV) $\cot(-\theta) = -\cot\theta$
   (V) $\sec(-\theta) = \sec\theta$
   (VI) $\text{cosec}(-\theta) = -\text{cosec}\,\theta$
2. T-ratios of $(90° - \theta)$ in terms of those of θ :
   (I) $\sin(90° - \theta) = \cos\theta$
   (II) $\cos(90° - \theta) = \sin\theta$
   (III) $\tan(90° - \theta) = \cot\theta$
   (IV) $\cot(90° - \theta) = \tan\theta$
   (V) $\sec(90° - \theta) = \text{cosec}\,\theta$
   (VI) $\text{cosec}(90° - \theta) = \sec\theta$
3. T-ratios of $(90° + \theta)$ in terms of those of θ :
   (I) $\sin(90° + \theta) = \cos\theta$
   (II) $\cos(90° + \theta) = -\sin\theta$
   (III) $\tan(90° + \theta) = -\cot\theta$
   (IV) $\cot(90° + \theta) = -\tan\theta$
   (V) $\sec(90° + \theta) = -\text{cosec}\,\theta$
   (VI) $\text{cosec}(90° + \theta) = \sec\theta$
4. T-ratios of $(180° - \theta)$ in terms of those of θ :
   (I) $\sin(180° - \theta) = \sin\theta$
   (II) $\cos(180° - \theta) = -\cos\theta$
   (III) $\tan(180° - \theta) = -\tan\theta$
   (IV) $\cot(180° - \theta) = -\cot\theta$
5. T-ratios of $(180° + \theta)$ in terms of those of θ :
   (I) $\sin(180° + \theta) = -\sin\theta$
   (II) $\cos(180° + \theta) = -\cos\theta$
   (III) $\tan(180° + \theta) = \tan\theta$
   (IV) $\cot(180° + \theta) = \cot\theta$
   (V) $\sec(180° + \theta) = -\sec\theta$
   (VI) $\text{cosec}(180° + \theta) = -\text{cosec}\,\theta$
6. T-ratios of $(270° - \theta)$ in terms of those of θ :
   (I) $\sin(270° - \theta) = -\cos\theta$
   (II) $\cos(270° - \theta) = -\sin\theta$
   (III) $\tan(270° - \theta) = \cot\theta$
   (IV) $\cot(270° - \theta) = \tan\theta$
   (V) $\sec(270° - \theta) = -\text{cosec}\,\theta$
   (VI) $\text{cosec}(270° - \theta) = -\sec\theta$

7. T-ratios of $(270° + \theta)$ in terms of those of θ :
   (I) $\sin(270° + \theta) = -\cos\theta$
   (II) $\cos(270° + \theta) = \sin\theta$
   (III) $\tan(270° + \theta) = -\cot\theta$
   (IV) $\cot(270° + \theta) = -\tan\theta$
   (V) $\sec(270° + \theta) = \text{cosec}\,\theta$
   (VI) $\text{cosec}(270° + \theta) = -\sec\theta$
8. T-ratios of $(360° - \theta)$ in terms of those of θ :
   (I) $\sin(360° - \theta) = -\sin\theta$
   (II) $\cos(360° - \theta) = \cos\theta$
   (III) $\tan(360° - \theta) = -\tan\theta$
9. T-ratios of $(360° + \theta)$ in terms of those of θ :
   (I) $\sin(360° + \theta) = \sin\theta$
   (II) $\cos(360° + \theta) = \cos\theta$
   (III) $\tan(360° + \theta) = \tan\theta$
   (IV) $\cot(360° + \theta) = \cot\theta$
   (V) $\sec(360° + \theta) = \sec\theta$
   (VI) $\text{cosec}(360° + \theta) = \text{cosec}\,\theta$
10. T-ratios of $(n \times 360° + \theta)$ in terms of those of θ :
   (I) $\sin(n \times 360° + \theta) = \sin\theta$
   (II) $\cos(n \times 360° + \theta) = \cos\theta$
   (III) $\tan(n \times 360° + \theta) = \tan\theta$
   (IV) $\cot(n \times 360° + \theta) = \cot\theta$
   (V) $\sec(n \times 360° + \theta) = \sec\theta$
   (VI) $\text{cosec}(n \times 360° + \theta) = \text{cosec}\,\theta$

- Relations between Trigonometric Ratios :

(I) $\text{cosec}\,\theta = \dfrac{1}{\sin\theta}$ or $\text{cosec}\,\theta \times \sin\theta = 1$

(II) $\sec\theta = \dfrac{1}{\cos\theta}$ or $\sec\theta \times \cos\theta = 1$

(III) $\cot\theta = \dfrac{1}{\tan\theta}$ or $\cot\theta \times \tan\theta = 1$

(IV) $\tan\theta = \dfrac{\sin\theta}{\cos\theta}$

(V) $\cot\theta = \dfrac{\cos\theta}{\sin\theta}$

Trigonometric Identities

A trigonometric identity is a trigonometric equation which is true for all values of the variable (s).

Important Trigonometrical Identities

1. $\sin^2\theta + \cos^2\theta = 1$
2. $\sin\theta = \sqrt{1 - \cos^2\theta}$
3. $\cos\theta = \sqrt{1 - \sin^2\theta}$
4. $\sec^2\theta - \tan^2\theta = 1$
5. $\sec^2\theta = 1 + \tan^2\theta$
6. $\tan^2\theta = \sec^2\theta - 1$
7. $\text{cosec}^2\theta - \cot^2\theta = 1$
8. $\text{cosec}^2\theta = 1 + \cot^2\theta$
9. $\cot^2\theta = \text{cosec}^2\theta - 1$
10. $\sin\theta.\ \text{cosec}\,\theta = 1$
11. $\sin\theta = \dfrac{1}{\text{cosec}\,\theta}$
12. $\text{cosec}\,\theta = \dfrac{1}{\sin\theta}$
13. $\cos\theta.\ \sec\theta = 1$
14. $\cos\theta = \dfrac{1}{\sec\theta}$
15. $\sec\theta = \dfrac{1}{\cos\theta}$
16. $\tan\theta.\ \cot\theta = 1$
17. $\tan\theta = \dfrac{1}{\cot\theta}$
18. $\cot\theta = \dfrac{1}{\tan\theta}$
19. $\tan\theta = \dfrac{\sin\theta}{\cos\theta}$
20. $\cot\theta = \dfrac{\cos\theta}{\sin\theta}$

Trigonometric Ratios of Specific Angles

Note :

(I) $\sin 18° = \left(\dfrac{\sqrt{5}-1}{4}\right)$

(II) $\cos 18° = \dfrac{\sqrt{10+2\sqrt{5}}}{4}$

(III) $\cos 36° = \left(\dfrac{\sqrt{5}+1}{4}\right)$

(IV) $\sin 36° = \dfrac{\sqrt{10-2\sqrt{5}}}{4}$

(V) $\sin 15° = \dfrac{\sqrt{3}-1}{2\sqrt{2}} = \cos 75°$

(VI) $\cos 15° = \dfrac{\sqrt{3}+1}{2\sqrt{2}} = \sin 75°$

(VII) $\sin 22\dfrac{1°}{2} = \dfrac{\sqrt{2-\sqrt{2}}}{2}$

(VIII) $\cos 22\dfrac{1°}{2} = \dfrac{\sqrt{2+\sqrt{2}}}{2}$

Some Important Formulae

1. $\sin(A + B) = \sin A.\ \cos B + \cos A \sin B$
2. $\sin(A - B) = \sin A.\ \cos B - \cos A \sin B$
3. $\cos(A + B) = \cos A.\ \cos B - \sin A \sin B$
4. $\cos(A - B) = \cos A.\ \cos B + \sin A \sin B$

5. $2 \sin A. \cos B = \sin (A + B) + \sin (A - B)$
6. $2 \cos A. \sin B = \sin (A + B) - \sin (A - B)$
7. $2 \sin A. \sin B = \cos (A - B) - \cos (A + B)$
8. $2 \cos A. \cos B = \cos (A + B) + \cos (A - B)$
9. $\sin C + \sin D = 2 \sin\left(\frac{C+D}{2}\right).\cos\left(\frac{C-D}{2}\right)$
10. $\sin C - \sin D = 2 \cos\left(\frac{C+D}{2}\right).\sin\left(\frac{C-D}{2}\right)$
11. $\cos C + \cos D = 2 \cos\left(\frac{C+D}{2}\right).\cos\left(\frac{C-D}{2}\right)$

Solved Examples

Example 1. What is the value of $\sec^2 D - \tan^2 D$?

Sol. Give that, the angles A, B, C and D of a quadrilateral ABCD are in the ratio 1 : 2 : 4 : 5

$\therefore x + 2x + 4x + 5x = 360°$

(since, sum of all interior angles in any quadrilateral is 360°)

$\Rightarrow 12x = 360°$

$\therefore x = 30°$

Hence, required angles of a quadrilateral ABCD are 30°, 60°, 120° and 150°, respectively.

$\sec^2 D - \tan^2 D = \sec^2 (150°) - \tan^2 (150°)$

$= \sec^2 (90° + 60°) - \tan^2 (90° + 60°)$

$= \text{cosec}^2 60° - \cot^2 60°$

$$= \left(\frac{2}{\sqrt{3}}\right)^2 - \left(\frac{1}{\sqrt{3}}\right)^2 = \frac{4}{3} - \frac{1}{3} = \frac{3}{3} = 1$$

Example 2. If $\sin \theta + 2 \cos \theta = 1$, where $0 < \theta < \pi/2$, what is $2\sin \theta - \cos \theta$ equal to ?

Sol. $\sin \theta + 2\cos \theta = 1$

On squaring both sides, we get

$(\sin \theta + 2\cos \theta)^2 = 1$

$\Rightarrow \sin^2\theta + 4\cos^2 \theta + 4\sin \theta \cos \theta = 1$

$\Rightarrow (1 - \cos^2 \theta) + 4(1 - \sin^2\theta) + 4\sin \theta \cos \theta = 1$

$\Rightarrow -(\cos^2 \theta + 4\sin^2 \theta) + 4\sin \theta \cos\theta = 1 - 5$

$\Rightarrow \cos^2 \theta + 4\sin^2 \theta - 4\sin \theta \cos \theta = 4$

$\Rightarrow (2\sin \theta - \cos \theta)^2 = 4 \Rightarrow 2\sin \theta - \cos \theta = 2$

Example 3. If $\cos x + \sec x = 2$, then what $\cos^n x + \sec^n x$ equal to, where n is a positive integer ?

Sol. $\cos x + \sec x = 2$ ...(i)

on squaring both sides, we get

$\cos^2 x + \sec^2 x + 2 = 4$

$\Rightarrow \cos^2 x + \sec^2 x = 2$ ...(ii)

On cubing Eq. (i), we get

$\cos^3 x + \sec^3 x + 3(\cos x + \sec x) = 8$

$\Rightarrow \cos^3 x + \sec^3 x + (3 \times 2) = 8$

$\Rightarrow \cos^3 x + \sec^3 x = 2$ ...(iii)

From Eqs. (i), (ii) and (iii)

$\cos^n x + \sec^n x = 2$

Example 4. If $5 \sin \theta + 12 \cos \theta = 13$, then what is $5 \cos \theta - 12 \sin \theta$ equal to ?

Sol. $\because 5\sin \theta + 12 \cos \theta = 13$

On squaring both sides, we get

$\Rightarrow 25 \sin^2 \theta + 144 \cos^2 \theta + 120 \sin\theta \cos \theta = 169$

$\Rightarrow 25(1 - \cos^2 \theta) + 144 (1 - \sin^2 \theta) + 120 \sin\theta \cos \theta = 169$

$\Rightarrow 25 - 25 \cos^2 \theta + 144 - 144 \sin^2\theta + 120 \sin\theta \cos \theta = 169$

$\Rightarrow 25 \cos^2 \theta + 144\sin^2 \theta - 120 \sin\theta \cos \theta = 169 - 169$

$\Rightarrow (5\cos \theta - 12 \sin \theta)^2 = 0$

$\therefore 5\cos \theta \; 12 \sin \theta = 0$

Exercise

1. If $\tan 5\pi/3 = x$, then the value of x is
(a) $-\sqrt{3}$ (b) 1
(c) 1/2 (d) $\sqrt{3}/2$

2. If $\sin (A/2) = x$, then the value of x is
(a) $\sqrt{[(1 + \cos A)/2]}$
(b) $\sqrt{[(1 - \cos A)/2]}$
(c) $\sqrt{[(1 - \sin A)/2]}$
(d) $\sqrt{[(1 + \sin A/2]}$

3. If $\cos A \cot A/(1 - \sin A) = x$, then the value of x is
(a) 1 – cosecA (b) 1 + cosecA
(c) 1 + secA (d) 1– secA

4. If $\tan (-7\pi/4) = x$, then the value of x is
(a) – 1/2 (b) $-\sqrt{3/2}$
(c) $\sqrt{3/2}$ (d) 1

5. If $(\cot A \cot B + 1) / (\cot B - \cot A) = x$, then the value of x is
(a) cot (A + B) (b) cot (A – B)
(c) tan (A – B) (d) tan (A + B)

6. If $2\sec^2 A = x$, then the value of x is
(a) 1/(1 + cos A) + 1/(1 – cos A)
(b) 1/(1 + tan A) + 1(1 + sin A)
(c) 1(1 + sin A) + 1/(1 – sin A)
(d) 1/(1 + cot A) + 1/(1 – cos A)

7. What is the value of $\cos 4\pi/3$?
(a) + 1/2 (b) $\sqrt{3}/2$
(c) – 1/2 (d) $-\sqrt{3}/2$

8. $\tan^3 A$ is equal to
(a) $3\tan A - \tan 3A(1 - 3\tan^2 A)$
(b) $3\tan A + \tan 3A(1 - 3\tan^2 A)$
(c) $3\tan A - \tan 3A(1 + 3\tan^2 A)$
(d) $3\tan A + \tan 3A(1 + 3\tan^2 A)$

9. $\sin A/(1 + \cos A)$ is equal to
(a) $(\text{cosec}A - \cot A)$
(b) $(\text{cosec}A + \cot A)$
(c) $\sqrt{[(\text{cosec}A - \cot A)]}$
(d) $\sqrt{[(\text{cosec}A + \cot A)]}$

10. If $\cos\frac{11\pi}{6} = x$, then the value of x is
(a) $\sqrt{3}/2$ (b) $1/2$
(c) 2 (d) $\sqrt{3}/2$

11. If $(\tan A - \tan B)/(1 + \tan A \tan B) = x$, then the value of x is
(a) $\tan(A - B)$ (b) $\tan(A + B)$
(c) $\cot(A - B)$ (d) $\cot(A + B)$

12. If $\tan^2 A + \cot^2 A + 2 = x$, then the value of x is
(a) $\tan^2 A\,\text{cosec}^2 A$
(b) $\sec A\,\text{cosec}A$
(c) $\sec^2 A\,\text{cosec}^2 A$
(d) $\tan A\,\text{cosec}A$

13. If $\cos(-4\pi/3) = x$, then the value of x is
(a) $\sqrt{3}/2$ (b) $1/2$
(c) $-\sqrt{3}/2$ (d) $-1/2$

14. If $(\cot A\cot B - 1)/(\cot B + \cot A) = x$, then the value of x is :
(a) $\cot(A - B)$ (b) $\tan(A + B)$
(c) $\cot(A + B)$ (d) $\tan(A - B)$

15. $\sin(A + B) - \sin(A - B)$ is equal to
(a) $2\sin A\cos B$ (b) $2\cos A\cos B$
(c) $2\cos A\sin B$ (d) $2\sin A\sin B$

16. $2 - (\cos A + \sin A)^2$ is equal to
(a) $(\text{cosec}A - \sin A)^2$
(b) $\cos A - \sin A$
(c) $\text{cosec}A - \sin A$
(d) $(\cos A - \sin A)^2$

17. $2\sin[(C+D)/2].\cos[(C-D)/2]$ is equal to
(a) $\sin C - \sin D$
(b) $\cos C + \cos D$
(c) $\cos C - \cos D$
(d) $\sin C + \sin D$

18. $\tan A\,\text{cosec}^2 A$ is equal to
(a) $(1 + \tan^2 A)\cot A$
(b) $(1 - \tan^2 A)\cot A$
(c) $\sqrt{[(1 + \tan^2 A)\cot A]}$
(d) $\sqrt{[(1 - \tan^2 A)\cot A]}$

19. If $\cot 4\pi/3 = x$, then the value of x is
(a) 1 (b) $1/\sqrt{3}$
(c) $\sqrt{3}$ (d) 1

20. If $\tan(A/2) = x$, then the value of x is
(a) $\sqrt{[(1 + \cos A)/(1 - \cos A)]}$
(b) $(1 - \cos A)/(1 + \cos A)$
(c) $(1 + \cos A)/(1 - \cos A)$
(d) $\sqrt{[(1 - \cos A)/(1 + \cos A)]}$

21. If $\tan^2 A / (\sec A - 1)^2 = x$, then the value of x is :
(a) $(1 - \text{cosec}A) / (1 + \text{cosec}A)$
(b) $(1+ \cos A)/(1 - \cos A)$
(c) $(1- \cos A) / (1 + \cos A)$
(d) $(1+ \text{cosec}A)(1 - \text{cosec}A)$

22. If $\cos 135° = x$, then the value of x is :
(a) $-1/\sqrt{2}$ (b) $-\sqrt{3}/2$
(c) $-1/2$ (d) 2

23. If $\sqrt{(1-\sin^2 A)} = x$, then the value of x is :
(a) $\tan A$ (b) $\cos A$
(c) $\text{cosec } A$ (d) $\sec A$

24. What is the value of $\frac{\sin A \tan A}{(1-\cos A)}$?
(a) $1 - \sec A$ (b) $1 + \sec A$
(c) $1 + \cot A$ (d) $1 - \cot A$

25. If $\sin 240° = x$, then the value of x is :
(a) $2/\sqrt{3}$ (b) $\sqrt{2}$
(c) 2 (d) $-\sqrt{3/2}$

26. If $\sqrt{(1+\tan^2 A)} = x$, then the value of x is :
(a) $\sin A$ (b) $\text{cosec } A$
(c) $\sec A$ (d) $\cos A$

27. If $\tan(A/2) = x$, then the value of x is :
(a) $\sin A/(1-\cos A)$
(b) $\sin A/(1+\cos A)$
(c) $\sqrt{[\sin A/(1+\cos A)]}$
(d) $\sqrt{[\sin A/(1-\cos A)]}$

28. If $2\sec A - (1 + \sin A) / \cos A = x$, then the value of x is :
(a) $\text{cosec}A/(1+\sin A)$
(b) $\cos A/(1+\sin A)$
(c) $\cos A(1+\sin A)$
(d) $\text{cosec}A\,(1+\sin A)$

Answers with Explanations

1. (a) $x = \tan 5\frac{\pi}{3} = \tan\left(\pi + \frac{2\pi}{3}\right)$

$= \tan\frac{2\pi}{3} = \tan\left(\pi - \frac{\pi}{3}\right)$

$= -\tan\frac{\pi}{3}$

$= -\tan 60° = -\sqrt{3}$

2. (b) $x = \sin(A/2)$

$= \sqrt{\frac{(1-\cos A)}{2}}$

3. (b) $x = \frac{\cos A \cot A}{(1-\sin A)}$

$= \frac{\cos A.\frac{\cos A}{\sin A}}{(1-\sin A)}$

$= \frac{\cos^2 A}{\sin A\,(1-\sin A)}$

$= \frac{1-\sin^2 A}{\sin A\,(1-\sin A)}$

$= \frac{(1-\sin A)(1+\sin A)}{\sin A.(1-\sin A)}$

$= \frac{1+\sin A}{\sin A} = \frac{1}{\sin A} + 1$

$= 1 + \text{cosec}A = \text{R.H.S.}$

4. (d) $x = \tan\left(\frac{-7\pi}{4}\right)$

$= \tan\left(\frac{-7\pi}{4}\right) \because \tan(-\theta) = -\tan\theta$

$= -\tan\left(\pi + \frac{3\pi}{4}\right) = -\tan\left(\frac{3\pi}{4}\right)$

$= -\tan 135° = -\tan(90° + 45°)$

$= +\cot 45° = 1$

5. (b) It is given that

$$x=\frac{\cot A\cot B+1}{\cot B-\cot A}$$

$$=\frac{\frac{\cos A}{\sin A}.\frac{\cos B}{\sin B}+1}{\frac{\cos B}{\sin B}-\frac{\cos A}{\sin A}}$$

$$=\frac{\frac{\cos A.\cos B+\sin A\sin B}{\sin A.\sin B}}{\frac{\sin A.\cos B-\cos A.\sin B}{\sin A.\sin B}}$$

$$=\frac{\cos(A-B)}{\sin(A-B)}=\cot(A-B)$$

6. (c) $x=2\sec^2 A=\frac{2}{\cos^2 A}$

$$=\frac{2}{1-\sin^2 A}$$

$$=\frac{1-\sin A+1+\sin A}{(1-\sin A)(1+\sin A)}$$

$$=\frac{1}{1+\sin A}+\frac{1}{1-\sin A}$$

7. (c) $\cos\frac{4\pi}{3}=\cos\left(\pi+\frac{\pi}{3}\right)$

$=-\cos\pi/3=-\cos 60^\circ=-1/2$

8. (a) $\tan 3A=\frac{3\tan A-\tan^3 A}{1-3\tan^2 A}$

$3\tan A-\tan^3 A=\tan 3A(1-3\tan^2 A)$

or $\tan 3A(1-3\tan^2 A)=3\tan A-\tan^3 A$

$\tan^3 A=3\tan A-\tan 3A(1-3\tan^2 A)$

9. (a) $\sin A/(1+\cos A)$

$$=\frac{\sin A(1-\cos A)}{(1+\cos A)(1-\cos A)}$$

$$=\frac{\sin A(1-\cos A)}{1-\cos^2 A}$$

$$=\frac{\sin(1-\cos A)}{\sin^2 A}$$

$$=\frac{(1-\cos A)}{\sin A}$$

$$=\frac{1}{\sin A}-\frac{\cos A}{\sin A}$$

$=\operatorname{cosec} A-\cot A$

10. (a) $\cos\frac{11\pi}{6}=x$ or $x=\cos\frac{11\pi}{6}$

$$=\cos\left(\pi+\frac{5\pi}{6}\right)=-\cos\frac{5\pi}{6}$$

$$=-\cos\left(\pi-\frac{\pi}{6}\right)=+\cos\pi/6$$

$=\cos 30^\circ=\sqrt{3}/2$

11. (a) $x=\frac{\tan A-\tan B}{1+\tan A.\tan B}$

$x=\tan(A-B)$

12. (c) $x=\tan^2 A+\cot^2 A+2$

$=(1+\tan^2 A)=1+\sec^2 A$

$=\sec^2 A+\operatorname{cosec}^2 A$

$$=\frac{1}{\cos^2 A}+\frac{1}{\sin^2 A}$$

$$=\frac{\sin^2 A+\cos^2 A}{\cos^2 A.\sin^2 A}$$

$$=\frac{1}{\cos^2 A.\sin^2 A}$$

$=\sec^2 A.\operatorname{cosec}^2 A$

13. (d) $\cos\left(-\frac{4\pi}{3}\right)=x$

$$x=\cos\frac{4\pi}{3}=\cos\left(\pi+\frac{\pi}{3}\right)$$

$$=-\cos\frac{\pi}{3}=-1/2$$

14. (c) $x=\frac{(\cot A.\cot B-1)}{\cot B+\cot A}$

$=\cot(A+B)$

15. (c) $\sin(A+B)-\sin(A-B)$

$=\sin A.\cos B+\cos A\sin B$

$-\sin A\cos B+\cos A.\sin B$

$=2\sin B.\cos A$

16. (d) $2-(\cos A+\sin A)^2$

$=1+1-(\cos^2 A+\sin^2 A+2\sin A.\cos A)$

$=1+1-1-2\sin A.\cos A$

$=\sin^2 A+\cos^2 A-2\sin A\cos A$

$=(\cos A-\sin A)^2$

17. (d) $2\sin[(C+D/2)].\cos[(C-D/2)]$

$=\sin C+\sin D$

18. (a) $\tan A.\operatorname{cosec}^2 A$

$=\tan A.(1+\cot^2 A)$

$=\tan A+\tan A.\cot A.\cot A)$

$=(\tan A+\cot A)$

$$=\left(\tan A+\frac{1}{\tan A}\right)$$

$$=\left(\frac{\tan^2 A+1}{\tan A}\right)=(1+\tan^2 A)\times\frac{1}{\tan A}$$

$=(1+\tan^2 A).\cot A$

19. (b) $\cot\left(\frac{4\pi}{3}\right)=x$

$$\frac{1}{\tan\left(\frac{4\pi}{3}\right)}=x$$

$$\frac{1}{\tan\left(\pi+\frac{\pi}{3}\right)}=x$$

$$\frac{1}{\tan\frac{\pi}{3}}=x \text{ or } x=\frac{1}{\tan 60^0}$$

$$=\frac{1}{\sqrt{3}}$$

20. (d) $x=\tan\left(\frac{A}{2}\right)=\frac{\sin\frac{A}{2}}{\cos\frac{A}{2}}$

$$=\frac{2\sin\frac{A}{2}\cos\frac{A}{2}}{2\cos^2\frac{A}{2}}=\frac{\sin A}{1+\cos A}$$

$$=\frac{\sqrt{1-\cos^2 A}}{\sqrt{1+\cos A}.\sqrt{1+\cos A}}$$

$$=\frac{\sqrt{1-\cos A}.\sqrt{1+\cos A}}{\sqrt{1+\cos A}.\sqrt{1+\cos A}}$$

$$=\frac{\sqrt{1-\cos A}}{\sqrt{1+\cos A}}$$

21. (b) $x=\frac{\tan^2 A}{(\sec A-1)^2}$

$$=\frac{\frac{\sin^2 A}{\cos^2 A}}{\left(\frac{1-\cos A}{\cos A}\right)^2}=\frac{1-\cos^2 A}{(1-\cos A)^2}$$

$$=\frac{(1-\cos A)(1+\cos A)}{(1-\cos A)(1-\cos A)}$$

$$=\frac{1+\cos A}{1-\cos A}$$

22. (a) If $\cos 135° = x$, then

$x = \cos 135° = \cos (180° - 45)$

$$= -\cos 45 = -\frac{1}{\sqrt{2}}$$

23. (b) $x = \sqrt{(1-\sin^2 A)}$

$$= \sqrt{\cos^2 A}$$

$$\left[\begin{array}{l}\because \sin^2 A + \cos^2 A = 1 \\ \therefore \cos^2 A = 1 - \sin^2 A\end{array}\right]$$

$= \cos A$

24. (b) $\dfrac{\sin A \tan A}{1-\cos A}$

$$= \frac{\sin A \cdot \sin A}{(1-\cos A)\cos A}$$

$$= \frac{\sin^2 A}{(1-\cos A)(\cos A)}$$

$$= \frac{1-\cos^2 A}{(1-\cos A)\cos A}$$

$$= \frac{(1-\cos A)(1+\cos A)}{(1-\cos A)\cos A}$$

$$= \frac{1+\cos A}{\cos A}$$

$$= \left(\frac{1}{\cos A} + \frac{\cos A}{\cos A}\right)$$

$= (1 + \sec A)$.

25. (d) $x = \sin 240° = \sin (180° + 60°)$

$\because \sin(\pi + \theta) = -\sin\theta$

$$= -\sin 60° = \frac{-\sqrt{3}}{2}$$

26. (c) $x = \sqrt{(1+\tan^2 A)}$

$$= \sqrt{1+\frac{\sin^2 A}{\cos^2 A}}$$

$$= \sqrt{\frac{\sin^2 A + \cos^2 A}{\cos^2 A}}$$

$$= \sqrt{\frac{1}{\cos^2 A}}$$

$[\because \sin^2 A + \cos^2 A = 1]$

$$= \sqrt{\sec^2 A} = \sec A$$

27. (b) $\tan (A/2) = x$

or $x = \tan\left(\dfrac{A}{2}\right)$

$$= \frac{\sin A/2}{\cos A/2}$$

$$= \frac{2\sin A/2.\cos A/2}{2\cos A/2.\cos A/2}$$

$$= \frac{\sin A}{2\cos^2 A/2} = \frac{\sin A}{1+\cos A}$$

28. (b) $2\sec A - (1+\sin A)/\cos A$

$$= \frac{2}{\cos A} - \frac{(1+\sin A)}{\cos A}$$

$$= \frac{2-1-\sin A}{\cos A}$$

$$= \frac{1-\sin A}{\cos A} \times \frac{(1+\sin A)}{(1+\sin A)}$$

$$= \frac{1-\sin^2 A}{\cos A(1+\sin A)}$$

$$= \frac{\cos^2 A}{\cos A(1+\sin A)}$$

$$= \frac{\cos A}{1+\sin A}$$

14 ALGEBRA

Some Important Algebraic Identities

(i) $(a + b)^2 = a^2 + b^2 + 2ab$

(ii) $(a - b)^2 = a^2 + b^2 - 2ab$

(iii) $(a + b)^2 = (a - b)^2 + 4ab$

(iv) $(a - b)^2 = (a + b)^2 - 4ab$

(v) $a^2 - b^2 = (a + b)(a - b)$

(vi) $(a + b)^3 = a^3 + b^3 + 3ab(a + b)$

(vii) $(a - b)^3 = a^3 - b^3 - 3ab(a - b)$

(viii) $(a^3 + b^3) = (a + b)(a^2 - ab + b^2)$

(ix) $(a^3 - b^3) = (a - b)(a^2 + ab + b^2)$

(x) $(a + b + c)^2 = a^2 + b^2 + c^2 + 2(ab + bc + ca)$

(xi) $a^3 + b^3 + c^3 - 3abc$

$= (a + b + c)(a^2 + b^2 + c^2 - ab - bc - ca)$

$= \frac{1}{2}(a + b + c)[(a - b)^2 + (b - c)^2 + (c - a)^2]$

Note :

$a^3 + b^3 + c^3 - 3abc = 0,$

$$\text{If } \left\{\begin{array}{l}\text{(i) } a+b+c=0 (a \neq b \neq c) \\ \text{(ii) } a^2+b^2+c^2-ab-bc-ca=0 \\ (i.e., a=b=c)\end{array}\right\}$$

(xii) $a^2 + b^2 + c^2 - ab - bc - ca$

$= \frac{1}{2}[(a - b)^2 + (b - c)^2 + (c - a)^2]$

(xiii) If $ax^2 + bx + c = 0$

then, $x = \dfrac{-b \pm \sqrt{b^2 - 4ac}}{2a}$

Some Important Results

- $(x - a)$ is a factor of $f(x)$ if $f(a) = 0$

  $(x + a)$ is a factor of $f(x)$ if $f(-a) = 0$

  $(ax - b)$ is a factor of $f(x)$ if $f\left(\frac{b}{a}\right) = 0$

  $(ax + b)$ is a factor of $f(x)$ if $f\left(-\frac{b}{a}\right) = 0$

  Hint: We put the divisor equal to zero and find the value of x. For example, if divisor is $(x - a)$, then $x - a = 0$

  $\Rightarrow x = a$

  If $f(x) = 0$ when $x = a$ then $f(x)$ is exactly divisible by $(x - a)$

- If $f(x)$ is divided by $(x - a)$, the remainder is $f(a)$.

  If $f(x)$ is divided by $(x + a)$, the remainder is $f(-a)$.

  If $f(x)$ is divided by $(ax - b)$, the remainder is $f\left(\frac{b}{a}\right)$.

  If $f(x)$ is divided by $(ax + b)$, the remainder is $f\left(-\frac{b}{a}\right)$.

- Remainder on dividing $(x^n - 1)$ by $(x - 1)$ is $1^n - 1 = 0$

  $\therefore$ $(x^n - 1)$ is always divisible by $(x - 1)$.

  $(x^n - 1)$ is divisible by $(x + 1)$ for even values of n.

  $\therefore$ $(x^n - 1)$ is not divisible by $(x + 1)$ for odd values of n.

- $(x^{ab} - 1)$ is always divisible by $(x^a - 1)$ and $(x^b - 1)$. [Logic : $(x^{ab} - 1) = (x^a)^b - 1)$]

  $(x^{abc} - 1)$ is always divisible by $(x^a - 1)$, $(x^b - 1)$ and $(x^c - 1)$.

- $(x^n + 1)$ is divisible by $(x + 1)$ for all odd values of n.

  $(x^n + 1)$ is not divisible by $(x + 1)$ for all even values of n.

  $(x^n + 1)$ is not divisible by $(x - 1)$ for all values of n.

- $(x^n - y^n)$ is always divisible by $(x - y)$.

  $(x^n - y^n)$ is divisible by $(x + y)$ for even values of n.

Solved Examples

Example 1. When $(x^3 - 2x^2 + px - q)$ is divided by $(x^2 - 2x - 3)$, the remainder is $(x - 6)$. What are the values of p, q, respectively ?

Sol.

$$\begin{array}{r} x \\ x^2-2x-3\overline{)x^3 - 2x^2 + px - q} \\ x^3 - 2x^2 - 3x \\ - \quad + \quad + \\ \hline (p+3)x - q \end{array}$$

By given condition,

$(p + 3)x - q = x - 6$

$\Rightarrow p + 3 = 1, q = 6$

$\Rightarrow p = -2, q = 6$

Example 2. If $x = 1+\sqrt{2}$, then what is the value of $x^4 - 4x^3 + 4x^2$?

Sol. Given, $x = 1+\sqrt{2}$

$\therefore$ $x^4 - 4x^3 + 4x^2 = x^2(x^2 - 4x + 4) = x^2(x-2)^2$

$= (1+\sqrt{2})^2 (1+\sqrt{2}-2)^2$

$= (1+\sqrt{2})^2 (\sqrt{2}-1)^2 = (1+\sqrt{2})^2 (\sqrt{2}-1)^2$

$= (1+2+2\sqrt{2})(2+1-2\sqrt{2})$

$= (3+2\sqrt{2})(3-2\sqrt{2})$

$= (3)^2 - (2\sqrt{2})^2 = 9 - 8 = 1$

Example 3. For what value of k, $(x + 5)$ is a factor of $6x^2 + kx + 10$?

Sol. Let $f(x) = 6x^2 + kx + 10$

If $(x + 5)$ is a factor of $f(x)$, then

$f(-5) = 0$

[since, zero of $(x + 5)$ is -5 *i. e.*, $x + 5 = 0$ $x = -5$]

$6(-5)^2 + k(-5) + 10 = 0$

$\Rightarrow$ $6 \times 25 - 5k + 10 = 0 \Rightarrow 5k = 150 + 10 = 160$

$\therefore$ $k = 32$

Example 4. One of the factors of the polynomial $x^4 - 7x^3 + 5x^2 - 6x + 81$ is ?

Sol. Let $f(x) = x^4 - 7x^3 + 5x^2 - 6x + 81$

By trial method,

$x^4 - 7x^3 + 5x^2 - 6x + 81$

$= x^3(x-3) - 4x^2(x-3) - 7x(x-3) - 27(x-3)$

$= (x-3)(x^3 - 4x^2 - 7x - 27)$

So, $(x - 3)$ is one of the factors of the given polynomial.

Exercise

1. Factorise $x^2 + 3x - 18$
(a) $(x + 18)(x - 2)$
(b) $(x - 1)(x + 18)$
(c) $(x + 6)(x - 3)$
(d) $(x - 6)(x + 3)$

2. The value of x for which the expressions $11x + 7$ and $17x - 1$ become equal is............
(a) $-4/3$ (b) $3/4$
(c) $4/3$ (d) $-3/4$

3. The sum of a non-zero number and thrice its reciprocal is 13/2. Find the number.
(a) 6 (b) 7
(c) 8 (d) 9

4. If $(7x - 13) - (12x + 3) = 14$, then the value of x is ______ .
(a) -6 (b) 6
(c) 2/5 (d) $-2/5$

5. The value of x for which the expressions $19 - 5x$ and $19x + 5$ become equal is ....
(a) 7/12 (b) 7/12
(c) 12/7 (d) 12/7

6. The value of x for which the expressions $15x + 4$ and $13x - 2$ become equal is ....
(a) -1 (b) 1
(c) -3 (d) 3

7. Coefficient of x^2 in $4x^3 - 2x^2 + 2x - 3$ is:
(a) 6 (b) -2
(c) 3 (d) -3

8. On dividing $221a^2b^2$ by $13b^2$, we get.............. .
(a) $17a^2$ (b) $17b^2$
(c) $13a^2b^2$ (d) 13

9. Which of the following is correct?
(a) $(3x + 4y)(4x - 3y) = 12x^2 - 7xy - 12y^2$
(b) $(3x + 4y)(4x - 3y) = 12x^2 + 251xy - 12y^2$
(c) $(3x + 4y)(4x - 3y) = 12x^2 - 7xy + 12y^2$
(d) $(3x + 4y)(4x - 3y) = 12x^2 + 7xy - 12y^2$

10. If $x + y = 12$ and $x^2 + y^2 = 94$, then xy is :
(a) 25 (b) 50
(c) 144 (d) 238

11. Expand and simplify : $(2x + 5)^2(4x - 1) - (3x^3 - 16x^2 + 25x - 21)$
(a) $13x^3 + 92x^2 - 55x + 4$
(b) $13x^3 - 92x^2 - 55x - 4$
(c) $13x^3 + 92x^2 + 55x - 4$
(d) $13x^3 - 92x^2 + 55x + 4$

12. If $a - b = 6$ and $ab = 16$, then $a^3 - b^3$ is :
(a) 504 (b) 702
(c) 728 (d) 511

13. Find the roots of the quadratic equation $6x^2 - 11x - 35 = 0$:
(a) $5/3, -7/2$
(b) $-5/3, 7/2$
(c) $-3/5, 2/7$
(d) $3/5, -2/7$

14. Expand and simplify $(x + 5)^2 + (x - 3)^2$:
(a) $2(x^2 + 2x - 17)$
(b) $2(x^2 - 2x + 17)$
(c) $2(x^2 - 2x - 17)$
(d) $2(x^2 + 2x + 17)$

15. Which of the following is correct ?
(a) $(4x + 5y)(5x - 4y) = 20x^2 + 9xy - 20y^2$
(b) $(4x + 5y)(5x - 4y) = 20x^2 + 41xy - 20y^2$
(c) $(4x + 5y)(5x - 4y) = 20x^2 - 9xy + 20y^2$
(d) $(4x + 5y)(5x - 4y) = 20x^2 - 41xy + 20y^2$

Answers with Explanations

1. (c) $x^2 + 3x - 18$
$\Rightarrow x^2 + 6x - 3x - 18$
$\Rightarrow x(x + 6) - 3(x + 6)$
$\Rightarrow (x + 6)(x - 3)$

2. (c) $11x + 7 = 17x - 1$
$17x - 11x = 7 + 1$
$6x = 8$
$\Rightarrow x = \frac{8}{6} = \frac{4}{3}$

3. (a) Let the number be x.
$$x + \frac{3}{x} = \frac{13}{2}$$
$\Rightarrow x^2 + 3 = \frac{13}{2}x$
$\Rightarrow 2x^2 + 6 = 13x$
$\Rightarrow 2x^2 - 13x + 6 = 0$
$\Rightarrow 2x^2 - 12x - x + 6 = 0$
$\Rightarrow 2x(x - 6) - 1(x - 6) = 0$
$\Rightarrow (x - 6)(2x - 1) = 0$
$x - 6 = 0$ or $2x - 1 = 0$
$x = 6$ or $x = 1/2$
Hence, the value of x is 6.

4. (a) $(7x - 13) - (12x + 3) = 14$
$7x - 13 - 12x - 3 = 14$
$-5x - 16 = 14$
$-5x = 14 + 16 = 30$
$x = -\frac{30}{5} = -6$

5. (b) $19 - 5x = 19x + 5$
$19 - 5 = 19x + 5x$
$14 = 24x$
$x = \frac{14}{24} = \frac{7}{12}$

6. (c) $15x + 4 = 13x - 2$
$\Rightarrow 15x - 13x = -2 - 4$
$\Rightarrow 2x = -6$
$\therefore x = -3$

7. (b) $4x^3 - 2x^2 + 2x - 3$
Coefficient of $x^2 = -2$

8. (a) $\frac{221a^2b^2}{13b^2} = 17a^2$

9. (d) $(3x + 4y)(4x - 3y)$
$(3x + 4y)(4x - 3y) = 3x(4x - 3y) + 4y(4x - 3y)$
$\Rightarrow 12x^2 - 9xy + 16xy - 12y^2$
$= 12x^2 + 7xy - 12y^2$

10. (a) $x + y = 12$
Squaring both sides
$\Rightarrow (x + y)^2 = 12^2$
$\Rightarrow x^2 + y^2 + 2xy = 144$
$\Rightarrow 94 + 2xy = 144$
$\Rightarrow 2xy = 144 - 94 = 50$
$\therefore xy = \frac{50}{2} = 25$

11. (c) $(2x + 5)^2 \times (4x - 1) - (3x^3 - 16x^2 + 25x - 21)$
$= (4x^2 + 20x + 25)(4x - 1)$
$= 4x(4x^2 + 20x + 25) - 1(4x^2 + 20x + 25) - 3x^3 + 16x^2 - 25x + 21$
$= 16x^3 + 80x^2 + 100x - 4x^2 - 20x - 25 - 3x^3 + 16x^2 - 25x + 21$
$= (16 - 3)x^3 + (40 - 4 + 16)x^2 + (100 - 10 - 25)x - 25 + 21$
$= 13x^3 + 92x^2 + 55x - 4 = 0.$

12. (a) $a - b = 6$
$(a - b)^2 = (6)^2$
$\Rightarrow a^2 + b^2 - 2ab = 36$
$\Rightarrow a^2 + b^2 - 2 \times 16 = 36$
$\Rightarrow a^2 + b^2 = 68$
$\therefore a^3 - b^3 = (a - b)(a^2 + b^2 + ab)$
$= 6 \times (68 + 16)$
$= 6 \times 84$
$= 504.$

13. (b) $6x^2 - 11x - 35 = 0$
$6x^2 - 21x + 10x - 35 = 0$
$3x(2x - 7) + 5(2x - 7) = 0$
$(2x - 7)(3x + 5) = 0$
$2x - 7 = 0$ or $3x + 5 = 0$
$x = \frac{7}{2}$ or $x = \frac{-5}{3}$

14. (d) The expression, $(x + 5)^2 + (x - 3)^2$
$= (x^2 + 25 + 10x) + (x^2 + 9 - 6x)$
$= x^2 + 25 + 10x + x^2 + 9 - 6x$
$= 2x^2 + 34 + 4x$
$= 2x^2 + 4x + 34$
$= 2(x^2 + 2x + 17).$

15. (a) $(4x + 5y)(5x - 4y)$
$= 4x(5x - 4y) + 5y(5x - 4y)$
$= 20x^2 - 16xy + 25xy - 20y^2$
$= 20x^2 + 9xy - 20y^2.$

15 DATA INTERPRETATION

TABULATION

Tabulation is one of the most important devices for the presentation of the data in a condensed and comprehensive form. The candidate is required to understand the given information and thereafter answer the given questions on the basis of comparative analysis of the data.

Here the data collected by the investigator are arranged in a systematic form in a *table* called *tabular form.*

- A statistical table is the logical listing of related quantitative data in vertical columns and horizontal rows of numbers with sufficient explanatory and qualifying words, heading and notes to make clear the full meaning of data and their origin.
- The interpretation of data of the tables is done on the basis of assessment of numerical figures in the light of inter-related column captions and style of the table. In fact, more attention is focussed on the relative position of different items in a table and questions are answered mostly regarding.
- Maximum and Minimum value
- Average value
- Percentage
- Maximum/Minimum rate of increase/decrease
- Items showing eccentric behaviour.

BAR-GRAPHS

Simple Bar Diagram

A simple bar diagram is constructed for an immediate comparison. It is advisable to arrange the given data set in an ascending or descending order and plot the data variables accordingly. However, time series data are represented according to the sequencing of the time period.

- A simple bar diagram can represent only one characteristic at a time.

In a Bar Graph,

- The width of each bar can be any, but widths of all the bars is same.
- Space between these bars should be same.

  The width of the bar has no special meaning except to make it pictorially more attractive.

Multiple Bar Diagram

Multiple bar diagrams are constructed to represent two or more than two variables for the purpose of comparison.

PIE-DIAGRAM

Pie-diagram : A pie diagram is a pictorial representation of the numerical data by non-intersecting adjacent sectors of the circle such that area of each sector is proportional to the magnitude of the data represented by the sector.

- In this method of data representation, the total quantity is distributed over a total angle of 360°, which is one complete circle or Pie.
- Since 1 percent of the total value is equal to

  $$\frac{360}{100} = 3.6°$$

  Degree of any component part

  $$= \frac{\text{Component value}}{\text{Total value}} \times 100$$

Solved Examples

Directions (Q. 1-2) : Study the table carefully to answer the questions that follow :

Total number of students studying in various colleges over the years :

Year	College				
	A	B	C	D	E
2001	1125	1200	1170	1090	1114
2002	1345	1265	1342	1238	1278
2003	1290	1348	1560	1346	1662
2004	1785	1440	1660	1546	1784
2005	1890	1802	1864	1790	1986
2006	2000	2100	2200	1996	2265
2007	2160	2346	2178	2061	2448

Example 1. What is the average number of students studying in the college E over the given years ?

(a) 1656 (b) 1791

(c) 1710 (d) 1581

Sol. (b) Average number of students studying in the college E over the given years

$= 1114 + 1278 + 1662 + 1784 + 1986 + 2265 + 2448$

$= \frac{12537}{7} = 1791.$

Example 2. The number of students studying in college B in the year 2003 is approximately what percent of the total number of students studying in various colleges in that year ?

(a) 31 (b) 37

(c) 19 (d) 23

Sol. (c) Required percentage $= \frac{1348}{7206} \times 100$

$= 18.70\% = 19\%$ (approx.)

Directions (Q. 3-4) : The following Pie-chart shows the marks scored by a student in different subjects in an examination. If the total marks obtained by the student be 648, answer the questions given below :

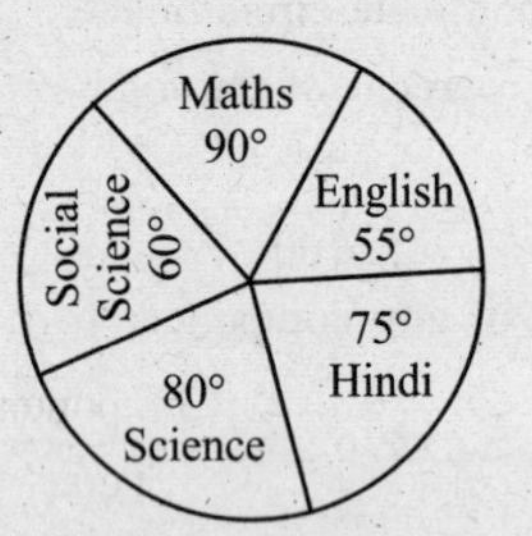

Example 3. The marks scored in English, Science and Social science exceed the marks scored in Hindi and Mathematics by :

(a) 50 (b) 52

(c) 53 (d) 54

Sol. (d) Angle represented by required difference

$= [(E + S + S.Sc) - (H + M)]$

$= 55° + 80° + 60° - 75° - 90° = 30°$

$\therefore$ Required marks $= \frac{30}{360} \times 648 = 54.$

Example 4. The marks scored in Hindi and Maths exceed the marks scored in English and Social science by:

(a) 50 (b) 85

(c) 95 (d) 75

Sol. (a) Angle represented by

$= (H + M) - (E + S.Sc.)$

$= 75° + 90° - (55° + 60°) = 50°$

Directions (Q. 5-6) : Study the following graph carefully and answer the questions given below :

Production of Pulses in Rabi and Khariff Season

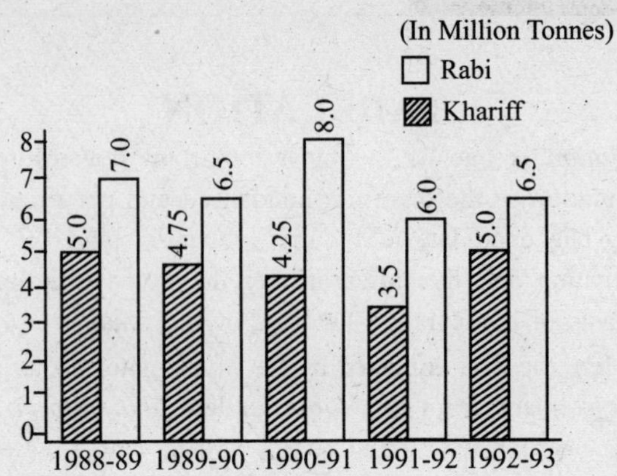

Example 5. What was the average of khariff production of the given years ? (In million tonnes)

(a) 4 (b) 5

(c) 4.5 (d) 5.5

Sol. (c) The average Khariff production of the given

years $= \frac{5 + 4.75 + 4.25 + 3.5 + 5}{5}$

$= \frac{22.5}{5} = 4.5$ million tons.

Example 6. What is the difference between the Rabi production in 1990-91 and the average Rabi production of the given years ? [In million tonnes]

(a) 2.5 (b) 20

(c) 1.2 (d) 15

Sol. (c) Average Production of Rabi

$= \frac{7 + 6.5 + 8 + 6 + 6.5}{5} = \frac{34}{5}$

$= 6.8$ million tons

In 1990-91 the production of Rabi

$= 8$ million tons.

$\therefore$ Required difference

$= 8 - 6.8 = 1.2$ million tons.

Exercise

Directions (Q. 1-5): Study the following table carefully and answer these questions.

Distribution of students according to Professional courses :

S.No.	Course	Faculty			
		Arts		Science	
		Girls	Boys	Girls	Boys
1.	Business Management	30	50	25	70
2.	Typewriting	25	190	20	35
3.	Costing	30	120	15	60
4.	Typewriting and Costing	15	100	5	10

1. The percentage of students of Arts faculty doing costing only is :
(a) 26.8% (b) 28%
(c) 30% (d) 30.2%

2. If 60% of boys and 80% of girls are successful in the courses taken by them, what is the combined pass percentage ?
(a) 62% (b) 64.12%
(c) 64.125% (d) 65%

3. Taking all the courses together by what number the boys exceed girls ?
(a) 450 (b) 460
(c) 470 (d) 480

4. What is the ratio of boys and girls of arts faculty doing costing ?
(a) 3 : 1 (b) 4 : 1
(c) 1 : 2 (d) 1 : 3

5. What is the ratio of boys of arts and science faculties doing type-writing and costing.
(a) 10 : 1 (b) 2 : 5
(c) 4 : 1 (d) 1 : 8

Directions (Q. Nos. 6-10): Read the table and answer the following questions :

City	I	II
P	65	15,610
Q	25	25,002
R	85	24,000
S	50	28,000
T	75	75,000

6. How many film-watchers in the city R see only one film in a week ?
(a) 13,600 (b) 13,500
(c) 36,000 (d) 14,000

7. Which city has the highest number of film-watchers who see only one film in a week ?
(a) P (b) R
(c) S (d) T

8. A city with the lowest number of film-watchers is :
(a) P (b) Q
(c) R (d) S

9. The highest number of film-watchers in any given city is :
(a) P (b) R
(c) T (d) S

10. The total number of all film-watchers in the five cities who see only one film in a week is :
(a) 4,26,324 (b) 4,20,324
(c) 4,60,324 (d) 4,65,325

Directions (Q. Nos. 11-15): The circle graph given here shows the spendings by a family on various items during the year 1998. Study the graph and answer the questions.

[Percent of money spent by a family on various items during 1998]

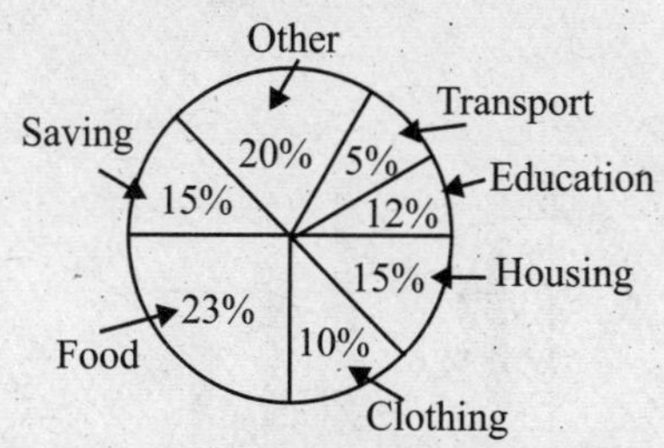

11. If the total amount spent during the year 1998 was ₹ 46000/- the amount spent on Food was :
(a) ₹ 20,00 (b) ₹ 10,580
(c) ₹ 23,000 (d) ₹ 2,300.

12. If the total amount spent was ₹ 46000/- how much was spent on Clothing and Housing together ?
(a) ₹ 11,500 (b) ₹ 1,150
(c) ₹ 10,000 (d) ₹ 15,000.

13. The ratio of the total amount of money spent on Housing to that spent on Education was :
(a) 5 : 2 (b) 2 : 5
(c) 4 : 5 (d) 5 : 4.

14. Graph shows that the maximum amount was spent on :
(a) Food
(b) Housing
(c) Clothing
(d) Others

15. If the total expenditure of the family for the year 1998 was ₹ 46,000/- the family saved during the year :
(a) ₹ 1,500
(b) ₹ 15,000
(c) ₹ 6,900
(d) ₹ 3,067

Directions (Q. Nos. 16-20): The following questions are based on the Pie-chart.

[The percentage expenses on various items during book production and sale]

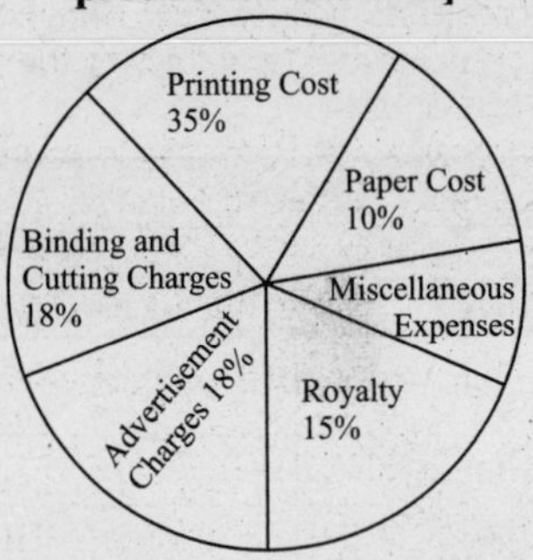

16. The central angle for the sector on 'Paper-cost' is :

(a) $22\frac{1}{2}°$ (b) 16°
(c) 54.8° (d) 36°.

17. If the 'Printing-cost' is ₹ 17,500, the royalty paid is :

(a) ₹ 8,750 (b) ₹ 7,500
(c) ₹ 3,150 (d) ₹ 6,300.

18. If the 'Miscellaneous expenses' are ₹ 6000, how much more are "Binding and Cutting charges" than 'Royalty' ?

(a) ₹ 6,000 (b) ₹ 5,500
(c) ₹ 4,500 (d) ₹ 10,500.

19. The central angle corresponding to the sector on "Printing cost" is more than that of "Advertisement charges" by :

(a) 72° (b) 61.2°
(c) 60° (d) 54.8°.

20. The "Paper cost" is approximately what percent of "Printing cost" ?

(a) 20.3% (b) 28.6%
(c) 30% (d) 32.5%.

Directions (Q. Nos. 21-25): Study the following graph carefully to answer the questions :

Percent of money spent on various items and savings by a family during 2001

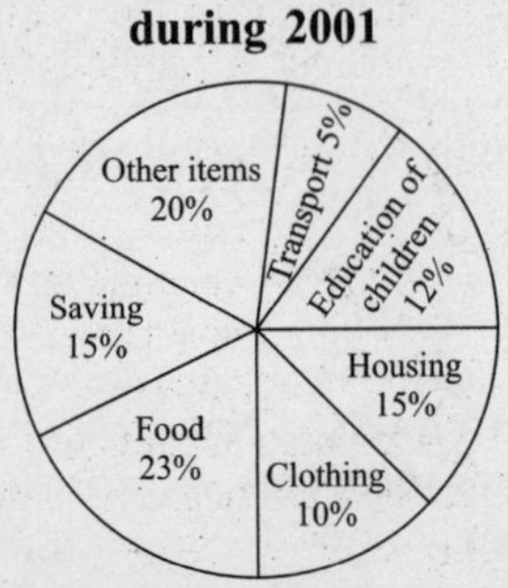

21. Maximum expenditure of the family was on :

(a) Food
(b) Housing
(c) Education
(d) Other items.

22. The total savings of the family for the year, here equal to the expenditure on :

(a) Food
(b) Clothing
(c) Housing
(d) Other items including transport.

23. What percent of the income was spent on Transport and Other items together ?

(a) 25% (b) 20%
(c) 30% (d) 32%.

24. If the total income of the family was ₹ 100,000, how much money was spent on the Education of the children ?

(a) ₹ 10,000 (b) ₹ 12,000
(c) ₹ 15,000 (d) ₹ 23,000.

25. If the total income for the year was ₹ 100,000 the difference of the expenses between Housing and Transport was ;

(a) 15,000 (b) 12,000
(c) 7,000 (d) 10,000.

Directions (Q. 26-30): Study the following Bar graph and answer the questions given below :

Number of Male and Female Employees Working on Each Floor of the Organisation

Y axis = No. of employees
X axis = Floor number

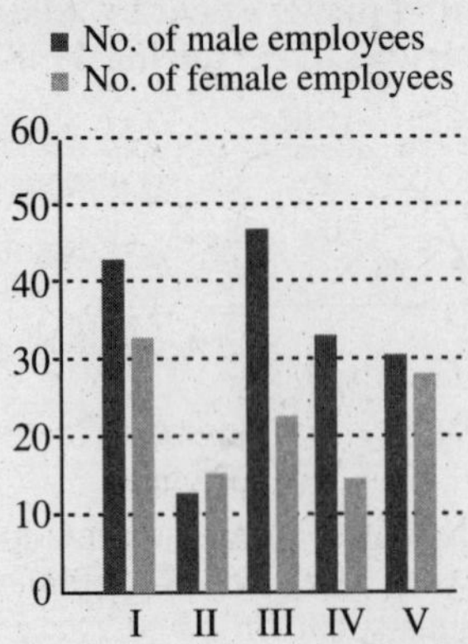

26. The number of male employees working on floor II is approximately what percent of the number of female employees working on floor V ?

(a) 15% (b) 35%
(c) 45% (d) 55%

27. What is the difference between the total number of male employees working on floor I and III together and the total number of male employees working on Floor II and V together ?

(a) 42 (b) 44
(c) 46 (d) 48

28. What is the respective ratio between the number of male employees on Floor III and the number of female employees on Floor II ?

(a) 7 : 3 (b) 8 : 3
(c) 8 : 5 (d) 10 : 3

29. The total number of employees working on Floor II is approximately what percent of the total number of employees working on Floor V ?

(a) 27 (b) 33
(c) 57 (d) 69

30. What is the total number of female employees in the organisation ?

(a) 124 (b) 122
(c) 126 (d) 128

Directions (Q. 31-35): Study the following Bar-graph carefully and answer the questions given below :

Number of Students Enrolled in three Different Courses in Six Different Years

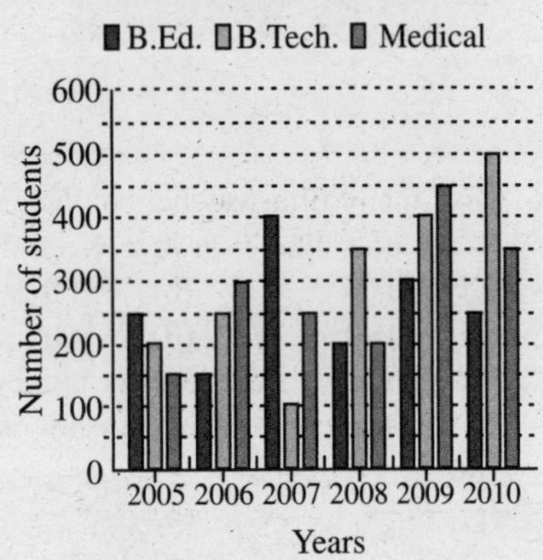

31. Number of students enrolled in B.Ed. in the year 2005 and 2009 together was approximately what percent of total number of students enrolled in Medical over all the years together ?

(a) 32 (b) 37
(c) 42 (d) 46

32. What was the average number of the students enrolled in B.Tech. over all the years together ?

(a) 400 (b) 300
(c) 900 (d) 1100

33. What was the respective ratio between the number of students enrolled in medical in the year 2010 and the number of students enrolled in B.Ed. in the year 2007 ?

(a) 8 : 5 (b) 7 : 8
(c) 5 : 8 (d) 7 : 9

34. In which year was the difference between the students enrolled in B.Ed. and B.Tech. second highest ?

(a) 2005 (b) 2006
(c) 2008 (d) 2009

35. What was the percentage increase in number of students enrolled in B.Tech. in the year 2008 as compared to previous year ?

(a) 150 (b) 250
(c) 350 (d) 450

Directions (Q. 36-40): Following graph shows wheat production, in thousand tonnes from 1999 to 2004. Answer the questions given below.

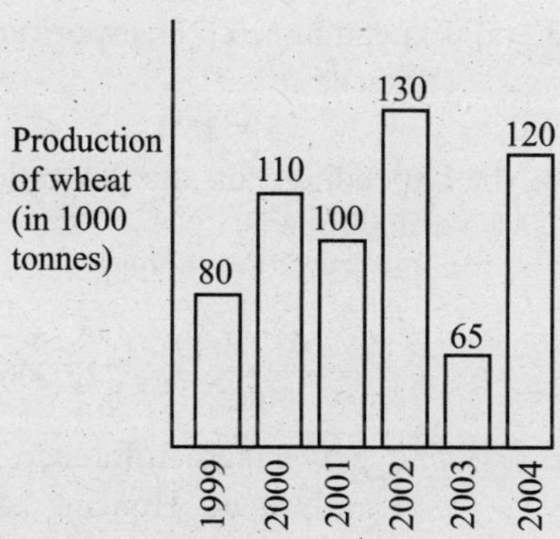

36. What is the percent increase in production in 2000 as compared to 1999 ?

(a) 45 (b) 37.5
(c) 52 (d) 51.

37. Which year's production is 50% of the sum of production of 1999 and 2004 ?

(a) 1999 (b) 2001
(c) 2003 (d) 2004

38. If the production during 2005 is more than the average production of the given years, which is the minimum production during 2005 ?

(a) 1,04,000 tonnes
(b) 1,34,000 tonnes
(c) 1,21,000 tonnes
(d) 1,00,830 tonnes.

39. How many year's production is more than the average production ?

(a) Three (b) Two
(c) One (d) Four.

40. Sum of production during 'odd' years is how many times that of the 'even' years ?

(a) 1.8 times (b) 8 times
(c) 2.5 times (d) 0.68 times.

Directions (Q. 41-45): Study the following Line-graph carefully and answer the questions given below :

Amounts Invested (in ₹ thousands) by three people in Schemes over the Years

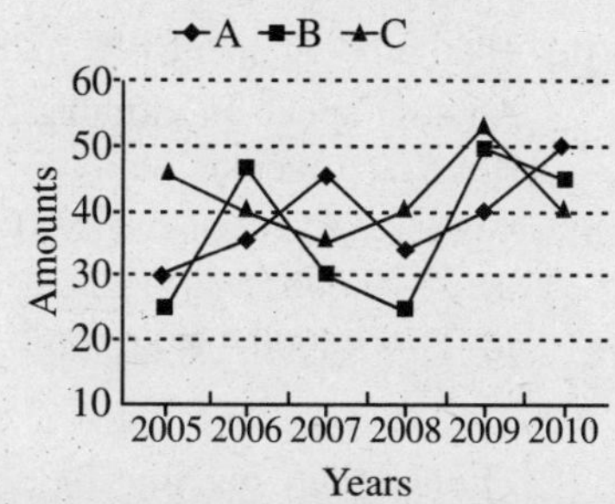

41. The amount invested by A in the year 2006 is approximately what percent of the total amount invested by him over all the years together ?

(a) 15 (b) 19
(c) 21 (d) 8

42. What is the average amount invested in the year 2009 by all the three people together ?

(a) ₹ 28,350 (b) ₹ $48,333\frac{1}{3}$
(c) ₹ $32,333\frac{1}{3}$ (d) ₹ 45,000

43. What is the percent decrease in the amount invested by C in the year 2007 from the previous year ?

(a) ₹ 1,000 (b) ₹ 10,000
(c) ₹ 1,00,000 (d) ₹ 100

44. What is the percent decrease in the amount invested by C in the year 2007 from the previous year ?

(a) 11.3 (b) 11.7
(c) 12.5 (d) 13.5

45. What is the respective ratio of total amount invested by B in the years 2008 and 2010 together to the total amount invested by C in those two years together ?

(a) 7 : 8 (b) 14 : 15
(c) 6 : 7 (d) 12 : 13

Directions (Q. 46-50): Study the Line-graph carefully and answer the questions given below :

Number of Players (in hundreds) participated in a sports event in three different sports in six different years

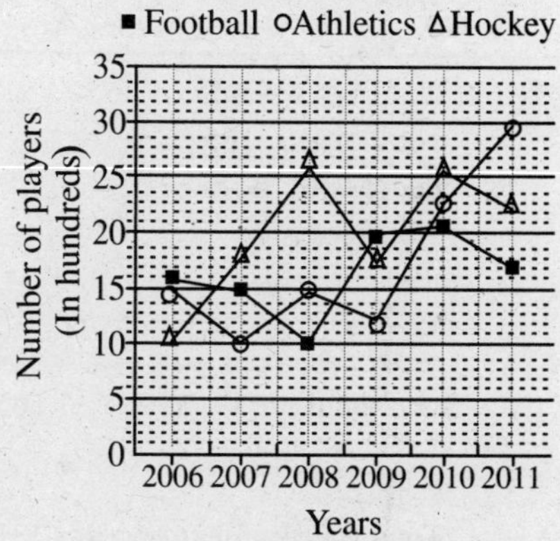

46. What was the difference between the number of players participated in athletics in the year 2010 and the number of players participated in Hockey in the year 2009 ?

(a) 660 (b) 600
(c) 700 (d) 580

47. What was the approximate average number of players participated in hockey over all the years together ?

(a) 2034 (b) 2104
(c) 2046 (d) 2146

48. Total number of players participated in all the sports together in the year 2007 was approximately what percentage of the total number of players participated in football over all the years together ?

(a) 49 (b) 51
(c) 44 (d) 35

49. What was the percent decrease in the number of players participated in football in the year 2008 as compared to previous year ?

(a) 30 (b) 34
(c) 44 (d) 48

50. If 23 percent of the players participated in athletics in the year 2006 found positive in dopping test, what was number of players participated in athletics in the year 2006 found negative in doping test ?

(a) 1026 (b) 1048
(c) 1078 (d) 1064

Answers

1. (a) Required percentage

$$= \frac{\text{(Girls+Boys) of costing}}{\text{(Girls+Boys) of Arts}} \times 100$$

$$= \frac{150}{560} \times 100$$

= 26.8%

2. (c) Total boys = 635,
Total girls = 165
∴ Successful boys
= 60% of 635

$$= \frac{60}{100} \times 635 = 381$$

∴ Successful girls = 80% × of 165

$$= \frac{80}{100} \times 165 = 132$$

Total successful students = 381 + 132
Total students = 800

$$\text{Reqd. percentage} = \frac{613}{800} \times 100$$

= 64.125%

3. (c) Boys exceed girls
= 635 – 165 = 470

4. (b) Required Ratio $= \frac{120}{30} = 4:1.$

5. (a) Required Ratio = 100 : 10 = 10 : 1

6. (a) In city R, the percentage of film-watchers who see two or more films a week = 100 – 85 = 15%
∴ 15% of total viewers = 24000
85% of total viewers

$$= \frac{24000 \times 85}{15} = 13600.$$

7. (d) For city S, the number

$$= \frac{50}{50} \times 28000 = 28000$$

Obviously, city T has the highest number of one film watchers.

8. (a) Lowest number of film-watchers is = P

9. (c) From the above solution, it is obviously city T.

10. (a) Total number of film watchers
= 225000 + 28990 + 8334 + 136000 + 28000
= 426324

11. (b) Total amount spent = ₹ 46,000
Amount spent on Food
= 23% of 46,000

$$= \frac{23}{100} \times 46{,}000 = ₹\ 10{,}580.$$

12. (a) Total amount spent = ₹ 46,000
Amount spent on clothing and Housing together
= (10% + 15%) of ₹ 46,000

$$= \frac{25}{100} \times 46000 = ₹\ 11{,}500$$

13. (d) $\dfrac{\text{Expenditure on Housing}}{\text{Expenditure on Education}}$

$$= \frac{15\%}{12\%} = \frac{15}{12} = \frac{5}{4} = 5:4.$$

14. (a) Maximum expenditure is 23% and it is on Food.

15. (c) Total expenditure = ₹ 46,000
Amount saved = 5% of ₹ 46,000

$$= \frac{15}{100} \times ₹\ 46{,}000 = ₹\ 6{,}900.$$

16. (d) ∵ 100% = 360°

$$\therefore\ 1\% = \frac{360°}{100}$$

$$\therefore\ 10\% = \frac{360° \times 10}{100} = 36°.$$

17. (b) ∵ 35% total cost = ₹ 17,500
∴ 15% of total cost

$$= ₹\ \frac{17500 \times 15}{35}$$

= ₹ 75,00.

18. (c) Difference in percent cost of 'Binding and Cutting charges' and 'Royalty' = 18 – 15 = 3
Now, ∵ 4% of total cost
= ₹ 6000
∴ 3% of total cost

$$= ₹\ \frac{6000 \times 3}{4}$$

= ₹ 4,500.

19. (b) Difference in percent expenses on Printing cost and Advertisement charges
= 35 – 18 = 17
Now, 1% = 3.6°
∴ 17% = 3.6° × 17
= 61.2°.

20. (b) The required percent

$$= \frac{10 \times 100}{35} = 28.6 \text{ (approx.)}$$

21. (a) Maximum expenditure of family is on Food *i.e.* 23%.

22. (a) It is obvious from the chart.

23. (a) Expenditure on Transport and Other items
= 20 + 5 = 25%.

24. (b) Expenditure on the Education of children
= 12% of ₹ 100000

$$= \frac{12 \times 100000}{100} = ₹\ 12{,}000.$$

25. (d) The percentage difference in expenditure on Housing and Transport = 15 – 5 = 10%.
∴ The required difference
= 10% of ₹ 1,00,000 = ₹ 10,000.

26. (d) Required percent

$$= \frac{16 \times 100}{28}\% = 57.1\% \simeq 55\%$$

27. (b) Required difference
= (42 + 48) ~ (16 + 30)
= (90 ~ 46) = 44

28. (b) Required ratio = 48 : 18 = 8 : 3

29. (c) Total number of employees working on Floor II
= (16 + 18) = 34
Total number of employees working on Floor V
= (30 + 29) = 59
∴ Required percent

$$= \left(\frac{34}{59} \times 100\right)\% = 57.62\% \simeq 57\%$$

30. (b) Total number of female employees
$= (35 + 18 + 25 + 16 + 28) = 122$

31. (a) Number of students enrolled in B.Ed. in the year 2005 and 2009
$= (250 + 300) = 550$
Total number of students enrolled in medical over all the years
$= (150 + 300 + 250 + 200 + 450 + 350) = 1700$
$\therefore$ Required percent
$$= \left(\frac{550}{1700} \times 100\right)\% = 32.35\% \simeq 32\%$$

32. (b) Required average number
$$= \frac{(200+250+100+350+400+500)}{6}$$
$$= \frac{1800}{6} = 300$$

33. (b) Required ratio $= 35 : 400 = 7 : 8$

34. (c) Difference in year 2005
$= (250 - 200) = 50$
Difference in year 2006
$= (250 - 150) = 100$
Difference in year 2008
$= (350 - 200) = 150$
Difference in year 2007
$= (400 - 100) = 300$
Difference in year 2009
$= (400 - 300) = 100$
Difference in year 2010
$= (500 - 250) = 250$
$\therefore$ In 2008, the difference in third highest.

35. (b) Required increase percent
$$= \left(\frac{350-100}{100} \times 100\right)\% = 250\%$$

36. (b) Percentage increase in the production of wheat in 2000 in comparison to 1999
$$= \frac{110-80}{80} \times 100 = 37.5$$

37. (b) Total production in 1999 and 2004
$= (80 + 120)$ thousand tonnes
Production of wheat in 2001
$= 100$ thousand tonnes.

38. (d) Average production
$$= \frac{80+110+100+130+65+120}{6}$$
$$= \frac{605}{6} \text{ thousand tonnes}$$
$= 100.83$ thousand tonnes.

39. (a) Three

40. (d) Total production of odd years
$= 80 + 100 + 65 = 245$ thousand tonnes
Total production of even years
$= 110 + 130 + 120 = 360$ thousand tonnes
$\therefore$ Required difference
$$= \frac{245}{360} = 0.68 \text{ times.}$$

41. (a) Required percent
$$= \frac{35}{(30+35+45+35+40+50)} \times 100\%$$
$$= \frac{3500}{235}\% = 14.89\% \simeq 15\%$$

42. (b) Average amount
$$= \frac{(40+50+55)}{3} \times 1000$$
$$= \left(\frac{145}{3} \times 1000\right) \Rightarrow ₹\,48{,}333\frac{1}{3}$$

43. (c) Required amount $= ₹\,(25 + 30 + 45) + 1{,}000$
$= ₹\,1{,}00{,}000$

44. (c) Required decrease percent
$$= \frac{(40-35)}{40} \times 100\% = 12.5\%$$

45. (a) Required ratio $= (25 + 45) : (40 + 40)$
$= 70 : 80 = 7 : 8$

46. (b) Required difference $= (23 - 17) \times 100$
$= (6 \times 100) \Rightarrow 600$

47. (a) Required average number
$$= \frac{(11+18+27+17+26+23)}{6} \times 100$$
$$= \frac{12200}{6} = 2033.33 \simeq 2034$$

48. (c) Total number of players participated in all the sports together in the year 2007
$= (10 + 15 + 18) = 43$
Total number of players participated in football over all the years
$= (16 + 15 + 10 + 19 + 21 + 17) \Rightarrow 98$
$\therefore$ Required percent
$$= \frac{4300}{98}\% = 43.87\% \simeq 44\%$$

49. (b) Required decrease
$$= \frac{(15-10)}{15} \times 100\% = 33\frac{1}{3}\% \simeq 34\%$$

50. (c) Required number
$$= \left(14 \times 100 \times \frac{77}{100}\right) \Rightarrow 1078$$

English

1 TENSES

Tense is that form of a verb which shows the time and state of an action or event.

There are three main tenses

1. The Present Tense
2. The Past Tense
3. The Future Tense

1. The Present Tense

The present tense indicates action in the present.

- **Present Indefinite Tense :** The Present Indefinite or Simple Present Tense is used

➢ To express a habitual action

I get up everyday at 7 O'clock.

➢ To express general truths

The sun sets in the west.

➢ To indicate a future event that is part of a plan or arrangement

We leave for Indore next Wednesday.

- **Present Continuous Tense:** The Present Continuous Tense is used.

➢ For an action going on at the time of speaking

The boys are playing cricket.

➢ For a temporary action which may not be actually happening at the time of speaking.

I am reading "Romeo Juliet."

➢ For an action that is planned or arranged to take place in the near future.

My father is arriving day after tomorrow.

Exception : The following verbs are not used in the continuous form

(a) **Verbs of Emotion:** want, wish, desire, feel, like, love, hate, hope, refuse, prefer.

(b) **Verbs of Perception:** see, hear, smell, recognize.

(c) **Verbs of Appearance:** appear, look, seem.

- **Present Perfect Tense :** The Present Perfect Tense is used

➢ To indicate complete activities in the immediate past

(i) He has just finished the Match.

(ii) The Bus has just started.

➢ To express past actions the time of which is not given and not definite

(i) I have never known him to be pessimistic.

(ii) Mr. Vikas has been to Europe.

- **Present Perfect Continuous Tense :** The Present Perfect Continuous Tense is used for an action which began at some time in the past and is still going on.

(i) He has been fishing for two hours.

2. The Past Tense

➢ The past tense shows that the action took place in the past.

- **Past Indefinite Tense :** The past Indefinite or Simple past Tense is used

➢ To indicate an action completed in the past

(i) The boy left college an hour ago.

➢ To denote past habits

He practiced many hours everyday.

- **Past Continuous Tense :** The Past Continuous Tense is used

➢ To denote an action going on at some time in the past

(i) We were watching the movie all evening.

➢ With always, continually, etc. for persistent habits in the past

(i) She was continually neglecting her duty.

- **Past Perfect Tense :** The Past Perfect Tense is used

➢ To describe an action completed before a certain moment in the past

(i) I called him at 5 am, I had found him got up at 8 am.

When two actions happened in the past and it may be necessary to show which action happened earlier than the other

(i) I had completed my work before the officer came.

- **Past Perfect Continuous Tense :** The Past Perfect Continuous Tense is used

➢ To describe an action that began before a certain point in the past and continued upto that time

(i) At that time he had been writing a short story for three months.

3. The Future Tense

The future tense shows that the action is going to take place in the future. The future tense needs the auxiliary verb will or shall.

- **Future Indefinite Tense :** The Future Indefinite or Simple Future Tense is used

➢ For an action that has still to take place.

(i) Day after tomorrow will be Friday.

- **Future Continuous Tense :** The Future Continuous Tense represents an action as going on at some time in Future.

(i) I shall be writing the letter then.

- **Future Perfect Tense :** The Future Perfect Tense is used

➢ To indicate the completion of an action by a certain future time.

(i) Before you go to meet him, he will have left the office.

- **Future Perfect Continuous Tense :** The Future Perfect Continuous Tense indicates an action represented as being in progress over a period of time that will end in the future.

(i) When he completes his school, he will have been studying at IIT.

Exercise

Directions : Pick out the most effective word from the given words to fill in the blank to make the sentence meaningfully complete.

1. They told us that man .... a social animal.
(a) is (b) was
(c) had been (d) will be
2. The population of the world .... very fast now.
(a) rises (b) rose
(c) is rising (d) will rise
3. It .... last week.
(a) has not rained
(b) did not rained
(c) will not be raining
(d) did not rain
4. The little girl confessed that she .... the glass.
(a) broke (b) had broken
(c) breaks (d) will break
5. She was tired because she .... very hard.
(a) is working
(b) was working
(c) has been working
(d) had been working
6. When I .... may bath I went to have a sleep.
(a) had taken (b) took
(c) have taken (d) take
7. Ruby .... very long hair when she was a child.
(a) has (b) will have
(c) didn't have (d) used to have
8. The child .... any food until he has remembered his lesson.
(a) would not get
(b) will not get
(c) gets
(d) had got
9. If I .... his number, I would phone him.
(a) know
(b) known
(c) knew
(d) did not know
10. I asked Babita if Savitri .... already been married.
(a) has (b) have
(c) had (d) would have
11. Payal told me that she .... out for a walk every morning.
(a) went (b) goes
(c) had gone (d) has gone
12. If they .... early, they would have caught the train.
(a) left
(b) have left
(c) had left
(d) would have left
13. She told her mother that Sonam .... her there the previous day.
(a) met (b) meets
(c) had met (d) would meet
14. She .... in Kolkata for three years before the year 1992.
(a) was living
(b) has been living
(c) would have been living
(d) had been
15. The Principal .... the peon to let the girl come in.
(a) said to (b) has said
(c) ordered to (d) ordered
16. She talks as if she .... mad.
(a) is (b) was
(c) were (d) had
17. Sushma said that she .... finished her work by 9 am.
(a) said to (b) has
(c) had (d) would have
18. I order her about as if she .... my wife.
(a) is (b) was
(c) had (d) were
19. Sarika said that she would go home ....
(a) tomorrow
(b) yesterday
(c) the previous day
(d) the next day
20. I .... many countries before I returned from England.
(a) saw
(b) have seen
(c) had seen
(d) had been seeing
21. I .... the newspaper when Rohit came.
(a) is reading (b) read
(c) has read (d) was reading
22. I shall tell you when she ....
(a) will come (b) come
(c) comes (d) is coming
23. Mr. Singh helped us more than he .... his own students.
(a) helped (b) has helped
(c) helps (d) is helping
24. They worked hard lest they .... in the examination.
(a) will fail (b) failed
(c) should fail (d) fail
25. Her mother told him that the sun .... in the east.
(a) rose (b) is rising
(c) will rise (d) rises

Answers

1. (a)	**2.** (c)	**3.** (d)	**4.** (b)	**5.** (d)	**6.** (a)	**7.** (d)	**8.** (b)	**9.** (c)	**10.** (c)
11. (b)	**12.** (c)	**13.** (c)	**14.** (d)	**15.** (d)	**16.** (c)	**17.** (d)	**18.** (d)	**19.** (d)	**20.** (c)
21. (d)	**22.** (c)	**23.** (c)	**24.** (c)	**25.** (d)					

2 COMMON ERRORS

These types of questions are intended to test the knowledge of the students about the understanding of the basic rules of English Grammar. The knowledge of basic rules of grammar relating to Articles, Nouns, Pronouns, Adjectives, Verb, Adverbs, Conjunctions, Prepositions, Subject-Verb Agreement are, therefore, necessary to solve this type of questions.

NOUNS

A Noun is a word used as the name of a person, place or thing.

Kinds of Nouns

1. **Proper Noun :** A proper noun is the name of a particular person or place. *e.g.,* Anamika, Kolkata, India.

Note : Proper nouns are always written with a capital letter at the beginning.

2. **Common Noun :** A common noun is a name given in common to every person or thing of the same class or kind. *e.g.,* student, mother, bird.

3. **Collective Noun :** A collective noun is the name of a group of persons or things taken together and spoken of as a whole, as unit. *e.g.,* team, army, jury, fleet.

4. **Material Noun :** A material noun is the name of metal or substance, of which things are made of. *e.g.,* gold, cotton, wood.

5. **Abstract Noun :** An abstract noun is usually the name of a quality, action or state considered apart from the object to which it belongs. *e.g.,* kindness, laughter, childhood.

Some Important Rules

Rule 1

Some nouns like furniture, information, poetry, scenery, machinery, work, wood, paper, glass, dust, traffic, electricity, food, grass, luggage, advice etc. are always singular.

Rule 2

Some nouns have the singular and the plural alike. As : sheep, deer, swine, species etc. *e.g.,*

(i) It is a rare species.
(ii) There are many species of dogs.

Rule 3

Nouns expressing number like dozen, score, hundred thousand etc. are used in singular with numerical adjective. *e.g.,*

(i) She bought three dozen oranges.
(ii) I gave him five hundred rupees.

Rule 4

Some nouns like cattle, poultry, people, police gentry, peasantry, electorate etc. are always plural. *e.g.,*

(i) Cattle are not allowed to enter this ground.
(ii) There are few gentry in this town.

Rule 5

Some nouns like committee, jury, family, crowd, government, audience etc. are used as singulars when they are thought of as a unit but they are used as plurals when their members are thought of. *e.g.,*

(i) The committee are divided and there is bitterness among the members.
(ii) The audience are requested to take their seats.

Rule 6

When the plural noun is a proper name for some single object or some collective unit, it is used as singular. *e.g.,*

(i) The United States has a big navy.

Rule 7

If a noun is used both before and after a preposition, it is in singular always. *e.g.,*

(i) Woman after woman climbed the rostrum to speak against the cruel practices of dowry and bride burning.

Rule 8

A plural noun is used after one of, either of, neither of and each of. *e.g.,*

(i) Neither of the girls has come yet.

Rule 9

The plural of compound nouns are formed by forming plural of the principal word. *e.g.,*

(i) None of the passers-by helped him.

Rule 10

Plural formation is done in both the parts of the compound nouns of man and woman. *e.g.,*

(i) None of the men-servants was present yesterday.

Possessive Case

Rule 11

The possessive case is chiefly used with the names of living things. *e.g.,*

(i) The cart's wheel was broken. (Incorrect)
The wheel of the cart was broken. (Correct)
(ii) Ravi's brother is my friend.

Rule 12

If else is used with anybody, somebody, nobody etc. the possessive sign is put to. *e.g.,*

(i) This shirt is not mine, it is somebody else's.
(ii) I follow your suggestion and nobody else's.

Rule 13

When two nouns are in opposition, the possessive sign is put to the latter only. *e.g.,*

(i) That is Dinkar the poet's house.
(ii) He is going to James Watt the scientist's country.

Rule 14

With compound nouns the possessive sign is attached only to the last word. *e.g.,*

(i) Her mother-in-law's health is not good these days.
(ii) His maid-servant's son has broken the pot.

PRONOUNS

A Pronoun is a word used in place of a noun.

Kinds of Pronouns

1. **Personal Pronouns :** I, we, you, he, me, her, them etc.
   (a) If a pronoun acts as a subject of a verb, it is in Nominative/ Subjective Case and if it acts as an object of a verb, it is in Objective Case.
   Nominative Case– I, we, you, her, she, it, they
   Objective Case–me, us, you, him, her, it, them
   (b) A pronoun is used in Objective Case after let. *e.g.,*
   (i) Let him and me do this.
   (c) A pronoun is used in Objective Case after a preposition. *e.g.,*
   (i) They laughed at her and me.
   (d) Nominative Case is used after than if the comparison is between two nominatives. *e.g.,*
   (i) As a student of science you are far better than her.
   (e) Objective Case is used after than if the comparison is between two objects. *e.g.,*
   (i) She loves you more than me.
   (f) Good manners require that the order of personal pronouns in a sentence should be 231 *i.e.,* the second person should come before the third and the third person before the first. *e.g.,*
   (i) You and he will follow it.
   (ii) You, he and I are going to Delhi.
2. **Distributive Pronouns :** Each, either, neither.
   (a) **Either** and **Neither** are used for two persons or things. *e.g.,*
   (i) Either of them can do this.
   (ii) Neither of you will go there.
   (b) **Each** is used for two or more than two persons/things. *e.g.,*
   (i) Each of the students contributed fifty rupees.
   (ii) Each of the two boys is doing his work.
3. **Demonstrative Pronouns :** This, that, these, those, such etc.
   (a) **This** and **these** are used for the persons/things which are near the speaker.
   This is used for one person/thing and those is used for more than one person/thing. *e.g.,*
   (i) This bat is a present for you.
   (ii) These flowers are beautiful.
   (b) **That** and **those** are used for the persons/things which are away from the speaker.
   That is used for one person/thing and those is used for more than one person/thing. *e.g.,*
   (i) That boy is my friend.
   (ii) Those skirts are mine.
4. **Indefinite Pronouns :** One, some, any, everybody, somebody, anybody, everyone, someone, anyone, no-one, everything, something, anything, nothing etc.
   (a) In referring to **anybody, every-body, everyone, anyone, each** etc., the pronoun he or she is used according to the context. *e.g.,*
   (i) I shall be glad to help everyone of the boys in his studies.
   (ii) Everyone of the Miss World contestants tried to improve herself through rigorous training.
   (b) The indefinite pronoun 'one' should be used throughout, if used as all, i.e. its nominative-one, objective - one, Possessive-one's and Reflexive-one-self should be used *e.g.,*
   (i) One should take care of one's house.
   (ii) One should help oneself.
5. **Reflexive Pronouns :** Myself, yourself, himself, herself, ourselves, itself, etc.
   (a) A reflexive pronoun or an object must be put after resign, revenge, exert, apply, adjust, pride. *e.g.,*
   (b) Verbs such as be, break, burst, feed, hide, make, open, qualify, rest, roll, speed, stop, turn are usually not followed by a reflexive pronoun. *e.g.,*
   (i) He has qualified for the match.
   (ii) You should keep a distance from bad boys.
   (c) A reflexive pronoun cannot be used as a substitute for the subject. *e.g.,*
   Rohit and myself decided to join the army. (Incorrect)
   Rohit and I decided to join the army. (Correct)
6. **Emphatic Pronouns :** When yourself, themselves etc. are used for the sake of emphasis, they are called Emphatic Pronouns. *e.g.,*
   (i) I myself went to finalise the deal.
   (ii) They themselves admitted their guilt.
7. **Relative Pronouns :** Who, Whom, Whose, Which, That
   (a) **Who** is used for persons only and **which** is used for things without life and for animals. *e.g.,*
   (i) This is the man who brought the news.
   (ii) The horse which I recently bought is an Arab.
   (b) **That** is used for persons and things. *e.g.,*
   (i) This is the man that brought the news.
   (ii) The horse that I recently bought is an Arab.
   (c) **Who/Which** is used in both defining and non-defining cases. That is used in defining case. *e.g.,*
   (i) The cow which she has bought is black.
   (d) **That** is used after superlative degree, all, same, only, none, nothing. *e.g.,*
   (i) He was the most eloquent speaker that I ever heard.
   (e) **Who** is used in Nominative Case i.e. it is followed by a verb while whom is used in Objective Case i.e. it is not followed by a verb. *e.g.,*
   (i) The girl whom I met today was his friend.
8. **Interrogative Pronouns :** Who, Whom, Whose, Which, That etc.
   (a) **Who** is used for persons only.
   Who was knocking at the door?

(b) **Which** is used for both persons and things. It implies selection. *e.g.,*
Which of them has said so?

9. **Exclamatory Pronoun:** What,
When interrogative word **what** is used to express surprise, it is called Exclamatory Pronoun. *e.g.,*
What! you don't know Modi?

10. **Reciprocal Pronouns:** Each other, one another
Each other is used for two persons/things and **one another** is used for more than two persons/things.
But in modern use there is no difference in the use of **each other** and **one another**. *e.g.,*
They all loved one another.

ADJECTIVES

An **Adjective** is a word which qualifies a noun or a pronoun.

Kinds of Adjectives

1. ***Proper Adjectives*:** Adjectives formed from Proper Nouns are called Proper Adjectives, *e.g.,*

Proper Nouns	Proper Adjectives
India	Indian
Turkey	Turkish
Shakespeare	Shakespearian

A Proper Adjective must begin with a capital letter.

2. ***Possessive Adjectives*:** My, our, your, his, her, their, its are called Possessive Adjectives.
Possessive Adjectives are always used before noun. *e.g.,*
My book, Your brother, His horse

3. ***Distributive Adjectives*:** Each, every, either, neither are called Distributive Adjectives.

(a) **Each** is used for two or more than two things/persons *e.g.,*
Each boy must take his turn.

(b) **Every** is used for more than two persons/things. *e.g.,*
He gave every girl the same dress.

(c) **Either** and **Neither** are used for two persons/things. *e.g.,*
Neither of the two ministers was available for comments.

4. ***Demonstrative Adjectives:*** Demonstrative Adjectives are of two kinds:

(a) **Definite:** this, that, these, those, such, same.
These Adjectives point out a particular person or thing exactly.

(b) **Indefinite:** a, an, a certain, certain, some, any, any other, another, other.
These adjectives point out persons or things in a certain sense, but not exactly.

5. ***Numeral Adjectives*:** Numeral Adjectives are of two kinds :

(I) **Definite:** These adjectives denote exact number or order of persons/things.

(a) Those which denote exact number of persons/things are called Cardinals.

(b) Those which denote the serial order in which a person or thing stands are called Ordinals. *e.g.,*

(c) Ordinals are used before Cardinals, if they both are to be used in a sentence. *e.g.,*

(i) The first three pages of this book.

(ii) The last two scenes of this movie.

(II) **Indefinite:** These adjectives denote number of some kind without saying precisely what the number is. *e.g.,*
Many, enough, all, most, various, numerous, several etc.

NOTE : *If Definite and Indefinite both Numeral Adjectives are to be used together, Indefinite Numeral Adjectives should be used before Definite Numeral Adjectives.*

6. ***Quantitative Adjectives*:** These adjectives show the quantity or degree of a thing. *e.g.,*
Much, little, whole, some, enough, all etc.

(a) Much, little, whole are always used for quantity.

(b) All, some, enough, sufficient, most are used for both quantity and number.

7. ***Qualitative Adjectives*:** These adjectives show what quality or in what state persons or things are. *e.g.,*
Big, small, sick, good etc.

8. **Interrogative Adjectives:** These adjectives are used to ask questions. *e.g.,*

(i) Which picture do you like most ?

(ii) Whose wife is she ?

9. ***Exclamatory Adjectives*:** What is called Exclamatory Adjective when it is used to express surprise. *e.g.,*

(i) What an idea!

(ii) What a piece of work is man!

DEGREES OF COMPARISON

Positive Degree

The Positive Degree of an Adjective is the Adjective in its simple form. It is used when no comparison is made. *e.g.,*
Rekha is a good singer.

Comparative Degree

The Comparative Degree of an Adjective is used when the quality of two persons or things are compared *e.g.,*
My mango is sweeter than his mango.

Superlative Degree

The Superlative Degree of an Adjective denotes the highest degree of quality and is used when more than two persons or things are compared. *e.g.,*
He is the most intelligent boy in the class.

Some Important Facts

(a) **Senior, superior, junior, prior, inferior, posterior** are followed by to instead of than. *e.g.,*
All his colleagues are senior than him. (*Incorrect*)
All his colleagues are senior to him. (*Correct*)

(b) **Interior, exterior, minor, major** etc. are the Adjectives of Positive Degree Neither more/most is used before them nor then/to is used after them. *e.g.,*
His age is a matter of minor importance.

(c) **After Comparatively** or **Relatively** Positive Degree is used. *e.g.,*
The wind is comparatively faster today. (*Incorrect*)
The wind is comparatively fast today. (*Correct*)

(d) Before **enough** Positive Degree is used. *e.g.,*
He is smarter enough to get selected for this prestigious post. (*Incorrect*)

He is smart enough to get selected for this prestigious post. (*Correct*)

ADVERB

An Adverb is a word which modifies the meaning of a verb, an adjective or another adverb.

Kinds of Adverbs

(A) According to their use, adverbs are divided into three classes :

1. **Simple Adverb:** These adverbs modify the meaning of a verb, an adjective, or an adverb. *e.g.,*
   She can hardly believe it.
2. **Interrogative Adverb:** These adverbs are used for asking questions. *e.g.,*
   Why is she not playing ?
3. **Relative Adverb:** These adverbs are the same in form as Interrogative Adverbs, but instead of asking question, they join two sentences together.
   These adverbs relate to some antecedent, expressed or understood. *e.g.,*
   (i) Let me know the time when you will come. (The antecedent expressed)
   Let me know when you will come. (the antecedent understood.)
   (ii) I remember the house where I was born.

(B) According to their meaning, adverbs may be divided into the following classes:

1. **Adverbs of time:** These are the adverbs which tell us when does an action takes place. *e.g.,*
   I hurt my knee yesterday.
2. **Adverbs of Place:** These are the adverbs which tell us where does an action takes place. *e.g.,*
   She left her bag here.
3. **Adverbs of Frequency:** These are the adverbs which tell us how often an action takes place. *e.g.,*
   I have called you twice.
4. **Adverbs of Degree or Quantity:** These are the adverbs which tell us how much or in what degree or to what extent. *e.g.,*
   He is kind enough to help her.

Position of Adverbs

1. **Always, often, seldom, never, just, ever, usually, hardly, already, nearly,** etc. are used before the main verb.*e.g.,*
   (i) I have told often him to write neatly. (*Incorrect*)
   I have often told him to write neatly. (*Correct*)
   (ii) He never talks ill of his friends.
   (iii) Imran always comes late.
2. Adverbs of Time/Place/Manner are generally placed after the verb or after the object if there is one. *e.g.,*
   (i) He does his work carefully.
   (ii) She looked everywhere.
   (iii) I met her yesterday.

Note : *Adverb of Manner is used before the object if a clause starting with who/which/that is used after the object. e.g.,*
She received warmly all those who had come in time.

3. If adverbs of time/place/manner, all are to be used in a sentence, the normal order is adverb of manner, adverb of place, adverb of time. *e.g.,*
   He danced in the city hall well last night. (*Incorrect*)
   He danced well in the city hall last night. (*Correct*)

Note : *With come/go/arrive etc. adverb of manner is used after adverb of place.*

4. Adverbs of quantity are usually used before the word that they qualify. *e.g.,*
   (i) The party was too dull.
   (ii) She is quite cool.

Note : But enough is always placed after the word to which it qualifies.

CONJUNCTIONS

A **Conjunction** is a word which joins two or more than two words, phrases, clauses or sentences.

Some Important Rules

***Rule* 1**

Scarcely/Hardly is always followed by **when/before**. *e.g.,*
Scarcely had he gone out of the office then he came. (*Incorrect*)
Scarcely had he gone out of the office when he came. (*Correct*)

***Rule* 2**

Lest is followed by **should. Not** is not used with it. *e.g.,*
Be careful lest you will fall. (Incorrect)
Be careful lest you should fall. (*Correct*)

***Rule* 3**

Both is followed by **and** *e.g.,*
Both Sonu as well as Pawan have done their work. (Incorrect)
Both Sonu and Pawan have done their work. (Correct)

***Rule* 4**

Rather and **other** are always followed by **than.** *e.g.,*
I have no other choice but to do it. (Incorrect)
I have no other choice than to do it. (Correct)

***Rule* 5**

And is not used before a Relative Pronoun. *e.g.,*
He is an intelligent boy and who is my friend. (Incorrect)
He is an intelligent boy who is my friend. (Correct)

***Rule* 6**

That, as to etc. are not used before Interrogative words (where, who, what, whom etc.). *e.g.,*
They asked her that where she had been. (Incorrect)
They asked her where she had been. (Correct)

***Rule* 7**

Seldom or **never** and **Seldom or ever** are used. *e.g.,*
We seldom or ever see those forsaken who trust in God. (Incorrect)
We seldom or never see those forsaken who trust in God. (Correct)

Exercise –1

Directions (1-30) : In each of the following questions, some of the sentences have errors and some are correct. Find out which part of a sentence has an error and blacken the option corresponding to it (a,b,c). If a sentence is free from errors, then your answer is (d) i.e. No error.

1. The minister for Education (a) / vehemently refused (b)/ the allegation that he had taken bribes. (c)/ No error. (d)
2. If I were Zubin (a) / I would not attend (b)/ the wedding, come what may. (c)/ No error. (d)
3. He says that (a) / he reads novels (b)/ to pass away the time. (c)/ No error. (d)
4. He left for Mumbai on Sunday (a) / arriving there (b)/ on Monday. (c)/ No error. (d)
5. No sooner did the teacher (a) / enter the class room (b)/ the students got up. (c)/ No error. (d)
6. It is (a) / nothing else (b)/ than pride. (c)/ No error. (d)
7. To the ordinary man, in fact, the pealing of bells (a) / is a monotonous jangle and a nuisance (b)/ tolerably only when mitigated by remote distance and sentimental association. (c)/ No error. (d)
8. The increasing mechanisation of life (a) / have led us farther away from daily contact with nature and (b)/ the crafts of the farm (c)/ No error. (d)
9. If you have a way with words, (a) / a good sense of design and administration ability (b)/ you may enjoy working in the high pressure world of advertising. (c)/ No error. (d)
10. Last week's sharp hike in the wholesale price of beef (a) / is a strong indication for (b)/ higher meat costs to come. (c)/ No error. (d)
11. Supposing if (a) / it rains (b)/ what shall we do? (c)/ No error. (d)
12. The captain along with his team (a) / are practising very hard (b)/ for the forthcoming match. (c)/ No error. (d)
13. It was him (a) / who came running (b)/ into the classroom. (c)/ No error. (d)
14. The capital of Yemen (a) / is situating (b)/ 2190 meters above the sea level. (c)/ No error. (d)
15. Ram was (a) / senior to (b)/ Sam in college. (c)/ No error. (d)
16. You are (a) / always doing (b)/ this mistake. (c)/ No error. (d)
17. He has (a) / a large family (b)/ to care. (c)/ No error. (d)
18. These poisonous gases (a) / will effect (b)/ our health. (c)/ No error. (d)
19. The only Indian (a) / to win the Nobel Prize for the Literature (b)/ was Rabindranath Tagore. (c)/ No error. (d)
20. After his illness, (a) / the patient was (b)/ sick with life. (c)/ No error. (d)
21. I told him (a) / that I availed (b)/ the opportunity. (c)/ No error. (d)
22. I think (a) / he owns an expensive (b)/ painting by Hussain. (c)/ No error. (d)
23. It is time (a) / we should have done (b)/ something useful. (c)/ No error. (d)
24. He will tell you (a) / about it when (b)/ he will come back. (c)/ No error. (d)
25. A large sign near (a) / the entrance warns the visitors (b)/ to beware about bears. (c)/ No error. (d)
26. I am going (a) / to have this certificate (b)/ attest by the Director. (c)/ No error. (d)
27. Ravi (a) / told to his friend (b)/ to buy a car. (c)/ No error. (d)
28. I would (a) / accept the offer (b)/ if were you. (c)/ No error. (d)
29. I am more lonelier (a) / here than (b)/ I was in the USA. (c)/ No error. (d)
30. May I know (a) / to who (b)/ I am speaking? (c)/ No error. (d)

Answers

1. (a)	2. (d)	3. (c)	4. (d)	5. (c)	6. (c)	7. (c)	8. (b)	9. (b)	10. (b)
11. (a)	12. (b)	13. (a)	14. (b)	15. (d)	16. (d)	17. (c)	18. (b)	19. (b)	20. (c)
21. (b)	22. (d)	23. (c)	24. (b)	25. (c)	26. (c)	27. (2)	28. (d)	29. (a)	30. (b)

Exercise –2

Directions (1-30) : In each of the following questions some of the sentences have errors and some are correct. Find out which part of a sentence has an error and blacken the option corresponding to it (a,b,c). If a sentence is free from errors, then your answer is (d) i.e. No error.

1. The way to increase the production of the food (a)/ is to bring more land (b)/ under cultivation. (c)/ No error. (d)
2. The girls watched intently (a)/ as the model applied her make up (b)/ with a practiced hand. (c)/ No error. (d)
3. If he is a millionaire (a)/ he would help (b)/ the millennium project. (c)/ No error. (d)
4. The Prime Minister along with his Cabinet colleagues (a)/ have been welcomed by the Chief Minister (2)/ at a formal ceremony. (c)/ No error. (d)
5. The political candidate talked (a)/ as if she has already been elected (b)/ to the presidency. (c)/ No error. (d)
6. Several guests noticed Mr. Sharma (a)/collapsing in his chair

(b)/and gasping for breath. (c)/ No error. (d)

7. This is our second reminder (a)/ and we are much surprised (b)/ at receiving no answer from you. (c)/ No error. (d)
8. You should (a)/ be always greatful (b)/ to your mentor. (c)/ No error. (d)
9. The furnitures (a)/ had become (b)/ old and rusty. (c)/ No error. (d)
10. Most people (a)/ are afraid of (b)/ swine flu these days. (c)/ No error. (d)
11. I may not be able (a)/ to attend (b)/ to the function. (c)/ No error. (d)
12. He is (a)/ residing here (b)/ since 1883. (c)/ No error. (d)
13. At his return (a)/ we asked him (b)/ many questions. (c)/ No error. (d)
14. The chief guest (a)/ entered into (b)/ the room. (c)/ No error. (d)
15. She is (a)/ very angry (b)/ on him. (c)/ No error. (d)
16. She is one of the (a)/ best mothers (b)/ that has ever lived. (c)/ No error. (d)
17. John, I and Hari (a)/ have finished (b)/ our studies. (c)/ No error. (d)
18. Neither the mouse (a)/ nor the lion (b)/ were caught. (c)/ No error. (d)
19. After you will returns (a)/ from New Delhi (b)/ will meet you (c)/ No error. (d)
20. When I was young, (a)/ I used to collect stamps (b)/ as a hobby. (c)/ No error. (d)
21. A senior doctor (a)/ expressed concern (b)/ about physicians recommended the vaccine. (c)/ No error. (d)
22. We have discussing (a)/ all the known mechanisms (b)/ of physical growth. (c)/ No error. (d)
23. Children enjoy listening to (a)/ ghosts stories (b)/ especially on Halloween night. (c)/ No error. (d)
24. (a)I/ have (b)/ many works to do. (c)/ No error. (d)
25. There are so many filths (a)/ all around (b)/ the place. (c)/ No error. (d)
26. A great many student (a)/ have been declared (b)/ successful. (c)/ No error. (d)
27. We are going to launch (a)/ this three-crores project (b)/ within the next few months. (c)/ No error. (d)
28. I hope to go to shopping (a)/ this weekend (b)/ if the weather permits. (c)/No error. (d)
29. The lawyer asked (a)/ if it was worth to take (b)/ the matter to court. (c)/ No error. (d)
30. After a carefully investigation (a)/ we discovered (b)/ that the house was infested with termites. (c)No error (d)

Answers

1. (a)	2. (c)	3. (a)	4. (b)	5. (b)	6. (d)	7. (d)	8. (b)	9. (a)	10. (a)
11. (c)	12. (a)	13. (a)	14. (b)	15. (c)	16. (c)	17. (a)	18. (c)	19. (a)	20. (d)
21. (c)	22. (a)	23. (b)	24. (c)	25. (a)	26. (a)	27. (b)	28. (d)	29. (b)	30. (a)

3 DETERMINERS AND ARTICLES

The word 'determiner' is not found in traditional grammar books. Half of what we now call determiners used to be a separate class, the articles. The other half, even though they work in the same way as articles do, used to be lumped in with adjectives. So, we had 'real' adjectives and also things called demonstrative adjectives, possessive adjectives etc.

Modern grammarians and linguists make a clear distinction between adjectives and determiners, because they have different sorts of meanings and different uses. Adjectives tell us about the qualities of the thing referred to (red pens, a black dog, beautiful girls).

The most common determiners are as follows

(i) Articles : a, an, the.

(ii) Quantifiers : all, few, many, several, some.

(iii) Possessives : her, his, its, my, our, their, your.

(iv) Demonstratives : this, that, these, those.

(v) Numerals : one, three, hundred, etc.

(vi) Negative : no

The determiner, along with the adjective, usually indicates whether a noun is singular or plural, masculine or feminine. In other words, it indicates Number and Gender. This means that most determiners have several different forms.

Determiners are words which quantify or identify nouns, determiners are followed by a noun.

The most common determiners in alphabetical order are as follows : a (n), all, another, any, both, certain, each, either, enough, every, few, half, last, least, less, little, many, more, most, much, neither, next, no, other, own, plenty, same, several, some, such, that/those, the, this/these, whole. To these must be added the numerals (cardinal and ordinal) and the possessives (e.g., my/mine, our/ours, Ram's).

The adjectives; a, an and the; are called Articles.

There are two kinds of articles

(I) Indefinite article—A/An

(II) Definite article—The

Use of Indefinite Articles–A/An

1. The article **An** is used before a word beginning with a vowel sound. e.g.,
   (i) She is an intelligent girl.
   (ii) You are an honest man.
2. The article **A** is used before a word beginning with a consonant sound. e.g.,
   (i) He is a university student.
   (ii) He is a one-eyed main.
3. **A/An** is used before a singular countable noun when it is mentioned for the first time representing no particular person or thing. e.g.,
   (i) He has an axe.
   (ii) A boy came to my office.
4. **A** is used before a singular countable noun which is used as the representative of a class of things or persons. e.g.,
   (i) A lion is a fierce animal.
   (ii) A pupil should obey his teacher.
5. **A** is used to make a common noun of a proper noun. e.g.,
   (i) My neighbour is a Daniel.
   (ii) She is a singer.
6. **A/An** is used in exclamations before singular countable nouns. e.g.,
   (i) What an interesting movie!
   (ii) What a lovely morning!
7. **A** is used in its original sense of one or any. e.g.,
   (i) She wants a car.
   (ii) He bought a book.

Use of Definite Article – The

The definite article **The** is used

1. When we talk about a particular person or thing or one already mentioned. e.g.,
   (i) Give me the book which you bought yesterday.
   (ii) The dress you want is out of stock.
2. When a singular noun represents a whole class. e.g.,
   (i) The lotus is a beautiful flower.
   (ii) The banyan is a useful tree.
3. Before the first noun in 'noun + preposition + noun' construction. e.g.,
   (i) She likes the sweets of Jaipur.
4. Before names of mountain-ranges. e.g. The Alps, The Himalayas, The Vindhyas
5. Before names of groups of islands. e.g., The Andamans, The Herbrides, The West Indies.
6. Before names of rivers, oceans, gulfs, deserts and forests. e.g., The Ganga, The Nile, The Arabian Sea, The Indian Ocean, The Persian Gulf, The Sahara, The Black Forest
7. Before names of religious and mythological books. e.g., The Veda, The Ramayana,
8. Before names of newspapers and magazines. e.g., The Hindustan Times, The Statesman
9. Before names of heavenly bodies, directions and things unique of their kind. e.g., The sun, The east, The north, The equator
10. Before names of historical buildings, places and events. e.g., The Taj Mahal, The Pyramids, The Kaba, The French Revolution
11. Before musical instruments. e.g.,
    (i) He can play the guitar.
    (ii) She is fond of playing on the piano.
12. Before religious communities and political parties. e.g., The Muslims, The BJP, The Congress Party, The Janata Dal
13. Before names of ships, aeroplanes and trains. e.g., The Vikrant, The Shatabdi Express, The Rajdhani Express.

14. Before the words denoting physical positions. e.g.,
The top, The bottom, The back, The inside, The front
15. Before parts of body. e.g.,
(i) He was hit on the head.
(ii) You caught me by the arm.
16. Before names of government departments and armed forces. e.g.,
The Judiciary, The Legislative, The Executive,
The Army, The Navy, The Air Force
17. Before the dates of months. e.g.,
The 6th February, The 21st of December

Omission of Articles

The articles; **a, an** and **the**; are omitted

1. Before names of days and months, e.g.,
(i) She will go on Monday.
(ii) They are getting married in January.
2. Before names of subjects e.g.,
(i) She has no interest in mathematics.
(ii) Biology is his favourite subject.
3. Before names of festivals and seasons. e.g.,
(i) He will go to Canada in winter.
(ii) She celebrated Christmas with her friends.
But,
(iii) He will go to Canada in the winter season.
(iv) She went to Delhi in the Diwali holidays.
4. Before the names of persons, villages, cities, districts, states and countries. e.g.,
(i) Anjali is a beautiful girl.
(ii) London is a big city.
(iii) Paris is the capital of France.
5. After possessive adjectives (my, our, your, his, her, their, its) and nouns in possessive case (Ram's, lion's). e.g.,
(i) This is Rahul's car.
(ii) That is my book.
6. Before school, college, church, prison, hospital, bed, market, when these places are visited or used for their primary purpose. e.g.
(i) She goes to church on Sunday.
(ii) The criminal was sent to prison.
(iii) I go to bed at 10 pm.
7. Before the nouns used after rank of/ title of. e.g.,
(i) He was promoted to the rank of Colonel.
(ii) He was given the title of Nawab.

Exercise

1. Complete the sentence by putting an appropriate determiner.
You should always carry .... umbrella with you.
(a) a (b) an
(c) any (d) a few

2. Supply an appropriate determiner.
I have .... glass of milk every morning.
(a) the (b) a
(c) any (d) some

3. Supply an appropriate determiner.
My neighbour is .... honest person.
(a) a (b) an
(c) the (d) any

Directions (Q. 4–10) : Insert appropriate determiners where necessary.

4. Have you got any .... coffee?
(a) much (b) little
(c) some (d) more

5. This is .... only remaining copy.
(a) a (b) an
(c) the (d) a few

6. She kicks the ball with .... left foot.
(a) a (b) two
(c) the (d) her

7. .... say one thing, some say another.
(a) A few (b) Much
(c) More (d) Some

8. .... of philosophy is concerned with questions that have no answer.
(a) More (b) Many
(c) Much (d) Any

9. Have you got .... sugar?
(a) little (b) much
(c) any (d) few

10. Many are called but .... are chosen.
(a) less (b) a little
(c) a few (d) few

Direction (Q. 11– 20) : Find out the part which has an error in each of the following sentences. If there is no error in a sentence, the answer is (d).

11. Sunil is a best student (a)/ in our class (b)/ at present, (c)/No error (d).

12. Important Congress dissident source said as (a)/ one stage that Raman Rao and Chandra Shekhar (b)/ had been asked the dissident group to suggest suitable names. (c)/ No error (d)

13. A cell is the smallest (a)/ identifiable unit of life (b)/ and cannot be seen with a naked eye. (c)/ No error (d).

14. Children who have had (a)/ good Pre-school Education are most likely (b)/ to out do other children at school. (c)/ No error (d).

15. The burglars were caught just as (a)/ they were about to (b)/ escape from the jail. (c)/ No error (d)

16. On my request Jatin (a)/ introduced me to his friend (b)/who is singer and scientist. (c)/No error (d)

17. I am not wealthy (a)/so I cannot afford (b)/ to buy a expensive car. (c)/ No error (d)

18. The teacher drew (a)/ an attention of the boys (b)/ to the importance of regular practice. (c)/ No error (d)

19. First European sailor (a)/to come to India in (b)/modern times was Vasco-Da-Gama. (c)/ No error (d).

20. It was by the mistake (a)/ that he caught (b)/ her hand. (c)/ No error (d)

Direction (Q. 21–40) : Choose the most appropriate article to fill in the blanks.

21. I bought .... horse, an ox and a buffalo.
(a) the (b) an
(c) a (d) no article

22. Do you see .... blue sky?
(a) the (b) an
(c) a (d) No article

23. Why do you throw .... tea?
(a) the (b) an
(c) a (d) No article

24. Let us discuss .... matter seriously.
(a) the (b) an
(c) a (d) no article

25. The guide knows .... way.
(a) the (b) an
(c) a (d) no article

26. Where is .... servant? I want a glass of water.
(a) the (b) an
(c) a (d) no article

27. He is .... unlucky man.
(a) the (b) an
(c) a (d) no article

28. It is .... unit of measurement.
(a) the (b) an
(c) a (d) no article

29. It is .... hour's distance from here.
(a) the (b) an
(c) a (d) no article

30. I want to be .... MP.
(a) the (b) an
(c) a (d) no article

31. The lion is .... king of beasts.
(a) the (b) an
(c) a (d) no article

32. I eat an egg .... day.
(a) the (b) an
(c) a (d) no article

33. .... Ganga is a sacred river.
(a) The (b) An
(c) A (d) No article

34. Give me .... umbrella which you bought yesterday.
(a) the (b) an
(c) a (d) no article

35. He died without .... heir.
(a) the (b) an
(c) a (d) no article

36. She is .... real Hitler.
(a) the (b) an
(c) a (d) no article

37. A bird in hand is worth two in .... bush.
(a) the (b) an
(c) a (d) no article

38. He looks as stupid as .... owl.
(a) the (b) an
(c) a (d) no article

39. It is very difficult to get .... taxi at such a time.
(a) the (b) an
(c) a (d) no article

40. Thieves stole the money from .... box.
(a) the (b) an
(c) a (d) no article

Answers

1. (b)	2. (b)	3. (b)	4. (b)	5. (c)	6. (d)	7. (d)	8. (b)	9. (a)	10. (c)
11. (a)	12. (a)	13. (c)	14. (b)	15. (c)	16. (c)	17. (c)	18. (b)	19. (a)	20. (a)
21. (c)	22. (a)	23. (a)	24. (a)	25. (a)	26. (a)	27. (b)	28. (c)	29. (b)	30. (b)
31. (a)	32. (c)	33. (a)	34. (a)	35. (b)	36. (c)	37. (a)	38. (b)	39. (c)	40. (a)

4 SPELLING TEST

Some spelling rules are as follows: The knowledge of grammatical rules is essential to write perfect English but the knowledge of accurate spelling is also equally important.

Final Consonant

Rule 1

One-syllable words ending in single vowel + single consonant double the consonant before a suffix beginning with a vowel. e.g.,

(i) big + er = bigger

(ii) swim + ing = swimming

Rule 2

Words of two or three syllables ending in single vowel + single consonant double the final consonant if the last syllable is stressed. e.g.,

(i) control + er = controller

(ii) permit + ed = permitted

Rule 3

Consonant 'l' is doubled in the words ending in single 'l' before a suffix beginning with a vowel. e.g.,

(i) signal + ing = signalling

(ii) quarrel + ed = quarrelled

Rule 4

When the suffix 'full' is added to a word, one 'l' is removed. e.g.

(i) use + full = useful

If the word to which the suffix 'full' is added ends in 'll', one 'l' is removed from the word also. e.g.,

(i) skill + full = skilful

(ii) will + full = wilful

Final 'e'

Rule 5

Words ending in silent 'e' drop the 'e' before a suffix beginning with a vowel. e.g.,

(i) hope + ing = hoping

(ii) live + ed = lived

(iii) drive + er = driver

(iv) tire + ing = tiring

If the suffix begins with a consonant, 'e' is not dropped. e.g.,

(i) hope + full = hopeful

(ii) sincere + ly = sincerely

Exercise

Directions (Q. 1–60) : In each of the following words group, choose the correctly spelt word.

1. (a) Sattlite (b) Satellite (c) Sattelite (d) Satelite
2. (a) Embarasment (b) Embarassment (c) Embarrasment (d) Embarrassment
3. (a) Ocasion (b) Ocassion (c) Occasion (d) Occassion
4. (a) Distilry (b) Distillry (c) Distillery (d) Distilery
5. (a) Efflorascence (b) Efflorescence (c) Eflloresence (d) Eflorescence
6. (a) Commettee (b) Committe (c) Comittee (d) Committee
7. (a) Posesion (b) Possession (c) Posession (d) Possesion
8. (a) Forefiet (b) Forefeit (c) Forfeit (d) Forfiet
9. (a) Aliennate (b) Allienate (c) Alienate (d) Alienatte
10. (a) Greivance (b) Grievance (c) Griveance (d) Grieveance
11. (a) Comemorate (b) Commemmorate (c) Comemmorate (d) Commemorate
12. (a) Exemple (b) Exampel (c) Example (d) Exampal
13. (a) Inteligensia (b) Inteligentsia (c) Intelligensia (d) Intelligentsia
14. (a) Beligrent (b) Belligerent (c) Belligrent (d) Belligerent
15. (a) Dielectic (b) Diallectic (c) Dilectic (d) Diallectic
16. (a) Coruppt (b) Curropt (c) Corrupt (d) Currupt
17. (a) Variegated (b) Varegated (c) Varigated (d) Variagated
18. (a) Psychology (b) Sycology (c) Psykology (d) Sychology
19. (a) Liesure (b) Leisure (c) Leasure (d) Lesiure
20. (a) Accesible (b) Accessibel (c) Accessible (d) Acessible
21. (a) Desicate (b) Desiccate (c) Dessicate (d) Dessiccate
22. (a) Tresspas (b) Trespass (c) Tresspas (d) Trwspas
23. (a) Pasanger (b) Pessenger (c) Pesanger (d) Passenger
24. (a) Argumant (b) Arguemant (c) Argument (d) Arguement
25. (a) Tariff (b) Tarriff (c) Tarif (d) Tarrif
26. (a) Mustach (b) Moustach (c) Mustache (d) Moustache
27. (a) Jewelery (b) Jewellry (c) Jwellry (d) Jewellery
28. (a) Sedantry (b) Sedentery (c) Sedentary (d) Sedantary
29. (a) Grametic (b) Grammetic (c) Grammatic (d) Gramatic
30. (a) Idiosynrcrecy (b) Idiosyncrasy (c) Idiosyncracy (d) Idiosyrcracy
31. (a) Blisfull (b) Blissful (c) Blisful (d) Blissfull
32. (a) Leftinent (b) Leutinent (c) Lieutenant (d) Liutenent
33. (a) Aproched (b) Aproached (c) Appraoched (d) Approached
34. (a) Amacher (b) Ameture (c) Amateur (d) Ametur
35. (a) Comentry (b) Commentry (c) Commentery (d) Commentary
36. (a) Itinerary (b) Itinerery (c) Itinery (d) Ittinerary
37. (a) Commission (b) Comision (c) Comission (d) Commision

38. (a) Appearent (b) Appareant (c) Apparant (d) Apparent
39. (a) Scripturi (b) Skripture (c) Scripture (d) Scripcher
40. (a) Nuisance (b) Neusense (c) Neusance (d) Nuisence
41. (a) Acquiescence (b) Aquicence (c) Acquisence (d) Acquissence
42. (a) Massenger (b) Messenger (c) Messanger (d) Massanger
43. (a) Guerila (b) Gurilla (c) Gorila (d) Gorilla
44. (a) Assignmante (b) Assignment (c) Asignment (d) Asienement
45. (a) Harasment (b) Harassment (c) Harrassment (d) Harrasment
46. (a) Sustinence (b) Sustenance (c) Sustenence (d) Sustinance
47. (a) Bizarre (b) Bizaree (c) Bizare (d) Bizzare
48. (a) Achievment (b) Acheivment (c) Achievement (d) Achevement
49. (a) Perseverance (b) Preservatance (c) Perseverence (d) Preserverence
50. (a) Coreander (b) Coriander (c) Coriandar (d) Coreandor
51. (a) Sovereignty (b) Soveriegnty (c) Sovereignity (d) Soveriegnity
52. (a) Kalidoscope (b) Kalaidoscope (c) Kaleidoscope (d) Kaliedoscope
53. (a) Addultration (b) Adultration (c) Addulteration (d) Adulteration
54. (a) Acurrate (b) Accurate (c) Acurate (d) Accuratte
55. (a) Gorgean (b) Georgian (c) Gorgian (d) Georgeaen
56. (a) Buisness (b) Bussiness (c) Business (d) Buisiness
57. (a) Examplary (b) Exemplary (c) Examplery (d) Exemplery
58. (a) Rapprochmant (b) Rapprochment (c) Raproachment (d) Rapproachement
59. (a) Sabotage (b) Sabbotage (c) Sabotaze (d) Sabatage
60. (a) Forecast (b) Forcaust (c) Forcast (d) Forecaste

Answers

1. (b)	2. (d)	3. (c)	4. (c)	5. (b)	6. (d)	7. (b)	8. (c)	9. (c)	10. (b)
11. (d)	12. (c)	13. (d)	14. (d)	15. (d)	16. (c)	17. (a)	18. (a)	19. (b)	20. (c)
21. (b)	22. (b)	23. (d)	24. (c)	25. (a)	26. (d)	27. (d)	28. (c)	29. (c)	30. (b)
31. (b)	32. (c)	33. (d)	34. (c)	35. (d)	36. (a)	37. (a)	38. (d)	39. (c)	40. (a)
41. (a)	42. (b)	43. (d)	44. (b)	45. (b)	46. (b)	47. (a)	48. (c)	49. (a)	50. (b)
51. (a)	52. (c)	53. (d)	54. (b)	55. (b)	56. (c)	57. (b)	58. (d)	59. (a)	60. (a)

5 PREPOSITIONS

Definition

Preposition is a word placed before a Noun or Pronoun, denotes the relation, the person or thing referred by it, has with something else.

Rule

There is one very simple rule about prepositions, and unlike most rules, this rule has no exception.

Kinds of Prepositions

Preposition is divided into four parts.

1. **Simple Prepositions :** e.g., at, in, from, for, of, off, on, out, till, to, up, with through, down, by etc. These are called simple prepositions.
2. **Compound Prepositions :** About, beside, inside, along, below outside etc. are called compound prepositions.
3. **Phrasal Prepositions :** When two more words are joined to make a preposition it is called phrasal prepositions.
4. **Participle Prepositions :** When present participle is used without Noun/Pronoun/present participle it is called participle preposition e.g., concerning, pending regarding, considering, touching etc.
   (i) Pending enquiry into the matter, he was transferred from the office.
   (ii) Considering the quality, the prices are reasonable.

Use of Some Important Prepositions

1. **At/In/On**

   These are very commonly used prepositions

   Note: The use of these preposition in reference of 'Time'

   (i) 'At' is used for precise time,
   (ii) 'In' is used for months years, centuries and long periods,
   (iii) 'on' is used for days and date

At	In	On
Precise Time	Months, Years, Centuries and Long Periods	Days, Dates
At 3 o'clock	In May	On Sunday
At 10.30 am	In summer	On Tuesdays
At sunrise	In the next century	On Independence Day
At the moment	in the past/future	On New Year's Eve

Examples

(i) The shop closes at midnight
(ii) Where will you be on Independence Day?
(iii) There should be a lot of progress in the next century.
(iv) Her birthday is on 26 April.

Expression	Example
At night	The stars shine at night
At the weekend	I don't usually work at the weekend
At the same time	We finished the test at the same time

Examples

We should not use; 'at, in, on' with 'last, next, every'.

(a) I went to Mexico last May. (not in last May)
(b) I go home every Easter. (not at every Easter).

The use of these prepositions in reference of 'Place'

(a) 'At' is used for a point.
(b) 'On' is used for a surface.

At	In	On
Point	Enclosed Space	Surface
At the corner	In the garden	On the wall
At the door	In India	On the door
At the end of the road	In my pocket	On the floor
At the entrance	In my wallet	On the carpet
At the altar	In a car	On a page

Look at the following examples

(a) Rima is waiting for you at the bus stop.
(b) The shop is at the end of the lane.
(c) I live on the 4th floor at 21 Diamond Street in Kolkata.
(d) Do you work in a company?
(e) I have a meeting in Delhi.
(f) Do you live in India?
(g) Saturn is in the solar system.
(h) The author's name is on the cover of the book.
(i) There are no prices on this menu.
(j) You are standing on my foot.
(k) There was a 'no smoking' sign on the wall.

Please note that these three prepositions are most commonly used, in writing and speaking, so students must learn the use of these prepositions well.

Comparing At, In, To, Into

A. 'At' shows stationary position or existing state while 'in' shows movement

   Examples

   (a) She is at School.
   (b) The Bus is in motion.

B. 'At' for small place, town etc. while 'in' for big place, town, city, country etc.

   Example

   (a) He lives at Alwar in Uttar Pradesh.

C. 'At' is used for point of time and 'in' is used for period of time

   Example

   (a) The train will arrive at six in the morning.

D. 'In' shows existing state of things while 'into' shows movement

   (a) He jumped into the river.
   (b) There are three students in the class.
   (c) They climbed into the lorry.
   (d) He is swimming in the river.

   'In can also be used as an adverb Come in = Enter : e.g., Get in (into the train).

E. 'To' and 'Into' are used as following:

To

(a) In the direction of : Turn to the right.

(b) Until : From Monday to Friday; Five minutes to ten.

(c) With indirect object; Please give it to me.

Into

(a) To the inside of : We stepped into room.

2. On/Onto

'On' can also be used for both existing position and movement

Examples

(i) He was sitting on his bag.

(ii) Snowfall on the hills.

(iii) His number is on the gate.

(iv) He went on board ship.

'On' can also be used as an adverb

1. Go on

2. Come on

'Onto' is used when there is movement involving a change of level

Example

(a) People climbed onto their roofs.

3. With/By

'with' is used for instruments and 'by' is used for agents.

Example

(i) The snake was killed by him with a stick.

4. Since/For/From

'Since' is often used with period of time i.e., present perfect or past perfect tense. 'Since' is used to denote point of time and never for period of time, as; Since 6 O' Clock/ last night/last Monday/since morning/ evening/ Monday/ January/ 2005 etc.

Examples

(i) It has been raining since 2 O'clock.

(ii) He had been ill since Monday.

(iii) He left school in 1983. I haven't seen him since.

'For' is used to express period of time; two hours/ two days/ two years/ a long time/ some time/ for ever etc.

Examples

(a) Boil it for five minutes

(b) He lived in this house for six months.

For is also used with present perfect tense or past perfect tense for an action which extends up to the time of speaking

Examples

(a) He has worked here for a year.

(b) He worked for three hours.

'From' is normally used with 'to or till/ until'

Example

(a) Most people work from eight to six.

'From' can also be used for place,

Examples

(a) He is from Lucknow.

(b) Where do you come from?

5. For/ During

'During' is used with known periods of time, i.e., – periods known by name, such as Christmas, Easter or periods which have been already defined:

(i) during the Middle ages,

(ii) during the summer,

(iii) during his childhood.

Examples

(a) It rained all Monday but stopped raining during the night.

(b) She was ill for a week and during that week she ate nothing.

'For' may be used to denote purpose and may also be used before known periods

Examples

(a) I went there for the summer.

(b) I rented my house for my holidays.

'For' has various other uses

Examples

(a) He asked for ten. I paid six for it.

(b) I bought one for Kuku.

6. Below/ Under/ Beneath

'Below' and 'under' both mean-lower than (in level) and sometimes either can be used. But 'under' usually denotes physical contact and 'below' denotes space between the things.

Example

(a) He put the books under the pillow.

'Below' and 'under' may also mean junior in rank

Examples

(b) He is under me; means that I am superior to him.

(c) He is working under me.

'Below' is used meaning – opposite to 'above'.

Examples

(d) The temperature can fall below 15 degree Celsius.

(e) Rainfall has been below average this year.

Beneath/Something that is beneath another thing is under the other thing

Examples

(f) I could see the muscles of his shoulders beneath his T-shirt.

(g) I found pleasure in sitting beneath the trees ...

(h) ... the frozen grass crunching beneath his feet.

'Beneath' could also mean 'unworthy as per status' or 'in lower strata in social class'

Examples

(i) It is beneath his dignity to beg for money. (unworthy of him)

(j) She married beneath her. (into a lower social class)

7. Ago and Before

'Ago' is used for past events while 'before' is used in reference to two events

Examples

(i) He came three days ago.

(ii) The train had left before he reached the station.

8. Beside/ Besides

Beside and Besides have altogether different meanings. Don't confuse beside with besides beside = at the side of

Examples

(i) He was sitting besides Sarla.

Besides = in addition to/ as well as

(ii) We camped beside a lake.

Examples

(a) He has a car besides a motor cycle.

(b) Besides doing the cooking I help Ram.

9. Of/Off

'Of' and 'Off' are used in following situations referring

(i) **Location** east of here; the middle of the road,

(ii) **Possession** a friend of mine; the sound of music,

(iii) **Part of a group** one of us; a member of the team,

(iv) **Measurement** a cup of milk; two metres of snow,

(v) **Not** on ways from; e.g., Please keep off the grass.

(vi) **At some distance** from e.g., There are islands off the coast.

Examples

(a) He is a member of our family

(b) He is off duty now.

But 'over' also means – 'covering'/ 'on the other side of' / 'across'

Examples

(a) I put a cloth over her. (covering)

(b) He lives over this mountain. (on the other side of)

(c) There is a bridge over the railway line. (across)

(d) He put a blanket over the dead body.

'Above' and have none of these meanings.

'Over' can mean higher in rank

(e) He is over me. (means; He is my immediate boss.)

'Over' is also used with meals/ food/ drink

Examples

(a) We had a chat over a cup of tea. (while drinking tea)

(b) The matter was decided over the lunch.

'Above' is also used meaning 'earlier' or 'previous'

Examples

(a) He lives at the above address. (Previously mentioned)

(b) For details please see (P–1) above. (Previously mentioned)

10. In/With

'In is used in following situations:

Examples

(i) Place thought of as an area : in London; in Europe.

(ii) Large units of time; That happened in March, in 1992.

(iii) By means of : write in pencil; speak in English.

(iv) A member of : He is in the orchestra; in the navy.

(v) With reference to : lacking in ideas; rich in oil.

'With' is used in following situations:

1. Accompanying : He came with her: I have my keys with me.
2. By means of; using : I repaired the shoes with glue.
3. Because of : We were paralysed with fear.

11. By and Before

'By' a time/by a date' usually implies before that time or date

Examples

(i) The train starts at 7:15, so you would better be at the station by 7:00 ('by 7:00' implies – 'before 7:00'.)

By + a time expression structure is often used with future perfect tense

Examples

(ii) By the end of July I'll have really those books.

'Before' can be used as a preposition or as a conjunction or as an adverb

Examples

(iii) Before signing this agreement let us discuss each and every point thread bare. (preposition)

(iv) Before you sign this you can discuss it with your father. (conjunction)

(v) I've seen her somewhere before. (adverb)

12. But and except

Both 'but' and 'except' have the same meaning and are usually interchangeable. After 'nobody/ none/ nothing/ nowhere' etc. usually 'but' is used:

Examples

(i) Nobody but Shyam knew the way.

(ii) Nothing but the best is sold in our shop.

Note 'Except' is used when the prepositional phrase comes later in a sentence. Look at the following examples:

Example

(a) Nobody knew the way except Shyam.

Note After 'but' and 'except' bare infinitive (infinitive without 'to') is used.

13. To and Towards

The preposition 'to' indicates movement with the aim of a specific destination, which can be a place or an event, e.g.,

(a) I'm going to the USA tomorrow.

(b) I need to go to the bank.

(c) Can you tell me the way to the station?

(d) Are you going to the party?

(e) I've never been to a cricket match.

(f) What time did you go to work?

Here some important Preposition are given.

1. Abundance of (wealth)
2. Accustomed to (work)
3. Attain to (a position)
4. Accede to (a request)
5. Absolved from (a promise, a sin)
6. Adhere to (principles)
7. Afraid to (A ghost)
8. Accession to (throne)
9. Absorbed in (study)
10. Acquaintance with (a person)
11. Comply with (one's wishes)
12. Cured of (a disease)
13. Comply with (wishes)
14. Despair of (success)
15. Desirous (doing something)
16. Devoid of (quality)
17. Eligible for (a post)
18. Excuse for (a fault)
19. Exchange a thing (with a person)
20. Fatal to (one's cause)
21. Fearful of (death)
22. Greedy of (money)
23. Heir to (ancestral property)
24. Hopeful of (success)
25. Hostile to (a person)
26. Innocent of (a crime)
27. Intimate with (a person)
28. Insist on a (thing)
29. Impertinent to (elders)
30. Invite to (dinner)
31. Jealous of (a person)
32. Keep to (the left, the point)
33. Match for (a person)
34. Key to (success)
35. Match for (a person)
36. Motive for (an action)

37. Need of (a thing)
38. Occur to (mind)
39. Overwhelmed with (sorrow, grief)
40. Passion for (study)
41. Peculiar to (a person or a thing)
42. Persist in (doing)
43. Pleased with (a person)
44. Proud of (a thing)
45. Pride (on a thing)
46. Refrain from (doing some wrong)
47. Repent of (a mistake)
48. Rob (a person) of (a thing)
49. Sentence of (punishment)
50. Short of (money)
51. Shocked at (a loss)
52. Sure of (some fact)
53. Sacred to (a cause)
54. Triumph over (difficulties)
55. Vain of (beauty)
56. Wanting in (wisdom)
57. Worthy of (a reward)
58. Yield to (an enemy)
59. Sacred to (a cause)
60. Work at (subject)
61. Stick to (point)
62. Suspect of something (point)
63. Touch upon (subject)

Exercise

Directions (Q. 1–35) : In the following questions, choose the appropriate option to fill in the blanks in given sentences.

1. The poor have to work .... morning to evening.
(a) in (b) to
(c) from (d) before

2. I go .... swimming every morning.
(a) to (b) for
(c) at (d) in

3. Never laugh............ the disables.
(a) on (b) from
(c) to (d) at

4. Please wait .... me, I am coming within five minutes.
(a) for (b) by
(c) from (d) to

5. He fell .... love with Sakshi.
(a) by (b) for
(c) in (d) with

6. I got your parcel .... Tuesday.
(a) since (b) for
(c) to (d) on

7. She was married .... en early age.
(a) for (b) of
(c) at (d) in

8. They will go to Bengaluru .... plane.
(a) on (b) in
(c) by (d) from

9. I am grateful .... my friends for their moral support.
(a) for (b) to
(c) of (d) with

10. This watch is a gift .... my uncle.
(a) by (b) from
(c) of (d) in

11. They will leave the place .... 10 pm.
(a) in (b) since
(c) for (d) at

12. The box belonged .... the landlord.
(a) of (b) with
(c) to (d) for

13. Children are fond .... chocolates and computer games.
(a) for (b) of
(c) with (d) in

14. His father died .... cancer.
(a) in (b) of
(c) by (d) for

15. She has great love .... her children.
(a) for (b) of
(c) by (d) with

16. Listen .... what your teachers say.
(a) at (b) in
(c) to (d) for

17. This book is a collection .... Shakespeare's poem.
(a) for (b) of
(c) with (d) by

18. She wants to get rid .... the brown fox.
(a) for (b) to
(c) with (d) of

19. You cannot see germs .... naked eyes.
(a) by (b) with
(c) for (d) in

20. He was fast asleep .... his bed.
(a) into (b) in
(c) by (d) for

21. We have a very good news .... him.
(a) for (b) of
(c) to (d) with

22. They have been reading .... 7 o'clock.
(a) for (b) in
(c) since (d) at

23. The four brothers always quarrelled .... themselves.
(a) to (b) between
(c) for (d) among

24. These boys go to college .... college bus.
(a) by (b) on
(c) to (d) for

25. He was fined .... driving negligently.
(a) to (b) of
(c) by (d) for

26. He is often late .... his dinner.
(a) for (b) at
(c) to (d) in

27. Try to reach the village .... the sunset.
(a) before (b) by
(c) from (d) of

28. A jeep hit him while he was going .... the main road.
(a) on (b) across
(c) behind (d) through

29. The case was put .... the judge and the judge decides it within a year.
(a) at (b) from
(c) before (d) of

30. She is suffering .... fever.
(a) with (b) of
(c) through (d) from

31. Chairs are made .... wood.
(a) of (b) from
(c) on (d) through

32. There are tall beautiful coconut trees .... the river.
(a) along (b) at
(c) into (d) over

33. Mount Abu is about five thousand feet .... the sea-level.
(a) above (b) along
(c) after (d) behind

34. Ramesh fell down while he was running .... a bus.
(a) into
(b) after
(c) over
(d) through

35. The shopkeeper does not have the toys, I was looking ....
(a) by
(b) about
(c) for
(d) to

Answers

1. (c)	**2.** (b)	**3.** (d)	**4.** (a)	**5.** (c)	**6.** (d)	**7.** (c)	**8.** (c)	**9.** (b)	**10.** (b)
11. (d)	**12.** (c)	**13.** (b)	**14.** (b)	**15.** (a)	**16.** (c)	**17.** (b)	**18.** (d)	**19.** (b)	**20.** (b)
21. (a)	**22.** (c)	**23.** (d)	**24.** (a)	**25.** (d)	**26.** (a)	**27.** (a)	**28.** (b)	**29.** (c)	**30.** (d)
31. (a)	**32.** (a)	**33.** (a)	**34.** (b)	**35.** (c)					

6 SYNONYMS AND ANTONYMS

WORD	SYNONYMS	ANTONYMS
abbreviate	shorten, condense	lengthen, increase
ability	skill, aptitude	incompetence, inability
able	capable, qualified	incapable
above	overhead	below
abundant	ample, sufficient	scanty, insufficient
accurate	correct, right	wrong
achieve	accomplish, attain	fail
active	energetic, animated, lively	lethargic, idle, sluggish
add	increase, total	subtract
adequate	sufficient, enough, ample	insufficient, sparse
adjourn	postpone, recess	recommence, continue
adult	grown-up	child
after	following, next	before
afraid	frightened, scared	courageous, brave
aggressive	assertive, pushy, militant	passive, peaceful
always	forever	never
amateur	beginner, novice	professional
antagonize	provoke, embitter	soothe, tranquilize
apparent	obvious, evident	hidden, obscure
approve	accept, ratify, endorse	disapprove, censure
arrogant	haughty, stuck-up	humble, modest
artificial	fake, synthetic	real, authentic
ask	question, inquire	answer
atrocious	dreadful, contemptible, vile	kind, wonderful
authentic	genuine, real, factual	false, artificial
average	ordinary, fair	unusual, exceptional
awful	dreadful, atrocious	pleasant
awkward	clumsy,	gracefu
ban	prohibit, forbid, outlaw	allow, permit
barren	unproductive, infertile	fertile, productive
bashful	shy, timid	outgoing, assured
beautiful	pretty, attractive, lovely	ugly
before	prior,	after, behind
beginning	start, initiate	finish, end
believe	trust, accept	doubt, distrust
below	under, lower	above
beneficial	helpful,	harmful, adverse
best	finest, choice	worst
birth	beginning	death, end
blend	combine, mix	separate
bottom	base, foundation	top
brave	courageous, bold, heroic	cowardly, timid
break	fracture, burst	repair, heal
brief	short, concise	long
broad	wide,	narrow
busy	active, occupied, working	idle, inactive

WORD	SYNONYMS	ANTONYMS
buy	purchase	sell
calm	quiet, tranquil, still	excited, turbulent
capture	apprehend, seize, arrest	free, release
care	concern,	neglect
careful	cautious, watchful	careless, reckless
cease	stop, discontinue	continue, recommence
certain	positive, sure, definite	uncertain, unsure
charming	delightful, appealing, enchanting	obnoxious, gross, vulgar
chilly	cool, nippy	warm
chubby	plump, pudgy	thin, skinny
clarify	explain, simplify	confuse
close	shut, fasten	open
close	near,	far
coarse	bumpy, rough	fine, smooth
colossal	enormous, immense, mammoth	tiny, insignificant, trivial
combine	blend, unite, join	separate
comical	amusing, funny, humorous	tragic, sorrowful
complex	complicated, intricate	simple
competent	capable, qualified	incompetent, inept
comprehend	grasp	confuse, misinterpret
complete	conclude, finish	incomplete
complex	complicated, intricate	simple
compress	crush, condense, squeeze	expand
concrete	real, tangible, solid	abstract, flimsy
concur	cooperate	disagree
condemn	censure, denounce	approve
condense	compress, concentrate	expand, enlarge
confess	acknowledge	deny
confine	contain, enclose, restrain	free, release
conflict	differ, clash	agree
conflict	fight, battle, struggle	peace, harmony
conform	comply, submit	dissent, dispute
confuse	complicate, muddle, jumble	clarify
congested	stuffed	empty, unfilled
connect	attach	separate, disconnect
conscientious	scrupulous, virtuous	neglectful, careless
conscious	aware, cognizant	unaware, unconscious
consecutive	successive, continuous	interrupted
conservative	cautious, restrained	radical, extreme
considerate	mindful	thoughtless, selfish
constantly	always, continually	scarcely, seldom
contaminate	infect	purify
contented	satisfied, pleased	dissatisfied, unhappy
continue	persist, persevere	discontinue, stop
convalesce	recover, heal	relapse
convenient	handy, accessible	inconvenient
conventional	traditional	unusual
correct	accurate, right, proper	wrong, incorrect
courage	bravery, valor	cowardice
courteous	polite, civil	rude
cover	conceal, hide	expose
cozy	comfortable, snug, homey	uncomfortable

WORD	SYNONYMS	ANTONYMS
cranky	irritable	good-humored
crazy	daft, mad	sane
cruel	mean, heartless, ruthless	kind, humane
cry	sob, weep	laugh
dally	linger	rush
damage	hurt, impair, harm	remedy, repair
dangerous	unsafe, hazardous, perilous	safe
daring	bold, audacious	cautious
dark	black	light
dawn	daybreak, sunrise	evening
dead	lifeless, deceased	alive, active
decay	rot, spoil	bloom, flourish
deduct	subtract, remove	add
defend	shield	attack, assault
defy	resist, challenge	obey, comply
delicate	dainty	sturdy
demolish	destroy, wreck	restore
denounce	blame, censure, indict	commend
dense	thick, heavy, compressed	sparse, empty
depart	leave, exit	arrive
deposit	place	withdraw
desolate	barren, forsaken	dense, verdant
despise	detest, loathe	love
destitute	penniless	wealthy
destroy	ruin, wreck, devastate	restore
detach	unfasten, remove	attach
deter	hinder, prevent	encourage
determined	sure, convinced, resolute	doubtful
die	expire, perish	live
different	distinct, unlike	same, alike
difficult	hard, challenging	easy
dilute	thin	strengthen
diminish	curtail, lessen, decrease	increase, amplify
dirty	soiled, messy	clean
disagree	differ, dispute	agree
dispute	debate, oppose	agree
diverse	different, distinct	same, similar
divide	separate, split	unite
docile	tame, gentle	wild, stubborn
dormant	sleeping, inactive	awake, active
doubt	dispute	believe
drab	dull, lifeless	bright
drastic	severe, extreme, tough	mild, moderate
dreadful	unpleasant	splendid, super
dry	arid, parched	wet
dubious	doubtful, questionable	certain
dull	blunt, dreary	sharp, bright
dumb	stupid, dense	smart
early	beforetime	late
easy	simple	hard
eccentric	peculiar, unusual	normal

WORD	SYNONYMS	ANTONYMS
ecstasy	joy, rapture, elation	sadness, depression
empty	drain, unload	fill encourag
encourage	urge	discourage
enemy	opponent, foe	ally, friend
enjoy	appreciate	dislike, hate
enlarge	magnify	reduce, shrink
enormous	vast, immense, colossal	tiny, microscopic
enough	sufficient, ample, plenty	insufficient
entirely	wholly, completely, solely	partly
eternal	always, perpetual, everlasting	temporary, passing
evident	apparent, obvious, clear	doubtful, vague
evil	bad, wrong, wicked	good
exceptional	outstanding	ordinary, commonplace
excite	provoke, incite	compose, calm
exhilarated	ecstatic, elated	depressed, dejected, sad
explicit	exact, distinct, unmistakable	indefinite, unclear
exquisite	charming, lovely	revolting, repulsive
exterior	outside, outer	interior
extravagant	extreme, excessive, luxurious	meager
fabulous	marvelous, amazing	unexciting
face	confront, meet	avoid
fair	honest, just, impartial	unjust, unfair
fake	phony, artificial	real, genuine
false	incorrect, untrue	true
fancy	ornate, fussy	simple, plain
fantastic	incredible, outrageous	ordinary, usual
fast	quick, swift	slow
fat	chubby, plump, stout	thin
fatal	deadly, mortal, killing	
fatigue	tire, exhaust	
feasible	attainable, practical	impossible
feeble	weak, frail	strong
ferocious	savage, brutal, savage	tame, gentle
fertile	productive	unproductive, barren
fiction	fantasy, untruth, myth	truth
fill	pack	empty
fix	mend, repair	break
flaw	defect, fault, blemish	perfection
flimsy	frail, fragile, delicate	sturdy, strong
flippant	sassy	polite, respectful
fluid	liquid	solid
foe	adversary, opponent	friend
follow	succeed, trail	lead, precede
forbid	ban, bar	encourage
forgive	pardon, excuse, absolve	
former	earlier	latter
fraction	portion, segment	whole
frank	candid, straightforward, blunt	evasive
frenzy	fury, rage	serenity, calmness
fresh	unused, new	old, stale
friend	comrade, buddy	enemy

WORD	SYNONYMS	ANTONYMS
frigid	frosty	warm, hot
frivolous	trivial, unimportant, silly	important, serious
front	fore	back
full	stuffed	empty
furious	enraged, infuriated	calm, placid
future	tomorrow	past
gain	acquire, obtain, receive	lose
gallant	chivalrous, stately	ungentlemanly
gather	collect, accumulate, compile	scatter, disperse
gaudy	showy, garish, vulgar	tasteful, refined
gaunt	scrawny, skinny, thin	overweight, plump
generous	giving, selfless, big-hearted	selfish, stingy
gentle	tender, mild	rough, harsh
genuine	real, authentic, sincere	fake, phony
gigantic	immense, colossal, enormous	tiny, minute
give	donate, present, offer	take, receive
glad	happy, pleased, delighted	sad, unhappy
gloomy	dark, dismal, depressing	cheery, bright
glorious	splendid, magnificent, superb	terrible, awful
good	nice, fine, well-behaved	bad, awful
gorgeous	ravishing, dazzling, stunning	hideous, unattractive
gratitude	thankfulness, appreciation	ungratefulness
great	outstanding, remarkable	insignificant, unimportant
handy	useful, convenient, skillful	inconvenient, inept
hard	firm, solid, difficult	soft, easy
hate	loathe, detest	love
help	aid, assist	hinder, thwart
high	elevated, lofty	low
hold	grasp, grip, retain	release, discharge
honest	truthful, sincere, frank	untruthful, insincere
hospitable	welcoming, cordial, gracious	rude, unfriendly
hostile	antagonistic, aggressive, militant	friendly, cordial
huge	vast, immense, great	small, tiny
humble	modest, unpretentious	vain, showy
humiliate	embarrass, disgrace, dishonor	honor, dignify
identical	alike, duplicate	different, varied
idle	inactive, lazy	busy, ambitious
ignorant	uninformed, unaware	knowledgeable
immaculate	spotless, pure	dirty, filthy
immature	childish, inexperienced	mature, adult
immune	resistant, exempt	susceptible
impartial	neutral, unbiased, fair	prejudiced
impatient	eager, anxious, intolerant	patient
imperative	compulsory, crucial, mandatory	unnecessary, optional
imperfect	marred, defective, faulty	perfect, flawless
impetuous	impulsive, rash, reckless	restrained, careful
important	significant, meaningful	unimportant, meaningless
independent	self-reliant, autonomous	dependent, unsure
inferior	lesser, substandard	superior
infuriate	enrage, agitate, provoke	soothe, clam
ingenious	clever, creative, original	unoriginal, dull

WORD	SYNONYMS	ANTONYMS
innocent	guiltless, blameless	guilty
insane	crazy, deranged, mad	sane
insufficient	inadequate, deficient	adequate, enough
intelligent	bright, sensible, rational	ignorant, dense
interesting	provocative, engrossing	dull, boring
intermittent	sporadic, periodic	regular, continual
internal	inner, inside	external, outer
intolerant	bigoted, prejudiced	understanding, accepting
intriguing	fascinating, enthralling	uninteresting, dull
irrelevant	inappropriate, unrelated	relevant, pertinent, applicable
irritate	annoy, agitate, provoke	soothe, calm
join	connect, unite, link	separate, disconnect, detach
jolly	merry, jovial, joyful	sad, grim, glum
jubilant	overjoyed, delighted, elated	dejected, depressed
keep	save, protect, guard	discard, lose
kind	considerate, tender, thoughtful	mean, cruel, inconsiderate
lament	mourn, grieve	rejoice, celebrate
large	big, massive, huge	small, little
last	final, end	first, beginning
least	fewest, minimum, smallest	most, maximum
legible	readable, clear	illegible, unreadable
lenient	lax, unrestrained, easy	harsh, strict
listless	lethargic, tired	active, energetic
logical	sensible, sane, rational	illogical, unreasonable
long	lengthy	short
loose	slack, limp	tight
lure	attract, seduce, entice	repel
luxurious	extravagant, elegant	meager, scanty
magnify	expand, enlarge, exaggerate	reduce, minimize
mandatory	required, compulsory	optional
maneuver	manipulate, handle, scheme	
maximum	greatest, uppermost, highest	minimum, least
meager	scanty, sparse, poor	abundant, generous
mean	unkind, malicious, nasty	pleasant, nice
mediocre	fair, moderate, so-so	outstanding
mend	repair, fix	break
migrant	drifting, traveling, transient	stationary, immovable
militant	combative, aggressive, warlike	peaceful
minor	lesser, inferior, secondary	major
mirth	merriment, fun, laughter	gloom, sadness
mischievous	naughty, impish	well-behaved, angelic
misfortune	hardship, catastrophe, mishap	good luck, fortune
mobile	moveable, changeable	immobile, stationary
moderate	temperate, lenient, medium	extreme, harsh
momentous	important, powerful, outstanding	unimportant, insignificant
monotonous	boring, tedious dreary, humdrum	interesting
moral	ethical, virtuous, righteous	immoral, unethical
morbid	appalling, awful, ghastly	pleasant
morose	gloomy, sullen, moody, glum	cheerful, optimistic
mourn	grieve, lament, bemoan	rejoice
mysterious	elusive, occult, secret	obvious, known

WORD	SYNONYMS	ANTONYMS
naughty	bad, disobedient, wrong	good, appropriate
neat	clean, orderly, tidy	sloppy, disorderly
negligent	careless, derelict, inattentive	conscientious, careful
nervous	ruffled, flustered, perturbed	composed, calm
neutral	impartial, unprejudiced	prejudiced, partial
new	unused, fresh, modern	old, antique
nice	pleasing, desirable, fine	unpleasant, naughty
nonchalant	indifferent, lackadaisical, blase	concerned, apprehensive
normal	ordinary, typical, usual	abnormal, unusual
numerous	several, abundant, considerable	few, scanty
obey	mind, heed, comply	disobey, resist
oblivious	unconscious, preoccupied, dazed	mindful, aware
obnoxious	offensive, abominable, repulsive	pleasant, pleasing
observe	examine, study, scrutinize	ignore, disregard
obsolete	extinct, dated, antiquated	stylish, vogue, current
obstinate	stubborn, bullheaded, adamant	maneuverable, flexible
odd	peculiar, weird, strange	usual, ordinary
offend	displease, affront, disgust	please, delight
ominous	threatening, menacing	
opaque	obscure, murky, unclear	transparent, clear
open	begin, unfold, originate	close
opponent	enemy, rival, foe	ally, friend
optimistic	hopeful, confident	pessimistic
optional	voluntary, elective	required
ordinary	usual, average	unusual, remarkable
outrageous	preposterous, shocking	warranted, acceptable
outstanding	extraordinary, distinguished	insignificant, inconsequential
painstaking	meticulous, precise, fastidious	careless, negligent
passive	compliant, submissive, yielding	forceful
past	former, previous, preceding	future
patience	tolerance, perseverance	impatience
peculiar	weird, bizarre	normal, conventional
perfect	flawless, accurate	imperfect, faulty
permanent	enduring, lasting	temporary, changing
perpetual	eternal, endless, incessant	short-lived, fleeting
persuade	convince, influence	dissuade, deter
plausible	believable, reasonable, logical	unbelievable
plentiful	ample, enough, abundant	scarce, insufficient
pliable	supple, flexible, compliant	rigid, closed-minded
polite	gracious, refined, courteous	rude, discourteous
poor	destitute, needy, impoverished	rich, wealthy
portion	part, segment, piece	whole, total
possible	conceivable, feasible, plausible	impossible, unachievable
precarious	dangerous, uncertain, shaky	sure, safe
precious	cherished, valuable, prized	cheap, worthless
prejudiced	biased, opinionated, influenced	impartial
premature	early, hasty	late, delayed
premeditated	planned, intended, calculated	spontaneous, accidental
preserve	uphold, guard, save	destroy, neglect
pretty	lovely, beautiful, attractive	homely, unattractive
prevalent	customary, widespread	uncommon, unusual

WORD	SYNONYMS	ANTONYMS
prevent	thwart, prohibit, hinder	permit, allow
probable	likely, apt, liable	improbable, doubtful
proficient	skilled, adept, competent	inefficient, inept
profit	gain, earnings, benefit	loss
prohibit	forbid, bar, restrict	allow, permit
prominent	distinguished, eminent	unknown, not renowned
prompt	punctual, timely	late, slow
prosperous	thriving, successful, flourishing	unsuccessful, fruitless
proud	arrogant, elated	modest, ashamed
push	shove, propel	pull
qualified	competent, suited, capable	unfit, unsuited
question	interrogate, inquire, ask	answer
quiet	silent, hushed, tranquil	noisy, rowdy
quit	cease, stop, withdraw	continue, remain
racket	noise, commotion, disturbance	peace, quiet
radiant	luminous, shining, lustrous	dim, not illuminated
raise	hoist, elevate	lower
ratify	approve, confirm, endorse	veto, refuse
rational	logical, level-headed, sensible	irrational, crazy
ravage	devastate, ruin, damage	restore, revitalize
raze	destroy, demolish	build, construct
recreation	amusement, pleasure, pastime	work, labor
reduce	lessen, decrease, diminish	increase, enlarge, amplify
refute	contradict, dispute	agree, concur
regular	routine, customary, steady	irregular, abnormal
regulate	control, oversee, handle	decontrol
relentless	persistent, merciless, unyielding	lenient, sympathetic
relevant	pertinent, suitable, apropos	irrelevant, insignificant
reliable	trustworthy, steadfast, stable	undependable, unreliable
reluctant	unwilling, hesitant	willing, accommodating
remote	secluded, isolated, distant	close, accessible
repulsive	hideous, offensive, gruesome	pleasing, alluring
reputable	honorable, upstanding, honest	dishonest, untrustworthy
resist	oppose, withstand, defy	comply, conform
retaliate	avenge, revenge, reciprocate	
reveal	show, disclose, divulge	hide, conceal
ridiculous	nonsensical, foolish, preposterous	sensible, believable
risky	hazardous, perilous, chancy	safe, sound
rowdy	boisterous, rambunctious	well-mannered, genteel
rude	impolite, discourteous	polite, mannerly
sad	unhappy, dejected, gloomy	happy, glad
same	identical, alike, equivalent	different, diverse
savage	uncivilized, barbarous	civilized, gentle, tame
save	preserve, conserve, keep	spend, discard
scarce	scanty, rare, sparse	plentiful, abundant
scrawny	skinny, gaunt, spindly	husky, chubby
scrupulous	meticulous, ethical, fastidious	unethical, careless
seize	apprehend, grab, snatch	release, free
separate	divide, segregate, partition	unite, join
serene	peaceful, tranquil, calm	disturbed, upset
serious	grave, solemn, pensive	flighty, fickle

WORD	SYNONYMS	ANTONYMS
shrewd	clever, cunning, crafty	unthinking, careless
shy	bashful, timid	bold, aggressive
sick	ill, ailing	well, healthy
slim	slender, thin, svelte	stout, stocky
sluggish	listless, lethargic, inactive	quick, speedy
small	little, insignificant, trivial	large, important
smooth	slick, glossy, level	rough
sociable	friendly, cordial, gregarious	unfriendly, aloof
sorrow	woe, anguish, grief	joy, ecstasy
special	exceptional, notable, particular	ordinary, usual
spontaneous	instinctive, automatic, natural	planned, rehearsed
stable	steady, unchanging, settled	unsettled
stationary	fixed, immobile, firm	movable, portable
stimulate	rouse, stir, motivate	stifle, suppress
stop	quit, cease, terminate	start, begin
strenuous	vigorous, laborious	effortless, easy
strict	stringent, severe, stern	lenient
strong	powerful, mighty, potent	weak
stupid	unintelligent, dense, foolish	knowledgeable, smart
subsequent	following, succeeding, latter	preceding, previous
successful	thriving, prosperous, triumphant	failing, unsuccessful
sufficient	ample, enough, adequate	lacking, insufficient
superb	magnificent, exquisite	inferior, mediocre
suppress	restrain, inhibit, squelch	foster, encourage
surplus	excess, additional, extra	lack, deficit
swift	fast, speedy, hasty	slow, sluggish
synthetic	man-made, artificial	natural
tall	high, lofty	short
tangible	concrete, definite	vague, ambiguous
taut	tense, tight, stiff	relaxed
tender	delicate, gentle, affectionate	harsh, rough
terrible	dreadful, horrible, vile	wonderful, superb
thaw	melt, defrost	freeze
thrifty	economical, frugal, prudent	wasteful, extravagant
thrive	prosper, flourish, develop	fail, fade, shrivel
total	whole, entire, complete	partial
trivial	insignificant, worthless	important, crucial
turbulent	tumultuous, blustering, violent	clam, peaceful
turmoil	commotion, disturbance, fracas	quiet, tranquility
unbiased	impartial, unprejudiced, fair	prejudiced, partial
upset	perturb, ruffle, agitate	soothe, calm
urgent	crucial, important, imperative	unimportant, trivial
vacant	unoccupied, empty	filled, occupied
vague	unclear, obscure, indistinct	clear, definite
valiant	courageous, brave, heroic	cowardly, fearful
vibrate	shake, quiver, tremble	firm, steady
vicious	malicious, spiteful, ferocious	kind, humane
victory	triumph, win, success	defeat
virtuous	moral, righteous, angelic	sinful, wicked
vulgar	offensive, uncouth, coarse	refined, tasteful
wealth	riches, prosperity, assets	poverty

WORD	SYNONYMS	ANTONYMS
weary	tired, fatigued, lethargic	energetic, lively
wholehearted	earnest, sincere	insincere
wild	uncivilized, savage, reckless	tame, calm
win	triumph, succeed, prevail	lose
wise	knowing, scholarly, smart	dull, uneducated
wonderful	marvelous, incredible, splendid	ordinary, blah
worn	used, impaired, old	new, fresh
wrong	incorrect, untrue, mistaken	correct, right
yield	produce, bear, provide	keep, retain
zenith	peak, pinnacle, apex	bottom, base

Exercise –1

Directions : (Q. No. 1-50) ***Choose the correct synonym for the word given in capital letters.***

1. TRIUMPH
(a) Joy (b) Excitement
(c) Gain (d) Victory

2. APPORTIONMENT
(a) Allotment (b) Bestowal
(c) Delivery (d)Presentation

3. PREDICT
(a) Explain (b) Foretell
(c) Assert (d) Observe

4. DOCILE
(a) Stubborn (b) Stupid
(c) Gentle (d) Vague

5. KID
(a) Regulate (b) Divert
(c) Entertain (d) Cheat

6. ARTIFACT
(a) Synthetic (b) Man-made
(c) Natural (d) Exact copy

7. AMPLE
(a) Sufficient (b) Swift
(c) Detailed (d) Huge

8. PILFER
(a) Destroy (b) Damage
(c) Steal (d) Snatch

9. RESILIENT
(a) Flexible (b) Proud
(c) Separable (d) Rigid

10. CAVIL
(a) Appreciate (b) Amuse
(c) Quibble (d) Munch

11. LOQUACIOUS
(a) Sad (b) Secretive
(c) Quiet (d) Talkative

12. CELIBATE
(a) Saint (b) Widower
(c) Bachelor (d) Teetotaller

13. LUDICROUS
(a) Absurd (b) Clear
(c) Simple (d) Dismal

14. LETHAL
(a) Dreary (b) Dreadful
(c) Deadly (d) Strange

15. GAMBIT
(a) Expression (b) Trick
(c) Explanation (d) Appeal

16. EXPOSE
(a) Open (b) Revel
(c) Declare (d) Conceal

17. DELETERIOUS
(a) Morose (b) Devious
(c) Harmful (d) Remorseful

18. AUTHENTIC
(a) Apparent (b) Intricate
(c) Stable (d) Factual

19. INFINITE
(a) Strange (b) Endless
(c) Indefinite (d) Vague

20. BAULK
(a) Identify (b) Prevent
(c) Encourage (d) Verify

21. ADMONISH
(a) Threaten (b) Praise
(c) Appeal (d) Support

22. PENCHANT
(a) Like (b) Eagerness
(c) Disability (d) Dislike

23. BARTER
(a) Deal (b) Return
(c) Lend (d) Exchange

24. RANGE
(a) Level (b) Expanse
(c) Grade (d) Standing

25. HAGGLE
(a) Postpone (b) Accept
(c) Bargain (d) Reject

26. REVISE
(a) Edit (b) Alter
(c) Correct (d) Reconsider

27. ACCUSE
(a) Absolve (b) Exonerate
(c) Vindicate (d) Impeach

28. UNICONSCIONABLE
(a) Distasteful (b) Unmanageable
(c) Excessive (d) Unmindful

29. DANK
(a) Dangerous (b) Ugly
(c) Plunder (d) Damp

30. DIVVY
(a) Selfless (b) Foolish
(c) Follower (d) Pioneer

31. APOGEE
(a) Climax (b) Beginning
(c) Middle (d) Bottom

32. ADVERSITY
(a) Crisis (b) Misfortune
(c) Failure (d) Helplessness

33. LIMP
(a) Kneel (b) Bend
(c) Falter (d) Stoop

34. MASSACRE
(a) Stab (b) Slaughter
(c) Murder (d) Assassinate

35. COMBAT
(a) Quarrel (b) Fight
(c) Conflict (d) Feud

36. ABSCOND
(a) Turn (b) Flee
(c) Manage (d) Avoid

37. PROFOUND
(a) Profuse (b) Boundless
(c) Deep (d) Fathomless

38. OVERSEE
(a) Supervise (b) Glance
(c) Contest (d) Look

39. COMPUNCTION
(a) Anger (b) Appreciate
(c) Regret (d) Wonder

40. DILETTANTE
(a) Opponet (b) Specialist
(c) Amateur (d) Expert

41. HOODLUM
(a) Pioneer (b) Criminal
(c) Devotee (d) Scholar

42. FOSTER
(a) Encourage (b) Fabricate
(c) Foment (d) Nurture

43. FILTHY
(a) Healthy (b) Ugly
(c) Dirty (d) Angry

44. SOPORIFIC
(a) Lethargic (b) Merry
(c) Soothing (d) Impressive

45. ABOMINATION
(a) Revulsion (b) Disgust
(c) Criticism (d) Attack

46. BURLESQUE
(a) Insult (b) Irritate
(c) Mock (d) Annoy

47. SOLICIT
(a) Beseech (b) Demand
(c) Claim (d) Require

48. PRUNE
(a) Lend (b) Reduce
(c) Expand (d) Prolong

49. VOGUE
(a) Fashion (b) Rejection
(c) Order (d) Satisfaction

50. DELEGATE
(a) Officer (b) Participant
(c) Member (d) Representative

Answers

1. (d)	2. (a)	3. (b)	4. (c)	5. (d)	6. (b)	7. (a)	8. (c)	9. (a)	10. (c)
11. (d)	12. (c)	13. (a)	14. (c)	15. (b)	16. (b)	17. (c)	18. (d)	19. (b)	20. (b)
21. (a)	22. (a)	23. (d)	24. (b)	25. (c)	26. (b)	27. (d)	28. (c)	29. (d)	30. (d)
31. (a)	32. (b)	33. (c)	34. (b)	35. (b)	36. (b)	37. (c)	38. (a)	39. (c)	40. (c)
41. (b)	42. (d)	43. (c)	44. (c)	45. (b)	46. (c)	47. (a)	48. (c)	49. (a)	50. (d)

Exercise–2

Direction : (Q. No. 1-58) ***In each of the following questions, choose the alternative which is opposite in meaning to the given word.***

1. OUTMODED
(a) Polished (b) Practicable
(c) Stylish (d) Fashionable

2. BRIDGE
(a) Divide (b) Bind
(c) Release (d) Open

3. TRANQUIL
(a) Impatient (b) Agitated
(c) Vociferous (d) Noisy

4. MALFORMED
(a) Fetid (b) Sketchy
(c) Curvaceous (d) Shapely

5. KNOWLEDGE
(a) Ignorance (b) Illiteracy
(c) Foolishness
(d) Backwardness

6. NADIR
(a) Progress (b) Liberty
(c) Zenith (d) Modernity

7. HOLY
(a) Offesive (b) Orthodox
(c) Simple (d) Obnoxious

8. LISSOME
(a) Ungainly (b) Huge
(c) Pungent (d) Crude

9. ALLEVIATION
(a) Exaggeration
(b) Exasperation
(c) Magnification
(d) Intensification

10. MINION
(a) Master (b) Quorum
(c) Majority (d) Host

11. LANGUID
(a) Smart (b) Energetic
(c) Fast (d) Ferocious

12. BAULK
(a) Admire (b) Strengthen
(c) Clamour (d) Encourage

13. STRINGENT
(a) Magnanimious (b) Lanient
(c) Vehement (d) General

14. IGNORE
(a) Support (b) Favour
(c) Redress (d) Accept

15. WRECK
(a) Make (b) Build
(c) Restore (d) Relieve

16. FLACCID
(a) Upright (b) Taut
(c) Uneven (d) Tough

17. AVOIDANCE
(a) Possession (b) Passion
(c) Pursuit (d) Power

18. RESPITE
(a) Tension (b) Exertion
(c) Regularity (d) Delay

19. GRATUITY
(a) Annuity (b) Grave
(c) Discount (d) Wages

20. ALIENATE
(a) Gather (b) Identify
(c) Assemble (d) Unite

21. EVANESCENT
(a) Blooming (b) Growing
(c) Twinkling (d) Teasing

22. MALICIOUS
(a) Boastful (b) Indifferent
(c) Kind (d) Generous

23. SAGACIOUS
(a) Casual (b) Cunning
(c) Foolish (d) False

24. PERSUASIVE
(a) Demoralizing
(b) False
(c) Discouraging
(d) Unconvincing

25. ZEST
(a) Restive (b) Callous
(c) Indifference (d) Distaste

26. REPEL
(a) Attract (b) Concentrate
(c) Attend (d) Continue

27. BANISH
(a) Abandon (b) Harbour
(c) Intrude (d) Drop

28. REWARD
(a) Demotion (b) Forfeiture
(c) Penalty (d) Retribution

29. FOSTER
(a) Repress (b) Curb
(c) Check (d) Control

30. AUSPICIOUS
(a) Spicy
(b) Unfavourable
(c) Conspicuous
(d) Condemnatory

31. CONVEX
(a) Flat (b) Protuberant
(c) Full (d) Indented

32. MANAGE
(a) Direct (b) Avail
(c) Bungle (d) Wild

33. ARID
(a) Plentiful (b) Productive
(c) Humid (d) Agreeble

34. TENTATIVE
(a) Immediate (b) Urgent
(c) Developed (d) Final

35. STUBBORN
(a) Willing (b) Consenting
(c) Pliable (d) Easy

36. LIABILITY
(a) Treasure (b) Debt
(c) Assets (d) Property

37. JEER
(a) Mourn (b) Praise
(c) Mock (d) Sneer

38. ADEQUATE
(a) Profuse (b) Abounding
(c) Scanty (d) Abundant

39. CONTENTED
(a) Rash (b) Narrow-minded
(c) Gloomy (d) Disappointed

40. CONCEAL
(a) Unfold (b) Revel
(c) Open (d) Discover

41. ROUGHLY
(a) Exactly (b) Completely
(c) Pointedly (d) Largely

42. LIBERALISM
(a) Humanism (b) Dynamism
(c) Sectarianism (d) Totalitarianism

43. MISERLY
(a) Generous (b) Liberal
(c) Spendthrift (d) Charitable

44. SELDOM
(a) Rarely (b) Daily
(c) Often (d) Never

45. AMALGAMATE
(a) Generate (b) Repair
(c) Materialise (d) Separate

46. FRAILTY
(a) Emaciation (b) Strength
(c) Health (d) Boldness

47. PROHIBIT
(a) Accept (b) Permit
(c) Agree (d) Grant

48. EMBRACE
(a) Suspect (b) Harm
(c) Reject (d) Hurt

49. BASHFUL
(a) Daring (b) Boastful
(c) Upright (d) Confident

50. WONDER
(a) Stock (b) Amusement
(c) Expectation (d) Surprise

51. DENSITY
(a) Brightness (b) Clarity
(c) Intelligence (d) Rarity

52. APPOINTMENT
(a) Disappointment
(b) Suspension
(c) Dismissal
(d) Discharge

53. ALLURE
(a) Repulse (b) Develop
(c) Entice (d) Decoy

54. CRASS
(a) Gross (b) Refined
(c) Coarse (d) Dense

55. REPRAISAL
(a) Relief (b) Forgiveness
(c) Exemption (d) Relaxation

56. FRIEND
(a) Rival (b) Acquaintance
(c) Foe (d) Competitor

57. JUSTIFY
(a) Regular (b) Infuriate
(c) Absolve (d) Vindicate

58. MONOLOGUE
(a) Dialogue (b) Prologue
(c) Epilogue (d) Catalogue

Answers

1. (d)	**2.** (d)	**3.** (b)	**4.** (d)	**5.** (a)	**6.** (c)	**7.** (c)	**8.** (a)	**9.** (b)	**10.** (a)
11. (b)	**12.** (d)	**13.** (b)	**14.** (c)	**15.** (c)	**16.** (b)	**17.** (c)	**18.** (b)	**19.** (d)	**20.** (b)
21. (a)	**22.** (d)	**23.** (c)	**24.** (d)	**25.** (d)	**26.** (a)	**27.** (b)	**28.** (c)	**29.** (a)	**30.** (b)
31. (d)	**32.** (c)	**33.** (c)	**34.** (d)	**35.** (c)	**36.** (c)	**37.** (b)	**38.** (c)	**39.** (d)	**40.** (b)
41. (a)	**42.** (d)	**43.** (a)	**44.** (c)	**45.** (d)	**46.** (b)	**47.** (b)	**48.** (c)	**49.** (d)	**50.** (c)
51. (d)	**52.** (c)	**53.** (a)	**54.** (b)	**55.** (b)	**56.** (c)	**57.** (a)	**58.** (a)		

7 ONE WORD SUBSTITUTION

One word substitution questions are designed to test a candidate's vocabulary as well as his ability to express in fewer words. The candidate is required to select the alternative which can be substituted for the given words/sentence.

Words and their Substitutes

Word/Sentence	Substitute
Voluntary giving up of throne in favour of someone	Abdication
Allowance paid to wife on legal separation	Alimony
A lover of others	Altruist
One who can use either hand with ease	Ambidextrous
Animals which live both on land and in water	Amphibian
One who is out to destroy all government law and order	Anarchist
One who studies the evolution of mankind	Anthropologist
A person appointed by two parties to solve a dispute	Arbitrator
A place for ammunition and weapons	Arsenal
A person who does not believe in God	Atheist
The life history of a person written by himself	Autobiography
A nation that is in a war-like mood	Belligerent
The practice of having two wives or two husbands at a time	Bigamy
The act of speaking disrespectfully about sacred things	Blasphemy
Government by the officials	Bureaucracy
A person who is bad in spelling	Cacographist
One who feeds on human flesh	Cannibal
One who draws maps	Cartographer
One who teaches dancing	Choreographer
A critical judge of any art and craft	Connoisseur
Persons living at the same time	Contemporaries
Nursery where children are cared for while their parents are at work	Creche
A religious war	Crusade
Centre of attraction	Cynosure
A room for several people to sleep in, especially in a college or public institution	Dormitory
Fit to be eaten	Edible
A poem of lamentation	Elegy
A person who leaves his own country and goes to live in another	Emigrant
Lasting one day	Ephemeral
Words which are inscribed on the grave or the tomb in the memory of the buried	Epitaph
One who is very selective in one's taste	Fastidious
One who believes in fate	Fatalist
One who works for welfare of the women	Feminist
The plants of particular region	Flora
Easily broken	Fragile
One who runs away from justice or the law	Fugitive
Murder of race	Genocide
Animals which live in flocks	Gregarious
A place for housing aeroplanes	Hangar
One who acts against religion	Heretic

A place for bees	Hive
Holding office without any remuneration	Honorary
Incapable of being read	Illegible
A person who comes to one country from another in order to settle there	Immigrant
A person who cannot be easily approached	Inaccessible
A sound that cannot be heard	Inaudible
Incapable of being corrected	Incorrigible
That cannot be erased	Indelible
One who is free from all mistakes and failures	Infallible
Murder of an infant	Infanticide
Liable to catch fire easily	Inflammable
A person who is unable to pay his debts	Insolvent or bankrupt
One who supervises in the examination hall	Invigilator
One who is too strong to be overcome	Invincible
A place for dogs	Kennel
One who cuts precious stones	Lapidist
One who is skilled in foreign language	Linguist
One who, talks continuously	Loquacious
The first speech delivered by a person	Maiden speech
One who dies for a noble cause	Martyr
Murder of mother	Matricide
A place where money is made	Mint
A hater of mankind	Misanthrope
A hater of womankind	Misogynist
The practice of marrying one at a time	Monogamy
A place where dead bodies are kept for post mortem	Mortuary
A person having same name as another	Namesake
A strong desire to return home, home sickness	Nostalgia
One new to anything, inexperienced	Novice or tyro
An account of one's achievements in the newspaper after one's death	Obituary
One who is all powerful	Omnipotent
One, who knows everything	Omniscient
One who eats everything	Omnivorous
One who has lost parents	Orphan
The study of ancient writing	Paleography
A remedy for all diseases	Panacea
Murder of father	Patricide
A person who looks at the dark side of things	Pessimist
A lover of mankind	Philanthropist
One, who does not care for art and literature	Philistine
Literary theft or passing off an author's original work as one's own	Plagiarism
The practice of marrying more than one husband at a time	Polyandry
The practice of marrying more than one wife at a time	Polygamy
One who speaks many languages	Polyglot
That can be carried easily	Portable
Child born after the death of his father, or the book published after the death of writer	Posthumous
Fit to drink	Potable
An act of separation from other persons to avoid infection	Quarantine
Murder of a king or queen	Regicide
Violating or profaning religious things/places	Sacrilege

A place for the sick to recover health	Sanatorium
A person who walks in sleep	Somnambulist
A person who talks in sleep	Somniloquist
Murder of sister	Sororicide
One who is habitual drunkard	Sot, toper
A place for horses	Stable
Murder of oneself	Suicide
One who does not take any intoxicating drink	Teetotaller
Government by religious principles	Theocracy
A person/student who absents himself from class or duty without permission	Truant
Murder of wife	Uroxicide
One extremely fond of one's wife	Uxorious
A fault that may be forgiven	Venial
Able to adapt oneself readily to many situations	Versatile
One who offers one's services	Volunteer

Exercise

Directions (Q. 1–47) : In each of the following questions, choose the alternative which can be substituted for the given words/ sentence.

1. A man who does a thing for pleasure and not as a profession
(a) Veteran (b) Player
(c) Connoisseur (d) Amateur
2. That which can be interpreted in any way
(a) Ambient (b) Ambivalent
(c) Amphibious (d) Ambiguous
3. A light sailing boat built especially for racing.
(a) Dinghy (b) Canoe
(c) Yacht (d) Frigate
4. A person who rarely speaks the truth
(a) Scoundrel (b) Liar
(c) Crook (d) Hypocrite
5. The practice of marrying more than one wife at a time
(a) Polyandry (b) Polygamy
(c) Matrimony (d) Celibacy
6. Animals living on land and in water as well
(a) Ambiguous (b) Amphibian
(c) Amorphous (d) Ambivalent
7. An instrument for viewing objects at a distance
(a) Microscope (b) Telescope
(c) Periscope (d) Keleidoscope
8. Be the embodiment or perfect example of
(a) Signify
(b) Characterise
(c) Personify (d) Masquerade
9. A man who operates on sick people
(a) Physician
(b) Operator
(c) Surgeon
(d) Physiotherapist
10. A man of odd habits
(a) Eccentric (b) Cynical
(c) Introvert (d) Moody
11. One whose attitude is : eat, drink and be merry
(a) Epicurean (b) Cynic
(c) Materialistic (d) Stoic
12. One who pretends illness to escape duty
(a) Truant (b) Malingerer
(c) Hypocrite (d) Concubine
13. Use of more words than needed to express the meaning
(a) Circumlocution
(b) Verbatim
(c) Ventriloquism
(d) Pleonasm
14. A person who is always dissatisfied
(a) Heretic (b) Felon
(c) Malcontent (d) Surrogate
15. Loss of power to move in any or every part of the body
(a) Rheumatism (b) Paralysis
(c) Eczema (d) Leprosy
16. A group of three novels or plays, each complete in itself
(a) Triplet (b) Triumvir
(c) Trilogy (d) Trivet
17. A house for storing grains
(a) Cellar (b) Store
(c) Godown (d) Granary
18. A person claiming to be superior in culture and intellect to others
(a) Intellectual (b) Aristocrat
(c) Elite (d) Highbrow
19. Responsible according to law
(a) Liable (b) Eligible
(c) Legalised (d) Legitimate
20. Decision made upon a political question by the votes of all qualified persons
(a) Veto (b) Suffrage
(c) Pubiscite (d) Franchise
21. A person who is made to bear the blame due to others
(a) Innocent (b) Scapegoat
(c) Ignoramus (d) Nincompoop
22. Person holding a scholarship at a university
(a) Intellectual (b) Pedant
(c) Scholar (d) Bursar
23. Member of a band of robbers
(a) Dacoit (b) Brigand
(c) Thief (d) Pirate
24. A speech by an actor at the end of a play
(a) Epilogue (b) Monologue
(c) Duologue (d) Prologue
25. The line which a plough cuts in the ground
(a) Vale (b) Trench
(c) Furrow (d) Trough

26. A person who forsakes religion
(a) Charlatan (b) Apostle
(c) Renegade (d) Apotheosis
27. To mediate between two parties in a dispute
(a) Interfere (b) Interact
(c) Interrups (d) Intercede
28. The place where bricks are baked
(a) Foundry (b) Mint
(c) Cemetery (d) Kiln
29. The branch of medical science which deals with the problems of the old
(a) Oncology (b) Geriatrics
(c) Obstetrics (d) Endocrinology
30. Indifference to pleasure or pain
(a) Docility (b) Stoicism
(c) Patience (d) Reticence
31. Equal in rank, merit or quality
(a) Chum (b) Contemporary
(c) Peer (d) Colleague
32. A field or a part of a garden where fruit-trees grow
(a) Park (b) Nursery
(c) Yard (d) Orchard
33. A woman of lax moral
(a) Prostitute (b) Harlot
(c) Concubine (d) Hostess
34. Present opposing arguments or evidence
(a) Rebut (b) Criticise
(c) Rebuff (d) Reprimand
35. A person who makes and sells ladies' hats, etc.
(a) Draper (b) Tinker
(c) Milliner (d) Farrier
36. A person who enters without any invitation
(a) Burglar (b) Intruder
(c) Thief (d) Vandal
37. The period between two reigns
(a) Lapse (b) Interregnum
(c) Stasis (d) Anachronism
38. Lack of enough blood
(a) Amnesia (b) Insomnia
(c) Anaemia (d) Allergy
39. A man who is having the qualities of woman
(a) Loquacious (b) Celibate
(c) Effeminate (d) Epicurean
40. One who does not know how to save money
(a) Reckless (b) Lavish
(c) Careless (d) Spendthrift
41. One who comes from a country area and is often considered to be stupid
(a) Villager (b) Rustic
(c) Bumpkin (d) Philanderer
42. Walk in a vain, self-important way
(a) Jog (b) Trek
(c) Trudge (d) Strut
43. A person working in the same place with another
(a) Comrade (b) Colleague
(c) Assistant (d) Contemporary
44. Place which provides both board and lodging
(a) Cafe (b) Inn
(c) Restaurant (d) Motel
45. A small shop that sells fashionable clothes, cosmetics etc.
(a) Booth (b) Stall
(c) Boutique (d) Store
46. A short journey made by a group of persons together
(a) Hike (b) Excursion
(c) Picnic (d) Stroll
47. Creature having both male and female organs
(a) Sodomite (b) Homosexual
(c) Masochist (d) Hermaphrodite

Direction (Q. 48–52) : In each of the following questions, find out which one of the words given below the sentence can most appropriately replace the group of words italicised in the sentence.

48. He does *unpaid work* for the Red Cross.
(a) honorific (b) honest
(c) honorary (d) honourable
49. The education in primitive Gurukuls comprised mainly of telling the stories *of old time Gods or heroes.*
(a) ode (b) epic
(c) allegory (d) legend
50. In the olden days the king was considered *all powerful.*
(a) veteran (b) omnipotent
(c) omnivorous (d) omniscient
51. *Those who pass through this gate without permission* will be prosecuted.
(a) Bypassers (b) Culprits
(c) Absconders (d) Trespassers
52. *The shelter for cow* ought to be clean and well ventilated.
(a) hutch (b) byre
(c) hangar (d) kennel

Answers

1. (d)	2. (d)	3. (c)	4. (b)	5. (b)	6. (b)	7. (b)	8. (c)	9. (c)	10. (a)
11. (a)	12. (b)	13. (d)	14. (c)	15. (b)	16. (c)	17. (d)	18. (d)	19. (d)	20. (c)
21. (b)	22. (c)	23. (b)	24. (a)	25. (c)	26. (c)	27. (d)	28. (d)	29. (b)	30. (b)
31. (c)	32. (d)	33. (d)	34. (a)	35. (c)	36. (b)	37. (b)	38. (c)	39. (c)	40. (d)
41. (c)	42. (d)	43. (b)	44. (b)	45. (c)	46. (b)	47. (d)	48. (c)	49. (d)	50. (b)
51. (d)	52. (b)								

8 ACTIVE AND PASSIVE VOICE

Voice is the form of a verb that shows whether the subject of the verb does something or has something done to it. The verb has two voices—Active and Passive.

Active Voice: A Verb is said to be in the Active Voice when the person or thing denoted by the subject acts.

For example,

(i) Aryan writes a letter. The sentence indicates the subject 'Aryan' does something. So, it is in Active Voice.

Passive Voice: A Verb is said to be in the Passive Voice when the person or thing denoted by the subject does not act, but suffers the action done by something/someone.

For example,

(i) A letter is written by Aryan. In this sentence, the written verb indicates that something is done by Aryan. So, the verb here is in Passive voice.

Rules to Change the Voice

To change a sentence from Active to Passive Voice the following steps are involved:

♦ To change the object into a subject: if object is the pronoun change it as follows

me	=	I
you	=	you
her	=	she
us	=	we
him	=	he
it	=	it
whom	=	who

♦ Change the subject into object by using 'by'

I	=	by me
We	=	by us
You	=	by you
He	=	by him
She	=	by her
It	=	by it
They	=	by them
Who	=	by whom

♦ The verb is changed according to the tense.

Rules for Change of Voice Exemplified

Present Indefinite Tense

(*Change into–Is/Am/Are + Past Participle of Verb*)

Active	Passive
He speaks French.	French is spoken by him.
Does he speak French?	Is French spoken by him?
He does not speak French.	French is not spoken by him.
Does he not' speak French?	Is French not spoken by him?

Present Continuous Tense

(*Change into–Is/Am/Are+Being+Past participle of Verb*)

Active	Passive
He is painting the wall.	The wall is being painted by him
Is he painting the wall?	Is the wall being painted by him?
He is not painting the wall.	The wall is not being painted by him.
Is he not painting the wall?	Is the wall not being painted by him?

Present Perfect Tense

(Change into—Has/Have + Been + Past Participle of Verb)

Active	Passive
You have spoken the truth.	The truth has been spoken by you.
Have you spoken the truth?	Has the truth been spoken by you?
You have not spoken the truth.	The truth has not been spoken by you.
Have you not spoken the truth?	Has the truth not been spoken by you?

Past Indefinite Tense

(Change into–Was/Were + Past Participle of Verb)

Active	Passive
England won victory.	Victory was won by England.
Did England win victory?	Was victory won by England?
England did not win victory.	Victory was not won by England.
Did England not win victory?	Was victory not won by England?

Past Continuous Tense

(Change into–Was/Were + Being + Past Participle of Verb)

Active	Passive
Rohit was reading a book.	A book was being read by Rohit.
Was Rohit reading a book?	Was a book being read by Rohit?
Rohit was not reading a book.	A book was not being read by Rohit
Was Rohit not reading a book?	Was a book not being read by Rohit?

Past Perfect Tense

(Change into–Had + Been + Past Participle of Verb)

Active	Passive
Students had purchased Bags.	Bags had been purchased by students.
Had students purchased Bags?	Had Bags been purchased by students?
Students had not purchased Bags.	Bags Had not been purchased by students.
Had students not purchased Bags?	Had Bags not been purchased by students?

Future Indefinite Tense

(Change into–Shall be/Will be + Past Participle of verb)

Active	Passive
War will destroy everything.	Everything will be destroyed by war.
Will war destroy everything?	Will everything be destroyed by war?
War will not destroy everything.	Everything will not be destroyed by war.
Will war not destroy everything?	Will everything not be destroyed by war?

Future Perfect Tense

Active	Passive
Shila will have completed work.	Work will have been completed by Shila.
Will Shila have completed work?	Will work have been completed by Shila?
Shila will not have completed work.	Work will not have been completed by Shila.
Will Shila not have completed work?	Will not work have been completed by Shila?

Verb followed by modals

In those sentences which carry modals like can, could, should, would, must etc., 'be' is used between the modal and the third form of verb in the passive voice.

Active voice : I can do this work.
Passive voice : This work can be done by me.
Active voice : May I help you ?
Passive voice : May you be helped by me?

Imperative Sentence

In changing imperative sentence to passive voice, the following rules are observed :

(i) Let + new object + be/not be + 3rd form

(ii) According to the idea of the sentence, we use phrases like you are requested to/advised to/ordered to, etc.

(iii) Kindly or please is deleted.

Active Voice	Passive Voice
Shut the door.	Let the door be shut.
Do not starve the man.	Let the man not be starved.
Get out of my sight.	You are ordered to get out of my sight.

Exercise

Direction (Q. 1–14): In each of the following questions a sentence has been given in Active or Passive Voice. Out of the four alternatives you have to select the one which best expresses the same sentence in Passive or Active Voice.

1. Poverty obliged him to steal.
(a) He was by poverty obliged to steal.
(b) He was to steal obliged by poverty.
(c) He was obliged by poverty to steal.
(d) He was obliged to steal.

2. People speak different languages in India.
(a) Different languages have been spoken in India.
(b) Different languages are spoken in India.
(c) Different languages were spoken in India.
(d) Different languages had been spoken in India.

3. Darjeeling grows tea.
(a) Tea grows in Darjeeling.
(b) Tea is grown in Darjeeling.
(c) Let the tea be grown in Darjeeling.
(d) Tea is being grown in Darjeeling.

4. Do not insult the weak.
(a) The weak should not be insulted.
(b) Let the weak not be insulted.
(c) The weak you should not insult.
(d) The weak insulted should not be.

5. Mona was writing a letter to her rather.
(a) A letter was written to her father by Mona.
(b) A letter has been written to her father by Moan.
(c) A letter was being written by Mona to her father.
(d) A letter was written by Mone to her father.

6. Who taught her such things ?
(a) Who was she taught such things by ?
(b) She was taught such things by who ?
(c) By whom she was taught such things ?
(d) By whom was she taught such things ?

7. I shall order the carriage.
(a) The carriage will be ordered.
(b) The carriage by me order.
(c) The carriage I will ordered.
(d) The carriage ordered by me.

8. You will have finished this work by tomorrow.
(a) This work will have been finished tomorrow.
(b) This work will be finished by tomorrow.
(c) This work will finished tomorrow.

9. The manager will give you a ticket.
(a) A ticket the manager will give you.
(b) A ticket will be given by manager.
(c) A ticket by the manager will be given to you.
(d) A ticket will give you the manager

10. A tiger may be helped even by a little mouse.
(a) A little mouse may even help a tiger.
(b) Even a little mouse may help a tiger.
(c) A little mouse can even help a tiger.
(d) Even a little mouse-ought to help a tiger.

11. The passive voice of 'We make Ice cream from milk' is
(a) Ice cream is being made from milk
(b) Ice cream has been made from milk

(c) Ice cream was made from milk
(d) Ice cream is made from milk by us

12. Which is the correct passive voice of the following sentence?
You have painted the window.
(a) The window was painted
(b) The window has been painted by you
(c) The window is painted
(d) The window be painted

13. Change the following into Passive Voice
'Do not insult your elders'.
(a) Let not your elders be insulted
(b) Your elders let not be insulted
(c) Let your elders not be insulted by you
(d) Let us not insult your elders.

14. Point out the sentence in passive voice
(a) The striking students were throwing stones
(b) Twenty lessons have been finished
(c) The murderer hide the knife
(d) The enemy will have sunk the ship by now

Answers

1. (d) **2.** (b) **3.** (b) **4.** (b) **5.** (c) **6.** (d) **7.** (a) **8.** (d) **9.** (b) **10.** (c)
11. (d) **12.** (b) **13.** (c) **14.** (b)

9 DIRECT AND INDIRECT SPEECH

Direct Speech

When we convey the words of a person in his actual words, this is called Direct Speech. We use inverted commas to mark off the exact words of the speaker.

Indirect Speech

When we convey the words of a person without using his exact words, this is called Indirect Speech.

Reporting Verb : It is the verb of the sentence which is outside inverted commas.

Reported Speech : It is the matter quoted within inverted commas.

When Direct Speech is transformed into Indirect Speech, changes are made in the following :

1. Reported verb
2. Inverted commas
3. Tense
4. Reported verb and Reported Speech
5. Adverbs of Time and Place

1. Change of Reporting Verbs

(a) In **Assertive sentences** the Reporting verb is changed into **tell** or **told**.

(b) In **Interrogative sentences** the Reporting verbs is changed into **asked** or **inquired of.**

(c) In **Imperative** sentences the Reporting verb is changed into **ordered, advised, requested, forbade, suggested** etc. according to the sense of the sentence.

(d) In **Exclamatory sentences** the reporting verb is changed **into exclaimed with joy, exclaimed with sorrow, exclaimed with surprise** etc. according to the sense of the sentence.

(e) In **Optative** sentence (prayers and wishes) the Reporting verb is changed into **wished** and **prayed.**

2. Removal of Inverted Commas

(a) In **Assertive** sentences **that** is used in place of inverted commas.

(b) **Interrogative** sentences

(i) In the sentences which start with **Auxiliary verbs** (do, did, is, are, was, were, can, may etc) if or whether is used in place of inverted commas.

(ii) In sentences which start with **question words** (who, by, what, where, etc), inverted commas are replaced by question word itself.

(c) In **Imperative** sentences to or not to is used in place of inverted commas.

(d) In **Exclamatory** sentences **that** is used in place of inverted commas.

(e) In **Optative** sentences **that** is used in place of inverted commas.

3. Change of Tense

(a) If the **Reporting verb** is in **Present** or **Future Tense,** the tense of Reported speech does not change.

(i) She will say to me, "I need your help".
She will tell me that she needs my help.

(b) If the **Reporting verb** is in the **Past Tense,** the tense of Reported Speech changes as

Direct	Indirect
Simple Present	Simple Past
Present Continuous	Past Continuous
Present Perfect	Past Perfect
Present Perfect Continuous	Past Perfect Continuous
Simple Past	Past Perfect
Past Continuous	Past Perfect Continuous
Past Perfect	No change
Past Perfect Continuous	No change

(i) He said to me, "I don't believe you".
He told me that he didn't believe me.

(ii) He said to the mother, "I have done my home work".
He told the mother that he had done his home work.

(iii) He said, "I wrote a letter".
He said that he had written a letter".

(iv) He said, "I shall meet her".
He said that he would meet her.

(v) We said to them, "We can defeat you".
We told them that we could defeat them.

4. Change of Pronoun

(a) First person of the Reported speech changes according to the subject of the Reporting verb.

(b) Second person of the Reported speech changes according to the object of the Reporting verb.

(c) Third person does not change.

Remember it as

1	2	3
First Person	Second Person	Third Person
S (Subject)	O (Object)	N (No Change)

1 → First Person S → Subject
2 → Second Person O → Subject
3 → Third Person N→No change

e.g.,

(i) They say to me, " We help you".
They tell me that they help me.

(ii) I said to Manoj, "You can meet her".
I told Manoj that he could meet her.

(iii) Rani said to me, "He is my friend".
Rani told me that he was her friend.

5. Change of Adverbs of Time and Place

Word expressing nearness in time or place are generally changed into words expressing distance. As

Now	becomes	**Then**
ago	comes	**before**
this	becomes	**that**
today	becomes	**that day**
yesterday	becomes	**the day before**
last night	becomes	**the night before**

e.g.,

(i) She said to me, "I shall do it next month".
She told me that she would do it the following month.

(ii) They said, "It is not so humid today as it was yesterday".
They said that it was not so humid that day as it had been the day before.

Exercise

Directions (Q. 1–30) : In each of the following questions, a sentence has been given in Direct/ Indirect Speech. Out of the given alternatives choose the one which best expresses the same sentence in Indirect/Direct Speech.

1. He said, "I saw a book here."
(a) He said that he saw a book here.
(b) He said that he saw a book there.
(c) He said that he had seen a book here.
(d) He said that he had seen a book there.

2. He said, "I have often told you not to waste your time."
(a) He said that he had often told not waste your time.
(b) He said that he had often told him not to waste his time.
(c) He said that he had often suggested to him not to waste his time.
(d) He told that he had often told him not to waste his time.

3. Pinki said to Gaurav, "Will you help me in my work just now?"
(a) Pinki asked Gaurav if he would help her in her work just then.
(b) Pinki questioned to Gaurav that will you help me in my work just now.
(c) Pinki told Gaurav whether he will help her in her work just now.
(d) Pinki asked to Gaurav that will he help her in her work just now.

4. He said to me, "What time to the officer close?"
(a) He wanted to know that time the offices close.
(b) He asked me what time the offices closed.
(c) He asked me what time the offices closed.
(d) He asked me what time the offices did close.

5. He said, "What a beautiful scene!"
(a) He said that what a beautiful scene it was.
(b) He wondered that it was a beautiful scene.
(c) He exclaimed what a beautiful scene it was.
(d) He exclaimed that it was very beautiful scene.

6. Rajan said, "O that I were a child against!"
(a) Rajan exclaimed with wonder that he was a child again.
(b) Rajan wondered that were he a child again
(c) Rajan strongly wished that he had been a child again.
(d) Rajan prayed that he were a child again.

7. Sarita said to me. "I will do it now or never."
(a) Sarita told me that I would do it then or never
(b) Sarita told me that she would do it now or never
(c) Sarita told me that she will do that now or never
(d) Sarita told me that she would do it then or never

8. I said to my brother, "Let us go to some hill station for a change."
(a) I asked my brother to go to some hill station for a change.
(b) I asked my brother if he would go to some hill station for a change.
(c) I permitted my brother to go to some hill station for a change.
(d) I suggested to my brother that we should go to some hill station for a change.

9. The Manager said, "Well, what can I do for you?"
(a) The Manager asked what he could do for him.
(b) The Manager wondered what he could do for him.
(c) The Manager wanted to know what he could do for him.
(d) The manager said that he couldn't to anything for him.

10. She said to him, "Why don't you go today?"
(a) She said to him that why he don't go today
(b) She asked him if he was going that day
(c) She asked him why he did not go today
(d) She asked him why he did not go that day

11. He said, "May God grant peace to the departed soul!"
(a) He wished by God to grant peace to the departed soul.
(b) He wished that God may grant peace to the departed soul
(c) He prayed that might God grant peace to the departed soul
(d) He prayed that God would grant peace to the departed soul

12. Mahendra Singh Dhoni said, "Sachin, you have done well".
(a) Mahendra Singh Dhoni exclaimed with joy that Sachin had done well
(b) Mahendra Singh Dhoni called Sachin and exclaimed that he had done well
(c) Mahendra Singh Dhoni congratulated Sachin, saying that he had done well
(d) Mahendra Singh Dhoni praised Sachin for his having done well

13. "Are you alone, my son?" asked a soft voice close behind me.
(a) A soft voice from by back asked if I was alone.
(b) A soft voice said to me are you alone son.
(c) A soft voice asked that what I was doing there alone.
(d) A soft voice behind me asked if I was alone.

14. He said to me, "Where is the post office?"
(a) He wanted to know where the post office was.
(b) He asked me that where the post office was.
(c) He asked me where the post office was.
(d) He asked me where was the post office.

15. He said, "I must go next week."
(a) He said that he must go next week.
(b) He said that he must go the following week.
(c) He said that he would have to go the following week.
(d) He said that he was to go the following week.

16. He said, "The mice will play, when the cat is away".
(a) He said that the mice will play when the cat is away.

(b) He said that the mice would play when the cat was away.
(c) He said that the mice would play when the cat would be away.
(d) He said that the mice shall play, when the cat is away.

17. He said to her, "Don't read so fast."
(a) He told her not to read so fast.
(b) He advised her don't read so fast.
(c) He requested her not to read so fast.
(d) He ordered her not to read so fast.

18. The sage said, "God helps those who help themselves."
(a) The sage said that God helps those who help themselves.
(b) The sage said that God helped those whose helped themselves.
(c) The sage said that God helps those who helped themselves.
(d) The sage said that God helped those who help themselves.

19. He said, "I clean my teeth twice a day."
(a) He said that he cleaned his teeth twice a day.
(b) He said that he cleans his teeth twice a day.
(c) He said that he used to clean his teeth twice a day.
(d) He said that he is used to cleaning his teeth twice a day.

20. "Please don't go away", she said.
(a) She said to please her and not go away.
(b) She told me not to go away.
(c) She begged that I not go away.
(d) She begged me not to go away.

21. He said, "Will you listen to such a man?"
(a) He asked them will you listen to such a man.
(b) He asked them are you listening to such a man.
(c) He asked them whether they would listen to such a man.
(d) He asked them whether they will listen to such a man.

22. The teacher said, "Be quiet, boys."
(a) The teacher said that they boys should be quiet.
(b) The teacher called the boys and ordered them to be quiet.
(c) The teacher urged the boys to be quiet.
(d) The teacher commanded the boys that they be quiet.

23. He said to them, "Don't make a noise."
(a) He told them that don't make a noise.
(b) He told them not to make noise.
(c) He told them not to make a noise.
(d) He asked them not to make a noise

24. "If you don't keep quiet I shall shoot you", he said to her in a calm voice.
(a) He warned her to shoot if she didn't keep quiet calmly.
(b) He said calmly that I shall shoot you if you don't be quiet.
(c) He warned her calmly that he would shoot her if she didn't keep quiet.
(d) Calmly he warned her that be quiet or else he will have to shoot her.

25. My friend said to me, "Has your father returned from Kolkata?"
(a) My friend said to me that my father has returned from Kolkata.
(b) My friend asked me if my father had returned from Kolkata.
(c) My friend told me that his father had returned from Kolkata.
(d) My friend enquired me if his father had returned form Kolkata.

26. Rajesh said, "I bought a car yesterday."
(a) Rajesh said that I have bought a car the previous day.
(b) Rajesh told that he had bought a car yesterday.
(c) Rajesh said that he bought a car the previous day.
(d) Rajesh said that he had bought a car the previous day.

27. He said, "Where shall be I be this time next year!"
(a) He asked that where should he be that time next year.
(b) He wondered where he should be that time the next year.
(c) He contemplated where shall he be that time the following year.
(d) He wondered where he would be that time the following years.

28. The employer said to the workman, "Icannot pay you higher wages."
(a) The employer told the workman that he could not be paid higher wages.
(b) The employer told the workman that he could not pay him higher wages.
(c) The employer forbade the workman to pay higher wages.
(d) The employer warned the workman that he cannot pay him higher wages.

29. "I don't know the way. Do you?" he asked.
(a) He said that he didn't know the way and did I know it.
(b) He told that he was not knowing the way, but wondered if I knew.
(c) He said that he didn't know the way and asked me if I did.
(d) He asked me if I knew the way which he didn't.

30. My cousin said, "My room-mate snored throughout the night."
(a) My cousin said that her room-mate had snored throughout the night.
(b) My cousin told me that her room-mate snored throughout the night.
(c) My cousin complained to me that her room-mate is snoring throughout the night.
(d) My cousin felt that her room-may be snoring throughout the night.

Answers

1. (d)	**2.** (b)	**3.** (a)	**4.** (c)	**5.** (d)	**6.** (c)	**7.** (d)	**8.** (d)	**9.** (c)	**10.** (d)
11. (d)	**12.** (c)	**13.** (d)	**14.** (c)	**15.** (c)	**16.** (a)	**17.** (a)	**18.** (a)	**19.** (b)	**20.** (d)
21. (c)	**22.** (c)	**23.** (d)	**24.** (c)	**25.** (b)	**26.** (d)	**27.** (d)	**28.** (b)	**29.** (c)	**30.** (a)

10 IDIOMS AND PHRASES

It will not be wrong to say that idioms and phrases are the soul of a language. The idiomatic words and phrases are usually independent of the dictionary definitions and often go against grammatical rules. Candidates generally commit errors in the use of idioms and phrases because they do not know their exact meaning. Every student, therefore should try to do the best of his/her capacity to achieve excellence in this field. Important Idioms and Phrases along with their meaning are given below:

- **At daggers drawn** (*having open enmity*): These days the two friends are at daggers drawn.
- **At home in** (*familiar*): He is at home in English.
- **At one's finger ends** (*ready with knowledge of something*): The names of all boys in the class are at my finger ends.
- **At the eleventh hour** (*at the last moment*): He came to me for help at the eleventh hour.
- **A white lie** (*a harmless lie*) : To save the child from a beating by the father, the mother had to tell a white lie.
- **Well-to-do** (*rich*): He belongs to a well-to-do family.
- **At a stone's throw** (*very near*) : My house is at a stone's throw from the college.
- **At sea** (*weak*): He is at sea in all subjects.
- **Break out** (*spread*): Cholera breaks out in a dirty city.
- **Bag and baggage** (*completely leaving nothing behind*) : Last year he left his village bag and baggage.
- **To bell the cat** (*to face risk*): All cry against the officer but nobody has the courage to bell the cat.
- **To bring up** (*to rear*): Parents bring up their children.
- **To burn the midnight oil** (*to work hard till late in night*): He bums the midnight oil and must win a scholarship.
- **By leaps and bounds** (*quickly*) : India can progress by leaps and bounds if we work together.
- **Bone o f contention** (*cause of quarrel*): Parental property often becomes a bone of contention between brothers.
- **Carry out** (*to obey*): The servant must carry out the orders of his master.
- **Come off** (*to happen*): His marriage comes on next Monday.
- **Call off** (*to withdraw*) : The workers have called off then strike.
- **To cut a sorry figure** (*to feel insulted*): He had to cut a sorry figure in his first speech.
- **To call a spade a spade** (*to be frank and truthful*):
  Political leaders never call a spade a spade.
- **A child's play** (*easy job*) : To win a scholarship in the Matriculation Examination is not a child's play.
- **Dispose of** (*to sell*): He has disposed of his old cycle.
- **Drawn game** (*in which no party wins*): The well-contested match turned out to be a drawn game.
- **To deal with** (*to behave*): He deals kindly with his friends.
- **To deal in** (to have trade in): My father is a doctor and his father deals in cloth.
- **To do without** (*to dispense with*) : I cannot do without tea.
- **Heart and soul** (*with full energy*) : He threw himself heart and soul into work.
- **Hale and hearty** (*very healthy*): Mohan was ill yesterday but today he is hale and hearty.
- **Hard and fast** (*strict*): There are no hard and fast rules in English grammar.
- **Hand in glove with** (*to have close relationship*): The two cousins are hand in glove with each other.
- **Hue and cry** (*a loud noise*): On seeing a snake he raised a hue and cry.
- **Hard up** (*in difficulties of money*): Help him because he is hard up these days.
- **A hair breadth escape** (*a narrow escape*) : He had a hair breadth escape in the car accident.
- **To hold good** (*to be true*) : The law of gravitation holds good everywhere.
- **In the long run** (*in the end*): Honesty pays in the long run.
- **In the nick of time** (*just in time*): The doctor reached the patient in the nick of time and saved him.
- **In full swing** (*in good progress*): Spring is in full swing these days.
- **In cold blood** (*without incitement from the other party*): Gandhiji was killed in cold blood.
- **Ins and outs** (*full details*): The head-clerk knows the ins and outs of office work.
- **In a fix** (*in confusion*): I am in a fix and want your help.
- **Get through** (*pass*) : An intelligent boy always gets through an examination.
- **To give a piece or a bit of one's mind** (*to scold*): The teacher gives the late comers a bit of his mind.
- **To get rid of** (*to be relieved of*) : I soon got rid of bad friends.

- **A mare's nest** (*seeming interesting but of no value; a complicated situation*): A good number of innovations turn out to be mare's nests on investigation.
- **A moot point** (*a matter that is undecided and open to discussion*) : Whether the menace of terrorism can be settled by offence or dialogue is a moot point.
- **To make a clean breast of** (*to tell the whole thing without concealing anything*): The best way to relieve yourself of mental tension is to make a clean breast of yourself.
- **To make a mess of something** (*to spoil*): If you try to do too many things too soon, you shall make a mess of everything.
- **To make a mountain of a molehill/To make much ado about nothing** (*to exaggerate something trivial*): Political business works upon the principle of making a mountain of a molehill.
- **To make both ends meet** (*to sustain one's life*) : In a well-structured society making both ends meet is the minim guarantee.
- **To fight with one's back to the wall** (*to make a desperate attempt in a no-way-out situation*): Even the most timid of persons wages a fierce battle when he has to fight with his back to the wall.
- **To flog a dead horse** (*to try in a hopeless condition*): Those who are reactive flog a dead horse when the calamity has actually struck.
- **Gift of the gab** (*eloquence*): An imposter always uses the gift of the gab to deceive innocent people.
- **To get into hot water** (*To be caught into trouble*): Why to blame others? You got into hot water yourself.
- **To get on one's nerves** (*to irritate*) : The actor had decided to look composed, but media persons got on his nerves with their personal questions.
- **To get the jitters** (*to become nervous*): Even the most well-prepared of the students get the jitters on examination day.
- **To give someone a rope** (*to give someone freedom of action or initiative*): If a manager wants innovation talent to bud, he will have to give them a rope.
- **To go begging/go to dogs** (*to do in vain*): At one stroke of misfortune, your entire effort could go a begging/ go to dogs.
- **To go** (at something) **hammer and tongs** (*to try at something with full energy*): Piecemeal steps will not solve the problem of population; the government must go at it hammer and tongs.
- **To go berserk** (*to become uncontrolled and violent*): Mob psychology works in a way that the entire gathering will go berserk if just a few turn violent.
- **Hush money** (*bribe*) : The secret cameras of the investigators have revealed the deep penetration of the hush money into the system.
- **Left-handed compliment** (*criticism in the form of praise*) : Indian Cricket team is a bunch of individually talented players.It is a left-handed compliment.
- **Long and short** (*summary*): The long and short of every holy book is that man should realise his worth.
- **Man of parts** (*having great qualities*): A man of parts always acts as a source of inspiration to many.

Exercise

1. Find the meaning of the following idiom.
   The read between the lines
   (a) to suspect
   (b) to read carefully
   (c) to understand the hidden meaning of the word
   (d) to do useless things
2. Select the most appropriate meaning of the given idiom.
   A bird of passage
   (a) A person of great importance
   (b) An evil person
   (c) A person who travels widely
   (d) A weak person
3. Find the meaning of the following idiom.
   He is in the habit of fishing in troubled waters.
   (a) putting others in trouble
   (b) indulging in evil conspirancies
   (c) aggravating the situation
   (d) taking advantage of troubled for personal profit

Direction : In each of the following questions, some alternatives are given or suggested for the idiom/phrase in italics in the sentence. Choose the one which best expresses the meaning of the idiom/phrase in italics.

4. She rejected his proposal of marriage point-blank.
   (a) directly (b) pointedly
   (c) abruptly (d) briefly
5. We should guard against our green-eyed friends.
   (a) rich
   (b) jealous
   (c) handsome
   (d) enthusiastic
6. The leader was popular with the audience as he had the gift of gab.
   (a) a charismatic personality
   (b) the ability to speak impressively
   (c) pleasing manners
   (d) an attractive appearance
7. He is under duress to finish the work in time.
   (a) under pressure
   (b) under request
   (c) under orders
   (d) under obligation
8. By signing this bond I have burnt all my boats.
   (a) relieved myself of worries
   (b) risked everything

(c) utilized all my resources
(d) tried my best

9. If you rub him the wrong way, he is bound to react,
(a) annoy him
(b) abuse him
(c) flatter him
(d) encourage him

10. He is in the habit of chewing the cuds.
(a) accusing others
(b) crying oVer split milk
(c) forgetting things
(d) to muse on

11. There was opposition to the new policy by the rank and file of the Government.
(a) the majority
(b) the ordinary members
(c) the cabinet members
(d) the official machinery

12. Bappi Lahiri's orchestra brought the house down.
(a) disappointed the audience
(b) was liked by the audience
(c) evoked tremendous applause
(d) created noise pollution

13. Dowry is a burning question of the day.
(a) a relevant problem
(b) a dying issue
(c) an irrelevant problem
(d) a widely debated issue

14. There is no love lost between the two neighbours.
(a) close friendship
(b) intense dislike
(c) a love-hate relationship
(d) cool indifference

15. He was cut to the quick when he leamt that his best friend had betrayed him.
(a) parted suddenly
(b) collapsed immediately
(c) was deeply hurt
(d) became angry

16. If you pass this difficult examination, it will be a feather in your cap.
(a) you will get a very good job
(b) you will feel proud of it
(c) your parents will be very happy
(d) you will get a scholarship for higher studies

17. I did not mind what he was saying, he was only talking through his hat.
(a) talking insultingly
(b) talking irresponsibly
(c) talking ignorantly
(d) talking nonsense

18. We should give a wide berth to bad characters,
(a) keep away from
(b) publicly condemn
(c) give publicly to
(d) not sympathise with

19. The boy turned a deaf ear to the pleading of all his well-wishers.
(a) listened carefully
(b) was deadly opposed
(c) posed indifference
(d) did not pay any attention

20. Sumit had to look high and low before he could find his scooter key.
(a) nowhere
(b) always
(c) everywhere
(d) somewhere

21. He is a plain, simple and sincere man. He will always call a spade a spade.
(a) say something to be taken seriously
(b) resist from making controversic statement
(c) find meaning or purpose in your action
(d) be out spoken in language

22. At a party, he is always in high spirits.
(a) talkative
(b) cheerful
(c) drunk
(d) uncontrollable

Answers

1. (c)	**2.** (c)	**3.** (d)	**4.** (a)	**5.** (b)	**6.** (b)	**7.** (a)	**8.** (b)	**9.** (a)	**10.** (d)
11. (b)	**12.** (c)	**13.** (d)	**14.** (b)	**15.** (c)	**16.** (b)	**17.** (d)	**18.** (a)	**19.** (d)	**20.** (c)
21. (d)	**22.** (b)								

11 SENTENCE IMPROVEMENT

Sentence Improvement or Phrase Replacement is basically related to Common Errors, or it may be taken as an improved version of questions on Spotting the Errors. The only difference between the two types of questions is that in case of questions relating to Common Errors a candidate has to spot the error only, but in case of questions relating to Sentence Improvement one has to find out the correct alternative for the erroneous part. The questions in this section may be related to Grammatical Norms, Word Usage, Idioms/Phrases, Subject-Verb Agreement, Tenses, Gerunds, Prepositions etc. General questions are framed on accepted rules of Grammar and Usage. But most of the questions are asked on exceptional rules. Earlier, the questions of simple nature pertaining to the use of Articles, Prepositions, Common rules of Tenses etc. were asked but not the emphasis has been shifted to Auxiliaries, Infinitives, Gerunds, Subject-Verb Agreement, Uses of Idioms/Phrases, Uncommon Structure etc. which may pose some problems for general candidates. Errors, thus, may be in Grammar, Appropriate word usage or Idioms. There may be a necessary word missing or there may be a word which should be deleted.

In order to solve questions on Sentence Improvement correctly, one must be acquainted with the rules of English Grammar and Usage, viz., Article, Noun, Pronoun, Adjective, Verb, Adverb, Voice, Mood, Preposition, Conjunction, Syntax, Tense, Infinitives, Gerund, Participle etc.

Exercise

Directions (1-10): In the following questions, a sentence is given which may need improvement. Alternatives are given at (a), (b) and (c) below, which may be a better option. In case no improvement is needed, your answer is (d).

1. A taller Sikh rushed forward than any of his comrades :
   (a) A Sikh, taller than any of his comrades, rushed forward.
   (b) A Sikh rushed forward taller than any of his comrades.
   (c) A Sikh rushed forward than any of his comrades taller.
   (d) No improvement
2. An author in the reign of Queen Anne who was famous lived in a cottage :
   (a) An author in the reign, who was famous, of Queen Anne lived in a cottage.
   (b) In the reign of Queen Anne, an author lived in a cottage, who was famous.
   (c) An author who was famous in the reign of Queen Anne lived in a cottage.
   (d) No improvement
3. In the absence of your support, he would have lost the election:
   (a) Lacking your support, he would have lost the election.
   (b) But for your support, he would have lost the election.
   (c) He would have lost the election, if you had not supported him.
   (d) No improvement
4. My uncle is enough rich to buy a car :
   (a) My uncle is rich enough to buy a car.
   (b) My uncle is richer enough to by a car.
   (c) My uncle is enough richer to buy a car.
   (d) No improvement
5. Walking along the road, an old man ran over the lorry:
   (a) Walking along the road, an old man ran behind the lorry.
   (b) Running along the road, the lorry ran over an old man.
   (c) The lorry ran over an old man walking along the road.
   (d) No improvement
6. He has for good left India :
   (a) He has left for good India.
   (b) He has left India for good.
   (c) Good he has left India.
   (d) No improvement
7. We are credibly informed that the murderer has given himself up :
   (a) We are informed that the murderer has credibly given himself up.
   (b) We are informed that the murderer has given credibly himself up.
   (c) We are informed that credibly the murderer has given up himself.
   (d) No improvement
8. We generally select **one of the most intelligent student of the school** for this award :
   (a) one of the most intelligent students of the school
   (b) one of the intelligent most students of the school
   (c) one of the intelligent most student of the school
   (d) No improvement
9. My friend lives in a nearby street **whose name** I have forgotten :
   (a) the name of which
   (b) which name
   (c) of which name
   (d) No improvement

10. He both won a medal and a scholarship:
   (a) He won a medal and a scholarship both.
   (b) Both he won a medal and a scholarship.
   (c) He won both a medal and a scholarship.
   (d) No improvement

Directions (11-30): In the following questions, a sentence is given, the bold part of which may need improvement. Alternatives are given at (a), (b) and (c) below, which may be a better option. In case no improvement is needed, your answer is (d).

11. With these extra people you can **work** easily with this job:
   (a) deal
   (b) improve
   (c) cope
   (d) no improvement
12. I visited my aunt just **before a week:**
   (a) a week before
   (b) a week earlier
   (c) a week ago
   (d) no improvement
13. Foreigners often **come across with** serious difficulties in studying English :
   (a) have to come across with
   (b) come cross with
   (c) come across
   (d) no improvement
14. He **work hard** will succeed :
   (a) who will work hard
   (b) who will be working hard
   (c) who works hard
   (d) no improvement
15. It is high time you **started** revising your lessons :
   (a) start
   (b) had started
   (c) will start
   (d) no improvement
16. It took her a long time to get **past** her failure in the medical examination :
   (a) through
   (b) over
   (c) by
   (d) No improvement
17. The boy wanted to ask his father for money, but waited for a **propitious** occasion :
   (a) protective
   (b) prophetic
   (c) prospective
   (d) no improvement
18. I did not agree with him; he appeared to be **so** bigoted for me to concur :
   (a) much
   (b) very
   (c) too
   (d) no improvement
19. As soon as she noticed the workmen, she asked them what they **have been** doing:
   (a) have done
   (b) had been
   (c) are doing
   (d) no improvement
20. He was asleep before the mother tucked him **off :**
   (a) through
   (b) away
   (c) in
   (d) no improvement
21. Sordid and sensational books tend to **vitiate** the public taste :
   (a) divide
   (b) distract
   (c) distort
   (d) No improvement
22. **By studying** AIDS has engaged many researchers in the last decade:
   (a) Important study
   (b) Now that the study
   (c) The study of
   (d) No improvement
23. His Master's thesis **was highly estimated** and is now being prepared for publication :
   (a) was highly discussed
   (b) was highly commended
   (c) is highly appraised
   (d) No improvement
24. No sooner had she realized her blunder **than she began to take** corrective measures:
   (a) then she began to take
   (b) than she began taking
   (c) when she began to take
   (d) No improvement
25. A good scholar **must be precise and possess originality :**
   (a) must be precise and original
   (b) must be possess precision and original
   (c) must be precision and possess originality
   (d) No improvement
26. The ship **ran over** when it crashed into an iceberg :
   (a) got over
   (b) gave up
   (c) went down
   (d) No improvement
27. His wife was **contentious :**
   (a) contagious
   (b) quarrelsome
   (c) content
   (d) No improvement
28. Historians feel there is an **earnest** need for the review of history textbooks every five years and a revision of the same every ten years:
   (a) imperative
   (b) indispensable
   (c) urgent
   (d) No improvement
29. My car broke **off** on my way to the office :
   (a) out
   (b) in
   (c) down
   (d) No improvement
30. Freedom is a wonderful thing **for** Jimmy was eager to experience it :
   (a) though
   (b) and
   (c) but
   (d) No improvement

Answers with Explanations

1. (a) A sikh, taller than any of his comrades, rushed forward.
2. (c) An author who was famous in the reign of Queen Anne lived in a cottage.
3. (c) He would have lost the election, if you had not supported him.
4. (a) My uncle is rich enough to buy a car.
5. (c) The lorry ran over an old man walking along the road.
6. (b) He has left India for good.

7. (d) **Give yourself up to somebody** means : to offer yourself to be captured.

8. (a) one of the most intelligent students of the school.

9. (a) the name of which

10. (c) He won both a medal and a scholarship.

11. (c) **To cope with** means : manage: to deal successfully with something difficult.

12. (c) Here, a **week ago** should be used.

13. (c) Here, **come across** should be used.

14. (c) Here, Adjective clause i.e. who works hard (Simple Present) should be used.

15. (d) No improvement

16. (b) over

17. (d) No improvement

18. (c) too

19. (b) had been

20. (c) **Tuck somebody in/up** means: to make somebody feel comfortable in bed by pulling the covers up around them.

21. (b) distract

22. (c) The study of

23. (b) was highly commended

24. (d) No improvement

25. (a) must be precise and original

26. (c) went down

27. (b) quarrelsome

28. (d) No improvement

29. (c) down

30. (b) and

12 COMPREHENSION

Read the following passages (1-6) and answer the questions that follow.

PASSAGE-1

The superintendence, direction and control of preparation of electoral rolls for, and the conduct of, elections to Parliament and State Legislatures and elections to the offices of the President and the Vice - President of India are vested in the Election Commission of India. It is an independent constitutional authority.

Independence of the Election Commission and its insulation from executive interference is ensured by a specific provision under Article 324 (5) of the Constitution that the Chief Election Commissioner shall not be removed from his office except in like manner and on like grounds as a Judge of the Supreme Court and conditions of his service shall not be varied to his disadvantage after his appointment.

In C.W.P. No. 4912 of 1998 (Kushra Bharat Vs. Union of India and Others), the Delhi High Court directed that information relating to Government dues owed by the candidates to the departments dealing with Government accommodation, electricity, water, telephone and transport etc. and any other dues should be furnished by the candidates and this information should be published by the election authorities under the commission.

1. The text of the passage reflects or raises certain questions:
(a) The authority of the commission cannot be challenged.
(b) This would help in stopping the criminalization of Indian politics.
(c) This would reduce substantially the number of contesting candidates.
(d) This would ensure fair and free elections.

2. According to the passage, the Election Commission is an independent constitutional authority. This is under Article No.
(a) 324 (b) 356
(c) 246 (d) 161

3. Independence of the Commission means:
(a) have a constitutional status.
(b) have legislative powers.
(c) have judicial powers.
(d) have political powers.

4. Fair and free election means:
(a) transparency
(b) to maintain law and order
(c) regional considerations
(d) role for pressure groups

5. The Chief Election Commissioner can be removed from his office under Article :
(a) 125 (b) 352
(c) 226 (d) 324

ANSWERS

1. (d) **2.** (a) **3.** (a) **4.** (b) **5.** (d)

PASSAGE-2

All political systems need to mediate the relationship between private wealth and public power. Those that fail risk a dysfunctional government captured by wealthy interests. Corruption is one symptom of such failure with private willingness-to-pay trumping public goals. Private individuals and business firms pay to get routine services and to get to the head of the bureaucratic queue. They pay to limit their taxes, avoid costly regulations, obtain contracts at inflated prices and get concessions and privatised firms at low prices. If corruption is endemic, public officials – both bureaucrats and elected officials – may redesign programmes and propose public projects with few public benefits and many opportunities for private profit. Of course, corruption, in the sense of bribes, pay-offs and kickbacks, is only one type of government failure. Efforts to promote 'good governance' must be broader than anti-corruption campaigns. Governments may be honest but inefficient because no one has an incentive to work productively, and narrow elites may capture the state and exert excess influence on policy. Bribery may induce the lazy to work hard and permit those not in the inner circle of cronies to obtain benefits. However, even in such cases, corruption cannot be confined to 'functional' areas. It will be a temptation whenever private benefits are positive. It may be a reasonable response to a harsh reality but, over time, it can facilitate a spiral into an even worse situation.

1. The governments which fail to focus on the relationship between private wealth and public power are likely to become:
(a) Functional
(b) Dysfunctional
(c) Normal functioning
(d) Good governance

2. One important symptom of bad governance is:
(a) Corruption
(b) High taxes
(c) Complicated rules and regulations
(d) High prices

3. When corruption is rampant, public officials always aim at many opportunities for:
(a) Public benefits
(b) Public profit
(c) Private profit
(d) Corporate gains

4. Productivity linked incentives to public/private officials is one of the indicatives for:
(a) Efficient government
(b) Bad governance
(c) Inefficient government
(d) Corruption

5. The spiralling corruption can only be contained by promoting:
   (a) Private profit
   (b) Anti-corruption campaign
   (c) Good governance
   (d) Pay-offs and kick-backs

ANSWERS

1. (b) **2.** (a) **3.** (c) **4.** (a) **5.** (a)

PASSAGE-3

After almost three decades of contemplating Swarovski-encrusted navels on increasing flat abs, the Mumbai film industry is on a discovery of India and itself. With budgets of over 30 crore each, four soon to be released movies by premier directors are exploring the idea of who we are and redefining who the other is. It is a fundamental question which the bling-bling, glam-sham and disham-disham tends to avoid. It is also a question which binds an audience when the lights go dim and the projector rolls: as a nation, who are we? As a people, where are we going?

The Germans coined a word for it, zeitgeist, which perhaps Yash Chopra would not care to pronounce. But at 72, he remains the person who can best capture it. After being the first to project the diasporic Indian on screen in Lamhe in 1991, he has returned to his roots in a new movie. Veer Zaara, set in 1986, where Pakistan, the traditional other, the part that got away, is the lover and the saviour. In Subhas Ghai's Kisna, set in 1947, the other is the English woman. She is not a memsahib, but a mehbooba. In Ketan Mehta's The Rising, the East India Englishman is not the evil oppressor of countless cardboard characterisations, which span the spectrum from Jewel in the Crown to Kranti, but an honourable friend.

This is Manoj Kumar's Desh Ki dharti with a difference: there is culture, not contentious politics; balle balle, not bombs: no dooriyan (distance), only nazdeekiyan (closeness).

All four films are heralding a new hero and heroine. The new hero is fallible and vulnerable, committed to his dharma, but also not afraid of failure - less of a boy and more of a man. He even has a grown up name: Veer Pratap Singh in Veer-Zaara and Mohan Bhargav in Swades. The new heroine is not a babe, but often a babe, dressed in traditional Punjabi clothes, often with the stereotypical body type as well, as in Bride and Prejudice of Gurinder Chadha.

1. Which word Yash Chopra would not be able to pronounce?
   (a) Bling + bling (b) Zeitgeist
   (c) Montaz (d) Dooriyan
2. Who made Lamhe in 1991?
   (a) Subhash Ghai
   (b) Yash Chopra
   (c) Aditya Chopra
   (d) Sakti Samanta
3. Which movie is associated with Manoj Kumar?
   (a) Jewel in the Crown
   (b) Kisna
   (c) Zaara
   (d) Desh Ki dharti
4. Which is the latest film by Yash Chopra?
   (a) Deewar
   (b) Kabhi Kabhi
   (c) Dilwale Dulhaniya Le Jayenge
   (d) Veer Zaara
5. Which is the dress of the heroine in Veer-Zaara?
   (a) Traditional Gujarati Clothes
   (b) Traditional Bengali Clothes
   (c) Traditional Punjabi Clothes
   (d) Traditional Madras Clothes

ANSWERS

1. (b) **2.** (b) **3.** (d) **4.** (d) **5.** (c)

PASSAGE-4

Gandhi's overall social and environmental philosophy is based on what human beings need rather than what they want. His early introduction to the teachings of Jains, Theosophists, Christian sermons, Ruskin and Tolstoy, and most significantly the Bhagavad Gita, was to have profound impact on the development of Gandhi's holistic thinking on humanity, nature and their ecological interrelation. His deep concern for the disadvantaged, the poor and rural Perhaps the moral principle for which Gandhi is best known is that of active non-violence, derived from the traditional moral restraint of not injuring another being. The most refined expression of this value is in the great epic of the Mahabharata, (c. 100 BCE to 200 CE), where moral development proceeds through placing constraints on the liberties, desires and acquisitiveness endemic to human life. One's action is judged in terms of consequences and the impact it is likely to have on another. Jainas had generalized this principle to include all sentient creatures and biocommunities alike. Advanced Jaina monks and nuns will sweep their path to avoid harming insects and even bacteria. Non-injury is a non-negotiable universal prescription.

1. Which one of the following have a profound impact on the development of Gandhi's holistic thinking on humanity, nature and their ecological interrelations?
   (a) Jain teachings
   (b) Christian sermons
   (c) Bhagavad Gita
   (d) Ruskin and Tolstoy
2. Gandhi's overall social and environmental philosophy is based on human beings':
   (a) need (b) desire
   (c) wealth (d) welfare
3. Gandhiji's deep concern for the disadvantaged, the poor and rural population created an ambience for an alternative:
   (a) rural policy
   (b) social thinking
   (c) urban policy
   (d) economic thinking
4. Colonial policy and modernization led to the destruction of:
   (a) major industrial infrastructure
   (b) irrigation infrastructure
   (c) urban infrastructure
   (d) rural infrastructure
5. Gandhi's active non-violence is derived from:
   (a) Moral restraint of not injuring another being